MEGARRY'S MANUAL

OF

THE LAW OF REAL PROPERTY

A MANUAL OF

THE LAW OF
REAL PROPERTY

BY

THE RT. HON. SIR ROBERT MEGARRY,
M.A., LL.D. (Cantab.), Hon. LL.D. (Hull, Nottingham,
The Law Society of Upper Canada, and London),
Hon. D.U. (Essex), F.B.A.
*an Honorary Fellow of Trinity Hall, Cambridge;
a Bencher of Lincoln's Inn; sometime the
Vice-Chancellor of the Supreme Court*

EIGHTH EDITION

BY

A. J. OAKLEY
M.A., LL.B. (Cantab.),
T.E.P.,
*of Lincoln's Inn, Barrister,
Fellow of Trinity Hall,
Cambridge*

LONDON
SWEET & MAXWELL LIMITED
2002

First Edition	1946	By R. E. MEGARRY
Second Impression, revised	1947	" "
Third Impression, revised	1949	" "
Fourth Impression	1951	" "
Second Edition	1955	" "
Second Impression	1960	" "
Third Edition	1962	" "
Second Impression	1967	" "
Fourth Edition	1969	By P. V. BAKER
Second Impression	1972	" "
Third Impression	1973	" "
Fifth Edition	1975	" "
Sixth Edition	1982	By D. J. HAYTON
Second Impression	1989	" "
Seventh Edition	1993	By R. E. MEGARRY and M. P. THOMPSON
Second Impression	1994	" "

Published in 2002 by Sweet & Maxwell Limited
of 100 Avenue Road, London NW3 3PF
Computerset by Interactive Sciences Ltd, Gloucester
Printed in Great Britain by The Bath Press, Bath, Avon.

A CIP catalogue record for this book
is available from The British Library

ISBN 0 421 717904

FOREWORD

I am deeply indebted to Tony Oakley for shouldering the whole burden of editing this new edition of the Manual, and for doing it so admirably. At one time I had hoped to play some part in it myself, but in the end, to my great regret, I contributed little of any substance. From the first, I always felt much sympathy for those embarking on a study of the law of real property. As an undergraduate, the subject seemed to me to be complex, endless and dull; worse, it was also remote from ordinary life, in contrast with subjects such as contract, tort and crime. When I unexpectedly began to teach law, I soon found that clarity of structure and directness of language usually provided a gateway for the puzzled, reluctant or confused; and this I sought to achieve, in place of the learned obscurity too often to be found elsewhere. The war delayed publication, but in 1946 the first edition of this book appeared, and later editions have continued in the same course. My regrets at contributing so little to this edition are the greater because it must be rare for someone in his nineties to be given the chance of editing what he wrote in his twenties.

Lincoln's Inn   R.E.M.
St. Swithin's Day, 2002

PREFACE

I was delighted when Sir Robert Megarry, an Honorary Fellow of the Cambridge College of which I am myself a Fellow, asked me to prepare the eighth edition of this work. Unfortunately, for a variety of reasons, its preparation has taken a great deal longer than either he wished or I intended. However, the delay has at least meant that it has been possible to incorporate the provisions of the recently enacted Land Registration Act 2002 and the Commonhold and Leasehold Reform Act 2002, something which would not have been possible if this edition had been published as originally scheduled.

Previous editions of this work have, very understandably in the light of the fact that the first edition was published as long ago as 1946, been written largely from the perspective of the system of unregistered conveyancing. That is not to say that the system of registered conveyancing was not fully covered in those editions, but we both agreed at the outset that one of the principal objectives of this edition must be to place registered land in its proper and pre-eminent position today. The principal changes in this respect are to the introductory Chapter 1 and to Chapter 4, which deals with the structure of modern land law. In the latter chapter, features that are common to both systems of conveyancing are discussed first, followed by separate discussions of each of the two systems. I hope that this change will make this work more accessible to students whose courses sadly now contain no discussion of unregistered conveyancing whatsoever. Discussion of the law as it stood prior to the 1925 legislation has been eradicated except where it remains relevant in this new century. The structure of the work is otherwise unchanged, although it is questionable whether future editions will need such a detailed treatment of settlements under the Settled Land Act 1925, now that no more settlements of this type can be created.

In the nine years which have passed since the publication of the previous edition, there has been more significant legislation than in any period since the decade in which the 1925 legislation was enacted. Three major statutes whose subject-matter is central to this work have had to be incorporated: the Landlord and Tenant (Covenants) Act 1995, the Trusts of Land and Appointment of Trustees Act 1996 and the Land Registration Act 2002. A considerable number of further legislative reforms have also been made. In the past year, there have been two important decisions of the House of Lords, in *Royal Bank of Scotland Plc v. Etridge (No. 2)* and in *Pye (J.A.) Oxford Ltd v. Graham* (the speeches in the latter decision were actually handed down while the proofs were being read). The Court of Appeal and the Chancery Division have also produced a considerable number of relevant decisions. The fact that it has been necessary to discuss both the current and the future systems of registered conveyancing and to double the length of the discussion of leasehold covenants so as to deal with both "old leases" and "new leases" has meant that this edition is some sixty pages longer than its predecessor.

Sir Robert read the first three chapters when they were originally produced and made a large number of helpful suggestions, both as to substance and to style: the latter were particularly valuable in assisting my efforts to write in the style for which this work is justifiably famous. He was unfortunately unable to read any of the remaining chapters until the proof stage, when I asked him to read Chapter 4, the chapter which has changed the most. His further suggestions were equally helpful and have virtually all been incorporated. The publishers decided to alter the format of this work; this initially came as rather a shock but, once two further amendments to the new format had been made at the proof stage, I have to admit that the work appears much more modern and will undoubtedly be easier to use.

I would like to thank Sir Robert for inviting me to prepare this edition, for which I alone am responsible, and I hope that he is not too disappointed with the result. I would also like to thank both him and the publishers for the patience which they have displayed while awaiting its production, and to thank the publishers for producing the tables and index. I would also like to thank my colleagues in the Faculty of Law at Cambridge University for keeping me up to date by means of the excellent lecture outlines that they have produced in recent years. Last, but by no means least, I would like to acknowledge with deep gratitude the very considerable assistance which I have derived from the excellent sixth edition of *Megarry & Wade: The Law of Real Property* produced by Mr Charles Harpum in 2000.

The law has been stated from the sources which were available to me on April 30, 2002, although it has proved possible to add some additional references at the proof stage.

11 Old Square   A.J.O.
Lincoln's Inn
July 9, 2002

CONTENTS

Foreword	v
Preface	vii
Contents	ix
Table of Cases	xv
Table of Statutes	li
Table of Statutory Instruments	lxxi
Abbreviations	lxxiii
Glossary	lxxv

1.	INTRODUCTION	1
	Sect. 1. Prefatory	1
	Sect. 2. The scope of the subject	4
	Sect. 3. Historical outline	15
	Sect. 4. Meaning of "real property"	17
	Sect. 5. Fixtures	19
	Sect. 6. Tenures and estates	24

2.	ESTATES	31
PART 1—CLASSIFICATION		31
	Sect. 1. Estates of freehold	31
	Sect. 2. Estates less than freehold	33
	Sect. 3. Seisin	35
PART 2—ESTATES OF FREEHOLD		37
	Sect. 1. Words of limitation	37
	Sect. 2. Nature of the estates of freehold	40

3.	LAW AND EQUITY	53
PART 1—GENERAL PRINCIPLES		53
	Sect. 1. The historical basis of equity	53
	Sect. 2. Equity follows the law	57
	Sect. 3. The nature of equitable rights	58
PART 2—SPECIES OF EQUITABLE RIGHTS		64
	Sect. 1. Trusts	64

Sect. 2. Other equitable rights 66
Sect. 3. Creation of equitable rights 67
Sect. 4. The borderline between personal and proprietary rights 70

4. THE STRUCTURE OF MODERN LAND LAW 73
PART 1—THE STRUCTURE PUT INTO PLACE BY THE 1925 LEGISLATION 73
PART 2—REGISTERED AND UNREGISTERED LAND TODAY 76
PART 3—ASPECTS COMMON TO BOTH SYSTEMS OF CONVEYANCING 78
Sect. 1. Reduction in the number of legal estates 78
Sect. 2. Extension of the doctrine of overreaching 84
Sect. 3. Registration of local land charges 91
Sect. 4. Human rights 92
PART 4—ASPECTS APPLYING ONLY TO UNREGISTERED CONVEYANCING 93
Sect. 1. Registration of land charges 93
Sect. 2. Effect of a conveyance 108
PART 5—ASPECTS APPLYING ONLY TO REGISTERED CONVEYANCING 111
Sect. 1. Introductory 111
Sect. 2. Interests in registered land 115
Sect. 3. Dealings with registered land 134
Sect. 4. Rectification and indemnity 138

5. DISPOSITIONS OF LAND 147
PART 1—CONTRACTS 147
Sect. 1. Contracts made before September 27, 1989 148
Sect. 2. Contracts made after September 26, 1989 148
Sect. 3. Effect of contracts 154
Sect. 4. Contracts in practice 155
PART 2—CONVEYANCING 158
Sect. 1. Unregistered title 158
Sect. 2. Registered title 166
PART 3—WILLS 172
Sect. 1. Freedom of testation 172
Sect. 2. Nature of a will 176
Sect. 3. The formalities of a will 177
Sect. 4. Operation of wills 183
Sect. 5. Construction of wills 187
PART 4—INTESTACY 192
PART 5—PERSONAL REPRESENTATIVES 198
Sect. 1. Introductory 198
Sect. 2. Devolution of property on personal representatives 199
Sect. 3. Number of personal representatives 200
PART 6—DISABILITIES 201
Sect. 1. Minors 201
Sect. 2. Mental patients 205
Sect. 3. Charities 206

6. FUTURE INTERESTS 209
PART 1—NATURE OF FUTURE INTERESTS 209
PART 2—THE RULE AGAINST PERPETUITIES 210
    Sect. 1. Vested and contingent interests 210
    Sect. 2. Classification of future interests 213
    Sect. 3. History of the rule 214
    Sect. 4. Operation of the rule 215
    Sect. 5. Exceptions from the rule 237
PART 3—THE RULE AGAINST INALIENABILITY 238
PART 4—THE RULE AGAINST ACCUMULATIONS 240
    Sect. 1. The statutory periods 241
    Sect. 2. Excessive accumulation 243
    Sect. 3. The rule in *Saunders v. Vautier* 244
    Sect. 4. Exceptions from the rule against accumulations 245

7. SETTLEMENTS 247
PART 1—BEFORE 1926 247
    Sect. 1. The strict settlement 247
    Sect. 2. Trusts for sale 250
PART 2—THE SETTLED LAND ACT 1925 251
    Sect. 1. Introduction 251
    Sect. 2. The essentials of settled land 252
    Sect. 3. How settlements had to be made, continue and determine 258
    Sect. 4. Powers of the tenant for life 268
    Sect. 5. Functions of Settled Land Act trustees 278
PART 3—TRUSTS FOR SALE AFTER 1925 279
PART 4—TRUSTS OF LAND 283
PART 5—TRUSTS AND TRUSTEES 289
    Sect. 1. Classification of trusts 289
    Sect. 2. Formalities for the creation of a trust 293
    Sect. 3. Formalities for transferring an interest under a trust 295
    Sect. 4. Trustees 296
    Sect. 5. Appointment of trustees 296
    Sect. 6. Retirement and removal of trustees 299
    Sect. 7. Vesting of trust property 300
    Sect. 8. Procedure for settlements 302

8. CO-OWNERSHIP 303
PART 1—JOINT TENANCY AND TENANCY IN COMMON 303
    Sect. 1. Nature of the tenancies: joint tenancies 303
    Sect. 2. Nature of the tenancies: tenancy in common 306
    Sect. 3. Estates in which the tenancies can exist 307
    Sect. 4. Mode of creating the tenancies: general 307
    Sect. 5. Mode of creating the tenancies: at law 308
    Sect. 6. Mode of creating the tenancies: in equity 313
    Sect. 7. Position of the beneficiaries 315
    Sect. 8. Position of land settled under the Settled Land Act 1925 326

Sect. 9. Determination of joint tenancies and tenancies in common   327
PART 2—PARTY WALLS   332

9. LANDLORD AND TENANT   337
PART 1—INTRODUCTORY   337
    Sect. 1. History   337
    Sect. 2. Terminology   338
PART 2—CREATION OF LEASES AND TENANCIES   339
    Sect. 1. Essentials of a lease or tenancy   339
    Sect. 2. Types of leases and tenancies   346
PART 3—ASSIGNMENT OF LEASES AND TENANCIES   353
PART 4—DETERMINATION OF TENANCIES   353
    Sect. 1. By expiry   354
    Sect. 2. By notice   354
    Sect. 3. By forfeiture   354
    Sect. 4. By surrender   364
    Sect. 5. By merger   365
    Sect. 6. By becoming a satisfied term   365
    Sect. 7. By enlargement   365
    Sect. 8. By disclaimer   366
    Sect. 9. By frustration   366
    Sect. 10. By repudiation   367
    Sect. 11. By rescission   367
PART 5—RIGHTS AND DUTIES OF THE PARTIES UNDER A LEASE OR TENANCY   367
    Sect. 1. Position in the absence of express provision   368
    Sect. 2. Position under a lease containing the usual covenants   374
    Sect. 3. Position under certain covenants usually found in leases   375
    Sect. 4. Statutory protection for tenants   380
PART 6—LEASEHOLD COVENANTS   381
    Sect. 1. General principles   381
    Sect. 2. Position of the original parties to an old lease   385
    Sect. 3. Position where the assignment of an old lease is effective at law   387
    Sect. 4. Position where the assignment of an old lease is effective only in equity   394
    Sect. 5. Restrictive covenants in an old lease   395
    Sect. 6. Position of landlord and tenant for the time being of a new lease   396
    Sect. 7. Position of former landlords and tenants of a new lease   400
    Sect. 8. Restrictive covenants in a new lease   405

10. INCORPOREAL HEREDITAMENTS   407
PART 1—RENTCHARGES   407
    Sect. 1. Nature of rentcharges   407
    Sect. 2. Creation and transfer of rentcharges   409
    Sect. 3. Means of enforcing payment   410
    Sect. 4. Extinguishment of rentcharges   411
    Sect. 5. Types of rent   412

Part 2—Easements and Profits 413
   Sect. 1. Nature of easements 413
   Sect. 2. Nature of a profit *à prendre* 421
   Sect. 3. Acquisition of easements and profits 424
   Sect. 4. Extinction of easements and profits 441
   Sect. 5. Species of easements 443
   Sect. 6. Species of profits *à prendre* 449
   Sect. 7. Rights of access 450

11. Restrictive Covenants 453
Part 1—Benefit 454
   Sect. 1. The benefit at law 454
   Sect. 2. The benefit in equity 456
Part 2—Burden 462
   Sect. 1. The burden at law 462
   Sect. 2. The burden in equity 468
Part 3—Enforcement 471
   Sect. 1. Determination 471
   Sect. 2. Town planning 473

12. Licences and Proprietary Estoppel 475
   Sect. 1. Nature of licences 475
   Sect. 2. Types of licences 475
   Sect. 3. Creation of licences 477
   Sect. 4. Revocation of licences 478
   Sect. 5. Transmission of benefit 480
   Sect. 6. Transmission of burden 480
   Sect. 7. Proprietary estoppel 483

13. Mortgages 491
Part 1—Nature of a Mortgage 491
Part 2—Creation of Mortgages 493
   Sect. 1. Legal mortgages and charges of unregistered land .. 493
   Sect. 2. Legal mortgages and charges of registered land ... 497
   Sect. 3. Equitable mortgages and charges 499
Part 3—Rights of the Parties under a Mortgage or Charge ... 501
   Sect. 1. Rights of the mortgagee or chargee—remedies for enforcing
      payment 501
   Sect. 2. Other rights of a mortgagee 513
   Sect. 3. Rights common to both parties 518
   Sect. 4. The right of the mortgagor or chargor to redeem ... 520
   Sect. 5. Other rights of the mortgagor or chargor 526
Part 4—Transfer of Rights 526
   Sect. 1. Death of mortgagor 526
   Sect. 2. Death of mortgagee 527
   Sect. 3. Transfer of equity of redemption *inter vivos* 527
   Sect. 4. Transfer of mortgages *inter vivos* 528

Sect. 5. Discharge of mortgages 529
PART 5—PRIORITY OF MORTGAGES 530
Sect. 1. Priorities as between mortgagees and beneficial co-owners 530
Sect. 2. Priorities as between mortgages of unregistered land 535
Sect. 3. Priorities as between mortgages of registered land 544

14. LIMITATION 547
PART 1—THE LENGTH OF THE PERIOD 549
PART 2—THE RUNNING OF TIME 550
Sect. 1. When time begins to run 550
Sect. 2. Postponement of the period 557
Sect. 3. Starting time running afresh 559
PART 3—THE EFFECT OF THE ELAPSE OF TIME 559
Sect. 1. Title to land 559
Sect. 2. Arrears of income 564

15. OWNERSHIP AND ITS LIMITS 565
PART 1—RIGHTS AND RESTRICTIONS AT COMMON LAW 565
Sect. 1. Rights 565
Sect. 2. Restrictions 568
PART 2—STATUTORY RESTRICTIONS 569
Sect. 1. Planning control 569
Sect. 2. Compulsory purchase 577
Sect. 3. Minerals 579
PART 3—PROTECTION OF TENANTS 580
Sect. 1. Business premises 581
Sect. 2. Agricultural land 584
Sect. 3. Dwellings 590
Sect. 4. Status 617

Index 621

TABLE OF CASES

AEG Unit Trust (Managers) Ltd's Deed, Re [1957] Ch. 415; [1957] 3 W.L.R. 95 246
AG Securities v. Vaughan [1990] 1 A.C. 417; [1988] 3 W.L.R. 1205 .... 304, 341
Abbey National Building Society v. Cann [1991] 1 A.C. 56; [1990] 2 W.L.R. 833 ... 62, 124, 125, 353, 498, 531
Abbey National Mortgages Plc v. Bernard (1996) 71 P. & C.R. 257; [1995] N.P.C. 118 509
Abbeyfield (Harpenden) Society Ltd v. Woods [1968] 1 W.L.R. 374; [1968] 1 All E.R. 352 341
Abbot, Re [1893] 1 Ch. 54 .... 225, 232, 233
Abbott v. Middleton (1858) 7 H.L.C. 68 187
Aberconway's Settlement Trusts, Re [1953] Ch. 647; [1953] 3 W.L.R. 183 277
Abigail v. Lapin [1934] A.C. 491 .... 62, 131, 545
Ackerley, Re [1913] 1 Ch. 510 192
Ackroyd v. Smith (1850) 10 C.B. 164 414
—— v. Smithson (1780) 1 Bro. C.C. 503 183
Adler v. Blackman [1953] 1 Q.B. 146; [1952] 2 All E.R. 945 348
Agra Bank Ltd v. Barry (1874–75) L.R. 7 H.L. 135 537
Ahmed v. Kendrick [1988] 2 F.L.R. 22; (1988) 56 P, & C.R. 121 .... 320, 330
Ailesbury's (Marquis of) Settled Estates, Re [1892] 1 Ch. 506 269
Alan Estates Ltd v. WG Stores Ltd [1982] Ch. 511; [1981] 3 W.L.R. 892 162
Albany Home Loans Ltd v. Massey [1997] 2 All E.R. 609; [1997] 2 F.L.R. 305 501
Aldin v. Latimer Clark Muirhead & Co [1894] 2 Ch. 437 .... 421, 476
Aldred's Case (1610) 9 Co. Rep. 57b 416
Alefounder's Will Trusts, Re [1927] 1 Ch. 360 .... 262, 267
Alfred F Beckett Ltd v. Lyons [1967] Ch. 449; [1967] 2 W.L.R. 421 423
Allen (Deceased) (No.1) [1953] Ch. 810; [1953] 3 W.L.R. 637 42
Allen v. Greenwood [1980] Ch. 119; [1979] 2 W.L.R. 187 445
—— v. Rochdale BC [2000] Ch. 221; [2000] 2 W.L.R. 182 364
Alliance & Leicester Plc v. Slayford [2001] 1 All E.R. (Comm) 1; [2001] C.P. Rep. 52 502
Alliance Building Society v. Pinwill [1958] Ch. 788; [1958] 3 W.L.R. 1 511
Allied Irish Banks v. Glynn [1973] I.R. 188 60
Allied London Investments Ltd v. Hambro Life Assurance Plc (1984) 269 E.G. 41 385
Allott, Re [1924] 2 Ch. 498 231
Alms Corn Charity, Re [1901] 2 Ch. 750 .... 63, 408
Alpenstow Ltd v. Regalian Properties Plc [1985] 1 W.L.R. 721; [1985] 2 All E.R. 545 131
Alvis v. Harrison 1991 S.L.T. 64; (1991) 62 P. & C.R. 10 444
Amec Developments Ltd v. Jury's Hotel Management (UK) Ltd (2001) 82 P. & C.R. 22; [2001] 1 E.G.L.R.
    81 470
Amsprop Trading Ltd v. Harris Distribution Ltd [1997] 1 W.L.R. 1025; [1997] 2 All E.R. 990 455
Anderson v. Stather (1845) 2 Coll.C.C. 209 525
Andrews v. Partington (1791) 3 Bro.C.C. 401 191
Angus & Co v Dalton (1877) 3 Q.B.D. 85 433
Ankerson v. Connelly [1907] 1 Ch. 678, affirming [1906] 2 Ch. 544 .... 443, 446
Ansruther-Gough-Calthorpe v. McOscar [1924] 716 378
Antoniades v. Villiers [1990] 1 A.C. 417; [1988] 3 W.L.R. 139 .... 440, 441
Arden, Re [1935] Ch. 326 57
Arden v. Arden (1885) L.R. 29 Ch. D. 702 541

Argyle Building Society v. Hammond (1985) 49 P. & C.R. 148; (1984) 81 L.S.G. 3425 139
Arkwright's Settlement, Re [1945] Ch. 195 272
Arlesford Trading Co v. Servansingh [1971] 1 W.L.R. 1080; [1971] 3 All E.R. 113 394
Armstrong's Will Trusts [1943] Ch. 400 90
Asco Developments v. Gordon (1978) 248 E.G. 683; [1978] E.G.D. 376 380
Ashburn Anstalt v. WJ Arnold & Co (No.1) [1989] Ch. 1; [1988] 2 All E.R. 147 .... 339, 346, 481, 482
Ashe v. Hogan [1920] 1 I.R. 159 .... 391, 560
Asher v. Whitlock (1865–66) L.R. 1 Q.B. 1 .... 548, 564
Ashfeild v. Ashfeild (1628) W.Jo. 157 203
Ashley Guarantee v. Zacaria [1993] 1 W.L.R. 62; [1993] 1 All E.R. 254 501
Aslan v. Murphy (No.1) and (No.2) [1990] 1 W.L.R. 766; [1989] 3 All E.R. 130 341
Assaf v. Fuwa [1955] A.C. 215; [1954] 3 W.L.R. 552 60
Assets Co Ltd v. Mere Roihi [1905] A.C. 176 140
Aston Cantlow and Wilmcote with Billesley Parochial Church Council v. Wallbank [2001] EWCA Civ 713;
    [2001] 3 W.L.R. 1323 93
Astor's Settlement Trusts, Re [1952] Ch. 534; [1952] 1 All E.R. 1067 239
Atkins Will Trusts, Re [1974] 1 W.L.R. 761; [1974] 2 All E.R. 1 217
Atkinson and Horsell's Contract, Re [1912] 2 Ch. 1 563
Att.-Gen. Ex rel Yorkshire Derwent Trust Ltd v. Brotherton [1992] 1 A.C. 425; [1991] 3 W.L.R. 1126 419
Att.-Gen. of the Duchy of Lancaster v. GE Overton (Farms) Ltd [1982] Ch. 277; [1982] 2 W.L.R. 397 568
Att.-Gen. of Hong Kong v. Humphreys Estate (Queen's Gardens) Ltd [1987] A.C. 114; [1987] 2 W.L.R. 343 487
Att.-Gen. of Southern Nigeria v. John Holt & Co (Liverpool) Ltd [1915] A.C. 599 417
Att.-Gen. v. Biphosphated Guano Co (1879) L.R. 11 Ch. D. 327 537
—— v. Blake [2001] 1 A.C. 268; [2000] 3 W.L.R. 625 470
—— v. British Museum, Trustees of [1903] 2 Ch. 598 568
—— v. Crispin (1784) 1 Bro.C.C. 386 228
—— v. Duke of Marlborough (1813) 3 Madd. 498 45
—— v. Lloyds Bank Ltd [1935] A.C. 382 189
Attwood v. Bovis Homes Ltd [2001] Ch. 379; [2000] 3 W.L.R. 1842; (2001) 82 P. & C.R. 2 .... 447, 448
Austen, In b. (1853) 2 Rob. Ecc. 611 182
Austen, Re [1929] 2 Ch. 155 255
Austerberry v. Oldham Corp (1885) L.R. 29 Ch. D. 750 .... 394, 462
Aynsley v. Glover (1875) 10 Ch. App. 283 435

BHP Petroleum Great Britain Ltd v. Chesterfield Properties Ltd [2001] EWCA Civ 1797; [2002] 2 W.L.R. 672;
    [2002] 1 All E.R. 821 .... 403, 404
BP Pension Trust v. Behrendt (1986) 18 H.L.R. 42; (1986) 52 P. & C.R. 117 361
BP Properties Ltd v. Buckler (1988) 55 P. & C.R. 337; (1987) 284 E.G. 375 .... 552, 559
Backhouse, Re [1921] 2 Ch. 51 225
Backhouse v. Bonomi (1861) 9 H.L.C. 503 417
Bacon v. Bacon [1947] P. 151; [1947] 2 All E.R. 327 254
Bagot's Settlement, Re [1894] 1 Ch. 177 305
Bailey (A Bankrupt), Re [1977] 1 W.L.R. 278; [1977] 2 All E.R. 26 324
Bailey v. Barnes [1894] 1 Ch. 25 .... 60, 61, 505
—— v. Stephens (1862) 12 C.B. (N.S.) 91 414
Baird v. Lord Advocate [1979] A.C. 666; [1979] 2 W.L.R. 369 241
Baker v. Merckel [1960] 1 Q.B. 657; [1960] 2 W.L.R. 492 364
Balfour v. Weston (1786) 1 T.R. 310 375
Ballard's Conveyance, Re [1937] Ch. 473 458
Ballard v. Dyson (1808) 1 Taunt 279 .... 443, 445
Banér v. Sweden (1989) 60 D. & R. 128 .... 92, 93
Bank of Baroda v. Shah [1988] 3 All E.R. 24; [1988] Fin. L.R. 403 530
Bank of Cyprus (London) Ltd v. Gill [1980] 2 Lloyd's Rep. 51 505
Bank of Ireland Home Mortgages Ltd v. Bell [2001] 2 All E.R. (Comm) 920; [2001] 2 F.L.R. 809 ...... 289, 322, 321,
                                                                                                       324
Bank of New South Wales v. O'Connor (1889) L.R. 14 App. Cas. 273 500
Bank of Scotland v. Grimes [1985] Q.B. 1179; [1985] 3 W.L.R. 294 509
Bankes v. Salisbury Diocesan Council of Education Inc [1960] Ch. 631; [1960] 2 W.L.R. 916 38
Bankes v. Small (1887) L.R. 36 Ch. D. 716 47
Banks v. Ripley [1940] Ch. 719 58
Bannister v. Bannister [1948] 2 All E.R. 133; [1948] W.N. 261 .... 254, 317
Barclay v. Barclay [1970] 2 Q.B. 677; [1970] 3 W.L.R. 82 283

Barclays Bank Ltd v. Stasek [1957] Ch. 28; [1956] 3 W.L.R. 760 520
—— v. Taylor [1974] Ch. 137; [1973] 2 W.L.R. 293 .... 129, 131, 500, 545
Barclays Bank Plc v. O'Brien [1994] 1 A.C. 180; [1993] 3 W.L.R. 786 .... 532, 533, 534
Barker v. Faulkner (1898) 79 L.T. 24 423
Barlow's Will Trusts, Re [1979] 1 W.L.R. 278; [1979] 1 All E.R. 296 42
Barnett v. Hassett [1981] 1 W.L.R. 1385; [1982] 1 All E.R. 80 98
Barnhart v. Greenshields (1853) 9 Moo P.C. 18 .... 61, 520
Barrett v. Hilton Developments Ltd [1975] Ch. 237; [1974] 3 W.L.R. 545 101
—— v. Lounova (1982) Ltd [1990] 1 Q.B. 348; [1989] 2 W.L.R. 137 372
—— v. Morgan [2000] 2 A.C. 264; [2000] 2 W.L.R. 284 365
Barrington (Viscount) v. Liddell (1852) 2 De G.M. & G. 480 245
Bartlett v. Barclays Bank Trust Co Ltd (No.2) [1980] Ch. 515; [1980] 2 W.L.R. 430 558
Barton v. Morris [1985] 1 W.L.R. 1257; [1985] 2 All E.R. 1032 331
Basham (Deceased), Re [1986] 1 W.L.R. 1498; [1987] 1 All E.R. 405 486
Bass Ltd's Application (1973) 26 P. & C.R. 156 472
Bass v. Gregory (1890) L.R. 25 Q.B.D. 481 .... 416, 448
Bassett v. Nosworthy (1673) Rep. T. Finch 102 59
Bassil v. Lister (1851) 9 Hare 177 246
Batchelor v. Marlow (No.2) [2001] EWCA Civ 1051; (2001) 82 P. & C.R. 36 417
Bateman v. Hotchkin (1847) 10 Beav. 426 245
Bathavon Rural DC v, Carlile 1958] 1 Q.B. 461; [1958] 2 W.L.R. 545 349
Bathurst (Earl) v. Fine [1974] 1 W.L.R. 905; [1974] 2 All E.R. 1160 .... 362, 363
Batt v. Adams [2001] 32 E.G. 90; [2001] 21 E.G.C.S. 164; (2001) 82 P. & C.R. 406 .... 551, 552, 554
Battersea Freehold & Leasehold Property Co Ltd v. Wandsworth LBC 2001) 82 P. & C.R. 12; [2001] 19 E.G.
    148 552
Battersea (Lord) v. Commissioners of Sewers for the City of London [1895] 2 Ch. 708 435
Battlespring v. Gates (1984) 11 H.L.R. 6; (1983) 268 E.G. 355 595
Baxendale v. Instow Parish Council [1982] Ch. 14; [1981] 2 W.L.R. 1055 566
—— v. McMurray (1867) 2 Ch. App. 790 447
Baxter v. Four Oaks Properties [1965] Ch. 816; [1965] 2 W.L.R. 1115 460
Bayley v. Great Western Railway (1884) L.R. 26 Ch. D. 434 426
Baynes & Co v. Lloyd & Sons [1895] 2 Q.B. 610 368
Beadle (Deceased), Re [1974] 1 W.L.R. 417; [1974] 1 All E.R. 493 177
Beale's Settlement Trusts, Re [1932] 2 Ch. 15 285
Bealey v. Shaw (1805) 6 East 208 433
Bean, Re [1944] P. 83; [1944] 2 All E.R. 348 177
Beaney (Deceased), Re [1978] 1 W.L.R. 770; [1978] 2 All E.R. 595 .... 205, 206
Beardman v. Wilson (1868) L.R. 4 C.P. 57 .... 352, 496
Beaumont Settled Estates, Re [1937] 2 All E.R. 353 280
Beesly v. Hallwood Estates [1961] Ch. 105; [1961] 2 W.L.R. 36, 162, CA; affirming [1960] 1 W.L.R. 549;
    [1960] 2 All E.R. 314 .... 162, 486
Belfast Corp v. OD Cars [1960] A.C. 490; [1960] 2 W.L.R. 148 576
Belgravia Insurance Co v. Meah1964] 1 Q.B. 436; [1963] 3 W.L.R. 1033 .... 359, 364
Bell Street Investments v. Wood (1970) 216 E.G. 585; [1970] E.G.D. 812 344
Bell v. Peter Browne & Co [1990] 2 Q.B. 495; [1990] 3 W.L.R. 510 105
Belvedere Court Management Ltd v. Frogmore Developments Ltd [1997] Q.B. 858; [1996] 3 W.L.R. 1008 612
Bence, Re [1891] 3 Ch. 242 226
Bendall v. McWhirter [1952] 2 Q.B. 466; [1952] 1 All E.R. 1307 98
Benn v. Hardinge (1992) 66 P. & C.R. 246 442
Benson v. Chester (1799) 8 T.R. 396 449
Bentley, Re (1885) 54 L.J. Ch. 782 257
Berenyi v. Watford BC (1980) 256 E.G. 271 377
Berkeley (Earl of), Re [1968] Ch. 744; [1968] 3 All E.R. 364 .... 241, 243
Berkeley Road (88), NW9, Re [1971] Ch. 648; [1971] 2 W.L.R. 307 332
Berkley v. Poulett [1977] 1 E.G.L.R. 86; (1977) 241 E.G. 911; [1977] E.G.D. 754 .... 20, 21
Bernard v. Josephs 1982] Ch. 391; [1982] 2 W.L.R. 1052 323
Bernstein (Lord) v. Skyviews and General Ltd [1978] Q.B. 479; [1977] 3 W.L.R. 136 568
Berry v Geen [1938] A.C. 575 244
Beswick v. Beswick [1968] A.C. 58; [1967] 3 W.L.R. 932 .... 16, 455
Bettison v. Langton [2001] UKHL 24; [2002] 1 A.C. 27; [2001] 2 W.L.R. 1605 449
Betty's Cafes Ltd v. Phillips Furnishing Stores Ltd (No.1)[1959] A.C. 20; [1958] 2 W.L.R. 513 583
Bevan v. Johnson [1990] 28 E.G. 113; [1990] 2 E.G.L.R. 33 .... 263, 271, 279

Bewick v. Whitfield (1734) 3 P.Wms. 267 51
Biggs v. Hoddinott [1898] 2 Ch. 307 521
Biles v. Caesar [1957] 1 W.L.R. 156; [1957] 1 All E.R. 151 198
Birchall, Re (1889) 40 Ch. D. 436 297
Billson v. Residential Apartments Ltd (No.1) [1992] 1 A.C. 494; [1992] 2 W.L.R. 15 .... 356, 357, 362, 363
Binions v. Evans [1972] Ch. 359; [1972] 2 W.L.R. 729 .... 254, 481, 482
Birch v. Wright (1786) 1 T.R. 378 507
Bircham & Co Nominees (2) v. Worrall Holdings Ltd (2001) 82 P. & C.R. 34 .... 67, 96
Bird v. Syme-Thompson [1979] 1 W.L.R. 440; [1978] 3 All E.R. 1027 .... 62, 125
Birmingham Citizens Permanent Building Society v. Caunt [1962] Ch. 883; [1962] 2 W.L.R. 323 508
Birmingham Corp v. West Midland Baptist (Trust) Association Inc [1970] A.C. 874; [1969] 3 W.L.R. 389 579
Birmingham Midshires Mortgage Services Ltd v. Sabherwal (Equitable Interest) (2000) 80 P. & C.R. 256 489
Birrell v. Carey (1989) 58 P. & C.R. 184 346
Bishop v. Bonham [1988] 1 W.L.R. 742; (1988) 4 B.C.C. 347 506
Bishop v. Plumley [1991] 1 W.L.R. 582; [1991] 1 All E.R. 236 173
Blacklocks v. JB Developments (Godalming) Ltd [1982] Ch. 183; [1981] 3 W.L.R. 554 .... 61, 124
Blackstone(David) Ltd v. Burnetts (West End) Ltd [1973] 1 W.L.R. 1487; [1973] 3 All E.R. 782 356
Blade v. Higgs (1865) 11 H.L.C. 621 566
Blaiberg and Abrahams, Re [1899] 2 Ch. 340 527
Bland v. Ingrams Estates Ltd (No.1) [2001] Ch. 767; [2001] 2 W.L.R. 1638 .... 359, 360, 364
—— v. Ingrams Estates Ltd (No.2) [2001] EWCA Civ 1088; [2002] 2 W.L.R. 361 .... 358, 359, 360, 363
—— v. Yates (1914) 58 S.J. 612 568
Blathwayt v. Baron Cawley [1976] A.C. 397; [1975] 3 W.L.R. 684 42
Bleakley v. Smith (1840) 11 Sim. 150 153
Bleckly (Deceased), Re [1951] Ch. 740; [1951] 1 All E.R. 1064 191
Bligh v. Martin [1968] 1 W.L.R. 804; [1968] 1 All E.R. 1157 552
Blount v. Layard [1891] 2 Ch. 681 567
Bocardo SA v. S & M Hotels Ltd [1980] 1 W.L.R. 17; [1979] 3 All E.R. 737 377
Bolton v. Buckenham [1891] 1 Q.B. 278 502
Bone v. Bone [1992] E.G.C.S. 81 479
Boosey v. Davis (1988) 55 P. & C.R. 83 552
Booth, Re [1926] P. 118 183
Boots The Chemist Ltd v. Street (1983) 268 E.G. 817; [1983] E.G.D. 251 61
Boreham v. Bignall (1850) 8 Hare 131 212
Borman v. Griffith [1930] 1 Ch. 493 .... 429, 430
Bostock's Settlement, Re [1921] 2 Ch. 469 58
Boston's Will Trusts, Re [1956] Ch. 395; [1956] 2 W.L.R. 700 279
Bothe v. Amos [1976] Fam. 46; [1975] 2 W.L.R. 838 319
Bourne v. Keane [1919] A.C. 815 239
Bourne's Settlement Trusts, Re [1946] 1 All E.R. 411 245
Boustany v. Piggott (1995) 69 P. & C.R. 298; [1993] E.G.C.S. 85 367
Bovill v. Endle [1896] 1 Ch. 648 524
Bowe, (Trustee of the Estate of) (A Bankrupt) v. Bowe [1998] 2 F.L.R. 439; [1997] B.P.I.R. 747 325
Bowen Burscarlet's Will Trusts, Re [1972] Ch. 463; [1971] 3 W.L.R. 742 195
Bowles.'s (Lewis) Case (1615) 11 Co. Rep. 79b 50
Bowring-Hanbury's Trustee v. Bowring-Hanbury [1943] Ch. 104 550
Boyer v Warbey (No.1) [1953] 1 Q.B. 234; [1953] 1 All E.R. 269 .... 388, 390, 395
Boyer's Settled Estates, Re [1916] 2 Ch. 404 254
Boyes v. Cook (1880) L.R. 14 Ch. D. 53 188
Boyle's Claim, Re [1961] 1 W.L.R. 339; [1961] 1 All E.R. 620 143
Bozon v. Williams (1829) 3 Y. & J. 151 500
Bradley v. Carritt [1903] A.C. 253 522
—— v. Peixoto (1797) 3 Ves. 324 43
Bradshaw (Deceased), Re [1950] Ch. 78; [1949] 2 All E.R. 905 283
Bradwell, Re [1952] Ch. 575;[1952] 2 All E.R. 286 243
Branchett v. Beaney, Coster & Swale BC [1992] 3 All E.R. 910; (1992) 24 H.L.R. 348 369
Brandon v. Robinson (1811) 18 Ves. 429 48
Brassington, In b. [1902] P. 1 180
Bravda, In the Estate of [1968] 1 W.L.R. 479; [1968] 2 All E.R. 217 185
Breams Property Investments Co v. Strouger 1948] 2 K.B. 1; [1948] 1 All E.R. 758 .... 348, 387
Brent's Case (1583) 2 Leon. 14 65
Brett v. Cumberland (1619) Cro.Jac. 521 392

Brew Brothers Ltd v. Snax (Ross) Ltd [1970] 1 Q.B. 612; [1969] 3 W.L.R. 657 378
Bridges v. Mees [1957] Ch. 475; [1957] 3 W.L.R. 215 123
Bridgett and Haye's Contract, Re [1928] Ch. 163 267
Bridgewater, In the Estate of [1965] 1 W.L.R. 416; [1965] 1 All E.R. 717 180
Bridgman v. Daw (1891) 40 W.R. 253 528
Bridle v. Ruby [1989] Q.B. 169; [1988] 3 W.L.R. 191; (1988) 56 P. & C.R. 155 431
Bright v. Walker (1834) 1 Cr.M. & R. 211 .... 431, 437, 438
Brikom Investments Ltd v. Seaford [1981] 1 W.L.R. 863; [1981] 2 All E.R. 783 370
Briscow v. Kenrick (1832) 1 L.J.Ch. 11 525
Bristol and West Building Society v. Henning [1985] 1 W.L.R. 778; [1985] 2 All E.R. 606 .... 62, 532
Bristow v. Boothby (1826) 2 Sim. & St. 465 237
Bristow v. Wood (1844) 1 Coll.C.C. 480 468
Britannia Building Society v. Earl [1990] 1 W.L.R. 422; [1990] 2 All E.R. 469 .... 510, 519
British Museum Trustees v. Finnis (1833) 5 C. & P. 460 419
British Railways Board v. Glass [1965] Ch. 538; [1964] 3 W.L.R. 913 445
Brocklebank v. Thompson [1903] 2 Ch. 344 415
Bromley Park Garden Estates Ltd v. Moss [1982] 1 W.L.R. 1019; [1982] 2 All E.R. 890 377
Brooks Settlement Trusts, Re [1939] Ch. 993 212
Broomfield v. Williams [1897] 1 Ch. 602 426
Brotherton v. Inland Revenue Commissioners [1978] 1 W.L.R. 610; [1978] 2 All E.R. 267 .... 212, 244
Brougham and Vaux's Settled Estates, Re [1954] Ch. 24; [1953] 3 W.L.R. 465 275
Brown, Re (1886) 32 Ch.D. 597 249
——, Re [1954] Ch. 39; [1953] 3 W.L.R. 877 43
—— v. Brash [1948] 2 K.B. 247; [1948] 1 All E.R. 922 594
—— v. Cole (1845) 14 Sim. 427 493
—— v. Gould [1972] Ch. 53; [1971] 3 W.L.R. 334 .... 43, 151, 291
—— v. Liverpool Corp [1969] 3 All E.R. 1345 371
—— v. Raindle (1796) 3 Ves. 256 330
Browne v. Flower [1911] 1 Ch. 219; [1908–10] All E.R. Rep. 547 .... 369, 416
—— v. Savage (1859) 4 Drew. 635 542
Bruce v. Marquess of Ailesbury [1892] A.C. 356 249
Brumfitt v. Roberts (1870) L.R. 5 C.P. 224 449
Brunner v. Greenslade [1971] Ch. 993; [1970] 3 W.L.R. 891 .... 460, 461
Bruton v. London & Quadrant Housing Trust [2000] 1 A.C. 406; [1999] 3 W.L.R. 150 .... 340, 352
Bryant v. Foot (1867) L.R. 2 Q.B. 161 .... 432, 433
Bryant v. Lefever (1878–79) L.R. 4 C.P.D. 172 .... 416, 434, 448
Buchanan-Wollaston's Conveyance, Re [1939] Ch. 738; [1939] 2 All E.R. 302;[1939] Ch. 217 ...... 282, 310
Buckby v. Coles (1814) 5 Taunt. 311 .... 415, 443
Buckinghamshire CC v. Moran [1990] Ch. 623; [1989] 3 W.L.R. 152 .... 548, 551, 552, 553
Buckland v. Butterfield (1820) 2 Brod. & B. 54 20
Budd Scott v. Daniell [1902] 2 K.B. 351 368
Bull v. Bull [1955] 1 Q.B. 234; [1955] 2 W.L.R. 78 .... 287, 304, 310, 323
Bulstrode v. Lambert [1953] 1 W.L.R. 1064; [1953] 2 All E.R. 728 425
Burchell v. Hornsby (1808) 1 Camp. 360 373
Burgess v. Rawnsley [1975] Ch. 429; [1975] 3 W.L.R. 99 .... 330, 331, 332
Burnett (Marjorie) Ltd v. Barclay (1980) 258 E.G. 642; 125 S.J. 199 351
Burns v. Anthony (1997) 74 P. & C.R. D41 552
Burns v. Burns 1984] Ch. 317; [1984] 2 W.L.R. 582 319
Burroughs-Fowler, Re [1916] 2 Ch. 251 41
Bushwall Properties Ltd v. Vortex Properties Ltd [1976] 1 W.L.R. 591; [1976] 2 All E.R. 283 151
Butler, Re [1918] 1 I.R. 394 184
Butler v. Fairclough (1917) 23 C.L.R. 78 545
—— v. Manchester Sheffield & Lincolnshire Railway Co (1888) L.R. 21 Q.B.D. 207 478

CIBC Mortgages Plc v. Pitt [1994] 1 A.C. 200; [1993] 3 W.L.R. 802 533
Cable v. Bryant [1908] 1 Ch. 259 .... 416, 448
Cadell v. Palmer (1833) 1 Cl. & F. 372 .... 215, 219, 221, 240
Caerphilly Concrete Products v. Owen [1972] 1 W.L.R. 372; [1972] 1 All E.R. 248 351
Caldy Manor Estate v. Farrell [1974] 1 W.L.R. 1303; [1974] 3 All E.R. 753 43
Calgary and Edmonton Land Co Ltd v. Dobinson [1974] Ch. 102; [1974] 2 W.L.R. 143 .... 99, 107
Calisher v. Forbes (1871–72) L.R. 7 Ch. App. 109 541
Callaway, Re [1956] Ch. 559; [1956] 3 W.L.R. 257 186

Camden (Maquis) v. Batterbury (1860) 7 C.B.N.S. 864 394
Campbell v. Holyland (1877–78) L.R. 7 Ch. D. 166; (1877) 26 W.R. 160 504
Campden Hill Towers Ltd v. Gardner [1977] Q.B. 823; [1977] 2 W.L.R. 159 .... 370, 371
Canas Property Co v. KL Television Services [1970] 2 Q.B. 433; [1970] 2 W.L.R. 1133 356
Canham v. Fisk (1831) 2 Cr. & J. 126 443
Cannon v. Villars (1878) 8 Ch.D. 415 444
Capital & Counties Bank Ltd v. Rhodes [1903] 1 Ch. 631 412
Capital Investments v. Wednesfield Urban DC [1965] Ch. 774; [1964] 2 W.L.R. 932 96
Cardigan v. Curzon-Howe (1885) L.R. 30 Ch. D. 5 269
Cargill v. Gotts [1981] 1 W.L.R. 441; [1981] 1 All E.R. 682 .... 447, 448, 567
Carnarvon's (Earl of) Chesterfield Settled Estates, Re [1927] 1 Ch. 138 277
Carnell v. Harrison [1916] 1 Ch. 328 203
Carne's Settled Estates, Re [1899] 1 Ch. 324 .... 254, 256
Carr v. Lynch [1900] 1 Ch. 613 151
Carr-Saunders v. Dick McNeil Associates Ltd [1986] 1 W.L.R. 922; [1986] 2 All E.R. 888 446
Carter v. Wake (1876–77) L.R. 4 Ch. D. 605 502
Cartwright, Re (1889) L.R. 41 Ch. D. 532 49
——, Re [1939] Ch. 90 90
Casborne v. Scarfe (1738) 1 Atk. 603 493
Castellain v. Preston (1882–83) L.R. 11 Q.B.D. 380 155
Castle Bytham (Vicar of), Ex p. [1895] 1 Ch. 348 38
Cater v. Essex CC [1960] 1 Q.B. 424; [1959] 2 W.L.R. 739 573
Catling, Re [1931] 2 Ch. 359 255
Cator v. Newton [1940] 1 K.B. 415 462
Cattell, Re [1914] 1 Ch. 177 242
Caunce v. Caunce [1969] 1 W.L.R. 286; [1969] 1 All E.R. 722 .... 9, 10, 62, 110, 320, 531
Cave v. Cave (1880) L.R. 15 Ch. D. 639 60
Celsteel Ltd v. Alton House Holdings Ltd (No.1) [1986] 1 W.L.R. 512; [1986] 1 All E.R. 608; [1985] 1 W.L.R.
    204; [1982] 2 All E.R. 562 .... 122, 482, 489
Celsteel Ltd v. Alton House Holdings Ltd (No.2) [1987] 1 W.L.R. 291; [1987] 2 All E.R. 240; CA; affirming
    [1986] 1 W.L.R. 666; [1986] 1 All E.R. 598 394
Centaploy Ltd v. Matlodge Ltd [1974] Ch. 1; [1973] 2 W.L.R. 832 348
Central Estates (Belgravia) Ltd v. Woolgar (No.2) [1972] 1 W.L.R. 1048; [1972] 3 All E.R. 610 .... 356, 363
Central London Commercial Estates Ltd v. Kato Kagaku Ltd [1998] 4 All E.R. 948; [1998] 3 E.G.L.R. 55 561,
    562
Centrovincial Estates Plc v. Bulk Storage Ltd (1983) 46 P. & C.R. 393; (1983) 268 E.G. 59 385
Chaffe v. Kingsley (2000) 79 P. & C.R. 404; [2000] 1 E.G.L.R. 104 428
Chalmers v. Pardoe [1963] 1 W.L.R. 677; [1963] 3 All E.R. 552 486
Chamberlaine v. Scally [1992] E.G.C.S. 90 364
Chamberlayne v. Brockett (1872) 8 Ch. App. 206 .... 237, 239, 240
Chambers Will Trusts, Re [1950] Ch. 267; 66 T.L.R. (Pt. 1) 595 230
Chambers v. Kingham (1878) 10 Ch. D. 743 365
—— v. Randall [1923] 1 Ch. 149 456
Chandler v. Bradley [1897] 1 Ch. 315 .... 263, 459
—— v. Kerley [1978] 1 W.L.R. 693; [1978] 2 All E.R. 942 479
Chaplin v. Chaplin (1773) 3 P. Wms. 229 408
—— v. Young (No. 1) (1863) 33 Beav. 330 507
Chapman and Hobbs (1885) 29 Ch. D. 1007 366
Chapman v. Edwards [1938] 2 All e.r. 507 414
—— v. Smith [1907] 2 Ch. 97 518
—— v. Tanner (1684) 1 Vern. 267 492
Chardon, Re [1928] Ch. 464 .... 229, 240
Charles Semon & Co Ltd v. Bradford Corp [1922] 2 Ch. 737 446
Charsley v. Jones (1889) 53 J.P. 280 370
Chartered Trust Plc v. Davies (1998) 76 P. & C.R. 396; [1997] 2 E.G.L.R. 83 367
Chartres, Re [1927] 1 Ch. 466 191
Chasemore v. Richards (1859) 7 H.L. Cas. 349 .... 416, 447, 566
Chatham Empire Theatre (1955) Ltd v. Ultrans Ltd [1961] 1 W.L.R. 817; [1961] 2 All E.R. 381 364
Chatsworth Properties v. Effiom [1971] 1 W.L.R. 144; [1971] 1 All E.R. 604 511
Chatsworth Estates Co v. Fewell [1931] 1 Ch. 224 471
Cheah Theam Swee v. Equiticorp Finance Group Ltd [1992] 1 A.C. 472; [1992] 2 W.L.R. 108 530
Cheese v. Lovejoy (No.2) (1876–77) L.R. 2 P.D. 251 [1876 H. 16.] 179, 180

Cheltenham & Gloucester Building Society v. Norgan [1996] 1 W.L.R. 343; [1996] 1 All E.R. 449 509
Cheltenham & Gloucester Plc v. Booker [1997] 1 F.L.R. 311; (1997) 29 H.L.R. 634; (1997) 73 P. & C.R. 412 .... 508, 509
—— v. Krausz [1997] 1 W.L.R. 1558; [1997] 1 All E.R. 21 510
Chester v. Buckingham Travel Ltd [1981] 1 W.L.R. 96; [1981] 1 All E.R. 386 375
Chesterfield's (Lord) Settled Estates, Re [1911] 1 Ch. 237 23
Chesterfield (Lord) v. Harris [1911] A.C. 623; affirming [1908] 2 Ch. 397 .... 415, 422
Cheverell Estates Ltd v. Harris [1998] 1 E.G.L.R. 27; [1998] 02 E.G. 127 387
Chhokar v. Chhokar [1984] Fam. Law 269; (1983) 80 L.S.G. 3243; (1983) 5 F.L.R. 313 .... 125, 287, 305, 323
Childers v. Childers (1857) 1 De G. and J. 482 294
China and South Seas Bank Ltd v. Tan [1990] 1 A.C. 536; [1990] 2 W.L.R. 56 .... 501, 505
Chowood Ltd v. Lyall (No.2) [1930] 2 Ch. 156 .... 139, 140
Chowood's Registered Land, Re [1933] Ch. 574 143
Chrisdell v. Johnson and Tickner (1987) 19 H.L.R. 406; (1987) 54 P. & C.R. 257 356
Christie v. Barker (1884) 53 L.J.Q.B. 537 410
Chudleigh's Case (1595) 1 Co. Rep. 113b 64
Church Commissioners for England v. Nodjoumi (1986) 51 P. & C.R. 155; (1985) 135 N.L.J. 1185 356
Church of England Building Society v. Piskor [1954] Ch. 553; [1954] 2 W.L.R. 952 353
Churston Settled Estates, Re [1954] Ch. 334; [1954] 2 W.L.R. 386 232
Citibank Trust v. Ayivor [1987] 1 W.L.R. 1157; [1987] 3 All E.R. 241 509
Citro (Domenico) (A Bankrupt), Re [1991] Ch. 142; [1990] 3 W.L.R. 880 324
City and Metropolitan Properties Ltd v. Greycroft [1987] 1 W.L.R. 1085; [1987] 3 All E.R. 839; (1987) 54 P. & C.R. 266 394
City of London Building Society v. Flegg [1988] A.C. 54; [1987] 2 W.L.R. 1266 ... 9, 10, 86, 87, 124, 310, 311, 313, 319, 320, 530
City of London Corp v. Fell [1994] 1 A.C. 458; [1993] 3 W.L.R. 1164 385
City Permanent Building Society v. Miller [1952] Ch. 840; [1952] 2 All E.R. 621 123
Cityland and Property (Holdings) Ltd v. Dabrah [1968] Ch. 166; [1967] 3 W.L.R. 605 .... 495, 522, 524
Claridge v. Tingey [1967] 1 W.L.R. 134; [1966] 3 All E.R. 935 .... 139, 142
Clark, In b. (1839) 2 Curt. 329 177
Clark v. Barnes [1929] 2 Ch. 368 430
Clarke v. Grant [1950] 1 K.B. 104; [1949] 1 All E.R. 768 .... 347, 349
—— v. Ramuz [1891] 2 Q.B. 456 155
Clarke (Richard) & Co Ltd v. Widnall [1976] 1 W.L.R. 845; [1976] 3 All E.R. 301 360
Clarke (W G) (Properties) v. Dupre Properties [1992] Ch. 297; [1991] 3 W.L.R. 579 .... 354, 360, 361
Claughton v. Charalambous [1998] B.P.I.R. 588 325
Clayhope Properties Ltd v. Evans and Jennings [1986] 1 W.L.R. 1223; [1986] 2 All E.R. 795 .... 100, 131
Clayton v. Corby (1842) 2 Q.B. 813 437
—— v. Ramsden [1943] A.C. 320; [1943] 1 All E.R. 16 42
Clayton's Deed Poll, Re [1980] Ch. 99; [1979] 3 W.L.R. 351 80
Cleaver (Deceased), Re 1981] 1 W.L.R. 939; [1981] 2 All E.R. 1018 176
Cleveland Petroleum Co Ltd v. Dartstone Ltd (No.1)[1969] 1 W.L.R. 116; [1969] 1 All E.R. 201 469
Clifford's Settlement Trusts, Re [1981] Ch. 63; [1980] 2 W.L.R. 749 191
Clifford v. Holt [1899] 1 Ch. 698 439
Clifton v. Viscount Bury (1887) 4 T.L.R. 8 569
Clore v. Theatrical Properties Ltd [1936] 3 All E.R. 483 480
Clough v. Killey [1996] N.P.C. 38; (1996) 72 P. & C.R. D22 .... 316, 317
Clout and Frewer's Contract [1924] 2 Ch. 230 297
Coates v. Diment [1951] 1 All E.R. 890 589
Coatsworth v. Johnson (1886) 55 L.J.Q.B. 220 344
Cockerill, Re [1929] 2 Ch. 131 43
Cocks v. Manners (1871) L.R. 12 Eq. 574 238
Cohen's Will Trusts [1936] 1 All E.R. 103 190
Colchester BC v. Smith [1992] Ch. 421; [1992] 2 W.L.R. 728 559
Colchester Estates (Cardiff) v. Carlton Industries Plc [1986] Ch. 80; [1984] 3 W.L.R. 693 380
Coldunell v. Gallon [1986] Q.B. 1184; [1986] 2 W.L.R. 466 530
Cole v. Kelly [1920] 2 K.B. 106 349
Colebrook's Conveyance, Re [1972] 1 W.L.R. 1397; [1973] 1 All E.R. 132 60
Colegrave v. Dias Santos (1823) 2 B. & C. 76 23
Coleman, Re [1936] Ch. 528 225
Coleman (Deceased), Re [1976] Ch. 1; [1975] 2 W.L.R. 213 .... 180, 181
Collings v. Lee [2001] 2 All E.R. 332; (2001) 82 P. & C.R. 3 .... 123, 316

Collins (Deceased) [1975] 1 W.L.R. 309; [1975] 1 All E.R. 321 194
—— (Deceased), Re [1990] Fam. 56; [1990] 2 W.L.R. 161 193
Collins v. Elstone [1893] P. 1 179
—— v. Slade (1874) 23 W.R. 199 443
Collison v. Lettsom (1815) 6 Taunt 224 388
Colls v. Home & Colonial Stores Ltd [1904] A.C. 179 .... 416, 440, 445
Colyer v. Finch (1856) 5 H.L.C. 905 538
Commercial Union Life Assurance Co Ltd v. Moustafa [1999] L. & T.R. 489; [1999] 2 E.G.L.R. 44 .... 386, 402
Commissioner for Railways v. Valuer General [1974] A.C. 328; [1973] 2 W.L.R. 1021 566
Commissioner of Stamp Duties (Queensland) v. Livingston [1965] A.C. 694; [1964] 3 W.L.R. 963 200
Commissioners of Sewers v. Glasse (1874–75) L.R. 19 Eq. 134 422
Congleton Corporation v. Pattison (1808) 10 East 130 388
Cook, In the Estate of [1960] 1 W.L.R. 353; [1960] 1 All E.R. 689 177
Cook, Re [1948] Ch. 212; [1948] 1 All E.R. 231 .... 283, 312
Coomber v. Howard (1845) 1 C.B. 440 375
Coombes v. Smith [1986] 1 W.L.R. 808; [1987] 1 F.L.R. 352 484
Coombs v. Wilkes [1891] 3 Ch. 77 151
Cooper v. Critchley 1955] Ch. 431; [1955] 2 W.L.R. 510 283
Cooperative Insurance Society Ltd v. Argyll Stores (Holdings) Ltd 1998] A.C. 1; [1997] 2 W.L.R. 898 368
Cooper's Conveyance Trusts, Re [1956] 1 W.L.R. 1096; [1956] 3 All E.R. 28 230
Copeland v. Greenhalf [1952] Ch. 488; [1952] 1 All E.R. 809 417
Corbet's Case (1585) 7 Co. Rep. 5a 449
Corbett v. Hill (1869–70) L.R. 9 Eq. 671 566
Cordell v. Second Clanfield Properties Ltd 1969] 2 Ch. 9; [1968] 3 W.L.R. 864 425
Cornish v. Brook Green Laundry [1959] 1 Q.B. 394; [1959] 2 W.L.R. 215 344
—— v. Stubbs (1869–70) L.R. 5 C.P. 334 478
Coronation Street Industrial Properties Ltd v. Ingall Industries Plc [1989] 1 W.L.R. 304; [1989] 1 All E.R.
  979 .... 388, 392, 394, 456
Cotching v. Bassett (1862) 32 Beav. 101 487
Cotterell v. Price [1960] 1 W.L.R. 1097; [1960] 3 All E.R. 315 555
Courtney & Fairbairn Ltd v. Tolaini Brothers (Hotels) Ltd [1975] 1 W.L.R. 297; [1975] 1 All E.R. 716 151
Cousins (Mortgages: Priority), Re (1886) L.R. 31 Ch. D. 671 63
Coventry (Deceased), Re [1980] Ch. 461; [1979] 3 W.L.R. 802 174
Coventry's (Earl of) Indentures, Re [1974] Ch. 77; [1973] 3 W.L.R. 122 232
Cowan v. Wrayford [1953] 1 W.L.R. 1340; [1953] 2 All E.R. 113 586
Cowcher v. Cowcher [1972] 1 W.L.R. 425; [1972] 1 All E.R. 943 313
Cox & Neve's Contract, Re [1891] 2 Ch. 109 63
Cox v. Bishop (1857) 8 De G.M. & G. 815 .... 391, 394, 397
—— v. Middleton (1854) 2 Drew 209 151
Crabb v. Arun DC (No.1) [1976] Ch. 179; [1975] 3 W.L.R. 847 .... 69, 424, 485, 486, 487, 488
Crago v. Julian [1992] 1 W.L.R. 372; [1992] 1 All E.R. 744 .... 68, 353
Crawley v. Crawley (1835) 7 Sim. 427 244
Cray v. Willis (1729) 2 P. Wms. 529 328
Credit Lyonnais Bank Nederland NV v. Burch [1997] 1 All E.R. 144; [1996] 5 Bank. L.R. 233 .... 533, 534
Cresswell v. Cresswell (1868) L.R. 6 Eq. 69 186
Cricklewood Property & Investment Trust Ltd v. Leightons Investment Trust Ltd [1945] A.C. 221; [1945] 1
  All E.R. 252 366
Cromwell Property Investment Co Ltd v. Western [1934] Ch. 322 524
Cross v. Jordan (1853) 8 Exch. 149 357
Crow v. Wood [1971] 1 Q.B. 77; [1970] 3 W.L.R. 516 .... 416, 417, 426
Crown Lands Commissioners v. Page [1960] 2 Q.B. 274; [1960] 3 W.L.R. 446 368
Croydon (Unique) Ltd v. Wright [2001] Ch. 318; [2000] 2 W.L.R. 683; [1999] 4 All E.R. 257 ...... 359, 363, 364
Cubitt v. Maxse (1872–73) L.R. 8 C.P. 704 418
Cubitt v. Porter (1828) 8 B. & C. 257 .... 333, 334
Cuckmere Brick Co v. Mutual Finance [1971] Ch. 949; [1971] 2 W.L.R. 1207 506
Cugny's Will Trusts, Re [1931] 1 Ch. 305 .... 265, 267
Cumberland Consolidated Holdings Ltd v. Ireland [1946] K.B. 264 155
Cumberland Court (Brighton) Ltd v. Taylor [1964] Ch. 29; [1963] 3 W.L.R. 313 529
Cumberland's (Countess of) Case (1610) Moo.K.B. 812 49
Cummins, Re, Cummins v. Thompson [1972] Ch. 62; [1971] 3 W.L.R. 580 319
—— v. Fletcher (1880) L.R. 14 Ch. D. 699 515
Curryer's Will Trusts, Re [1938] Ch. 952 226

Curtis v. Lukin (1842) 5 Beav. 147 .... 243, 246
Cuthbertson v. Irving (1859) 4 H. & N. 742; (1860) 6 H. & N. 135 352

DHN Food Distributors v. Tower Hamlets LBC [1976] 1 W.L.R. 852; [1976] 3 All E.R. 462 482
D (J), Re [1982] Ch. 237; [1982] 2 W.L.R. 373 205
DWS (Deceased), Re [2001] Ch. 568; [2000] 3 W.L.R. 1910; [2001] W.T.L.R. 445 186
Da Costa, Re [1912] 1 Ch. 337 42
Dallas, Re [1904] 2 Ch. 385 540
Dalton v. Henry Angus & Co (1880–81) L.R. 6 App. Cas. 740 .... 430, 431, 433, 438, 441
Damper v. Bassett [1901] 2 Ch. 350 440
Dance v. Triplow (1991) 63 P. & C.R. 1 435
Dances Way, West Town, Hayling Island, Re [1962] Ch. 490; [1962] 2 W.L.R. 815 .... 129, 140
Daniel v. North (1809) 11 East 372 431
—— v. Walker [2000] 1 W.L.R. 1382 93
Daniels, Re (1918) 87 L.J. Ch. 661 192
Dare v. Heathcote (1856) 25 L.J. Ex. 245 432
Dartstone Ltd v. Cleveland Petroleum Co Ltd (No.2) [1969] 1 W.L.R. 1807; [1969] 3 All E.R. 668 .... 96, 109, 396,
406, 470
Dashwood v. Magniac [1891] 3 Ch. 306 .... 49, 50
Davenport v. R. (1877) 3 App. Cas. 115 356
Davey v. Durrant (1857) 1 De G. & J. 535 505
Davies, In b. (1850) 2 Rob. Ecc. 337 178
Davies v. Beynon-Harris (1931) 47 T.L.R. 424 204
—— v. Du Paver [1953] 1 Q.B. 184; [1952] 2 All E.R. 991 .... 435, 438
—— v. Stephens (1836) 7 C. & P. 570 445
—— v. Sweet [1962] 2 Q.B. 300; [1962] 2 W.L.R. 525 151
Davis v. Richards and Wallington Industries Ltd [1990] 1 W.L.R. 1511; [1991] 2 All E.R. 563 315
—— v. Whitby [1974] Ch. 186; [1974] 2 W.L.R. 333 432
Davron Estates Ltd v. Turnshire Ltd (1982) 133 N.L.J. 937 155
Dawes v. Hawkins (1860) 8 C.B. (N.S.) 848 419
Dawnay v. Cashford (1697) Carth. 432 431
De Lusignan v. Johnson (1973) 230 E.G. 499; 117 S.J. 693; E.G.D. 76 135
De Sommery, Re [1912] 2 Ch. 622 232
Deacon v. South Eastern Ry. (1889) 61 L.T. 377 428
Dean, Re (1889) 41 Ch. D. 552 239
Deanplan Ltd v. Mahmoud [1993] Ch. 151; [1992] 3 W.L.R. 467 .... 364, 385, 387, 400
Dearle v. Hall (1828) 3 Russ. 1 .... 499, 540, 544, 545
Deen v. Andrews (1986) 52 P. & C.R. 17; [1986] 1 E.G.L.R. 262 21
Demetriou v. Poolaction (1991) 62 P. & C.R. 536; [1991] 25 E.G. 113; [1991] 1 E.G.L.R. 100 372
Dendy v. Evans [1909] 2 K.B. 894 363
Denley's Trust Deed, Re [1969] 1 Ch. 373; [1968] 3 W.L.R. 457 239
Dennis (A Bankrupt), Re [1993] Ch. 72; [1992] 3 W.L.R. 204 330
Dennis v. McDonald [1982] Fam. 63; [1982] 2 W.L.R. 275 .... 304, 323
—— v. Malcolm [1934] Ch. 244 120
Denny, Re [1947] L.J.R. 1029; 177 L.T. 291 331
Densham (A Bankrupt), Re [1975] 1 W.L.R. 1519; [1975] 3 All E.R. 726 317
Deptford High Street, (139) ex p. British Transport Commission, Re [1951] Ch. 884; [1951] 1 All E.R. 950 142
Deverall v. Wyndham 1989 21 H.L.R. 260; (1989) 58 P. & C.R. 12; (1989) 1 E.G..L.R. 57 377
D'Eyncourt v. Gregory (1866) L.R. 3 Eq. 382 21
Dickin and Kelsall's Contract, Re [1908] 1 Ch. 213 88
Dickinson v. Grand Junction Canal Co Ltd (1852) 7 Exch. 282 .... 416, 447
Diligent Finance Co v. Alleyne (1972) 23 P. & C.R. 346 102
.... Dillwyn v. Llewellyn (1862) 4 De G.F. & J. 264 .... 483, 487
Diment v. NH Foot Ltd [1974] 1 W.L.R. 1427; [1974] 2 All E.R. 785 431
Dinefwr BC v. Jones (1987) 19 H.L.R. 445; (1987) 284 E.G. 58 371
Dingle v. Coppen [1899] 1 Ch. 726 564
District Bank Ltd v. Webb (Practice Note) [1958] 1 W.L.R. 66 (Note); [1958] 1 W.L.R. 148 80
Dixon v. Muckleston (1872–73) L.R. 8 Ch. App. 155 538
—— v. Treasury Solicitor [1905] P. 42 180
—— v. Winch [1900] 1 Ch. 736 528
Dodds v. Walker [1981] 1 W.L.R. 1027; [1981] 2 All E.R. 609 349
Dodsworth v. Dodsworth (1973) 228 E.G. 1115; [1973] E.G.D. 233 .... 254, 285, 486, 487, 488

Dodwell & Co Ltd's Trust Deed, Re [1979] Ch. 301; [1978] 3 All E.R. 738 246
Doe d. Aslin v. Summersett (1830) 1 B. & Ad. 135 306
Doe d. Bryan v. Bancks (1821) 4 B. & Ald. 401 355
Doe d. Durant v. Doe (1830) 6 Bing. 574 348
Doe d. Freeman v. Bateman (1818) 1 B. & Ald. 168 463
Doe d. Hallen v. Ironmonger (1803) 3 East 533 306
Doe d. Hearle v. Hicks (1832) 1 CL. & F. 20 176
Doe d. Jeff v. Robinson (1828) 2 Man, & Ry. 249 48
Doe d. Lockwood v. Clarke (1807) 8 East 185 355
Doe d. Thomson v. Amey (1840) 12 A. & E. 476 345
Doe d. Wilson v. Phillips (1824) 2 Bing. 13 355
Doherty v. Allman (1877–78) L.R. 3 App. Cas. 709 48
Doland's Will Trusts, Re [1970] Ch. 267; [1969] 3 W.L.R. 614 186
Dolling v. Evans (1867) 36 L.J. Ch. 474 151
Dolphin's Conveyance, Re [1970] Ch. 654; [1970] 3 W.L.R. 31 460
Donnison v. People's Cafe Co (1881) 45 L.T. 187 151
Dougal v. McCarthy [1893] 1 Q.B. 736 347
Downes v. Grazebrook (1871) 3 Mer. 200 506
Dowty Boulton Paul Ltd v. Wolverhampton Corp (No.2) [1976] Ch. 13; [1973] 2 W.L.R. 618 .... 417, 448
Drake v. Gray [1936] Ch. 451 .... 457, 458
—— v. Whipp [1996] 1 F.L.R. 826; [1996] 2 F.C.R. 296 316
Drane v. Evangelou [1978] 1 W.L.R. 455; [1978] 2 All E.R. 437 369
Drewell v. Towler (1832) 3 B. & Ad. 735 448
Driscoll v. Church Commissioners for England [1957] 1 Q.B. 330; [1956] 3 W.L.R. 996 472
Du Cane and Nettlefold's Contract, Re [1898] 2 Ch. 96 88
Du Sautoy v. Symes [1967] Ch. 1146; [1967] 2 W.L.R. 342 106
Dudley and District Benefit Society v. Emerson [1949] Ch. 707; [1949] 2 All E.R. 252 519
Duke v. Robson [1973] 1 W.L.R. 267; [1973] 1 All E.R. 481 505
Dumpor's Case (1603) 4 C. Rep. 119b 356
Dunbar v. Plant [1998] Ch. 412; [1997] 3 W.L.R. 1261 331
Dungate v. Dungate [1965] 1 W.L.R. 1477; [1965] 3 All E.R. 818 559
Dunn, Re [1916] 1 Ch. 97 308
Dunn v. Fidoe [1950] 2 All E.R. 685; 66 T.L.R. (Pt. 2) 611 586
Dunraven (Earl of) v. Llewellyn (1850) 15 Q.B. 791 422
Duppa v. Mayo (1669) 1 Wms. Saund. 275 150
Durham & Sunderland Ry. V. Walker (1842) 2 Q.B. 940 425
Dyce v. Hay (1852) 1 Macq. 205 416
Dyer v. Dyer (1788) 2 Cox Eq. 92 .... 85, 292
Dyson v. Forster [1909] A.C. 98 455

E. & G.C. Ltd v. Bate (1935) 79 L.J. News 203 462
EWP v. Moore [1992] Q.B. 460; [1992] 2 W.L.R. 184 586
Ealing Corp v. Ryan [1965] 2 Q.B. 486; [1965] 2 W.L.R. 223 573
East Barnet Urban DC v. British Transport Commission [1962] 2 Q.B. 484; [1962] 2 W.L.R. 134 572
East Riding CC v. Park Estate (Bridlington) Ltd [1957] A.C. 223; [1956] 3 W.L.R. 312 575
Eastern Telegraph Co Ltd v. Dent [1899] 1 Q.B. 835 376
Easton v. Isted [1903] 1 Ch. 405 .... 416, 446
Ebbetts v. Conquest [1896] A.C. 490HL; affirming [1895] 2 Ch. 377 379
Eccles v. Bryant [1948] Ch. 93; [1947] 2 All E.R. 865 152
—— v. Cheyne (1856) 2 K. & J. 676 184
Ecclesiastical Commissioners for England v. Kino (1880) L.R. 14 Ch. D. 213 443
Ecclesiastical Commissioners for England's Conveyance, Re [1936] Ch. 430 455
Eckersley v. Platt (1866) L.R. 1 P. & D. 281 179
Edell v. Dulieu [1924] A.C. 38 586
Edmondson's Will Trusts, Re [1972] 1 W.L.R. 183; [1972] 1 All E.R. 444 190
Edwards Will Trusts, Re [1982] Ch. 30; [1981] 3 W.L.R. 15 200
Edwards v. Carter [1893] A.C. 360 203
—— v. Hastings [1996] N.P.C. 87 330
—— v. Tuck (1853) 3 De G.M. & G. 40 245
Egerton v. Harding 1975] Q.B. 62; [1974] 3 W.L.R. 437 .... 416, 417
Elias v. Mitchell [1972] Ch. 652; [1972] 2 W.L.R. 740 .... 129, 131, 283
Elite Investments v. TI Bainbridge Silencers (No.2) [1986] 2 E.G.L.R. 43; (1987) 283 E.G. 747 378

Elitestone Ltd v. Morris [1997] 1 W.L.R. 687; [1997] 2 All E.R. 513 20
Ellenborough Park, Re [1956] Ch. 131; [1955] 3 W.L.R. 892 .... 414, 417, 448
Elliott v. Boynton [1924] 1 Ch. 236 356
—— v. Johnson (1866) L.R. 2 Q.B. 120 .... 390, 394, 395
Ellis and Sons Amalgamated Properties v. Sisman [1948] 1 K.B. 653; [1948] 1 All E.R. 44 594
Elliston v. Reacher [1908] 2 Ch. 665, CA [1908] 2 Ch. 374 .... 460, 461
Elmcroft Developments Ltd v. Tankersley-Sawyer (1984) 15 H.L.R. 63; (1984) 270 E.G. 140 378
Elmdenc Estates Ltd v. White [1960] A.C. 528; [1960] 2 W.L.R. 359 599
Elsden v. Pick [1980] 1 W.L.R. 898; [1980] 3 All E.R. 235 586
Elwes v. Brigg Gas Co (1886) L.R. 33 Ch. D. 562 566
Elwes v. Maw (1802) 3 East 38 22
Emmet's Estate, Re (1879–80) L.R. 13 Ch. D. 484 191
Endacott, Re [1960] Ch. 232; [1959] 3 W.L.R. 799 239
Epps v. Esso Petroleum Co Ltd [1973] 1 W.L.R. 1071; [1973] 2 All E.R. 465 .... 118, 124, 139, 142, 145
Equities (39) v. Bank Leumi (UK) Ltd [1986] 1 W.L.R. 1490; [1987] 1 All E.R. 108 376
Equity & Law Home Loans Ltd v. Prestridge and Brown [1992] 1 W.L.R. 137; [1992] 1 All E.R. 909 .... 323, 324, 532
Ernest v. Vivian (1863) 33 L.J. Ch. 513 60
Errington Ex p. Mason, Re [1894] 1 Q.B. 11 528
Errington v. Errington and Woods [1952] 1 K.B. 290; [1952] 1 All E.R. 149 .... 480, 481
Escalus Properties Ltd v. Dennis [1996] Q.B. 231; [1995] 3 W.L.R. 524 .... 358, 363
Esselte AB v. Pearl Assurance Plc [1997] 1 W.L.R. 891; [1997] 2 All E.R. 41 582
Esso Petroleum Co Ltd v. Harper's Garage (Stourport) Ltd [1968] A.C. 269; [1967] 2 W.L.R. 871 .... 469, 523
—— v. Kingswood Motors (Addlestone) Ltd 1974] Q.B. 142; [1973] 3 W.L.R. 780 70
Espresso Coffee Machine Co Ltd v. Guardian Assurance Co [1959] 1 W.L.R. 250; [1959] 1 All E.R. 458 583
Evan's Contract, Re [1920] 2 Ch. 469 48
Evans v. Roper [1960] 1 W.L.R. 814; [1960] 2 All E.R. 507 588
—— v. South Ribble BC [1992] Q.B. 757; [1992] 2 W.L.R. 429 .... 344, 376
—— v. Walker (1876) L.R. 3 Ch. D. 211 .... 210, 216
Everest (Deceased), Re [1975] Fam. 44; [1975] 2 W.L.R. 33 179
Evers Trust, Re [1980] 1 W.L.R. 1327; [1980] 3 All E.R. 399 323
Eves v. Eves [1975] 1 W.L.R. 1338; [1975] 3 All E.R. 768 .... 316, 317, 319
Ewart v. Fryer [1901] 1 Ch. 499 .... 359, 364
—— v. Graham (1859) 7 H.L.C. 331 450
Expert Clothing Service & Sales Ltd v. Hillgate House Ltd [1986] Ch. 340; [1985] 3 W.L.R. 359 .... 356, 360, 361

Facchini v. Bryson 1952] 1 T.L.R. 1386; 96 S.J. 395 340
Fairclough v. Swan Brewery Co Ltd [1912] A.C. 565 521
Fairman v. Perpetual Investment Building Society [1923] A.C. 74 444
Fairweather v. St Marylebone Property Co Ltd [1963] A.C. 510; [1962] 2 W.L.R. 1020 .... 561, 562
Fane, Re [1913] 1 Ch. 404 233
Farmer v. Curtis (1829) 2 Sim.466 525
Farrand v. Yorkshire Banking Co (1889) L.R. 40 Ch. D. 182 537
Farrell v. Alexander [1977] A.C. 59; [1976] 3 W.L.R. 145 599
—— v. Green (1974) 232 E.G. 587 150
Faruqi v. English Real Estates Ltd [1979] 1 W.L.R. 963; (1979) 38 P. & C.R. 318 .... 157, 166
Fawcett and Holmes Contract, Re ((1889) L.R. 42 Ch. D. 150 469
Fawcett Properties Ltd v. Buckingham CC [1961] A.C. 636; [1960] 3 W.L.R. 831 573
Fawke v. Viscount Chelsea [1980] Q.B. 441; [1979] 3 W.L.R. 508 584
Fay v. Miller, Wilkins & Co [1941] Ch. 360 .... 151, 163
Featherstone v. Staples [1986] 1 W.L.R. 861; [1986] 2 All E.R. 461 586
Federated Homes Ltd v. Mill Lodge Properties Ltd [1980] 1 W.L.R. 594; [1980] 1 All E.R. 371 458
Feltham v. Cartwright (1839) 5 Bing. N.C. 569 478
Fenwick, In b. (1867) L.R. 1 P. & D. 319 179
Ferrand v. Wilson (1845) 4 Hare 344 245
Ferrishurst Ltd v. Wallcite Ltd [1999] Ch. 355; [1999] 2 W.L.R. 667 .... 125, 128
Feversham Settled Estates, Re [1938] 2 All E.R. 210 273
Ffinch v. Combe [1894] P. 191 178
Field, Re [1918] 1 I.R. 40 561
Finch, Re (1881) 17 Ch. D. 211 221
Finck v. Tranter [1905] 1 K.B. 427 513
Finn, In b. (1936) 53 T.L.R. 153 177

Finnemore (Deceased), Re [1991] 1 W.L.R. 793; [1992] 1 All E.R. 800 .... 179, 186
First Middlesbrough Trading and Mortgage Co Ltd v. Cunningham (1974) 28 P. & C.R. 69; (1974) 118 S.J.
    421 509
First National Bank Plc v. Thompson [1996] Ch. 231; [1996] 2 W.L.R. 293 499
First National Securities Ltd v. Hegerty [1985] Q.B. 850; [1984] 3 W.L.R. 769 ...... 320, 323, 330, 531
Fish, Re [1894] 2 Ch. 83 189
Fishenden v. Higgs and Hill (1935) 153 L.T. 128 446
Fisher v. Taylor's Furnishing Stores [1956] 2 Q.B. 78; [1956] 2 W.L.R. 985 583
——— v. Wiggs (1700) 12 Mod. 296 307
Fison's Will Trusts, Re [1950] Ch. 394; [1950] 1 All E.R. 501 526
Fitzgerald's Trustee v. Mellersh [1892] 1 Ch. 385 524
Fitzroy v. Duke of Richmond (1858) 28 L.J. Ch. 750 190
Fitzwalter, Re [1943] Ch. 285 272
Flather v. Hood (1928) 44 T.L.R. 698 586
Fletcher, Re [1917] 1 Ch. 339 412
Fletcher v. Ashburner (1779) 1 Bro. C.C. 497 283
Flexman v. Corbett [1930] 1 Ch. 672 375
Flynn (Deceased), Re (No.2) [1969] 2 Ch. 403; [1969] 2 W.L.R. 1148 559
Formby v. Barker [1903] 2 Ch. 539 .... 458, 469
Former King of Greece v. Greece (25701/94) (2001) 33 E.H.R.R. 21 92
Forsey and Hollebone's Contract, Re [1927] 2 Ch. 379 102
Foster v. Lyons & Co Ltd [1927] 1 Ch. 219 440
Foster v. Reeves [1892] 2 Q.B. 255 344
Fountain Forestry Ltd v. Edwards [1975] Ch. 1; [1974] 2 W.L.R. 767 200
Four-Maids Ltd v. Dudley Marshall (Properties) Ltd [1957] Ch. 317; [1957] 2 W.L.R. 931 507
Fowkes v. Pascoe (1875) 10 Ch. App. 343 292
Fowler v. Dale (1594) Cro.Eliz. 362 423
Fox v. Swann (1655) Sty. 482 377
Frances Holland School v. Wassef [2001] 29 E.G. 123; [2001] 2 E.G.L.R. 88 334
Frankland v. Capstick [1959] 1 W.L.R. 205; [1959] 1 All E.R. 209 586
Fraser, Re [1904] 1 Ch. 726 408
Fredin v. Sweden (A/192) (1991) 13 E.H.R.R. 784 .... 92, 93
Free Fishermen of Faversham, Re (1887) L.R. 36 Ch. D. 329 424
Freeman d.Vernon v. West (1763) 2 Wils. K.B. 165 36
Freer v. Unwins Ltd [1976] Ch. 288; [1976] 2 W.L.R. 609 .... 135, 141, 142, 144
Frewen, Re [1926] Ch. 580 256
Friary Holroyd and Healey's Breweries Ltd v. Singleton [1899] 2 Ch. 261CA; reversing [1899] 1 Ch. 86 .... 391, 394
Friends Provident Life Office v. British Railways Board [1996] 1 All E.R. 336; (1997) 73 P. & C.R. 9 385
Frogley v.Earl of Lovelace (1859) Johns. 333 476
Fuller v. Judy Properties Ltd (1992) 64 P. & C.R. 176; [1992] 1 E.G.L.R. 75; [1992] 14 E.G. 106 .... 359, 363
Fuller's Contract, Re [1933] Ch. 652 314
Fyfe v. Smith [1975] 2 N.S.W.L.R. 408 507

GMS Syndicate Ltd v. Gary Elliott Ltd 1982] Ch. 1; [1981] 2 W.L.R. 478 363
Gabriel Wade & English Ltd v. Dixon & Cardus Ltd [1937] 3 All E.R. 900 434
Gafford v. Graham 1999) 77 P. & C.R. 73; [1999] 3 E.G.L.R. 75 470
Gage, Re [1898] 1 Ch. 498 230
Gaite's Will Trusts, Re [1949] 1 All E.R. 459; 65 T.L.R. 194 216
Gallenga's Will Trusts [1938] 1 All E.R. 106 256
Gape, Re [1952] Ch. 743; [1952] 2 All E.R. 579 42
Gardiner, Re [1901] 1 Ch. 697 246
Gardner v. Hodgson's Kingston Brewery Co. Ltd [1903] A.C. 229 .... 435, 436, 441
Gare (Deceased), Re [1952] Ch. 80; [1951] 2 All E.R. 863 189
Garland v. Brown (1864) 10 L.T. 292 225
Garside, Re [1919] 1 Ch. 132 243
Garston v. Scottish Widows Fund & Life Assurance Society [1998] 1 W.L.R. 1583; [1998] 3 All E.R. 596 582
Gassiott, Re (1901) 70 L.J.Ch. 242 239
Gateward's Case (1607) 6 Co. Rep 59b 431
Gavaghan v. Edwards [1961] 2 Q.B. 220; [1961] 2 W.L.R. 948 153
Gaved v. Martyn (1865) 19 C.B. (N.S.) 732 436
Gearns v. Baker (1874–75) L.R. 10 Ch. App. 355 450
Gentle v. Faulker [1900] 2 Q.B. 267 377

George Wimpey & Co v. Sohn [1967] Ch. 487; [1966] 2 W.L.R. 414 .... 552, 563
Georgiades v. Edward Wolfe & Co [1965] Ch. 487; [1964] 3 W.L.R. 653 95
Gibbons, Re [1920] 1 Ch. 372 254
Gibson, Re [1949] P. 434; [1949] 2 All E.R. 90 178
Gilbert, In the Goods of [1893] P. 183 178
Gilbert v. Spoor [1983] Ch. 27; [1982] 3 W.L.R. 183 472
Gilbey v. Rush [1906] 1 Ch. 11 273
Giles, Re [1972] Ch. 544; [1971] 3 W.L.R. 640 186
Giles v. Walker (1890) L.R. 24 Q.B.D. 656 566
Gillett v. Holt [2001] Ch. 210; [2000] 3 W.L.R. 815 .... 484, 486, 48, 4887
Gilligan, Re [1950] P. 32; [1949] 2 All E.R. 401 180
Gissing v. Gissing [1971] A.C. 886; [1970] 3 W.L.R. 255 .... 316, 317, 318, 319
Gladstone v. Bower [1960] 2 Q.B. 384; [1960] 3 W.L.R. 575 586
Glass v. Kencakes [1966] 1 Q.B. 611; [1965] 2 W.L.R. 363 361
Glenorchy (Lord) v. Bosville (1733) Ca.t. Talb. 3 45
Glessing v. Green [1975] 1 W.L.R. 863; [1975] 2 All E.R. 696 162
Gloucester (Bishop of) v. Cunnington [1943] K.B. 101 593
Glynn v. Coghlan [1918] 1 I.R. 482 364
Goddard v. Lewis (1909) 101 L.T. 528 329
Godwin v. Schweppes Ltd [1902] 1 Ch. 926 426
Goldberg v. Edwards [1950] Ch. 247; 94 S.J. 128 426
Goldsack v. Shore [1950] 1 K.B. 708; [1950] 1 All E.R. 276 .... 480, 585
Good v. Parry [1963] 2 Q.B. 418; [1963] 2 W.L.R. 846 559
Goodman v. Gallant [1986] Fam. 106; [1986] 2 W.L.R. 236 .... 315, 316, 329
Goodright d. Charter v. Cordwent (1795) 6 T.R. 219 356
Goodright d. Humphreys v. Moses (1774) 2 Wm. Bl. 1019 60
Goodwin, Re [1969] 1 Ch. 283; [1968] 3 W.L.R. 558 174
Gordon v. Holland (1913) 82 L.J.P.C. 81 63
Gordon Grant & Co Ltd v. Boos [1926] A.C. 781 512
Gore and Snell v. Carpenter (1990) 60 P. & C.R. 456 330
Goring v. Bickerstaffe, Pollex. 31 214
Gorst v. Lowndes (1841) 11 Sim. 434 242
Gossage, In the Estate of [1921] P. 194 182
Gough v. Wood & Co [1894] 1 Q.B. 713; (1894) 10 T.L.R. 318 19
Grace Rymer Investments v. Waite [1958] Ch. 831; [1958] 3 W.L.R. 337 .... 135, 498
Graham v. Murphy [1997] 1 F.L.R. 860; [1997] 2 F.C.R. 441 .... 174, 175, 176
——— v. Philcox [1984] Q.B. 747; [1984] 3 W.L.R. 150 426
——— v. Seal (1918) 88 L.J.Ch. 31 524
Granada Theatres, Ltd v. Freehold Investment (Leytonstone), Ltd [1959] Ch. 592; [1959] 1 W.L.R. 570 391
Grand Junction Co v. Bates [1954] 2 Q.B. 160; [1954] 3 W.L.R. 45 364
Grangeside Properties v. Collingwoods Securities [1964] 1 W.L.R. 139; [1964] 1 All E.R. 143 .... 496, 520
Grant v. Edmondson [1931] 1 Ch. 1CA; affirming [1930] 2 Ch. 245 .... 388, 409, 410
Grant v. Edwards [1986] Ch. 638; [1986] 3 W.L.R. 114 317
Grant's Will Trusts, Re [1980] 1 W.L.R. 360; [1979] 3 All E.R. 359 240
Grantham v. Hawley (1615) Hob. 132 52
Grattan v. McNaughton [2001] W.T.L.R. 1305 .... 174, 187
Graves v. Weld (1833) 5 B. & Ad. 105 52
Greasley v. Cooke [1980] 1 W.L.R. 1306; [1980] 3 All E.R. 710 .... 485, 488
Great Western Ry. V. Smith (1876) 2 Ch. D. 235 359
Green v. Ashco Horticulturist, Ltd [1966] 1 W.L.R. 889; [1966] 2 All E.R. 232 426
——— v. Rheinberg (1911) 104 L.T. 149 61
Greene v. Church Commissioners for England [1974] Ch. 467; [1974] 3 W.L.R. 349 .... 95, 389, 397, 398
Greenfield v. Greenfield (1979) 38 P. & C.R. 570 331
Greenhi Builders Ltd v. Allen [1979] 1 W.L.R. 156; [1978] 3 All E.R. 1163 99
Green's Will Trusts, Re [1985] 3 All E.R. 455; (1984) 81 L.S.G. 3590 224
Greenwich District (Board of Works for) v. Maudslay (1869–70) L.R. 5 Q.B. 397 418
Greenwich LBC v. Discreet Selling Estates Ltd (1991) 61 P. & C.R. 405; [1990] 48 E.G. 113 356
Greenwood (James Newsome), Re [1903] 1 Ch. 749 44
Greenwood v. Greenwood [1939] 2 All E.R. 150 191
Greig v. Insole [1978] 1 W.L.R. 302; [1978] 3 All E.R. 449 70
Grey v. Inland Revenue Commissioners [1960] A.C. 1; [1959] 3 W.L.R. 759 .... 16, 294, 295, 296
——— v. Pearson (1857) 6 H.L. Cas. 61 187

Griffith v. Pelton (No.1) [1958] Ch. 205; [1957] 3 W.L.R. 522 395
Griffiths v. Vere (1803) 9 Ves. 127 243
—— v. Williams [1978] E.G.D. 919; (1978) 248 E.G. 947 .... 253, 254, 487, 488
Grigsby v. Melville [1974] 1 W.L.R. 80; [1973] 3 All E.R. 455 566
Grimwood v. Moss (1872) L.R. 7 C.P. 360 356
Grindal v. Hooper [1999] E.G.C.S. 150; (2000) 97(3) L.S.G. 35 .... 312, 331
Grossman v. Hooper [2001] EWCA Civ 615; [2001] 3 F.C.R. 662; [2001] 2 E.G.L.R. 82 152
Grover's Will Trusts, Re [1971] Ch. 168; [1970] 2 W.L.R. 574 196
Grubb v. Gwillim (1676) S.S. 347 66
Grymes v. Boweren (1830) 6 Bing. 437 22
Guildford Rural DC v. Fortescue [1959] 2 Q.B. 112; [1959] 2 W.L.R. 643 572

H (Deceased), Re [1990] 1 F.L.R. 441; [1990] Fam. Law 175 .... 186, 331
HE Dibble Ltd v. Moore [1970] 2 Q.B. 181; [1969] 3 W.L.R. 748 .... 21, 23
Habermann v. Koehler (No.1) (1997) 73 P. & C.R. 515; [1996] N.P.C. 45 124
Habermann v. Koehler (No.2) [2000] E.G.C.S. 125; Times, November 22, 2000 124
Habib Bank Ltd v. Habib Bank A.G. Zurich [1981] 1 W.L.R. 1265; [1982] 3 All E.R. 561 485
—— v. Tailor [1982] 1 W.L.R. 1218; [1982] 3 All E.R. 561 509
Hagee (London) Ltd v. AB Erikson and Larson 1976] Q.B. 209; [1975] 3 W.L.R. 272 .... 349, 581
Haines v. Welch (1868) L.R. 4 C.P. 91 373
Hair v. Gillman (2000) 80 P. & C.R. 108; [2000] 3 E.G.L.R. 74 .... 417, 426
Hakansson and Syuresson v. Sweden (1990) Series A No. 121 93
Hale (Deceased), Goods of [1915] 2 I.R. 362 182
Halifax Mortgage Services Ltd v. Stepsky [1996] Ch. 207; [1996] 2 W.L.R. 230, CA; affirming [1996] Ch. 1;
     [1995] 3 W.L.R. 701 533
Hall, In b. [1914] P. 1 186
Hall, Re sub nom: Hall v. Hall [1916] 2 Ch. 488 51
—— v. Hall [1982] 3 F.L.R. 379 319
—— v. Howard (1988) 20 H.L.R. 566; (1989) 57 P. & C.R. 226 371
Halley v. O'Brien [1920] 1 I.R. 330 153
Halliard Property Co Ltd v. Jack Segal Ltd [1978] 1 W.L.R. 377; [1978] 1 All E.R. 1219 362
Hallwood Estates v. Flack 66 T.L.R. (Pt. 2) 368; [1950] W.N. 268 594
Halsall v. Brizell [1957] Ch. 169; [1957] 2 W.L.R. 123 463
Hamilton v. Martell Securities Ltd [1984] Ch. 266; [1984] 2 W.L.R. 699 380
Hammersmith and Fulham LBC v. Monk [1992] 1 A.C. 478; [1990] 3 W.L.R. 1144 .... 306, 347
Hammond, Re [1938] 3 All E.R. 308 189
—— v. Mather (1862) 3 F. & F. 151 357
—— v. Mitchell [1991] 1 W.L.R. 1127; [1992] 2 All E.R. 109 .... 317, 319
Hamp v. Bygrave (1983) 266 E.G. 720; [1983] 1 E.G.L.R. 174; [1983] E.G.D. 1000 .... 20, 21
Hampshire v. Wickens (1877–78) L.R. 7 Ch. D. 555 .... 355, 374
Hanbury's Settled Estates, Re [1913] 2 Ch. 357 45
Hancock (Deceased), Re [1998] 2 F.L.R. 346; [1999] 1 F.C.R. 500 175
Hancock v. Watson [1902] A.C. 14 189
Handman and Wilcox's Contract, Re [1902] 1 Ch. 599 271
Hanmer v. Chance (1865) 4 De G.J. & S. 626 436
Hannah v. Peel [1945] K.B. 509 566
Hansford v. Jago[1921] 1 Ch. 322 429
Hanson, Re [1928] Ch. 96 .... 279, 281
Hardwick v. Johnson [1978] 1 W.L.R. 683; [1978] 2 All E.R. 935 479
Harewood v. Retese [1990] 1 W.L.R. 333; (1990) 134 S.J. 166 151
Hargreaves, Re (1890) L.R. 43 Ch. D. 401 216
Harker's Will Trusts, Re [1938] Ch. 323 50
Harley v. King (1835) 2 Cr.M. & R. 18 391
Harlow v. Hartog (1977) 245 E.G. 140 461
Harmer v. Jumbil (Nigeria) Tin Areas Ltd 1921] 1 Ch. 200 369
Harnett v. Maitland (1847) 16 M. & W. 257 373
Harpham v. Shacklock (1881–82) L.R. 19 Ch. D. 207 60
Harrington v. Bennett [2000] B.P.I.R. 630; [2000] E.G.C.S. 41; (2000) New Law Online Case 200035003 325
Harris v. Flower & Sons (1905) 74 L.J. Ch. 127; (1904) 91 L.T. 816 444
—— v. Goddard [1983] 1 W.L.R. 203; [1983] 3 All E.R. 242 .... 330, 331, 332
—— v. Jenkins (1883) L.R. 22 Ch. D. 481 440
Harrison v. Forth (1695) Prec. Ch. 51 63

Harrow LBC v. Johnstone [1997] 1 W.L.R. 459; [1997] 1 All E.R. 929 306
Hart v. O'Connor [1985] A.C. 1000; [1985] 3 W.L.R. 214 206
—— v. Windsor (1844) 12 M. & W. 68 369
Harte v. Frampton [1948] 1 K.B. 73; [1947] 2 All E.R. 604 596
—— v. Williams [1934] 1 K.B. 201 343
Harter v. Coleman (1882) 19 CH. D. 630 518
Harvey v. Pratt [1965] 1 W.L.R. 1025; [1965] 2 All E.R. 786 346
Haslemere Estates v. Baker [1982] 1 W.L.R. 1109; [1982] 3 All E.R. 525 .... 96, 99
Hastings and Thanet Building Society v. Goddard [1970] 1 W.L.R. 1544; [1970] 3 All E.R. 954 509
Hatten v. Russell (1888) L.R. 38 Ch. D. 334 89
Hawkins v. Rutter [1892] 1 Q.B. 668 413
Hayes Will Trusts, Re [1971] 1 W.L.R. 758; [1971] 2 All E.R. 341 200
Hayward (Deceased), Re [1957] Ch. 528 196
Hayward, Re [1928] Ch. 367 309
—— v. Cunnington (1668) 1 Lev. 231 450
—— v. Brunswick Permanent Benefit Building Society (1881–82) L.R. 8 Q.B.D. 403 .... 468, 469
Hazell v. Hazell 1972] 1 W.L.R. 301 319
Healey v. Hawkins [1968] 1 W.L.R. 1967; [1968] 3 All E.R. 836 436
Heard v. Pilley (1869) 4 Ch. App. 584 153
Heaseman v. Pearse (1871) 7 Ch. App. 275 237
Heath v. Drown [1973] A.C. 498; [1972] 2 W.L.R. 1306 583
—— v. Elliott (1838) 4 Bing.N.C. 388 422
Helier v. Casebert (1665) 1 Lev. 127 384
Hellawell v. Eastwood (1851) 6 Exch. 295 21
Hemmings v. Stoke Poges Golf Club Ltd [1920] 1 K.B. 720 357
Henderson v. Eason (1851) 17 Q.B. 701 304
Herbage Rents (Greenwich), Re [1896] 2 Ch. 811 410
Herbert Duncan Ltd v. Cluttons (1992) 63 P. & C.R. 135; [1992] 1 E.G.L.R. 101; [1992] 22 E.G. 110 581
Herbert, Re [1946] 1 All E.R. 421 277
Hereford's (Lord) Settled Estates, Re [1932] W.N. 34 252
Herklots Will Trusts, Re [1964] 1 W.L.R. 583; [1964] 2 All E.R. 66 285
Hewitt v. Loosemore (1851) 9 Hare 449 537
Hewlins v. Shippam (1826) 5 B. & C. 221 409
Hewson v. Shelley [1914] 2 Ch. 13 200
Heys, In b. [1914] P. 192 176
Hickman v. Peacey [1945] A.C. 304 185
Higgins v. Betts [1905] 2 Ch. 210 445
Hill v. Barclay (1811) 18 Ves. Jr. 56 358
—— v. Rochard [1983] 1 W.L.R. 478; [1983] 2 All E.R. 21 596
—— v. Tupper (1863) 2 H. & C. 121 .... 414, 476
Hill (Viscount) v. Bullock [1897] 2 Ch. 482 21
Hinckley and Country Building Society v. Henny [1953] 1 W.L.R. 352; [1953] 1 All E.R. 515 511
Hobbs v. Norton (1682) 1 Vern. 137 69
Hodges v. Jones [1935] Ch. 657 135
Hodgkinson, In b. [1893] P. 339 181
Hodgson v. Halford (1879) 11 Ch. D. 959 226
—— v. Marks [1971] Ch. 892; [1971] 2 W.L.R. 1263 .... 10, 62, 123, 125
Hodson and Howes' Contract, Re (1887) L.R. 35 Ch. D. 668 513
Hoffmann v. Fineberg [1949] Ch. 245; [1948] 1 All E.R. 592 .... 360, 361
Holaw (470) Ltd v. Stockton Estates Ltd (2001) 81 P. & C.R. 29; [2000] E.G.C.S. 89 125
Holding & Management Ltd v. Property Holding & Investment Trust Plc [1989] 1 W.L.R. 1313; [1990] 1 All E.R. 938 378
Holland v. Hodgson (1871–72) L.R. 7 C.P. 328 20
Holliday (A Bankrupt), Re [1981] Ch. 405; [1981] 2 W.L.R. 996 325
Hollington v. Rhodes [1951] 2 All E.R. 578 (Note); [1951] 2 T.L.R. 691 345
Hollis Hospital Trustees and Hague's Contract, Re [1899] 2 Ch. 540 .... 238, 411
Holman v. Exton (1692) Carth. 246 438
Holmes, Re (1885) L.R. 29 Ch. D. 786 540
—— v. Cowcher [1970] 1 W.L.R. 834; [1970] 1 All E.R. 1224 564
Holt's Settlement, Re [1969] 1 Ch. 100; [1968] 2 W.L.R. 653 215
Holy Monasteries v. Greece (A/301–A) (1995) 20 E.H.R.R. 1 .... 92, 93
Holyland v. Lewin (1884) L.R. 26 Ch. D. 266 184

Honeywood v. Honeywood (1874) L.R. 18 Eq. 306 .... 49, 50
Hooper, Re [1932] 1 Ch. 38 239
Hopgood v. Brown [1955] 1 W.L.R. 213; [1955] 1 All E.R. 550 .... 477, 482, 485, 489
Hopkinson v. Lovering (1883) L.R. Q.B.D. 92 391
Hopper v. Corporation of Liverpool (1944) 88 S.J. 213 230
Hopwood v. Cannock Chase DC [1975] 1 W.L.R. 373; [1975] 1 All E.R. 796 371
Horford Investments v. Lambert [1976] Ch. 39; [1973] 3 W.L.R. 872 592
Horlock v. Smith (1842) 6 Jur. 478 507
Horrill v. Cooper (1999) 78 P. & C.R. 336; [1998] E.G.C.S. 151 142
Horrocks v. Forray [1976] 1 W.L.R. 230; [1976] 1 All E.R. 737 479
Horsey Estate Ltd v. Steiger [1899] 2 Q.B. 79 .... 361, 387
Horsford, In the Goods of (1872–75) L.R. 3 P. & D. 211 .... 178, 180
Hounslow LBC v. Hare (1992) 24 H.L.R. 9; 89 L.G.R. 714 142
—— v. Minchinton (1997) 74 P. & C.R. 221; [1997] N.P.C. 44 552
—— v. Twickenham Garden Developments Ltd [1971] Ch. 233; [1970] 3 W.L.R. 538 .... 476, 479
House, Re [1929] 2 Ch. 166 310
Howard v. Duke of Norfolk (1681) 2 Swans. 454 219
—— v. Fanshawe [1895] 2 Ch. 581 358
—— v. Shaw (1841) 8 M. & W. 118 349
Howkins v. Jardine [1951] 1 K.B. 614; [1951] 1 All E.R. 320 586
Hua Chiao Commercial Bank v. Chiaphua Industries [1987] A.C. 99; [1987] 2 W.L.R. 179 .... 385, 388
Hubbard's Will Trusts, Re [1963] Ch. 275; [1962] 3 W.L.R. 682 225
Hubert v. Treherne (1842) 3 Man. & G. 743 153
Huckvale v. Aegean Hotels (1989) 58 P. & C.R. 163 .... 97, 443
Hudson v. Cripps [1896] 1 Ch. 265 .... 369, 461
Hughes v. Griffin [1969] 1 W.L.R. 23; [1969] 1 All E.R. 460 .... 552, 555
—— v. Robotham (1593) Cro. Eliz. 302 365
Hulbert v. Dale [1909] 2 Ch. 570 .... 433, 441
Humphreys v. Miller [1917] 2 K.B. 122 370
Hunt v. Carew (1649) Nels. 47 69
—— v. Luck [1902] 1 Ch. 428, CA; affirming [1901] 1 Ch. 45 .... 11, 61
Hunter and Hewlett's Contract, Re [1907] 1 Ch. 46 253
Hunter v. Canary Wharf Ltd [1997] A.C. 655; [1997] 2 W.L.R. 684 .... 92, 416
Hunter's Lease, Re [1942] Ch. 124 388
Huntingford v. Hobbs [1993] 1 F.L.R. 736; (1992) 24 H.L.R. 652 318
Hurlbatt, Re [1910] 2 Ch. 553 245
Hurrell v. Littlejohn [1904] 1 Ch. 689 .... 263, 270
Hurst v. Picture Theatres [1915] 1 K.B. 1 .... 476, 478
Hurt v. Bowmer [1937] 1 All E.R. 797 444
Hussein v. Mehlman [1992] 2 E.G.L.R. 287; [1992] 32 E.G. 59 367
Hussey v. Palmer [1972] 1 W.L.R. 1286; [1972] 3 All E.R. 744 .... 318, 319
Hutchinson v Mains (1832) Alc. & N. 155 334
Hutton v. Warren (1836) 1 M. & W. 466 49
—— v. Watling [1948] Ch. 398; [1948] 1 All E.R. 803; affirming [1948] Ch. 26; [1947] 2 All E.R. 641 ... 236
Hyde's Conveyance, Re (1952) 102 L.J. 58 282
Hyde v. Pearce [1982] 1 W.L.R. 560; [1982] 1 All E.R. 1029 552
Hyman v. Van den Burgh [1908] 1 Ch. 167 .... 435, 436, 439
Hynes v. Vaughan (1985) 50 P. & C.R. 444 20
Hypo-Mortgage Services Ltd v. Robinson [1997] 2 F.L.R. 71; [1997] 2 F.C.R. 422 125

IDC Group Ltd v. Clark [1992] 1 E.G.L.R. 187; [1992] 08 E.G. 108 .... 425, 443, 481
Idle v. Cook (1705) 1 P. Wms. 70 41
Imperial Loan Co Ltd v. Stone [1892] 1 Q.B. 599 206
Industrial Properties (Barton Hill) Ltd v. Associated Electrical Industries Ltd [1977] Q.B. 580; [1977] 2 W.L.R.
    726 .... 344, 352
Ingle v. Vaughan Jenkins [1900] 2 Ch. 368 412
Inglesant v. Inglesant (1872–75) L.R. 3 P. & D. 172 178
Inland Revenue Commissioners v. Williams [1969] 1 W.L.R. 1197; [1969] 3 All E.R. 614 217
International Drilling Fluids Ltd v. Louisville Investments (Uxbridge) Ltd [1986] Ch. 513; [1986] 2 W.L.R.
    581 377
International Tea Stores Co v. Hobbs [1903] 2 Ch. 165 .... 426, 427
Interoven Stove Co v. Hibbard and Painter (t/a Odell Hibbard & Co)[1936] 1 All E.R. 263 340

Inwards v. Baker [1965] 2 Q.B. 29; [1965] 2 W.L.R. 212 .... 69, 479, 482, 483, 485, 487, 489
Ipswich Permanent Money Club Ltd v. Arthy [1920] 2 Ch. 257 541
Irani Finance Ltd v. Singh [1971] Ch. 59; [1970] 3 W.L.R. 330 100
Ironside, Crabb and Crabb v. Cook, Cook and Barefoot (1981) 41 P. & C.R. 326 432
Irvine v. Moran (1992) 24 H.L.R. 1; [1991] 1 E.G.L.R. 261 371
Irwin, Re [1904] 2 Ch. 752 40
Itter (Deceased), Re (No.2) [1950] P. 130; [1950] 1 All E.R. 68 178
Ive's Case (1597) 5 Co. Rep. 11a 364
Ives (ER) Investment Ltd v. High [1967] 2 Q.B. 379; [1967] 2 W.L.R. 789 .... 97, 110, 463, 482, 489
Ivimey v. Stocker (1866) 1 Ch. App. 396 447
Ivory v. Palmer [1975] I.C.R. 340; 119 S.J. 405 254

JT Developments v. Quinn (1991) 62 P. & C.R. 33; [1991] 2 E.G.L.R. 257 487
Jackson, Re (1887) L.R. 34 Ch. D. 732 .... 314, 527
——, Re [1933] Ch. 237 188
—— v. Lever (1792) 3 Bro.C.C. 605 409
Jacobsson v. Sweden (A/163) (1990) 12 E.H.R.R. 56 92
Jaggard v. Sawyer [1995] 1 W.L.R. 269; [1995] 2 All E.R. 189 470
Jagger v. Jagger (1883) 25 Ch.D. 729 242
Jamaica Mutual Life Assurance Society v. Hillsborough 1989] 1 W.L.R. 1101; 133 S.J. 1032 461
James Jones & Sons Ltd v. Earl of Tankerville [1909] 2 Ch. 440 477
James v. James (1873) L.R. 16 Eq. 153 512
—— v. United Kingdom (1986) 8 E.H.R.R. 123; [1986] R.V.R. 139 .... 92, 93, 609
Javad v. Aqil [1991] 1 W.L.R. 1007; [1991] 1 All E.R. 243 .... 347, 349
Jeans, Re (1895) 72 L.T. 834 188
Jeune v. Queen's Cross Properties Ltd [1974] Ch. 97; [1973] 3 W.L.R. 378 .... 368, 379
Jefferys, Re [1939] Ch. 205 .... 256, 276
Jeff's Transfer, Re (No.2) [1966] 1 W.L.R. 841; [1966] 1 All E.R. 937 458
Jelley v. Buckman [1974] Q.B. 488; [1973] 3 W.L.R. 585 393
Jelley v. Iliffe [1981] Fam. 128; [1981] 2 W.L.R. 801 173
Jemmett and Guest's Contract, Re [1907] 1 Ch. 629 255
Jenner v. Turner (1880–81) L.R. 16 Ch. D. 188 44
Jennings Motors Ltd v. Secretary of State for the Environment [1982] Q.B. 541; [1982] 2 W.L.R. 131 572
Jennings v. Ward (1705) 2 Vern. 520 521
Jessamine Investment Co v. Schwartz [1978] Q.B. 264; [1977] 2 W.L.R. 145 .... 554, 594
Joel v. International Circus and Christmas Fair (1920) 123 L.T. 459 340
John Trenbeth Ltd v. National Westminster Bank Ltd (1980) 39 P. & C.R. 104; (1979) 253 E.G. 151 569
John Young & Co v. Bankier Distillery Co [1893] A.C. 691 567
John's Assignment Trusts [1970] 1 W.L.R. 955; [1970] 2 All E.R. 210 315
Johnsey Estates v. Webb [1990] 19 E.G. 84; [1990] 1 E.G.L.R. 80 385
Johnson's Settled Estate [1913] W.N. 222 257
Johnson v. Barnes (1872–73) L.R. 8 C.P. 527 .... 432, 441
—— v. Dodgson (1837) 2 M. & W. 653 153
—— v Evans (1889) 61 L.T. 18 524
Johnstone v. Holdway [1963] 1 Q.B. 601; [1963] 2 W.L.R. 147 425
Jones (Deceased), Re [1981] Fam. 7; [1981] 2 W.L.R. 106 181
Jones v. Challenger [1961] 1 Q.B. 176; [1960] 2 W.L.R. 695 .... 282, 323
—— v. Jones (1875–76) L.R. 1 Q.B.D. 279 44
—— v. Jones [1977] 1 W.L.R. 438; (1977) 33 P. & C.R. 147 .... 287, 304, 485
—— v. Lavington [1903] 1 K.B. 253 368
—— v. Read (1876) 10 I.R.C.L. 315 333
—— v. Rhind (1869) 17 W.R. 1091 537
—— v. Rhys-Jones (1974) 30 P. & C.R. 451 472
—— v. Smith (1841) 1 Hare 43 61
Jordan v. May [1947] K.B. 427; [1947] 1 All E.R. 231 20
Josephine Trust v. Champagne [1963] 2 Q.B. 160; [1962] 3 W.L.R. 1077 473
Josselyn v. Josselyn (1837) 9 Sim. 63 244
Joyner v. Weeks 1891] 2 Q.B. 31 379
Judd v. Brown [1998] 1 F.L.R. 360; [1997] B.P.I.R. 470; [1998] 325
Jull v. Jacobs (1876) 3 Ch. D. 703 186

K (Deceased), Re 1986] Ch. 180; [1985] 3 W.L.R. 234 .... 186, 187, 331

K (Enduring Powers of Attorney), Re [1988] Ch. 310; [1988] 2 W.L.R. 781 206
Kaur v. Gill [1988] Fam. 110; [1988] 3 W.L.R. 39; [1988] 2 All E.R. 28 98
Kay Green v. Twinsectra Ltd (No.1) [1996] 1 W.L.R. 1587; [1996] 4 All E.R. 546 612
Kaye v. Banks (1770) Dick. 431 50
Kelly, Re [1932] I.R. 255 220
—— v. Barrett [1924] 2 Ch. 379 .... 454, 461, 469
—— v. Battershell [1949] 2 All E.R. 830 461
Kelsen v. Imperial Tobacco Co [1957] 2 Q.B. 334 568
Kemeys-Tynte, Re [1892] 2 Ch. 211 272
Kemmis v. Kemmis [1988] 1 W.L.R. 1307; [1988] 2 F.L.R. 223 100
Kemp v. Derrett (1814) 3 Camp. 510 347
Kempthorne, Re [1930] 1 Ch. 268 .... 87, 283
Kennealy v. Dunne [1977] Q.B. 837; [1977] 2 W.L.R. 421 596
Kennedy v. De Trafford [1897] A.C. 180 505
Kenny v. Preen [1963] 1 Q.B. 499; [1962] 3 W.L.R. 1233 .... 368, 369
Keppell v. Bailey (1833) 2 My. & K. 517 416
Kerrison v. Smith [1897] 2 Q.B. 445 478
Kestell v. Langmaid [1950] 1 K.B. 233; [1949] 2 All E.R. 749 588
Ketley (A) Ltd v. Scott [1980] C.C.L.R. 37 523
Kilgour v. Gaddes 1904] 1 K.B. 457 431
Killick v. Roberts [1991] 1 W.L.R. 1146; [1991] 4 All E.R. 289 367
Kinch v. Bullard [1999] 1 W.L.R. 423; [1998] 4 All E.R. 650 332
King (Deceased), Re [1963] Ch. 459; [1963] 2 W.L.R. 629 393
King v. David Allen & Sons Billposting Ltd [1916] 2 A.C. 54 480
—— v. Malcott (1852) 9 Hare 692 384
—— v. Smith [1950] 1 All E.R. 553; [1950] W.N. 177 554
—— v. South Northamptonshire DC (1992) 24 H.L.R. 284; (1992) 64 P. & C.R. 35 372
King's Will Trusts, Re [1964] Ch. 542; [1964] 2 W.L.R. 913 200
Kingsalton Ltd v. Thames Water Developments Ltd [2001] EWCA Civ 20; [2002] 1 P. & C.R. 15 .... 93, 128, 129,
                                                                                                139, 141
Kingsbury v. Walter [1901] A.C. 187 227
Kingsmill v. Millard (1855) 11 Exch. 313 554
Kingsnorth Finance Co Ltd v. Tizard [1986] 1 W.L.R. 783; [1986] 2 All E.R. 54 .... 9, 10, 62, 63, 87, 110, 531
Kingswood Estate Co v. Anderson [1963] 2 Q.B. 169; [1962] 3 W.L.R. 1102 344
Kinnaird v. Trollope (No.1) (1888) L.R. 39 Ch. D. 636 528
Kirkham v. Smith (1749) Amb. 518 57
Kitcat v. King [1930] P. 266 185
Kitney v. MEPC Ltd [1977] 1 W.L.R. 981; [1978] 1 All E.R. 595 .... 114, 539
Kling v. Keston Properties Ltd (1985) 49 P. & C.R. 212; (1984) 81 L.S.G. 1683 125
Knapp's Settlement, Re [1895] 1 Ch. 91 191
Knibbs, In the Estate of [1962] 1 W.L.R. 852; [1962] 2 All E.R. 829 182
Knight v. Crockford (1794) 1 Esp. 190 153
Knightsbridge Estates Trust Ltd v. Byrne [1940] A.C. 613 affirming [1939] Ch. 441 ...... 238, 521, 522
Kreglinger v. New Patagonia Meat & Cold Storage Co Ltd [1914] A.C. 25 .... 493, 522
Kronheim v. Johnson (1877) 7 Ch. D. 60 294
Krubert (Deceased), Re [1997] Ch. 97; [1996] 3 W.L.R. 959 174

L v. K [1985] Fam. 144; [1985] 3 W.L.R. 202 217
Lace v. Chantler [1944] K.B. 368 346
Lacon v. Allen (1856) 3 Drew. 579 .... 500, 536
Ladyman v. Grave (1871) 6 Ch.App. 763 440
Laird v. Briggs (1881) 19 Ch.D. 22 437
Lake v. Craddock (1732) 3 P. Wms. 158 314
—— v. Gibson (1729) 1 Eq. Ca.Abr. 290 314
Lambeth LBC v. Archangel (2001) 33 H.L.R. 44; [2002] 1 P. & C.R. 18 559
—— v. Blackburn [2001] EWCA Civ 912; (2001) 33 H.L.R. 74; (2001) 82 P. & C.R. 39 .... 551, 552
—— v. Howard [2001] EWCA Civ 468; (2001) 33 H.L.R. 58 93
Land Settlement Association Ltd v. Carr [1944] K.B. 657 348
Landi (Deceased), Re [1939] Ch. 828 .... 305, 556
Langston, Re [1953] P. 100; [1953] W.L.R. 581 180
Lassence v. Tieney (1849) I Mac. & G. 551 189
Latec Investments Ltd v. Hotel Terrigal Pty Ltd (In Liquidation) (1965) 113 C.L.R. 265 61

Lawrence v. Jenkins 1872–73) L.R. 8 Q.B. 274 416
Layton v. Martin [1986] 2 F.L.R. 227; [1986] Fam. Law 212 485
Leach, Re 1[1912] 2 Ch. 422 44
—— v. Jay (1878) L.R. 9 Ch. D. 42 548
Leach's Will Trusts, Re [1948] Ch. 232; [1948] 1 All E.R. 383 183
Leahy v. Attorney General of New South Wales [1959] A.C. 457; [1959] 2 W.L.R. 722 240
Leake v. Robinson (1817) 2 Mer. 363 .... 227, 243
Lechmere and Lloyd, Re (1881) 18 Ch. D. 524 211
Lee v. Barrey [1957] Ch. 251; [1957] 2 W.L.R. 245 116
—— v. Gaskell (1875–76) L.R. 1 Q.B.D. 700 149
Leech v. Schweder (1874) 9 Ch. App. 463 414
Leeds Industrial Cooperative Society Ltd v. Slack [1924] A.C. 851; [1924] All E.R. Rep. 264 470
Leek and Moorlands Building Society v. Clark [1952] 2 Q.B. 788; [1952] 2 All E.R. 492 306
Leeman v. Mohammed [2001] EWCA Civ 198; (2001) 82 P. & C.R. 14 134
Leeman v. Stocks 1951] Ch. 941; [1951] 1 All E.R. 1043 153
Lee-Parker v. Izzet (No.1) [1971] 1 W.L.R. 1688; [1971] 3 All E.R. 1099 .... 123, 380
Leeward Securities Ltd v. Lilyheath Properties Ltd (1985) 17 H.L.R. 35; (1983) 271 E.G. 279 377
Legh's Settlement Trusts, Re [1938] Ch. 39 .... 211, 234
Leicester (Earl of) v. Wells-next-the-Sea Urban DC [1973] Ch. 110; [1972] 3 W.L.R. 486 459
Leigh v. Dickeson (1884–85) L.R. 15 Q.B.D. 60 350
—— v. Jack (1879–80) L.R. 5 Ex. D. 264 552
—— v. Taylor [1902] A.C. 157 HL 20, 21
Leigh's Settled Estates (No.1), Re [1926] Ch. 852 280
Leighton's Conveyance, Re [1937] Ch. 149; [1936] 1 All E.R. 1033; [1936] 1 All E.R. 667 .... 140, 142
Lemarge v. Goodban (1865) L.R. 1 P. & D. 57 179
Lemon v. Lardeur [1946] K.B. 613 349
Leonard v. Leonard [1902] P. 243 179
Lester v. Burgess (1973) 26 P. & C.R. 536 131
L'Estrange v. L'Estrange [1902] 1 I.R. 467 308
Letterstedt v. Broers (1883–84) L.R. 9 App. Cas. 371; [1881–85] All E.R. Rep. 882 300
Lever Finance v. Needleman's Trustee [1956] Ch. 375; [1956] 3 W.L.R. 72 .... 498, 511, 513
Leverhulme (No. 2), Re [1943] 2 All E.R. 274 219
Levermore v. Levermore [1979] 1 W.L.R. 1277; [1980] 1 All E.R. 1 100
Levy (Deceased), Re [1960] Ch. 346; [1960] 2 W.L.R. 278 244
Lewis (EH) & Son v. Morelli [1948] 2 All E.R. 1021; 65 T.L.R. 56 352
Lewis (Jenkins R) & Son, Ltd v. Kerman [1971] Ch. 477; [1970] 3 W.L.R. 673 364
Lewis, Re [1939] Ch. 232 384
—— v. Frank Love Ltd [1961] 1 W.L.R. 261; [1961] 1 All E.R. 446 521
—— v. Plunket [1937] Ch. 306 514
—— v. Thomas [1950] 1 K.B. 438; [1950] 1 All E.R. 116 419
Lewisham BC v. Maloney [1948] 1 K.B. 50; [1947] 2 All E.R. 36 97
Liberty's Will Trusts, Re [1937] Ch. 176 268
Liggins v. Inge (1831) 7 Bing. 682 443
Lim Teng Huan v. Ang Swee Chuan [1992] 1 W.L.R. 113; (1992) 64 P. & C.R. 233 488
Limond, Re [1915] 2 Ch. 240 185
Littledale v. Liverpool College [1900] 1 Ch. 19 552
Liverpool City Council v. Irwin [1977] A.C. 239; [1976] 2 W.L.R. 562 .... 371, 372
Liverpool Corp v. H Coghill & Son Ltd [1918] 1 Ch. 307 430
Llanover's (Baroness) Will, Re [1903] 2 Ch. 16 254
Llewellin, Re (1888) L.R. 37 Ch. D. 317 51
Lloyd, Re [1903] 1 Ch. 385 512
—— v. Banks (1868) 3 Ch. App. 488 .... 61, 541
—— v. Rosbee (1810) 2 Camp. 453 350
Lloyds Bank Ltd v. Jones [1955] 2 Q.B. 298; [1955] 3 W.L.R. 5 587
—— v. Marcan [1973] 1 W.L.R. 1387; [1973] 3 All E.R. 754; affirming [1973] 1 W.L.R. 339; [1973] 2 All
   E.R. 359 16
—— v. Pearson [1901] 1 Ch. 865 542
Lloyds Bank Plc v. Byrne & Byrne [1993] 1 F.L.R. 369; [1993] 2 F.C.R. 41 324
—— v. Carrick [1996] 4 All E.R. 630; [1996] 2 F.L.R. 600 .... 69, 316, 482, 484, 486, 489
—— v. Rosset [1991] 1 A.C. 107; [1990] 2 W.L.R. 867 .... 125, 316, 318, 319
Lobb v. Stanley (1844) 5 Q.B. 574 153
Lock v. Abercester Ltd [1939] Ch. 861 445

Lock v. Pearce [1893] 2 Ch. 271 360
Lodge v. Wakefield MDC [1995] 2 E.G.L.R. 124; [1995] 38 E.G. 136 554
Lohia v. Lohia [2001] EWCA Civ 1691 affirming [2001] W.T.L.R. 101 292
London & Blenheim Estates Ltd v .Ladbroke Retail Parks Ltd [1994] 1 W.L.R. 31; [1993] 4 All E.R. 157; CA;
    affirming [1992] 1 W.L.R. 1278; [1993] 1 All E.R. 307 417
London and Cheshire Insurance Co Ltd v. Laplagrene Property Co Ltd [1971] Ch. 499; [1971] 2 W.L.R. 257 123,
    125, 141
London and County (A&D) Ltd v. Wilfred Sportsman Ltd [1971] Ch. 764; [1970] 3 W.L.R. 418 .... 393, 394
London and Manchester Assurance Co v. O & H Construction [1989] 29 E.G. 65; (1990) 6 Const. L.J. 155;
    [1989] 2 E.G.L.R. 183 335
London & North Western Railway Co v. Evans [1893] 1 Ch. 16 417
London and South Western Ry v. Gomm (1882) 20 Ch. D. 562 .... 236, 468
London County and Westminster Bank Ltd v. Tompkins [1918] 1 K.B. 515 .... 492, 501
London CC v. Allen [1914] 3 K.B. 642 .... 454, 469
London (Corporation of) v Riggs (1880) 13 Ch.D. 798 444
London, Tilbury & Southend Ry etc (1889) 24 Q.B.D. 326 446
Long v. Blackall (1797) 7 T.R. 100 .... 214, 220
—— v. Gowlett [1923] 2 Ch. 177 426
Longrigg Burrough & Trounson v. Smith [1979] 2 E.G.L.R. 42; (1979) 251 E.G. 847; [1979] E.G.D. 472 .... 347, 349
Lonrho Ltd v. Shell Petroleum Co Ltd (No.2) [1982] A.C. 173; [1981] 3 W.L.R. 33 105
Lonsdale (Earl) v. Attorney General [1982] 1 W.L.R. 887; [1982] 3 All E.R. 579 580
Lonsdale (Earl of) v. Lowther [1900] 2 Ch. 687 272
Lotus Ltd v. British Soda Co Ltd 1972] Ch. 123; [1971] 2 W.L.R. 7 .... 417, 418
Louis v. Sadiq 59 Con. L.R. 127; (1997) 74 P. & C.R. 325; [1997] 1 E.G.L.R. 136 335
Lovesy v. Palmer [1916] 2 Ch. 233 151
Lowe v. Ashmore (JW) [1971] Ch. 545; [1970] 3 W.L.R. 998 421
Lowe's Will Trusts, Re [1973] 1 W.L.R. 882; [1973] 2 All E.R. 1136 28
Lowrie (A Bankrupt), Re [1981] 3 All E.R. 353 .... 324, 325
Lowson v. Coombes [1999] Ch. 373; [1999] 2 W.L.R. 720 318
Lucie-Smith v. Gorman [1981] C.L.Y. 2866 155
Luganda v. Services Hotels [1969] 2 Ch. 209; [1969] 2 W.L.R. 1056 341
Luker v. Dennis 1877–78] L.R. 7 Ch. D. 227 468
Lund v. Taylor (1975) 31 P. & C.R. 167; 239 E.G. 199 460
Lurcott v. Wakely [1911] 1 K.B. 905 378
Lyell v. Lord Hothfield [1914] 3 K.B. 911 431
Lyme Valley Squash Club Ltd v. Newcastle under Lyme BC [1985] 2 All E.R. 405 427
Lynton International Ltd v. Noble (1992) 63 P. & C.R. 452 131
Lyon & Co v. London City and Midland Bank [1903] 2 K.B. 135 21
Lysaght v. Edwards (1875–76) L.R. 2 Ch. D. 499 .... 67, 155
Lyus v. Prowsa Developments Ltd [1982] 1 W.L.R. 1044; [1982] 2 All E.R. 953 .... 135, 455, 482

MRA Engineering Ltd v. Trimster Co Ltd (1988) 56 P. & C.R. 1 .... 426, 427
Maber, Re [1928] Ch. 88 246
Macaulay's Estate, Re [1943] Ch. 435 (Note) 240
McAuley v. Bristol City Council [1992] Q.B. 134; [1991] 3 W.L.R. 968 372
McCarrick v. Liverpool Corp [1947] A.C. 219; [1946] 2 All E.R. 646 370
McCarthy & Stone, Ltd v. Julian S Hodge & Co, Ltd [1971] 1 W.L.R. 1547; [1971] 2 All E.R. 973 .... 60, 110, 543
McCartney v. Londonderry and Lough Swilly Railway Co Ltd [1904] A.C. 301 .... 447, 567
Macdonald v Scott [1893] A.C. 642 60
McDowell v. Hirschfield Lipson & Rumney [1992] 2 F.L.R. 126; [1992] Fam. Law 430 331
M'Fadden v Jenkyns (1842) 1 Ph. 153 193
McGrath v. Wallis 1995] 2 F.L.R. 114; [1995] 3 F.C.R. 661 318
Machu, Re (1882) L.R. 21 Ch. D. 838 44
Mackenzie v. Childers (1890) L.R. 43 Ch. D. 265 471
Mackley v. Nutting [1949] 2 K.B. 55; [1949] 1 All E.R. 413 353
Mackreth v. Symmons (1808) 15 Ves. 329 492
Macleay, Re (1875) L.R. 20 Eq. 186 .... 41, 43
M'Murdo, In b. (1867) L.R. 1 P. & D. 540 182
M'Naul's Estate, Re [1902] 1 I.R. 114 463
Maddison v. Alderson (1882–83) L.R. 8 App. Cas. 467 148
Maharaj v. Chand [1986] A.C. 898; [1986] 3 W.L.R. 440 .... 317, 479
Malayan Credit v Chia-Mph (Jack) 1986] A.C. 549; [1986] 2 W.L.R. 590 314

Malcolmson v. O'Dea (1863) 10 H.L.C. 593 423
Malone v. Harrison [1979] 1 W.L.R. 1353; 123 S.J. 804 173
Malpass (Deceased), Re [1985] Ch. 42; [1984] 3 W.L.R. 372 151
Mancetter Developments v. Garmanson and Givertz [1986] Q.B. 1212; [1986] 2 W.L.R. 87 221
Manchester Brewery Co v. Coombs [1901] 2 Ch. 608 344
Manchester City Council v. Cochrane [1999] 1 W.L.R. 809; (1999) 31 H.L.R. 810 606
Manjang v. Drammeh (1991) 61 P. & C.R. 194 427
Mann Crossman & Paulin Ltd v. Land Registry (Registrar) [1918] 1 Ch. 202 347
Mann, Re [1942] 2 All E.R. 193; [1942] P. 146 177
Manners v. Mew (1885) L.R. 29 Ch. D. 725 538
Manning v. Wasdale (1836) 5 A. & E. 758 .... 421, 447
Manning's (Matthew) Case (1609) 8 Co. Rep. 94b at 95b 42
Mansukhani v. Sharkey (1992) 24 H.L.R. 600; [1992] 33 E.G. 65 596
Manuel, In b. (1849) 13 Jur. 664 202
Marcroft Wagons Ltd v. Smith [1951] 2 K.B. 496; [1951] 2 All E.R. 271 340
Marcus, Re (1887) 56 L.J. Ch. 830 186
Mareva Compania Naviera SA v. International Bulk Carriers SA [1980] 1 All E.R. 213; [1975] 2 Lloyd's Rep. 509 .... 100, 132
Markfield Investments Ltd v. Evans [2001] 1 W.L.R. 1321; [2001] 2 All E.R. 238; (2001) 81 P. & C.R. 33 557
Markham v. Paget [1908] 1 Ch. 697 .... 368, 369
Marks v. Attallah (1966) 110 S.J. 709 .... 123, 124
Marriott v. Anchor Reversionary Co (1861) 3 De G.F. &J. 177 507
Marshall, In b. (1866) 13 L.T. 643 177
Marshall, Re [1920] 1 Ch. 284 205
—— v. Cave (1824) 3 L.J. (O.S.) Ch. 57 507
—— v. Green (1875–76) L.R. 1 C.P.D. 35 150
—— v. Taylor [1895] 1 Ch. 641 .... 560, 562
Marshfield, Re (1887) L.R. 34 Ch. D. 721 564
Marsland, Re [1939] Ch. 820 176
Marten v. Flight Refuelling Ltd (No.1) [1962] Ch. 115; [1961] 2 W.L.R. 1018 459
Martin v. Martin 1987] 54 P. & C.R. 238 316
—— v. Roe (1857) 7 E. & B. 237 22
—— v. Smith (1874) L.R. 9 Ex. 50 343
Martinez' Trusts (1870) 22 L.T. 403 297
Maryon Wilson's Instruments, Re [1971] Ch. 789; [1969] 3 W.L.R. 575 277
Mason v. Clarke [1955] A.C. 778; [1955] 2 W.L.R. 853 424
—— v. Hill (1833) 5 B. & Ad. 1 421
—— v. Shrewsbury & Hereford Ry. (1871) L.R. 6 Q.B. 578 447
Massey v. Midland Bank Plc [1995] 1 All E.R. 929; [1994] 2 F.L.R. 342 533
Master's Settlement, Re [1911] 1 Ch. 321 212
Matharu v. Matharu [1994] 2 F.L.R. 597; [1994] 3 F.C.R. 216; (1994) 68 P. & C.R. 93 .... 484, 488
Mathews v. Keble (1867) L.R. 4 Eq. 467; affirmed 3 Ch. App. 691 244
Matthews v. Goodday (1861) 31 L.J.Ch. 282 501
—— v. Smallwood [1910] 1 Ch. 777 .... 355, 356
May v. Belleville [1905] 2 Ch. 605 425
—— v. May (1881) 44 L.T. 412 254
Mayho v. Buckhurst (1617) Cro. Jac. 438 388
Mayn v. Mayn (1867) l.R. 5 Eq. 150 315
Mayo, Re [1943] Ch. 302 282
Medforth v. Blake [2000] Ch. 86; [1999] 3 W.L.R. 922 511
Meftah v. Lloyds TSB Bank Plc (No.2) [2001] 2 All E.R. (Comm) 741; [2001] 14 E.G.C.S. 146 506
Mellacher v. Austria (1989) Series A No. 192 92
Mellor v. Spateman (1669) 1 Wms.Saund. 339 450
—— v. Watkins (1874) L.R. 9 Q.B. 400 480
Mercer v. Denne [1905] 2 Ch. 538 416
Metropolitan Properties Co Ltd v. Cordery (1980) 39 P. & C.R. 10; (1979) 251 E.G. 567 356
Meyer v. Chartres (1918) 34 T.L.R. 589 63
Midland Bank Plc v. Chart Enterprises [1990] 44 E.G. 68; [1990] 2 E.G.L.R. 59 376
—— v. Cooke [1995] 4 All E.R. 562; [1997] 6 Bank. 147; [1995] 2 F.L.R. 915 .... 318, 319
—— v. Dobson [1986] 1 F.L.R. 171; [1986] Fam. Law 55 317
—— v. Farmpride Hatcheries Ltd [1981] E.G.D. 985; (1980) 260 E.G. 493 62
Midland Bank Plc v. Greene [1994] 2 F.L.R. 827; [1995] 1 F.C.R. 365 532

—— v. Pike [1988] 2 All E.R. 434 .... 288, 324
Midland Bank Trust Co Ltd v. Green (No.1) [1981] A.C. 513; [1981] 2 W.L.R. 28 ..... 59, 70, 95, 105, 106, 140, 389, 397, 398
—— v. Green (No.3) [1982] Ch. 529; [1982] 2 W.L.R. 1 105
—— v. Hett Stubbs & Kemp [1979] Ch. 384; [1978] 3 W.L.R. 167 105
Midland Railway Co's Agreement, Re [1971] Ch. 725; [1971] 2 W.L.R. 625 .... 346, 348
Midland Ry. V. Miles (1886) 33 Ch. D. 632 427
Midleton (Earl) v. Cottesloe (Baron) [1949] A.C. 418; [1949] 1 All E.R. 841 90
Mikeover Ltd v. Brady [1989] 3 All E.R. 618; (1989) 21 H.L.R. 513 341
Miles v. Bull (No.2) [1969] 3 All E.R. 1585; 21 P. & C.R. 23 .... 70, 129, 346
Miles v. Harford (1879) 12 Ch. D. 691 227
Miller v. Emcer Products [1956] Ch. 304; [1956] 2 W.L.R. 267 .... 368, 417
—— v. Hancock [1893] 2 Q.B. 177 444
Miller's Agreement, Re [1947] Ch. 615; [1947] 2 All E.R. 78 455
Millett v. Davey (1863) 31 Beav. 470 508
Mills v. Silver 1991] Ch. 271; [1991] 2 W.L.R. 324 .... 431, 433, 441
Milner's Safe Co Ltd v. Great Northern and City Railway Co (No.1) [1907] 1 Ch. 208 445
Minister of Health v. Bellotti [1944] K.B. 298; [1944] 1 All E.R. 238 476
Ministry of Housing and Local Government v. Sharp [1970] 2 Q.B. 223; [1970] 2 W.L.R. 802 106
Minshull v. Oakes (1858) 2 H. & N. 793 391
Mitchell v. Mosley [1914] 1 Ch. 438 566
Moffat v. Burnie (1853) 18 Beav. 211 307
—— v. Kazana [1969] 2 Q.B. 152; [1969] 2 W.L.R. 71 566
Mogridge v. Clapp [1892] 3 Ch. 382 .... 263, 270
Molton Finance, Re [1968] Ch. 325; [1967] 3 W.L.R. 1561 .... 99, 500
Monmouth Canal Co v. Harford (1834) 1 Cr.M. & R. 614 431
Monnickendam v. Leanse (1923) 39 T.L.R. 445 148
Monolithic Building Co, Re [1915] 1 Ch. 64 140
Monson (Lord) v. Bound [1954] 1 W.L.R. 1321; [1954] 3 All E.R. 228 586
Montague v. Long (1972) 24 P. & C.R. 240; 116 S.J. 712 21
Montagu's Settlement Trusts, [1987] Ch. 264; [1987] 2 W.L.R. 1192 61
Monti v. Barnes 1901] 1 Q.B. 205 .... 21, 24
Monypenny v. Dering (1852) 2 De G.M. & G. 145 226
Moodie v. Bannister (1859) 4 Drew. 432 559
Moody v. Steggles (1879) L.R. 12 Ch. D. 261 414
—— v. Stevenson [1992] Ch. 486; [1992] 2 W.L.R. 640 175
Moore and Hulme's Contract [1912] 2 Ch. 105 496
Moore, In b. [1892] P. 378 179
Moore (Martha Mary), Re [1901] 1 Ch. 936 219
Moore, Re (1888) L.R. 39 Ch. D. 116 44
——, Re [1906] 1 Ch. 789 257
—— v. Rawson (1824) 3 B. & C. 332 442
Moran (Christopher) Holdings Ltd v. Bairstow and Ruddock [2000] 2 A.C. 172; [1999] 2 W.L.R. 396 366
Morelle v. Wakeling [1955] 2 Q.B. 379; [1955] 2 W.L.R. 672 .... 114, 118, 135
Morgan v. Davies (1877–78) L.R. 3 C.P.D. 260 348
—— v. Fear [1907] A.C. 425 440
—— v. Gronow (1873) L.R. 16 Eq. 1 .... 232, 234
——, Re (1883) L.R. 24 Ch. D. 114 255
Morgan's Lease, Re [1972] Ch. 1; [1971] 2 W.L.R. 1503 .... 263, 270, 272
Morley v. Bird (1798) 3 Ves. 628 .... 308, 314
Morrells of Oxford Ltd v. Oxford United Football Club Ltd [2001] Ch. 459; [2001] 2 W.L.R. 128 .... 468, 469, 470
Morss v. Morss [1972] Fam. 264; [1972] 2 W.L.R. 908 254
Mortgage Corp Ltd v. Nationwide Credit Corp Ltd [1994] Ch. 49; [1993] 3 W.L.R. 769 .... 498, 545
Moss, Re (1886) L.R. 31 Ch. D. 90 524
Moule v. Garrett (1872) L.R. 7 Ex. 101 .... 392, 404
Mounsey v. Ismay (1865) 3 H. & C. 486 440
Mount Carmel Investments Ltd v. Thurlow [1988] 1 W.L.R. 1078; [1988] 3 All E.R. 129; (1989) 57 P. & C.R. 396 .... 559, 564
Mountford v. Hodkinson [1956] 1 W.L.R. 422; [1956] 2 All E.R. 17 586
Mowan v. Wandsworth LBC (2001) 33 H.L.R. 56; [2001] B.L.G.R. 228 93
Multiservice Bookbinding Ltd v. Marden [1979] Ch. 84; [1978] 2 W.L.R. 535 522
Mundy and Roper's Contract, Re [1899] 1 Ch. 275 88

Murly v. M'Dermott (1838) A. & E. 138 333
Murphy v. Brentwood DC [1991] 1 A.C. 398; [1990] 3 W.L.R. 414 106
Murray v. Hall (1849) 7 C.B. 441 304
Muskett v. Hill (1836) 5 Bing. N.C. 694 477
Mutual Life Assurance Society v. Langley 1886) L.R. 32 Ch. D. 460 540
Mykolyshyn v. Noah [1970] 1 W.L.R. 1271; [1971] 1 All E.R. 48 596

Nash v. Eads (1880) 25 S.J. 95 506
National & Provincial Building Society v. Ahmed [1995] 2 E.G.L.R. 127; [1995] 38 E.G. 138 510
National Carriers Ltd v. Panalpina (Northern) Ltd [1981] A.C. 675; [1981] 2 W.L.R. 45 366
National Guaranteed Manure Co Ltd v. Donald (1859) 4 H. & N. 8 415
National Provincial Bank Ltd v. Ainsworth [1965] A.C. 1175; [1965] 3 W.L.R. 1 .... 61, 71, 98, 124
National Westminster Bank Ltd v. Allen [1971] 2 Q.B. 718; [1971] 3 W.L.R. 495 100
——— v. Stockman [1981] 1 W.L.R. 67; [1981] 1 All E.R. 800 100
Neale v. Del Soto 1945] K.B. 144 .... 341, 592
Neaverson v. Peterborough R.D.C. [1902] 1 Ch. 557 434
Neeld (No.1), Re [1962] Ch. 643; [1962] 2 W.L.R. 1097 526
Neilson v. Poole (1969) 20 P. & C.R. 909 96
New Windsor Corp v. Mellor [1974] 1 W.L.R. 1504; [1974] 2 All E.R. 510 416
New Zealand Government Property Corp v. HM&S Ltd [1982] Q.B. 1145; [1982] 2 W.L.R. 837 22
Newbery v Turngiant Ltd (1991) 63 P. & C.R. 458 157
Newbury DC v. Secretary of State for the Environment [1981] A.C. 578; [1980] 2 W.L.R. 379 573
Newcomen v. Coulson (1877) L.R. 5 Ch. D. 133 444
Newis v. Lark (1571) 2 Plowd. 403 42
Newland (Deceased), Re [1952] P. 71; [1952] 1 All E.R. 841 182
Newman v. Keedwell (1978) 35 P. & C.R. 393; (1977) 244 E.G. 469 306
——— v. Real Estate Debenture Corp Ltd [1940] 1 All E.R. 131 369
——— v. Slade [1926] 2 K.B. 328 349
Newnham v. Willison (1988) 56 P. & C.R. 8 430
Newton v. Marsden (1862) 2 J. & H. 356 44
Newton Abbott Cooperative Society Ltd v. Williamson & Treadgold Ltd [1952] Ch. 286; [1952] 1 All E.R.
   279 .... 454, 459
Nichols v. Hawkes (1853) 10 Hare 342 409
Nicholson v. England [1926] 2 K.B. 93 559
Nickerson v. Barroughclough [1981] Ch. 426; [1981] 2 W.L.R. 773 427
Nicolls v. Sheffield (1787) 2 Bro.C.C. 215 237
Nielson-Jones v. Fedden 1975] Ch. 222; [1974] 3 W.L.R. 583 .... 330, 331
Nightingale v. Courtney 1954] 1 Q.B. 399; [1954] 2 W.L.R. 266 365
Nisbet and Potts Contract, Re [1906] 1 Ch. 386, CA; affirming [1905] 1 Ch. 391 .... 454, 560
Noakes & Co Ltd v. Rice [1902] A.C. 24 521
Noble v. Meymott (1851) 14 Beav. 471 296
Norfolk's (Duke of) Case (1681) 3 Ch. Ca. 1 214
Norfolk (Duke of) v. Arbuthnot (1879–80) L.R. 5 C.P.D. 390 433
Norris v. Wilkinson (1806) 12 Ves. 192 500
North v. Loomes [1919] 1 Ch. 378 294
North London Ry v. The Vestry of St. Mary, Islington (1872) 27 L.T. 672 419
Northern Bank v. Henry [1981] I.R. 1 62
Northern Counties of England Fire Insurance Co v. Whipp (1884) L.R. 26 Ch. D. 482; (1884) 32 W.R. 626 538
Northern Developments (Holdings) Ltd v. U.D.T. Securities Ltd [1976] 1 W.L.R. 1230; (1975) 120 S.J. 769 107
Norton and Las Casas Contract, Re [1909] 2 Ch. 59 90
Norton, Re [1929] 1 Ch. 84 280
Norwich & Peterborough Building Society v. Steed (No.2) [1993] Ch. 116; [1992] 3 W.L.R. 66 .... 139, 140
Nottage, Re [1895] 2 Ch. 649 239
Notting Hill Housing Trust v. Brackley [2001] EWCA Civ 601; [2002] H.L.R. 10; [2001] 35 E.G. 106 306
Nynehead Developments Ltd v. RH Fibreboard Containers Ltd [1999] 1 E.G.L.R. 7; [1999] 02 E.G. 139 367

Oak Cooperative Building Society v. Blackburn [1968] Ch. 730; [1968] 2 W.L.R. 1053 .... 102, 106
Oastler v. Henderson 1876–77) L.R. 2 Q.B.D. 575 364
O'Brien v. Robinson [1973] A.C. 912; [1973] 2 W.L.R. 393 371
Observatory Hill Ltd v. Camtel Investments SA [1997] 1 E.G.L.R. 140; [1997] 18 E.G. 126 335
Ocean Estates Ltd v. Pinder [1969] 2 A.C. 19; [1969] 2 W.L.R. 1359 548
Oceanic Village Ltd v. United Attractions Ltd [2000] Ch. 234; [2000] 2 W.L.R. 476 .... 396, 405, 406, 471

Ogle's Settled Estates, Re [1927] 1 Ch. 229 251
Oland's Case (1602) 5 Co. Rep. 116a 52
Old Grovebury Manor Farm Ltd v. W Seymour Plant Sales & Hire Ltd (No.2) [1979] 1 W.L.R. 1397; [1979]
    3 All E.R. 504 .... 361, 376
Oliver v. Hinton [1899] 2 Ch. 264 .... 61, 537
O'May v. City of London Real Property Co Ltd [1983] 2 A.C. 726; [1982] 2 W.L.R. 407 .... 583, 584
Onley v. Gardiner (1838) 4 M. & W. 496 437
Orakpo v. Manson Investments Ltd [1978] A.C. 95; [1977] 3 W.L.R. 229; (1978) 33 P. & C.R. 1; 121 S.J. 632;
    affirming [1977] 1 W.L.R. 347; [1977] 1 All E.R. 666 139
Orgee v. Orgee [1997] E.G.C.S. 152; [1997] N.P.C. 156; [1997] New Law Digest, Property Communication
    107 484
Orlebar, Re [1936] Ch. 147 277
Osborne v. Bradley [1903] 2 Ch. 446 461
Otter v. Lord Vaux (1856) 6 De G.M. & G. 638 524
—— v. Norman [1989] A.C. 129; [1988] 3 W.L.R. 321 593
Ough v. King [1967] 1 W.L.R. 1547; [1967] 3 All E.R. 859 446
Oughtred v. Inland Revenue Commissioners [1960] A.C. 206; [1959] 3 W.L.R. 898 295
Owen, Re [1894] 3 Ch. 220 501
—— v. Gadd [1956] 2 Q.B. 99; [1956] 2 W.L.R. 945 369
Owers, Re (No.2) [1941] Ch. 389 384
Oxford's (Earl of) Case (1615) 1 Rep. Ch. 1 56

P&A Swift Investments v. Combined English Stores Group Plc [1989] A.C. 632; [1988] 3 W.L.R. 313 ...... 387, 388,
                                                                                                        394, 456
Paddington Building Society v. Mendelsohn (1985) 50 P. & C.R. 244; [1987] Fam. Law 121 .... 62, 323, 392, 531,
                                                                                                        532
Pahl v. Trevor [1992] 1 E.G.L.R. 22; [1992] 25 E.G. 130 586
Palk v. Mortgage Services Funding Plc [1993] Ch. 330; [1993] 2 W.L.R. 415 .... 501, 502, 505, 528
—— v. Shinner (1852) 18 Q.B. 568 437
Palmer (Gavin) (Deceased) (A Debtor), Re [1994] Ch. 316; [1994] 3 W.L.R. 420 330
—— v. Bowman [2000] 1 W.L.R. 842; [2000] 1 All E.R. 22 .... 416, 447
—— v. Fletcher (1663) 1 Lev. 122 169
—— v. Hendrie (1859) 27 Beav. 349 512
—— v. Holford (1828) 4 Russ. 403 220
Papachelas v. Greece (2000) 30 E.H.R.R. 923 92
Paragon Finance Plc v. Nash [2001] EWCA Civ 1466; [2002] 1 W.L.R. 685; [2002] 522, 523
Parkash v. Irani Finance Ltd [1970] Ch. 101; [1969] 2 W.L.R. 1134 .... 131, 524, 545
Parker v. British Airways Board 1982] Q.B. 1004; [1982] 2 W.L.R. 503 566
—— v. Housefield (1834) 2 My. & K. 419 499
—— v. Mitchell (1840) 11 A. & E. 788 435
—— v. Parker (1863) 1 N.R. 508 254
—— v. Taswell (1858) 2 De G. & J. 559 343
Parker's Settled Estates, Re [1928] Ch. 247 280
Parker-Tweedale v. Dunbar Bank Plc (No.1) [1991] Ch. 12; [1990] 3 W.L.R. 767 506
Parkus v. Greenwood [1950] Ch. 644; [1950] 1 All E.R. 436 351
Parmee v. Mitchell [1950] 2 K.B. 199; [1950] 1 All E.R. 872 596
Parsons v.Parsons [1983] 1 W.L.R. 1390; (1984) 47 P. & C.R. 494 306
Partriche v. Powlet (1740) 2 Atk. 54 329
Pascoe v. Turner [1979] 1 W.L.R. 431; [1979] 2 All E.R. 945 .... 69, 483, 485, 487, 488
Patman v. Harland (1881) L.R. 17 Ch. D. 353 .... 101, 103, 104
Patten, Re [1929] 2 Ch. 276 277
Patterson, In b. (1898) 79 L.T. 123 182
Paul v. Nurse (1828) 8 B. & C. 486 391
Paul's Settlement Trusts, Re [1920] 1 Ch. 99 191
Pavledes v. Ryesbridge Properties (1989) 58 P. & C.R. 459 417
Payne, Re [1927] 2 Ch. 1 189
—— v. Cardiff Rural DC [1932] 1 K.B. 241 .... 504, 505
Peabody Donation Fund (Governors of) v. London Residuary Body (1988) 55 P. & C.R. 355; Times, July 25,
    1987 236
Peacock v. Custins [2001] 2 All E.R. 827; (2001) 81 P. & C.R. 34 444
Pearce v. Maryon-Wilson [1935] Ch. 188 461
Pearce v. Morris (1869) 5 Ch.App. 227 523

Pearks v. Moseley (1880) 5 App. Cas. 714 .... 212, 227, 229
Pearson v. Inland Revenue Commissioners [1981] A.C. 753; [1980] 2 W.L.R. 872 210
—— v. Spencer (1863) 3 B. & S. 761; affirming (1861) 1 B. & S. 571 428
Pease v. Courtney [1904] 2 Ch. 503 273
Pechar, Re [1969] N.Z.L.R. 574 186
Peck and the School Board for London [1893] 2 Ch. 315 430
Peech v. Best [1931] 1 K.B. 1 450
Peffer v. Rigg [1977] 1 W.L.R. 285; [1978] 3 All E.R. 745 135
Pembery v. Lamdin 1940] 2 All E.R. 434 378
Penang v. Beng Hong Oon [1972] A.C. 425; [1972] 2 W.L.R. 1 476
Penn v. Bristol and West Building Society [1995] 2 F.L.R. 938; [1996] 2 F.C.R. 729 330
Pennant's Will Trusts, Re [1970] Ch. 75; [1969] 3 W.L.R. 63 275
Pennial v. Harborne (1848) 11 Q.B. 386 380
Pennington v. Reliance Motor Works Ltd [1923] 1 K.B. 127 492
Penwarden v. Ching (1829) Moo. & M. 400 433
Perera v. Vandiyar [1953] 1 W.L.R. 672; [1953] 1 All E.R. 1109 369
Perez-Adamson v. Perez Rivas [1987] Fam. 89; [1987] 3 W.L.R. 500 100
Perrin v. Morgan [1943] A.C. 399 188
Perrott (JF) & Co v. Cohen [1951] 1 K.B. 705; [1950] 2 All E.R. 939 554
Perry Herrick v. Attwood (1857) 2 De G. & J. 21 538
Perry v. Barker (1806) 13 Ves. 198 512
—— v. Clissold [1907] A.C. 73 563
—— v. Eames [1891] 1 Ch. 658 440
Pertwee v. Townsend 1896] 2 Q.B. 129 410
Peter v. Russell (1716) Gilb.Eq. 122 .... 536, 538
Pettit v. Pettit [1970] A.C. 777; [1969] 2 w.l.r. 966 .... 315, 318
Petrie, Re [1962] Ch. 355; [1961] 3 W.L.R. 1348 217
Petrol Filling Station, Vauxhall Bridge Road, London, Re (1968) 20 P. & C.R. 1 522
Pettingall v. Pettingall (1842) 11 L.J.Ch. 176 239
Peyton v Mayor of London (1829) 6 H. & N. 454; (1829) 9 B. & C. 725 .... 418, 447
Phelan (Deceased), Re [1972] Fam. 33; [1971] 3 W.L.R. 888 179
Phelps (Deceased), Re [1980] Ch. 275; [1980] 2 W.L.R. 277 195
Phillips Trusts, Re [1903] 1 Ch. 183 542
Phillips v. Lamdin [1949] 2 K.B. 33; [1949] 1 All E.R. 770 23
—— v. Low [1892] 1 Ch. 47 429
—— Ltd v. Mobil Oil Co Ltd [1989] 1 W.L.R. 888; [1989] 3 All E.R. 97 .... 95, 389, 397, 398
—— v. Phillips (1862) 4 De G.F. & J. 208 60
Phillips-Higgins v. Harper [1954] 1 Q.B. 411; [1954] 2 W.L.R. 782 558
Phipps v. Ackers (1842) 9 Cl. & F. 583 212
—— v. Lovegrove (1873) L.R. 16 Eq. 80 542
—— v. Pears [1965] 1 Q.B. 76; [1964] 2 W.L.R. 996 .... 416, 426
Picken v. Matthews (1878–79) L.R. 10 Ch. D. 264 .... 191, 221
Pickford v. Brown (1856) 2 K. & J. 426 230
Pilcher v. Rawlins (1872) 7 Ch. App. 259 .... 59, 60, 537
Pine Valley Developments v. Ireland (A/222) (1992) 14 E.H.R.R. 319; Times, December 11, 1991 93
Pinero v. Judson (1829) 6 Bing. 206 348
Pinewood Estate, Farnborough, Re [1958] Ch. 280; [1957] 3 W.L.R. 256 .... 459, 460
Pinhorn v. Souster (1853) 8 Exch. 763 349
Pink v. Lawrence (1978) 36 P. & C.R. 98 315
Pinnington v. Galland (1853) 9 Exch. 1 427
Pipe, Re (1937) 106 L.J. Ch. 252 192
Pitts, Re [1931] 1 Ch. 546 186
Plant v. Bourne [1897] 2 Ch. 281 151
Plasterers' Co. v. Parish Clerk's Co. (1851) 6 Exch. 630 440
Platt v. Mendel (1884) L.R. 27 Ch. D. 246 503
Pledge v. White [1896] A.C. 187 516
Plimmer v. Wellington Corp (1883–84) L.R. 9 App. Cas. 699 .... 477, 479, 487
Plymouth Corp v. Harvey [1971] 1 W.L.R. 549; [1971] 1 All E.R. 623 360
Polden v. Bastard (1865–66) L.R. 1 Q.B. 156 429
Pollard v. Jackson 1994] 67 P. & C.R. 327; [1993] N.P.C. 94 551
Pollock, Re [1941] Ch. 219 186
Pomfret v. Ricroft (1669) 1 Wms. Saund. 321 416

Poole's Case (1703) 1 Salk. 368 22
Poplar Housing & Regeneration Community Association Ltd v Donoghue [2001] EWCA Civ 595; [2002] Q.B.
   48; [2001] 3 W.L.R. 183 93
Port v. Griffith [1938] 1 All E.R. 295 369
Porter v. Watts (1852) 21 L.J. Ch. 211 299
Portman v. Viscount Portman [1922] 2 A.C. 473 217
Post Office v. Aquarius Properties Ltd [1987] 1 All E.R. 1055; (1987) 54 P. & C.R. 61 379
Poster v. Slough Estates Ltd [1969] 1 Ch. 495; [1968] 1 W.L.R. 1515 .... 97, 109
Potter v. Duffield (1874) L.R. 18 Eq. 4 151
Potton Developments Ltd v. Thompson [1998] N.P.C. 49 20
Powell v. Cleland [1948] 1 K.B. 262; [1947] 2 All E.R. 672 596
—— v. McFarlane (1979) 38 P. & C.R. 452 .... 551, 552
—— v. Powell (1866) L.R. 1 P. & D. 209 180
Power's Settlement Trusts, Re [1951] Ch. 1074; [1951] 2 All E.R. 513 299
Pownall v. Graham (1863) 33 Beav. 242 219
Powys v. Blagrave (1854) 4 De G.M. & G. 448 49
Predeth v. Castle Phillips Finance Co [1986] 2 E.G.L.R. 144; (1986) 279 E.G. 1355 506
Prevost, Re [1930] 2 Ch. 383 240
Price Bros (Somerford) v. Kelly (J) Homes (Stoke on Trent) [1975] 1 W.L.R. 1512; [1975] 3 All E.R. 369 131,
    140
Price v. Hartwell [1996] E.G.C.S. 98 328
—— v. Hilditch [1930] 1 Ch. 500 446
—— v. Romilly [1960] 1 W.L.R. 1360; [1960] 3 All E.R. 429 587
Prior's Case, The, Y.B. 42 Edw. 3, Hil., pl. 13 (1368) 455
Pritchard v. Briggs [1980] Ch. 338; [1979] 3 W.L.R. 868 .... 67, 70, 96
—— v. Powell (1845) 10 Q.B. 589 422
Proctor v. Bishop of Bath and Wells (1794) 2 Hy. Bl. 358 .... 225, 226
—— v. Kidman (1986) 51 P. & C.R. 67 118
Property & Bloodstock Ltd v. Emerton [1968] Ch. 94; [1967] 3 W.L.R. 973 505
Property Discount Corp v. Lyon Group Ltd [1981] 1 W.L.R. 300; [1981] 1 All E.R. 379 99
Proudfoot v. Hart (1890) L.R. 25 Q.B.D. 42 378
Provincial Properties (London) v. Caterham and Warlingham Urban DC [1972] 1 Q.B. 453; [1972] 2 W.L.R.
   44 579
Prudential Assurance Co Ltd v. London Residuary Body 1992] 2 A.C. 386; [1992] 3 W.L.R. 279 346
—— v. Waterloo Real Estate [1999] 2 E.G.L.R. 85; [1999] 17 E.G. 131 551
Public Trustee v. Lawrence [1912] 1 Ch. 789 519
Pugh v. Savage [1970] 2 Q.B. 373; [1970] 2 W.L.R. 634 .... 414, 431, 437
Pwllbach Colliery Co Ltd v. Woodman [1915] A.C. 634 428
Pye (JA) (Oxford) Ltd v. Graham [2001] EWCA Civ 117; [2001] Ch. 804; [2001] 2 W.L.R. 1293 .... 93, 547, 552,
    553
Pyer v. Carter (1857) 1 H. & N. 916 429

Queen's Club Gardens Estate Ltd v. Bignell [1924] 1 K.B. 117 349
Quennell v. Maltby [1979] 1 W.L.R. 318 .... 507, 508
Quick v. Taff Ely BC [1986] Q.B. 809; [1985] 3 W.L.R. 981 .... 370, 371
Quicke v. Chapman [1903] 1 Ch. 659 426
Quigly v. Chief Land Registrar [1992] 1 W.L.R. 834; [1992] 3 All E.R. 940 120

R. v. Broke (1859) 1 F. & F. 514 418
—— v. Hancock [1990] 2 Q.B. 242; [1990] 2 W.L.R. 640 568
—— v. Hussey (1924) 18 Cr. App. R. 160 356
—— v. Minister of Housing and Local Government [1960] 1 W.L.R. 587; [1960] 2 All E.R. 407 577
—— v. West London Rent Tribunal Ex p. Napper [1967] 1 Q.B. 169; [1966] 2 W.L.R. 76 615
—— v. Williams (1735) Bunb. 342 313
—— (on the application of Alconbury Developments Ltd) v. Secretary of State for the Environment, Transport
   and the Regions [2001] UKHL 23; [2001] 2 W.L.R. 1389 93
Race v. Ward (1855) 4 E. & B. 702 .... 421, 423
Radcliffe, Re [1892] 1 Ch. 227 412
Raffety v. Scholfield [1897] 1 Ch. 937 155
Rainbow Estates Ltd v. Tokenhold Ltd [1999] Ch. 64; [1998] 3 W.L.R. 980 .... 368, 379
Rains v. Buxton (1880) L.R. 14 Ch. D. 537 551
Ramsbottom v. Wallis (1835) 5 L.J.Ch. 92 .... 503, 525

Ramsden v. Dyson (1866) L.R. 1 H.L. 129 .... 477, 483, 485
Rance v. Elvin (1985) 50 P. & C.R. 9 .... 416, 447
Rangeley v. Midland Railway Co (1867–68) L.R. 3 Ch. App. 306 413
Ransome, Re [1957] Ch. 348; [1957] 2 W.L.R. 556 243
Rapley (Deceased), Re [1983] 1 W.L.R. 1069; [1983] 3 All E.R. 248 182
Raval, Re [1998] 2 F.L.R. 718; [1998] B.P.I.R. 389 325
Ravenseft Properties Ltd v. Davstone (Holdings) Ltd [1980] Q.B. 12; [1979] 2 W.L.R. 898 378
Rawlplug Co Ltd v. Kamvale Properties Ltd (1968) 112 S.J. 723; (1969) 20 P. & C.R. 32 .... 108, 131
Ray v. Fairway Motors (Barnstable) (1969) 20 P. & C.R. 261; (1968) 112 S.J. 925 .... 443, 447
Rayner v. Preston (1880–81) L.R. 18 Ch. D. 1 155
Ray's Will Trusts, Re [1936] Ch. 520; [1936] 2 All E.R. 93 240
Reade, In b. [1902] P. 75 181
Recher's Will Trusts, Re [1972] Ch. 526; [1971] 3 W.L.R. 321 240
Record v. Bell [1991] 1 W.L.R. 853; [1991] 4 All E.R. 471 152
Red House Farms (Thorndon) Ltd v. Catchpole [1977] E.G.D. 798 552
Redding, In b. (1850) 2 Rob. Ecc. 339 177
Reeve v. Lisle [1902] A.C. 461 521
Regan & Blackburn v. Rogers [1985] 1 W.L.R. 870; [1985] 2 All E.R. 180 99
Regent Oil Co v. Gregory (JA) (Hatch End) [1966] Ch. 402; [1965] 3 W.L.R. 1206 .... 469, 495, 511
Regional Properties Co v. Sedgwick Forbes Bland Payne Group (1981) 257 E.G. 65 416
Regis Property Co Ltd v. Dudley [1959] A.C. 370; [1958] 3 W.L.R. 647 378
—— v. Redman [1956] 2 Q.B. 612; [1956] 3 W.L.R. 95 426
Reid v. Bickerstaff [1909] 2 Ch. 305 461
—— v. Dawson [1955] 1 Q.B. 214; [1954] 3 W.L.R. 810 585
Reilly v. Orange [1955] 2 Q.B. 112; [1955] 1 W.L.R. 616 435
Remon v. City of London Real Property Co. Ltd [1921] 1 K.B. 49 350
Renals v. Cowlishaw (1879) L.R. 11 Ch. D. 866, affirming (1878) L.R. 9 Ch. D. 125 .... 457, 459
Rendall v Andreae (1892) 61 L.J.Q.B. 630 384
Reynolds v. Ashby & Son Ltd [1904] A.C. 466 24
Rhodes v. Dalby [1971] 1 W.L.R. 1325; [1971] 2 All E.R. 1144 519
—— v. Whitehead (1865) 2 Dr. & Sm. 532 212
Rhone v. Stephens [1994] 2 A.C. 310; [1994] 2 W.L.R. 429 .... 462, 463, 464, 469
Rhyl Urban DC v. Rhyl Amusements Ltd 1959] 1 W.L.R. 465; [1959] 1 All E.R. 257 352
Rice v. Rice (1853) 2 Drew. 73 537
Richards v. Cooper (1842) 5 Beav. 304 525
—— v. Delbridge 1874) L.R. 18 Eq. 11 291
—— v. Morgan (1853) 4 Y. & C.Ex. 570 508
—— v. Rose (1853) 9 Exch. 221 428
—— v. Sydenham (1703) 2 Vern. 447 388
Richardson v. Graham [1908] 1 K.B. 39 .... 415, 443
—— v. Watson (1833) 4 B. & Ad. 787 .... 188, 189
Richerson (No.1), Re [1892] 1 Ch. 379 283
Rickett v. Green [1910] 1 K.B. 253 .... 393, 395
Ridge, Re (1886) L.R. 31 Ch. D. 504 49
Ridley v. Taylor [1965] 1 W.L.R. 611; [1965] 2 All E.R. 51 473
Ridout v. Pain (1747) Atk. 486 19
Riggs Ex p. Lovell, Re [1901] 2 K.B. 16 377
Right d. Jefferys v. Bucknell (1831) 2 B. & Ald. 278 499
Rignall Developments Ltd v. Halil [1988] Ch. 190; [1987] 3 W.L.R. 394; [1987] 1 E.G.L.R. 193 102
Riley (EJ) Investments Ltd v. Eurostile Holdings Ltd [1985] 1 W.L.R. 1139; [1985] 3 All E.R. 181 349
Rimington v. Cannon (1853) 12 C.B. 18 551
Rimmer v. Webster [1902] 2 Ch. 163 538
Risch v. McFee [1991] 1 F.L.R. 105; [1991] F.C.R. 168; (1991) 61 P. & C.R. 42 318
Rivers (Lord) v. Adams (1877–78) L.R. 3 Ex. D. 361 424
Roake v. Chadha [1984] 1 W.L.R. 40; [1983] 3 All E.R. 503 458
Robb, Re [1953] Ch. 459; [1953] 2 W.L.R. 819 241
Roberts v. Davey (1833) 4 B. & Ad. 664 355
—— v. James (1903) 89 L.T. 282 .... 431, 434
Robertson v. Hartopp (1890) L.R. 43 Ch. D. 484 .... 422, 441
Rochefoucauld v. Boustead (1897) 1 Ch. 196 .... 294, 295, 317
Rochford's Settlement Trusts, Re [1965] Ch. 111; [1964] 2 W.L.R. 1339 245
Rodenhurst Estates Ltd v. WH Barnes Ltd [1936] 2 All E.R. 3 .... 353, 391

Rodway v. Landy [2001] EWCA Civ 471; [2001] Ch. 703; (2000) New Law Online Case 2001018801 ...... 285, 287, 305, 326, 327
Rodwell v. Phillips (1842) 9 M & W 501 150
Roe v. Siddons (1889) L.R. 22 Q.B.D. 224 415
Rogers Question, Re [1948] 1 All E.R. 328 318
Rogers v. Hosegood [1900] 2 Ch. 388 .... 455, 456, 457
—— v. Humphreys (1835) 4 A. & E. 299 518
—— v. Mutch (1878) 10 Ch. D. 25 228
Ropaigealach v. Barclays Bank Plc [2000] Q.B. 263; [1999] 3 W.L.R. 17 .... 507, 509
Ropemaker Properties v. Noonhaven (No.1) [1989] 34 E.G. 40; [1989] 2 E.G.L.R. 50 363
Rose (Deceased), Re [1952] Ch. 499; [1952] 1 All E.R. 1217 291
Rossiter v. Miller (1877–78) L.R. 3 App. Cas. 1124 151
Rosslyn's Trust (Lady) (1848) 16 Sim. 391 243
Rous v. Jackson (1885) 29 Ch. D. 521 232
Rowhook Mission Hall (Horsham), Re [1985] Ch. 62; [1984] 3 W.L.R. 710 80
Rowson, In the Estate of [1944] 2 All E.R. 36 182
Roy v. Roy [1996] 1 F.L.R. 541; [1996] Fam. Law 280 .... 315, 329
Royal Bank of Scotland Plc v. Etridge (No.2) [2001] UKHL 44; [2001] 3 W.L.R. 1021; [2001] 4 All E.R. 449 ... 323, 532, 533, 534
Royal Bank of Scotland Plc v. Miller [2001] EWCA Civ 344; [2002] Q.B. 255; [2001] 3 W.L.R. 523 508
Royal Trust Co of Canada v. Markham [1975] 1 W.L.R. 1416; [1975] 3 All E.R. 433 509
Royse (Deceased), Re [1985] Ch. 22; [1984] 3 W.L.R. 784 .... 175, 186
Ruck v. Barwise (1865) 2 Dr. & Sm. 510 306
Rudge v. Richens (1872–73) L.R. 8 C.P. 358 512
Rugby Joint Water Board v. Walters [1967] Ch. 397; [1966] 3 W.L.R. 934 567
Rugby School (Governors of) v. Tannahill [1935] 1 K.B. 87; affirming 1934] 1 K.B. 695 ...... 360, 361
Russel v. Russel (1783) 1 Bro.C.C. 269 500
Russell, In b. (1890) 15 P.D. 111 180
Russell Road Purchase Moneys, Re (1871) L.R. 12 Eq. 78 34
Rust v. Goodale [1957] Ch. 33; [1956] 3 W.L.R. 749 519
Rutherford v. Maurer [1962] 1 Q.B. 16; [1961] 3 W.L.R. 5 585
Rutherford's Conveyance, Re [1938] Ch. 396 459
Rye v. Purcell [1926] 1 K.B. 446 .... 393, 395
—— v. Rye [1962] A.C. 496; [1962] 2 W.L.R. 361 427

Sainsbury (J) Plc v. Enfield LBC [1989] 1 W.L.R. 590; [1989] 2 All E.R. 817 457
Saint v. Jenner [1973] Ch. 275; [1972] 3 W.L.R. 888 444
St Catherine's College (Oxford) v. Dorling [1980] 1 W.L.R. 66; [1979] 3 All E.R. 250 592
St Edmundsbury and Ipswich Diocesan Board of Finance v. Clark (No.2) [1975] 1 W.L.R. 468; [1975] 1 All E.R. 772, CA; affirming [1973] 1 W.L.R. 1572; [1973] 3 All E.R. 903 .... 425, 444
Sallis v. Jones [1936] P. 43 180
Salmon (Deceased), Re [1981] Ch. 167; [1980] 3 W.L.R. 748 174
Salmon Ex p. Trustee, Re [1903] 1 K.B. 147 518
Salt v. Cooper (1880–81) L.R. 16 Ch. D. 544 57
—— v. Marquess of Northampton [1892] A.C. 1 521
Salvation Army Trustee Co Ltd v. West Yorkshire CC (1981) 41 P. & C.R. 179 487
Salvin's Indenture, Re [1938] 2 All E.R. 498 .... 414, 415
Samuel v. Jarrah Timber and Wood Paving Corp Ltd [1904] A.C. 323 .... 521, 522
Samuel Keller Holdings Ltd v. Martins Bank Ltd [1971] 1 W.L.R. 43; [1970] 3 All E.R. 950 .... 501, 506
Sanders v. Karnell (1858) 1 F. & F. 356 347
Saner v. Bilton (1878) 7 Ch. D. 815 373
Santley v. Wilde [1899] 2 Ch. 474 521
Sarson v. Roberts [1895] 2 Q.B. 395 370
Saunders v. Vautier (1841) 4 Beav. 115; affirmed Cr. & Ph. 240 .... 244, 311
Savage, In b. (1870) L.R. 2P. & D. 78 176
Savage v. Dunningham [1974] Ch. 181; [1973] 3 W.L.R. 471 319
Savory, In b. (1815) 15 Jur. 1042 177
Scala House & District Property Co v. Forbes 1974] Q.B. 575; [1973] 3 W.L.R. 14 .... 560, 561
Scatterwood v. Edge (1697) 1 Salk. 229 219
Scene Estate v. Amos [1957] 2 Q.B. 205; [1957] 2 W.L.R. 1017 585
Schär (Deceased), Re [1951] Ch. 280; [1950] 2 All E.R. 1069 328
Schnabel v. Allard [1967] 1 Q.B. 627; [1966] 3 W.L.R. 1295 349

Schwab (ES) & Co Ltd v. McCarthy (1976) 31 P. & C.R. 196 .... 125, 346, 364, 389
Schwann v. Cotton [1916] 2 Ch. 459 429
Sclater v. Horton [1954] 2 Q.B. 1; [1954] 2 W.L.R. 566 588
Scott v. Pape (1886) L.R. 31 Ch. D. 554 443
Scott-Whitehead v. National Coal Board (1987) 53 P. & C.R. 263; [1987] 2 E.G.L.R. 227 447
Searle, Re [1912] 1 Ch. 610 347
Seddon v. Bank of Bolton (1881–82) L.R. 19 Ch. D. 462 435
—— v. Smith (1877) 36 L.T. 168 551
Sedgwick Forbes Bland Payne Group v. Regional Properties Co See Regional Properties Co v. Sedgwick
    Forbes Bland Payne Group
Segal Securities Ltd v. Thoseby [1963] 1 Q.B. 887; [1963] 2 W.L.R. 403 356
Segelman (Deceased), Re [1996] Ch. 171; [1996] 2 W.L.R. 173 187
Sehota (Deceased), Re [1978] 1 W.L.R. 1506; [1978] 3 All E.R. 385 173
Sekhon v. Alissa [1989] 2 F.L.R. 94; [1989] Fam. Law 355 318
Selby v. Nettlefold (1873–74) L.R. 9 Ch. App. 111 444
Selim Ltd v. Bickenhall Engineering Ltd [1981] 1 W.L.R. 1318; [1981] 3 All E.R. 210 99
Selous, Re [1901] 1 Ch. 921 307
Selous Street Properties v. Oronel Fabrics (1984) 270 E.G. 643; (1984) 270 E.G. 743 385
Selwyn's Conveyance Hayman v. Soole [1967] Ch. 674; [1967] 2 W.L.R. 647 458
Sevenoaks, Maidstone and Tunbridge Railway Co v. London, Chatham and Dover Railway Co (1879) L.R. 11
    Ch. D. 625; (1879) 27 W.R. 672 81
Shah v. Shah [2001] EWCA Civ 527; [2002] Q.B. 35; [2001] 3 W.L.R. 31 .... 160, 342
Shams v. United Bank Ltd (May 24, 1994) on Lexis 533
Shannon, The v. Venner [1965] Ch. 682; [1965] 2 W.L.R. 718 425
Sharp v. Coates [1949] 1 K.B. 285; [1948] 2 All E.R. 871 95
—— v. Rickards [1909] 1 Ch. 109 515
Sharpe, Re, Ex p. Trustee of the Bankrupt's Property [1980] 1 W.L.R. 219; [1980] 1 All E.R. 198 .... 293, 318
Sharpe v. Foy (1868) 4 Ch. App. 35 63
Sharpe's Deed of Release, Re [1939] Ch. 51< 280
Shaw, Re [1957] 1 W.L.R. 729; [1957] 1 All E.R. 745 239
—— v. Foster (1871–72) L.R. 5 H.L. 321 154
—— v. Rhodes (1836) 1 My. & Cr. 135 244
Shayler v. Woolf [1946] Ch. 320; [1946] 2 All E.R. 54, affirming [1946] 1 All E.R. 464 ...... 455, 480
Shears v. Wells [1936] 1 All E.R. 832 104
Sheffield Masonic Hall Co Ltd v. Sheffield Corp [1932] 2 Ch. 17 446
Shelley's Case (1581) 1 Co. Rep. 88b 37
Shepard v. Jones (1882) L.R. 21 Ch. D. 469 508
Shepherd Homes Ltd v. Sandham (No.2) [1971] 1 W.L.R. 1062; [1971] 2 All E.R. 1267 468
Shiloh Spinners Ltd v. Harding (No.1) [1973] A.C. 691; [1973] 2 W.L.R. 28 .... 83, 97, 109, 353, 357, 463
Shrewsbury's (Countess of) (1600) Co. Rep. 13b 349, 373
Shropshire CC v. Edwards 1983] 46 P. & C.R. 270 457
Shurey, Re [1918] 1 Ch. 263 201
Shuttleworth v. Le Fleming (1865) 19 C.B. (N.S.) 687 .... 432, 441
Siddiqu v. Rashid [1980] 1 W.L.R. 1018; [1980] 3 All E.R. 184 596
Sifton v. Sifton [1938] A.C. 656 42
Sigsworth, Re [1935] Ch. 89 186
Sikes, Re [1927] 1 Ch. 364 190
Simons v. Leaker (1885) 15 Q.B.D. 629 438
Simmons, Re [1956] Ch. 125; [1956] 2 W.L.R. 16 274
—— v. Dobson [1991] 1 W.L.R. 720; [1991] 4 All E.R. 25 431
—— v. Midford [1969] 2 Ch. 415; [1969] 3 W.L.R. 168 21
Simper v. Foley (1862) 2 J. & H. 564 440
Simpson v. Foxon [1907] P. 54 179
—— v. Geoghegan [1934] W.N. 232 529
—— v. Godmanchester Corp [1897] A.C. 696 HL; affirming [1896] 1 Ch. 214 .... 414, 417, 447
Sinclair (Deceased), Re [1985] Ch. 446; [1985] 2 W.L.R. 795 181
Skinner v. Geary [1931] 2 K.B. 546; 29 L.G.R. 599 594
Slark v. Dakyns (1874) 10 Ch. App. 35 233
Sledmore v. Dalby (1996) 72 P. & C.R. 196; [1996] N.P.C. 16 .... 487, 488
Slingsby's Case (1587) 5 Co. Rep. 18b 316
Slipper v. Tottenham and Hampstead Junction Railway Co (1867) L.R. 4 Eq. 112 377
Smiley v. Townshend [1950] 2 K.B. 311; [1950] 1 All E.R. 530 379

Smirk v. Lyndale Developments Ltd [1975] Ch. 317; [1975] 2 W.L.R. 495 554
Smith v. Baxter [1900] 2 Ch. 138 .... 435, 439
—— v. City Petroleum Co Ltd [1940] 1 All E.R. 260 22
—— v. Egginton (1874) L.R. 9 C.P. 145 393
—— v. Evangelization Society (Inc) Trust [1933] Ch. 515 446
—— v. Green (1844) 1 Coll.C.C. 555 525
—— v. Jones [1952] 2 All E.R. 907; [1952] 2 T.L.R. 846 151
—— v. Jones [1954] 1 W.L.R. 1089; [1954] 2 All E.R. 823 .... 60, 61
—— v. Marrable (1843) 11 M. & W. 5 370
—— v. Matthews (1861) 3 De G.F. and J. 139 294
—— v. Morrison [1974] 1 W.L.R. 659; [1974] 1 All E.R. 957 70
—— v. River Douglas Catchment Board 1949] 2 K.B. 500; [1949] 2 All E.R. 179 .... 455, 467
—— v. Surman (1829) 9 B. & C. 561 150
Smith (Arthur) v. Bradford City Council (1982) 4 H.L.R. 86; 80 L.G.R. 713; (1982) 44 P. & C.R. 171 371
Smith (Colin) Music v. Ridge [1975] 1 W.L.R. 463; [1975] 1 All E.R. 290 594
Solomon v. Mystery of Vintners (1859) 4 H. & N. 585 430
Somerset (Duke of) v. Fogwell (1826) 5 B. & C. 875 .... 424, 476
Somerville and Turner's Contract, Re [1903] 2 Ch. 583 57
South Eastern Railway Co v. Cooper 1924] 1 Ch. 211 444
Southern v. Wollaston (1852) 16 Beav. 276 221
Southern Centre of Theosophy Inc v. South Australia [1982] A.C. 706; [1982] 2 W.L.R. 544 566
Sovmots Investments Ltd v. Secretary of State for the Environment [1979] A.C. 144; [1977] 2 W.L.R. 951 .... 426, 429
Sowerby v. Sowerby (1982) 44 P. & C.R. 192 100
Sowerby's Trusts (1856) 2 K. & J. 630 183
Spadee and Scalabrino v. Italy (1996) Series A No. 315B 92
Spark, In the Estate of [1941] P. 115 181
Speakman v. Speakman (1850) 8 Hare 180 220
Spearman Settled Estates, Re [1906] 2 Ch. 502 257
Spectrum Investment Co v. Holmes [1981] 1 W.L.R. 221; [1981] 1 All E.R. 6 .... 140, 171, 391, 561, 562
Spencer's Case (1583) 5 Co. Rep. 16a 390, 391, 394
Spencer's Settled Estates, Re [1903] 1 Ch. 75 251
Spicer, Re [1949] P. 441; [1949] L.J.R. 1588 182
Spiro. v Glencrown Properties Ltd [1991] Ch. 537; [1991] 2 W.L.R. 931 150
—— v. Lintern [1973] 1 W.L.R. 1002; [1973] 3 All E.R. 319 62
Spitzel's Will Trusts, Re [1939] 2 All E.R. 266 230
Sporrung and LSYMBOL 216 f 'Times New Roman Special G1' s 11nnruth v. Sweden (1982) Series A No. 52 93
Spyer v. Phillipson 1931] 2 Ch. 183 21
Squarey v. Harris Smith (1981) 42 P. & C.R. 118 427
Stable, Re [1919] P. 7 182
Staffordshire and Worcestershire Canal Navigation v. Bradley [1912] 1 Ch. 91 423
Stamford, Earl of, Re [1896] 1 Ch. 288 298
Stamford's (Lord) Settled Estates, Re (1890) L.R. 43 Ch. D. 84 268
Standard Chartered Bank Ltd v. Walker [1982] 1 W.L.R. 1410; [1982] 3 All E.R. 938 506
Standard Pattern Co Ltd v. Ivey [1962] Ch. 432; [1962] 2 W.L.R. 656 358
Standard Property Investment, Plc v. British Plastics Federation (1987) 53 P. & C.R. 25 102
Stanhope v. Earl Verney (1761) 2 Eden 81 59
Stanley (Ada), Re [1916] P. 192 182
State Bank of India v. Sood [1997] Ch. 276; [1997] 2 W.L.R. 421 .... 87, 90, 124
Steadman v. Steadman [1976] A.C. 536; [1974] 3 W.L.R. 56 154
Stedman v. Smith (1857) 8 E. & B. 1 334
Steed v. Whitaker (1740) Barn. Ch. 220 485
Steeds v. Steeds (1889) L.R. 22 Q.B.D. 537 314
Stent v. Monmouth DC (1987) 19 H.L.R. 269; (1987) 54 P. & C.R. 193 371
Stephens, Re [1904] 1 Ch. 322 .... 191, 245
—— v. Bridges (1821) 6 Madd. 66 365
—— v. Junior Army & Navy Stores Ltd 1914] 2 Ch. 516 356
—— v. Snell [1939] 3 All E.R. 622 423
Stern, Re [1962] Ch. 732; [1962] 2 W.L.R. 161 234
Stevens v. King [1904] 2 Ch. 30 183
Steyning and Littlehampton Building Society v. Wilson [1951] Ch. 1018; [1951] 2 All E.R. 452 511

Stock v. Wanstead and Woodford BC [1962] 2 Q.B. 479; [1961] 2 W.L.R. 868 106
Stocker v. Planet Building Society (1879) 27 W.R. 877 373
Stockholm Finance Ltd v. Garden Holdings Inc [1995] N.P.C. 162 124
Stockler v. Fourways Estates Ltd [1984] 1 W.L.R. 25; [1983] 3 All E.R. 501 100
Stokes v. Anderson [1991] 1 F.L.R. 391; [1991] F.C.R. 539 317
Storrs v. Benbow (1853) 3 De G.M. & G. 390 228
Stott v. Ratcliffe (1982) 126 S.J. 310 323
Strand & Savoy Properties Ltd, Re [1960] Ch. 582; [1960] 3 W.L.R. 1 347
Strand Securities v. Caswell [1965] Ch. 958; [1965] 2 W.L.R. 958 .... 123, 125, 130, 131, 346, 389, 500
Strathblaine Estates Ltd, Re [1948] Ch. 228; [1948] 1 All E.R. 162 41
Street v. Denham [1954] 1 W.L.R. 624; [1954] 1 All E.R. 532 98
—— v. Mountford [1985] A.C. 809; [1985] 2 W.L.R. 877 .... 340, 341, 581
Strode v. Russel (1708) 2 Vern 621 189
Stroud Building Society v. Delamont [1960] 1 W.L.R. 431; [1960] 1 All E.R. 749 519
Stroyan v. Knowles (1861) 6 H. & N. 454 418
Stuart v. Joy [1904] 1 K.B. 368 385
Sturges v. Bridgman (1879) 11 Ch. D. 852 430
Sudbrook Trading Estate Ltd v. Eggleton [1983] 1 A.C. 444; [1982] 3 W.L.R. 315 151
Suffield v. Brown (1864) 4 De G.J. & Sm. 185 .... 429, 448
Sugden v. Lord St Leonards (1875–76) L.R. 1 P.D. 154; [1874–80] All E.R. Rep. 21 179
Sullivan, Re [1930] 1 Ch. 84 195
Summers v. Salford Corp [1943] A.C. 283 370
Surtees v. Surtees (1871) L.R. 12 Eq. 400 308
Sutherland (Duke of) v. Heathcote [1892] 1 Ch. 475 421
Suttill v. Graham [1977] 1 W.L.R. 819; [1977] 3 All E.R. 1117 319
Swan v. Sinclair [1925] A.C. 227, HL; affirming [1924] 1 Ch. 254 442
Swans, The Case of (1592) 7 Co. Rep. 15b 566
Swansborough v. Coventry (1832) 2 M. & S. 362 429
Swiss Bank Corp v. Lloyds Bank Ltd [1982] A.C. 584; [1981] 2 W.L.R. 893; revrsng [1979] Ch. 548; [1979]
    3 W.L.R. 201 .... 70, 501
Sykes v. Harry [2001] EWCA Civ 167; [2001] Q.B. 1014; (2001) 82 P. & C.R. 35 .... 371, 372
Symson v. Turner (1700) 1 Eq. Ca. Abr. 383 66

TSB Bank Plc v. Botham [1996] E.G.C.S. 149; [1996] N.P.C. 133; (1997) 73 P. & C.R. D1 20
—— v. Camfield [1995] 1 W.L.R. 430; [1995] 1 All E.R. 951 532
—— v. Marshall [1998] 2 F.L.R. 769; [1998] 3 E.G.L.R. 100 323
Tadman v. Henman [1893] 2 Q.B. 168 352
Taggart v. Taggart (1803) 1 Sch. & Lef. 84 315
Tandon v. Trustees of Spurgeons Homes [1982] A.C. 755; [1982] 2 W.L.R. 735 609
Tanner v. Tanner (No.1) [1975] 1 W.L.R. 1346; [1975] 3 All E.R. 776 479
Tapling v. Jones (1865) 11 H.L.C. 290 .... 438, 440, 445
Target Home Loans v. Clothier & Clothier [1994] 1 All E.R. 439; (1993) 25 H.L.R. 48 509
Targett v. Torfaen BC [1992] 3 All E.R. 27; (1992) 24 H.L.R. 164 372
Tarn v. Turner (1888) L.R. 39 Ch. D. 456; (1888) 57 L.J. Ch. 452 523
Tassell v. Smith (1858) 2 De g. & j. 713 518
Taylor d. Smith v. Biddall, 2 Mod. 287 214
Taylor v. Caldwell (1863) 32 L.J. Q.B. 164; (1863) 3 B. & S. 826 476
—— v. Ellis [1960] Ch. 368; [1960] 2 W.L.R. 509 519
—— v. Russell [1892] A.C. 244 538
—— v. Stibbert (1794) 2 Ves. Jun. 437 61
—— v. Taylor 1875) L.R. 20 Eq. 155 196
—— v. Taylor (1968) [1968] 1 W.L.R. 378; [1968] 1 All E.R. 843 99
—— v. Twinberrow [1930] 2 K.B. 16 560
Taylors Fashions Ltd v. Liverpool Victoria Trustees Co Ltd[1982] Q.B. 133n 69, 477, 483, 484, 485, 486
Tecbild Ltd v. Chamberlain (1969) 20 P. & C.R. 633; (1969) 209 E.G. 1069 .... 551, 552
Tee v. Tee [1999] 2 F.L.R. 613; [1999] 3 F.C.R. 409 289
Teevan v. Smith (1881–82) L.R. 20 Ch. D. 724 .... 524, 525
Tehidy Minerals v. Norman [1971] 2 Q.B. 528; [1971] 2 W.L.R. 711 .... 430, 434, 442
Terry, Re (1918) 87 L.J. Ch. 577 50
Terunnanse v. Terunnanse [1968] A.C. 1086; [1968] 2 W.L.R. 1125 .... 476, 480
Tetsall, Re [1961] 1 W.L.R. 938; [1961] 2 All E.R. 801 190
Texaco Antilles v. Kernochan [1973] A.C. 609; [1973] 2 W.L.R. 381 461

Thames Guaranty Ltd v. Campbell [1985] Q.B. 210; [1984] 3 W.L.R. 109 315
Thames Manufacturing Co Ltd v. Perrotts (Nichol & Peyton) Ltd (1985) 50 P. & C.R. 1; (1984) 271 E.G.
  284 385
Thamesmead Town Ltd v. Allotey (1998) 30 H.L.R. 1052; (2000) 79 P. & C.R. 557; [1998] 3 E.G.L.R. 97 464
Thatcher v. CH Pearce & Sons (Contractors), Ltd [1968] 1 W.L.R. 748; 19 P. & C.R. 682 358
Thatcher v. Douglas (1996) 140 S.J.L.B. 36; [1995] N.P.C. 206; (1996) 146 N.L.J. 282 .... 122, 482, 489
Thellusson v. Woodford (1799) 4 Ves. 227; (1805) 11 Ves. 112 .... 215, 221, 240
Thirkell v. Cambi [1919] 2 K.B. 590 153
Thomas (John) (Deceased), Re [1939] Ch. 513 327
Thomas v. Fryer [1970] 1 W.L.R. 845; [1970] 2 All E.R. 1 596
——— v. Packer (1857) 1 H. & N. 669 347
——— v. Rose [1968] 1 W.L.R. 1797; [1968] 3 All E.R. 765 .... 95, 96
——— v. Sorrell (1673) Vaugh. 330 .... 475, 476
——— v. Sylvester (1872–73) L.R. 8 Q.B. 368 410
——— v. Thomas (1835) 2 Cr.M. & R. 34 415
——— v. Thomas (1902) 87 L.T. 58 217
Thompson and Cottrell's Contract, Re [1943] Ch. 97; [1943] 1 All E.R. 169 366
Thompson, Re [1906] 2 Ch. 199 234
——— Re [1934] Ch. 342 239
——— v. Park [1944] K.B. 408 478
Thorn v. Dickens [1906] W.N. 54 188
Thornber, Re [1937] Ch. 29 195
Thorndike v. Hunt (1859) 3 De G. & J. 563 59
Thorne v. Heard & Marsh [1895] A.C. 495 506
Thorneycroft v. Crockett (1848) 2 H.L.C. 239 516
Thornhill Road (90) Tolworth Surrey, Re [1970] Ch. 261; [1969] 3 W.L.R. 570 .... 276, 326
Thorpe v. Bestwick (1880–81) L.R. 6 Q.B.D. 311 185
——— v. Brumfitt (1873) 8 Ch. App. 650 414
Threlfall Ex p. Queen's Benefit Building Society, Re (1880–81) L.R. 16 Ch. D. 274 348
Throckmerton v Tracy (1555) 1 Plowd. 145 38
Thursby v. Plant (1670) 1 WMS. Saund. 230 385
Tichbourne v. Weir (1892) 67 L.T. 735 .... 391, 559, 560
Tickle v. Brown (1836) 4 A. & E. 369 .... 430, 436
Tickner v. Buzzacott [1965] Ch. 426; [1965] 2 W.L.R. 154 560
——— v. Hearn [1960] 1 W.L.R. 1406; [1961] 1 All E.R. 65 594
Tidey v. Mollett (1864) 16 C.B. (N.S.) 298 343
Tilbury v. Silva (1890) L.R. 45 Ch. D. 98 433
Tilney v. Norris (1700) 1 Ld.Raym. 553 383
Tiltwood, Sussex, Re [1978] Ch. 269; [1978] 3 W.L.R. 474 454
Timmins v. Moreland Street Property Co Ltd [1958] Ch. 110; [1957] 3 W.L.R. 678 151
Tito v. Waddell (No.2) [1977] Ch. 106; [1977] 3 W.L.R. 972 .... 395, 463, 560
Tiverton Estates Ltd v. Wearwell Ltd [1975] Ch. 146; [1974] 2 W.L.R. 176 131
Todrick v. Western National Omnibus Co Ltd [1934] Ch. 561 414
Tom's Settlement, Re [1987] 1 W.L.R. 1021; [1987] 1 All E.R. 1081 191
Toms v. Wilson (1863) 4 B. & S. 453 503
Tooker v. Smith (1857) 1 H. & N. 732 348
Toomes v. Conset (1745) 3 Atk. 261 521
Tootal Clothing Ltd v. Guinea Properties Management Ltd (1992) 64 P. & C.R. 452; [1992] 41 E.G. 117;
  [1992] 2 E.G.L.R. 452 152
Topfell Ltd v. Galley Properties Ltd [1979] 1 W.L.R. 446; [1979] 2 All E.R. 388 150
Torbay Hotel Ltd v. Jenkins [1927] 2 Ch. 225 461
Total Oil Great Britain Ltd v. Thompson Garages (Biggin Hill) Ltd [1972] 1 Q.B. 318; [1971] 3 W.L.R. 979 367
Tourville v. Naish (1734) 3 P. Wms. 307 59
Tower Hamlets LBC v. Miah [1992] Q.B. 622; [1992] 2 W.L.R. 761 606
Town & Country Building Society v. Julien (1992) 24 H.L.R. 312 509
Townley v. Watson (1844) 3 Curt. 761 178
Travis, Re [1900] 2 Ch. 541 243
Tredegar (Viscount) v. Harwood [1929] A.C. 72 377
Treloar v. Bigge (1873–74) L.R. 9 Ex. 151; (1874) 22 W.R. 843 376
——— v. Nute [1976] 1 W.L.R. 1295; [1977] 1 All E.R. 230 551
Tremayne v. English Clays Lovering Pochin & Co [1972] 1 W.L.R. 657; [1972] 2 All E.R. 234 434
Trenchard, Re [1902] 1 Ch. 378 276

Treweeke v. 36 Wolseley Road Pty Ltd (1973) 128 C.L.R. 274 443
Trickey v. Trickey (1832) 3 My. & Cr. 560 244
Trimmer v. Danby (1856) 25 L.J.Ch. 424 239
Trinder v. Trinder (1866) L.R. 1 Eq. 695 190
Trotter, Re [1899] 1 Ch. 764 186
Trustees, Executors and Agency Ltd v. Short (1888) 13 App. Cas. 793 564
Tse Kwong Lam v. Wong Chit Sen [1983] 1 W.L.R. 1394; [1983] 3 All E.R. 54 506
Tucker v. Hutchinson (1987) 54 P. & C.R. 106 .... 107, 108, 131
——— v. Vowles [1893] 1 Ch. 195 461
Tulk v. Moxhay (1848) 2 Ph. 774; (1848) 18 L.J. Ch. 83 .... 454, 459, 468
Turley v. Mackay [1944] Ch. 37 96
Turner's Will Trusts, Re [1937] Ch. 15 16
Turner v. Doe d. Bennett (1842) 9 M. & W. 643 349
——— v. Smith [1901] 1 Ch. 213 528
——— v. Wright (1860) 2 De G.F. & J. 234 49
Turnworth Down, Dorset, Re [1978] Ch. 251; [1977] 3 W.L.R. 370 442
Turton v. Turton [1988] Ch. 542; [1987] 3 W.L.R. 622 315
Twentieth Century Banking Corp Ltd v. Wilkinson [1977] Ch. 99; [1976] 3 W.L.R. 489 503
Tyler, Re [1891] 3 Ch. 252 237
Tyrell's Case (1557) 2 Dy. 155a 65
Tyrell's Estate, Re [1907] 1 I.R. 292 238
Tyrringham's Case (1584) 4 Co. Rep. 36b 422, 443

Underwood Ltd v. Burgh Castle Brick and Cement Syndicate [1922] 1 K.B. 343 149
Ungurian v. Lesnoff [1990] Ch. 206; [1989] 3 W.L.R. 840 .... 254, 317
Union Lighterage Co v. London Graving Dock Co[1902] 2 Ch. 557 .... 427, 430
Union of London and Smith's Bank Ltd's Conveyance, Re [1933] Ch. 611; 89 A.L.R. 797 .... 457, 458, 459
United Bank of Kuwait Plc v. Sahib [1997] Ch. 107; [1996] 3 W.L.R. 372 .... 69, 500
United Dominions Trust Ltd v. Shellpoint Trustees Ltd [1993] 3 All E.R. 301; (1992) 64 P. & C.R. 457; [1992]
    39 E.G. 144 358
Unity Joint Stock Mutual Banking Association v. King (1858) 25 Beav. 72 488
Universal Permanent Building Society v. Cooke [1952] Ch. 95; [1951] 2 All E.R. 893 .... 95, 352
University College of North Wales v. Taylor [1908] P. 140 177
Uratemp Ventures Ltd v. Collins [2001] UKHL 43; [2002] 1 A.C. 301; [2001] 3 W.L.R. 806 341
Uziell-Hamilton v. Keen (1971) 22 P. & C.R. 655 95

Valentini v. Canali (1890) L.R. 24 Q.B.D. 166 204
Van Haarlam v. Kasner Charitable Trust (1992) 64 P. & C.R. 214; [1992] 36 E.G. 135 .... 356, 361, 363
Vanderplank v. King (1843) 3 Hare 1 216
Vandersteen v. Agius (1993) 65 P. & C.R. 266; [1992] N.P.C. 108 581
Vandervell v. Inland Revenue Commissioners [1967] 2 A.C. 291; [1967] 2 W.L.R. 87 295
Vandervell's Trusts (No.2), Re [1974] Ch. 269; [1974] 3 W.L.R. 256 292
Vane v. Lord Barnard (1716) 2 Vern. 738 49
Vaudeville Electric Cinema Ltd v. Muriset [1923] 2 Ch. 74 21
Vaughan v. Hampson (1875) 33 L.T. 15 476
Vaux, Re [1939] Ch. 465 217
Verrall v. Great Yarmouth BC [1981] Q.B. 202; [1980] 3 W.L.R. 258 .... 478, 470
Villar, Re [1929] 1 Ch. 243 219
Vine v. Raleigh [1891] 2 Ch. 13 246
Viner v. Francis (1789) 2 Cox Eq. 190 190
Vinogradoff, Re [1935] W.N. 68 203
Vynior's Case (1610) 8 Co. Rep. 81b 176
Vyvyan v. Arthur (1823) 1 B. & C. 410 392

Wainwright v. Miller [1897] 2 Ch. 255 230
Wakefield, Re [1943] 2 All E.R. 29 526
Wakeman, Re [1945] Ch. 177 87
Walker, In b. (1912) 28 T.L.R. 466 205
Walker, Re [1905] 1 Ch. 160 205
——— v. Hall [1984] Fam. Law 21; (1983) 80 L.S.G. 2139; [1984] F.L.R. 126 318
——— v. Linom [1907] 2 Ch. 104 .... 536, 538
Walker v. Shore (1808) 15 Ves. 122 191

Walker v. Waller [1967] 1 W.L.R. 451; [1967] 1 All E.R. 305 .... 87, 320
Wallis & Simmonds (Builders), Re [1974] 1 W.L.R. 391; [1974] 1 All E.R. 561 .... 99, 500
Wallis Fashion Group Ltd v. CGU Life Assurance Ltd (2001) 81 P. & C.R. 28; [2000] L. & T.R. 520; [2000]
    2 E.G.L.R. 49 401
Wallis v. Harrison (1838) 4 M. & W. 538 480
Wallis's Cayton Bay Holiday Camp Ltd v. Shell-Mex and BP Ltd [1975] Q.B. 94; [1974] 3 W.L.R. 387 552
Walmsley and Shaw's Contract, Re [1917] 1 Ch. 93 430
Walsh v. Lonsdale (1882) 21 Ch. D. 9 .... 343, 344, 345
—— v. Oates [1953] 1 Q.B. 578; [1953] 2 W.L.R. 835 419
Waltham Forest LBC v. Thomas [1992] 2 A.C. 198; [1992] 3 W.L.R. 131 606
Walton Harvey Ltd v. Walker & Homfrays Ltd [1931] 1 Ch. 274 476
Ward v. Day (1863) 4 B. & S. 337; (1864) 5 B. & S. 364 356
—— v. Duncombe [1893] A.C. 369 .... 540, 542
—— v. Kirkland [1967] Ch. 194; [1966] 1 W.L.R. 601 .... 430, 448
—— v. Van der Loeff [1924] A.C. 653 216
—— v. Ward (1852) 7 Exch. 838 443
—— v. Ward (1870–71) L.R. 6 Ch. App. 789 306
Waring (Lord) v. London and Manchester Assurance Co Ltd [1935] Ch. 310 505
Warner v. Sampson 1959] 1 Q.B. 297; [1959] 2 W.L.R. 109; [1958] 1 Q.B. 404; [1958] 2 W.L.R. 212 .... 354, 361
Warr (Earl de la) v. Miles (1881) L.R. 17 Ch. D. 535 431
Warren v. Keen [1954] 1 Q.B. 15 373
Wasdale, Re [1899] 1 Ch. 163 541
Waterlow v. Bacon (1866) L.R. 2 Eq. 514 442
Waters v. Mynn (1850) 15 L.T. (O.S.) 157 520
Watkins v. Weston (1863) 3 De G.J. & S. 434 189
Watson (Deceased), Re [1999] 1 F.L.R. 878; [1999] 3 F.C.R. 595 197
Watson v. Gray (1880) L.R. 14 Ch. D. 192 332
Watson's Settlement Trusts, Re [1959] 1 W.L.R. 732; [1959] 2 All E.R. 676 216
Watts, Re [1931] 2 Ch. 302 232
Watt's Will Trusts, Re [1936] 2 All E.R. 1555 244
Watts v. Kelson (1870–71) L.R. 6 Ch. App. 166 .... 426, 429
—— v. Waller [1973] Q.B. 153; [1972] 3 W.L.R. 365 98
Wayling v. Jones [1995] 2 F.L.R. 1029; [1996] 2 F.C.R. 41; (1995) 69 P. & C.R. 170 488
Weatherell v. Thornburgh (1878) 8 Ch.D. 261 244
Weaver v. Mogford 1988] 31 E.G. 49; [1988] 2 E.G.L.R. 48 385
Webb, In b. (1855) Dea. & Sw. 1 178
Webb v. Bird (1862) 13 C.B. (N.S.) 841 .... 416, 448
—— v. Pollmount Ltd [1966] Ch. 584; [1966] 2 W.L.R. 543 .... 123, 389, 398
Webb's Lease, Re [1951] Ch. 808; [1951] 2 All E.R. 131 428
Wedd v. Porter [1916] 2 K.B. 91 373
Weg Motors v. Hales [1962] Ch. 49; [1961] 3 W.L.R. 558; 1961] Ch. 176; [1960] 3 W.L.R. 964 .... 236, 347, 381,
    393
Weigall v. Brome (1833) 6 Sim. 99 337
Wellcome v. Upton (1840) 6 M. & W. 536 432
Weld v. Bradbury (1715) 2 Vern 705 191
Wells, Re [1933] Ch. 29 .... 493, 521
—— v. Kingston upon Hull (1874–75) L.R. 10 C.P. 402 340
Wellsted's Will Trusts, Re [1949] Ch. 296; [1949] 1 All E.R. 577 .... 87, 275
West Bank Estates v. Arthur [1967] 1 A.C. 665; [1966] 3 W.L.R. 750 551
West Layton Ltd v. Ford [1979] Q.B. 593; [1979] 3 W.L.R. 14 377
West London Commercial Bank v. Reliance Permanent Building Society (1885) L.R. 29 Ch. D. 954 506
West v. Dobb (1869) L.R. 4 Q.B. 634 390
—— v. Williams [1899] 1 Ch. 132 544
Western Bank Ltd v. Schindler [1977] Ch. 1; [1976] 3 W.L.R. 341 510
Western Fish Products Ltd v. Penwith DC [1981] 2 All E.R. 204; 77 L.G.R. 185 486
Western v. MacDermott (1866) L.R. 1 Eq. 499 460
Westhoughton Urban DC v. Wigan Coal and Iron Co Ltd [1919] 1 Ch. 159 .... 455, 456
Westminster Bank Ltd v. Lee [1956] Ch. 7; [1955] 3 W.L.R. 376 .... 61, 98
Westminster City Council v. Clarke [1992] 2 A.C. 288; [1992] 2 W.L.R. 229 341
Westminster (Duke of) v. Guild 1985] Q.B. 688; [1984] 3 W.L.R. 630 372
Weston v. Arnold 1872–73] L.R. 8 Ch. App. 1084 .... 332, 333
Weston v. Henshaw [1950] Ch. 510 263

Westripp v. Baldock [1939] 1 All E.R. 279 471
Wetherill v. Wetherill (1863) 1 De G.J. & S. 134 219
Whaley, Re [1908] 1 Ch. 615 21
Wharton v. Masterman [1895] A.C. 186 244
Whatman v. Gibson (1838) 9 Sim. 196 468
Wheaton v.Maple & Co [1893] 3 Ch. 48 440
Wheeldon v. Burrows (1879) L.R. 12 Ch. D. 31; [1874–90] All E.R. Rep. 669 .... 427, 428, 429
Wheeler and De Rochow [1896] 1 Ch. 315 297
Wheeler v. Mercer [1957] A.C. 416; [1956] 3 W.L.R. 841 .... 35, 349, 581
Wheelwright v. Walker (1883) L.R. 23 Ch. D. 752 269
—— v. Walker (No. 2) (1883) 31 W.R. 912 270
Whitby v. Mitchell (1890) L.R. 44 Ch. D. 85; affirming (1889) L.R. 42 Ch. D. 494 248
White (Deceased), Re [1991] Ch. 1; [1990] 3 W.L.R. 187 178
White (William), Re [1901] 1 Ch. 570 216
White v. Bijou Mansions Ltd [1938] Ch. 351; [1937] Ch. 610 .... 104, 119, 455, 471
—— v. City of London Brewery Co (1889) L.R. 42 Ch. D. 237 507
—— v. Grand Hotel Eastbourne Ltd [1913] 1 Ch. 113 (affirmed on another point 84 L.J.Ch. 938) 444
—— v. Metcalf [1903] 2 Ch. 567 511
—— v. Taylor (No.2) [1969] 1 Ch. 150; [1967] 3 W.L.R. 1246 443
White Rose Cottage, Re [1965] Ch. 940; [1965] 2 W.L.R. 337; CA; reversing [1964] Ch. 483; [1964] 2 W.L.R.
    396 [1964] Ch. 483 .... 130, 513, 545
Whitehall Court Ltd v. Ettlinger [1920] 1 K.B. 680 375
Whiteley v. Delaney [1914] A.C. 132 524
Whittingham v. Whittingham [1979] Fam. 9; [1978] 2 W.L.R. 936 .... 99, 100
Whorwood, Re (1887) L.R. 34 Ch. D. 446 192
Wickham v. Hawker (1840) 7 M. & W. 63 421
Wightwick's Will Trusts, Re [1950] Ch. 260; [1950] 1 All E.R. 689 .... 238, 240
Wiles v. Banks (1985) 50 P. & C.R. 80 425
Wilkes v. Gee [1973] 1 W.L.R. 742; [1973] 2 All E.R. 1214 442
—— v. Spooner [1911] 2 K.B. 473 .... 59, 63, 470
William Brandt's Sons & Co v. Dunlop Rubber Co Ltd [1905] A.C. 454 499
Williams & Glyn's Bank Ltd v. Boland [1981] A.C. 487; [1980] 3 W.L.R. 138 .... 9, 10, 62, 87, 99, 110, 114, 124,
                                                                                              283, 304, 310, 313, 320, 531
Williams Bros Direct Supply v. Raftery [1958] 1 Q.B. 159; [1957] 3 W.L.R. 931 552
Williams (Deceased), Re [1985] 1 W.L.R. 905; [1985] 1 All E.R. 964 188
Williams v Burlington Investments (1977) 121 S.J. 424 96
—— v. Earle (1867–68) L.R. 3 Q.B. 739 388
—— v. Hensman (1861) 1 J. & H. 546 331
—— v. Morgan [1906] 1 Ch. 804 503
—— v. Staite [1979] Ch. 291; [1978] 2 W.L.R. 825 .... 486, 487
—— v. Tyley (1858) Johns. 530 179
—— v. Unit Construction Co. Ltd (1955) 19 Conv N.S. 261 458
—— v. Usherwood (1983) 45 P. & C.R. 235 .... 417, 560, 562
—— v. Wellingborough BC [1975] 1 W.L.R. 1327; [1975] 3 All E.R. 462 506
—— v. Williams (Sale of Matrimonial Home) [1976] Ch. 278; [1976] 3 W.L.R. 494 323
Williamson v. Naylor (1838) 3 Y. & C.Ex. 208 183
Willingale v. Maitland 1866–67) L.R. 3 Eq. 103 423
Willis (J) & Son v. Willis [1986] 1 E.G.L.R. 62; (1985) 277 E.G. 1133 486
Willmott v. Barber (1880) L.R. 15 Ch. D. 96 .... 483, 484
Wilmer's Trusts [1903] 2 Ch. 411 220
Wilson Bowden Properties Ltd v. Milner [1997] N.P.C. 187; (1997) New Law Digest, Property Communica-
    tion 128 488
Wilson, In b. [1952] P. 92 182
Wilson v. Clapham (1819) 1 Jac. & W. 36 155
—— v. Finch Hatton (1876–77) L.R. 2 Ex. D. 336 .... 367, 370
—— v. Tavener [1901] 1 Ch. 578 476
—— v. Wilson (1851) 1 Sim. (N.S.) 288 240
Wiltshear v. Cottrell (1853) 1 E. & B. 674 20
Wimbledon and Putney Commons Conservators v. Dixon (1875–76) L.R. 1 Ch. D. 362 445
Wingham, Re [1949] P. 187; [1948] 2 All E.R. 908 181
Winter Garden Theatre (London) Ltd v. Millenium Productions Ltd [1946] 1 All E.R. 678 .... 477, 478
Winter Garden Theatre (London) Ltd v. Millenium Productions Ltd [1948] A.C. 173; [1947] 2 All E.R. 331 478

Wirral BC v. Smith 80 L.G.R. 628; (1982) 43 P. & C.R. 312 199
Wisbech St Mary Parish Council v. Lilley [1956] 1 W.L.R. 121; [1956] 1 All E.R. 301 354
Wiscot's Case (1599) 2 Co. Rep. 60b 329
Witham v. Vane (1883) Challis R.P. 440 235
Witty, Re [1913] 2 Ch. 666 234
Wix, Re [1916] 1 Ch. 279 272
Wolfe v. Hogan [1949] 2 K.B. 194; [1949] 1 All E.R. 570 592
Wollaston v. Hakewill (1841) 3 Man. & G. 297 .... 352, 384
—— v. King (1868) L.R. 8 Eq. 165 233
Wolson, Re [1939] Ch. 780 184
Wolveridge v Steward (1833) 1 Cr. & M. 644 392
Wong v. Beaumont Property Trust [1965] 1 Q.B. 173; [1964] 2 W.L.R. 1325 428
Wood, Re [1894] 3 Ch. 381 217
—— v. Leadbitter (1845) 13 M. & W. 838 .... 476, 478
—— v. Smith [1993] Ch. 90; [1992] 3 W.L.R. 583; [1992] 3 All E.R. 556 177
Woodall v. Clifton [1905] 2 Ch. 257 .... 236, 388
Woodhouse & Co v. Kirkland (Derby) Ltd [1970] 1 W.L.R. 1185; [1970] 2 All E.R. 587 445
Woodstead Finance v. Petrou (1985) 136 N.L.J. 188; The Times, January 23, 1986 523
Woolf Project Management, Ltd v. Woodtrek, Ltd (1988) 56 P. & C.R. 134; [1988] 1 E.G.L.R. 179 108
Woollerton and Wilson Ltd v. Richard Costain Ltd [1970] 1 W.L.R. 411; [1970] 1 All E.R. 483 569
Woolley, Re [1903] 2 Ch. 206 313
Worcester, Re (1868) 3 Ch.App. 555 541
Wordingham v. Royal Exchange Trust Co Ltd [1992] Ch. 412; [1992] 2 W.L.R. 496 187
Wormald v. Maitland (1866) 35 L.J. Ch. 69 59
Worthing Corporation v. Heather [1906] 2 Ch. 532 235
Wright, Ex p. (1812) 19 Ves. 255 499
Wright, Re, [1949] Ch. 729; [1949] 2 All E.R. 605 377
—— v. Burroughes (1846) 3 C.B. 685 393
—— v. Dean [1948] Ch. 686; [1948] 2 All E.R. 415 .... 389, 403
—— v. Macadam [1949] 2 K.B. 744; [1949] 2 All E.R. 565 .... 417, 426, 427, 448
—— v. Wakeford (1811) 17 Ves. 454 177
—— v. Walford [1955] 1 Q.B. 363; [1955] 2 W.L.R. 198 596
—— v. Williams (1836) 1 M. & W. 77 438
Wrightson, Re [1908] 1 Ch. 789 300
Wroth v. Tyler [1974] Ch. 30; [1973] 2 W.L.R. 405 .... 62, 99
Wrotham Park Estate Co Ltd v. Parkside Homes Ltd [1974] 1 W.L.R. 798; [1974] 2 All E.R. 321 470
Wrout v. Dawes (1858) 25 Beav. 369 492
Wyatt v. Berry [1893] P. 5 178
—— v. Cole (1877) 36 L.T. 613 347
—— v. Harrison (1823) 3 B. & Ad. 871 .... 418, 447
Wycombe AHA v. Barnett (1982) 47 P. & C.R. 394 (1982) 264 E.G. 619 371
Wyld v. Silver [1963] 1 Q.B. 169; [1963] Ch. 243 59

Y.B. 5 Edw. 4, Mich., pl 16 58
Y.B. 22 Edw. 4, Pasch., pl. 18 58
Y.B. 14 Fen.8, Mich., pl. 5, fo 7 58
Yates, In the Estate of [1919] P. 93 182
Yates v. Jack (1866) 1 Ch. App. 295 446
Yaxley v. Gotts [2000] Ch. 162; [1999] 3 W.L.R. 1217 .... 69, 149, 154, 294, 296, 330, 485, 486
Yeap Cheah Neo v. Ong Cheng Neo (1875) L.R. 6 P.C. 381 238
Yellowly v. Gower (1855) 11 Exch. 274 373
Young (Deceased), Re [1951] Ch. 344; [1950] 2 All E.R. 1245 186
Young v. Ashley Gardens Properties Ltd [1903] 2 Ch. 112 376
—— v. Clarey [1948] Ch. 191; [1948] 1 All E.R. 197 .... 511, 512, 555
—— v. Dalgety [1987] 1 E.G.L.R. 116; (1987) 281 E.G. 427 .... 21, 22
—— v. Davies (1863) 2 Dr. & Sm. 167 186
—— v. Secretary of State for the Environment [1983] 2 A.C. 662; [1983] 3 W.L.R. 382 573
Youngmin v. Heath [1974] 1 W.L.R. 135; [1974] 1 All E.R. 461 384

Zetland (Marquess of) v. Driver 1939] Ch. 1 458
Zimbler v. Abrahams [1903] 1 K.B. 577 343
Zouch d. Abbot v. Parsons (1765) 3 Burr. 1794 203

TABLE OF STATUTES

1215 Magna Carta (16 John) 423

1236 Statute of Merton (20 Hen. 3, c.4)(Commons Act) 441

1258 Provisions of Oxford 54

1285 Statute of Westminister II (13 Edw. 1, c.
46)(Commons Act) 54, 441
c.24 *In Consimili Casu* 54
Statute De Donis Conditionalibus 32, 45, 46

1290 Statute of Quia Emptores 26, 27, 32, 33, 408,
413, 422

1324 Statute De Prerogativa Regis (17 Edw. 2,
St.1, cc. 9, 10) 205

1535 Statute of Uses (27 Hen. 8, c.10) 65, 66, 248,
249, 292

1539 Partition Act (31 Hen. 8, c. 1) 328

1540 Statute of Wills (32 Hen. 8, c. 1) 38
ss.1, 2 38
Grantees of Reversions Act (32 Hen. 8, c.
34)
ss.1, 2 393

1545 Statute of Uses (27 Hen. 8, c. 10) 15

1660 Tenures Abolition Act (12 Car. 2, c. 24) 27

1677 Statute of Frauds (29 Car. 2, c. 3) 68, 294
s.1 68
s.4 .... 148, 294
ss.7, 8 294
s.8 .... 294, 296
s.9 295

1698 Statute of Posthumous Children (10 Will.
3, c. 22) 214

1706 6 Anne, cc. 6, 7 (Duke of Marlborough) 47

1730 Landlord and Tenant Act (4 Geo. 2, c.
28)
s.1 350
ss.2, 4 358
s.5 410

1737 Distress for Rent Act (11 Geo. 2, c. 19)
s.11 349
s.18 350

1800 Accumulations Act (39 & 40 Geo. 3, c.
98) 241

1801 Inclosure (Consolidation) Act (41 Geo. 3,
c. 98) 441

1814 54 Geo. 3, c. 161 (Duke of Wellington) 47

1832 Prescription Act (2 & 3 Will. 4, c. 71) 430,
432, 433, 434, 435, 436, 438, 439,
440, 441
s.1 .... 430, 434, 435, 440
s.2 .... 430, 434, 435. 437, 440
s.3 .... 434, 439, 440
s.4 .... 434, 437, 439
s.5 .... 435, 436
s.6 436
s.7 .... 436, 437, 438, 439
s.8 .... 436, 437, 438, 439

1833 Fines and Recoveries Act (3 & 4 Will. 4, c.
74) 46
s.18 47
s.19 47
s.35 47
s.39 47
Inheritance Act (3 & 4 Will. 4, c. 106) 32

1837 Wills Act (7 Will. 4 & 1 Vict. c. 26) ... 39, 40,
184, 185
s.9 .... 177, 178
s.11 181
s.15 185
s.18 .... 180, 181
s.18A 181
s.20 179
s.21 178
s.22 181
s.24 .... 176, 190
s.25 183
s.27 192
s.28 .... 39, 40
s.32 183
s.33 .... 183, 184, 186
(2) 184
(4) 184
s.34 39

1839 Judgments Act (1 & 2 Vict. c. 110) 11

1840 Settled Estates Drainage Act (3 & 4 Vict. c.
55) 249

1845 Lands Clauses Consolidation Act (8 & 9
Vict. c. 18) 577
Settled Estates Drainage Act (8 & 9 Vict. c.
56) 249

1845   Real Property Act (8 & 9 Vict. c. 106)   68
       s.2   68
       s.3 ....   68, 353, 364
       s.5   455
       Inclosure Act (8 & 9 Vict. c. 118)   441
1851   Landlord and Tenant Act (14 & 15 Vict. c.
       25)   373
       s.1   373
       s.3   22
1852   Wills Act Amendment Act (15 & 16 Vict.
       c. 24)   177
       Common Law Procedure Act (15 & 16
       Vict. c. 76) 54, 358, 359
       s.210 ....   357, 358, 359
       ss.210–212   358
       s.212   359
       Inclosure Act (15 & 16 Vict. c. 79)   442
1856   Settled Estates Act (19 & 20 Vict. c.
       120)   249
1858   Chancery Amendment Act (Lord Cairns'
       Act) (21 & 22 Vict. c 27)   470
       s.2   57
1859   Law of Property Amendment Act (22 & 23
       Vict. c. 35)
       s.27   384
1860   Lincoln's Inn Act (23 & 24 Vict. c.
       clxxxiv)   566
1862   Land Registry Act (25 & 26 Vict. c. 53)   12,
                                                       76, 111
1864   Improvement of Land Act (27 & 28 Vict. c.
       114)   409
1868   Partition Act (31 & 32 Vict. c. 40)   328
1873   Supreme Court of Judicature (36 & 37
       Vict. c. 66) 54, 344
       s.25(4)   412
       (11)   344
       Supreme Court of Judicature Act (36 & 37
       Vict. c. 66)   56
1874   Vendor and Purchaser Act (37 & 38 Vict. c.
       78)
       s.1   63
       s.2   103
       Supreme Court of Judicature (Commence-
       ment) Act (37 & 38 Vict. c. 79)
       s.2   56
1875   Land Transfer Act (38 & 39 Vict. c. 87)   12,
                                                       111
       Agricultural Holdings (England) Act (38 &
       39 Vict. c. 92) 580, 584
1876   Commons Act (39 & 40 Vict. c. 92) 441, 442
       ss.10–12   442
       s.31   441
1877   Settled Estates Act (40 & 41 Vict. c. 18)   249
1881   Conveyancing Act (44 & 45 Vict. c. 41)
       s.5(1)   528
       s.6(1)   426
       s.7   163
       s.10   395
       s.11   395
       s.14   360
       s.18   518
       s.19(1)   515

1881   Conveyancing Act—cont.
       s.23   515
       s.44   410
       s.51 ....   38, 39
       s.58   458
       s.61   527
       s.65   365
1882   Settled Land Act (45 & 46 Vict. c. 38)   249
       s.26   274
       s.35   50
       s.54   263
       Conveyancing Act (45 & 46 Vict. c. 39)   63
       s.2   360
       s.3   63
       s.4   360
       s.11   365
1888   Land Charges Registration and Searches
       Act (51 & 52 Vict. c. 51)   11
1890   Lunacy Act (53 & 54 Vict. c. 29)   205
1892   Conveyancing Act (55 & 56 Vict. c. 13)
       s.3   377
1893   Law of Commons Amendment Act (56 &
       57 Vict. c. 57)
       ss.2, 3   441
1897   Land Transfer Act (60 & 61 Vict. c. 65)   12,
                                                   76, 111, 199
1898   Benefices Act (61 & 62 Vict. c. 48) 79, 115
1899   Bodies Corporate (Joint Tenancy) Act (62
       & 63 Vict. c. 20)   304
1909   Housing, Town Planning, etc., Act (9 Edw.
       7, c. 44)   569
1911   Conveyance Act (1 & 2 Geo. 5, c. 37)
       s.2   393
       s.3   519
1914   Deeds of Arrangement Act (4 & 5 Geo. 5,
       c. 47)   101
       s.1   101
       s.7   101
       s.8   101
       Sched. 1   101
1915   Increase of Rent and Mortgage Interest
       (War Restrictions) Act (5 & 6 Geo. 5,
       c. 98)   590
1918   Wills (Soldiers and Sailors) Act (7 & 8
       Geo. 5, c. 58)   204
       s.2   182
       s.3   183
       s.5   182
1920   Air Navigation Act (10 & 11 Geo. 5, c.
       80)
       s.9   569
       Increase of Rent and Mortgage Interest
       (Restrictions) Act (10 & 11 Geo. 5, c.
       17)
       s.13   581
1922   Law of Property Act (c. 16) 16, 28, 351
       s.14   105
       s.32   105
       s.128   28
       s.145   351
       Sched. 7   105
       Sched. 12, para. 1   28

1922   Law of Property Act—*cont.*
        Sched. 13, Pt. II 28
        Sched 15 351
                para. 7 236
1923   Agricultural Holdings Act (13 & 14 Geo.
        5, c. 9)
        s.12 584
        Benefices Act 1898 (Amendment) Meas-
        ure (14 & 15 Geo 5, No. 1) 79, 115
1924   Law of Property (Amendment) Act (15 &
        16 Geo. 5, c. 5) 16
        Sched. IX 409
1925   Settled Land Act (c. 18) 7, 16, 45, 51, 77, 80,
                84, 87, 89, 90, 91, 95, 108, 110,
                124, 126, 127, 129, 130, 132, 133,
                200, 201, 203, 206, 207, 214, 243,
                249, 251, 252, 253, 254, 255, 257,
                258, 259, 261, 264, 265, 266, 267,
                268, 269, 275, 279, 280, 282, 283,
                285, 289, 290, 297, 298, 300, 302,
                309, 310, 326, 327, 347, 409, 486,
                487, 541, 556, 557
        s.1 252
            (1) 254
        s.2(5) 265
        s.3 266
        s.4 .... 251, 258, 261
        s.5 .... 258, 261
            (3) 264
        s.6 260
        s.7(1) 266
            (2) 266
            (4) 266
            (5) 266, 267, 280
        s.8 .... 260, 266
            (4) 265
                (a) 266
        s.9 261
        s.10 264
        s.12 266
        s.13 .... 260, 261, 262, 263
        s.16 .... 268, 272
        s.17 267
        s.18 .... 89, 263
            (1) 263, 297
                (a) 263
                (b, (c) 263
        s.19(2) 326
            (3) 326
        s.24 277
        s.25 279
        s.27(1) 202, 290
        s.29 .... 206, 265
        s.30 .... 256, 257
        s.34 257
        s.35(1) 302
        s.36 .... 265, 267
            (1) 326
            (2) 327
            (4) 308, 310
            (6) 327
        s.38 270

1925   Settled Land Act —*cont.*
        ss.38–48 269
        s.39 270
        s.41 .... 51, 259, 270
        s.42 .... 51, 259, 271
        s.44 271
        s.45 271
        ss.45–47 51
        s.47 .... 51, 272
        s.48 .... 270, 271
        s.49(1) 434
        s.51 .... 269, 273
        s.52 272
        s.53 268
        s.58 274
        s.59 272
        s.64 274
        s.65 273
        s.66 50
        s.67 274
        s.68 275
        s.71 .... 269, 272
        s.72 .... 88, 89
        s.73 275
        s.75 .... 89, 90
        ss.83–87 274
        s.86(1) 259
            (2) 259
            (3) 259
            (5) 259
        s.91 259
        s.93 276
        s.97 269
        s.101 269
        s.104 .... 277, 278
        s.105 277
        s.106 276
        s.107 268
        s.108 276
        s.109 276
        s.110 .... 260, 270
            (1) 263
            (2) 264, 265
            (2) proviso 265
                (e) 265, 267
            (4) 90, 266
        s.117 273
            (1)(xxiv) 351
        s.119(3) 258, 259
        Sched. 2, para. 1 260
        Sched. 3 275
                Pt I 275
                Pt II 275
                Pt III 275
        Trustee Act (c. 19) 16, 77, 246, 296, 297, 384
        s.18(2) 300
        s.26(1) 384
            (1A) 384
            (2) 384
        s.31 246
        s.34 .... 310, 311
            (2) 297, 298, 311

1925   Trustee Act—*cont.*

s.35 302

(3) 302

s.36(1) 297, 198, 300

(6) 299

s.37(1)(c) 298

(2) 298

s.39(1) 299

s.40 .... 300, 302

(1) 300

(2) 301

(4) 301

(6) 300

s.41 297

ss.44–56 301

s.69(2) 297

Law of Property Act (c. 20) 8, 16, 46, 66, 68,
77, 80, 85, 86, 102, 105, 115, 156,
165, 215, 219, 221, 238, 241, 260,
281, 282, 284, 292, 294, 295, 309,
312, 328, 329, 330, 331, 350, 359,
365, 392, 393, 412, 494, 495, 496,
497, 502, 504, 505, 511, 515, 538,
540

Pt. I 105

s.1 .... 45, 78, 81, 213, 214

(1) **78**, 79, 342

(2) **78**, 79

(a) 110

(e) 463

(3) **79**, 110

(4) 79

(5) 84

(6) 201, 308

s.2 .... 84, 85, 87, 252

(1) 108

s.3(1) 411

(b)(ii) 311

(ii) proviso 267

s.4 238

(1) 110

(2) 212

(3) 462

s.5 529

s.7(1) 80

s.8(2) 411

s.14 105

s.19(2) 202, 309

(4) 203

(5) 203

(6) 202

s.20 298

ss.24–36 8

s.25 282

s.26 286

s.27 .... 86, 87, 281

(2) 87, 200, 201, 297

s.28 .... 87, 284

(3) 328

s.30 .... 288, 321

s.31 .... 281, 284, 503

s.32 .... 281, 284

1925   Law of Property Act—*cont.*

s.34(1) 308

(2) 309, 310

(3) 310

ss.34–36 284

s.35 309

s.36(1) 309, 310

(2) 308, 329, 331

s.38(2) 333

s.40 .... 68, 95, 148, 294

(1) 148

(2) 148

s.44 .... 63, 103

(3) 396

(4) 396

(5) 103, 104, 396

s.45(9) 160

s.46 156

s.47 155

s.48(1) 156

s.50 .... 108, 528

s.51 68

(1) 425

s.52 .... 79, 364

(1) 68, 160, 342, 342, 353

(2)(d) 342

s.53 409

(1) 499

(b) 294

(c) 153, 294, 295

(2) 289, 294, 196

s.54 .... 68, 79

(2) 68, 123, 126, 342

s.56 .... 455, 456("section 56")

s.60 .... 19, 39

(1) 38

(2) 39

(3), (4) 292

s.62 .... 345, 426, 429, 458("section 62")

(1) 23, 24, 426, 427

(2) 426

(4) 426

s.63 .... 61, 162

s.64 160

s.65 425

s.69 162

s.70 411

s.72(4) 328

s.76 .... 163, 164

(6) 163

s.77(1)(c) 392

s.78 .... 163, 456, 458("section 78")

(1) 458

s.79(1) 468, 469

s.84(1), (1C) 472

(2) 472

(7) 472

(12) 473

s.85(1) 494, 514

(2) 81, 495

s.86(1) 496, 514, 529

(2) 496

1925 Law of Property Act—*cont.*

s.86(3) 529
s.87 495
    (1) 81, 495, 497, 507
s.88(2) 502, 504
s.89(2) 502, 504
s.91 526
    (2) 502, 503, 513, 528
s.93 515
s.94(1) 543
    (c)
    (2) 543
s.95 .... 524, 526
    (4) 81
s.96 526
    (1) 514
    (2) 514
s.97 .... 536, 538, 539, 540
s.98 526
s.99 518
    (14) 519
    (17) 519
s.100 519
s.101 .... 504, 511
    (1) 505, 508, 511, 515
    (2) 505, 508, 511
ss.101–107 504
s.103 504
s.104 108
    (1) 506
    (2) 505
s.105 .... 108, 506
s.108 515
s.109 512
    (1) 511
    (2) 511
s.111 527
s.115(1) 529
    (2) 529
    (3) 524
s.116 529
s.121 .... 238, 410
    (2) 410
    (3) 410
    (4) 411
    (6) 411
s.122 .... 82, 408
    (2), (3) 411
s.130 .... 19, 39, 45
    (3) 46
s.135 49
s.137(1) 540
    (2) 541
    (3) 541
    (4), (5) 542
    (8) 542
    (9) 542
s.138 542
s.140(1) 393
s.141 .... 393, 395, 526
    (1) 387
s.142 .... 393, 395

1925 Law of Property Act—*cont.*

s.142(1) 387
    (2) 385
s.144 377
s.146 .... 360, 362, 380
    (1) 360
    (2) 359, 362, 363
    (4) 359, 363
    (8) 361
    (9) 362, 363
    (10)(a) 362
        (b) 362
    (12) 360
s.147 379
s.149(3) 347
    (5) 496
    (6) 350
        (a) 351
s.153 .... 365, 554
s.154 393
s.162 238
s.163 .... 221, 223, 229, 234
s.164 .... 244, 245
    (1) 246
ss.164–166 241
s.165 .... 245, 246
s.166 243
s.176 46
s.177 180
s.184 185
s.185 .... 365, 412
s.187(1) 414
s.191 412
s.196(3) 332
    (4) 332
s.198 .... 11, 94, 102, 104
s.199 .... 61, 63, 94, 105
s.205(1)(I) 362
    (ii) 149, 342, 427
    (v) 101
    (ix) 79, 82, 115
    (xxi) 539
    (xxiii) 342
    (xxvi) 351
    (xxvii) 81, 339
    (xxix) 279
Sched. 1, Pt. II, para. 3 260
        Pt. II, para. 5 260
        Pt. II, para. 6 .... 251, 260
        Pt. IV, para. 1(3) 327
        Pt. IV, para. 2 326
        Pt. V 333
Sched 2 .... 163, 164
        Pt. IX 392
Sched. 7 66
Land Registration Act (c. 21) ... 12, 16, 76, 77,
        78, 111, 118, 121, 122, 127, 128,
        129, 134, 136, 138, 139, 143, 258,
        259, 264, 335, 382, 397, 546, 562
s.2 115
    (1) 131, 545
s.3(xv) 129, 497

1925   Land Registration Act—*cont.*
s.3(xvi) 121, 497
  (xviii) 141
  (xxiii) 497
s.4 .... 118, 120
s.5 118
ss.5–12 114
s.6 119
s.7 119
  (1) 119
s.8 .... 118, 120
  (1)(a) 498
s.9 .... 119, 391
ss.9–11 561
s.10 119
s.11 .... 119, 391
s.12 119
s.13 120
s.18 134
s.18(4) 497
s.19(1) 118
  (2) 115, 118, 545
ss.19–23 135
s.20 .... 114, 118, 135, 346
  (1) 135, 545
  (4) 135, 172, 320
s.21 134
  (4) 497
s.22(1) 118, 545
s.23 .... 114, 118, 346
  (1) 545
  (5) 172
s.25 .... 134, 498
ss.25–27 121
s.26 498
  (1) 498
s.27 498
  (2) 498
s.29 .... 498, 544
s.30 546
  (1) 546
  (2) 546
  (3) 546
s.33 .... 114, 118, 346
s.34 498
  (1) 513
  (3) 504
  (4) 506
s.37 .... 136, 169
s.40 134
s.41 136
s.42 136
ss.48–51 130
ss.48–62 130
s.49(1)(j) 451
s.50 471
  (3) 473
s.53 120
s.54(1) 131
s.55(1) 131
s.56 121
  (3) 131

1925   Land Registration Act—*cont.*
s.57(1) 132
  (2) 132
  (4) 132
s.58(1) 132
  (3) 133
s.61 .... 130, 136
  (3) 132
s.64 130
  (1) 130, 132
s.65 .... 130, 498, 514
s.66 .... 134, 500, 545
s.69 .... 114, 118, 135, 346
  (1) 114
  (4) 168
s.70(1) 122
    (a) 138
    (f) 562
    (g) 482, 489, 562
  (2), (3) 129
s.75 .... 123, 137, 391, 561
  (1) 561
s.76 116
s.77 120
  (6) 144
s.79 391
s.82 .... 114, 131, 139
  (1) 139
  (3) 141
s.83 143
  (1) 143
  (3) 144
  (9) 145
    (c) 144
s.83(4) 144
  (5)(a) 144
    (b), (c) 144
  (6) 144
  (11) 145
s.85(3)(c) 144
  (8) 144
s.86(2) 124
  (3) 132
s.106(2) 124
    (a) 498
s.110(1) 113
  (2) 166
  (4) 144
s.112 112
s.112A 112
s.113 144
s.123(1) 117, 118
Land Charges Act (c. 22) ... 11, 16, 77, 78, 94,
                                  536
s.10 535
s.13(2) 345, 536
Administration of Estates Act (c. 23) ... 16, 77,
     192, 193, 194, 198 199, 281, 284,
                              526, 527
s.1 300
  (1) 199, 527
s.2(2) 200

1925 Administration of Estates Act—*cont.*
s.3(1) 199, 527
(2) 199
(3) 199
(4) 199
(5) 199
s.7 198
s.9 199
s.22 266
s.23 199
s.33(1) 192, 284
(2) 193
s.34(3) 193
s.35 526
s.36(2) 200
(4) 200
(7) 200
(8) 200
s.37 200
s.39(1) 200
(ii) 200
s.41 194
ss.45–47 19
s.46(1) 193, 195, 196, 198
(3) 195
(4) 193
s.47(1) 193, 196
(2) 196
(3) 197
(4) 193
s.47A 194
s.49 196
(1)(aa) 195
s.51(3) 182, 203
s.55(1)(x) 193
(xv) 199
(xviii) 200
Universities and College Estates Act (15 &
16 Geo. 5, c. 24) 207, 283
Supreme Court of Judicature Act (15 & 16
Geo. 5, c. 49)
s.44 344
s.46 359
1926 Law of Property (Amendment) Act (16 &
17 Geo. 5, c. 11) 80, 255
s.1 .... 255, 262
Sched. ... 80, 87, 261, 266, 286, 312, 327, 514
1927 Landlord and Tenant Act (17 & 18 Geo. 5,
c. 36) 376, 379, 584
Pt. I 581
ss.1–3 584
ss.4, 5 581
s.18(1) 379
s.19(1) 376
(1A) 401
s.25(1) 581
1929 Law of Property (Amendment) Act (19 &
20 Geo. 5, c. 9)
s.1 359
Age of Marriage Act (19 & 20 Geo. 5, c.
36) 216

1932 Law of Property (Entailed Interests) Act
(22 & 23 Geo. 5, c. 27) 82
s.2 82
Rights of Way Act (22 & 23 Geo. 5, c.
45) 419
Town and Country Planning Act (22 & 23
Geo. 5, c. 48) 569
1934 Petroleum (Production) Act (24 & 25 Geo.
5, c. 36) 580
1936 Land Registration Act (26 Geo. 5 & 1 Edw.
8, c. 26) 111
Tithe Act (26 Geo. 5 & 1 Edw. 8, c. 43) 83
s.3 83
Sched. 9 83
1938 Leasehold Property (Repairs) Act (1 & 2
Geo 6, c. 3) 99, 379, 380
s.1 380
Inheritance (Family Provision) Act (1 & 2
Geo. 6, c. 45) 173
Coal Act (1 & 2 Geo. 6, c. 52) 580
1939 Limitation Act (2 & 3 Geo. 6, c. 21) 547
s.9(1) 554
s.26(b) 558
Landlord and Tenant (War Damage) Act (2
& 3 Geo. 6, c. 72) 366
London Building Acts (Amendment) Act
(2 & 3 Geo. 6, c. xcvii) 335
1941 Landlord and Tenant (War Damage) Act (4
& 5 Geo. 6, c. 41) 366
1942 Landlord and Tenant (Requisitioned Land)
Act (5 & 6 Geo. 6, c. 13) 366
1943 Settled Land and Trustee Acts (Court's
General Powers) Act (6 & 7 Geo 6, c.
25)
s.2 274
Town and Country Planning (Interim
Development) Act (6 & 7 Geo. 6, c.
29) 569, 576
1944 Landlord and Tenant (Requisitioned Land)
Act (7 & 8 Geo. 6, c. 5) 366
Validation of War-Time Leases Act (7 & 8
Geo. 6, c. 34) 346
Town and Country Planning Act (7 & 8
Geo. 6, c. 47)
s.10 577
1945 Limitation (Enemies and War Prisoners)
Act (8 & 9 Geo. 6, c. 16) 559
Welsh Church (Burial Grounds) Act (8 & 9
Geo. 6, c. 27)
s.1 81
1946 Furnished Houses (Rent Control) Act (9 &
10 Geo. 6, c. 34) 614
Coal Industry Nationalisation Act (9 & 10
Geo. 6, c. 59) 580
1947 Agriculture Act (10 & 11 Geo. 6, c. 48) 584
s.73 585
Sched. 9 585
Town and Country Planning Act (10 & 11
Geo. 6, c. 51) 569, 570, 571, 576, 577,
578
s.5 571
s.19 578

1947	Town and Country Planning Act—*cont.*	
	s.38	577
1948	Statute Law Revision Act (11 & 12 Geo. 6, c. 62)	
	Sched. 2	441
	Agricultural Holdings Act (11 & 12 Geo. 6, c. 63)	584
	s.24	306
1949	Lands Tribunal Act (12, 13 & 14 Geo. 6, c. 42)	
	s.1(4)	472
	Civil Aviation Act (12, 13 & 14 Geo. 6, c. 67)	
	s.40	569
1952	Disposal of Uncollected Goods Act (15 & 16 Geo. 6 & 1 Eliz. 2, c. 43)	492
	Intestates' Estates Act (15 & 16 Geo. 6 & 1 Eliz. 2, c. 64)	192, 193, 194, 195
	s.1	193
	(4)	195
	s.4	103
	Sched. 2	194, 195
1954	Landlord and Tenant Act (2 & 3 Eliz. 2, c. 56)	
	Pt. I	607, 608, 609
	Pt. II	581
	Pt. III	584
	ss.1, 2	607, 608
	s.4	608
	s.5	608
	ss.6–9	608
	s.12	608
	s.13	608
	s.17	608
	s.23	581
	s.24	581
	s.24A	584
	s.25	582
	s.26	582
	s.27	582
	s.29	582
	s.30	582
	s.31A	583
	s.32	583, 584
	s.33	583
	s.34	583, 584
	s.35	583, 584
	s.37	584
	s.43	581
	s.46	581
	s.51	379, 380
	s.52	473
	Sched. 3	608
1957	Rent Act (5 & 6 Eliz. 2, c. 25)	598, 607, 614
1958	Adoption Act (6 & 7 Eliz. 2, c. 5)	
	s.16(2)	188
	s.17(2)	188
	s.59	188
	Sched 5, para. 4	188
1959	Rights of Light Act (7 & 8 Eliz. 2, c. 56)	
	s.2	440
	s.3	440
1959	Mental Health Act (7 & 8 Eliz. 2, c. 72)	205
1960	Charities Act (8 & 9 Eliz. 2, c. 58)	206
	s.29	207
	s.38(2), (3)	206
	Sched. 7	206
	Caravan Sites and Control of Development Act (8 & 9 Eliz. 2, c. 62)	574
	ss.1, 2	574
	ss.3, 5	574
	Sched. 1	574
1961	Land Compensation Act (9 & 10 Eliz. 2, c. 33)	577
	Pt. III	579
	Pt. IV	579
	s.5	579
	ss.6–9	579
	ss.15, 16	579
	Sched. 1	579
1963	Finance Act (c. 25)	
	s.14	372
	s.55	166, 171
	s.68	83, 372
	Sched. 14, Pt. V	83
	Sched. 14, Pt. VI	83
	Water Resources Act (c. 38)	568
1964	Universities and College Estates Act (c. 51)	207
	Perpetuities and Accumulations Act (c. 55)	16, 215, 217, 218, 219, 222, 223, 224, 225, 226, 227, 228, 229, 230, 231, 232, 233, 234, 235, 236, 238, 239, 241, 243
	s.1	224
	s.2	227
	(1)	217
	(2)	218
	(4)	218
	s.3(1)	218
	(2)	233
	(3)	233, 243
	(4)(a)	222
	(b)	222
	(5)	222
	(b)(iii)	233
	s.4(1)	223
	(2)	223
	(3)	229
	(4)	228
	(7)	223
	s.5	224
	s.6	226
	s.7	232
	s.8(1)	231
	(2)	231
	s.9(1)	236
	(2)	236
	s.10	236
	s.11	411, 462
	(1)	238
	s.12	231
	s.13(1)	241
	(2)	241

1964 Perpetuities   and   Accumulations
        Act—*cont.*
      ss.13, 14 241
      s.15(4) 239
            (5) 215, 221, 223, 229, 235
      Law of Property (Joint Tenants) Act (c.
            63) 16, 312
      s.1 312
      s.2 312
      s.3 312
1965 Compulsory Purchase Act (c. 56) 577
      s.5 578
      s.11 578
      Commons Registration Act (c. 64) ... 127, 442,
                                        449, 450
      s.1(1) 442
          (2) 442
      s.2(1) 442
      s.4(6) 442
      s.5(2) 442
      s.15 450
          (1) 449
      s.16 438
      s.22(1) 442
      Rent Act (c. 75) 591, 598
1966 Family Provision Act (c. 35)
      s.1 .... 193, 194
      Land Registration Act (c. 39) 111
1967 Land Commission Act (c. 1)
      s.86 579
      s.101 579
      Sched. 17 579
      Forestry Act (c. 10) 271
      Matrimonial Homes Act (c. 75) 16, 98
      Leasehold Reform Act (c. 88) ... 377, 607, 608
      s.1 609
          (4) 610
      ss.1–4 609
      s.5 .... 95, 389, 397, 609
          (5) 124, 130
      s.8 .... 609, 610
      s.9(1) 610
          (1A), (1B) 610
          (4) 610
      s.14 610
      s.15 610
      s.17 611
      s.18 611
      s.19 611
      s.20 610
      s.21 610
      s.22 609
      s.23 610
      s.28 611
      s.33 611
      s.39 .... 607, 608
      Sched. 2 611
      Sched. 3 609
      Sched. 3, para. 2 609
      Sched. 5 .... 607, 608
      Sched. 5, paras.3, 4 608

1968 Wills Act (c. 28)
      s.1 185
      Caravan Sites Act (c. 52) 574
      Town and Country Planning Act 1968 (c.
            72) 571
      Pt. I 571
1969 Housing Act (c. 33)
      s.82 610
      Family Law Reform Act (c. 46) 215
      s.1 .... 201, 242
      s.3(2) 196
          (3) 182
      s.9 201
      s.12 201
      s.15 .... 188, 189
      Law of Property Act (c. 59) 12, 16, 581
      s.3 584
      s.4 581
      s.7 583
      s.11 584
      s.23 .... 63, 103
      s.24 102
      s.25 .... 12, 103
          (9), (10) 104
      s.28 472
          (7) 473
1970 Administration of Justice Act (c. 31)
      s.36 509
          (1) 509
          (3) 509
      Matrimonial Proceedings and Property Act
            (c. 45)
      s.1 199
      s.37 319
      s.40 195
      Sched. 2, para. 5 199
1971 Powers of Attorney Act (c. 27)
      s.4(1) 513
      s.5(3) 513
      Land Registration and Land Charges Act
            (c. 54) 111
      s.1 144
      s.2 144
          (2), (4) 144
          (5) 145
      Tribunals and Inquiries Act (c. 62)
      s.1 585
      Sched. 1 585
1972 Defective Premises Act (c. 35)
      s.4 372
      s.6(3) 372
      Land Charges Act (c. 61) ... 11, 16, 77, 78, 94,
                        99, 130, 382, 397, 514, 536, 538
      s.1 94
          (6) 107
      s.2 94
          (4) 95, 535
      ss.2 – 4 94
      s.3(1) 101
          (7) 99
      s.4 105
          (5) 536, 539, 540

1972 Land Charges Act—*cont.*
    s.4(6), (7) 345
    s.5 99
      (4) 101
      (7), (8) 105
      (10) 107
    s.6 100
      (1) 100
        (d) 451
      (2) 101
      (4), (5), (6) 105
    s.7(1) 101
      (2) 105
    s.8 100
    s.9 106
    s.10(4) 106
      (6) 106
    s.11 107
      (5), (6) 106
    s.12 106
    s.17 99
      (1) 97, 101, 536
    s.18(6) 536
    Sched. 1, para. 4 105
    Sched. 2 94
    Agriculture (Miscellaneous Provisions) Act (c. 62)
    s.21 585
1973 Administration of Justice Act (c. 15)
    s.8(1) 509
      (2) 509
    Matrimonial Causes Act (c. 18)
    s.18(2) 195, 189, 323
    ss.22–25 .... 289, 323
    Land Compensation Act (c. 26) 577
    Pt. III 579
    Pt. IV 579
1974 Consumer Credit Act (c. 39) 508, 523
    s.8(2) 523
    s.16 523
    ss.58–61 523
    s.94 523
    s.126 523
    s.129 508
    s.135 508
    ss.137–139 523
    s.138(1) 523
    s.139 523
    s.173 523
      (3) 523
    s.189(1) 523
    Housing Act (c. 44)
    s.118 610
      (2) 611
    Rent Act (c. 51) 377, 614
    s.1 593
1975 Finance Act (c. 7)
    Pt III 96
    Sched. 4 96
    Inheritance (Provision for Family and Dependants) Act (c. 63) 40, 173, 175, 181, 187, 197

1975 Inheritance (Provision for Family and Dependants) Act—*cont.*
    s.1 173
      (1) 173, 174
      (2)(a) 174
        (b) 174
      (3) 173
    s.2 175
    s.3(1) 175
      (2) 174, 175
      (3), (4) 175
    s.4 174
    ss.5, 6 176
    s.9 175
    ss.10–12 175
    s.21 175
    s.25(1) 173, 175
      (4) 173
    Children Act (c. 72)
    Sched. 3, para. 43 223
    Local Land Charges Act (c. 76) 11, 77
    s.1 92
    s.2 92
    s.3 91
    s.9 91
    s.10 92
    Sched. 1 92
1976 Adoption Act (c. 36)
    ss.38–46 197
    s.44 197
    Race Relations Act (c. 74)
    ss.1–3 377
    ss.21–24 40
    s.22 377
    s.24 377
    Rent (Agriculture) Act (c. 80) 605
    ss.1, 2 604
    s.3 604
    s.4 605
    ss.6, 7 605
    s.13 605
    ss.27, 28 605
    Sched. 3, Pt. I 604
    Sched. 4 605
1977 Agricultural Holdings (Notices to Quit) Act (c. 12) 584
    Rentcharges Act (c. 30) 80, 408, 409, 411, 462
    s.2 82
      (1), (2) 409
      (3)(a) 409
        (b) 409, 462
        (c) 410
        (d) 409
      (4) 462
        (a) 410
        (b) 410
      (5) 410, 463
    s.3 82
      (1) 412
      (3), (4), (5) 412
    ss.8–10 412

1977 Torts (Interference with Goods) Act (c. 32)
ss.12, 13 492
Sched. 1 492
Finance Act (c. 36)
s.56 83
Administration of Justice Act (c. 38)
s.24 141
s.26 498
s.28 .... 193, 194
Rent Act (c. 42) ... 591, 592, 598, 599, 600, 603,
605, 608, 609, 610, 614
Pt. X 599
s.1 592
s.2 594
s.3 594
(5) 594, 599
s.4 593
s.5(1) 593
s.6 593
s.7 593
ss.8, 9 593
s.11 593
s.12 593
s.13 592
ss.14, 15 592
ss.19–21 .... 614, 615
s.19 615
s.21 592
s.22 592
s.25 593
s.26 593
ss.44, 45 598
s.67 598
s.70 599
ss.77, 78 615
s.79 615
s.81 615
s.98 .... 594, 595, 596
s.101 598
s.102A 615
s.103 .... 599, 615
s.104 616
s.105 616
s.106A 615
s.122 615
Sched. 1, Pt I 594
Pt. II 599
para. 13 594
Sched. 15, Pt. I 595
Pt. II 596, 597
Pt. III 596
Pt. V 596
Protection from Eviction Act (c. 43) 616
s.1 616
s.2 .... 356, 616
s.3 616
(2A) 615
s.3A 349, 616
s.5 349
Criminal Law Act (c. 45)
s.6 356

1977 National Health Service Act (c. 49)
s.54(1) 326
1978 Civil Liability (Contribution) Act (c. 47) ... 399
1979 Charging Orders Act (c. 53) 16
s.1 100
s.2 100
s.3 100
(3) 130
1980 Limitation Amendment Act (c. 24) 547
s.3(1) 554
Housing Act (c. 51) 111, 591, 597, 603, 605,
614
s.52 597
s.60 598
s.65 593
s.66 .... 596, 597
s.67 597
s.69 615
s.70 615
s.72 614
s.73 592
s.74 592
s.76 594
s.142 610
Sched. 22 610
Limitation Act (c. 58) 16, 118, 122, 136, 140,
143, 412, 506, 512, 547, 548, 549,
550, 553, 554, 556, 557, 559, 561,
562, 563, 564
s.2 549
s.5 549
s.11 549
s.15 549
(1) 549
(2) 553
(3) 553
s.16 .... 511, 555
s.17 559
s.18 556
s.19 .... 549, 564
s.20 .... 549, 555, 556
(5) 564
s.21(1) 556
(2) 556
(3) 556
s.27 47
s.28 557
(1) 557
(3) 558
s.29 .... 555, 559
s.30 559
s.32(1) 558
(2) 558
(3) 558
s.38(1) 564
(2) 557
(5) 553
(8) 555
Sched. 1, para. 1 551
para. 4 .... 553, 554
para. 5(1) 554
(2) 554

1980 Limitation Act—*cont.*
        Sched. 1, para. 6 554
                  para. 8 551
                  para. 8(2) 564
                  para. 8(4) 552
                  para. 9 557
                  para. 10 549
                  para. 11 549
                  para. 12 555
        Sched. 3, para. 1 145
      Local Government, Planning and Land Act
        (c. 65)
        Pt. XVII 574
        Sched. 32 574
      Highways Act (c. 66)(1980 Act) 419
        s.31(1) 419
            (2) 419
        s.33 419
        ss.116–123 419
1981 Supreme Court Act (c. 54) 56
        s.37(4) 100
        s.38 358
        s.49 344
        s.50 .... 57, 470
        s.113 .... 199, 266
        s.114 201
            (2) 201
            (4) 201
        s.116 199
        s.118 .... 199, 202
        s.119 198
        Sched. 5 194
      Acquisition of Land Act (c. 67) 577
1982 Greater London Council (General Powers)
        Act (c. 1)
        s.3(6) 334
      Civil Aviation Act (c. 16)
        s.76 569
      Forfeiture Act (c. 34) 187, 331
        s.2 187
        s.3 187
        s.5 187
      Administration of Justice Act (c. 53)
        s.17 .... 177, 178
        s.18 .... 180, 181
        s.19 .... 183, 184
        s.20(1) 187
            (2) 187
            (3), (4) 187
        s.21 188
        s.33(1) 184
        s.73(6) 181, 184
            (7) 181
1983 Mental Health Act (c. 20) 205
        s.93 205
        s.94 205
            (2) 205
        s.95 205
        s.96 205
        s.96(1) 47, 278
            (d) 205
            (e) 205

1983 Mental Health Act—*cont.*
        s.96(1)(k) 285
        s.99 .... 205, 285
        s.105 205
1984 County Courts Act (c. 28) 358
        s.23(d) 344
        s.136 358
        s.139(1) 357
            (2) 359
      Agricultural Holdings Act (c. 41) 584
      Finance Act (c. 43)
        s.109(1) 166, 171
      Inheritance Tax Act (c. 51) 96
        s.4(2) 185
        s.212(2) 95
        s.237 96
        Sched. 8, para. 3 .... 95, 96
1985 Companies Act (c. 6) 99
        s.35 352
        s.193 521
        s.396 .... 99, 112
        s.397 112
      Enduring Powers of Attorney Act (c. 29) ... 206
        s.1 206
        s.2 206
        s.3 206
        s.4 206
        s.6(5) 206
        Sched. 1 206
      Finance Act (c. 54) 570
      Administration of Justice Act (c. 61)
        s.55 358
      Insolvency Act (c. 65) 16
        Sched. 8, Pt. III 105
        Sched. 8, para. 5 .... 132, 136
      Housing Act (c. 68) 111, 116, 126, 598
        Pt. IV 606
        Pt. V 116, 124, 126, 607
        Pt. VI 372
        ss.79, 80 606
        s.81 606
        ss.82–84 606
        ss.87, 88 606
        s.89 606
        s.113 606
        s.118 607
        s.119 607
        s.127 607
        s.129 607
        s.131 607
        s.171A 116, 126
        s.264(5) 598
        s.270(3) 598
        s.276 598
        s.609 469
        s.610 473
        Sched. 2 606
      Landlord and Tenant Act (c. 70) 370
        s.3(3)(a) 391
        s.8 370
            (5) 370
        s.10 370

1985 Landlord and Tenant Act—*cont.*
      s.11 370
         (1)(a) 370
            (b) 371
         (1A) 371
         (2)(a) 371
            (b), (c) 371
         (3A) 371
         (6) 371
      ss.12–14 370
      s.17 .... 368, 379
      s.36 370
      s.38 370
      Housing (Consequential Provisions) Act
         (c. 71)
      Sched. 2 598
1986 Agricultural Holdings Act (c. 5) 373, 584,
                                           585, 589, 593
      s.1 585
      s.2 585
      ss.3, 4 586
      s.5 586
      s.10 .... 22, 593
      s.12 588
         (2) 588
         (4) 588
      s.13 588
      s.16 564
      s.21 373
      s.25 586
      s.26 586
      s.27 586
      s.27(1) 587
         (2) 587
         (3) 587
            (f) 589
         (4) 587
      ss.34–48 587
      s.60 588
         (4) 589
      s.61 588
         (4) 589
         (5) 589
      s.64 589
      ss.64–66 589
      s.78 589
      s.84 588
      s.86 94
      s.96 586
      Sched. 2 588
      Sched. 3 586
      Sched. 7 589
      Sched. 8 589
      Sched. 9 589
      Sched. 14, para. 49 585
      Land Registration Act (c. 26) 111
      s.1 120
      s.5(1) 546
      Finance Act (c. 41)
      s.100 .... 95, 96
      Insolvency Act (c. 45)
      s.283 330

1986 Insolvency Act—*cont.*
      s.314 47
      s.315 366
      s.335A(2) 288, 322, 325
         (3) 289, 322, 325
      s.336(2) 98
         (5) 325
      s.347 564
      Sched. 5 47
      Building Societies Act (c. 53)
      Sched. 4 506
      Sched. 4, para. 2 529
      Financial Services Act (c. 60) 149
      Housing and Planning Act (c. 63)
      Pt. I 607
      s.17 599
1987 Reverter of Sites Act (c. 15)
      s.1 .... 80, 281, 284
      Landlord and Tenant Act (c. 31) 607, 611
      Pt. I 611
      s.1(1) 612
         (2) 611
         (3), (4) 611
         (1) 611
         (2) 611
      s.5(1) 612
      s.12 612
      s.50 391
      Family Law Reform Act (c. 42)
      s.1 197
         (1) 204
      s.18 193
         (1) 197
         (2) 197
      s.19 204
         (1) 204
         (2) 204
1988 Income and Corporation Taxes Act (c. 1)
      s.15 372
      s.23 372
      Land Registration Act (c. 3) 111
      s.1 112
      Landlord and Tenant Act (c. 26) 376
      s.1 401
         (3) 376, 377
         (4) 376
         (5) 376, 377
      s.4 376
      Legal Aid Act (c. 34)
      s.16(6) 94
      Housing Act (c. 50) 591, 599, 600, 603, 604,
                                                       614
      s.1 .... 592, 600
      s.5 600
      s.7(4) 601
      s.8 600
      s.13 602
      s.14 602
      s.17 602
      s.18A 603
      s.20 .... 600, 603
      s.21 .... 602, 604

1988   Housing Act—*cont.*

    s.22 604

    s.24 605

       (2)(a) 605

    s.25 605

    s.26 605

    s.27 .... 356, 616

    s.28 616

    s.29 616

    s.30 616

    s.31 .... 349, 616

    s.32 349

    s.34 .... 597, 600

       (1) 599

       (3) 603

    s.36 615

    s.39 594

    s.45(1) 600

    s.116 .... 370, 371

    Sched. 1 592

          para. 1 600

          para. 13(1) 599

    Sched. 2 603

           Pt. I 601

           Pt. II 601

    Sched. 4 594

    Sched. 7, para. 9 605

    Sched. 17 605

1989   Common Land (Rectification of Registers) Act (c. 18) 442

    Law of Property (Miscellaneous Provisions) Act (c. 34) 16, 68, 69, 147, 148, 152

    s.1(1) 160

       (2)–(4) 160, 342

    s.2 .... 23, 68, 95, 330, 342, 343

       (1) 148, 149, 150

       (2) 150, 152

       (3) 153

       (4) 152, 289

       (5) 149, 154

         (a) 343

       (6) 149

       (7) 147, 148

       (8)–148

    s.5(3), (4) 147, 148

    Sched. 2 .... 1'48

    Companies Act (c. 40)

    s.93 .... 99, 112

    s.108 352

    Local Government and Housing Act (c. 42)

    s.149 594

    Sched. 10 603

1990   Town and Country Planning Act (c. 8) 570, 572, 573

    Pt. II 571

    Pt. V 573

    ss.36–45 571

    s.55(1) 572

       (2)(f) 573

       (3) 573

1990   Town and Country Planning Act —*cont.*

    s.57(4) 573

    s.58 574

    ss.65, 66 573

    s.69 573

    s.70 573

    ss.82–87 574

    ss.88, 89 574

    s.106(3) 469

    ss.137–148 578

    ss.149–160 578

    s.171A 575, 576

    s.171B 575, 576

    s.171C 575

    s.171D 575

    s.172 .... 574, 575

    s.173 574

    s.174 575

    s.175 575

    s.176 575

    s.177 575

    s.178 575

    s.179 575

    ss.183–186 575

    s.187 575

    s.187A 576

    s.187B 575

    s.188 575

    ss.198–210 576

    ss.211–214 576

    ss.220–225 576

    s.226 577

       (3)(b) 577

    ss.247–260 419

    s.289 575

    s.336(1) 572

    Sched. 7 574

    Sched. 13 578

    Planning (Listed Buildings and Conservation Areas) Act (c. 9) 570

    Pt. I 576

    Pt. II 576

    Planning (Hazardous Substances) Act (c.10) 570

    Planning (Consequential Provisions) Act (c. 11) 570

1991   Planning and Compensation Act (c. 34) 570, 577

    s.1 575

    s.2 576

    s.3 575

    s.4 .... 575, 576

    s.5 .... 574, 575

    s.6 575

    s.7 575

    s.8 575

    s.9 575

    s.13 .... 572, 574

    s.23 576

    s.28 574

    s.66 579

    s.67 578

1991 Planning and Compensation Act—*cont.*
        Sched. 5 574
        Sched. 14 579
      Water Resources Act (c. 57)
        s.24 568
        s.27 568
        s.221 568
1992 Access to Neighbouring Land Act (c. 23) ... 335,
                                                              450
        s.1 450
        ss.4, 5 451
      Charities Act (c. 41) 206
1993 Charities Act (c. 10) 206
        s.36 207
          (5) 207
          (6) 207
          (7) 207
        s.38 207
      Leasehold Reform, Housing and Urban
        Development Act (c. 28) ... 607, 608, 609,
                                                         612, 614
        s.1(1) 613
        s.3 612
        s.4 612
          (1) 612
        s.5(1) 612
          (5) 612
        s.6 612
        s.7 612
        s.9 613
        s.13 613
          (2) 612
        s.22 613
        s.23 613
        s.24 613
        s.32 613
        s.33 614
        s.36 613
        s.39 614
        Sched. 6 .... 613, 614
        Sched. 9 613
1994 Coal Industry Act (c. 21)
        ss.7, 8 580
      Law of Property (Miscellaneous Provi-
        sions) Act (c. 36) 163, 164, 165, 172
        s.1(2) 164
        s.2(1) 164
          (3)(b) 165
        s.3(1) 165
          (3) 165
        s.5 165
          (1) 165
        s.6 165
        s.7 165
1995 Finance Act (c. 4)
        s.155 584
      Agricultural Tenancies Act (c. 8) 581, 584,
                                                         589, 593
        s.1(1) 589
        s.5(1) 590
        s.6(1) 590
        s.7(1) 590

1993 Agricultural Tenancies Act—*cont.*
        s.9 590
        s.10 590
        s.13 590
        s.15 590
        s.17 590
        s.19 590
        s.20 590
      Landlord and Tenant (Covenants) Act (c.
        30) 339, 381, 384, 386, 388, 396, 397,
                       399, 400, 401, 402, 404, 405, 583
        s.1(3) 381
          (6) 381
        s.2(1) 397
        s.3(1) 345, 353, 397, 398
          (2) 398
          (3) 398
          (4) 398
          (5) 405
          (6)(a) 397, 403
            (b) 397
        s.4 398
        s.5(2) 400
        s.6(2) 403
        s.7(1), (2) 403
        s.8(1) 403
          (2) 403
          (3) 403
        s.9 399
          (6) 398
        s.10(1) 399
          (2) 399
          (3) 399
        s.11 .... 402, 561, 562
          (1) 404
          (2)–(4) 404
          (5)(b) 404
          (6) 404
        s.12 405
          (2), (3) 405
        s.13(1) 399
          (3) 399
        s.14 404
        s.15(1) 398
          (a) 398
          (b) 398
          (2) 398
          (3) 398
          (4) 398
          (6) 398
        s.16 401
          (1) 404, 405
          (3) 401
            (b) 401
          (5)(a) 401
            (b) 401
            (c) 401
        s.17 .... 386, 402
        s.19 402
        ss.19–20 .... 386, 402
        s.20(1) 386, 402
        s.21(2) 399

1995	Landlord and Tenant (Covenants) Act—*cont.*	
	s.22	401
	s.23(1)	399, 404
	(2)	399, 405
	(3)	399
	s.25(1)	396, 400, 404
	(2), (3)	396, 400
	s.26(1)	399
	s.27	399, 403
	s.28(1)	345, 353, 396, 397
	Sched. 1, paras.3, 4	583
	Law Reform (Succession) Act (c. 41)	
	s.2	173
1996	Treasure Act (c. 24)	568
	ss.1–3	568
	s.4	568
	(2)	568
	Family Law Act (c. 27)	98, 510
	s.30(1)	98
	(2)	98
	(3)	510
	(9)	98
	s.31(2)	98
	(3)	98
	(10)(b)	124
	(12)	543
	s.33(3)	98
	(6)	98
	s.34(2)	98
	s.35(13)	510
	s.36(15)	510
	s.55	510
	s.56	510
	Party Wall etc. Act (c. 40)	334, 335
	s.1(2)	334
	(3)	334
	(4)	334
	(5)	334
	(6)	334
	(7)	334
	s.2	335
	s.3	334
	s.4(1)	335
	(3)	335
	s.6	335
	(3)	335
	(7)	335
	s.7	335
	s.8	335
	(3), (4)	335
	s.10	335
	s.16	335
	s.20	334
	Trusts of Land and Appointment of Trustees Act (c. 47)	8, 32, 45, 52, 200, 206, 265, 267, 282, 283, 284, 285, 288, 289, 305, 309, 310, 321, 323, 324, 325, 326, 328, 487
	s.1	9, 16, 76, 86, 109, 124
	(1)	206, 283
	(3)	207, 283

1996	Trusts of Land and Appointment of Trustees Act—*cont.*	
	s.2(1)	51, 240, 251
	(4)	267
	s.2(5)	206
	s.3	86, 87, 100, 250
	s.4(1)	282, 283
	(2)	283
	(3)	283
	s.5(1)	309
	s.6(1)	52, 206, 282, 284
	(2)	284
	(3)	284
	(4)	284
	(5)	284
	s.7	284, 321, 325, 328
	(1)	285
	(3)	285, 328
	s.8(1)	52, 284, 285
	(2)	285
	s.9(1)	285
	(2)	286
	(3)	285
	(4)	286
	(7)	286
	(8)	286
	s.10(1)	285
	(3)(a)	285
	(b)	285
	s.11(1)	286
	(2)(a)	286
	(b)	286
	(c)	286
	(3)	286
	(4)	286
	s.12(1)	287, 305
	(2)	287, 305
	s.13	321, 325
	(1)	287, 305
	(2)	287, 305
	(3)	287, 305
	(4)	288, 305
	(5)(a)	287
	(b)	287
	(6)	287
	(7)(a)	287, 305
	(b)	287, 305
	s.14	285, 287, 288, 321, 328
	(1)	282, 320, 326
	(2)(a)	285
	s.15	282
	(1)	288, 322
	(2)	288, 322
	(3)	288, 322
	s.16(1)	284, 286, 328
	s.17	288
	s.19	299, 300, 311
	(1)	298
	(2)(a)	298
	(b)	298
	(3)	298
	s.20	298

1996 Trusts of Land and Appointment of Trustees Act—cont.
    s.22(3) 284, 285, 286, 288, 305, 322
    s.25(2) 183
    s.296 309
    Sched. 1, para. 1 .... 202, 290
           (1) 203, 309
           (2) 203, 309
           (5) 204
      para. 2 .... 202, 290
      para. 5 .... 39, 45
      para. 6 268
    Sched. 2, para. 1 .... 281, 284, 503
           (7) 281
      para. 2 284
           (2) 281
      para. 3 .... 284, 309
           (6) 281, 309
      para. 4 .... 284, 309
           (4) 281, 309
      para. 5 284
           (5) 281
      para. 6 284
           (6) 281
      para. 7 281
    Sched. 3, para. 4 .... 182, 203
      para. 4(8) 281
      para. 15(1), (2) 409
      para. 23 .... 322, 325
    Sched. 4 .... 183, 265, 279
  Housing Act (c. 52) 591, 603, 605, 606
    s.24 607
    s.96(1) 603
    s.107 613
    s.108 613
    s.112 614
    s.126 606
    ss.127, 128 606
    s.129 606
    ss.131–134 607
    Sched. 7 603
1997 Land Registration Act (c. 2) 111
    s.2 145
  Protection from Harassment Act (c. 40) ... 617
    s.1(1) 617
    s.2(1) 617
    s.3(1) 617
    s.4(1) 617
1998 Petroleum Act (c. 17) 580
  Human Rights Act (c. 42) 92, 93, 128, 129,
                              139, 357
    s.6 92
1999 Trustee Delegation Act (c. 15) 206
  Contracts (Rights of Third Parties) Act (c.
    31) 66, 70, 291, 454, 455
2000 Financial Services and Markets Act (c.
    8) 149
  Trustee Act (c. 29) 77, 185
    s.28(4)(a) 185

2000 Land Registration Act (c. 9) 12, 13, 16, 74,
        75, 77, 78, 83, 111, 113, 114, 115,
        116, 117, 118, 119, 120, 121, 125,
        128, 129, 130, 133, 134, 135, 136,
        137, 138, 142, 143, 259, 261, 264,
        320, 321, 335, 338, 345, 346, 382,
        389, 397, 398, 471, 482, 489, 498,
        500, 504, 506, 511, 514, 529, 545,
        546, 547, 549, 550, 553, 554, 555,
            556, 558, 559, 562, 564
    s.1 118
    s.3 115
      (2) 120
    s.4(1)(c)–(e) 115
      (2) 115
    s.5 117
    ss.6–7 118
    s.9(2), (3) 118, 120
    ss.9–10 114
    s.11(2)–(5) 118
      (4)(c) 550
      (6) 119
      (7) 119
    ss.11–12 .... 114, 118, 122, 125
    s.12(2)–(5) 119
      (6) 119
      (7) 119
    s.15(3) 121
    ss.15–22 120
    s.18(8) 119
    s.19 121
    s.23(1) 134, 135, 338
      (a) 498
      (b) 498
      (2) 134, 135
        (a) 529
        (b) 529
      (3) 529
    s.24(2) 136
    s.27(1) 135
    s.28 545
    ss.28–31 .... 114, 346
    s.29 .... 114, 122, 125, 135, 320
      (1) 129
      (4) 116
    s.30 .... 114, 122, 125, 545
    s.32 133
    s.33 133
    s.34 133
    s.35 133
    s.36 133
    s.40(1) 133
      (2) 133
      (3) 133
    s.41 133
    s.42 134
    s.43(1) 134
    s.44 134
    s.45 134
    s.48 544
      (1) 498
    ss.48–50 121

2000   Land Registration Act—*cont.*
    s.49 546
      (1) 546
      (2) 546
      (3) 546
      (4) 546
      (5) 546
    s.51 513
    s.52 130
      (1) 498
    s.53 529
    s.54 506
    s.60 116
    s.62 120
    s.65 .... 114, 142
    s.74 135
    s.77 .... 121, 133, 134
    s.91 113
    ss.91–94 113
    s.92 113
    s.93 113
      (5) 113
    s.94 113
    s.95 549
      (1) 137
      (2) 555
    s.97(2), (3), (4) 550
    s.102 143
    s.105 113
    s.106 113
    s.113 127
    s.114 .... 482, 489
    s.115 126
    s.116 117
    s.129(1) 114, 129, 135, 320, 346, 389, 497
    Sched. 1 .... 122, 1126, 346
      para. 1 126
      para. 2 126
        (1) 260
      para. 3 .... 126, 138, 482, 489
      paras. 4–6 126
      paras. 10–14 126
      para. 10 126
    Sched. 3 .... 122, 126, 346
      para. 1 126
      para. 2 126
        (1)(a) 260
      para. 3 .... 127, 138, 482, 489
      paras. 4–6 127
      paras. 10–14 126
      para. 10 127
    Sched. 4 142
      para. 1 142
      para. 2 142
      para. 3 143
        (2) 143
        (3) 143
      para. 4(a) 142
      para. 5 142
        (d) 473
      para. 6 143
        (2) 143

2000   Land Registration Act—*cont.*
    Sched. 4—*cont.*
      para. 6(3) 143
      para. 7(a) 142
      para. 8 143
    Sched. 5 113
      para. 5 114
    Sched. 6, para. 1 .... 137, 549
      para. 2 .... 137, 549
      para. 3 .... 137, 549
      para. 4 .... 137, 550
      para. 5 .... 137, 550
      paras.6, 7 .... 138, 550
      para. 8 137
        (1) 559
        (2) 558
        (3) 558
      para. 9 138
        (1) 562
        (2) 562
        (3) 562
        (4) 562
      para. 11(1) 550
        (2) 550, 564
        (3)(a) 557
      para. 12 .... 137, 550, 553, 556
      para. 13 550
      para. 14 555
    Sched. 8 143
      para. 1(1)(a) 143
        (2)(a) 120, 144
        (b) 144
        (c)–(h) 144
        (8) 145
      para. 2 144
      para. 3(1)
      para. 5(1) 144
        (2) 144
        (3) 144
      para. 6 144
      para. 9 145
      para. 10 145
    Sched. 11, para. 1 259
    Sched. 12 128
      paras.1–3 130
      para. 7 129
      para. 8 .... 127, 128
      para. 9 128
      para. 10 128
      para. 11 129
      para. 12 128
      para. 14(1) 121
        (2) 121
      para. 16 121
      para. 18(1) 128
2002   Commonhold and Leasehold Reform Act
    (c. 15) 28, 29, 464, 566, 609, 610, 612,
                          613, 614
    s.1 465
    s.2 466
    s.3 466
    s.4 465

2002   Commonhold and Leasehold Reform
          Act—*cont.*
          s.7(1), (2) 467
              (3) 467
          s.9(2) 467
              (3) 467
                  (a) 465
                  (b), (c) 465
                  (e) 465
          s.16 466
          ss.17, 18 466
          s.20(1) 466
              (3), (4) 466
          s.30(3)(b) 465
              (8) 465
          ss.30–32 465
          s.33(2) 4654
          ss.33–35 465
          s.34 465
          s.36 465
          s.37 465

2002   Commonhold and Leasehold Reform
          Act—*cont.*
          s.41 466
          ss.42–48 467
          ss.49–53 467
          s.59 467
          s.113 612
          s.116 612
          s.117 612
          s.118 613
          s.119 613
          s.123 614
          s.125 613
          s.127 614
          s.214 613
          s.135(1) 609
          s.138 609
          s.139 610
          Sched. 1 467
          Sched. 2, para. 1 465
          Sched. 3, Pt. 1 465

TABLE OF STATUTORY INSTRUMENTS

1925 Land Registration Rules (S.R. & O. 1925
        No. 1093) 111, 168
      r. 8 113
      r. 10 113
      r. 12 113
      rr. 13, 14 140
      rr. 56–58 132
      r. 58(1) 259
          (2) 259
      r. 60 .... 132, 133
      r. 72 169
      r. 74 168
      r. 76 168
      r. 78 168
      r. 83(2) 114, 135
      r. 98 168
      r. 131 .... '40
      r. 168 136
      r. 170 136
      r. 172 136
      rr. 174–177 136
      r. 212 .... 471, 473
      r. 213 133
      r. 215 131
      r. 236 132
      rr. 240–242 500
      r. 250 .... 122, 127, 138
      r. 258 122
      r. 262 498
      rr. 276, 277 140
      r. 278 116
      r. 299 113
          (3) 113
      r. 300 113
      Sched., Form 9 259
      Sched. 3 170
1965 Rules of the Supreme Court (SI 1965 No.
        1776)
      Ord. 6, r. 2 .... 359, 363
1968 Commons Registration (Time Limits)
        Order (SI 1968 No. 1470) 442
1969 Family Law Reform Act 1969 (Com-
        mencement No. 1) Order (SI 1969
        No. 1140) 201

1969 Commons Registration (New Land) Reg-
        ulations (SI 1969 No. 1843) 442
1970 Commons Registration (Objections and
        Maps) (Amendment) Regulations (SI
        1970 No. 384) 442
      Secretary of State for the Environment
        Order (SI 1970 No. 1681) 441
1971 Commons Commissioners Regulations (SI
        1971 No. 1727) 442
1974 Land Charges Rules (SI 1974 No. 1286)
      rr. 5, 6 107
      rr. 9–12 107
1977 Local Land Charges Rules (SI 1977 No.
        985)
      r. 3 91
      r. 6 92
      r. 10 92
      Sched. 1, Forms A, B 92
      Intestate Succession (Interest and Capital-
        isation) Order (SI 1977 No. 1491) ... 194
1983 Consumer Credit (Increase of Monetary
        Limits) Order (SI 1983 No. 1878) 523
1987 Town and Country Planning (Use Classes)
        Order (SI 1987 No. 764) 573
      Children Act 1975 and the Adoption Act
        1976 (Commencement No. 2) Order
        (SI 1987 No. 1242) 197
1988 Family Law Reform Act 1987 (Com-
        mencement No. 1) Order (SI 1988
        No. 425) (C. 11) 197
      Land Registration (Official Searches)
        Rules (SI 1988 No. 629)
      r. 3 134
      Notice to Quit etc. (Prescribed Informa-
        tion) Regulations (SI 1988 No.
        2201) 349
1989 Housing (Right to Buy) (Maximum Dis-
        count) Order (SI 1989 No. 513) 607
      Registration of Title Order (SI 1989 No.
        1347) 117
1990 References to Rating (Housing) Regula-
        tions (SI 1990 No. 434) 594, 607, 608
      Land Registration Act 1988 (Commence-
        ment) Order (SI 1990 No. 1359) 112

1992   Town and Country Planning (Use Classes) (Amendment) Order (SI 1992 No. 610) 573

Planning (Hazardous Substances) Regulations (SI 1992 No. 656) 570

Town and Country Planning (Use Classes) (Amendment) (No. 2) Order (SI 1992 No. 657) 573

Town and Country Planning (Control of Advertisements) Regulations (SI 1992 No. 666) 576

1993   Family Provision (Intestate Succession) Order (SI 1993 No. 2906) 193, 194

1995   Town and Country Planning (General Permitted Development) Order (SI 1995 No. 418) 573

1995   Landlord and Tenant (Covenants) Act 1995 (Notices) Regulations (SI 1995 No. 2964) 399, 403

1998   Civil Procedure Rules (SI 1998 No. 3132) 54

Pt. 25.1(f) 100, 132

Pt. 36 176

Pt. 55 PD

para. 2.2 358

para. 2.3 358

para. 2.4 .... 359, 363

Sched. 2

CCR Ord. 6

r. 3(2) 359, 363

ABBREVIATIONS

STATUTES

A.E.A.: Administration of Estates Act
A.H.A.: Agricultural Holdings Act
C.A.: Conveyancing Act
C. & L.R.A.: Commonhold and Leasehold Reform Act
E.C.H.R.: European Convention on Human Rights
H.A.: Housing Act
I.E.A.: Intestates' Estates Act
J.A.: Supreme Court of Judicature (Consolidation) Act
L.C.A.: Land Charges Act
L.P.A.: Law of Property Act
L.P.(Am.)A.: Law of Property Amendment Act
L.P.(M.P.)A.: Law of Property (Miscellaneous Provisions) Act
L.R.A.: Land Registration Act
L.R.H. & U.D.A.: Leasehold Reform, Housing and Urban Development Act
L.R.R.: Land Registration Rules
L. & T.A.: Landlord and Tenant Act
L. & T.(C.)A.: Landlord and Tenant (Covenants) Act
R.P.A.: Real Property Act
S.L.A.: Settled Land Act
T.A.: Trustee Act
T.L.A.T.A.: Trusts of Land and Appointment of Trustees Act

CASES

B.S.: Building Society
D.C.: District Council
I.R.C.: Commissioners of Inland Revenue
In b.: (*In bonis*) In the Goods of, In the Estate of
L.B.C.: London Borough Council
R.D.C.: Rural District Council
S.E.: Settled Estate(s)

S.T.: Settlement Trust(s)
W.T.: Will Trust(s)

BOOKS AND PERIODICALS

Bl. Comm.: Blackstone's Commentaries on the Laws of England (15th ed., 1809)
C.L.J.: Cambridge Law Journal
Challis R.P.: Challis's Law of Real Property (3rd ed., 1911)
Co.Litt.: Coke's Commentary upon Littleton (19th ed., 1832)
Conv. (N.S.) (or Conv.): The Conveyancer, New Series, 1936–
Conv. (O.S.): The Conveyancer, Old Series, 1916–36
Conv. Y.B.: Conveyancers' Year Book
Cru.Dig: Cruise's Digest of the Laws of England respecting Real Property (4th ed., 1835)
Gray, *Perpetuities*: Gray's Rule against Perpetuities (4th ed., 1942)
Gray & Gray: Elements of Land Law (3rd ed., 2001)
Halsbury: Halsbury's Laws of England (4th ed.)
Harv.L.R.: Harvard Law Review
H.E.L.: Holdsworth's History of English Law, 1922–66 (see (1945) 61 L.Q.R. 346)
Law Com.: Law Commission
Litt.: Littleton's Tenures: see Co.Litt.
L.J.News.: Law Journal Newspaper
L.Q.R.: Law Quarterly Review
L.R.Ann.Rep.: Land Registry Annual Report
L.S.G.: The Law Society's Gazette
Maitland, *Equity*: Maitland's Equity (2nd ed., 1936)
        Forms of Action: Maitland's Forms of Action at Common Law, 1936
M.L.R.: Modern Law Review
M. & W.: Megarry & Wade's Law of Real Property (6th ed., 2000)
N.L.J.: New Law Journal
P. & M.: Pollock & Maitland's History of English Law (2nd ed., 1898: reprinted with new
    introduction 1968)
Parker and Mellows: Parker and Mellows: The Modern Law of Trusts (7th ed., 1998)
Preston, *Estates*.: Preston's Elementary Treatise on Estates (1820–27)
Ruoff & Roper: Ruoff & Roper's Law and Practice of Registered Conveyancing (6th ed.,
    looseleaf)
Sanders, *Uses*: Sanders' Essay on Uses and Trusts (5th ed., 1844)
Shep.: Sheppard's Touchstone of Common Assurances (7th ed., 1820)
S.J.: Solicitors' Journal
Theobald, *Land*: Theobald's Law of Land (2nd ed., 1929)
Tudor L.C.R.P.: Tudor's Selection of Leading Cases on Real Property, Conveyancing and the
    Construction of Wills and Deeds (4th ed., 1898)
Williams R.P.: Williams' Principles of the Law of Real Property (23rd ed., 1920)
        V. & P.: Williams' Treatise on the Law of Vendor & Purchaser (4th ed., 1936)
W.P.: Working Paper

GLOSSARY

The object of this glossary is to provide a ready source of reference to the meanings of some of the more troublesome technical expressions used in the text. For the most part, brief but not necessarily exhaustive definitions have been given, with references by means of numerals in brackets to the pages of the text where further information can be obtained and the terms may be seen in their context. References which are essential to a proper understanding of the terms are in bold type. Where the text contains a convenient collection and explanation of a number of contrasting terms, a simple reference to the appropriate pages is given instead of setting out the definitions.

Abstract of title: an epitome of documents and facts showing ownership (**158**).
Ademption: the failure of a gift by will, *e.g.* because the property ceases to exist or belong to the testator (190).
Ad hoc settlement, trust for sale or trust of land: one with special overreaching powers (90).
Administrators: persons authorised to administer the estate of an intestate (198); compare Executors.
Advowson: a right of presenting a clergyman to a vacant benefice (79).
Alienation: the act of disposing of or transferring.
Allodial land: land not held of a lord (24).
Ante-nuptial: before marriage.
Appendant: attached to land by operation of law (422); compare Appurtenant.
Approvement: the appropriation of a portion of the manorial waste free from rights of common (441).
Appurtenant: attached to land by act of parties (411); compare Appendant.
Assent: an assurance by personal representatives vesting property in the person entitled (199).
Assignment: a disposition or transfer, usually of a lease.
Assurance: the documentary or other evidence of a disposition or transfer.

Beneficial owner: a person entitled for his own benefit and not, *e.g.* as trustee.
Beneficiaries: those entitled to benefit under a trust or will.
Bona vacantia: goods without an owner.

Cestui que trust: a beneficiary under a trust.

Cestui que use: a person to whose benefit property was conveyed (64).

Cestui que vie: a person for whose life an estate *pur autre vie* lasted (48).

Charge: an incumbrance securing the payment of money.

Commonhold: a freehold tenure which enables freeholds to be acquired by the owners of individual units in buildings which are divided horizontally (28).

Consolidation: a requirement that a mortgagor shall not redeem one mortgage without another (515).

Contingent: operative only upon an uncertain event (**210**); compare Vested.

Conversion: a change in the nature of property either actually or notionally (**283**).

Conveyance: an instrument (other than a will) transferring property.

Corporeal: accompanied by physical possession (67); contrast Incorporeal.

Covenant: a promise contained in a deed.

Deed: a document which shows that it is intended to be a deed and has been signed and delivered (160).

Deed poll: a deed with only one party (161); compare Indenture.

Defeasance: the determination of an interest on a specified event.

Demise: a transfer, usually by the grant of a lease.

Determine: terminate, come to an end.

Devise: a gift of real property by will.

Distrain, distress: the lawful extra-judicial seizure of chattels to enforce a right, *e.g.* to the payment of rent (375).

Dominant tenement: land to which the benefit of a right is attached (413); compare Servient tenement.

Emblements: crops still growing which an outgoing tenant may take (52).

Engross: prepare a fair copy (159).

En ventre sa mère: conceived but not born.

Equities: equitable rights (61).

Equity of redemption: the sum of a mortgagor's rights in the mortgaged property (**493**).

Escrow: a document which upon delivery will become a deed (162).

Estate: 1. the *quantum* of an interest in land (26).

         2. an area of land (26).

         3. the whole of the property owned by a deceased person (26, 198).

Estovers: wood which a tenant may take for domestic or other purposes (50).

Execute: 1. to perform or complete, *e.g.* a deed.

         2. to convert, *e.g.* to transform the equitable interest under a use into a legal estate (65).

Executors: persons appointed by a testator to administer his estate (198); compare Administrators.

Executory trust: a trust the details of which remain to be set out in some further document (314).

Fee: base (46), conditional (41), determinable (41), simple (32), tail (45).

Feoffee to uses: a person holding property to the use of another (64).

Feoffment: a conveyance by livery [delivery] of seisin (67).

Fine: a premium or a lump sum payment, *e.g.* for the grant of a lease.

Foreclosure: proceedings by a mortgagee which free mortgaged property from the equity of redemption (502).

Freehold: 1. socage tenure (28).
        2. commonhold tenure (28).
        3. an estate of fixed but uncertain duration (**31**, **32**).

General equitable charge: an equitable charge on a legal estate not protected by a deposit of documents of title (95).

Good consideration: natural love and affection for near relatives (60).

Hereditaments: inheritable rights in property (67).

Heritable issue: descendants capable of inheriting.

Hold over: remain in possession after the termination of a tenancy (347).

Hotchpot: the bringing into account of benefits already received before sharing in property (196).

Human rights: the rights conferred by the European Convention on Human Rights (**92**).

Improved value: the value of land together with improvements to it.

In capite: in chief, immediately holding of the Crown (25).

Inclosure: the appropriation of the whole of a manorial waste free from rights of common (441).

Incorporeal: not accompanied by physical possession (67); contrast Corporeal.

Incumbrance: a liability burdening property.

Indenture: a deed between two or more parties (161); compare Deed poll.

Infant: a person under 18 years of age.

In gross: existing independently of a dominant tenement (422).

Instrument: a legal document.

Intestacy: the failure to dispose of property by will.

Issue: descendants of any generation.

Jointure: provision by a husband for his widow, usually under a settlement (247).

Jus accrescendi: right of survivorship (303).

Lapse: the failure of a gift.

Letters of administration: the authorisation to persons to administer the estate of a deceased person (198).

Licence: a permission, *e.g.* to enter on land (475).

Limitation, words of: words delimiting the estate granted to some person previously mentioned (**37**); compare Purchase, words of.

Marriage articles: the preliminary agreement for a marriage settlement (314).

Mere equities: rights to equitable relief that fall short of being rights in land (60).

Merger: the fusion of two or more estates or interests (365).

Mesne: intermediate, middle (25).

Minor: see Infant.

Minority: the state of being an infant.

Nuncupative: oral (of wills) (182).

Overreach: to transfer rights from land to the purchase money paid for the land (5, 6).

Parol: by word of mouth.
Particular estate: an estate less than a fee simple (213).
Per capita: by heads; one share for each person (195); compare *Per stirpes*.
Personal representatives: executors or administrators (198).
Per stirpes: by stocks of descent: one share for each line of descendants (195); compare *Per capita*.
Portions: provisions for children, especially lump sums for the younger children under a settlement (247).
Possibility of reverter: the grantor's right to land if a determinable fee determines (41).
Post-nuptial: after marriage.
Prescription: the acquisition of easements or profits by long user (430).
Privity of contract: the relation between parties to a contract (381).
Privity of estate: the relation between landlord and tenant under a legal lease (381).
Probate: the formal confirmation of a will, granted by the court to an executor (198).
Puisne mortgage: a legal mortgage not protected by a deposit of title deeds (94).
Pur autre vie: for the life of another person (48).
Purchase, words of: words conferring an interest on the person that they mention (37); compare Limitation, words of.
Purchaser: a person who takes land by virtue of a disposition by another person and not by operation of law.

Que Estate: dominant tenement (432).

Remainder: the interest of a grantee subject to a prior particular estate (213).
Rent: chief rent (413), fee farm rent (413), ground rent (123), quit rent (413), rack rent (123), rent of assize (413), rentcharge (412), rent seck (412), rent service (412).
Restrictive covenant: a covenant restricting the use of land (453).
Reversion: the interest remaining in a grantor after granting a particular estate (213).
Riparian owner: the owner of land adjoining a watercourse (567).
Root of title: a document from which ownership of unregistered land is traced (63).

Satisfied term: a term of years created for a purpose which has since been fulfilled (365).
Seisin: the feudal possession of land by a freeholder (**35**).
Servient tenement: land burdened by a right such as an easement (413); compare Dominant tenement.
Settlement: provisions for persons to enjoy property in succession (or the instruments making such provisions) (247).
Severance: the conversion of a joint tenancy into a tenancy in common (328).
Severance, words of: words showing that a property is to be held in undivided (distinct) shares (308).
Spes or *Spes successionis*: a possibility of succeeding to property.
Squatter: a person occupying land without any title to it (559).
Statutory owner: persons with the powers of a tenant for life under the Settled Land Act 1925 (256).

Statutory trusts: certain trusts imposed by statutes, especially—
      1. the trust for sale of land under co-ownership before 1997 (**281**).
      2. the trust of land under co-ownership after 1996 (**283**).
      3. the trusts for issue on intestacy (**195**).
Sub-mortgage: a mortgage of a mortgage (528).
Sui juris: "of his own right", *i.e.* subject to no disability.

Tenement: anything which may be held by a tenant.
Tenure: the set of conditions upon which a tenant holds land (24); compare Estate.
Term of years: a period with a defined minimum for which a tenant holds land (81).
Terre tenant: a freehold tenant in possession (410).
Title: the evidence of a person's right to property.
Trust: bare (85), completely constituted (291), constructive (293), executed (288), executory
    (314), express (290), implied (292), incompletely constituted (291), precatory (290),
    resulting (291).
Trust corporation: one of certain companies with a large paid-up capital, or one of certain
    officials (85).

Undivided share: the interest of a tenant in common (307).
Use: benefit (64).
User: use, enjoyment (Note: *not* the person who uses).

Vested: unconditionally owned (**210**); compare Contingent.
Vesting assent (259), declaration (300), deed (258), instrument (258).
Voluntary conveyance: a conveyance not made for valuable consideration.
Volunteer: a person taking under a disposition without having given valuable
    consideration.

Waste: ameliorating (48), equitable (49), permissive (49), voluntary (49).

Chapter 1

INTRODUCTION

Sect. 1. Prefatory

What is generally described as the English law of real property applies to all land in England and Wales. It has never applied to any other part of the United Kingdom, although it has provided the basis for the systems of many countries in the common law world, from Ireland and the common law jurisdictions of the United States of America to Australia and New Zealand. The subject, traditionally described by Oliver Cromwell as "an ungodly jumble", is justly recognised as a difficult one for beginners. This is partly because of the intricate interlocking of its component parts and partly because of the complexity of the language, which involves the use of many technical terms. An excellent illustration of both these difficulties is the precise meaning of the expression "real property" itself.[1] For these reasons, those coming new to the subject must not expect to understand everything at a first reading. In this subject, more than any other, it is economical of time and effort to read fast and often. Much that is almost incomprehensible at first will become clear on a second reading and perhaps obvious on a third. In order to understand complex ideas expressed in unfamiliar language it is necessary to master the language as soon as possible, and for this purpose a generous use should be made of the glossary which immediately precedes this page.

1. Objects of learning the subject

The objects of learning the law of real property are:

> (i) to acquire a knowledge of the rights and liabilities attached to interests in land; and

> (ii) to lay a foundation for the study of conveyancing.

(a) Real property and conveyancing

It is not easy to distinguish accurately between real property and conveyancing. In general, it can be said that the former is static, the latter dynamic; real property deals with the rights

---

[1] See below, pp. 17–19.

and liabilities of landowners, conveyancing with the art of creating and transferring rights in land. Yet inevitably the two overlap, and often the exact place at which to draw the line is ultimately a matter of taste. But, although this is a book on the law of real property, it is built upon a conveyancing foundation. In deciding what to include and what to exclude, conveyancing has played a large part. The reader's knowledge of land law has to be carried to the point where it will be possible for him to embark with profit on a study of conveyancing; the joints must be true and the overlapping restrained within due limits. It is, indeed, best to regard real property and conveyancing not as two separate though closely related subjects, but as two parts of the one subject of land law; it is convenience of teaching rather than any essential difference of nature that dictates the division.

(b) History

Conveyancing necessarily influences any book on real property in another way, namely, by making it essential to include some historical element. A conveyancer must deal with both ownership and incumbrances. In other words, he must see not only that his client gets what he has agreed to buy but also that he gets it free from any burdens such as mortgages or rights of way which would make it less valuable. (In parenthesis, it must be noted that this division between ownership and incumbrances is not rigid; what in one transaction appears as an incumbrance may appear in another as the subject-matter of ownership. If A owns a mortgage on X's land, the mortgage is regarded as an incumbrance if X sells his land, but as the subject-matter of ownership if A sells his mortgage. Nevertheless, in any particular transaction the distinction is clear). A conveyancer acting for a client who is purchasing property must investigate the title to the land, both as to ownership and as to incumbrances. Incumbrances binding the land may well have been created considerably more than a hundred years before the conveyancing transaction in question, and the ownership of the land sometimes has to be investigated for at least the preceding 15 years. Those who are engaged in this work must consequently know the law not only as it is but also as it was.

2. Registered and unregistered land

Modern conveyancing is based upon the 1925 property legislation, which came into force some 76 years ago on January 1, 1926. The title to land may either be registered at the Land Registry, or else be unregistered. In the case of registered land, the register of titles sets out, subject to various classes of interests which override registration,[2] the current state of the title, and only to an extremely limited extent is any knowledge of the pre-1926 law required. Comparatively little attention therefore will be paid to it on subjects that fall within the system of registration of title.[3] In the case of unregistered land, although a purchaser now need only investigate the vendor's title as far back as a good "root of title" (such as a conveyance on sale) at least 15 years old,[4] it is of course perfectly possible for the root of title in question to predate the 1925 legislation. Further, it is also necessary to investigate the incumbrances binding the land, one particular type of which (covenants restricting the use of

---

[2] See below, pp. 13, 121 *et seq.*
[3] Where more detailed knowledge is required, see the fifth (1984) or earlier editions of Megarry and Wade, *The Law of Real Property* (the current (sixth) edition of which, by C. Harpum, is cited as "M. & W.") or the fifth (1975) or earlier editions of this book.
[4] Below, p. 10.

the land[5]) will not infrequently have been created in the latter part of the nineteenth century. It is nevertheless relatively uncommon for any detailed knowledge of the pre-1926 law to be required, although attention will be paid to such parts of it as are likely to be relevant. However, now that any transfer of unregistered land on sale or by way of gift obliges the transferee to register the title, registered land is increasingly predominant, and so the emphasis of this edition of this book will be on registration of title.

3. The common law basis of the subject

The law of real property is part of the common law of England. The phrase "common law" or "at law", which will frequently be encountered, is used in three senses:

    (i) in contrast with local custom;

    (ii) in contrast with statute law; and

    (iii) in contrast with equity.

The third is the most usual sense, the second less usual, the first comparatively rare: the context will normally make it plain which is meant. A word must be said on the third meaning. As will be seen later,[6] certain rights could be enforced in the common law courts (*i.e.* the King's ordinary courts), and these were known as legal rights. Other rights were not protected by the common law courts, but in time came to be protected by the Chancellor, the King's Chief Minister, exercising a residual jurisdiction of the Crown to intervene where the common law courts could not or would not do justice, if he deemed this to be equitable. It was the Chancellor who first compelled trustees to carry out their trusts, and remedied wrongs which the common law courts would not redress because of non-compliance with some formal requirement. Rights enforced by the Chancellor were known as equitable rights, for the court presided over by the Chancellor, the Court of Chancery, was often described as the Court of Equity. Equitable rights were (and, in the case of unregistered land, still are) inferior to legal rights, in that a legal right would be enforced against everyone, whereas an equitable right would be enforced only against a person whom the Chancellor considered was unable in good conscience to deny liability (the enforceability of rights in registered land does not normally depend on whether they are legal or equitable). Thus not only would a trustee be compelled to carry out his trust but also, if he gave or sold the trust property to a third person who knew that the trustee was committing a breach of trust, the equitable rights of the beneficiaries under the trust would be enforced against that third person, who would thus be compelled to carry out the trust.

Ultimately, by virtue of what is known as the equitable doctrine of notice, equitable rights became enforceable against the whole world except a bona fide purchaser for value of a legal estate without notice of the equitable right, or someone claiming title under such a person.[7] In the language of more spacious days, he was "equity's darling", the one person whom equity preferred to the holder of an equitable right. Legal rights, on the

---

[5] Below, pp. 453 *et seq.*
[6] Below, pp. 53 *et seq.*
[7] See below, pp. 59 *et seq.*, where this is more fully discussed.

other hand, were enforceable against everyone, without this exception. Rights in unregistered land continue to be governed by these rules, although some equitable rights now have to be protected by registration to be enforceable against a purchaser for value.[8] On the other hand, rights in registered land are enforceable against a purchaser for value, or someone claiming title under such a person, only if they fall within one of the classes of interests which override registration or have been protected on the register; where they are not enforceable, the purchaser in question is sometimes jocularly described as "the Registrar's darling".

The common law affecting real property has in the course of time been profoundly affected by equity. Today most questions on real property law fall for decision in the Chancery Division of the High Court; yet this is merely a procedural arrangement which must not be allowed to obscure the common law basis of the law of real property, though much affected by statute law.

Sect. 2. The scope of the subject

1. The complex functions of land

A principal reason for the complexity of the law of real property lies in the physical nature of land itself. Land is both virtually indestructible and uniquely immovable, with the result that various people can have different interests in it and rights over it. This is not generally true in the case of chattels. Thus, if a person buys a car, he does not find that it is subject to obligations such as a prohibition on driving it to Exeter, or a limit to what can be carried in it or what alterations he may make to it. He may, of course, by contract impose such obligations on himself, but they will not flow from his ownership of the car. Nor will such a person find that by reason of owning the car he has acquired rights over other people's property, such as a right to drive over their land. Again, he will not find that the boundaries of his car are uncertain or that it is liable to be compulsorily purchased. Nor will he find that another person has a life interest in the car or a 99-year tenancy or a 21-year sub-tenancy of it.

In contrast, because of the nature of land, it is quite feasible that an owner of land may be concerned with matters of this nature. Land may be settled upon A for life, then to A's eldest son for life and, finally to A's eldest grandson absolutely. Alternatively, it may be leased to X for 99 years, X may sub-lease it to Y for 21 years, and Y may further sub-lease it to Z for a year. Laws have to regulate not only the relationships both between A and those entitled to the land after him (who are generally described as remaindermen), and between X, Y and Z, but also the position of a purchaser of the property in which they are interested. Land is also especially apt for satisfying concurrent needs, whether of spouses or businessmen. Land may be owned by H and W as joint tenants or by P and Q as tenants in common. In the former case, by virtue of what is known as the *jus accrescendi* (right of survivorship), the survivor of the two will become the sole owner; whereas in the latter instance the share of the first to die will pass under his will or, if he has left no will, under the rules governing his intestacy.

---

[8] See below, pp. 93 *et seq.*

Land may also be subject to adverse rights. For example, a neighbour may have a right of light over the land. The land may also be subject to covenants restricting its user, as by limiting the number of buildings that may be erected upon it or prohibiting their use except as private dwellings. Land also provides ideal security for a loan of money where it is lent on the basis of a mortgage or charge of it.

Land and any buildings thereon, which are treated as part of the land under the maxim *quicquid plantatur solo, solo cedit* (whatever is attached to the soil becomes part of it), are divisible vertically (such as into semi-detached or terraced houses) or horizontally (such as into maisonettes and flats), thus creating many problems as to mutual rights and obligations. Further difficulties arise from the unique inelasticity of the supply of land, something which has provoked much legislation.

2. Legal estates and interests and equitable interests

Before 1926, there were many different legal estates and legal interests that could exist in land, and a corresponding range of estates and interests could exist in equity. Since 1925, only two legal estates in land can exist, and the number of legal interests has been limited. The two legal estates are the "fee simple absolute in possession" and the "term of years absolute". In lay terms, A will be called the "owner" of Greenacre. In legal terminology, A holds the fee simple absolute in possession in Greenacre. If A has granted a lease to B (for instance for 21 years), A's fee simple is still "in possession", for "possession" includes the right to receive the rent from the land. Although B has a "term of years absolute" in the land, he will commonly be called the leaseholder or tenant of it.

Legal interests are rights over someone else's land, such as easements (*i.e.* rights of way or rights of light), rentcharges (*i.e.* rights to a rent where there is no lease or tenancy), legal charges (*i.e.* certain types of mortgage), and rights of entry (*i.e.* the right reserved by the grantor of a lease to enter the land and end the lease if the tenant fails to comply with his obligations thereunder). All other interests are equitable. These include the right to enforce restrictive covenants (such as an undertaking that the land will not be built upon) and interests under trusts. Further, any of the estates and interests that can exist at law may instead exist in equity, something which will occur where they have been created without the necessary formalities.

For unregistered land, legislation has reduced the number of estates and interests which will bind a purchaser of the land without notice of them. For registered land, as mentioned above, the enforceability of rights does not normally depend on whether they are legal or equitable.

3. The estate owner and overreaching

Before 1926, the legal estate in land could be divided between two or more persons in succession, so that X might have a legal life estate and Y the fee simple subject to that life estate. Since 1925, this is no longer possible. The entire legal estate in fee simple will be vested in one or more persons and the life interest can exist only in equity behind a trust of the legal estate. However, by following the correct procedure, the owner of the fee simple can sell the land free from the rights that others have in it; yet their rights will not be destroyed, for they will be transferred to the purchase money and this will be held by the trustees of the trust. The process whereby rights in the land are detached from it and attached instead to the proceeds of sale is known as "overreaching".[9] This is quite distinct from the process whereby equitable rights are held to be void as against a purchaser of unregistered land without notice of them or a purchaser of registered land when such rights are neither overriding interests nor protected on the register of titles. That process destroys the equitable rights in question, whereas rights that are overreached are merely transferred, not invalidated.

4. Settlements

Some of the complications of land law arise from cases where land has been settled upon a succession of persons. A somewhat complex (and not very realistic) example may be taken so as to give a bird's eye view of the matter, though many readers will probably not fully comprehend the example until most of this book has been read. Until 1997, such settlements could take effect either in accordance with the provisions of the Settled Land Acts or behind an express trust for sale. Since 1996 it is no longer possible to create settlements in accordance with the Settled Land Acts. Although existing settlements of this type nevertheless continue, the choice now is between an express trust for sale and a trust of land which is not a trust for sale.

(a) Beneficial interests

By his will a testator gives Greenacre to his son H for life, subject thereto to H's wife W for life, and subject thereto for such child of H and W as H shall appoint by deed during his lifetime or by his will absolutely, but in default of appointment to the first of the sons of H and W to attain 21 years of age absolutely. This provision gives H what is known as a life interest in possession and W what is known as a life interest in remainder. H is also given what is known as a special power of appointment which enables him to appoint Greenacre to any child of H and W absolutely, for an estate in fee simple. Each child of H and W is what is known as an "object" of the power of appointment, taking no estate or interest in the land but having a mere hope (often known as a *spes*, the Latin word for hope) that the power will be exercised in his or her favour. Each of the sons of H and W has what is known as a contingent absolute interest in remainder, the contingency being the attainment of 21 years of age; and the interest of each son is subject to the exercise of the power of appointment and to the interest of any older sons. When a son attains the age of 21, he acquires what is known as a vested absolute interest in remainder. This is subject to the interests of H and W and to any exercise of the power of appointment. Because the testator has not disposed of the whole of his estate in fee simple (it is possible that H and W will die without any children or without any son who attains the age of 21 and without H exercising his power of appointment), the testator retains what is known as an estate in fee simple in reversion; if none of the children of H and W obtains an estate in fee simple, the land will fall back into the estate of the testator and will devolve in accordance with the remaining provisions of his will or, if they do not deal with the land, it will pass under the rules of intestacy, which determine who inherits the assets of someone who dies without leaving a will. Given the number of different beneficial interests in Greenacre thus created, the land would be virtually unsaleable if a purchaser had to deal with everyone who had any such interest in it: hence the need for the settlement to take effect in one of the ways already mentioned.

---

[9] Below, p. 84.

(b) Settlements under the Settled Land Acts

The Settled Land Acts made it possible for a purchaser to acquire Greenacre in fee simple, free from the interests of H, W, their children, and the testator's estate, without having to deal with anyone except the tenant for life for the time being (initially H and, after his death, W). Under the Settled Land Act 1925 the estate in fee simple is vested in the tenant for life on trust for himself and all the other beneficiaries under the settlement. He therefore has full powers of management and control of the land, including the power to convey the estate vested in him to any purchaser. However, the purchaser will take free from the interests of the other beneficiaries only if those interests are protected by being overreached, *i.e.* transferred from the land into the proceeds of sale. This requires the purchaser to pay the purchase moneys to the trustees of the settlement (who must be at least two in number or a trust corporation) rather than to the tenant for life for the time being. As will be seen below, rights in the land existing outside the settlement, such as easements and mortgages, will not be overreached and will not be affected.[10] As already mentioned, no further settlements of this type can now be created.

(c) Express trusts for sale

The alternative to settlements under the Settled Land Act 1925 were express trusts for sale, which can still be created. Such trusts enable exactly the same beneficial interests to take effect. The difference is that the estate in fee simple is vested in the trustees for sale rather than in the tenant for life for the time being. An express trust for sale is created by conveying the land to two, three or four trustees (or to a trust corporation) to hold it on trust to sell it but with a power to postpone sale. Normally the trustees will be expected to retain the land under the power of postponement, rather than to sell it, but by refusing to concur in exercising the power to postpone sale, any one trustee can compel the others to sell. While the trustees do retain the land, they will have full power to manage and control it. When they do sell it, they will convey to the purchaser the estate in fee simple that is vested in them and will receive and hold the purchase money on trust for all the beneficiaries under the trust for sale. The interests of the latter will thus be overreached into the purchase money provided that it has been paid to the trustees, being at least two in number or a trust corporation. Rights in the land existing outside the express trust for sale, such as easements and mortgages, will not be overreached and will not be affected.[11] In the days when there was a choice between creating a settlement under the Settled Land Acts and an express trust for sale, an important factor in the decision was who the creator of the settlement wished to be able to make decisions and exercise powers. This is not a factor in the present choice between an express trust for sale and a trust of land other than an express trust for sale.

(d) Trusts of land

Since 1996 it has been possible for exactly the same beneficial interests to take effect under a trust of land which is not an express trust for sale. Such a trust works in exactly the same way as an express trust for sale. The difference is that the trustees now have only a power rather than a duty to sell the land so that the agreement of all the trustees is necessary for a sale: one alone cannot force a sale. This is obviously likely to be an important factor in the choice between the two.

---

[10] See generally below, pp. 87, 88.
[11] See generally below, pp. 85, 86.

(e) Rights not overreached

In the case of all three types of settlements that have been discussed, rights in the land existing outside the settlement are not affected by the process of overreaching and are therefore potentially binding on any purchaser of the land. He will therefore be as concerned to discover the existence of any such rights as a purchaser of land which is not settled. Thus tenancies, mortgages, easements and other rights existing when the settlement was made will continue to bind the land even when it has been sold by the tenant for life or by the trustees; a purchaser will take free from them only if he can do so under the rules which have already been discussed.[12] A purchaser for value of registered land will be able to do so only if the rights in questions neither fall within one of the classes of interests which override registration nor have been protected on the register of titles. A purchaser for value of unregistered land will be able to do so only if the rights in question are equitable interests of which he has no notice. The position is exactly the same in respect of any such rights created by the tenant for life or trustees in the course of managing the land while it was settled and in respect of any beneficial interests which have not been overreached because the purchase money was not paid to the requisite number of trustees.[13]

5. Co-ownership

(a) Fragmentation of title

As well as being held for persons in succession, land may be held for persons concurrently: ownership may be divided not only vertically but also laterally. Even though Greenacre may be free from any successive interests in it, it may be held by two or more co-owners. There might be dozens of co-owners of the fee simple in Greenacre, either as joint tenants or tenants in common. Joint tenants tended to become reduced in numbers, for when one died, the *jus accrescendi* (right of survivorship) would in effect carry his interest to his fellow joint tenants. On the other hand, tenants in common tended to increase in number, since when one died his interest would pass under his will or intestacy, perhaps to his ten children. Land might be owned by dozens of tenants in common living in different parts of the world; and even if all of them could be traced, some might be minors or mental patients. Until 1926, a would-be purchaser of such land might face such formidable and expensive difficulties that he would abandon his venture.

(b) Integration of title

In 1925 the problem was resolved.[14] There can never now be more than four co-owners of the legal estate. They must hold the legal estate as joint tenants, so that on death the legal estate remains in the survivors, by the *jus accrescendi*. They can appoint others to be joint tenants of the legal estate with themselves so long as their number does not exceed four. The Law of Property Act 1925[15] provided that the legal estate should be held by the joint tenants on trust for sale with power to postpone sale, thus enabling the property to remain unsold for a long time. However, as a result of the Trusts of Land and Appointment of Trustees Act

---

[12] Above, pp. 3–4.
[13] See below, pp. 84–91.
[14] Below, pp. 307–315.
[15] L.P.A. 1925, ss.34–36.

1996,[16] all such trusts for sale have since the end of 1996 been converted into trusts of land and all subsequent joint tenancies also take effect as trusts of land. Consequently, the legal estate is now held by the joint tenants as trustees of the land with *power* to sell it but no longer on any *trust* for sale. The discretion whether to sell or retain the land continues but the emphasis is now on retention rather than sale. Both before and after this reform, the joint tenants have held and may hold the legal estate on trust for any number of co-owners. They may be minors or mental patients, or live in remote countries, and have equitable interests which may be joint tenancies or tenancies in common. So long as a purchaser pays his purchase moneys to the joint tenants holding the legal estate as trustees and takes a conveyance of the legal estate from them, he obtains a good legal title, free from all the equitable interests of the beneficial co-owners. They are instead overreached and become interests in the proceeds of sale.[17]

(c) Undisclosed title

Difficulties can however arise when there is an undisclosed co-owner. If H purchases a house and his wife W contributes one-third of the purchase price, the course envisaged by the draftsmen of the 1925 property legislation was that the house should be conveyed to H and W as joint tenants to hold on trust for sale (now, of course, under a trust of land) for themselves as tenants in common in equity, as to two-thirds and one-third respectively. The draftsmen did not envisage, or at any rate did not specifically provide for, the possibility of the house instead being conveyed to H alone with nothing to reveal W's contribution. She will still be entitled to a one-third share as a tenant in common in equity but there will be nothing to disclose this to a purchaser of the legal estate. If such a purchaser, P, pays the purchase moneys to H, thinking him to be solely entitled, W's equitable rights will not be overreached, for the purchase moneys will not have been paid to the necessary number of trustees (either at least two persons or a trust corporation). In these circumstances, not envisaged by the 1925 property legislation, the courts have decided that W's rights will bind P unless he has taken free of them under the relevant general principles.[18] If the land in question is registered land, P will take free from W's rights unless they fall within one of the classes of interests which override registration or have been protected on the register of titles. If W is in actual occupation of the land, she will have such an interest by virtue of her actual occupation, and so her rights will bind P.[19] But if the marriage has broken up and she has left the house permanently, she will not have such an interest and her rights will bind P only if she has protected them on the register. If, on the other hand, the land in question is unregistered land, P will take free from W's rights only if he can show that he is a bona fide purchaser for value of the legal estate without notice of them.[20] P will obviously have had no actual knowledge of W's rights, for otherwise he would have paid the purchase moneys to the appropriate number of trustees in order to overreach her rights. However, he will be treated as having notice of those rights if they would have come to his knowledge had he made such inquiries and inspections as he ought reasonably to have made.[21] These concepts have produced difficulties with both registered and unregistered land. In the case of registered

---

[16] T.L.A.T.A. 1996, s.1.
[17] *City of London B.S. v. Flegg* [1988] A.C. 54.
[18] *Caunce v. Caunce* [1969] 1 W.L.R. 286; *Williams & Glyn's Bank v. Boland* [1981] A.C. 487.
[19] *Williams & Glyn's Bank v. Boland* [1981] A.C. 487.
[20] *Caunce v. Caunce* [1969] 1 W.L.R. 286.
[21] *Kingsnorth Finance Co. Ltd v. Tizard* [1986] 1 W.L.R. 783.

land, the limits of actual occupation are still unclear. While it is clear that W will still be regarded as being in actual occupation during a temporary absence, as while in hospital or away on holiday, it is unclear whether and, if so, for how long she will be regarded as being in actual occupation if she left intending never to return. In the case of unregistered land, the courts have encountered difficulties in deciding what inquiries and inspections P ought reasonably to have made. At one time the tendency was for this obligation to be construed somewhat narrowly. It was therefore held that, if H was in possession of the property, it was unreasonable to require P to make inquiries of H's wife or of other occupiers where their presence was consistent with H being the sole owner.[22] However, this view has now been discredited, and failure to inquire of other occupiers will at least in some cases constitute notice.[23] These difficulties are considered more fully later.[24] However, it must be stressed that they only arise where there is a sole legal owner other than a trust corporation. Where the purchaser has paid the purchase moneys either to at least two persons or to a trust corporation, the rights of all co-owners will be overreached whether or not they are in actual occupation of the land and whether or not their presence on the land is inconsistent with the trustees being the sole owners.[25] Consequently, if the house had instead been conveyed to H and a third party T, payment by P of the purchase moneys to H and T would overreach W's rights into the proceeds of sale even if she was completely unaware of the transaction or wholly opposed to it. Her rights would not bind P and she would have to give up possession of the house to him.

6. The modern system of unregistered conveyancing

(a) Investigation of a vendor's title

A purchaser of land must investigate the title of the vendor in order to confirm that the vendor is able to convey it. Where the land in question is unregistered land, he does this by examining the documents under which the vendor holds the land, going back to a "good root of title" at least 15 years old. A good root of title is a document which deals with the whole legal and equitable interest in the land, describes the land adequately, and contains nothing to throw any doubt on the title. If the title consists of a series of conveyances on sale made 4, 14 and 30 years ago, the purchaser must go back to the 30-year-old conveyance. If he fails to do this (such as by accepting the 14-year-old conveyance as the root of title), he will be fixed with constructive notice of all that he would have discovered had he investigated the title for the full period.

(b) Investigation of third party rights in the land

In addition to confirming that the vendor has power to convey the land, the purchaser must see that there are no burdens on the land such as tenancies, easements or mortgages that will affect him. For this purpose, he must consider any third party rights which are disclosed by his investigation of title, and also inspect the land and make due inquiries of any tenant or

---

[22] *Caunce v. Caunce* [1969] 1 W.L.R. 286.
[23] *Hodgson v. Marks* [1971] Ch. 892; *Williams & Glyn's Bank v. Boland* [1981] A.C. 487; *Kingsnorth Finance Co. Ltd v. Tizard* [1986] 1 W.L.R. 783.
[24] Below, pp. 61 *et seq.*
[25] *City of London B.S. v. Flegg* [1988] A.C. 54.

other person in occupation of it.[26] In addition, he must search two registers, the land charges register and the appropriate local land charges register.

(i) Land charges: The existence of the Land Charges Register is intended to avoid many of the difficulties of the equitable doctrine of notice by making certain equitable rights in unregistered land readily discoverable by being registered therein. This system, begun in a very restricted form in 1839, was much extended in 1888, and further important extensions were made in 1925. The present statute is the Land Charges Act 1972, replacing the Land Charges Act 1925. If such a right is duly registered, all persons are deemed to have actual notice of it for all purposes.[27] If it is not registered, it will normally be void against a purchaser for value, even if he knows of it.[28] What is decisive is thus the indisputable state of the register and not the arguable state of the purchaser's mind. Equitable interests registrable in this way include equitable easements, mortgages and restrictive covenants. In addition, the system has been extended to certain legal interests, such as mortgages not protected by a deposit of the title deeds. Such interests do not, of course, depend on notice for their protection, but nevertheless they are made void against a purchaser for value if they are not registered. Land charges are registered against the names of the persons who created them, in a national computerised system at Plymouth.

(ii) Local land charges: The existence of the system of Local Land Charges Registers, one of which is maintained by each district council in England and Wales, each London borough, and the Common Council of the City of London, is intended to make charges of a local public nature over both registered and unregistered land equally discoverable by being registered therein. The present statute is the Local Land Charges Act 1975 (replacing provisions in the Land Charges Act 1925). Charges so registrable include prohibitions or restrictions on the use of land under planning law, and charges for the cost of making up a private road. Registration is against the address of the land and not the name of the landowner.

(iii) Searches: Because local land charges are registered against the address of the land, the obligation of the purchaser to search the local land charges register presents no special problems other than the time it takes. Such registers are not computerised and have to be searched manually by employees of the local authority which maintains them. The time that this takes is one of the two principal causes of delay in conveyancing transactions (the other is the time that it often takes for a purchaser who needs mortgage finance to obtain it). However, the Land Charges Register, being a names register, sometimes creates very considerable difficulties for a purchaser obliged to search it. He will be bound by all the land charges registered against the name of anyone who has held the legal title to the land in question since 1925; registration remains valid indefinitely. He will know the names of all the estate owners back to the good root of title at least 15 years old with which the vendor has to provide him and so he can search against their names. But usually he will not know and cannot discover who were the estate owners prior to the root of title and so he cannot search against their names; yet he will be bound by land charges registered against those names.

---

[26] *Hunt v. Luck* [1902] 1 Ch. 428.
[27] See Judgments Act 1839; Land Charges Registration and Searches Act 1888; L.P.A. 1925, s.198.
[28] L.P.A. 1925, s.198.

Since 1969, however, a person who is adversely affected by such a charge may obtain compensation out of public funds.[29]

7. The system of registered conveyancing

(a) Investigation of a vendor's title and of third party rights in the land

A purchaser of registered land is equally obliged to investigate the title of the vendor in order to confirm that the vendor is able to convey it and to ensure that there are no burdens on the land such as tenancies, easements or mortgages that will affect him. His obligation to inspect the land and make due inquiries of any tenant or other person in occupation of the land and to search the Local Land Charges Register is the same as that of the purchaser of unregistered land. But the latter's obligations to examine the documents under which the vendor holds the land, going back to a "good root of title" at least 15 years old, and to search the land charges register are, in the case of registered land, replaced by the obligation to examine the register of titles. A brief consideration of the rationale and basis of the system of registration of title is the easiest way to explain what this will and will not reveal, and the extent to which the purchaser can rely on the contents of the register.

(b) The rationale and history of the system

Although modern legislation has mitigated the defects of the ancient system of investigating title to some extent, in other respects it has aggravated them, particularly because of the extensions made to the system of registration of land charges in 1925. Further, the system of unregistered conveyancing has always involved much duplication of work; a purchaser has to investigate the title anew even though many previous purchasers have fully investigated it and found it satisfactory. Under the system of registration of title, there is an official investigation of title and thereafter the land can be transferred without any further investigation of title. The register also notes certain rights held for the benefit of the land, and contains entries that protect certain rights adverse to the land. The first attempts to introduce a system of registration of title merely provided for the voluntary registration of titles.[30] However, in 1897 the registration of title on dealings with land in the County and City of London became compulsory.[31] Not until the Land Registration Act 1925 came into force did the compulsory registration of title on dealings with land become more extensive and the system was not greatly extended until after the Second World War. Since then, the system has been gradually extended throughout England and Wales, reaching over 12 million registered titles today, and it is expected that in time the system will entirely replace unregistered conveyancing. This extension made it possible to end the limited and unsatisfactory system for the registration of deeds for land in Middlesex and Yorkshire that had been established early in the eighteenth century as a safeguard against the loss, destruction or suppression of deeds; and these registers were closed in, respectively, 1940 and 1976.[32] The present system of registered conveyancing will be substantially amended when the already enacted Land Registration Act 2002 comes into force.

---

[29] L.P.A. 1969, s.25.
[30] Land Registry Act 1862; Land Transfer Act 1875.
[31] Land Transfer Act 1897.
[32] See M. & W. (5th ed.), p. 170.

(c) Registrable interests

At present two estates in land are capable of being registered: the fee simple absolute in possession, and a term of years absolute which has more than 21 years to run. A legal rentcharge can also be registered; however, since 1977 there have been substantial restrictions on the creation of any new ones. Further legal estates and interests will be able to be registered when the Land Registration Act 2002 comes into force. Any legal interests in land which are not registrable interests either fall within one of the classes of interests which override registration or have to be protected on the register of titles. On registration, a land certificate is issued to the owner of the estate or interest in question, who thereupon becomes the "registered proprietor" of it. He then becomes the holder of the legal estate or interests subject only to any interests which override registration and any interests protected by entries on the register of titles, and free from all other interests. The land certificate shows the title that is recorded in the register of title maintained at the appropriate District Land Registry. The certificate and the register are divided into three parts.

(i) The property register: this describes the property by reference to a filed plan, and notes certain rights held for the benefit of the property.

(ii) The proprietorship register: this sets out the name of the registered proprietor. It also records any restrictions on his powers of disposition (such as that no disposition will be effective unless the purchase money is paid to at least two trustees or a trust corporation).

(iii) The charges register: this notes the existence of subsidiary registered titles, such as a term of years absolute which is a registrable interest and of the type of mortgage most commonly used in registered conveyancing, the registered charge. It also contains notices protecting certain incumbrances on the title, such as other types of leases and mortgages, restrictive covenants and easements.

(d) Interests which override registration

These are various classes of interests that will bind a purchaser even though they have not been protected by any entry on the register of titles. In general, they are rights which usually can easily be discovered by inspecting the land, making inquiries of occupiers and searching the local land charges register (as has been mentioned, the land charges register plays no part in registered conveyancing). Interests which override registration include: certain types of easements; the rights of any person in actual occupation of the land where his rights are not disclosed after inquiry of him; legal terms of years absolute which are not long enough to be registrable interests and which are granted at a rent without taking a lump sum premium (technically known as a fine); and local land charges. These categories will be reduced when the Land Registration Act 2002 comes into force and willl be progressively reduced thereafter.

Although in most respects the system of registered conveyancing is plainly an improvement on the old system of unregistered conveyancing, the existence of interests which override registration means that it is not free from difficulties. One particular difficulty lies in the protection given to the rights of a person in actual occupation of the land by virtue of the fact that he has an interest of this type. An example is the case, considered above,[33] of

---

[33] See above, p. 9.

a house bought with money provided partly by H and partly by W but conveyed into the sole name of H. This, and other potential difficulties, are considered later.[34]

(e) Conclusiveness of registration

A further important difference between the two systems of conveyancing lies in the greater security of title given to the owner of registered land. If a vendor V forges deeds that show him to be the owner of unregistered land when in fact he has no title thereto, a conveyance by V to a purchaser P vests nothing in P; a person cannot transfer what is not his (*nemo dat quod non habet*). But the result is different if the land is registered and V forges a transfer of it in his favour or uses the forged deeds to become the first registered proprietor of the land. In that case if he later sells the registered land to P, on registration of the transfer P will become the estate owner, and both his title and the title of any third party to whom he sells it will be valid. This is because, subject to the possibility of the register being rectified, the registration of P as the registered proprietor is conclusive.

(f) Rectification and indemnity

As has just been indicated, the court and the registrar have wide powers to rectify the register where there has been an error or omission, although these powers are considerably restricted if the registered proprietor is in possession, as P is likely to be in the example just considered.[35] On the other hand, there are corresponding provisions for compensation out of public funds if any person suffers loss by reason of any rectification of the register, or by reason of an error or omission in the register which is not rectified.[36] There are no similar provisions for compensation in the case of unregistered land.

8. The concurrent systems of conveyancing

In principle, the intention is that all land will ultimately become registered land. After successive extensions over nearly a century, the whole of England and Wales is now subject to the compulsory registration of title. This has been the case since 1990. But that does not mean that all land is now registered land. Until April 1, 1998 registration was not required except on the conveyance on sale of the fee simple absolute or the grant or assignment of a lease with more than 21 years to run. Much land therefore remained unregistered because it had not been sold or leased for more than 21 years since registration became compulsory in the area in question. Since April 1, 1998 registration has also been required when either of these estates is the subject of a first legal mortgage or a gift. This means that all land held by natural persons will become registered at the very latest on the death of those persons, effectively within a generation from 1998. Fee incentives have also been introduced to encourage voluntary first registration. However, unregistered land vested in companies or other corporations or bodies, which of course may never die, may remain unsold for centuries. However, consideration is now being given to the possibility of requiring that, at some point in the future, all land will be required to be registered by some specified date. Further, sales and gifts of unregistered land are usually still carried out under the system of

---

[34] See below, pp. 124, 127.

[35] See the unreported *Haigh* case, discussed in Ruoff & Roper, *The Law and Practice of Registered Conveyancing* (6th ed., 1991) (cited as "Ruoff & Roper"), 2–08 (murderer dissolves victims in acid bath and obtains registered title to a victim's land by forgery).

[36] See below, pp. 143 *et seq.*

unregistered conveyancing, although the purchaser or donee must then register his title within two months after completion. A knowledge of both systems of law will thus be needed for a while yet, although admittedly to an ever-decreasing extent; the outcome of the considerations at present being given will determine whether it will be required indefinitely.

9. A balance of interests

The complexity of land law is in large measure due to the complexity of the rights in land which have grown up to meet many different human needs. A single plot of land may be subject to a wide variety of rights, and the extent and validity of these rights may be tested from time to time, especially when the land is sold. The interests of a purchaser would be served if all such rights were made void against him if not registered. Yet such a provision would be oppressive, not only in the scale of registration that would be required but also in respect of rights that could not reasonably be expected to be registered. The question is therefore one of balance.

Sect. 3. Historical outline

The history of the law of property in land can be divided into six periods.

1. Formulation of principles

This was the early period during which the courts of common law formulated many of the fundamental rules of land law. A number of important statutes were passed during this period, which extended from the Norman Conquest to the end of the fourteenth century.

2. Growth of equity

This was the period from about 1400 to 1535, when the jurisdiction of the Chancellor to give relief in cases not covered by the common law rules was firmly established and developed.

3. The Statute of Uses

This was the period from 1535 to the middle of the seventeenth century, when the great changes made by the Statute of Uses 1535 were being worked out.

4. Development of trusts and the rules against remoteness

This encompassed the end of the seventeenth century and the eighteenth century, when trusts—which had been considerably restricted by the Statute of Uses 1535—were once more enforced. The modern form of a strict settlement of land, by which land was "kept in the family" from one generation to another, was fully developed during this period, as were rules preventing interests vesting in persons at remote future dates.

5. Statutory reforms

This period consists of the nineteenth and twentieth centuries, when far-reaching reforms were made by Parliament. Many reforms were made during the nineteenth century, particularly between 1832 and 1845 and again between 1881 and 1890. Yet, important though these were, they could not rival the 1925 property legislation in complexity and comprehensiveness. The Law of Property Act 1922 laid the foundation for the Acts of 1925, but most of it—together with extensive amendments of the law made by the Law of Property (Amendment) Act 1924—was repealed and replaced before it came into force. The provisions of these two Acts and of much of the earlier reforms were consolidated and divided up into six Acts. These Acts and the unrepealed portions of the Act of 1922 all came into force on January 1, 1926. What is known as "the 1925 property legislation" thus consists of:

the few unrepealed portions of the Law of Property Act 1922;

the Settled Land Act 1925;

the Trustee Act 1925;

the Law of Property Act 1925;

the Land Registration Act 1925;

the Land Charges Act 1925; and

the Administration of Estates Act 1925.

In addition, some amending statutes were subsequently passed, altering details in the principal Acts. This process has been particularly notable in the case of the Land Registration Act 1925, which has been amended by many Land Registration Acts, the most recent of which was in 1997.

The genesis of the 1925 property legislation is important when construing it. The Acts of 1925 are all consolidating Acts, and a consolidating Act is presumed to change the law no more than the language necessarily requires. However, the Acts of 1922 and 1924 are professedly amending Acts, so that the presumption is not that the Acts of 1925 have not changed the old law, but that they have not changed the changes in that law made by the Acts of 1922 and 1924. Accordingly, where the Acts of 1922 and 1924 have left the old law unchanged, the Acts of 1925 are presumed not to have changed the law.[37] But where the Acts of 1922 and 1924 have changed the old law, it is those provisions which, though repealed, must first be construed.[38] Since 1925 a number of statutes directed to specific reforms have appeared. These include the Perpetuities and Accumulations Act 1964, the Law of Property (Joint Tenants) Act 1964, the Matrimonial Homes Act 1967, the Law of Property Act 1969, the Charging Orders Act 1979, the Limitation Act 1980, the Insolvency Act 1985, the Law of Property (Miscellaneous Provisions) Act 1989, and the Trusts of Land and Appointment of Trustees Act 1996. Furthermore, in 1972 the Land Charges Act 1925 was replaced by a new consolidating Act, the Land Charges Act 1972. The Land Registration Act 1925 will be replaced by the already enacted Land Registration Act 2002, probably sometime in 2003, in

---

[37] See, *e.g. Beswick v. Beswick* [1968] A.C 58.
[38] *Re Turner's W.T.* [1937] Ch. 15; *Grey v. Inland Revenue Commissioners* [1960] A.C. 1; *Lloyds Bank Ltd v. Marcan* [1973] 1 W.L.R. 339 at 344 (affirmed [1973] 1 W.L.R. 1387).

order to introduce the reforms necessary for the development of a system of electronic conveyancing.

6. Social control and registration of title

This period overlaps the last. It consists of the last 76 years. During this period Parliament enacted drastic provisions, sometimes varying with the political party in power, which curtailed and restricted the rights of landowners in the interests of tenants and the public. During this period there has also been a great extension of the compulsory registration of title, especially since 1965, culminating, as has already been seen, in the whole of England and Wales becoming subject to compulsory registration in 1990.

Sect. 4. Meaning of "real property"

1. Land

The natural division of physical property is into land (sometimes called "immovables") and other objects known as chattels or "movables". This simple distinction is inadequate. In the first place chattels may become attached to land so as to lose their character of chattels and become part of the land itself.[39] Secondly, a sophisticated legal system of property has to provide not simply for the ownership of physical property, but also for the ownership of a wide variety of interests in such physical property, and also for the ownership of interests in non-physical or intangible property such as shares in companies or copyright.[40] Thirdly, for historical reasons English law has developed a distinction between "real property" (or "realty") and personal property (or "personalty") which only approximately corresponds to that between land and other types of property.

2. History

In early law, property was deemed "real" if the courts would restore to a dispossessed owner the thing itself, the "*res*", and not merely give compensation for the loss.[41] Thus if X forcibly evicted Y from land which was classified as "freehold" under the feudal system of land-holding imposed on all land in England after the Norman Conquest in 1066,[42] Y could bring a "real" action whereby he could obtain an order from the court that X should return the land to him. But if X took Y's sword or glove from him, Y could bring only a personal action which gave X the choice of either returning the article or paying the value of it. Consequently, a distinction was made between real property, which could be specifically recovered, and personal property, which was not thus recoverable. The classification of property as realty or personalty might have been expected to be that of nature, between immovable and movable property, in other words between land and chattels. The early lawyers did indeed

---

[39] For "fixtures", see below, p. 20.
[40] For interests in land, see below, p. 24.
[41] 3 H.E.L. 3, 4; and see T.C. Williams (1888) 4 L.Q.R. 394.
[42] See below, p. 31.

draw this distinction, but in accordance with what they regarded as interests in land. They regarded leasehold interests in land as falling outside the feudal system of landholding and, consequently, only freehold interests in land were classified as real property, leases being classified, along with chattels, as personal property.

3. Reasons for distinction

In early times there were no opportunities for investing in stocks and shares such as there are today. Money was therefore often employed in buying land and letting it out on lease on order to obtain an income from the capital, or in buying a lease for a lump sum which could be recovered out of the produce of the land. Further, the relationship between landlord and tenant was regarded as being mainly contractual, the tenant agreeing to pay rent and the landlord agreeing to allow the tenant to occupy the land.[43] These conceptions were far removed from the feudal system of landholding, which at least initially was based on a personal relationship between feudal lord and feudal tenant that was totally absent from the relationship between freehold landlord and leasehold tenant. Hence leaseholds remained outside that system and so were classified as personalty[44]; indeed, for a long time they were hardly regarded as being rights in the land at all.

4. Subsequent developments

As a result of the classification of leaseholds as personalty, at first a dispossessed leaseholder had no right to recover his land from anyone except the lessor who had granted him the lease. Against third parties, he remained without remedy until late in the thirteenth century, when he was enabled to recover damages but not possession. This did not prejudice the investor lessee, who was basically only interested in his monetary investment. Not until 1468 was this rule seriously questioned. By that time the number of leasehold tenants had substantially increased as a result of changes made to the feudal system of landholding in 1290. The typical tenant had become a subsistence farmer who had insufficient capital to purchase a freehold; his need for continued possession of his land was imperative. But when subsequently in 1499 it was finally decided that leasehold tenants were entitled to recover the land itself from anyone,[45] leaseholds had become too firmly established as personalty for this change to make any difference to their status. This produces the curious result that, even today, if a testator dies leaving a will giving all his realty to R and all his personalty to P, the leaseholds will be included in the property passing to P, the reason lying in a rule which ceased to exist some 500 years ago.

5. Formal classification

Although leaseholds are still classified as personalty, they differ from most of the other kinds of personalty in that they fall under the heading of "land" or "immovables" as opposed to

---

[43] See 3 H.E.L. 213–216.
[44] 2 P. & M. 106.
[45] 2 Challis R.P. 63.

"pure personalty" or "movables" such as furniture or stocks and shares. They are accordingly classified as "chattels real", the first word indicating their personal nature (cattle were the most important chattels in early days, hence the name), the second showing their connection with land.[46] The three types of interests may therefore be classified thus:

Land   {   (i)   Realty.
                 (ii)   Chattels real.[47]

Personalty   {   (iii)   Pure personalty.

Although, strictly speaking, a book with a title that refers only to real property should exclude leaseholds, it has long been customary and convenient to include them, and that course is adopted here.

6. Modern distinction

Before 1926 the classification of leaseholds as personalty had a number of significant consequences. For example, if a person died intestate (*i.e.* without a will), all his realty passed to his heir, while his personalty was divided between certain of his relatives. Again, realty could be the subject-matter of a now virtually obsolete estate known as an estate in fee tail or entail, under which the land in question could descend only to the descendants of the original tenant in fee tail, while personalty could not. However, the property legislation of 1925 abolished most of the remaining differences between the law governing realty and that governing personalty.[48] Consequently, since 1925 realty and personalty both pass on intestacy to certain relatives of the deceased; and until the end of 1996, after which time entails could no longer be created, both kinds of property could be entailed. Thus the modern emphasis is on the distinction between land and other property, though the term "real property" still has some significance and is still widely used.

Sect. 5. Fixtures

In law, the word "land" extends to a great deal more than "land" in everyday speech. The general rule is *quicquid plantatur solo, solo cedit* (whatever is attached to the soil becomes part of it). Thus if a building is erected on land and objects are attached to the building, the word "land" prima facie includes the soil, the building and the objects affixed to it; and the owner of the land becomes the owner of the building, even if it was built with bricks stolen by the builder.[49] The word "fixtures" has traditionally been the name used to denote anything that has become so attached to land as to form in law part of the land. A mortgage or devise of Greenacre or a contract to sell it thus passes rights to the fixtures on Greenacre to the mortgagee or devisee or purchaser. In contrast, such transactions pass no such rights to

---

[46] See *Ridout v. Pain* (1747) 3 Atk. 486 at 492.
[47] For other chattels real, of no importance today, see Co. Litt. 118b and M. & W. (5th ed.), p. 16.
[48] See A.E.A. 1925, ss.45–47; L.P.A. 1925, ss.60, 130.
[49] *Gough v. Wood & Co.* (1894) 10 T.L.R. 318.

chattels on the land which have not become fixtures. However, the courts now seem to be moving towards acceptance of a new threefold classification, dividing those elements which will pass with the land (chattels of course will continue not to do so) into fixtures, and objects which have become part and parcel of the land.[50] Confining the expression "fixtures" to its everyday meaning, and consequently no longer having to describe buildings as "fixtures", will not only have linguistic advantages but may well also assist in resolving borderline cases.[51]

A. *Objects that will Pass with the Land*

1. The elements

In deciding whether or not an object has become a fixture (or, in the new terminology, part and parcel of the land), there are two main elements to be considered, namely:

    (i) the degree of annexation; and

    (ii) the purpose of annexation.

2. Degree of annexation

The degree of annexation used unquestionably to be the primary element but, because of the ever-increasing technical skills of removing objects which are attached to buildings, it may well now have given way to the purpose of annexation,[52] except possibly in relation to buildings themselves. The test is whether some physical connection with the land, or with a building on it, can be shown. If, on the other hand, the object in question merely rests on the ground by its own weight, it will be regarded as a chattel; the traditional example of the latter is a "dutch barn", which rests on timber laid on the ground.[53] A building which cannot be removed from land without destroying it will be regarded as part and parcel of the land, even if it rests on concrete pillars and is not itself attached to the ground.[54] A pre-fabricated building which can be removed in sections may remain a chattel and be no fixture,[55] whereas an article attached to land may be a fixture even if it is not very difficult to remove it.[56] Although now less decisive, the degree of annexation remains important as showing where the burden of proof lies[57]: if the article is securely fixed, the burden lies on those who contend that it is not a fixture.

3. Purpose of annexation

The purpose of the annexation is now the main factor; the modern tendency, save possibly in the case of buildings, is to regard the degree of annexation as being chiefly of importance as evidence of the purpose of annexation.[58] The more securely an object is affixed and the

---

[50] *Elitestone Ltd v. Morris* [1997] 1 W.L.R. 687 at 690–692.
[51] See S. Bridge [1997] C.L.J. 498.
[52] *Berkley v. Poulett* [1977] 1 E.G.L.R. 86 at 89; *Hamp v. Bygrave* [1983] 1 E.G.L.R. 174 at 177; *TSB Bank Plc v. Botham* (1996) 73 P. & C.R. D1 at D2.
[53] See *Wiltshear v. Cottrell* (1853) 1 E. & B. 674.
[54] See *Elitestone Ltd v. Morris* [1997] 1 W.L.R. 687.
[55] *Potton Developments Ltd v. Thompson* [1998] N.P.C. 49.
[56] See *Buckland v. Butterfield* (1820) 2 Brod. & B. 54; *Jordan v. May* [1947] K.B. 427.
[57] *Holland v. Hodgson* (1872) L.R. 7 C.P. 328 at 335.
[58] *Leigh v. Taylor* [1902] A.C. 157 at 162. See also *Hynes v. Vaughan* (1985) 50 P. & C.R. 444.

more damage that would be caused by its removal, the more likely it is that the object was intended to form a permanent part of the land.[59] It therefore follows that an object which is not affixed at all is unlikely to be held to be a fixture.[60] In determining the purpose of annexation, the question to be asked is: "Was the intention to effect a permanent improvement of the land or building as such; or was it merely to effect a temporary improvement or to enjoy the chattel as a chattel?"[61] In the first case, the chattel is a fixture, in the second it is not. Thus, a wall composed of blocks of stone, or statues forming part of a general architectural design,[62] or movable dog-grates substituted for fixed grates,[63] or tapestries and portraits in a room designed as an Elizabethan room, have all been held to be fixtures.[64] In each case, the evident intention was to effect a permanent improvement to the land. But tapestry attached by tacks to wooden strips fastened to the wall by two-inch nails,[65] panelling screwed into wooden plugs let into the wall, a collection of stuffed birds attached to movable wooden trays in glass cases attached to the walls of a bird gallery,[66] and pictures recessed into panelling[67] have all been held not to form part of the premises. Although in these cases there was a substantial degree of annexation, the only way in which the chattels could be properly enjoyed was to attach them to the house in some way, and thus it was easy to infer an intent to affix them for the better enjoyment of them as chattels and not for the permanent improvement of the building.[68] So, too, a drainpipe serving a house and laid in adjoining land has been held not to be a fixture; it was put there for the commodious occupation of the house and not for the benefit of the land in which it lay.[69] Similar articles may in individual cases remain chattels or become fixtures, depending on the circumstances, such as tip-up seats fastened to the floor of a cinema or theatre,[70] statues, and tapestries.[71]

B. The Right to Remove Objects which would Normally Pass with the Land

If, according to the above rules, an article is a chattel, it can be removed by the person bringing it on to the land or by his successors in title. If, on the other hand, it is a fixture or has become part and parcel of the land, then prima facie it cannot be removed from the land and must be left for the owner in fee simple. However, there are some important exceptions to this rule. Questions of the right to remove fixtures arise between the following parties.

---

[59] *Spyer v. Phillipson* [1931] 2 Ch. 183 at 209, 210.
[60] *H.E. Dibble Ltd v. Moore* [1970] 2 Q.B. 181; *Berkley v. Poulett* [1977] E.G.D. 754; *Deen v. Andrews* (1985) 52 P. & C.R. 17. Contrast *Hamp v. Bygrave* [1983] E.G.D. 1000, not citing *Berkley v. Poulett* [1997] E.G.D. 754.
[61] See *Hellawell v. Eastwood* (1851) 6 Exch. 295 at 312.
[62] *D'Eyncourt v. Gregory* (1866) L.R. 3 Eq. 382. See now *Berkley v. Poulett* [1977] E.G.D. 754.
[63] *Monti v. Barnes* [1901] 1 Q.B. 205.
[64] *Re Whaley* [1908] 1 Ch. 615.
[65] *Leigh v. Taylor* [1902] A.C. 157.
[66] *Viscount Hill v. Bullock* [1897] 2 Ch. 482.
[67] *Berkley v. Poulett* [1977] E.G.D. 754.
[68] See *Young v. Dalgety Plc* [1987] 1 E.G.L.R. 116 (carpeting and light fittings).
[69] *Simmons v. Midford* [1969] 2 Ch. 415; contrast *Montague v. Long* (1972) 24 P. & C.R. 240 (bridge over river).
[70] Contrast *Lyon Co. v. London City Midland Bank* [1903] 2 K.B. 135 with *Vaudeville Electric Cinema Ltd v. Muriset* [1923] 2 Ch. 74.
[71] Compare *Re Whaley* [1908] 1 Ch. 615 with *Leigh v. Taylor* [1902] A.C. 157, and *D'Eyncourt v. Gregory* (1866) L.R. 3 Eq. 382 with *Berkley v. Poulett* [1977] E.G.D. 754.

1. Limited right of removal

(a) Landlord and tenant

Prima facie, all fixtures that are attached by the tenant or become part and parcel of the land during his tenancy are "landlord's fixtures", *i.e.* they must be left for the landlord. But the exceptions which have arisen nearly swallow up the rule, and articles which can be removed under these exceptions are known as "tenant's fixtures". These can be removed while the tenancy continues, and even after it has ended if the tenant remains in possession as a tenant under some statutory or other right.[72] If the tenancy is brought to an end by a notice which does not allow enough time for the tenant to remove his "tenant's fixtures", he is allowed a reasonable time in which to do so.[73] When removing them, the tenant must make good any damage that has been caused to the property either on their removal or on their original installation.[74]

The following articles have been held capable of being removed by a tenant, though in some cases it is not clear whether the article is removable because it has never become anything other than a chattel or because, although a fixture or part and parcel of the land, it is nevertheless a "tenant's fixture".

(i) Trade fixtures: "Trade fixtures" are articles attached by the tenant for the purpose of his trade or business; these have long been removable by him.[75] Vats, fixed steam engines and boilers, a shed for making varnish, shrubs planted by a market gardener and the fittings of a public house have all been held to come within the category of trade fixtures.[76] A tenant does not surrender his right of removal by surrendering his existing tenancy in return for the grant of a new tenancy.[77] Nor is the value of any tenant's fixtures taken into account for the purposes of a rent review.[78]

(ii) Ornamental and domestic fixtures: The exception of what are known as "ornamental and domestic fixtures" appears to be rather more limited than the previous one. It seems to extend only to chattels perfect in themselves which can be removed without substantial injury to the building.[79] An article which can be moved entire is more likely to fall within this exception than one which cannot.[80] Thus while a conservatory on brick foundations has been held not to be removable, looking glasses, ornamental chimney pieces, window blinds, stoves, grates and kitchen ranges have all been held to be removable during the tenancy.

(iii) Agricultural fixtures: At common law, buildings and other articles used for the purposes of agriculture were not regarded as being removable by an agricultural tenant,[81] for agriculture was regarded as a normal use of land and not as a trade. But by statute[82] a tenant of an agricultural holding who has erected buildings or attached fixtures to the land for this

---

[72] *New Zealand Government Property Corporation v. H.M. & S. Ltd* [1982] Q.B. 1145.
[73] *Smith v. City Petroleum Co. Ltd* [1940] 1 All E.R. 260. See G. Kodilinye [1987] Conv. 253.
[74] *Mancetter Developments Ltd v. Garmanson Ltd* [1986] Q.B. 1212.
[75] *Poole's Case* (1703) 1 Salk. 368.
[76] See M. & W. 14–318.
[77] *New Zealand Government Property Corporation v. H.M. & S. Ltd* [1982] Q.B. 1145.
[78] See *Young v. Dalgety Plc* [1987] 1 E.G.L.R. 116.
[79] *Martin v. Roe* (1857) 7 E. & B. 237 at 244.
[80] *Grymes v. Boweren* (1830) 6 Bing. 437.
[81] *Elwes v. Maw* (1802) 3 East 38.
[82] A.H.A. 1986, s.10, replacing provisions in statutes from L. & T.A. 1851, s.3, onwards.

purpose may remove them before, or within two months after, the determination of the tenancy, provided that the following conditions are observed:

(i) one month's written notice is given to the landlord;

(ii) all rent due is paid and all the tenant's obligations under the tenancy are satisfied by him;

(iii) no avoidable damage is done in the removal, and any damage done is made good; and

(iv) the landlord is allowed to retain the articles in question if he pays a fair price for them.

(b) Tenant for life and remainderman

If land is settled on A for life with remainder to B, on the death of A the question arises whether articles which A has attached to the land or which have become part and parcel of the land during his lifetime can be removed and treated as part of A's estate or whether they must be left for B. The position here is similar to that between landlord and tenant. Prima facie, all such articles must be left for B, with the common law exceptions of trade, ornamental and domestic fixtures[83]; but the statutory exception for agricultural fixtures does not apply.

2. No right of removal

(a) Devisee and personal representative

If the land is given by will, the rule is that all articles which are either fixtures or have become part and parcel of the land pass under the devise; the testator's personal representatives are not entitled to remove them for the benefit of those otherwise entitled to the testator's estate, whether they are ornamental, trade or any other kind of fixture.[84]

(b) Vendor and purchaser

Without exception, all articles which are either fixtures or have become part and parcel of the land at the time of a contract of sale must be left for the purchaser[85] unless the contract contains an express stipulation to the contrary (a more informal agreement would now be likely to be void for lack of formality[86]). The transfer or conveyance will be effective to pass all such articles to the purchaser without express mention.[87] It will not, however, be effective to pass structures or erections which are still chattels; these will only pass as the result of an express stipulation to this effect.

(c) Mortgagor and mortgagee

If land is mortgaged, all articles which are either fixtures or have become part and parcel of the land are included within the security without any need for special mention; the exceptions

---

[83] See *Re Hulse* [1905] 1 Ch. 406 at 410.
[84] See *Re Lord Chesterfield's S.E.* [1911] 1 Ch. 237.
[85] *Colegrave v. Dias Santos* (1823) 2 B. &; C. 76; *Phillips v. Lamdin* [1949] 2 K.B. 33.
[86] L.P.(M.P.)A 1989 s.2; see below, p. 147.
[87] L.P.A. 1925, s.62(1); H.E. *Dibble Ltd v. Moore* [1970] 2 Q.B. 181.

as between landlord and tenant do not apply.[88] The mortgagor is not even entitled to remove any articles which he has affixed to the land after the date of the mortgage which are fixtures or have become part and parcel of the land, although he can of course remove articles afffixed to the land which have not become fixtures.[89]

Sect. 6. Tenures and estates

The underlying basis of English land law is that all land in England and Wales is held from the Crown. This was a direct consequence of the imposition after the Norman Conquest of England in 1066 of what is known as the feudal system, a system progressively extended to Wales thereafter. Obviously only a very small part of this land is in the actual occupation of the Crown; the rest is occupied by freehold and leasehold tenants who hold either directly or indirectly from the Crown.[90] *Nulle terre sans seigneur* (no land without a lord); there was never in England and Wales (as there was in other countries in which a feudal system was imposed) any land owned by a subject which was not held of some lord: in technical terms, there has never been any allodial land in England and Wales.[91]

1. Lord and tenant

The basis of the imposition of the feudal system in 1066 was that the victorious Norman Conqueror, William I, regarded, at least for this purpose, the whole of England as his by right of conquest. To reward his principal followers (and also to give them some incentive for staying in England and thereby enabling him to preserve his military force more or less intact), he granted each of them certain lands to be held by them from him as their overlord. He also confirmed on this same basis the landholdings of the relatively few members of the Anglo-Saxon aristocratic classes who had survived the Conquest and had submitted to him.[92]

These lands were not granted in the way in which land is usually sold today, by way of an out-and-out transfer, but were to be held from the Crown in return for and subject to the performance of certain services. Thus, a large area of land in (say) Lancashire might be granted to X on terms that he did homage and swore fealty to the King (an entirely formal but nevertheless important condition) and that he provided the King with fifty armed horsemen to fight for the Crown for 40 days in each year; it was by means of grants of this type that the King preserved his military force. A larger area of land in (say) Yorkshire might be granted to Y on similar terms with the additional condition that he supported the King's train in his coronation. X and Y would in practice grant some of the land granted to them on to their own principal followers in return for being or providing the necessary number of horsemen, and would also grant other land to agricultural labourers in return for carrying out the necessary work on the land retained by them. At the lower end of the feudal ladder, the basic agricultural unit was a manor, held by the lord of the manor, usually a Norman, from his immediate feudal lord in return for providing (say) five horseman. Smallholdings of land

---

[88] *Monti v. Barnes* [1901] 1 Q.B. 205; L.P.A. 1925, s.62(1).
[89] *Reynolds v. Ashby & Son* [1904] A.C. 466.
[90] 1 P. & M. 232, 233.
[91] Co. Litt. 1b.
[92] Williams R.P. 12.

on the manor would be granted by the lord to his own immediate servants and to agricultural labourers in return for the services which he himself needed. In days when land and its rents and profits constituted nearly the whole tangible wealth of the country,[93] it was more usual to secure the performance of services by the grant of land in return for those services than it was to secure them by payment; the whole social organisation was based on landholding in return for services.[94]

Within this system, those who held directly of the King (such as X and Y in the example above) were known as "tenants in capite" or "tenants in chief". Those who in fact occupied the land, whether tenants in chief or agricultural labourers, were called "tenants in demesne", whereas those persons (if any) who occupied the rungs on the feudal ladder between the King and the tenant in demesne were called "mesne lords" or "mesnes".[95] Each feudal lord, from the King down to the lord of the smallest manor, had an obligation to hold a court for his feudal tenants, which was the forum for disputes between them over their respective landholdings. It was from the court of this type that the King held for his tenants in chief that a centralised system of justice and the first royal law courts (the courts which later became known as the courts of common law) subsequently began to emerge about a hundred years after the Conquest.

2. Services

In the decades following the Conquest the services mentioned in the example above became standardised to a considerable extent. In descending order of importance, there was one set of services known as grand sergeanty, which included the performance of some honourable service for the King in person; there was another set of services known as knight service which included the provision of armed horsemen for battle; and there was a set of services known as socage,[96] which included performing agricultural services of a fixed type and duration. Each set of services was known as a tenure, for it showed how the land was held (*tenere*, to hold). All of those who held by grand sergeanty and most of those who held by knight service were Normans rather than Anglo-Saxon. The basic tenure for the non-military classes of both nationalities was therefore socage, one form of which (common socage) constituted a residuary category applicable in the absence of proof to the contrary. All these tenures, together with the tenures by which land was held by ecclesiastical corporations, were eventually classified as "free tenures", which is the origin of the modern expression "freehold".

Once the royal law courts had evolved about a hundred years after the Conquest, tenants with free tenures were encouraged by the Crown to take disputes over their landholdings to the royal courts. As a result, the courts held by their feudal lords for this purpose were progressively undermined and virtually disappeared. However, for long they retained exclusive jurisdiction over some other forms of tenure, with sets of services which included the obligation simply to carry out agricultural work for a feudal lord without restriction of type or time. These tenures were originally held by common serfs, and the most common form at

---

[93] Challis R.P. 1.
[94] Williams R.P. 10.
[95] Pronounced "demain" (domain) and "mean".
[96] From "soc" meaning either "plough-share" or, more probably, "seek", for the tenant must seek his lord's "soke" or court.

that time was known as "villeinage"; in contrast with the tenures already discussed, they were classified as "unfree tenures". In the absence of any protection by the royal courts, the tenant was protected only by the custom of the manor in question as laid down in that manor's feudal court. It gradually came to be established that land held on an unfree tenure could be transferred only by a surrender and admittance made in the lord's court. The transaction was recorded on the court rolls and the transferee was given a copy of the entry to prove his title; he thus held "by copy of the court roll", and the tenure became known as "copyhold".

3. Time

A further essential variant was obviously the length of time for which the land in question was actually held. The grants made by William the Conqueror were in principle only for the tenant's lifetime, although he and his successors usually in practice had little option other than to renew the grant to the tenant's heir after his death. Such a grant of land for life (for as long as the tenant lives) has always been possible and still is. It subsequently also became accepted that land could be granted in fee tail (for as long as the tenant or any of his descendants lives), something which remained possible until 1996, or in fee simple (for as long as the tenant or any of his heirs, whether descendants or not, lives). This last form of grant is now overwhelmingly predominant.

Each of these possible lengths of tenancy was known as an estate, a word derived from status.[97] Thus the Crown might grant land to A for an estate in fee simple and A might in turn grant that land to B for the latter to hold for his lifetime. But the Crown remained entitled to that land as feudal overlord; A was both tenant in chief of the Crown and B's mesne lord, while B was tenant in demesne. Both A and B owned estates in land, yet neither owned any of the land itself: each continued to hold it from the Crown. Indeed, until the Statute of Quia Emptores 1290, a feudal tenant had no right to grant land in the modern sense, by out-and-out transfer. All he could do as of right was to turn himself into a feudal lord. However, that statute, which is still in force, prevented a feudal tenant from granting his land to a tenant to hold from him ("sub-infeudation"). Instead, he had to transfer his whole interest to someone who would replace him in the existing feudal tenancy of the land. The Statute enabled him to do this as of right and so drop out of the feudal ladder. As a result, although all the land in England and Wales is still held from the Crown, ownership of the largest estate in land, the fee simple, has come more and more to resemble ownership of the land itself. Even today, however, it is technically true to say that a subject can own only an estate, not the land itself.

For the sake of completeness, it should be mentioned that, in both popular speech and legal parlance, the word "estate" is often used in other senses. Thus it may describe an area of land ("the Blank Estate is for sale") or assets generally ("the testator left a net estate of £50,000"). The context will usually leave little doubt about which sense is intended.

4. Basic doctrines

There are thus two basic doctrines in the law of real property. These are known as:

---

[97] 2 H.E.L. 351, 352.

(i) the doctrine of tenure: all land is held of the Crown, either directly or indirectly, on one or other of the various tenures; and

(ii) the doctrine of estates: a subject cannot own land, but can merely own an estate in it, authorising him to hold it for some period of time.

In short, the tenure answers the question "How is the land held?"; the estate answers the question "For how long is it held ?".

5. Effects of doctrines

This doctrine of estates, coupled with the permanence of land as opposed to mere destructible chattels, is one reason why the law relating to land is so much more complex than the law governing chattels. At common law, it can in general be said that only two distinct legal rights can exist at the same time in chattels, namely possession and ownership. If A lends his watch to B, the ownership of the watch remains vested in A, while B has possession of it. But in the case of land, a large number of legal rights could and still can exist at the same time. Thus the position of Greenacre in 1920 might have been that A was entitled to the land for life, B to a life estate in remainder (*i.e.* after A's death), and C to the fee simple in remainder. At the same time, D might own a lease for 99 years, subject to a sub-lease in favour of E for 21 years, and the land might be subject to a mortgage in favour of F, a rentcharge in favour of G, easements such as rights of way in favour of H, J and K, and so on, almost *ad infinitum*. Before 1926, all these estates, and interests could exist as legal rights and most, but not all, can exist as legal rights today.

It may thus be said that in the case of pure personalty, the unit of ownership is the chattel or other thing itself; either it is owned by one person (or several persons jointly or in common with each other), or it is not owned at all. In the case of land, however, the unit of ownership is not the land itself (which is necessarily held from the Crown) but the estates and interests which have been artificially created in the land. In popular speech, one may refer to X's ownership of Greenacre, but technically one should speak of X owning a lease of Greenacre, or holding Greenacre in fee simple. This conception of the subject-matter of ownership being an abstract estate rather than the corporeal land was a remarkable and distinctive achievement of early English legal thought; it contributed greatly both to the triumphant flexibility of the English system and to its undoubted complexity.

6. The modern significance of tenure and estates

The modern significance of the doctrine of tenure, which is now greatly attenuated, will be briefly described here. The modern significance of the doctrine of estates, which is still substantial, is considered in much greater detail in the next chapter.

(a) Free feudal tenures

Today, only one free feudal tenure survives, the original residuary category of common socage. With the benefit of hindsight, the process of reducing the number of tenures may be seen as beginning with the Statute Quia Emptores 1290, still in force today, which prohibited the creation of any new tenures by anyone except the Crown. The first tenures actually to be abolished, by the Tenures Abolition Act 1660, were grand sergeanty and knight service; they therefore became common socage, a fate which the 1925 property legislation, by means of the Law of Property Act 1922, also imposed on all the other free tenures and all the regional variations of common socage. The process of attrition of tenures also brought about the disappearance of all intermediate tenures, and so the courts will now readily act on the presumption that all land held by free tenure (now universally described as "freehold land") is held directly of the Crown.[98]

(b) Unfree feudal tenures

Prior to the 1925 property legislation, provision had already been made by a series of statutes during the nineteenth century for the enfranchisement of the only surviving unfree feudal tenures, copyholds, by converting them into land held by common socage. But the various copyhold tenures themselves remained substantially unaltered until 1926 when the Law of Property Act 1922[99] converted all remaining copyhold land into land of freehold tenure. However, while virtually all the incidental rights conferred on the parties to free tenures had become irrelevant centuries before the 1925 property legislation and they could therefore simply be abolished,[1] some of the incidental rights conferred on the parties to unfree tenures remained important and effective in 1925 and could not be abolished without causing injustice, particularly to feudal lords. Some were abolished forthwith subject to the payment of compensation.[2] Others were preserved for ten years. But a few will continue indefinitely unless and until they are abolished by written agreement between lord and tenant; they should therefore be listed here. They are: first, any rights of the lord or tenant to mines and minerals; secondly, any rights of the lord in respect of fairs, markets and sporting; thirdly, any tenant's rights of common (such as to pasture beasts on the waste land of the manor); and, fourthly, any liability of lord or tenant for the upkeep of dykes, ditches, sea walls, bridges and the like.

(c) Present freehold tenures

The developments outlined above have ensured that only one feudal tenure is left today, namely common socage, now universally described as freehold tenure; little or nothing now remains of the former rights and obligations between feudal lord and tenant. However, statute will create a wholly new freehold tenure, commonhold, when the Commonhold and Lease-hold Reform Act 2002 comes into force.[3] This tenure, which will only be able to be created in respect of registered land held for an estate in fee simple, will provide a means of providing for freehold ownership of buildings such as blocks of flat which are horizontally divided with individuals owning different units on one or more floors (at present ownership of such units is only practicable under a long lease). Basically each owner of a "commonhold unit" will automatically be a member of the "commonhold association" which will own the common parts. Much of the detail of how this new tenure will work is to be contained in statutory instruments which had not yet been published when this edition had to go to press. In practice, commonhold will be almost entirely limited to new buildings and the decision as

---

[98] See, e.g. Re Lowe's W.T. [1973] 1 W.L.R. 882.
[99] s.128, Sched. 12, para.1.
[1] A survival is escheat where the trustee in bankruptcy of a landowner disclaims, or a corporation holding land is dissolved.
[2] L.P.A. 1922, Sched. 12, para.1; Sched. 13, Pt. II, as amended.
[3] See below, pp. 464 et seq.

to whether or not to utilise it rather than the existing system will be that of the developer. Whether or not commonhold becomes the norm and, if so, when remains to be seen.

(d) Present leasehold tenures

In contrast with feudal freehold tenures, leasehold land has greatly increased in importance,[4] with rights and obligations between landlord and tenant that are always important and sometimes complex and extensive. Although leaseholds have always stood outside the feudal system of tenures, they have long been the only important form of tenure. While an alternative form of tenure will come into existence when the Commonhold and Leasehold Reform Act 2002 comes into force,[5] it has already been seen[6] that this legislation will apply only to buildings such as blocks of flat which are horizontally divided with individuals owning different units on one or more floors. Consequently, it will not apply even prospectively to the vast majority of the situations in which land is leased and units in the overwhelming majority of existing buildings which are horizontally divided will continue to be the subject-matter of long leases.

---

[4] See below, pp. 33–35 and Chap. 9 (pp. 337–406).
[5] See below, pp. 464 *et seq.*
[6] Above.

Chapter 2

ESTATES

PART 1—CLASSIFICATION

The nature of an estate has already been discussed[1]; it is essentially an interest in land of defined duration. It is now necessary to consider the different kinds of estate. In doing this, much of the discussion will be in the past tense, for as will be seen[2] some of the estates can no longer exist as such, although some, but not all, of the corresponding rights can still exist as interests (instead of estates) in land.

Estates were divided into two classes:

    (i) estates of freehold; and

    (ii) estates less than freehold.[3]

It should be noted that "freehold" here has nothing to do with freehold (or socage) tenure. It is merely that the same word is used to express sometimes the quality of the tenure, and sometimes the quantity of the estate. "Freehold", as normally used by the man in the street, unconsciously combines these senses; thus when a house agent advertises "a desirable freehold residence", he refers to a fee simple estate in land of freehold tenure.

Sect. 1. Estates of freehold

1. The three estates of freehold

The three estates of freehold were:

    (i) a fee simple;

    (ii) a fee tail; and

    (iii) a life estate.[4]

---

[1] Above, rr. 24 *et seq.*
[2] Below, p. 78.
[3] 1 Preston, Estates, 22.
[4] Co. Litt. 43b.

The basic feudal estate was the life estate. The grants made by William the Conqueror were in principle only for the tenant's lifetime, although he and his successors usually in practice had little option other than to renew the grant to the tenant's heir after his death. It has always remained possible to create life estates and life interests are not uncommon even today. However, the basic feudal estate became heritable in the course of the twelfth century and became alienable as a result of the Statute Quia Emptores 1290; only thereafter is it really appropriate to describe it as a fee simple. The fee tail had in the meantime been introduced by statute in 1285[5]; it was abolished prospectively by statute with effect from the end of 1996,[6] although existing fees tail nevertheless continue. Before considering the estates in any detail a brief account of each must be given.

(a) Fee simple

Originally a fee simple was an estate which endured for as long as the original tenant or any of his heirs survived. "Heirs" comprised any blood relations, although originally ancestors were excluded; not until the Inheritance Act 1833 could a person be the heir of one of his descendants. Thus when the basic feudal estate first became heritable, it would terminate if the original tenant died without leaving any descendants or collateral blood relations (such as brothers or cousins), even if before his death the land had been conveyed to another tenant who was still alive, something which at that stage required the permission of the feudal lord. But by 1306, it was settled that where a tenant in fee simple alienated the land, which by then[7] did not require the permission of anyone,[8] the fee simple would continue as long as there were heirs of the new tenant and so on, irrespective of any failure of the original tenant's heirs.[9] Thenceforward a fee simple was virtually eternal.[10]

(b) Fee tail

A fee tail was an estate which continued for as long as the original tenant or any of his descendants survived. Thus if the original tenant died leaving no relatives except a brother, a fee simple would continue, but a fee tail would come to an end. The terms "fee tail", "estate tail", "entail" and "entailed interest" are often used interchangeably, although "fee tail" was the correct expression for legal entails,[11] which could only be created prior to 1926, and "entailed interest" is usually reserved for equitable entails, which all existing fees tail necessarily are.[12]

(c) Life estate

As its name indicates, a life estate lasted only for the length of the life or lives in question. The name "life estate" usually denoted that the measuring life was that of the life tenant or tenants, for example when the grant was to A for life or to A and B for their joint lives or to A and B until the death of the survivor. The alternative form of life estate, where the

---

[5] Statute De Donis Conditionalibus 1285.
[6] T.L.A.T.A. 1996.
[7] As a result of the Statute Quia Emptores 1290.
[8] Save in the case of tenants in chief who, because the Statute Quia Emptores 1290 did not bind the Crown, continued to require the permission of the King until 1326, when Edward III conceded the point.
[9] Y.B. 33–35 Edw. I (R.S.) 362.
[10] 1 Preston, Estates, 429; but see T. Cyprian Williams (1930) 69 L.J. News. 369, 385; 70 ibid., 4, 20; (1931) 75 S.J. 843 at 847.
[11] Litt. 13; 1 Preston, Estates, 420; Challis R.P. 60.
[12] See below, p. 45.

measuring life was that of some person other than the tenant or tenants, is known as an estate *pur autre vie* (pronounced "per *oh*ter vee", and meaning "for the life of another"), for example to A for so long as B lives.

A common feature of all estates of freehold was that the duration of the estate was fixed but uncertain.[13] Nobody could say when the death would occur of a man and his heirs, or a man and all his descendants, or a man alone. But the duration was not wholly indefinite; the estate was bound to determine if some pre-ordained event occurred. In the case of the fee simple and the fee tail, the word "fee" denoted (a) that the estate was an estate of inheritance, *i.e.* an estate which, on the death of the tenant, was capable of descending to his heir[14]; and (b) that the estate was one which might continue for ever.[15] A life estate, on the other hand, was not a fee. It was not an estate of inheritance and it could not continue for ever. On the death of the tenant, an ordinary life estate determined, and an estate *pur autre vie* did not descend to the tenant's heir, but until 1926 passed under the special rules of "occupancy"[16]; since then it has devolved under the tenant's will or intestacy. Life estates were sometimes called "mere freeholds" or "freeholds," as opposed to "freeholds of inheritance".

Each estate of freehold could exist in a number of varied forms which will be considered in due course.

2. Reversions and remainders

Before it became possible, as a result of the Statute Quia Emptores 1290, to alienate an estate in fee simple without the permission of the tenant's feudal lord, a tenant who granted a lesser estate, such as a life estate or estate in fee tail would have done so by granting a feudal tenancy to the prospective life tenant or tenant in fee tail and so become the latter's feudal lord. This process, known as subinfeudation, was prohibited by the Statute. Thereafter, a tenant in fee simple who created a life estate or an estate in fee tail had to carve the lesser estate out of his own estate. The estate thus created was called a "particular" estate" in fee simple, as it was a mere part (*particula*) of the estate in fee simple. That estate remained vested in the tenant, and was known as a "reversion", since the land would revert into his possession by operation of law when the life estate or fee tail ended. If instead some further life estate or fee tail had been created, subject to the particular estate and so taking effect when it expired, that further estate was classified as a "remainder", since the land remained away from the tenant instead of reverting to him. Estates in land could thus be said to be held either "in reversion" or "in remainder". There could be many estates in remainder, but only one in reversion. An estate is said to be held "in possession" when the tenant has an immediate right either to the possession and enjoyment of the land itself or to receive the rents and profits of it, as under a lease or tenancy of the law.

Sect. 2. Estates less than freehold

At first, the three estates of freehold were the sole estates recognised by law; the only other lawful right to the possession of land was known as a tenancy at will,[17] under which the tenant could be ejected at any time, and which therefore hardly ranked as an estate at all.

[13] Williams R.P. 65.
[14] 1 Preston, Estates, 262, 419; Challis R.P. 218.
[15] 1 Preston, Estates, 419, 480.
[16] See M. & W. (5th ed.), pp. 93–94.
[17] Challis R.P. 63.

Terms of years grew up outside this system of estates; the lack of protection given to them by the courts, and early doubts whether terms for longer than 40 years were valid,[18] placed leaseholders in a position of inferiority from which they never recovered. Although by the sixteenth century terms of years had become recognised as legal estates[19] and were fully protected, yet they ranked below the three estates of freehold.[20] Leaseholders were regarded as holding their land in the name of their landlords, the possession of the leasehold tenant being regarded as the possession of the landlord.[21]

Like the estates of freehold, leasehold estates may be held in possession, in reversion or in remainder. The grant of a lease of land that is already held on lease takes effect as a lease of the reversion, giving the right to possession of the land only when the prior lease ends. Such leases are called "reversionary leases". When instead a leaseholder grants a sub-lease of the land (which cannot last longer than his own lease), he is said to hold the "leasehold reversion" while the sub-lease still exists. It should also be noted that the right of the freeholder to his estate in fee simple while that estate is the subject-matter of a lease is also a reversion, usually described as a "freehold reversion" (this does not prevent the freehold estate from being an estate in possession in the meantime).

Today, the various forms of leasehold estate are of the first importance. Nevertheless, it is still not easy to find any satisfactory common element in them; perhaps it is not possible to evolve a more precise definition than "an estate not a freehold". The principal categories are as follows. They are dealt with more fully later.[22]

1. Fixed term of certain duration

The tenant may hold the land for a fixed term of certain duration,[23] as under a lease for 99 years. The possibility of the term being extended or curtailed under some provision in the lease to this effect does not affect the basic concept, which is one of certainty of duration in the absence of steps being taken for extension or curtailment. A lease "for 99 years if X so long lives" also fell under this head; it was not an estate of freehold,[24] for although X might well die before the 99 years had run, the maximum duration of the lease was fixed. For all practical purposes, there was no chance of X outliving the 99 years, so that the duration of the lease would be the same as an estate granted "to X for life"; yet in law the former was less than freehold and the latter freehold. Partly as a result of the intervention of statute, such leases are comparatively rare today.[25]

2. Fixed term with duration capable of being rendered certain

A lease of land "to A from year to year", with no other provision as to its duration, will continue indefinitely unless either landlord or tenant takes some step to determine it. Such a lease is known as "a yearly periodic tenancy". But either party can give half a year's notice to determine it at the end of a year of the tenancy, and thus ensure its determination on a fixed date. This, coupled with the fact that originally the lease was for an uncertain term of uncertain duration, classifies the estate as less than freehold. The same applies to shorter

---

[18] See Co. Litt. 45b, 46a.
[19] Challis R.P. 64.
[20] Co. Litt. 43b; and see *Re Russell Road Purchase Moneys* (1871) L.R. 12 Eq. 78 at 84.
[21] 1 Preston, Estates, 205, 206.
[22] Below, pp. 346–353.
[23] 1 Preston, Estates 203.
[24] 1 Cru.Dig. 47.
[25] See below, p. 350.

periodic tenancies such as quarterly, monthly, and weekly periodic tenancies, save that in their case the notice to determine them is a full period rather than half a period.[26] It is not possible for a periodic tenancy to have a period of more than a year.

3. Uncertain period of uncertain duration

A tenancy at will arises where a landlord agrees that to a tenant occupying the land indefinitely until his right to do so is determined by either of them at any time: it is thus less than freehold. In the same way, a tenancy at sufferance, which arises where a tenant remains in occupation of the leased property after the end of a lease without the permission of his landlord, is less than freehold.[27] Indeed, such tenancies are arguably not estates at all.[28] Both will be converted into the appropriate periodic tenancy if the landlord accepts rent from the tenant.

4. Position of leaseholds today

As has been seen, leaseholds were at first regarded as mere contractual rights to occupy land.[29] Despite their subsequent recognition as legal estates, they always remained outside the feudal system of landholding. Today, it is possible to regard leasehold as a tenure. Only in the case of leaseholds does there now arise a relationship of lord and tenant which has any practical importance. The one remaining feudal tenure, socage, has been shorn of all the incidents of any consequence, whereas in the case of leaseholds a valuable rent is nearly always payable, and the lord usually has power to forfeit the lease if the tenant does not fulfil his obligations. Further, the position as regards creating successive interests in leaseholds is substantially the same as for land held in socage. Thus just as socage land may be given "to A for life, remainder to B for life, remainder to C in fee simple", so leasehold land may be given "to A for life, remainder to B for life, remainder to C absolutely". Nevertheless, leaseholds also retain the principal characteristic of an estate, for they mark out the length of time for which the land is held. Consequently, although it may be true that for all practical purposes leaseholds have completed the transition from contract via estate to tenure, it is better to regard them as being in a class by themselves, having features of both estates and tenures. The details of leaseholds will be considered later.[30]

Sect. 3. Seisin

1. Meaning

One distinction between freeholders and owners of estates less than freehold which was formerly of considerable importance was that only a freehold could carry seisin with it. It is difficult to define seisin satisfactorily.[31] It has nothing to do with the word "seizing", with its implication of violence. To medieval lawyers it suggested the very opposite: peace and quiet. A man who was put in seisin of land was "set" there and continued to "sit" there.[32] Seisin thus denotes quiet possession of land, but quiet possession of a particular kind.

---

[26] For these tenancies see below, pp. 347–349.
[27] For these tenancies see below, p. 350.
[28] Consider *Wheeler v. Mercer* [1957] A.C. 416 at 427, 428; M. & W., p. 792.
[29] Above, p. 17.
[30] Below, Chap. 9, pp. 337 *et seq.*
[31] See, generally, Maitland's *Collected Papers*, Vol. 1, pp. 329, 358, 407.
[32] 2 P. & M. 30.

2. Freeholder

Although at first the term was applied to the possession of a leaseholder as well as that of a freeholder, during the fifteenth century it became confined to those who held an estate of freehold.[33] A leaseholder merely had possession: only a freeholder could be seised.[34] And since the possession of a leaseholder was regarded as the possession of the freeholder from whom he held, a freeholder remained seised even after he had granted a term of years and had given up physical possession of the land: receipt of the rent was evidence of seisin. Further, only land of freehold tenure carried seisin with it. A copyholder could not be seised, even if he held a fee simple.

From this it will be seen that a person was seised only if:

(i) he held an estate of freehold;

(ii) the land was land of freehold tenure; and

(iii) either he had taken physical possession of the land, or a leaseholder or copyholder held the land from him.

3. Definition

Although it seems impossible to frame a satisfactory definition of seisin, to call it "that feudal possession of land which only the owner of a freehold estate in freehold land could have" is to express the most important elements. A man might be seised of many plots of land at the same time, whether or not he had granted any leases of them, for the requirement of physical possession did not mean that the person seised had to be in continuous occupation: seisin was not lost merely because he went away on a visit. Once seisin was acquired, it continued until another person acquired it.

4. Importance

The original importance of seisin was that:

(i) feudal services could be claimed only from the tenant seised of the land[35];

(ii) real actions (ones in which the land itself could be recovered and not merely damages) could be brought only against the tenant seised (such actions were little used after the seventeenth century and had all been abolished by 1854)[36];

(iii) curtesy and dower (the rights of a surviving spouse under the rules for intestacy before 1926) could be claimed only out of property of which the deceased had been seised[37]; and

(iv) conveyances of freehold land could until the sixteenth century be made only by a "feoffment[38] with livery of seisin"—this was a solemn ceremony carried out by the parties entering on the land, and the feoffor, in the presence of witnesses, delivering

---

[33] Challis R.P. 99.
[34] Litt. 324; Co. Litt. 17a, 200b.
[35] Challis R.P. 100.
[36] *Freeman d. Vernon v. West* (1763) 2 Wils. K.B. 165 at 166.
[37] See M. & W. (5th ed.), pp. 543–546.
[38] Pronounced "feffment"; and similarly for "feoffor" and "feoffee".

the seisin to the feoffee either by some symbolic act, such as handing him a twig or sod of earth, or by uttering some words such as "Enter into this land and God give you joy", and leaving him in possession of the land.

For these and other reasons, the common law abhorred an abeyance of seisin. Any transactions whereby one person lost seisin without transferring it to another was void.

Seisin survived the 1925 property legislation only to the extent that pre-existing rights to curtesy and dower continued (all such rights must long since have ended as a result of the death of the surviving spouse in question) and in respect of a few surviving feudal services of a ceremonial nature, most of which have to do with the coronation (there have only been two coronations since 1925; it remains to be seen whether future monarchs claim these services).

PART 2—ESTATES OF FREEHOLD

The two main points to be considered concerning estates of freehold are:

(i) the words required to create each of the estates; and

(ii) the characteristics of each estate.

Sect. 1. Words of limitation

"Words of limitation" is the phrase used to describe the words which limit (*i.e.* delimit, or mark out) the estate to be taken. Thus in a conveyance today "to A in fee simple", the words "in fee simple" are words of limitation; for they show what estate A is to have.

1. *Inter vivos*

The rule at common law was that a freehold estate of inheritance could be created in a conveyance *inter vivos* (*i.e.* a transfer of land between living persons) only by a phrase which included the word "heirs". A life estate could be created without using this word, but a fee simple or fee tail could not[39]: no other word would do. "Heirs" was the sanctified word of limitation, and had a magic which no other word possessed. Thus a gift "to A and his heirs" gave (and still gives) A a fee simple. It is important to note that, precisely because the words "and his heirs" are words of limitation, the reference to A's heirs gave no estate in the land to those heirs. They merely delimit or mark out the estate which A is to take.[40] Words which do confer estates or interests on persons referred to are instead known as words of purchase. "Purchase" is here being used in the technical sense as referring to any transaction, whether for value or not, whereby property is acquired by the act of parties to it, such as a sale or gift, and not merely by operation of law, as on an intestacy.

---

[39] Co. Litt. 20a, 20b.
[40] Under the rule in *Shelley's Case* (1581) 1 Co. Rep. 88b, abolished in respect of deeds executed and wills taking effect after 1925, a gift "to A for life, remainder to his heirs" also gave A a fee simple, the latter words also being treated as words of limitation.

2. Wills

In the case of gifts by will, the attitude of the courts was different. A conveyance was a solemn transaction that was enforced by the courts of law, whereas wills were less formal and were at first enforced by the Court of Chancery; and that court looked to the intent rather than the form. When the Statute of Wills 1540 compelled the common law courts to give effect to wills, both the words of the statute (authorising the testator to dispose of land "at his free will and pleasure"[41]) and the practice of Chancery encouraged the courts to interpret wills liberally. Thus strict words of limitation were not required in wills. Provided the intention of the testator was clear, it would be effectuated.[42]

3. Words of limitation for a fee simple

(a) Conveyances inter vivos to natural persons

At common law, the proper expression to employ was "and his heirs" following the grantee's name, for example "to A and his heirs".[43] "Heir" in the singular would not do, and the word "and" could not be replaced by "or"[44]: "to A or his heirs" gave A a mere life estate, and so did expressions not containing the word "heirs", such as "to A for ever", or "to A in fee simple".[45] Since 1881 the words "in fee simple" have also sufficed to pass the fee simple.[46] Since 1925, there has been no need for any words of limitation whatever, since the grantee takes "the fee simple or other the whole interest which the grantor had power to convey in such land, unless a contrary intention appears in the conveyance."[47] However, in practice, the words "in fee simple" are always inserted to make it clear that there is no contrary intention; were they not, the document in question could never constitute a valid root of title because it would not show what estate was being transferred.

(b) Conveyances inter vivos to corporations

At common law, different rules applied which depended on whether the corporation was a corporation aggregate or a corporation sole. A corporation aggregate consists of two or more persons united together under some name to form a new legal person potentially having perpetual existence, such as a Dean and Chapter, or a limited company. No words of limitation whatever were needed in such a case; a conveyance to the corporation, for instance "to the Alpha Co. Ltd", sufficed to pass the fee simple, for there was no reason to give it any other estate.[48] A corporation sole, on the other hand, comprises only one natural person. Thus the Queen, a bishop or a parson are all corporations sole in their official capacities. In such cases, a life estate to the individual holder of the office was a conceivable alternative to a fee simple, and so to create a fee simple a formula had to be used which indicated that the corporation rather than the individual should benefit.[49] This formula was "and his successors", for example "to the Vicar of Bray and his successors".[50] Failure to use this phrase

---

[41] Statute of Wills 1540, ss.1, 2.
[42] *Throckmerton v. Tracy* (1555) 1 Plowd. 145 at 162, 163.
[43] 2 Preston, Estates, 1.
[44] Co. Litt. 8b; Challis R.P. 221, 222.
[45] Litt. 1.
[46] Conveyancing Act 1881, s.51.
[47] L.P.A. 1925, s.60(1).
[48] 2 Preston, Estates, 43–47.
[49] See *Ex p. Vicar of Castle Bytham* [1895] 1 Ch. 348 at 354.
[50] Co. Litt. 8b, 94b; and see *Bankes v. Salisbury Diocesan Council of Education Incorporated* [1960] Ch. 631.

resulted in a mere life estate passing to the individual.[51] The statutory reforms of 1881 and 1925 also apply to corporations sole.[52]

(c) Gifts by will before 1838

Before 1838, no formal words of limitation were required in a will, but it was necessary for the will to show an intent to pass the fee simple.[53] Thus "to A for ever", "to A and his heir", or "to A to dispose at will and pleasure" all sufficed to pass the fee simple.[54] But it was for the devisee to show that a fee simple was intended to pass; a devise "to A" prima facie carried merely a life estate.[55]

(d) Gifts by will after 1837

By the Wills Act 1837[56] the fee simple or other the whole interest of which the testator has power to dispose passes in a gift by any will made or confirmed after 1837[57] unless a contrary intention is shown. This is the same rule as that subsequently adopted for conveyances *inter vivos* after 1925.

4. Words of limitation for a fee tail

Since no further entails have been able to be created fees since the end of 1996, either by deed or by will,[58] no detailed discussion of this topic is necessary. The rules were comparable to those for fees simple, with the additional complication that it was possible to restrict the descendants of the original tenant in fee tail who could take to his or her descendants of a particular sex or by a particular spouse, known as "a tail male", a "tail female" and "a tail special" respectively; an unrestricted fee tail was known as "a tail general".

(a) Conveyances inter vivos

At common law what was required was the word "heirs" followed by some words of procreation,[59] *i.e.* words which confined "heirs" to descendants of the original grantee; an example is "to A and the heirs of his body". The word "heirs" was essential, but any words of procreation sufficed. This formula created a tail general. For a tail male or tail female, the word "male" or "female" had to precede "heirs"; for a tail special, the words "begotten upon (or by) B" were added. After 1881 the words "in tail" (but not "in fee tail") with the appropriate modifications also sufficed to pass a fee tail.[60]

(b) Gifts by will before 1926

The rule before 1926 was that in a will any words showing an intent to create a fee tail sufficed, even if no technical expressions were used.

---

[51] A gift "to the Vicar of Bray and his heirs" perhaps gave a fee simple to the current vicar as an individual rather than as a body corporate. 2 Preston, Estates, 48; Co. Litt. 94b, n.(5).
[52] L.P.A. 1925, s.60(2).
[53] 2 Preston, Estates, 68.
[54] See, generally, 6 Cru.Dig., Chap. XI.
[55] 2 Preston, Estates, 78.
[56] s.28.
[57] s.34.
[58] T.L.A.T.A. 1996, Sched. 1, para. 5.
[59] 2 Preston, Estates, 477, 478.
[60] Conveyancing Act 1881, s.51; L.P.A. 1925, ss.60, 130.

(c) Gifts by will after 1925

After 1925, informal expressions no longer sufficed to create a fee tail in a will. Instead, expressions which created a fee tail in a conveyance *inter vivos* had to be employed.

5. Words of limitation for a life estate

(a) Conveyances inter vivos

In a conveyance before 1926, a life estate was created either by words showing an intention to create a life estate, such as "to A for life", or by the use of expressions insufficient to create a fee simple or fee tail, such as "to A" or "to A for ever" or "to A and his seed".[61] After 1925, a fee simple (or the whole of the interest that the grantor has power to convey, if it is less than a fee simple) passes unless a contrary intention is shown.[62] Thus to create a life estate, words showing an intention to do so must normally be used, such as "to A for life".

(b) Wills

Before the Wills Act 1837, a gift of land passed only a life estate unless an intention to create a fee simple or fee tail was shown. That Act provided that the fee simple passes unless a contrary intention is shown,[63] so that in this case also, words showing an intent to pass only a life interest are now essential.

Sect. 2. Nature of the estates of freehold

1. The fee simple

The fee simple is the most ample estate which can exist in land. Although in theory it still falls short of absolute ownership, in practice it amounts to this, for nearly all traces of the old feudal burdens have disappeared. A fee simple normally exists in a defined area of land, and all that is above or below it; but it can exist in the upper storey of a building, without the soil beneath it, and it may even be movable, shifting from plot to plot within a defined area (such as as settled by lot annually), or varying with boundary changes, as where the sea gradually invades or retreats.[64] Subject to provisions against racial discrimination,[65] a tenant in fee simple has long been free to dispose of his estate in whatever way he thinks fit, *inter vivos* since 1290[66] and by will since 1540.[67]

A fee simple (and for that matter a fee tail or a life estate) may be absolute or modified; a modified fee simple is any fee simple except a fee simple absolute. There are four types of fee.

---

[61] *Re Irwin* [1904] 2 Ch. 752.
[62] Above, p. 38.
[63] s.28; see above, p. 39.
[64] See Co. Litt. 48b; below.
[65] See Race Relations Act 1976, ss.21–24.
[66] Tenants in chief could not do so until 1326.
[67] Subject to certain restrictions removed in 1661 and now subject to possible claims under the Inheritance (Provision for Family and Dependants) Act 1975 (see below, pp. 172 *et seq.*).

(a) Fee simple absolute

This is the type normally encountered in practice. It is an estate which can potentially continue for ever. "Fee" denotes inheritability,[68] "simple" excludes fees tail, and "absolute" distinguishes modified fees.

(b) Determinable fee

A determinable fee is a fee simple which will automatically determine on the occurrence of some specified event which may never occur. If the event is bound to happen at some time, the estate created is not a determinable fee. Thus before 1926 a grant "to A and his heirs until B dies" gave A an estate *pur autre vie*, and a grant "to C and his heirs" for a fixed term of years gave C a mere tenancy for a term of years. A grant to X and his heirs until a specified lease was made, or to Y and his heirs "as long as such a tree stands", however, created determinable fees.[69] The estates of X and Y might continue for ever, but if the specified state of affairs came about, the fee determined and the land reverted to the original grantor. The grantor thus had a "possibility of reverter", *i.e.* a possibility of having an estate at a future time. If the occurrence of the determining event became impossible, the possibility of reverter was destroyed and the fee simple became absolute,[70] as where land was given "to A and his heirs until B marries" and B died a bachelor.

Determinable fees are rarely encountered in practice with two exceptions. First, under marriage settlements,[71] which are themselves an increasingly rare phenomenon, the settlor typically grants land to himself until the solemnisation of the marriage to avoid any difficulties in recovering it if the marriage does not in the end take place. Secondly, under family settlements, including marriage settlements, land is very occasionally settled until the bankruptcy of the beneficiary in question,[72] although it is more usual for a life estate rather than a fee simple to be settled in this way. But a fee simple limited to a corporation does not determine merely because the corporation is dissolved.[73]

(c) A fee simple upon condition

In making a grant of a fee simple, a clause may be added providing that the fee simple is not to commence until some event occurs, or that it is to determine on the occurrence of some event. Conditions of the first type are conditions precedent[74]: a gift "to X in fee simple if he attains 21" is a gift of a fee simple with a condition precedent that X must attain 21 before he can take the land. These limitations are dealt with under future interests.[75] A condition subsequent is one which operates to defeat an existing interest, for example a devise of land to X "on the condition that he never sells it out of the family".[76] Here the land passes to X, but it is liable to be forfeited if the condition is broken: in such circumstances, X is said to have a vested interest, liable to be divested.

---

[68] See above, p. 32.
[69] *Idle v. Cook* (1705) 1 P.Wms. 70 at 78.
[70] Challis R.P. 83, 254.
[71] Below, p. 215.
[72] Who must be a person other than the settlor; *Re Burroughs-Fowler* [1916] 2 Ch. 251.
[73] *Re Strathblaine Estates Ltd* [1948] Ch. 228.
[74] Pronounced "preeseedent" with the accent on the second syllable.
[75] Below, pp. 209, *et seq.*
[76] *Re Macleay* (1875) L.R. 20 Eq. 186.

(d) The distinction between (b) and (c)

The difference between a determinable fee and a fee simple defeasible by condition sub-sequent is not always easy to discern. The essential distinction is that the determining event in a determinable fee is included in the words marking out the limits of the estate, whereas a condition subsequent is a clause added to a limitation of a complete fee simple absolute which seeks to defeat it. Thus a devise to a school in fee simple "until it ceases to publish its accounts" would create a determinable fee, whereas a devise to the school in fee simple "on condition that the accounts are published annually" creates a fee simple defeasible by condition subsequent.[77] Words such as "while", "during", "as long as", "until" and so on are apt for the creation of a determinable fee, whereas words which form a separate clause of defeasance, such as "provided that", "on condition that", "but if", or "if it happen that", operate as a condition subsequent.[78]

It will be seen that the difference is primarily one of wording; the determining event may be worked into the limitation in such a way as to create either a determinable fee or a fee simple defeasible by condition subsequent, whichever the grantor wishes. The question is whether the words limit the utmost time of continuance of the estate, or whether they mark an event which, if it takes place in the course of that time, will defeat the estate: in the first case the words form a limitation, in the second a condition. In short, a limitation marks the bounds or compass of the estate, a condition defeats the estate before it attains its boundary.

There are some practical differences between the two forms of fee.

(i) Determination: A determinable fee automatically determines when the specified event occurs, for the natural limits of its existence have been reached.[79] A fee simple upon condition merely gives the grantor (or whoever is entitled to his realty, if the grantor is dead) a right to enter and determine the estate when the event occurs; until entry is made, the fee simple continues.[80]

Since a right of forfeiture arises from a condition subsequent, the condition is void (and so the grantee takes a fee simple absolute) unless it can be seen from the outset distinctly and precisely what events will cause a forfeiture.[81] The concepts of continuing to reside in Canada[82] and of marrying a person "not of Jewish parentage and of the Jewish faith"[83] have been held to be uncertain, whilst the concepts of continuing in permanent residence in England[84] and of being or becoming a Roman Catholic have been held to be sufficiently certain.[85] This strict rule for conditions subsequent may be contrasted with the more relaxed rule for conditions precedent, where the question is one not of forfeiture but of entitlement. Thus under a gift to the eldest son of X who is "a member of the Church of England",[86] or an option to purchase given to "any friends of mine",[87] the impossibility of defining who is

---

[77] See *Re Da Costa* [1912] 1 Ch. 337.
[78] See 1 Sanders, Uses 156; Shep. 121.
[79] *Newis v. Lark* (1571) 2 Plowd. 403.
[80] *Matthew Manning's Case* (1609) 8 Co.Rep. 94b at 95b.
[81] *Sifton v. Sifton* [1938] A.C. 656.
[82] *ibid.*
[83] *Clayton v. Ramsden* [1943] A.C. 320.
[84] *Re Gape* [1952] Ch. 743: "permanent residence" is a concept used in the doctrine of domicile in the conflict of laws.
[85] *Blathwayt v. Baron Cawley* [1976] A.C. 397.
[86] *Re Allen* [1953] Ch. 810.
[87] *Re Barlow's W.T.* [1979] 1 W.L.R. 278.

or is not a "member" or "friend" will not invalidate the gift for any person who on any possible meaning of the words is indisputably a "member" or "friend". The courts are reluctant to hold a provision void for uncertainty.[88]

(ii) Remoteness: Determinable limitations made up to and including July 15, 1964, some of which are likely still to be in existence despite the intervening years, were probably valid no matter how far in the future the determining event might occur and bring the estate to an end.[89] Conditions subsequent made up to and including that date were void if there was at the date when the condition was imposed any possibility that the condition might not be fulfilled until after the end of the perpetuity period, a relevant life or lives in being plus 21 years. Such a possibility rendered the intended conditional estate absolute. Both determinable limitations and conditions subsequent made since July 16, 1964 will under the present law become void if the determining event has not in fact happened or the condition has not been fulfilled by the end of the perpetuity period, statutory relevant lives in being plus 21 years or, if specified as such, any fixed number of years up to 80.[90]

(iii) Existence at law: A determinable fee cannot, it seems, exist as a legal estate after 1925; but a fee simple subject to a condition subsequent apparently can.[91]

(iv) Flexibility: A determinable fee is more flexible than a fee simple upon condition. There are certain restrictions upon the conditions on which a fee simple may be made liable to be defeated. A condition subsequent will be void, and the fee simple will consequently be absolute, if the condition infringes any of the following rules.

(i) It must not take away the power of alienation. One of the incidents of ownership is the right to sell or otherwise dispose of the property. A condition against alienation is said to be repugnant to this right, and contrary to public policy, if it substantially takes away the tenant's power of alienation; such conditions are thus void.[92] For example, conditions prohibiting all alienation, or all alienation during the life of some person, or alienation to anyone except X, have all been held void.[93] But certain partial restraints have been held valid; thus where land was devised to A "on the condition that he never sells it out of the family", the condition was held valid on the grounds that it did not prohibit any form of alienation except sale, it did not prohibit sales to members of the family, and it bound only A and not subsequent owners of the land.[94] Moreover, a mere covenant not to alienate is not repugnant to the power of alienation; the covenantee may recover damages (which might be nominal) for breach of the covenant, but the alienation is valid and gives rise to no right of forfeiture.[95]

(ii) It must not be directed against a course of devolution prescribed by law. A condition rendering a fee simple liable to be defeated if the tenant dies intestate, becomes bankrupt, or has the estate seized in execution, is void, for on each of

---

[88] See *Brown v. Gould* [1972] Ch. 53 at 56.
[89] Below, p. 229.
[90] *ibid.*
[91] Below, pp. 79–80.
[92] *Bradley v. Peixoto* (1797) 3 Ves. 324.
[93] See *Re Cockerill* [1929] 2 Ch. 131.
[94] *Re Macleay* (1875) L.R. 20 Eq. 186; *cf. Re Brown* [1954] Ch. 39; and see (1954) 70 L.Q.R. 15.
[95] *Caldy Manor Estates Ltd v. Farrell* [1974] 1 W.L.R. 1303.

these events the law prescribes that a fee simple shall devolve in a particular way, and this course of devolution cannot be altered by condition.[96]

(iii) It must not be illegal, immoral or otherwise contrary to public policy. The condition under this head most frequently encountered is a condition in restraint of marriage. Partial restraints, prohibiting marriage with a Papist, or a Scotsman, or a person who had been a domestic servant, have been held good.[97] But total restraints (or restraints which are virtually total, such as against marrying a person who has not freehold property worth £500 per annum in 1795) are void unless the intent is not merely to restrain marriage but simply to provide for the tenant until marriage,[98] or unless the tenant has already been married once.[99]

A determinable fee, on the other hand, is not so strictly confined. A devise of freeholds on trust for X "until he shall assign charge or otherwise dispose of the same or some part thereof or become bankrupt . . . or do something whereby the said annual income or some part thereof would become payable to or vested in some other person" has been held to give X a determinable fee.[1] On any of the events occurring X's estate would determine; if he died before any of them occurred, the fee simple would become absolute, for it would then cease to be possible for any of them to occur. But although a fee may thus be made determinable on alienation or on bankruptcy or on similar events, a limitation would probably be void if it were contrary to public policy for the fee to be determinable on the stated event, such as if the event is the return to X of his wife who is separated from him.

(v) Effect of condition or limitation becoming void or impossible: If a condition subsequent is void or becomes impossible, the donee takes a fee simple absolute, free from any condition[2]; but if a fee is made determinable upon an event contrary to law, the whole gift fails.[3]

(e) A base fee

A base fee is a particular kind of determinable fee which may arise as a result of an attempt by a tenant in fee tail to deal with his estate. The two essentials of a base fee are (a) that it continues only so long as the original grantor or any heirs of his body are alive; and (b) that there is a remainder or reversion after it.[4] Such estates are dealt with below.[5]

(f) Nature of modified fees

In general, the owner of a modified fee has the same rights over the land as the owner of a fee simple absolute: thus the common law refused to restrain him from committing acts of waste,[6] such as opening and working mines. Equity, on the other hand, would intervene to

---

[96] *Re Machu* (1882) 21 Ch.D. 838 (bankruptcy).
[97] *Jenner v. Turner* (1880) 16 Ch.D. 188 (domestic servant).
[98] See *Jones v. Jones* (1876) 1 Q.B.D. 279.
[99] *Newton v. Marsden* (1862) 2 J. & H. 356.
[1] *Re Leach* [1912] 2 Ch. 422.
[2] *Re Greenwood* [1903] 1 Ch. 749.
[3] Consider *Re Moore* (1888) 39 Ch.D. 116 (personalty).
[4] See below, pp. 46, 214.
[5] Below, p. 46.
[6] For waste, see below, p. 47.

prevent the commission of equitable waste, *i.e.* acts of wanton destruction,[7] whereas the owner of a fee simple absolute is under no such restraint.

At common law the owner of a modified fee could not convey a fee simple absolute but merely a fee liable to determination, for a man cannot convey more than he has. Statute has qualified this position.[8] Further, such a fee may become enlarged into a fee simple absolute, for example by the determining event becoming impossible[9]; and there are special rules for the enlargement of base fees.[10]

2. The fee tail

Since no further fees tail can now be created, the characteristics of this estate can be discussed much more briefly.

(a) Origin

The fee tail was created by the Statute *De Donis Conditionalibus* 1285 in order to prevent a gift of land to X and the heirs of his body being destroyed as a result of X alienating the land in fee simple as soon as any issue was born to him, something which he had previously been entitled to do. By doing so, he would not only defeat the expectations of the issue inheriting which had motivated the gift in the first place but would also destroy any possibility of the land reverting to the donor when X's line died out. The Statute provided that, notwithstanding any act of the original tenant in fee tail or his issue, the land was bound to descend to the next person in line as intended. While this did not prevent a tenant in fee tail from alienating the land, the estate so created could be defeated by his issue after his death or, if he had no issue, by the person next entitled to the land or, in default of any such person, by the donor or whoever had inherited the latter's assets.

(b) Rights of a tenant in fee tail

In general, a tenant in fee tail whose estate is in possession has the same rights of enjoyment of the land as a tenant in fee simple. He may thus commit all kinds of waste, including equitable waste, even if he is restrained from barring the fee tail by statute.[11] Since 1925, it has not been possible for a legal fee tail to exist[12] so all existing estates in fee tail must take effect behind a trust. This means that the legal estate in fee simple must be vested in some trustees or trustee (who may be the tenant in fee tail himself) on trust for the person entitled in fee tail and everyone else interested in the land after him. This does not impair the benefits accruing from the land; only the bare legal ownership is affected. After 1925, it was also possible to entail personal property as well as real property.[13]

(c) Prospective abolition

The Trusts of Land and Appointment of Trustees Act 1996 prohibited the creation of any further entails after the end of 1996.[14] Existing entails nevertheless continue. They will usually have taken effect as settlements under the Settled Land Act 1925 although it is also

---

[7] *Re Hanbury's S.E.* [1913] 2 Ch. 357 at 365.
[8] Below, p. 270.
[9] Above, p. 41.
[10] Below, pp. 46, 47.
[11] *Lord Glenorchy v. Bosville* (1733) Ca.t.Talb. 3 at 16; *Att.-Gen. v. Duke of Marlborough* (1818) 3 Madd. 498.
[12] L.P.A. 1925, s.1; below, pp. 78–81.
[13] L.P.A. 1925, s.130.
[14] Sched. 1, para. 5.

theoretically possible for them to have taken effect behind an express trust for sale of land. Any attempt to create an estate in fee tail after 1996 has the effect of conferring an absolute interest on the first tenant in fee tail.[15]

(d) The barring of fees tail

For nearly two centuries following the Statute *De Donis Conditionalibus* 1285 donors of land who created estates in fee tail were able to secure the unbroken descent of their land to the successive issue of the first tenant in fee tail. However, freedom of alienation was ultimately secured by the ingenuity of practitioners and the acquiescence of the courts. The process of alienation is described as "barring the entail", in other words preventing all persons entitled to the land in the future from taking. The devices developed for this purpose in the fifteenth and sixteenth centuries, which were known as fines and recoveries, were ultimately legitimated by the Fines and Recoveries Act 1833. This provided that a fee tail could be barred by any conveyance or other transfer by which a fee simple could be disposed of, except a will. Finally, under the Law of Property Act 1925,[16] it also became possible to bar a fee tail by any will made or confirmed after 1925 but only where the estate of the tenant in fee tail had come into possession and he was of full age. Both these methods can still be utilised in appropriate circumstances by existing tenants in fee tail.

(e) The effect of barring a fee tail

(i) Creation of a fee simple absolute: Between 1833 and 1926, a conveyance or other transfer was fully effective to bar the fee tail in question only if it was enrolled (this requirement was removed after 1925[17]). When that requirement existed and was satisfied, the transfer would give the transferee a fee simple absolute if it was executed by a tenant in fee tail whose estate was in possession. It would also do so if it was executed by a tenant in fee tail whose estate had not yet come into possession provided that he had obtained the consent of the person known as "the protector of the settlement", who in practice would be whoever held the freehold estate which was in possession at the time. This remains the position today. The result of barring a fee tail by will when this is possible has the same effect.

(ii) Creation of a base fee: A transfer which was not enrolled when this was still necessary, or which was executed without the consent of the protector of the settlement by a tenant in fee tail whose estate had not yet come into possession would give the transferee the particular type of determinable fee simple known as a base fee. This is a fee simple which would last as long as the fee tail would have lasted had it not been barred, in other words for as long as there continued to be issue of the original tenant in fee tail. If all his issue died out, the base fee would automatically determine and the land would pass to the person next entitled to it or, in default of any such person, to the donor or whoever has inherited his assets. This also remains the position today.

(iii) Enlargement of a base fee: There were and are a number of ways in which a base fee can be enlarged into a fee simple absolute:

[15] *ibid.*
[16] s.176.
[17] L.P.A. 1925, s.130(3).

  (i) by the former tenant in fee tail making a further transfer either with the consent of the protector of the settlement or when that consent is no longer necessary because his estate has come into possession[18];

 (ii) by the former tenant in fee tail barring the entail by will after his estate has come into possession;

(iii) by the holder of the base fee acquiring all the remaining interests in the land[19]; and

(iv) by twelve years possession of the land after the estate of the former tenant of tail has come into possession.[20]

(f) Unbarrable entails

Certain entails cannot be barred. If the descendants of the original tenant in fee tail who can take are restricted to his or her descendants by a particular spouse (known as "a tail special"), then the fee tail cannot be barred after the death of the specified spouse without leaving any issue capable of inheriting the fee tail. The tenant in fee tail then becomes "a tenant in tail after possibility of issue extinct", the last three words usually being omitted for brevity.[21] Nor is it possible to bar fees tail created by the Crown for services rendered to the Crown to which the Crown is entitled subject to the fee tail[22] or fees tail made unbarrable by special Acts of Parliament, such as the fee tail given to reward the first Duke of Marlborough and the first Duke of Wellington.[23] Nor can fees tail be barred by infants,[24] persons of unsound mind or bankrupts, although the receiver of a person of unsound mind[25] and the trustee in bankruptcy of a bankrupt can do so.[26]

(3) The life estate

Until 1926 an interest in land for life was able to exist as a legal estate but since 1925 it has not been able to do so and has therefore to take effect as an equitable interest.[27] In general, the law which governed legal life estates prior to 1926 equally applies to the corresponding life interests after 1925.

(4) Types of life estate

The two types of life estate were the ordinary estate for the life of the tenant and the estate *pur autre vie*.

(a) Estate for the life of the tenant

The normal type of life estate was one for the life of the tenant. This arose either:

---

[18] Fines and Recoveries Act 1833, ss.19, 35; *Bankes v. Small* (1887) 36 Ch.D. 716.
[19] Fines and Recoveries Act 1833, s.39.
[20] Limitation Act 1980, s.27.
[21] Fines and Recoveries Act 1833, s.18.
[22] Fines and Recoveries Act 1833, s.18.
[23] 6 Anne, cc. 6, 7, 1706; 54 Geo. 3, c. 161, 1814.
[24] See below, p. 215.
[25] Mental Health Act 1983, s.96(1).
[26] Insolvency Act 1986, s.314, Sched. 5. The former disability of married women is obsolete.
[27] Below, p. 78.

(i) by express limitation, as by a grant "to A for life"[28]; or

(ii) by operation of law, as in the case of a surviving spouse's rights on an intestacy before 1926 to curtesy and dower.[29]

(b) Estate pur autre vie

An estate *pur autre vie* was an estate for the life of someone other than the tenant,[30] the person whose life measured the duration of the estate being called the *cestui que vie* (pronounced "setty ker vee"). An estate *pur autre vie* could arise either:

(i) by the owner of a life estate assigning it to another: *nemo dat quod non habet* (nobody can give what he does not have), so that the assignor could create no interest which would last for longer than his own life; or

(ii) by express grant, for example "to A for the life of X".

Both types of life estate were estates of freehold, but neither was a freehold of inheritance, for they were not capable of descending to the tenant's heir on his death. A life estate ceased automatically when the tenant died, and although an estate *pur autre vie* continued during the life of the *cestui que vie* despite the tenant's death, before 1926 it did not descend to the tenant's heir as such but passed on intestacy according to special rules of occupancy. Since 1925 it passes like other property under a will or intestacy.

Both types of life estate could be made determinable or subject to conditions subsequent[31] and were in general subject to similar rights and burdens.

(5) Position of a tenant for life at common law

In considering the position of a tenant for life at common law, an important part is played by the law of waste (particularly as to timber and minerals), and the rules governing emblements and fixtures.

(a) Waste

Although the law of waste is of importance in other connections, notably in the law of landlord and tenant, it is most suitably considered in relation to life interests, where it is applicable both to ordinary life interests and to interests *pur autre vie*. Technically, waste consists of any act which alters the nature of the land, whether for the better or for the worse, for example the conversion of arable land into a wood or vice versa. Four types of waste must be considered, namely, ameliorating, permissive, voluntary and equitable.

(i) Ameliorating waste: Alterations which improve the land, such as converting dilapidated store buildings into dwellings, or a farm into a market garden, constitute ameliorating waste. Since the decision of the House of Lords in *Doherty v. Allman*[32] in 1878 the court is unlikely to grant an injunction to restrain such waste or to award any damages.

---

[28] Above, p. 40.
[29] See below, p. 192.
[30] See, generally, *Doe d. Jeff v. Robinson* (1828) 2 Man. & Ry. 249.
[31] *Brandon v. Robinson* (1811) 18 Ves. 429; and see *Re Evans's Contract* [1920] 2 Ch. 469; see also above, pp. 41–44.
[32] 3 App.Cas. 709 (conversion of dilapidated barracks into dwelling-houses by tenant for years).

(ii) Permissive waste: This consists of the failure to do that which ought to be done, as by the non-repair of buildings or the failure to clean out a ditch or moat so as to prevent the foundations becoming rotten.[33] But mere non-cultivation of land is not permissive waste.[34] A tenant for life is not liable for permissive waste unless an obligation to repair is imposed upon him by the terms of the limitation under which he holds.[35]

(iii) Voluntary waste: Voluntary waste is positive in nature: "the committing of any spoil or destruction in houses, lands, etc., by tenants, to the damage of the heir, or of him in reversion or remainder."[36] Literally, this would include equitable waste, but the term voluntary waste is usually reserved for such voluntary waste as does not amount to equitable waste. Such acts as opening and working a mine in the land (but not merely working a mine already open),[37] or cutting timber,[38] are examples of voluntary waste. Timber consists of oak, ash and elm trees which are at least 20 years old and not too old to have a reasonable quantity of usable wood in them. Other trees may rank as timber by local custom, such as beech in Buckinghamshire and willow in Hampshire; and custom may also prescribe some qualification other than an age of 20 years for the trees to be considered timber.[39]

A tenant for life is liable for voluntary waste unless his interest was granted to him by an instrument exempting him from liability for voluntary waste, as under a grant "without impeachment of waste".[40] Where there is such an exception the tenant is said to be "unimpeachable of waste": otherwise he is said to be "impeachable of waste". Thus if nothing is said about waste, the tenant is impeachable; in practice, however, he is usually made unimpeachable.

(iv) Equitable waste: "Equitable waste is that which a prudent man would not do in the management of his own property."[41] Acts of wanton destruction, such as stripping a house of all its lead, iron, glass, doors, boards, etc., to the value of £3,000,[42] or pulling down houses, or cutting timber planted for ornament or shelter (unless this is necessary for the preservation of part of the timber), fall under the head of equitable waste. A tenant for life is liable for equitable waste unless the document conferring his interest upon him shows an intention to allow him to commit equitable waste. It is not enough that his interest has been given to him without impeachment of waste: he must show that it is intended that he should be allowed to commit equitable as well as voluntary waste.[43]

(b) Timber

Although largely governed by the general law of waste, the rights of a tenant for life with regard to timber and minerals are important enough to merit separate treatment.

There are many relevant factors regarding timber.

---

[33] See, *e.g. Powys v. Blagrave* (1854) 4 De G.M. & G. 448.
[34] *Hutton v. Warren* (1836) 1 M. & W. 466 at 472.
[35] *Re Cartwright* (1889) 41 Ch.D. 532.
[36] *Bacon's Abridgement* (7th ed.), Vol. 8, p. 379, definition of waste.
[37] See *Dashwood v. Magniac* [1891] 3 Ch. 306 at 360.
[38] *Honywood v. Honywood* (1874) L.R. 18 Eq. 306.
[39] *ibid.*, at 309; *Countess of Cumberland's Case* (1610) Moo.K.B. 812.
[40] *Re Ridge* (1886) 31 Ch.D. 504 at 507.
[41] *Turner v. Wright* (1860) 2 De G.F. & J. 234 at 243.
[42] *Vane v. Lord Barnard* (1716) 2 Vern. 738.
[43] L.P.A. 1925, s.135.

(i) Estovers: Whether impeachable of waste or not, a tenant for life can take reasonable estovers (or botes) from the land. These consist of wood and timber taken as:

(i) house-bote, for repairing the house or burning in it;

(ii) plough-bote, for making and repairing agricultural implements; and

(iii) hay-bote, for repairing fences.

The tenant's right to house-bote does not entitle him to cut down timber in excess of his present needs in order to use it for any repairs which may become necessary in the future, nor does it authorise him to sell the timber, even if he employs the proceeds in repairing, or the timber proves unfit for repairs.[44]

(ii) Timber estate: On a timber estate (an estate cultivated mainly for the produce of saleable timber which is cut periodically), the tenant can cut and sell timber according to the rules of proper estate management even if he is impeachable of waste. The reason for this rule is that the timber properly cut on such an estate is part of the annual fruits of the land rather than part of the inheritance.[45]

(iii) Timber planted for ornament or shelter: As has been seen,[46] it is equitable waste to cut timber planted for ornament or shelter, and only a tenant unimpeachable of equitable waste is permitted to do this.

(iv) Trees: In general, a tenant for life, even if he is impeachable of waste, may cut dotards (dead trees not fit for use as timber) and all trees which are not timber, such as in most cases willows or larches.[47] But there are a number of exceptions to this. It is voluntary waste to cut trees which would be timber but for their immaturity (unless the cutting is necessary to thin them out and so allow proper development) or to cut fruit trees in a garden or orchard.[48] Further, it is voluntary waste to cut wood which a prudent man would not cut, such as willows which help to hold a river bank together; and it is equitable waste to cut trees planted for ornament or shelter, or to grub up an entire wood. Where by reason of abnormal circumstances, such as extraordinary gales or wartime conditions, trees are severed before they are ripe for cutting, the court will direct that the tenant for life is to receive only part of the proceeds, the balance being held in trust for those entitled after his death.[49]

(v) Normal rules: Subject to the above special rules, the position is that a tenant for life who is unimpeachable of waste may cut and sell timber and keep all the proceeds.[50] But if the tenant is impeachable of waste, his only right to cut timber is that given to him by statute.[51] This authorises him to cut and sell timber ripe and fit for cutting, provided:

(i) the consent of the trustees of the settlement under which he holds his life interest, or an order of the court, is obtained; and

---

[44] Co. Litt. 41b, 53b.
[45] *Honywood v. Honywood* (1874) L.R. 18 Eq. 306 at 309, 310; *Dashwood v. Magniac* [1891] 3 Ch. 306.
[46] Above.
[47] *Re Harker's W. T.* [1938] Ch. 323.
[48] *Kaye v. Banks* (1770) Dick. 431.
[49] *Re Terry* (1918) 87 L.J. Ch. 577.
[50] *Lewis Bowles's Case* (1615) 11 Co.Rep.79b.
[51] S.L.A. 1925, s.66, replacing S.L.A. 1882, s.35.

(ii) three-quarters of the proceeds are set aside as capital money: this means that the trustees hold this portion of the price on trust for all persons having any interest in the land, paying only the interest to the tenant for life. The remaining quarter of the proceeds is paid to the tenant for life.

(vi) Ownership of severed timber: Until timber is severed, a tenant for life has no claim to it, so that if land is sold with the uncut timber on it, the life tenant cannot claim any share of the price even though he could lawfully have cut the timber.[52] Once the timber is severed it belongs to the life tenant if he was entitled to cut it, whether the severance was effected by the tenant, a stranger or an act of God, such as a storm; but if he was not entitled to sever it, it belongs not to him but to the owner of the next vested estate or interest of inheritance.[53]

(c) Minerals

The mineral rights of a tenant for life depend on two factors, namely, whether the mine was already open when his tenancy began, and whether he is impeachable of waste.

(i) Right to work mines: A tenant for life may work a mine and take all the proceeds unless:

    (i) he is impeachable of waste; and

    (ii) the mine was not open when his tenancy began.

Where both these conditions are satisfied, he cannot work the mine at all, for to open and work an unopened mine is voluntary waste. But it is not waste to continue working a mine already open,[54] even if new pits are made on different parts of the same plot of land to pursue the same or a new vein; for the grantor, by opening or allowing the opening of the mines, has shown an intent that the minerals should be treated as part of the profits of the land.

(ii) Right to lease mines under the Settled Land Act 1925: This legislation,[55] which now applies only to settlements created before 1997,[56] authorises a tenant for life to grant mining leases for one hundred years or less, whether the mine is open or not, and whether or not the tenant is impeachable of waste. In each case, subject to any contrary intention in the settlement, the tenant for life is entitled to three-quarters of the rent, except that if he is impeachable of waste and the mine is unopened, he is entitled to only one-quarter. The balance of rent is capital money, and is held for the benefit of all those interested under the settlement.[57]

(iii) Right to lease mines under trusts for sale and trusts of land: A tenant for life under any type of trust for sale prior to 1997 had no power to grant mining leases; nor does a tenant for life under a trust of land created after 1996. If anyone has this power, it will be the trustees in question. Until 1997, whether or not they had it depended on the wording of the trust

---

[52] *Re Llewellin* (1888) 37 Ch.D. 317.
[53] *Bewick v. Whitfield* (1734) 3 P.Wms. 267.
[54] See *Re Hall* [1916] 2 Ch. 488 at 493.
[55] ss.41, 42, 45–47, replacing earlier Acts; see below, pp. 270 *et seq.*
[56] T.L.A.T.A., s.2 (1).
[57] S.L.A. 1925, s.47.

instrument in question. The trustees of a trust of land will have this power[58] in the absence of any contrary provision in the trust instrument.[59] The Trusts of Land and Appointment of Trustees Act 1996 does not say who is entitled to the rent but, since it authorises the trustees to grant the lease in question, there seems to be no basis on which any apportionment can be made. If this is indeed the case, the tenant for life will unquestionably benefit at the expense of the remaining beneficiaries. The trustees will therefore have to take this consequence into account when granting the mining lease in question and endeavour to protect the remaining beneficiaries by obtaining some part of the consideration payable for the lease by way of lump sum (technically known as a fine). Since failure to do so could render the trustees liable for breach of trust, if they can only grant a mining lease on terms which do not protect the remaining beneficiaries, they would be well advised to seek the directions of the court before doing so.

(d) Emblements and fixtures

A tenant cannot foresee the date on which an estate *pur autre vie* or for his own life will determine, and so to encourage him to cultivate his land by assuring him of the fruits of his labour, the law gives him a right to emblements (pronounced *em*-blem-ents). This means that the tenant's personal representatives, or in the case of an estate *pur autre vie* the tenant himself, may enter the land after the life estate has determined and reap the crops which the tenant himself has sown.[60] This applies only to annual crops artificially produced, such as corn, hemp and flax, and not to things such as fruit trees and timber; further, it extends only to the crops actually growing at the determination of the tenancy.[61] Where the end of the tenancy is brought about by the tenant's own act (such as where a life estate is granted to a widow until remarriage and she remarries) there is no right to emblements.[62]

Prima facie any fixtures attached to the land by a tenant for life must be left after his death for the person next entitled to the land; but trade fixtures and ornamental and domestic fixtures are excepted.[63]

---

[58] T.L.A.T.A., s.6 (1).
[59] T.L.A.T.A., s.8 (1).
[60] Co. Litt. 55b; *Grantham v. Hawley* (1615) Hob. 132.
[61] *Graves v. Weld* (1833) 5 B. & Ad. 105 at 119.
[62] *Oland's Case* (1602) 5 Co.Rep. 116a.
[63] See above, p. 23.

Chapter 3

LAW AND EQUITY

PART 1—GENERAL PRINCIPLES

The difference between Law and Equity, which has already been mentioned in brief outline,[1] must now be considered in greater detail.

Sect. 1. The historical basis of equity

1. The common law courts

The existence of equity can best be explained historically. At the end of the thirteenth century the principal courts were (a) many local courts, organised on a geographical basis for each shire and hundred and some boroughs, where justice was dispensed on a communal basis; (b) the courts held by each feudal lord for his tenants, which dealt principally with disputes concerning land; and (c) the Royal courts, which had emerged from the feudal court held by the King for his tenants in chief (also known as the King's Council), and which by this time had become known as the Courts of Common Law, consisting of the Court of King's Bench, the Court of Common Pleas, and the Court of Exchequer. These Courts, which had initially only dealt with matters of interest to the King, had by this time begun to take over a substantial part of the jurisdiction of the local courts and the jurisdiction of the feudal courts relating to freehold tenures. Until the fifteenth century, each of the Royal courts had had its own proper sphere, but in the course of that century their jurisdiction came to overlap so much that a claimant could usually choose to litigate in any of the three of them. By this time, they had attracted virtually all the litigation of the country. Although many of the local courts survived into the eighteenth century, most of them were by then in decline, or moribund, while the feudal courts remained in existence only for the purpose of dealing with certain matters relating to unfree tenures.

2. The writ system

In general, no action could be commenced in any of the common law courts until a writ had been issued by the Chancellor. The Chancellor, who was usually an ecclesiastic, was the head

[1] Above, p. 3.

of the King's Secretarial Department. As keeper of the Great Seal with which writs were sealed, he was at the head of the English legal system.

The writs issued by the Chancellor differed for each different kind of action. Since 1852, anyone claiming to be entitled to some remedy, such as the recovery of possession of land of which he had been dispossessed, or the payment of money owed to him, has been able to issue proceedings claiming the appropriate relief. From 1856 until April 25, 1999, he did so by issuing a writ in a form which left it to him to state his claim in his own words.[2] Since April 26, 1999,[3] he does so instead by issuing a claim form, which similarly leaves it to him to state his claim in his own words. The same writ and claim form could be filled up with a claim for the possession of land as for payment of a debt, or damages for trespass to land: since 1852 there has been no special form which has to be used for any specific type of action. But in medieval days this was not so. Each different kind of action had its own writ, often with its own special procedure.[4] Often causes of action which seemed very similar in principle had separate writs. Thus if a tenant of land died and before his heir could enter the land a stranger took it, the heir could bring an action against the stranger for possession of the land. If the heir were a son of the tenant the action had to be started by a writ of *mort d'ancestor*; if he was a grandson a writ of *aiel* had to be used, while if he was the great-grandson a writ of *besaiel* was required. No action could succeed unless the correct writ was chosen.

The selection of the correct writ was thus of great importance. Even after the Common Law Procedure Act 1852 replaced the old writs by a single form of writ for all actions, it was still necessary, until the Judicature Acts 1873–1875 came into force, to observe the form of action based on the old writs which was appropriate to the case. Sometimes there were two or more writs appropriate to the claimant's proceedings. Where this was so, one writ usually had procedural advantages over the other or others. A writ which had already been settled was known as a writ *de cursu*, a writ "of course", obtainable as a matter of course simply on paying the prescribed fee. But sometimes there was no known writ to fit the case, and the claimant would have to ask for the invention of a new writ.

At first new writs were invented with comparative freedom. But it did not follow that the courts would accept each new writ as being valid. Even if a suitor had surmounted the first obstacle by obtaining a writ from the clerks in the Chancellor's office, he might still fall at the second fence by failing to obtain the court's recognition of its validity. Nevertheless the Register of Writs rapidly increased in size during the latter half of the twelfth century and the first half of the thirteenth: many new writs became writs *de cursu*, duly recognised by the courts.

This power to invent new writs was assailed by the barons. Recognising that the power to invent new remedies was a power to create new rights and duties, they procured the making of the Provisions of Oxford 1258, in which the Chancellor swore that he would seal no writ, except a writ *de cursu*, without the command of the King and his Council. Had this undertaking remained fully effective, it would have stifled the growth of the common law. But the Statute of Westminster II 1285 provided in the famous Chapter 24, *In Consimili Casu*, that the clerks in Chancery should have a limited power to invent new writs.[5] If there already

---

[2] As a result of the Common Law Procedure Act 1852.

[3] As a result of the Civil Procedure Rules 1998.

[4] Maitland, Forms of Action, 5.

[5] It is controversial how far the statute was responsible for this development: see S.F.C. Milsom, *Historical Foundations of the Common Law* (2nd ed.), pp. 284, 344, collecting the literature.

existed one writ and in a like case (*in consimili casu*), falling under like law and requiring like remedy, there was none, the clerks in the Chancellor's office were authorised to agree in making a writ, or else they were to refer the matter to the next Parliament. Consequently a suitor whose grievance was not covered by a writ *de cursu*, or one in *consimili casu*, was still left without a remedy unless he could persuade Parliament to intervene.

3. Petitions to the King referred to the Chancellor

The result of this was that there were a number of cases where claimants could obtain no remedy from the courts. In addition to the problems associated with writs, there was the possibility that a rich and powerful adversary would bribe or intimidate the members of the jury, which by this time had replaced earlier more archaic methods of trial as the means of deciding disputed issues of fact. The only way to obtain relief was then to petition the King's Council; for the King, as the Fountain of Justice, was regarded as having a residue of judicial power left in his hands after the Courts of Common Law had emerged from his Council. Such petitions were initially heard by the King's Council itself, of which the Chancellor was an important member. As keeper of the King's Conscience (at this stage he was usually a bishop), he was particularly well fitted to deal with such petitions, and during the reigns of Edward II and III (1307–1377) many petitions were referred to him for decision. Thereafter petitions were often addressed to the Chancellor alone rather than to the King's Council. But although the Chancery became recognised as a court during the fourteenth and fifteenth centuries, the Chancellor continued to take decisions on those petitions either in the name of the King's Council or else with the advice of the judges and the serjeants-at-law. Not until 1474, it seems, did the Chancellor make a decree on his own authority; but after that date such decrees became frequent.[6]

4. The Court of Chancery

In this way there gradually came into existence what became known as the Court of Chancery, in which the Chancellor, acting independently of the King's Council, sat as a judge administering a system of justice which came to be called equity. By the middle of the sixteenth century the typical Chancellor was a lawyer rather than a bishop and no non-lawyer was appointed to the office of Chancellor after the end of the seventeenth century. Initially the rules of equity had varied according to the views of each Chancellor, but under Lord Ellesmere (1596–1617) they began to develop into a code of principles, and the work of Lord Nottingham (1673–1682) in systematising the rules earned him the title of the Father of equity. By the time Lord Eldon retired in 1827 the rules of equity had become as fixed as those of the common law.

In the course of time various subsidiary officials were appointed to assist the Chancellor (including the Master of the Rolls and, later, Vice-Chancellors), a system of appeals grew up, and finally in 1875 the Chancery system was merged with the common law courts to form the present Supreme Court of Judicature. In short, what was once a method of petitioning the King for justice in exceptional cases gradually became a way of starting an action before a regular court of justice. But there were important differences between Chancery and the common law courts. The latter decided cases according to strict common law rules, and technicalities often played an important part. Chancery, on the other hand, mitigated the rigour of the common law, deciding cases in the light of what had seemed just and equitable

---

[6] 1 H.E.L. 400–404.

to generations of Chancellors, and technical pleas were usually unsuccessful. Further, the common law courts were mainly concerned with enforcing the strict rights of the claimant regardless of his conduct, whereas Chancery was a court of conscience. In Chancery, the court might cleanse the conscience of the parties, compelling a defendant to disgorge any ill-gotten gains by acting *in personam* (against his person), such as by imprisoning him; and a remedy might be withheld from a claimant who was guilty of unconscionable conduct. There were also important differences in the remedies available. In the courts of common law a claimant might recover his land or be awarded damages, but he could not obtain orders for the specific performance of contracts, or injunctions (orders compelling the defendant to do or not do something on pain of imprisonment) or various other remedies that were available only in Chancery. The Court of Chancery might even grant an injunction to restrain a claimant who had succeeded in a court of common law from inequitably enforcing his judgment.[7] There was thus a marked difference between legal rights, the name for rights enforced by the courts of law, and equitable rights, enforced only by equity. This will be examined later.[8]

5. Fusion of the courts of law and equity

By the Supreme Court of Judicature Act 1873,[9] with effect from 1875 the superior courts of law and equity were fused into one Supreme Court of Judicature, divided into a High Court and Court of Appeal: the final court of appeal, the House of Lords, remained and still remains outside the Supreme Court of Judicature. For convenience, the High Court was divided into five Divisions, each of which had certain matters assigned to it. In 1880 the Common Pleas Division and Exchequer Division were merged into the Queen's Bench Division, and in 1972 the Probate, Divorce and Admiralty Division was re-named the Family Division, with some adjustments of jurisdiction. There are now three Divisions:

> the Chancery Division;
>
> the Queen's Bench Division; and
>
> the Family Division.

The Queen's Bench Division primarily hears common law cases, the Chancery Division primarily hears equity cases, and the Family Division primarily deals with matrimonial matters and minors, although overlaps between the Queen's Bench Division and the Chancery Division have become increasingly common. But it is important to notice that the three are only divisions of one court, the High Court, and not separate courts; each division of the High Court has jurisdiction to enforce both legal and equitable rights and give both legal and discretionary equitable remedies. This means that it is no longer necessary to go to two separate courts to enforce legal and equitable rights or to obtain legal and equitable remedies. If a point of equity arises in an action in the Queen's Bench Division, for example, the court can deal with it; and it will not be fatal to an action if it is started in the wrong division, for the case will be transferred to the proper division.

---

[7] Earl of Oxford's Case (1615) 1 Rep.Ch. 1.

[8] Below, pp. 58 *et seq.*

[9] Which, by the Supreme Court of Judicature (Commencement) Act 1874, s.2, came into force on November 1, 1875. See now Supreme Court Act 1981.

Law and equity nevertheless remain distinct: the systems have not been fused, although they are now both administered by the same court.[10] Apart from registered land,[11] a legal right is still enforceable against a purchaser without notice, while an equitable right is not. Equitable rights in property of all types are still enforceable only by equitable remedies, though there is now power to award damages in place of or in addition to an order for specific performance or an injunction.[12] Indeed, the distinction between the two systems is emphasised by the provision that where there is any conflict between the rules of law and those of equity, the rules of equity shall prevail. Conflicts rarely occur: but there have been cases where this provision has been operative, and the most important will be considered later.[13] The Court of Chancery is a ghost, but like many other English legal ghosts, its influence can be seen on every side.

Sect. 2. Equity follows the law

In equity, there could exist a whole range of equitable estates or interests corresponding to the legal estates and interests in land. A fee simple, a fee tail, a life estate, a mortgage, an easement (such as a right of light) and nearly every other interest might be either legal or equitable. Thus if A granted a lease to B to hold on trust for C, B had a legal lease and C an equitable lease. If the fee simple owner of Greenacre granted Y a lease for 99 years, Y's lease would be legal if it was granted by deed, equitable if merely in writing. If a person held an equitable interest it would usually be found either that his interest arose under a trust or else that it was created without employing the formalities necessary at law.

Certain interests could exist only in equity: if Greenacre was bound by a restrictive covenant, this could never cast a legal burden on anyone who subsequently acquired the land, although it might well bind him in equity. But apart from these cases, there was a strict parallel in law and in equity. In most cases the maxim "equity follows the law" applied: "the Chancery moulded equitable estates and interests after the fashion of the common law estates and interests."[14] The courts tended to treat an interest in the land in the same way whether it was legal or equitable.[15] Thus equitable fees tail had to be barred in the same way as legal fees tail[16]; equitable interests passed on intestacy to the same persons as legal estates; an equitable tenant for life was in the same position as regards equitable waste as a legal tenant for life, and so on. But in certain matters, equity considered that there was good reason for refusing to follow the law, often to avoid hardship. Thus equity allowed someone who mortgaged his land to secure the repayment of a loan made to him to recover the property which he had mortgaged if he paid all that was due, even though he no longer had any right under the common law so to do because the due date for repayment had already passed.

With regard to words of limitation, equity followed the law in part only. If the grantor used informal words showing a clear intention to create a fee simple, such as a limitation on trust for A "absolutely",[17] these were as effective to create a fee simple in equity as the formal

---

[10] *Salt v. Cooper* (1880) 16 Ch.D. 544 at 549.
[11] Where enforceability does not depend on whether rights are legal or equitable; see above, p. 5.
[12] Supreme Court Act 1981, s.50, replacing Chancery Amendment Act 1858 (Lord Cairns' Act), s.2.
[13] Below, pp. 343 *et seq.*
[14] Maitland, equity, 108.
[15] See *Re Somerville and Turner's Contract* [1903] 2 Ch. 583 at 588.
[16] *Kirkham v. Smith* (1749) Amb. 518.
[17] *Re Arden* [1935] Ch. 326.

words required by the common law. But if strict conveyancing language was employed, the limitation was construed in the same way as a legal limitation, and in the absence of proper words of limitation as at common law only a life estate passed. This was so even if a general intention to pass some other interest could be gathered from the instrument,[18] although in this case if the court was asked to rectify the instrument and not merely construe it, words of limitation necessary to carry out the grantor's intention would be inserted.[19]

It will thus be seen that in some important points equity refused to follow the law. Nevertheless it has been said with some justice that "the cases, where the analogy fails, are not numerous; and there is scarcely a rule of law or equity, of a more ancient origin, or which admits of fewer exceptions, than the rule, that equity followeth the law."[20]

Sect. 3. The nature of equitable rights

1. Distinction between legal and equitable rights

At first sight it might seem that as long as a person had a right which would be enforced by some court, it mattered little which court it was. But there is a great difference between legal and equitable rights. This is sometimes expressed by saying that "legal rights are rights *in rem*, equitable rights are rights *in personam*." A legal interest in unregistered land is a right in the land itself, so that whoever acquires the land is bound by that right, whether or not he knew of it. Equity, on the other hand, would enforce equitable rights only against certain persons. For example, if land was conveyed to T in fee simple on trust for A in fee simple, there was at first no court which would compel T to carry out his trust. The Chancellor, however, began to intervene on behalf of A if T was guilty of a breach of trust, and so A's interest, being enforceable in equity but not at law, was merely equitable. It was a right *in personam* enforceable against T alone, so that if he died or conveyed the land to another, the trust would not be enforced against the new tenant.

Then successive extensions were made. In 1465 it was laid down that a trust would be enforced against anyone who took a conveyance of the land with notice of the trust.[21] In 1483 the Chancellor said that he would enforce a trust against the trustee's heir,[22] and in 1522 it was said that a trust would be enforced against anyone to whom the land had been given.[23] After it had been decided that other persons, such as the executors and creditors of the trustees, would be bound by the trust, it finally became established as one of the most important rules of equity that trusts and other equitable rights would be enforced against everyone except a bona fide purchaser of a legal estate for value without notice of these rights, or somebody claiming through such a person. Equitable rights thus gradually came to look less and less like mere rights *in personam* and more and more like rights *in rem*. Although it is possible still to regard them as rights *in personam*, it is perhaps best to treat them as hybrids, being neither entirely one nor entirely the other. They have never reached the status of rights *in rem*, yet the class of persons against whom they will be enforced is too large for them to be regarded as mere rights *in personam*.

---

[18] *Re Bostock's Settlement* [1921] 2 Ch. 469.
[19] *Banks v. Ripley* [1940] Ch. 719.
[20] Co. Litt. 290b, n. 1, xvi.
[21] Y.B. 5 Edw. 4, Mich., pl. 16.
[22] Y.B. 22 Edw. 4, Pasch., pl. 18.
[23] Y.B. 14 Hen. 8, Mich., pl. 5, fo. 7.

The difference between legal and equitable rights as regards a purchaser without notice of unregistered land may be illustrated as follows. In 1920 X bought the fee simple in Greenacre. In 1921 he granted a legal easement, a right of way, across one corner to L, and a similar equitable easement of way across the other corner to E.[24] As long as X still owned Greenacre, no substantial difference appeared between the rights of L and E: both were enforceable against X. But as soon as the land was conveyed to a third party, Y, the distinction between the rights of L and E became apparent. Even if Y purchased the land without notice of L's easement, it bound him, for it was a right *in rem*.[25] But if Y could prove that he was a bona fide purchaser for value of a legal estate without notice of E's easement, he took free from it.

This doctrine of purchaser without notice, which has historically been so fundamental to property law (the "polar star of equity"[26]) and is still significant except in relation to registered land, must now be considered more fully.

2. The purchaser without notice

The plea of bona fide purchase of a legal estate for value without notice is "an absolute, unqualified, unanswerable defence".[27] The onus of proof lies on the person setting it up: it is a single plea, and cannot be regarded as a plea of a purchase for value, to be met by a reply of notice.[28] The principal points are as follows.

(a) Bona fide

The purchaser must act in good faith. Although this is a separate requirement from the absence of notice,[29] there is no clear example of it doing more than emphasising the requisite innocence of notice.

(b) Purchaser for value

The words "for value" are included to show that value must have been given, because "purchaser" in its technical sense does not necessarily imply this. A "purchaser" is a person who acquires property by act of parties, as under a gift *inter vivos* or by will, and not by mere operation of law, as by descent on intestacy. "Value" includes money, money's worth (for example other land, or stocks and shares) and marriage (acquiring the land in consideration of entering into a particular marriage).[30] The value need not be full value,[31] but it must all have been actually paid or given before the purchaser receives notice of the equity.[32] "Money or money's worth" usually consists of some present consideration in the sense used in the law of contract, but it also includes the satisfaction of an existing debt.[33] "Marriage", however, extends only to a future marriage: an ante-nuptial agreement (*i.e.* a promise made in consideration of future marriage) is deemed to have been made for value, but a promise

---

[24] Dates before 1926 have been used because an equitable easement of way created after 1925 over unregistered land requires registration as a land charge: see above, p. 11; below, pp. 93, 97.

[25] See, *e.g. Wyld v. Silver* [1963] Ch. 243 (purchaser bound by undiscovered legal rights of others to hold an annual fair or wake on the land even though none had been held for over 80 years).

[26] *Stanhope v. Earl Verney* (1761) 2 Eden 81 at 85, *per* Lord Henley L.C.

[27] *Pilcher v. Rawlins* (1872) 7 Ch.App. 259 at 269.

[28] *Wilkes v. Spooner* [1911] 2 K.B. 473 at 486.

[29] *Midland Bank Trust Co. Ltd v. Green* [1981] A.C. 513 at 528.

[30] *Wormald v. Maitland* (1866) 35 L.J.Ch. 69 at 73.

[31] *Bassett v. Nosworthy* (1673) Rep.t. Finch 102; *Midland Bank Trust Co. Ltd v. Green* [1981] A.C. 513.

[32] *Tourville v. Naish* (1734) 3 P.Wms. 307.

[33] See *Thorndike v. Hunt* (1859) 3 De G. & J. 563.

made in respect of a past marriage (a post-nuptial agreement) is not. When an ante-nuptial marriage settlement is made, valuable consideration is deemed to have been given both by the spouse and by the unborn issue of the marriage.[34] "Good consideration" (the natural love and affection which a person has for his near relatives, usually his children) formerly also amounted to value in certain circumstances but now no longer suffices, although it is sometimes still significant for other purposes. "Purchaser" is not confined to a person who acquires a fee simple; it includes, for example, mortgagees and lessees, who are purchasers *pro tanto* (to the extent of their interests).[35]

(c) Of a legal estate

The purchaser normally must show that he has acquired some legal estate in the land and not merely an equitable interest.[36] If the purchaser acquires a mere equitable interest, that interest is necessarily later in time than any pre-existing equitable interests, and as between competing equitable interests the first in time normally prevails; where part of the equitable interest is already vested in the owner of the pre-existing equitable interest, the subsequent purchaser can take only what remains.[37]

There are three qualifications to this rule.

(i) Better right to legal estate: A purchaser without notice who acquires only an equitable interest will nevertheless take free from pre-existing equitable interests if his purchase gives him the better right to a legal estate. Thus if a legal estate is conveyed not to the purchaser but to a trustee on trust for him and the trustee is also without notice, the purchaser takes free from pre-existing equitable interests.[38]

(ii) Subsequent acquisition of legal estate: A purchaser without notice who at the time of his purchase fails to obtain either a legal estate or the better right to one will nevertheless prevail over a pre-existing equitable interest if he subsequently acquires a legal estate, even if by then he has notice of that equitable interest. As between himself and the owner of the prior equitable interest, there is equal equity, and the legal estate will prevail.[39] But if the purchaser knowingly acquires the legal estate in breach of trust, he will not take free from the interests of the beneficiaries under that trust.[40]

(iii) Mere equities: Although a purchaser of an equitable interest without notice of prior equitable interests does not take free from them, he takes free from any "mere equities" of which he has no notice.[41] Mere equities fall short of being actual interests in the land, and in the main are rights to equitable relief in respect of property. They include the right to have a transaction set aside for fraud,[42] or to have an instrument rectified for mistake.[43] Mere equities are not purely personal rights. They are ancillary to the land, and the benefit of them

---

[34] *Macdonald v. Scott* [1893] A.C. 642 at 650.
[35] See *Goodright d. Humphreys v. Moses* (1774) 2 Wm.Bl. 1019.
[36] See *Pilcher v. Rawlins* (1872) 7 Ch.App 259 at 268, 269.
[37] *Phillips v. Phillips* (1862) 4 De G.F. & J. 208 at 216; *Cave v. Cave* (1880) 15 Ch.D. 639; below, p. 535.
[38] See *Assaf v. Fuwa* [1955] A.C. 215.
[39] *Bailey v. Barnes* [1894] 1 Ch. 25; and see below, p. 535.
[40] *Harpham v. Shacklock* (1881) 19 Ch.D. 207; *McCarthy & Stone Ltd v. Julian S. Hodge & Co. Ltd* [1971] 1 W.L.R. 1547.
[41] *Phillips v. Phillips* (1862) 4 De G.F. & J. 208; *Cave v. Cave* (1880) 15 Ch.D. 639 at 647; *Allied Irish Banks Ltd v. Glynn* [1973] I.R. 188.
[42] *Ernest v. Vivian* (1863) 33 L.J.Ch. 513.
[43] *Smith v. Jones* [1954] 2 All E.R. 823; *Re Colebrook's Conveyance* [1972] 1 W.L.R. 1397.

will pass with the land to a purchaser.[44] The burden of them will also pass with the land, but they will not bind a purchaser of an equitable interest without notice of them as he is acquiring the entire equitable interest, and the mere equities are only burdens on that interest.[45] For brevity, equitable interests in unregistered land are often included in the term "equities", but they are not "mere" equities.

(d) Without notice

There are three kinds of notice.

(i) Actual notice: A person has actual notice of all facts of which he has[46] actual knowledge, however that knowledge was acquired; but he is not regarded as having actual notice of facts which have come to his ears only in the form of vague rumours.[47] As seen above, statute has made a number of rights registrable as land charges, and registration of them constitutes actual notice.[48]

(ii) Constructive notice: A person has constructive notice of all facts of which he would have acquired actual notice had he made those inquiries and inspections which he ought reasonably to have made, the standard of prudence being that of men of business under similar circumstances.[49] A purchaser has constructive notice of a fact if he:

i) had actual notice that there was some incumbrance and a proper inquiry would have revealed what it was; or

ii) has, whether deliberately or carelessly, abstained from making those inquiries that a prudent purchaser would have made.[50]

A purchaser's duties of prudence fall under two main heads, namely inspecting the land and investigating the title.

Inspection of land.   It has long been accepted that a purchaser should inspect the land with the object of discovering whether it is affected by any adverse interest (such as a right of way that is suggested by a footpath over the land) and whether any of the land is occupied by any other person.[51] A purchaser has constructive notice of all the equitable rights[52] of a tenant in occupation of any of the land, though not of the rights of that tenant's landlord.[53]

Where the vendor is not in sole occupation of the land himself but there are others who occupy it as well, there are sometimes questions as to whether a purchaser is to be treated as having constructive notice of the rights of those other occupants. At one time the view was that a purchaser was not required to make inquiries of any occupants whose presence was

---

[44] L.P.A. 1925, s.63 (below, p. 130); *Boots the Chemist Ltd v. Street* [1983] E.G.D. 251.
[45] See *National Provincial Bank Ltd v. Ainsworth* [1965] A.C. 1175 at 1238, 1253; *Westminster Bank Ltd v. Lee* [1956] Ch. 7; see also *Latec Investments Ltd v. Hotel Terrigal Pty. Ltd* (1965) 113 C.L.R. 265.
[46] For facts forgotten, see *Re Montagu's Settlement* [1987] Ch. 264 at 284.
[47] *Lloyd v. Banks* (1868) 3 Ch.App. 488; *Barnhart v. Greenshields* (1853) 9 Moo.P.C. 18 at 36.
[48] Above, p. 13; more fully, below, p. 93.
[49] L.P.A. 1925, s.199; *Bailey v. Barnes* [1894] 1 Ch. 25 at 35.
[50] *Jones v. Smith* (1841) 1 Hare 43 at 55; *Oliver v. Hinton* [1899] 2 Ch. 264.
[51] *Taylor v. Stibbert* (1794) 2 Ves.Jun. 437 at 440; *Barnhart v. Greenshields* (1853) 9 Moo.P.C. 18 at 32, 33.
[52] Including at least some mere equities: see *Green v. Rheinberg* (1911) 104 L.T. 149 and *Blacklocks v. J.B. Developments (Godalming) Ltd* [1982] Ch. 183 at 196, and contrast *Smith v. Jones* [1954] 1 W.L.R. 1089.
[53] *Hunt v. Luck* [1902] 1 Ch. 428.

consistent with the vendor being in occupation: the presence of the vendor's spouse would normally be explicable in terms of the vendor being in occupation, and as being a mere shadow of that occupation.[54] This view facilitated conveyancing by reducing the burden of inquiries that a purchaser had to make, but it also failed to give proper protection to any rights that those occupants might have.[55] In particular, in recent years it has become increasingly common for a wife to own some equitable interest in the matrimonial home (for example through having contributed to the purchase price), even though the house has been put in the husband's sole name; and the husband may sell or mortgage the house without disclosing his wife's interest.[56] There has thus been some criticism of the "easy-going practice of dispensing with enquiries as to occupation beyond that of the vendor".[57]

Today, the approach is different. A purchaser who omits to inquire of any occupier of the land or any part of it will probably be held to have constructive notice of all the rights of that occupier, at all events so far as his occupation is in conflict with the vendor's title.[58] This approach has many difficulties for purchasers, especially mortgagees. Some houseowners have large families of varying ages, and some houses have "floating populations", making full inquiries burdensome. Again, a mortgagee may be held to have constructive notice of the rights of an estranged wife who only intermittently occupies the matrimonial home and is absent when the mortgagee inspects the house under an appointment arranged by the husband, the mortgagor.[59] The wide publicity given to cases in which the equitable interests of spouses have been held to bind mortgagees[60] has ensured that no mortgagee is likely to lend money on the security of residential property without at the very least the consent of the spouse or partner of the mortgagor. Indeed, mortgagors who have neither spouses nor partners encounter very considerable difficulties in convincing mortgagees of that fact. However, this has not resolved the position of mortgagees in respect of equitable interests held by other members of a family and by "floating populations". In at least the latter respects, the limits of the new approach have yet to be worked out.

Sometimes the position is affected by the doctrine of estoppel. Where an occupier has represented to the purchaser (whether by words, conduct or silence) that the property will pass free from any claim by the occupier, the occupier will be precluded from claiming any interest adverse to a purchaser who has relied on the representation.[61] Similarly, the owner of an equitable interest who permits the legal owner to mortgage the land without disclosing that interest will be precluded from claiming any priority for his interest over the mortgage.[62]

Investigation of title.   A purchaser has constructive notice of all rights which he would have discovered had he investigated the title to the land for the period prescribed by law in

---

[54] *Caunce v. Caunce* [1969] 1 W.L.R. 286; *Bird v. Syme-Thompson* [1979] 1 W.L.R. 440 at p. 444.

[55] See *Northern Bank Ltd v. Henry* [1981] I.R. 1.

[56] See, *e.g. Hodgson v. Marks* [1971] Ch. 892.

[57] See *Williams & Glyn's Bank Ltd v. Boland* [1981] A.C. 487 at 508, *per* Lord Wilberforce; and see *Hodgson v. Marks* [1971] Ch. 892.

[58] *Midland Bank Ltd v. Farmpride Hatcheries Ltd* [1981] E.G.D. 985 (directors residing in their company's property).

[59] *Kingsnorth Finance Co. Ltd v. Tizard* [1986] 1 W.L.R. 783, a case in which there was notice of the wife's rights from other sources. See the criticism at [1986] Conv. 283 (M.P. Thompson).

[60] Particularly *Williams & Glyn's Bank Ltd v. Boland* [1981] A.C. 487 (registered land).

[61] *Abigail v. Lapin* [1934] A.C. 491; *Spiro v. Lintern* [1973] 1 W.L.R. 1002; *Midland Bank Ltd v. Farmpride Hatcheries Ltd* [1981] E.G.D. 985. See also *Wroth v. Tyler* [1974] Ch. 30 at 47.

[62] *Bristol and West B.S. v. Henning* [1985] 1 W.L.R. 778; *Paddington B.S. v. Mendelsohn* (1985) 50 P. & C.R. 244 (registered land); *Abbey National B.S. v. Cann* [1991] 1 A.C. 56 at 94. For criticism, see (1986) 49 M.L.R. 245; [1986] Conv. 57 (M. P. Thompson); (1986) 16 Fam.Law 315 (J. Martin).

the case of an open contract, *i.e.* one which *inter alia* prescribes no special length of title. This period was originally at least 60 years, but it has been successively reduced by statute: in 1874 to at least 40 years, in 1925 to at least 30 years, and in 1969 to at least 15 years.[63] The period is "at least" 15 years, so that the purchaser must call for a good root of title which is at least 15 years old, and see all documents subsequent thereto which trace dealings with the property. A good root of title is a document which deals with the whole legal and equitable interest in the land, describes the property adequately, and contains nothing to throw any doubt on the title. Thus if the title consists of a series of conveyances respectively 3, 14, 41 and 45 years old, as well as older deeds, a purchaser under an open contract (a contract which contains no express provision as to the title which the vendor is obliged to provide) can require the production of the conveyance 41 years old and all subsequent conveyances. If in fact he fails to investigate the title at all, or else investigates it for only part of this period (for example because he has agreed to accept a shorter title), he is fixed with constructive notice of everything that he would have discovered had he investigated the title for the full statutory period.[64]

(iii) Imputed notice: If a purchaser employs an agent, such as a solicitor, any actual or constructive notice which the agent receives may be imputed to the purchaser.[65] Before the Conveyancing Act 1882, notice received by an agent in a previous transaction was occasionally imputed to a purchaser; but this discouraged the employment of local solicitors with knowledge of local affairs[66] and was modified by the Act. Only actual or constructive notice which the agent acquires as such in the particular transaction in question is now imputed to a purchaser.[67] Where the same solicitor acts for both parties, any notice he acquires may be imputed to both parties, except where he enters into a conspiracy with one to conceal something from the other.[68]

(e) Successors in title

The protection given to a purchaser without notice extends also to his successors in title, even if they take with notice[69]; for otherwise the owner of the equitable interest could, by widely advertising his right, make it difficult for the purchaser without notice to dispose of the land for as much as he had paid for it. To this rule there is one exception, which prevents it being abused. If a person bound by the interest sells to a purchaser without notice and later acquires the property again, he cannot shelter behind the immunity of that purchaser.[70] But this exception can be evaded by the simple expedient of the property being reacquired by the person's wife or son,[71] provided, of course, that the latter actually provides the purchase money and is therefore not holding the property on trust for the person who was bound.

---

[63] Vendor and Purchaser Act 1874, s.1; L.P.A. 1925, s.44; L.P.A. 1969, s.23.
[64] See *Re Cox and Neve's Contract* [1891] 2 Ch. 109 at 117, 118.
[65] *Re The Alms Corn Charity* [1901] 2 Ch. 750.
[66] See *Re Cousins* (1886) 31 Ch.D. 671.
[67] L.P.A. 1925, s.199, replacing C.A. 1882, s.3. See *Kingsnorth Finance Co. Ltd v. Tizard* [1986] 1 W.L.R. 783.
[68] *Sharpe v. Foy* (1868) 4 Ch.App. 35; *Meyer v. Chartres* (1918) 34 T.L.R. 589.
[69] *Harrison v. Forth* (1695) Prec.Ch. 51; *Wilkes v. Spooner* [1911] 2 K.B. 473.
[70] *Gordon v. Holland* (1913) 82 L.J.P.C. 81.
[71] See *Wilkes v. Spooner* [1911] 2 K.B. 473.

PART 2—SPECIES OF EQUITABLE RIGHTS

Sect. 1. Trusts

1. Origin

Everyone today is familiar with the nature of trusts, whereby the ownership of property is vested in one or more persons (the trustees) who hold it for the benefit of others (the beneficiaries). The ancestor of the trust is the use, which had substantially the same nature. The word "use" was not derived from the Latin "*usus*" but from the Latin "*opus*" in the phrase "*ad opus*" (on his behalf) via the Old French "*al oes*" or "*al ues*" and hence "to the use of": thus land was conveyed "to A and his heirs to the use of B and his heirs".[72]

Although there are records of uses having been created even before the Norman Conquest, the only uses found for some time after the Conquest appear to have been merely temporary uses, so that a landowner could secure the protection of his land and his family while he went on a crusade. In about 1225 the Franciscan friars came to England. The rules of their Order prevented them from owning property, and so land was conveyed, for example, to some town to the use of the friars.[73] After this, uses of a permanent nature became more common, and by the middle of the fourteenth century they were frequent.

2. Enforced by equity

After early hesitations, the common law courts refused to recognise uses. If land was conveyed by A "to B and C and their heirs to the use of D and his heirs", B and C were technically described as the feoffees to uses (there would usually be more than one to avoid the difficulties which would otherwise have arisen if a sole feoffee to uses had died) and D was technically described as the *cestui que use* (pronounced "setty ker use"). The common law courts therefore refused to compel B and C to hold the land for the benefit of D. B and C were the persons with the seisin,[74] and the common law would take notice only of their rights; D had no interest which the common law would recognise, for "uses were but imaginations".[75] Nevertheless, many uses were created in reliance on the honour and good faith of feoffees to uses, and sometimes they failed in their duty and committed breaches of trust. Towards the end of the fourteenth century the Chancellor's aid was sought, and although there is no record of a decree in favour of a *cestui que use* until 1446, relief was probably being given by the first quarter of the fifteenth century.[76]

3. Duties

The duties of the feoffees to uses towards their *cestui que use* were threefold: they were bound:

(i) to permit him to take the profits of the land ("pernancy of profits");

(ii) to dispose of the land in accordance with his instructions; and

---

[72] Maitland, equity, 24.
[73] 2 P. & M. 231–238.
[74] See above, p. 35.
[75] Chudleigh's Case (1595) 1 Co.Rep. 113b at 140a; and see Maitland, equity, 28.
[76] Ames, Lectures on Legal History, 237.

(iii) to take all necessary proceedings to protect or recover the land.[77]

Although at first the *cestui que use* was regarded as merely having a right to compel the feoffees to uses to carry out their duties, the rights of the *cestui que use* were so extensive that it was soon recognised that he had an estate in the land.[78] The legal estate was in the feoffees to uses, the equitable estate in the *cestui que use*: the former had the husk, the latter the kernel. With some qualifications, it could be said in Chancery that "the equity is the land."

4. Legal and equitable interests

Frequently the legal and equitable interests in property go together; a person who has had the legal fee simple in Blackacre conveyed to him normally receives the equitable fee simple as well. But although there is often no need to consider separately the legal and equitable estate in land, in some cases this is the only way to arrive at a proper understanding of the subject.[79] One of the fundamental principles of English law is the ability of the beneficial owner of a legal estate (*i.e.* someone who has the equitable interest as well as the legal estate for his own benefit) to separate the legal from the equitable interest.

5. The Statute of Uses 1535

By conveying lands to feoffees to uses it was possible to evade most of the feudal taxes to which feudal lords were in principle entitled, as these fell only upon the person or persons who were seised of land. All that was needed was the selection of suitable and sufficient feoffees so that the land was never vested in a single feoffee to uses whose death would give rise to the feudal taxes which had to be paid by anyone who inherited freehold land (these liabilities were particularly stringent if the person in question was an infant since the feudal lord then also acquired the right to manage the land for his own benefit during the infant's minority). The evasion seriously affected all feudal lords but principally the King, who alone was always lord and never tenant. After various manoeuvres, in 1535 "the Statute of Uses was forced upon an extremely unwilling parliament by an extremely strong-willed king".[80] The effect of this was to "execute" all uses to which it applied, taking the legal estate out of the feoffees to uses and converting the equitable interests of the *cestui que use* into corresponding legal estates. Thereafter, if land was conveyed by A "to B and C and their heirs to the use of D and his heirs", the effect was to vest the legal fee simple in D, so that when D died or, if an infant, attained his majority, the relevant feudal taxes would all be payable.

6. The use upon a use

Soon after the statute was passed it was held that, where property was conveyed on two successive uses ("a use upon a use"), the second use was void at common law.[81] The final result of the decisions to this effect was that, if land was conveyed by A "to B and C and their heirs to the use of D and his heirs to the use of E and his heirs", the first use was executed by the Statute of Uses but the second use was void. This gave the whole legal and equitable

---

[77] 4 H.E.L. 431.
[78] *Brent's Case* (1583) 2 Leon. 14 at 18.
[79] Consider, *e.g.* joint tenancies and tenancies in common; below, pp. 303 *et seq.*
[80] Maitland, equity, 34; the King in question was Henry VIII.
[81] *Tyrrel's Case* (1557) 2 Dy. 155a.

interest to D and nothing to B, C or E. Initially, successive uses were not created deliberately; in the cases which established this rule, the second use (that in favour of E and his heirs in the example above) had been created by implication. However, after the restoration of the monarchy in 1660, most of the relevant feudal taxes were abolished,[82] and so the purpose for which the Statute of Uses had been passed became irrelevant. There was therefore no reason to prevent the situation which had existed prior to that statute from being recreated, and successive uses were intentionally employed for this purpose. Since the person entitled under the second use was then as unprotected at common law as all *cestui que use* had been before the Statute of Uses, by 1676 the Chancellor had come to enforce second uses as trusts. [83] Thereafter, the effect of the conveyance set out above was that D held the legal estate on trust for E. In time, the shorter formula "unto and to the use of B and C and their heirs in trust for D and his heirs" came to be employed as the usual means of creating trusts. The Statute of Uses nevertheless survived until its repeal by the Law of Property Act 1925[84] so this formulation continued to be necessary until 1926.

7. After 1925

A trust of land is now created by conveying land "to A and B in fee simple in trust" for the intended beneficiaries. The legal estate is thus in A and B, while those named as beneficiaries will have equitable interests.[85] Since 1925 life interests and entails have been able to exist only as equitable interests under a trust of the legal estate in fee simple.

Sect. 2. Other equitable rights

The Chancellor did not confine his intervention to the enforcement of uses or trusts, though that always remained the most important part of his jurisdiction. There were other important areas of real property and leases in which he intervened.

1. Mortgages

If A conveyed his land to B as security for a loan, equity would allow A at any time after repayment of the loan fell due, despite any contrary provisions in the mortgage, to recover his land by paying B what was due to him under the loan, namely the outstanding principal sum, interest thereon and costs. The development of this equitable right of redemption, exercisable after expiry of the legal date for redemption, is described later.[86]

2. Restrictive covenants

The basic rule of common law, now modified by the Contracts (Rights of Third Parties) Act 1999, was that a contract is normally binding upon and enforceable by the parties alone. But during the nineteenth century it was held that if a landowner covenants for the benefit of neighbouring landowners not to use his land in a certain way, the covenant could be enforced in equity against successors in title of the covenantor, thus imposing an equitable burden on

---

[82] Above, p. 27.
[83] *Grubb v. Gwillim* (1676) 73 S.S. 347; *Symson v. Turner* (1700) 1 Eq. Ca. Abr. 383. For a full treatment of the Statute of Uses and developments therefrom, see M. & W. (5th ed.), pp. 1164–1175.
[84] Sched. 7.
[85] For the categories of trusts today, see below, pp. 289 *et seq.*
[86] Below, p. 493.

his land.[87] This is confined to covenants that are negative in nature prohibiting certain acts, such as building on the land in question; it does not apply to positive covenants, requiring the landowner to carry out some action on the land in question, such as maintaining a garden.

3. Estate contracts

Where a person enters into a valid contract for the purchase of an estate in land, he is at once considered to have an equitable interest in that land, even before he has paid the price and has had the estate of the vendor conveyed to him.[88] This also applies to an option to purchase an interest in land, but not to a mere right of pre-emption.[89] If P has an option to purchase land, he has the right, on exercising the option, to compel the landowner to sell the land to him in accordance with the terms of the option, and neither the landowner nor his successors in title can deal with the land in such a way as to defeat the option. If instead P has a right of pre-emption (often called a right of first refusal), he has no more than the right to be offered the land if the landowner decides to sell it; and although the right will become an interest in the land as soon as the landowner makes Pan offer which cannot be withdrawn before the time by which it has to be accepted[90]; until then it is no more than a mere *spes* (hope).[91]

Sect. 3. Creation of equitable rights

Equitable rights in land arose under three heads:

> (i) Lack of formality—where the proper formalities for the creation or conveyance of a legal estate were not observed;
>
> (ii) Lack of capacity—where the grantor had power only to create or convey an equitable interest;
>
> (iii) Lack of intention—where the grantor provided that only an equitable interest should arise;

1. Lack of formality

(a) At common law

At law, in order to create or transfer a legal estate, certain formalities had to be observed.

(i) Freeholds: The original rule was that "Corporeal hereditaments lie in livery, incorporeal hereditaments lie in grant". A corporeal hereditament was an inheritable right in realty which was accompanied by physical possession of the land, for example a fee simple in possession; for such estates, a feoffment with livery of seisin was essential.[92] An incorporeal hereditament was an inheritable right in land not accompanied by physical possession, such as a fee

---

[87] Below, p. 453 *et seq.*

[88] *Lysaght v. Edwards* (1876) 2 Ch.D. 499; below, p. 154.

[89] *Pritchard v. Briggs* [1980] Ch. 338; below, p. 95.

[90] *Pritchard v. Briggs* [1980] Ch. 338; *Bircham & Co. Nominees (2) v. Worrall Holdings Ltd* (2001) 82 P. & C.R. 34.

[91] See *Pritchard v. Briggs* [1980] Ch. 338, criticised in this respect at (1980) 96 L.Q.R. 488 (H.W.R.Wade). The right of pre-emption is nevertheless registrable: below, p. 95.

[92] Above, p. 36.

simple in remainder or an easement; for such interests, a feoffment was inappropriate but a deed of grant was essential. By the beginning of the seventeenth century it had become possible to use a deed for both corporeal and incorporeal hereditaments, and feoffments with livery of seisin generally ceased to be employed. This practice was subsequently formalised, ultimately by the Real Property Act 1845,[93] which specifically provided that a deed was an alternative to a feoffment of corporeal hereditaments and that, if a feoffment was employed, it would be void unless evidenced by a deed. Feoffment by livery of seisin was finally abolished by the Law of Property Act 1925[94] and as a result no legal estate in freehold land can now be created otherwise than by deed.[95]

(ii) Leaseholds: Leases for a term of years were not hereditaments and at first could be created orally, but the Statute of Frauds 1677[96] made writing necessary in nearly all cases. The Real Property Act 1845[97] made a deed essential for most leases. This remains the position under the Law of Property Act 1925; a lease can be created otherwise than by deed only if it is for three years or less at a rent taking effect in possession immediately.[98]

Thus since the Real Property Act 1845 it has been substantially true to say that without a deed no legal estate can be created or transferred.[99]

(b) In equity

Equity, on the other hand, was not so strict. In two important respects, what was ineffective at law might be effective in equity.

(i) Contract: In accordance with the maxim "equity treats that as done which ought to be done", equity regarded a specifically enforceable contract to create or convey an interest in land as being as effective as if the transaction had been properly carried out. With certain exceptions, such as leases for three years or less at a rent taking effect in possession immediately, such a contract would not take effect at law because of the absence of a deed.[1] Equity, however, treated an attempt to convey or create a legal estate which failed at law through lack of a deed as being a contract to carry out the transaction, and thus, if it was specifically enforceable, as being effective in equity. Formerly, a transaction of this type would be specifically enforceable if it was supported either by sufficient evidence of it in writing (such as a letter referring to it) signed by the person against whom it was being enforced or by what was known as a sufficient act of part performance.[2] In this way, many informal transactions took effect in equity, including leases and mortgages by deposit of the relevant documents evidencing title (title deeds in the case of unregistered land; the land certificate in the case of registered land).[3] Now, however, under the Law of Property (Miscellaneous Provisions) Act 1989, contracts for the sale or disposition of land or any interest in land must actually be in writing, incorporating all the terms of the contract, and must be signed by all the parties.[4] Where these much more stringent requirements are

[93] s.2.
[94] s.51.
[95] L.P.A. 1925 s.52(1).
[96] s.1.
[97] s.3.
[98] L.P.A. 1925, s.54(2).
[99] *Crago v. Julian* [1992] 1 W.L.R. 372; see below, pp. 342, 353.
[1] L.P.A. 1925, ss.52(1), 54; for the leases, see below, p. 342.
[2] L.P.A. 1925, s.40; below, p. 148.
[3] Below, p. 499.
[4] s.2.; see below, p. 148.

satisfied, equity continues to regard the transaction as being as effective as if it had been properly carried out. But informal transactions which do not satisfy these requirements are no longer effective as such. This is the position of mortgages by deposit of the documents evidencing title, which no longer take effect as mortgages.[5] It is questionable whether Parliament would have adopted this oblique method of removing the theoretical foundation of an important range of long-established equitable interests if it had really intended to abolish them but it has clearly succeeded in doing so. In the Report which led to the 1989 Act, the Law Commission envisaged the adaptation of the doctrine of proprietary estoppel[6] so as to prevent informal transactions from losing their status in equity[7]; this has happened in appropriate circumstances where contracts have failed to comply with the requisite formalities[8] but not where other informal transactions have been entered into.[9]

(ii) Proprietary estoppel: Proprietary estoppel is an important equitable doctrine of considerable antiquity.[10] The essence of the doctrine is that if A has acted to his detriment in reliance on the belief or expectation that he owns or will acquire an interest in O's land, and O has either encouraged that belief or expectation or has acquiesced in A's action, it is unconscionable for O to deny a proper fulfilment of A's belief or expectation.[11] An equity arises in A's favour and it is then in the court's discretion as to how that equity should be satisfied.[12] Thus if O knows that A is spending money on improving O's land in the belief that the land is A's, O's silence may result in the land being held to be A's,[13] or A may be held to have some lesser right.[14] Equity is at its most flexible here.[15] In the example just given, A is potentially prejudiced not by any lack of formality but by his own mistaken belief. However, the doctrine is equally applicable where a party to an informal contract has incurred detriment on the basis of an agreement that he would thereby acquire an interest in the land of the other party.[16] But the doctrine not assist a person who has entered into some other form of informal transaction such as a mortgage by deposit of the documents evidencing his title.[17] Nor does the doctrine assist a person who has entered into a transaction which is formally valid but has subsequently failed to protect it in the appropriate way.[18]

2. Lack of capacity

If X owned only an equitable interest, such as a right under a trust, he had no power to create a legal interest out of it. So far as the common law was concerned, he had no interest in land at all, and thus could create nothing that the common law would recognise. But he could transfer his equitable interest or create a new equitable interest out of it, as by mortgaging it or declaring a sub-trust.

---

[5] *United Bank of Kuwait plc v. Sahib* [1997] Ch. 107.
[6] Below; and see below, p. 154.
[7] See (1987) Law Com. No. 164, para. 5.4.
[8] *Yaxley v. Gotts* [2000] Ch. 162.
[9] *United Bank of Kuwait plc v. Sahib* [1997] Ch. 107.
[10] See *Hunt v. Carew* (1649) Nels. 47; *Hobbs v. Norton* (1682) 1 Vern. 137.
[11] *Taylors Fashions Ltd. v. Liverpool Victoria Trustees Co. Ltd* [1982] Q.B. 133N.
[12] *Crabb v. Arun D.C.* [1976] Ch. 179.
[13] *Pascoe v. Turner* [1979] 1 W.L.R. 431.
[14] *Inwards v. Baker* [1965] 2 Q.B. 29.
[15] See *Crabb v. Arun D.C.* [1976] Ch. 179 at 189. On the doctrine generally, see below, pp. 477, 483 *et seq.*
[16] *Yaxley v. Gotts* [2000] Ch. 162.
[17] *United Bank of Kuwait plc v. Sahib* [1997] Ch. 107.
[18] *Lloyds Bank plc v. Carrick* [1996] 4 All E.R. 630.

3. Lack of intention

Even if a deed was employed, and the grantor had power to create or convey a legal interest, no legal estate would pass if the grantor expressly provided that only an equitable interest should be created or transferred.

Sect. 4. The borderline between personal and proprietary rights

The boundary between rights that are merely personal and rights in the land itself is not always distinct. A fundamental rule of the common law was that a contract binds only the parties to it, creating merely personal rights and liabilities; and subject to the Contract (Rights of Third Parties) Act 1999, which permits someone who is expressly named in the contract as benefitting from it to enforce it, this is still the case. But as has been seen,[19] when equity intervened to grant specific performance of a contract to sell land, the purchaser's rights came to be treated as equitable rights in the land itself: the purchaser's personal rights became proprietary.[20]

This well-settled impact of remedies upon rights has now been carried further. Under the law of tort, merely personal rights may sometimes become enforceable against third parties, and so produce something of the same effect as if they were rights in land. If G Ltd, the owner of a garage, covenants with P Ltd that for five years G Ltd will sell only P Ltd's petrol at the garage (this is known as a "solus" agreement), and that if G Ltd sells the garage a similar covenant will be extracted from his purchaser, the obligations of G Ltd to P Ltd are merely personal: unless the restrictions are for the benefit of some land owned by P Ltd in the vicinity, which will not usually be the case, they cannot be enforced against others under the equitable doctrine of restrictive covenants.[21] So if T Ltd then buys all the shares in G Ltd and makes G Ltd sell the garage to a subsidiary of T Ltd, the subsidiary, not being a party to the covenant, is not bound by it. Yet if T Ltd and its subsidiary have committed the tort of wrongful interference in the execution of the contract between G Ltd and P Ltd, the court may grant a mandatory injunction compelling the subsidiary to transfer the garage back to G Ltd, to be held subject to the covenant.[22] In this way the merely personal rights of P Ltd against G Ltd have in effect been enforced against third parties in respect of the garage. But mere uncertainties or suspicions about the contract are not enough[23]; actual knowledge must be shown.[24] Nor is there any tort if the interference is justifiable.[25] Thus if V contracts to sell land to X and then contracts to sell the same land to Y, X will be justified in requiring V to convey the land to him, despite the interference with Y's contract; for X has the prior right.[26] Again, a person who interferes with a contract appears to be justified in doing so if the contract is void against him for want of registration.[27]

---

[19] Above, p. 68.

[20] See *Swiss Bank Corporation v. Lloyds Bank Ltd* [1979] Ch. 548 at 565 (reversed on a different point: [1982] A.C. 584).

[21] Below, p. 453.

[22] *Esso Petroleum Co. Ltd v. Kingswood Motors (Addlestone) Ltd* [1974] Q.B. 142.

[23] *Smith v. Morrison* [1974] 1 W.L.R. 659.

[24] *Greig v. Insole [1978] 1 W.L.R. 302; Swiss Bank Corporation v. Lloyds Bank Ltd* [1979] Ch. 548 at 575 (reversed on other grounds [1982] A.C. 584).

[25] *Greig v. Insole* [1978] 1 W.L.R. 302 at 340–342; and see (1977) 41 Conv.(N.S.) 318 (R.J. Smith).

[26] See *Pritchard v. Briggs* [1980] Ch. 338 at 415.

[27] Consider *Miles v. Bull (No. 2)* [1969] 3 All E.R. 1585 at 1590; *Midland Bank Trust Co. Ltd v. Green* [1981] A.C. 513.

Such cases are not yet recognised as forming part of property law, but they illustrate the effect of remedies on rights, and the need to look outside the sometimes narrow bounds of property law, for example in protecting the rights of contractual licensees.[28] In general, a right can be admitted to the category of property rights only if it is definable, identifiable by third parties, capable in its nature of being transferred to and taken over by third parties, and has some degree of permanence or stability.[29] What is relevant is the nature of the right and not the remedy which exists for its enforcement.[30]

[28] See below, p. 480.
[29] *National Provincial Bank Ltd v. Ainsworth* [1965] A.C. 1175 at 1248.
[30] *ibid.*

Chapter 4

THE STRUCTURE OF MODERN LAND LAW

PART 1—THE STRUCTURE PUT INTO PLACE BY THE 1925 LEGISLATION

The structure of modern land law was put into place by the 1925 legislation, whose dominant policy was to facilitate the transfer of land by easing the burden on purchasers without defeating the interests of others unfairly. A fundamental principle underlying the legislation, but nowhere explicitly stated in it, was to distinguish between commercial interests and family interests. Examples of commercial interests are leases, rights of way and mortgages; such rights are almost invariably created for money or money's worth. Examples of family interests are the rights of beneficiaries under a trust or settlement (this includes the beneficial rights of co-owners of land); such rights are not usually created for money or money's worth. Broadly speaking, with some exceptions intentionally created in 1925 and a few further exceptions not envisaged by the 1925 legislation which have been created subsequently by both the courts and the legislature, it was intended that:

(1) commercial interests should bind the successors in title of the person who created them; and

(2) family interests should upon sale or other disposition giving rise to the payment of a capital sum be overreached, that is to say transferred from the land to that capital sum, and so should not bind the successors in title of the person who created them.

The different methods by which these objectives were achieved have already been considered in outline, but it is convenient to consider them together here. It has already been seen that the title to land may either be registered at the Land Registry or else be unregistered.[1] While the treatment of commercial interests inevitably had to differ, depending on whether the land in question was registered or unregistered, the intention of the draftsmen of the 1925 legislation, admittedly not wholly achieved, was that family interests should be treated in the same way whether the land in question was registered or unregistered. Three distinct classes of interests therefore have to be considered.

[1] Above, p. 2.

1. Commercial interests in unregistered land

A purchaser of a legal estate in unregistered land for value without notice of adverse claims generally takes subject to those which are legal but free from those which are equitable. The dominant policy of the 1925 legislation was put into effect in two ways.

(a) Reduction in number of legal estates

The reduction by the 1925 legislation of the number of legal estates and interests which can exist in land substantially improved the position of a purchaser of unregistered land for value.[2]

(b) Extension of registration of land charges

The width of constructive and imputed notice sometimes made it difficult for the innocent purchaser of a commercial interest for value to establish that he had no notice, and offered scope for argument. The extension of registration of land charges to three legal commercial interests in unregistered land and the vast majority of equitable commercial interests in unregistered land made the question not one of notice but one of the state of the register; and this was discoverable by a search. The extension of the system of registration of land charges often substituted certainty for contention. But some equitable commercial interests in unregistered land were intentionally not made registrable and the courts have subsequently held not to be registrable some interests which the draftsmen of the 1925 legislation probably expected to be registrable. Commercial interests in unregistered land which are not registrable continue to bind a purchaser without notice only if they are legal interests.[3]

2. Commercial interests in registered land

Save for the fact that only legal estates and interests in land are capable of being registrable interests (interests registered on the Land Register with their own separate title),[4] the enforceability of rights in registered land does not normally depend on whether they are legal or equitable. The dominant policy of the 1925 legislation was put into effect in the following ways.[5]

(a) Protection of commercial interests

Some commercial interests in registered land are registrable interests; an example is a legal lease for more than a specified period (21 years at present, seven years when the Land Registration Act 2002 comes into force). Such interests are protected by virtue of the fact that their existence is noted on the register of the freehold title. Most mortgages of registered land take effect as registered charges; at present they give rise to the issue of a charge certificate which is protected by being noted on the register; but charge certificates will be abolished when the Land Registration Act 2002 comes into force. Other commercial interests in registered land either automatically bind the successors in title of the registered proprietor (an

---

[2] Above, p. 59.
[3] Above, pp. 11, 59 *et seq.*
[4] At present, only estates in fee simple absolute, leases for more than 21 years, and rentcharges can be so registered. Leases for more than seven years, franchises and profits in gross will also be registrable when L.R.A. 2002 comes into force.
[5] See below, p. 111.

example is shorter legal leases[6]) by overriding registration or only bind the successors in title of the registered proprietor if they are protected by an entry on the register (this is the way in which mortgages of registered land will be protected when the Land Registration Act 2002 comes into force). The purchaser of a commercial interest who protects his interest in the appropriate way is completely protected. Further, registrable interests which have not been registered, and interests which should have been protected by registration but have not been will override registration and so automatically bind the successors in title of the registered proprietor if their holder is in actual occupation of the registered land (admittedly not particularly likely in the case of the holder of a commercial interest) or, at present, in receipt of its rents and profits (the receipt of rent and profits will not have this effect when the Land Registration Act 2002 comes into force).

(b) Protection of purchasers

A purchaser of registered land for value is only bound by interests which override registration and by interests which have been protected by an entry on the register. Interests which should have been so protected but have not been (and which do override registration for the reason set out above) do not bind any purchaser for value, even if he has notice of them. This simplifies the task of a purchaser by enabling him to obtain the title to the land that is shown in the Land Register rather than the title which appears to him to be disclosed by his examinations of often bulky title deeds.

3. Family interests

The dominant policy of the 1925 legislation was given effect to by making all family interests in both registered and unregistered land overreachable. This was done in the following ways.

(a) Extension of overreaching

When two or more persons are beneficially entitled to land (or for that matter to pure personalty) in succession (that is to say one after another) the property in question is said to be subject to a settlement; the simplest possible example of a settlement is where a testator leaves his property to his wife for life and subject to that to his children equally. The 1925 legislation made all the beneficial interests which arise under settlements of land overreachable. In other words, a purchaser for value of both registered and unregistered land will take free of all family interests arising under any settlement of that land provided that he pays the purchase money to at least two trustees or a trust corporation. He is protected in this way, while the beneficiaries of the settlement are protected by the fact that their rights are thus overreached and so transferred to the purchase money received by the trustees or the trust corporation.

(b) Simplification of title for co-ownership

The ownership of land by co-owners, and particularly by tenants in common (persons who hold undivided shares in land, of which there can be a large number of different sizes), often led to difficulties in making title to the land in question. These difficulties were met by a combination of prohibiting the ownership of a legal estate by tenants in common and

---

[6] At present for 21 years or less; for seven years or less when L.R.A. 2002 comes into force.

providing for the legal estate instead to be vested in trustees on trust for sale (since 1996 on a trust of land[7]). The trustees could then make a good title to the land, and the rights of the co-owners would be overreached and so transferred to the purchase money received from the purchaser. This enables the purchaser to take free of the interests of all the co-owners, who are in turn protected by the fact that their rights are overreached.[8]

PART 2—REGISTERED AND UNREGISTERED LAND TODAY

In 1925 the immense majority of the land in England and Wales was unregistered. Although registration of title had been possible since 1862,[9] registration was on a voluntary basis and few titles were registered until the Land Transfer Act 1897 made registration compulsory in the County and City of London. Consequently, apart from those titles which had been registered voluntarily, only land in the County and City of London which had been the subject since 1897 of a transaction triggering first registration was registered.

The draftsmen of the 1925 legislation did not propose universal registration of title. They instead proposed that the much modified system of registered conveyancing introduced by the Land Registration Act 1925 should exist side by side with the equally modified system of unregistered conveyancing for an experimental period of 10 years, during which the two systems of conveyancing could be prepared.[10] This was because the legal profession was divided between those who accepted that universal registration of title was inevitable and those who thought that the already much amended system of unregistered conveyancing required only a little further amendment to make it perfect.[11] The proposed legislation was therefore designed to win the support of both sides, which it did.

During the 10-year review period only two county boroughs[12] became, at their own request, new areas of compulsory registration. After that period had concluded, the County of Middlesex and one further county borough[13] were designated areas of compulsory registration. No further extensions took place until 1952, by which time it had become accepted that registered conveyancing was the system of the future. By 1964 compulsory registration had been extended to three further counties[14] and 11 further county boroughs; and, following a decision in that year to accelerate the process, by 1978 the areas of compulsory registration covered three-quarters of the population of England and Wales. Finally, as from December 1, 1990, the whole of England and Wales became subject to compulsory registration.

This does not mean that all land in England and Wales is now registered. Until 31 March, 1998, titles to land in areas of compulsory registration had to be registered only on the conveyance on sale of the fee simple absolute or the grant or assignment of a lease with more than 21 years to run. Since 1 April, 1998, titles have also had to be registered if either of these estates is the subject of a first legal mortgage or a gift. This means that all land in England

---

[7] T.L.A.T.A. s.1.
[8] See above, p. 7.
[9] Land Registry Act 1862.
[10] Memorandum prefixed to Law of Property Bill 1922: see 154 H.C.Deb (5th ser.) 102, 103 (1922).
[11] C. Sweet (1912) 28 L.Q.R. 24.
[12] Eastbourne and Hastings.
[13] Croydon.
[14] Surrey, Kent and Berkshire.

and Wales held directly by natural persons will become registered at the very latest on the death of those persons, effectively within a generation from 1998. Fee incentives have also been introduced to encourage voluntary first registration. However, land held on family settlements is likely to remain unregistered for very much longer (first registration is not triggered merely by a change of trustees) and land vested in companies or other corporations or bodies (which of course may never die) may remain unsold and unmortgaged for centuries. The Land Registry has so far expressly eschewed any suggestion that, at some point in the future, all land will be required to be registered by some specified date. However, this is apparently going to be reviewed in the next five years. Thus, although an ever-increasing proportion of the land in England and Wales is now registered, the system of unregistered conveyancing remains in existence, admittedly to an ever-decreasing extent; and unless the Land Registry changes its present position, it may well remain in existence indefinitely.

It is important to understand which parts of the 1925 legislation apply to which system of conveyancing.

(i) The Law of Property Act 1925, which contains the fundamental reforms to the pre-existing land law made by the 1925 legislation, applies to both registered and unregistered land.

(ii) So do three other statutes which form part of the 1925 legislation:

(a) the Settled Land Act 1925, which governs a form of settlement which has, since 1996, not been able to be created, although existing settlements continue;

(b) the Trustee Act 1925, now substantially amended and supplemented by the Trustee Act 2000, which deals with the administrative powers of trustees; and

(c) the Administration of Estates Act 1925, which deals with the administration of the property of deceased persons and contains the rules which determine who inherits the property of someone who dies without making a will.

(iii) The Land Registration Act 1925, which created the current system of registered conveyancing and will be replaced by the Land Registration Act 2002 when it comes into force, applies only to registered land.

(iv) The Land Charges Act 1972, which has replaced the Land Charges Act 1925, which created the current system of registration of land charges, applies only to unregistered land.

(v) The Local Land Charges Act 1975, which deals with charges imposed on land by local authorities, either restricting the uses to which the land can be put or imposing financial liabilities relating to matters such as roads and sewers, applies to both registered and unregistered land (the similarity between the title of this Act and the Land Charges Act 1972, which applies only to unregistered land, is a frequent cause of confusion).

The basic rules of land law contained in the Law of Property Act 1925, the decided cases which have interpreted it, and the pre-existing and subsequent case law governing those aspects of those basic rules with which the Law of Property Act 1925 did not deal, therefore apply to both registered and unregistered land. It was the intention of the draftsmen of the

1925 legislation that these basic rules should be unaffected by whether the land in question was registered and unregistered. This remains the case, although, as will be seen in the remaining sections of this chapter, this objective was not achieved in a number of respects, probably by accident rather than by design. However, the Land Registration Act 2002, which when it comes into force will replace the Land Registration Act 1925 in the same way as the Land Charges Act 1972 replaced the Land Charges Act 1925, will specifically change the basic rules of land law in respect of registered land only. This fundamental change to the structure imposed by the 1925 legislation is controversial but is being put into effect.

Part 3 of this chapter contains a discussion of certain aspects of the structure of modern land law which are common to both registered and unregistered land, principally the reduction in the number of legal estates and interests which formed such a fundamental part of the reforms to the basic rules of land law made by the 1925 legislation. Parts 4 and 5 deal with aspects of that structure which apply to only one of the two systems of conveyancing.

PART 3—ASPECTS COMMON TO BOTH SYSTEMS OF CONVEYANCING

Sect. 1. Reduction in the number of legal estates

Section 1 of the Law of Property Act 1925 reduced the number of legal estates that can exist in land to two, and the number of classes of legal interests to five. The distinction, broadly, is that a legal estate confers full rights to use and enjoy land as one's own, while a legal interest is a right over the land of another. The terms of the first three subsections of section 1 are as follows:

"1—(1) The only estates in land which are capable of subsisting or of being conveyed or created at law are—

    (a) An estate in fee simple absolute in possession;

    (b) A term of years absolute.

(2) The only interests or charges in or over land which are capable of subsisting or of being conveyed or created at law are—

    (a) An easement, right, or privilege in or over land for an interest equivalent to an estate in fee simple absolute in possession or a term of years absolute;

    (b) A rentcharge in possession issuing out of or charged on land being either perpetual or for a term of years absolute;

    (c) A charge by way of legal mortgage;

    (d) Land tax, tithe rentcharge,[15] and any other similar charge on land which is not created by an instrument;

    (e) Rights of entry exercisable over or in respect of a legal term of years absolute, or annexed, for any purpose, to a legal rentcharge.

---

[15] These four words have been repealed: below, p. 83.

(3) All other estates, interests, and charges in or over land take effect as equitable interests."

It should be noted that the section does not provide that the estates and interests mentioned in subsections (1) and (2) are necessarily legal, but merely that they alone can be legal. If they are to be legal the proper formalities must be employed, *i.e.* a deed must be used except in the creation of leases at a rack rent taking effect in possession for a term not exceeding three years.[16]

The incidents of equitable interests are probably similar to those attaching to corresponding legal estates before 1926. Thus the position of a tenant for life as regards waste seems to have remained unchanged despite the conversion of his legal life estate into an equitable life interest at the beginning of 1926. There is no express provision on this point but "equity follows the law".[17]

The general scheme of the section is to deal with the legal rights of ownership in the land itself in subsection (1) and with legal rights over the land of another in subsection (2). However, this is complicated by the definition of "land" given by the Act. "Land" is defined as including, unless the context otherwise requires, any corporeal or incorporeal hereditament, and among the latter is mentioned an advowson.[18] An advowson is the right of presenting a clergyman to a living[19] and, oddly enough, is a species of real property. By reading subsection (1) in the light of the definition of "land", it seems clear that a fee simple absolute in possession in an advowson is a legal estate, and so is a term of years absolute in an advowson.

It will be noted that the rights mentioned in subsection (1) are called legal estates and those mentioned in subsection (2) are called legal interests or charges. This is a convenient distinction between rights over a person's own land and rights over the land of another, but both types of right are referred to in the Act as "legal estates", and have the same incidents attached to them as attached to legal estates before 1926.[20] The title "estate owner" is given to the owner of a legal estate.[21] Before 1926, equitable rights in land were frequently and properly called equitable estates, but they should now be called equitable interests, and the name "estate" reserved for legal rights.

The various legal estates and interests must now be examined more closely.

1. "Fee simple absolute in possession"

The meaning of "fee simple" has already been considered.[22]

(a) Absolute

"Absolute" is used to distinguish a fee simple which will continue for ever from a modified fee,[23] such as a determinable fee or a base fee. A fee simple defeasible by condition

---

[16] L.P.A. 1925, ss.52, 54; below, p. 343.
[17] Above, p. 57.
[18] L.P.A. 1925, s.205(1)(ix).
[19] It is subject to important restrictions, *e.g.* no advowson may be sold after two vacancies of the benefice have occurred since July 14, 1924: see Benefices Act 1898; Benefices Act 1898 (Amendment) Measure 1923.
[20] L.P.A. 1925, s.1(4).
[21] *ibid.*
[22] Above, p. 31.
[23] See above, p. 40.

subsequent[24] would also not be "absolute" but for the Law of Property (Amendment) Act 1926. A fee simple defeasible by condition subsequent used to arise most frequently in connection with rentcharges until the Rentcharges Act 1977 prohibited the creation of legal rentcharges in most cases. In some parts of the country, particularly Manchester and the north-west of England, it was a common practice to sell a fee simple for a comparatively small sum in cash and a perpetual rentcharge (an annual sum charged on the land). The remedies for non-payment of a rentcharge include a right to enter on the land temporarily in order to collect sufficient rents and profits to satisfy the annual payment; further, in a number of cases an express right of re-entry was reserved by the conveyance, entitling the grantor to enter and determine the fee simple, and thus regain his old estate, when the annual payment is a specified number of days in arrears. The express reservation of such a right of re-entry clearly made the fee simple less than absolute, and it was thought by some that even a temporary right of entry might have this effect. This meant that those who had purchased land in this way before 1926 and had obtained legal estates suddenly found that as from January 1, 1926 their estates might no longer be legal; indeed, where they were not, it was far from clear exactly who did have the legal estate. Further, the complicated provisions of the Settled Land Act 1925 probably applied.[25]

To remedy this state of affairs the Law of Property (Amendment) Act 1926[26] provided that "a fee simple subject to a legal or equitable right of entry or re-entry is for the purposes of [the Law of Property Act 1925] a fee simple absolute". While this undoubtedly meets the difficulty it was meant to deal with, the wide terms in which it was drawn appear to have done more than was intended. The effect of a condition subsequent annexed to a fee simple is to give rise to an implied right of re-entry exercisable on breach of the condition, and until the right of re-entry is exercised the fee simple continues.[27] Consequently, by virtue of this amending Act, every fee simple defeasible by condition subsequent appears to rank as a legal estate (unless created under a trust), even though it is far from being "absolute" in the ordinary sense of the word. Further, by statute, certain land held for special purposes, such as schools or highways, is divested and reverts to (usually) the grantor when the special purpose is at an end. Such a fee simple was nevertheless declared to be absolute.[28] But, as a result of subsequent legislation, at the end of the special purpose the legal estate now remains vested in the existing owners, though they hold it on a trust of land for those entitled to the right of reverter.[29]

(b) In possession

"In possession" means that the estate is a present estate and not in remainder or in reversion.[30] It includes not only physical possession of the land but also the receipt of rents and profits or the right to receive them, if any. Thus a fee simple is still "in possession" even though the owner has granted a lease, for he is entitled to the rent reserved by the lease. But if land has been granted "to A for life, remainder to B in fee simple", the interests of both A and B are necessarily equitable, for a life interest cannot now be legal and B's fee simple

---

[24] Above, p. 41.
[25] Below, pp. 251 *et seq.*
[26] Sched., adding words to L.P.A. 1925, s.7(1).
[27] Above, p. 42.
[28] L.P.A. 1925, s.7(1).
[29] Reverter of Sites Act 1987, s.1, resolving the difficulty shown by *Re Clayton's Deed Poll* [1980] Ch. 99 and *Re Rowhook Mission Hall, Horsham* [1985] Ch. 62. See [1987] Conv. 408 (D. Evans).
[30] See *District Bank Ltd v. Webb* [1958] 1 W.L.R. 148.

is not in possession.[31] However, a mortgagor's legal estate is not converted into an equitable interest merely by the mortgagee exercising his power to take possession of the mortgaged property.[32]

2. "Term of years absolute"

(a) Term of years

"Term of years" is defined as including a term of less than a year, or for a year or years and a fraction of a year, or from year to year.[33] In effect "term of years" seems to mean a term for any period having a fixed and certain duration as a minimum. Thus, in addition to a tenancy for a specified number of years (such as "to X for ninety-nine years"), such tenancies as a yearly tenancy or a weekly tenancy are "terms of years" within the definition, for there is a minimum duration of a year or a week respectively. But a lease "for the life of X" cannot exist as a legal estate, and the same, perhaps, applies to tenancies at will or at sufferance (if they are estates at all[34]), for their duration is wholly uncertain.

(b) Absolute

"Absolute" This word has very little effect since, by virtue of the definition section, a term of years is not prevented from being absolute merely by being liable to determination by notice, re-entry, operation of law or by a provision for cesser on redemption or in any other event (other than the dropping of a life, or the determination of a determinable life interest).[35] This means that a term of years may be absolute even if it contains a clause enabling the parties to determine it at certain specified periods, such as at the end of the first five or 10 years, or if it provides (as is almost always the case) that the landlord may determine it if the rent is not paid or a covenant is broken. A lease is determined by "operation of law" pursuant to the doctrine of satisfied terms[36] and to a proviso for cesser on redemption in a mortgage (although, today the type of mortgages which contain such provisos are virtually obsolete).[37]

It will be seen from this discussion that by the express provisions of statute a term of years absolute may consist of a tenancy which is neither a "term of years" nor "absolute" according to the natural meaning of the words, such as a monthly tenancy liable to be forfeited for non-payment of rent. "Absolute" really has very little meaning here.

Unlike a fee simple absolute, a term of years absolute may be a legal estate even though not "in possession". A lease to commence in five years' time may thus be legal, although there is now a 21-year limit to the length of time which may elapse between the grant of a lease and the commencement of the term.[38] There is no limit to the length of a term of years absolute; terms of 3,000 years can arise in the case of mortgages, although mortgages of this type are today virtually obsolete.[39] But there is no such thing as a lease in perpetuity.[40]

---

[31] See, however, the Welsh Church (Burial Grounds) Act 1945, s.1, for a curious qualification of L.P.A. 1925, s.1.
[32] L.P.A. 1925, s.95(4). See below, p. 506.
[33] *ibid.*, s.205(1)(xxvii).
[34] See above, p. 35.
[35] L.P.A. 1925, s.205(1)(xxvii).
[36] Below, pp. 365, 495.
[37] Below, p. 495.
[38] Below, p. 347.
[39] See L.P.A. 1925, ss.85(2), 87(1).
[40] See *Sevenoaks, Maidstone and Tunbridge Ry. v. London, Chatham and Dover Ry.* (1879) 11 Ch.D. 625 at 635.

3. "An easement, right, or privilege in or over land for an interest equivalent to an estate in fee simple absolute in possession or a term of years absolute"

This head includes both easements and, it seems, profits *à prendre*.[41] An easement confers the right to use the land of another in some way, or to prevent it from being used for certain purposes. Thus rights of way, rights of water and rights of light may exist as easements. A profit *à prendre* gives the right to take something from the land of another, such as peat, fish or wood. These rights can be legal only if they are held for interests equivalent to one of the two legal estates. Thus a right of way for 21 years may be legal but a right of way for life must be equitable.

4. "A rentcharge in possession issuing out of or charged on land being either perpetual or for a term of years absolute"

A rentcharge is a right which, independently of any lease or mortgage, gives the owner the right to a periodical sum of money, with the payment of which some land is burdened,[42] as where the fee simple owner of Blackacre charges the land with a payment of £50 per annum to X. With some exceptions, no new legal rentcharges have been able to be created since August 21, 1977, and any existing legal rentcharges will be extinguished 60 years after they first became payable and in any case by July 22, 2037.[43]

(a) "In possession"

Under the subsection a rentcharge to start at a date subsequent to that on which it was granted could not be legal, even if it was perpetual or for a term of years absolute. But the Law of Property (Entailed Interests) Act 1932[44] declared that a rentcharge was "in possession" notwithstanding that the payments were limited to commence or accrue at a date subsequent to its creation, unless the rentcharge was limited to take effect in remainder after or expectant on the failure or determination of some other interest.[45] Thus if X conveyed land to Y in consideration of a perpetual rentcharge becoming payable one year after the conveyance, the rentcharge could nevertheless have been legal; but if a perpetual rentcharge was granted "to A for life, remainder to B absolutely", B's interest could only be legal after A's death.

(b) Issuing out of or charged on land

"Land" includes another rentcharge.[46] Thus if P charged his fee simple estate in Blackacre with the payment to Q of £100 per annum in perpetuity, Q could, until August 21, 1977, have created a legal rentcharge of £50 per annum in favour of R, charged on his rentcharge of £100.

(c) "Being either perpetual or for a term of years absolute"

"Perpetual" is used here in place of "fee simple absolute" used in 2(a) above. This verbal difference seems to be of no practical importance.

---

[41] For easements and profits, see below, pp. 413 *et seq.*
[42] For rentcharges, see below, pp. 407 *et seq.*
[43] Rentcharges Act 1977, ss.2, 3. See below, pp. 409–410.
[44] s.2.
[45] See (1932) 73 L.J. News. 321.
[46] L.P.A. 1925, ss.122, 205(1)(ix); see below, p. 406.

5. "A charge by way of legal mortgage"

This needs no comment here save to point out that this is one of the methods (in fact the way almost universally used) of creating a legal mortgage today; the other method, to grant a term of years absolute on certain conditions, is now virtually obsolete and will no longer be able to be used in the case of registered land when the Land Registration Act 2002 comes into force. Both forms are dealt with later.[47]

6. "Land tax, tithe rentcharge, and any other similar charge on land which is not created by an instrument"

This group comprises periodical payments with which land is burdened by operation of law (such as by statute) and not by some conveyance or other voluntary act of parties. The words "land tax, tithe rentcharge" have now been repealed,[48] but they are printed here in order to explain the word "similar".

Land tax was a small annual tax on land first imposed in 1692. It was abolished in 1963.[49]

Tithe rentcharge was abolished by the Tithe Act 1936. It was a type of rentcharge imposed by statute in lieu of the former right of parsons and others to one-tenth of the produce of land. Under the Act of 1936, tithe owners were compensated with government stock, and the land formerly burdened with tithe rentcharge was subjected to a "tithe redemption annuity" payable to the Crown; this was originally payable for 60 years[50] but the obligation was subsequently extinguished on October 2, 1977.[51] Although a tithe redemption annuity was not expressly stated to be a legal interest, it clearly fell within that category as being a "similar charge on land which is not created by an instrument".

7. "Rights of entry exercisable over or in respect of a legal term of years absolute, or annexed, for any purpose, to a legal rentcharge"

As already mentioned,[52] a legal term of years absolute is usually made subject to an express right of the landlord to re-enter if the tenant fails to pay rent or comply with the covenants (such a right will only rarely be implied). Such a right may be a legal right. This is also the case for any right of entry or re-entry attached to a legal rentcharge. If the rent is not paid, a temporary right of entry to collect payment out of the rents and profits is implied; and profits and many rentcharges have the benefit of an express right to re-enter and determine the legal estate of the person liable to pay the annual sum in the event of non-payment). By contrast, a right reserved on an assignment of a lease for the benefit of the assignor (who retains no other interest in the land enabling him to re-enter and retake the land in the event of a breach of covenant by the assignee is merely an equitable interest,[53] even, perhaps, if the right is reserved only for a defined or indefinite term.[54]

---

[47] Below, pp. 494, 497.
[48] Tithe Act 1936, Sched. 9; Finance Act 1963, Sched. 14, Pt. VI.
[49] Finance Act 1963, s.68, Sched. 14, Pt. V, VI.
[50] Tithe Act 1936, s.3.
[51] Finance Act 1977, s.56. See M. & W. (5th ed.), pp. 830–833 for further details about tithe, tithe rentcharge and tithe redemption annuity.
[52] Above, p. 81.
[53] *Shiloh Spinners Ltd v. Harding* [1973] A.C. 691. For assignments of leases, see below, p. 353.
[54] *ibid.*, at 726.

8. Concurrent legal estates

Any number of legal estates may exist concurrently in the same piece of land.[55] Thus A may have the legal fee simple in Greenacre, subject to a legal mortgage in favour of B, a legal rentcharge in favour of C, a legal lease in favour of D, and so on.

Sect. 2. Extension of the doctrine of overreaching

It has already been seen that a fundamental principle underlying the 1925 legislation was that all family interests should be capable of being overreached into any capital sum paid by way of purchase money for the land or an interest therein.

1. The scope of the doctrine

(a) Settlements

It has already been seen that when two or more persons are beneficially entitled to property of any type in succession, that is to say one after another, the property in question is said to be subject to a settlement. The 1925 legislation made all interests which arise under settlements of land overreachable. A purchaser for value of both registered and unregistered land will take free of all family interests arising under settlements provided that he pays the purchase money to at least two trustees or a trust corporation. If he does so, the family interests in question are overreached and transferred to the purchase money received from the purchaser.

Settlements created after 1996 necessarily take effect under a trust of land. Before 1997, settlements could take effect in two ways: under an express trust for sale and under the Settled Land Act 1925. Express trusts for sale, whenever created, have since 1996 been trusts of land. Settlements which took effect under the Settled Land Act 1925 before 1997 are still governed by that legislation. The overreaching of interests arising under trusts of land is governed by section 2 of the Law of Property Act 1925. The overreaching of interests arising under settlements under the Settled Land Act 1925 is governed by that legislation.

(b) Co-ownership

Co-ownership of land does not, without more, give rise to a settlement although it is obviously possible for individual interests under a settlement to be jointly owned. Thus where a testator leaves his property to his wife for life and subject to that to his children equally, the interest in remainder of the children is thus co-owned. However, the beneficial interests of co-owners of land now take effect under an implied trust of land under which up to four co-owners of the land hold it on trust for all of the co-owners. Before 1997 these beneficial interests took effect behind an implied trust for sale but implied trusts for sale that arose then now take effect as trusts of land. Provided that a purchaser pays the purchase money to at least two trustees or a trust corporation, the rights of the co-owners are similarly overreached and transferred to the purchase money received from the purchaser. The overreaching of the beneficial interests of co-owners of land is also governed by section 2 of the Law of Property Act 1925.

---

[55] L.P.A. 1925, s.1(5).

(c) Bare trusts

A bare, or simple, trust also does not constitute a settlement. Such a trust arises when a trustee or trustees hold property (whether legal or equitable) on trust for a person who is of full age and absolutely beneficially entitled, the nature of the trust not being prescribed by the settlor but being left to the construction of the law, as where X conveys land "to T in fee simple on trust for A in fee simple". In such a case, T is bound to permit A to occupy the land or receive the rents and profits and must obey A's instructions about the disposition of the land. A bare trust may also arise where on a purchase of land the money is provided by one person but the conveyance is made to another. Thus where P, wishing to keep his name out of the transaction, provides N with the money to buy the land, N holds on a bare trust for P.[56] Since 1996 beneficial interests arising under bare trusts have also been able to be overreached (prior to 1997 it was necessary for the beneficiary to join in the sale). This is because a bare trust is included in the definition of a trust of land. Provided that a purchaser pays the purchase money to at least two trustees or a trust corporation, the rights of the beneficiary or beneficiaries are similarly overreached and transferred to the purchase money received from the purchaser. The overreaching of beneficial interests arising under bare trusts is therefore now also governed by section 2 of the Law of Property Act 1925.

(d) Other examples

Overreaching also occurs:

(i) where a mortgagee sells the mortgaged property in the exercise of a power of sale arising as a result of a default by the mortgagor in making his repayments or in some other respect, in which case the interests in the mortgaged property of the mortgagor and any one claiming through him are overreached and transferred to the purchase money received from the purchaser (the mortgagee will of course first deduct from that purchase money the principal sum, interest and costs owed to him); and

(ii) where the personal representatives of a deceased person sell land owned by him at the date of his death, in which case the potential beneficial interests of those entitled under his will or intestacy (it will not be known if they actually have any until the administration of the estate is completed and the net value of the deceased's assets is known) are overreached and transferred to the purchase money received from the purchaser.

These last two examples of overreaching will be considered separately in the relevant chapters.

2. Overreaching under the Law of Property Act 1925

Where overreaching takes place under the Law of Property Act 1925, it will be the trustees who will be entering into the transaction by which the interests of the beneficiaries are overreached.

---

[56] See *Dyer v. Dyer* (1788) 2 Cox Eq. 92 at 93.

(a) Until 1997

Until 1997 overreaching was only possible under the Law of Property Act 1925 under some form of trust for sale, either an express trust for sale or a trust for sale implied as a result of beneficial co-ownership. Indeed, in one sense, it could be said that a disposition by trustees for sale had no overreaching effect; for by the equitable doctrine of conversion, so long as the land remained unsold, the rights of the beneficiaries were already deemed to be rights in the purchase money into which it would ultimately be converted. It could thus be said that a sale or other transaction by trustees for sale did not transfer the rights of the beneficiaries from the land to the purchase money, for strictly they never were attached to the land in the first place. This view rather overstated the impact of the doctrine of conversion, particularly when the beneficiaries were in possession of the land, as was highly likely in the case of beneficial co-ownership.[57] It was therefore both convenient and less misleading to use the term "overreaching" as including the process by which the beneficiaries had their rights in what is money in theory but land in fact transferred to what is money both in theory and in fact.

(b) Since 1996

Since 1996 overreaching has been possible under the Law of Property Act 1925 under a trust of land, which is defined[58] as including an express trust for sale of land, a bare trust of land and what is now implied as a result of beneficial co-ownership of land. The doctrine of conversion no longer exists, having been abolished except in respect of trusts created by will where the testator died before 1997,[59] and so, except in respect of the latter trusts, it can now no longer be argued that a disposition by express trustees for sale of land has no overreaching effect.

(c) The effect of overreaching under the Law of Property Act 1925

A disposition by trustees of land under the Law of Property Act 1925 is effective to overreach the equitable rights of the beneficiaries thereunder; there is no power to overreach legal estates, nor, apparently, to overreach rights already existing when the trust of land was created. A purchaser of a legal estate from the trustees is not concerned with the rents and profits of the land until sale or the proceeds of sale thereafter, even if the trusts are declared by the instrument which created the trust of land.[60]

(d) Payment of capital money

For beneficial interests to be overreached,[61] the proceeds of sale or other capital money must be paid to or applied by the direction of:

> (i) all the trustees of the trust of land, who must be either two or more in number or a trust corporation (the definition of "trust corporation" includes certain officials such as the Public Trustee and certain companies with sufficient paid-up capital (at present £250,000)[62]); or

---

[57] (1984) 100 L.Q.R. 86 (S. Anderson); and see below, p. 322.
[58] T.L.A.T.A. 1996, s.1.
[59] T.L.A.T.A. 1996, s.3.
[60] L.P.A. 1925, s.27; below, p. 280.
[61] *City of London B.S. v. Flegg* [1988] A.C. 54.
[62] See Parker & Mellows: 464–467.

(ii) a sole personal representative.[63]

There is no provision for payment into court. Overreaching will also occur where a transaction would normally give rise to the payment of capital money, even though no capital money is actually payable to or received by the trustees or personal representative in question. This has been held to occur where a mortgage secures only the existing indebtedness of the trust.[64] It would presumably also occur where no capital money was payable on the sale of an estate, either because the vendor had agreed to defer payment of the purchase price or, more implausibly, because the property was being leased back to the vendor and the lump sum payable for the lease back cancelled out the purchase price.

Where these requirements are satisfied, the interests of the beneficiaries will be overreached, whether or not they are aware of the transaction, and, if they are aware of the transaction, whether or not they are in favour of it[65]; the only exception to this rule is where the consent of the beneficiary in question is made a prerequisite of the transaction being entered into.[66] However, a beneficiary may obtain an injunction to restrain a sale if there is only one trustee[67]; one trustee will suffice if the transaction is of a type under which no capital money arises, such as the grant of a lease at a rent where no lump sum is payable.[68] Where capital money is paid to only one trustee, there is no overreaching; but if the land is registered land a beneficiary in actual occupation under a trust of land will have an interest which overrides registration and so will be binding upon the purchaser.[69] In the case of unregistered land, a purchaser will in all cases be bound by the beneficial interest unless he is a bona fide purchaser for value of a legal estate without notice.[70]

(e) Capital money as land

Until 1997 proceeds of sale or other capital money arising under a trust for sale could be applied in the same way as capital money arising from settled land.[71] This did not convert the rights of the beneficiaries into rights in land; they remained rights in pure personalty[72] and any land acquired under this provision had to be conveyed to the trustees for sale to hold on trust for sale.[73] Since 1996, as a result of the abolition of the doctrine of conversion (except in respect of trusts created by will where the testator died before 1997),[74] the rights of the beneficiaries are rights in land even before sale and, after sale, remain rights in land in the event that further land is acquired with the proceeds of sale.

3. Overreaching under the Settled Land Act 1925

In settlements under the Settled Land Act 1925, the legal title to their subject-matter will be vested not in the trustees of the settlement but in what the Act describes as the "tenant for

---

[63] L.P.A. 1925, ss.2, 27; L.P.(Am.)A. 1926, Sched.
[64] *State Bank of India v. Sood* [1997] Ch. 276.
[65] *City of London B.S. v. Flegg* [1988] A.C. 54.
[66] See below, p. 285.
[67] *Walker v. Waller* [1967] 1 W.L.R. 451; for the appointment of additional trustees, see below, p. 296.
[68] L.P.A. 1925, s.27(2); L.P.(Am.)A. 1926, Sched.
[69] *Williams & Glyn's Bank Ltd v. Boland* [1981] A.C. 487; below, pp. 123, 127.
[70] *Kingsnorth Finance Co. Ltd v. Tizard* [1986] 1 W.L.R. 783; above, pp. 61 *et seq.*
[71] L.P.A. 1925, s.28 (now repealed); *Re Wellsted's W.T.* [1949] Ch. 296. *cf. Re Wakeman* [1945] Ch. 177. See Thompson, *Co-ownership*, pp. 7, 8.
[72] *Re Kempthorne* [1930] 1 Ch. 268.
[73] L.P.A. 1925, s.28 (now repealed).
[74] T.L.A.T.A. 1996, s.3.

life", the person entitled under the settlement to an interest in possession for the time being, whether or not that interest is actually a life interest. If there is no such person or the person in question is an infant, the legal title will instead be vested in what are described as the "statutory owner", who usually will be the trustees of the settlement. It is therefore the tenant for life or statutory owner, rather than the trustees of the settlement as such, who will be entering into the transaction by which the interests of the beneficiaries are overreached.

(a) Rights under the settlement[75]

A conveyance is effectual to pass the land or other interest concerned "discharged from all the limitations, powers, and provisions of the settlement, and from all estates, interests, and charges subsisting or to arise thereunder"; it is immaterial whether or not a purchaser has notice of these rights. In short, the purchaser takes the land free from all the rights under the settlement. The Act then makes certain qualifications to this rule: the land is to pass to the purchaser discharged from the above rights, "but subject to and with the exception of"[76]:

> (i) All legal estates and charges by way of legal mortgage having priority to the settlement.

In nearly every case this provision is mere surplusage, for no power is given to overreach rights prior to the settlement and so the qualification is unnecessary. If X makes a legal mortgage of land and later settles the land, the tenant for life has no power to overreach the mortgage, which continues to bind the land.

> (ii) All legal estates and charges by way of legal mortgage which have been conveyed or created for securing money actually raised at the date of the deed.

This is a true exception, for it excludes something which otherwise would have been included in the overreaching provision. Thus if a tenant for life creates a legal mortgage to pay for improvements or raise portions, and the mortgagee has actually paid the money, the mortgage cannot be overreached even though it is an interest arising under the settlement. "Mortgagees who have actually lent their money on the security of the land are regarded as strangers to the settlement, and are not to have the security which they bargained for on the land itself transferred to the purchase money at the will of the tenant for life."[77] If the money has not in fact been paid (for instance, where a legal term of years has been created to secure portions which have not been raised) the right is overreached.[78]

> (iii) All leases and grants of other rights (except annuities, limited owner's charges and general equitable charges[79]) which at the date of the deed are—
>
> (a) binding on the successors in title of the tenant for life, and
> (b) duly registered if capable of registration.

[75] S.L.A. 1925, s.72.
[76] See *Re Dickin and Kelsall's Contract* [1908] 1 Ch. 213 at 221.
[77] *Re Mundy and Roper's Contract* [1899] 1 Ch. 275 at 289, *per* Chitty L.J.
[78] See *Re Du Cane and Nettlefold's Contract* [1898] 2 Ch. 96 at 108.
[79] For these rights, see below, pp. 94, 97.

This also is a true exception, but unlike the previous provisions it is not confined to legal rights. It thus apparently applies to a restrictive covenant creating a mere equitable burden on the land.

(b) Rights prior to the settlement

Having dealt with the exceptions to the rule that all rights arising under the settlement can be overreached, the Act proceeds to the converse case, namely the exceptions to the rule that rights prior to the settlement cannot be overreached. The Act[80] provides that:

    (i) an annuity,

    (ii) a limited owner's charge, and

    (iii) a general equitable charge

will be overreached on a disposition under the Act even if they have been duly protected by registration; these rights are treated as if they had been created by the settlement even if in fact they arose before it came into existence. They are all rights which can be represented in terms of money and so will not suffer from being transferred to the purchase money.

(c) Summary

It cannot be said that the overreaching provisions are very happily drawn. For those who wish to have a bird's eye view of their effect (necessarily at the expense of some accuracy) the position may be represented as follows:

    (i) there is in general no power to overreach legal rights;

    (ii) subject to the three exceptions set out above, there is no power to overreach equitable rights already existing when the settlement was made;

    (iii) there is power to overreach all the equitable rights of the beneficiaries under the settlement, including derivative rights, such as the rights of a mortgagee of the beneficial interest of a tenant for life.

(d) Payment of capital money

Notwithstanding anything to the contrary in the settlement, for beneficial interests to be overreached any capital money payable in respect of the transaction must be paid either:

    (i) to, or by the direction of, all the trustees of the settlement, who must be either two or more in number or a trust corporation, or

    (ii) into court.[81]

It is for the tenant for life to decide which of the two methods of payment is to be adopted.[82] Presumably, as in the case of trusts of land, overreaching will also occur where a transaction

---

[80] S.L.A. 1925, s.72.
[81] S.L.A. 1925, s.18.
[82] *ibid.*, s.75; *Hatten v. Russell* (1888) 38 Ch.D. 334 at 345.

would normally give rise to the payment of capital money, even though no capital money is actually payable to or received by the trustees or paid into court.[83]

Where these requirements are satisfied, the interests of the beneficiaries will be overreached whether or not they are aware of the transaction and, if they are aware of the transaction, whether or not they are in favour of it; this is because, in the case of settlements under the Settled Land Act 1925, it is not possible to impose restrictions on the dispositive powers of the tenant for life.[84] If a purchaser fails to pay his money in accordance with these provisions, and pays it, for example, to the tenant for life, he will not get a good discharge and will be unable to make a good title to a subsequent purchaser.[85] Where no capital money arises on a transaction (as where a lease is granted at a rent where no lump sum is payable), a disposition in favour of a bona fide purchaser for value of a legal estate takes effect under the Act and thus has an overreaching effect even though there are no trustees.[86]

(e) Capital money as land

The capital money and any investments representing it are for all purposes of disposition, transmission and devolution (but not otherwise, such as for fiscal purposes[87]) treated as land, and are held for and go to the same persons, in the same manner and for the same estates, interests and trusts, as the land whence they arise would have been held and have gone under the settlement.[88] Thus where a tenant for life had become absolutely entitled to the land, a will of his that effectively disposed of personalty alone could not carry any capital money[89]; whereas an option under the settlement to purchase the land can be exercised so as to obtain the capital money.[90] In short, the state in which the settled property happens to be at any given moment, whether it is land, investments or money, cannot affect the rights of the beneficiaries or those claiming under them.

4. Under ad hoc settlements

The original intention of the 1925 legislation was that a conveyance under a settlement under a trust for sale or under the Settled Land Act 1925 should overreach not only the interests of the beneficiaries but also prior equitable interests as well. This provision was attacked in Parliament, and ultimately a workable scheme was produced and duly embodied in the 1925 legislation.

Clearly some equitable interests cannot be overreached; thus a restrictive covenant (such as against building) and an equitable easement (such as a right of way which takes effect only in equity) cannot become corresponding rights in the purchase money. But dispositions under certain special settlements under (until 1997) trusts for sale, under (since 1996) trusts of land, and under the Settled Land Act 1925, described in each case by the label "ad hoc", have a special wider overreaching effect than that set out above. Dispositions under ad hoc settlements overreach, in addition to the rights of the beneficiaries under the settlement, annuities, limited owner's charges and general equitable charges (dispositions under settlements under

---

[83] By analogy with *State Bank of India v. Sood* [1997] Ch. 276.
[84] See below, p. 269.
[85] *Re Norton and Las Casas' Contract* [1909] 2 Ch. 59. For purchases made without knowing that the land is settled, see below, p. 263.
[86] S.L.A. 1925, s.110(4).
[87] Earl of *Midleton v. Baron Cottesloe* [1949] A.C. 418.
[88] S.L.A. 1925, s.75.
[89] *Re Cartwright* [1939] Ch. 90.
[90] *Re Armstrong's W.T.* [1943] Ch. 400.

the Settled Land Act 1925 do this anyway, so that this is only an advantage in the case of, until 1997, ad hoc trusts for sale and of, since 1996, ad hoc trusts of land). Certain other equities, such as a widow's right of dower, which must by now be entirely obsolete are also overreached to obtain this wider effect the settlement in question must have "guaranteed" trustees, *i.e.* either trustees appointed or approved by the court, or a trust corporation. The idea is that such trustees are likely to be particularly trustworthy and that this will console those whose rights are overreached but would not normally have been overreached. That is the theory; in practice, because the additional overreaching powers are so meagre, little use has ever been made of such special settlements, which are effectively obsolete. It therefore seems inappropriate to consider them any further.

5. Summary of overreaching provisions

In broad outline, the position may be summarised as follows:

> (i) A conveyance until 1997 under an ordinary trust for sale or since 1996 under an ordinary trust of land overreaches the rights of the beneficiaries thereunder.

> (ii) A conveyance under an ordinary settlement under the Settled Land Act 1925 overreaches—

> (a) the rights of the beneficiaries thereunder, and
> (b) annuities, limited owner's charges and general equitable charges.

> (iii) A conveyance until 1997 under an ad hoc trust for sale or since 1996 under an ad hoc trust of land or under an ad hoc settlement under the Settled Land Act 1925 overreaches—

> (a) the rights of the beneficiaries thereunder;
> (b) annuities, limited owner's charges and general equitable charges; and
> (c) certain other equities, such as a widow's right of dower.

Sect. 3. Registration of local land charges

A register of local land charges is kept by each district council, each London Borough, and the Common Council of the City of London.[91] These registers are divided into 12 Parts[92] and the charges are registered against the land itself.[93] Official searches may be made.[94] This system, which applies to both registered and unregistered land, is quite distinct from the system of registration of land charges, which applies only to unregistered land and is operated on a national basis by the Land Charges Department of the Land Registry.[95] Another particularly significant distinction is that land charges are registered against the name of the person who is the owner of the relevant estate in it at the time of registration, thus necessitating, at least in principle, a series of searches against the names of all the successive owners of that estate since 1925.

---

[91] Local Land Charges Act 1975, s.3.
[92] Local Land Charges Rules 1977 (S.I. 1977 No.985), r. 3.
[93] *ibid.*, r. 6.
[94] Local Land Charges Act 1975, s.9.
[95] Below, pp. 93–108.

There is a wide range of interests that are registrable as local land charges.[96] In general, these interests are charges acquired by statute by a local authority or, in some cases, by a government department; and they have the general nature of being public rights, rather than the private rights registrable in the Land Charges Department of the Land Registry. They may for the most part be classified as being either financial or restrictive. Some examples may be given: charges for making up a road that are imposed on the frontagers; the cost of certain sewerage works; prohibitions or restrictions on the use of land imposed or enforceable by a local authority or government department; closing or demolition orders for houses; conditions in a planning permission; and tree preservation orders. But some private rights are registrable, such as light obstruction notices.[97]

Failure to register a local land charge no longer makes it void against a purchaser. Instead, the charge remains valid, but the purchaser is normally entitled to compensation for any loss that he suffers; and similarly for omissions from an official search certificate.[98]

Sect. 4. Human rights

"The law of property has always said much more than is commonly supposed about the subject of human rights",[99] and international human rights standards have always been able to "be taken into account in shaping the common law".[1] However, it was not until the Human Rights Act 1998 incorporated the European Convention on Human Rights ("the Convention") into English law with effect from October 2, 2000 that it was possible formally to challenge established rules of English property law on the basis that their utilisation by a public body infringed human rights.[2]

The essential provision of the Convention is to be found in Article 1 of its First Protocol: "Every natural or legal person is entitled to the peaceful enjoyment of his possessions. No one shall be deprived of his possessions except in the public interest and subject to the conditions provided for by law and by the general principles of international law. The preceding provisions shall not, however, in any way impair the right of a State to enforce such laws as it deems necessary to control the use of property in accordance with the general interest or to secure the payment of taxes or other contributions or penalties". Deprivation of possessions can only be impugned when it is committed by a public authority. [3]

The decisions of the European Court of Human Rights have in general distinguished between deprivation of property,[4] which normally necessitates the payment of compensation,[5] and mere control of land use, which carries no inherent right to compensation.[6]

---

[96] *ibid.*, ss.1, 2. See J.F. Garner, *Local Land Charges* (10th ed., 1987).
[97] *ibid.*, s.1, Sched. 1; Local Land Charges Rules 1977, r. 10, Sched. 1, Forms A, B. For these notices, see below, p. 396.
[98] Local Land Charges Act 1975, s.10.
[99] K.J. Gray: (1994) 47(2) *Current Legal Problems* 157, 211.
[1] *Hunter v. Canary Wharf Ltd* [1997] A.C. 655 at 714 *per* Lord Cooke.
[2] J. Howell [1999] Conv. 287.
[3] H.R.A. 1998, s.6.
[4] *Allan Jacobsson v. Sweden* (1989) Series A No. 163, paras 54, 57 (town planning measure); *Mellacher v. Austria* (1989) Series A No. 192, para. 44 (statutory rent control); *Fredin v. Sweden* (1991) Series A No. 192, paras 47–48 (environmental conservation); *Spadee and Scalabrino v. Italy* (1996) Series A No. 315B, para. 28 (restraint on eviction from residential property; *Papachelas v. Greece* (2000) 30 E.H.H.R. 923 (expropriation of land for road building).
[5] *James v. United Kingdom* (1986) Series A No. 98, para. 54; *Holy Monasteries v. Greece* (1994) Series A No. 301, para. 71; *Former King of Greece v. Greece* (2000) Judgment of November 23, 2000, para. 89.
[6] *Banér v. Sweden* (1989) 60 D.R. 128 at 142 (regulation of land use presumptively legitimate).

However, there is a blurred borderline between the two.[7] The court has to determine whether a "fair balance" has been struck between what have been described as "the demands of the general interest of the community and the requirements of the protection of the individual's fundamental rights"; what is said to be crucial is whether the individual landowner has been singled out to bear an "individual and excessive burden" in relation to some community-directed obligation which should have been shared more widely.[8] Relevant criteria are legality[9] and proportionality.[10]

The need to "take a responsible attitude when it is right to raise a Human Rights Act point" has been emphasised by the judiciary.[11] Nevertheless, a number of challenges have been made to the rules of English property law since the Human Rights Act 1998 came into force.[12] However, the only one which has so far succeeded has been the successful challenge by the freehold owners of a field to their continuing liability to keep the chancel of a parish church in repair[13]; they were so liable because the field had been rectorial property since 1743. It was held that the parochial church council constituted a public authority and that the imposition of liability was a form of taxation which did not satisfy Article 1 because it operated arbitrarily. It was also held that the way in which these owners were singled out from other neighbouring landowners was discriminatory within Article 14 of the Convention. The successful challenge to this antiquated and somewhat esoteric liability is hardly surprising; even so, it is subject to an appeal to the House of Lords. All the other challenges have failed and it is extremely unlikely that many others will be successful. Those which have failed to date will each be discussed in the relevant place.

PART 4—ASPECTS APPLYING ONLY TO UNREGISTERED CONVEYANCING

Sect. 1. Registration of land charges

The system of registration of land charges, already considered in outline,[14] must now be examined in some detail. The registers in question are maintained by the Land Charges

---

[7] *Sporrung and Lönnruth v. Sweden* (1982) Series A No. 52 para. 63 (de facto expropriation); *Banér v. Sweden* (1989) 60 D.R. 128 at 139–140 (regulation of land assimilated to a deprivation of possessions); *Fredin v. Sweden* (1991) Series A No. 192, para. 45 (removal of all meaningful use of the property); *Pine Valley Developments Ltd v. Ireland* (1991) Series A, No. 222, para. 56 (land could still be farmed or leased).

[8] *Sporrung and Lönnruth v. Sweden* (1982) Series A No. 52 paras 69, 73; *James v. United Kingdom* (1986) Series A No. 98, para. 50; *Hakansson and Syuresson v. Sweden* (1990) Series A No. 121, para. 151; *Fredin v. Sweden* (1991) Series A No. 192, para. 51; *Holy Monasteries v. Greece* (1994) Series A No. 301, para. 70.

[9] *Aston Cantlow and Wilmcote with Billesley P.C.C. v. Wallbank* [2001] 3 W.L.R. 1323 (arbitrariness of application).

[10] *James v. United Kingdom* (1986) Series A No. 98, para. 50.

[11] *D (A Child) v. Walker* [2000] 1 W.L.R. 1382 at 1387 *per* Lord Woolf M.R.

[12] *Pye (J.A.) Oxford Ltd v. Graham* [2001] Ch. 804 (loss of title as a result of adverse possession); *Kingsalton Ltd v. Thames Water Developments Ltd* [2002] 1 P. & C.R. 15 (power to deny rectification of the Land Register); *Aston Cantlow and Wilmcote with Billesley P.C.C. v. Wallbank* [2001] 3 W.L.R. 1323 (liability to keep chancel in repair); see also *R. (Alconbury Developments Ltd) v. Secretary of State for the Environment* [2001] 2 W.L.R. 1389 (ability of Secretary of States to determine planning appeals); *Poplar Housing and Regeneration Community Association Ltd v. Donoghue* [2001] 3 W.L.R. 183 (power of Housing Association to evict); *Mowan v. Wandsworth B.C.* (2001) 33 H.L.R. 56 and *Lambeth L.B.C. v. Howard* (2001) 33 H.L.R. 58 (both landlord and tenant disputes).

[13] *Aston Cantlow and Wilmcote with Billesley P.C.C. v. Wallbank* [2001] 3 W.L.R. 1323.

[14] Above, p. 11.

Department of the Land Registry under the Land Charges Act 1972, replacing the Land Charges Act 1925. They are held in a computerised form at Plymouth. The two basic principles of the system of registration of land charges are that for any registrable interest:

(i) due registration of the interest constitutes actual notice of the interest registered[15]; and

(ii) non-registration makes the interest void against certain purchasers.[16]

(1) Registrable interests

Five separate registers and an index are kept in the Land Charges Department of the Land Registry.[17] The first of these registers is much more important than the others.

(a) Land charges

Land charges,[18] strictly so-called, are divided into six classes, A, B, C, D, E and F. The most important classes are C and D (which are subdivided) and F.[19] Most of the interests are equitable interests affecting another's land.

(i) Class A: Class A consists of charges imposed on land by some statute, but which come into existence only when some person makes an application. Thus where a landlord who is not entitled to land for his own benefit has to pay compensation to an agricultural tenant, the landlord may apply to the Minister of Agriculture, Fisheries and Food for a charge on the land for the amount of compensation.[20] Class A charges are registrable whenever created.

(ii) Class B: Class B consists of charges which are similar to those in Class A except that they are not created on the application of any person, but are automatically imposed by statute. Most charges thus imposed are registrable as local land charges, and so few are registrable in Class B. An example is a charge on property recovered or preserved for a legally aided litigant in respect of unpaid contributions to what is now known as the legal services commission.[21]

(iii) Class C: Class C land charges are divided into four categories.

C(i): A puisne mortgage. A puisne (pronounced "puny") mortgage is a legal mortgage not protected by a deposit of documents relating to the legal estate affected. This has been made registrable because, while a mortgagee who takes the title deeds puts a subsequent mortgagee or purchaser on inquiry by virtue of the fact that the mortgagor will not be able to produce them, a mortgagee who does not obtain the deeds does not do so. He thus needs to protect his mortgage and is able to do so by registering a land charge under this head.

C(ii): A limited owner's charge. This is an equitable charge which a tenant for life or statutory owner acquires under any statute by discharging inheritance tax or other liabilities to which the statute gives special priority. Inheritance tax is payable on the death of a tenant for life of any form of settlement. If the land remains settled thereafter, the person next entitled to the land may prefer to find the money necessary to pay the inheritance tax out of

[15] L.P.A. 1925, ss.198, 199.
[16] See below, pp. 104 *et seq.* for the details.
[17] L.C.A. 1972, s.1.
[18] *ibid.*, ss.2–4.
[19] *ibid.*, s.2.
[20] A.H.A. 1986, s.86. For a full list of such charges, see L.C.A. 1972, Sched. 2.
[21] Legal Aid Act 1988, s.16(6).

his own pocket instead of leaving the burden to fall on the settled property itself, something which would normally require it to be sold. If he does pay the inheritance tax himself, he is entitled to a charge on the land in the same way as if he had lent money to the estate on mortgage.[22] Such a charge is registrable under this head.

C(iii): A general equitable charge.   This is any equitable charge which:

(i) is not included in any other class of land charge;

(ii) is not protected by a deposit of documents relating to the legal estate affected; and

(iii) does not arise, or affect any interest arising, under a trust of land or settlement under the Settled Land Act 1925 (and so is overreachable).

This is a residuary class which catches equitable charges not registrable elsewhere, such as the right of an unpaid vendor to a charge on the land for the unpaid purchase money (technically known as an unpaid vendor's lien).[23] It includes equitable mortgages of a legal estate and certain annuities created after 1925.[24] It does not include either equitable mortgages of an equitable interest under a settlement under the Settled Land Act 1925 or a trust of land or other charges on the proceeds of sale of land.[25]

C(iv): An estate contract.   This is a contract to convey or create a legal estate, made by a person who either owns a legal estate or is entitled at the date of the contract to have a legal estate conveyed to him. Oral contracts formerly sufficed if sufficiently supported by evidence in writing or part performance,[26] but contracts made after July 27, 1989, must be in writing.[27] It suffices if the person who makes the contract owns any legal estate in the land, even if it is less substantial than the estate he has agreed to convey or create, as where a yearly tenant agrees that if he acquires the reversion he will grant his sub-tenant a lease for 10 years.[28]

In addition to ordinary contracts, options to purchase, rights of pre-emption[29] and other like rights are expressly included by the statute. Thus an option given to a tenant to purchase the freehold reversion is registrable,[30] and so is an option to renew a lease, even though such an option runs with the land at law[31] so that there seems little point in making it registrable.[32] An obligation to offer to surrender a lease to the landlord before seeking to assign it is also included,[33] and so is a tenant's notice exercising his statutory right to purchase the freehold or take an extended lease.[34] However, rights of pre-emption do not become registrable until the vendor makes the purchaser an offer which cannot be withdrawn before the time by which

---

[22] Inheritance Tax Act 1984, s.212(2); L.C.A. 1972, s.2(4), as amended by Inheritance Tax Act 1984, Sched. 8, para. 3. See Finance Act 1986, s.100.

[23] *Uziell-Hamilton v. Keen* (1971) 22 P. & C.R. 655. For the lien, see below, p. 492.

[24] Below, p. 97.

[25] *Georgiades v. Edward Wolfe & Co. Ltd* [1965] Ch. 487 (estate agent's commission charged on proceeds of sale not a C(iii) land charge); and see *Thomas v. Rose* [1968] 1 W.L.R. 1797.

[26] L.P.A. 1925, s.40; *Universal Permanent B.S. v. Cooke* [1952] Ch. 95 at 104.

[27] L.P.(M.P.)A. 1989, s.2; above, p. 68.

[28] *Sharp v. Coates* [1949] 1 K.B. 285.

[29] See above, p. 67.

[30] *Midland Bank Trust Co. Ltd v. Green* [1981] A.C. 513.

[31] *Phillips v. Mobil Oil Co. Ltd* [1989] 1 W.L.R. 888.

[32] See (1981) 125 S.J. 816 (M.P. Thompson).

[33] *Greene v. Church Commissioners for England* [1974] Ch. 467.

[34] Leasehold Reform Act 1967, s.5; below, p. 608.

it has to be accepted.[35] At least some conditional contracts seem to be registrable,[36] and it has been held that a contract with an agent to convey the land to whoever the agent directs is also included.[37] But a contract with an agent to make an estate contract is not registrable,[38] nor is a notice to treat under the process for the compulsory acquisition of land.[39] A boundary agreement is registrable only if it clearly transfers land.[40]

(iv) Class D: Class D land charges fall into three categories.

D(i): Inland Revenue charges.   Originally this class comprised charges for estate duty on death (often called "death duty"). But in 1975 estate duty was replaced by the different system of capital transfer tax,[41] and after 1984 this tax, in a revised form, was renamed "inheritance tax".[42] The tax creates a charge on land in favour of the Board of Inland Revenue, though it does not apply to leaseholds or undivided shares in land under a trust of land which were owned by the deceased beneficially.[43] This type of charge is therefore chargeable only on freeholds, and must be registered in order to bind purchasers. However, in practice such charges have rarely been registered and today are normally no longer necessary. This is because the personal representatives of the deceased now have to pay whatever inheritance tax is due before they can obtain a grant of representation, so that by the time the Board of Inland Revenue discover that the deceased has died the tax will already have been paid. Consequently it is only where the personal representatives have under-declared the tax payable that there will be any need for the registration of this type of charge.

D(ii): Restrictive covenants.   Under this head, any covenant or agreement restrictive of the user of land may be registered, provided it:

(i) was entered into after 1925, and

(ii) is not between a lessor and a lessee.

Restrictive covenants in leases are never registrable even where they relate not to the demised land but to adjoining land owned by the lessor[44] (this is the most natural interpretation of the legislation but may well not have been the intention of the legislature since it means that a tenant who is the holder of a restrictive covenant over adjoining land of his landlord has no effective way of protecting his rights thereunder against a subsequent purchaser). As between landlord and tenant, the position depends on whether the lease was created before 1996 or after 1995. Where the lease was created before 1996, the landlord and the tenant for the time being can always enforce restrictive covenants against one another provided that the tenant has a legal, rather than an equitable lease, and they can sometimes also do so as against the original tenant or landlord. As between landlord and equitable tenant and landlord and sub-tenant, the question, as usual, is one of notice. Where the lease was created after 1995, the

---

[35] *Pritchard v. Briggs* [1980] Ch. 338; *Bircham & Co. Nominees (2) Ltd v. Worrall* (2001) 82 P. & C.R. 34.
[36] See *Haslemere Estates Ltd v. Baker* [1982] 1 W.L.R. 1109 at 1118; and see *Williams v. Burlington Investments Ltd* (1977) 121 S.J. 424.
[37] *Turley v. Mackay* [1944] Ch. 37, doubted in *Thomas v. Rose* [1968] 1 W.L.R. 1797.
[38] *Thomas v. Rose* [1968] 1 W.L.R. 1797.
[39] *Capital Investments Ltd v. Wednesfield U.D.C.* [1965] Ch. 774.
[40] *Neilson v. Poole* (1969) 20 P. & C.R. 909.
[41] Under Finance Act 1975, Pt. III, Sched. 4.
[42] Under Capital Transfer Act 1984, now named Inheritance Tax Act 1984: see Finance Act 1986, s.100.
[43] Inheritance Tax Act 1984, s.237; and see Sched. 8, para. 3.
[44] *Dartstone Ltd v. Cleveland Petroleum Co. Ltd* [1969] 1 W.L.R. 1807.

landlord and the tenant for the time being can always enforce restrictive covenants against one another whether the tenant has a legal or an equitable lease, and they can occasionally also do so as against the original tenant or landlord but on fewer occasions than hitherto. The landlord can also always enforce restrictive covenants against sub-tenants.

All restrictive covenants made before 1926 (other than those in leases which are in the position set out above) also still depend upon notice and are therefore enforceable against everyone except a purchaser for value of a legal estate without notice. This rule is considerably more significant than most of those relating to the pre–1926 law since many thousands of restrictive covenants created in the second half of the nineteenth century remain in force today.

D(iii): Equitable easements.   Any "easement, right or privilege over or affecting land" is registrable under this head, provided:

  (i) it is merely equitable, and

  (ii) it was created or arose after 1925.

Thus a perpetual easement created without using a deed and an easement for life, being equitable, are both registrable.[45] Similarly, a specifically enforceable contract to create an easement is also registrable as an equitable easement,[46] or perhaps as an estate contract.[47] Equitable profits *à prendre* also seem to be included under this head.[48]

The apparent width of the term "right or privilege" is restricted by the context. The modern approach has been to construe this head narrowly. It has therefore been held, controversially, that this head does not include a requisition of land under Defence Regulations,[49] an interest arising under the doctrine of equitable proprietary estoppel,[50] a right to remove fixtures at the end of a lease[51] or an equitable right of entry to secure compliance with the covenants contained in an assignment of a lease.[52] The result is that a number of both formal and informal rights fall outside the system of registration of land charges and so remain within the scope of the old doctrine of notice. It is questionable whether this was the intention of the 1925 legislation.

(v) Class E: Annuities created but not registered before 1926.[53] An annuity is a rentcharge or an annuity for life or lives, or for an estate determinable on a life or lives (such as to X for 99 years if he so long lives) not created by a marriage settlement or a will.[54] It is highly unlikely that anyone granted an annuity before 1926 can still be alive so this class must now be virtually, if not completely, obsolete. It has already been seen that annuities of these types created after 1925 are registrable in Class C(iii) as general equitable charges.

[45] See above, pp. 67, 79.
[46] *E. R. Ives Investment Ltd v. High* [1967] 2 Q.B. 379 at 403 (contrast at 395, 396); [1986] Conv. 31 at 34–37 (M.P. Thompson).
[47] *Huckvale v. Aegean Hotels Ltd* (1989) 58 P. & C.R. 163 at 165; (1947) 11 Conv.(n.s.) 165 at 176 (E.O. Walford); and see *E. R. Ives Investment Ltd v. High* [1967] 2 Q.B. 379 at 397.
[48] *E. R. Ives Investment Ltd v. High* [1967] 2 Q.B. 379 at 395.
[49] *Lewisham Borough Council v. Maloney* [1948] 1 K.B. 50.
[50] *E. R. Ives Investment Ltd v. High* [1967] 2 Q.B. 379; but see below, p. 110.
[51] *Poster v. Slough Estates Ltd* [1969] 1 Ch. 495 at 506, 507.
[52] *Shiloh Spinners Ltd v. Harding* [1973] A.C. 691; above, p. 83.
[53] For annuities registered before 1926, see below, p. 101.
[54] L.C.A. 1972, s.17(1).

(vi) Class F: A spouse's statutory right to occupy a house owned by the other spouse. In a series of cases in the 1950s,[55] a controversial[56] doctrine was evolved under which a wife who had been deserted by her husband was held to have an equitable right to remain in occupation of the matrimonial home vested in her husband. This right, which was held to be a mere equity[57] rather than an equitable interest, was enforceable against her husband and everyone else except a bona fide purchaser for value of a legal or equitable interest in the house.[58] In 1965, the House of Lords held that this "deserted wife's equity" did not exist, and that the wife had a mere personal right that would not bind a purchaser.[59] This led to the enactment of the Matrimonial Homes Act 1967 (now part of the Family Law Act 1996) which gave statutory rights of occupation to both husbands and wives.

The statutory "rights of occupation" conferred by the Act arise automatically, and are not dependent on desertion or anything else. The rights are given only to a spouse who has neither the legal fee simple nor a term of years in the matrimonial home, and either has no right to occupy it (whether by virtue of any estate, interest, contract or statute) or else has only an equitable interest in it, or in the proceeds of sale.[60] The statutory rights are the right not to be excluded from the home, and the right, with the leave of the court, to enter into occupation of it.[61] The rights are a charge on the other spouse's estate or interest in the home as from the date when that spouse acquired the home, or the date of the marriage, or January 1, 1968, whichever is the latest.[62] These rights are registrable as a Class F land charge even before the court has granted any leave to enter into occupation of the home[63]; and once registered, the rights will bind purchasers, and also the trustee in bankruptcy of the owning spouse.[64] But a registration effected not for the protection of rights of occupation but for some ulterior purpose (such as to put financial pressure on the other spouse) is improper and will be set aside.[65]

The statutory rights of occupation are not absolute. They end when the marriage ends, and the court has wide powers at any time to restrict or terminate them, or to prohibit, suspend or restrict the exercise of the right of occupation by either spouse, including the owning spouse.[66] In making orders under the Act the court has a wide discretion, and must consider all the circumstances of the case, including in particular the financial resources of the spouses, the housing needs of and the effect of any order on the spouses and any relevant child.[67] The court may also take into account the position of a purchaser from the owning spouse[68] and may decline to make an order against him even if he has not taken the matrimonial home free of the Class F charge.[69]

While married couples are living together, it is unusual for any rights of occupation to be registered. Registration, when discovered, is likely to be seen as a hostile act, and it is not the

---

[55] *Bendall v. McWhirter* [1952] 2 Q.B. 466; *Street v. Denham* [1954] 1 W.L.R. 624.
[56] See (1952) 68 L.Q.R. 379 (R.E.M.).
[57] See above, p. 60.
[58] *Westminster Bank Ltd v. Lee* [1956] Ch. 7.
[59] *National Provincial Bank Ltd v. Ainsworth* [1965] A.C. 1175. See also below, p. 480.
[60] Family Law Act 1996, s.30(1), (9).
[61] *ibid.*, s.30(2).
[62] *ibid.*, s.31(2), (3).
[63] *Watts v. Waller* [1973] Q.B. 153; [1976] Current Legal Problems 26 at 31–33, 43–50 (D.J. Hayton).
[64] Insolvency Act 1986, s.336(2).
[65] *Barnett v. Hassett* [1981] 1 W.L.R. 1385.
[66] Family Law Act 1996, s.33(3).
[67] *ibid.*, s.33(6).
[68] *ibid.*, s.34(2).
[69] *Kaur v. Gill* [1988] Fam. 110, effectively codified by Family Law Act 1996, s.34(2).

practice of the Land Registry to inform the owning spouse of any registration.[70] This is liable to create difficulties for an owning spouse who sells the home without knowing that a Class F Charge has been registered; it is also possible for such a charge to be registered between contract and completion. In both cases, registration of the charge will in practice prevent the sale from being completed.[71] A prudent purchaser will therefore obtain the written concurrence of the non-owning spouse to any sale before contracting, both for this reason and in case that spouse claims some beneficial interest in the home.[72]

(vii) Companies: Most charges on land created by a company for securing money (including a charge created by deposit of title deeds[73]) require registration within 21 days in the Companies Charges Register maintained under the Companies Act 1985 and earlier legislation which that Act replaced.[74] For floating charges and charges created before 1970, this suffices, and takes effect as registration under the Land Charges Act 1972[75]; other charges require registration in both registers.[76]

(b) Pending actions

This head comprises pending land actions and petitions in bankruptcy. A pending land action (often called a *lis pendens*) is any action or proceeding pending in court relating to land or any interest in land or charge on it.[77] This definition is not so wide as it may seem. It is confined to claims for some proprietary right in specific land.[78] This includes a claim to an easement over the land,[79] an application for an access order,[80] and an application for leave to bring proceedings for forfeiture of a lease which would terminate the lease.[81] But it does not include an action for damages for breach of a repairing covenant in a lease (even if coupled with a claim for a mandatory order to effect the repairs),[82] an action to restrain a nuisance emanating from land,[83] or a claim to restrain the sale of land[84] or to receive the proceeds of sale if it is sold.[85] Nor does it include a claim based on equitable proprietary estoppel brought merely in the hope that, if it succeeds, the court will satisfy the estoppel by granting some form of proprietary right in the land to the claimant.[86]

---

[70] See Ruoff and Roper, 39–11.
[71] See *Wroth v. Tyler* [1974] Ch. 30.
[72] See *Williams & Glyn's Bank Ltd v. Boland* [1981] A.C. 487; (1974) 38 Conv. 110 (D.J. Hayton).
[73] *Re Wallis & Simmonds (Builders) Ltd* [1974] 1 W.L.R. 391.
[74] Companies Act 1985, s.396, as inserted by Companies Act 1989, s.93 (when brought into force); see *Re Molton Finance Ltd* [1968] Ch. 325.
[75] L.C.A. 1972, s.3(7); see *Property Discount Corporation Ltd v. Lyon Group Ltd* [1981] 1 W.L.R. 300.
[76] See [1982] Conv. 43 (D. M. Hare and T. Flanagan).
[77] L.C.A. 1972, ss.5, 17.
[78] *Calgary and Edmonton Land Co. Ltd v. Dobinson* [1974] Ch. 102; and see *Whittingham v. Whittingham* [1979] Fam. 9.
[79] *Greenhi Builders Ltd v. Allen* [1979] 1 W.L.R. 156.
[80] See below, p. 408.
[81] *Selim Ltd v. Bickenhall Engineering Ltd* [1981] 1 W.L.R. 1318 (under Leasehold Property (Repairs) Act 1938; below, p. 347).
[82] *Regan & Blackburn Ltd v. Rogers* [1985] 1 W.L.R. 870.
[83] See *Calgary and Edmonton Land Co. Ltd v. Dobinson* [1974] Ch. 102, at 105.
[84] *Calgary and Edmonton Land Co. Ltd v. Dobinson* [1974] Ch. 102.
[85] *Taylor v. Taylor* [1968] 1 W.L.R. 378.
[86] *Haslemere Estates Ltd v. Baker* [1982] 1 W.L.R. 1109. For proprietary estoppel, see above, p. 68; below, p. 483.

A claim in divorce proceedings for a property adjustment order is registrable if it specifies the particular land claimed,[87] or, if it does not, when the land is specified on the application for registration.[88] But there is no *lis pendens*, and so nothing is registrable, before the proceedings have been commenced[89]; and a registration will be vacated when the proceedings have terminated on the making of the order, even if other proceedings to set aside the order have been commenced.[90] Registration lasts for five years, and it may be renewed for successive periods of five years if the *lis* is still pending.[91]

(c) Writs and orders affecting land

This register[92] is confined to writs and orders enforcing judgments and orders of the court; it does not include writs commencing an action relating to land. There are three heads.

(i) Writs and orders affecting land issued or made by a court for the purpose of enforcing a judgment or recognisance: This head includes access orders,[93] and also charging orders, whereby the land of a judgment debtor is charged with the payment of the money due.[94] A charging order may now be made against a beneficial interest under a trust of land.[95] Before 1997 such an interest was not "land",[96] and so a charging order against it still appeared not to be registrable[97] but since the abolition of the doctrine of conversion[98] such a charging order must now be registrable. What was formerly known as a *Mareva injunction*[99] and is now known as a freezing injunction,[1] is not registrable, for it merely prevents a litigant from disposing of his assets pending trial.[2]

(ii) An order appointing a receiver or sequestrator of land: Sometimes a receiver is appointed in cases where no charging order can be made[3]; and in a dispute between the landlord and tenants of a block of flats, a receiver may be appointed to manage the flats pending trial.[4]

(iii) A bankruptcy order: Such an order is registrable whether or not the bankrupt's estate is known to include land.[5]

Registration remains effective for five years, but may be renewed for successive periods of five years.[6]

---

[87] *Whittingham v. Whittingham* [1979] Fam. 9.
[88] *Perez-Adamson v. Perez-Rivas* [1987] Fam. 89.
[89] *Kemmis v. Kemmis* [1988] 2 F.L.R. 223 at 239.
[90] *Sowerby v. Sowerby* (1982) 44 P. & C.R. 192.
[91] L.C.A. 1972, s.8.
[92] *ibid.*, s.6.
[93] See below, p. 450.
[94] Charging Orders Act 1979, s.3.
[95] *ibid.*, ss.1, 2. See *National Westminster Bank Ltd v. Stockman* [1981] 1 W.L.R. 67.
[96] See below, p. 283; and see *Irani Finance Ltd v. Singh* [1971] Ch. 59.
[97] Contrast *National Westminster Bank Ltd v. Allen* [1971] 2 Q.B. 718 (joint judgment against both joint tenants).
[98] T.L.A.T.A. 1996, s.3.
[99] See *Mareva Compania Naviera S.A. v. International Bulk Carriers S.A.* [1975] 2 Lloyd's Rep. 509.
[1] As a result of the Civil Procedure Rules 1998, Pt. 25.1(f).
[2] *Stockler v. Fourways Estates Ltd* [1984] 1 W.L.R. 25.
[3] See *Levermore v. Levermore* [1979] 1 W.L.R. 1277; Supreme Court Act 1981, s.37(4).
[4] *Clayhope Properties Ltd v. Evans* [1986] 1 W.L.R. 1223.
[5] L.C.A. 1972, s.6(1), as amended by Insolvency Act 1985, Sched. 8, para. 21.
[6] L.C.A. 1972, s.8.

(d) Deeds of arrangement[7]

The Deeds of Arrangement Act 1914[8] elaborately defines deeds of arrangement. For the present purpose, a deed of arrangement may be taken as any document whereby control over a debtor's property is given for the benefit of his creditors generally, or, if he is insolvent, for the benefit of three or more creditors. A common example is an assignment by a debtor of all his property to a trustee for all his creditors, made in the hope of his trading out of his actual or expected insolvency.

Registration is effective for five years and may be renewed for successive periods of five years.[9] The registration may be effected by the trustee of the deed or by any creditor assenting to or taking the benefit of the deed.[10]

(e) Annuities[11]

This register, opened in 1855, was closed in 1925.[12] It is highly unlikely that anyone granted an annuity before 1926 can still be alive so this register must now be virtually, if not completely, obsolete.

2. Mode of Registration

(a) Land charges

All land charges must be registered in the name of the estate owner whose estate is to be affected.[13] The estate owner is the owner of a legal estate.[14] Normally this does not give rise to any difficulty as the estate owner usually creates the charge. Charges created by beneficiaries of their beneficial interests under trusts are not registrable.[15] However in one common case there is a trap. If V contracts to sell land to P who then contracts to sell it to S, it is against V, the estate owner, and not P, that S must register his estate contract; registration against P will not be effective even if P later acquires the legal estate.[16] Yet S will often be ignorant of the identity and even the existence of V. To be safe S should stipulate for the name of the estate owner to be disclosed as soon as contracts are exchanged.[17]

(b) Other registers

Pending actions and writs and orders affecting land are registrable in the name of the estate owner or other person whose estate or interest is intended to be or is affected.[18] It will be noted that this is not limited to estate owners. Deeds of arrangement are registrable in the name of the debtor.[19]

---

[7] *ibid.*, s.7.
[8] *ibid.*, s.1.
[9] *ibid.*, s.8.
[10] *ibid.*, s.7.
[11] *ibid.*, s.1, Sched. 1.
[12] See M. & W. (5th ed.), pp. 172, 173. For the registration of annuities created after 1925, see above, p. 95.
[13] L.C.A. 1972, s.3(1).
[14] *ibid.*, s.17(1), applying the definition in L.P.A. 1925, s.205(1)(v).
[15] See above, p. 95.
[16] *Barrett v. Hilton Developments Ltd* [1975] Ch. 237.
[17] See *Patman v. Harland* (1881) 17 Ch.D. 353 at 359.
[18] L.C.A. 1972, ss.5(4), 6(2).
[19] *ibid.*, s.7(1).

(c) The name

Registration should be against the estate owner's full correct name as it appears in the conveyance to him, even if he is generally known by another name, or another name appears in his birth certificate[20] (in the event of any doubt, there is no reason why registration should not be made in more than one name). This ensures that the name will appear in its correct place in the index and will be revealed on a search made in the correct name. A registration in a name which may fairly be described as a version of the correct name (for example "Frank" for "Francis") is not a nullity but will bind all except those who make an official search in the correct name and obtain a certificate which does not disclose the entry.[21] But registration is ineffective if it omits one of the names of the estate owner.[22] If the estate owner is dead and his estate has not yet been administered, registration should be effected not against his name but against the names of his personal representatives or, if there are none and he died intestate, against the President of the Family Division.[23]

3. Effects of registration and non-registration

(a) Effect of registration

(i) Notice: By the Law of Property Act 1925,[24] registration under the Land Charges Acts constitutes actual notice of the interest registered to all persons and for all purposes connected with the land affected. There are statutory exceptions to this rule[25] (in particular, it does not apply to a purchaser entering into a contract for the sale of land, where only actual or imputed knowledge suffices.[26] However, this exception only regulates the position as between vendor and purchaser: if the purchaser completes such a contract, he will have notice and so will be bound). But the general effect of this provision is to prevent any person claiming to be a purchaser without notice of a registered interest.

(ii) Names register: The most serious defect of the system from the point of view of a purchaser is that the registers are registers of the names of persons; an incumbrance is registered against the name of the estate owner at the time and not against the land. Thus on a purchase of 14 Newcastle Street it is not possible to search against 14 Newcastle Street, and a search must be made against the names of all previous owners of the land. The rights most likely to concern a purchaser, namely, Classes C, D and F, only became registrable after 1925 (Class F only in 1968), but in course of time the cost of searches has become considerable. It assists if each purchaser in turn preserves the certificate of the search he made when purchasing the land, and hands the certificates on with the title deeds so that the subsequent purchasers can rely upon them; there can of course now be only one more purchaser since any purchase will trigger compulsory registration of title.

---

[20] *Standard Property Investment Plc. v. British Plastics Federation* (1987) 53 P. & C.R. 25.

[21] See *Oak Co-operative B.S. v. Blackburn* [1968] Ch. 730, where the system of indexing is described. See below, p. 89, for searches.

[22] *Diligent Finance Co. Ltd v. Alleyne* (1972) 23 P. & C.R. 346.

[23] See [1979] Conv. 249 (A.M. Prichard); [1986] Conv. 237 (J.E. Adams); (1986) 83 L.S.Gaz. 2127 (E.J. Pryer). A reform proposed at one stage was to validate registration against the name of the deceased: (1989) Law Com. No. 184, para. 2.7.

[24] s.198.

[25] See below, p. 103 (compensation scheme), p. 514 (mortgage deeds).

[26] L.P.A. 1969, s.24, removing for land charges (but not local land charges) the difficulty arising from *Re Forsey and Hollebone's Contract* [1927] 2 Ch. 379: see *Rignall Developments Ltd v. Halil* [1987] 1 E.G.L.R. 193.

(iii) Compensation scheme: In 1956, when 30 years had elapsed since 1926, it became possible that the names of persons against whom charges were registered were contained in documents of a date earlier than the root of title (which at that time had to be at least 30 years old) which the purchaser was consequently not entitled to see. This possibility increased with each passing year and the situation was further aggravated in 1969 when the minimum length of title which had to be shown was reduced to 15 years.[27] The problem is that, despite the fact that a purchaser may be unable to discover the relevant names, he will nevertheless be deemed to have actual notice of the charges registered against those names. Since it has at all times been impossible to reorganise the registers on a territorial basis, the only long-term solution was to press on with the extension of compulsory registration of title.[28] Since 1990 this has extended to the whole of England and Wales and since April 1, 1998 has been triggered by gifts as well as sales, and this continues.[29] As an interim measure financial compensation at public expense was introduced for purchasers saddled with registered but undisclosed and undiscoverable land charges. The two main requirements are that the purchaser should not have any actual or imputed knowledge of the charge (the deemed actual notice from registration is disregarded), and that the estate owner against whom the charge is registered should not be a party to any transaction in the title which the purchaser was entitled to see or be concerned with any event in its devolution.[30]

(iv) Lessees: The doctrine that registration constitutes notice *per se* may work especial hardship in the case of lessees. Where a lease is granted by a tenant in fee simple at a low rent in consideration of a lump sum (technically known as a "fine"), the lessee usually stipulates that he shall be entitled to investigate the lessor's title, whereas if the lease is granted at a rent which reflects the occupation value of the property (technically known as a "rack rent"), the lessee usually takes it for granted that the lessor is able to grant the lease and so does not investigate his title. Further, by statute,[31] under an open contract[32] for the grant of a lease the lessee is not entitled to investigate the freeholder's title; this is also the case when an existing lease is assigned. This causes two problems.

(i) In respect of leases granted before 1926, of which there are many still in existence, an assignee of a lease is fixed with notice of all that he would have discovered had he made a full investigation of the freehold title (this is on the grounds that he could have insisted on a provision in the contract entitling him to investigate this title). This rule, known as the rule in *Patman v. Harland*,[33] has been abolished for leases granted after 1925.[34]

(ii) In respect of all leases granted after 1925, the prospective lessee will be able to search against the name of the lessor, but if he is not entitled to investigate the lessor's title he will not know the names of the previous owners of the land and so will not be able to discover land charges such as restrictive covenants registered against their names. Nevertheless, since registration is notice to all persons and for

[27] L.P.A. 1969, s.23; above, pp. 62–63.
[28] See Report of Committee on Land Charges 1956 (Cmd. 9825).
[29] See above, p. 14; below, p. 117.
[30] L.P.A. 1969, s.25. For the first claim, see Chief Land Registrar's Report (1988–1989) para. 56.
[31] L.P.A. 1925, s.44, replacing Vendor and Purchaser Act 1874, s.2.
[32] Below, p. 155.
[33] The rule to the contrary in *Patman v. Harland* (1881) 17 Ch.D. 353 was abolished.
[34] L.P.A. 1925, s.44(5).

all purposes connected with the land,[35] the lessee is deemed to have notice of the covenants and, to make matters worse, is excluded from the compensation scheme.[36]

(iii) An assignee of any lease, whenever granted, will as of right know only the name of the person who was owner of the land at the time when the lease was granted (because this will be on the lease) and the current owner (who will be receiving the rent). Although he will therefore be able to search against those two names, he will not know the names of anyone else who has owned the land, whether before or after the grant of the lease; and since the person assigning the lease to him is unlikely to know them either, a contractual provision entitling the assignee to investigate the lessor's title may not help either. Consequently, the assignee will be even more vulnerable to undiscoverable land charges such as restrictive covenants.

The position may be summarised thus:

(i) Lease and restrictive covenant both made before 1926: any assignee of the lease is caught by *Patman v. Harland*.

(ii) Lease and restrictive covenant both made after 1925: both the original lessee and any assignee of the lease are caught by the provisions for the registration of land charges.

(iii) Restrictive covenant made before 1926, lease made after 1925: here alone is the position of the original lessee and any assignees improved; they are safe unless they have obtained notice in some other way, for *Patman v. Harland* does not apply and the restrictive covenant, being made before 1926, is not registrable.[37]

(b) Effect of non-registration

(i) Categories: The effect of non-registration varies according to the interest. There are two main categories:

(i) the incumbrance may be void against a purchaser for value of any interest in the land; or

(ii) the incumbrance may be void against a purchaser for money or money's worth of a legal estate in the land.

There are two differences between (i) and (ii): a purchaser of an equitable interest is protected by (i) but not by (ii); and, since marriage is "value" but is not "money or money's worth", in the case of land settled on an ante-nuptial marriage settlement the spouses and their issue will be protected by (i) but not by (ii). In each case "purchaser" has an extended meaning and includes a lessee, mortgagee or other person taking an interest in land for value.

---

[35] *ibid.*, s.198. This prevails over s.44(5): see *White v. Bijou Mansions Ltd* [1937] Ch. 610 at 619.
[36] L.P.A. 1969, s.25(9), (10). For the scheme see above, p. 103.
[37] See, *e.g. Shears v. Wells* [1936] 1 All E.R. 832.

(ii) Effect: The effect of non-registration may be expressed as follows.[38]

(i) In general, whichever register is concerned, non-registration of any registrable matter in the appropriate register makes it void against a purchaser for value of any interest in the land.

(ii) If, however, a land charge falls within Class C(iv) (estate contracts) or Class D, and was created after 1925, non-registration makes it void only against a purchaser of a legal estate for money or money's worth.

(iii) Bankruptcy petitions (registrable as pending actions) and the title of trustees in bankruptcy under bankruptcy orders (registrable as writs and orders) are void only against a bona fide purchaser of a legal estate for money or money's worth.

(iv) Any other pending action is void against a purchaser for value of any interest in the land, provided he had no express notice of it.

(iii) "Void": The courts have given full and literal effect to the word "void"; "void" really does mean void. An unregistered interest will be void against a purchaser even if he had full knowledge of it, even if he was not acting in good faith, and even though the owner of the interest was in possession of the land concerned.[39] In the leading case,[40] a son was the tenant of a farm owned by his father. The father then granted the son an option for 10 years to purchase the farm at a fixed price. Some six years later, after the farm had nearly doubled in value and family disputes had arisen, the father conveyed the farm to his wife for £500, with the common intention of defeating the son's option, which had not been registered. It was held that the option was void against the wife. The son had a claim for breach of contract against the father,[41] a claim for conspiracy against the father and the wife[42] (provided a sufficient intent to injure was shown[43]), and a claim against his solicitor for negligence in failing to register the option[44]: but he had no claim to the farm. Had the land been registered, the actual occupation of it by the son would have conferred adequate protection[45]; but there is no corresponding provision for unregistered land. A section of the Law of Property Act 1925[46] provides that the interest of any person in possession or in actual occupation of land is not to be prejudiced by Part I of the Act; but Part I does not contain the provisions relating to land charges.[47] In any case, the section is confined to interests to which the person is entitled "in right of such possession or occupation", and that would not include the option above. By construing "void" simply and strictly all concerned are relieved of the burden of litigious inquiries into the motives and state of mind of the purchaser; a clear and definite system for the protection of title to land is not to be destroyed by reading into the Act

---

[38] L.C.A. 1972, ss.4, 5(7), (8), 6(4), (5), (6), 7(2), Sched. 1, para. 4, as amended by Insolvency Act 1985, Sched. 8, para. 21, Sched. 10, Pt. III.
[39] L.P.A. 1925, s.199; *Midland Bank Trust Co. Ltd v. Green* [1981] A.C. 513.
[40] *ibid.*
[41] *ibid.*, at 526.
[42] *Midland Bank Trust Co. Ltd v. Green (No. 3)* [1982] Ch. 529; but see [1985] C.L.J. 280 at 293–295 (M.P. Thompson).
[43] See *Lonrho Ltd v. Shell Petroleum Co. Ltd* [1982] A.C. 173 at 189.
[44] *Midland Bank Trust Co. Ltd v. Hett, Stubbs & Kemp* [1979] Ch. 384: see *Midland Bank Trust Co. Ltd v. Green* [1981] A.C. 513 at 526; but contrast *Bell v. Peter Browne & Co.* [1990] 2 Q.B. 495.
[45] Below, p. 123.
[46] s.14.
[47] Originally it did: see L.P.A. 1922, ss.14, 32, Sched. 7. The change seems to have been an oversight.

provisions to protect a person who has failed to protect himself by registering his land charge.[48]

4. Searches and priority notices

(a) Searches

The means by which an intending purchaser of land can discover registrable incumbrances is by a search. This may be made in person,[49] which today means travelling to Plymouth and looking at the screen on which the results of the computerised search of the Land Charges Register appear. However, it is advisable to obtain an official certificate of search, since:

(i) it is conclusive in favour of a purchaser or intending purchaser whose application correctly specifies the persons[50] and the land,[51] and so frees him from registered rights which it fails to disclose[52];

(ii) it protects a solicitor or trustee who makes it from liability for any error in the certificate[53]; and

(iii) it provides protection against incumbrances registered in the interval between search and completion. If a purchaser completes his transaction before the expiration of the fifteenth working day after the date of the certificate he is not affected by any entry made after the date of the certificate and before completion, unless it is made pursuant to a priority notice[54] entered on the register before the certificate was issued.[55]

If the official certificate of search mistakenly fails to disclose a charge properly registered before the search, the owner of the charge will be wrongly deprived of his rights and may suffer loss. Damages for negligence against those responsible may be obtained,[56] though in the absence of fraud, individual employees of the Registry are not liable for any discrepancy between what is shown by the official search certificate as the particulars in the request for search and those actually stated in the request for a search.[57]

A single search is effective for all divisions of all five registers: but this does not include local land charges which have to be the subject of a separate search of the registers maintained by the relevant local authority.

(b) Priority notices

Special provision has been made to provide for a rapid sequence of transactions, such as the creation of a restrictive covenant followed immediately by the creation of a mortgage before there has been time to register the covenant. Thus if V is selling land to P, who is both raising

---

[48] See *Midland Bank Trust Co. Ltd v. Green* [1981] A.C. 513 at 528, 530.
[49] L.C.A. 1972, s.9.
[50] See *Oak Co-operative B.S. v. Blackburn* [1968] Ch. 730; above, p. 102.
[51] See *Du Sautoy v. Symes* [1967] Ch. 1146.
[52] L.C.A. 1972, s.10(4): see *Stock v. Wanstead and Woodford B.C.* [1962] 2 Q.B. 479 (local land charge).
[53] L.C.A. 1972, s.12.
[54] See below.
[55] L.C.A. 1972, s.11(5), (6). For corresponding provisions for registered land, see below, p. 108.
[56] See *Ministry of Housing and Local Government v. Sharp* [1970] 2 Q.B. 223 (local land charge), not invalidated by *Murphy v. Brentwood D.C.* [1991] 1 A.C. 398: see at 486.
[57] L.C.A. 1972, s.10(6).

the purchase money by means of a loan on mortgage from M and entering into a restrictive covenant back in favour of V, both the relevant documents, the conveyance of the land from V to P which will also contain the grant of the restrictive covenant by P to V, and the mortgage of the land by P to M, will have to take effect simultaneously. P will need the funds being lent to him by M in order to be able to pay the purchase price to V. M will not release the funds without his mortgage and V will not convey the land without having received the purchase money. In practice, both documents will be executed in advance and will be held in escrow (to the order of the party executing them) pending receipt of the sum in question.

In such a case, V cannot register the restrictive covenant against the name of P before the mortgage to M takes effect because the restrictive covenant and the mortgage come into existence simultaneously. On the face of things, that means that the restrictive covenant, although valid as against P, will be void against M, a purchaser for money or money's worth of a legal estate. However, V can avoid this result by availing himself of the machinery of the priority notice. To do this, he must give a priority notice to the registrar at least 15 days before the creation of the restrictive covenant, and then, if he registers his land charge within 30 days of the entry of the priority notice in the register, the registration dates back to the moment of the creation of the restrictive covenant, *i.e.* to the execution of the conveyance from V to P; once again, days on which the registry is not open to the public are excluded.[58] The priority notice must be given 15 days before completion in order to allow the expiry of the 15 days' period of protection given to those who made official searches before the priority notice was lodged.[59]

Priority notices are not, of course, confined to restrictive covenants, but apply to all land charges.

5. The vacation of entries

An entry on the various registers at the Land Registry may be effected merely by making an application in the proper form[60]; registration is automatic, without the Land Registry investigating whether there is anything to justify the entry. As registration may effectively paralyse dealing with the land by the owner, provision is made for the court to order the vacation (*i.e.* removal) of any entries on the registers. There is an inherent jurisdiction to do this,[61] and also a wide statutory jurisdiction which now applies to all the registers and not only the land charges register.[62] This jurisdiction may be used to vacate entries not only of unjustified claims but also of interests that have ceased to be effective, such as contracts which have expired or have been rescinded (however, in these cases the person registering the charge will usually apply to have the entry cancelled).[63] There is also power to vacate the entry of a pending land action if the proceedings are not being prosecuted in good faith.[64] Applications under this jurisdiction can be made speedily, without any need first to issue a claim form, by the owner making an application to the court, and the jurisdiction is

---

[58] *ibid.*, s.11.
[59] Above.
[60] Land Charges Rules 1974, rr. 5, 6.
[61] *Calgary and Edmonton Land Co. Ltd v. Dobinson* [1974] Ch. 102.
[62] L.C.A. 1972, s.1(6); *Northern Developments (Holdings) Ltd v. U.D.T. Securities Ltd* [1976] 1 W.L.R. 1230; and see *Tucker v. Hutchinson* (1987) 54 P. & C.R. 106 at 112.
[63] See Land Charges Rules 1974, rr. 9–12.
[64] L.C.A. 1972, s.5(10).

exercised with a certain robustness.[65] Sometimes the court will refuse to order the entry to be vacated only if the person who has made the entry is prepared to undertake to pay the landowner damages if at the trial it is established that the entry was wrongly made.[66]

Sect. 2. Effect of a conveyance

Before summarising the effect of a conveyance of unregistered land on the legal and equitable interests in that land, the greater complexity of equitable interests requires them to be considered first; yet it must at all times be remembered that legal interests bind the whole world unless they can be overreached and, as between themselves, rank in the order of their creation.

1. Equitable interests

In determining whether or not a purchaser of land takes subject to equitable interests in it, there are three major heads to consider;

    (i) overreaching;

    (ii) non-registration of land charges; and

    (iii) the purchaser without notice.

The broad picture is that the expansion of (i) and (ii) has reduced but not destroyed the importance of (iii).

(a) Overreaching

The system of overreaching, whereby rights in land become corresponding rights in the purchase money, has been considered mainly in relation to settlements under the Settled Land Act 1925 and trusts of land.[67] But there are other overreaching conveyances which take effect if the purchase money is paid to trustees or others in accordance with the law.[68]

    (i) If a mortgagee exercised his power of sale on some default by the mortgagor, this overreaches the rights of all subsequent mortgagees (even if legal) and of the mortgagor, and these become attached to the money in the hands of the mortgagee, under a trust, though subject to the mortgagee's right to repayment of his loan, interest thereon and costs.[69]

    (ii) A conveyance by personal representatives overreaches the rights of the beneficiaries under the will or intestacy.[70]

    (iii) A conveyance made under an order of the court, such as to remove incumbrances, overreaches all equitable interests and powers which are bound by the order.[71]

---

[65] *The Rawlplug Co. Ltd v. Kamvale Properties Ltd* (1969) 20 P. & C.R. 32 at 40; *Woolf Project Management Ltd v. Woodtrek Ltd* [1988] 1 E.G.L.R. 179.
[66] See *Tucker v. Hutchinson* (1987) 54 P. & C.R. 106, citing the cases (all on registered land).
[67] Above, pp. 84, 91.
[68] L.P.A. 1925, s.2(1).
[69] *ibid.*, ss.2(1), 104, 105; below, p. 505.
[70] Below, p. 200.
[71] L.P.A. 1925, ss.2(1), 50.

(b) Non-registration of land charges

If a land charge is not duly registered it is void against a purchaser; the charge is overridden and destroyed, not overreached. The varying details of this have already been considered.[72]

(c) The purchaser without notice

The doctrine of purchaser without notice, though greatly reduced in its ambit, can still apply in a somewhat motley collection of cases, in all of which the equitable interests in question have been held to be capable of binding the whole world other than a bona fide purchaser for value of a legal estate without notice. The various situations can perhaps be classified as follows.

(i) Excluded interests: Some interests have been expressly made not registrable, as apparently being otherwise protected.

(i) A mortgage protected by a deposit of documents relating to the legal estate affected is not registrable[73]; the absence of the deeds will normally put a subsequent purchaser on inquiry, and so, if the mortgage is equitable (as it will be if it is not created by deed), he cannot claim to be a purchaser without notice.

(ii) Restrictive covenants and equitable easements are not registrable if they arose before 1926, or, in the case of restrictive covenants, if they are between a lessor and a lessee,[74] when the lease will normally disclose them to a purchaser. However, where the covenant binds not the lessor's reversion in the land, but other land of his, a purchaser of that other land will usually not see the lease and so will take free of covenants in question (this result has been criticised).[75]

(ii) Omitted interests: Some interests, without being expressly excluded, have simply been omitted from the provisions for overreaching and registration.

(i) Equitable rights of entry have not been made registrable. Thus the grant of a right to enter land and remove fixtures from it is not registrable,[76] nor is a right reserved on an assignment of a lease for the assignor (who retains no interest in the land) to re-enter the land and retake it for breach of covenant.[77]

(ii) Until 1997, where A held land on trust for B absolutely (B being *sui juris*) there was nothing to make B's equitable interest under the bare trust either registrable or overreachable.[78] However, since 1996 bare trusts are trusts of land and so can now be overreached.[79]

---

[72] Above, pp. 102 *et seq.*
[73] Above, p. 94.
[74] Above, p. 97.
[75] *Dartstone Ltd v. Cleveland Petroleum Co. Ltd* [1969] 1 W.L.R. 1807 above, p. 96.
[76] *Poster v. Slough Estates Ltd* [1969] 1 Ch. 495.
[77] *Shiloh Spinners Ltd v. Harding* [1973] A.C. 691.
[78] Consider *Hodgson v. Marks* [1971] Ch. 892. A must obey B's directions.
[79] T.L.A.T.A. 1996, s.1.

(iii) The fringes of overreaching and non-registration: Various equitable interests which appear to fall within the provisions for overreaching or non-registration will nevertheless been held to fall outside their operation.

(i) An overreachable interest will not be overreached if the statutory requirements are not observed,[80] as where the purchase money is not properly paid to the trustees.[81]

(ii) A registrable interest will not be void against a purchaser who merely gives value (such as marriage) where the statute requires money or money's worth to be given,[82] as for estate contracts and post–1925 restrictive covenants.[83]

(iii) An equitable easement for an uncertain period, such as so long as certain foundations stand on certain land, created by proprietary estoppel or acquiescence, has been held not to be registrable as an equitable easement on the ground that it could not have existed at law before 1926.[84]

2. Legal and equitable interests: a summary

In the briefest possible form, the effect of a conveyance on sale on legal and equitable interests in the land may be shown as follows.

(a) The purchaser takes subject to all legal rights.

(i) Exceptions: He takes free from—

(i) the few legal rights which are void against him for want of registration; and

(ii) the few legal rights which are overreached.

(b) The purchaser takes subject to all equitable rights.

Exceptions: He takes free from—

(i) equitable rights which are void against him for want of registration: notice is irrelevant;

(ii) the many equitable rights which are overreached, such as under a settlement under the Settled Land Act 1925 or a trust of land: again, notice is irrelevant; and

(iii) other equitable rights, relatively few in number, in respect of which he can show either that he is a bona fide purchaser of a legal estate for value without notice, or else that he claims through such a person.

---

[80] Consider *Caunce v. Caunce* [1969] 1 W.L.R. 286; (1969) 33 Conv. 240 (J. F. Garner); also *Williams & Glyn's Bank Ltd v. Boland* [1981] A.C. 487.
[81] Consider *Kingsnorth Finance Co. Ltd v. Tizard* [1986] 1 W.L.R. 783.
[82] See *McCarthy & Stone Ltd v. Julian S. Hodge & Co. Ltd* [1971] 1 W.L.R. 1547 (no legal estate); [1976] *Current Legal Problems* 26 (D.J. Hayton).
[83] Above, p. 103.
[84] *E. R. Ives Investment Ltd v. High* [1967] 2 Q.B. 379. L.P.A. 1925, ss.1(2)(a), 1(3), 4(1) (as cited at 395), seem to provide little support.

PART 5—ASPECTS APPLYING ONLY TO REGISTERED CONVEYANCING

Sect. 1. Introductory

1. History

Today, registration of title is of great and increasing importance; but it is by no means new. Acts were passed in 1862 and 1875,[85] providing for voluntary registration of title, but not until the Land Transfer Act 1897 made registration of title compulsory on dealings with land in the County of London were any substantial numbers of titles registered. The present principal Act is the ill-drafted Land Registration Act 1925, which, with a series of amending Acts, may be cited as the Land Registration Acts 1925 to 1997.[86] These Acts are supplemented by the Land Registration Rules 1925, as amended, and a number of other statutory rules.[87] All this legislation will be repealed by the Land Registration Act 2002 when it comes into force[88]; it is expected that this will occur sometime in 2003. By then the necessary amendments will have been made to the Land Registration Rules, which will presumably also be replaced in their entirety (no new Rules had been published by the time that this edition went to press). The vast majority of the work of conveyancing today is estimated to concern registered land, which will become increasingly and overwhelmingly predominant.

2. Basis of the system

The basic idea is to replace the separate investigation of title that takes place on every purchase by a title guaranteed by the State. In the case of unregistered land, a purchaser must satisfy himself from the abstract or epitome of title, the deeds, his requisitions on title, his searches and his inspection of the land that the vendor has power to sell the land and that it is subject to no undisclosed incumbrances. In the case of registered land, on the other hand, the purchaser can discover from the mere inspection of the register whether the vendor has power to sell the land and what the more important incumbrances are; the other incumbrances must be investigated in much the same way as in the case of unregistered land. The complexity of rights in land is such as to render it impossible to make the transfer of registered land as simple as the transfer of shares registered in the books of a company, but the present system of registration of title may be said to go almost as far on that road as is practicable.

3. Classification of rights

The system of registration of title in no way amounts to a separate code of land law although a few of the rules of the substantive law do differ depending on whether land is registered or unregistered, and several more will do so when the Land Registration Act 2002 comes into force. In the main it is concerned with the conveyancing aspects of land law, *i.e.* actual or potential transfers of rights existing under the general law, and in the main it leaves the basis

---

[85] Land Registry Act 1862; Land Transfer Act 1875.
[86] See Land Registration Act 1936; Land Registration Act 1966; Land Registration and Land Charges Act 1971; Land Registration Act 1986, Land Registration Act 1997. See also Administration of Justice Act 1977; Land Registration Act 1988; and certain Acts on special subjects, such as Housing Acts 1980 and 1985.
[87] They are printed in the standard work, Ruoff & Roper, *The Law and Practice of Registered Conveyancing* (looseleaf), Appendix B.
[88] This new legislation followed Law Com. No. 254 and is described in Law Com. No. 271.

of this unaffected. In this connection, the differing classes of interests in land must be distinguished.

(a) Unregistered land

In very broad terms, on a purchase of unregistered land, rights in the land fall into three main categories:

(i) the estate or interest that the purchaser is buying;

(ii) rights adverse to the land which, being legal, will bind the purchaser except in the few cases where they are overreached or are void for want of registration;

(iii) other rights adverse to the land which are equitable, and so, if not overreached or void for want of registration, will bind the purchaser unless he takes the estate for value in good faith without notice of them.

(b) Registered land

On a purchase of registered land, there is a similar but not exactly corresponding division:

(i) the estate or interest that the purchaser is buying will usually be a registrable interest: a legal estate or interest which is registrable with its own title (legal easements, profits *à prendre*, mortgages and rights of entry are not registrable interests and after completion the purchaser will have to protect them as minor interests on his vendor's registered title);

(ii) rights adverse to the land which will override registration and so, if they are not overreached, will bind the purchaser whether or not their existence is disclosed by the register or otherwise;

(iii) other rights adverse to the land which will not bind the purchaser if they are overreached or if he purchased for value under a registered disposition and they have not been protected by some entry on the register.

4. Other registrations

If the title to land is registered, there is no question of registration in the land charges register, for entries on the land register take the place of this. But entries must still be made in the local land charges registers. Further, most charges created by a company for securing money require registration in the companies charges register in addition to protection by an entry on the land register.[89]

5. Open register

On December 3, 1990, the land register was opened to public inspection, with the right to obtain copies of it.[90] Previously, nobody could inspect it or obtain copies of the entries on the register without the authority of the registered proprietor of the land,[91] though on a sale or other disposition (except a lease or charge) the vendor was obliged to give the purchaser an

---

[89] Companies Act 1985, ss.396, 397, as inserted by Companies Act 1989, s.93.
[90] L.R.A. 1988, s.1; S.I. 1990 No. 1359.
[91] L.R.A. 1925, ss.112, 112A.

authority to inspect the register.[92] Further, an index map, a parcels index and a list of pending applications were[93] (and still are) open to public inspection, making it possible to discover whether or not any particular property has been or is about to be registered.

6. Electronic conveyancing

The Land Registration Act 2002[94] has created a framework by which it will in due course be possible to create and to transfer interests in registered land electronically. The Act has done so by enabling the formal documents to be executed electronically[95] and by providing for an electronic communications network which will be secure.[96] Access to the network is to be controlled by the Land Registry. This is because it is envisaged that the execution of the formal documents and their registration will be a simultaneous process to be initiated by conveyancers.[97] The Land Registry will also be obliged to make arrangements for access to the network by persons who wish to do their own conveyancing.[98] Both conveyancing practitioners and the Land Registry will have to develop new ways of working if the system is to be established. It is therefore envisaged that it will be introduced in stages, starting with only the simplest transactions and gradually progressing. This will be regulated by rules which the Act gives the Lord Chancellor power to make.[99] He has also been given power, subject to appropriate consultation, to make electronic conveyancing compulsory[1]; this is because some of the benefits of electronic conveyancing can be maximised only if it is used universally. However, compulsory electronic conveyancing will only become feasible when it has become the predominant way of carrying out transactions; consequently, this is likely to be many years away.

7. Dispute resolution

Under the present law, objections to applications to register titles and to the registration of dispositions of registered land are resolved by the Chief Land Registrar,[2] subject to an appeal to the High Court.[3] He also has the power to refer disputes directly to the High Court if he feels this to be appropriate.[4] This jurisdiction is in practice now exercised by the solicitor to the Land Registry. The Land Registration Act 2002 has created a new office, that of an adjudicator to the Land Registry,[5] who will have these powers in respect of disputes which the solicitor to the Land Registry has not been able to resolve by agreement. The adjudicator will also have two wholly new jurisdictions: first, he will hear appeals against any refusal by the Land Registry to give access to the electronic communications network; secondly, he will have the power to make an order rectifying or setting aside a document which disposes of a registered estate or charge in some way which would be reflected on the register[6]: the

---

[92] *ibid.*, s.110(1).
[93] L.R.R. 1925, rr. 8, 10, 12; the new L.R.R. will presumably deal with this.
[94] L.R.A 2002, ss.91–95.
[95] L.R.A 2002, s.91.
[96] L.R.A 2002, s.92 & Sched. 5.
[97] L.R.A 2002, s.93.
[98] L.R.A 2002, s.92 & Sched. 5.
[99] L.R.A 2002, s.95.
[1] L.R.A 2002, s.93.
[2] L.R.R., r. 299; the new L.R.R. will presumably deal with this.
[3] L.R.R., r. 300; the new L.R.R. will presumably deal with this.
[4] L.R.R., r. 299 (3); the new L.R.R. will presumably deal with this.
[5] L.R.A 2002, s.107.
[6] L.R.A 2002, s.108.

absence of any such power in the Chief Land Registrar at present means that all such matters have had to be referred to the High Court. The solicitor to the Land Registry also in practice exercises the jurisdiction of the Chief Land Register to order rectification of the register,[7] a jurisdiction which will continue to be vested in him when the Land Registration Act 2002 comes into force.[8]

8. Fundamental principles

Two linked principles are fundamental to registered land.

(a) Registration confers title

In unregistered conveyancing, the vendor's estate in the land passes to the purchaser as soon as the conveyance is executed. In registered conveyancing, the execution of the transfer by the vendor confers no estate on the purchaser. It is registration that vests the title in the purchaser in accordance with the register.[9] Registration is treated as having effect "as of" the day when the purchaser delivers the relevant documents to the appropriate District Registry of the Land Registry.[10]

(b) Registration is conclusive

Registration is conclusive of title. When a title is first registered, the registration confers a new statutory title on the registered proprietor, even if his previous title was defective or he had no title at all, as where he claims under forged title deeds. The act of registration confers the statutory title on the proprietor,[11] and gives him "a new root of title".[12] He holds this title subject to any interests protected by entries on the register and to any interests which override registration. In principle he holds free from all other interests,[13] even if he has full notice of them; the doctrine of notice for unregistered land has no application to registered land, even by analogy.[14] In practice, however, the first registered proprietor will have acquired title to the land in question under the system of unregistered conveyancing and he will continue to be bound by any interests to which he took subject under that system even if they neither override registration nor are protected on the register at the time of first registration. Subject to this qualification and to interests which override registration, the register is conclusive and can be relied on by subsequent registered proprietors. A second or subsequent registered proprietor who purchases the land for valuable consideration which is other than nominal (valuable consideration at present includes marriage consideration but will not do so when the Land Registration Act 2002 comes into force[15]) does indeed acquire title free from all interests other than those which are protected on the register or override registration but free from all other interests,[16] even if he has full notice of them. The one qualification to this doctrine is that there are limited powers to rectify the register in order to correct errors; but

---

[7] L.R.A. 1925, s.82; below, p. 138.
[8] L.R.A. 2002, s.65 & Sched. 5, para. 5.
[9] L.R.A. 1925, s.69(1); L.R.A. 2002, ss.29, 30.
[10] L.R.R. 1925, r. 83(2); the new L.R.R. will presumably deal with this.
[11] L.R.A. 1925, ss.5–12; L.R.A. 2002, ss.9–10.
[12] *Kitney v. MEPC Ltd* [1977] 1 W.L.R. 981 at 993.
[13] L.R.A. 1925, ss.20, 23, 33, 69 (see *Morelle Ltd v. Wakeling* [1955] 2 Q.B. 379 at 411); L.R.A. 2002, ss.11–12.
[14] *Williams & Glyn's Bank Ltd v. Boland* [1981] A.C. 487 at 504.
[15] L.R.A. 2002, s.132(1).
[16] L.R.A. 1925, ss.20, 23, 33, 69; and see *Morelle Ltd v. Wakeling* [1955] 2 Q.B. 379 at 411; L.R.A. 2002, ss.28–31, 129(1).

normally these are subject to the payment of compensation to any person thereby suffering loss.[17] Subject to this, a registered title is indefeasible.

Sect. 2. Interests in registered land

The three types of interest in registered land (namely registrable interests, interests which override registration and interests which require protection on the register) will now be considered in turn.

1. Registrable interests

(a) Interests which can be registered

The only interests in respect of which a proprietor can be registered are estates and interests capable of subsisting as legal estates[18] but not all of them are capable of being registered. At present, the following are registerable:

(i) a fee simple absolute in possession in any "land" as defined in the Law of Property Act 1925[19]: this therefore includes a fee simple absolute in possession in an advowson (the right of presenting a clergyman to a living[20]);

(ii) a term of years absolute with more than 21 years to run in any land: this therefore includes a term of years absolute in an advowson (other leases are not registrable interests but they either override registration or require protection on the register; and they nevertheless take effect as if they were registered dispositions)[21]; and

(iii) a legal rentcharge.

Of the remaining legal estates, legal mortgages take effect as registered charges, easements and profits *à prendre* are either interests which override registration or interests which require protection, and rights of entry do not require protection apart from the interest over which they are exercisable. When the Land Registration Act 2002 comes into force, the categories of terms of years absolute in possession which are registrable interests will be increased[22] and two further legal estates will become registrable interests.[23] The estates capable of being registered will then be:

(i) a fee simple absolute in possession in any "land" as defined in the Law of Property Act 1925[24]—this will continue to include a fee simple absolute in possession in an advowson (the right of presenting a clergyman to a living[25]);

---

[17] See below, pp. 138 *et seq.*
[18] L.R.A. 1925, s.2.; L.R.A. 2002, s.3.
[19] L.P.A. 1925, s.205(1)(ix).
[20] Such rights are subject to important restrictions, *e.g.* no advowson may be sold after two vacancies of the benefice have occurred after July 14, 1924: see Benefices Act 1898; Benefices Act 1898 (Amendment) Measure 1923.
[21] L.R.A. 1925, s.19(2).
[22] L.R.A. 2002, s.4 (1)(c), (d), (e) and (2).
[23] L.R.A. 2002, s.3.
[24] L.P.A. 1925, s.205(1)(ix).
[25] Such rights are subject to important restrictions, *e.g.* no advowson may be sold after two vacancies of the benefice have occurred after July 14, 1924: see Benefices Act 1898; Benefices Act 1898 (Amendment) Measure 1923.

(ii) a term of years absolute in any land so defined which has more than seven years to run "land" still including a term of years absolute in an advowson: unless they fall within the next category, other leases are not registrable interests but are either override registration or require protection on the register, though they will continue to take effect as if they were registered dispositions[26];

(iii) a term of years absolute for seven years or less which takes effect in possession more than three months after its grant or is granted pursuant to the Housing Act 1985[27];

(iv) a legal rentcharge;

(v) a legal franchise (a grant from the Crown such as the right to hold a market or fair)—at present such rights are minor interests; and

(vi) a legal profit *à prendre* in gross (a right with an existence independent of any land of its owner, such as the right to hunt, fish or shoot game)—at present such rights either override registration or require protection but their present value can be such that it has been thought appropriate that their owners should have the option of treating them as registered interests.

(b) The register

The register for each individual registered title is divided into three parts.

(i) The property register: This describes the land and the estate for which it is held, refers to a map or plan showing the land, and contains notes of interests held for the benefit of the land, such as easements or restrictive covenants of which the registered land is the dominant tenement, and other like matters. The boundaries shown on the map are general and are not so exact as to show on which side of a hedge or fence they run unless stated by the register to be "fixed"[28] or, when the Land Registration Act 2002 comes into force, "determined".[29]

(ii) The proprietorship register: This states the nature of the title (*i.e.* whether it is absolute, good leasehold, qualified or possessory)[30] states the name, address and description of the registered proprietor, and sets out any limitations on his right to deal with the land; at present, these can take the form of cautions, inhibitions or restrictions but only restrictions will survive when the Land Registration Act 2002 comes into force.[31]

(iii) The charges register: This notes the existence of subsidiary registered titles, such as leases registered with their own title, and contains entries relating to rights adverse to the land, such as mortgages or restrictive covenants (such entries take the form of notices[32]).

The Land Registry, which is now a self-financing Executive Agency,[33] has its headquarters in Lincoln's Inn Fields in London. The registers of individual titles are kept at the appropriate

---

[26] L.R.A. 2002, s.29(4).
[27] Either under s.171A or Pt. 5.
[28] L.R.A. 1925, s.76; L.R.R. 1925, r. 278; *Lee v. Barrey* [1957] Ch. 251.
[29] L.R.A. 2002, s.60.
[30] See below, pp. 118–120.
[31] Below, pp. 129–134.
[32] See below, p. 129.
[33] As from July 1990: see L.R.Ann.Rep. 1990–1991.

District Land Registry; there are some 20 of these, dispersed throughout the country. The three parts of the register in respect of each property are kept together. A copy of these entries is included in what is known as a "Land Certificate", which is given to each registered proprietor as a record of his title for retention until he disposes of the land or, at present, charges it[34] (on first registration, the title deeds which constituted proof of the unregistered title are usually returned, stamped with a notice of registration). But the registered proprietor's proof of title is the register itself and not his Land Certificate, which may well be out of date as a result of entries having been made in the register since the certificate was last presented to the relevant District Land Registry to enable some disposition to be registered.

(c) Compulsory and voluntary registration

(i) The compulsory areas: During the years 1897 to 1990, the areas in which registration of title is compulsory were gradually extended, with a marked acceleration from 1965 onwards.[35] Since December 1, 1990, the whole of England and Wales has been subject to compulsory registration of title.[36]

(ii) Ambit of compulsory registration: By no means all the land in the country has a registered title. Registration is compulsory only on the conveyance on sale of a fee simple, or on the grant or assignment of a lease in the relevant categories, made after the area became a compulsory area[37] or, since 1 April, 1998, if either of these estates is the subject of a first legal mortgage or a gift. In the case of rentcharges, the holder has the choice of treating his interest either as a registrable interest or otherwise and this will also be the case for franchises and profits *à prendre* in gross when the Land Registration Act 2002 comes into force. Under that Act, the Lord Chancellor will also have power, after consultation, to increase still further the categories of leases which will trigger first registration by making even shorter leases registrable (it is envisaged that all leases for more than three years will eventually be registrable interests).[38] (The decision to make leases between seven and 21 years in length registrable never mind the further reduction envisaged, has been criticised on the grounds of the increased incidence of stamp duty and because of doubts as to whether the Land Registry will be able to cope with the work involved.) The Lord Chancellor will also have power to provide that the grant or assignment of some or all rentcharges, franchises and profits *à prendre* in gross will also require first registration[39]; this is less controversial.

(iii) Extent of compulsory registration: Much land is still unregistered and some of that land is likely to remain unregistered indefinitely. Although all land held directly by natural persons will become registrable within a generation from April 1, 1998, land held on family settlements is likely to remain unregistered for very much longer (first registration is not required merely by a change of trustees); and land vested in companies or other corporations or bodies, which of course may never die, may remain unsold and unmortgaged for centuries.

---

[34] See below, p. 134.
[35] See the map in L.R.Ann.Rep. 1990–1991.
[36] S.I. 1989 No. 1347.
[37] L.R.A. 1925, s.123(1).
[38] L.R.A. 2002, s.118.
[39] L.R.A. 2002, s.5.

(iv) Non-registration: Where registration is compulsory, the transaction will be void as to the legal estate unless application to register it is made within two months[40]; but the registrar has power to extend this period for "sufficient cause".[41] In default of due registration, the vendor or lessor will hold the legal estate on a bare trust for the purchaser or lessee. There is no default in registration if an application is made but it misdescribes the land or omits part of it[42]; and where a freehold title is registered, the time limit does not at present appear to apply to leases carved out of it,[43] although it will do so when the Land Registration Act 2002 comes into force.

(v) Voluntary registration: A voluntary application for registration may be made in respect of any registrable interest.[44] There were formerly restrictions on such applications if the land in question was outside the compulsory areas of registration but these disappeared when the whole of England and Wales became subject to compulsory registration. Since then, fee incentives have been introduced to encourage voluntary first registration with a view to reducing still further the land that still remains unregistered.

(d) Titles

There are four classes of title with which an applicant for registration may be registered.[45]

(i) Absolute: In the case of freeholds, an absolute title vests in the first registered proprietor, by force of statute and without any conveyance, a fee simple in possession (in equity[46] as well as at law) together with all rights and privileges (such as easements) belonging thereto, subject only to:

    (i) entries on the register;

    (ii) interests which override registration, except so far as the register states that the land is free from them;

    (iii) when the Land Registration Act 2002 comes into force, interests acquired under the Limitation Act 1980 of which he has notice; and

    (iv) as between himself and those entitled to interests which require protection on the register, to those interests of which he has notice, if he is not entitled to the land for his own benefit; thus trustees for sale who are registered as proprietors will still hold subject to the claims of the beneficiaries.[47]

In principle he holds free from all other interests,[48] even if he has full notice of them. In practice, however, the first registered proprietor will have acquired title to the land in question under the system of unregistered conveyancing and he will continue to be bound by

---

[40] L.R.A. 1925, s.123(1); L.R.A. 2002, ss.6–7.

[41] *ibid.*, a power which has to date been used generously.

[42] *Proctor v. Kidman* (1985) 51 P. & C.R. 67.

[43] See L.R.A. 1925, ss.19(1), (2), 22(1).

[44] L.R.A. 1925, ss.4, 8; L.R.A. 2002, s.1.

[45] L.R.A. 2002, ss.9(2), (3) (there is no explicit statement of this in L.R.A. 1925).

[46] The inference to the contrary from *Epps v. Esso Petroleum Co. Ltd* [1973] 1 W.L.R. 1071 at 1075, 1078, is very slender; and see (1974) 38 Conv.(n.s.) 236 (S.N.L. Palk).

[47] L.R.A. 1925, s.5; L.R.A. 2002, s.11(2)–(5).

[48] L.R.A. 1925, ss.20, 23, 33, 69 (see *Morelle Ltd v. Wakeling* [1955] 2 Q.B. 379 at 411); L.R.A. 2002, ss.11–12.

any interests to which he took subject under that system even if they neither override registration nor have been protected on the register at the time of first registration.

In the case of leaseholds, an absolute title similarly vests the leasehold in the first registered proprietor subject to the rights set out above, and in addition to:

(v) all the covenants, obligations and liabilities incident to the lease.[49]

An absolute title in the case of leaseholds guarantees not only that the registered proprietor is the owner of the lease but also that the lease was validly granted. Easements, restrictive covenants and other incumbrances affecting the superior title (but not mortgages or charges) also appear on the leasehold title,[50] so that, in contrast with unregistered land,[51] a purchaser of the lease is free from the risk of being bound by incumbrances which he cannot discover.

(ii) Good leasehold: A good leasehold title applies only to leaseholds. It is the same as an absolute title, save that the lessor's right to grant the lease is not guaranteed.[52] If it appears that the lessor was never entitled to grant the lease, the lessee is protected if he has an absolute title, but unprotected if he has a good leasehold title. Since a lessee cannot investigate the freehold title unless he stipulates for this in the contract,[53] he usually cannot give the registrar evidence of the freehold title where it is or appears to be unregistered, and so he can apply only for a good leasehold title. The registrar may nevertheless be able to grant an absolute title if the title to the freehold is in fact registered, and, though unknown to the lessee, his landlord is the registered proprietor.

(iii) Qualified: In the case of freeholds, a qualified title has the same effect as an absolute title except that the property is held subject to some defect or right specified in the register. This title is granted when an absolute title has been applied for but the registrar has been unable to grant it owing to some defect in the title. A qualified title to leaseholds has the same effect as an absolute or good leasehold title, as the case may be, except for the specified defect.[54]

(iv) Possessory: In the case of either freeholds or leaseholds, first registration with possessory title has the same effect as registration with an absolute title, save that the title is subject to all rights existing or capable of arising at the time of first registration.[55] In short, the title is guaranteed as far as all dealings after the date of registration are concerned, but no guarantee is given as to the title prior to first registration, which must accordingly be investigated by a purchaser in the same way as if the land were not registered.

At present, application may be made in the first instance for any of the above titles except a qualified title, which can be applied for only if an absolute title is refused.[56] There is no equivalent provision in the Land Registration Act 2002; when this legislation comes into force, it appears that the registrar will be free to decide which class of title to confer.

---

[49] L.R.A. 1925, s.9; L.R.A. 2002, s.12(2)–(5).
[50] See Ruoff & Roper 5–09; and see *White v. Bijou Mansions Ltd* [1937] Ch. 610 (affirmed [1938] Ch. 351).
[51] See above, p. 103.
[52] L.R.A. 1925, s.10; L.R.A. 2002, s.12(6).
[53] Above, p. 103.
[54] L.R.A. 1925, ss.7, 12; L.R.A. 2002, ss.11(6), 12(7).
[55] L.R.A. 1925, ss.6, 11; L.R.A. 2002, ss.11(7), 12(8).
[56] See L.R.A. 1925, s.7(1).

(e) Conversion of titles

Where there has been registration with any title other than absolute, the title may be converted subsequently, either on application by the proprietor or by the registrar of his own motion. There are various categories.[57]

(i) Good leasehold: a good leasehold title may be converted to absolute if the registrar is satisfied as to the title to the freehold and to any intermediate leasehold.

(ii) Possessory: a possessory title may be converted to absolute or (if leasehold) to good leasehold if the registrar is satisfied as to the title, or if the possessory title has been registered for at least 12 years and he is satisfied that the proprietor is in possession.

(iii) Qualified: a qualified title may be converted to absolute or (if leasehold) to good leasehold if the registrar is satisfied as to the title.

Any person (other than the proprietor) who suffers loss by any conversion of title is entitled to indemnity as if a mistake had been made in the register.[58]

(f) Application for first registration

With the exceptions set out above, an application for registration may be made by any estate owner, including those holding the estate as a trustee. Further, anyone entitled to call for a legal estate to be vested in him (except a mere purchaser under a contract, or a mortgagee) can apply for registration.[59] Thus if A holds land on a bare trust for B, B can apply for registration without first requiring a conveyance to be executed in his favour, though normally A will have to join or concur in the application.

The registrar examines the title and inquires into any objections that may be made to the proposed registration. At present, he has power to accept a defective title if in his opinion it is "a title the holding under which will not be disturbed".[60] When the Land Registration Act 2002 comes into force, he will have power to register an absolute title if he is of the opinion that the title is "such as a willing buyer could properly be advised by a competent professional adviser to accept"[61]; and in applying that test, he may disregard the fact that a title is defective if in his opinion it is "a title the holding under which will not be disturbed".[62] There is no appeal to the court from a refusal to register a title as absolute,[63] though it may be possible to challenge the registrar's action or inaction on an application for judicial review.[64]

(g) Cautions against first registration

Any person interested in unregistered land who thinks that he may be prejudiced by an application to register any title to it may lodge a caution against first registration with the registrar.[65] This entitles him to be informed by the registrar of any application to register the title. Thus a person who claims that the execution by him of a conveyance of his unregistered

---

[57] L.R.A., s.77, as inserted by L.R.A. 1986, s.1; L.R.A. 2002, s.62.
[58] L.R.A., s.77; L.R.A. 2002, Sched. 8, para. 1(2)(a); below, p. 143.
[59] L.R.A. 1925, ss.4, 8; L.R.A. 2002, s.3(2).
[60] L.R.A. 1925, s.13.
[61] L.R.A. 2002, s.9(2).
[62] L.R.A. 2002, s.9(3).
[63] *Dennis v. Malcolm* [1934] Ch. 244, considered in *Quigly v. Chief Land Registrar* [1992] 1 W.L.R. 834 at 837.
[64] *Dennis v. Malcolm* [1934] Ch. 244. at 253.
[65] L.R.A. 1925, s.53; L.R.A. 2002, ss.15–22.

land was obtained by fraud may lodge a caution against first registration to prevent the grantee registering the title without his knowledge. The notice given to the cautioner requires him to make his objections to the registration or conversion within a fixed time, usually 14 days. Abuse of this procedure is discouraged by a provision that any person who causes damage to another by unreasonably lodging a caution is liable to pay him compensation.[66] When the Land Registration Act 2002 comes into force, the registrar will for the first time be required to keep a register of cautions against first registration[67]; at present details are kept on a "caution title". Cautions against first registration are sometimes registered by holders of registrable interests which are not subject to compulsory registration. All cautions of this and any other type which are in existence when the Land Registration Act 2002 comes into force will continue to be effective indefinitely.[68] However, that Act will only permit a person who has a fee simple absolute in possession or a term of years absolute with more than seven years to run to register a caution during the first two years after it comes into force[69]; at that point any such cautions registered during that two-year period will cease to have effect.[70] The purpose of this provision is to ensure that registering a caution against first registration is no longer regarded as a substitute for voluntary first registration.

(h) Registered charges

The normal, but not the only, way of mortgaging registered land is to effect a registered charge by deed. Once registered, this operates as a charge by way of legal mortgage.[71] A registered charge is *sui generis*. It is not an interest which overrides registration or a minor interest, and it is not a registrable interest for which a land certificate can be issued to the mortgagee. At present, a charge certificate is issued to the mortgagee instead, and the land certificate is retained in the registry for the duration of the mortgage. When the Land Registration Act 2002 comes into force, charge certificates will be discontinued and registered charges will simply be protected on the register in the same way as other interests which require such protection; it will therefore no longer be necessary for the land certificate to be retained in the registry. That Act will also formally reduce the number of ways in which it is possible to mortgage registered land, although this will make little difference in practice since registered charges are already almost always used. Registered charges and the other types of mortgages will be considered in due course.[72]

2. Interests which override registration

(a) Nature

The Land Registration Act 1925 describes interests which override registration as "overriding interests" and defines them as "all the incumbrances, interests, rights, and powers not entered on the register but subject to which registered dispositions are", by the Act, "to take effect".[73] The Land Registration Act 2002 does not use the expression "overriding interests" but provides for two classes of interests which will have the same effect as overriding interests

[66] L.R.A. 1925, s.56; L.R.A. 2002, s.77.
[67] L.R.A. 2002, s.19.
[68] *ibid.*, Sched. 12, para. 16.
[69] *ibid.*, s.15(3), Sched. 12, para. 14(1).
[70] *ibid.*, Sched. 12, para. 14(2).
[71] L.R.A. 1925, ss.25–27; L.R.A. 2002, ss.48–50.
[72] See below, p. 497.
[73] L.R.A. 1925, s.3(xvi). The words omitted relate only to land registered before 1926.

have at present. These are respectively called "unregistered interests which override first registration"[74] and "unregistered interests which override registered dispositions".[75] Interests which override registration bind the proprietor even though he has no knowledge of them and the register does not refer to them. In general, they are the kinds of rights which a purchaser of unregistered land would not expect to discover from a mere examination of the abstract and title deeds, but for which he would make inquiries and inspect the land. Many are legal rights but some are equitable. Yet it is to be emphasised that for incumbrances on registered land, the issue in deciding whether or not a purchaser is bound is not whether the rights are legal or equitable, but whether they override registration or require protection on the register. It should be noted that the changes which the Land Registration Act 2002 will make to the present law governing interests which override registration are extremely significant and are one of the respects in which the law will most change.

(b) Interests which override registration under the present law

The Land Registration Act 1925[76] sets out in 12 paragraphs a list of "subsisting" interests which it classifies as "overriding interests". Only the most important of them will be considered here.

(i) Paragraph (a): rights of common, public rights, profits *à prendre*, rights of way, watercourses, rights of water and other easements "not being equitable easements required[77] to be protected by notice on the register".[78] These final words have caused difficulties since nowhere in the Land Registration Act 1925 are equitable easements required to be protected by notice on the register. As a result it could be and has been contended that all equitable easements override registration. However, it has been held that none in fact do so; however, an equitable easement of way openly exercised and enjoyed for the benefit of adjoining land has nevertheless been held to override registration.[79] This paragraph catches both legal and equitable profits *à prendre* whenever and however they are acquired, legal easements which existed at first registration, and easements acquired as a result of an implied grant or reservation or by prescription after first registration: "easements, rights and privileges adversely affecting registered land" can be acquired by prescription in the same way as if the land was not registered.[80] However, a legal easement can be acquired as a result of an express grant or reservation after first registration only if it is created by registered disposition and is therefore entered on the register: an easement created merely by deed will take effect only as an equitable easement; consequently, this paragraph does not apply to legal easements created by express grant or reservation after first registration.

(ii) Paragraph (f): rights acquired or being acquired under the Limitation Acts.[81] A title to registered land may at present be acquired under these Acts by adverse possession in the same way as for unregistered land, though the operation of the Acts is different. For

---

[74] L.R.A. 2002, ss.11, 12 and Sched. 1.
[75] L.R.A. 2002, ss.29, 30 and Sched. 3.
[76] L.R.A. 1925, s.70(1).
[77] In the sense of needing protection, it seems: there is no express requirement.
[78] L.R.A. 1925, s.70(1).
[79] *Celsteel Ltd v. Alton House Holdings Ltd* [1985] 1 W.L.R. 204 (in C.A. [1986] 1 W.L.R. 512), relying on L.R.R. 1925, r. 258; *Thatcher v. Douglas* (1996) 146 N.L.J. 282.
[80] L.R.R. 1925, r. 250; the new L.R.R. will presumably deal with this.
[81] See Limitation Act 1980; below, pp. 547 *et seq.*

unregistered land, the adverse possession extinguishes the title of the landowner,[82] whereas for registered land the adverse possessor acquires no legal title until he has been registered as proprietor; until then, the registered proprietor holds the land on a bare trust for him.[83] The adverse possessor may be registered with any of the four possible titles.[84]

(iii) Paragraph (g): rights of every person "in actual occupation" of the land, or in receipt of the rents and profits, unless the rights are not disclosed when inquiry is made of him. There are some statutory exceptions; these and other aspects of this important and difficult provision will be given detailed consideration shortly.[85]

(iv) Paragraph (h): where the title is not absolute, all estates, rights, interests and powers excepted from the effect of registration, such as rights existing at the time of first registration where only a possessory title has been granted.

(v) Paragraph (i): rights under local land charges unless and until registered or protected on the register.

(vi) Paragraph (k): legal[86] leases for not more than 21 years, granted at a rent without taking a fine. This paragraph therefore does not include leases of this type created by signed writing unless they are for three years or less and take immediate effect in possession (the latter leases are legal even if created orally[87]). However, nearly all leases will, except registrable interests entered on the register, will take effect as overriding interests under paragraph (g) above, even if they are for more than 21 years.[88]

(c) "Actual occupation or receipt of rent and profits" under the present law

As mentioned above. paragraph (g) is both important and difficult. It reads: "The rights of every person in actual occupation of the land or in receipt of the rents and profits thereof, save where enquiry is made of such person and the rights are not disclosed". The two main elements of this definition must be examined in turn.

(i) "Rights": The word "rights" here includes all proprietary rights, whether legal or equitable. Thus it includes a contract for the purchase of land,[89] including an option and, possibly, a right of pre-emption (a right of first refusal); an option to purchase the freehold reversion on a lease[90]; an unpaid vendor's lien[91]; a purchaser's lien for his deposit[92]; the rights of a beneficiary under a bare trust, whether arising as a result of a conveyance by the beneficiary to the trustee[93] or arising as a result of a transfer induced by the fraudulent misrepresentation of the transferee[94]; the rights of a beneficiary under an express or implied statutory trust for sale or other type of trust of land (bare trusts and trusts for sale have since

---

[82] See below, p. 559.
[83] L.R.A. 1925, s.75. See *Bridges v. Mees* [1957] Ch. 475.
[84] L.R.A. 1925, s.75.
[85] Below.
[86] *City Permanent B.S. v. Miller* [1952] Ch. 840.
[87] L.P.A. 1925, s.54(2).
[88] See *Strand Securities Ltd v. Caswell* [1965] Ch. 958.
[89] *Bridges v. Mees* [1957] Ch. 475.
[90] *Webb v. Pollmount Ltd* [1966] Ch. 584.
[91] *London and Cheshire Insurance Co. Ltd v. Laplagrene Property Co. Ltd* [1971] Ch. 499.
[92] *Lee-Parker v. Izzet* [1971] 1 W.L.R. 1688.
[93] *Hodgson v. Marks* [1971] Ch. 892; *Marks v. Attallah* (1966) 110 S.J. 709.
[94] *Collings v. Lee* [2001] 2 All E.R. 332.

1996 both been types of trusts of land[95]); and rights protected by equitable proprietary estoppel[96] (controversially, this is the case even if the right in question is a right that would not otherwise be proprietary such as a licence). Even a right which is either a registrable interest which is required to be registered or a minor interest which is required to be protected by an entry on the register[97] may instead override registration if the requirement of actual occupation is satisfied[98]; and derivative interests, carved out of interests which override registration (such as a lease granted by the occupying beneficiary under a bare trust), have the protection conferred by those interests.[99]

On the other hand, rights which are merely personal and not proprietary cannot override registration even if they relate to land[1]; nor can rights that have been overreached[2] or could have been overreached had any contemporaneous capital money been payable[3]; nor can "mere equities" unless they are ancillary to some interest in land, or dependent on it.[4] There are also certain rights, with little in common, which by statute cannot override registration under paragraph (g) and therefore require protection on the register. These include the rights of beneficiaries of a settlement under the Settled Land Act 1925[5]; rights under a mortgage which is not a registered charge[6]; a notice by a tenant exercising his statutory right to acquire the freehold or an extended lease[7]; and a spouse's statutory rights to occupy the matrimonial home.[8]

(ii) Actual occupation or receipt of rents and profits: Nothing can override registration under paragraph (g) unless not only is it within the category of rights considered above, but also the owner of the right is "in actual occupation of the land or in receipt of the rents and profits thereof".

Whether a person is "in actual occupation" is a question of fact[9] and degree. There must be some degree of permanence and continuity, and not a mere fleeting[10] or irregular[11] presence. However, actual occupation will not be destroyed by temporary absences, for example in hospital or on holiday, although there must be some point, as yet unidentified, when the absence will cease to be temporary. Prolonged but intermittent car parking on an unidentified part of the land will not suffice,[12] nor will a purchaser of a house be in actual occupation of it merely because, by permission, he has taken preparatory steps before

---

[95] T.L.A.T.A. 1996, s.1.
[96] *Habermann v. Koehler (No. 1)* (1996) 73 P. & C.R. 515 at 520, 522–523; *(No. 2)* (2000) *The Times*, November 22, 2000.
[97] See below, pp. 129 *et seq.*
[98] *Williams & Glyn's Bank Ltd v. Boland* [1981] A.C. 487.
[99] *Marks v. Attallah* (1966) 110 S.J. 709.
[1] *National Provincial Bank Ltd v. Ainsworth* [1965] A.C. 1175 at 1238, 1240.
[2] *City of London B.S. v. Flegg* [1988] A.C. 54.
[3] *State Bank of India v. Sood* [1997] Ch. 276.
[4] See *National Provincial Bank Ltd v. Ainsworth* [1965] A.C. 1175 at 1238, 1240; *Blacklocks v. J.B. Developments (Godalming) Ltd* [1982] Ch. 183 (rectification); and see (1976) 40 Conv. N.S. 209 (A.R. Everton).
[5] L.R.A. 1925, s.86(2).
[6] *ibid.*, s.106(2); see below, p. 498.
[7] Leasehold Reform Act 1967, s.5(5); but there is no corresponding provision for such rights under the Housing Act 1985, Pt. V.
[8] Family Law Act 1996, s.31(10)(b).
[9] *Williams & Glyn's Bank Ltd v. Boland* [1981] A.C. 487 at 506, 508, 511 ("a plain factual situation").
[10] *Abbey National B.S. v. Cann* [1991] 1 A.C. 56 at 93.
[11] *Stockholm Finance Ltd v. Garden Holdings Inc.* [1995] N.P.C. 162 (Saudi Princesses in Hampstead Garden Suburb).
[12] *Epps v. Esso Petroleum Co. Ltd* [1973] 1 W.L.R. 1071.

completion, such as carrying out building works[13] or laying carpets or moving furniture in.[14]

Mere physical presence may not be enough. Where a sole proprietor's spouse lives in a house with him or her, the spouse will be in actual occupation if he or she is entitled to some proprietary interest in the house,[15] but otherwise will be there merely by virtue of the actual occupation of the sole proprietor.[16] A purchaser will thus be at risk if he fails to make inquiry of all who are normally present on the premises, apart from young children[17]; and the presence of furniture or other articles that suggest that the vendor is not the sole occupier may be important.[18] But the paragraph specifically provides that an overriding interest cannot be claimed by anyone who, on inquiry, fails to reveal his rights.[19]

Despite the most careful inspections and inquiries, a purchaser may nevertheless be bound by the rights of some undiscovered third party whose occupation of the land has been deliberately concealed by the vendor or who is absent but has not been absent for long enough to have lost his overriding interest.[20] To make matters worse, actual occupation of any part of the land in the registered title protects rights held by the occupier in the whole of it[21]; this is a tremendous potential problem when a building is in multiple occupation. Discovering exactly who is in receipt of the rents and profits also has its own difficulties, particularly now that rights held by the recipient in the whole of the land in the registered title are protected; but it has at least been held that the rights of a landlord who is not actually in receipt of rent and profits, because he either takes no steps to enforce their payment[22] or permits rent free occupation,[23] are not protected.

The date for determining whether a person is in actual occupation is the date when the purchase is completed and the relevant documents executed, even though the estate will not vest in the purchaser until the title is registered.[24] If the occupation later ceases before there has been any relevant dealing with the land, the validity of the interest which overrides registration remains unimpaired.[25]

(d) Interests which override registration under the Land Registration Act 2002

As has already been mentioned, the Land Registration Act 2002 provides[26] for two classes of interests which will override registration in the same way as overriding interests do at present which are respectively called "unregistered interests which override first registration" and "unregistered interests which override registered dispositions". The classes of interests are contained in the Schedules to the Act.

---

[13] See *Lloyds Bank Plc. v. Rosset* [1991] 1 A.C. 107, where the point was left undecided: see at 134.
[14] *Abbey National B.S. v. Cann* [1991] 1 A.C. 56 at 94.
[15] *Hodgson v. Marks* [1971] Ch. 892; see at 932.
[16] *Bird v. Syme-Thompson* [1979] 1 W.L.R. 440 ("as a shadow of occupation by the owner": 444).
[17] *Hypo-Mortgage Services Ltd v. Robinson* [1997] 2 F.L.R. 71.
[18] See *Chhokar v. Chhokar* (1983) 5 F.L.R. 313 at 317; [1989] Conv. 342 (P. Sparkes).
[19] *Holaw (470) Ltd v. Stockton Estates Ltd* (2001) 81 P. & C.R. 404.
[20] See *Kling v. Keston Properties Ltd* (1985) 49 P. & C.R. 212 at 222; and see *Hodgson v. Marks* [1971] Ch. 892 at 923.
[21] *Ferrishurst Ltd v. Wallcite Ltd* [1999] Ch. 355.
[22] *E. S. Schwab & Co. v. McCarthy* (1976) 31 P. & C.R. 196.
[23] *Strand Securities Ltd v. Caswell* [1965] Ch. 958.
[24] *Abbey National B.S. v. Cann* [1991] 1 A.C. 56; *Lloyds Bank Plc. v. Rosset* [1991] 1 A.C. 107. See above, p. 96.
[25] *London and Cheshire Insurance Co. Ltd v. Laplagrene Property Co. Ltd* [1971] Ch. 499.
[26] In ss.11 and 12 and ss.29 and 30 respectively.

(i) Unregistered interests which override first registration: Schedule 1 to the Land Registration Act 2002 sets out in 14 paragraphs a list of unregistered interests which will override first registration. Only the most important of them will be considered here. Paragraphs 10 to 14 will cease to have effect 10 years after Schedule 1 comes into force.[27]

(a) Paragraph 1: legal leases for not more than seven years unless they take effect in possession more than three months after their grant or are granted pursuant to the Housing Act 1985[28] (the excluded categories are registrable interests). This paragraph therefore does not catch leases of this type created by signed writing unless they are for three years or less and take immediate effect in possession (the latter leases are legal even if created orally[29]). However, all leases where the lessee is in physical possession of the land, unless they are registrable interests which are entered on the register, will override registration under paragraph 2 below, even if they are for more than seven years.

(b) Paragraph 2: interests of every person in actual occupation, except for an interest in a settlement under the Settled Land Act 1925. This provision will be considered shortly.[30]

(c) Paragraph 3: legal easements and profits *à prendre*.

(d) Paragraphs 4, 5, 6 and 10: customary rights, public rights, local land charges and franchises (Paragraph 10 will cease to have effect 10 years after Schedule 1 comes into force).

(ii) Unregistered interests which override registered dispositions: Schedule 3 to the Land Registration Act 2002 also sets out in 14 paragraphs a list of unregistered interests which will override registered dispositions; however, the scope of several of the paragraphs is considerably more restricted. Only the most important of them will be considered here. Paragraphs 10 to 14 will cease to have effect 10 years after Schedule 3 comes into force.[31]

(a) Paragraph 1: legal leases for not more than seven years unless they take effect in possession more than three months after their grant or are granted pursuant to the Housing Act 1985[32] or are for some other reason registrable interests. This paragraph therefore does not catch leases of this type created by signed writing unless they are for three years or less and take immediate effect in possession (the latter leases are legal even if created orally[33]). However, all leases where the lessee is in physical possession of the land will, unless they are registrable interests which are entered on the register, will override registration under paragraph 2 below, even if they are for more than seven years.

(b) Paragraph 2: interests of every person in actual occupation, except for

    (i) an interest under a settlement subject to the Settled Land Act 1925;

    (ii) an interest of a person who failed to disclose the interest upon inquiry when he could reasonably have been expected to do so;

    (iii) an interest of a person whose occupation would not have been obvious on a

[27] L.R.A. 2002, s.117.
[28] Either under s.171A or Pt. 5.
[29] L.P.A. 1925, s.54(2).
[30] Below.
[31] L.R.A. 2002, s.117.
[32] Either under s.171A or Pt. 5.
[33] L.P.A. 1925, s.54(2).

reasonably careful inspection of the land and of which the purchaser had no actual knowledge; and

(iv) a lease taking effect in possession more than three months after its grant which has not yet done so.

This provision will also be considered shortly.[34]

(c) Paragraph 3: Legal easements or profits *à prendre*, except for those not registered under the Commons Registration Act 1965 of which the purchaser had no actual knowledge and which would which not have been obvious on a reasonably careful inspection of the land over which they are exercised; the exception does not apply where they have been exercised within the preceding year. This paragraph catches both legal and equitable profits *à prendre* whenever and however they are acquired, legal easements which existed at first registration, and easements acquired as a result of an implied grant or reservation and by prescription after first registration ("easements, rights and privileges adversely affecting registered land" can be acquired by prescription in the same way as if the land was not registered[35]). However, a legal easement can only be acquired as a result of an express grant or reservation after first registration if it is created by registered disposition and therefore entered on the register (an easement created merely by deed will take effect only as an equitable easement); consequently, this paragraph does not catch any legal easements created by express grant or reservation after first registration.

(d) Paragraphs 4, 5, 6 and 10: customary rights, public rights, local land charges and franchises (Paragraph 10 will cease to have effect ten years after Schedule 3 comes into force).

(iii) "Actual occupation" under the Land Registration Act 2002: The first point to note is that the Land Registration Act 2002 will not protect any interests by virtue of the fact that their holder is in receipt of rent and profits save when they were already protected when that Act comes into force.[36]

An "interest" will presumably be interpreted in the same way as "rights" have been under the present law, although the Act specifically provides that rights of pre-emption (rights of first refusal) are from the moment of their creation capable of binding successors in title,[37] thus resolving an uncertainty in the present law.

The impact of actual occupation on first registration will be comparable with its impact under the present law, with the following four differences: there will be only one statutory exception, the interests of beneficiaries of a settlement under the Settled Land Act 1925; the interests of occupiers which are not revealed on inquiry will be protected; actual occupation of only part of the land in the registered title will protect only the interests held by the occupier in that part, not as at present in the whole of it; and a person will only be in actual occupation if he, or his agent or employee, is physically present there (the first two of these changes will increase the impact of actual occupation, while the last two will decrease it).

The impact of actual occupation on registered dispositions will have similar differences from the present law save that the interests of occupiers which are not revealed on inquiry

---

[34] Below.
[35] L.R.R. 1925, r. 250; the new L.R.R. will presumably deal with this.
[36] L.R.A., Sched. 12, para. 8; see below.
[37] L.R.A. 2002, s.115.

when they might reasonably have been expected to do so will not be protected. The impact of actual occupation on registered dispositions will be further reduced in that two more categories of interests will not be protected: interests of persons whose occupation would not have been obvious on a reasonably careful inspection of the land and of which the purchaser does not actually know (it is the occupation which has to be obvious, not the interest of the occupier); and leases taking effect in possession more than three months after their grant which have not yet done so. Although it is admittedly unlikely that a failure to reveal interests will be held to have been reasonably expected, precisely what is meant by occupation which is not obvious on a reasonably careful inspection is susceptible of very considerable debate and may require consideration of the authorities on unregistered land which consider of whom a purchaser is expected to make inquiries.[38]

(iv) Transitional provisions: Schedule 12 of the Land Registration Act 2002 contains a number of provisions dealing with interests which at present override registration but will not do so when the Land Registration Act 2002 comes into force.

Easements, profits *à prendre*,[39] and leases [40] which overrode registration at the time when they came into existence[41] will continue to do so indefinitely despite the fact that they would not do so if they came into existence after the Act comes into force. Legal easements and profits *à prendre* of any type which come into existence during the first three years after the Act comes into force will also always override registration.[42] And rights which overrode registration by virtue of the receipt of rents and profits at the time when the Act comes into force[43] will continue to do so for as long as the person in question continues to receive the rents and profits. These provisions are uncontroversial. However, no transitional provision has been made for protecting the interests which an actual occupier of only part of the land in the registered title at present has in the whole of it[44]; the protection given to the interests which he has in the part which he does not occupy will simply disappear when the Act comes into force. This loss of protection may be challenged under the Human Rights Act 1998 on the basis that it infringes the right of every person thereunder to the peaceful enjoyment of his possessions.[45] However, any such challenge may well be defeated on the grounds that the rights so protected can and should be protected on the register before the Land Registration Act 2002 comes into force; further, a challenge to the Land Registration Act 1925 under the Human Rights Act 1998 has already been rejected on the basis that the power in question (to refuse to rectify the register) had been "given for the legitimate aim in the public interest in enhancing the land registration system".[46]

Rights acquired by adverse possessors in land before the Act comes into force, whether before or after the first registration of the land in question, will no longer take effect under a bare trust. Instead, the Land Registration Act 2002 confers on such adverse possessors a right to be registered as proprietors.[47] Where the adverse possessor is in actual occupation of

---

[38] Above, pp. 61–63.
[39] L.R.A. 2002, para. 9.
[40] L.R.A. 2002, para. 12.
[41] Some easements and profits *à prendre* which come into existence within two years of the Act coming into force will also do so; *ibid.*, para. 10.
[42] *ibid.*, para. 10.
[43] *ibid.*, para. 8.
[44] *Under Ferrishurst Ltd v. Wallcite Ltd* [1999] Ch. 355, above p. 125.
[45] E.C.H.R., Protocol 1, art. 1.
[46] *Kingsalton Ltd v. Thames Water Developments Ltd* [2002] 1 P. & C.R. 15 at para. 45.
[47] *ibid.*, para. 18(1).

the land in question, this will protect him indefinitely because his right will override registration by virtue of his actual occupation. However, where he is not in actual occupation, his right will only override registration for three years after the Act comes into force.[48] The destruction of these acquired rights after the three-year period may also be challenged under the Human Rights Act 1998.[49] However, this challenge is even less likely to succeed. Quite apart from the rejection of the challenge already made to the Land Registration Act 1925 under the Human Rights Act 1998 on the basis that the power in question had been "given for the legitimate aim in the public interest in enhancing the land registration system",[50] a successful adverse possessor who is out of possession should be conscious of the need to protect his rights, and a three-year period should be more than enough for this purpose.

(e) Entries on the register

Under the present law, the Registrar may make entries on the register stating that the land is free from or subject to certain overriding interests. His only obligation is to enter a notice of the existence of any easement, right, privilege or benefit created by an instrument (and not, for example, an easement created by prescription) which appears on the title at the time of first registration.[51] There does not seem to be any equivalent provision in the Land Registration Act 2002 but one may well be provided by the new Rules when they appear.

3. Interests which require protection on the register

(a) Definition

The Land Registration Act 1925 Act describes interests which require protection on the register as "minor interests"[52] and elaborately defines them[53]; the Land Registration Act 2002 does give any collective name to interests which require protection on the register. Interests which override registration obviously do not require protection on the register and any registrable interests which have been registered and registered charges are necessarily on the register anyway. All other interests require protection by an entry on the register, otherwise they will not bind a purchaser for valuable consideration (which at present includes marriage consideration but will not do so when the Land Registration Act 2002 comes into force[54]) under a registered disposition of a registered or registrable estate or interest.[55] Interests which require protection on the register are divided into two classes:

(i) those which will not bind a purchaser even when protected by an entry on the register, but which will be overreached, such as the equitable interests of beneficiaries of a settlement under the Settled Land Act 1925 or a trust of land (which includes both express trusts for sale and bare trusts); and

(ii) those which will bind a purchaser provided they are protected in the appropriate way, such as restrictive covenants.

---

[48] *ibid.*, paras 7, 11.
[49] E.C.H.R., Protocol 1, art. 1.
[50] *Kingsalton Ltd v. Thames Water Developments Ltd* [2002] 1 P. & C.R. 15 at para. 45.
[51] L.R.A. 1925, s.70(2), (3). See *Re Dances Way, West Town, Hayling Island* [1962] Ch. 490.
[52] *Elias v. Mitchell* [1972] Ch. 652.
[53] L.R.A. 1925, s.3(xv); L.R.A. 2002, s.29(1).
[54] L.R.A. 2002, s.132(1).
[55] *Miles v. Bull (No. 2)* [1969] 3 All E.R. 1585; contrast *Barclays Bank Ltd v. Taylor* [1974] Ch. 137, where the purchaser took an equitable interest only.

(b) The manner of protection on the register

Under the present law, a minor interest may be protected by a notice, a caution against dealings, an inhibition or a restriction.[56] Notices appear on the charges register of the registered title in question, the other three on the proprietorship register. Notices and restrictions normally can be entered only when the land certificate is at the relevant District Land Registry.[57] Under the Land Registration Act 2002, minor interests will only be able to be protected by notices and restrictions but these will be able to be entered whether or not the land certificate is at the relevant District Land Registry. All entries on the register made before the Land Registration Act 2002 comes into force will continue to have effect indefinitely so existing cautions against dealings and inhibitions remain valid.[58]

(i) Notices under the present law—effect of a notice: In general, the effect of the entry of a notice is to ensure that any subsequent dealing with the land will take effect subject to the right protected by the notice[59]; the mere entry of a notice will not, of course, give validity to an invalid claim. A notice also serves to fix the registered proprietor with knowledge of the claim as from the moment of entry.

A wide and varied range of rights can be protected by notice.[60] These include leases for more than 21 years, land charges within the Land Charges Act 1972 (including a spouse's right of occupation of the matrimonial home within Class F, the right of a tenant under a long leasehold to serve notice for the acquisition of the freehold or an extended lease,[61] and Inland Revenue charges for inheritance tax[62]), legal rentcharges, legal easements, creditors' rights under a bankruptcy petition (when the notice is called a "creditors' notice"[63]), charging orders,[64] access orders,[65] and the right of a beneficiary under a settlement under the Settled Land Act 1925 or a trust of land to ensure that there are at least two trustees (though the beneficial interests themselves are not included).

Normally before the notice can be entered, the land certificate must be produced to the Registrar. Thus unless the land is already charged so that the certificate has been deposited at the Land Registry,[66] a notice cannot be entered without the co-operation of the registered proprietor. But this does not apply to Class F land charges (a spouse's right of occupation of the matrimonial home), creditor's notices, Inland Revenue charges for inheritance tax, or leases at a rent without a fine.[67]

(ii) Cautions against dealings under the present law—effect of a caution: Like cautions against first registration, considered above,[68] the main function of a caution against dealings

---

[56] L.R.A. 1925, ss.48–62.
[57] *ibid.*, s.64(1).
[58] L.R.A. 2002, Sched. 12, paras 1–3.
[59] *ibid.*, s.52. See *Re White Rose Cottage* [1964] Ch. 483.
[60] L.R.A. 1925, ss.48–51, as amended.
[61] Leasehold Reform Act 1967, s.5(5); see below, p. 549.
[62] See above, p. 79.
[63] L.R.A. 1925, s.61.
[64] Charging Orders Act 1979, s.3(3); see above, p. 83.
[65] See below, p. 408.
[66] L.R.A. 1925, s.65.
[67] *ibid.*, s.64, as amended. See *Strand Securities Ltd v. Caswell* [1965] Ch. 958; above, pp. 79, 81 and 83.
[68] Above, p. 101.

is to ensure that the cautioner receives notice of a proposed transaction. Such cautions are sometimes used when the proprietor will not co-operate in the entry of a notice. Once a caution against dealings has been lodged, no dealing will be registered until notice has been served on the cautioner, warning him that registration will be effected unless he objects within (usually) 14 days.[69] A caution may be lodged by any person who claims any interest in registered land, including a beneficiary under a trust of land[70] (though not a person with a mere contractual right to a share in the proceeds of sale[71]), and a tenant in a block of flats for which a receiver has been appointed.[72] The application must be supported by a statutory declaration.[73] Failure by the Registrar to disclose a caution on an official search does not deprive the cautioner of his protection against subsequent purchasers or chargees.[74] Conversely, the lodging of a caution does not of itself give the cautioner any priority over earlier chargees.[75]

If the cautioner does duly object, the situation is resolved in accordance with the dispute resolution procedures already discussed.[76] The Chief Land Registrar may order the caution to be vacated, or refuse to do so; or he may allow the dealing to be registered subject to a notice protecting the cautioner's interest, or subject to the cautioner commencing legal proceedings within a fixed time. A person who lodges a caution without reasonable cause is liable to pay such compensation as is just to anyone who thereby suffers damage, although only the court, not the Chief Land Registrar, can so order.[77] There is also both a general and a statutory jurisdiction[78] for the court on application to rectify the register by vacating the caution. This jurisdiction will be exercised fairly robustly,[79] even if difficult questions of construction or law are involved,[80] but in case of doubt the court may order the entry to be vacated unless the cautioner undertakes to pay damages to the proprietor if the entry is later found to be unjustified.[81]

Interests protected by cautions take effect only as equitable interests,[82] and so where there is conflict between two or more of them they will normally take effect in the order of creation according to the general law[83]; the order in which they were protected by cautions does not affect this. Thus if A contracts to purchase land, and before he has protected his contract on the register B contracts to purchase the same land and enters a caution, A will have priority over B[84]; the priority of cautions confers no priority of interests.

---

[69] L.R.A. 1925, s.55(1).
[70] *ibid.*, s.54(1); *Elias v. Mitchell* [1972] Ch. 652.
[71] *Lynton International Ltd v. Noble* (1991) 63 P. & C.R. 452.
[72] *Clayhope Properties Ltd v. Evans* [1986] 1 W.L.R. 1223; see above, p. 84.
[73] L.R.R. 1925, r. 215, Form 14; the new L.R.R. will presumably deal with this.
[74] *Parkash v. Irani Finance Ltd* [1970] Ch. 101.
[75] *Barclays Bank Ltd v. Taylor* [1974] Ch. 137.
[76] Above, p. 96.
[77] L.R.A. 1925, s.56(3).
[78] *Lester v. Burgess* (1973) 26 P. & C.R. 536 (where an order operates *in personam*, rather than on the register); L.R.A. 1925, s.82; below, p. 111.
[79] *Rawlplug Co. Ltd v. Kamvale Properties Ltd* (1968) 20 P. & C.R. 32; and see *Price Bros. (Somerford) Ltd v. J. Kelly Homes (Stoke-on-Trent) Ltd* [1975] 1 W.L.R. 1512.
[80] *Alpenstow Ltd v. Regalian Properties Plc.* [1985] 1 W.L.R. 721.
[81] *Tiverton Estates Ltd v. Wearwell* [1974] 2 W.L.R. 176; *Tucker v. Hutchinson* (1987) 54 P. & C.R. 106.
[82] L.R.A. 1925, s.2(1).
[83] See below, p. 480.
[84] *Barclays Bank Ltd v. Taylor* [1974] Ch. 137 (equitable mortgagee and contract for sale); and see *Abigail v. Lapin* [1934] A.C. 491 at 502; *Strand Securities Ltd v. Caswell* [1965] Ch. 958 at 991.

(iii) Inhibitions under the present law: An inhibition is an order of the court, or an entry made by the Registrar, which inhibits the registration of any dealing with the land, either for a fixed time or until some event occurs, or generally until further order or entry.[85] Any person interested may apply for an inhibition,[86] including the proprietor, as where his land certificate has been stolen. The entry is made after making such inquiries, giving such notices and holding such hearings as are thought expedient; and a notice or restriction may be placed on the register instead of an inhibition.[87] Inhibitions used to be rare since they are intended for use when there is no other way of protecting a claim. However, when a bankruptcy order is made, a "bankruptcy inhibition" is automatically registered, preventing any disposition of the land until a trustee in bankruptcy has been registered.[88] And when what was formerly known as a *Mareva injunction*[89] and is now known as a freezing injunction[90] is made in order to prevent a litigant from disposing of his assets pending trial, the court will invariably order the registration of an inhibition against any land which he owns beneficially. The rise in bankruptcies and in the use of freezing injunctions has made inhibitions much more common.

(iv) Restrictions under the present law—Effect of a restriction: A restriction is similar to an inhibition in that it prevents any dealing with the land unless some condition has been complied with.[91] It differs from an inhibition in that the entry is normally made on the application of the registered proprietor himself (or with his consent),[92] either voluntarily or under the duty of trustees to protect their beneficiaries. If the registered proprietor fails to apply for the entry of restrictions, any other person may apply with his consent[93]; but the land certificate must be produced unless it is already in the registry.[94] In practice, the registrar sees that suitable restrictions are framed and entered. A restriction is a friendly entry, whereas inhibitions and cautions are hostile.

Restrictions are appropriate for the protection of the rights of beneficiaries under a settlement under the Settled Land Act 1925 or a trust of land. Thus for land settled under the Settled Land Act 1925, there will be a restriction which prevents the registration of any disposition by the tenant for life which is not authorised by the Settled Land Act 1925, or one in which capital money arises unless it is paid to the trustees, being at least two in number or a trust corporation, or into court.[95] In the case of land subject to a trust of land, there will be a restriction which prevents the registration of any disposition by the trustees in which capital money arises unless it is paid to at least two trustees or to a trust corporation. Restrictions are used in many other cases, such as restricting any disposition of a charity's land without the consent of the Charity Commissioners.[96] In this case, and where there are two or more registered proprietors but the survivor, not being solely beneficially

---

[85] L.R.A. 1925, s.57(1).
[86] *ibid.*
[87] *ibid.*, s.57(2), (4).
[88] *ibid.*, s.61(3), as amended by Insolvency Act 1985, Sched. 8, para. 5.
[89] See *Mareva Compania Naviera S.A. v. International Bulk Carriers S.A.* [1975] 2 Lloyd's Rep. 509.
[90] As a result of the Civil Procedure Rules 1998, Pt. 25.1(f).
[91] L.R.A. 1925, s.58(1).
[92] *ibid.*
[93] L.R.R. 1925, r. 236; the new L.R.R. will presumably deal with this.
[94] L.R.A. 1925, s.64(1).
[95] *ibid.*, s.86(3); L.R.R. 1925, rr. 56–58; the new L.R.R. will presumably deal with this. See below, p. 260.
[96] L.R.R. 1925, r. 60; the new L.R.R. will presumably deal with this.

entitled, will be unable to give a valid receipt for the purchase money on a sale, the registrar is required to enter a suitable restriction.[97]

(v) Notices under the Land Registration Act 2002—definition: A notice is defined as an entry on the register in respect of the burden of an interest affecting a registered estate or charge.[98] Some interests cannot be protected by a notice[99]: these include interests under either a settlement under the Settled Land Act 1925 or a trust of land (because they will be overreached on a disposition); a lease granted for three years or less which is not a registrable interest (because it is an overriding interest); and covenants in a lease relating to the subject-matter of the lease (which are binding under the general law[1]).

The fact that the notice is registered will not mean that the interest in question is valid but, if it is, its priority will be protected.[2] Notices will be able to be agreed notices or unilateral notices. The former will only be able to be registered on the application of or with the consent of the registered proprietor unless the Registrar is satisfied of the validity of the interest in question.[3] Following the registration of the latter, the Registrar will have to notify the registered proprietor of its registration.[4] He will be able to apply to have the registration cancelled and, if the beneficiary of the notice does not object within a prescribed period, it will have to be cancelled.[5] Objections will be resolved in accordance with the dispute resolution procedures already discussed.[6] The Adjudicator and the courts will presumably have all the powers which the Chief Land Registrar and the courts at present have in respect of cautions against dealings. A person who fails to exercise reasonable care when applying for the entry of a notice will be potentially liable to anyone who suffers damage thereby.[7]

(vi) Restrictions under the Land Registration Act 2002—definition: A restriction is defined as an entry in the register regulating the circumstances in which a disposition of a registered estate or charge may be the subject of an entry in the register.[8] It may prohibit any disposition or a specific type of disposition either indefinitely, for a specified period or until the occurrence of a specified event,[9] which include the giving of notice, the obtaining of consent and the making of an order by the court or registrar.[10]

When a restriction has been entered, no entry will be able to be made on the register otherwise than in accordance with the terms of the restriction, although the registrar will, on the application of a person who appears to him to have a sufficient interest in the restriction, be able to disapply or modify it.[11] The registrar will himself be able to enter a restriction if it appears to him that it is necessary or desirable to do so for the purpose of preventing

---

[97] L.R.A. 1925, s.58(3); L.R.R. 1925, rr. 60, 213; the new L.R.R. will presumably deal with this. See below, p. 290.
[98] L.R.A. 2002, s.32.
[99] L.R.A. 2002, s.33.
[1] See below, pp. 348 *et seq.*
[2] L.R.A. 2002, s.32.
[3] L.R.A. 2002, s.34.
[4] L.R.A. 2002, s.35.
[5] L.R.A. 2002, s.36.
[6] Above, p. 96.
[7] L.R.A. 2002, s.77.
[8] L.R.A. 2002, s.40(1).
[9] L.R.A. 2002, s.40(2).
[10] L.R.A. 2002, s.40(3).
[11] L.R.A. 2002, s.41.

invalidity or unlawfulness in relation to dispositions, protecting a right or claim or for securing compliance with the overreaching rules[12] and will have to do the latter when he registers two or more persons as registered proprietors.[13] Restrictions will be notifiable unless they are registered on the application of or with the consent of the registered proprietor or the Registrar is satisfied of the validity of the interest in question.[14] Following the registration of a notifiable restriction, the Registrar will have to notify the registered proprietor of its registration.[15] As in the case of notices, objections will be resolved in accordance with the dispute resolution procedures already discussed.[16] The adjudicator and the courts will presumably have all the powers which the Chief Land Registrar and the courts at present have in respect of cautions against dealings. A person who fails to exercise reasonable care when applying for the entry of a restriction will be potentially liable to anyone who suffers damage thereby.[17]

(c) Official searches

A purchaser may discover any entries which protect interests which require protection on the register by making an official search of the register; and he may obtain an official search certificate.[18] This certificate will protect the purchaser during the "priority period", *i.e.* the period of 30 working days after the application for the search.[19] This protection operates by providing that if the purchaser's application for registration is delivered to the registry during the priority period, any entries made during that period will be postponed to him,[20] thereby protecting him against last minute entries.[21] A second search made during the priority period will not extend that period, but merely create its own priority period.[22]

Sect. 3. Dealings with registered land

In general, the registered proprietor can deal with or dispose of his land to the same extent as an owner with an unregistered title. The Land Registration Act 1925 expressly authorises a wide range of dealings.[23] The Land Registration Act 2002 states that the registered proprietor has power to make a disposition of any kind permitted by the general law other than mortgages by lease or sub-lease (which will therefore be abolished prospectively in respect of registered land when that Act comes into force) and has power to charge his estate at law[24] (sub-mortgages of registered land will also be prohibited, no matter what type the mortgage is).[25] The most important dispositions are outlined below.

[12] L.R.A. 2002, s.42.
[13] L.R.A. 2002, s.44.
[14] L.R.A. 2002, s.43(1).
[15] L.R.A. 2002, s.45.
[16] Above, p. 96.
[17] L.R.A. 2002, s.77.
[18] Land Registration (Official Searches) Rules 1988 (No. 629), r. 3; the new L.R.R. will presumably deal with this.
[19] *ibid.*, rr. 2, 3; the new L.R.R. will presumably deal with this. For corresponding provisions for unregistered land, see above, p. 90.
[20] Land Registration (Official Searches) Rules 1988, above, r. 5; the new L.R.R. will presumably deal with this.
[21] See *Leeman v. Mohammed* (2001) 82 P. & C.R. 14.
[22] Land Registry Notice (1981) 131 N.L.J. 881; the new L.R.R. will presumably deal with this.
[23] See L.R.A. 1925, ss.18, 21, 25, 40, 66.
[24] L.R.A. 2002, s.23(1).
[25] L.R.A. 2002, s.23(2).

1. Transfer *inter vivos*

(a) Transfer

The transfer of registered land *inter vivos* is effected by a simple form of transfer[26] which must be lodged at the appropriate District Land Registry together with the land certificate. The registrar makes the necessary entries on the register and the land certificate, and returns the latter to the new proprietor if the whole of the land has been sold. If part only has been sold, the original certificate is amended and returned to the vendor, and a new certificate for the part sold is issued to the purchaser.

(b) Title

No legal estate passes until the title is registered,[27] though registration is treated as occurring when the purchaser delivers the relevant documents to the appropriate District Land Registry.[28] It is registration that confers on the transferee the legal estate,[29] despite any defect in the transferor's title or any irregularity in the transfer.[30] With the land, the transferee takes all easements and other rights for the benefit of the land.[31] Correspondingly the transferee takes subject to all entries on the register and to interests which override registration. However, where the disposition is made for valuable consideration (which at present includes marriage consideration but will not do so when the Land Registration Act 2002 comes into force[32]), he takes free from all other estates and interests,[33] even if he has express notice of them.[34] It is otherwise if the transferee contracts to take the land "subject to" some other interest, for the court will not permit the Act to be used as an instrument of fraud.[35] A transfer made without valuable consideration has the same effect as a transfer for value, except that the transferee takes subject to any interests which require protection on the register that bind the transferor even if they have not been protected.[36]

2. Mortgages

Mortgages of registered land may at present be created by a registered charge, by a lease or sub-lease, by an unregistered mortgage, or by deposit of the land certificate. However, the Land Registration Act 2002 will prospectively abolish mortgages of registered land by lease or sub-lease[37] and sub-mortgages of registered land will also be prohibited, no matter what type the mortgage is.[38] These different types of mortgages are considered later.[39]

---

[26] See below, p. 169.
[27] L.R.A. 1925, ss.19–23 (see *Grace Rymer Investments Ltd v. Waite* [1958] Ch. 831 (charge)); L.R.A. 2002, s.74.
[28] L.R.R. 1925, r. 83(2); L.R.A. 2002, s.74.
[29] L.R.A. 1925, ss.20, 69 (*Morelle Ltd v. Wakeling* [1955] 2 Q.B. 379 at 411); L.R.A. 2002, s.27(1).
[30] *Morelle Ltd v. Wakeling* [1955] 2 Q.B. 379.
[31] L.R.A. 1925, s.20. This is implicit in L.R.A. 2002.
[32] L.R.A. 2002, s.131(1).
[33] L.R.A. 1925, s.20(1) (see *Freer v. Unwins Ltd* [1976] Ch. 288); L.R.A. 2002, s.29.
[34] *Hodges v. Jones* [1935] Ch. 657 at 671; *De Lusignan v. Johnson* [1974] E.G.D. 76. Contrast *Peffer v. Rigg* [1977] 1 W.L.R. 285, which is unlikely to be followed, particularly after L.R.A. 2002 comes into force.
[35] *Lyus v. Prowsa Developments Ltd* [1982] 1 W.L.R. 1044.
[36] L.R.A. 1925, s.20(4); L.R.A. 2002, s.29.
[37] L.R.A. 2002, s.23(1).
[38] L.R.A. 2002, s.23(2).
[39] See below, pp. 497 *et seq.*

3. Transfer on Death

On the death of a sole registered proprietor, his personal representatives may either[40]:

(i) apply for registration themselves, on producing to the registrar the grant of probate or letters of administration; or

(ii) without being themselves registered, transfer the land direct either to a purchaser or to the person entitled under the will or intestacy; in this case, both the transfer or assent and the probate or letters of administration must be lodged with the application for registration.

The name of a joint proprietor will be removed from the register on proof of death.[41]

4. Bankruptcy

The steps at present taken on bankruptcy, so far as they affect registered land, are briefly as follows.

(i) A bankruptcy petition is presented; this is protected by the entry of a creditors' notice, which prevents the debtor from selling the land free from the claims of the creditors.

(ii) A bankruptcy order is made; this is protected by a bankruptcy inhibition, which prevents the registered proprietor from dealing with the land at all.

(iii) The registered proprietor is adjudicated bankrupt. His trustee in bankruptcy (or, until a trustee is appointed, the official receiver) may be registered as proprietor in place of the bankrupt on production of an office copy of the adjudication, a certificate of his appointment as trustee and a declaration that the land is part of the bankrupt's estate.[42]

Under the Land Registration Act 2002, bankruptcy inhibitions will necessarily be replaced by restrictions (because inhibitions will be abolished). Other matters will be governed by the new Rules.[43]

5. Limitation and Prescription

(a) Limitation under the Land Registration Act 1925

At present a title to registered land may be acquired under the Limitation Act 1980 in the same way as in the case of unregistered land. This occurs when a person, his predecessors in title, and earlier adverse possessors dispossessed by him or them having between them been in adverse possession for a continuous period of 12 years. The 12-year period starts to run again as against holders of superior titles when the inferior title would have determined but for the adverse possession and holders of interests under trusts which are not in possession have a further six-year period in which to recover the land after their interests

---

[40] L.R.A. 1925, ss.37, 41; L.R.R. 1925, rr.168,170. The new L.R.R. will deal with this (L.R.A. 2002, s.24(2)).
[41] L.R.R. 1925, r. 172. The new L.R.R. will deal with this (L.R.A. 2002, s.24(2)).
[42] L.R.A. 1925, ss.42, 61, as amended by Insolvency Act 1985, Sched. 8, para. 5; L.R.R. 1925, rr. 174–177. The new L.R.R. will deal with this (L.R.A. 2002, s.24(2)).
[43] L.R.A. 2002, s.24(2).

come into possession. However, in the case of registered land, no legal title is acquired by the adverse possessor until he has been registered as proprietor; until then, the registered proprietor holds the land on trust for him.[44] Registration of the adverse possessor's title may be made with absolute, qualified, good leasehold or possessory title as the case may be, but interests not extinguished by the adverse possession such as easements and restrictive covenants are not affected and retain their existing priorities.

(b) Limitation under the Land Registration Act 2002

The Land Registration Act 2002 will totally change the present law when it comes into force. This change has been made because of what the Law Commission has described[45] as "considerable public disquiet" over the operation of the existing law. Adverse possession of itself, for however long, will not bar the title of the registered proprietor.[46] The new system will be as follows.

(i) Ten-year period: When a person is in adverse possession of registered land or has been evicted from that land during the last six months by the registered proprietor, and he and his predecessors in title (but not earlier adverse possessors dispossessed by him or them) have been in adverse possession for 10 years, he will be able to apply to the registrar to be registered as proprietor.[47] However, no application will be able to be made during any period while the registered proprietor is an enemy, detained in enemy territory, or is suffering from mental disability.[48] No one will be regarded as having been in adverse possession during any period while the land has been held for persons by way of succession.[49]

(ii) Procedure thereafter: The registrar will then notify this application to the registered proprietor, any registered chargee, and the registered proprietor of any superior title.[50] Anyone who is notified will be able to serve a notice on the registrar within a period to be laid down by the new Rules.[51] If no one does so, the applicant will be registered as proprietor.[52] If a notice is served, the applicant will only be able to be registered as proprietor at this stage in one of the following three circumstances: first, if it would be unconscionable because of an equity by estoppel for the registered proprietor to seek to dispossess the applicant and the circumstances are such that the applicant ought to be registered as proprietor; secondly, if he is for some other reason entitled to be registered as proprietor (for example, as being entitled under the will or intestacy of the deceased proprietor or having purchased the land without having taken a transfer); and, thirdly, if he is the owner of adjoining property, the boundary has not been determined, and for the 10-year period he reasonably believed that the land to which the application relates belonged to him.[53] If the applicant and the server of the notice cannot reach agreement as to whether any of these

---

[44] L.R.A. 1925, s.75. For limitation, see below, pp. 547 *et seq.* Contrast unregistered land, where the adverse possessor acquires an entirely new estate: below, p. 559.
[45] Law. Com. No. 271, para. 24.
[46] L.R.A. 2002, s.95(1).
[47] L.R.A. 2002, Sched. 6, para. 1.
[48] *ibid.,* para. 8.
[49] *ibid.,* para. 12.
[50] *ibid.,* para. 2.
[51] *ibid.,* para. 3.
[52] *ibid.,* para. 4.
[53] *ibid.,* para. 5.

circumstances has arisen, the registrar will have to refer the matter to the Adjudicator in accordance with the dispute resolution procedures already discussed.[54]

(iii) Further two-year period: Save in these three circumstances, the registered proprietor will then have a further period of two years from the date of the application to evict the adverse possessor. If he does not commence proceedings by then, a further application by the same applicant or his successors in title to be registered as proprietor after that two year period will be successful.[55]

(iv) Effect of registration: The adverse possessor will obtain the same class of title as the previous registered proprietor. Following registration, the priorities of existing interests in the registered land will be preserved save in the case of registered charges, which will only bind the adverse possessor if he is registered in one of the three circumstances set out above (the reason for the general exclusion of registered charges is that the chargee will be one of the persons entitled to be notified).[56]

(v) Precautions: When the Land Registration Act 2002 comes into force, registered proprietors will need to ensure that the register contains an address other than the address of the property in question (up to three addresses will be able to be included) otherwise the notification sent by the registrar will be received by the adverse possessor and by no one else other than any registered chargees and holders of superior titles! Further, owners of unregistered land who consider that they may have a potential problem with adverse possessors will be well advised to apply for voluntary registration of title to bring their land within the new system.

(c) Prescription

"Easements, rights and privileges adversely affecting registered land" are capable of being acquired by prescription in the same way as if the land were not registered.[57] Such rights override registration under the Land Registration Act 1925[58] and will continue to do so under the Land Registration Act 2002.[59]

Sect. 4. Rectification and indemnity

Although in general it may be said that a registered proprietor has a title guaranteed by the State, the guarantee is not absolute but relative. There is power to rectify the register so as to correct mistakes, and a registered proprietor may lose some or all of his land by rectification. If he does, he will instead have a right to compensation by way of indemnity. His title is, in effect, insured by the state: he will have either the land or compensation. The existing statutory provisions for rectification have been completely recast by the Land Registration Act 2002. The existing statutory provisions for indemnity were amended as recently as 1997 and will not be further changed by the Land Registration Act 2002 when it comes into force, although the provisions of the latter Act are in a different form.

---

[54] Above, p. 113.
[55] L.R.A. 2002, Sched. 6, paras 6, 7.
[56] *ibid.*, para. 9.
[57] L.R.R. 1925, r. 250. For prescription, see below, pp. 430 *et seq.*
[58] L.R.A. 1925, s.70(1)(a).
[59] L.R.A. 2002, Sched. 1, para. 3; Sched. 3, para. 3.

1. Rectification under the Land Registration Act 1925

(a) Jurisdiction

The statutory power to rectify the register under section 82 of the Land Registration Act 1925 is confined[60] to eight statutory grounds. Rectification may be ordered by the court, or, except on the first two grounds, by the registrar.[61] It is important to emphasise that the fact that the court or the registrar may order rectification under one or more of the statutory grounds does not mean that the order must be made. Whether or not rectification is ordered is a matter of discretion.[62] In exercising its discretion, the court will consider factors such as the relative good faith and blameworthiness of the parties,[63] and both the availability of an indemnity and the impact on the future utilisation of the land on the alternative hypotheses that rectification is and is not ordered[64]; undertakings offered by the parties may also be relevant to the court's decision.[65] Rectification or non-rectification cannot be ordered on terms,[66] although any undertaking by one party which are accepted by the other party will in practice take effect as terms.

(b) Human rights

The power to refuse rectification and the inability to order rectification or non-rectification on terms has been challenged on the grounds that it infringes the right of every person under the Human Rights Act 1998 to the peaceful enjoyment of his possessions.[67] However, the power to refuse rectification was justified on the basis that "it is given for the legitimate aim in the public interest in enhancing the land registration system"[68] and the criticism of the inability to order rectification or non-rectification on terms was rejected on the basis that the present provisions for indemnity are "reasonably related to the value of the property lost".[69]

(c) Grounds

The eight grounds for rectification may be summarised as follows. In some cases, two or more of the grounds are applicable.[70]

(i) Entitlement: where the court has decided that a person is entitled to an estate, right or interest in the land, and as a consequence of the decision considers that rectification is required, and so orders. As well as an order for the registration of some person other than the existing registered proprietor as proprietor of some or all of the land,[71] an order may be made to rectify the register by entering notices, cautions or restrictions to protect some right.[72]

---

[60] *Norwich & Peterborough B.S. v. Steed* [1993] Ch. 116.
[61] L.R.A. 1925, s.82(1), setting out the grounds in the eight lettered paragraphs considered below.
[62] *Argyle B.S. v. Hammond* (1985) 49 P. & C.R. 148.
[63] *Claridge v. Tingey* [1967] 1 W.L.R. 134; *Kingsalton Ltd v. Thames Water Developments Ltd* [2002] 1 P. & C.R. 15 at paras 27–28.
[64] *Epps v. Esso Petroleum Co. Ltd* [1973] 1 W.L.R. 1071; *Kingsalton Ltd v. Thames Water Developments Ltd* [2002] 1 P. & C.R. 15 at paras 27–28.
[65] *Kingsalton Ltd v. Thames Water Developments Ltd* [2002] 1 P. & C.R. 15 at paras 31–35.
[66] *ibid.*, at paras 31, 46, 58.
[67] E.C.H.R., Protocol 1, art.1.
[68] *Kingsalton Ltd v. Thames Water Developments Ltd* [2002] 1 P. & C.R. 15 at para. 45.
[69] *ibid.*, para. 30.
[70] See, *e.g. Chowood Ltd v. Lyall (No. 2)* [1930] 2 Ch. 156 (grounds (a), (g) and (h), and perhaps (b)).
[71] *Kingsalton Ltd v. Thames Water Developments Ltd* [2002] 1 P. & C.R. 15.
[72] *Orakpo v. Manson Investments Ltd* [1977] 1 W.L.R. 347 (in H.L. [1978] A.C. 95).

(ii) Person aggrieved: where any person is aggrieved by the making or omission of an entry, or any default or unnecessary delay in making an entry. Rectification to expunge a caution may be ordered summarily on motion where there is no serious question to be tried.[73]

(iii) Consent: where all persons interested consent.

(iv) Fraud: where the court or the registrar is satisfied that any entry has been obtained by fraud. The requisite fraud is some actual dishonesty of the person obtaining the entry, and not (unless he knew of it at the time) the fraud of a predecessor in title of his.[74] But it is no fraud for the proprietor merely to take advantage of some legal right, as where statute invalidates some adverse interest.[75]

(v) Duplication: where two or more persons are mistakenly registered as proprietors of the same registered estate or charge.

(vi) Mortgage: where a mortgagee has been registered as proprietor of the land instead of as proprietor of a charge, and a right of redemption still exists.

(vii) Non-owner: where a legal estate has been registered in the name of a person who, if the land had not been registered, would not have been the estate owner. This applies to the registration of a proprietor whose title has been extinguished under the Limitation Act 1980[76] and to a proprietor who has been registered as a result of a transaction which was void because of forgery or *non est factum*, or because the transferor had no title or no power to convey.[77]

(viii) "Just": In any other case where it is deemed just to rectify the register by reason of any error or omission in it, or by reason of any entry made under a mistake. "Mistake" is given a very wide meaning, and it covers the case where a title is registered for more land than the applicant owns[78]; but where a charge is correctly entered, there can be no rectification merely because the charge was obtained by fraud.[79] However, this power does not confer a general discretion to rectify merely because it seems just, but applies only in the circumstances already listed.[80] It therefore merely re-emphasises that the fact that the court or the registrar may order rectification under one or more of the statutory grounds does not mean that it must do so. In so far as any earlier authorities suggested that rectification could be ordered under this head when it could not be ordered under any of the others,[81] those authorities will presumably no longer be followed.

In addition, there are minor powers to correct or amend the register, such as for clerical errors or fixing boundaries.[82]

---

[73] *Price Bros. (Somerford) Ltd v. J. Kelly Homes (Stoke-on-Trent) Ltd* [1975] 1 W.L.R. 1512.

[74] See *Assets Co. Ltd v. Mere Roihi* [1905] A.C. 176 at 210; and see *Re Leighton's Conveyance* [1936] 1 All E.R. 667 (in C.A. [1937] Ch. 149).

[75] *Re Monolithic Building Co.* [1915] 1 Ch. 643 at 669; *Midland Bank Trust Co. Ltd v. Green* [1981] A.C. 513 at 531.

[76] *Spectrum Investment Co. v. Holmes* [1981] 1 W.L.R. 221.

[77] *Norwich & Peterborough B.S. v. Steed* [1993] Ch. 116 at 132.

[78] *Chowood Ltd v. Lyall (No. 2)* [1930] 2 Ch. 156.

[79] *Norwich & Peterborough B.S. v. Steed* [1993] Ch. 116.

[80] *Norwich & Peterborough B.S. v. Steed* [1993] Ch. 116 at 135.

[81] *Re Dances Way, West Town, Hayling Island* [1962] Ch. 490 (decision that, on an application made on this ground, the registrar has jurisdiction to determine the extent of a right of way).

[82] See, *e.g.* L.R.R. 1925, rr. 13, 14, 131, 276, 277.

(d) Proprietor in possession

The width of the overlapping grounds for rectification considered above is subject to an important qualification. The register cannot be rectified on any of the grounds "so as to affect the title of the proprietor who is in possession".[83] This is the nearest approach to indefeasibility in the Act. "Possession" seems to mean "physical occupation". The term is defined in the Act as including (unless the context otherwise requires) the right to receive the rents and profits[84] but it is now clear that that definition is not applicable here,[85] (for it were, every registered proprietor would be in possession and so every case would fall into this category rather than under the heads already discussed[86]). Instead, every registered proprietor is deemed by virtue of his registration to have possession of the registered land unless and until he is physically dispossessed.[87] The reason for this qualification is that, while monetary compensation will usually be adequate in place of the rents and profits which are all that a registered proprietor whose title is rectified under the heads already discussed will have been receiving, for a proprietor in physical occupation it is no substitute for the land itself.

This protection for the proprietor in possession is subject to four exceptions.[88]

(i) "Overriding interests": giving effect to interests which override registration. Every registered title is subject to all interests which override registration, and so rectification to give effect to them will not affect the rights of the proprietor. An interest which overrides registration existing at the time of first registration is not affected if the proprietor later goes out of possession.[89]

(ii) Order of court: giving effect to an order of the court. The purpose of this exception, added in 1977, may well have been to enable the court to order rectification against a proprietor in possession where the property had been transferred to him in order to defraud the transferor's creditors or to defeat the potential claims of his spouse and dependants on his divorce or death.[90] However, the wording of the provision is certainly not limited to this; it also enables the court to order the registration of a trustee in bankruptcy in place of the bankrupt and to order the registration of new trustees appointed pursuant to its statutory jurisdiction. And, contrary to what was previously thought, it has now been held that the addition of this exception means that the court no longer has any absolute fetter against ordering rectification against a registered proprietor in possession.[91] However, that does not mean that any fundamental change has been made to the policy of the Act, so that the two remaining factors set out below continue to be highly relevant when the court is deciding whether or not to exercise its discretion.[92] It is therefore not thought that it gives the court any general discretion to order rectification against a proprietor in possession.

(iii) Proprietor's fraud or lack of care: the proprietor "has caused or substantially contributed to the error or omission by fraud or lack of proper care". This wording, amended

---

[83] L.R.A. 1925, s.82(3), as amended by Administration of Justice Act 1977, s.24.
[84] L.R.A. 1925, s.3(xviii); and see *Freer v. Unwins Ltd* [1976] Ch. 288 at 294, a dictum which has not been followed.
[85] *Kingsalton Ltd v. Thames Water Developments Ltd* [2002] 1 P. & C.R. 15 at para. 21.
[86] See (1968) 84 L.Q.R. 528 at 539, 540 (S. Cretney and G. Dworkin); Ruoff & Roper 40–10.
[87] *Kingsalton Ltd v. Thames Water Developments Ltd* [2002] 1 P. & C.R. 15 at para. 21.
[88] L.R.A. 1925, s.82(3), as amended by Administration of Justice Act 1977, s.24.
[89] *London and Cheshire Insurance Co. Ltd v. Laplagrene Property Co. Ltd* [1971] Ch. 499.
[90] See *Kingsalton Ltd v. Thames Water Developments Ltd* [2002] 1 P. & C.R. 15 at para. 54.
[91] *ibid.*, at paras 18, 42, 54.
[92] *ibid.*

in 1977, now excludes innocent mistakes such as misdescribing the land when applying for first registration[93]; but it includes intentionally misleading the registrar.[94]

(iv) Unjust not to rectify: where "for any other reason, in any particular case, it is considered that it would be unjust not to rectify the register" against the proprietor. The question is not whether to order rectification would be "just", but whether refusing to order it would be "unjust": a positive case of injustice must be shown. This wide and general ground requires a broad survey of all the relevant facts. Thus rectification has been refused under this head where the true owner of the land had no real use for it, so that an indemnity would be adequate to satisfy him, and the registered proprietor had spent money on the land.[95] The court may also, as before, take account of the relative blameworthiness of the parties[96] and of the availability of an indemnity on the alternative hypotheses that rectification is and is not ordered.[97]

(e) Effect of rectification

On rectification, a new edition of the register is issued, and the rectification takes effect then, without relating back to any earlier date.[98]

2. Rectification under the Land Registration Act 2002

The provisions of the Land Registration Act 2002 in respect of what it describes as alteration of the register are contained in Schedule 4.[99] The present law has been recast to reflect the present practice in relation to rectification and amendment of the register. Rectification is defined much more narrowly and is limited to the situation where a mistake is to be corrected and where the correction also prejudicially affects the title of the registered proprietor.[1] Rectification will become just one particular form of alteration.

(a) Alterations which do not amount to rectification

The court will be able to order[2] and the registrar will be able to make[3] an alteration to the register as distinct from a rectification of it for the purposes of correcting mistakes, bringing the register up to date, and giving effect to any estate, right or interest excepted from the effect of registration; and the registrar also has power to remove superfluous entries. Rules may make provision for the circumstances in which there is a duty to make alterations of this type.[4] They will obviously enable clerical errors to be amended but will also enable effect to be given to interests which override registration, since such alterations do not prejudice the registered proprietor who is bound by such interests both before and after the alteration.

---

[93] See, *e.g. Claridge v. Tingey* [1967] 1 W.L.R. 134.
[94] See *Re Leighton's Conveyance* [1936] 1 All E.R. 667 (in C.A. [1937] Ch. 149).
[95] *Re 139 High Street, Deptford* [1951] Ch. 884; see at 892; *Epps v. Esso Petroleum Co. Ltd* [1973] 1 W.L.R. 1071 at 1082, 1083.
[96] *Hounslow L.B.C. v. Hare* (1992) 24 H.L.R. 9 at 26; *Horrill v. Cooper* [1998] E.G.C.S. 151.
[97] *Epps v. Esso Petroleum Co. Ltd* [1973] 1 W.L.R. 1071.
[98] *Freer v. Unwins Ltd* [1976] Ch. 288.
[99] L.R.A. 2002, s.65.
[1] L.R.A. 2002, Sched. 4, para. 1.
[2] *ibid.*, para. 2.
[3] *ibid.*, para. 5.
[4] *ibid.*, paras 4(a), 7(a).

(b) Alterations which do amount to rectification

The court[5] and the registrar[6] will be able to order rectification of the register.

(i) Registered proprietors not in possession: Unless there are exceptional circumstances which justify not doing so, the court and the registrar will be obliged to order rectification as against a registered proprietor who is not in possession.[7] Possession clearly means physical occupation since in this Act possession is not defined as including the receipt of rents and profits, although it would have been preferable if this had been spelt out. There will therefore be considerably less discretion not to order rectification in such circumstances than under the present law, although the authorities on the Land Registration Act 1925 may nevertheless continue to be relevant in deciding when there are such exceptional circumstances.

(ii) Registered proprietors in possession: The court and the registrar will not be able to order rectification as against a registered proprietor who is in possession unless he has by fraud or lack of proper care caused or substantially contributed to the mistake or it would for any other reason be unjust for rectification not to be made.[8] These are two of the exceptions in the Land Registration Act 1925, and the authorities already considered will clearly continue to be relevant. No provision is made for the court to order rectification, as it can at present, against a proprietor in possession where the property had been transferred to him in order to defraud the transferor's creditors or to defeat the potential claims of his spouse and dependants on his divorce or death. This is less than satisfactory. Presumably the person seeking to reverse the effect of the transfer will have to be ordered to retransfer the property himself.

(iii) Effect of rectification: Rectification will continue to be of only prospective effect.[9]

3. Indemnity

Indemnity is governed by section 83 of the Land Registration Act 1925, which was substantially reformed in 1997 with prospective effect from April 1, 1998. Indemnity under the Land Registration Act 2002 will be governed by Schedule 8.[10] The latter Act will not make any further reforms but its provisions are in a different form. The right to indemnity falls under three heads: the grounds, exceptions, and determination.

(a) Grounds

The grounds on which a person may claim indemnity may be put under four heads.

(i) Rectification: loss by reason of any rectification of the register.[11] There is no indemnity for rectification which does not cause any loss but merely gives effect to a loss previously suffered, as where it gives effect to an overriding interest[12] such as a title acquired by an adverse possessor under the Limitation Act 1980,[13] or the rights of a person in actual occupation of the land when the proprietor acquired his registered title.[14] However, where the

---

[5] *ibid.*, para. 3.
[6] *ibid.*, para. 6.
[7] *ibid.*, paras 3(3), 6(3).
[8] *ibid.*, paras 3(2), 6(2).
[9] *ibid.*, para. 8.
[10] L.R.A. 2002, s.102.
[11] L.R.A. 1925, s.83(1); L.R.A. 2002, Sched. 8, para. 1(1)(a).
[12] For these, see above, pp. 121 *et seq.*
[13] *Re Chowood's Registered Land* [1933] Ch. 574.
[14] *Re Boyle's Claim* [1961] 1 W.L.R. 339 (boundary dispute).

title of a proprietor claiming in good faith under a forged disposition is rectified, he is deemed to have suffered loss by reason of the rectification and to be entitled to indemnity.[15] Since April 1, 1998, indemnity may also be paid to a person in whose favour the register is rectified who nevertheless suffers loss. (This is possible because the rectification has only prospective effect and so adverse terms of an overriding interest such as a lease created between the mistake and the rectification may continue to bind him after rectification[16]).

(ii) Non-rectification: loss by reason of an error or omission in the register which is not rectified. Thus if F by forgery obtains registration as proprietor of A's land, and then sells it to B, A will be entitled to indemnity if he cannot obtain rectification against B because B is a registered proprietor in possession.[17]

(iii) Conversion of title: loss suffered by anyone except the registered proprietor by reason of any entry made on the conversion of titles.[18]

(iv) Errors: loss by reason of various errors or omissions. These include errors in official searches or inaccuracies in various documents, and also the loss or destruction of documents lodged at the registry.[19]

(b) Exceptions

The main provision is that no indemnity is payable where the applicant or a predecessor in title of his (except under a disposition for value protected on the register) has suffered loss wholly or partly as a result of his own fraud or wholly as a result of his own lack of proper care.[20] Prior to April 1, 1998, any lack of proper care deprived the applicant of any indemnity; a consequence of the reform made with effect from that date is that any indemnity paid where the applicant has suffered loss partly as a result of his own lack of proper care is reduced to such extent as is just and equitable having regard to his share of the responsibility.[21] There are also exceptions for certain minerals and costs.[22]

(c) Determination

Liability and amount are both determined by proceedings in court against the registrar; and payment is made out of moneys provided by Parliament.[23] The indemnity is for the amount of the loss, together with a reasonable amount for costs and expenses properly incurred by the claimant, though not the costs of any proceedings brought by the claimant against third parties (such as those who caused the loss) without the registrar's consent.[24] But where an estate or interest in land, or a charge on it, has been lost, the amount of the indemnity is restricted to its value. For rectification, the amount is the value immediately before rectification. For non-rectification it is the value when the error or omission causing the loss was

---

[15] L.R.A. 1925, s.83(4); L.R.A. 2002, Sched. 8, para. 1(2)(b).
[16] *Freer v. Unwins Ltd* [1976] Ch. 288.
[17] See above, p. 141.
[18] L.R.A. 1925, s.77(6); L.R.A. 2002, Sched. 8, para. 1(2)(a).
[19] L.R.A. 1925, ss.83(3), 110(4), 113; L.R.A. 2002, Sched. 8, para. 1(2)(c)–(h); see below, p. 546 (tacking).
[20] L.R.A. 1925, s.83(5)(a); L.R.A. 2002, Sched. 8, para. 5(1), (3).
[21] L.R.A. 1925, s.83(6); L.R.A. 2002, Sched. 8, para. 5(2).
[22] L.R.A. 1925, s.83(5)(b), (c); L.R.A. 2002, Sched. 8, para. 2; Act of 1971, s.2; for costs, see below.
[23] Act of 1971, ss.1, 2. In 1993–1994, there were 50 claims amounting in all to £1,520,000, with a further £336,000 in costs: see Ruoff & Roper 40–32.
[24] L.R.A. 1925, s.85(3)(c), (8); L.R.A. 2002, Sched. 8, para. 3(1); Act of 1971, s.2(2), (4).

made.[25] This may be much less than its present value[26] but the restriction is less harsh than it appears because the registry pays interest on the sum from the time that the mistake is made.[27] Claims for indemnity are barred after six years, though time begins to run only when the claimant knew of the existence of the claim, or but for his own default might have known of it.[28] Formerly, when the claim arose from registration with an absolute or good leasehold title, the six years ran from the date of registration, though there were some exceptions for infants, remaindermen, restrictive covenants and mortgages.[29] However, this has not been the case since April 1, 1998.[30]

Where an indemnity is paid, the registrar may recover the amount of it from any person who caused or substantially contributed to the loss by his fraud.[31]

---

[25] L.R.A. 1925, s.83(6); L.R.A. 2002, Sched. 8, para. 6.
[26] See *Epps v. Esso Petroleum Co. Ltd* [1973] 1 W.L.R. 1071 at 1081 (1959 values for non-rectification in 1973).
[27] Apparently on the basis of Act of 1971, s.2(5). Rules may be made in this respect under L.R.A. 2002 (see Sched. 8, para. 9).
[28] L.R.A. 1925, s.83(11); L.R.A. 2002, Sched. 8, para. 1(8); Limitation Act 1980, Sched. 3, para. 1.
[29] L.R.A. 1925, s.83(11); see *Epps v. Esso Petroleum Co. Ltd* [1973] 1 W.L.R. 1071.
[30] L.R.A. 1997, s.2.
[31] L.R.A. 1925, s.83(9); L.R.A. 2002, Sched. 8, para. 10.

Chapter 5

DISPOSITIONS OF LAND

Land may be disposed of in a variety of ways. The most common dispositions *inter vivos* are by sale, though gifts and settlements are sometimes made. On a sale, the formal conveyance or transfer of the land is almost always preceded by a contract for sale. Then on death, land may pass under the owner's will or, if none, under the rules for intestacy; and in each case, the executors or administrators of the estate of the deceased (his "personal representatives") have an important part to play. Finally, there are various disabilities which restrict certain persons or bodies in owning or disposing of land. In this chapter, these subjects will be considered under six headings:

1. Contracts;

2. Conveyancing;

3. Wills;

4. Intestacy;

5. Personal representatives; and

6. Disabilities.

PART 1—CONTRACTS

The law governing contracts for the sale or disposition of any interest in land was substantially reformed in 1989. Under the Law of Property (Miscellaneous Provisions) Act 1989[1] contracts made before September 27, 1989, continue to be governed by the old law, but all other contracts are subject to the new law.[2] Although the former law is now of very little importance, in order that decisions made thereunder may be understood, it must be briefly summarised before turning to the new law.

---

[1] Cited as L.P.(M.P.)A. 1989. It is discussed at [1989] Conv. 431 (P. H. Pettit).
[2] L.P.(M.P.)A. 1989, ss.2(7), 5(3), (4).

Sect. 1. Contracts made before September 27, 1989

Before September 27, 1989, a contract for the sale or disposition of land or any interest in land could be validly made in any way. Although such contracts were usually made in writing, an oral contract was perfectly valid. But unless an oral contract was sufficiently evidenced in writing, or supported by a sufficient act of part performance, it could not be enforced by action.[3] Although deprived of its most important remedy, such a contract remained valid, and it could be enforced by any means except an action, as where a vendor forfeited (*i.e.* kept) the deposit paid by a purchaser who later defaulted.[4] The law as to writing and part performance gave rise to much litigation.[5]

1. Evidenced in writing

The law required the agreement, "or some memorandum or note thereof", to be in writing, and to be signed by or on behalf of "the party to be charged",[6] namely, the person against whom the action was to be brought. Any form of evidence of the contract sufficed if it was in writing; and it might come into existence long after the contract was made, and be made up of two or more connected documents. But the writing was required to state all the terms of the contract that the parties had agreed. Where the evidence in writing was signed by one party (V) but not by the other (P), V could not sue P, but P could sue V; for V was the party to be charged.

2. Part performance

If a party to an oral contract for the sale or disposition of land or any interest in land had carried out a sufficient act of part performance of that contract, equity would enforce it for him against the other party. The principle behind the doctrine[7] was that, if the plaintiff had partly performed the contract, it would have been fraudulent for the defendant to plead the lack of evidence as a defence. The acts done by the plaintiff raised an equity in his favour, and in satisfying that equity the court had to choose "between undoing what has been done (which is not always possible, or, if possible, just) and completing what has been left undone."[8] Part performance differed from evidence in writing in that the act of part performance had to have been done by the plaintiff, whereas the evidence in writing had to have been signed by the defendant. What was required for part performance was some act which sufficiently indicated that there was some contract of the kind alleged. Thus if V agreed to sell land to P, and then allowed P to take possession of the land, the handing over of possession was a sufficient act of part performance both by V and by P.

Sect. 2. Contracts made after September 26, 1989

For any contract made after September 26, 1989, the Act of 1989 repealed the law both as to evidence in writing and part performance.[9] Instead, it provided that "a contract for the sale

---

[3] L.P.A. 1925, s.40.
[4] *Monnickendam v. Leanse* (1923) 39 T.L.R. 445.
[5] For details, see M. & W. (5th ed.), pp. 571–598.
[6] L.P.A. 1925, s.40(1), replacing part of Statute of Frauds 1677, s.4; and see below, p. 293.
[7] It had been recognised by L.P.A. 1925, s.40(2).
[8] *Maddison v. Alderson* (1883) 8 App.Cas. 467 at 476, *per* Earl of Selborne L.C.
[9] L.P.(M.P.)A. 1989, ss.2(1), (7), (8), 5(3), (4), Sched. 2.

or other disposition of an interest in land can only be made in writing and only by incorporating all the terms which the parties have expressly agreed in one document or, where contracts are exchanged, in each."[10] A contract which does not comply with this provision is wholly void, and not merely unenforceable by action. The terms of this provision will be considered in turn, together with the requirement as to signature.

1. Sale or other disposition

(a) Transactions included

"The sale or other disposition" of an interest in land includes every type of disposition, whether sale, lease, mortgage or anything else[11]; and it applies both to disposing of existing interests and to the creation of new interests. It includes the sale of fixtures separately from the land to a stranger,[12] but not to the sale of fixtures to the landlord by a tenant who is entitled to remove them,[13] for in substance this is merely a waiver by the tenant of his right of removal, and so is no sale of either land or goods.[14]

(b) Exceptions

There are three classes of contract to which these statutory provisions do not apply[15]:

(i) short leases—a lease for not more than three years at the best rent reasonably obtainable without taking a fine[16];

(ii) public auctions—a contract made in the course of a public auction;

(iii) financial services—a contract regulated under what is now the Financial Services and Markets Act 2000, which has replaced the Financial Services Act 1986; this Act controls the conduct of investment business.

Further, these statutory provisions do not affect the creation or operation of resulting, implied or constructive trusts.[17] It has now been held that estoppel interests take effect behind a constructive trust.[18] Consequently, if a party to an agreement with a landowner which does not satisfy the statutory formalities acts to his detriment on the strength of an assurance by the landowner that he will thereby acquire an interest in the land, he will be able to claim that interest on the basis that the landowner is estopped from denying the existence of that interest and is therefore a constructive trustee of the land for him.[19]

2. Interest in land

"Interest in land" is widely defined. It means "any estate, interest or charge in or over land or in or over the proceeds of sale of land".[20] Interests under a trust for sale of land are thus

---

[10] L.P.(M.P.)A. 1989, s.2(1).
[11] *ibid.*, s.2(6); L.P.A. 1925, s.205(1)(ii).
[12] See *Underwood Ltd v. Burgh Castle Brick and Cement Syndicate* [1922] 1 K.B. 123.
[13] See above, p. 22.
[14] *Lee v. Gaskell* (1876) 1 Q.B.D. 700.
[15] L.P.(M.P.)A. 1989, s.2(5).
[16] See below, p. 342.
[17] L.P.(M.P.)A. 1989, s.2(5).
[18] *Yaxley v. Gotts* [2000] Ch. 162.
[19] *Yaxley v. Gotts* [2000] Ch. 162.
[20] L.P.(M.P.)A. 1989, s.2(6).

plainly included, but the Act does not apply to annual crops, such as corn or potatoes, which require the periodical application of labour for their production; these are known as *fructus industriales*.[21] *Fructus naturales*, on the other hand, are sometimes included. This term applies to the natural products of the soil, such as grass and timber, and also the products of those plants and trees which, although needing attention at first, do not require it each year to produce a crop,[22] such as fruit from fruit trees.[23] *Fructus naturales* are treated as land within the statute unless either they are to be severed by the vendor and not the purchaser,[24] or else the contract binds the purchaser to sever them as soon as possible.[25]

3. Made in writing

The Act requires the contract to be "made" in writing and not merely "evidenced" in writing.[26] An oral agreement is thus void, and cannot constitute a binding contract. Under an option to buy land, it could be said that there is no contract of purchase until the purchaser has exercised his option; but for the purposes of the Act the option is treated as being a conditional contract to sell the land, so that if the option satisfies the Act it is immaterial that the notice exercising it does not.[27] One consequence of this is that an option granted in 1988 and exercised in 2001 will be subject to the old law and not the new, even though not until 2001 did any obligation to buy and sell arise.

4. All the terms

(a) The terms

The writing must incorporate "all the terms which the parties have expressly agreed".[28] This does not extend to terms implied by law, such as the term that on a sale with vacant possession, vacant possession must be given at completion[29]; and perhaps the omission of an express term to this effect would be no breach of the statute.[30] Terms may be incorporated in a document either by being set out in it or by reference to some other document.[31] Formerly, although a memorandum in writing which did not accord with the true contract was bad if a term solely for the benefit of one party, or to his detriment, was omitted, that party could cure the defect by offering to waive the term if it was for his benefit, or to perform it if it was for his detriment.[32] But no such cure seems possible now that the contract must include all the express terms.

(b) Certainty

The terms of the contract are sufficiently stated if they fall within the principle *id certum est quod certum reddi potest* (that is certain which can be made certain). The only three essential terms are the parties, the property to be sold and the price; a contract which contains no more

---

[21] See *Duppa v. Mayo* (1669) 1 Wms. Saund. 275.
[22] *Marshall v. Green* (1875) 1 C.P.D. 35 at 40.
[23] *Rodwell v. Phillips* (1842) 9 M. & W. 501.
[24] *Smith v. Surman* (1829) 9 B. & C. 561.
[25] *Marshall v. Green* (1875) 1 C.P.D. 35 (and see the summary of decisions at 42).
[26] L.P.(M.P.)A. 1989, s.2(1).
[27] *Spiro v. Glencrown Properties Ltd* [1991] Ch. 537.
[28] L.P.(M.P.)A. 1989, s.2(1).
[29] See *Topfell Ltd v. Galley Properties Ltd* [1979] 1 W.L.R. 446.
[30] See *Farrell v. Green* (1974) 232 E.G. 587.
[31] L.P.(M.P.)A. 1989, s.2(2).
[32] See M. & W. (5th ed.), pp. 581, 582.

than these three terms is known as an open contract. All other necessary terms, such as the time for completion and the title to be shown by the vendor, can be implied by the general law although the immense majority of contracts contain express provisions dealing with these and many other matters. A contract which contains no express provisions as to, for example, the title to be shown by the vendor, is described as a contract which is open as to title.

(i) As for certainty of the parties, while it is essential that the document should disclose each party to the contract, or his agent,[33] it suffices if, without being named, each party is so described that his identity cannot be fairly disputed,[34] such as if the document refers to the "proprietor"[35] of the property, or states that "the vendor will convey as legal personal representative".[36] But references to the "vendor"[37] or "landlord"[38] or "my clients"[39] are not sufficient by themselves, for these descriptions may fit many persons; the proprietor of land is not the only person who can be the vendor, for many other persons such as mortgagees or even complete strangers may enter into a contract to sell the land.[40]

(ii) As for certainty of the property to be sold, when the land to be sold is sufficiently described, parol evidence is admissible to identify it and its boundaries.[41] However, where a contract is to be completed in stages, it must be stated which part is to be conveyed first.[42] In the absence of any statement to the contrary, it is assumed that the vendor is contracting to sell an estate in fee simple free from incumbrances of which the purchaser is not already aware.[43] Where the contract states that something less than the vendor's entire interest in the property is to pass (such as where a lease is being sold), the contract must state exactly what interest the purchaser is buying.[44]

(iii) And as for certainty of the price, this will be sufficiently certain if it is stated by reference to a formula which the court is capable of applying[45] but not where the parties have merely agreed to agree the price.[46] If the parties refer the decision as to the price to a third party, they will be presumed to have intended him to determine a fair and reasonable price by objective criteria, thus enabling the court to do so in his stead if he declines, in the absence of a clear indication that he was intended to determine it by subjective criteria, in which case the court cannot determine it in his stead.[47]

---

[33] *Davies v. Sweet* [1962] 2 Q.B. 300.
[34] *Carr v. Lynch* [1900] 1 Ch. 613 at 615.
[35] *Rossiter v. Miller* (1878) 3 App.Cas. 1124.
[36] *Fay v. Miller, Wilkins & Co.* [1941] Ch. 360; but see (1941) 57 L.Q.R. 452.
[37] *Potter v. Duffield* (1874) L.R. 18 Eq. 4.
[38] *Coombs v. Wilkes* [1891] 3 Ch. 77.
[39] *Lovesy v. Palmer* [1916] 2 Ch. 233.
[40] *Donnison v. People's Cafe Co.* (1881) 45 L.T. 187.
[41] *Plant v. Bourne* [1897] 2 Ch. 281; *Harewood v. Retese* [1990] 1 W.L.R. 333.
[42] *Bushwall Properties Ltd v. Vortex Properties Ltd* [1976] 1 W.L.R. 591.
[43] *Timmins v. Moreland Street Property Co. Ltd* [1958] Ch. 110.
[44] *Dolling v. Evans* (1867) 36 L.J. Ch. 474; *Cox v. Middleton* (1854) 2 Drew 209.
[45] *Smith v. Jones* [1952] 2 All E.R. 907; *Brown v. Gould* [1972] Ch. 53.
[46] *Courtney Ltd v. Tolaini Brothers Ltd* [1975] 1 W.L.R. 297.
[47] *Sudbrook Trading Estate Ltd v. Eggleton* [1983] 1 A.C. 444; *Re Malpass* [1985] 1 Ch. 42.

Any other express terms of the contract must equally be certain or be capable of being rendered certain. A lack of certainty as to any express term, whether essential or not, will render the entire contract void for uncertainty.

(c) Rectification

Where a document does not satisfy the requirements of the Act of 1989, it can sometimes be rectified by the court so as to cure the defect. Thus a term omitted by mistake can be inserted or mistaken language altered; but strong and convincing proof of the mistake must be adduced. Rectification normally operates retrospectively, so that the document takes effect as if it had originally been in its correct form; but where a contract satisfies the Act of 1989 only by reason of the rectification of one or more documents, the contract comes into being at the time specified in the order of the court.[48]

5. "One document"

Save where contracts are exchanged, the terms expressly agreed must be incorporated in one document. However, the absence of terms which have not been agreed will not invalidate the document provided that the parties intended to be bound with or without those terms.[49] The agreed terms may be incorporated in a document either by being set out in it or by reference to some other document,[50] so that the terms may be found in two or more documents provided one of them sufficiently refers to the others. Where contracts are exchanged, which is what generally occurs in order to enable each party to have a copy signed by the other party, the usual practice is to prepare identical documents, and then, when both parties are ready to bind themselves, to exchange the document signed by the vendor for the document signed by the purchaser.[51] Where both parties are legally represented, traditionally the purchaser's solicitor sends the document signed by the purchaser to the vendor's solicitor together with any deposit payable, and on receipt the vendor's solicitor sends the document signed by the vendor to the purchaser's solicitor. However, because one or both parties is likely to be involved in a related sale or purchase in which contracts have to be exchanged more or less simultaneously, exchanges of contracts are now generally carried out over the telephone in accordance with Formulae laid down by The Law Society[52] on the basis of undertakings by the solicitors involved. However, whether contracts are exchanged or not, the statute does not invalidate an independent collateral warranty (for example as to title) given to induce the signing of the contract.[53] It has also been held that the statute does not invalidate an agreement which is supplemental to a contract (such as to grant a lease) which has been duly carried out and so is no longer executory[54] but this has since been doubted.[55]

---

[48] L.P.(M.P.)A. 1989, s.2(4).
[49] *Grossman v. Hooper* [2001] 2 E.G.L.R. 82.
[50] *ibid.*, s.2(2).
[51] See *Eccles v. Bryant* [1948] Ch. 93.
[52] To be found in the *Encyclopaedia of Forms and Precedents* (5th ed., Vol. 35, 1997 Reissue), as Form 10, in paras 1472–1482.
[53] *Record v. Bell* [1991] 1 W.L.R. 853.
[54] *Tootal Clothing Ltd v. Guinea Properties Management Ltd* [1992] 2 E.G.L.R. 452.
[55] *Grossman v. Hooper* [2001] 2 E.G.L.R. 82.

6. Signed

"The document incorporating the terms or, where contracts are exchanged, one of the documents incorporating them (but not necessarily the same one) must be signed by or on behalf of each party to the contract."[56]

(a) Signature

The words in brackets in this provision permit the continuance of the practice of exchanging contracts, with each part signed by only one party. Under the current law, both parties will normally sign at the end of the document or, where contracts are exchanged, on the part which is to be given to the other party. Under the previous law, when only a note or memorandum was required, the courts gave an extended meaning to the word "signed"; provided the name of the signatory appeared in some part of the document in some form, whether in writing, typewriting, print or otherwise, there was a sufficient signature if that person had shown in some way that he recognised the document as an expression of the contract.[57] Thus memoranda in the handwriting of A which began "I, A, agree"[58] or "A agrees"[59] or "sold A",[60] without any further signature, were held to have been sufficiently signed by A on the ground that he had shown by his writing that he recognised the existence of the contract mentioned in the document (but the mere occurrence of a person's name in a document written by him did not necessarily amount to a signature; thus if A wrote out a document beginning "Article of agreement made between A and B" and ending "As witness our hands," without any signatures, the statute was not satisfied[61]; for the names had to have been inserted in such a way as to "have the effect of authenticating the instrument",[62] or "to govern what follows"[63]). However, such documents will only constitute valid contracts today if the other party also signs the same document or an identical copy of it because only in such circumstances can the requirements of the present law be satisfied.

(b) Agents

Where a party does not himself sign the contract, signature "on behalf of" him suffices. No provision is made about the mode in which an agent must receive his authority, and so it need not be given in writing[64] (this rule made more sense under the previous law than it does now and, although not expressly altered by the Act, could conceivably now be rejected by the courts). But the mere existence of an agency is not enough; it must be shown that the agent had authority to sign the same kind of contract as that which in fact he signed.[65] The same person may be given authority to sign on behalf of both parties, as where a solicitor acts for both of them,[66] a course of conduct which is most unwise for the solicitor in question because of possible conflicts of interest and which is not permitted anyway by the current solicitors' practice rules unless both parties are already established clients. An auctioneer was formerly

---

[56] L.P.(M.P.)A. 1989, s.2(3).
[57] See *Halley v. O'Brien* [1920] 1 I.R. 330 at 339; and see *Leeman v. Stocks* [1951] Ch. 941.
[58] *Knight v. Crockford* (1794) 1 Esp.190.
[59] *Bleakley v. Smith* (1840) 11 Sim. 150.
[60] *Johnson v. Dodgson* (1837) 2 M. & W. 653.
[61] *Hubert v. Treherne* (1842) 3 Man. & G. 743.
[62] *Ogilvie v. Foljambe* (1817) 3 Mer. 53 at 62, *per* Grant M.R.
[63] *Lobb v. Stanley* (1844) 5 Q.B. 574 at 582, *per* Coleridge J.
[64] *Heard v. Pilley* (1869) 4 Ch.App. 584; contrast L.P.A. 1925, s.53(1)(c) (below, p. 295).
[65] See *Thirkell v. Cambi* [1919] 2 K.B. 590 at 598.
[66] *Gavaghan v. Edwards* [1961] 2 Q.B. 220.

treated as having authority to sign a note or memorandum on behalf of each party at an auction,[67] but now that such contracts no longer have to be in writing anyway,[68] this is now of little importance save to the extent that the note or memorandum constitutes evidence of what was actually agreed.

7. Abolition of part performance

Although there has been no express abolition of the doctrine of part performance, which had developed uncertainties,[69] it is plain that that doctrine no longer exists. As an oral agreement for the sale or other disposition of an interest in land cannot be a contract, there is no contract that can be partly performed. This may well cause hardship.[70] If V orally agrees to grant or sell some interest in land to P, V can refuse to perform the agreement, however many and costly the acts that P has done in part performance of the agreement. This may be mitigated in some degree by the doctrine of proprietary estoppel,[71] to which the doctrine of part performance was related,[72] and it has been held that in such circumstances the operation of the doctrine gives rise to a constructive trust,[73] to whose creation the Act expressly does not apply.[74] In such circumstances the court is obviously likely to regard the oral agreement, though void as a contract, as providing evidence of the appropriate way of satisfying P's equity and has indeed done so.[75] However, the court is not obliged to follow this course; the type of interest to be given to P depends on the court's discretion and, as a result, the doctrine of proprietary estoppel is more uncertain in its operation than the doctrine of part performance was since it will not necessarily lead to the enforcement of the agreement actually made between the parties.[76]

Sect. 3. Effect of contract

Once a contract for the sale of land has been made, the parties have many rights and become subject to many obligations. The detailed law on the subject is generally regarded as falling within the province of conveyancing rather than real property, but an outline of one particular aspect must be given here.[77]

1. The purchaser as owner in equity

As soon as a specifically enforceable contract for the sale of land has been made, the purchaser becomes "the real and beneficial owner of it".[78] Nearly all contracts for the sale of land are specifically enforceable, and equity treats that as done which ought to be done. The purchaser is under many obligations, not least that of paying the purchase money at

---

[67] See M. & W. (5th ed.), p. 587.
[68] Above, p. 149.
[69] See *Steadman v. Steadman* [1976] A.C. 536; Law Com. No. 164, para. 1.9.
[70] See also below, p. 499.
[71] See above, p. 69; below, p. 483; Law Com. No. 164, paras 5.4, 5.
[72] See (1985) 36 N.I.L.Q. 358 at 359–364 (M. P. Thompson).
[73] *Yaxley v. Gotts* [2000] Ch. 162.
[74] L.P.(M.P.)A. 1989, s.2(5).
[75] In *Yaxley v. Gotts* [2000] Ch. 162.
[76] See above, p. 148.
[77] See the much fuller outline in M. & W., pp. 675–726.
[78] *Shaw v. Foster* (1872) L.R. 5 H.L. 321 at 338, *per* Lord Cairns.

completion, and he normally has no right to possession until then; but in equity (though not at law) the land is his.

2. The vendor as trustee

On the same grounds, the vendor becomes a trustee of the land for the purchaser, and so is under a duty to take reasonable care of it.[79] Thus he is liable to the purchaser if he damages the land himself,[80] or if he fails to take reasonable care to prevent it being damaged by third parties[81] or by natural events.[82] His trusteeship is qualified by the various rights that he has, such as the right to retain possession until completion; but his powers to act as the owner in matters such as changing tenancies is suspended.[83]

3. Passing of risk

For similar reasons, the risk of anything happening to the property pass to the purchaser as soon as the contract is made, unless it otherwise provides. Thus, if a house is destroyed by fire between contract and completion, the purchaser must still pay the vendor the full price, for the risk was his.[84] The purchaser should therefore either insure the house himself or arrange to take over the benefit of the vendor's policy. He can do this if the insurers consent and he pays the vendor a proportionate part of the premium, but probably only if the consent is obtained before and payment is made at the time of the contract. In this case, the vendor will become liable to pay the insurance moneys to the purchaser on completion.[85] Otherwise the loss will fall on the purchaser, for he must pay the purchase money on completion, and as the vendor has suffered no loss, his insurers need not pay him.[86] However, these unsatisfactory provisions, which often led to a duplication of insurance,[87] usually do not apply today, for the Standard Conditions of Sale[88] that are generally used provide otherwise. Under these, the vendor retains the risk until completion; he is under no obligation to the purchaser to insure; the provision for taking over the benefit of the vendor's policy is excluded; further, the purchaser is given a right, which does not arise other than by an express provision of this type, to rescind the contract if the physical state of the property has made it unusable for its purpose at the date of the contract as a result of damage against which the vendor could not reasonably have insured or which he cannot legally make good.[89]

Sect. 4. Contracts in practice

1. Cases where it is usual to have a contract

Whenever a transaction involves a payment of a capital sum, it is usual for it to be governed by a contract. Thus where land is being sold in fee simple, or a lease at a ground rent (a rent

---

[79] *Wilson v. Clapham* (1819) 1 Jac. & W. 36 at 38.
[80] *Cumberland Consolidated Holdings Ltd v. Ireland* [1946] K.B. 264 (abandonment of much rubbish on land).
[81] *Clarke v. Ramuz* [1891] 2 Q.B. 456 (trespasser removes soil); *Davron Estates Ltd v. Turnshire Ltd* (1982) 133 N.L.J. 937 (squatters).
[82] *Lucie-Smith v. Gorman* [1981] C.L.Y. 2866 (burst pipe from failure to turn off water in winter).
[83] *Raffety v. Scholfield* [1897] 1 Ch. 937 at 945.
[84] *Lysaght v. Edwards* (1876) 2 Ch.D. 499 at 507; *Rayner v. Preston* (1881) 18 Ch.D. 1. See criticisms at [1984] Conv. 43 (M. P. Thompson).
[85] L.P.A. 1925, s.47.
[86] See *Castellain v. Preston* (1883) 11 Q.B.D. 380.
[87] See Law Com. W.P. No. 109, paras 2.1–2.44.
[88] For these, see below, p. 156.
[89] See para. 5 of the Conditions.

representing the value of the land without the buildings on it or a nominal rent payable as a result of a purchase of a long lease of, typically, a flat for a lump sum technically described as a fine) is being assigned in consideration of a capital payment, a formal contract is normally made. If, on the other hand, no capital payment is involved, there is usually no contract, such as on the grant or assignment of a lease at a rack rent (a rent representing the full value of the land and buildings). And a mortgage, although involving a capital payment, is rarely preceded by a contract as such, although some institutional lenders require the intending borrower to countersign and return a copy of their written offer, something which has the effect of creating a binding contract between them.

2. Types of contract

There are three main types of contract.

(a) Open contracts

As has already been seen, in these contracts only the essential terms (the parties, the property to be sold and the price) have been expressly agreed. The remaining terms, such as the time for completion and the title to be shown by the vendor, are implied by the general law.

(b) Contracts by correspondence

In the case of contracts by correspondence for the sale of land, the Law of Property Act 1925[90] provides that the Statutory Form of Conditions of Sale 1925, made by the Lord Chancellor, are to govern the contract, subject to any modification or contrary intention expressed in the correspondence.[91] Such contracts were comparatively infrequent even prior to the Act, and now that they must be in writing signed by both parties[92] they are likely to become even more rare; but they are not impossible, as where a copy of a letter signed by one party is signed by the other. However, it is no longer possible, as it was prior to the Act, for a valid contract to be formed by an exchange of letters because in this case there will be neither one contract signed by both parties nor two identical contracts signed by each of them.

(c) Formal contracts

It is always open to the parties to make a contract in such terms as they see fit, subject to the rule that certain provisions contrary to the policy of the law are void, such as any provision that the conveyance should be prepared by a solicitor appointed by the vendor.[93] In practice, various standard forms of conditions have been settled, the most recent being the Standard Conditions of Sale,[94] introduced in 1990 and subsequently amended on a number of occasions. Standard forms of conditions, with such emendations as are desirable to fit the particular case, are usually employed, since they avoid the labour of preparing a set of

---

[90] s.46.

[91] See (1974) 90 L.Q.R. 55 (A. M. Prichard).

[92] Above, p. 148.

[93] L.P.A. 1925, s.48(1).

[94] These conditions were originally an amended conflation of *The Law Society's Conditions of Sale* (20th ed.) and the *National Conditions of Sale* (20th ed.). The original version is discussed in [1990] Conv. 179 (J. E. Adams). The current 3rd edition appears in the *Encyclopaedia of Forms and Precedents* (5th ed., Vol. 35, 1997 Reissue), as Form 7, in paras 1416–1451. There is also a National Conveyancing Protocol which sets out the steps to be taken by each party: the current 3rd edition is set out *loc. cit.* Form 1 in paras 1300–1316. It envisages the use of a number of further forms providing information about the property, its fixtures and so forth which are also set out *loc. cit.* Forms 3–6 paras 1323–1415.

conditions for each case. It is common for standard forms of conditions to be supplemented by special conditions on a variety of matters, as by precluding the purchaser from objecting to certain defects in the vendor's title.[95]

This division of the types of contract is not rigid; thus the parties may agree a few special conditions and leave the rest to the rules of the general law, thereby creating a contract which is in part formal and as to the remainder an open contract. A contract which contains no express provisions as to, for example, the title to be shown by the vendor, is described as a contract which is open as to title. This is actually the position under the Standard Conditions of Sale when the property to be sold is an estate in fee simple.

3. Terms of contract

The following are examples of the matters usually dealt with in a formal contract for the sale of land.

1. Provision for the payment of a deposit (usually 10 per cent of the purchase money) and for the payment of interest on the purchase money if completion is delayed.

2. Where the title is unregistered, any variations to general law relating to the length and nature of the title to be deduced by the vendor, and any special conditions as to title, such as as to making no objections to some specified defect in title or flaw in the evidence of title. Where the title is registered, the title number of the property, the class of title and copies of documents referred to on the register, such as as imposing restrictive covenants.[96]

3. The time within which the matters affecting the title must be dealt with.

4. The date and place for completion of the sale.

5. Power for the vendor to rescind the contract or re-sell the property in certain circumstances, such as the purchaser's insistence on objections to the title, or his failure to perform the contract.

6. Power for either party to serve a notice to complete if the contract is not completed on the date specified in the contract. Such a notice sets a further period of time for completion and entitles the party serving the notice to rescind the contract in default of compliance.

4. Preliminaries to contract

Whenever time permits, the proposed purchaser will usually send the proposed vendor "Inquiries before Contract", in order to obtain information on the state of the property. At the same time there will often be negotiations about the precise terms of the proposed contract. In addition, the purchaser will make the necessary searches before signing the contract.[97] The vendor may also be well advised to do the same in case some land charge has been registered against him without his knowledge[98]; for, unless he contracts to sell expressly subject to the land charge, he will have to discharge it before completion.

---

[95] As should have been done in *Faruqi v. English Real Estates Ltd* [1979] 1 W.L.R. 963.
[96] See *Faruqi v. English Real Estates Ltd* [1979] 1 W.L.R. 963.
[97] See above, pp. 106, 134.
[98] See *Newbury v. Turngiant Ltd* (1992) 63 P. & C.R. 458.

Part 2—Conveyancing

Conveyancing may be regarded as the application of the law of real property in practice. It is an immense subject, and only a very brief outline of a few of the chief features can be given here.[99] Although conveyancing does not form part of the subject of real property, every student should have some idea of the relationship between the two subjects. The work of a conveyancer is twofold. First, he investigates titles by examining documents and making inquiries and searches. Secondly, he drafts conveyances and other legal documents. The drafting of legal documents demands great skill, though books of forms or "precedents" are widely used. The steps taken after a contract has been made will depend on whether the title is registered or unregistered. The steps are considerably more complex when the title is unregistered than when it is registered, something which was one of the principal factors which led to the decision to make the system of registered conveyancing predominant.

Sect. 1. Unregistered title

1. From contract to completion

The usual sequence of events on the sale of a freehold by V to P are as follows; most of the steps are normally taken by the solicitors for the parties rather than by the parties in person. Formal contracts invariably contain a detailed timetable for the completion of each stage. Under open contract, each stage merely has to be completed within a reasonable time, a most unsatisfactory rule which allows matters to drag on more or less indefinitely.

(a) Delivery of abstract or epitome of title

Within the time mentioned in the contract, V must deliver to P the abstract of title or epitome of title. Abstracts of title are now rare. These documents provide a consecutive story of the derivation of the title, consisting in part of a condensed version of the various documents and in part of a recital of the relevant events, such as the births, deaths and marriages which affect the title. An abstract starts with a good root of title[1] and traces the devolution of the property down to V. Thus a very simple abstract might consist of:

  (i) a summary of a conveyance by A to B;

  (ii) a recital of B's death;

  (iii) a recital of probate of B's will being granted to X and Y;

  (iv) a summary of the assent by X and Y in favour of V.

However, once photocopiers became commonly available, it became customary instead to provide an epitome of the title, stating briefly the essential facts in the derivation of title, and supporting this by photocopies of the documents mentioned in the epitome. Today most epitomes of title consist of nothing more than a list in chronological order of the documents which have been photocopied.

---

[99] See generally M. & W., pp. 150–174, 261–290.
[1] Above, p. 10.

(b) Consideration of abstract

P then examines the abstract or epitome of title and considers the validity of the title shown. If an epitome of title supported by photocopies of the title deeds has been sent, he will be able to verify V's title at that stage. Where an abstract of title is used, this will not be possible until the title deeds are produced at completion.

(c) Requisitions on title

P's examination of the abstract or epitome usually discloses a number of points upon which he requires further information. This further explanation is obtained by means of "requisitions on title", a series of written questions which P delivers to V. Requisitions usually consist of a mixture of genuine objections or requests for information (example as to the date of some death, or as to the existence of some incumbrance which the abstract does not disclose), and statements of the obvious, such as that V, having agreed to sell free from incumbrances, must discharge a mortgage or obtain the concurrence of the mortgagee to the sale of the property free from the mortgage. Requisitions also usually seek confirmation of the answers to the inquiries on draft contract sent before conclusion of the contract.[2]

(d) Replies to requisitions

V then answers the requisitions within the agreed time. If his answers are unsatisfactory on any point, P may make further requisitions.

(e) Draft conveyance

P next prepares a draft conveyance in the form which he thinks it should take. He sends this draft to V for his approval; V makes in red ink any emendations he considers necessary, returns it to P, who makes any further amendments in green ink, and so on until the conveyance is agreed. P then engrosses the conveyance (*i.e.* prepares a fair copy of it) and sends it to V for execution.

(f) Searches

A few days before the date fixed for completion, P searches the Land Charges Register once more. He will also then search the Land Registry Parcels Map so as to ensure that the land which is to be sold is not already part of a registered title.

(g) Completion

Completion[3] then takes place, usually at the office of V's solicitor, before expiry of the priority period afforded by the official search certificate.[4] This involves V delivering to P the engrossment of the conveyance duly executed by V; only if P is entering into some obligation towards V, as by binding himself to observe restrictive covenants, will the conveyance be executed by P as well. In addition to receiving the conveyance, P is entitled to receive the pre-existing title deeds. However, V may retain any deed which:

---

[2] Above, p. 157.
[3] For variations in the process of completion, for both unregistered and registered land, see [1991] Conv. 15, 81, 185 (D. G. Barnsley).
[4] See above, p. 106.

(i) relates to other land retained by him; or

(ii) creates a trust which is still subsisting; or

(iii) relates to the appointment or discharge of trustees of a subsisting trust.[5]

If V retains any deeds, he must give P an acknowledgment of P's rights to production of the deeds and, unless V is a mortgagee or trustee of the land, an undertaking for their safe custody.[6]

In return, P pays V the purchase money either in cash, although in modern conditions this would be very unusual, or by banker's draft although, where both parties are legally represented, the vendor's solicitor will normally accept a cheque drawn on the purchaser's solicitor's client account. The exact amount due is settled by the "completion statement" which apportions the outgoings up to the exact day of completion; in modern conditions the only outgoings which normally have to be apportioned are council tax, water and sewage rates, and any ground rent and residents' association charges (the statutory undertakers will normally read the meters on the date of completion and bill each party separately).

(h) The passing of title

Legal title to the property will pass as soon as the deed is delivered to P. Following completion, P must attend to the stamping of the conveyance, if the value of the transaction is such that this is necessary, within 30 days and apply to the Land Registry for first registration of the title within two months. Failure to comply with the latter deadline causes the conveyance to cease to have effect in relation to the legal title, which will revest in V who will thereafter hold it on trust for P unless and until the Land Registry grants an extension of time or the title is eventually registered.

2. The conveyance: precedent and details

A conveyance of a legal estate must be by deed.[7] Formerly a deed required to be signed, sealed and delivered, but now the requirement of sealing, which had become an unimportant formality, has been abolished.[8] Instead, an instrument will be a deed only if[9]:

(i) it makes it clear on its face that it is intended to be a deed, usually by using the expression "signed as a deed by" each person who is executing it;

(ii) it is signed either by the person making it (or one of the parties to it) in the presence of a witness who attests the signature, or else at his direction and in his presence and the presence of two witnesses who each attest the signature (however, if the signatory holds out the document as a deed, it does not matter if the purported witness did not actually attest the signature but signed later on provided that there is nothing to place the other party to the conveyance on inquiry[10]); and

(iii) it is delivered[11] as a deed by him or by a person authorised to do so on his behalf.

[5] L.P.A. 1925, s.45(9).
[6] For the effect, see L.P.A. 1925, s.64.
[7] L.P.A. 1925, s.52(1); and see above, p. 67.
[8] L.P.(M.P.)A. 1989, s.1(1).
[9] *ibid.*, s.1(2)–(4).
[10] *Shah v. Shah* [2001] 3 W.L.R. 31.
[11] For delivery, see below, p. 162.

Commencement and date	THIS CONVEYANCE is made the 1st day of June 2002
Parties	BETWEEN John Bull of No.1 Weelkes Street Farnaby in the County of Tye Composer (hereinafter called "the vendor") of the one part and Orlando Gibbons of No. 1 Morley Street Dowland in the County of Tallis Organist (hereinafter called "the purchaser") of the other part
Recitals	WHEREAS— (1) The vendor is the estate owner in respect of the fee simple of the property hereby assured for his own use and benefit absolutely free from incumbrances (2) The vendor has agreed with the purchaser to sell to him the said property free from incumbrances for the price of £249,000
Testatum	NOW THIS CONVEYANCE WITNESSETH that in
Consideration	consideration of the sum of £249,000 now paid by the purchaser
Receipt clause	to the vendor (the receipt whereof the vendor hereby
Operative words	acknowledges) the vendor With Full Title Guarantee hereby conveys unto the purchaser
Parcels	ALL THAT messuage or dwellinghouse with the yard gardens offices and outbuildings thereto belonging known as No. 1 Byrd Street Purcell in the County of Norcome which premises are more particularly delineated and coloured pink on the plan annexed to these presents
Habendum	TO HOLD the same unto the purchaser in fee simple
Certificate of value	IT is hereby certified that the transaction hereby effected does not form part of a larger transaction or a series of transactions in respect of which the amount or value or the aggregate amount or value of the consideration exceeds £250,000
Testimonium	IN WITNESS WHEREOF the parties to these presents have hereunto set their hands the day and year first above written
Attestation Clause	Signed as a deed by the vendor in the presence of Edward Elgar Legal Executive JOHN BULL with Messrs. Delius, Field and Stanford solicitors EDWARD ELGAR

In considering the very simple form of conveyance set out above, the following points should be noticed.

(a) Commencement

The old practice was for the initial words to be "This Indenture". An indenture was a deed with the top of the parchment indented, *i.e.* having an irregular edge. The deed was written out twice on a single sheet of parchment, which was then severed by cutting it with an irregular edge; the two halves of the parchment thus formed two separate deeds which could be fitted together to show their genuineness. This contrasted with a "deed poll", a deed to which there was only one party, which at the top had been polled, or shaved even. The modern practice is for the commencement to describe the general nature of the document, such as "This Conveyance", "This Mortgage" and the like.

(b) Date

Whatever date is in fact inserted in the conveyance, the document takes effect from the date upon which it was signed and delivered by the parties to it.[12] A deed which has been signed but not delivered is ineffective; delivery is effected formally by uttering words such as "I deliver this as my act and deed", or informally by doing some act showing that the deed is intended to be operative. A deed may be delivered in escrow, *i.e.* delivered on the condition that it is not to become operative until some stated event occurs.[13] Usually a vendor of land will execute the conveyance some days before completion and deliver it to his solicitor in escrow, the condition being the completion of the purchase by the purchaser.[14] On satisfaction of the condition, the deed operates retrospectively to the date of delivery in escrow, though only as between the parties to it and not as to third parties.[15]

(c) Parties

If any other person is an essential party to the transaction, such as a mortgagee who is releasing the property from his mortgage, he will be included as a party.

(d) Recitals

These are of two types:

(i) Narrative recitals: which deal with matters such as how the vendor became entitled to the land; and

(ii) Introductory recitals: which explain how and why the existing state of affairs is to be altered, e.g. that the parties have agreed for the sale of the property.

(e) Testatum

This is the beginning of the operative part of the conveyance.

(f) Consideration

The consideration is stated to show, *inter alia*, that the transaction is not a voluntary one.[16]

(e) Receipt clause

This is inserted to save a receipt being given. Further, a solicitor who produces a conveyance containing such a clause which has been duly executed by the vendor thereby demonstrates that he has authority from the vendor to receive the purchase money.[17]

(h) Operative words

These effect the actual conveyance of the property. They transfer all the rights which the vendor has in the land, or has power to convey.[18] A most important part of them is the phrase

---

[12] *Norton on Deeds* (2nd ed., 1928), p. 189.
[13] See *Beesly v. Hallwood Estates Ltd* [1961] Ch. 105.
[14] *Glessing v. Green* [1975] 1 W.L.R. 863.
[15] *Alan Estates Ltd v. W.G. Stores Ltd* [1982] Ch. 511.
[16] This excludes the possibility of a resulting trust.
[17] L.P.A. 1925, s.69.
[18] *ibid.*, s.63, obviating the former "All the estate" clause.

"With Full Title Guarantee". These imply covenants for title, in other words contractual undertakings by the vendor as to the nature of the title which he is conveying to the purchaser. These covenants are implied in order to shorten conveyances and other documents. The law governing covenants for title was reformed by the Law of Property (Miscellaneous Provisions) Act 1994 which came into force on July 1, 1995. Prior to that covenants for title were governed by the Law of Property Act 1925, under which the equivalent phrase implying the equivalent covenants for title was "As Beneficial Owner". Since the covenants for title implied before July 1, 1995 are likely to be the subject of proceedings for many years yet, it is necessary to consider both the former and the present law. It involves some consideration of the subject of covenants for title.

(i) Conveyances before July 1995

(i) The covenants: The Law of Property Act 1925[19] provides that where for valuable consideration a person conveys and[20] is expressed to convey land "as beneficial owner" the following covenants for title are implied:

    (i) good right to convey: the vendor has power to convey the land;

    (ii) quiet enjoyment: the purchase shall have quiet enjoyment of the land[21];

    (iii) freedom from incumbrances: the land is free from any incumbrances other than those subject to which the conveyance is expressly made; and

    (iv) further assurance: the vendor will execute such assurances and do such things as are necessary to cure any defect in the conveyance;

In the case of a sale of a lease, the following additional covenants are implied:

    (v) that the lease is valid; and

    (vi) that the rent has been paid and the covenants in the lease duly performed.[22]

Where a person instead conveys and is expressed to convey (whether or not for value) "as settlor" the only covenant implied is one for further assurance, binding that person and those claiming under him; and where a person instead conveys "as trustee", "as mortgagee", "as personal representative", or "under an order of the court" the only covenant implied is that the grantor has not himself encumbered the land.[23]

(ii) Enforceability of the covenants: The rules for enforcing covenants for title implied by the Law of Property Act 1925 are as follows.

The benefit of the covenants runs with the land, so that each person in whom the land is for the time being vested is entitled to enforce the covenant.[24] Thus if V enters into the covenants with P, and later P sells the land to Q, Q is entitled to enforce the covenants for

---

[19] s.76, Sched. 2, replacing C.A. 1881, s.7.
[20] See *Fay v. Miller, Wilkins & Co.* [1941] Ch. 360 (vendor must in fact be what he is expressed to be).
[21] See below, p. 368.
[22] L.P.A. 1925, s.76, Sched. 2.
[23] *ibid.*, s.76, Sched. 2.
[24] *ibid.*, ss.76(6), 78.

title against V even though Q was not a party to the conveyance from V to P which created the obligations.

As regards the burden of the covenant, the person liable is the person entering into the covenant. He does not, however, always make himself responsible for the acts of everyone. If land is conveyed "as beneficial owner" the general rule is that the vendor makes himself responsible for the acts and omissions of:

(i) himself, and

(ii) those claiming through, under, or in trust for him, and

(iii) those through whom he claims otherwise than by purchase for money or money's worth, and those claiming under them.[25]

Thus if V conveyed land to P for value "as beneficial owner" prior to July 1995 and P today discovers undisclosed incumbrances, he can sue V on the covenants for title if those incumbrances were created by V, or those claiming through, under or in trust for V, or those through whom V claims otherwise than by purchase for money or money's worth, and those claiming under them. This last phrase means that V will not be responsible for the acts of someone from whom he bought the land, but that he will be responsible for the acts of somebody who made a voluntary conveyance of the land to him, or gave it to him under a marriage settlement. Further, the covenants are subject to the usual 12-year limitation period. Consequently, liability can only be imposed under the first covenant set out above, good right to convey, and under the two leasehold covenants during the 12 years following the conveyance. But time will not start to run under the other covenants until the purchaser is actually dispossessed or requires further assurance.

Where a person creates a mortgage "as beneficial owner", the covenants for title implied are absolute[26]; the mortgagor thus makes himself responsible for the acts of everyone.

As stated under (**i**) above, the liability on the covenants implied by using phrases other than "as beneficial owner" is limited to the grantor's own acts.

(j) Conveyances after June 1995

(**i**) **The covenants:** The Law of Property (Miscellaneous Provisions) Act 1994[27] provides that where for valuable consideration or otherwise a person effects or purports to effect a disposition of any interest in land, including grants of rights such as easements which were not within the previous system, or for that matter any other property and is expressed to do so "with full title guarantee" the following covenants for title are implied:

(i) that he has the right to dispose of the property as he purports to[28];

(ii) that he will at his own cost do all that he reasonably can do to pass the title which he purports to give[29];

---

[25] *ibid.*, Sched. 2; *David v. Sabin* [1893] 1 Ch. 523 at 532, 533. And see M. & W., pp. 162–163.
[26] L.P.A. 1925, s.76, Sched. 2.
[27] s.1(2).
[28] s.2(1).
[29] *ibid.*

    (iii) that the property is free from all charges, incumbrances and third party rights other than those of which he neither knew nor could reasonably be expected to know.[30]

In the case of a lease, the following additional covenant is implied

    (iv) that the lease is subsisting and that there are no subsisting breaches of the tenant's obligations which would render the lease liable to forfeiture.[31]

However, he is not liable for any matter to which the disposition is expressly made subject or for anything actually known or which was a necessary consequence of facts known by the transferee.[32] There is a presumption that the property disposed of is the estate in fee simple or, in the case of a lease of unregistered land, the unexpired portion of the lease.[33]

    Where the disposition is a mortgage of a lease or of property subject to a rentcharge, the following additional covenant is implied:

    (v) that the mortgagor will fully and promptly observe and perform all the obligations under the lease imposed on him in his capacity as tenant or imposed by the rentcharge which are enforceable by the owner of the rentcharge as such.[34]

Where a person instead effects or purports to effect a disposition of any interest in land or any other property and is expressed to do so "with limited title guarantee", the position is the same save that, instead of the covenant in (iii) above, he covenants that he has not, since the last disposition for value, encumbered the property or allowed the property to become encumbered by means of any incumbrance or charge which is still existing and that he is not aware that anyone else has done so either.[35]

(ii) Enforceability of the covenants: The rules for enforcing covenants for title implied by the Law of Property Act (Miscellaneous Provisions) Act 1994 are as follows.

    The benefit of the covenants runs with the land, so that each person in whom the land is for the time being vested is entitled to enforce the covenant.[36] Thus, as before, if V enters into the covenants with P, and later P sells the land to Q, Q is entitled to enforce the covenants for title against V even though Q was not a party to the conveyance from V to P which created the obligations.

    As regards the burden of the covenant, the person liable is the person entering into the covenant and his liability is absolute.[37] The covenants in (i), (iii) and (iv) above will be breached if at all at the date of the disposition so the 12-year limitation period will run from then. However, breach of the covenants in (ii) and (v) above will not occur until the obligation in question is not complied with so time will only start to run then.

---

[30] s.3(1).
[31] s.5(1).
[32] s.6.
[33] s.2(3)(b).
[34] s.5.
[35] s.3(3).
[36] s.7.
[37] *ibid.*

(k) Parcels

The parcels describe what is conveyed; often the conveyance employs a plan for this purpose, but this is not essential, for instance if an accurate verbal description can be given, or the property can be described by reference to a plan on an earlier conveyance. The purchaser is entitled on completion to all fixtures attached to the land at the date of the contract,[38] for they are part of it; and the conveyance will transfer them with the land, without special mention.

(l) Habendum

This shows that the purchaser is to hold the land for his own benefit and not upon trust for a third party. It also contains the usual words of limitation.[39] It is followed by the acknowledgment and undertaking[40] where these are to be included.

(m) Certificate of value

This certifies that the total consideration does not exceed the next threshold for stamp duty, thus establishing the rate of stamp duty to which the conveyance is subject or, if it does not exceed £60,000, an exemption from it.[41]

(n) Testimonium

and

(o) Attestation clause

These need no comment.

Sect. 2. Registered title

1. From contract to completion

On the sale of a freehold estate in registered land by V to P, the sequence of steps (normally taken by their solicitors) is as follows.

(a) Inspection

Now that the register is an open register,[42] P no longer requires V's authority to inspect it. But V must supply copies or abstracts of any documents noted on the register, for example as imposing restrictive covenants burdening the title.[43] If the registered title is only possessory or qualified then the pre-registration title or the qualification must be investigated as for unregistered land.[44] In every case, any possible interests which override registration[45] must be carefully investigated.

---

[38] For fixtures, see above, pp. 19 *et seq.*
[39] Above, pp. 37 *et seq.*
[40] Above, p. 160.
[41] Finance Act 1963, s.55, as amended by Finance Act 1984, s.109(1). The rates of stamp duty are set out in the Finance Act which implements each year's Budget.
[42] See above, p. 112.
[43] See *Faruqi v. English Real Estates Ltd* [1979] 1 W.L.R. 963 (restrictive covenants not disclosed on first registration).
[44] L.R.A. 1925, s.110(2).
[45] See above, pp. 121 *et seq.*

(b) Examination of title

The entries on the register must be examined to see that the purchaser will obtain what he is expecting. The register provides an instant title (subject to interests which override registration) so there is obviously no need to examine past history.

(c) Requisitions on title

If P's official search of the register reveals any untoward entries, such as a recent entry of a caution in favour of X, or if a copy of a document noted on the register is not supplied, then P will raise requisitions on these matters, as well as requiring confirmation of the answers given to his earlier inquiries on draft contract.

(d) Replies to requisitions

V then answers the requisitions. If his answers are unsatisfactory on any point then P may make further requisitions until he is satisfied that he is obtaining what he contracted to purchase.

(e) Draft transfer

P next fills in a standard form of draft transfer with such special clauses as he considers appropriate to give effect to the contract. He sends this to V for approval. When the draft transfer has been agreed (usually an easy matter), P sends a fair copy to V to be used as the engrossment for execution by V.

(f) Searches

A few days before the date fixed for completion P makes an official search of the register to ensure that nothing has been entered against the title since the last search.

(g) Completion

Before expiry of the priority period of 30 working days afforded by the official search certificate,[46] completion will take place. It is possible that, as in the case of unregistered land, P will attend upon V to receive the duly executed transfer and the land certificate in return for P's cash payment, banker's draft or solicitor's cheque for the moneys due under V's completion statement. However, given that in the case of registered land there are no title deeds which P's solicitor needs to examine, where both parties are legally represented completion normally takes place in accordance with The Law Society's Code for Completion by Post.[47] P's solicitor will transfer the necessary sum to V's solicitor's client account to be held to the order of P's solicitor and, once the funds have arrived in that account or on the agreed completion date, if later, V will complete the transaction, after which he will hold the transfer rather than the funds to the order of P's solicitor, notify P's solicitor by telephone or by fax and send the transfer to him by post or, in practice, through a document exchange service.

(h) The passing of title

In contrast with unregistered land, the legal title does not pass until P is registered as proprietor, though registration will take effect from the day when he lodged his application

---

[46] See above, p. 134.
[47] To be found in the *Encyclopaedia of Forms and Precedents* (5th ed., Vol. 35, 1997 Reissue), as Form 11, in paras 1483–1491.

to register the transfer with the appropriate District Land Registry[48]; and P must ensure that this is done before the priority period expires. Before doing so, he will have to attend to the stamping of the conveyance, if the value of the transaction is such that this is necessary.

(2) The Transfer: precedent and details

A registered proprietor can dispose of his registered estate, or deal with it, only as authorised by statute.[49] The forms set out in the Schedule to the Land Registration Rules 1925 (or when the Land Registration Act 2002 comes into force, the forms set out in the Schedule to the revised Rules) must be used in all matters to which they are capable of being applied or adapted, with any alterations or additions which are necessary or desired and the registrar allows.[50] Some additions are expressly allowed, and others are customarily accepted. Thus expressions such as "as beneficial owner" and other words apt for creating covenants for title were authorised until July 1995,[51] and additions such as a receipt for the purchase money also used to be customary. However, the present Land Registry forms include both the two phrases which are now apt for creating covenants for title and various forms of receipt by means of boxes which have to be ticked if they are to be utilised. The registrar has a wide discretion to refuse to register an instrument, as where it is not in the proper form, or is lacking in clarity, or is inconsistent with the principles of registered land; and he may require modifications.[52]

The following is the present Land Registry Form (Form TR1) for the transfer of the whole of a registered title (different forms are employed for other forms of transfer).[53]

---

[48] See above, p. 116–117.
[49] L.R.A. 1925, s.69(4).
[50] L.R.R. 1925, r. 74. Many of the rules prescribe particular forms for particular transactions.
[51] ibid., r. 76; and see above, p. 163.
[52] ibid., r. 78.
[53] See Ruoff & Roper, Vol. II, p. B/100/15, para.B–298J. This and the other forms are required by r. 98.

Transfer of whole
of registered title

HM Land Registry

TR1

(If you need more room than is provided for in a panel, use continuation sheet CS and staple to this form.)

---

1. Stamp duty

> *STAMPED*
> *£249,000*

Place "X" in the box that applies and complete the box in the appropriate certificate.

[ ] I/We hereby certify that this instrument falls within this category [ ] in the Schedule to the Stamp Duty (Exempt)

[X] It is certified that the transaction effected does not form part of a larger transaction or of a series of transactions in respect of which the amount or value or the aggregate amount or value of the consideration exceeds the sum of

£ *250,000*

---

2. Title number(s) of the Property *(leave blank if not registered)*

FT 034567   Norcome District Land Registry

---

3. Property

1 Byrd Street, Purcell, in the County of Norcome

If this transfer is made under section 37 of the Land Registration Act 1925 following a not-yet-registered dealing with part only of the land in a title, or is made under rule 72 of the Land Registration Rules 1925, include a reference to the last preceding document of title containing a description of the property.

---

4. Date   *1st June 2002*

---

5. Transferor *(Give full names and Company's Registered Number if any)*

John Bull

---

6. Transferee for entry on the register *(Give full names and Company's Registered Number if any: for Scottish Co. Reg. Nos., use an SC prefix. For foreign companies give territory in which incorporated.)*

Orlando Gibbons and Shirley Gibbons

Unless otherwise arranged with Land Registry headquarters, a certified copy of the transferee's constitution (in English or Welsh) will be required if it is a body corporate but is not a company registered in England and Wales or Scotland under the Companies Acts.

---

7. Transferee's intended address(es) for service in the U.K. *(including postcode)* for entry on the register

℅ John Blow & Co., 3 High Street, Tallis TA1 0XJ

---

8. The Transferor transfers the property to the Transferee

---

9. Consideration *(Place "X" in the box that applies. State clearly the currency unit if other than sterling. If none of the boxes applies, insert an appropriate memorandum in the additional provisions panel.)*

[X] The Transferor has received from the Transferee for the property the sum of *(in words and figures)*

Two hundred and forty-nine thousand pounds (£249,000)

[ ] *(insert other receipt as appropriate)*

[ ] The Transfer is not for money or anything which has a monetary value

10. The Transferor transfers with *(place "X" in the box that applies and add any modifications)*

[X] full title guarantee   [ ] limited title guarantee

11. Declaration of trust *Where there is more than one transferee, place "X" in the appropriate box*

[X] The transferees are to hold the property on trust for themselves as joint tenants

[ ] The transferees are to hold the property on trust for themselves as tenants in common in equal shares

[ ] The transferees are to hold the property *(complete as necessary)*

12. Additional Provision(s) *Insert here any required or permitted statement, certificate or application and any agreed covenants, declarations, etc.*

The transferees covenant to observe the Restrictive
Covenants on the Registered Title

13. *The Transferors and all other necessary parties should execute this transfer as a deed using the space below. Forms of execution are given in Schedule 3 to the Land Registration Rules 1925. If the transfer contains transferees' covenants or declarations or contains an application by them (e.g. for a restriction), it must also be executed by the Transferees.*

Signed as a Deed by   John Bull

In the presence of   Edward Elgar
                                 Delius Field and Stanford
                                 Solicitors

Signed as a Deed by   Orlando Gibbons

In the presence of   John Blow
                                 John Blow & Co.
                                 Solicitors

Signed as a Deed by   Shirley Gibbons

In the presence of   John Blow

(a) Stamp duty

If stamp duty is payable, the Transfer is stamped by the Stamp Office in the box at the top of the form. The appropriate box is ticked below. The first one is used where no stamp duty is payable because of the nature of the transaction, such as the transfer of property held on trust to new trustees. The second one is used where the transaction is such that stamp duty is prima facie payable. It comprises the Certificate of Value certifying that the total considera-tion does not exceed the next threshold for stamp duty, thus establishing the rate of stamp duty to which the conveyance is subject or, if it does not exceed £60,000, an exemption from it.[54] That threshold is then written in the box at the bottom.

(b) Title Number(s) of the Property

This contains the title number or numbers of the Registered Title and the name of the relevant District Land Registry.

(c) Property

This contains the address of the Property.

(d) Date

This contains the date on which the transfer takes effect (this is unlikely to be the date on which the vendor signed it; the date is inserted when the sale is actually completed). As between the parties to it, it takes effect from the date when it is signed and delivered.[55] But no legal estate passes until the transfer is registered, though when it is, it takes effect "as of" the date when the application for registration was lodged at the appropriate District Land Registry.[56]

(e) Transferor; (f) Transferee for entry on the Register; (g) Transferee's intended address for service in the U.K. for entry on the Register

These are self-explanatory. Where there are more than four joint vendors or joint purchasers only four of their names will appear here; they will hold the Property on a trust of land for themselves and the others. The address usually given is that of the property itself although for various reasons it is sometimes prudent to give the address of the transferee's solicitors.

(h) The Transferor transfers the property to the Transferee

These are the Operative Words which give the Transfer its effect; they do not of course pass the legal title but merely give the Transferee the right to be registered as proprietor in place of the Transferor. The Transferee obtains whatever title the Transferor had in the land described in the Register.

(i) Consideration

The appropriate box must be ticked. If a payment has been made, this constitutes the Transferor's receipt for the sum in question (it will be for the complete purchase price rather

---

[54] Finance Act 1963, s.55, as amended by Finance Act 1984, s.109(1). The rates of stamp duty are set out in the Finance Act which implements each year's Budget.
[55] *Spectrum Investment Co. v. Holmes* [1981] 1 W.L.R. 221.
[56] Above, pp. 116–117, 167.

than for the sum paid on completion; any deposit paid will have been deducted from the complete purchase price and further credits and debits will have been made in respect of the apportionment of outgoings). So far as the Transferee is concerned, a disposition made without valuable consideration is subject not only to entries on the register and interests which override registration but also to all interests which require protection, even if not protected.[57]

(j) The Transferor transfers with

If covenants for title are being given, the appropriate box must be ticked and any modifications to the covenants implied by the Law of Property (Miscellaneous Provisions) Act 1994 written below.

(k) Declaration of trust

Where there is more than one purchaser, they will, where there are four or less of them, hold the legal title as joint tenants on a trust of land for themselves as either joint tenants or tenants in common in equity. The first or second box is ticked accordingly. The third box is utilised where there are more than four joint purchasers (in which case, it will be stated that the four transferees whose names appear on the Transfer are holding for all the joint purchasers in the appropriate way) or where the trustees are not or are not all beneficiaries of the trust in question (in which case, the name if any of the settlement in question will be inserted).

(l) Additional Provisions

This will contain the details of any rights or obligations which are being created or reserved. Examples are where the vendor is reserving some right, such as a right of way, over the property or where the purchaser is entering into any covenants, whether restrictive or otherwise, with the vendor.

(m) The Transferors and all other necessary parties should execute this transfer as a deed using the space below

All the parties who need to sign the Transfer will do so here in the manner appropriate to their juridical nature (companies execute deeds in a different manner from natural persons). No Transferees will need to sign unless a trust is being declaring a trust in (k) above or some obligation is being entered into with the Transferor in (l) above.

PART 3—WILLS

Sect. 1. Freedom of testation

From the fourteenth century until 1939 there was in general[58] no restriction upon a testator's power to dispose of property as he thought fit save that in certain circumstances surviving spouses had a right to a life interest in a proportion of his real property[59]: for good reasons or bad he might give all the rest of his property to charities or other causes and leave the

---

[57] L.R.A. 1925, ss.20(4), 23(5).
[58] For the limited restrictions that there were, see M. & W., pp. 585–586.
[59] Dower in the case of a widow; curtesy in the case of a widower.

remaining members of his family and his dependants penniless. This was changed by the Inheritance (Family Provision) Act 1938, which, after amendment, was replaced and extended by the Inheritance (Provision for Family and Dependants) Act 1975. Most legal systems outside the common law world give a testator's descendants and sometimes also his surviving spouse the right to challenge any will which does not leave specified proportions of his property to them. However, the English legislation instead instead makes dispositions subject to the court's discretionary power to vary their effect. Initially, the legislation applied only to wills and claims could only be made by members of the testator's family. However, it now applies to intestacies as well and claims can also be made by cohabitees, de facto members of the deceased's family and other dependants.

1. Ambit of the Act

The 1975 Act applies to the estate of any person who on or after April 1, 1976, has died domiciled in England and Wales. It enables certain persons to make an application to the court on the ground that reasonable provision has not been made for them out of the deceased's estate.[60]

(a) Applicants

The persons who can apply are the following[61]:

    (i) the wife or husband of the deceased, including a polygamous wife[62];

    (ii) anyone who lived in the same household as the deceased as his husband or her wife for a period of at least two years prior to his death[63];

    (iii) a former wife or husband who has not remarried, including a remarriage that is void or voidable;

    (iv) a child of the deceased, including a child who is *en ventre sa mère*, illegitimate or adopted;

    (v) any other person who was treated by the deceased as a member of the family in relation to any marriage to which the deceased was at any time a party; and

    (vi) any other person who immediately before the death of the deceased was being maintained, either wholly or partly, by the deceased.

(b) "Maintained"

Under the last head above, a person is to be treated as being maintained by the deceased, whether wholly or partly, if the deceased (otherwise than for full valuable consideration) was making a substantial contribution towards the applicant's reasonable needs.[64] For persons living together other than as husband and wife, this requires the balancing of the respective contributions to the household expenses that they were making on a settled basis at the death

---

[60] Inheritance (Provision for Family and Dependants) Act 1975 ("the Act of 1975"), s.1(1).
[61] *ibid.*, ss.1(1), 25(1), (4).
[62] *Re Sehota* [1978] 1 W.L.R. 1506.
[63] Law Reform (Succession) Act 1995, s.2, which added this class to s.1 of the Act of 1975.
[64] Act of 1975, s.1(3).

of the deceased.[65] If one was the sole owner of the home, the provision of rent free accommodation for the other is a major factor which is subject to reduction to the extent that the applicant contributed to the acquisition and maintenance of the home[66] (persons living together as husband and wife for the requisite period are now in a different category and are no longer obliged to prove dependency).

2. Applications

(a) Time

Any application under the Act must be made not later than six months from the first grant of probate or letters of administration; but the court has a discretion to extend the period,[67] as may be done if a new will or codicil is found. The burden lies on the applicant to show sufficient grounds for extending the time.[68]

(b) No "reasonable financial provision"

The ground for making an application is that the disposition of the estate of the deceased by his will, or on his intestacy (or under both combined), does not make reasonable financial provision for the applicant.[69] The meaning of this falls under two heads.

> (i) For a surviving spouse (unless separated under a decree of judicial separation), it means such financial provision as it would be reasonable in all the circumstances for a husband or wife to receive, whether or not it is required for his or her maintenance.[70] Consequently, a surviving spouse can be awarded capital payments as well as or in addition to whatever is required for his or her maintenance. In such cases, the court must have regard to the provision which the spouse might reasonably have expected to receive if the marriage had been ended by divorce instead of death[71] although it has now been made clear that this factor, though important, is only one of a number of factors which the court must take into account.[72]

> (ii) For all other applicants, it means such financial provision as it would be reasonable in all the circumstances for the applicant to receive for his or her maintenance,[73] thus restricting the amount to income payments rather than payments of capital, although the increasing trend is for those income payments to be capitalised by reference to annuity tables so as to enable the applicant to purchase an annuity if he or she so wishes.[74]

The test is objective: it is not whether the deceased acted unreasonably but whether any provision made was in fact not reasonable in the light of the facts at the date of the hearing[75];

---

[65] *Jelley v. Iliffe* [1981] Fam. 128; *Bishop v. Plumley* [1991] 1 W.L.R. 582; and see *Malone v. Harrison* [1979] 1 W.L.R. 1353.
[66] *ibid.*
[67] Act of 1975, s.4.
[68] See *Re Salmon* [1981] Ch. 167.
[69] Act of 1975, s.1(1).
[70] *ibid.*, s.1(2)(a).
[71] *ibid.*, s.3(2).
[72] *Re Krubert* [1997] Ch. 97; *Grattan v. McNaughton* [2001] 1 W.T.L.R. 1305.
[73] *ibid.*, s.1(2)(b).
[74] *Graham v. Murphy* [1997] 1 F.L.R. 860.
[75] See *Re Goodwin* [1969] 1 Ch. 283; *Re Coventry* [1980] Ch. 461.

(consequently, unexpected windfalls occurring after the deceased's death can be taken into account[76]). A will does not fail to make reasonable financial provision for a beneficiary merely because he can take nothing under it because he murdered the testator.[77]

(c) "Net estate"

It is the "net estate" of the deceased that is available to satisfy any order under the Act. This consists of all the property of which the deceased had power to dispose by will, but after deducting his funeral, testamentary and administration expenses, and his debts and liabilities, including any inheritance tax.[78] Property over which the deceased had a power of appointment[79] is included if the power is general but not if it is special; and the court may order the deceased's interest under a joint tenancy which had passed from him by survivorship on his death to be treated as if he had had a one-half share in the property in question.[80] The court may also order the inclusion of property which has been subject to certain devices for evading the Act.[81]

3. Order

The court exercises a very wide discretion under the Act of 1975.

(a) Circumstances

If the court is satisfied that the disposition of the estate of the deceased does not make reasonable financial provision for the applicant, the court must consider all the relevant circumstances of the case when deciding whether to make an order, and what order to make. These circumstances include the present and future financial resources and financial needs of the applicant, of other possible applicants and of the beneficiaries of the deceased's estate, any obligation or responsibility of the deceased to any applicant or beneficiary, and any physical or mental disability that they have.[82] For spouses, children and persons maintained there are further special considerations.[83] Statements by the deceased, whether oral or written, are admissible as evidence of the facts stated.[84]

(b) Terms of order

The court has a wide discretion as to the provisions which are to be made out of the net estate.[85] The order may provide for the payment of a lump sum or of some or all of the income of the estate, or for making periodical payments or for transferring or settling property, or for varying marriage settlements. As has already been mentioned, in the case of claims by applicants who are entitled only to maintenance (all applicants other than surviving spouses), the increasing trend is for those maintenance payments to be capitalised by reference to annuity tables so as to enable the applicant to purchase an annuity if he or she so wishes.[86] There are also powers to vary or discharge orders for periodical payments, and

[76] *Re Hancock* [1998] 2 F.L.R. 346.
[77] *Re Royse* [1985] Ch. 22.
[78] Act of 1975, s.25(1).
[79] See below, p. 232.
[80] Act of 1975, ss.9, 25(1).
[81] *ibid.*, ss.10–12, 25(1).
[82] *ibid.*, s.3(1).
[83] *ibid.*, s.3(2)–(4). See *Moody v. Stevenson* [1992] 2 W.L.R. 640.
[84] *ibid.*, s.21.
[85] *ibid.*, s.2.
[86] *Graham v. Murphy* [1997] 1 F.L.R. 860.

to make interim orders in case of immediate need.[87] If any provision is ordered, the costs of the applicant on the standard basis and the costs of the personal representatives of the deceased on the indemnity basis are normally[88] paid out of the part of the deceased's estate which is not awarded to the applicant.[89]

Sect. 2. Nature of a will

1. A will is ambulatory

Until the death of the testator, a will has no effect at all, but operates as a mere declaration of his intention, which may be changed from time to time. For this reason, a will is said to be "ambulatory"; a beneficiary under it has merely a "*spes*", and not any interest in property. This distinguishes a will from a conveyance, settlement or other dealing *inter vivos*, which operates either at once or at some fixed time in the future and confers an interest in property.

A will is also ambulatory in that it "speaks from death", *i.e.* it is capable of disposing of all property owned by the testator at his death, even if acquired after the date of the will.[90]

2. A will is revocable

Notwithstanding any declaration in the will itself or any other document, a will can be revoked at any time.[91] However, although a binding contract not to revoke a will does not prevent its revocation,[92] and will prima facie be construed as not extending to revocation by marriage,[93] such a contract binds the testator's assets, so that if the will is revoked, the beneficiaries thereunder can compel the person to whom the assets have passed to hold them on trust for them in accordance with the terms of the contract.[94]

3. Codicils

A codicil is similar to a will and is governed by the same rules. A testamentary document is usually called a codicil if it is supplementary to a will and adds to, varies or revokes provisions in the will: if it is an independent instrument, it is called a will. Although sometimes indorsed on a will, a codicil may be a separate document, and can stand by itself even after the revocation of the will to which it is supplementary.[95] Codicils are construed in such a way as to disturb the provisions of a will no more than is absolutely necessary to give effect to the codicil.[96]

---

[87] *ibid.*, ss.5, 6.
[88] In the absence of any relevant Offer under Pt. 36 of the Civil Procedure Rules.
[89] *Graham v. Murphy* [1997] 1 F.L.R. 860.
[90] Wills Act 1837, s.24; see further, below, p. 190.
[91] *Vynior's Case* (1610) 8 Co.Rep. 81b.
[92] *In b. Heys* [1914] P. 192.
[93] *Re Marsland* [1939] Ch. 820.
[94] *Re Cleaver* [1981] 1 W.L.R. 939.
[95] *In b. Savage* (1870) L.R. 2 P. & D. 78.
[96] *Doe d. Hearle v. Hicks* (1832) 1 Cl. & F. 20.

Sect. 3. The formalities of a will

1. Formal wills

The present rules governing the execution of a formal will are as follows.[97]

(a) Writing

The will must be in writing. Any form of writing, printing, typewriting and the like may be employed. No special form of words need be used: all that is required is an intelligible document.

(b) Signature by testator

The will must be signed by the testator, or by someone else in his presence and by his direction. The testator's signature may be made in any way, provided there is an intention to execute the will. Thus initials,[98] a stamped name, a mark,[99] a signature in a former or assumed name,[1] or "your loving Mother",[2] all suffice. But a seal is not enough and was not even when deeds required a seal, for the will must be signed and sealing is not signing.[3] Similar principles apply to signature by someone on behalf of the testator. Thus the signature of his own name instead of that of the testator is sufficient.[4] But it is essential that the signature should be made in the testator's presence and authorised by him, either expressly or by implication.[5]

Effect will be given to dispositions contained in a document which has not been executed as a will if the document is incorporated in a will. For this to be the case:

   (i) the will must clearly identify the document to be incorporated;

   (ii) the will must refer to the document as being already in existence and not as one subsequently to be made; and

   (iii) the document must in fact be in existence when the will is executed.[6]

(c) Position of signature

Before 1983, it was necessary for the signature to appear at the end of the will.[7] Any material which followed the signature in time or in space would be refused probate. This requirement caused various difficulties,[8] and the position has now been simplified. For those dying after 1982, the signature may be placed in any position in the will, provided that "it appears that the testator intended by his signature to give effect to the will",[9] and that he was not, for

---

[97] Wills Act 1837, s.9, as substituted by Administration of Justice Act 1982, s.17.
[98] *In b. Savory* (1815) 15 Jur. 1042.
[99] *In b. Finn* (1936) 53 T.L.R. 153 (thumb-mark).
[1] *In b. Redding* (1850) 2 Rob. Ecc. 339.
[2] *In b. Cook* [1960] 1 W.L.R. 353.
[3] *Wright v. Wakeford* (1811) 17 Ves. 454.
[4] *In b. Clark* (1839) 2 Curt. 329.
[5] *In b. Marshall* (1866) 13 L.T. 643.
[6] See *University College of North Wales v. Taylor* [1908] P. 140.
[7] Wills Act 1837, s.9; Wills Act Amendment Act 1852.
[8] See M. & W. (5th ed.), p. 507.
[9] Administration of Justice Act 1982, s.17, substituting a new s.9 of the Wills Act 1837.

example, merely identifying the document.[10] Thus T's will is duly signed if, as part of a single operation, he writes "My will by T" and then the dispositive words.[11]

(d) Presence of witnesses

The testator must either make or acknowledge the signature in the presence of two witnesses present at the same time. Whether the signature to the will is made by the testator or by someone in his presence and by his direction, there is no need for witnesses to be present at the time of the signature if they are present when the testator subsequently makes a proper acknowledgment of the signature. But either the signature or the acknowledgment must be made in the simultaneous presence of two witnesses. An express acknowledgment is desirable but not essential,[12] and an acknowledgment by a third party is effective if it can be shown that it should be taken to be the acknowledgment of the testator.[13]

It is desirable but not essential that the witnesses should be of full age and sound intelligence; yet a blind person cannot be a witness, for the will cannot be signed in his "presence".[14]

(e) Signature by witnesses

The witnesses must then sign in the presence of the testator. No form of attestation is necessary although a proper attestation clause showing that the will has been executed in accordance with the statutory requirements will facilitate the grant of probate. All that is necessary is that after the testator's signature has been made or acknowledged in the joint presence of two witnesses, they should sign their names or acknowledge their signatures in the testator's presence.[15] There is no need for the witnesses to sign in each other's presence,[16] although it is both desirable and usual.

2. Formal wills: alterations

Every obliteration, interlineation or other alteration made after a will has been executed must itself be executed in the same way as a will; in default, it is ineffective unless it revokes any part of the will by rendering it illegible.[17] No alteration will therefore be effective unless it is signed or initialled by the testator and the witnesses.[18]

An obliteration or erasure of part of a will, even though unattested, is effective to revoke that part, since it amounts to a destruction of that part[19]; and the same applies to the pasting of paper over part of a will,[20] provided the words are not decipherable by any natural means, such as by the use of magnifying glasses or by holding the will up to the light.[21] The court will not permit physical interference with the will, as by using chemicals or removing paper

---

[10] Contrast *In b. Mann* [1942] P. 146 with *In b. Bean* [1944] P. 83 and *Re Beadle* [1974] 1 W.L.R. 417 (the envelope cases).
[11] *Wood v. Smith* [1992] 3 All E.R. 556.
[12] See *In b. Davies* (1850) 2 Rob. Ecc. 337.
[13] *Inglesant v. Inglesant* (1874) L.R. 3 P. & D. 172.
[14] *In b. Gibson* [1949] P. 434.
[15] Wills Act 1837, s.9, as substituted by Administration of Justice Act 1982, s.17, permitting acknowledgment by a witness and so reversing *Wyatt v. Berry* [1893] P.5.
[16] *In b. Webb* (1855) Dea. & Sw. 1.
[17] Wills Act 1837, s.21.
[18] *Re White* [1991] Ch. 1.
[19] See *Townley v. Watson* (1844) 3 Curt. 761; and see below.
[20] *In b. Horsford* (1874) L.R. 3 P. & D. 211.
[21] *Ffinch v. Combe* [1894] P. 191.

pasted over the words[22]; and an obliteration is not ineffective merely because the original words can be deciphered by making another document, such as an infra-red photograph.[23]

3. Formal wills: revocations

A will or codicil may be revoked by another will or codicil, by destruction, or by marriage.

(a) By another will or codicil

A revocation clause expressly revoking all former wills is effective provided it is contained in a document executed with the proper formalities.[24] This is so even if the testator had been misled as to the effect of the clause,[25] but not if the testator did not know of the presence of the clause.[26] A will is not revoked merely because a later will is entitled (as is usual) "This is the last will and testament of me" or some similar phrase.[27]

A will is revoked by implication if a later will is executed which merely repeats the former will or is inconsistent with it, although if the repetition or inconsistency is merely partial, those parts of the former will which are neither repeated in the later will nor inconsistent with it remain effective.[28] Any number of testamentary documents may be read together, each being effective except so far as subsequently varied or revoked; the sum total constitutes the testator's will.[29]

(b) By destruction animo revocandi

A will is revoked if it is destroyed by the testator, or by some person in his presence and by his direction, with intent to revoke it.[30] There are thus two elements, an act of destruction and an *animus revocandi* (intention to revoke).

(i) Destruction: It is not necessary that the will should be completely destroyed; there must, however, be some burning, tearing or other destruction of the whole will or some essential part of it, as by cutting off the signature of the testator or the witnesses.[31] It is not enough for the testator to draw a line through part of the will, indorse it "all these are revoked" and kick it into the corner.[32] Destruction of part of a will normally revokes that part alone,[33] unless the part destroyed is so important as to lead to the conclusion that the rest cannot have been intended to stand alone.[34]

If a will has been destroyed without being revoked (for example because an *animus revocandi* was lacking), it can be proved by means of a draft or copy, or even by oral evidence.[35] A will in the testator's possession which cannot be found at his death is presumed

---

[22] *In b. Horsford* (1874) L.R. 3 P. & D. 211; contrast *In b. Gilbert* [1893] P. 183.
[23] *In b. Itter* [1950] P. 130.
[24] Wills Act 1837, s.20.
[25] *Collins v. Elstone* [1893] P. 1.
[26] *In b. Moore* [1892] P. 378; and see *Re Phelan* [1972] Fam. 33.
[27] *Simpson v. Foxon* [1907] P. 54.
[28] *Lemage v. Goodban* (1865) L.R. 1 P. & D. 57.
[29] *In b. Fenwick* (1867) L.R. 1 P. & D. 319. For distributive revocation, see *Re Finnemore* [1991] 1 W.L.R. 793.
[30] Wills Act 1837, s.20.
[31] *Williams v. Tyley* (1858) Johns. 530.
[32] *Cheese v. Lovejoy* (1877) 2 P.D. 251.
[33] *Re Everest* [1975] Fam. 44.
[34] *Leonard v. Leonard* [1902] P. 243.
[35] *Sugden v. Lord St. Leonards* (1876) 1 P.D. 154.

to have been destroyed by him *animo revocandi* and cannot be proved unless the presumption is rebutted by evidence of non-revocation.[36]

(ii) Intention: The testator must have an *animus revocandi* at the time of destruction. If a will is intentionally torn up by a testator who is drunk[37] or believes the will to be ineffective, it is not revoked, for an intent to destroy the document is no substitute for the requisite intent to revoke the will. "All the destroying in the world without intention will not revoke a will, nor all the intention in the world without destroying: there must be the two."[38]

Revocation of a will may be conditional, in which case the will remains unrevoked until the condition has been fulfilled. One particular kind of conditional revocation is known as dependent relative revocation. If revocation is relative to another will and intended to be dependent upon the validity of that will, the revocation is ineffective unless that other will takes effect. Thus if a will is destroyed by a testator who is about to make a new will, and the evidence shows that he intended to revoke the old will only if he executed the new one, the old will remains valid if the new will is never executed.[39] Another example arises in the case of revival; if Will No. 1 is revoked by Will No. 2, any subsequent revocation of Will No. 2 will not be sufficient to revive Will No. 1,[40] so that if the testator revokes Will No. 2 in the mistaken belief that he is thereby reviving Will No. 1, the doctrine of dependent relative revocation applies and the revocation of Will No. 2 is ineffective.[41] Again, if a testator obliterates a legacy and by unattested writing substitutes a new legacy, the old legacy remains effective if the court is satisfied that it was revoked only on the (erroneous) supposition that the new legacy would be effective.[42]

(c) By marriage

Marriage automatically revokes all wills made by the parties to the marriage.[43] There are two exceptions to this.

(i) Certain appointments: An appointment by will under a power of appointment is not revoked by the marriage of the testator unless, in default of appointment, the property would pass to his personal representatives[44] and so become part of his estate. The general intention of this provision is that if the testator's new "family" will get the property even if the will is revoked, there is no harm in allowing the marriage to revoke it. But if the property would pass out of the "family" in default of appointment, the will is allowed to stand so far as it exercises the power of appointment, and no farther.[45]

(ii) Contemplation of marriage: A will made after 1925 that is expressed to be made in contemplation of a marriage is not revoked by the solemnisation of the particular marriage contemplated.[46] The contemplation may be inferential, such as a gift "to my fiancée" X,[47] but

---

[36] *Eckersley v. Platt* (1866) L.R. 1 P. & D. 281.
[37] *In b. Brassington* [1902] P. 1.
[38] *Cheese v. Lovejoy* (1877) 2 P.D. 251 at 253, *per* James L.J.
[39] *Dixon v. Treasury Solicitor* [1905] P. 42.
[40] Below, p. 143.
[41] *Powell v. Powell* (1866) L.R. 1 P. & D. 209; *In b. Bridgewater* [1965] 1 W.L.R. 416.
[42] *In b. Horsford* (1874) L.R. 3 P. & D. 211.
[43] Wills Act 1837, s.18, as substituted by Administration of Justice Act 1982, s.18.
[44] See below, p. 198.
[45] *In b. Russell* (1890) 15 P.D. 111; *In b. Gilligan* [1950] P. 32.
[46] L.P.A. 1925, s.177.
[47] *In b. Langston* [1953] P. 100; *Re Coleman* [1976] Ch. 1.

a mere general contemplation ("made in contemplation of marriage") is not enough,[48] nor is a contemplation expressed in relation to only some gifts in the will and not the will as a whole.[49] Wills made after 1982 are subject to similar provisions, with some variations.[50] It is now required that it should appear from the will that when it was made the testator was expecting to be married to a particular person, and that he intended that the will should not be revoked by the marriage. Further, if this intention applies only to some disposition in the will, the marriage will not revoke that disposition, nor, unless a contrary intention appears, will it revoke the rest of the will.

Where a testator dies after 1982, and his marriage is dissolved, annulled or declared void, any gift in his existing will to his former spouse will lapse,[51] and any appointment of his former spouse as an executor or trustee of the will is ineffective.[52] If a life interest lapses in this way, any remainder is accelerated.[53] A lapse under these provisions does not prejudice any right of the former spouse to apply for financial provision under the Inheritance (Provision for Family and Dependants) Act 1975.[54]

4. Formal wills: revival

A will revoked by destruction animo revocandi can never be revived.[55] Any other will can be revived, but only by re-execution with the proper formalities or by a codicil showing an intention to revive it.[56] If a will has been revoked by a subsequent will, the first will is thus not revived merely by the revocation of the latter will.[57] If a will is first partially revoked, then wholly revoked, and then revived, the revival does not extend to the part partially revoked unless an intention to this effect is shown.[58]

5. Informal wills: general

Cetain persons are excepted from the rules that a testator must be of full age and must comply with the usual formalities.[59]

6. Informal wills: privileged testators

(a) A soldier in actual military service

The testator must not merely be in an army; when he makes the will he must be actually serving in connection with military operations which are or have been taking place or are believed to be imminent.[60] Thus service at a camp in England in August 1940 sufficed,[61] and so did service in Northern Ireland in 1978 during an armed and clandestinely organised insurrection.[62] A soldier is deemed to be in actual military service from the moment he

[48] *Sallis v. Jones* [1936] P. 43.
[49] *Re Coleman*, above.
[50] Wills Act 1837, s.18, as substituted by Administration of Justice Act 1982, ss.18, 73(7).
[51] See *Re Sinclair* [1985] Ch. 446.
[52] Wills Act 1837, s.18A, inserted by Administration of Justice Act 1982, ss.18, 73(6).
[53] *ibid.*
[54] *ibid.* See above, p. 172.
[55] *In b. Reade* [1902] P. 75.
[56] Wills Act 1837, s.22.
[57] *In b. Hodgkinson* [1893] P. 339.
[58] Wills Act 1837, s.22.
[59] *ibid.*, s.11.
[60] *Re Wingham* [1949] P. 187.
[61] *In b. Spark* [1941] P. 115.
[62] *Re Jones* [1981] P. 7.

receives mobilisation orders until the full conclusion of the operations. "Soldier" includes both officers and other ranks, a female army nurse,[63] and a member of the Air Force,[64] or Women's Auxiliary Air Force.[65]

(b) A mariner or seaman at sea

This includes both members of the Royal Navy and merchant seamen, and extends to a female typist employed on a liner.[66] It includes an admiral directing naval operations on a river,[67] a master mariner in his ship lying in the Thames before starting on her voyage,[68] and a seaman whose ship is permanently stationed in harbour.[69] It also extends to a seaman on shore leave from his ship, or under orders to join a new ship.[70]

(c) A member of Her Majesty's Naval or Marine Forces so circumstanced that, had he been a soldier, he would have been in actual military service[71]

This enables a member of the navy or marines who has been called up to make an informal will before his departure even though he has not joined his ship.[72]

7. Informal wills: extent of the privilege

A will made by a testator who at the time of making the will comes within one of the above categories has the following privileges.

(a) The will can be made or revoked even though the testator is a minor

This is certainly the case with personalty but a minor has not since 1925 been able to dispose of realty by will if he is unmarried and, since 1996, also has no issue[73] (the curtailment of the privilege in this respect was probably accidental).

(b) The will can be made or revoked informally

The will may be made in writing, with or without witnesses or signature, or it may be nuncupative; thus informal words of farewell spoken at a railway station may suffice.[74] The testator need not know that he is making a will, provided he gives deliberate expression to his wishes as to the destination of his property on his death,[75] such as "If I stop a bullet everything of mine will be yours".[76] Those entitled to make an informal will (including minors[77]) may also revoke a will, even if it has been made formally, in an informal manner, such as by an unattested letter to a relative asking that the will should be burned, "for I have already cancelled it".[78]

---

[63] *In b. Stanley* [1916] P. 192.
[64] Wills (Soldiers and Sailors) Act 1918, s.5.
[65] *In b. Rowson* [1944] 2 All E.R. 36.
[66] *In b. Hale* [1915] 2 I.R. 362.
[67] *In b. Austen* (1853) 2 Rob. Ecc. 611.
[68] *In b. Patterson* (1898) 79 L.T. 123.
[69] *In b. M'Murdo* (1867) L.R. 1 P. & D. 540.
[70] *In b. Newland* [1952] P. 71; *In b. Wilson* [1952] P. 92. Contrast *Re Rapley* [1983] 1 W.L.R. 1069.
[71] Wills (Soldiers and Sailors) Act 1918, s.2.
[72] *In b. Yates* [1919] P. 93.
[73] See A.E.A. s.51(3), altered by T.L.A.T.A., Sched. 3, para.4; below p. 203.
[74] *In b. Yates* [1919] P. 93.
[75] *In b. Spicer* [1949] P. 441.
[76] *Re Stable* [1919] P. 7; contrast *In b. Knibbs* [1962] 1 W.L.R. 852.
[77] Family Law Reform Act 1969, s.3(3).
[78] *In b. Gossage* [1921] P. 194.

These privileges have always applied to wills of personalty, and were extended to wills of realty in respect of testators who died after February 6, 1918.[79] A will properly made under the above conditions remains valid indefinitely unless revoked, even after the military or other service is over.[80]

Sect. 4. Operation of wills

1. Lapse: general rule

A legacy or bequest (*i.e.* a testamentary gift of personalty) or a devise (*i.e.* a testamentary gift of realty) is said to lapse if the beneficiary dies before the testator. In such a case, unless a contrary intention is shown, the gift fails and the property comprised in it falls into residue. This means that it passes under any general or residuary gift in the will,[81] such as "all the rest of my property I leave to X". If there is no residuary gift, or if the gift which lapses is itself a gift of all or part of the residue, there is a partial intestacy and the property passes to the persons entitled on intestacy.[82]

2. Lapse: exclusion of the general rule

The general rule as to lapse is excluded in four cases, one of which is now obsolete.

(a) Moral obligation

A legacy which is intended to satisfy some moral obligation recognised by the testator and is therefore not merely given as an act of bounty, has always been outside the doctrine of lapse and so can be claimed by the legatee's personal representatives in the event that he predeceases the testator.[83] Examples are legacies made in order to pay debts which are barred by lapse of time[84] or under the bankruptcy laws[85] or made with the intention of paying the debts of someone for whom the testator felt morally responsible.[86]

(b) Fees tail

By section 32 of the Wills Act 1837, subject to any contrary intention in the will, there used to be no lapse if property was given to a person in fee tail and he predeceased the testator, leaving issue living at the testator's death capable of inheriting under the entail. No more fees tail can now be created and as a result this provision has been repealed.[87]

(c) Gifts to issue

By section 33 of the Wills Act 1837, as amended for testators dying after 1982,[88] subject to any contrary intention in the will a gift to a child or remoter descendant of the testator who predeceased him, but left issue surviving him, takes effect as a gift to the issue living at the

[79] Wills (Soldiers and Sailors) Act 1918, s.3.
[80] *Re Booth* [1926] P. 118.
[81] Wills Act 1837, s.25.
[82] *Ackroyd v. Smithson* (1780) 1 Bro.C.C. 503; below, pp. 192 *et seq.*
[83] *Stevens v. King* [1904] 2 Ch.30.
[84] *Williamson v. Naylor* (1838) 3 Y. & C.Ex. 208.
[85] *Re Sowerby's Trusts* (1856) 2 K. & J. 630.
[86] *Re Leach* [1948] Ch. 232.
[87] T.L.A.T.A. 1996, s.25(2), Sched. 4.
[88] Administration of Justice Act 1982, s.19.

testator's death[89]; and they take in equal shares *per stirpes*.[90] For these purposes, illegitimacy is disregarded; and a person *en ventre sa mère* at the testator's death and born alive thereafter is treated as being alive at the testator's death.[91]

(d) Class gifts

The membership of a class of beneficiaries, such as "all my children", is normally ascertained at a testator's death, and those dying before the testator fail to become members of the class. Strictly, there is therefore no question of lapse: it is merely that nothing has ever been given to those who predecease the testator. However, where the testator dies after 1982,[92] subject to any contrary intention in the will, where there is a gift to a class of persons consisting of children or remoter descendants of the testator, and a member of the class predeceases the testator but leaves issue who do survive the testator, the gift takes effect as if the class included the issue living at the testator's death.[93]

(e) Exceptions

In three cases the provisions of the Wills Act 1837 do not apply to prevent a lapse.

(i) Appointments under special powers: Section 33 of the Wills Act 1837 does not apply to an appointment by will under a special power,[94] for it is confined to cases where property is devised or bequeathed. It does, however, apply to appointments under general powers for the exercise of such powers amounts to a devise or bequest.[95]

(ii) Interests terminable on donee's death: The original version of section 33 of the Wills Act 1837 did not preserve gifts which would in any case terminate as a result of the donee's death at or before the testator's death, such as gifts of a life interest or in joint tenancy.[96] This exclusion does not appear in the present version of that section but it is not thought that the position has changed since the nature of the gift is likely to be held to manifest the necessary contrary intention.

(iii) Certain contingent gifts: Nor did the original version of section 33 of the Wills Act 1837 preserve a contingent gift such as a bequest "to X as and when he is 25" if X died aged 24, even if he would have attained the requisite age had he in fact outlived the testator.[97] This exclusion again does not appear in the present version of that section but, for the same reasons, it is not thought that the position has changed.

3. Lapses: *Commorientes*

Where a devisee or legatee dies at nearly the same time as the testator, it is necessary to determine which survived the other in order to know whether or not the gift has lapsed. Similar questions between *commorientes* (those dying together) arise on intestacy and in respect of joint tenancies. Before 1926, there was no means of settling the question if there was no evidence of the order of deaths. Thus if two people perished in a shipwreck, in the

---

[89] *ibid.*, s.33(1). For the previous law, see M. & W. (5th ed.), p. 519.
[90] Below, p. 195.
[91] Wills Act 1837, s.33(4), as substituted by Administration of Justice Act 1982, ss.19, 73(6).
[92] For the previous law, see M. & W. (5th ed.), p. 521.
[93] Wills Act 1837, s.33(2), as substituted by Administration of Justice Act 1982, ss.19, 73(6).
[94] *Holyland v. Lewin* (1883) 26 Ch.D. 266; below, p. 201.
[95] *Eccles v. Cheyne* (1856) 2 K. & J. 676.
[96] See *Re Butler* [1918] 1 I.R. 394.
[97] *Re Wolson* [1939] Ch. 780.

absence of evidence of survivorship the estate of one could not benefit under the will or intestacy of the other, for it was impossible for the personal representatives to establish the survivorship essential to their case. In the case of deaths after 1925, however, where it is uncertain which survived the other, for all purposes affecting the title to property the younger is deemed to have survived the elder, subject to any order of the court.[98] This rule applies equally to cases of simple uncertainty, as where one of the parties is on a ship which founders with all hands on an uncertain date and the other dies at home during that period, and to common disasters, such as virtually simultaneous deaths in an air-raid,[99] terrorist bomb or car-crash. But for the purpose of inheritance tax, the old rule remains, and each is deemed to have died simultaneously, so that there is no second liability for inheritance tax on the death of the notional survivor.[1]

4. Gifts to witnesses

(a) Invalidation of gift

The Wills Act 1837[2] provides that the attestation of a beneficiary or his or her spouse is not to invalidate the will, but the beneficiary can claim no benefit under the will, either as to realty or personalty. This rule also used to prevent executors from charging for administering the estate pursuant to a charging clause in the will in the event that they, their spouses, other members of their firm, or their spouses had attested the will. But this aspect of the rule was reversed with effect from February 1, 2001 by the Trustee Act 2000,[3] which for this purpose treats sums payable under charging clauses as remuneration for services rather than gifts under the will in question.

(b) Limits of the rule

This rule does not apply in the following cases.

(i) Informal wills: where no witnesses at all are necessary for the validity of the will, as where the testator is a soldier in actual military service.[4]

(ii) Enough other witnesses who are not beneficiaries: where, in respect of deaths after May 29, 1968, the will would have been validly executed without regard to the attestation by the beneficiary or his or her spouse.[5]

(iii) Signed not as a witness: where the person has signed the will not as a witness but merely, for example, to show that he agrees with the testator's leaving him less than his brothers and sisters.[6]

(iv) Subsequent marriage: where the marriage of the beneficiary to the witness occurred after the date of the will.[7]

---

[98] L.P.A. 1925, s.184. For an exception, see below, p. 195 (intestate spouses).
[99] *Hickman v. Peacey* [1945] A.C. 304.
[1] Inheritance Tax Act 1984, s.4(2).
[2] s.15.
[3] T.A. 2000, s.28(4)(a).
[4] *Re Limond* [1915] 2 Ch. 240.
[5] Wills Act 1968, s.1, reversing *Re Bravda* [1968] 1 W.L.R. 479.
[6] *Kitcat v. King* [1930] P. 266.
[7] *Thorpe v. Bestwick* (1881) 6 Q.B.D. 311.

(v) Fiduciary gifts: where the gift to the witness is to him as a trustee and not beneficially.[8]

(vi) Confirmation: where the gift is made or confirmed by any will or codicil not attested by the beneficiary. Thus if there is a gift by will confirmed by codicil, a beneficiary who witnesses only one document is entitled to the gift since he can claim under the other document.[9]

(vii) Secret trusts: where the beneficiary takes not under the will but under a secret trust in his favour binding property given by the will to another person.[10]

(viii) Dependant relative revocation: where there was a gift in similar terms to the same legatee in a previous will which was not witnessed by him or his spouse, it may be able to be saved by the doctrine of dependant relative revocation.[11]

(c) Effect

Where the rule applies, the effect is that the will is treated as if it had omitted the offending gift. Where the gift is of a limited interest, the effect is to accelerate the subsequent interests. Hence if property is given to A for life, with remainder to B, the effect of A attesting the will is that B is entitled to the property as soon as the testator dies.[12] Similarly if property is given to X, Y and Z as joint tenants, and X attests the will, Y and Z are entitled to the whole of the property.[13] The notional omission of the offending gift also means that a gift expressed to take effect if the offending gift fails is also void.[14]

5. Gifts to persons unlawfully causing the death

At common law, a person who unlawfully kills another can take no benefit under his victim's will[15]; and under the victim's intestacy the killer's prospective interest devolves as if he did not exist.[16] He is not deemed to predecease the victim and so the gift to him does not lapse. His children therefore cannot take in his place under section 33 of the Wills Act 1837 and so they are excluded as well; nor can they take under the intestacy rules.[17] The rule applies to murder[18] even where there is a finding of diminished responsibility,[19] though not where the killer is found not guilty by reason of insanity.[20] In its application to manslaughter, a crime which varies almost infinitely in seriousness, there are two qualifications. First, the courts have confined the rule to cases of deliberate, intentional and unlawful violence or threats of violence.[21] Secondly, for manslaughter and any other unlawful killing except murder, such as

---

[8] *Cresswell v. Cresswell* (1868) L.R. 6 Eq. 69.
[9] *Re Marcus* (1887) 56 L.J.Ch. 830; *Re Trotter* [1899] 1 Ch. 764.
[10] *Re Young* [1951] Ch. 344.
[11] *Re Finnemore* [1991] 1 W.L.R. 793.
[12] *Jull v. Jacobs* (1876) 3 Ch.D. 703.
[13] *Young v. Davies* (1863) 2 Dr. & Sm. 167.
[14] *Re Doland's W.T.* [1970] Ch. 267.
[15] *In b. Hall* [1914] P. 1; *Re Pollock* [1941] Ch. 219.
[16] *Re Sigsworth* [1935] Ch. 89; *Re Callaway* [1956] Ch. 559. For another application of the rule, see below, p. 331.
[17] *Re DWS* [2001] W.T.L.R. 445.
[18] *Re Pollock* [1941] Ch. 219.
[19] *Re Giles* [1972] Ch. 544; *Re Royse* [1985] Ch. 22.
[20] *Re Pitts* [1931] 1 Ch. 546; compare *Re Pechar* [1969] N.Z.L.R. 574.
[21] *Re K.* [1986] Ch. 180 at 186; *Re H.* [1990] 1 F.L.R. 441.

infanticide or causing death by reckless driving, statute[22] has empowered the court to modify the rule if satisfied that in all the relevant circumstances "the justice of the case" requires this, provided application to the court is made within three months after the conviction.[23] Murder apart, the rule does not preclude certain applications for financial provision being made, for example, under the Inheritance (Provision for Family and Dependants) Act 1975.[24]

6. Rectification

Formerly the court had no power to rectify a will, however clear it was that some clerical blunder had been made in it, as in writing or typing it from a draft. But in respect of deaths after 1982, the court now has a limited power to rectify a will, confined to cases where the court is satisfied that the will fails to carry out the testator's intention in consequence of a clerical error or a failure to understand his instructions.[25] This includes a solicitor's inadvertent omission of a clause when drafting a revised version of a will.[26] For a claim for rectification to succeed, convincing evidence is necessary.[27] No application for rectification may be made more than six months after probate or letters of administration are first taken out unless the court extends the time[28]; and there is protection for personal representatives who distribute the estate after the six months have run without considering the possibility of time being extended.[29]

Sect. 5. Construction of wills

The construction of wills is a vast subject; only a few of the more important rules can be mentioned here.

1. General rule

The cardinal rule of construction is that effect must be given to the intention of the testator as expressed in the will, the words being given their natural meaning except so far as that leads to absurdities or inconsistencies.[30] The will alone must be looked at, and, in general, no evidence can be received to contradict the meaning of the words used in the will. "The will must be in writing, and the only question is, what is the meaning of the words used in that writing."[31] If the rule were otherwise, the requirement that a will should be in writing might largely be set at nought.

However, although words will usually be given their natural meaning, or the most appropriate of their several natural meanings, there is nothing to prevent words from being construed in some special sense if the will clearly shows that they are used in that sense; and in recent times the courts have been rather more ready to perceive that the testator has used

---

[22] Forfeiture Act 1982.
[23] *ibid.*, ss.2, 5. See *Re K.* [1986] Ch. 180.
[24] *ibid.*, ss.3, 5; above, pp. 172 *et seq.*
[25] Administration of Justice Act 1982, s.20(1).
[26] *Wordingham v. Royal Exchange Trust Co. Ltd* [1992] 2 W.L.R. 496.
[27] *Re Segelman* [1996] Ch. 171; *Grattan v. McNaughton* [2001] W.T.L.R. 1305.
[28] Administration of Justice Act 1982, s.20(2).
[29] *ibid.*, s.20(3), (4).
[30] See *Abbott v. Middleton* (1858) 7 H.L.C. 68 at 114.
[31] *Grey v. Pearson* (1857) 6 H.L.C. 61 at 106, *per* Lord Wensleydale.

words otherwise than according to their "strict" meaning.[32] Furthermore, statute may require a particular meaning to be given. For example, in wills made after 1969 a provision for the benefit of a child or relation of any kind is to be construed as including those illegitimately related, unless the contrary intention appears.[33] Again, if the will was made after 1949 or confirmed after April 1, 1959, children who were formally adopted before the testator died are included.[34]

2. Extrinsic evidence

Since only the words of the will may be considered, extrinsic evidence (*i.e.* evidence not gathered from the will itself) is normally inadmissible. However, this is subject to certain qualifications.

(a) Surrounding circumstances

Evidence of facts and circumstances existing when the will was made is always admissible. "You may place yourself, so to speak, in [the testator's] arm-chair."[35] Thus extrinsic evidence is admissible to show that certain words had a peculiar meaning to the testator by the custom of the district or the usage of the class of persons to which he belonged. Again, nicknames, or symbols used by the testator in his trade, may be explained; thus it may be shown that a gift for "mother" was intended for the testator's wife, whom he always described thus,[36] or that a gift by a childless testator to "my children" was intended for his step-children.[37]

(b) Equivocations

(i) Ambiguity: Evidence of the testator's intention has always been admissible to explain an equivocation. There is said to be an equivocation or ambiguity in a will when there is a description of a person or thing which can apply equally well to two or more persons or things. Thus if a testator devises his close (enclosed land) "in the occupation of W" and he has two such closes, there is an equivocation.[38]

By statute extrinsic evidence (including evidence of the testator's intention) is admissible to assist in the interpretation of a will in so far as (i) any part of the will is meaningless, or (ii) the language in any part of the will is ambiguous on the face of it,[39] or (iii) evidence (not being evidence of the testator's intention) shows that any of the language is ambiguous in the light of surrounding circumstances.[40]

(ii) Effect of extrinsic evidence: Once extrinsic evidence of the testator's intention is admitted, it will be given effect to even if it shows that someone apparently outside the scope of the gift was intended. Thus in one case[41] a testatrix gave part of her property "to my nephew Arthur Murphy". She had two legitimate nephews of that name, and extrinsic

---

[32] See *Perrin v. Morgan* [1943] A.C. 399 (meaning of "money").
[33] Family Law Reform Act 1969, s.15. This does not affect the meaning of "heir" (or entailed interests but such interests cannot now be created anyway).
[34] Adoption Act 1958, ss.16(2), 17(2), 59, Sched. 5, para. 4.
[35] *Boyes v. Cook* (1880) 14 Ch.D. 53 at 56, *per* James L.J.
[36] Consider *Thorn v. Dickens* [1906] W.N. 54 (where the entire will consisted of the words "All for mother").
[37] *Re Jeans* (1895) 72 L.T. 834.
[38] *Richardson v. Watson* (1833) 4 B. & Ad. 787.
[39] See *Re Williams* [1985] 1 W.L.R. 905.
[40] Administration of Justice Act 1982, s.21.
[41] *Re Jackson* [1933] Ch. 237.

evidence was admitted to explain this ambiguity. The evidence admitted showed that the testatrix intended to benefit an illegitimate nephew called Arthur Murphy, and it was held that he took to the exclusion of the two legitimate nephews. Had there been only one legitimate and one illegitimate nephew, there would have been no ambiguity, for "nephew" then prima facie meant "legitimate nephew" (it does not now[42]); consequently no extrinsic evidence would have been admitted and the legitimate nephew would have taken.[43]

(iii) Uncertainty: If extrinsic evidence fails to resolve an ambiguity, the gift is void for uncertainty.[44] The same applies where the description is on the face of it indefinite, such as a gift by a testator "to one of the sons of X", X having at the time several sons.[45]

3. Contradictions

(a) Inconsistency

Extrinsic evidence is not admissible to explain a contradiction in a will, such as a gift of "one hundred pounds (£500) to X". In such a case, the rule is that the second expression prevails over the first[46] since it is the latest in the testator's mind; this contrasts with a deed, where the former of two inconsistent expressions prevails, for what has once been done cannot be undone. Before resorting to such a rule of thumb, however, the court tries to reconcile the two provisions in some way.[47]

(b) Engrafted gift

An important example of such a reconciliation is what was originally known as the rule in *Lassence v. Tierney*.[48] It is now more commonly known as the rule in *Hancock v. Watson*.[49] This rule, which applies to deeds as well as to wills,[50] has been stated as follows: "If you find an absolute gift to a legatee in the first instance, and trusts are engrafted or imposed on that absolute interest which fail, either from lapse or invalidity or any other reason, then the absolute gift takes effect so far as the trusts have failed to the exclusion of the residuary legatee or next of kin as the case may be."[51] Thus suppose a gift to X of a fee simple or an absolute interest in personalty, with a direction later in the will or in a codicil that the property given to X shall be held for X for life with remainder to his children. If the gift to the children wholly or partly fails (for example through there being no children or through the perpetuity rule being infringed), the gift of the fee simple or absolute interest to X takes effect, instead of the property passing under a residuary gift or as on intestacy.[52] For the rule to apply, there must be an initial absolute gift which is subsequently cut down; one continuous limitation containing both gift and restrictions will normally not bring the doctrine into play,[53] nor will

---

[42] Family Law Reform Act 1969, s.15.
[43] *Re Fish* [1894] 2 Ch. 83.
[44] *Richardson v. Watson*, above.
[45] *Strode v. Russel* (1708) 2 Vern 621 at 624, 625.
[46] *Re Hammond* [1938] 3 All E.R. 308.
[47] See, *e.g. Re Gare* [1952] Ch. 80; and see below, p. 315.
[48] (1849) 1 Mac. & G. 551.
[49] [1902] A.C. 14.
[50] See *Att.-Gen. v. Lloyds Bank Ltd* [1935] A.C. 382.
[51] *Hancock v. Watson* [1902] A.C. 14 at 22, *per* Lord Davey.
[52] See *Watkins v. Weston* (1863) 3 De G.J. & S. 434.
[53] *Re Payne* [1927] 2 Ch. 1.

a gift in which the names of the beneficiaries are immediately followed by the words "subject to the provisions hereinafter contained".[54]

4. A will speaks from death: general

There are two aspects of the rule that a will speaks from death: statute applies it to property, and the courts have applied it to persons.

5. A will speaks from death: as to property

As already mentioned,[55] a will is ambulatory. Subject to any contrary intention, it is to be construed, with reference to the property in it, as if it had been executed immediately before the testator's death.[56] A will is therefore capable of disposing of all property owned by the testator at his death even if he acquired it only after making his will. Thus a gift of "my shares in the XYZ Co. Ltd" includes not only those owned when the will was made but also those acquired subsequently[57]; and a devise of land carries with it all fixtures attached to the land, even if they were affixed after the will was made.[58]

However, while the rule applies to all generic descriptions (*i.e.* descriptions of a class of objects which may increase or decrease) and is not confined to general or residual gifts, it has no application to a gift of a specific object existing at the date of the will. Thus if a testator makes a will giving "my piano" to X and subsequently sells his piano and buys another, X has no claim to it.[59] The bequest is said to have been adeemed, a term applied to the failure of a gift by the property concerned ceasing to exist, or ceasing to belong to the testator, between the date of his will and his death.

6. A will speaks from death: as to persons

It is only in some respects that a will is construed as speaking from death as to persons.

(a) Class gifts

A class gift is a gift of property to all who come within some description, the property being divisible according to the number of persons in the class, such as a gift of £10,000 "equally between X's children who attain full age".[60]

(i) Class fixed at death: The rule of construction adopted by the courts in determining the effect of class gifts is the same as in other cases, namely, to carry out the intention of the testator as expressed in the will. In the absence of any such intention being expressed, such as a gift to children "whenever born",[61] the primary rule is that, if any member of the class is in existence at the testator's death, membership of the class is fixed at that moment, so that persons dying before the testator[62] or born after his death are excluded.[63] Thus under a gift to "all of my sisters", the sisters alive at the testator's death take to the exclusion of any born afterwards. In short, the will speaks from death.

---

[54] *Re Cohen's W.T.* [1936] 1 All E.R. 103.
[55] Above, p. 176.
[56] Wills Act 1837, s.24.
[57] *Trinder v. Trinder* (1866) L.R. 1 Eq. 695; contrast *Re Tetsall* [1961] 1 W.L.R. 938 ("my 750 shares").
[58] For fixtures, see above, pp. 19 *et seq.*
[59] *Re Sikes* [1927] 1 Ch. 364.
[60] See below, p. 227.
[61] *Re Edmondson's W.T.* [1972] 1 W.L.R. 183.
[62] *Fitzroy v. Duke of Richmond* (1858) 28 L.J.Ch. 750.
[63] *Viner v. Francis* (1789) 2 Cox Eq. 190.

(ii) Rule excluded: There are, however, a number of secondary rules which should be mentioned.[64]

    (a) No member living. If no member of the class is alive at the testator's death, the gift prima facie includes all members born at any future date.[65] Thus if a testator gives property "equally among A's children", a child born after the testator's death can claim a share only if A had no children at the testator's death.

    (b) Life interest existing. If a life interest precedes the class gift (such as "to X for life, remainder to Y's children"), all those alive when the life interest ceases are entitled to share in the gift.[66] Further, those who survive the testator but die before the life interest ceases are included and their shares will pass under their wills or intestacies.[67] Similarly, if a valid direction for accumulation is made, the class does not close until the accumulations cease.[68]

    (c) Reversionary interest given. Again, if a reversionary interest[69] is given by will, the class remains open until the interest falls into possession. Thus if property is settled on S for life with remainder to T absolutely, and T dies in S's lifetime, leaving his interest to X's children, all of X's children born before S's death are entitled to share in the gift.[70]

    (d) Conditional gift. If a gift is contingent upon the beneficiaries fulfilling some condition, such as attaining the age of 21 years, the rule in *Andrews v. Partington*[71] applies, and the class remains open until one member has fulfilled the condition; it then closes.[72] If one member has fulfilled the condition at the testator's death, the class is ascertained then.[73]

(iii) The principle: The principle behind these rules (which apply to realty and personalty alike) has been said to be one of convenience rather than of construing the testator's intention.[74] As soon as any member of a class is entitled to call for his share, the class must be closed, for otherwise the size of the share to be given to him cannot be ascertained. But subject to this requirement, the class is kept open for as long as possible. Thus if property is given to A for life, remainder to all the testator's grandchildren who attain the age of 21 years, the class remains open until A has died and a grandchild is 21 years old; neither event by itself suffices to close the class.[75] The rules apply to settlements *inter vivos* as well as wills; and although they yield to a contrary intention, the standard is high, so that nothing will oust them except an intention which is inescapably incompatible with their operation.[76]

---

[64] See the summary in *Re Chartres* [1927] 1 Ch. 466 at 471, 472.
[65] *Weld v. Bradbury* (1715) 2 Vern 705.
[66] *Re Knapp's Settlement* [1895] 1 Ch. 91 at 96.
[67] *Greenwood v. Greenwood* [1939] 2 All E.R. 150.
[68] *Re Stephens* [1904] 1 Ch. 322.
[69] See below, p. 163.
[70] *Walker v. Shore* (1808) 15 Ves. 122.
[71] (1791) 3 Bro.C.C. 401.
[72] *Re Bleckly* [1951] Ch. 740.
[73] *Picken v. Matthews* (1878) 10 Ch.D. 264.
[74] *Re Emmet's Estate* (1880) 13 Ch.D. 484 at 490. See generally (1954) 70 L.Q.R. 61 (J. H. C. Morris).
[75] *Re Paul's S.T.* [1920] 1 Ch. 99.
[76] *Re Clifford's S.T.* [1981] Ch. 63; see *Re Tom's Settlement* [1987] 1 W.L.R. 1021.

(b) Gifts to individuals

In the case of gifts to individuals, the date of the will, and not the date of the testator's death, is normally the relevant time. Thus a gift "to the eldest son of my sister" is a gift to the eldest at the date of the will; if he dies before the testator, the gift lapses and the eldest son at the testator's death has no claim. Similarly, a bequest "to Lord Sherborne" is a gift to the holder of the title at the date of the will.[77] But like all rules of construction, this yields to a contrary intention, and a legacy "to the Lord Mayor of London for the time being" operates as a gift to the person holding that office at the testator's death,[78] while a gift "to the Mayor of Lowestoft for the benefit of poor and needy fisherman of Lowestoft" takes effect as a gift to the Mayor of Lowestoft for the time being, and not as a gift to a particular person who is Mayor at a particular time.[79]

7. Exercise of powers of appointment

A general devise or bequest (such as "I give all my property to X") operates to exercise a general power of appointment unless a contrary intention is shown by the will.[80] On the other hand, a special power (which for this purpose includes a power to appoint to "anyone except X"[81]) is not exercised by a general bequest or devise unless the will shows a contrary intention, as by referring to the power or to the property concerned.[82]

Part 4—Intestacy

The rules relating to intestacy must now be considered. If the deceased died wholly intestate, leaving no effective will, these rules govern the devolution of all his property, while if he died partly testate and partly intestate, they apply to all the property which does not pass under his will.

Before 1926, realty and personalty descended differently but since 1925 they have devolved in the same way under the code laid down in the Administration of Estates Act 1925, which was substantially modified by the Intestates' Estates Act 1952 in respect of deaths after 1952. Today, only the post-1952 rules[83] require consideration.

By the Administration of Estates Act 1925,[84] all property of an intestate, whether real or personal, which does not already consist of money is held on trust to be sold. The personal representatives of the deceased have power to postpone sale for such periods as they think proper. However, unless required for the purpose of administration for want of other assets, "personal chattels" (see below) are not to be sold without special reason, and reversionary interests (such as an interest in a trust fund which will not fall into the intestate's estate until the life interest of some third person has ceased) are similarly not to be sold without special reason.

---

[77] *Re Whorwood* (1887) 34 Ch.D. 446.
[78] *Re Daniels* (1918) 87 L.J.Ch. 661.
[79] *Re Pipe* (1937) 106 L.J.Ch. 252.
[80] Wills Act 1837, s.27.
[81] Contrast below, p. 231.
[82] *Re Ackerley* [1913] 1 Ch. 510 at 515.
[83] For the earlier rules, see M. & W. (4th ed.), pp. 509–523; and for a full review of the existing rules, see Law Com. W.P. No. 108 (1988).
[84] s.33(1).

Out of the fund thus produced, the personal representatives must pay all funeral, testamentary and administration expenses, debts and other liabilities, and set aside a fund to meet any pecuniary legacies[85] in cases where the deceased was only partly intestate. The residue must then be distributed to the persons beneficially entitled. The rules for this distribution were in the main laid down by the Administration of Estates Act 1925 (it was in this respect that the Act of 1925 was most modified by the Intestates' Estates Act 1952, which did much to improve the position of a surviving spouse[86]). References to sections of the Act of 1925 are to the sections as they stand amended (the rules stated apply to deaths after 1966[87]).

1. The surviving spouse

The rights of the surviving spouse,[88] whether widow or widower, depend on whether the intestate left issue or any "near relations", a convenient term to describe the parents and brothers and sisters of the whole blood or their issue; but any of them who die before attaining the age of 18 years or marrying thereunder are then disregarded.[89] As usual, "issue" means any descendant however remote; and it has since 1988 been in general irrelevant whether any relationship is legitimate or illegitimate.[90] The surviving spouse's rights depend on whether the intestate left issue; or left no issue but "near relations"; or left neither.[91] The three heads will be taken in turn.

(a) Head 1: issue

If the intestate left issue (whether or not there are also any "near relations") the surviving spouse takes the following interests.

(i) The personal chattels absolutely. "Personal chattels" are elaborately defined. They include horses, cars, domestic animals, plate, linen, china, books, pictures, prints, furniture, jewellery, "articles of household or personal use or ornament", and wines and consumable stores, but not chattels used for business purposes, money, or securities for money.[92] Roughly speaking, the phrase includes everything that goes to make a home, and rather more besides, but not the house itself: the phrase has a meaning quite distinct from "personalty" or "personal property".

(ii) A fixed net sum, which is raised periodically by statutory instrument[93] (at present it is £125,000[94]), free of inheritance tax and the costs of administering the estate, with six per cent interest thereon from the date of death until it is paid or appropriated.[95] Both the fixed net sum and the interest thereon are charged on the residuary estate, though the interest is payable primarily out of income and not capital.[96]

---

[85] A.E.A. 1925, ss.33(2), 34(3).
[86] See I.E.A. 1952, s.4; Family Provision Act 1966, s.1; Administration of Justice Act 1977, s.28.
[87] But certain of the amounts have since been varied, as will be seen below.
[88] See *Re Collins* [1990] Fam. 56 (a divorcee is still a "spouse" until the decree absolute).
[89] A.E.A. 1925, ss.46(1), 47(1), (4).
[90] Family Law Reform Act 1987, s.18.
[91] A.E.A. 1925, s.46(1).
[92] *ibid.*, s.55(1)(x).
[93] *ibid.*; Family Provision Act 1966, s.1; Administration of Justice Act 1977, s.28.
[94] Family Provision (Intestate Succession) Order 1993 (SI 1993 No. 2906).
[95] *ibid.*, s.46(1), as substituted by Intestates' Estates Act 1952, s.1.
[96] A.E.A. 1925, s.46(1), (4).

(iii) A life interest in half the remainder of the residuary estate, thereby providing income but not capital.

(b) Head 2: near relations but no issue

If the intestate left one or more "near relations" but no issue, the surviving spouse takes the following interests.

(i) The personal chattels absolutely.

(ii) A higher fixed net sum, which is also raised periodically by statutory instrument[97] (at present it is £200,000[98]), free of inheritance tax and the costs of administering the estate, with interest as above.

(iii) Half the residuary estate absolutely, thereby providing capital.

(c) Head 3: neither issue nor near relations

If the intestate left no issue and no "near relations", the surviving spouse is entitled to the entire residuary estate absolutely.

These provisions are subject to a number of subsidiary rules.

(i) Purchase of life interest: Within 12 months of probate or letters of administration being first taken out (or within such extended period as the court may grant), a surviving spouse who takes a life interest may (even if a minor) by notice in writing to the personal representatives elect that his or her life interest shall be purchased for a capital sum reckoned in accordance with special rules.[99] If the surviving spouse is the sole personal representative, written notice must be given to the Senior Registrar of the Family Division.[1]

(ii) Purchase of matrimonial home: The surviving spouse may by writing require the personal representatives (even if he or she is one of them) to appropriate to him or her any dwelling-house forming part of the residuary estate in which he or she was resident at the death of the intestate; usually this will be the matrimonial home.[2] This does not apply where the intestate's interest in the house is a mere tenancy which would determine (or could be determined by the landlord) within two years of his death, nor where the house is part of larger property held by the intestate unless the court is satisfied that the exercise of the surviving spouse's right is not likely to diminish the value of assets in the residuary estate or make them more difficult to dispose of. These provisions of the Act of 1952 in effect give the surviving spouse a power to compel the personal representatives to exercise in respect of the house the general discretionary power of appropriation conferred by the Act of 1925.[3] The property appropriated is taken, at a proper valuation when appropriated (not at the death),[4] to have satisfied to that extent the property to which the surviving spouse is absolutely entitled. However, if the house is worth more than the surviving spouse's interest such spouse can still require the house to be transferred to him or her partly in satisfaction

---

[97] *ibid.*; Family Provision Act 1966, s.1; Administration of Justice Act 1977, s.28.
[98] Family Provision (Intestate Succession) Order 1993 (S.I. 1993 No. 2906).
[99] See Intestate Succession (Interest and Capitalisation) Order 1977 (S.I. 1977 No. 1491).
[1] A.E.A. 1925, s.47A; Supreme Court Act 1981, Sched. 5.
[2] I.E.A. 1952, Sched. 2.
[3] By s.41.
[4] *Re Collins* [1975] 1 W.L.R. 309.

of his or her interests in the estate and partly for money.[5] The personal representatives must not unnecessarily sell the house within 12 months after probate or letters of administration are first taken out, and the surviving spouse's right to require an appropriation is exercisable only during that period or any extension granted by the court.[6]

(iii) Partial intestacy: Under the Act of 1952, the fixed net sum of (at present) £125,000 or £200,000 mentioned above must be diminished by the value of any beneficial interest acquired by the surviving spouse under the will of the deceased.[7] If, for example, the surviving spouse is given a life interest under the will, and the rest of the property is undisposed of, the spouse may at once claim the fixed net sum in question less the actuarial value of the life interest.[8] Alternatively, the surviving spouse may prefer to disclaim the testamentary life interest and take under the intestacy alone.[9]

(iv) Separation: If husband and wife are separated by a decree of judicial separation and the separation is continuing, any property in respect of which either of them dies intestate will devolve as if the other were already dead.[10]

(v) *Commorientes* Although the general rule laid down for *commorientes*[11] applies in general to intestacy, the Act of 1952 modified its application as between husband and wife. When the intestate and his or her spouse die in circumstances rendering it uncertain which survived the other, the rules of intestacy apply as if the spouse had not survived the intestate.[12] Thus if the wife, W, is younger than the husband, H, and both perish in a common disaster, then for the purposes of H's intestacy W will be treated as not having survived him. This avoids W taking benefits under H's intestacy which would almost instantly pass under her will or intestacy (probably to her side of the family if she had no issue). H's property accordingly passes as if no spouse had survived him, and so does W's. This exception to the general rule is confined to intestacy as between spouses; it does not affect wills, nor does it apply to other relations, such as issue.

2. The issue

Subject to the rights of the surviving spouse, if any, the property is held on the statutory trusts for the issue.[13] Under these trusts, the property is held upon trust for all the children of the deceased living at his death in equal shares, subject to three qualifications.

(a) Subject to representation

This means subject to the rule that issue of a deceased child stand in his shoes and take his share; descent is thus *per stirpes* (through the stocks of descent) and not *per capita* (one share for each head).

---

[5] *Re Phelps* [1980] Ch. 275.
[6] I.E.A. 1952, Sched. 2.
[7] A.E.A. 1925, s.49(1)(aa).
[8] *Re Bowen-Buscarlet's W.T.* [1972] Ch. 463.
[9] See *Re Sullivan* [1930] 1 Ch. 84; *Re Thornber* [1937] Ch. 29.
[10] Matrimonial Causes Act 1973, s.18(2), replacing Matrimonial Proceedings and Property Act 1970, s.40, applying to deaths after July 31, 1970.
[11] See above, p. 184.
[12] A.E.A. 1925, s.46(3), added by I.E.A. 1952, s.1(4).
[13] A.E.A. 1925, s.46(1).

(b) Subject to the rule that no issue attains a vested interest until he is 18 years old[14] or married

This in effect means that if a minor dies without having married, the property must be dealt with from that moment as if the minor had never existed.[15] Thus if X dies leaving a widow and minor son, the widow takes a life interest in half of the residue. If the son dies before either marrying or attaining his majority, the widow forthwith takes absolutely either half the residue, or all, depending on whether any "near relations" survived X.

(c) Subject to hotchpot

There are two rules governing this.

(i) *Inter vivos*: If they wish to share in the distribution of the estate, children (but not remoter issue) must bring into account any money or property which the deceased has in his lifetime paid them or settled for their benefit by way of advancement or upon marriage.[16] For example, if the estate is worth £160,000 and there are three children, one of whom has received an advancement of £20,000 in the intestate's lifetime, that child can claim only £40,000 out of the £160,000; the other two children each receive £60,000. Had the first child received an advancement of £100,000 he could not be compelled to refund any part of it for distribution between the others. The obligation to bring property into hotchpot is subject to any contrary intention appearing from the circumstances of the case. In determining what advances must be brought into hotchpot, a distinction must be made between payments made to start a child in life, and casual or periodical sums paid in the ordinary course of events, or so as to relieve the child from temporary difficulties; the former alone need be brought into hotchpot.[17]

(ii) Partial intestacy: In the case of partial intestacy, issue of the deceased, whether children or remoter descendants, must, subject to any contrary intention shown by the deceased, bring into hotchpot any benefit received by him or his issue under his will.[18] Thus if a grandchild of the deceased has received £10,000 from him, neither he nor his parent need bring it into hotchpot if it was an advancement made *inter vivos* (for he is not a child of the deceased), but it must be brought into account if it is given him by will.

If no issue attains a vested interest, then, subject to the claims of the surviving spouse (if any), the relatives of the deceased are entitled in the following order[19]; any member of one class who takes a vested interest excludes all members of subsequent classes.

3. The parents

The parents of the deceased are entitled in equal shares absolutely; if one is dead, the survivor is entitled absolutely.

---

[14] Family Law Reform Act 1969, s.3(2).
[15] See A.E.A. 1925, s.47(2).
[16] *ibid.,* s.47(1).
[17] See *Taylor v. Taylor* (1875) L.R. 20 Eq. 155 at 157; *Re Hayward* [1957] Ch. 528.
[18] A.E.A. 1925, s.49; see *Re Grover's W.T.* [1971] Ch. 168.q.
[19] A.E.A. 1925, s.46(1).

4. The brothers and sisters of the whole blood, who hold on the statutory trusts.

5. Those other than "near relations"

A division must be made here, for at this point the "near relations" end. Those included in the foregoing classes may take an interest even though the intestate left a surviving spouse; those in the subsequent classes cannot.

> *(a) The brothers and sisters of the half blood,* on the statutory trusts.
>
> *(b) The grandparents,* if more than one in equal shares.
>
> *(c) The uncles and aunts of the whole blood,* on the statutory trusts.
>
> *(d) The uncles and aunts of the half blood,* on the statutory trusts.
>
> *(e) The Crown* (or the Duchy of Lancaster or Duke of Cornwall) as *bona vacantia* in lieu of any right to escheat.

A number of points arise on the foregoing list.

(i) Statutory trusts: The statutory trusts for the brothers, sisters, uncles and aunts are the same as those for the issue of the deceased, save that the provisions relating to hotchpot do not apply.[20] Thus deceased brothers, sisters, uncles and aunts are represented by their descendants, whose interests in every case are contingent upon their attaining full age or marrying. "Uncles" and "aunts" include only blood relations, and so the wife of a mother's brother, though called "aunt", has no claim: marriage is not blood.

(ii) Illegitimate children: Where the intestate dies after April 3, 1988, it does not matter if the claimant, or anyone through whom his relationship is deduced, is illegitimate.[21] For these purposes, however, there is a rebuttable presumption that the father of an illegitimate person (and anyone related to him solely through his father) predeceased him.[22]

(iii) Adopted children: A formal adoption order (as distinct from a mere *de facto* adoption) puts both child and adoptive parents in the same position for all subsequent intestacies as if the child were their child, born in lawful wedlock, and not the child of any other person.[23] This does not apply to the descent of a peerage or of property limited to devolve with it.[24]

(iv) Crown discretion: In practice, the Crown modifies its strict rights under head No. 9. It makes provision for dependants of the deceased (although they anyway now have the right to claim reasonable financial provision out of the estate of the deceased under the Inheritance (Provision for Family and Dependants) Act 1975 and, given that in such circumstances the Crown has been held to have no relevant needs or any moral claim to the estate,[25] any provision ordered by the court is likely to be on the generous side). The Crown also makes

---

[20] A.E.A. 1925, s.47(3).
[21] Family Law Reform Act 1987, ss.1, 18(1); S.I. 1988 No. 425.
[22] *ibid.*, s.18(2).
[23] Adoption Act 1976, ss.38–46; S.I. 1987 No. 1242.
[24] *ibid.*, s.44.
[25] *Re Watson* [1999] 1 F.L.R. 878.

provision for others, whether related to the deceased or not, for whom he might reasonably have been expected to have made provision. This purely discretionary power, which the Act of 1925 confirmed,[26] was made all the more necessary by the Crown's increased prospects of succeeding to property of an intestate thereafter[27] (before 1926, any relation, however remote, could take on intestacy whereas now no relation more remote than a first cousin can ever do so).

PART 5—PERSONAL REPRESENTATIVES

Sect. 1. Introductory

1. Vesting of property

The beneficial devolution of property on death has been considered above; it is now necessary to discuss the means by which the property becomes vested in those beneficially entitled. The general rule today is that all property first vests in the personal representatives of the deceased, who in due course (and normally within the "executor's year", *i.e.* one year from the death) are required to transfer to the beneficiaries any of the property not required in the due administration of the estate, such as for payment of debts. In this context "estate" is used not in the technical sense of an estate in land, but as a collective expression for the sum total of the assets and liabilities of the deceased.

2. Executors

"Personal representatives" is a phrase which includes both executors and administrators. If a person makes a will, he may (but need not) appoint one or more persons to be his executor or executors, with the duty of paying debts, inheritance tax and funeral expenses, and ultimately of distributing the estate to those entitled. The executor derives his powers from the will,[28] although he must obtain confirmation of his position by "proving the will", *i.e.* obtaining a grant of probate from the court. If a sole or only surviving executor who has obtained probate dies, having himself appointed an executor, the latter, on proving the original executor's will, becomes executor of the original testator also. This "chain of representation" may be continued indefinitely until broken by failure to appoint an executor, or failure of an executor to obtain a grant of probate.[29]

3. Administrators

If a person dies without having appointed an executor, or if none of the executors he has appointed is able and willing to act, application must be made to the court by some person or persons interested in the estate for "letters of administration" appointing an administrator or administrators. The duties of an administrator are substantially the same as those of an executor. If the deceased left no will, simple administration is granted; if he left a will, the grant is of administration *cum testamento annexo* ("with the will annexed").[30] A grant may

---

[26] A.E.A. 1925, s.46(1).
[27] See N. D. Ing, Bona Vacantia (1971), pp. 104–109.
[28] *Biles v. Caesar* [1957] 1 W.L.R. 156.
[29] See A.E.A. 1925, s.7.
[30] Supreme Court Act 1981, s.119.

be limited in any way the court thinks fit,[31] so that there may be a grant confined to settled land, or a grant "save and except" settled land,[32] or a grant *durante minore aetate* ("during the minority" of the sole executor).[33] There is no "chain of representation" for administrators. If a sole or last surviving administrator dies without completing the administration of the estate, application must be made for a grant of administration *de bonis non administratis* (more shortly, *de bonis non*), which is a grant "in respect of the goods left unadministered".

Sect. 2. Devolution of property on personal representatives

1. The background

Before the Land Transfer Act 1897, all personalty (including leaseholds) vested in the personal representatives, whilst all realty passed immediately to the heir or devisee as the case might be. The Act made the "personal" representatives also "real" representatives, so that a testator's realty as well as his personalty vested in his executors.

2. Vesting

The Administration of Estates Act 1925 substantially repeats the provisions of the Land Transfer Act 1897. In the case of deaths after 1925, all land owned by the deceased, whether freehold or leasehold, vests in the personal representatives,[34] with the following exceptions:

(i) fees tail, unless disposed of by the deceased's will[35];

(ii) property to which the deceased was entitled as a joint tenant[36];

(iii) property to which the deceased was entitled as a corporation sole[37];

(iv) interests which ceased on the death of the deceased, such as an interest for his life.[38]

Property subject to a general power of appointment exercised by the will of the deceased passes to his personal representatives.[39] On an intestacy, both realty and personalty vest in the Probate judge (*i.e.* the President of the Family Division of the High Court of Justice as senior Probate judge) until administration is granted.[40]

3. Assents

Since 1925 any land which is not needed by the personal representatives (such as for the payment of debts) has to be transferred to the person entitled to it by a document known as an assent. No assent made after 1925 will pass a legal estate in land unless it is in writing and

---

[31] *ibid.*, s.113.
[32] See A.E.A. 1925, s.23.
[33] Supreme Court Act 1981, ss.116, 118.
[34] A.E.A. 1925, ss.1(1), 3(1). For legal estates in settled land, see below, pp. 265–268.
[35] *ibid.*, s.3(3).
[36] *ibid.*, s.3(4).
[37] *ibid.*, s.3(5).
[38] *ibid.*, s.1(1).
[39] *ibid.*, s.3(2).
[40] *ibid.*, ss.9, 55(1) (xv), as amended by Administration of Justice Act 1970, s.1, Sched. 2, para. 5. See, *e.g. Wirral B.C. v. Smith* (1982) 43 P. & C.R. 312.

signed by the personal representatives.[41] A written assent is also required when a legal estate is not transferred but is to be held in a different capacity, as where personal representatives, having completed the administration of the deceased's estate, begin to hold as trustees under any trusts in the will.[42] But an assent to the vesting of an equitable interest still need not be in writing, and may be inferred from conduct.[43] A bona fide purchaser for value is no longer concerned with the terms of the will; he can rely on the grant of probate or letters of administration, coupled with an assent or conveyance executed by the personal representatives, as constituting his title[44] (this is of course only relevant to unregistered land; a purchaser of registered land will simply rely on the registration of the personal representatives as proprietor).

4. Ownership of assets

While the administration of the deceased's estate is proceeding, the personal representatives are the legal and equitable owners of all assets not specifically devised and bequeathed. The beneficiaries entitled to the residue of the deceased's estate have no interest, legal or equitable, in any specific assets. They merely have the right to compel the personal representatives to administer the estate properly.[45]

5. Powers

Personal representatives now have all the powers of a trustee of land[46] (thus in relation to land settled under the Settled Land Act 1925 they have all the powers given by that Act to the tenant for life and the trustees under the Settled Land Act 1925).[47] On a sale they will thus overreach all the beneficial interests under the will or intestacy into the proceeds of sale (this will be the case even if there is only one personal representative[48]). Although they should sell the property only if this is necessary for the purposes of administration, a conveyance to a purchaser for value in good faith is not invalidated merely because he knows that all the debts and other liabilities have been met.[49] Nor is a conveyance to a purchaser for value in good faith invalidated merely because the probate or letters of administration under which the personal representatives acted are subsequently revoked.[50]

Personal representatives have joint and several powers over pure personalty but they have only joint authority over realty and leaseholds.[51]

Sect. 3. Number of personal representatives

1. Maximum

No grant of probate or letters of administration can be made to more than four personal

---

[41] A.E.A. 1925, s.36(2), (4).
[42] *Re King's W.T.* [1964] Ch. 542, a controversial decision.
[43] *Re Edwards' W.T.* [1982] Ch. 30 at 40.
[44] A.E.A. 1925, ss.36(4), (7), 39(1).
[45] *Commissioner of Stamp Duties (Queensland) v. Livingston* [1965] A.C. 694; *Re Hayes' W.T.* [1971] 1 W.L.R. 758 at 764.
[46] A.E.A. 1925, s.39 (1)(ii), as substituted by T.L.A.T.A..
[47] Below, pp. 268 *et seq.*
[48] L.P.A. 1925, s.27(2).
[49] A.E.A. 1925, ss.36(8), 55(1) (xviii).
[50] *ibid.*, ss.37, 55(1)(xviii), retrospectively confirming *Hewson v. Shelley* [1914] 2 Ch. 13.
[51] A.E.A. 1925, s.2(2); *Fountain Forestry Ltd v. Edwards* [1975] Ch. 1.

representatives in respect of the same property.[52] If a testator appoints more than four executors, they must decide among themselves who will apply for probate.

2. Minimum

Unlike trustees of land, there is no provision preventing a sole personal representative from giving a valid receipt for purchase money; a sole personal representative, whether original or by survivorship, has full power to give valid receipts for capital money or any other payments.[53] However, if any person interested in the estate is a minor or has a life interest in it, the court must normally not appoint a sole administrator, other than a trust corporation.[54] A sole executor can act under such circumstances, but the court has power to appoint additional personal representatives.[55]

PART 6—DISABILITIES

Certain persons are subject to disabilities as to the interests in land which they can hold, create or alienate. Formerly, the list of such persons was more extensive than it is today, including married women, certain convicts and aliens.[56] These disabilities no longer exist, and this Part will be confined to those disabilities that remain.

Sect. 1. Minors

A minor (formerly called an infant[57]) is a person who has not attained full age. For centuries,[58] a person attained full age or "majority" at the first moment of the day preceding the twenty-first anniversary of his birth.[59] With effect from January 1, 1970, the age of majority was reduced to 18 years,[60] and this is now reached at the first moment of the eighteenth anniversary of birth.[61] The following are the main points to note.

1. Ownership of land

Since 1925, a minor has not been able to hold a legal estate in land,[62] although he may still hold equitable interests.

2. Attempted conveyance to a minor

From 1926 to 1996 an attempt to convey a legal estate to a minor alone or jointly with other minors operated as a contract for value to make a proper settlement under the Settled Land

---

[52] Supreme Court Act 1981, s.114.
[53] L.P.A. 1925, s.27(2).
[54] Supreme Court Act 1981, s.114(2).
[55] *ibid.*, s.114(4).
[56] See M. & W. (5th ed.), pp. 1020–1027.
[57] See Family Law Reform Act 1969, s.12.
[58] See 3 H.E.L. 510, 511 for the development of the rule in the Middle Ages.
[59] See, *e.g. Re Shurey* [1918] 1 Ch. 263.
[60] Family Law Reform Act 1969, s.1; S.I. 1969 No. 1140.
[61] Family Law Reform Act 1969, s.9.
[62] L.P.A. 1925, s.1(6).

Act 1925 by means of a vesting deed and trust instrument, and in the meantime to hold the land in trust for the minor or minors[63] while an attempted conveyance of a legal estate to a minor jointly with a person of full age vested the legal estate in the person of full age on trust for sale for himself and the minor.[64] These provisions did not apply to a conveyance to a minor as mortgagee or trustee, for which special provisions were made.[65] Since 1996, an attempt to convey a legal estate to a minor alone or jointly with other minors operates as a declaration of trust in favour of the minor or minors while an attempted conveyance of a legal estate to a minor jointly with a person of full age vests the legal estate in the person of full age on a trust of land for himself and the minor.[66] These provisions apply to a conveyance to a minor as mortgagee but not to a minor as trustee, for which special provision is made.[67]

3. Mortgages

Since 1925 a minor has not been able to be a legal mortgagee. Between 1926 and 1996, an attempt to grant a legal mortgage to one or more persons who were all minors operated as an agreement for value to execute a proper mortgage when the minor or minors was of full age, and in the meantime to hold the beneficial interest in trust for those intended to benefit,[68] while a mortgage to a minor and other persons of full age operated, so far as the legal estate was concerned, as if the minor had not been named, although his beneficial interest was not affected.[69] Since 1996, attempts to create mortgages in favour of any minor have been treated in the same way as attempts to convey any other legal estate to such a person.

4. Personal representatives

A minor can be neither an executor[70] nor an administrator.[71] If a minor would, but for his minority, be entitled to be an administrator, or is appointed sole executor, he cannot take a grant until he is of full age; in the meantime a grant may be taken by someone on his behalf, for example his guardian. In the case of administration, the grant must be made to at least two persons or a trust corporation on the minor's behalf, since a minor is interested in the estate.[72] If a minor is appointed one of several executors, the rest of whom are of full age, he must wait until he attains his majority, when he can join in the grant of probate previously made to the others.

5. Trustees

No minor can be appointed a trustee after 1925. This applies to trusts of any property, real or personal. The effect of a purported conveyance of a legal estate in land to a minor as trustee is governed by different and not identically worded statutory provisions depending on whether it was made before 1997 or after 1996 but is substantially the same:

---

[63] S.L.A. 1925, s.27(1) (a statutory exception to the equitable rule that an imperfect voluntary conveyance will not be treated as a declaration of trust: below, p. 291).
[64] L.P.A. 1925, s.19(2).
[65] See below.
[66] T.L.A.T.A., Sched. 1, paras 1 and 2.
[67] See below.
[68] L.P.A. 1925, s.19(6).
[69] ibid.
[70] Supreme Court Act 1981, s.118.
[71] In b. Manuel (1849) 13 Jur. 664.
[72] See above.

(i) If the minor is a sole trustee, the conveyance operates as a declaration of trust by the grantor; the effect is the same if the conveyance is to two or more trustees, all of whom are minors.[73]

(ii) If the minor is one of two or more trustees, at least one of whom is of full age, the conveyance operates as if the minor were not named, although this does not prejudice any beneficial interest thereby given to him.[74]

These provisions do not prevent a minor from becoming a trustee of property other than a legal estate in land in other ways, such as under a resulting or constructive trust.[75]

6. Settled land

From 1926 to 1996, land to which a minor was entitled in possession was deemed to be settled land.[76] This was so even if the minor was absolutely entitled. In such a case, both the legal estate and the statutory powers were vested in the trustees of the settlement as statutory owner.[77] Since 1997, if a minor becomes entitled in possession to a legal estate in land other than under a purported conveyance, such as under a will or intestacy, it will be held on trust for him until he becomes of age by, at least initially, the personal representatives.[78]

7. Voidable dispositions

Any disposition by a minor of any interest in land is voidable at the option of the minor (but not of the grantee[79]) on the minor attaining his majority,[80] or within a reasonable time thereafter.[81] If the minor dies under age, his personal representatives may avoid the disposition within a reasonable time.[82] As the disposition is voidable and not void, it is binding if the minor fails to repudiate it within a reasonable time after attaining his majority.[83] However, the land itself can of course be dealt with by the holder of the legal title, whoever that is, provided that the overreaching rules are complied with, in which case the minor's interest is overreached into what ever capital money is paid.

8. Transfer on death

Although normally any equitable interest vested in a minor will pass on his death under his will (only if he is privileged as a soldier or mariner) or (in every other case) under his intestacy, there is one exception. By the Administration of Estates Act 1925, s.51(3), if a minor who died between 1926 and 1996 without ever having married was entitled at his death under a settlement under the Settled Land Act 1925 to a vested equitable interest in land in fee simple, or an absolute interest in property settled to devolve with such land or as freehold land, he was deemed to have had an entailed interest. Since 1996,[84] if a minor who dies

---

[73] L.P.A. (1925), s.19(4) (until 1997); T..L.A.T.A., Sched. 1, para.1(1) (after 1996).
[74] L.P.A. (1925), s.19(5) (until 1997); T..L.A.T.A., Sched. 1, para.1(2) (after 1996).
[75] *Re Vinogradoff* [1935] W.N. 68.
[76] Below, p. 256.
[77] Below, p. 256.
[78] T..L.A.T.A., Sched. 1, para.1(2).
[79] *Zouch d. Abbot v. Parsons* (1765) 3 Burr. 1794.
[80] *Ashfeild v. Ashfeild* (1628) W.Jo. 157.
[81] *Carnell v. Harrison* [1916] 1 Ch. 328.
[82] 4 Cru.Dig. 69.
[83] *Edwards v. Carter* [1893] A.C. 360.
[84] A.E.A. s.51(3) was amended by T.L.A.T.A, Sched. 3, para. 4.

without ever having married and also without issue is entitled at his death under a trust or settlement to a vested equitable interest in land in fee simple, or an absolute interest in property devolving such land or as freehold land, he is deemed to have a life interest (the result is different because it is no longer possible to create entailed interests[85]).

The objects of this somewhat strange subsection appear to be:

(i) to make it unnecessary always to take out a grant of administration to the minor's estate; and

(ii) to make the land revert to the donor.

This was certainly the effect of the provision between 1926 and April 3, 1988 and has again been since 1996. If D had settled land on A for life with remainder to B (a minor) in fee simple, and B had died a minor between 1926 and April 3, 1988 without having married, he would have been deemed to have had an entailed interest; since he could have had no legitimate children, his notional entailed interest would have come to an end on his death[86] and D would have become entitled to the fee simple, subject to A's life interest. Where B instead dies a minor after 1996 without having married and without issue, he is deemed to have had a life interest and, on the determination of that interest on his death, D equally becomes entitled to the fee simple, subject to A's life interest. The justification for this result is that it is probably closer to D's intentions than that the land should pass under B's intestacy to, for example, his father or uncle. During the intervening period, from April 4, 1988 until December 31, 1996, the position was complicated by the fact that illegitimate children were able to inherit entailed interests,[87] so that if B had died a minor without having married but with surviving issue, the entailed interest would have passed to the relevant child and D's reversion would have been subject to that interest; where B had no surviving issue, the result would have been the same as above. However, at no time would any grant of probate or administration to B's estate have been needed in respect of the land.

Read literally, this provision restricts the power of disposition over realty given by the Wills (Soldiers and Sailors) Act 1918 to minors who are soldiers or members of the Air Force in actual military service, or mariners at sea[88] by depriving them of any testamentary power over realty until they marry or, since 1996, have issue, since a minor could not before 1997 bar an entail by will[89] and since 1997 his life interest will determine on his death.

9. Leases

A purported grant of a legal lease to a minor is governed by the provisions which have already been discussed. However, there is nothing to stop him from enjoying the rights to which he is entitled under the grant (occupation or, where the property is sub-let, the rent paid by the sub-lessee) subject to the obligations attached to the lease. Further, unless he repudiates the lease within a reasonable time after attaining his majority, he is bound by it.[90] But even if he repudiates the lease, he cannot recover the rent he has paid.[91]

---

[85] T.L.A.T.A., Sched. 1, para. 1(5).
[86] But consider Family Law Reform Act 1987, s.19.
[87] Family Law Reform Act 1987, s.1(1), 19(1), 19(2).
[88] Above, p. 181.
[89] Above, p. 46.
[90] *Davies v. Beynon-Harris* (1931) 47 T.L.R. 424.
[91] *Valentini v. Canali* (1890) L.R. 24 Q.B.D. 166.

Sect. 2. Mental patients

If a person is suffering from a mental disorder there are two points to consider: first, some control may have to be exercised over his person, and secondly, someone must be appointed to manage his property. Only the second of these points is relevant here.

1. Control over property

(a) Jurisdiction

Ever since the statute De Prerogativa Regis 1324 the Crown has exercised a jurisdiction over the property of mental patients (formerly called lunatics, and then persons of unsound mind). The current statute is the Mental Health Act 1983.[92] At present the jurisdiction is exercised by one or more nominated judges of the Chancery Division. In practice, the work is done by an office of the Supreme Court called "the Court of Protection" under a Master, subject to appeal to the judge.[93] The jurisdiction is exercisable over any person who is "incapable, by reason of mental disorder, of managing and administering his property and affairs".[94] The normal course of events is for the Court of Protection to appoint a receiver for the patient (usually a near relation), and for the receiver to exercise wide powers under the supervision of the court, including the disposition of property, the management of a business and the conduct of litigation.[95]

(b) Settlements

As well as managing the property in the interests of the patient, the court is empowered to make dispositions and other transactions for the benefit of the patient's family or other persons for whom he might have been expected to provide whether in his lifetime or at his death.[96] Thus the court may authorise the making of a settlement[97] or a will[98] by the patient.

2. Capacity

(a) After proceedings

If a receiver has been appointed, the patient ceases to have any capacity to deal with his property.[99] He remains the owner but control has been taken from him. Thus even in a lucid interval any disposition by him is void,[1] although a will made during a lucid interval is valid.[2]

(b) Before proceedings

If there are no proceedings on foot in the Court of Protection, a voluntary disposition of property by the patient is absolutely void unless made with a sufficient understanding of the

---

[92] Replacing Mental Health Act 1959, which in turn replaced Lunacy Act 1890.
[93] Mental Health Act 1983, ss.93, 94, 105.
[94] *ibid.*, s.94(2).
[95] *ibid.*, s.99.
[96] *ibid.*, ss.95, 96.
[97] *ibid.*, s.96(1)(d).
[98] *ibid.*, s.96(1)(e). See *Re D.(J.)* [1982] Ch. 237 for the principles.
[99] *Re Walker* [1905] 1 Ch. 160; *Re Marshall* [1920] 1 Ch. 284.
[1] *Re Walker* [1905] 1 Ch. 160.
[2] *In b. Walker* (1912) 28 T.L.R. 466; *Re Beaney* [1978] 1 W.L.R. 770 at 772.

effect of the gift.[3] A disposition for value is normally not void, but voidable, *i.e.* it remains valid until set aside. However, if the disposition is made during a lucid interval, or takes effect in favour of a person not aware of the mental disorder, it is valid.[4]

3. Enduring powers of attorney

The Enduring Powers of Attorney Act 1985, which was modified in some respects which are not relevant for present purposes by the Trustee Delegation Act 1999, has now provided a means of avoiding some of the expense and complication of applying for the appointment of a receiver. Under this Act, a power of attorney may now be granted which, unlike an ordinary power of attorney, will not be revoked by any supervening mental incapacity of the donor.[5] Such a power must be granted in the prescribed form, and be executed by both donor and donee[6]; and such a power may be granted even by a donor who is suffering from a mental disorder, provided he understands the nature and effect of the power.[7] It may confer an authority which either is general or is limited to specified matters.[8] If the attorney believes that the donor is, or is becoming, mentally incapable, he must promptly apply to the Court of Protection for registration of the power, giving notice of the application to the donor and specified relatives, and so enabling them to object on certain specified grounds.[9] Any supervening incapacity precludes the attorney from exercising any of his powers except under the authority of the court.[10] The Act thus enables a patient to arrange for his affairs to be managed by a person of his own choice, subject to safeguards.

Sect. 3. Charities

Formerly there were complex and far-reaching restrictions on gifts of land to a charity and dispositions of land by a charity. The former were abolished by the Charities Act 1960[11] and the latter have been drastically curtailed by what is now the Charities Act 1993[12] and the Trusts of Land and Appointment of Trustees Act 1996. The present position is as follows.

1. Powers of disposition of trustees of charities

Until 1997 land held on charitable trusts was settled land, and the trustees had all the powers given by the Settled Land Act 1925 to a tenant for life and trustees of the settlement.[13] Since 1996 trustees of charities instead hold land on a trust of land[14] and so have all the powers of an absolute owner[15] subject to the restrictions on their exercise now laid down in the Charities Act 1993. However, dispositions by certain charities (such as the Universities and Colleges of Oxford, Cambridge and Durham) are not governed by the Trusts of Land and

---

[3] *Re Beaney* [1978] 1 W.L.R. 770.
[4] *Imperial Loan Co. Ltd v. Stone* [1892] 1 Q.B. 599; *Hart v. O'Connor* [1985] A.C. 1000.
[5] Enduring Powers of Attorney Act 1985, s.1.
[6] *ibid.*, s.2.
[7] *Re K.* [1988] Ch. 310.
[8] Enduring Powers of Attorney Act 1985, s.3.
[9] *ibid.*, ss.4, 6(5), Sched. 1.
[10] *ibid.*, s.1.
[11] Charities Act 1960, s.38(2), (3), Sched. 7.
[12] Re-enacting the Charities Act 1992.
[13] S.L.A. 1925, s.29. See below, pp. 268 *et seq.*
[14] T.L.A.T.A. 1996, ss.1(1), 2(5).
[15] *ibid.*, s.6(1).

Appointment of Trustees Act 1996[16] and continue to be governed by the Universities and Colleges Estates Acts 1925 and 1964 which impose restrictions somewhat similar to those imposed on tenants for life of settlements under the Settled Land Act 1925.

2. Restrictions on dispositions

Prior to 1993, charities could not make dispositions of land which formed part of their permanent endowment or which was or had been occupied for the purposes of the charity without an order from the court or the Charity Commissioners, which was in practice only forthcoming subject to safeguards ensuring that the trustees acted in the best interests of the charity in question; investment land, on the other hand, was freely disposable.[17] Since 1992, these rules no longer apply; land of any type may be sold leased or otherwise disposed of without an order of the court or of the Charity Commissioners provided that the trustees have obtained and considered a written report on the proposed disposition from a qualified surveyor, advertised the proposed disposition for such period and in such manner as the surveyor has advised, and are satisfied that the terms are the best reasonably obtainable.[18] Comparable provisions apply to mortgages[19] but leases for seven years or less are subject to less stringent requirements.[20] Where the land in question is expressly held on trust for the purposes of the charity, it is also required that public notice be given and any representations received within one month duly considered,[21] unless the purpose of the transaction is to acquire replacement property or in the case of the grant of a lease not exceeding two years.[22] However, neither set of restrictions has ever applied to exempt charities, which include many universities and a number of other bodies such as the principal London museums.

[16] *ibid.*, s.1(3).
[17] Charities Act 1960, s.29.
[18] Charities Act 1993, s.36.
[19] *ibid.*, s.38.
[20] *ibid.*, s.36(5).
[21] *ibid.*, s.36(6).
[22] *ibid.*, s.36(7).

Chapter 6

FUTURE INTERESTS

PART 1—NATURE OF FUTURE INTERESTS

1. Alienability of land

In feudal times land was the basis of wealth and status; and many men had dynastic ambitions. A landowner with full power to dispose of the fee simple in his lands would often seek to keep the land in his family by tying it up so that his heirs could not alienate it. From early days, however, the policy of the law was to make land freely alienable, so that it could be used to the fullest advantage; and this conflicted with the desire of landowners to keep land in the family. The creation of an estate in fee tail was the most direct way of doing this; but by the fifteenth century the courts had evolved means whereby the fee tail could be barred and converted into a fee simple.[1] Again, if a fee simple was granted with a condition that the land was not to be alienated, the courts held the condition to be void.[2] Further, the feudal system required that there should always be some person who was holding the land and so was liable for the feudal services.[3] Thus the courts of common law held that a limitation which left a gap in the holding of the land after a tenant for life died (such as pending the birth or marriage of some person) was void.

2. Future Interests

Out of these conflicting elements arose the law of future interests. Today, that law is far from simple; but formerly it was far more complicated. There is now rarely any need to consider in any detail the rules which failed to survive 1925, but something must be said of them, if only to make intelligible some of the case law that is still relevant to the present law. Today, future interests are mainly governed by three rules: the rule against perpetuities, the rule against inalienability, and the rule against accumulations. The first two rules prevent property from being tied up for longer than the perpetuity period: this at present consists of a life or lives in being, with a further 21 years or, in the case of the rule against perpetuities, a fixed period of up to 80 years. The rule against perpetuities is directed against remoteness of vesting: a future interest is void if it will take longer than the perpetuity period before it

---

[1] Above, p. 46.
[2] Above, p. 41.
[3] Above, p. 36.

becomes a vested interest. The rule against inalienability prevents property from being made inalienable for longer than the perpetuity period. The rule against accumulations is similarly directed against the duration of restrictions, rather than remoteness of vesting. It prevents the compulsory accumulation of income for, at present, longer than one of the available accumulation periods: these are shorter than the perpetuity period. However, the Law Commission's current proposals envisage[4] that the periods both for the rule against perpetuities and, with one exception, for the rule against accumulations, but not that for the rule against inalienability, should be changed to a fixed period of 125 years. The three rules will be considered in turn.[5]

3. Tying up capital

Originally, the law did not prevent dispositions of the land itself being restrained, provided the relevant period was not exceeded. But the introduction of the system of overreaching,[6] first in the drafting of some settlements and then by statutes in the nineteenth century, meant that the land itself was always alienable, though if it was sold, the restraints attached to the purchase money instead. The rules governing future interests were thereafter no longer required to secure the free alienability of land; but they continued to prevent a settlor or testator from tying up either the land or the capital money representing it for an unreasonably long period.

PART 2—THE RULE AGAINST PERPETUITIES

Sect. 1. Vested and contingent interests

One of the fundamentals of the rule against perpetuities is the distinction between vested and contingent interests.

1. Vested interests

A future interest in land is an interest which confers a right to the enjoyment of the land at a future time, such as a right to the land after the death of a living person. A future interest may be either vested or contingent. "Vested", when used by itself (as here), means "vested in interest", *i.e.* that there is a present fixed right of future enjoyment. This contrasts with a right "vested in possession", which carries with it a right of present enjoyment. Thus if land is devised on trust for X for life with remainder to his first and other sons successively for life, each son obtains a vested interest at birth, and it is immaterial that the interests of the younger sons may not vest in possession until long after X's death.[7]

2. Conditions for vesting

A future interest is vested if two conditions are satisfied:

(i) that the person or persons entitled to the interest are ascertained; and

---

[4] Law Comm. No. 251 (1998). Earlier and now abandoned proposals were made in Law Comm. No. 133 (1993).
[5] Below.
[6] Above, p. 5.
[7] See *Evans v. Walker* (1876) 3 Ch.D. 211; and see *Pearson v. I.R.C.* [1981] A.C. 753.

(ii) that the interest is ready to take effect forthwith upon the determination of all the preceding estates and interests.[8]

(a) Conditions satisfied

Thus, if land is given "to A for life, remainder to B for life, remainder to C in fee simple", the interests of A, B and C are all vested. A has the only interest which is vested both in interest and in possession. The interests of B and C are not vested in possession. But if A's life interest were to terminate forthwith, an ascertained person, B, is ready to take the land, and so B's interest is vested. Even if A is aged 23 and B 97, so that it is most improbable that B's interest will ever vest in possession, B nevertheless has a vested interest; an interest may be vested even if there is no certainty of its taking effect in possession at any time, for otherwise no future life interest or fee tail would be vested. If land is given to X in fee tail, remainder to Y in fee simple, Y's remainder is vested, not because X's fee tail is bound to determine at some time (for this is not the case), but because the whole fee simple has been split up between X and Y, and Y has been invested with a portion of it.

(b) Person not ascertained

If the person to take is not ascertained his interest is contingent, even though it is bound to take effect at some time. For example, if property is given "to A and B for their joint lives, with remainder to the survivor", the death of one before the other is bound to occur at some time, yet since it is uncertain who will be the survivor, the remainder is contingent.[9] Similarly, a gift to the heir of a living person is contingent, for until that person dies his heir cannot be ascertained.

(c) Interest not ready

Although the gift is in favour of a specified person, it will not be vested if it is made to depend upon some event occurring, such as "to A upon attaining 25 or marrying", or "to B if he returns to take up permanent residence in England". In such cases, the interests of A and B are contingent until the event occurs, when they become vested.

3. Size of interest

(a) Under the general law

For most purposes[10] an interest will be vested even if the size of the beneficiary's interest has not been finally ascertained. For example, where land is devised in trust for "A for life, reminder to all his children who shall attain the age of 18 years", each child obtains a vested interest on attaining his majority; but these vested interests are liable to open to let in each child who subsequently attains full age.[11] Thus if X and Y are the only children who have attained their majority, they each have a vested interest in one-half of the property, subject to that interest being partially divested in favour of subsequent children. When Z becomes 18, the shares of X and Y each fall to one-third and Z has the other third; and so on for any other children. X and Y, having vested interests, can dispose of their shares either *inter vivos* or by

---

[8] Fearne C.R. 9, 216; *Re Legh's S.T.* [1938] Ch. 39 at 52. For the purposes of the rule against perpetuities, there is an additional condition: see below, p. 212.
[9] See *Re Legh's S.T.* [1938] Ch. 39.
[10] For an exception, see below.
[11] See *Re Lechmere and Lloyd* (1881) 18 Ch.D. 524.

will, although even in the hands of the transferee the shares will be liable to be diminished by other children attaining full age. But any child of A who dies before he is 18 never has any interest in the property.[12]

(b) For the purposes of the rule against perpetuities

A long line of cases has established that the size of a beneficiary's interest must be ascertained before the interest is vested for the purposes of the rule.[13] Thus, but for a statutory reform which took effect in 1926 and was amended in 1964, a gift to trustees for such of the children of X as attained the age of 25 (X being alive at the date of the gift and having no child aged 25 or more) would be totally void because, as will be seen, a child might attain the age of 25 outside the period allowed by the rule.[14] It mattered not that one or more children attained the age within the period, because until it was known how many children would ultimately reach the given age, the size of the share to be taken by each beneficiary was uncertain. This aspect of vesting is considered more fully later.[15]

4. Vesting subject to divesting

A remainder may be vested and yet subject to some provision which may operate to defeat the remainder completely. For example, if land is held on trust for A for life, remainder on trust for A's issue as A shall appoint, and in default of appointment on trust for all A's children equally, the remainder to the children is vested, subject to being divested to the extent of any appointment made by A.[16] In cases of doubt, the law favours early vesting, and every interest is construed as being vested forthwith if that is possible; if not, it is treated as becoming vested as soon as possible. A gift by will to X "if" or "when" he is 25 is prima facie contingent, but the addition of a gift over to Y if X dies before he is 25 indicates that X is intended to have all that is not given to Y, and so X's interest will prima facie be construed as being vested subject to being divested.[17]

5. Assignability

In the sense that all vested interests give a present right to future enjoyment, the name "future interests" is hardly appropriate. If land is given "to X for life, reminder to Y in fee simple", Y has a present interest in fee simple which is future only as to the possession of the land. Y can sell, give away, devise or otherwise dispose of his fee simple at any time he wishes. Nevertheless, for convenience, vested interests which are not coupled with a right of present enjoyment are usually dealt with under the head of future interests. Contingent interests are more clearly entitled to be described as future interests, for until the contingency occurs, the person entitled has no estate but merely a possibility of acquiring one. They can, however, be assigned, devised or otherwise disposed of.[18]

---

[12] *Rhodes v. Whitehead* (1865) 2 Dr. & Sm. 532.
[13] See, *e.g. Pearks v. Moseley* (1880) 5 App. Cas. 714.
[14] *Boreham v. Bignall* (1850) 8 Hare 131.
[15] Below, pp. 227 *et seq.*
[16] *Re Master's Settlement* [1911] 1 Ch. 321; and see *Re Brooks' S.T.* [1939] Ch. 993.
[17] The rule in *Phipps v. Ackers* (1842) 9 Cl. & F. 583; *Brotherton v. I.R.C.* [1978] 1 W.L.R. 610.
[18] L.P.A. 1925, s.4(2).

Sect. 2. Classification of future interests

The two main categories of interests which are relevant for the purposes of the rule against perpetuities are reversions, and remainders. These will be considered in turn.

1. Reversions

(a) Nature of reversions

A "particular estate" in land may be defined as some estate or interest less than a fee simple, *i.e.* either a fee tail, a life interest or a term of years: it is a mere part (*particula*) of the fee simple. If the owner of an estate in land creates one or more particular estates out of his own estate, the residue of his original estate which he retains is known as a reversion. Thus if a tenant in fee simple grants a life interest or a lease for a term of years, the fee simple which he retains is a reversion. If, on the other hand, the tenant creates a particular estate and by the same instrument disposes of some or all of the residue of his estate to one or more other persons, the interests of those other persons are not reversions but remainders. In the case of a reversion, the land reverts to the grantor when the particular estate determines; in the case of a remainder, it remains away from him for the benefit of some third party. It follows that while there may be many remainders created out of one estate, there can be but one reversion. Thus if X, a tenant in fee simple, grants land "to A for life, remainder to B for life, remainder to C for life", he retains the reversion in fee simple, and yet has created two remainders, namely those of B and C. Further, a reversion arises by operation of law, a remainder by act of parties.

(b) All reversions are vested

From its very nature, it follows that a reversion is always a vested interest[19]; the grantor, or, if he is dead, his representatives, stand ready to receive the land as soon as the particular estate determines. A freehold reversioner on a term of years has an estate which is vested both in interest and in possession, for the grant of a lease does not deprive the grantor of seisin, and he therefore has what is properly called a freehold in possession subject to the term. From this point of view, a reversion on a lease is not a reversion or, indeed, a future interest at all; but from a more practical point of view such interests are generally treated as reversions today. A possibility of reverter[20] cannot be a reversion as it is a mere possibility of having an estate and not an estate.

(c) Reversions after 1925

Before 1926 a reversion could be legal or equitable, according to whether the estate out of which it was created was legal or equitable. After 1925, a reversion upon a fee tail or life interest is necessarily equitable because both the fee tail or life interest and the reversion thereon are not within the list of legal estates and interests in section 1 of the Law of Property Act 1925; the land will therefore be held on trust[21] to give effect, successively, to the fee tail or life interest and to the reversion (a reversion upon a term of years, however, can still exist as a legal estate, because if the owner of a legal fee simple absolute in possession grants a lease, his estate remains a legal estate, for "possession" includes the right to receive the rents

---

[19] Challis R.P. 67.
[20] Above, p. 41.
[21] Since 1996 on a trust of land. See below, pp. 283 *et seq.*

and profits, if any; and if the owner of a legal term of years absolute grants a sublease, there is nothing in this to render his estate any the less legal; any number of legal estate can exist concurrently in the same land[22]).

2. Remainders

In addition to reversions, before 1926 three principal types of future interest could exist, legal remainders, legal executory interests, and future trusts. Because since 1925 any future interest must necessarily take effect behind a trust, again because it is not within the list of legal estates and interests in section 1 of the Law of Property Act 1925, after 1925, therefore, all future interests must necessarily be equitable. Legal remainders and legal executory interests existing before 1926 were automatically converted into equitable interests. Thus the comparatively simple law of future trusts, free from feudal rules and statutory modifications, now applies to all future interests. In all cases, the land will either be settled land and subject to the Settled Land Act 1925, or else be subject to a trust for sale or, since 1996, a trust of land. This means that there is full freedom to dispose of the land itself, notwithstanding the rights of the beneficiaries, for their rights will be transferred from the land to the purchase money which represents it.[23]

Sect. 3. History of the rule

1. Development

The rule against remoteness that finally emerged to govern future trusts kept future interests in land within reasonable and intelligible limits by allowing settlors to leave the ultimate ownership uncertain for a maximum period of a lifetime plus a further 21 years. This corresponded to the practice under what was known as a strict settlement: if land was settled on H for life with remainder to his eldest son in tail, the longest period that could elapse before the entail could be barred was H's lifetime plus his son's minority, which, until the reduction of the age of majority with effect from 1970, was 21 years.[24]

Many years passed before the rule was finally settled. As early as 1662 the limitation of a term of years to several living persons in succession had been held good,[25] and in 1679 an executory devise which might not have vested until the expiration of a lifetime plus 21 years was held valid.[26] But the rule became firmly established only by stages. The *Duke of Norfolk's Case*[27] in 1685 settled beyond doubt that a future trust bound to take effect, if at all, during a life in being was valid. In 1797 it was settled that a child *en ventre sa mère* (conceived but not born) might be treated as a life in being,[28] thus extending the period by a possible further nine months or so; and by then it had become accepted that the effect of a statute of 1698[29] was that the period of 21 years after the life in being also might be extended to cover a further period of gestation, if it existed. In 1805 it was finally settled that

---

[22] Above, p. 84.
[23] Above, pp. 5, 84 *et seq.*
[24] Above, p. 201.
[25] *Goring v. Bickerstaffe*, Pollex. 31.
[26] *Taylor d. Smith v. Biddall*, 2 Mod. 287.
[27] 3 Ch.Ca. 1.
[28] *Long v. Blackall*, 7 T.R. 100.
[29] Statute of Posthumous Children 1698.

the lives in being might be chosen at random and be unconnected with the property,[30] and by 1833 the rule was completed by the decision of the House of Lords in *Cadell v. Palmer*[31] that the period of 21 years was an absolute period without reference to any minority, but that the periods of gestation could be added only if in fact gestation existed.

2. Statutory reform

The rule was invented and developed by the judges without the intervention of Parliament. In the main it achieved a sound solution to the problem of perpetuity, but its undue rigidity produced anomalies requiring reform. Minor amendments were made by the Law of Property Act 1925, followed by revolutionary alterations under the Perpetuities and Accumulations Act 1964 ("the Act of 1964").[32] The Law Commission has now proposed further revolutionary alterations.[33] As is customary, these statutes did not (and the Law Commission's current proposals will not) sweep away the old law, but built (and will build) upon it. Thus an understanding of the old law is still essential in order to appreciate the changes. Moreover, the former law still governs future interests taking effect under past dispositions, for the Act of 1964, which came into force on July 16, 1964, applies in general only to instruments taking effect after July 15, 1964.[34] Many instruments prior to the Act of 1964 created special powers of appointment which are still exercisable, and the exercise of such powers is governed by the old law. If the current proposals of the Law Commission are enacted, the present law will also continue to govern future interests taking effect under dispositions between July 16, 1964 and whenever the new legislation comes into force and under wills made before the latter date.[35]

Sect. 4. Operation of the rule

The rule may be stated as follows:

(i) A limitation of any interest in any property, real or personal, is void at common law if by any possibility it might become vested after the perpetuity period has expired.

(ii) The perpetuity period originally consisted of a life or lives in being at the time of the gift, together with a further period of 21 years[36]; and where gestation actually exists, the period or periods of gestation may be added.

(iii) However, under the Act of 1964, a fixed period of up to 80 years may be selected instead and, whether or not it is, it is possible to "wait and see" whether or not a limitation which is void at common law does vest within the perpetuity period.

(iv) Under the current proposals of the Law Commission, if enacted, a fixed period of 125 years will become the only perpetuity period and it will continue to be possible

---

[30] *Thellusson v. Woodford* (1805) 11 Ves. 112.

[31] 1 Cl. & F. 372.

[32] Based on the Fourth Report of the Law Reform Committee (Cmnd. 18, 1956).

[33] Law Comm. No. 251 (1998). Earlier and now abandoned proposals were made in Law Comm. No. 133 (1993).

[34] s.15(5). See *Re Holt's Settlement* [1969] 1 Ch. 100 (order of court).

[35] This has been criticised: see Sparkes (1998) 12 T.L.I. 148.

[36] This is unaffected by the reduction of the age of majority to 18 under the Family Law Reform Act 1969.

to "wait and see" whether or not a limitation which is void at common law does vest within that period.

The principal points must now be considered in some detail.[37]

1. Meaning of "vest"

The meaning of "vest" has already been considered.[38] The rule does not require that an interest should be incapable of vesting in possession after the period has run, but only that it should be incapable of becoming vested in interest outside the period.[39] Thus if land is devised on trust for X for life with remainder to his first and other sons successively for life, the limitations are valid even if X was a bachelor at the time of the gift. Each of X's sons obtains a vested interest at birth, and these interests are not invalidated by the fact that some of the sons may not be entitled to possession of the property until after the period has run.[40] It is thus immaterial that if X was a bachelor at the time of the gift and his eldest son outlives him by 50 years, the interest of the second son will not vest in possession until 29 years after the perpetuity period has expired.

2. No "wait and see" at common law

In general,[41] the unreformed rule deals with possibilities, not probabilities or actual events. Every limitation must be considered at the time when the instrument creating it takes effect. Thus a deed must be considered at the time when it is executed, while a will must be considered at the moment of the testator's death.[42] If at the relevant moment there is the slightest possibility that the perpetuity period may be exceeded, the limitation is void, even if it is most improbable that this in fact will happen and even if, as events turn out, it does not.[43] For example, if property is given "to A (a bachelor) for life, remainder to his widow for life, remainder to the eldest of his brothers living at the widow's death", the remainder to the brother is bad if A's parents are alive. It is just possible that A will marry someone who was not alive at the time of the gift, and if A's wife survived him for more than 21 years, the property might become vested outside the period in a brother born after the date of the gift. This possibility renders the gift to the brother void, even if A is very old and unlikely to marry or in fact marries someone alive at the time of the gift, and even if A's parents are so old that they are most unlikely to have any more children. For the purposes of the unreformed rule, no person is ever deemed too old to have children,[44] though for other purposes the courts take a more realistic view of preternatural fertility[45]; but statute prevents the lawful marriage (and so lawful issue) of a person under the age of 16 years.[46] Again, a gift of property to certain persons "if the minerals under the said farm should be worked" offends the perpetuity

---

[37] For a full consideration of the rule, see Maudsley, *Modern Law of Perpetuities* (1979) and Morris & Leach, *The Rule against Perpetuities* (2nd ed., 1962, with Supp. 1964). The classic text for the old law is *Gray on Perpetuities* (4th ed., 1942).

[38] Above, p. 210.

[39] *Evans v. Walker* (1876) 3 Ch.D. 211.

[40] *Re Hargreaves* (1890) 43 Ch.D. 401.

[41] See below, pp. 218, 234, for qualifications of this rule.

[42] *Vanderplank v. King* (1843) 3 Hare 1 at 17.

[43] These words were approved in *Re Watson's S.T.* [1959] 1 W.L.R. 732 at 739.

[44] See *Ward v. Van der Loeff* [1924] A.C. 653 (persons aged 66).

[45] See, *e.g. Re White* [1901] 1 Ch. 570.

[46] *Re Gaite's W.T.* [1949] 1 All E.R. 459 (Age of Marriage Act 1929); but see (1949) 13 Conv. (N.S.) 289 (J.H.C. Morris).

rule and is void because of the possibility that the minerals will be worked after the perpetuity period has expired.[47]

It is immaterial that the gift may never vest at all; the question is whether if it does vest, it is capable of vesting outside the period. A gift to the first son of X, a bachelor, may never vest at all, for X may never have a son. But this possibility does not render the gift void for perpetuity; the gift is incapable of vesting outside the perpetuity period, for if X does have a son, the son must be born or conceived during X's lifetime, and X is the life in being. In short, the gift is bound to vest, if it vests at all, within the perpetuity period. Again, a gift by will "to the first of my daughters to marry after my death" is valid, even though no daughter may marry; for if any daughter does marry, she must do so in her own lifetime, and since the testator is dead when the gift takes effect, no further daughters can be born and all those who are alive or *en ventre sa mère* rank as lives in being. Had the gift been made by deed, it would have been void, for the donor might have had further daughters after the date of the gift (who would not have been lives in being) and one of these might have been the first to qualify for the gift by marrying more than 21 years after the death of the donor and all his other daughters.

A gift which would otherwise be too remote may be validated by the insertion of an express clause confining its vesting to the proper period. Thus a gift by a testator to such of his issue as should be living when some gravel pits should become exhausted is void as it stands, even if it is highly probable that the pits will be worked out in five or six years and even if they have been by the time that the court rules on the matter.[48] The gift would have been valid, however, if worded "to such of my issue living 21 years after my death or when the gravel pits are exhausted, whichever first happens"; and a gift to bodies existing "when the residue of my estate is realised" has been construed as being confined to the "executor's year",[49] *i.e.* one year from death.[50] But a clause seeking to confine the vesting within the period must do so clearly; a void gift is not validated merely by the addition of words providing that the vesting shall be postponed only "so far as the rules of law and equity will permit".[51]

3. Future parenthood

The Act of 1964 has replaced the rigid rule that no person is too old to have children with a statutory presumption:

> (i) that a male can have a child at the age of 14 or over, but not under that age, and
>
> (ii) that a female can have a child at the age of 12 or over, but not under that age or over the age of 55.[52]

This presumption may be rebutted by showing that in a particular case a living person will or will not be able to have a child at the time in question.[53] "Having a child" extends to

---

[47] *Thomas v. Thomas* (1902) 87 L.T. 58.
[48] *Re Wood* [1894] 3 Ch. 381.
[49] See above, p. 164.
[50] *Re Petrie* [1962] Ch. 355; and see *Re Atkins' W.T.* [1974] 1 W.L.R. 761.
[51] *Portman v. Viscount Portman* [1922] 2 A.C. 473; contrast *Re Vaux* [1939] Ch. 465; and see *I.R.C. v. Williams* [1969] 1 W.L.R. 1197 at 1202.
[52] s.2(1).
[53] *ibid.*, See *L. v. K.* [1985] Fam. 144.

having a child "by adoption, legitimation or other means".[54] If events falsify the presumptions, the High Court has a general discretion to make such order as it thinks fit for placing the persons interested in the property in the position in which they would have been if the presumptions had not been applied.[55]

4. "Wait and see" under the Act of 1964

(a) The new rule

The common law rule had one great advantage: one can see at the outset whether the gift is good or bad. But it frequently frustrated the intentions of settlors and testators by striking down limitations which almost certainly would have vested within the period. To meet these cases the Act of 1964 introduced the rule of "wait and see" for limitations in instruments taking effect after July 15, 1964,[56] which would have been void at common law. For such a gift the Act provides that it is not to be treated as if it were subject to the rule against perpetuities until "it becomes established that the vesting must occur, if at all, after the end of the perpetuity period".[57] Until then, the gift is valid. It is now permissible to look at actual rather than possible events, so that the disposition does not become void until it is clear that it is going to vest, if it vests at all, outside the period.

(b) Examples

The previous example[58] of a gift "to the first of my daughters to marry" was bad at common law if the gift was made by deed and the donor had at the time no daughter who was married. Even if he had unmarried daughters at that time the gift would be bad, for he might have had further daughters, one of whom might have been the first daughter to marry, and that marriage might have occurred more than 21 years after the death of the donor and of all his daughters living at the date of the deed. But under the Act it is possible wait and see whether one of his daughters, whether living at the date of the deed or still unborn, marries within the period, that is the period which ends 21 years after the death of the donor and any daughters living at the date of the deed. If no daughter marries within that period the gift will fail, even though an after-born daughter marries thereafter.

Similarly, a gift by a testator to such of his issue as should be living when some gravel pits should become exhausted, which is void at common law, will be valid if the pits in fact become exhausted within 21 years of the death of the survivor of those of his issue who are living at his death.

(c) Consequences

The practical consequences of the new are not so great as one might suppose from so radical an amendment of the rule. First, the great majority of limitations in fact comply with the old rule, and it was not expected that the Act would bring about a relaxation of the standards of drafting (nor has it done so). Secondly, the new rule does not extend the period: it does not enable a donor to do anything which he cannot achieve within the framework of the common law rule by the use of an express clause confining the vesting to the proper period, such as

---

[54] s.2(4).
[55] s.2(2).
[56] See above, p. 183.
[57] s.3(1).
[58] Above, p. 185.

a period expiring 21 years after the death of all the descendants of King George VI living at the date when the instrument comes into effect.

The Law Commission's current proposals envisage the continuation of "wait and see".

5. The perpetuity period

The perpetuity period must be considered as it stands at common law, as it has been varied by the Law of Property Act 1925, as it stands under the Act of 1964, and as it will stand if the Law Commission's current proposals are enacted.

(a) At common law

(i) Lives in being: For a person to be a life in being for the purposes of the rule, it is unnecessary that he should receive any benefit from the gift or that he should be in any way connected with the beneficiaries.[59] Nor is there any restriction upon the number of lives selected, provided it is reasonably possible to ascertain who they are; "for let the lives be never so many, there must be a survivor, and so it is but the length of that life".[60] "If a term be limited to one for life, with twenty several remainders for lives to other persons successively, who are all alive and in being, so that all the candles are lighted together, this is good enough".[61] For example, gifts by a testator to such of his descendants as are living 21 years after the death of the last survivor of the members of a given school at the testator's death,[62] or 20 years after the death of the last survivor of all the lineal descendants of Queen Victoria living at the testator's death,[63] have been held valid. In the latter case, the testator died in 1926 when there were some 120 lives in being and it was reasonably possible to follow the duration of their lives; a similar limitation today might well be void for uncertainty,[64] though the living descendants of King George VI (the father of the present Queen) may still safely be selected[65] (provisions of this type are known as "royal lives clauses"). One potential difficulty about such clauses today is the fact that "descendants" now includes illegitimate descendants, who are not necessarily identifiable. But there seems no reason why future "royal lives clauses" should not be expressly restricted to legitimate descendants. The Law Commission's proposals will, if enacted, give trustees of existing trusts with "royal lives clauses" the option of opting for a 125-year period instead if they execute a deed stating that it is not reasonably practicable to ascertain whether the perpetuity period has ended (this is the one of only two proposals which will have retrospective effect).

From one point of view, everyone alive at the time of the gift is a life in being in the literal sense; but a gift depending on the dropping of all those lives would be void for uncertainty. Thus the only lives in being which have to be considered in relation to the perpetuity rule are those which are implicated in the gift, being mentioned in it either expressly or by implication in a way that is relevant to its vesting, governing the time when the gift is to vest. In the above examples, lives in being have been expressly mentioned; but this is not always the case. If a testator gives property to such of his grandchildren as attain the age of 21, his children can be taken as lives in being. At the time when the rule against remoteness was developed, all of them were bound to have been born within nine months of the testator's death (this is no

---

[59] *Cadell v. Palmer* (1833) 1 Cl. & F. 372.
[60] *Scatterwood v. Edge* (1697) 1 Salk. 229.
[61] *Howard v. Duke of Norfolk* (1681) 2 Swans. 454 at 458, *per* Lord Nottingham L.C.
[62] *Pownall v. Graham* (1863) 33 Beav. 242 at 245, 247.
[63] *Re Villar* [1929] 1 Ch. 243.
[64] Consider *Re Moore* [1901] 1 Ch. 936.
[65] See *Re Leverhulme* [1943] 2 All E.R. 274.

longer the case due to the recent developments in genetics whereby peoples' sperm and eggs can be frozen, thus enabling their children to be born far in the future), and a gift to grandchildren presupposes the existence of children. The gift is therefore good, for no grandchild can take longer than 21 years from his or her parent's death to reach the age of 21. But a gift to the grandchildren of a living person is bad, unless the class is restricted in some way, such as to those living at the death of a life in being[66]; the living person might have another child after the date of the gift and then, long after all those alive at the date of the gift had died, that child might have a child.

Consequently, it can be said that everyone who is alive at the time of the gift and is implicated in its vesting, should be treated as a life in being. Others, the duration of whose lives have no bearing on the vesting of the gift, should be ignored. In the case of limitations made *inter vivos*, the date of the instrument, and, in the case of wills, the date of the testator's death, is the time when the period starts running and the facts must be ascertained; to be a life in being, a person must be alive at that moment.

The lives must be human lives, and not the lives of animals.[67]

(ii) No lives: If the limitation is made without reference to lives in being, the period is 21 years. A gift by a testator to all his issue living 50 years after his death, or to all the children of X (who is alive) living 28 years after the testator's death, is void.[68] It is true that in the first case the testator's children and in the second X could be taken as lives in being, but in neither case has the period selected any relation to their lives; it is a period in gross, and neither the immediate death nor the prolonged life of the testator's children or of X will alter the date of vesting. Consequently the gifts must be treated as if there were no lives in being, with the result that the period is 21 years.

(iii) Child *en ventre sa mère*: For the purposes of the perpetuity rule, a child *en ventre sa mère* is treated as if it had been born. Two cases can arise:

(a) A child may be *en ventre sa mère* at the beginning of the period, *i.e.* at the time of the gift. In this case, the child is treated as a life in being.[69] Thus if a testator gives property for life to the child with which his wife is pregnant, with a remainder contingent upon certain circumstances existing at that child's death, the remainder is good; for the contingency must be resolved at the child's death and the child is treated as the life in being.[70]

(b) A child may be *en ventre sa mère* during the period. In this case, the period is extended as far as is necessary to include the period of gestation. Thus if property is given to the first of A's sons to be 21 years old, the gift is valid even if A's only son was unborn at A's death; the perpetuity period in such a case is A's lifetime plus the period of gestation and 21 years.

It will be seen from this that two periods of gestation may arise in the same case; both are allowed. If property is given to Jane's eldest child for life, with remainder to the first son of that child to be 21, and Jane is pregnant with her first child at the time of the gift, the

---

[66] *Wetherell v. Wetherell* (1863) 1 De G.J. & S. 134 at 139, 140.
[67] See *Re Kelly* [1932] I.R. 255 at 260, 261.
[68] *Speakman v. Speakman* (1850) 8 Hare 180; *Palmer v. Holford* (1828) 4 Russ. 403.
[69] *Re Wilmer's Trusts* [1903] 2 Ch. 411 at 421.
[70] *Long v. Blackall* (1797) 7 T.R. 100.

remainder does not infringe the perpetuity rule even though Jane's child may be a son who dies leaving his wife pregnant of an only son. Jane's child is treated as a life in being, and the perpetuity period will be extended to cover the period of gestation of the child's son.[71]

These rules do not allow the addition of any period or periods of nine months or so in all cases; they apply only where gestation actually exists.[72]

(b) Under the Law of Property Act 1925

A frequent cause of gifts failing was that they were made contingent upon the beneficiary attaining an age greater than 21. Thus property might be given "to the first of A's children to attain the age of 25". In certain circumstances, the gift would be good: if A was dead at the time of the gift, he could have no further children, and since every possible claimant was a life in being, the gift would be valid.[73] Further, even if A was alive, if one of his children had attained the age of 25 at the date of the gift, the limitation was valid as being an immediate gift to an ascertained person.[74] But if A was alive and no child had attained the age of 25, the gift was bad. This was so even if a child had attained the age of 24, for there was no certainty that he would not die before his twenty-fifth birthday, and a child born after the date of the gift might be the first child to reach the age of 25.[75]

To deal with cases such as this, section 163 of the Law of Property Act 1925 laid down that in certain circumstances the age of 21 might be substituted for the offending age. This might be done only if:

(i) the limitation was contained in an instrument executed after 1925, or in the will of a testator dying after 1925, but in either case before July 16, 1964[76]; and

(ii) the limitation would otherwise be void; and

(iii) the excess is in the age of the beneficiary or class of beneficiaries.

The first point needs no illustration. The second may be illustrated by considering the limitation mentioned above, namely, "to the first of A's children to attain the age of 25". Before 1926, if A was alive and no child had reached the age of 25, the gift failed; if made after 1925, section 163 substituted "21" for "25" and the gift was good, the first child to attain the age of 21 taking the property at that age. But if A had been dead, the gift would have been valid without the aid of section 163 and so "25" remained undisturbed. In the result, if A's eldest child was aged 19 at the time of the gift, whether he had to wait two years or six before becoming entitled depended upon whether A was alive or dead. The third point may be illustrated by cases where vesting was postponed for a fixed period of years. A gift to the testator's issue living 50 years after his death was void before 1926[77] and was not validated by section 163, for the "50" is not the age of a beneficiary.

---

[71] See *Thellusson v. Woodford* (1805) 11 Ves. 112 at 143, 149, 150.
[72] *Cadell v. Palmer* (1833) 1 Cl. & F. 372 at 421, 422.
[73] *Southern v. Wollaston* (1852) 16 Beav. 276.
[74] *Picken v. Matthews* (1878) 10 Ch.D. 264.
[75] See, *e.g. Re Finch* (1881) 17 Ch.D. 211.
[76] Except in the case of an instrument made in the exercise of a special power of appointment created before July 16, 1964: Act of 1964, s.15(5).
[77] See above, p. 220.

(c) The Act of 1964

(i) Lives in being: Whether the introduction of the "wait and see" principle required any alteration in the rules for ascertaining the lives in being is controversial. Probably no alteration was needed, since the lives in being at common law are not confined to those which necessarily succeed in restricting the vesting of the gift to the perpetuity period, but include any lives sufficiently implicated in the vesting, whether or not they succeed in saving the gift.[78] Unfortunately, some took the view that at common law the only lives that rank as lives in being are those which save the gift by confining its vesting to the perpetuity period; only "salvation lives" count as lives in being. In consequence, where a gift is void at common law there are necessarily no salvation lives, and so there would be no lives in being which could save the gift on waiting and seeing.[79]

The draftsman of the Act of 1964 appears to have acted on this latter view. The Act provides four categories of lives, all of whom must be both in being and ascertainable at the date of the gift. Further, lives in the second and third categories which are defined by description are to be disregarded if they are so numerous as to render it impracticable to ascertain the death of the survivor.[80] If there are no lives in the four categories which satisfy the preceding conditions, the "wait and see" period is 21 years from the date of the gift.[81]

The four categories are as follows.[82]

    (a) The donor: "the person by whom the disposition was made".

    (b) A donee: "a person to whom or in whose favour the disposition was made, that is to say—

       (i) in the case of a disposition to a class of persons, any member or potential member of the class;

      (ii) in the case of an individual disposition to a person taking only on certain conditions being satisfied, any person as to whom some of the conditions are satisfied and the remainder may in time be satisfied;

      [(iii)and (iv) concern special powers of appointment, discussed below[83]];

      (v) in the case of any power, option or other right, the person on whom the right is conferred."

    (c) A donee's parent or grandparent.

    (d) The owner of a prior interest.

In many cases these complicated provisions produce the same lives in being as the common law rule, but there are divergences. Often more lives are available under the Act. Thus a gift "to A's first grandson to attain 21" where A is alive and without such a grandson at the date

---

[78] (1964) 80 L.Q.R. 486 at 495–501 (J. H. C. Morris and H. W. R. Wade); (1981) 97 L.Q.R. 593 (R. L. Deech); (1986) 102 L.Q.R. 250 (J. Dukeminier). This was the assumption of the Law Reform Committee: above, p. 215.
[79] (1965) 81 L.Q.R. 106 (D. E. Allan); (1970) 86 L.Q.R. 357 (R. H. Maudsley); Maudsley, *Modern Law of Perpetuities*, pp. 87 *et seq.*
[80] s.3(4)(a).
[81] s.3(4)(b).
[82] s.3(5).
[83] Below, pp. 231 *et seq.*

of the gift is void at common law. Under the "wait and see" rule, the lives in being are the donor (under (a) above), A and any existing children of A and their existing spouses (under (c) above), and any existing grandchildren (under (b)(ii) above), so that it is necessary to wait and see whether a grandchild reaches 21 within 21 years of the death of the survivor of all those lives.

(ii) Statutory age reduction: For instruments taking effect after July 15, 1964,[84] the Act of 1964 has replaced the Law of Property Act 1925, s.163,[85] by a more flexible provision. It operates where a disposition satisfies the following conditions.

(a) It is limited by reference to the attainment by any person or persons of a specified age exceeding 21 years.[86] The corresponding provision of section 163 applied only to the excessive age of a beneficiary; the new provision applies to the excessive ages of others as well, as in a gift to an unborn person "living when A's eldest son attains 25".

(b) It is apparent when the disposition is made, or becomes apparent later—

(i) that it would otherwise be void for remoteness, but
(ii) that it would not be so void if the specified age had been 21 years.

(c) It is not saved by the "wait and see" rule.

If these conditions are satisfied, the disposition is treated as if it had been limited by reference to the greatest age which would have prevented it from being void.[87] Here again the new provision diverges from section 163, for under that section the reduction was to a uniform 21 years in every case.

Thus if there is a gift by will to A's children at 25, and A is alive at the date of the testator's death, one first "waits and sees" whether the gift is valid without alteration. This will be so if A's children were all alive at the testator's death, or were all over four at A's death. If, however, A's youngest child was not alive at the testator's death but was a year old at A's death, it is thought that the vesting age will immediately be reduced to 22 years. However, it may be that the age will only be reduced by enough to enable the oldest child who has not yet attained the age of 25 to take, with further reductions if they prove to be necessary.[88] Either way, there are potential difficulties if a child has attained the age to which the age is reduced during "wait and see" but has then died without attaining the age originally specified before it is reduced: does the reduction have retrospective effect to enable him to take posthumously?

Unlike section 163, the provision also caters for gifts which specify two or more ages. If there is a gift by will to A's sons who attain 30 and his daughters who attain 25, and on A's death after the testator his youngest son is eight and his youngest daughter is three, the vesting ages will be reduced to 29 for sons and 24 for daughters.[89]

---

[84] Except instruments made in the exercise of a special power of appointment created before July 16, 1964; s.15(5).
[85] Above, p. 221.
[86] Act of 1964, s.4(1).
[87] *ibid.*, s.4(1), (7), added by Children Act 1975, Sched. 3, para. 43.
[88] See [1969] C.L.J. 286 (M. J. Prichard). For class gifts, see below, pp. 227 *et seq.*
[89] See s.4(2). This assumes that A was the last surviving statutory life in being.

(iii) Surviving spouses: A gift to such of the children of A as are living at the death of the survivor of A and his widow frequently failed at common law because of the possibility that A might marry a person not born at the date of the gift but who might survive A by more than 21 years. The Act of 1964 eliminated this notorious trap of the "unborn widow". If a gift which refers to the death of the survivor of a person in being and his or her spouse is not saved by the "wait and see" rule, it is to be treated "as if it had instead been limited by reference to the time immediately before the end of" the perpetuity period.[90] Thus, in the example above, if A is survived by his widow, the gift will vest 21 years after the death of A if the widow is then still living, so that the children then living will take an interest vested in interest (the widow's life interest will nevertheless continue until her eventual death) even if one or more of those children subsequently dies before the widow.

(iv) Alternative fixed period: The Act of 1964 contained one completely new concept. As an alternative to the perpetuity period based on lives in being, it is permissible to specify a fixed period of years not exceeding 80 as the perpetuity period[91] and this is what is now usually done. The period must be expressly specified. It cannot be left to be implied, as in a gift by will to such of the testator's descendants are living 80 years after his death; but it suffices if two dates are specified from which the period between can be calculated.[92] The proper course is to use some expression such as "which I specify as the perpetuity period for this gift". It will be noted that this period can be used with much the same effect as "royal lives clauses" at common law, although the latter will generally provide a period longer than 80 years. However, nothing in the Act affects the validity of "royal lives clauses" or similar perpetuity clauses where the gift must vest, if at all, within the specified period.

(d) The Law Commission's proposals

The Law Commission[93] has proposed the introduction of a universal fixed period of 125 years. If a gift does not vest in interest by the end of that period, it will become void and the provisions of the settlement dependant on its not vesting will then take effect (of course, it may become clear long before the end of the 125 years that a gift is never going to vest, as where a person whose children are the beneficiaries of the gift dies childless; in that case, the provisions of the settlement dependant on its not vesting will take effect at that point). Age reduction to save a gift by treating it as if it had been limited by reference to the greatest age which would have prevented it from being void will continue; in practice this will have to be done, if at all, after 104 years have passed; the problems to which this type of age reduction potentially gives rise have not been resolved.

The principal reason and justification for this proposal and the consequential abandonment of lives in being is the fact that it can no longer be guaranteed that children will be born no later than nine months after the death of their parents. The recent developments in genetics whereby peoples' sperm and eggs can be frozen enables their children to be born far in the future; in such circumstances, the link between lives in being and the next generation on which the rule against remoteness has so far been based is broken. This difficulty does not arise with fixed periods of years; a child or grandchild will either be born by the end of it or will not have been; any born thereafter will simply not be able to take in the case of an

---

[90] Act of 1964, s.5.
[91] *ibid.*, s.1.
[92] *Re Green's W.T.* [1985] 3 All E.R. 455.
[93] Law Comm. No. 251 (1998).

individual gift (and in the case of a class gift will be excluded from the class in the manner discussed below).

6. Separate application

Where a deed or will contains two or more limitations, the rule is applied to each limitation separately. Thus, if there is a gift "to A for life, remainder to his eldest son for life, remainder to B's eldest grandson in fee simple", the perpetuity rule must be applied to each of the three limitations separately. If all are valid, no difficulty arises; but if one or more are bad, the following rules must be applied.

(a) Prior limitation

No limitation is void merely because it is followed by a void limitation.[94] A gift "to A for life" standing by itself is clearly good, and it is not invalidated merely because a limitation which infringes the rule is added, such as "to A for life, remainder to be first of his descendants to marry a Latvian". In such a case, A takes a life interest, and after his death the property reverts to the grantor or passes under his will or intestacy, unless the remainder is saved by the Act of 1964.

(b) Subsequent limitation

A limitation which is subsequent to and dependent upon a void limitation is itself void.[95] A limitation is not void merely because it follows a void limitation; it is invalidated by the rule only if in addition to following the void limitation it is also dependent upon it.[96] Thus if a testator devises property in fee simple "to the first of X's sons to become a clergyman, but if X has no such son, to Y in fee simple", and when the testator dies X is alive, the first part of the gift is void since the requisite event might occur more than 21 years after the death of lives in being. The gift to Y is subsequent to and dependent upon this void limitation; not until X and all his sons have died without any son having become a clergyman could it be said that Y is entitled. Thus even though the gift to Y is in favour of a living person, at common law it failed as being dependent upon a void limitation.[97]

On the other hand, if property is given "to A for life, remainder for life to any wife he may marry, remainder for life to any husband whom such wife may marry, remainder to such of A's children as attain the age of 21", the gifts to A and his wife are both valid, for A is a life in being and his wife must be ascertained in his lifetime. But at common law the limitation to the wife's husband was void for perpetuity, since A's wife may not be alive at the time of the gift and may marry more than 21 years after A's death. Nevertheless, the gift to A's children is valid, for although it follows a void limitation, it has its own independent date of vesting which cannot exceed the perpetuity period.[98]

The precise meaning of "dependent" in this context is obscure. Sometimes it seems to mean no more than "contingent", so that there is no special rule as to "dependence". But sometimes a remainder which seems plainly vested is struck down as being "dependent" upon a prior void limitation.[99] Such cases can be explained on the principle that if a testator

---

[94] *Garland v. Brown* (1864) 10 L.T. 292.
[95] *Re Abbott* [1893] 1 Ch. 54; *Re Hubbard's W.T.* [1963] Ch. 275.
[96] See *Re Coleman* [1936] Ch. 528.
[97] *Proctor v. Bishop of Bath and Wells* (1794) 2 Hy. Bl. 358.
[98] See *Re Coleman* [1936] Ch. 528.
[99] *Re Backhouse* [1921] 2 Ch. 51.

intends the remainder not to take effect until the prior limitation ends, it would be contrary to that intention to allow the remainder to take immediate effect merely because the prior limitation is void for perpetuity. The remainder accordingly falls with the prior limitation. Thus if a testator gives property for life to the first son of A (a bachelor) to marry, and then to B, he may well have intended no immediate gift to B. Further, where a void limitation stands between two or more valid limitations, the limitation following the void limitation will be held dependent on it, and so invalid, unless it will "dovetail in and accord with" the prior limitations.[1]

(c) The Act of 1964

The whole doctrine of "dependence" was so unsatisfactory and obscure that the Act of 1964 abolished it for gifts made after July 15, 1964. Such a gift is not void merely because it is "ulterior to and dependent upon" a void gift. It is only the doctrine of dependence which has been abolished. If the ultimate gift is contingent, the contingency must be satisfied before it can vest. Thus of the gifts mentioned above, that to B is dependent only; but the gift "but if X has no such son, to Y" is contingent as well as dependent. The Act further provides that the existence of the prior void gift will no longer prevent the acceleration of the vesting of the subsequent gift.[2]

7. Alternative contingencies

Where a gift expresses two alternative contingencies upon which the property may vest, and one contingency is too remote but the other is not, the gift is good if in fact the valid contingency occurs.[3] Thus in one case,[4] a testator gave property to his grandchildren and issue of his grandchildren living "on the decease of my last surviving child or on the death of the last surviving widow or widower of my children as the case may be whichever shall last happen." It was held that this gift did not infringe the perpetuity rule as it stood, and that if in fact one of the testator's children outlived all the other children and their spouses, the gift would be valid. There were two alternatives:

(i) that one of the testator's children (a life in being) would be the last survivor, or

(ii) that the spouse of one of the testator's children (not necessarily a life in being) would be the last survivor;

if the former actually occurred, the gift did not infringe the rule. To this extent, there is a "wait and see" in the perpetuity rule even at common law.

The foregoing applies only if the two alternative contingencies are expressed in the gift.[5] If only one contingency is expressed in the gift and that may be too remote, the gift fails even if there are in fact two contingencies. Thus in *Proctor v. Bishop of Bath and Wells*,[6] only one contingency was expressed, namely that, if no son of X became a clergyman, Y should be entitled. In fact, two contingencies were implicit in the gift, namely:

---

[1] *Monypenny v. Dering* (1852) 2 De G.M. & G. 145 at 182.
[2] s.6.
[3] *Hodgson v. Halford* (1879) 11 Ch.D. 959.
[4] *Re Curryer's W.T.* [1938] Ch. 952.
[5] *Re Bence* [1891] 3 Ch. 242.
[6] Above, p. 193.

(i) X might leave no son; this must be known at X's death, which would be within the period;

(ii) X might leave one or more sons, who might become clergymen more than 21 years after X's death, which would be outside the period.

Nevertheless, the gift to Y was void *ab initio*, for the only contingency expressed was a void one. Had the gift over been worded "but if no son of X shall become a clergyman, or if X shall leave no son, to Y in fee simple", the gift to Y would have been valid if X had died leaving no son, *i.e.* if the valid contingency had occurred.[7]

The Act of 1964 has not specifically altered these rules, but its general "wait and see" provisions will apply if the unduly remote contingency occurs, or if there is only one composite contingent gift.

8. Class gifts

A class gift is a gift of property to all who come within some description, the property being divisible in shares varying according to the number of persons in the class.[8] Thus gifts of property "to my children who shall live to be 25", or "to all the nephews and nieces of my late husband who were living at his death, except A and B" are class gifts. But gifts of property to be equally divided between "the five daughters of X", or "my nine children", or a gift of £2,000 "to each of my daughters", are not class gifts, for a distinct one-fifth or one-ninth share or the sum of £2,000 is given to each child, exactly as if he or she had been named.

(a) At common law

The perpetuity rule applies at common law to class gifts in the following way. If a single member of the class might possibly take a vested interest outside the period, the whole gift fails, even as regards those members of the class who have already satisfied any required contingency.[9] A class gift cannot be good as to part and void as to the rest: "the vice of remoteness affects the class as a whole, if it may affect an unascertained number of its members".[10] Until the total number of members of the class has been ascertained, it cannot be said what share any member of the class will take, and this state of affairs will continue as long as it is possible for any alteration in the number to be made.

Thus if before 1926 personalty was given "to A for life and after his death to be equally divided between all his children who shall attain the age of 25", an intent being shown to include every child of A, the remainder was void even as regards children alive at the time of the gift, who were thus lives in being.[11] This was so even if A was in fact many years past the age of child-bearing,[12] for in theory other children might be born, and since one of these might not be 25 until more than 21 years after the death of all lives in being at the time of the gift, the period might be exceeded.

---

[7] *Miles v. Harford* (1879) 12 Ch.D. 691 at 703.
[8] *Pearks v. Moseley* (1880) 5 App. Cas. 714 at 723; *Kingsbury v. Walter* [1901] A.C. 187 at 192.
[9] *Leake v. Robinson* (1817) 2 Mer. 363.
[10] *Pearks v. Moseley* (1880) 5 App. Cas. 714 at 723.
[11] *Leake v. Robinson* (1817) 2 Mer. 363.
[12] Nowadays s.2 of the Act of 1964 lays down sensible child-bearing age presumptions: above p. 217.

(b)   The class-closing rules

Sometimes a class gift is saved by the operation of the class-closing rules that have already been considered.[13] Subject always to a sufficient contrary intention, these rules close the class as soon as any member of it is entitled to claim his share, and exclude anyone who subsequently becomes a member of the class. Thus at common law a devise "equally between all my grandchildren who marry" would prima facie be void for perpetuity if any child of the testator survived him. But if one or more grandchildren married before the testator died, each of the grandchildren then living would become entitled to his share on marrying, with the prospect of that share being increased from the prospective shares of any of the other living grandchildren who died without marrying. The gift would thus take effect as a gift to lives in being, to the exclusion of grandchildren born after the testator's death.

Where there is no class gift but individual gifts to each member of a class,[14] such as £5,000 to each of X's children, or to each of Y's children to attain full age, the only persons who can take are children of X who are alive when the testator dies or the children of Y whose minorities had ended by then: for if other children could take, the estate could not be distributed, and so a rule of convenience excludes them.[15] But where A is given a life interest in the estate prior to the gifts to the children, all children who qualify before A's death will be included,[16] for this causes no inconvenience.

(c)   Statutory class reduction

Where the class closing rules do not save a gift at common law but the gift is made after July 15, 1964, the Act of 1964 may save the gift by excluding from the class those members whose presence makes the gift void for perpetuity. In such cases, the common law rule that a class gift cannot be partly good and partly bad does not apply. The Act provides that, where it becomes apparent that the inclusion of potential members of the class would cause the gift to be void for remoteness, those members are to be excluded from the class, unless this would exhaust the class.[17] Thus under a devise "to A for life with remainder equally among his grandchildren whenever born", the last two words oust the class-closing rules, and at common law the gift is void for perpetuity unless A predeceased the testator. But under the Act, one must wait until the end of the perpetuity period to see how many grandchildren have been born, and then they alone will take, to the exclusion of any future-born grandchildren. This type of statutory class reduction will continue to be possible under the Law Commission's current proposals if they are enacted. This is how children born after the end of the relevant perpetuity period as a result of the utilisation of frozen sperm and eggs can be excluded and so disregarded both under the Act of 1964 and the Law Commission's current proposals; the trustees therefore will not need to make any inquiries as to the existence of frozen sperm and eggs and will be able to distribute the gift to the existing members of the class as soon as the perpetuity period ends. Since this cannot be done in the case of gifts made before July 16, 1964, in such cases the trustees will presumably need to inquire and, in principle, the existence of frozen sperm and eggs will render the gift void (whether a court would actually reach such a conclusion in practice is, however, rather questionable).

[13] Above, p. 190.
[14] See *Storrs v. Benbow* (1853) 3 De G.M. & G. 390.
[15] *Rogers v. Mutch* (1878) 10 Ch.D. 25.
[16] *Att.-Gen. v. Crispin* (1784) 1 Bro.C.C. 386.
[17] Act of 1964, s.4(4).

(d) Age reduction

If a class gift contained in an instrument executed after 1925, or in the will of a testator dying after 1925, but in either case before July 16, 1964[18] would be void at common law because it specified an age over 21, it may still be saved by age reduction under section 163 of the Law of Property Act 1925, which will reduce the age to 21 for all the members of the class. And if a class gift contained in an instrument to which the Act of 1964 applies would be void at common law for this reason despite the class-closing rules and it is not saved by the "wait and see" principle, it may still be saved by age reduction under the Act of 1964.[19] If a will governed by the 1964 Act gives property "to all X's children who attain the age of 25", and X dies 10 years later leaving children aged three and one, the age will be reduced. It is thought that the reduction will be to 22 for each child, but it may be that it is only to 24 for the elder child. In either case, there are potential difficulties about members of the class who have attained the age to which the age is reduced during "wait and see" but have then died without attaining the age originally specified before it is reduced: does the reduction have retrospective effect to include them in the class posthumously?[20] This latter type of age reduction will continue to be possible under the Law Commission's current proposals if they are enacted; the problems just adverted to have not been resolved.

(e) Class and age reduction

Under the Act of 1964, the provisions for class reduction may be combined with those for age reduction. If property is given to A (a bachelor) for life, with remainder "equally between all of A's children who attain 25 together with all the children of any child of A who dies under 25, such children taking their parents' share", the gift to the compound class is void at common law[21] and would not be saved by reducing the age to 21: for an unborn grandchild might attain 21 after the expiration of the perpetuity period. If the gift is not saved under the "wait and see" principle, the grandchildren will be excluded under the class reduction provisions, and under the age reduction provisions the age will be reduced so far as is necessary.[22] Class and age reduction will also continue to be possible under the Law Commission's current proposals if they are enacted.

9. Determinable and conditional interests[23]

(a) Determinable interests at common law

"The rule against perpetuities is not dealing with the duration of interests but with their commencement, and as long as the interest vests within lives in being and 21 years it does not matter how long that interest lasts."[24] Thus it can be said that the perpetuity rule does not invalidate a limitation at common law merely because it provides that an interest shall cease at some future date outside the perpetuity period. Accordingly it has been held that where property is given to an unborn person "for life or until she becomes a member of the Roman Catholic Church" or "for life or until marriage", the specified event may occur outside the

---

[18] Except in the case of an instrument made in the exercise of a special power of appointment created before July 16, 1964: Act of 1964, s.15(5).
[19] Above, p. 223.
[20] See [1969] C.L.J. 286 (M. J. Prichard).
[21] *Pearks v. Moseley* (1880) 5 App. Cas. 714.
[22] Act of 1964, s.4(3).
[23] See also above, pp. 41 *et seq.*
[24] *Re Chardon* [1928] Ch. 464 at 468.

perpetuity period but the limitation was nevertheless valid at common law.[25] The better view was thought to be that it is immaterial that the determinable interest is a fee simple and the event on which it will determine may not happen for centuries, such as where property is conveyed to the X Co. Ltd in fee simple until the premises are used otherwise than as a biscuit factory; this was because, when the event occurs, no new estate arises; the fee simple of X Co. Ltd terminates, and the grantor's possibility of reverter (a vested interest which after 1925 can only be an equitable interest) takes effect. However, the opposite view was taken in 1944,[26] when the rule was held to apply and the holder of the determinable fee was held to take a fee simple absolute. This view was criticised[27] and ignored in a later case.[28] There may well be determinable fees created by instruments to which the 1964 Act (which has resolved this conflict of authorities) does not apply so this question may still one day have to be resolved.

A similar rule applied to resulting trusts at common law.[29] Where land is conveyed to trustees in trust for an orphans' home, and on failure of that trust, in trust for the then owner of other land, the initial gift is good but the gift over is plainly void for perpetuity at common law. Instead, there will be a resulting trust for the grantor's estate, and this will not be void for perpetuity.[30]

(b) Conditional interests at common law

A condition may be either precedent or subsequent.[31]

A condition precedent is one which must be fulfilled before the beneficiary is entitled to a vested interest, for example "to X and his heirs when he marries". In such a case the perpetuity rule applies, for a new interest is limited to arise when the event occurs; consequently, if the condition might be fulfilled outside the perpetuity period the whole gift failed at common law.[32]

A condition subsequent is one which authorises the grantor or his representatives to determine an existing interest. Thus a gift of land to X in fee simple "on condition that he never sells it out of the family" gives the grantor a right of re-entry if the condition is broken. If such a condition infringes the perpetuity rule it is void, but the interest which it was to defeat is not invalidated. Thus at common law, if there was a valid gift by a testator to his grandchildren followed by a clause providing for the forfeiture of the interest of any grandchild who should forsake the Jewish faith or marry outside the faith, all the beneficiaries took absolute interests. The forfeiture clause was void since it might not take effect until the perpetuity period had expired, but there was nothing to invalidate the gift to the grandchildren.[33]

It will be noticed that a breach of a condition subsequent gives rise to a right of re-entry, so that some active step must be taken to determine the estate; a determinable limitation, on

---

[25] *Wainwright v. Miller* [1897] 2 Ch. 255; *Re Gage* [1898] 1 Ch. 498.
[26] In *Hopper v. Corporation of Liverpool* (1944) 88 S.J. 213.
[27] In 1945 Conv. Y.B. at 203–206.
[28] *Re Chambers' W.T.* [1950] Ch. 267.
[29] Any beneficial interest of which the settlor fails to dispose remains in him under a resulting trust: see below, p. 291.
[30] *Re Cooper's Conveyance Trusts* [1956] 1 W.L.R. 1096.
[31] Above, p. 41.
[32] See, *e.g. Pickford v. Brown* (1856) 2 K. & J. 426.
[33] *Re Spitzel's W.T.* [1939] 2 All E.R. 266.

the other hand, requires no future activity, for the estate automatically determines by force of the original limitation.[34]

(c) The Act of 1964

Where the Act of 1964 applies, however, the "wait and see" principle may save both conditions precedent and conditions subsequent. Where it does not do so, the position remains the same as at common law; the gift subject to the condition precedent will fail and the holder of the gift subject to the condition subsequent will take an absolute interest. Further, the Act has assimilated the rules for determinable and conditional interests by providing that the rule against perpetuities does apply to possibilities of reverter and resulting trusts created by dispositions made after the Act as if they were in the form of conditions subsequent.[35] So if after "waiting and seeing" the determining event has not occurred within the perpetuity period, then the interest subjected to the condition becomes absolute. The position will remain the same under the Law Commission's current proposals if they are enacted.

10. Powers

Settlements often authorise trustees, tenants for life and others to do things which they would not otherwise be entitled to do. One class of such powers may authorise acts of administration, such as the sale or leasing of the settled land.[36] Other powers, known as overriding powers of appointment, which are now extremely common, may authorise an alteration of the beneficial interests. The application of the rule against perpetuities to powers is somewhat complicated.

(a) Administrative powers

(i) At common law: In general, an administrative power which was exercisable outside the perpetuity period was void, such as a power to lease or sell during the lifetime of an unborn person.[37]

(ii) The Act of 1964: It was generally thought that the extension of the rule to administrative powers was unwarranted, and that it ought to be confined to the invalidation of the remote vesting of beneficial interests. Accordingly the Act provides that the rule is not to operate to invalidate a power conferred on trustees and other persons "to sell, lease, exchange or otherwise dispose of any property for full consideration, or to do any other act in the administration (as opposed to the distribution) of any property".[38] Exceptionally, this provision is retrospective to the extent that it applies to the exercise of a power after July 15, 1964, even if the settlement or will which conferred the power took effect before then.[39] The law will remain the same if the current proposals of the Law Commission are enacted.

(b) Powers of appointment

A power of appointment is a power for the person to whom it is given ("the donee of the power") to appoint property to such persons ("the objects of the power") as he may select.

---

[34] See above, pp. 41 *et seq.*
[35] s.12.
[36] See below, p. 241.
[37] *Re Allott* [1924] 2 Ch. 498.
[38] s.8(1).
[39] s.8(2). For the general rule, see above, p. 215.

(i) Special, general and intermediate powers: A power is a "special power" if the donee's choice is restricted to a limited class of objects, such as X's children; a "general power" arises if his choice is unrestricted and so he himself could benefit; an "intermediate power" arises where his choice is unrestricted save for excluded persons—usually in practice, the donor and his wife.

(a) *At common law.* For the purposes of the perpetuity rule, the general test is whether or not the donee of the power is as free to dispose of the property as an absolute owner is. Thus for this purpose a joint power of appointment has been held special,[40] and so has a power to appoint with the consent of X,[41] unless, perhaps X's consent is a requisite merely to the exercise of the power and he has no control over the amounts appointed or the persons to benefit, in which case the power may be general. Whether an intermediate power such as one to appoint "to anyone except Z" is general or special for this purpose is doubtful. An unrestricted power to appoint by will alone (where the donee, of course, is unable to appoint to himself) is treated as being special in determining whether the power itself is valid, but as being general in determining whether an appointment is valid.[42]

(b) *The Act of 1964.* The Act of 1964 has codified the distinction between special, general and intermediate powers. It adopts the formulation worked out in the cases, and resolves the doubts which have been mentioned. In dispositions taking effect after July 15, 1964, a power is treated as a special power unless it is expressed to be exercisable by one person only, and it could be exercised by him so as to transfer the property to himself without the consent of any other person or compliance with any condition (apart from a mere formal condition relating only to the mode of exercise of the power).[43] Under this provision, a sole power to appoint "to anyone except X" is general unless X is the donee of the power. However, the exceptional position of general testamentary powers has been left unchanged. The law will remain the same if the current proposals of the Law Commission are enacted.

(ii) Validity of the power: In the application of the perpetuity rule to powers of appointment, two separate points have to be considered:

(a) Does the power itself infringe the rule?

(b) If it does not, does the appointment made under the power infringe the rule?

(c) A special power

A special power of appointment is subject to the ordinary rule relating to powers and is thus void if it could be exercised outside the period; time runs from the date when the instrument creating the power took effect[44] and the donor's bounty gave the objects their hope of benefit. Thus if the donee of the power will not necessarily be ascertained within the period (if at all) or is capable of exercising the power when the period has expired, the power is bad.[45] But

---

[40] *Re Churston S.E.* [1954] Ch. 334; *Re Earl of Coventry's Indentures* [1974] Ch. 77.
[41] *Re Watts* [1931] 2 Ch. 302.
[42] *Morgan v. Gronow* (1873) L.R. 16 Eq. 1; *Rous v. Jackson* (1885) 29 Ch.D. 521.
[43] s.7.
[44] *Re De Sommery* [1912] 2 Ch. 622.
[45] *Re Abbott* [1893] 1 Ch. 54.

a power exercisable only by a person living when it was created can never be void for remoteness.

If a power complies with these conditions, it is not void merely because an appointment which offends the rule might be made under it.[46] Thus where a living person is given power to appoint to his issue, he might make an appointment to his great-great-grandchildren, but this possibility does not invalidate either the power itself or an appointment which in fact complies with the rule.

The Act of 1964 applies the new "wait and see" principle to powers created by instruments taking effect after July 15, 1964. The power is to be treated as void only if and so far as it is not fully exercised within the perpetuity period.[47] If the objects of the power are in existence at the creation of the power and are reasonably ascertainable they are included among the lives in being.[48]

The proposals of the Law Commission will, if enacted, apply the 125-year perpetuity period to powers and, where a pre-existing power is exercised after the new legislation comes into force, its effect (as well as its validity) will be measured as if the appropriate perpetuity period had been, for this and for no other purpose, 125 years (this is the other proposal which will have retrospective effect).

If a power is void for remoteness, a gift in default of appointment (such as "but if no appointment shall be made, to X and Y equally") is not thereby invalidated; provided it does not itself infringe the rule, it is valid.[49]

(d) A general power

For the purposes of the perpetuity rule, at common law a general power to appoint by deed is so nearly akin to absolute ownership that principles similar to those appropriate to absolute ownership are applied: the perpetuity rule is satisfied if the power must be acquired within the period, if at all, even if the power might be exercised outside the period.[50] But if the power is exercisable only by will, it is treated as a special power and so will be bad if it might be exercised outside the period.[51]

Here, too, the Act of 1964 applies the "wait and see" principle. A general power created by an instrument taking effect after July 15, 1964, will not be void on the ground that it might be acquired at too remote a time, but will be valid unless and until it becomes established that it will not be exercisable within the period.[52] Under the Act of 1964, a general testamentary power, being special, is treated as being void only if and so far as it is not fully exercised within the perpetuity period.[53]

The current proposals of the Law Commission will, if enacted, be equally applicable to general powers.

(e) Validity of appointments

If the power itself is void, clearly no valid appointment can be made under it. But even if the power itself is valid, an appointment made under it may nevertheless be too remote.

[46] *Slark v. Dakyns* (1874) 10 Ch.App. 35.
[47] s.3(3).
[48] s.3(5)(b)(iii). For lives in being, see above, p. 219.
[49] *Re Abbott* [1893] 1 Ch. 54.
[50] See *Re Fane* [1913] 1 Ch. 404.
[51] *Wollaston v. King* (1868) L.R. 8 Eq. 165.
[52] s.3(2).
[53] See above, p. 232.

(i) A special power: In the case of a special power of appointment, the property is fettered from the moment the power is created. It can be said at once that either an appointment will be made in favour of one or more of the designated class of persons or else it will pass to those nominated to take in default of appointment, or, if none, to the grantor. The perpetuity period therefore starts to run from the creation of the power.[54] However, as has been seen,[55] the mere fact that the power authorises the making of an appointment which may be too remote does not invalidate it, and until the appointment has been made, it cannot be seen if in fact it is too remote. Consequently, contrary to the general rule in matters of perpetuity, even at common law "the principle seems to be to wait and see".[56] When the appointment is ultimately made, it must be examined to see whether the interests appointed are bound to vest (if at all) within 21 years of the dropping of the lives of persons who were living or *en ventre sa mère*[57] at the time of the creation of the power and not at the time of the appointment. Further, the facts existing at the time of the appointment must be taken into account when deciding this point. In short, in ascertaining the lives in being the relevant time is that of the creation of the power; in ascertaining the facts of the case, the relevant time is that of the making of the appointment.

Some examples of the position apart from the Act of 1964 may make this clearer.

(a) Devise to A for life with power to appoint to his children: A appoints to his son B "when he is 23": B was unborn at the testator's death but aged three at the time of the appointment. A is the only life in being, but since the property is bound to vest (if at all) within 20 years of his death, the appointment is good. Had B been under the age of two at the time of the appointment, then if it had been made before 1926 it would have been void; if it was made after 1925, B would have taken when he was 21.[58]

(b) Marriage settlement upon C for life, remainder as he should appoint among his issue: C appoints in favour of his daughter D, postponing the vesting of her interest until her marriage: D is unmarried at the date of the appointment. The appointment is void. A few years later, D marries and C then executes a document confirming the void appointment. D is entitled to the property, since the confirmation operates as a fresh appointment, and taking the facts existing at the time of the appointment, the property has vested during the lifetime of a person alive at the date of the settlement, namely C.[59]

(c) Deed giving property to F for life with power to appoint to his issue: F appoints by will in favour of his grandchildren G and H (neither of whom was alive at the date of the gift) for their joint lives as tenants in common, with remainder to the survivor. The interest for their joint lives is valid but the remainder is void.[60]

---

[54] *Re Thompson* [1906] 2 Ch. 199.
[55] Above, p. 233.
[56] *Re Witty* [1913] 2 Ch. 666 at 673, *per* Cozens-Hardy M.R.
[57] *Re Stern* [1962] Ch. 732.
[58] L.P.A. 1925, s.163; above, p. 221.
[59] This is based on *Morgan v. Gronow* (1873) L.R. 16 Eq. 1.
[60] *Re Legh's S.T.* [1938] Ch. 39.

The Act of 1964 has enlarged the scope of "wait and see" in relation to the exercise of special powers, as well as providing for age reduction and class reduction. If the powers in the example given above are created after July 15, 1964,[61] the result will be as follows.

(a) If B is under two years old at the time of the appointment, he will take when he is 23 if in fact he attains that age within the period, for example if A lives until B is five. But if A dies before B is two, B will take at whatever age he is when 21 years have elapsed after A's death.[62]

(b) The first appointment to D will be valid unless and until it appears that D will not marry within the perpetuity period, running from the date of the settlement.

(c) The remainder is valid if it in fact vests within the period, *i.e.* 21 years after the death of the survivor of the donor, F, and any of F's children living at the date of the deed and any persons who were then their spouses.

As has already been mentioned, the proposals of the Law Commission will, if enacted, apply the 125 year perpetuity period to powers and, where a pre-existing power is exercised after the new legislation comes into force, its validity (as well as its effect) and validity will be measured as if the appropriate perpetuity period, for this and for no other purpose, had been 125 years. Age reduction and class reduction will continue as under the 1964 Act.

(ii) A general power: Since the property is unfettered until the appointment has been made, the donee of the power being able to deal with it as he wishes, the perpetuity period does not begin to run until the date of the appointment. Thus for the purposes of the perpetuity rule there is no difference between the exercise of a general power and a conveyance by an absolute owner.

The difference between appointments under general and special powers may be summarised thus. In both cases, the relevant facts are those existing at the time of the appointment; but the time at which the perpetuity period must be ascertained is the creation of the power in the case of a special power, and the exercise of the power in the case of a general power.

11. Contracts, covenants and options

The rule against perpetuities is essentially a rule relating to property, and so it has only a limited application to contracts, covenants and options.

(a) At common law

(i) Personal obligations: The rule against remoteness does not apply to contracts in so far as they create mere personal obligations, such as to pay mining royalties.[63] The rule is directed against the vesting of interests in some specific property at too remote a date, and personal contracts do not do this. Further, even if a contract confers a right to an interest in some specific property exercisable at too remote a date, the rule did not prevent damages[64]

---

[61] The Act does not apply to appointments made after July 15, 1964, under a special power created earlier: s.15(5).

[62] See above, p. 223.

[63] *Witham v. Vane* (1883) Challis R.P. 440.

[64] *Worthing Corporation v. Heather* [1906] 2 Ch. 532.

or specific performance[65] being awarded against a party to the contract; for the court is merely enforcing his personal obligations and not any rights of property.

(ii) Proprietary interests: Where, however, the claimant's case depends not on a personal obligation but on the existence of an interest in specific property, the rule applies. Thus if a lease for 99 years confers on the lessee and his assigns an option to purchase a freehold at any time during the lease[66] (an option appurtenant to the lease), or a corporation is given an option to purchase or take a lease of land[67] (an option in gross), an action to enforce the option against a successor in title of the person who granted the option cannot be based on any personal obligation, and must depend on the burden of the option running with the land. The rule accordingly makes the option unenforceable against the successor unless its exercise is confined within the period.

(iii) Covenants to renew lease: Exceptionally, a covenant in a lease giving the tenant the right to an extension of the term is not void merely because it can be exercised outside the perpetuity period.[68] An option to renew a lease (unlike an option to purchase the reversion) has traditionally been regarded as "touching and concerning"[69] the land held under the lease so as to run with it and form part of the tenant's present interest. But a contract made after 1925 to renew a lease for more than 60 years from its termination is void.[70]

(b) The Act of 1964

The Act of 1964 has made three changes in relation to dispositions in instruments taking effect after July 15, 1964.

(i) Personal obligations: The Act reverses the rule that damages or specific performance may be obtained against an original contracting party even though the proprietary interest conferred by the contract is void for perpetuity. A disposition *inter vivos* which creates an interest in property is void between the original contracting parties wherever it would be void for perpetuity against a third party.[71]

(ii) Options appurtenant to leases: The rule against remoteness does not apply to an option for a lessee to purchase the freehold or superior leasehold title which is exercisable only by the lessee or his successors in title and which ceases to be exercisable not later than a year after the end of the lease.[72]

(iii) Options in gross An option to acquire for value any interest in land is subject to a specially short perpetuity period of 21 years only.[73] The "wait and see" principle applies, so that even if no time limit is specified in the instrument conferring the option, it will remain exercisable for 21 years.

---

[65] *Hutton v. Watling* [1948] Ch. 26, 398.
[66] *Woodall v. Clifton* [1905] 2 Ch. 257.
[67] *London and South Western Ry v. Gomm* (1882) 20 Ch.D. 562.
[68] *Woodall v. Clifton* [1905] 2 Ch. 257 at 265, 268; *Weg Motors Ltd v. Hales* [1962] Ch. 49.
[69] See below, p. 387. This does not make the covenant enforceable against third parties.
[70] L.P.A. 1922, Sched. 15, para. 7; below, p. 351.
[71] s.10.
[72] s.9(1).
[73] s.9(2). But see *Governors of Peabody Donation Fund v. London Residuary Body* (1988) 55 P. & C.R. 355 (exemption from rule provided by statutory scheme).

(c) The Law Commission's proposals

The Law Commission's current proposals will, if enacted, make the perpetuity rule inapplicable to options, thus permitting perpetual options in all cases.

Sect. 5. Exceptions from the rule

The preceding section has indicated some cases to which the rule against perpetuities does not apply, namely:

    (i) personal obligations;

    (ii) covenants for renewal of a lease; and

    (iii) covenants in a lease for the purchase of the landlord's reversion.

The Law Commission's current proposals will, if enacted, remove all options from the scope of the rule against perpetuities.

There are certain other existing exceptions, which will continue under the Law Commission's current proposals if enacted.

1. Certain limitations after fees tail

No more entailed interests can now be created so the Law Commission's proposals are irrelevant to this exception. However, it remains relevant in respect of continuing fee tail. A limitation which is bound to take effect, if at all, during the continuance, or at the moment of the determination, of fee tail is not rendered void by the rule, even though the fee tail may continue for longer than the perpetuity period.[74] Thus a gift to X in fee tail, with remainder to such of Y's issue as are alive when the fee tail determines, is valid, even though the persons entitled to take the remainder may not be ascertained for several hundred years.[75] The fee tail can always be barred by the tenant in fee tail, and so he is not fettered by the remainder. This exception, however, does not protect limitations which can or must vest when an interval has elapsed after the determination of the fee tail.[76] If property is given to trustees in trust for A in fee tail, remainder to the first of the great-grandchildren of B to attain the age of 30, A's fee tail is valid but the remainder is void, for it might very well vest many years after the period has run and the fee tail has determined.

2. Certain gifts to charities

The general rule is that a gift to a charity is subject to the rule in the same way as any other gift.[77] However, if there is a gift to one charity followed by a gift over to another charity on a certain event, the gift over is not void merely because the event may occur outside the perpetuity period. Thus if property is given to Charity A with a proviso that it shall go to Charity B if Charity A fails to keep the testator's tomb in repair, the gift over is valid.[78] To this extent alone are charities exempted from the rule against remoteness.[79]

---

[74] *Nicolls v. Sheffield* (1787) 2 Bro.C.C. 215.
[75] See *Heaseman v. Pearse* (1871) 7 Ch.App. 275 at 282, 283.
[76] See *Bristow v. Boothby* (1826) 2 Sim. & St. 465.
[77] *Chamberlayne v. Brockett* (1872) 8 Ch.App. 206.
[78] *Re Tyler* [1891] 3 Ch. 252; and see below, pp. 239, 240.
[79] See also the exemption from the rule against inalienability, below, p. 240.

3. Certain rights of entry and re-entry

The right to re-enter and determine a lease if a covenant is broken, which most leases give to the landlord, is excepted from the perpetuity rule.[80] Again, the statutory remedies for enforcing payment of a rentcharge[81] or any like powers or remedies conferred by any instrument were expressly excepted from the rule in 1925.[82] For rentcharges created after July 15, 1964, the Act of 1964 extends the exemption to all powers and remedies for enforcing rentcharges.[83] Further, the Law of Property Act 1925[84] sets out a list of certain rights retrospectively excepted from the rule, such as a right to enter or use the surface of land in order to work minerals or execute repairs. A right of re-entry in respect of a fee simple is not within this exception and will accordingly be void if it is exercisable outside the perpetuity period.[85]

4. Mortgages

"The rule has never been applied to mortgages", and thus a clause postponing the mortgagor's right to redeem the property is not invalid merely because the right is postponed for longer than the perpetuity period.[86]

PART 3—THE RULE AGAINST INALIENABILITY

1. The rule

It is a fundamental principle of English law that property cannot be rendered inalienable. Thus a devise of land to be retained in perpetuity as a family burial ground is void.[87] This is not affected by the property being subject to powers to sell or otherwise dispose of it where the restrictions would apply to the purchase money, so that there would be a fund which in one form or another must be held indefinitely to order to provide income under the terms of the gift. A gift is bad if effect can be given to it only by holding the property for ever and applying the income for the purposes specified.[88] The rule is sometimes called "the rule against trusts of perpetual duration", or "the rule that gifts which tend to a perpetuity are void". This rule will not be affected in any way by the Law Commission's current proposals.

2. The period

Although property cannot be made inalienable for ever, or for a period to which no clear or definite limit is set,[89] it appears to be settled that a limitation making property inalienable is valid if it is limited to a maximum period of a life or lives in being at the time of the gift,

---

[80] *Re Tyrell's Estate* [1907] 1 I.R. 292 at 298.
[81] Below, p. 410.
[82] L.P.A. 1925, s.121.
[83] s.11(1).
[84] s.162.
[85] *Re Trustees of Hollis' Hospital and Hague's Contract* [1899] 2 Ch. 540; L.P.A. 1925, s.4; and see above, pp. 41, 229–231.
[86] *Knightsbridge Estates Trust Ltd v. Byrne* [1939] Ch. 441 at 463 *per* Greene M.R.; on appeal, [1940] A.C. 613.
[87] *Yeap Cheah Neo v. Ong Cheng Neo* (1875) L.R. 6 P.C. 381.
[88] See *Cocks v. Manners* (1871) L.R. 12 Eq. 574 at 585, 586.
[89] *Re Wightwick's W.T.* [1950] Ch. 260.

with a further 21 years.[90] This period is borrowed from the rule against perpetuities, considered above.[91] In practice, if it is wished to make the property inalienable for longer than a fixed period of years not exceeding 21 or "for such period as the law allows", which means 21 years, it is necessary to use "royal lives clauses" or similar perpetuity clauses. This period is not affected by the Perpetuities and Accumulations Act 1964.[92] Thus the "wait and see" principle, the 80-year period, and the statutory list of lives in being do not apply to the rule against inalienability. Nor will the 125-year period proposed by the Law Commission be applicable either.

3. Purpose trusts

The rule has no application to a trust for abstract or impersonal objects or purposes (as distinct from persons) where there is nobody who can enforce it; for such trusts are void.[93] Where there is a trust for some non-charitable purpose, such as preserving the independence and integrity of newspapers,[94] or pursuing inquiries into a new alphabet,[95] or providing "some useful memorial" of the testator,[96] the trust is void because there is no beneficiary or other person who can enforce it. Such trusts are sometimes called "trusts of imperfect obligation". There are a few accepted exceptions in which testamentary trusts for maintaining individual animals,[97] for erecting or maintaining a tomb or other funerary monument,[98] or for the saying of masses in circumstances where this is not charitable[99] have been held valid, the duration in each case having been limited to the perpetuity period; these authorities will be applied but not extended.[1] There are also some cases of doubtful authority which are unlikely to be followed; thus a trust for the furtherance of fox hunting was upheld[2] and trusts to endow an annual cup for yacht racing[3] and to keep a portrait in repair[4] would have been upheld had they been limited to the perpetuity period. Further, what at first appears to be merely a purpose trust may be enforceable by persons for whose benefit it was imposed, as where land is given on the terms that for the perpetuity period it is to be maintained as a sports ground for the benefit of identifiable employees of a company.[5] On the other hand, where the trust is wholly charitable in nature, it is not void for lack of anyone to enforce it, for the Attorney General can do this; and it is exempt from the rule against inalienability.[6] This may be employed to secure indirectly the carrying out of some purpose such as the maintenance of a tomb indefinitely.[7]

---

[90] See *Re Dean* (1889) 41 Ch.D. 552 at 557.
[91] Above, p. 210.
[92] See s.15(4), where the sense requires "remoteness" to mean "inalienability".
[93] *Re Denley's Trust Deed* [1969] 1 Ch. 373.
[94] *Re Astor's S.T.* [1952] Ch. 534.
[95] *Re Shaw* [1957] 1 W.L.R. 729.
[96] *Re Endacott* [1960] Ch. 232.
[97] *Pettingall v. Pettingall* (1842) 11 L.J.Ch. 176 (horse); *Re Dean* (1889) 41 Ch.D. 552 (horses and dogs).
[98] *Trimmer v. Danby* (1856) 25 L.J.Ch. 424; *Re Hooper* [1932] 1 Ch. 38.
[99] *Bourne v. Keane* [1919] A.C. 815 at 874–875.
[1] *Re Endacott* [1960] Ch. 232 at 250–251.
[2] *Re Thompson* [1934] Ch. 342.
[3] *Re Nottage* [1895] 2 Ch. 649.
[4] *Re Gassiott* (1901) 70 L.J.Ch. 242.
[5] *Re Denley's Trust Deed* [1969] 1 Ch. 373.
[6] *Chamberlayne v. Brockett* (1872) 8 Ch.App. 206; compare the rule against perpetuities: above, p. 237.
[7] Above, p. 237.

4. Immediate gifts

Where property is given to an unincorporated association, such as a members' club, it must be decided whether the gift is made to all the members of the association, both present and future, or whether it is an immediate gift to all the existing members of the association. This depends on the terms of the gift and the rules of the association: either may impose a trust or obligation to hold the property for the benefit of all present and future members. If it does this, the gift is void for inalienability unless it is confined to the perpetuity period.[8] Otherwise the gift will take effect as an absolute gift to the existing members; and as each of them can call forthwith for his distributive share, no question of inalienability arises.[9] The same applies to a gift to the trustees of an association for its general purposes where the trustees are free to alienate the property forthwith.[10] Further, an immediate gift of income for an indefinite period to a company does not infringe the rule merely because it is to cease at an indefinite future date (such as when a tomb is no longer in good repair), for the company is always free to assign the right to the future income, and nothing is inalienable.[11]

5. Charities

Charities are exempt from the rule against inalienability; no gift for charitable purposes is void merely because it renders property inalienable in perpetuity.[12]

PART 4—THE RULE AGAINST ACCUMULATIONS

The rule against accumulations resembles the rule against inalienability in that it is directed against remoteness of control over a vested interest rather than against interests which may vest at too distant a date. At common law, the rule was that a direction to accumulate was valid if it was confined to the perpetuity period applicable to the rule against remoteness.[13] This rule was applied in *Thellusson v. Woodford*.[14] Mr. Thellusson had by his will directed that the income of his property should be accumulated during the lives of his sons, grandsons and their issue who were living at his death, and that on the death of the survivor, the accumulated fund should be divided among certain of his descendants. This direction, being confined to lives in being, was held valid. (At that time this was generally regarded as the perpetuity period applicable to the rule against remoteness, the additional period of 21 years not yet having been firmly established.[15]) However, it was calculated that the accumulated fund would amount to many millions of pounds and many of the members of Parliament did not relish either the prospect of Thelluson's descendants potentially becoming as wealthy as the Crown or the fact that the decision entitled their parents to keep them out of the capital which they expected to inherit for their entire lifetimes. Consequently, Parliament intervened

---

[8] *Re Macaulay's Estate* [1943] Ch. 435n; *Re Grant's W.T.* [1980] 1 W.L.R. 360 ("the Labour Party property committee").

[9] See *Re Ray's W.T.* [1936] 2 All E.R. 93 at 97, 98; and see *Leahy v. Att.-Gen. for New South Wales* [1959] A.C. 457 at 477.

[10] *Re Prevost* [1930] 2 Ch. 383 (the London Library); *Re Recher's W.T.* [1972] Ch. 526.

[11] *Re Chardon* [1928] Ch. 464; *Re Wightwick's W.T.* [1950] Ch. 260.

[12] *Chamberlayne v. Brockett* (1872) 8 Ch.App. 206 at 211; contrast the rule against remoteness, above, p. 237.

[13] *Wilson v. Wilson* (1851) 1 Sim. (N.S.) 288 at 298.

[14] (1799) 4 Ves. 227; (1805) 11 Ves. 112.

[15] This did not occur until the decision of the House of Lords in *Cadell v. Palmer* (1833) 1 Cl. & F. 372.

to prevent further directions of this nature by enacting the ill-drafted Accumulations Act 1800 (hence the Act is often called "the Thellusson Act"). In the event that the current proposals of the Law Commission are enacted, this Act will be repealed and the common law rule will be restored, save that the applicable period will become the 125 years which the Law Commission proposes should be the perpetuity period applicable to the rule against remoteness (this will not apply to charitable trusts, where accumulation will still be permitted for only 21 years).

Sect. 1. The statutory periods

1. The periods

The present law is contained in the Law of Property Act 1925,[16] and the Perpetuities and Accumulations Act 1964.[17] If the disposition took effect before July 16, 1964, a direction or power[18] to accumulate may be validly given for any one (but not more) of the following periods:

(i)   the life of the grantor or settlor;

(ii) 21 years from the death of the grantor, settlor or testator;

(iii) the minority or respective minorities of any person or persons living or *en ventre sa mère* at the death of the grantor, settlor or testator;

(iv) the minority or respective minorities only of any person or persons who under the limitations of the instrument directing accumulation would for the time being, if of full age, be entitled to the income directed to be accumulated.

For dispositions taking effect after July 15, 1964, two further periods have been added[19]:

(v)   21 years from the date of the making of the disposition;

(vi) the minority or respective minorities of any person or persons in being at that date.

As has already been mentioned, the Law Commission has proposed that accumulation should be permitted throughout the 125 years which it has proposed as the perpetuity period applicable to the rule against remoteness save in the case of charitable trusts. It is felt that it is not consistent with the public nature of charitable trusts for all income to be withdrawn from the charitable purpose in question for such a long time so a direction to charitable

---

[16] ss.164–166.
[17] ss.13, 14.
[18] *Re Robb* [1953] Ch. 459; Act of 1964, s.13(2). *Re Robb* was disapproved in *Re Earl of Berkeley* [1968] Ch. 744, but not so as to affect this point: *Baird v. Lord Advocate* [1979] A.C. 666 at 675.
[19] Act of 1964, s.13(1).

trustees to accumulate income will be limited to 21 years. The effect of excessive accumulations, which are discussed below, will remain the same as at present.

2. Choice of periods

Under the present law the question which period has been chosen in each particular case is one of construction.[20] The first two and the fifth periods cause little difficulty. Of the first, it should be noted that it is the only period of a life available for accumulation, and that it must be the life of the grantor or settlor himself and not of some third person. The second period is a fixed term of years which starts to run at the beginning of the day after the testator's death and expires at the end of the twenty-first anniversary of his death.[21] Thus if a testator directs accumulations to start at the end of an interval after his death and continue for 21 years, he exceeds the second period. The second period was of little use save in wills. Now, the fifth period allows the 21 years to run from the date of the settlement.

The third, fourth and sixth periods are all minorities. Minority now ends at the age of 18.[22] The periods differ in the following respects.

(i) The third and sixth periods are confined to the minorities of persons alive or *en ventre sa mère* at the death of the grantor, settlor or testator, or at the date of the settlement, as the case may be. The fourth period is not.

(ii) The third and sixth periods are not restricted to the minorities of those who are prospectively entitled to any benefit under the gift, whereas the fourth period is confined to the minorities of those who can say "but for my minority I would be entitled to the income being accumulated".[23]

(iii) The third and sixth periods can never exceed a single minority; for even if accumulation is directed during a large number of minorities, the period is in effect merely the longest of these minorities. Under the fourth period, on the other hand, accumulation during successive minorities is possible.

An example may make this clear.[24] A testator devises the residue of his property between all the children of his sons, whether born before or after his death, the income of their shares to be accumulated during their respective minorities. At the testator's death, there is only one child of his sons alive, and she is a minor named D. The whole of the income must be accumulated during this minority, the direction to accumulate falling within the fourth period; for if she was of full age she would for the time being be entitled to the whole of the income. After D attains her majority, a child, C, is born to one of the testator's sons. C becomes entitled to one half of the estate, subject to the same liability, *i.e.* that his share may be partially divested by the birth of other children. During the minority of C, the income from his share must be accumulated, even though the income from the whole of the residuary estate has already been accumulated once. If D had not been born until after the testator's

---

[20] *Jagger v. Jagger* (1883) 25 Ch.D. 729.

[21] *Gorst v. Lowndes* (1841) 11 Sim. 434.

[22] Family Law Reform Act 1969, s.1. The period of 21 years in the second and fifth periods is not affected, nor is the validity of directions for accumulation in dispositions made before 1970 with reference to the previous period of minority ending at the age of 21.

[23] *Jagger v. Jagger* (1883) 25 Ch.D. 729 at 733, as corrected in *Re Cattell* [1914] 1 Ch. 177 at 189.

[24] See *Re Cattell* [1914] 1 Ch. 177.

death, there could have been no accumulation under the fourth period until her birth, for not until then would her minority have commenced.

3. Purchase of land

Where after June 27, 1892, accumulation is directed for the sole purpose of purchasing land, only the fourth period may be selected. But this restriction does not apply to accumulations to be held as capital money under the Settled Land Act 1925 or any of the Acts which it replaced.[25]

4. Ambit of rules

These rules apply whether the limitations are contained in a deed or a will, whether the accumulation is at compound or, it seems, merely simple interest,[26] and whether it is the whole or merely part of the income of a fund that is to be accumulated.[27] Yet there is no accumulation if income is merely retained to meet possible future deficiencies in the income required for paying annuities, and is not added to capital.[28]

Sect. 2. Excessive accumulation

1. Exceeding perpetuity period

If the period for which accumulation is directed may exceed the perpetuity period, the direction to accumulate is totally void, such as where accumulation was directed until a lease with over 60 years to run had "nearly expired".[29] This applies even to accumulations for the benefit of charities.[30] The "wait and see" provisions of the Act of 1964 apply to a power to accumulate but not, it seems, to a direction to accumulate, unless, perhaps, the direction can be treated as being a power that is subject to a duty to exercise it.[31]

2. Exceeding accumulation period

If the period for which accumulation is directed cannot exceed the perpetuity period but exceeds the relevant accumulation period, the direction to accumulate is good *pro tanto*, and only the excess over the appropriate accumulation period is void; the statutory provisions are merely restrictive of the wider powers formerly enjoyed.[32]

Which is the appropriate period depends on the circumstances.[33] Thus, where accumulation is directed for the lifetime of any person (other than the settlor in the case of an *inter vivos* settlement), accumulation will take place for 21 years from the date of the settlement or, as the case may be, from the testator's death, if the named person so long lives.[34] This uses

---

[25] L.P.A. 1925, s.166; see above, p. 90.
[26] See *Re Garside* [1919] 1 Ch. 132.
[27] *Re Travis* [1900] 2 Ch. 541.
[28] *Re Earl of Berkeley* [1968] Ch. 744.
[29] *Curtis v. Lukin* (1842) 5 Beav. 147.
[30] *Re Bradwell* [1952] Ch. 575.
[31] s.3(3).
[32] *Leake v. Robinson* (1817) 2 Mer. 363 at 389.
[33] See *Re Ransome* [1957] Ch. 348 at 361.
[34] *Griffiths v. Vere* (1803) 9 Ves. 127. In the case of a settlement inter vivos made before July 16, 1964, the first period was the most appropriate, and accumulation continued during the period common to the lives of the settlor and the named person: *Re Lady Rosslyn's Trust* (1848) 16 Sim. 391.

the second or fifth period, and these periods are also the most appropriate whenever accumulation is directed for a period of years. The same applies where accumulation is directed until X is 25,[35] or from the time Y remarries until her death,[36] or from the death of either A or B until the death of the survivor. In each of these cases, if accumulation is still continuing 21 years after the date of the settlement or the death of the testator, it must cease forthwith, even if it has been proceeding for only a short period, for example two years.[37]

Again, if property is given by will to all the children of X (a living person) who attain their majority, and accumulation of the whole fund is directed while any child of X is a minor, the first two periods are clearly not intended and the fourth is not appropriate, for the accumulation is directed to continue for as long as any child is a minor, even if some of the children are 18; the latter children, though of full age, are not entitled to the income to be accumulated within the wording of the fourth period. Consequently the third period is the most appropriate, and so far as it is exceeded the direction is void; accumulation will therefore cease as soon as all children living at the testator's death are 18.[38]

3. Surplus income

The income for any period during which accumulation is invalidly directed passes to the person who would have been entitled had no excessive accumulation been directed.[39] Thus if there is a gift of a vested interest subject only to an excessive trust for accumulation, the vested interest will carry any income not validly accumulated. For example, where property is given by will to X, subject to a direction that the income exceeding a certain figure is to be accumulated during X's life for the benefit of Y, the accumulation must cease 21 years after the testator's death, and the surplus income will go to X.[40] But otherwise, the income reverts to the settlor or his estate, or in the case of a gift by will, passes under any residuary gift, or, in default, to the persons entitled on intestacy.[41]

Sect. 3. The rule in *Saunders v. Vautier*

Under the rule in *Saunders v. Vautier*,[42] a beneficiary of full age who has an absolute indefeasible interest in property may at any time, notwithstanding any direction to accumulate, require the transfer of the property to him and terminate any accumulation; a man may do as he likes with his own, and the same applies to a charity.[43] Thus if property is given to A with a direction to accumulate the income for his benefit until he is 24, A can demand payment of both the original property and the accumulations as soon as he is of full age.[44] The rule applies, however, only if the beneficiary or beneficiaries seeking to put an end to the accumulation together comprise every person who has any vested or contingent interest in the property.[45] Thus it will not apply if there is a gift to a class of persons or charities not yet

---

[35] *Crawley v. Crawley* (1835) 7 Sim. 427.
[36] *Weatherell v. Thornburgh* (1878) 8 Ch.D. 261.
[37] *Shaw v. Rhodes* (1836) 1 My. & Cr. 135.
[38] *Re Watts' W.T.* [1936] 2 All E.R. 1555.
[39] L.P.A 1925, s.164.
[40] *Trickey v. Trickey* (1832) 3 My. & Cr. 560. See also *Brotherton v. I.R.C.* [1978] 1 W.L.R. 610.
[41] *Mathews v. Keble* (1867) L.R. 4 Eq. 467 at 473, 474 (affirmed 3 Ch.App. 691).
[42] (1841) 4 Beav. 115; affirmed Cr. & Ph. 240.
[43] *Wharton v. Masterman* [1895] A.C. 186; contrast *Re Levy* [1960] Ch. 346.
[44] *Josselyn v. Josselyn* (1837) 9 Sim. 63. A took at 21; today he would take at 18.
[45] *Berry v. Geen* [1938] A.C. 575.

determined, or to beneficiaries whose interests are contingent or liable to be defeated by some event occurring.

Sect. 4. Exceptions from the rule against accumulations

The rule against accumulations does not apply in the following cases.[46]

1. Payment of debts

Payment of debts is a provision for accumulation for the payment of the debts of any person,[47] whether the settlor, testator or anyone else.[48] An accumulation for the payment of the debts of the settlor or testator is valid even if it may exceed the perpetuity period[49]; such a direction can cause little mischief, for the creditors may terminate the accumulation at any time by demanding payment. But an accumulation to pay the debts of any other person must be confined within the perpetuity period. This exception includes all debts, whether existing or contingent, provided the accumulation is directed bona fide for their payment; thus it extends to accumulations to discharge a mortgage or to provide for liability under a leasehold covenant not yet broken.[50] It does not extend to debts not in existence when the instrument directing accumulation took effect, such as estate duty or inheritance tax payable on the death of a tenant for life.[51]

2. Portions

This is a provision for accumulation for raising portions (lump sums) for any issue of the grantor, settlor or testator or any person to whom an interest is limited under the settlement.[52] This is an exception from the rule against accumulations only; such accumulations must be confined to the perpetuity period. The meaning of "portions" here is not clear. It is not confined to sums raised out of real estate, nor to provisions for the benefit of the younger children of a marriage.[53] It does not, however, apply where there is no existing obligation to use the fund for portions but a mere future discretionary power,[54] nor where the direction is to accumulate the income from the whole of a testator's estate, for "it is not raising a portion at all, it is giving everything."[55]

3. Timber or wood

This is a provision for accumulating the produce of timber or wood.[56] Although excepted from the accumulation rules, such a direction will be void if it exceeds the perpetuity period.[57]

---

[46] See L.P.A. 1925, ss.164, 165.

[47] *ibid.*, s.164.

[48] *Viscount Barrington v. Liddell* (1852) 2 De G.M. & G. 480.

[49] *Bateman v. Hotchkin* (1847) 10 Beav. 426.

[50] *Re Hurlbatt* [1910] 2 Ch. 553.

[51] *Re Rochford's S.T.* [1965] Ch. 111.

[52] L.P.A. 1925, s.164; see also below, p. 247.

[53] *Re Stephens* [1904] 1 Ch. 322.

[54] *Re Bourne's S.T.* [1946] 1 All E.R. 411.

[55] *Edwards v. Tuck* (1853) 3 De G.M. & G. 40 at 58, *per* Lord Cranworth L.C.

[56] L.P.A. 1925, s.164. This exception is said to be due to the need for naval timber in 1800.

[57] *Ferrand v. Wilson* (1845) 4 Hare 344.

4. Maintenance of property

This is a provision for maintaining property at its present value. Directions to devote surplus income to maintaining buildings in a proper state of repair, or to apply a fixed annual sum to keep up an insurance policy to replace the capital lost by not selling leaseholds, are outside the rule against accumulations. Although income is added to capital, the payments are merely to keep up the property and not add to it, so that there is no true accumulation.[58] But they must be confined to the perpetuity period.[59]

5. Minority

This refers to accumulations made during a minority under the general law or any statutory power. While the person entitled to any trust property is a minor, a statutory power is given to the trustees to apply the income for his maintenance; subject thereto, they are bound to accumulate the residue of the income.[60] It is expressly provided that the period of such accumulation is to be disregarded when determining the period for which accumulations are permitted.[61] Thus, if a testator directs accumulation for 21 years after his death and the beneficiary at the end of the period is a minor, the accumulations both for the 21 years and during the minority are valid.[62]

6. Certain commercial contracts

This refers to transactions which cannot fairly be described as settlements or dispositions. Many commercial transactions involve a measure of accumulation, such as partnership agreements which provide for the accumulation of certain profits, and investment trusts which capitalise part of their income. Such transactions are outside the Act,[63] which merely provides that no person may "settle or dispose" of property in breach of the Act.[64] Many of them are also outside the perpetuity rule as creating merely personal obligations.

7. Corporations

With regard to settlements made by a corporation, the statute applies only to natural persons and not to corporations.[65]

---

[58] *Vine v. Raleigh* [1891] 2 Ch. 13; *Re Gardiner* [1901] 1 Ch. 697.
[59] *Curtis v. Lukin* (1842) 5 Beav. 147.
[60] T.A. 1925, s.31.
[61] L.P.A. 1925, s.165.
[62] *Re Maber* [1928] Ch. 88.
[63] See *Bassil v. Lister* (1851) 9 Hare 177 at 184; *Re A.E.G. Unit Trust (Managers) Ltd's Deed* [1957] Ch. 415.
[64] L.P.A. 1925, s.164(1).
[65] *Re Dodwell & Co. Ltd's Trust* [1979] Ch. 301.

Chapter 7

SETTLEMENTS

PART 1—BEFORE 1926

It is now necessary to turn from matters of substance to matters of machinery. The last chapter discussed the rules regulating the various future interests in land which can be created, and this chapter will examine how land which is the subject of future interests is managed and disposed of. The starting point is to consider settlements.

When two or more persons are beneficially entitled to land (or for that matter to pure personalty) in succession, that is to say one after another, the property in question is said to be subject to a settlement (the simplest possible example of a settlement is where a testator leaves his property to his wife for life and subject to that to his children equally). Historically, settlements were most often made on the occasion of a marriage, providing for the spouses and the future issue of the marriage by giving the property to the husband for life, with remainders to the children in order of seniority for an estate in fee tail subject to the payment to the wife of an annual sum. But not all settlements were marriage settlements and today few are. For most purposes it can be taken that a settlement exists whenever future interests in property have been created.

By the middle of the nineteenth century two methods of settling land were firmly established: these were what was then known as the strict settlement and the trust for sale.

Sect. 1. The strict settlement

1. Principal provisions

A strict settlement was the type of settlement employed "to keep land in the family". Provided that the various rules of law and equity were observed, the settlor might create such limitations as he thought fit; but the type of settlement most frequently encountered was the marriage settlement, giving a life interest to the husband and estates in fee tail to the children in order of seniority. Provision was also made for the wife by giving her a jointure (an annual income during widowhood), and for the younger children whose estate in fee tail never vested in possession by giving them portions (lump sums of money to assist them in their careers and in matrimony). This form of settlement was adopted because it made provision for all the members of the family and yet preserved the land as a unit. The device of giving the husband a mere life estate with remainder to his son for an estate in fee tail (the son, of course, being unborn at the time of the settlement, which was made shortly before the marriage) was adopted as being the best way of keeping the land in the family. If an estate in fee tail had been given to the husband, he could at once have converted it into an estate in fee simple by barring it; and under what eventually became known as the rule in *Whitby v. Mitchell*,[1] a succession of life estates to the husband, his son, the son's son and so on was invalid after the first gift to an unborn person.

2. Alienation

(a) Settlement and resettlement

The effect of such a settlement was to render the land substantially inalienable until the eldest son became able to bar the estate in fee tail on attaining his majority. Shortly after the son's twenty-first birthday he was usually persuaded (often by some financial inducement) to bar the estate in fee tail with his father's consent; the land was then resettled on the husband for life, remainder to the son for life, remainder to the son's son for an estate in fee tail. The land was thus tied up for another generation. This process of settlement and resettlement prevented any person of full age from having more than a life estate; and the tenant in possession of the land was always a tenant for life. The tenant for life could alienate his life estate, but that was all; no matter how desirable or necessary it was, he had no power to sell the estate in fee simple in any part of the land, or to grant leases which would be binding after his death. If improvements to the property were required, he could effect them only if he paid for them out of his own pocket. Unless he was unimpeachable of waste,[2] the discovery of valuable minerals beneath the land was of little importance to him, for he could not open mines; and even if he was unimpeachable of waste, he could not grant mining leases with an adequate security of tenure for the lessee. In short, for many purposes the land was sterilised.

(b) Powers in settlement

These defects were frequently met by a series of provisions in the settlement. Many powers were given to the tenant for life, such as powers to grant specified leases which would be binding on his successors. He was also empowered to sell the estate in fee simple provided that the purchase money was paid to trustees to hold on the trusts of the settlement; his own rights and the rights of his son and the other beneficiaries were thus overreached.[3] Usually the bulk of the land would be retained and not sold, but a power of sale was useful for emergencies.

(c) Legal estate

The legal estate in settled land might be either split up between the beneficiaries or vested in trustees, according to the way in which the settlement was made. For example, a conveyance "to T and his heirs to the use of A for life, remainder to B and the heirs of his body, remainder to C and his heirs" gave A a legal life estate, B a legal estate in fee tail and C a legal estate in fee simple, the uses in their favour being executed under the Statute of Uses 1535. If the gift to T and his heirs had instead been worded "unto and to the use of T and his heirs in trust

---

[1] (1890) 44 Ch.D. 85.
[2] Above, p. 48.
[3] Above, p. 5.

for A for life . . .", the Statute of Uses 1535 would have executed only the first use in favour of Y and his heirs. Consequently, the legal estate in fee simple would have been in T, and A, B and C would have had merely equitable interests. In the first case, the settlement conferred the desired powers upon A by means of legal powers also executed under the Statute of Uses 1535; the settlement took effect as if the land had been given to A for life and then, subject to such sales, leases and other authorised dealings as A made, to B for an estate in fee tail with remainder to C for an estate in fee simple. In the second case, the powers conferred upon A would be merely equitable, but T was bound to give effect to any authorised disposition made by A, and the court would compel him to create or transfer the necessary legal estate.[4]

(d) Absence of powers

Although it was thus possible for a settlement to provide the necessary powers, in many cases this was not done, especially where the settlement was made by will. In such cases the land could not be dealt with unless the expense of obtaining a private Act of Parliament was incurred. Further, even if the powers were inserted, difficulties sometimes arose over the construction to be put upon them; and in any case the deed or will creating the settlement became of formidable length.

3. Intervention of statute

This position was dealt with by a series of statutes passed in the nineteenth century. Starting with Acts such as the Settled Estates Drainage Acts 1840 and 1845 which contained certain limited improvements, the legislature proceeded to enact the Settled Estates Acts 1856 and 1877, which enabled the court to authorise a number of dealings, and even enabled the tenant for life to grant certain leases without application to the court. These comparatively timid measures remained the law until the enactment of the Settled Land Act 1882, which was passed as the result of a period of agricultural depression and had as its paramount object the well-being of settled land. "The leading purpose of the Legislature was to prevent the decay of agricultural and other interests occasioned by the deterioration of lands and buildings in the possession of impecunious life-tenants."[5] The general scheme of the Act was to give the tenant for life under the settlement wide powers of dealing with the land free from the limitations of the settlement without making any application to the court, and to protect the rights of the beneficiaries in the case of a sale by shifting the settlement from the land to the purchase money, which had to be paid into court or into the hands of the trustees. A purchaser was not concerned with the rights of the beneficiaries, even if he had full knowledge of them; those rights were not destroyed, but, being overreached, were transformed from rights in the land to rights in the money paid for it. This Act formed the basis of the current legislation, the Settled Land Act 1925. However, that legislation governs only settlements created before 1997; no further settlements thereunder can now be created.[6]

---

[4] See *Re Brown* (1886) 32 Ch.D. 597 at 601.
[5] *Bruce v. Marquess of Ailesbury* [1892] A.C. 356 at 363, *per* Lord Watson.
[6] T.L.A.T.A. 1996, s.2(1).

Sect. 2. Trusts for sale

1. Origin

Compared with strict settlements, settlements by way of trust for sale are of comparatively recent origin.[7] It is true that trusts for sale created by will can be traced back for some 500 years, but most of the earliest of these trusts seem to have been designed to raise sums of money, for example for the payment of debts, rather than to provide for persons by way of succession. Trusts for sale created *inter vivos* are more recent in origin; it was less than 200 years ago that marriage settlements by way of trust for sale appear to have become at all common. The purpose of such trusts for sale usually differed greatly from that of a strict settlement. Where the property to be settled was a family estate on which the beneficiaries would reside and over which the tenant for life would wish to exercise direct control, the settlor usually employed a strict settlement which would keep the land in the family. Where, however, the property was in the nature of an investment, such as a row of shops, there would be no desire to keep it in the family in any particular form, nor would the tenant for life wish to live on it or manage it. In such cases, a trust for sale would be employed, the primary object of such a settlement being to produce a regular income for the beneficiaries.

2. Retention unsold

For these reasons, in a trust for sale the legal estate was vested in the trustees upon trust to sell the land and hold the income until sale and the proceeds thereafter upon specified trusts for the beneficiaries. The trustees were usually given power to postpone sale in their discretion, and to manage the land until sale. Thus as long as the land produced a satisfactory income, it could be retained, and the trustees did not have to sell until market conditions made an advantageous sale possible. Often the consent of the beneficiaries entitled in possession was made a prerequisite of any sale. And the purchase money arising on any sale was usually directed to be invested in stocks, shares and other securities.

3. Conversion

The effect of creating a trust for sale was that even before sale, the rights of the beneficiaries were deemed to be rights in personalty. Equity treated that as done which ought to be done, and since there was a binding obligation to sell the land sooner or later, the beneficiaries were treated as having forthwith interests in the purchase money into which the land was to be converted: this is known as the equitable doctrine of conversion. For this reason, trusts for sale were often referred to as "personalty settlements", in common with settlements of stocks and shares and other personal property; and the doctrine (which has in this respect now been abolished[8]) had important consequences, not least in relation to wills.[9] They were also sometimes called "traders' settlements", since they were more appropriate to the urban property of business men than the rural estates of the landed gentry.

---

[7] See generally (1927) 3 Camb. L.J. 59 (J.M. Lightwood).
[8] T.L.A.T.A. 1996, s.3.
[9] Below, p. 283.

PART 2—THE SETTLED LAND ACT 1925

Sect. 1. Introduction

The Settled Land Act 1925 governs those settlements created before 1997 which fell within the definition of settled land contained therein. Such settlements are better described as settlements under the Settled Land Act 1925 than strict settlements because the definition in that Act was broad enough to catch a number of arrangements which were not intended to have created settlements at all, never mind strict settlements. No further settlements under the Settled Land Act 1925 have been able to be created since 1996 since settlements created thereafter which fall within the definition of settled land instead take effect as trusts of land.[10] Existing settlements continue until no land or personal chattels, usually heirlooms, settled so as to devolve with it are subject to the settlement or until those settlements cease to fall within the definition of settled land as a result, for example, of the death of a life tenant and the vesting in possession of the interests of remaindermen who are absolutely beneficially entitled.

It should be noted that, in respect of this legislation, the term "settlement" sometimes means the documents by which the land was settled, but more usually means the state of affairs resulting from them[11]; the context usually indicates which.

The basic structure of a settlement under the Settled Land Act 1925 is that the legal estate in the settled land is virtually always[12] vested in the person interested in possession under the settlement for the time being; this person is described in the Act as "the tenant for life", whether or not his beneficial interest is actually a life interest. Only in two exceptional circumstances discussed below is the legal estate vested not in the tenant for life but in a person or persons described as "the statutory owner", usually but not always, the trustees of the settlement. Consequently, on the creation of the settlement, the legal estate in the settled land had to be conveyed to the tenant for life or to the statutory owner, unless, of course, it was already vested in the tenant for life,[13] as would be the case where the owner of property settled it upon himself as tenant for life, with remainders over. ("With remainders over" is a concise way of referring to the remainders following the life interest without setting them out in detail.) The legal estate did not have to be so vested before 1926 but, in the case of pre-1926 strict settlements, the legal estate in the settled land was automatically vested in the tenant for life or statutory owner at the first moment of 1926.[14]

The tenant for life has wide and unfettered powers of sale, exchange, leasing, mortgaging and otherwise dealing with the settled land. Those beneficially entitled under the settlement other than the tenant for life are protected by the fact that:

(1) the tenant for life is a trustee for those beneficiaries;

(2) in the case of the most important powers, the tenant for life must give notice to the trustees of his intention to exercise them;

---

[10] T.L.A.T.A. 1996, s.2(1).
[11] See *Re Spencer's S.E.* [1903] 1 Ch. 75 at 79; *Re Ogle's S.E.* [1927] 1 Ch. 229 at 233.
[12] For the two exceptions, see below.
[13] S.L.A. 1925, s.4.
[14] L.P.A. 1925, Sched. 1, Pt. II, para.6.

(3) in a few exceptional cases the tenant for life must not exercise his powers without the leave of the trustees or an order of the court; and

(4) the other party to any transaction entered into with the tenant for life which gives rise to the payment of capital moneys will only obtain a title free from the interests of the other beneficiaries if he pays those moneys to the trustees of the settlement and so enables their beneficial interests to be overreached.

Sect. 2. The essentials of settled land

The three essential points which have to be considered are therefore:

(1) whether the land is settled land;

(2) who is the tenant for life; and

(3) who are the trustees.

1. Definition of settled land

(a) "Settlement"

Before 1997 land was settled land if "it is or is deemed to be the subject of a settlement".[15] A settlement under the Settled Land Act 1925 was any deed, will, agreement, Act of Parliament[16] or other instrument (including, it seems, an order of the court[17]) or any number of instruments whereby one of the following requirements was satisfied.[18]

(i) Succession: The land stood limited in trust for any persons by way of succession. In addition to cases such as limitations "to A for life, remainder to B in fee simple", this definition seems to be wide enough to have covered the following cases which are somewhat superfluously set out in the section as independent heads, namely, where land was limited in trust for any person in possession:

(i) for an entailed interest, whether or not capable of being barred or defeated;

(ii) for an estate in fee simple or for a term of years absolute subject to an executory gift over (such as a devise to trustees in trust for "A in fee simple but for B in fee simple when B marries");

(iii) for a base or determinable fee, including a fee determinable by condition, or any corresponding interest in leasehold land;

or where:

(iv) land was limited in trust for any person for an estate in fee simple or for a term of years absolute contingently on the happening of an event (such as a devise to trustees in trust for X in fee simple if his brothers die under the age of 21 years).

[15] *ibid.*, s.2.
[16] See, *e.g. Re Lord Hereford's S.E.* [1932] W.N. 34.
[17] See below, pp. 253–254.
[18] S.L.A. 1925, s.1.

In all these cases there is an element of succession sufficient to satisfy the definition in (i). Thus if S settled land upon trust for X for an estate in fee tail, the land stood limited in trust for persons by way of succession and the limitations arose under the settlement; for any estate or interest not disposed of under the settlement and remaining in or reverting to the settlor or anyone deriving title under him was deemed to arise under the settlement, with the consequence that S's fee simple reversion upon X's estate in fee tail was deemed to arise under the settlement.[19]

(ii) Minors: The land stood limited in trust for a minor in possession for an estate in fee simple or for a term of years absolute.

(iii) Family charges: The land stood charged, whether voluntarily or in consideration of marriage or by way of family arrangement, with the payment of any sums for the benefit of any persons.

(b) "Limited in trust"

It will be seen that under heads **(i)** (succession) and **(ii)** (minors), but not **(iii)** (family charges), it was necessary for the land to be "limited in trust" if it was to fall within the definition; if there was no trust, or if the trust was an immediate binding trust for sale,[20] the land was not settled land. In all cases where property was given by will, there was necessarily a trust for the beneficiaries by reason of the legal estate first vesting in the testator's personal representatives. Where the disposition was made *inter vivos* it would be made either:

(i) by a proper vesting deed and trust instrument, whereupon the legal estate vested in the tenant for life as trustee, or

(ii) by a single instrument, in which case the legal estate would remain in the settlor and only an equitable interest would be transferred; for none of the interests mentioned in **(i)** was capable of existing at law (except, it seems, a fee simple determinable by condition[21] where the right of entry was equitable), and in **(ii)**, by reason of a minor's inability after 1925 to hold a legal estate in land, no legal estate passed. Consequently, on the principle that there is a trust if the legal estate is in one person and the equitable interest in another, the grantor would hold the land in trust even without any express limitation in trust.[22]

Under head **(iii)**, no limitation by way of trust was required. Whether the estate which is subject to family charges was conveyed directly to the beneficiary or whether it was held in trust for the beneficiary, the land was nevertheless settled land.

(c) Licences and equities

Sometimes a person is given the right to occupy or reside in property rent free for his life. Prior to 1997 if this gave him a life interest, and it had been given to him under a "settlement", he would be tenant for life under the Settled Land Act 1925 and have the extensive powers that that Act confers. But if the gift was construed as giving him a mere

---

[19] See *Re Hunter and Hewlett's Contract* [1907] 1 Ch. 46.
[20] See below, p. 279.
[21] See above, p. 41.
[22] See *Griffiths v. Williams* [1977] E.G.D. 919 at 926.

licence or permission to reside not amounting to an interest in land, he would not be tenant for life or have those powers.[23] At one time distinctions were made between a mere permission to reside in a house for life and the grant of a right to occupy it for life; and only in the latter case was there a life interest.[24] As will be seen,[25] the borderline between licence and tenancy is far from clear, and the policy of the courts was not to restrict the class of persons who constituted tenants for life within the Act.[26] The tendency was thus to construe such limitations as creating tenancies for life within the Act.[27] Thus when V conveyed a cottage to P on the oral understanding (duly reflected in the price) that V could occupy the cottage rent free for life, V was held to be a tenant for life under a constructive trust who fell within the Settled Land Act 1925.[28] The result was similar when under an agreement in writing an employer permitted an employee's widow to occupy a cottage rent free for life, a purchaser from the employer agreeing (at a reduced price) to take the cottage subject to the widow's right of occupation.[29]

In these cases little or no attention appears to have been given to whether there was a "settlement", nor whether an oral "agreement" could be one.[30] While an order of the court might suffice as evidence of a binding agreement which constitutes a "settlement",[31] it never became clear whether in cases of proprietary estoppel[32] the order itself could be a "settlement" if it gave the claimant a life interest as the resolution of his claim.[33] The fear that to give the claimant a life interest would confer on him all the powers of a tenant for life as well, and so give him more extensive rights than the court considered just, on at least one occasion induced the court to give him some other relief instead.[34] Previous editions of this work[35] considered it probable that the definition of a "settlement" would be held to include an order of the court. It is highly unlikely that this point will now ever have to be resolved.

(d) Family Charges

For a settlement to arise under this head, all that was required was that the sum of money in question should have been charged on the land either voluntarily, or in consideration of marriage, or by way of family arrangement; the Act did not apply if the charge was created for money or money's worth, as where a tenant in fee simple sold his land and took a charge on it as part of the price. But subject to this requirement, it was immaterial whether the provision was present or future, whether it was for capital or annual sums, or whether it was for a limited period (such as for life) or in perpetuity. Thus if a testator devised land to

---

[23] *Griffiths v. Williams* [1978] E.G.D. 919 at 925, 926.

[24] See *Parker v. Parker* (1863) 1 N.R. 508; *May v. May* (1881) 44 L.T. 412.

[25] See below, pp. 340, 475.

[26] See *Re Baroness Llanover's Will* [1903] 2 Ch. 16 at 24.

[27] *Re Carne's S.E.* [1899] 1 Ch. 324; *Re Baroness Llanover's Will* [1903] 2 Ch. 16; and see *Re Boyer's S.E.* [1916] 2 Ch. 404; *Re Gibbons* [1920] 1 Ch. 372 at 377. Contrast *Morss v. Morss* [1972] Fam. 204.

[28] *Bannister v. Bannister* [1948] 2 All E.R. 133; and see *Ungurian v. Lesnoff* [1990] Ch. 206.

[29] *Binions v. Evans* [1972] Ch. 359, a case that "stretched to the very limit" the application of the Act: *Ivory v. Palmer* [1975] I.C.R. 340 at 347, *per* Cairns L.J. On these cases, see generally (1977) 93 L.Q.R. 561 (J.A. Hornby).

[30] See *Griffiths v. Williams* [1977] E.G.D. 919 at 925, 926. The words "agreement . . . or other instrument" in S.L.A. 1925, s.1(1) look unpromising.

[31] *Bacon v. Bacon* [1947] P. 151 at 158.

[32] See above, p. 69; below, p. 483.

[33] Consider *Morss v. Morss* [1972] Fam. 264.

[34] *Dodsworth v. Dodsworth* [1973] E.G.D. 233.

[35] See 7th ed., p. 236.

trustees on trust to pay a perpetual annuity to X, and subject thereto on trust for A in fee simple, the land became settled land.[36]

(i) Resulting inconvenience: Prior to 1926 a settlement only arose under this head if the sum of money itself was limited to persons by way of succession. Consequently, the effect of the Settled Land Act 1925 was that at the beginning of 1926 much land which had previously not been settled land was forthwith converted into settled land. In a number of cases this caused hardship to those who had purchased such land before 1926. The practice in such cases had been that, unless the land could be freed from the charges (as by the owners of the charges all releasing them in return for a share of the purchase money), the vendor conveyed the land to the purchaser subject to the charges but with an indemnity against them, *i.e.* the vendor agreed to pay the charges himself and so ensure that they would not be enforced against the land. In cases where this had been done, the astonished purchaser found (if, indeed, he could understand the matter at all) that at the beginning of 1926 his land had become settled land and that it could be sold only after compliance with the troublesome Settled Land Act procedure which, as will be seen later, required the appointment of trustees and the execution of a vesting deed.

(ii) Means of escape: To meet this situation, the Law of Property (Amendment) Act 1926, s.1, provided that where a person of full age is beneficially entitled in possession to land in fee simple or for a term of years absolute subject to charges of this kind, he can nevertheless create or convey a legal estate subject to the charges in the same way as if the land were not settled land. This applies whether the charges arose before 1926 or after 1925, and whether the person entitled to the land is the tenant under the settlement or a purchaser from him; but it applies only if the sole reason for the land being deemed settled land is that it is subject to the charges and not, for example, when it is also the subject-matter of an estate in fee tail. Where the Amendment Act applies, a vendor may thus sell the land either (i) free from the charges, by making use of the Settled Land Act procedure, or (ii) subject to the charges, by virtue of the Amendment Act.

2. Definition of tenant for life

(a) Tenant for life

The Settled Land Act 1925[37] gives an elaborate definition of "tenant for life". The definition includes not only a person entitled to a life interest but also a tenant in fee tail, a tenant in fee simple subject to a gift over or to family charges, a tenant for years terminable on life (unless at a rent[38]), a tenant *pur autre vie*, and a person entitled to the income of land for his own or any other life.

In addition to falling within the above category, a person must also be of full age and beneficially entitled in possession.[39] Thus a trustee for another person, or somebody who is entitled only to a future interest in the land, cannot be a tenant for life under the Act. The practical effect of the definition is that where there is some person of full age beneficially entitled to either the possession of settled land or the whole of the income from it, that person

---

[36] *Re Austen* [1929] 2 Ch. 155.
[37] ss.19, 20.
[38] *Re Catling* [1931] 2 Ch. 359.
[39] *Re Morgan* (1883) 24 Ch.D. 114 at 116; *Re Jemmett and Guest's Contract* [1907] 1 Ch. 629.

will be the tenant for life. The position where two or more persons are thus entitled jointly or in common is dealt with later.[40]

(b) Where the tenant for life is an infant

A legal estate cannot be vested in a minor after 1925 and it was undesirable to give him the statutory powers. Consequently, where the tenant for life was a minor the legal estate and the statutory powers were vested in the statutory owner, consisting of:

(i) a personal representative if the land was vested in him and no vesting instrument[41] had been executed, such as where the settlement had been made by the will of a testator who had just died; but otherwise

(ii) the trustees of the settlement.

(c) Cases where there was no tenant for life

Although there would normally be a tenant for life under the above provisions, there were some cases where there was no tenant for life, as where land was given to trustees on trust to pay X a fixed annuity[42] or a definite fraction of the income,[43] with a direction to accumulate the balance, or where there was an immediate discretionary trust, such as a direction to trustees to pay the income to such one or more members of a class of persons as they thought fit, no member being entitled as of right to any of the income.[44] In these cases the legal estate and statutory powers were in the statutory owner, consisting of:

(i) any person of full age upon whom the settlement expressly conferred the powers; if none,

(ii) the trustees of the settlement.

3. Definition of trustees of the settlement

The trustees of the settlement are defined by section 30 of the Settled Land Act 1925. There are five heads, which had to be applied in turn; thus if there were any trustees under one head, they excluded any under a subsequent head. The definition is as follows:

(i) The persons who, under the settlement, were trustees with power to sell the land (even if this power was subject to the consent of anyone) or with power of consenting to or approving the exercise of a power of sale.

For example, if in a settlement on A for life, with remainders over, there was a trust giving X and Y a general[45] power to sell the land, this would make them trustees of the settlement, in preference even to any other persons expressly appointed Settled Land Act trustees. X and Y would in fact have had no power to sell the land for, as will be seen,[46] this power would

---

[40] Below, p. 326.
[41] For vesting instruments, see below, p. 258.
[42] *Re Jefferys (No. 2)* [1939] Ch. 205.
[43] *Re Frewen* [1926] Ch. 580.
[44] *Re Gallenga's W.T.* [1938] 1 All E.R. 106.
[45] See *Re Carne's S.E.* [1899] 1 Ch. 324.
[46] Below, p. 275.

have been taken away from them and given to the tenant for life. Nevertheless, the attempt to give them the power sufficed to make them trustees of the settlement.

(ii) The persons declared by the settlement to be trustees thereof for the purposes of the Settled Land Acts 1882 to 1890, or 1925, or any of them.

This is the head under which the trustees of the settlement would usually have been found, for cases under head (i) were rare. It was not sufficient to appoint X and Y "trustees of the settlement"[47]: the appointment would be ineffective unless words such as "for the purposes of the Settled Land Act 1925" were added.

(iii) Persons who, under the settlement, are trustees with power of sale or of consenting to or approving a sale, or upon trust for sale, of other land held under the same settlement and upon the same trusts.

(iv) Persons who, under the settlement, are trustees with a future power of sale, or under a future trust for sale, or with a power of consenting to or approving the exercise of such a future power of sale, even if the power or trust does not take effect in all events.

Thus if there was a settlement of Greenacre and Brownacre which gave trustees a power of sale over Greenacre alone, clause (iii) made those trustees Settled Land Act trustees of both properties.[48] Again, if Redacre was settled on A for life with remainder to X and Y on trust for sale, clause (iv) made X and Y Settled Land Act trustees.[49]

(v) The persons appointed by deed by those able to dispose of the whole equitable interest in the settled land.

For example, if land was settled on A for life, remainder to B in fee tail, remainder to C in fee simple, A and B between them could dispose of the whole equitable interest in the land by barring the estate in fee tail, and so they could appoint trustees of the settlement.[50]

Where a settlement arose under a will or intestacy and there were no trustees under any other provisions, the personal representatives of the deceased were trustees of the settlement until other trustees were appointed.[51] This useful provision dealt with the most frequent cause of a lack of trustees, namely a will made without proper legal advice. Where even this provision failed (such as where there was a home-made settlement created *inter vivos*) the court had power to appoint trustees on the application of any person interested under the settlement.[52]

---

[47] Consider *Re Bentley* (1885) 54 L.J. Ch. 782.
[48] *Re Moore* [1906] 1 Ch. 789.
[49] *Re Johnson's S.E.* [1913] W.N. 222.
[50] *Re Spearman S.E.* [1906] 2 Ch. 502.
[51] S.L.A. 1925, s.30. This rarely applied on intestacies since trusts for sale then normally arose: above, p. 192.
[52] S.L.A. 1925, s.34.

Sect. 3. How settlements had to be made, continue and determine

1. The basic rule

The provisions of the Settled Land Act 1925 are couched in terms of unregistered convey-ancing, although the Act does admittedly expressly provide that it takes effect subject to the provisions of the Land Registration Act 1925.[53] The scheme of the legislation is for every settlement made after 1925 to be made by two documents, a trust instrument and a vesting instrument (this was not the case prior to 1926). The trust instrument sets out the details of the settlement, with which a purchaser of the settled land will not normally be concerned. His only concern is to ensure that any beneficial interests which there may be are duly over-reached. In the case of unregistered land, the need for overreaching and the manner in which this can be done is revealed by the vesting instrument. This constitutes the relevant title deed containing all the information to which a purchaser is entitled. In this context, the contents of the trust instrument are said to be "behind the curtain" formed by the vesting instrument, and the curtain is one behind which the purchaser is not entitled to peep. In the case of registered land, the vesting instrument will take the form of a registered disposition of the land, which will lead to the registration as proprietor of the tenant for life or statutory owner subject to a restriction which will ensure that any beneficial interests are duly overreached. This scheme must now be examined in greater detail.

2. Settlements *inter vivos*

Every settlement of a legal estate in land made *inter vivos* after 1925 and before 1997 had to be made by two deeds, a trust instrument and a principal vesting instrument.[54] The contents of these deeds were as follows.

In the case of both registered and unregistered land, the trust instrument generally took the form of a deed, although signed writing was in fact sufficient. This document:

(i) declared the trusts affecting the settled land;

(ii) bore any ad valorem stamp duty payable in respect of the settlement;

(iii) appointed trustees of the settlement;

(iv) contained the power, if any, to appoint new trustees of the settlement; and

(v) set out, either expressly or by reference, any powers intended to be conferred by the settlement in extension of those conferred by the Act.

In the case of unregistered land the principal vesting instrument had to be a deed which:

(i) described the settled land, either specifically or generally;

(ii) declared that the settled land was vested in the person or persons to whom it was conveyed, or in whom it was declared to be vested, upon the trusts from time to time affecting the settled land;

(iii) stated the names of the trustees of the settlement;

[53] S.L.A. 1925, s.119(3).
[54] S.L.A. 1925, ss.4, 5.

(iv) stated the names of any persons empowered to appoint new trustees of the settlement; and

(v) stated any additional or larger powers conferred by the trust instrument.

It will be noticed that the last three particulars in each document were similar, the only difference being that whereas the trust instrument actually made the appointment and conferred the powers, the vesting deed merely recited what had been done by the trust instrument. The first two particulars in each of the deeds were, of course, completely dissimilar. The second requirement of a vesting deed was worded so as to cover two cases:

(i) where the vesting deed acted as a conveyance from the settlor to the tenant for life or statutory owner, as where X settled property on A for life with the remainders over; and

(ii) where the same person was both settlor and tenant for life, so that there is no transfer of the legal estate, as where Z on his marriage settled property on himself for life with remainders over.

In the case of registered land the principal vesting instrument took the form of a registered transfer of the land. Its precise contents varied depending on what Land Registry Form was in use at the relevant time but as a minimum stated the title number, the name of the tenant for life or statutory owner, who of course had to be registered as proprietor,[55] and revealed the fact that the settled land was subject to a settlement under the Settled Land Act 1925, thus enabling the appropriate restriction to be registered[56] in order to protect the interests of the remaining beneficiaries, which cannot override registration,[57] by ensuring that they are overreached. The restriction provides that except under an order of the registrar, no disposition will be registered unless it is authorised by the Settled Land Act 1925,[58] and that no disposition under which capital money arises is to be registered unless the money is paid to the trustees of the settlement (being not less than two nor more than four in number, or a trust corporation), or into court.[59]

The provision in the Settled Land Act 1925 which expressly provides that it takes effect subject to the provisions of the Land Registration Act 1925[60] will cease to have effect when the Land Registration Act 2002 comes into force.[61] However, since no more settlements under the Settled Land Act 1925 can now be created, only in the relatively unlikely event that land is added to an existing settlement will any further land subject to the Settled Land Act 1925 have to be dealt with. In this event, the situation will remain the same. However, the only specific provisions of the Land Registration Act 2002 dealing with settlements under the Settled Land Act 1925 are those which state that the interests of beneficiaries thereunder

[55] S.L.A. 1925, ss.41, 86(1), (5), 91.
[56] ibid., s.86(3).
[57] ibid., s.86(2); above, p. 132.
[58] Or by any extended power under the settlement: L.R.R. 1925, r. 58(2).
[59] See L.R.R. 1925, r. 58(1); Sched., Form 9.
[60] S.L.A. 1925, s.119(3).
[61] L.R.A. 2002, Sched. 11, para.1.

cannot override registration.[62] Remaining matters will presumably be dealt with by the new Land Registration Rules.

3. Settlements by will

Where land was settled by the will of a testator dying after 1925 and before 1997, the position was effectively the same whether the land was registered or unregistered. The will was treated as the trust instrument and the testator's personal representatives, after providing for debts and inheritance tax, held the land on trust to execute a vesting instrument in favour of the tenant for life or statutory owner on being required to do so.[63] The vesting instrument might be either a vesting deed or a vesting assent. A vesting assent is a document merely in writing containing the same particulars as a vesting deed[64]; it attracts no stamp duty, whereas a vesting deed, being a deed, must carry a stamp. Personal representatives in practice thus used a vesting assent. The only difference between registered and unregistered land was that, in the case of registered land, the person in favour of whom the personal representatives assented then had to present the assent to the Land Registry so that he could be registered as proprietor subject to the necessary restriction.

4. Settlements made before 1926

A deed creating a settlement existing at the beginning of 1926 was treated as a trust instrument. The Act provided that as soon as was practicable the trustees of the settlement might, and at the request of the tenant for life or statutory owner must, execute a vesting instrument.[65] Normally this would convey no estate but merely declare that the legal estate in the settled land was vested in the tenant for life or statutory owner, for in nearly all cases the Law of Property Act 1925 automatically vested the legal estate in him at the beginning of 1926[66]; but if in fact the legal estate was outstanding, the vesting instrument operated to convey it.

It is unlikely that much land settled before 1926 is still settled. If it is, it is highly likely still to be unregistered land (if it is registered land, the fact that it was settled before 1926 is irrelevant since any purchaser can rely on the register). A purchaser of unregistered land settled before 1926 is entitled to see and consequently obliged to examine the trust instrument (this is one of the two important cases where the trust instrument is not kept behind the curtain).[67] Despite the existence of a vesting deed, a purchaser of land which was originally settled before 1926 must therefore verify from the settlement that the vesting deed included the land in question and that the proper persons are tenant for life and trustees of the settlement.[68]

5. Section 13

(a) The rule

Some provision had to be made to prevent evasions of the requirement that there should be a vesting instrument. Whilst a vesting instrument is not invalidated merely by some error in

---

[62] L.R.A. 2002, Sched. 1, para.2(1); Sched. 3, para.2(1)(a).
[63] S.L.A. 1925, ss.6, 8.
[64] *ibid.*, s.8.
[65] *ibid.*, Sched. 2, para.1.
[66] L.P.A. 1925, Sched. 1, Pt. II, paras 3, 5, 6.
[67] For the other case, see below, p. 262.
[68] S.L.A. 1925, s.110.

the statements required to be contained in it,[69] the absence of any vesting instrument at all usually makes it impossible to deal with the land.

First, a settlement *inter vivos* of a legal estate in land made otherwise than by two deeds could not transfer or create a legal estate. The tenant for life or statutory owner, however, could require the trustees of the settlement to execute a vesting deed.[70] Thus, if A purported to convey his fee simple to B in fee simple on trust for B for life with remainder to C in fee simple, no legal estate passed to B and so B could not dispose of any legal estate.

Secondly, section 13 of the Settled Land Act 1925 (sometimes called the "paralysing section" or the "freezing section") in effect provides that, where a tenant for life or statutory owner has become entitled to have a vesting instrument executed in his favour, no disposition of a legal estate can be made until a vesting instrument has been executed in accordance with the Act. Until this has been done, any purported disposition of the land *inter vivos* by any person operates only as a contract for valuable consideration to carry out the transaction after the requisite vesting instrument has been executed. This applies even if the legal estate is already vested in the tenant for life, as where he is the settlor, or where the transitional provisions have vested it in him automatically.

(b) Exceptions

There are four exceptions to this rule.

(i) Disposition by personal representative: The section does not apply where the disposition is made by a personal representative.[71] For example, if A settled land on himself for life with remainders over but never executed a vesting deed, the legal estate would on his death duly pass to his personal representatives, who could dispose of the land without a vesting instrument being executed, for example if part of the land had to be sold to raise money for inheritance tax.

(ii) Purchaser taking free of the settlement: The section does not apply where the disposition is made to a purchaser who takes free of the settlement. Section 13 is couched in terms of unregistered land; such a purchaser is a purchaser for value of a legal estate without notice of the tenant for life or statutory owner having become entitled to a vesting instrument.[72] For example, if by a deed executed before 1997 A settled unregistered land on himself for life with remainders over, and subsequently, suppressing the deed, sells the land to a purchaser who is ignorant of the settlement, the purchaser will obtain a good title even though no vesting deed has ever been executed. In the case of registered land, the position of such a purchaser is even stronger because of the principle that in registered conveyancing the register is paramount. If a registered proprietor created similar trusts before 1997 and has failed to secure the registration of the appropriate restriction, the register will continue to show him as the registered proprietor subject to no restriction. If he then sells the land to a purchaser for value, the latter will take free from the interests of the beneficiaries even if he knows of them, for they have not been protected on the register and do not override registration. This will continue to be the position under the Land Registration Act 2002 when it comes into force, save that value will no longer include marriage consideration.

---

[69] *ibid.,* s.5.
[70] *ibid.,* ss.4, 9.
[71] *ibid.,* s.13.
[72] S.L.A. 1925, as amended by L.P.(Am.)A. 1926, Sched.

(iii) Settlement at an end: The section does not apply where the settlement has come to an end before a vesting instrument has been executed. Thus where at the end of 1925 X was a tenant in fee tail in possession free from any trusts or incumbrances, it was held that if, before any vesting instrument had been executed, he barred the estate in fee tail and so terminated the settlement, it was unnecessary for a vesting instrument to be executed before he conveyed the land to a purchaser.[73] When the land ceases to be settled, the fetters of section 13 drop off. However, in practice there does not seem to be any situation in which this exception can now operate.

(iv) Section 1 of the Amending Act: Section 13 does not apply where advantage is taken of section 1 of the Law of Property (Amendment) Act 1926. As has already been seen,[74] in a limited class of cases this provision allows settled land to be dealt with as if it were not settled.

(c) Operation of the provisions

An illustration of the operation of these provisions is given by the case of a settlor who attempts to make a settlement *inter vivos* after 1925 and before 1997 in favour of his son and family by a single document. In such a case:

(i) the document is ineffective to transfer or create any legal estate, which thus remains vested in him;

(ii) the document is treated as a trust instrument;

(iii) as soon as it is practicable the trustees of the settlement may, and at the request of the tenant for life or statutory owner must, execute a principal vesting deed, which will operate to take the legal estate out of the settlor and vest it in the tenant for life or statutory owner;

(iv) until a vesting deed has been duly executed, section 13 in principle prevents any disposition of the land being made although in practice until it has been the settlor can defeat the settlement at any time if he conveys unregistered land to a purchaser for value without notice of the settlement or transfers registered land to a purchaser for value with or without notice of the settlement;

(v) if a vesting deed is executed, it must be executed by the trustees—the settlor cannot execute it and thus correct his error, even if the legal estate is still vested in him; if there are no trustees and no persons able and willing to appoint trustees, an application must be made to the court for the appointment of trustees; and

(vi) even after a vesting deed has been executed the settlement is not so satisfactory as one made in the proper manner, for the document creating the settlement, although treated as the trust instrument, is not behind the curtain (this is the other of the two important exceptions to the rule that a purchaser is not concerned with the trust instrument[75]; a purchaser must examine the document creating the settlement to see that it includes the land in question and that the proper persons are tenant for life and trustees of the settlement).

[73] *Re Alefounder's W.T.* [1927] 1 Ch. 360.
[74] Above, p. 255.
[75] For the first exception, see above, p. 260.

6. Dispositions under settlements: section 18

(a) Unauthorised transactions

Once a vesting instrument has been duly executed, section 13 ceases to apply, but the land is subject to section 18. Under this, until the trustees of the settlement have been duly discharged, any disposition by the tenant for life or statutory owner is void if it is not authorised by the Act, any other statute, or any additional or larger powers mentioned in the vesting instrument, except so far as it binds the tenant for life's own beneficial interest.[76] Further, where any capital money is payable, a conveyance to a purchaser takes effect only if the capital money is paid to (or by the direction of) the trustees of the settlement, being at least two in number or a trust corporation, or into court.[77] Thus if a tenant for life of unregistered land, dishonestly concealing the fact that the land is settled land, mortgages it to raise money for his personal purposes, the mortgage is void against other beneficiaries under the settlement both because it is not authorised by the Act and because the money is not paid to the trustees of the settlement[78]; and unlike section 13, section 18 makes no exception for a purchaser of unregistered land without notice. Such concealment occurred where a tenant for life, having previously bought the land, sold it to somebody else (his father) who then made the settlement; the tenant for life afterwards mortgaged the land by suppressing all the transactions subsequent to his purchase and the mortgage was held to be void.[79] However, this situation could not arise in the case of registered land, because the tenant for life could not suppress his registration as proprietor as such subject to a restriction; consequently the mortgagee would necessarily become aware of the need to pay the capital money to the trustees of the settlement.

(b) Protection against irregularity

On any disposition, a purchaser dealing in good faith[80] with a tenant for life or statutory owner is to be conclusively taken, as against all persons entitled under the settlement, to have given the best price, consideration or rent that could reasonably be obtained by the tenant for life or statutory owner "and to have complied with all the requisitions of this Act".[81] Although this provision has been held to apply only where the purchaser knew that he was dealing with a tenant for life,[82] the better view is that such knowledge is immaterial,[83] and that the remedy of the beneficiaries is not against the mortgagee or other purchaser but against the tenant for life for breach of his fiduciary duties.[84] In any case, the language of the statutory protection seems to be confined to irregularities in authorised transactions,[85] and not as extending to transactions that are wholly unauthorised, such as the grant of an oral tenancy by a tenant for life.[86]

---

[76] S.L.A. 1925, s.18(1)(a).
[77] *ibid.*, s.18(1)(b), (c).
[78] *Weston v. Henshaw* [1950] Ch. 510.
[79] *ibid.*
[80] See *Chandler v. Bradley* [1897] 1 Ch. 315.
[81] S.L.A. 1925, s.110(1).
[82] *Weston v. Henshaw* [1950] Ch. 510.
[83] *Re Morgan's Lease* [1972] Ch. 1.
[84] *Mogridge v. Clapp* [1892] 3 Ch. 382 (on S.L.A. 1882, s.54, the predecessor of S.L.A. 1925, s.110(1)).
[85] See, *e.g. Hurrell v. Littlejohn* [1904] 1 Ch. 689 (rent under proper lease).
[86] See *Bevan v. Johnson* [1990] 2 E.G.L.R. 33 (tenancy held void under s.18(1) without mention of s.110(1)).

7. Subsidiary vesting deed

Where a settlement of land is already in existence and other land is brought into the settlement, a subsidiary vesting deed is required to convey the land to the tenant for life or statutory owner. (It is not now possible to settle any further land on the trusts of an existing settlement under the Settled Land Act 1925 but land which is purchased with the existing settled property or with the proceeds of its sale still has to be the subject-matter of a subsidiary vesting deed.) The contents of a subsidiary vesting deed are as follows[87]:

(i) particulars of the last or only principal vesting deed affecting land subject to the settlement;

(ii) a statement that the land conveyed is to be held upon and subject to the same trusts and powers as the land comprised in the principal vesting deed;

(iii) the names of the trustees of the settlement; and

(iv) the name of any person entitled to appoint new trustees of the settlement.

There is no need to refer to the trust instrument or any additional powers conferred by it.

8. The "curtain" principle

This principle is only relevant to unregistered land. In the case of registered land any purchaser can rely on the register and has no need to see anything else; he is at no risk from interests which override registration because both the Land Registration Act 1925 and the Land Registration Act 2002 provide that the interests of the beneficiaries of a settlement under the Settled Land Act 1925 cannot override registration.

(a) The curtain

The purpose of a vesting instrument is to provide a purchaser with all that he needs to know. It is therefore provided that "a purchaser of a legal estate in settled land" is not entitled to see the trust instrument,[88] and he is also bound and entitled to assume that the particulars required to be set out in the vesting instrument are correct,[89] such as the persons who are the tenant for life and the trustees. Further, a vesting deed is not invalidated merely by any error in the particulars required to be contained in it.[90]

(b) Errors

No statutory provision is made for cases in which there is some error in the vesting instrument. Thus if land has been settled on W for life or until remarriage, with remainder to X in fee simple, W will cease to be a tenant for life on remarriage and so has no power to sell the land. If she nevertheless purports to sell it, the purchaser cannot discover from the vesting instrument that she is no longer tenant for life, and is bound to assume from the vesting instrument that she still is. While the legal estate remains vested in her, she probably can still convey it; but she cannot overreach the equitable interests, and these will bind the purchaser. Such problems are unlikely to occur in practice, for truth will out when the

---

[87] S.L.A. 1925, s.10.
[88] *ibid.*, s.110(2).
[89] *ibid.*
[90] *ibid.*, s.5(3).

purchaser seeks to pay the purchase money to the trustees. If such a case did arise, the Act[91] and case law[92] give some support to the view that the protection given to a purchaser of a legal estate "in settled land"[93] would probably apply to land which merely appears to be settled land. In any case, the purchaser might also be treated as being a purchaser without notice of the interests under the trust instrument which statute precludes him from inspecting.[94]

(c) Exceptions

In three cases a purchaser may and should inspect the trust instrument.[95] Two cases are where the principal vesting instrument gives effect to a settlement made before 1926, or to an imperfect settlement made after 1925.[96] The third, less important, case is an example of a "deemed" settlement, where a minor became entitled under an intestacy before 1997. There used to be a fourth case, another "deemed" settlement, where land was held on trust for charitable, ecclesiastical or public purposes.[97] However, the Trusts of Land and Appointment of Trustees Act 1996 provides that such land no longer is or is deemed to be settled under the Settled Land Act 1925 even if it was deemed to be so settled before 1997.[98] The three surviving cases all have (and the fourth used to have) the increased risk of error that comes from vesting instruments being executed after the settlement arose.

9. Duration and determination of settlements

(a) Determination of interest of tenant for life

When a tenant for life dies, or his interest comes to an end in some other way (such as by forfeiture or surrender), the settlement may still continue or it may come to an end depending on whether, after the determination of his interest, it does or does not satisfy the definition of a settlement under the Settled Land Act 1925. In each case, provision has been made for the execution of a document that, in the case of unregistered land, will reveal to a purchaser which has occurred without any need for him to look behind the curtain (in the case of registered land the relevant document will instead enable the correct entries to be made on the register). Provision has also been made for the devolution of the legal estate vested in the tenant for life.

> (i) If the settlement continues, the document will be a vesting deed or vesting assent (a document containing all the particulars required in a vesting deed[99]), and this will vest the legal estate in the next tenant for life, subject in the case of registered land to his subsequent registration as proprietor—the restriction on the register will continue.

---

[91] See s.110(2)(e), which requires a purchaser of a legal estate "in settled land" to assume the correctness of statements in a "deed of discharge", which *ex hypothesi* shows that the land is no longer settled: see below, p. 266.

[92] See *Re Cugny's W.T.* [1931] 1 Ch. 305 (on S.L.A. 1925, s.36; below, p. 265).

[93] S.L.A. 1925, s.110(2); see above.

[94] See [1984] Conv. 354 (P.A. Stone), and compare [1985] Conv. 377 (R. Warrington).

[95] S.L.A. 1925, s.110(2), proviso.

[96] Above, pp. 227, 229.

[97] S.L.A. 1925, s.29 (now repealed by T.L.A.T.A. 1996, Sched. 4).

[98] s.2(5).

[99] *ibid.*, s.8(4).

(ii) If the settlement ends, the document will usually be an ordinary conveyance or an ordinary assent which will not state the names of the trustees of the settlement. This will vesting the legal estate in the person entitled, subject again in the case of registered land to his subsequent registration as proprietor—the restriction on the register will this time disappear. A bona fide purchaser for value of a legal estate in unregistered land is bound and entitled to assume that the person in whom the land was thereby vested holds the land free from all rights under the settlement.[1] A bona fide purchaser for value of registered land claiming under a registered disposition will simply rely on the absence of any restriction on the register.

The court has wide powers to make an appropriate order if there is any difficulty in obtaining the execution of the requisite document.[2] Occasionally the document required will not be a vesting instrument, conveyance or assent but a deed of discharge, which transfers no legal estate. The two main categories will be considered in turn.

(b) Settlement continuing thereafter

Land once settled remains settled so long as:

(i) any limitation, charge or power of charging under the settlement still exists or is capable of being exercised, or

(ii) the person beneficially entitled in possession is an infant,

unless in either case the land is, following the determination of the interest of the tenant for life, held on express trust for sale.[3] Once land is either held on express trust for sale or else vested in a person of full age free from all actual or possible rights under the settlement, the settlement under the Settled Land Act 1925 is at an end.

If the tenant for life dies, but the land remains settled land, the legal estate will vest in the trustees of the settlement who, as his special personal representatives, will take out probate or letters of administration to his estate, limited to the settled land.[4] They will then vest the legal estate by means of a vesting assent in the next tenant for life.[5] Where the tenant for life is still alive but has ceased to be tenant for life (as where his life interest has been determined by forfeiture or surrender), he must by vesting deed vest the legal estate in the next tenant for life.[6] Where a minor who is entitled in possession attains his majority, the legal estate must be vested in him (normally by the statutory owner[7]) by a vesting deed if the settlement is continuing and by an ordinary conveyance if it is not.[8] In all three cases the new tenant for life will, in the case of registered land, have to procure his subsequent registration as proprietor subject to the existing restriction, which will continue.

---

[1] *ibid.*, s.110(4).
[2] *ibid.*, s.12.
[3] S.L.A. 1925, s.3; L.P.(Am.)A. 1926, Sched.
[4] S.L.A. 1925, s.7(1); A.E.A. 1925, s.22; Supreme Court Act 1981, s.113.
[5] S.L.A. 1925, s.8.
[6] *ibid.*, ss.7(4), 8(4)(a).
[7] See above, p. 256.
[8] S.L.A. 1925, s.7(2), (5).

(c) Settlement not continuing thereafter

Where the settlement comes to an end on the death of the tenant for life, the legal estate vests in his ordinary personal representatives, who will take out a grant of probate or letters of administration.[9] They will then vest the legal estate in the person absolutely entitled, or in trustees of land, by means of an ordinary (and not vesting) assent. If those entitled are tenants in common of full age, the personal representatives should vest the legal estate in them on a trust of land by an ordinary assent.[10] But if one of them is a minor, the personal representatives should instead vest it in the former trustees of the settlement on trust for the tenants in common by an ordinary assent, even if they are the same persons as those former trustees.[11] If the settlement comes to an end for some reason other than the death of the tenant for life, as where another person has become absolutely entitled, the tenant for life must convey the legal estate to that other person by an ordinary conveyance.[12] In all these cases the person to whom the legal estate is conveyed will, in the case of registered land, have to procure his subsequent registration as proprietor; the existing restriction will be removed.

However, if the settlement does not continue because the tenant for life has become absolutely entitled to the settled land, as where he has purchased the interests of all the other beneficiaries, or the last remaining interest under the settlement is that of an annuitant who has died, the former trustees of the settlement must instead execute a deed of discharge, declaring that they are discharged from the trust so far as the land is concerned.[13] This entitles a purchaser of unregistered land to assume that the land has ceased to be settled land and is subject to no trust of land.[14] In the case of registered land, the tenant for life will be able to use the deed of discharge to procure the removal of the existing restriction and a purchaser will be able to rely on its absence. This means that, if the tenant for life secures the removal of the restriction by means of a forged deed of discharge, a purchaser from him will obtain a good title on registration of a transfer in his favour—the interests of the beneficiaries will not longer be protected on the register and do not override registration. But in such cases there might well be a valid claim to rectification of the register.[15]

If a settlement comes to an end before any vesting instrument has been executed,[16] no deed of discharge is required.[17] In the case of both registered and unregistered land, the real state of the title will then revert to what it has throughout appeared to be.

(d) Absence of relevant property

Existing settlements under the Settled Land Act 1925 continue until no land or personal chattels, usually heirlooms, settled so as to devolve with it (together referred to as "relevant property") are subject to the settlement.[18] Although the Trusts of Land and Appointment of Trustees Act 1996, unlike the draft bill prepared by the Law Commission, does not specifically so provide, an existing settlement under the Settled Land Act 1925 clearly does not end

---

[9] *Re Bridgett and Hayes' Contract* [1928] Ch. 163.
[10] L.P.A. 1925, s.3(1)(b)(ii), proviso.
[11] S.L.A. 1925, s.36; *Re Cugny's W.T.* [1931] 1 Ch. 305; the word "vesting" at 309 is an obvious slip.
[12] S.L.A. 1925, s.7(5).
[13] *ibid.*, s.17.
[14] *ibid.*, and see s.110(2)(e).
[15] See above, p. 138.
[16] As in *Re Alefounder's W.T.* [1927] 1 Ch. 360; above, p. 262.
[17] See S.L.A. 1925, s.17.
[18] T.L.A.T.A. 1996, s.2(4).

simply because part of the existing relevant property is sold, whether or not the proceeds of its sale are reinvested in further land.[19] It is thought that such a settlement also continues if all the relevant property is exchanged for other relevant property[20] or is sold at a time when the tenant for life or statutory owner has already contracted to purchase other relevant property.[21] However, if all the relevant property is sold in any other circumstances, the settlement under the Settled Land Act 1925 will end. At that point, the settlement will necessarily hold no land and the trustees will be holding the proceeds of sale on the trusts of the settlement. If those proceeds of sale are subsequently invested in land, the settlement will take effect not as a settlement under the Settled Land Act 1925 but as a trust of land.[22] Consequently, title to that land will have to be taken and retained by the trustees rather than being vested in the tenant for life or statutory owner.

Sect. 4. Powers of the tenant for life

The tenant for life has wide and unfettered powers of sale, exchange, leasing, mortgaging and otherwise dealing with the settled land. As has already been mentioned, those beneficially entitled under the settlement other than the tenant for life are protected by the fact that:

(1) the tenant for life is a trustee for those beneficiaries;

(2) in the case of the most important powers, the tenant for life must give notice to the trustees of his intention to exercise them;

(3) in a few exceptional cases the tenant for life must not exercise his powers without the leave of the trustees or an order of the court; and

(4) the other party to any transaction entered into with the tenant for life which gives rise to the payment of capital moneys will only obtain a title free from the interests of the other beneficiaries if he pays those moneys to the trustees of the settlement and so enables their beneficial interests to be overreached.

In general, what follows applies to statutory owners as well as to tenants for life.

1. The tenant for life as trustee

The tenant for life has the legal estate in the settled land as well as the statutory powers vested in him, and he holds both the estate and the powers on trust for himself and the other beneficiaries under the settlement.[23] This emphasises the dual capacity of a tenant for life: he holds two interests in the land, the legal estate as trustee and his own equitable interest beneficially.[24] In relation to the exercise of his statutory powers, because he is deemed to be a trustee for the other beneficiaries he is bound to consider their interests.[25] This enables the

---

[19] See Barraclough and Matthews, *A Practitioner's Guide to the Trusts of Land and Appointment of Trustees Act* (1996), para. 2.4.

[20] *ibid.*

[21] By analogy with the position of trusts for sale before 1997; see *Re Wakeman* [1945] Ch. 177.

[22] T.L.A.T.A. 1996, Sched. 1, para. 6.

[23] S.L.A. 1925, ss.16, 107.

[24] See generally *Re Liberty's W.T.* [1937] Ch. 176.

[25] *ibid.*, s.53; *Re Lord Stamford's S.E.* (1890) L.R. 43 Ch.D. 84 at 95.

court to intervene if he seeks to sell at a price infinitely below the value of the property[26] or
to make an investment which, although not outside his powers, is undesirable. Nevertheless,
provided the transaction is a proper one, it will not be invalidated merely because the motive
of the tenant for life is not very commendable, (for instance that "he is selling out of ill will
or caprice, or because he does not like the remainderman, because he desires to be relieved
from the trouble of attending to the management of land, or from any other such object, or
with any such motive"[27]).

Subject to these restrictions, the tenant for life is in general unfettered in the exercise of
his powers. They cannot be taken away or cut down either directly or indirectly, nor can he
curtail or divest himself of them or effectively contract not to exercise them. Additional or
larger powers can be conferred by the settlor on the tenant for life, and the Act in no way
restricts such powers. The tenant for life is thus normally in complete control of the land,
even if he is "a spendthrift, who has ruined himself by his own extravagance and folly, who
has brought disgrace on the family name, and who has exposed the family estate to
destruction for the rest of his life."[28]

The position of the tenant for life as trustee will be further considered later.

2. Powers exercisable upon giving notice[29]

If the tenant for life intends to make a sale, exchange, lease, mortgage or charge, or to grant
an option, he must give written notice to the trustees of the settlement, and, if known, to their
solicitor. The notice must be given by registered letter or recorded delivery posted at least one
month before the transaction or the contract therefor, and is invalid unless when it is given
the trustees consist of two or more persons or a trust corporation; thus if there are no trustees,
a tenant for life is not entitled to exercise these powers. The object of this provision for giving
notice seems to be to enable the trustees to prevent any fraudulent dealing by applying to the
court for an injunction.[30] In fact, however, it affords comparatively little protection, for:

(i) the trustees are apparently under no obligation to interfere with an improper
transaction[31];

(ii) except in the case of a mortgage or charge, a general notice suffices, such as "take
notice that I intend from time to time to exercise any or all of my powers under the
Settled Land Act 1925." In such cases, however, the tenant for life must, at the
request of a trustee of the settlement, give reasonable information as to any sales,
exchanges or leases effected, in progress or immediately intended[32];

(iii) any trustee may by writing accept less than one month's notice or waive it
altogether[33]; and

(iv) a person dealing in good faith with the tenant for life is not concerned to inquire
whether notice has been given.[34] Even if there are no trustees, a bona fide purchaser

[26] *Wheelwright v. Walker (No. 1)* (1883) 23 Ch.D. 752 at 762.
[27] *Cardigan v. Curzon-Howe* (1885) 30 Ch.D. 531 at 540, *per* Chitty J.
[28] *Re Marquis of Ailesbury's S.E.* [1892] 1 Ch. 506 at 535, *per* Lindley L.J.
[29] S.L.A. 1925, ss.38–48, 51, 71, 101.
[30] *Wheelwright v. Walker (No. 1)* (1883) 23 Ch.D. 752.
[31] S.L.A. 1925, s.97.
[32] S.L.A. 1925, s.101.
[33] *ibid.*
[34] *ibid.*

for value of a legal estate gets a good title if the transaction is one on which no capital money is payable, such as the grant of a lease for which no premium is payable.[35]

Each of the powers in respect of which notice is normally required must now be examined.

(a) Power to sell

A tenant for life may sell the settled land or any part thereof, or any easement, right or privilege of any kind over the land.[36] He may, for example, sell to a railway company the right to tunnel under the land. With certain qualifications, he must obtain the best consideration in money that can reasonably be obtained. In one case[37] a tenant for life was made an offer by another beneficiary, but being unwilling to sell to him, proposed to sell to a third party for a lower price; the court restrained the tenant for life from selling for less than the price offered by the beneficiary, or from selling at all without informing the beneficiary of the proposed price and giving him two days in which to increase his offer. But there is no need for the sale to be by auction. Further, a purchaser is protected by the provision that if he deals in good faith with the tenant for life, he is to be conclusively taken, as against all the beneficiaries, to have given the best consideration reasonably obtainable and to have complied with all the requirements of the Act. This applies both to sales and other dealings such as leases,[38] and applies whether the transaction has been completed or is still the subject of an executory contract.[39] Thus a purchaser who made a good bargain and bought for £2,000 property which he forthwith resold for £3,000 was held to be protected.[40]

(b) Power to exchange

Settled land, or any part of it, or any easement, right or privilege over it, may be exchanged for other land or any easement, right or privilege.[41] For "equality of exchange" (*i.e.* to adjust any difference in value) capital money may be paid or received.

(c) Power to lease

(i) The power: The settled land, or any part of it, or any easement, right or privilege over it, may be leased for any period not exceeding:

   (i) 999 years for building or forestry;

   (ii) 100 years for mining;

   (iii) 50 years for any other purpose.[42]

These periods apply even to settlements made before 1926, when the permissible periods were shorter. A building lease is one made partly in consideration of erecting, improving,

---

[35] *Mogridge v. Clapp* [1892] 3 Ch. 382; *Re Morgan's Lease* [1972] Ch. 1.
[36] S.L.A. 1925, ss.38, 39. See below, p. 326, for joint tenants for life.
[37] *Wheelwright v. Walker (No. 2)* (1883) 31 W.R. 912.
[38] S.L.A. 1925, s.110; above, p. 263.
[39] *Re Morgan's Lease* [1972] Ch. 1.
[40] *Hurrell v. Littlejohn* [1904] 1 Ch. 689.
[41] S.L.A. 1925, ss.38, 40.
[42] *ibid.*, s.41.

adding to or repairing buildings, or an agreement to do this[43]; the advantage to the settled land is that in return for a reduced rent the lessee must leave on the land at the end of his lease the new or improved buildings. By the Forestry Act 1967, a forestry lease means a lease to the Minister of Agriculture, Fisheries and Food for purposes authorised by the Act.

(ii) Conditions of lease: Every lease of settled land must comply with the following conditions.[44]

    (i) It must be made by deed.

    (ii) It must be made to take effect in possession not more than one year after its date, or in reversion after an existing lease with not more than seven years to run at the date of the new lease. Thus if a tenant for life grants a lease to commence in 14 months' time, it is invalid unless it is to commence after the determination of an existing lease.

    (iii) It must reserve the best rent reasonably obtainable in the circumstances, regard being had to any fine (*i.e.* a premium or lump sum) taken, and to any money laid out or to be laid out for the benefit of the land. Any fine is capital money. A lease granted by a tenant for life in return for a bribe or the release from a claim for damages against him personally has accordingly been held not to comply with the statutory requirements.[45] A nominal or reduced rent may be reserved for not longer than the first five years of a building lease or the first 10 years of a forestry lease; and in the case of mining or forestry leases, there are wide powers to vary the rent, for example according to the value of the minerals or trees taken.[46]

    (iv) It must contain a covenant by the lessee for payment of rent and a condition of re-entry (*i.e.* a provision for forfeiture of the lease) on rent not being paid within a specified time not exceeding 30 days.

    (v) A counterpart (*i.e.* copy) of the lease must be executed by the lessee and delivered to the tenant for life; it is sufficient evidence that this has been done if the tenant for life duly executes the lease.

It will be seen that normally a lease must be by deed and notice must be given to the trustees. In certain cases, however, these requirements are relaxed. A lease at the best rent reasonably obtainable without a fine and not exempting the lessee from liability for waste has two privileges:

    (i) if it is for not more than 21 years, it may be made without giving notice to the trustees; and

    (ii) if it is for not more than three years, it may also be made merely in writing and not by deed,[47] though not orally.[48]

---

[43] *ibid.*, s.44.
[44] *ibid.*, s.42. For defective leases, see M. and W. (5th ed.), pp. 364, 365; (1971) 87 L.Q.R. 338 (D.W. Elliott).
[45] *Re Handman and Wilcox's Contract* [1902] 1 Ch. 599.
[46] S.L.A. 1925, ss.44, 45, 48.
[47] S.L.A. 1925, s.42.
[48] *Bevan v. Johnson* [1990] 2 E.G.L.R. 33.

As a corollary to his power to grant leases, a tenant for life has wide powers of accepting surrenders of leases and of varying or waiving the terms of any lease.[49] These powers are exercisable without notice to the trustees.

(iii) Rent from leases: The normal rule is that the tenant for life is entitled to the whole of the rent from leases of the settled land.[50] But as seen above,[51] this does not apply to mining leases, where the capital value of the land is being diminished. The general rule as to rent from mining leases granted under the Act is that, subject to any contrary intention in the settlement, the tenant for life is entitled to three-quarters of the rent unless he is impeachable of waste and the mine is an unopened one, when he is entitled to only one-quarter of the rent; the balance in each case is capital.[52] These provisions, however, apply only to rent from leases granted under the Act, so that if the lease is granted under an express power in the settlement,[53] or if the lease or a contract therefor[54] was made before the land was settled or resettled,[55] the tenant for life is entitled to the whole of the income. As has been seen, the rules as to the tenant for life working the minerals himself are different from the rules as to leases.[56] Where the tenant for life has not a life interest but some interest such as a fee simple subject to a gift over, he may be unimpeachable of waste even if the settlement is silent on the subject; the owner of a mere life interest, on the other hand is impeachable unless the settlement exempts him from liability for waste.[57]

(d) Power to mortgage or charge

In the absence of a contrary provision in the settlement, a tenant for life has no power to mortgage or charge the legal estate for his own benefit. If he wishes to raise money for his own use, he can of course do so by mortgaging his beneficial interest, consisting of his life interest, fee tail or whatever interest he has. The legal estate, on the other hand, can be mortgaged only for certain specified purposes for the benefit of the settled land or those entitled under the settlement, such as to pay for improvements, discharge incumbrances or provide money which is required to be raised under the provisions of the settlement, such as portions.[58]

(e) Power to grant options

A tenant for life may grant an option in writing to purchase or take a lease of all or any part of the settled land or of any easement, right or privilege over it. But:

(i) the price or rent must be the best reasonably obtainable and must be fixed at the time of granting the option[59]; a tenant for life thus has no power to agree to sell at a price to be fixed by arbitration;

---

[49] S.L.A. 1925, ss.52, 59.
[50] See, *e.g. Re Wix* [1916] 1 Ch. 279.
[51] Above, p. 51.
[52] S.L.A. 1925, s.47; *Re Fitzwalter* [1943] Ch. 285.
[53] *Earl of Lonsdale v. Lowther* [1900] 2 Ch. 687.
[54] *Re Kemeys-Tynte* [1892] 2 Ch. 211.
[55] *Re Arkwright's Settlement* [1945] Ch. 195.
[56] He can keep the whole of the profits unless he is impeachable of waste and the mine is unopened, when he cannot work it at all: above, p. 51.
[57] Above, pp. 44, 45, 48.
[58] S.L.A. 1925, ss.16, 71. For portions, see above, pp. 247–248.
[59] See *Re Morgan's Lease* [1972] Ch. 1, where the option was contained in an existing lease.

(ii) the option must be made exercisable within an agreed number of years not exceeding 10; and

(iii) the option may be granted with or without any consideration being paid, but if any is paid, it is capital money.[60]

3. Powers exercisable only with consent

In the following cases, the tenant for life can exercise his powers only with the consent of the trustees of the settlement or under an order of the court.

(a) Power to dispose of the principal mansion house

If the tenant for life wishes to make a disposition whether by sale, lease, exchange or otherwise[61] of the principal mansion house, if any, and the pleasure-grounds and park,[62] and the lands, if any, usually occupied therewith, the consent of the trustees or an order of the court is required:

(i) if the settlement was made before 1926 and does not expressly provide to the contrary; or

(ii) if the settlement was made after 1925 and expressly requires such consent or order to be obtained.[63]

In other cases, no consent is required, but the usual notice must be given.

If a house is usually occupied as a farmhouse, or if the site of a house and the pleasure-grounds and park and lands, if any, usually occupied therewith do not together exceed 25 acres, the house is not deemed a principal mansion house.[64] In other cases, it is a question of fact whether at a given moment a house is a principal mansion house. Where two separate establishments are comprised in the same settlement, there may be two principal mansion houses, or one may be subsidiary to the other, as where one is used as the main residence and the other as a shooting-box.[65] Again, a house may cease to be a principal mansion house, as where it is let as a school; and if the tenant for life then uses a smaller house on the estate as his home, that may become a principal mansion house.[66]

(b) Power to cut and sell timber

This has already been dealt with.[67] It is only if the tenant for life is impeachable of waste that he requires the consent of the trustees or an order of the court and three-quarters of the proceeds are capital money; if he is unimpeachable, he needs no consent or order and may keep all the proceeds.

---

[60] S.L.A. 1925, s.51.
[61] ibid., s.117.
[62] See Pease v. Courtney [1904] 2 Ch. 503.
[63] S.L.A. 1925, s.65.
[64] ibid.
[65] Gilbey v. Rush [1906] 1 Ch. 11 at 21.
[66] Re Feversham S.E. [1938] 2 All E.R. 210.
[67] Above, p. 49.

(c) Power to compromise claims

Subject to the consent in writing of the trustees, the tenant for life has a wide power to compromise and settle disputes relating to the settled land or any part thereof.[68]

(d) Power to sell settled chattels

With the leave of the court the tenant for life may sell any chattels settled to devolve with the land,[69] as furniture, pictures and the like sometimes are.

(e) Power to effect any proper transaction

The court has a statutory jurisdiction to authorise the tenant for life to effect any transaction not otherwise authorised by the Act or the settlement if it is for the benefit of the land or the beneficiaries and is a transaction which an absolute owner could validly effect.[70] This power even permits the court to sanction alterations in the beneficial interests under the settlement.[71]

4. Other powers of a tenant for life

(a) Power to effect improvements

The power to effect improvements is complex.[72]

(i) Making the improvements: A tenant for life may of course effect improvements to the land at his own expense, but if he wishes the cost to be borne either temporarily or permanently by capital money, or to be raised by a mortgage or charge of the settled land, he must comply with the Act. He no longer needs prior approval of a scheme,[73] but he must first ascertain that the proposed improvements are within the list of those authorised by the Act. He must then obtain the appointment of a surveyor or engineer, for capital money cannot be applied in paying for improvements unless:

 (1) if the money is in the hands of the trustees,

  (a) a certificate is furnished by a competent engineer or able practical surveyor employed independently of the tenant for life, certifying—

   (i) that the work or some specific part thereof has been properly executed; and

   (ii) the amount properly payable in respect thereof; or

  (b) an order of the court directs or authorises payment:

 (2) if the money is in court,

  (a) a report or certificate of the Minister of Agriculture, Fisheries and Food is given; or

  (b) a report of a competent engineer or able practical surveyor approved by the court is given; or

---

[68] S.L.A. 1925, s.58.
[69] *ibid.*, s.67.
[70] S.L.A. 1925, s.64; Settled Land and Trustee Acts (Court's General Powers) Act 1943, s.2.
[71] *Re Simmons* [1956] Ch. 125.
[72] S.L.A. 1925, ss.83–87; and see M. and W. (5th ed.), pp. 372–377.
[73] As he did under S.L.A. 1882, s.26.

(c) such other evidence as the court thinks fit is given.

(ii) Repayment: When the improvements are paid for out of capital, the question arises whether or not the tenant for life must repay the money. This depends on the nature of the improvements. A long list is set out in the Third Schedule to the Act, which is divided into three parts:

(i) If the improvement falls within Part I (such as drainage or erection of bridges) or is authorised by the settlement, repayment cannot be ordered. In the case of agricultural land, ordinary repairs reasonably required for proper farming are somewhat surprisingly included under this head if effected after April 1948.[74]

(ii) If the improvement falls within Part II (such as the restoration or reconstruction of buildings damaged or destroyed by dry rot), the trustees or the court have a discretion to order repayment by instalments.

(iii) If the improvement falls within Part III (such as the installation of artificial light in a building), the trustees or the court must order repayment by instalments.

The number of the instalments is within the discretion of the court or the trustees, except that the trustees may not order more than 50 half-yearly instalments.

(b) Power to select investments for capital money

Capital money must be applied in one or more of the 21 methods specified in the Act.[75] These include investment in trustee securities, paying for improvements, and the purchase of land held in fee simple or on a lease with 60 years or more unexpired.[76] The tenant for life may select which of these methods of application is to be employed, in default of which the trustees make the choice.

5. Position of the tenant for life

(a) The tenant for life as trustee

As already seen,[77] the tenant for life is a trustee both of the land and of his powers. This has consequences if he wishes to acquire any or all of the settled land for himself. It is a settled rule of equity that any acquisition of trust property by a trustee, either directly or indirectly, is voidable by any beneficiary, no matter how fair the transaction may be, for otherwise the trustee might be in a position where his interest conflicts with his duty.[78] To avoid this difficulty, the Settled Land Act 1925[79] authorises the trustees of the settlement to exercise all the powers of a tenant for life in carrying out any transaction whereby the tenant for life acquires any interest in the settled land.[80]

---

[74] See the cases cited in *Re Lord Brougham and Vaux's S.E.* [1954] Ch. 24; [1954] Camb.L.J. 63 (H.W.R. Wade).

[75] S.L.A. 1925, s.73.

[76] See *Re Wellsted's W.T.* [1949] Ch. 296.

[77] Above, p. 268.

[78] See Oakley, *Constructive Trusts* (3rd ed.), pp. 137–151.

[79] s.68.

[80] See *Re Pennant's W.T.* [1970] Ch. 75. If the tenant for life is also one of the trustees, he should join in the conveyance to himself as one of the conveying parties: *ibid.*

Where any question arises as to the exercise of any of the powers of the tenant for life, the court, on the application of anyone interested, may make such order as it thinks fit.[81] But the court will not intervene where joint tenants for life are in honest disagreement.[82]

(b) No powers can be given to anyone else

Any power, other than a power of revocation or appointment, which the settlement purports to give to anyone except the tenant for life, is exercisable not by that person but by the tenant for life as if it were an additional power conferred by the settlement.[83] Thus if land is devised "to X and Y in fee simple with power to sell, on trust for A for life and then for B absolutely" the power of sale purported to be given to X and Y is divested from them and given to A; this is so even though A already has a statutory power of sale. But the abortive attempt to give a power of sale to X and Y may not be wholly ineffective, for it may make them Settled Land Act trustees.[84]

(c) The statutory powers cannot be ousted, curtailed or hampered

(i) The Act prevails The settlor may confer additional powers on the tenant for life, and such powers are exercisable in the same way as if they were conferred by the Act.[85] Further, nothing in the Act in any way restricts powers which the settlement gives to the tenant for life or purports to give to the trustees to be exercised with the approval of the tenant for life: the powers given by the Act and the settlement are cumulative. But in other respects, so far as the settlement and the Act conflict in relation to powers exercisable under the Act, the Act prevails.[86] Thus if the settlement provides that no sale shall be made without the consent of some specified person, this provision is inconsistent with the unfettered power of sale given by the Act, and the latter prevails.[87]

In particular, it is enacted that any provision in any document is void to the extent to which it purports or tends to prevent or discourage the tenant for life from exercising his statutory powers or from requiring the land to be vested in him.[88] This applies even when the attempt to restrain the exercise of the powers is made by way of determinable limitation, as where land is settled on "Y for life until he ceases permanently to reside in the property". Notwithstanding anything in a settlement, the exercise of a statutory power can never cause a forfeiture.

(ii) Conditions of residence: These provisions are most frequently invoked by conditions of residence, such as a proviso in the settlement that the tenant for life shall forfeit his interest on ceasing to reside on the settled land. In such cases, if the tenant for life ceases to reside for some reason other than the exercise of his statutory powers (as where he moves out to allow a relation to live there rent-free), the proviso for forfeiture is operative and he loses his interest.[89] But if the reason for his ceasing to reside is that he has exercised his statutory powers, as by leasing or selling the land, there is no forfeiture and he continues to be entitled

---

[81] S.L.A. 1925, s.93.
[82] *Re 90 Thornhill Road, Tolworth, Surrey* [1970] Ch. 261.
[83] S.L.A. 1925, s.108.
[84] Above, p. 256.
[85] S.L.A. 1925, s.109.
[86] *ibid.*, s.108.
[87] *Re Jefferys (No. 2)* [1939] Ch. 205. Contrast trusts of land: below, p. 285.
[88] S.L.A. 1925, s.106.
[89] *Re Trenchard* [1902] 1 Ch. 378.

as tenant for life, receiving the rent from the lease or the income from the purchase money.[90] These provisions may also apply where the settlement provides a fund for the payment of outgoings while the tenant for life occupies the land. If his occupation ceases because he has exercised his statutory power of leasing, the payments from the fund will still continue.[91] If instead he sells the land, thus taking it out of the settlement, he has no claim to any of the income of the fund, for none has been given to him[92]; but if the settlement had given him any surplus income not required for the outgoings until the land is sold, he would have been entitled to the whole of the income for life, for it had all become surplus and the provision for the income to cease on sale is void.[93]

(d) The tenant for life cannot assign, release or contract not to exercise his powers[94]

(i) Exercise of powers: Once a person has become a tenant for life, he is incapable of divesting himself of his powers, even if he parts with his entire beneficial interest, as he is entitled to do; it is he, and not the assignee of his beneficial interest, who alone can exercise the statutory powers.[95] However, in three cases the statutory powers may become exercisable by someone other than the tenant for life.

(1) *Extinguishment of interest.* Where the interest of the tenant for life has been assured, with intent to extinguish it, to the person next entitled under the settlement, the statutory powers cease to be exercisable by the tenant for life and become exercisable as if he were dead.[96] Thus if land is settled on A for life, remainder to B for life, remainder to C in fee simple, the effect of A surrendering his life interest to B is to make the statutory powers exercisable by B instead of A, and A must forthwith convey the legal estate to B by a vesting deed. If B then surrenders his life interest to C, he must convey the legal estate to C, but by an ordinary conveyance, for the land ceases to be settled land.[97] This exception does not apply if there is an intervening limitation which might take effect, such as to D for life, remainder to the sons of D, remainder to E for life, and D, aged 80 and childless, surrenders to E.[98]

(2) *Order of court.* If the tenant for life:

(i) has ceased to have a substantial interest in the land, whether by bankruptcy, assignment or otherwise, and

(ii) either consents to an order being made or else has unreasonably refused to exercise his statutory powers,

any person interested in the land may apply to the court for an order authorising the trustees to exercise any or all of the statutory powers in the name and on behalf of the tenant for life.[99] Such an order prevents the tenant for life from exercising any of the powers affected by the

---

[90] *Re Orlebar* [1936] Ch. 147.
[91] *Re Patten* [1929] 2 Ch. 276.
[92] *ibid.,* contrast *Re Aberconway's S.T.* [1953] Ch. 647.
[93] *Re Herbert* [1946] 1 All E.R. 421.
[94] S.L.A. 1925, s.104.
[95] *Re Earl of Carnarvon's Chesterfield S.E.* [1927] 1 Ch. 138 at 145, 146.
[96] S.L.A. 1925, s.105.
[97] See above, p. 265.
[98] *Re Maryon-Wilson's Instruments* [1971] Ch. 789.
[99] S.L.A. 1925, s.24.

order, but until it has been registered[1] the order does not affect those dealing with the tenant for life. Such an order vests neither the legal estate nor the statutory powers in the trustees, who do not become the statutory owner; the order merely authorises the trustees to exercise the powers on behalf of the tenant for life and in his name.

(3) *Mental patients.* Where the tenant for life is a mental patient, his receiver may, in his name and on his behalf under an order of the Court of Protection, exercise his statutory powers.[2]

(ii) Position of assignees: Where an assignment of the beneficial interest of a tenant for life is made after 1925, the consent of the assignee is not required for the exercise of the statutory powers by the tenant for life, even if the assignment is made for money or money's worth.[3] But for the application of capital money affected by the assignment for any purpose other than for investment in trustee securities, the consent of the assignee is necessary if the assignment so provides or takes effect by operation of the law of bankruptcy, and the trustees have notice of this. Further, unless the assignment otherwise provides, notice of any intended transaction must be given to the assignee. If the land is sold the rights of the assignee are transferred to the capital money which represents the land; and provision is made for obtaining consents in any cases of difficulty.

Sect. 5. Functions of Settled Land Act trustees

It may be useful to collect together the principal functions of Settled Land Act trustees. They are:

(i) to receive and hold capital money[4];

(ii) to receive notice from the tenant for life of his intention to effect certain transactions[5];

(iii) to give consent to certain transactions[6];

(iv) to act as special personal representatives on the death of a tenant for life[7];

(v) to act as statutory owner if the tenant for life is an infant or there is no tenant for life[8];

(vi) to exercise the powers of the tenant for life if he wishes to acquire the settled land for his own benefit[9];

(vii) to exercise the powers of the tenant for life where he has no substantial beneficial interest and either consents to such exercise or unreasonably refuses to exercise his powers[10]; and

---

[1] As "an order affecting land" (above, p. 100); or under L.R.A. 1925 or 2002.
[2] Mental Health Act 1983, s.96(1). For mental patients, see above, p. 205.
[3] S.L.A. 1925, s.104.
[4] Above, pp. 84 *et seq.*
[5] Above, p. 269.
[6] Above, p. 273.
[7] Above, p. 266.
[8] Above, p. 256.
[9] Above, p. 275.
[10] Above, pp. 277–278.

(viii) to exercise a general supervision over the well-being of the settled land.[11]

From the point of view of those acquiring interests in the settled property, the first of the functions set out above is crucial since it is the receipt of any capital money by the trustees which triggers overreaching and therefore enables the purchaser to take the settled property or interest therein which he is purchasing free from the interests of those beneficially entitled under the settlement. The detail of the overreaching provisions of the Settled Land Act 1925 has already been considered.[12]

PART 3—TRUSTS FOR SALE AFTER 1925

1. What is a trust for sale

It has been seen[13] that after 1925 land could not be settled land if it was subject to an "immediate binding trust for sale". Between 1925 and 1977, whenever land was limited in trust for persons by way of succession or for some other reason fell within the definition of settled land, it was governed by the Settled Land Act 1925 (and still is if the settlement is still continuing) unless it could be shown that it was subject to a trust for sale of this nature. The meaning of the phrase is of great importance. Because many settlements created before 1997 are still, it is still necessary to establish whether they were subject to the Settled, in which case they still will be. Consequently, this phrase must be exam

(a) There had to be a trust for sale

There had to be a trust and not a mere power of sale. Thus a conveyance to trustees on trust for persons giving the trustees a power of sale, made the land settled land; the conveyance an imperfect settlement and the trustees could not and cannot sell.[14] However, a trust to retain or sell the land"[15] in a disposition or settlement coming into operation after 1925 is construed as a trust for sale with power to postpone sale.[16]

(b) The trust for sale had to be "immediate"

A trust to sell at some future date, such as when X attained the age of 25, did not prevent land from being settled land.[17] But if there was a trust for sale which was immediately operative, this took the land out of the Settled Land Act 1925, even if the trustees had power to postpone the sale and even if a sale could not be made without the request or consent of some person.[18]

---

[11] See *Re Boston's W.T.* [1956] Ch. 395 at 405.
[12] Above, pp. 84 *et seq.*
[13] Above, p. 253.
[14] Above, pp. 260, 278.
[15] Above, p. 250.
[16] L.P.A. 1925, s.25 (now repealed by T.L.A.T.A. 1996, Sched. 4).
[17] *Re Hanson* [1928] Ch. 96; and see *Bevan v. Johnson* [1990] 2 E.G.L.R. 33.
[18] L.P.A. 1925, s.205(1)(xxix).

(c) The trust for sale had to be "binding"

The interpretation of the word "binding" gave rise to considerable difficulty, especially in cases where the land was first subject to the Settled Land Act 1925 and then to a trust for sale, as where it was limited to A for life with remainder to trustees for sale. Three views were put forward:

(i) That it meant a trust for sale capable of binding, in the sense of overreaching, as many interests as possible. Thus if an equitable interest created under the earlier settlement could not be overreached by the trustees for sale then the trust for sale was not "binding".[19]

(ii) That the word "binding" was inserted to emphasise that a revocable trust for sale was excluded, or else that the word was mere surplusage.[20]

(iii) That a "binding" trust for sale was one which was capable of binding the whole legal estate which had been settled.[21] If the legal estate was vested in the trustees for sale as such, the trust for sale was "binding", even if equitable interests such as charges under a former settlement were still outstanding. But where such equitable charges were outstanding when the tenant for life died, this would normally prevent the trustees for sale from requiring the special personal representatives to vest the legal estate in them[22] and as a result the trust for sale would not be "binding".[23]

It seems safe to say that the first alternative is now generally recognised as being wrong,[24] and that although the second view is innocuous, the third is probably correct. The issue is largely technical: on any view there is clearly a power of sale and the sole question, which can of course still arise today, is as to who is able to exercise it.

2. How a trust for sale comes into being

Since 1996 the only way in which a trust for sale has been able to arise has been expressly, by land being deliberately limited on trust for sale. Before 1997, trusts for sale also arose by operation of statute in five situations. Since 1996 these situations have instead given rise to trusts of land and in four of the five situations statutory trusts for sale which were in existence on January 1, 1997 were converted into trusts of land.

(a) Express trusts for sale

With a view to keeping the trusts off the title, the general practice for many years has been to employ two documents to create an express trust for sale, namely, a conveyance on trust for sale and a trust instrument; it was this practice which suggested the vesting deed and trust instrument of the Settled Land Act 1925. Although today two documents are almost invariably employed to create a trust for sale *inter vivos*, there is nothing in the 1925

---

[19] *Re Leigh's S.E. (No. 1)* [1926] Ch. 852. See above, p. 90, for ad hoc trusts for sale with wider overreaching powers.
[20] *Re Parker's S.E.* [1928] Ch. 247 at 261.
[21] See *Re Beaumont S.E.* [1937] 2 All E.R. 353; *Re Sharpe's Deed of Release* [1939] Ch. 51.
[22] S.L.A. 1925, s.7(5).
[23] *Re Norton* [1929] 1 Ch. 84; and see *Re Parker's S.E.* [1928] Ch. 247.
[24] *ibid.*

legislation to make this essential. In the case of testamentary trusts for sale, the usual position before 1926 was that the will was the sole document concerned. After 1925, a written assent is required to vest the legal estate in the trustees for sale, so that now there will usually be two documents in such cases. But even if a trust for sale is created by a single document, it is now provided that a purchaser of the legal estate from the trustees for sale is not concerned with the trusts affecting the rents and profits of the land until sale and the proceeds of sale thereafter, whether or not the trusts are declared by the same instrument as that by which the trust for sale is created.[25]

(b) Statutory trusts for sale before 1997

Until January 1, 1997 a trust for sale was imposed by statute in a number of cases. For example:

  (i) if two or more persons were entitled to land as joint tenants or tenants in common, a trust for sale was normally imposed by the Law of Property Act 1925[26];

 (ii) the Administration of Estates Act 1925 imposed a trust for sale on the property of a person dying intestate[27];

(iii) if trustees lent money on mortgage and the property became vested in them free from the right of repayment (such as by foreclosure), they held it upon trust for sale[28] (this preserved the character of the trust property; the money was pure personalty, and under the doctrine of conversion, the rights of the beneficiaries under a trust for sale were treated as being interests in pure personalty, even if the subject-matter of the trust was land);

 (iv) land held for special purposes, such as schools or highways, was held on trust for sale for (usually) the grantor when the special purpose came to an end[29]; and

  (v) if the trustees of a personalty settlement invested trust funds in the purchase of land, they held it on trust for sale unless the settlement otherwise provided.[30]

(c) Statutory trusts for sale after 1996

Statutory trusts for sale which existed on January 1, 1997 were converted into trusts of land on that date[31] with the sole exception of statutory trusts for sale which had already arisen as a result of the trustees of a personalty settlement investing trust funds in the purchase of land.[32] Consequently, the only situation in which a statutory trust for sale can still be in existence is where land was purchased by the trustees of a personalty settlement prior to

---

[25] L.P.A. 1925, s.27 (now amended by T.L.A.T.A. 1996, Sched. 3, para.4(8)).
[26] Below, p. 302.
[27] Above, p. 192.
[28] L.P.A. 1925, s.31 (now amended by T.L.A.T.A. 1996, Sched. 2, para.1).
[29] Reverter of Sites Act 1987, s.1.
[30] *ibid.*, s.32; see *Re Hanson* [1928] Ch. 96.
[31] T.L.A.T.A. 1996, Sched. 2, paras 1(7), 3(6), 4(4), 5(5), 6(6), 7.
[32] *ibid.*, para.2(2).

January 1, 1997; in such circumstances, unless the settlement otherwise provided, they held that land on statutory trust for sale from the outset and still do so.

3. Position of trustees for sale

Since 1996, a trust for sale of land has been a trust of land and the position of trustees for sale of land is therefore generally the same as that of all other trustees of land discussed below. However, in one respect the position of trustees for sale of land is not the same as that of other trustees of land. The very essence of a trust for sale is that a duty to sell is imposed on the trustees. Admittedly the Law of Property Act 1925 implied a power to postpone sale in every trust for sale of land, even one created before 1926,[33] in the absence of an express provision to the contrary and the 1996 Act also implies such a power to postpone, in this case even if there is an express provision to the contrary.[34] Consequently, trustees for sale can now never be liable in any way if they postpone sale indefinitely in the exercise of their discretion.[35]

Superficially this appears no different from the position under other trusts of land, where the trustees have all the powers of an absolute owner of land[36] and, consequently, a power of sale. However, there is in fact a difference. The exercise of powers requires unanimity whereas a duty can be imposed by a minority of the trustees on an unwilling majority.[37] Consequently, if any one of the trustees of an express trust for sale of land wishes to sell, the land has to be sold; unanimity is required for the exercise of their power to postpone. On the other hand, all the trustees of a trust of land which is not a trust for sale must agree before selling that land; they are under no duty to sell and unanimity is required for the exercise of their power to sell.

The authorities prior to 1997 established that a minority of the trustees could not force a sale where this sale would have defeated the spirit or object of the trust or amounted to a breach of contract,[38] an aspect which had become increasingly important in cases of beneficial co-ownership.[39] However, all these authorities concerned trusts for sale which were implied by statute to give effect to beneficial co-ownership; beneficial co-ownership now gives rise to an implied statutory trust of land which is not a trust for sale. There has never been a reported case where the courts have taken into account these factors and denied a sale to a minority of the trustees of an express trust for sale. It is true that the court can now in principle order a postponement against the wishes of a minority, or for that matter of the majority, of the trustees on the application of any trustee or other person who has an interest in the property.[40] The 1996 Act lays down a list of matters which are relevant to the determining of the application.[41] However, it is likely that, if these matters are very evenly balanced, the court will be more likely to order a sale in the case of an express trust for sale than in the case of other trusts of land simply because the settlor or testator has expressly imposed a duty of sale upon trustees.

[33] L.P.A. 1925, s.25 (now repealed).
[34] T.L.A.T.A. 1996, s.4(1).
[35] *ibid.*
[36] *ibid.*, s.6(1).
[37] *Re Mayo* [1943] Ch. 302. Contrast joint tenants for life of settlements under S.L.A. 1925: below, p. 326.
[38] See *Re Buchanan-Wollaston's Conveyance* [1939] Ch. 738; *Re Hyde's Conveyance* (1952) 102 L.J. News. 58; *Jones v. Challenger* [1961] 1 Q.B. 176.
[39] Below, p. 322.
[40] T.L.A.T.A. 1996, s.14(1).
[41] *ibid.*, s.15.

4. The doctrine of conversion

Until 1997 it was settled that the rights of a beneficiary under a trust for sale were to be regarded as being rights not in the land itself but in the proceeds of sale on the basis of the equitable maxim that equity looks on that as done which ought to be done. The trustees were bound by the trust for sale to convert the land into money, sooner or later; and so, on the simple principle that it would be wrong that the precise moment when the trustees carried out their administrative duty of selling should alter the devolution of the beneficial interests,[42] the nature of those interests remain unchanged throughout.[43] This doctrine had many important effects, particularly on the devolution of property on death. (Until 1926 realty and personalty devolved in different ways on an intestacy and until 1997, if a testator died leaving all his realty to R and all his personalty to P, it was P who took the testator's interests under an ongoing trust for sale[44] although R would do so if the trust for sale had in effect ended by the testator becoming solely entitled before his death.[45])

However, during the second half of the twentieth century there was some judicial reluctance to apply the doctrine relentlessly, particularly in relation to modern statutes drafted without overt regard to its impact[46] and also where the real concern of the beneficiaries of the trust for sale was with the land itself (as where it was their home) and not merely with the proceeds of sale under a trust for sale imposed by statute.[47] This culminated in the abolition of the doctrine of conversion by the 1996 Act in relation to trusts for sale arising both before and after its commencement[48] save for testamentary trusts for sale created by the will of a testator who died before 1997.[49] But both the doctrine of conversion and the equitable maxim on which it is based remain important in other areas of property law.

PART 4—TRUSTS OF LAND

1. What is a trust of land?

The expression "trust of land" was given a statutory definition by the Trusts of Land and Appointment of Trustees Act 1996[50] ("the 1996 Act"). It embraces all trusts of property which consists of or includes land[51] other than (i) settlements under the Settled Land Act 1925 which were in existence prior to January 1, 1997 and are still in existence and (ii) land to which the Universities and College Estates Act 1925 applies.[52] It therefore includes express trusts for sale, bare trusts and the statutory trusts of land imposed in a number of situations which until January 1, 1997 gave rise to statutory trusts for sale, namely:

---

[42] *Re Richerson* [1892] 1 Ch. 379 at 383.
[43] See *Fletcher v. Ashburner* (1779) 1 Bro.C.C. 497; M. and W. (5th ed.), pp. 315–317.
[44] *Re Kempthorne* [1930] 1 Ch. 268.
[45] *Re Cook* [1948] Ch. 212.
[46] *Elias v. Mitchell* [1972] Ch. 652; *Re Bradshaw* [1950] Ch. 78; *Cooper v. Critchley* [1955] Ch. 431.
[47] *Barclay v. Barclay* [1970] 2 Q.B. 677 at 684, 685; *Williams and Glyn's Bank Ltd. v. Boland* [1981] A.C. 487 at 507.
[48] T.L.A.T.A. 1996, s. 4(1), (3).
[49] *ibid.*, s.4(2).
[50] See [1997] Conv. 401 (A.J. Oakley); [1997] Conv. 411 (N. Hopkins); 61 M.L.R. (1998) 56 (A. Clements).
[51] T.L.A.T.A. 1996, s.1(1).
[52] *ibid.*, s.1(3).

   (i) if two or more persons are entitled to land as joint tenants or tenants in common, a trust of land is normally imposed by the Law of Property Act 1925,[53] as amended by the 1996 Act[54];

  (ii) the Administration of Estates Act 1925,[55] as amended by the 1996 Act,[56] imposes a trust of land on the land of a person dying intestate;

 (iii) if trustees lend money on mortgage and the property becomes vested in them free from the right of repayment (such as by foreclosure), they hold it on a trust of land[57];

 (iv) land held for special purposes, such as schools or highways, is held on a trust of land for (usually) the grantor when the special purpose comes to an end[58]; and

  (v) if the trustees of a personalty settlement invest trust funds in the purchase of land after December 31, 1996, they held it on a trust of land unless the settlement otherwise provides.[59]

The 1996 Act defines "beneficiaries" more restrictively than the general law by excluding from that category persons who are merely annuitants.[60] This must be borne in mind when considering both the powers of the trustees and the rights of the beneficiaries.

2. Powers of trustees of land

Trustees of land are given, subject to contrary stipulation in the trust instrument,[61] all the powers of an absolute owner[62] and it is specifically provided that they can purchase land[63] by way of investment, for occupation by any beneficiary, or for any other reason.[64] They must, however, have regard to the rights of the beneficiaries,[65] although a purchaser need not be concerned to see that they have complied with this requirement.[66] They can also compel absolutely entitled beneficiaries to take a conveyance of the legal title.[67] The power which trustees for sale had before 1997 to partition land[68] now applies to all trusts of land,[69] again subject to contrary stipulation in the trust instrument.[70] This enables them to divide any land to which beneficiaries of full age are absolutely entitled in undivided shares[71] between those

---

[53] L.P.A. 1925 ss.34–36; below, p. 303.
[54] T.L.A.T.A. 1996, Sched. 2, paras 3, 4.
[55] A.E.A. 1925, s.33(1); above, p. 192.
[56] T.L.A.T.A. 1996, Sched. 2, para.5.
[57] L.P.A. 1925, s.31, as amended by T.L.A.T.A. 1996, Sched. 2, para.1.
[58] Reverter of Sites Act 1987, s.1, as amended by T.L.A.T.A. 1996, Sched. 2, para.6.
[59] L.P.A. 1925, s.32, as amended by T.L.A.T.A. 1996, Sched. 2, para. 2; see *Re Hanson* [1928] Ch. 96.
[60] T.L.A.T.A. 1996, s.22(3).
[61] *ibid.*, s.8(1).
[62] *ibid.*, s.6(1).
[63] *ibid.*, s.6(3).
[64] *ibid.*, s.6(4).
[65] *ibid.*, s.6(5).
[66] *ibid.*, s.16(1).
[67] *ibid.*, s.6(2).
[68] Under L.P.A. 1925, s.28 (which has been repealed).
[69] T.L.A.T.A. 1996, s.7.
[70] *ibid.*, s.8(1).
[71] See below, p. 306.

beneficiaries.[72] However, this requires either the consent of each of these beneficiaries,[73] although a purchaser need not be concerned to see that they have consented,[74] or, apparently, an order of the court.[75]

3. Curtailment of powers

It has already been seen that the trust instrument can reduce the powers of trustees from those of an absolute owner and take away the power to partition.[76] The trust instrument can also make the exercise of any of the powers of an absolute owner and the power to partition subject to the requirement that the consent of specified persons, usually but not necessarily beneficiaries, should first be obtained[77] (consent of the relevant beneficiaries is a prerequisite of partition anyway unless, apparently, it is ordered by the court). Any consent required from a minor must be obtained from one of his parents or his guardian[78] but any consent required from a mental patient can only be obtained from his receiver.[79]

If the consent of more than two persons is required, a bona fide purchaser for value is protected if the consent of any two such persons is obtained[80] and he need not concern himself with the consent of any minor[81] (but he will need the consent of the receiver of any mental patient unless two other persons have consented). But this protection is given only to such a purchaser: the trustees will be guilty of a breach of trust if they do not obtain the full number of consents stipulated from the appropriate persons. However, the court has power[82] to dispense with consents which cannot be obtained due to the absence of a person or the lack of a receiver[83] or where consent is unreasonably refused.[84] Under the previous legislation it was not required that the need for a consent be explicitly stated. This was able to be inferred, where, for example, the trust instrument gave a beneficiary a right to the land itself at a future date.[85] However, the 1996 Act only envisages needs for consent to be required by the trust instrument so it may no longer be possible for their need to be inferred in this way.

4. Delegation

The trustees have a power, which cannot be taken away by the trust instrument, to delegate revocably or irrevocably by power of attorney to one or more of the beneficiaries of full age entitled to an interest in possession in land (other than persons who are merely annuitants[86]) any of their functions as trustees which relate to that land.[87] They must delegate jointly, although any one trustee can revoke a revocable delegation,[88] and if a delegate ceases to be

[72] T.L.A.T.A. 1996, s.7(1).
[73] ibid., s.7(3).
[74] ibid., s.16(1).
[75] Under s.14; see *Rodway v. Landy* [2001] Ch. 703, where partition was denied.
[76] ibid., s.8(1).
[77] ibid., s.8(2). Contrast land subject to the Settled Land Act 1925: above, p. 276.
[78] ibid., s.10(3)(b).
[79] Under Mental Health Act 1983, s.99.
[80] T.L.A.T.A. 1996, s.10(1).
[81] ibid., s.10(3)(a).
[82] Under s.14(2)(a).
[83] Mental Health Act 1983, s.96(1)(k).
[84] *Re Beale's S.T.* [1932] 2 Ch. 15.
[85] *Re Herklots' W.T.* [1964] 1 W.L.R. 583, considered in *Dodsworth v. Dodsworth* [1973] E.G.D. 233.
[86] T.L.A.T.A. 1996, s.22(3).
[87] ibid., s.9(1).
[88] ibid., s.9(3).

beneficially entitled to an interest in possession a revocable delegation to him is revoked automatically.[89] It is presumed in favour of anyone dealing with a person to whom functions have so been delegated that that he qualified to be a delegate in the absence of knowledge to the contrary and that absence of knowledge is also conclusively presumed in favour of any purchaser whose interest depends on the validity of the delegation if he makes a statutory declaration to that effect not later than three months after the completion of the purchase.[90] Delegates are in the same position and have the same duties and rights as the trustees in respect of the functions delegated to them (although they cannot sub-delegate or give a good receipt for capital sums)[91] and the trustees are only liable for the acts of delegates if they did not exercise reasonable care in deciding to delegate the function in question to the delegate in question.[92]

5. Consultation

Subject to contrary stipulation in the trust instrument,[93] the trustees are under an obligation, when exercising any of their functions relating to land subject to the trust (other than their right to compel absolutely entitled beneficiaries to take a conveyance of the legal title[94]), so far as is practicable to consult the beneficiaries of full age entitled to interests in possession in the land (other than persons who are merely annuitants[95]). The trustees must, so far as is consistent with the general interests of the trust, give effect to the wishes of those beneficiaries or, in the event that they are not all in agreement, to the wishes of the majority by value.[96]

Before 1997 this obligation to consult was confined to trusts for sale which were implied by statute, in which case it could not be ousted by contrary stipulation, or which manifested an intention that the obligation was to apply.[97] This remains the position for trusts of land created by wills made before 1997[98]. It also remains the position for trusts of land which were created as trusts for sale before 1997 or which were created after 1996 by reference to trusts for sale created before 1997 unless the settlor (or the survivor(s) of joint settlors) executes a deed stating that the obligation is to apply[99] (once executed, such a deed is irrevocable[1]).

Even when the obligation to consult arises, the trustees are not actually obliged to follow the wishes of the beneficiaries, nor need a purchaser be concerned to see that the trustees have complied with the obligation.[2]

6. Occupation of the trust property

A beneficiary who is beneficially entitled to an interest in possession under a trust of land (other than a person who is merely an annuitant[3]) is entitled by reason of his interest to

---

[89] *ibid.*, s.9(4).
[90] *ibid.*, s.9(2).
[91] *ibid.*, s.9(7).
[92] *ibid.*, s.9(8).
[93] *ibid.*, s.11(2)(a).
[94] *ibid.*, s.11(2)(c).
[95] *ibid.*, s.22(3).
[96] *ibid.*, s.11(1).
[97] L.P.A. 1925, s.26 as amended by L.P.(Am.)A. 1926, Sched.
[98] T.L.A.T.A. 1996, s.11(2)(b).
[99] *ibid.*, s.11(3).
[1] *ibid.*, s.11(4).
[2] *ibid.*, s.16(1); this was also the case prior to 1997 (L.P.A. 1925, s.26 as amended by L.P.(Am.)A. 1926, Sched.)
[3] T.L.A.T.A. 1996, s.22(3).

occupy the land at any time when the purposes of the trust include making the land available for his occupation or the land is held by the trustees so as to be so available.[4] This right does not extend to land which is either unavailable or unsuitable for occupation by any particular beneficiary.[5]

At common law, where two or more persons are entitled to occupy land, the basic rule is that each of them is entitled to physical possession of every part of the land and to the use and enjoyment of it "in proper manner".[6] From this rule is derived the further rule that such co-owners are not obliged to pay rent to one another simply because only one of them happens to be in occupation.[7] Hitherto it has only been in quite exceptional circumstances that the courts have refused to allow a co-owner to exercise his right to occupation and use.[8] However, where two or more beneficiaries of a trust of land are entitled to occupy land under the 1996 Act, the trustees may exclude or restrict the entitlement of any one or more of them but not of all of them.[9] It has been held that this provision entitles the trustees to permit or the court to order[10] occupation of different parts of the land by different beneficiaries where such distinct occupation is feasible.[11] This is done by restricting each beneficiary from occupying specific parts of the land, thus enabling joint occupation of areas such as entrances, corridors, stairways and lifts and individual occupation of the remainder of the land by the different beneficiaries.[12] The trustees must not exercise the power to exclude or restrict occupation unreasonably[13] or so as to prevent any person who is in occupation from continuing to occupy the land unless he consents or the court so orders.[14]

The trustees may also from time to time impose reasonable conditions on any beneficiary in relation to his occupation of the land,[15] although not in a manner which is likely to result in the beneficiary ceasing to occupy the land unless he consents or the court so orders.[16] In particular the trustees may require the occupying beneficiary to pay outgoings and expenses,[17] to assume obligations in relation to the land or to any activity conducted thereon[18] and, where another beneficiary's entitlement to occupy has been excluded or restricted, to pay compensation to the latter either directly or by forgoing in his favour other benefits under the trust to which the occupying beneficiary would otherwise have been entitled.[19] Reasonable conditions also include requiring the beneficiaries to pay the costs of any necessary adaptation of any premises where different beneficiaries have been allowed to occupy different parts of them.[20]

---

[4] *ibid.*, s.12(1).
[5] *ibid.*, s.12(2).
[6] *Bull v. Bull* [1955] 1 Q.B. 234 at 237.
[7] *Jones v. Jones* [1977] 1 W.L.R. 438.
[8] *Chhokar v. Chhokar* (1984) 5 F.L.R. 313.
[9] T.L.A.T.A. 1966, s.13(1).
[10] Under s.14.
[11] *Rodway v. Landy* [2001] Ch. 703.
[12] This was done in *Rodway v. Landy* [2001] Ch.703.
[13] T.L.A.T.A., s.13(2).
[14] *ibid.*, s.13(7)(a). The court did so order in *Rodway v. Landy* [2001] Ch. 703.
[15] *ibid.*, s.13(3).
[16] *ibid.*, s.13(7)(b).
[17] *ibid.*, s.13(5)(a).
[18] *ibid.*, s.13(5)(b).
[19] *ibid.*, s.13(6).
[20] *Rodway v. Landy* [2001] Ch. 703.

In exercising these different powers, the trustees are to have regard to the intentions of the settlor or testator, the purposes for which the land is held, and the circumstances and wishes of each of the beneficiaries who is entitled to occupy the land.[21]

7. Dispute resolution

"Any person who is a trustee of land or has an interest in property subject to a trust of land" may apply to the court for an order relating to the exercise by the trustees of any of their functions, including an order directing them to consult or relieving them from their obligation to do so, or declaring the nature or extent of anyone's interest in the trust property.[22] This provision obviously extends to mortgagees, who have an interest in the mortgaged land; it also extends to a person who is merely an annuitant and to trustees in bankruptcy of beneficiaries and annuitants. It presumably also extends to a creditor who has a charging order against the interest of a beneficiary; under the previous legislation[23] the similar expression "person interested" was held to include such a creditor.[24] The 1996 Act specifically provides that the provision also extends to trusts of the proceeds of sale of land and the trustees of such trusts.[25]

In determining an application by anyone other than a trustee in bankruptcy, the matters to which the court has to have regard include: first, the intentions of the settlor or testator; secondly, the purposes for which the land is held; thirdly, the welfare of any minor who occupies or might reasonably be expected to occupy any land subject to the trust as his home; and, fourthly, the interests of any secured creditor of any beneficiary[26] (other than a person who is merely an annuitant[27]). Where the application concerns the occupation of any trust property, the court must additionally have regard to the circumstances and wishes of each of the beneficiaries who is entitled to occupy the land.[28] In any other case other than one concerning the occupation of any trust property or one relating to the trustees' right to compel absolutely entitled beneficiaries to take a conveyance of the legal title,[29] the court must instead additionally have regard to the circumstances and wishes of the beneficiaries of full age entitled to interests in possession in the land[30] (other than persons who are merely annuitants[31]).

However, where the application is made by a trustee in bankruptcy, the court must instead make such order as it thinks just and reasonable having regard to the following matters: first, the interests of the bankrupt's creditors; secondly, where the application concerns a dwelling-house which is or has been the home of the bankrupt, his spouse or his former spouse, the conduct of the spouse or former spouse in so far as it contributed to the bankruptcy, the needs and financial resources of the spouse or former spouse, and the needs of any children; and, thirdly, all the circumstances of the case other than the needs of the bankrupt.[32] On any application made more than a year after the appointment of the trustee in bankruptcy, the

---

[21] *ibid.*, s.13(4).
[22] *ibid.*, s.14.
[23] L.P.A. 1925, s.30 (now repealed).
[24] *Midland Bank Plc. v. Pike* [1988] 2 All E.R. 434.
[25] T.L.A.T.A. 1996, s.17.
[26] *ibid.*, s.15(1).
[27] *ibid.*, s.22(3).
[28] *ibid.*, s.15(2).
[29] This interpretation of was confirmed in *The Mortgage Corporation v. Shaire* [2000] 1 F.L.R. 973 at 991.
[30] *ibid.*, s.15(3).
[31] *ibid.*, s.22(3).
[32] Insolvency Act 1986, s.335A(2).

court must assume, unless the circumstances of the case are exceptional, that the interests of the bankrupt's creditors outweigh all other considerations.[33]

It has been held that the matters to which the court is to have regard are not exclusive but inclusive and that other matters may also be of relevance.[34]

All the reported decisions to date concerning proceedings of this type have been disputes between or involving co-owners. It therefore seems more appropriate to deal with these decisions in the chapter on co-ownership.[35] It should however be emphasised at this stage that it has been held[36] that in disputes between husband and wife where there are no third party interests the only relevant legislation is the Matrimonial Causes Act 1973,[37] not the 1996 Act.

PART 5—TRUSTS AND TRUSTEES

Much of the law of trusts and trustees is more appropriate to text-books on equity and trusts than to a book on real property. But some account must be given here of the general points that most concern the law of land, in addition to the special provisions for settled land and land held on trust for sale.

Sect. 1. Classification of Trusts

1. Conveyancing classification

From the point of view of a conveyancer, a trust whose subject-matter is land falls under one of two heads:

  (i) trusts of land, which now include express trusts for sale and bare trusts; or

  (ii) settlements under the Settled Land Act 1925.

All these types of trusts have already been dealt with.

2. Equity's classification

In equity, trusts have been classified in a number of ways. A traditional classification which has a statutory basis[38] is to distinguish between express, resulting, implied and constructive trusts. Previous editions of this work have also classified separately trusts which are imposed by statute. Although the editor of this edition regards these trusts as examples of express trusts, they will nevertheless be set out first and the traditional classification will be examined thereafter.

(a) Trusts imposed by statute

Various trusts are imposed by statute. Thus:

---

[33] *ibid.*, s.335A(3).
[34] *Bank of Ireland Home Mortgages Ltd. v. Bell* [2001] 2 F.L.R. 809 at 815 (para.24).
[35] Below, p. 321.
[36] In *Tee v. Tee* [1999] 2 F.L.R. 613.
[37] ss.22–25.
[38] L.P.A. 1925, s.53(2); L.P.(M.P.)A 1989, s.2(4).

(i) a statutory trust of land is imposed in the case of joint tenancies and tenancies in common (prior to 1997 what was imposed was a statutory trust for sale)[39];

(ii) where a person dies intestate, in certain cases his personal representatives hold his property on a statutory trust of land for his surviving spouse and relatives (prior to 1997 what was imposed was a statutory trust for sale)[40];

(iii) from 1926 to 1996 an attempt to convey a legal estate to a minor operated as a contract for value to make a proper settlement under the Settled Land Act 1925 and in the meantime to hold the land in trust for the minor or minors[41];

(iv) since 1996, an attempt to convey a legal estate to a minor operates as a declaration of trust in favour of the minor[42]; and

(v) a statutory trust of land is created when property on the security of which trustees have lent money becomes vested in them by foreclosure, or where trustees of a personalty settlement exercise a power conferred thereby to invest money in the purchase of land.[43]

Both (i) and (ii) are referred to in the 1925 legislation as "the statutory trusts". Although other trusts imposed by statute are in a sense "statutory" trusts, they are usually not thus referred to, and to avoid confusion they are perhaps better called "trusts imposed by statute".

(b) Express trusts

Express trusts are those expressly created by the settlor or testator (or, in the opinion of the editor of this edition, imposed by statute). Trusts created by a settlor or testator must be formally valid, must satisfy the "three certainties", must have a human beneficiary capable of enforcing them, and must be completely constituted.

(i) Formal validity: The formalities required for the creation of a trust and for the transfer of an interest under a trust are considered below.[44]

(ii) The three certainties[45]: The first certainty is that there must be imperative words of trust. At one time merely precatory words, expressing only a hope or request, were sometimes held to suffice. But today precatory words are no longer enough unless the instrument as a whole shows an intention to create a trust. The word "trust" need not be used, but there must be language showing an imperative obligation. Secondly, there must be certainty of subject-matter, both as to the property to be held on trust and as to the beneficial interest to be taken by each beneficiary. Thirdly, except in the case of charitable trusts, there must be certainty of objects. It must be possible to ascertain who the beneficiaries are. A trust for "my

---

[39] Below, p. 303.
[40] Above, p. 192.
[41] S.L.A. 1925, s.27(1) (a statutory exception to the equitable rule that an imperfect voluntary conveyance will not be treated as a declaration of trust: below, p. 291).
[42] T.L.A.T.A., Sched. 1, paras 1 and 2.
[43] Above, pp. 281, 284; below, p. 502.
[44] Below, pp. 293, 294.
[45] Parker and Mellows, pp. 82–105.

old friends" is uncertain as to the concept of the persons who are to be regarded as the donor's "old friends".[46]

The result of the absence of any of the certainties is as follows. If there is no certainty as to the subject-matter to be held on trust, the transaction is wholly ineffective. If that certainty is present, but there is no certainty of words, the person entitled to the property holds it beneficially, free from any trust. If both these certainties are present, but there is uncertainty of objects, there is a resulting trust for the settlor. The same applies where there is uncertainty of subject-matter as regards the beneficial interest, unless any beneficiary can establish a claim to the whole.

(iii) The beneficiary requirement[47]: Except in the case of charitable trusts and some further anomalous exceptions which will be applied but not extended, it is necessary that there is some human beneficiary capable of enforcing the trust. The absence of any such beneficiary renders the trust ineffective and there is a resulting trust for the settlor.

(iv) Completely and incompletely constituted trusts[48]: A trust is completely constituted as soon as the trust property is vested in the trustee upon the trusts; until then it is incompletely constituted. The importance of the distinction is that a completely constituted trust may be enforced by any of the beneficiaries, even if they have provided no consideration for the creation of the trust and are therefore what equity describes as volunteers. On the other hand, if the trust is incompletely constituted it cannot be enforced by volunteers but only by beneficiaries who have given valuable consideration, although volunteers may nevertheless be able to enforce a contract or covenant with the settlor to which they are parties or third parties[49] and thereby obtain financial compensation. A trust may be completely constituted either by the trust property being effectually vested in the trustees upon the requisite trusts, or else by a "present irrevocable declaration of trust" being made by the settlor. In the latter case the settlor need not expressly declare that he holds the property on trust, but he must do something equivalent to this. An ineffective transfer to trustees will not be construed as being a declaration of trust except where the settlor has done all in his power to vest the property in the trustees,[50] and so there is no equity to perfect an imperfect transfer.[51]

(c) Resulting trusts

A resulting trust is said to exist where, on a conveyance of property, a trust arises by operation of equity.[52] Three cases must be considered.

(i) Trusts not exhaustive: Where a disposition of property is made by the owner and all or part of the equitable interest is not effectively disposed of, there is a resulting trust for the owner. If the property is conveyed expressly on trust, for example "to X on trust", there is no difficulty; a trustee can take no benefit from the fact that the declared trusts do not exhaust the beneficial interest, and so much of the equitable interest as is not disposed of results to the grantor. Thus if G conveys property to X on trust for a beneficiary who is dead, there is

---

[46] See *Brown v. Gould* [1972] Ch. 53 at 57.

[47] Parker and Mellows, pp. 105–123.

[48] *ibid.*, pp. 124–162.

[49] See Contracts (Rights of Third Parties) Act 1999.

[50] *Re Rose* [1952] Ch. 499.

[51] *Richards v. Delbridge* (1874) L.R. 18 Eq. 11 (attempted gift of lease by indorsement). For a statutory exception, see above, p. 203.

[52] See generally Parker and Mellows, pp. 238–265.

a resulting trust of the entire beneficial interest in favour of G. Similarly if G conveys property to X on trust for Y for life without specifying any gifts in remainder, there is a resulting trust of the beneficial interest in favour of G subject to Y's life interest. What a person fails effectually to dispose of remains automatically vested in him.[53]

(ii) Voluntary conveyance: Before 1926, on a conveyance by G to X made without any consideration and without expressing any use, there was a resulting use to G in fee simple which the Statute of Uses 1535 promptly executed, thereby making the conveyance totally ineffective. The Law of Property Act 1925[54] provides that, in a voluntary conveyance executed after 1925, no resulting trust for the grantor is to be implied merely by reason that the property is not expressed to be conveyed for the use or benefit of the grantee. Because of the presence in this provision of a double negative, its effect has been disputed.[55] However, it has now been held that, as stated in previous editions of this work, its effect is to prevent any corresponding resulting trust of land arising after 1925.[56] However, this does not prevent a resulting trust for the grantor from arising where it appears that the grantee was intended to take as a trustee, as where the property is conveyed on express trusts which fails to exhaust the entire beneficial interest; and in other cases there will be presumed to be a resulting trust, though the presumption is easily rebutted.[57]

(iii) Purchase in the name of another: Where a conveyance is made to one person, but the purchase money is provided by another as purchaser, there is a resulting trust in favour of the person providing the purchase money. If V conveys land to P, A being the real purchaser and as such providing the purchase money, prima facie P holds on a resulting trust for A.[58] Nevertheless, this is only a presumption which can be rebutted by evidence that P was intended to benefit.[59] It may also be displaced by the presumption of advancement. That presumption arises if P is the wife, child or ward of A. It is itself rebuttable, and it does not apply to other relationships, as where A is the wife, child, mother, stepmother or aunt of P.[60]

(d) Implied trusts

Previous editions of this work have stated that an implied trust arises where, without any conveyance of the property in question having been made, two people enter into such a relationship with each other that equity implies that one holds on trust for the other. Thus if one person agrees for value to make a settlement or conveyance of his estate, equity forthwith deems him to be a trustee of that estate for the beneficiaries or the purchaser. Again, under a contract for the sale of land the vendor holds it on an implied trust for the purchaser, subject to certain important rights which protect the vendor.[61] The editor of this edition instead regards both these trusts as constructive trusts and considers that the terms "implied trust" and "resulting trust" are synonymous; according to this view there is no separate category of implied trusts.

---

[53] See *Re Vandervell's Trusts (No. 2)* [1974] Ch. 269 at 288, 289, 294 (not affected on appeal).
[54] s.60(3), (4).
[55] Parker and Mellows, pp. 254–255.
[56] *Lohia v. Lohia* [2001] W.T.L.R. 101.
[57] See *Re Vandervell's Trusts (No. 2)* [1974] Ch. 269.
[58] See *Dyer v. Dyer* (1788) 2 Cox Eq. 92 at 93.
[59] *Fowkes v. Pascoe* (1875) 10 Ch.App. 343.
[60] See Parker and Mellows, pp. 243–247.
[61] Above, p. 154.

(e) Constructive trusts[62]

Constructive trusts are trusts which arise by operation of equity, usually but not always as a consequence of a breach of some pre-existing fiduciary relationship. The best known type of constructive trust arises where a trustee or other fiduciary makes a profit as a result of his fiduciary position. He will hold the profit on constructive trust for the person to whom he owes his fiduciary duty. If a person receives property knowing that it is subject to a trust and that the transfer to him was in breach of trust, he will hold it subject to the trusts as a constructive trustee. If instead he receives the property innocently but later, after getting knowledge of the trusts, he deals with it inconsistently with the trusts, he will similarly be a constructive trustee. Further, a person who dishonestly acts as an accessory to a trustee who commits a breach of trust is often said to be liable as a constructive trustee even if he receives none of the trust property; however, a trust cannot exist without any trust property so such a person is better described as being liable to account as a trustee. The editor of this edition also regards as constructive trusts the trusts which were classified as implied trusts in previous editions.

Although the principal categories of constructive trusts are those set out above, they have expanded into other fields, including cases of fraud and, more recently, estoppel. Today there is a tendency for the courts to hold that a constructive trust exists in a variety of other cases where equity and good conscience require it. Indeed, some jurisdictions now treat constructive trusts as being a general remedy in cases of inequitable conduct[63] but English law has yet to adopt this approach and is unlikely to do so.

(f) Uncertainties of classification

It will have been observed that this edition of this work has adopted a different classification from previous editions. There are other variants; some commentators treat "constructive trusts" as including all except express trusts; and secret trusts, trusts created by testators[64] whose existence and/or terms are not revealed on the face of their wills, have been classified in every conceivable way. In practice, except for the distinction between express trusts and other trusts, which can affect the formal validity of the trust, the category into which a trust falls of no great importance; the division is frequently little more than a convenient way of setting out the nature of the different forms of trust.

Sect. 2. Formalities for the creation of a trust[65]

1. Pure Personalty

An enforceable trust of pure personalty can be validly created by word of mouth, whether the owner is declaring himself a trustee of the property or is transferring it to a third party on trust for the beneficiaries.[66]

---

[62] See Parker and Mellows, pp. 266–378.
[63] See *Re Sharpe* [1980] 1 W.L.R. 219 at 225.
[64] And by those who die intestate.
[65] See Parker and Mellows, pp. 44–62.
[66] See *M'Fadden v. Jenkyns* (1842) 1 Ph. 153.

2. Land

(a) Evidenced by writing

Before 1677, a trust of land could be created by word of mouth, but since then the Statute of Frauds 1677[67] and more recently the Law of Property Act 1925[68] have provided that a declaration of trust respecting any land or any interest therein must be evidenced either by writing signed by some person able to declare the trust, or else by his will. The chief points to note on this provision are as follows:

(i) "Any land". This includes leaseholds (and included copyholds before they were abolished).

(ii) "Evidenced". The actual words in both statutes are "manifested and proved". It is settled that this does not require that the declaration should actually be made in writing, but that it suffices if an oral declaration is supported by some signed acknowledgement or declaration in existence when the action is begun, such as a letter,[69] or a recital in a deed, even if this was made some time after the trust was declared.[70] The writing must show not only that there is a trust but also what its terms are.[71]

(iii) "Some person able to declare the trust". This means the owner of the beneficial interest, so that if a trust is declared of an equitable interest held under an existing trust, the writing must be signed by the beneficiary; the signature of the trustees is not sufficient.[72] There is no provision for signature by an agent.[73]

Failure to comply with these requirements renders the trust unenforceable rather than void. Consequently, the beneficiary can bring seek to enforce the trust and it is only if the absence of writing is pleaded that he will be unable to do so.[74]

(b) Exceptions

To these requirements, there are two important exceptions:

(i) Resulting, implied or constructive trusts: The statutory requirements do not affect the creation of resulting, implied or constructive trusts[75] (operation is restrictively interpreted; a disposition of an interest under one of these types of trust must nevertheless comply with the statutory requirements[76]). It has now been held that estoppel interests take effect behind a constructive trust.[77] Consequently, if a landowner declared orally that he was holding land on trust for another and that other acted to his detriment on the strength of that assurance, it

---

[67] ss.7, 8.
[68] s.53(1)(b).
[69] *Childers v. Childers* (1857) 1 De G. and J. 482.
[70] *Rochefoucauld v. Boustead* [1897] 1 Ch. 196 at 206.
[71] *Smith v. Matthews* (1861) 3 De G.F. and J. 139; and see above, p. 148.
[72] *Kronheim v. Johnson* (1877) 7 Ch.D. 60.
[73] Contrast transfers, below.
[74] *North v. Loomes* [1919] 1 Ch.378 (actually a decision on Statute of Frauds 1677, s.4 (subsequently L.P.A. 1925, s.40) which also required only evidentiary writing).
[75] L.P.A. 1925, s.53(2), replacing Statute of Frauds 1677, s.8.
[76] *Grey v. I.R.C.* [1960] A.C. 1 (actually an authority on s.53(1)(c)).
[77] *Yaxley v. Gotts* [2000] Ch. 162 (party to void contract for the sale of land estopped from denying its validity).

appears that he would be able to enforce that trust against the landowner on the basis that the latter was estopped from denying the trust and was therefore a constructive trustee of the land for him.

(ii) Fraud: The court will not permit the statutory requirements to be used as an engine of fraud. "It is a fraud on the part of a person to whom land is conveyed as a trustee, and who knows it was so conveyed, to deny the trust and claim the land himself. Consequently, notwithstanding the statute, it is competent for a person claiming land conveyed to another to prove by parol evidence that it was so conveyed upon trust for the claimant, and that the grantee, knowing the facts, is denying the trust and relying upon the form of conveyance and the statute, in order to keep the land himself."[78] The grantee would therefore be an express trustee. It appears that the grantor could now alternatively rely on the doctrine of equitable proprietary estoppel to claim that the grantor was a constructive trustee for him.[79]

Sect. 3. Formalities for transferring an interest under a trust

By the Law of Property Act 1925,[80] a disposition[81] of an existing equitable interest or trust must either be in writing signed by the person disposing of it or his agent authorised in writing, or else be made by will. On this, the following points should be noted.

1. "In writing"

A parol assignment supported by evidence thereof in writing is not enough. Unlike the rule for the creation of trusts, the rule here requires the assignment itself to be written, and is thus not a mere rule of evidence.

2. "Signed by the person disposing of it or his agent authorised in writing"

This should be contrasted with:

  (i) the rule for the creation of a trust of land, where the signature of an agent is not enough[82]; and

  (ii) the rule for contracts for the disposition of land, where the signature of an agent suffices even if his authority was given only by word of mouth.[83]

3. Scope

The rule applies to pure personalty as well as land. Although a trust of pure personalty is enforceable even if it is not evidenced in writing, once the trust has been created, a disposition of any interest under it is void unless it is in writing. Whether a declaration of a sub-trust is a disposition is a matter of some controversy. The general view is that it is (and so requires writing) unless the sub-trustee has retained some interest under the trust or some active duties under the sub-trust.

---

[78] *Rochefoucauld v. Boustead* [1897] 1 Ch. 196 at 206, *per* Lindley L.J.
[79] Above.
[80] s.53(1)(c), replacing Statute of Frauds 1677, s.9.
[81] See *Grey v. I.R.C.* [1960] A.C. 1 (oral direction); *Oughtred v. I.R.C.* [1960] A.C. 206 (oral agreement); but see *Vandervell v. I.R.C.* [1967] 2 A.C. 291 (oral directions extended to legal estate).
[82] Above.
[83] Above, p. 153.

4. Effect of non-compliance

Failure to comply with these requirements renders the disposition wholly void and its subject-matter remains vested in the person disposing of it.

5. Exceptions

To these requirements, there are the same two important exceptions:

(i) Resulting, implied or constructive trusts: The statutory provisions do not affect the creation or operation of resulting, implied or constructive trusts[84] (as before operation is restrictively interpreted; a disposition of an interest under one of these types of trust must nevertheless comply with the requirements[85]). And if the holder of an equitable interest purported to assign it orally to someone who acted to his detriment on the strength of that purported assignment, it appears that he would be able to enforce that assignment on the basis that the assignor was estopped from denying its existence and therefore held the equitable interest on constructive sub-trust for him.[86]

(ii) Fraud: The court will not permit the statutory provisions to be used as an engine of fraud. Consequently, if the owner of an equitable interest, such as the interest of a beneficial co-owner of land, purported to assign it for value and later sought to raise the statutory formalities in order to claim that he was still beneficially entitled, he would hold his beneficial interest on constructive sub-trustee for the person to whom he had purported to assign it. It appears that the assignee could now achieve the same result by relying on the doctrine of equitable proprietary estoppel.[87]

Sect. 4. Trustees

The Trustee Act 1925, as amended, makes general provision for the appointment, replacement, retirement and removal of trustees, and also for the vesting of the trust property when a change is made. These heads will be taken in turn.

Sect. 5. Appointment of trustees

1. Original appointment

(a) Appointment

Trustees are usually appointed by the settlor when creating the trust. If he neither makes an appointment nor makes any provision for one, the court may appoint trustees; once the trust has been created, the settlor has no power of making an appointment unless he has reserved such a power. A person appointed trustee need not accept the trust even if he had agreed to do so before it was created, provided he disclaims the trust before he has accepted it either expressly or by acting as trustee.[88] A disclaimer should preferably be express but it may be

---

[84] L.P.A. 1925, s.53(2), replacing Statute of Frauds 1677, s.8.
[85] *Grey v. I.R.C.* [1960] A.C. 1.
[86] By analogy with *Yaxley v. Gotts* [2000] Ch. 162; above.
[87] Above.
[88] See *Noble v. Meymott* (1851) 14 Beav. 471.

inferred from conduct[89]; and although the presumption is in favour of acceptance, a person appointed a trustee who maintains a complete inactivity in relation to the trust for a long period may be held thereby to have disclaimed the trust.[90] Disclaimer retrospectively divests the person appointed both of his office and of the trust property.[91]

(b) Maximum number

Since 1925 not more than four trustees of a settlement subject to the Settled Land Act 1925 or, until 1997, a trust for sale or, since 1996, a trust of land have been able to be appointed. If more than four are named as trustees, the first four who are able and willing to act become trustees to the exclusion of the others.[92] These provisions apply only to land; and in general there is no limit to the number of trustees of pure personalty.

(c) Minimum number

There is no minimum number of trustees even in the case of land. But in the case of settlements under the Settled Land Act 1925 or trusts of land, a sole trustee cannot, notwithstanding any contrary provision, give a valid receipt for capital money unless that trustee is a trust corporation.[93] This restriction, however, does not affect the right of a sole personal representative acting as such to give valid receipts for purchase money,[94] for example where a sole administrator sells under the trust which is imposed on all the property of an intestate.[95]

2. Replacement

(a) The power

Even if there are properly appointed trustees when the trust is created, it may later become necessary to appoint new trustees, such as owing to the death of trustees. The events upon which new trustees can be appointed may be specified in the trust instrument. This is not usual, however, and reliance is normally placed on the statutory provisions, which apply notwithstanding any such express provision[96] unless a contrary intention is shown.[97] By the Trustee Act 1925[98] a new trustee or trustees may be appointed if a trustee "is dead; or remains outside the United Kingdom for a continuous period exceeding 12 months; or desires to be discharged from all or any of his trusts or powers; or refuses to act; or is unfit to act; or is incapable of acting; or is a minor; or is removed under a power in the trust instrument".

(b) Mode of appointment

The appointment must be in writing and must be made[99]:

---

[89] Re Birchall (1889) 40 Ch.D. 436.
[90] Re Clout and Frewer's Contract [1924] 2 Ch. 230 (29 years' inactivity).
[91] Re Martinez' Trusts (1870) 22 L.T. 403.
[92] T.A. 1925, s.34(2).
[93] S.L.A. 1925, s.18(1); L.P.A. 1925, s.27(2); see above, pp. 84 et seq.
[94] L.P.A. 1925, s.27(2).
[95] Above, p. 192.
[96] See Re Wheeler and De Rochow [1896] 1 Ch. 315.
[97] T.A. 1925, s.69(2).
[98] s.36(1), replacing earlier provisions.
[99] ibid., ss.36(1), 41, replacing earlier provisions.

(i) by the person or persons nominated by the trust instrument for the purpose of appointing new trustees; in default of there being any such person able and willing to act,

(ii) by the remaining trustees; in default of any,

(iii) by the personal representatives of the last remaining trustee; in default of any,

(iv) by the court.

Since 1996, if there is no person nominated by the trust instrument for the purpose of appointing new trustees and the beneficiaries under the trust are of full age and capacity and are between them absolutely entitled to the property subject to the trust,[1] they may give a direction to any trustee to retire[2] and/or give a direction to the trustees or to the personal representatives of the last trustee to appoint the persons specified in the direction.[3] Where a trustee is directed to retire, once reasonable arrangements have been made for the protection of any rights of his in connection with the trust, he must by deed retire provided that there will thereafter be either a trust corporation or two persons to act as trustees and either another person is to be appointed or the continuing trustees by deed give their consent.[4] Similar provisions apply where it is necessary to replace a trustee who is incapable of exercising his functions as such by reason of mental disorder and there is no one able and willing to appoint a replacement.[5]

(c) Who may be appointed

It is expressly provided that the person making the appointment may appoint himself.[6] Even if he appoints a person whom the court would not normally appoint, such as a beneficiary, or the husband of a beneficiary, or the solicitor to the trustees or beneficiaries, the appointment will not thereby be rendered invalid[7]; but an appointment of a minor as trustee, whether of realty or personalty, is void.[8] Where a single trustee was originally appointed, the appointment of a single trustee in his place is valid,[9] except that in the case of settlements under the Settled Land Act and of trusts of land, a sole trustee (not being a trust corporation) cannot be appointed under the statutory power if, after his appointment, he would be unable to give receipts for capital money,[10] as would be the case if there were no other trustee. There is never any obligation to appoint more than two trustees even if originally more than two were appointed.[11] The appointment may increase the number of trustees, provided that in the case of settlements under the Settled Land Act and of trusts of land, the number is not increased above four.[12]

---

[1] T.L.A.T.A. 1996, s.19(1).
[2] *ibid.*, s.19(2)(a)
[3] *ibid.*, s.19(2)(b).
[4] *ibid.*, s.19(3).
[5] *ibid.*, s.20.
[6] T.A. 1925, s.36(1).
[7] *Re Earl of Stamford* [1896] 1 Ch. 288.
[8] L.P.A. 1925, s.20.
[9] T.A. 1925, s.37(1)(c), replacing earlier provisions.
[10] *ibid.*, s.37(2).
[11] *ibid.*, s.37(1)(c), replacing earlier provisions.
[12] *ibid.*, s.34(2).

3. Additional trustees

Even though no occasion has arisen for the appointment of new trustees, if there are not more than three trustees and none of them is a trust corporation, one or more additional trustees may be appointed, provided the effect of the appointment is not to increase the number above four. The appointment must be made by the same persons and in the same way as an appointment of new trustees, except that there is no provision for an appointment by the personal representatives of the last remaining trustee, or for the appointor to appoint himself.[13]

Sect. 6. Retirement and removal of trustees

1. Retirement

A trustee may retire:

(i) If another trustee is appointed in his place; this has already been considered.[14]

(ii) If no new trustee is being appointed in his place, provided that after his discharge there will be left to act in the trust either a trust corporation or two or more persons (until 1997 it had to be two or more individuals). The retirement is effected by a deed declaring the trustee's desire to retire; this is executed by the retiring trustee, the continuing trustees and the person entitled to appoint new trustees, all of whom must concur in the retirement.[15]

(iii) If authorised to do so by an express power in the trust instrument.

(iv) With the consent of all the beneficiaries if they are all of full age and capacity and are between them absolutely entitled to the property subject to the trust (in these circumstances they can now of course direct him to retire if there is no person nominated by the trust instrument for the purpose of appointing new trustees[16]).

(v) With the leave of the court; this method should be employed only in cases of difficulty, for if the trustee applies to the court without good cause he may have to pay his own costs.[17]

2. Removal

A trustee may be removed:

(i) Under the power to appoint new trustees considered above.[18]

(ii) Under any express power to do so contained in the trust instrument.

(iii) Since 1996, the beneficiaries may remove any trustee if there is no person nominated by the trust instrument for the purpose of appointing new trustees and they

[13] *ibid.*, s.36(6); *Re Power's S.T.* [1951] Ch. 1074.
[14] Above, p. 298.
[15] T.A. 1925, s.39(1), replacing earlier provisions.
[16] T.L.A.T.A. 1996, s.19.
[17] *Porter v. Watts* (1852) 21 L.J.Ch. 211.
[18] Above, p. 298.

are of full age and capacity and are between them absolutely entitled to the property subject to the trust.[19]

(iv) Under the court's inherent jurisdiction to remove a trustee where it is necessary for the safety of the trust property or the welfare of the beneficiaries,[20] as where the trustee has been inactive for a long while, or his interests conflict with those of the beneficiaries, or there has been friction with the beneficiaries on the mode of administering the trust.[21]

Sect. 7. Vesting of trust property

Some trustees have no property vested in them, as is often the case with trustees of settlements subject to the Settled Land Act 1925; in such cases, no question of the devolution of trust property arises. But where property is vested in trustees, questions of the transfer of the trust property arise on their death, retirement or removal, or on the appointment of new trustees.

1. On death

Where there is a plurality of trustees, they are always made joint tenants or joint owners of the trust property, whether it is real or personal. The advantage of this is that on the death of one trustee the estate or interest vested in him passes to the surviving trustees by the doctrine of survivorship.[22] If a sole surviving trustee dies the estate or interest held on trust vests in his personal representatives notwithstanding any provision in his will.[23] Until new trustees are appointed, the personal representatives may exercise any power or trust exercisable by the former trustee, without being obliged to do so[24]; and they may appoint new trustees.[25]

2. On appointment of new trustees

(a) Vesting declaration

On an appointment of new trustees, the trust property has to be vested in the new trustees jointly with any continuing trustees. Formerly, a formal conveyance of the trust property by the persons in whom it was vested was necessary; if A and B were trustees and C was appointed a new trustee on A's death, B had to convey the trust property to himself and C jointly.[26] But by section 40 of the Trustee Act 1925,[27] if an appointment of new trustees is made by deed, a declaration therein by the appointor that the property shall vest in the trustees (a "vesting declaration") is sufficient to vest the property in them. This applies to all deeds executed after 1881[28]; and if the deed is executed after 1925, a vesting declaration is implied in the absence of an express provision to the contrary.[29]

---

[19] T.L.A.T.A. 1996, s.19.
[20] *Re Wrightson* [1908] 1 Ch. 789 at 803.
[21] *Letterstedt v. Broers* (1884) 9 App.Cas. 371.
[22] Above, p. 4; below, p. 304.
[23] A.E.A. 1925, s.1.
[24] T.A. 1925, s.18(2).
[25] *ibid.*, s.36(1).
[26] See M. and W. (4th ed.), p. 458.
[27] Replacing earlier provisions.
[28] T.A. 1925, s.40(6).
[29] *ibid.*, s.40(1).

These provisions apply even if the trust property is not vested in the appointor. He has a statutory power to transfer what he has not got. Thus where A and B are the trustees and X has the power to appoint new trustees, if A dies and X appoints C a trustee in his place, the deed of appointment will vest the property in B and C jointly.

(b) Exceptions

In certain cases the trust property cannot be transferred by a vesting declaration, either express or implied. These cases are when the property consists of:

(i) land which the trustees hold by way of mortgage for securing trust money;

(ii) land held under a lease with a provision against assigning or disposing of the land without consent, unless the requisite consent has first been obtained, or the vesting declaration would not be a breach of covenant or give rise to a forfeiture;

(iii) any share, stock or other property which is transferable only in books kept by a company or other body, or in a way directed by statute[30]; or

(iv) registered land.

In these excepted cases the trust property must be transferred by the method appropriate to the subject-matter, such as in the case of shares and registered land, by a duly registered transfer.[31] The reason for the inclusion of (1) is to avoid bringing the trusts on to the title, for otherwise, when the borrower sought to repay the loan, he would have to investigate the trust documents to see that he was paying the right persons; and (2) is included to avoid accidental breaches of the terms of the lease.

(c) Vesting orders

The court has a wide jurisdiction to make vesting orders where this is desirable.[32]

3. On retirement or removal

Where a trustee retires or is discharged from a trust without a new trustee being appointed, and the transaction is effected by deed, the trust property can be divested from the former trustee and vested solely in the continuing trustees by means of a vesting declaration. This applies only if the deed is executed by the retiring trustee, the continuing trustees and any person with power to appoint new trustees; if the deed is executed after 1925, a vesting declaration is implied.[33] There are the same exceptions as in the case of vesting declarations on the appointment of new trustees. This special provision is necessary since survivorship operates only on death and not on retirement.

---

[30] *ibid.*, s.40(4), replacing earlier provisions.
[31] See *Ruoff and Roper*, pp. 32–13.
[32] T.A. 1925, ss.44–56.
[33] T.A. 1925, s.40(2), replacing earlier provisions.

Sect. 8. Procedure for settlements

1. One document

Although it is undesirable, a trust of land may be created by only one instrument. In this case, when a new trustee is appointed, the appointment may be made by a single document. This may be merely in writing. In the case of unregistered land it should be by deed so that the legal estate may be vested in the new and continuing trustees by virtue of section 40 of the Trustee Act 1925,[34] thus avoiding the necessity of a separate conveyance; in addition, a memorandum must be indorsed on or annexed to the instrument creating the trust of land, stating the names of those who are the trustees after the appointment is made,[35] and not merely the names of the new trustees. In the case of registered land, whether the appointment is made in writing or by deed, it will be necessary for the registered land to be transferred by the existing trustees into the names of the continuing and the new trustees (or, if there are no surviving trustees, by the personal representative of the last surviving trustee into the names of the new trustees or, in the last resort, by an order of the court).

2. Two documents

Normally, however, a trust of land is created by two documents. In this case, and in the case of land settled under the Settled Land Act 1925, the procedure is more complicated. There must be[36]:

(i) An appointment to go with the trust instrument. This may be either in writing or by deed.[37]

(ii) In the case of unregistered land,

(a) a deed to go with the conveyance creating the trust of land or the vesting instrument, which purchasers can see.

(b) an indorsement on the conveyance creating the trust of land or on the vesting instrument, stating the names of those who are the trustees after the appointment.

---

[34] Above, p. 300.
[35] T.A. 1925, s.35(3).
[36] *ibid.*, 35; S.L.A. 1925, s.35(1); and see above, p. 280.
[37] T.A. 1925, s.35; S.L.A. 1925, s.35.

Chapter 8

CO-OWNERSHIP

Little has so far been said about cases where two or more persons are entitled to the simultaneous enjoyment of land. Formerly, there were four types of such ownership: joint tenancy; tenancy in common; co-parcenary; and tenancy by entireties. The two latter types are obsolete; but joint tenancies and tenancies in common are important, and must be considered in some detail. The terms "co-ownership", "concurrent interests", and "estates and interests in community" may each be used to include these forms of co-ownership. The main provisions are those governing joint tenancies and tenancies in common, and they will be considered together; but party walls fall into a different category, and they will be considered separately.

PART 1—JOINT TENANCY AND TENANCY IN COMMON

Sect. 1. Nature of the tenancies: joint tenancies

"A gift of lands to two or more persons in joint tenancy is such a gift as imparts to them, with respect to all other persons than themselves, the properties of one single owner."[1] Although as between themselves joint tenants have separate rights, as against everyone else they are in a position of a single owner. The intimate nature of joint tenancy is shown by the two principal features, the right of survivorship and the "four unities".

1. The right of survivorship

(a) The right

The right of survivorship is the distinguishing feature of a joint tenancy. On the death of one joint tenant, his interest in the land passes to the other joint tenants by the *jus accrescendi* (right of survivorship), and this process continues until there is but one survivor, who then holds the land as sole owner.[2] This *jus accrescendi* takes precedence over any disposition made by a joint tenant's will, and the same principle applies if a joint tenant dies intestate;

---

[1] Williams R.P. 143.
[2] Litt. 280.

a joint tenancy cannot pass under a will or intestacy.[3] For this reason it has been said that each joint tenant holds nothing and yet holds the whole[4]: he will become entitled to nothing or to all, according to whether or not he survives his fellows. But if he acts in his lifetime he may convert his interest into a tenancy in common.[5]

(b) Corporations

The common law held that although a corporation could be a tenant in common, no joint tenancy could exist between a corporation and a natural person. A corporation never died, and the natural person would thus have no effective right of survivorship. However, Parliament provided in 1899 that a corporation should be able to acquire and hold any property in joint tenancy in the same manner as if it were an individual.[6] This provision became necessary as banks and other corporations were taking up the work of acting as trustees.

(c) Trustees

Trustees are always made joint tenants because of the convenience of the trust property passing automatically by the *jus accrescendi* to the surviving trustees when one trustee dies. If trustees were made tenants in common, a conveyance of the trust property to the surviving trustees by the personal representatives of the deceased trustee would be necessary. Although the *jus accrescendi* of a joint tenancy is often unsuitable for beneficial owners because it introduces an element of chance, it is ideal for trustees.

2. The four unities must be present

The four unities of a joint tenancy are the unities of possession, interest, title and time.[7]

(a) Unity of possession

Each joint tenant is as much entitled to possession of any part of the land as the others.[8] No tenant can point to any part of the land as his own to the exclusion of the others; if he could, there would be separate ownership and not joint tenancy. In this respect, the position is similar to that of partners; no partner can point to any particular asset of the business as being his, for each is entitled to possession of all the assets.

(i) **Right to occupy:** Unity of possession is common to both forms of co-ownership. If one co-owner of land under a trust of land is in sole occupation of any or all of the land, the others cannot evict him[9]; and he is not liable to pay any rent or compensation to them[10] unless he excludes them from possession.[11] But if he lets the land, he must account to the others if he receives more than his just share.[12] At common law, if he was not in occupation, he appeared to have no right to insist on being let into possession, though the trustees might in their

---

[3] Litt. 287.
[4] *Murray v. Hall* (1849) 7 C.B. 441 at 455n.: he holds "*per mie* [nothing] *et per tout*".
[5] Below, p. 328.
[6] Bodies Corporate (Joint Tenancy) Act 1899.
[7] See *A.G. Securities v. Vaughan* [1990] 1 A.C. 417 at 474. Their initial letters form the convenient mnemonic P.I.T.T.
[8] Litt. 288: *Bull v. Bull* [1955] 1 Q.B. 234.
[9] *Bull v. Bull* [1955] 1 Q.B. 234, criticised at [1955] C.L.J. 155, but accepted in *Williams & Glyn's Bank Ltd v. Boland* [1981] A.C. 487.
[10] *Jones v. Jones* [1977] 1 W.L.R. 438.
[11] *Dennis v. McDonald* [1982] Fam. 63.
[12] *Henderson v. Eason* (1851) 17 Q.B. 701.

discretion permit beneficiaries entitled in possession to occupy the land in lieu of receiving the rents and profits.[13] However, under the Trusts of Land and Appointment of Trustees Act 1996 ("the 1996 Act") a beneficiary who is beneficially entitled to an interest in possession under a trust of land (other than a person who is merely an annuitant[14]) is entitled by reason of his interest to occupy the land at any time when the purposes of the trust include making the land available for his occupation or the land is held by the trustees so as to be so available.[15] This right does not extend to land which is either unavailable or unsuitable for occupation by any particular beneficiary.[16]

(ii) Right to exclude: Before 1997, it was only in quite exceptional circumstances that the courts refused to allow a co-owner to exercise his right to occupation and use.[17] However, where two or more beneficiaries of a trust of land are entitled to occupy land under the 1996 Act, the trustees may exclude or restrict the entitlement of any one or more of them but not of all of them.[18] It has been held that this provision entitles the trustees to permit occupation of different parts of the land by different beneficiaries where such distinct occupation is feasible.[19] The trustees must not exercise this power unreasonably[20] or so as to prevent any person who is in occupation from continuing to occupy the land unless he consents or the court so orders.[21] They may, however, from time to time impose reasonable conditions on any beneficiary in relation to his occupation of the land,[22] although not in a manner which is likely to result in the beneficiary ceasing to occupy the land unless he consents or the court so orders.[23] In exercising these different powers, the trustees are to have regard to the intentions of the settlor or testator, the purposes for which the land is held, and the circumstances and wishes of each of the beneficiaries who is entitled to occupy the land.[24]

(b) Unity of interest

The interest of each joint tenant is the same in extent, nature and duration, for in theory of law they hold but one estate. This means[25]:

    (i) that although in theory of law each joint tenant has the whole of the property, the rents and profits of the land are divided equally between all the joint tenants;

    (ii) that there can be no joint tenancy between those with interests of a different nature, such as a freeholder and a leaseholder;

    (iii) that there can be no joint tenancy between those whose interests are similar but of different duration, such as a tenant in fee simple and a tenant in fee tail; and

---

[13] See *Re Bagot's Settlement* [1894] 1 Ch. 177; *Re Landi* [1939] Ch. 828 at 836; (1955) 19 Conv. 146 (F.R. Crane).
[14] T.L.A.T.A. 1996, s.22(3).
[15] *ibid.*, s.12(1).
[16] *ibid.*, s.12(2).
[17] *Chhokar v. Chhokar* (1984) 5 F.L.R. 313.
[18] T.L.A.T.A. 1966, s.13(1).
[19] *Rodway v. Landy* [2001] Ch. 703.
[20] T.L.A.T.A., s.13(2).
[21] *ibid.*, s.13(7)(a).
[22] *ibid.*, s.13(3).
[23] *ibid.*, s.13(7)(b).
[24] *ibid.*, s.13(4).
[25] See Co.Litt. 188a; 2 Bl.Com. 181.

(iv) that any legal act, such as surrendering a lease or giving notice under a contractual power to determine it,[26] or giving a statutory notice,[27] can be done only by all the joint tenants jointly: one alone cannot effectually bind the estate, for the whole estate is not his. In the case of the type of leases known as periodic tenancies (such as leases from week to week or from year to year) this rule somewhat paradoxically means that a notice to quit may be valid even if given by only one of the joint periodic tenants[28]; this has been held to be the case even if an ouster injunction is in force against the giver of the notice.[29] This is because such leases expire at the end of each period unless all concerned, either expressly or tacitly, concur in their continuation,[30] and so a notice given by one of joint landlords[31] or one of joint leaseholders[32] shows that there is no unanimity in a continuation.

(c) Unity of title

Each joint tenant must claim his title to the land under the same act or document.[33] This requirement is satisfied if all the joint tenants acquired their rights by the same conveyance or if they simultaneously took possession of land and acquired title to it by adverse possession.[34]

(d) Unity of time

The interest of each joint tenant must vest at the same time. This does not necessarily follow from the existence of unity of title. It is difficult to find any realistic modern example of a situation where there is unity of title without unity of time. Before 1926, if land was conveyed "to A for life, remainder to the heirs of B and C as joint tenants" and B and C died at different times in A's lifetime, B's heir and C's heir took the remainder in fee simple not as joint tenants but as tenants in common; they could not take as joint tenants because, although there was unity of title, there was no unity of time.[35] Today the equivalent would be a remainder to the statutory next of kin of B and C as joint tenants but it is hardly likely that anyone would ever make a gift in such peculiar terms. The requirement for there to be unity of time has never applied to class gifts so if land is settled on trust for the children of D as joint tenants each will acquire an interest at birth; the disparity of time does not prevent them from taking as joint tenants.[36] However, in practice, class gifts are invariably made to persons as tenants in common.

Sect. 2. Nature of the tenancies: tenancy in common

A tenancy in common differs greatly from a joint tenancy.

[26] *Leek and Moorlands B.S. v. Clark* [1952] 2 Q.B. 788.
[27] *Newman v. Keedwell* (1978) 35 P. & C.R. 393 (counter-notice under A.H.A. 1948, s.24: below, p. 528).
[28] *Hammersmith and Fulham L.B.C. v. Monk* [1992] 1 A.C. 478.
[29] *Harrow L.B.C. v. Johnstone* [1997] 1 All E.R. 929; see also *Notting Hill Housing Trust v. Brackley* [2001] E.G. 106.
[30] Below, pp. 347–349.
[31] *Doe d. Aslin v. Summersett* (1830) 1 B. & Ad. 135; *Parson v. Parsons* [1983] 1 W.L.R. 1390.
[32] *Hammersmith and Fulham L.B.C. v. Monk* [1992] 1 A.C. 478; *Harrow L.B.C. v. Johnstone* [1997] 1 All E.R. 929; *Notting Hill Housing Trust v. Brackley* [2001] E.G. 106.
[33] Co. Litt. 189a, 299b.
[34] *Ward v. Ward* (1871) 6 Ch.App. 789; below, p. 547.
[35] Co. Litt. 188a; 2 Bl.Com. 181.
[36] *Ruck v. Barwise* (1865) 2 Dr. & Sm. 510; *Doe d. Hallen v. Ironmonger* (1803) 3 East 533.

1. The tenants hold in undivided shares

Unlike joint tenants, tenants in common hold in undivided shares: each tenant in common has a distinct fixed share in property which has not yet been divided among the co-tenants.[37] There is no *jus accrescendi*; the share of each tenant is fixed once and for all and is not affected by the death of one of his fellows. When a tenant in common dies, his interest passes under his will or intestacy, for his undivided share is his to dispose of as he wishes.[38]

2. Only the unity of possession is essential

Although the four unities of a joint tenancy may be present in a tenancy in common, the only unity which is essential is the unity of possession. In particular, it should be noted that the unity of interest may be absent and the tenants may hold unequal interests, so that one tenant in common may be entitled to a one-fifth share and the other to four-fifths, or one may be entitled for life and the other in fee simple.[39]

Sect. 3. Estates in which the tenancies can exist

In general, before 1926 joint tenancies and tenancies in common could both exist either at law or in equity (*i.e.* as legal estates or as equitable interests), and in possession or in remainder, in any of the estates of freehold or in leaseholds.[40] After 1925, the position is substantially the same except that a tenancy in common can no longer exist at law; this is dealt with below.[41] Further, since only fees simple absolute in possession and terms of years absolute can exist at law, even joint tenancies of all other estates must necessarily also be equitable; an example is a joint life interest.

Co-ownership of a life interest is not unusual. If land is given to A and B as joint tenants for their lifetimes, they enjoy it jointly for their joint lives and the survivor enjoys the whole for the rest of his life.[42] If A and B instead hold as tenants in common for their lifetimes or have converted their joint tenancy into a tenancy in common (a process which is known as severing the joint tenancy and which can have fiscal benefits), the survivor is entitled only to the appropriate proportion of the property for the rest of his life. And, if X and Y are joint tenants for the life of X (a situation which could either have been created expressly or have arisen as a result of X assigning his life interest to himself and Y), X becomes sole tenant of the whole for the rest of his life if he is the survivor, whereas Y takes nothing if he is the survivor; the estate which he acquires by survivorship is one which comes to an end at the moment he receives it.

Sect. 4. Mode of creating the tenancies: general

The key to a proper understanding of joint tenancies and tenancies in common is always to consider the legal estate separately from the equitable interest.[43] Thus it may be found that

---

[37] *Fisher v. Wiggs* (1700) 12 Mod. 296 at 302.
[38] Challis R.P. 368.
[39] Co.Litt. 189a; Williams R.P. 148; 2 Bl.Com. 191.
[40] Williams R.P. 143.
[41] Below, p. 308.
[42] *Moffat v. Burnie* (1853) 18 Beav. 211.
[43] Despite *Re Selous* [1901] 1 Ch. 921, criticised in Williams V. & P. 501, 502.

at law A and B are joint tenants, while in equity they are tenants in common. In such a situation, the effect of A's death on the legal joint tenancy is that B becomes solely entitled. In equity, on the other hand, A's share passes under his will or intestacy. In the result, B holds the legal estate on trust for himself as to his share and for A's personal representatives as to A's share. The mode of creating joint tenancies and tenancies in common must now be considered.

Sect. 5. Mode of creating the tenancies: at law

1. Presumption of joint tenancy

At law, the presumption has always been in favour of a joint tenancy,[44] because before 1926 that had advantages for feudal lords, for tenants, and for conveyancers. The rule was thus that if land was conveyed to two or more persons a joint tenancy of the legal estate was created unless either one of the unities was absent or words of severance had been employed.

(a) Absence of unities

The four unities have already been considered. If there was unity of possession but one or more of the other unities were missing, the parties took as tenants in common; if there was no unity of possession, the parties took as separate owners.

(b) Words of severance

Any words in the grant showing that the tenants were each to take a distinct share in the property amounted to words of severance and thus created a tenancy in common. Words which have been held to have this effect include: "share and share alike"; "to be divided amongst"; "equally"; and "between". Further, words showing that the tenants were to take unequal interests (such as "two-thirds to A and one-third to B") sufficed to create a tenancy in common; and even if there were no clear words of severance, the gift taken as a whole might show that a tenancy in common was intended.[45] Thus, if under a settlement on children there was provision for making advances out of capital, any advance to a child would have to be debited against that child's share, and this could not be done unless the child was a tenant in common and so had a distinct share.[46]

2. A legal tenancy in common cannot exist after 1925

The absence of a unity or the presence of words of severance still leads to the creation of a tenancy in common but not at law. Since 1925, a tenancy in common has not been able to take effect at law[47]; for this reason a legal joint tenancy can no longer be severed and converted into a legal tenancy in common.[48] As explained below, a tenancy in common can still exist in equity, but at law the only form of co-ownership possible after 1925 is a joint tenancy. Thus a conveyance today "to A, B and C in fee simple as tenants in common" (all being of full age) will vest the legal estate in A, B and C as joint tenants, although in equity

---

[44] *Morley v. Bird* (1798) 3 Ves. 628.
[45] *e.g. Surtees v. Surtees* (1871) L.R. 12 Eq. 400.
[46] See *L'Estrange v. L'Estrange* [1902] 1 I.R. 467 at 468, 469; *Re Dunn* [1916] 1 Ch. 97.
[47] L.P.A. 1925, ss.1(6), 34(1), 36(2); S.L.A. 1925, s.36(4).
[48] Below, p. 328.

they will be tenants in common.[49] If A is a minor, his rights in equity will not be affected but the legal estate will vest in B and C on trust for all three of them.[50] If A, B and C are all minors, the legal estate will now remain in the grantor who will hold it on trust for the minors or, if the purported conveyance was to them as trustees for other persons, on trust for those persons[51] (before 1996 the legal estate would equally have remained in the grantor but it was not clear whether he would have been deemed to have made an agreement for value to execute a settlement under the Settled Land Act 1925 in their favour and in the meantime to hold the land in trust for them, or whether the transaction would have been void[52]).

3. The legal estate is now held on a trust of land

(a) The trusts imposed by the Law of Property Act 1925

From 1926 to 1996, subject to the special provisions relating to land subject to the Settled Land Act 1925,[53] land was held upon what were described in the Law of Property Act 1925 as the "statutory trusts" wherever there was beneficial co-ownership, in other words whenever it was conveyed to or held by two or more persons beneficially, whether as tenants in common[54] or joint tenants.[55] The "statutory trusts" could be summarised thus: upon trust to sell the land, and stand possessed of the net proceeds of sale and of the net rents and profits until sale upon such trusts and subject to such powers and provisions as may be requisite for giving effect to the rights of those interested in the land,[56] whether beneficially or as trustees.[57]

(b) The trusts imposed by the 1996 Act

Since 1996, land is instead held on a trust of land[58] whenever it was conveyed to or held by two or more persons beneficially, whether as tenants in common[59] or joint tenants.[60] Statutory trusts for sale which were implied before 1997 now take effect as trusts of land.[61] The 1996 Act does not utilise the expression "statutory trusts" as such but that does not alter the fact that the trusts which it imposes are statutory.

(c) Beneficial not fiduciary co-ownership

Both before 1997 and after 1996, the trusts in question are imposed by statute only where the co-ownership is beneficial and not merely fiduciary. Thus they apply where land is conveyed to A and B to hold jointly, or to hold on trust for C and D jointly, but not where A and B are to hold on trust for E absolutely, for then the only co-ownership is not beneficial.

---

[49] L.P.A. 1925, s.34(2).
[50] T.L.A.T.A. 1996, s.2(6), Sched. 1, para. 1(2). Although the law was less clear before 1997, this was thought also to have been the position then; see L.P.A. 1925, s.19(2) (now repealed).
[51] T.L.A.T.A. 1996, s.296, Sched. 1, para. 1(1).
[52] See above, p. 201.
[53] Below, p. 326.
[54] L.P.A. 1925, s.34(2).
[55] *ibid.*, s.36(1).
[56] *ibid.*, s.35 (now repealed).
[57] *Re Hayward* [1928] Ch. 367.
[58] T.L.A.T.A. 1996, Sched. 2, paras 3, 4.
[59] L.P.A. 1925, s.34(2).
[60] *ibid.*, s.36(1).
[61] T.L.A.T.A. 1996, s.5(1) and Sched. 2, paras 3(6), 4(4).

(d) Scope of the trusts

While the trusts in question are imposed both where land is beneficially limited to and held in trust for persons as joint tenants,[62] on a literal interpretation of the legislation they are imposed only when land is "expressed" to be conveyed in undivided shares to persons of full age.[63] Theoretical difficulties therefore arose before 1997 where land was conveyed in undivided shares to persons who included a minor. However, this problem has now been resolved by the 1996 Act.[64] Such difficulties also arose before 1997 and still do today in a number of situations where the undivided shares arise extraneously; an example is where land is conveyed to A alone but he and B are beneficially entitled as tenants in common because they contributed to the purchase price in unequal shares[65] (the fact that these difficulties have survived the enactment of the 1996 Act is one of the very few respects in which that legislation may justifiably be criticised). However, without paying undue attention to these difficulties the courts have managed to carry out the evident general intention of the legislation by recourse to statutory provisions which, on their face, have nothing whatever to do with the matter.[66] As a result, it is now generally accepted that, despite the literal interpretation of the legislation, whenever there is beneficial co-ownership, however it arose, the land will be held on the trusts imposed by statute[67] unless the land is settled under the Settled Land Act 1925.[68]

4. The legal estate cannot be vested in more than four persons

The position here is clear in the case of tenancies in common and rather less clear in the case of joint tenancies; each type of tenancy will be dealt with separately.[69]

(a) Tenancies in common

If land is conveyed to trustees on trust for tenants in common, the general prohibition against the number of trustees exceeding four applies.[70] If the conveyance is expressed to be made to the tenants in common themselves, and they are of full age, statute provides for it to operate as a conveyance "to the grantees, or, if there are more than four grantees, to the four first named in the conveyance, as joint tenants upon the statutory trusts."[71] Further, a gift of land by will to, or in trust for,[72] tenants in common operates as a gift to the Settled Land Act trustees of the will, or, if, as is now virtually inevitable, there are none, to the testator's personal representatives, upon a trust of land[73]; and the number of Settled Land Act trustees or personal representatives cannot exceed four. If all the beneficiaries are of full age and absolutely entitled, they can instead require the legal estate to be vested in themselves (or not

---

[62] L.P.A. 1925, s.36(1).

[63] *ibid.*, s.34(2).

[64] See above, p. 309.

[65] This occurred in *Bull v. Bull* [1955] 1 Q.B. 234.

[66] L.P.A. 1925, s.36(1), relied on in *Re Buchanan-Wollaston's Conveyance* [1939] Ch. 217 at 222 (Ch.D.), [1939] Ch. 738 at 744 (C.A.); S.L.A. 1925, s.36(4), relied on in *Bull v. Bull* [1955] 1 Q.B. 234.

[67] See *Williams & Glyn's Bank Ltd v. Boland* [1981] A.C. 487; *City of London B.S. v. Flegg* [1988] A.C. 54 at 77, 78.

[68] Below, p. 326.

[69] Elaborate transitional provisions were enacted with the object of ensuring that the legal estate should vest in suitable persons on January 1, 1926.

[70] Trustee Act 1925, s.34.

[71] L.P.A. 1925, s.34(2); for minors, see above p. 201.

[72] *Re House* [1929] 2 Ch. 166.

[73] L.P.A. 1925, s.34(3).

more than four of them) as joint tenants on trust for themselves as tenants in common.[74] Since 1997, in such circumstances, if there is no person appointed by the trust instrument for the purpose of appointing new trustees, they have also been entitled to require the legal estate to be vested in up to four other persons of their choice on the same trusts.[75]

(b) Joint tenancies

There are no provisions dealing expressly with the number of persons in whom the legal estate can be vested when two or more persons are beneficially entitled as joint tenants. But the trust of land arising in such cases involves the general provision that, in a trust of land made or coming into operation after 1925, the number of trustees must not exceed four,[76] and "where more than four persons are named as such trustees, the first four named (who are able and willing to act) shall alone be the trustees".[77] In the case of a gift of land by will to joint tenants, the general prohibition against more than four trustees of land coupled with the fact that there is a trust of land prevents the personal representatives from vesting the legal estate in more than four persons. If all the beneficiaries are of full age and absolutely entitled, they can instead require the legal estate to be vested in themselves (or not more than four of them) as joint tenants, this time on trust for themselves as joint tenants.[78] Since 1997, in such circumstances, if there is no person appointed by the trust instrument for the purpose of appointing new trustees, they too have also been entitled to require the legal estate to be vested in up to four other persons of their choice on the same trusts.[79]

5. End of the trusts imposed by statute

The trusts imposed by statute will cease to affect the land in question if the beneficial interests are overreached into the proceeds of sale (although in these circumstances the trusts themselves will continue in respect of those proceeds of sale) and in the event that the land becomes vested legally and beneficially in one person.

(a) Overreaching

The trusts of land created by statute in the case of beneficial co-ownership take effect in the same way as all other trusts of land in the manner already considered.[80] Further, the overreaching provisions apply. Consequently, provided that a purchaser pays his purchase money to trustees of land (being at least two in number or a trust corporation) he will take free from the rights of the beneficiaries, irrespective of whether or not they are in occupation of the land.[81] To a purchaser who does this, it is immaterial whether in equity there are three or thirty people entitled, or whether they are joint tenants or tenants in common. However, in practice, on a conveyance of land to joint tenants or tenants in common, it is usual for the conveyance to be made on an express trust of land, in which case there is no need to have recourse to the trusts imposed by statute.

---

[74] *Saunders v. Vautier* (1841) Cr. & Ph. 240; L.P.A. 1925, s.3(1)(b)(ii).
[75] T.L.A.T.A. 1996, s.19.
[76] T.A. 1925, s.34.
[77] *ibid.*, s.34(2).
[78] *Saunders v. Vautier* (1841) Cr. & Ph. 240; L.P.A. 1925, s.3(1)(b)(ii).
[79] T.L.A.T.A. 1996, s.19.
[80] Above, pp. 283 *et seq.*
[81] *City of London B.S. v. Flegg* [1988] A.C. 54.

(b) Union in one person

If the whole legal estate and equitable interest becomes vested in one person, the trust imposed by statute comes to an end,[82] as where A and B are joint tenants at law and in equity and A dies. In such circumstances the Schedule to the Law of Property (Amendment) Act 1926 provides that nothing in the Law of Property Act 1925 is to affect the right of a survivor of joint tenants who is solely and beneficially interested to deal with his legal estate as if it were not held on what is now a trust of land. Thus B, as the sole legal and beneficial owner of the land, can make title by himself despite the fact that a sole trustee of land is unable to give a proper receipt for purchase money.

(i) **Potential severances:** Formerly there was in these circumstances a practical difficulty in satisfying a purchaser that B was in fact solely beneficially entitled. An act of severance might have occurred in A's lifetime,[83] causing A and B to become tenants in common, so that what was then the trust for sale imposed by statute continued to exist after A's death. Because it was impossible for B to prove affirmatively that this had not happened, any purchaser was potentially at risk of being bound by any severed beneficial interest formerly held by A; such an interest would not be overreached by a conveyance from B alone and the purchaser could not claim to have taken free of it under the equitable doctrine of notice. Consequently, he would insist upon the appointment of a second trustee to receive the purchase money together with B.

(ii) **Unregistered land:** So far as unregistered land is concerned, this difficulty was overcome by the Law of Property (Joint Tenants) Act 1964, which is retrospective to January 1, 1926.[84] It provides that in favour of a purchaser of a legal estate, a survivor of two or more joint tenants is "deemed to be solely and beneficially interested if he conveys as beneficial owner[85] or the conveyance includes a statement that he is so interested."[86] Where the survivor has himself died, his personal representatives have similar powers. The Act does not apply if, before the conveyance by the survivor, a memorandum recording the severance is indorsed on or annexed to the conveyance which vested the land in the joint tenants[87]; in the absence of such a memorandum the purchaser can safely assume that no severance has occurred unless he has actual notice that there has been a severance.[88] Nor does the Act apply where a bankruptcy petition or bankruptcy order has been registered[89] against the name of the deceased joint tenant.

(iii) **Registered land:** The Law of Property (Joint Tenants) Act 1964 does not apply to registered land.[90] At the time when the legislation was enacted, it was assumed, wrongly as it turned out,[91] that the interest of a beneficial co-owner under a trust for sale could not take effect as an interest which overrides registration and therefore would bind a purchaser only where it had been protected on the register. Consequently, it was thought that in the absence

---

[82] *Re Cook* [1948] Ch. 212.
[83] See below, pp. 328 *et seq.*
[84] s.2.
[85] Above, pp. 162–163. A conveyance with full title guarantee also suffices.
[86] s.1.
[87] *ibid.*
[88] *Grindal v. Hooper* [1999] E.G.C.S. 150.
[89] Above, pp. 99–100.
[90] s.3.
[91] See above, p. 123.

of any entry on the register any purchaser for value would take free of any severed beneficial interest that there might be. Further, the system put into place by the legislation could not have worked in the case of registered land since there would have been nothing on which any memorandum of severance could have been indorsed. However, it has now been established[92] that the interest of a beneficial co-owner under a trust for sale can override registration and since 1996 the interest of a beneficial co-owner under a trust of land has also been able to do so. Purchasers of registered land from a sole surviving trustee of land who have any reason to suspect that anyone other than him is in actual occupation of the land or in receipt of its rents and profits therefore have no alternative but to do what purchasers of unregistered land formerly had to do, namely to insist upon the appointment of a second trustee to receive the purchase money together with him. However, the risk of such purchasers being bound by severed beneficial interests will anyway be considerably reduced when the Land Registration Act 2002 comes into force because of the reforms which it will make to the categories of interests which override registration.[93]

6. Benefit to purchaser

It will be noticed that the three main changes introduced by the 1925 legislation all assist the purchaser. The prohibition of a legal tenancy in common and the limitation of the number of tenants of the legal estate to four means that purchasers are no longer exposed to the burden of having to investigate the titles of each of, say, 30 legal tenants in common, some of whom might own a sixty-eighth share, and who might be so scattered about the world that it took six months to get all their signatures to the conveyance.[94] Further, the overreaching effect of a conveyance by trustees of land enables a purchaser to ignore the equitable rights of the beneficiaries.

Sect. 6. Mode of creating the tenancies: in equity

1. Preference for tenancy in common

Despite the feudal and conveyancing advantages of a joint tenancy, equity did not favour it. Equity looked to the beneficial interests of the co-tenants, and preferred the certainty and equality of a tenancy in common to the element of chance which the *jus accrescendi* of a joint tenancy introduced. "Survivorship is looked upon as odious in equity"[95]; not least is this the case because few laymen contemplate that a gift to two or more persons gives rise to such a right.[96] This preference for a tenancy in common was manifested by equity holding that a tenancy in common would exist in equity not only in those cases where it existed at law, but also in certain other cases where an intention to create a tenancy in common could be discerned. Tenancies in common can no longer exist at law but equity still holds that a tenancy in common will exist in the remaining cases. However, outside those cases, equity follows the law so that when legal title is transferred to two or more adult persons, they will be legal and beneficial joint tenants.[97]

---

[92] In *Williams & Glyn's Bank Ltd v. Boland* [1981] A.C. 487.
[93] See above, pp. 121–129.
[94] See (1929) 15 Conv. (O.S.) 83 (A.H. Cosway); and see *City of London B.S. v. Flegg* [1988] A.C. 54 at 77.
[95] *R. v. Williams* (1735) Bunb. 342 at 343.
[96] See *Re Woolley* [1903] 2 Ch. 206 at 211.
[97] *Cowcher v. Cowcher* [1972] 1 W.L.R. 425 at 430.

(a) Purchase money provided in unequal shares

If two or more persons together purchase property and provide the money in unequal shares, the purchasers are presumed to take as tenants in common in shares proportionate to the sums advanced.[98] Thus if A finds one-third and B two-thirds of the price, they are presumed to be tenants in common as to one-third and two-thirds respectively. If, on the other hand, the purchasers provide the money in equal shares, they are presumed to be joint tenants. These presumptions can be rebutted by evidence of circumstances showing that those providing the purchase money equally intended to take as tenants in common or vice versa.

(b) Loan on mortgage

Where two or more persons advance money on mortgage, whether in equal or unequal shares, equity presumes a tenancy in common in the land between the mortgagees. "If two people join in lending money upon a mortgage, equity says, it could not be the intention, that the interest in that should survive. Though they take a joint security, each means to lend his own and take back his own."[99] "It is obvious, however, that this proposition cannot be put higher than a presumption capable of being rebutted."[1] Yet it should be noted that the "joint account clause" which is normally inserted in mortgages to make the mortgagees appear as joint tenants to the outside world and so simplify the mechanism of discharging the mortgage[2] does not affect this presumption of a tenancy in common in the relationship of the mortgagees as between themselves.[3]

(c) Partnership assets

Where partners acquire land as part of their partnership assets, they are presumed to hold it as tenants in common.[4] *Jus accrescendi inter mercatores locum non habet*: the right of survivorship has no place between merchants. The rule extends to any joint undertaking with a view to a profit, even if there is no formal partnership between the parties. Equity adopted this view despite the fact that the legal estate was held on a joint tenancy (it of course now has to be anyway). In equity the partners were nevertheless presumed to be entitled in undivided shares, so that the surviving partners (or whoever held the legal estate) would be compelled to hold the legal estate on trust for those entitled to the property of a deceased partner as far as his share was concerned.[5] This is also the case where a tenancy of business premises is granted to joint tenants for each to occupy separate but unequal areas.[6]

(d) Executory trusts

Executory trusts are trusts where the details have not been set out but a further document is to be drawn up to give effect to the settlor's intention.

(i) **Marriage articles:** "Marriage articles" are the preliminary agreement for a marriage settlement and create executory trusts, while the marriage settlement itself creates executed trusts. In such cases there was a tenancy in common where any intention to create such a

---

[98] *Lake v. Gibson* (1729) 1 Eq.Ca.Abr. 290 at 291; and see below, p. 293.
[99] *Morley v. Bird* (1798) 3 Ves. 628 at 631, *per* Arden M.R.
[1] *Steeds v. Steeds* (1889) 22 Q.B.D. 537 at 541, *per* Wills J.
[2] Below, p. 527.
[3] *Re Jackson* (1887) 34 Ch.D. 732.
[4] *Lake v. Craddock* (1732) 3 P.Wms. 158; *Malayan Credit Ltd v. Jack Chia-MPH Ltd* [1986] A.C. 549.
[5] See *Re Fuller's Contract* [1933] Ch. 652.
[6] *Malayan Credit Ltd v. Jack Chia-MPH Ltd* [1986] A.C. 549.

tenancy could be found or presumed. "Joint tenancy as a provision for the children of a marriage, is an inconvenient mode of settlement",[7] for no child could rely upon having a distinct share for his family until he had severed his joint tenancy (*i.e.* converted it into a tenancy in common) nor could any advance to a child be set against his share until this had been done.[8] Accordingly the court would readily infer that a provision in marriage articles or other executory trusts for the benefit of a class of children was intended to be a provision for them as tenants in common, despite the absence of words of severance.[9]

(ii) Pension trusts: Marriage articles are now rare, presumably because, in so far as marriage settlements are still created at all, they are highly likely to be set up at least partly for the purpose of tax avoidance, something which requires all the documents involved to have been carefully thought out and prepared in advance. The only executory trusts commonly found today are those relating to occupational pension schemes which are commonly established by an interim deed of trust which provides for the subsequent execution of a definitive deed, something which often only occurs some years later.[10] However, no beneficiary under the trusts of an occupational pension scheme is a co-owner of any interest thereunder with any of the other beneficiaries so there is no room or need for any of the sort of inferences which have been drawn in the case of marriage articles.

2. Nature of tenancies in common since 1925

Strictly speaking, there have not been able to be any "tenancies" in common since 1925 because those interested hold no estate or interest in the land but are entitled merely as beneficiaries under, since 1996, a trust of land; the 1925 legislation throughout refers not to "tenancies in common" but to "undivided shares". In general, however, the rights of these beneficiaries correspond to the rights of tenants in common before 1926, and the same applies to those entitled in equity as joint tenants.

Sect. 7. Position of the beneficiaries

1. Extent of the beneficial interests

(a) Express trusts

Many cases of co-ownership arise pursuant to an express trust, declared in the will or in the conveyance to the co-owners or to trustees to hold for them. If the relevant document states that the parties are to be beneficial joint tenants, or are to be tenants in common, showing the size of their shares, that conclusively determines the matter,[11] subject only to any question of rescission or rectification[12]; and for this the burden of proof is heavy.[13] Thus a conveyance to two or more persons expressly as joint tenants makes them joint tenants, each with an equal potential share, even if their contributions to the purchase money were not only unequal

---

[7] *Taggart v. Taggart* (1803) 1 Sch. & Lef. 84 at 88.
[8] Above, p. 308.
[9] See *Mayn v. Mayn* (1867) L.R. 5 Eq. 150.
[10] See *Davis v. Richards & Wallington Industries Ltd* [1990] 1 W.L.R. 1511.
[11] *Pettitt v. Pettitt* [1970] A.C. 777 at 813; *Pink v. Lawrence* (1978) 36 P. & C.R. 98; *Goodman v. Gallant* [1986] Fam. 106; *Turton v. Turton* [1988] Ch. 542; *Roy v. Roy* [1996] 1 F.L.R. 541.
[12] *Re Johns' Assignment Trusts* [1970] 1 W.L.R. 955; *Thames Guaranty Ltd v. Campbell* [1985] Q.B. 210; *cp. Roy v. Roy* [1996] 1 F.L.R. 541.
[13] See *Thames Guarantee Ltd v. Campbell* [1985] Q.B. 210.

but wholly disproportionate.[14] As an express trust of land must at least be evidenced in writing,[15] the question will normally be merely[16] one of construing the document or documents. Contradictory expressions such as "as beneficial joint tenants in equal shares"[17] can usually be resolved without resort to the quaint rule that, if all else fails, the first words prevail in a deed but the last in a will.[18]

(b) Other types of trusts

In the absence of any express trust, a resulting, implied or constructive trust may nevertheless arise; and these are exempt from the statutory requirement of writing.[19] In the cases, the division between resulting and constructive trusts is somewhat blurred[20] (even in the event that implied trusts constitute a category distinct from resulting trusts,[21] such trusts play no role in this area of the law). Of the two, it might appear more natural first to consider resulting trusts, which are implied by equity, and constructive trusts, which are imposed by equity as a result of the conduct of the parties, only afterwards. However, since an affirmative answer to what has been described as "the first and fundamental question which must always be resolved"[22] will, when coupled with some act of detrimental reliance, lead to the imposition of a constructive trust, it is in fact necessary to consider constructive trusts first.

(c) Constructive trusts

Constructive trusts of this type are imposed by equity to prevent the holder of the legal title from reneging on some sort of agreement or bargain which he has made[23]; such constructive trusts are quite distinct from the traditional categories of constructive trusts which have already been considered.[24]

(i) Express common agreement: The first and fundamental question referred to is "whether, independently of any inference to be drawn from the conduct of the parties in the course of sharing the house as their home and managing their joint affairs, there has at any time prior to acquisition, or exceptionally at some later date,[25] been any agreement, arrangement or understanding between them that the property is to be shared beneficially."[26] It appears that this will only be the case where there is evidence of express discussions between the parties, however, imprecise and however imperfectly remembered. However, agreements in this context do not necessarily correspond with contractual agreements and the presence or absence of express common intention is judged objectively.[27] An express agreement that one party should bear all the household expenses in order to enable the other party to pay the mortgage instalments will now be interpreted as an agreement of this type.[28]

---

[14] *Goodman v. Gallant* [1986] Fam. 106.
[15] Above, pp. 293–294.
[16] "Merely" is sometimes an overstatement.
[17] *Martin v. Martin* (1987) 54 P. & C.R. 238 ("in equal shares" prevailed).
[18] *Slingsby's Case* (1587) 5 Co.Rep. 18b at 19a; see above, p. 189.
[19] See above, p. 294.
[20] *Drake v. Whipp* [1996] 1 F.L.R. 826; *Collings v. Lee* [2001] 2 All E.R. 332.
[21] See above, p. 292.
[22] *Lloyds Bank Plc v. Rosset* [1991] A.C. 107 at 132.
[23] *Lloyds Bank plc v. Carrick* [1996] 4 All E.R. 630; *Clough v. Killey* (1996) 72 P. & C.R. D22.
[24] Above, p. 293.
[25] As in *Clough v. Killey* (1996) 72 P. & C.R. D22.
[26] *Lloyds Bank Plc v. Rosset* [1991] A.C. 107 at 132.
[27] *Lloyds Bank Plc v. Rosset* [1991] A.C. 107 at 133; *Eves v. Eves* [1975] 1 W.L.R. 1338.
[28] See *Gissing v. Gissing* [1971] A.C. 886 at 903, 909.

(ii) Detrimental reliance: As a general rule, when there is an agreement or express common intention that land is to be held on trust, a beneficiary cannot enforce any trust if the statutory requirement of evidence in writing[29] is not satisfied. But if the intended beneficiary, in reliance on the agreement or express common intention, acts to his detriment in relation to the property in the reasonable belief that he is entitled to a beneficial interest under the trust, it would be inequitable to allow the legal owner to rely on the statute as defeating the claim of the beneficiary[30]; the statute cannot be used as an instrument of fraud.[31] However, there has to be some link between the common intention and the acts of detriment relied on.[32] The court will accordingly give effect to the intended trust by imposing a constructive trust on the property to the same effect.[33] This process has much in common with the doctrine of proprietary estoppel.[34]

(iii) Quantum of beneficial interest: In such cases, the size of the interest taken by the beneficiary depends on what was agreed, either in fact or by inference; it does not, as in the case of resulting trusts, depend on the size of whatever contribution was made to the purchase or improvement of the property made by the beneficiary in reliance on the agreement.[35] Nor are the acts of reliance confined, as in the case of resulting trusts, to direct or indirect payments towards the purchase price, but include other acts carried out in reliance on the express common intention,[36] such as doing heavy work to the house and grounds,[37] making substantial contributions to the general household expenses, and even staying at home to look after children.[38] Difficulties which have yet to be resolved are what happens when one of the parties has failed to provide the whole of whatever contribution was envisaged and where an express common intention envisaging a beneficial interest but no contribution is followed by acts of detriment in reliance on the existence of the beneficial interest. Are the beneficial interests to be quantified in the proportions envisaged quite irrelevant of the scale of the acts of detrimental reliance?

(d) Resulting trusts

Resulting trusts of this type bear a closer resemblance to the traditional categories of resulting trusts which have already been considered.[39]

(i) Basic principles: The presumption of a resulting trust depends on common intention and on the making of contributions (these two elements can take a number of forms). When property is purchased with money provided by A and B, and there is a common intention (whether expressed or, more usually, inferred[40]) that each of them is to have a beneficial

---

[29] Above, pp. 293–294.

[30] *Gissing v. Gissing* [1971] A.C. 886 at 905; *Midland Bank Plc v. Dobson* [1986] 1 F.L.R. 171.

[31] *Rochefoucauld v. Boustead* [1897] 1 Ch. 196; *Bannister v. Bannister* [1948] 2 All E.R. 133.

[32] *Grant v. Edwards* [1986] Ch. 638.

[33] *Gissing v. Gissing* [1971] A.C. 886; *Midland Bank Plc v. Dobson* [1986] 1 F.L.R. 171; and see *Maharaj v. Chand* [1986] A.C. 898 at 907.

[34] See *Grant v. Edwards* [1986] Ch. 638 at 656, 657; *Stokes v. Anderson* [1991] 1 F.L.R. 391 at 398–400. For proprietary estoppel, see below, pp. 434 *et seq.*

[35] See *Re Densham* [1975] 1 W.L.R. 1519 at 1524; *Eves v. Eves* [1975] 1 W.L.R. 1338; and see *Ungarian v. Lesnoff* [1990] Ch. 206 (life interest).

[36] *Clough v. Killey* (1996) 72 P. & C.R. D22.

[37] *Eves v. Eves* [1975] 1 W.L.R. 1338; *Clough v. Killey* (1996) 72 P. & C.R. D22.

[38] *Grant v. Edwards* [1986] Ch. 638; and see the wide language at 657. See also *Hammond v. Mitchell* [1991] 1 W.L.R. 1127.

[39] Above, pp. 291–292.

[40] See *Gissing v. Gissing* [1971] A.C. 886 at 902.

interest in it, there will be presumed to be a resulting trust for them in shares proportionate to their contributions, whether the property is conveyed to one or both of them or to some third party. Thus if a house is conveyed to A alone, but the price is provided as to nine-tenths by A and as to one-tenth by B, A will be presumed to hold the house on resulting trust as to nine-tenths for himself and as to one-tenth for B.[41] This will be the case whether the contributions are in cash or by way of mortgage advances for whose repayment A or B is solely responsible.[42] However, no resulting trust will be inferred where money is provided by way of gift or loan[43]; and the presumption of a resulting trust may be rebutted. This may occur either because there is evidence of contrary intention[44] or where there is a presumption of advancement,[45] though as between husband and wife that presumption is of little weight today,[46] at least while they are both still alive.

(ii) Common intention: It has already been seen that express common intention coupled with any act of detrimental reliance leads to the imposition of a constructive trust rather than the presumption of a resulting trust and to a quantum of beneficial interest potentially superior to that obtainable under a resulting trust. Consequently, it is only in the absence of an express common intention that any beneficiary will need to fall back on a resulting trust. Where the common intention instead has to be inferred, it will have to be inferred from the contributions and the circumstances in which they were made; the main weight is thus on the contributions. The question is what in fact the inferred common intention was, and not what the court considers it might or ought to have been.[47] It is doubtful whether a common intention can be inferred from anything less than contributions to the purchase price.[48]

(iii) Direct contributions to the purchase price: Contributions to the purchase price are sometimes made outright (such as contributions to the deposit[49] and to other initial payments of funds found by the purchasers themselves) but often they take the form of regularly bearing a share of the mortgage repayments on the property; merely occasional payments are not enough.[50] However, minor contributions appear to suffice. Thus, where the deposit was provided by a husband's parents, the wife was held thereby to have made a direct contribution of one half of that deposit on the basis that that sum was a gift to both of them; it was then inferred that they had clearly "agreed to share everything" and she was held to be entitled to 50 per cent of the property.[51]

(iv) Indirect contributions to the purchase price: Indirect contributions to the purchase price also suffice. Thus where A purchased property out of the profits of a family business

[41] *Re Rogers' Question* [1948] 1 All E.R. 328; *Walker v. Hall* [1984] F.L.R. 126 (purchase in joint names).
[42] *Huntingford v. Hobbs* [1993] 1 F.L.R. 736.
[43] *Hussey v. Palmer* [1972] 1 W.L.R. 1286; *Re Sharpe (a Bankrupt)* [1980] 1 W.L.R. 219; contrast *Risch v. McFee* (1991) 61 P. & C.R. 42 (loan becoming a contribution).
[44] *Sekhon v. Alissa* [1989] 2 F.L.R. 94; *cp. Lowson v. Coombes* [1999] Ch. 373 (illegal contrary intention).
[45] Above, p. 292.
[46] *Pettitt v. Pettitt* [1970] A.C. 777 at 793, 811, 824; *cp.* at 813, 815; *McGrath v. Wallis* [1995] 2 F.L.R. 114 at 115; *Lowson v. Coombes* [1999] Ch. 373.
[47] *Gissing v. Gissing* [1971] A.C. 886, esp. at 898; and see *Pettitt v. Pettitt* [1970] A.C. 777.
[48] See *Lloyds Bank Plc v. Rosset* [1991] A.C. 107 at 133, where "constructive" seems to be used in the sense of "resulting".
[49] See *Midland Bank Plc v. Cooke* [1995] 2 F.L.R. 915.
[50] *Gissing v. Gissing* [1971] A.C. 886 at 900, 906. For endowment mortgages, see Thompson, *Co-ownership*, 52.
[51] *Midland Bank Plc v. Cooke* [1995] 2 F.L.R. 915.

to which B's unpaid work in the business had substantially contributed, B was entitled to a beneficial interest in the property.[52]

(v) Contributions of other types: At one time the court sometimes considered that contributions of other types, such as doing work on the house and grounds,[53] bearing some of the household expenses, purchasing chattels for use in the house, and even staying home to look after children, sufficed.[54] Such contributions do indeed constitute sufficient detrimental reliance for the imposition of a constructive trust. But, in the context of resulting trusts, it is now settled that nothing will do except contributions to the purchase of the property, whether direct or indirect.[55] Thus even very substantial sums expended or time spent on renovating, improving and redecorating the property, never mind relatively trivial sums expended on paying the rates, is not enough by itself.[56] However, some form of judicial relief from the harshness of this result is apparently available to anyone who has actually made some form of contribution to the purchase price, no matter how trivial, since this apparently enables contributions of other types to be taken into account in determining what the common intention of the parties was.[57] And an inferred arrangement that one party should bear all the household expenses in order to enable the other party to pay the mortgage instalments may well still be held to be sufficiently related to the acquisition of the property for the inference to be drawn that each party was intended to have a beneficial interest.[58]

(e) Subsequent improvements

By statute,[59] subsequent contributions towards improvements to the property (as distinct from its original acquisition) may now be invoked[60] in order to alter the balance of beneficial ownership as between husband and wife, but not as between others. Any substantial contribution in money or money's worth made by a husband or wife to the improvement of real or personal property in which either or both of them have a beneficial interest will entitle the contributor to such a share or enlarged share as is agreed or, in default, as seems "just" in all the circumstances.

2. Protection of beneficiaries' interests

Where all the co-owners hold the legal title on trust for themselves, only they will be able to deal with the legal title and, while all remain alive, require no protection from one another. In the case of registered land, the interests of the beneficial co-owners will anyway normally be protected by the entry of a restriction on the register.[61] (This will ensure that on a sale the purchase money will be properly paid to the trustees and the beneficial interests of the co-owners will be overreached and become corresponding rights in the proceeds of sale.[62])

---

[52] *Re Cummins* [1972] Ch. 62; *Bothe v. Amos* [1976] Fam. 46.
[53] *Eves v. Eves* [1975] 1 W.L.R. 1338.
[54] *Hazell v. Hazell* [1972] 1 W.L.R. 301; *Hussey v. Palmer* [1972] 1 W.L.R. 1286 at 1289, 1290 (constructive trust); *Hall v. Hall* [1982] 3 F.L.R. 379 at 381. See generally (1976) 92 L.Q.R. 489 (F.Webb).
[55] *Gissing v. Gissing* [1971] A.C. 886; *Burns v. Burns* [1984] Ch. 317.
[56] *Lloyds Bank Plc v. Rosset* [1991] A.C. 107; *Hammond v. Mitchell* [1991] 1 W.L.R. 1127. See also *Savage v. Dunningham* [1974] Ch. 181 (tenancy: rent).
[57] *Midland Bank Plc v. Cooke* [1995] 2 F.L.R. 915.
[58] See *Gissing v. Gissing* [1971] A.C. 886 at 903, 909.
[59] Matrimonial Proceedings and Property Act 1970, s.37.
[60] See *Suttill v. Graham* [1977] 1 W.L.R. 819 at 824.
[61] Above, pp. 132–134.
[62] See *City of London B.S. v. Flegg* [1988] A.C. 54.

Any purported conveyance[63] or mortgage[64] of the entire property, effected by one joint tenant forging the signature of the other or others takes effect only as against his own beneficial interest. The position where there is a sole survivor of joint tenants has already been considered.[65]

What is the position of beneficial co-owners who are not on the legal title, something which is highly likely where their beneficial interests have arisen under a resulting or constructive trust? The intention of the 1925 property legislation was that on any disposition of the land their beneficial interests would be overreached into the proceeds of sale. This will happen when there is a disposition by two trustees or a trust corporation whether the beneficiaries wish their interests to be overreached or not.[66] This is so even as to any of the beneficiaries who are in "actual occupation" of registered land (their interests, having been overreached, are no longer "subsisting" in the land, and so cannot override registration of the title of the purchaser[67]). In the case of registered land, the beneficial co-owners will therefore be completely protected where a restriction has been entered on the register. However, this is not particularly likely where their beneficial interests arise under a resulting or constructive trust unless the land was co-owned already and no similar protection is ever available in the case of unregistered land. Consequently, whenever there is a sole trustee of land, the interests of beneficial co-owners who are not on the legal title are potentially vulnerable.

The 1925 property legislation did not state the effect of a disposition by a sole trustee of land. However, the courts have decided that in these circumstances the overreachable but unoverreached interests of the beneficial co-owners are treated as if they were commercial interests rather than family interests.[68] Consequently, those interests will be destroyed if the land reaches the hands of a bona fide purchaser for value of a legal estate without notice in the case of unregistered land[69] and a bona fide purchaser for value claiming under a registered disposition in the case of registered land[70] (when the Land Registration Act 2002 comes into force, value will not include marriage consideration in the case of registered land[71]).

In the case of unregistered land, there is no way in which a beneficial co-owner can protect himself from the risk of his interest being destroyed as a result of a disposition by a sole trustee unless he goes to the court[72] and asks for a second trustee to be appointed.[73] However, most beneficiaries of resulting and constructive trusts will be in occupation of the land. If this is the case, it is only in the most exceptional circumstances (such as where the trustee has removed all signs of a beneficiary's existence) that a purchaser will not have constructive notice of his presence and a purchaser who has notice will obviously be unable to take free of his interest.

In the case of registered land, assuming that no restriction has been registered, the beneficial co-owner can also go to the court and ask for a second trustee to be appointed. In practice, however, all that it is necessary for him to do is to register a caution against dealings

[63] *Ahmed v. Kendrick* (1988) 56 P. & C.R. 121.

[64] *First National Securities Ltd v. Hegerty* [1985] Q.B. 850.

[65] Above, p. 312.

[66] See *City of London B.S. v. Flegg* [1988] A.C. 54.

[67] *ibid.*; above, pp. 122 *et seq.*

[68] *Caunce v. Caunce* [1969] 1 W.L.R. 286 (unregistered land); *Willliams & Glyn's Bank Ltd v. Boland* [1981] A.C. 487 (registered land).

[69] *Caunce v. Caunce* [1969] 1 W.L.R. 286.

[70] L.R.A. 1925, s.20(4); L.R.A. 2002, s.29.

[71] L.R.A. 2002, s.129(1)

[72] Under T.L.A.T.A. 1996, s.14(1); see above, p. 288 and below.

[73] See *Walker v. Waller* [1967] 1 W.L.R. 451.

(cautions against dealings will be replaced by notifiable restrictions when the Land Registration Act 2002 comes into force). Where this has not been done, the beneficial co-owner will nevertheless be protected when he is in actual occupation of the land, which most beneficiaries of resulting and constructive trusts will be, because in that case his beneficial interest will override the registration of any purchaser. However, the protection so provided will be less when the Land Registration Act 2002 comes into force because the actual occupation will then have to be obvious on a reasonably careful inspection of the land[74] rather than at present a simple question of fact. Consequently, it will then be possible, as in the case of unregistered land, for a purchaser to take free because the trustee has removed all signs of a beneficiary's existence.

Nevertheless, only in very exceptional circumstances will a beneficial co-owner be at risk when he is in occupation of the land. Generally speaking, therefore, it is only where the beneficial co-owners of land held by a sole trustee are not in occupation of the land that there is any serious risk that their interests will be destroyed.

3. Dispute resolution

(a) Occupation trusts

The imposition, from 1926 until 1996, of a trust for sale and, since 1996, of a trust of land in cases of co-ownership has meant that there have been many trusts holding land whose main purpose is not the provision of financial benefits but to provide the means of occupying the property, usually a house. Such trusts may, for brevity, be called "occupation trusts", in contrast with what may be called "financial trusts", trusts holding land whose main purpose is to provide financial benefits for their beneficiaries. This has been and is the purpose of most express trusts for sale, under which the beneficiaries obtain income until sale and capital thereafter. (There is no formal classification of this kind, but the distinction is useful in relation to the resolution of disputes over the property, usually but not exclusively over selling the property and over orders for sale.[75])

(b) The 1996 Act

Under the 1996 Act, "any person who is a trustee of land or has an interest in property subject to a trust of land" may apply to the court for an order relating to the exercise by the trustees of any of their functions, including an order directing them to consult or relieving them from their obligation to do so, or declaring the nature or extent of anyone's interest in the trust property.[76] Anyone who is, or claims to be, a beneficial co-owner of land is therefore entitled to apply to the court for an order establishing the existence and extent of his beneficial interest. Both the trustees and the beneficial co-owners are also entitled to apply to the court for an order relating to the way in which the trustees should exercise their functions. In practice, by far the most likely function in respect of which such an order will be sought is the trustees' power of sale (indeed, before 1997, this was the only function in respect of which such an order could be sought[77]). However, the powers conferred on trustees by the 1996 Act to partition the land[78] and to permit and restrict occupation[79] have also been the

---

[74] Above, p. 127.
[75] Formerly under L.P.A. 1925, s.30 (now repealed), now under T.L.A.T.A 1996, s.14; see above, p. 288.
[76] T.L.A.T.A. 1996, s.14.
[77] Under L.P.A. 1925, s.30 (now repealed).
[78] T.L.A.T.A. 1996, s.7, above p. 284.
[79] ibid., s.13, above p. 286.

subject of applications and the trustees' obligations to consult the beneficiaries specifically referred to in this provision are obviously likely to be the subject of applications in the future.

In determining an application by anyone other than a trustee in bankruptcy, the matters to which the court is to have regard include: first, the intentions of the settlor or testator; secondly, the purposes for which the land is held; thirdly, the welfare of any minor who occupies or might reasonably be expected to occupy any land subject to the trust as his home; and, fourthly, the interests of any secured creditor of any beneficiary.[80] Where the application concerns the occupation of any trust property, the court must additionally have regard to the circumstances and wishes of each of the beneficiaries who is entitled to occupy the land.[81] In any case other than one concerning the occupation of any trust property or one relating to the trustees' right to compel absolutely entitled beneficiaries to take a conveyance of the legal title,[82] the court must additionally have regard to the circumstances and wishes of the beneficiaries of full age entitled to interests in possession in the land.[83]

However, where the application is made by a trustee in bankruptcy, the court must instead make such order as it thinks just and reasonable having regard to the following matters: first, the interests of the bankrupt's creditors; secondly, where the application concerns a dwelling-house which is or has been the home of the bankrupt, his spouse or his former spouse, the conduct of the spouse or former spouse in so far as it contributed to the bankruptcy, the needs and financial resources of the spouse or former spouse, and the needs of any children; and, thirdly, all the circumstances of the case other than the needs of the bankrupt.[84] On any application made more than a year after the appointment of the trustee in bankruptcy, the court must assume, unless the circumstances of the case are exceptional, that the interests of the bankrupt's creditors outweigh all other considerations.[85]

It has been held that the matters to which the court is to have regard are not exclusive but inclusive and that other matters may also be of relevance.[86]

(c) Sales

This is the situation in which occupation trusts differ most from financial trusts. In the case of a financial trust, none of the matters to which the court must have regard is likely to impede the trustees from exercising their power of sale if they wish to do so or if the majority of the beneficiaries of full age entitled to interests in possession of the land or a trustee in bankruptcy of a beneficiary wishes them to do so; the sale will merely convert one form of financial asset into another. Even more so is this the case where the financial trust in question is an express trust for sale; in such cases it is hard to envisage any reason why the trustees should not carry out their duty to sell the property in the event that they are no longer unanimous about continuing to exercise their power to postpone sale.[87] But where there is an occupation trust, a sale will often defeat the purpose of the trust by making one or more of the co-owners homeless and so different considerations apply.

---

[80] *ibid.*, s.15(1); by s.22(3) "beneficiary" does not include an annuitant.
[81] *ibid.*, s.15(2).
[82] This interpretation was confirmed in *The Mortgage Corporation v. Shaire* [2000] 1 F.L.R. 973 at 991.
[83] T.L.A.T.A. 1996, s.15(3); by s.22(3) "beneficiary" does not include an annuitant.
[84] Insolvency Act 1986, s.335A(2), inserted by T.L.A.T.A. 1996, Sched. 3, para. 23.
[85] *ibid.*, s.335A(3), inserted by T.L.A.T.A. 1996, Sched. 3, para. 23.
[86] *Bank of Ireland Home Mortgages Ltd v. Bell* [2001] 2 F.L.R. 809 at 815 (para. 24).
[87] Above, p. 282.

(i) Applications by a co-owner: The first point that must be made is that, where the dispute is between husband and wife in the course of divorce proceedings and there are no third party interests, the only relevant legislation is the Matrimonial Causes Act 1973,[88] not the 1996 Act (this was also the view generally adopted before 1997[89]).

On an application for sale made by one of the co-owners other than in the course of divorce proceedings, the position before 1997 was as follows. The law started from the position that the purpose of an occupation trust was for occupation of the property by its co-owners; consequently, an occupying co-owner could not be evicted by the others.[90] However, where the purpose of the trust was the provision of a family or matrimonial home for a married or unmarried couple, that purpose was regarded as ending when the couple separated, and so it would no longer prevent a sale.[91] A sale was therefore usually, but not always, ordered unless the occupying co-owner paid a proper rent or compensation[92] for his occupation.[93] But where the purpose or the trust was to provide a family home for a man and woman and their children, the house would not cease to be occupied as a family home merely because the man left it; therefore, he would be refused an order for sale.[94]

It has been accepted that the 1996 Act has given scope for some change in the court's practice,[95] although this has been in the context of applications brought by secured creditors rather than by one of the co-owners. While the court now clearly has to consider all the matters to which it is directed to have regard and not, as before 1997, merely those matters which it considers relevant, there seems no obvious reason why a consideration of those matters should lead to any changes being made in the court's previous practice when the only interested parties are the co-owners themselves. At any rate, it seems that the court will continue to regard the purpose of providing a family home as at an end when a couple separate and there are no longer any infant children.[96] Where the court is unable or unwilling to order sale, it is possible instead for the land to be partitioned between the co-owners or for the occupation of different parts of it by different co-owners to be permitted.[97]

(ii) Applications by creditors: Most creditors who make applications will be secured creditors, that is to say mortgagees of either the co-owned property or the beneficial interest of one of the co-owners. It is important to note that the liability of co-owners under a mortgage or a further advance may be different for a number of reasons: the advance may have been obtained as a result of the undue influence of one co-owner over the other[98] or behind the back of the other co-owner[99] or by forging the latter's signature.[1] In all such cases the mortgage or further advance takes effect only against the beneficial interest of the co-owner who obtained it but the beneficial interest of the other co-owner remains bound to

[88] ss.22–25; *Tee v. Tee* [1999] 2 F.L.R. 613.
[89] *Williams v. Williams* [1976] Ch. 278.
[90] *Bull v. Bull* [1955] 1 Q.B. 234; above, p. 254.
[91] *Jones v. Challenger* [1961] 1 Q.B. 176; *Bernard v. Josephs* [1982] Ch. 391.
[92] Above, p. 305.
[93] *Dennis v. McDonald* [1982] Fam. 63; contrast *Stott v. Ratcliffe* (1982) 126 S.J. 310 (no order).
[94] *Re Evers' Trust* [1980] 1 W.L.R. 1327; and see *Chhokar v. Chhokar* [1984] F.L.R. 313 at 327.
[95] *The Mortgage Corporation v. Shaire* [2000] 1 F.L.R. 973, not following *TSB Bank plc v. Marshall* [1998] 2 F.L.R. 769; *Bank of Ireland Home Mortgages Ltd v. Bell* [2001] 2 F.L.R. 809.
[96] *Bank of Ireland Home Mortgages Ltd v. Bell* [2001] 2 F.L.R. 809 at 815–816 (para. 28).
[97] Below.
[98] *Royal Bank of Scotland plc v. Etridge (No. 2)* [2001] 4 All E.R. 449, below, p. 532.
[99] *Equity & Law Home Loans Ltd v. Prestridge* [1992] 1 W.L.R. 137, below, p. 532.
[1] *First National Securities Ltd v. Hegarty* [1985] Q.B. 850; cp. *Paddington B.S. v. Mendelsohn* (1985) 50 P. & C.R. 244. See below, p. 531.

the extent that any previous mortgage was binding on him.[2] The interests of secured creditors are one of the matters to which the court is directed to have regard. However, it is also possible that an application for sale may be made by an unsecured creditor who has obtained a charging order against either the co-owned property or the beneficial interest of one of the co-owners.[3] The interests of such a creditor are not one of the matters to which the court is directed to have regard and it is unlikely that they would order a sale at his suit if the co-owner in question had other unsecured creditors, since to do so would give him a priority over them which he would not enjoy in the event of the co-owner's bankruptcy (mortgagees have an automatic priority over unsecured creditors).

On an application for sale made by a creditor, whether secured or unsecured, the position before 1997 was as follows. The court had a discretion whether to make the order, and had to balance the conflicting interests. The interests of the creditors usually prevailed over those of any other co-owners or occupants of the property and so an order for sale was normally made.[4] Only in exceptional circumstances did the interests of children and families in occupation prevail.

However, it has been held that the 1996 Act has given scope for some change in the court's practice in this respect since the interests of any secured creditor is merely one of the five factors to which the court has to have regard and the court is not directed to have regard to the interests of unsecured creditors at all. In particular, there is no indication that the interests of secured creditors are to be given priority over the welfare of any minor who occupies the property as his home.[5] Consequently, where the mortgage debt of a deceased co-owner exceeded the value of his 25 per cent beneficial interest so that that interest was, in effect, the property of the mortgagee, sale was not ordered provided that the other co-owner continued to discharge her own much lower mortgage debt and to pay interest at 1.25 per cent above base rate on the value of the beneficial interest of the other co-owner (not on the much higher amount of his mortgage debt).[6] On the other hand, sale was ordered where the mortgage debt exceeded the value of the entire property and the co-owner resisting sale had no possibility of compensating the mortgagee for being kept out of its money.[7] In neither of these two cases was the property occupied by minors as their home; where it is so occupied, it is clearly likely that even greater changes will be made to the court's previous practice. It remains to be seen how the courts will balance the interests of such minors against the interests of secured creditors; their interests will presumably prevail over the interests of unsecured creditors.

(iii) Applications by trustees in bankruptcy: On an application made by the trustee in bankruptcy of a bankrupt co-owner, the position before 1997 was the same as when an application was made by a creditor. The court equally had a discretion whether to make the order, and had to balance the conflicting interests. However, the interests of the creditors to whom the trustee in bankruptcy owed his fiduciary duties again usually prevailed over those of any other co-owners or occupants of the property, and so an order for sale was normally made.[8] Only rarely did the circumstances justify refusing an immediate order for sale, as by

---

[2] *Equity & Law Home Loans Ltd v. Prestridge* [1992] 1 W.L.R. 137, below, p. 532.
[3] Such a person presumably has an interest by analogy with the previous legislation ("person interested" held to be within L.P.A. 1925, s.30 in *Midland Bank v. Pike* [1988] 2 All E.R. 434).
[4] *Lloyds Bank plc v. Byrne* [1993] 1 F.L.R. 369.
[5] *The Mortgage Corporation v. Shaire* [2000] 1 F.L.R. 973 at 988.
[6] *ibid.*, at 994–995.
[7] *Bank of Ireland Home Mortgages Ltd v. Bell* [2001] 2 F.L.R. 809 at 815–817.
[8] *Re Bailey* [1977] 1 W.L.R. 278; *Re Lowrie* [1981] 3 All E.R. 353; *Re Citro* [1991] Ch. 142.

postponing the sale of a house for five years while children were being educated.[9] Further, statute provided that, where a bankrupt and his spouse or former spouse were the co-owners of a dwelling-house and the trustee in bankruptcy applied for an order for sale at least a year after the dwelling vested in him, the court had to assume (unless the circumstances of the case are exceptional) that the interests of the bankrupt's creditors outweighed all other considerations.[10]

This provision has been re-enacted by the 1996 Act.[11] Consequently, whatever effect the courts give to the factors to which it has to have regard during the first year following bankruptcy[12] (which are different from those to which it has to have regard on applications by anyone other than a trustee in bankruptcy), thereafter the position is very clear.[13] The presence of exceptional circumstances is a necessary condition to displace the assumption that the interests of the creditors outweigh all other considerations but the presence of exceptional circumstances does not debar the court from making an order for sale.[14] Consequently, once a year has passed, it is almost inevitable that sale will be ordered.

In the modern cases the exceptional circumstances typically relate to the person circumstances of one of the co-owners, such as a medical or mental condition.[15] However the categories of exceptional circumstances are not to be categorised or defined; the court must make a value judgment after looking at all the circumstances.[16] Neither the fact that the other co-owner has been keeping up the mortgage payments, thus benefitting the bankrupt's estate, nor the fact that the other co-owner has also applied for an order for sale in order to complete a sale which he has already negotiated, nor the fact that any delay in sale might cause a mortgagee to step in and sell at a lower price constitute exceptional circumstances.[17] In the absence of such circumstances, a sale can be ordered even though its effect will be that the entire proceeds of sale will be consumed by the trustee's fees and expenses; that is not an exceptional circumstance and such a sale is still for the benefit of the creditors.[18]

(d) Partition and divided occupation

In disputes between co-owners, it is possible for an application to be made for partition of the land[19] or for the co-owners to be permitted to occupy different parts of it.[20] Such an application may be made either outright or by way of counterclaim to an application for an order for sale. Where premises were owned by two doctors and occupied for the purposes of their medical practice, an application by one doctor for an order for sale was met by a counterclaim for partition or for an order that the two doctors be permitted to occupy different

---

[9] *Re Holliday* [1981] Ch. 405 (bankrupt's own petition: creditors not pressing for payment); contrast *Re Lowrie* [1981] 3 All E.R. 353 (immediate sale, completion only postponed for three months).

[10] Insolvency Act 1986, s.336(5).

[11] *ibid.*, s.335A(3), inserted by T.L.A.T.A. 1996, Sched. 3, para. 23.

[12] *ibid.*, s.335A(2), inserted by T.L.A.T.A. 1996, Sched. 3, para. 23.

[13] *Harrington v. Bennett* (2000) New Law Online Case 200035003.

[14] *Re D.R. Raval* [1998] B.P.I.R. 389.

[15] *Judd v. Brown* [1997] B.P.I.R. 470; *Re D.R. Raval* [1998] B.P.I.R. 389; *Claughton v. Charalamabous* [1998] B.P.I.R. 588.

[16] *Claughton v. Charalamabous* [1998] B.P.I.R. 588.

[17] *Harrington v. Bennett* (2000) New Law Online Case 200035003.

[18] *Trustee of the Estate of Bowe v. Bowe* [1997] B.P.I.R. 747; *Harrington v. Bennett* (2000) New Law Online Case 200035003.

[19] Under T.L.A.T.A. 1996, s.7; above, p. 284.

[20] Under *ibid.*, s.13; above, p. 286.

parts of the premises.[21] The court was unable to order sale[22] and did not order partition,[23] presumably because of the impossibility of partitioning the entrance and a central corridor. But each doctor was restricted from occupying specific parts of the premises, thus procuring joint occupation of the entrance and central corridor and individual occupation of the units on either side of the corridor.[24] The court also ordered the doctors to contribute to the costs of adapting the property.[25]

(e) Consultation

The 1996 Act specifically envisages[26] that applications may be made for an order directing the trustees to consult the beneficiaries or relieving them from their obligation to do so. No such application has yet been the subject of a reported decision.

Sect. 8. Position of land settled under the Settled Land Act 1925

The position of two or more persons who are together entitled in possession under a settlement subject to the Settled Land Act 1925[27] depends upon whether in equity they are entitled as joint tenants or in undivided shares.

1. Joint tenants

If two or more persons of full age are entitled as joint tenants of land subject to the Settled Land Act 1925, they together constitute the tenant for life.[28] If any of them is a minor, such one or more of them as for the time being is or are of full age constitute the tenant for life[29]; if they are all minors, the legal estate and statutory powers are vested in the statutory owner[30] until one of them is of full age. Because the land is settled subject to the Settled Land Act 1925, there is no trust of land. All the joint tenants in whom the land is vested must concur in exercising the power of sale and other statutory powers. The court will not compel a dissident tenant to concur unless he is acting in bad faith.[31]

2. Undivided shares

(a) Trust of land

If two or more tenants in common become entitled in possession to settled land, the land forthwith ceases to be settled land and, since 1997, becomes subject to a trust of land (until 1996 to a trust for sale). The Settled Land Act trustees can require the legal estate to be conveyed to them if it is not already vested in them.[32] Until 1996 they held it on the statutory trusts, namely on trust for sale, with power to postpone sale, holding the income until sale and

---

[21] *Rodway v. Landy* [2001] Ch. 703.
[22] National Health Service Act 1977, s.54(1) makes unlawful any sale of the goodwill of a medical practice.
[23] *Rodway v. Landy* (2000) New Law Online Case 2001018801 (Ch.D.); the application for partition was not pursued on appeal.
[24] *Rodway v. Landy* [2001] Ch. 703.
[25] *ibid.*
[26] In s.14(1).
[27] Before 1926 the position was different.
[28] S.L.A. 1925, s.19(2).
[29] *ibid.*, s.19(3).
[30] Above, p. 256.
[31] *Re 90 Thornhill Road, Tolworth, Surrey* [1970] Ch. 261. Contrast trusts of land, above, p. 288.
[32] S.L.A. 1925, s.36(1); L.P.A. 1925, Sched. 1, Pt. IV, para. 2.

the proceeds thereafter upon such trusts and subject to such provisions are as requisite for giving effect to the rights of the persons interested in the land.[33] Since 1997, they hold it on a trust of land. Thus if land is settled on A for life, remainder to B and C in equal shares as tenants in common for life, remainder to the children of B and C in fee simple, when A dies the land will be held upon what is now a trust of land and the legal title must be vested in the Settled Land Act trustees as trustees of land.

(b) Land ceasing to be settled

This provision that the legal estate shall be vested in the Settled Land Act trustees and not in the persons beneficially entitled applies even if the land ceases to be settled at the moment when the tenants in common become entitled in possession. Thus if land is settled on A for life, remainder to his children in fee simple in equal shares as tenants in common, the land ceases to be settled land on the death of A, for it is no longer settled for persons by way of succession. Nevertheless, A's personal representatives must convey the legal estate to the Settled Land Act trustees as joint tenants on a trust of land, and not to the children.[34] To this extent the land retains traces of its former status as settled land. But the children may instead, if they are *sui juris*, require the legal estate to be vested in themselves[35] or, if there is no person appointed by the trust instrument for the purpose of appointing new trustees, on up to four other persons, in each case on a trust of land.[36]

(c) Overreaching powers

The Settled Land Act trustees hold on a special form of trust of land which enables them to overreach not only the rights under that trust but also any other rights existing under a former settlement and not protected by a legal mortgage, even if these rights are prior to the trust of land.[37] For example, if land is settled on A for life, subject to an equitable rentcharge for B, with remainder to C and D as tenants in common, on the death of A the Settled Land Act trustees will hold the land on a trust of land with power to overreach B's rentcharge even though it has priority to the trust of land.

Sect. 9. Determination of joint tenancies and tenancies in common

Joint tenancies and tenancies in common may be determined by partition or by union in a sole tenant; joint tenancies may also be determined by severance, which converts them into tenancies in common.

1. Partition

(a) No power at common law

Joint tenants and tenants in common have always been able to make a voluntary partition of the land concerned if all agreed; their co-ownership thus comes to an end as a result of each of them becoming sole tenant of the piece of land allotted to him. But at common law there was no right to compel a partition.

---

[33] S.L.A. 1925, s.36(2), (6).
[34] *Re Thomas* [1939] Ch. 513.
[35] Above, p. 310.
[36] Above, p. 311.
[37] S.L.A. 1925, s.36(2); L.P.A. 1925, Sched. 1, Pt. IV, para. 1(3), as amended by L.P.(Am.)A. 1926, Sched.

(b) Statutory powers

The 1996 Act,[38] extending similar powers given to trustees for sale by the Law of Property Act 1925[39] to all trusts of land, gives trustees of land power to divide any land to which beneficiaries of full age are absolutely beneficially entitled in undivided shares between those beneficiaries. However, this requires either the consent of each of these beneficiaries,[40] although a purchaser need not be concerned to see that they have consented,[41] or, apparently, an order of the court.[42]

2. Union in a sole tenant

Joint tenancies and tenancies in common may be determined by the entirety of the land becoming vested in a sole tenant. Thus where one of two surviving joint tenants dies, the other becomes sole tenant and the joint tenancy is at an end. Similarly if one joint tenant or tenant in common acquires the interests of all his fellows, as by purchase, the co-ownership is at an end.

Because in theory each joint tenant has the whole of the land, the appropriate way for one joint tenant to transfer his rights to another is by a release operating to extinguish rather than to convey any rights, and so requiring no words of limitation; but any sort of conveyance will be construed as a release,[43] and it has now been retrospectively provided that the transaction can also be effected by grant.[44] A tenant in common, on the other hand, cannot release his share to his fellows, but has to convey it by some assurance by which a sole tenant could have conveyed his land, for "a release supposes the party to have the thing in demand".[45]

Co-ownership in land is also extinguished if the land is sold to a purchaser, for the co-ownership is transferred from the land to the proceeds of sale.

3. Severance

The common law mitigated the uncertainty of the *jus accrescendi* by enabling a joint tenant to destroy the joint tenancy by severance, thereby becoming a tenant in common. "The duration of all lives being uncertain, if either party has an ill opinion of his own life, he may sever the joint tenancy by a deed granting over a moiety [*i.e.* conveying one-half] in trust for himself; so that survivorship can be no hardship, where either side may at pleasure prevent it."[46] This right of severance is unrestricted and absolute save where a joint tenant has by his conduct estopped himself from severing, in which case any attempted severance will be ineffective.[47] The expression "severance" strictly includes partition, but the word is normally used to describe the process whereby a joint tenancy is converted into a tenancy in common, and it is used in this sense here. Although no joint tenant owned any distinct share in the land, yet each had a potential share equal in size to that of his companions, and so depending upon the number of joint tenants at the time in question. Thus if there were five joint tenants, each had the right to sever his joint tenancy and become tenant in common of one undivided fifth

---

[38] T.L.A.T.A. 1996, s.7.
[39] L.P.A. 1925, s.28(3) (now repealed). This replaced the successive Partition Acts of 1539, 1540 and 1868.
[40] T.L.A.T.A. 1996, s.7(3).
[41] *ibid.*, s.16(1).
[42] Under s.14; see *Rodway v. Landy* [2001] Ch. 703, where partition was denied (above, p. 325).
[43] See *Re Schär* [1951] Ch. 280.
[44] L.P.A. 1925, s.72(4).
[45] Litt. s.304, n.1.
[46] *Cray v. Willis* (1729) 2 P.Wms. 529, *per* Verney M.R.
[47] *Price v. Hartwell* [1996] E.G.C.S. 98.

share; if one joint tenant died before the severance each of the survivors had a potential quarter share, and so on. The potential shares in land conveyed to two or more persons as beneficial joint tenants will always be equal, even if they contributed unequally to the purchase price. Consequently, if those interests are severed, their interests in common will also be equal.[48]

Before 1926, a joint tenancy could be severed both at law and in equity. Since 1925, a legal joint tenancy can never be severed so as to create a legal tenancy in common; but this does not prevent one joint tenant from releasing his interest to the others nor does it affect the right to sever a joint tenancy in equity.[49] A severance can be effected by any of the methods which would have been effective in equity in the case of personalty before 1926.[50] These methods all involve destroying one of the unities. Unity of time cannot be destroyed and severance of the unity of possession means partition; but severance of the unity either of title or of interest converts a joint tenancy into a tenancy in common. It is also now possible to use a further method of severance created by the Law of Property Act 1925.[51] A joint tenancy can therefore now be severed in the following ways.

(a) By acquiring another estate in the land

Although it is not fatal to a joint tenancy that one of the tenants is initially given some further estate in the land than his joint tenancy, the subsequent acquisition of an additional estate in the land destroys the unity of interest and severs the joint tenancy.[52] Thus if land is granted to A, B and C as joint tenants for life, with remainder to C in fee simple, the mere existence of C's fee simple remainder does not destroy his tenancy for life. However, if A acquires C's fee simple, A's life estate merges in the fee simple and severs his joint tenancy for life (this will not of course affect the legal title which will continue to be held by A, B and C as joint tenants on a trust of land). It should be noted, however, that this method of severance requires that some estate different from the estate held in joint tenancy should be acquired. Thus in the above example if A instead releases his interest to B, B takes A's one-third share as a tenant in common, but his beneficial joint tenancy with C in the remaining two-thirds is not affected.

(b) By alienation

If a joint tenant alienates his interest *inter vivos*,[53] his joint tenancy is severed and the person to whom the interest is transferred takes it as tenant in common with the other joint tenants, for he has no unity of title with them.[54] Such a severance does not affect the other joint tenants, who remain joint tenants *inter se*. Thus if A, B and C are joint tenants, and A sells his interest to X, X becomes beneficial tenant in common of one-third and B and C remain joint tenants of two-thirds. (This will again not affect the legal title which will continue to be held by A, B and C as joint tenants on a trust of land unless and until A, B and C convey it to B, C and X.) If B then dies, C alone profits by the *jus accrescendi* in equity, X and C being

---

[48] *Goodman v. Gallant* [1986] Fam. 106; *Roy v. Roy* [1996] 1 F.L.R. 541.
[49] L.P.A. 1925, s.36(2).
[50] *ibid.*
[51] *ibid.*
[52] *Wiscot's Case* (1599) 2 Co.Rep. 60b.
[53] Above, pp. 303–304.
[54] *Partriche v. Powlet* (1740) 2 Atk. 54; and see *Goddard v. Lewis* (1909) 101 L.T. 528, collecting many of the authorities.

left as tenants in common as to one-third and two-thirds respectively; but the legal title will be held by the survivors of whoever held it prior to B's death.

An involuntary alienation suffices, as where a joint tenant becomes bankrupt and his interest vests in his trustee in bankruptcy.[55] However, where the estate of a deceased person is insolvent, his administrator in bankruptcy cannot claim his share of a joint tenancy which was subject to the *jus accrescend* on his death.[56] Partial alienation is also enough, as where a joint tenant mortgages his beneficial interest or leases it, provided that the lease really does take effect as a lease rather than a licence.[57] A purported conveyance[58] or mortgage[59] of the entire property, effected by one joint tenant forging the signature of the other, severs the forger's joint tenancy and takes effect only as against his beneficial interest. However, this is not the case when the purported conveyance is in favour of a person who is aware of the forgery; such a conveyance is a total sham and has no effect whatever.[60]

(c) By mutual agreement

Prior to the reform of the formalities rules governing contracts for the sale of land in 1989,[61] an agreement by a joint tenant to alienate his beneficial interest or simply to sever that interest severed his equitable joint tenancy if the agreement was specifically enforceable,[62] and even if it was not when it was made with the only other joint tenants instead of with a third party.[63] This remains the situation since the reform of those rules but such an agreement will in principle now only be valid if it is in writing and signed by all the parties to it.[64] However, it has now been held that estoppel interests take effect behind a constructive trust.[65] Consequently, if the other party to an oral agreement by a joint tenant to sever his interest acted to his detriment in reliance on that agreement, it appears that he would be able to enforce it on the basis that the joint tenant was estopped from denying the agreement and was therefore a constructive sub-trustee of the land for him. However, the agreement must be for an immediate severance, not a severance at some time in the future[66]; but the making of mutual wills, which are irrevocable in equity without the consent of the other party, does amount to a severance (those making mutual wills normally leave their assets to one another with a substitutionary gift to the same third party). Mere negotiations for an agreement have never been enough,[67] nor is a mere unilateral declaration of a desire to sever[68] unless it takes effect as a notice in writing under the Law of Property Act 1925.[69]

---

[55] Insolvency Act 1986, s.283; *Re Dennis* [1993] Ch. 72.
[56] *Re Palmer* [1994] Ch. 316.
[57] Below, pp. 339 *et seq.*
[58] *Ahmed v. Kendrick* (1988) 56 P. & C.R. 121.
[59] *First National Securities Ltd v. Hegerty* [1985] Q.B. 850.
[60] *Penn v. Bristol & West Building Society* [1996] 2 F.C.R. 729.
[61] Above, p. 148.
[62] *Brown v. Raindle* (1796) 3 Ves. 256.
[63] *Burgess v. Rawnsley* [1975] Ch. 429. See [1976] C.L.J. 20 (D. J. Hayton).
[64] L.P.(M.P.)A. 1989, s.2.
[65] *Yaxley v. Gotts* [2000] Ch. 162 (party to oral contract for the sale of land estopped from denying its validity).
[66] *Harris v. Goddard* [1983] 1 W.L.R. 203. *Edwards v. Hastings* [1996] N.P.C. 87.
[67] *Gore v. Carpenter* (1990) 60 P. & C.R. 456; but see *Burgess v. Rawnsley* [1975] Ch. 429.
[68] See *Nielson-Jones v. Fedden* [1975] Ch. 222, and contrast *Burgess v. Rawnsley* [1975] Ch. 429. See now below, p. 331.
[69] Below.

(d) By a mutual course of dealing

A severance can be made by means of any course of dealing between all the joint tenants which sufficiently indicates an intention that they are to become tenants in common.[70] There has to be a course of dealing which shows that all concerned are treating their interests as being tenancies in common with immediate effect, as where the joint tenants authorise the trustees to pay one of the tenants his share.[71] The burden of proof lies on the person seeking to establish a severance,[72] and it is not enough merely to show that the joint tenants have engaged in lengthy negotiations about the possibility of one buying the other out,[73] or that the joint tenants of a house have converted it into maisonettes so that each can live separately,[74] or that partners have included the farmhouse and land which they hold as joint tenants in their partnership accounts.[75]

(e) By homicide

Nobody can benefit in law by his crime.[76] Hence if one joint tenant is guilty of the murder or deliberate and violent manslaughter[77] of another joint tenant, the criminal is treated as having severed the joint tenancy and so he forfeits the interest which he would otherwise have taken by survivorship.[78] However, despite the severance, the Forfeiture Act 1982 gives the court the power to grant relief against forfeiture in cases of homicide other than murder[79] and has done so.[80] A survivor of a suicide pact is also within this principle but is entitled to relief in full.[81]

(f) By notice in writing

This is the method created by the Law of Property Act 1925. "Where a legal estate (not being settled land) is vested in joint tenants beneficially, and any tenant desires to sever the joint tenancy in equity, he shall give to the other joint tenants a notice in writing of such desire", whereupon the parties concerned are to be treated in equity as if there had been an actual severance.[82] This provision is limited in its operation. Settled land is expressly excluded, thus preventing it becoming subject to a trust of land,[83] and it appears to be confined to land, thus excluding pure personalty.[84] It plainly applies where A and B hold the legal estate on trust for themselves jointly, but, read literally, not where they hold it on trust for themselves and others, or where other trustees hold it on trust for them. But the court may be able to read "vested in joint tenants beneficially" as being "vested in any persons for joint tenants

---

[70] *Williams v. Hensman* (1861) 1 J. & H. 546 at 557; *Burgess v. Rawnsley* [1975] Ch. 429 at 440, 447; *McDowell v. Hirschfield Lipson & Rumney and Smith* [1992] 2 F.L.R. 126.
[71] *Williams v. Hensman* (1861) 1 J. & H. 546.
[72] *Re Denny* [1947] L.J.R. 1029.
[73] *McDowell v. Hirschfield Lipson & Rumney and Smith* [1992] 2 F.L.R. 126.
[74] *Greenfield v. Greenfield* (1979) 38 P. & C.R. 570.
[75] *Barton v. Morris* [1985] 1 W.L.R. 1257.
[76] See above, p. 186.
[77] *ibid.*
[78] *Re K.* [1986] Ch. 180.
[79] Forfeiture Act 1982.
[80] *Re K* [1986] Ch. 180; *Re H* [1990] 1 F.L.R. 441.
[81] *Dunbar v. Plant* [1998] Ch. 412.
[82] L.P.A. 1925, s.36(2); *Harris v. Goddard* [1983] 1 W.L.R. 203 at 209. *Grindal v. Hooper* [1999] E.G.C.S. 150.
[83] See above, p. 326.
[84] *Nielson-Jones v. Fedden* [1975] Ch. 222; but see below.

beneficially", and so cure this strange omission. The suggestion[85] that joint tenancies of pure personalty could be severed in equity by a notice in writing before 1926 and consequently joint tenancies of both land and pure personalty still can be so severed would remove both these limitations but does not appear to be any acceptable way of doing so. A notice given to one but not all of the other joint tenants seems to be ineffective as having been given not to "the other joint tenants" but only to one of them.

No form for such a notice is prescribed. A notice which is posted is effective if the letter is delivered to the other joint tenant's last known abode or business address, even if he does not receive it[86] and a notice sent by registered post to one of these addresses is effective even if it is not delivered unless it is returned.[87] A writ or originating summons commencing legal proceedings, or an affidavit in the proceedings may suffice if a claim to an immediate interest in the property is asserted, even if the proceedings are not pursued.[88] However, a divorce petition which makes no immediate claim but prays for a property adjustment order to be made in the future is not enough.[89]

4. Operation of the present law

An example illustrating the present position may be useful. In 1997 X purported to convey land to A, B, C, D, and E in fee simple; all were of full age. The legal estate vested in A, B, C, and D on a trust of land; in equity, A, B, C, D and E were tenants in common if there were words of severance or if it was one of equity's special cases, but otherwise joint tenants. If they were joint tenants and A died, B, C, and D would then hold the legal estate on a trust of land for B, C, D and E as joint tenants; E would not automatically fill the vacancy at law, but could, of course, be appointed by the remaining trustees to be a new trustee in place of A. If B afterwards sold and transferred his interest to P, then B, C and D would continue to hold the legal estate but thereafter on trust for P as tenant in common of a quarter and C, D and E as joint tenants of three-quarters. If C then severed his joint tenancy (such as by agreement in writing with D and E), the legal estate would remain in B, C and D as before, on trust for P and C as tenants in common of one-quarter each, and D and E as joint tenants of half. On D's death, B and C would hold the legal estate on trust for P, C and E as tenants in common as to one-quarter, one-quarter and one-half respectively.

PART 2—PARTY WALLS

1. Categories

Where a wall separates land owned by A from land owned by B, the wall may either be in the sole ownership of one party, free from any rights of the other, or else be a party wall. A wall may even be in sole ownership for part of its height and a party wall for the rest.[90] There appears to be no precise legal definition of the term "party wall". There are now three possible meanings.[91]

---

[85] *Burgess v. Rawnsley* [1975] Ch. 429 at 440 *per* Lord Denning M.R.
[86] *Kinch v. Bullard* [1999] 1 W.L.R. 423, applying L.P.A. 1925, s.196(3).
[87] *Re 88 Berkeley Road, NW9* [1971] Ch. 648, applying L.P.A. 1925, s.196(4).
[88] *Burgess v. Rawnsley* [1975] Ch. 429 at 447.
[89] *Harris v. Goddard* [1983] 1 W.L.R. 203.
[90] *Weston v. Arnold* (1873) 8 Ch.App. 1084.
[91] See *Watson v. Gray* (1880) 14 Ch.D. 192 at 194, 195.

(i) *Divided*: the wall is divided longitudinally into two strips, one belonging to each of the neighbouring owners.

(ii) *Divided with easements*: the wall is divided as in (b), but each half is subject to an easement of support in favour of the owner of the other half.

(iii) *Ownership subject to easement*: the wall belongs entirely to one of the adjoining owners, but is subject to an easement or right in the other to have it maintained as a dividing wall.

Before 1926, there was also a fourth category, where the two adjoining owners were tenants in common of the wall. The category had the disadvantage that either owner could insist upon a partition. Had no special provision been made, all party walls in this category would after 1925 have become subject to a trust for sale. It was consequently provided that all party walls in this category should thereafter be deemed to be severed vertically, and that the owner of each part should have such rights of support and user over the rest of the wall as were requisite for giving the parties rights similar to those which they would have enjoyed had they been tenants in common of the wall.[92] The practical effect of this provision was to translate all party walls in this category into the second category.

2. Characteristics

The general rule is that ownership of a party wall follows the ownership of the land on which it is built. "As a matter of law, the property in the wall followed the property in the land upon which it stood".[93] As has already been mentioned, a wall may even be in sole ownership for part of its height and a party wall for the rest.[94]

(a) Divided

Where the wall is built on the boundary, so that substantially half the soil on which it stands is A's and half B's, there is a presumption that the case falls into the first category, the wall being regarded as divided into two walls each of half the thickness.[95] However, cases of this category are rare; they have an unsatisfactory aspect in that either owner, acting with reasonable care, can remove his half of the wall and leave a structure which is perhaps incapable of standing alone.[96]

(b) Divided with easements

Where each owner has exercised dominion over the same wall and the exact boundary cannot be shown, there is now a presumption that they are deemed to be severed vertically, and that the owner of each part shall have such rights of support and user over the rest of the wall as are requisite for giving the parties rights similar to those which they would have enjoyed had they been tenants in common of the wall.[97] Neither owner is under any positive obligation to repair his half nor can he pull down a wall of this kind except for the purpose of rebuilding

---

[92] L.P.A. 1925, s.38(2), Sched. 1, Pt. V.
[93] *Jones v. Read* (1876) 10 I.R.C.L. 315 at 320, *per* Palles C.B.
[94] *Weston v. Arnold* (1873) 8 Ch.App. 1084.
[95] *Murly v. M'Dermott* (1838) 8 A. & E. 138 at 142.
[96] See *Cubitt v. Porter* (1828) 8 B. & C. 257 at 264.
[97] L.P.A. 1925, s.38(2), Sched. 1, Pt. V.

it with all reasonable dispatch[98]; nor can either prevent the other from enjoying any part of the wall, as by covering the top with broken glass or replacing it with part of a shed.[99]

(c) Ownership subject to easement

Where the wall is built entirely on A's land, the presumption was that the wall was A's.[1] However, only if it can be proved that an appropriate easement has been created can this category be established (otherwise the wall will not be a party wall).

3. The Party Wall, etc. Act 1996

The Party Wall, etc. Act 1996 extended to the whole of England and Wales provisions that had previously existed in some parts of the country, particularly London, for many years.[2] The Act defines "party wall" by reference to its function not to its ownership. A wall will be a party wall either where it forms part of a building and the wall projects beyond the boundary into the land of the adjoining owner or where it is built on the land of one owner but separates buildings belonging to different owners.[3] The Act requires that a landowner who wishes to carry out any of a number of specified works must serve a notice of specified kinds on the adjoining landowner (for these purposes landowner includes a purchaser and a person in possession other than as a mortgagee or as a tenant from year to year or any lesser period[4]).

(a) New party wall

Where what the landowner wishes to do is to erect is a new party wall of the first or second categories (in practice inevitably of the second category),[5] the adjoining landowner can either consent by a further notice served within 14 days of receipt of the relevant notice, in which case the wall will be built on the land of both of them and the cost will be apportioned between them in regard to their respective intended user of it,[6] or not so consent, in which case the wall has to be built entirely on the land of the landowner serving the notice and at his expense.[7] If the landowner serving the notice instead wishes to erect a new party wall of the third category, he can do so as of right one month after serving the notice.[8] Any wall thus built entirely on the land of the landowner serving a notice can have foundations which extend under the land of the adjoining landowner[9] but the latter must be compensated for any damage caused thereby or otherwise.[10]

(b) Works to existing party wall

Where what the landowner wishes to do is to repair an existing party wall or carry out a variety of other works in respect of it, once he has served his notice[11] he has a series of rights

---

[98] *Cubitt v. Porter* (1828) 8 B. & C. 257.
[99] *Stedman v. Smith* (1857) 8 E. & B. 1 at 6, 7.
[1] *Hutchinson v. Mains* (1832) Alc. & N. 155.
[2] *e.g.* the London Building Acts 1930 to 1982: see Greater London (General Powers) Act 1982, s.3(6).
[3] Party Wall, etc. Act 1996, s.20.
[4] *ibid.*, (a statutory tenant is not included; *Frances Holland School v. Wassef* [2001] 2 E.G.L.R. 88).
[5] *ibid.*, s.1(2)
[6] *ibid.*, s.1(3).
[7] *ibid.*, s.1(4).
[8] *ibid.*, s.1(5).
[9] *ibid.*, s.1(6).
[10] *ibid.*, s.1(7).
[11] *ibid.*, s.3.

so to do subject to making good any damage caused to the walls or the buildings of the adjoining landowner.[12] However, the latter has the right to respond to the relevant notice by serving a counter notice setting out such requirements as to the nature of the works as are reasonable for his own convenience[13] and these must generally be complied with.[14]

(c) Excavations

Where what the landowner wishes to do is to excavate within a specified distance of any building or structure on the land of an adjoining landowner,[15] he must at his own expense underpin or strengthen the foundations of any buildings or structures on the adjoining land.[16] Unless the adjoining owner consents to the excavation within 14 days of receipt of the relevant notice, a dispute is deemed to have arisen between the parties.[17]

All disputes between adjoining landowners arising under this legislation are resolved by a form of arbitration carried out by persons described by the Act as "surveyors" (who will usually actually be surveyors). They are required to make an "award" determining such matters as the right to carry out the works, the time and manner of their execution and any incidental matters.[18] In the case of registered land, it might be expected that there is some provision for the registration of any such award so as to bind successors in title but surprisingly there is not[19] either under the Land Registration Act 1925 or under the Land Registration Act 2002 (unless the new Land Registration Rules provide to the contrary).

Very extensive rights are conferred on a person carrying out works under this Act, including rights of entry, by force if accompanied by a police officer, and rights of removal of furniture or fittings,[20] although 14 days' advance notice must be given except in emergencies[21] and the adjoining landowner must as always be compensated for any loss or damage done.[22] Further, failure to comply with the requirements of the Act amounts to an actionable nuisance[23] and in exceptional circumstances the court may apparently even order the removal or reversal of any unauthorised works.[24] On the other hand, an adjoining landowner or occupier who knowingly refuses to permit the exercise of rights given by the Act is guilty of a criminal offence.[25] The rights thus conferred are considerably more extensive than those given by the Access to Neighbouring Land Act 1992[26] to a landowner who needs to enter adjoining land in order to carry out works which are reasonably necessary for the protection of his own land; such a landowner will therefore now only rely on that Act if he cannot bring himself within the provisions of the Party Wall, etc. Act 1996.

---

[12] ibid., s.2.
[13] ibid., s.4(1).
[14] ibid., s.4(3).
[15] ibid., s.6 (depending on the purpose of the excavation, the distance is either three metres or six metres).
[16] ibid., s.6(3).
[17] ibid., s.6(7).
[18] ibid., s.10.
[19] Observatory Hill Ltd v. Camtel Investments S.A. [1997] 1 E.G.L.R. 140.
[20] Party Wall, etc. Act 1996, s.8.
[21] ibid., s.8(3), (4).
[22] ibid., s.7.
[23] See Louis v. Sadiq [1997] 1 E.G.L.R. 136 (on the London Building Acts (Amendment) Act 1939).
[24] cp. London and Manchester Assurance Co. Ltd v. O & H Construction Ltd [1989] 2 E.G.L.R. 183 (also on the London Building Acts (Amendment) Act 1939).
[25] Party Wall, etc. Act 1996, s.16.
[26] Below, p. 450.

Chapter 9

LANDLORD AND TENANT

PART 1—INTRODUCTORY

Before considering leases and tenancies in detail, some mention will be made of their history and terminology.

Sect. 1. History

1. Leases

A lease, as generally understood today, is a document creating an interest in land for a fixed period of certain duration,[1] usually but not necessarily in consideration of the payment of rent. This has not always been so.

2. Leases for lives

The owner of a life estate in land was able to recover the land itself if he was dispossessed, whereas until the end of the fifteenth century a tenant for a term of years could not do so if he was dispossessed by someone other than his landlord. One result of this was that in early times it was a common practice for a lessee to take a lease of land for the duration of a specified number of lives, instead of for a specified term of years. Thus, instead of a lease for 99 years, a tenant would take a lease for the life of the survivor of X, Y and Z. The tenant had an estate *pur autre vie*, which, being an estate of freehold and classified as real property,[2] entitled him to recover the land if he was dispossessed. The disadvantage of the uncertainty of the period was outweighed by the advantages it gave to the tenant and sometimes to the landlord. The rent payable was usually fairly small, but a lump sum, technically known as a fine, was paid when the lease was granted. A further fine was payable when, on the dropping of the lives, the tenant exercised the right the lease invariably gave him to replace them and so extend the lease. If the lessor was a corporation such as a monastery or college, the fines were treated as income by the then members of the corporation, to the disadvantage of their successors. Leases for life finally lost their popularity when legislation in the first half of the

---

[1] See above, p. 33.
[2] *Weigall v. Brome* (1833) 6 Sim. 99; above, pp. 19, 32.

nineteenth century compelled corporations to add such fines to their capital.[3] Nowadays a lease for life is converted into a 90-year determinable term.[4]

3. Leases for fixed terms of years

Leases for fixed terms of years are used today for more purposes than one.

The usual type of lease is the occupational lease, where the tenant holds at a rent or in consideration of a fine, or both, and occupies the property himself, as his residence or as his place of business, or sub-lets it. This type of lease is dealt with in this chapter.

Sometimes leases are granted as a mere conveyancing device. Such leases are granted without a fine and at no rent, in order to provide security for the payment of money. The only relevant modern example is where a mortgage is created as a result of the grant of a lease or sub-lease by the mortgagor to the mortgagee. This method of creating mortgages is in fact virtually obsolete and it will no longer be possible to mortgage registered land by this method when the Land Registration Act 2002 comes into force.[5] Leases of this kind are dealt with under mortgages.[6]

Sect. 2. Terminology

It is important to be familiar with the terms used in the law of leases. A lease is sometimes referred to as a "demise" and the premises in question as the "demised premises". The term "tenancy" is normally used for interests lasting for a relatively short period only, while "lease" usually indicates a more enduring interest. There is no hard-and-fast division, and in this chapter "lease" normally includes "tenancy". "Lease" and "term of years" are virtually synonymous terms today (before 1926 a term of years could only be regarded as one kind of lease, since leases for lives were by no means unknown but today they have nearly all disappeared[7]). "Lease" is often used interchangeably for the document and the "term of years" or "leasehold interest" created by it, although strictly it merely means the document.

The grantor of a lease is known as the lessor, the person to whom it is granted as the lessee. On the grant of a lease, the lessor retains a reversion, which he may assign. Similarly, the lessee may assign the lease, provided that this has not been prohibited. Instead of assigning the lease (*i.e.* transferring the property for the whole of the period for which it is held), the owner of the lease may grant a sub-lease (or underlease) for some shorter period, the parties to this sub-lease being known as the sub-lessor and sub-lessee respectively. Where the original lessor and original lessee have both assigned their interests, the new owners of the reversion and the lease are sometimes called the lessor and lessee, although it is better to keep these expressions for the original parties to the lease, and refer to the owners for the time being, whether original or by assignment, as the landlord and the tenant.

These expressions may be illustrated as follows:

---

[3] See Radcliffe, *Real Property* (2nd ed., 1928), p. 28.
[4] Below, p. 350.
[5] L.R.A. 2002, s.23(1).
[6] See below, p. 494.
[7] Below, p. 350.

X   ⇒   Y
⇓   99
A   ⇒   B
          ⇓   21
          C   ⇒   D

This diagram is the usual way of representing the following events. X grants a 99 years' lease to A and then assigns the reversion to Y. B takes an assignment of A's lease and grants a sub-lease to C for 21 years, C assigning his sub-lease to D. As to the 99 years' lease, X is the "lessor", Y is the "assignee of the reversion" or "landlord", and A the "lessee". B is in a dual position; as to the 99 years' lease, he is the "assignee" or "tenant" and as to the 21 years' lease he is the "sub-lessor" or "landlord". C is the "sub-lessee", and D the "assignee" of the sub-lease, or the "sub-tenant".

For the purpose of enforcing covenants in leases created before 1996, it is important to note that "privity of contract" exists between X and A and between B and C, whilst "privity of estate" potentially exists between Y and A, and then Y and B (having the same estates as were originally vested in X and A), and between B and D. However, "privity of estate" will only actually exist if all the relevant grants and assignments have been carried out with the formalities required by the common law rather than merely having taken effect in equity.[8] The enforcement of covenants in leases granted after 1995 is instead governed by the Landlord and Tenant (Covenants) Act 1995 ("the 1995 Act"). In the absence of contrary agreement, covenants in such leases are enforceable only as between current landlords and current tenants, so only as between Y and B and between B and D, and this is the case whether or not all the relevant grants and assignments have been carried out with the formalities required by the common law.[9]

PART 2—CREATION OF LEASES AND TENANCIES

Sect. 1. Essentials of a lease or tenancy

No lease or tenancy can be created unless four conditions are satisfied. They are:

   (i) that the premises are sufficiently defined;

   (ii) that the tenant has the right to exclusive possession of the premises during the term;

   (iii) that the requirements as to duration are satisfied; and

   (iv) that the proper formalities have been observed.

Under a tenancy there is nearly always a requirement to pay rent, but this is not actually essential.[10] In recent years there has been much litigation on whether or not a tenancy has

---

[8] See below, pp. 387, 394.
[9] See below, pp. 396–397.
[10] *Ashburn Anstalt v. Arnold* [1989] Ch. 1; and see L.P.A. 1925, s.205(1)(xxvii).

been created, for whereas a tenancy of a dwelling-house can be protected by what are collectively described as the Rent Acts (although the more recent statutes have insteaed been called Housing Acts),[11] a mere licence to occupy the dwelling cannot. Many landlords have therefore sought to grant licences in lieu of tenancies, with varying success.

The four heads will be considered in turn.

1. Premises sufficiently defined

A lease or tenancy can exist only in relation to defined premises. Thus a contract by the owner of a building to store goods in them, though with liberty to change the rooms in which they are stored, at his convenience, can create no tenancy since no rights are given over any particular area.[12] But where the premises are clearly defined, the mere imposition of severe restrictions on the use that can be made of them will not negative a tenancy.[13]

2. Right to exclusive possession

In determining whether a tenancy has been granted, the essential question is whether there has been the grant of a right to the exclusive possession of the premises. If there has, then provided the other requirements for a tenancy are satisfied, a tenancy will have been created.[14]

(a) Right

The question is not whether it was intended to confer a right to exclusive possession, nor whether exclusive possession is in fact enjoyed, but whether a right to exclusive possession has in fact been given[15]; and this has to be determined from the substance of the transaction as a whole, though disregarding any provisions which are mere pretences or shams[16]; such provisions are inserted in order to try to prevent the occupier from obtaining statutory protection against eviction. "The manufacture of a five-pronged implement for manual digging results in a fork even if the manufacturer, unfamiliar with the English language, insists that he intended to make and has made a spade"[17] and "A cat does not become a dog because the parties have agreed to call it a dog".[18] What must be considered is what the parties have in fact done, and not what they intended, or pretended, to do. It does not even matter that the grantor of the right had no title to grant a lease if, as between himself and the grantee, he is estopped from denying the existence of a right to exclusive possession.[19] However, the intention of the parties is important in deciding whether or not they intended to enter into legal relations, or whether the transaction was a mere family arrangement or act of friendship or generosity.[20]

---

[11] For these, see below, pp. 590 *et seq.*
[12] *Interoven Stove Co. Ltd v. Hibbard* [1936] 1 All E.R. 263; and see *Wells v. Kingston-upon-Hull Corporation* (1875) L.R. 10 C.P. 402.
[13] *Joel v. International Circus and Christmas Fair* (1920) 124 L.T. 459.
[14] *Street v. Mountford* [1985] A.C. 809. The authorities are fully considered in Megarry's *Rent Acts* (11th ed., 1989 and subsequent Supplements).
[15] *Street v. Mountford* [1985] A.C. 809.
[16] See below.
[17] *Street v. Mountford* [1985] A.C. 809 at 819.
[18] *Antoniades v. Villiers* [1990] 1 A.C. 417 at 444.
[19] *Bruton v. London & Quadrant Housing Trust* [2000] 1 A.C. 406; see M. Dixon [2000] C.L.J. 25.
[20] See *Facchini v. Bryson* [1952] 1 T.L.R. 1386 at 1389; and see *Marcroft Wagons Ltd v. Smith* [1951] 2 K.B. 496. See also *Street v. Mountford* [1985] A.C. 809 at 826 as to other relationships.

(b) Exclusive possession

The right must be to "exclusive" possession, entitling the tenant to exclude all others (including the landlord) from the premises during the term.[21] Lodgers are not tenants, because the owner and his staff have unrestricted access to the room or rooms to provide attendance or services, and although the lodger has the right to be there he cannot call the place his own.[22] The same applies to occupants of old people's homes,[23] a local authority's hostel for homeless men,[24] and hotel rooms and bed-sitting rooms.[25] On the other hand, the fact that bathroom and lavatory facilities are shared with other persons does not prevent the occupier from having exclusive possession of the room or rooms that he occupies provided he can exclude all others from those premises during the term.[26] In technical terms, his lease of those premises will be coupled with an easement or a licence to use the bathroom and lavatory. The same would be true of shared kitchen facilities. However, in the context of whether or not the occupier has statutory protection from eviction, shared kitchen facilities,[27] but not shared bathroom and lavatory facilities,[28] prevent his accommodation from being a dwelling; but the fact that he has no cooking facilities and never eats there does not have this effect[29] nor does the fact that the premises have no bed, provided that he does normally sleep there.[30]

(c) Pretences or shams

In determining whether or not a tenancy has been granted, the court will ignore any provisions in the agreement which are mere pretences or shams seeking to negative a tenancy.[31] Thus provisions in a "licence" to occupy a small room which negated any right to exclusive possession, allowed the licensor (who retained a set of keys) to use and authorise others to use the room, and conferred no right to occupy the room from 10.30 until noon each day have been held to be mere pretences which did not prevent a tenancy arising.[32] Again, where a cohabiting couple simultaneously made separate agreements to occupy a small flat on terms that they had no exclusive possession and that the use of the flat was to be in common with the landlord and others authorised by him, the two agreements, being interdependent, were held to make the couple the joint holders of a lease.[33] But independent agreements made at different times and on different terms which gave four persons the exclusive right to use a flat in common with each other made them mere licensees; and, lacking the four unities,[34] they could not in any case have been joint tenants.[35]

---

[21] *Street v. Mountford* [1985] A.C. 809.
[22] *ibid.*, at 818.
[23] *Abbeyfield (Harpenden) Society Ltd v. Woods* [1968] 1 W.L.R. 374.
[24] *Westminster City Council v. Clarke* [1992] 2 A.C. 288.
[25] *Luganda v. Services Hotels Ltd* [1969] 2 Ch. 209 at 219.
[26] *Westminster City Council v. Clarke* [1992] 2 A.C. 288.
[27] *Neale v. Del Soto* [1945] K.B. 144.
[28] *ibid.*; *Westminster City Council v. Clarke* [1992] 2 A.C. 288.
[29] *Uratemp Ventures Ltd v. Collins* [2001] 3 W.L.R. 806.
[30] *ibid*; see S. Bright [2002] C.L.J. 146.
[31] *Street v. Mountford* [1985] A.C. 809 at 825; *A.G. Securities v. Vaughan* [1990] 1 A.C. 417 at 462.
[32] *Aslan v. Murphy (No. 1)* [1990] 1 W.L.R. 766; and see *Street v. Mountford* [1985] A.C. 809 at 825.
[33] *Antoniades v. Villiers* [1990] 1 A.C. 417. But consider *Mikeover Ltd v. Brady* (1989) 21 H.L.R. 513 (no joint tenancy as no joint obligation to pay the rent: *sed quaere*).
[34] See above, p. 304.
[35] *A.G. Securities v. Vaughan* [1990] 1 A.C. 417.

3. Requirements as to duration

The general nature of an estate less than freehold has already been considered,[36] and details of the requisite duration of each particular type of lease or tenancy are set out below.[37] A lease cannot be for an uncertain period such as the duration of a war.[38]

4. Requisite formalities—legal issues

To create a legal estate after 1925, a lease or tenancy must not only grant a term of years absolute within section 1(1) of the Law of Property Act 1925[39] but must also be made with the proper formalities.

(a) Leases and tenancies

A lease cannot create a legal estate unless it is made by deed.[40] It will be recalled[41] that an instrument will be a deed only if[42]—

    (i) it makes it clear on its face that it is intended to be a deed, usually by using the expression "signed as a deed by" each person who is executing it;

    (ii) it is signed either by the person making it (or one of the parties to it) in the presence[43] of a witness who attests the signature, or else at his direction and in his presence and the presence of two witnesses who each attest the signature; and

    (iii) it is delivered[44] as a deed by him or by a person authorised to do so on his behalf.

But there is an exception for a lease which—

    (i) takes effect in possession (*i.e.* starts immediately),

    (ii) is for a term not exceeding three years, whether or not the lessee is given power to extend the term, and

    (iii) is at the best rent reasonably obtainable without taking a fine.[45]

If all three conditions are complied with, a legal lease or tenancy can be created either orally or by writing which does not satisfy the requirements of a deed.

(b) Contracts for leases and tenancies

Since September 26, 1989,[46] the general rules has been that a contract to grant a lease or tenancy is void unless it is actually made in writing and signed by all the parties.[47] However,

---

[36] Above, p. 33.
[37] Below, pp. 346–353.
[38] Below, p. 346.
[39] Above, p. 81.
[40] L.P.A. 1925, ss.52(1), 205(1)(ii), (xxiii).
[41] Above, p. 160.
[42] L.P.(M.P.)A. 1989, s.1(2)–(4).
[43] The witness can sign later if the person making the deed intends that he is to do so; *Shah v. Shah* [2001] 3 W.L.R. 1.
[44] For delivery, see above, p. 162.
[45] L.P.A. 1925, ss.52(1), (2)(d), 54(2); but see below, p. 353 (assignment).
[46] For the pre-existing law, see above, p. 147.
[47] L.P.(M.P.)A. 1989, s.2; see above, p. 148.

contracts for leases or tenancies within the above exception are also exempt from this requirement,[48] and so may be made either orally or by writing which does not satisfy this requirement.

5. Requisite formalities—equitable leases

(a) Informal lease void at law

A lease which did not satisfy the above requirements was void at law and passed no legal estate. However, although at law the lease was ineffective to create any tenancy, a tenancy at law might arise independently of the lease. For if the tenant took possession with the landlord's consent, a tenancy at will arose; and as soon as rent was paid and accepted, the tenancy at will was converted into a yearly or other periodic tenancy (depending on the way the rent was paid[49]), on such of the terms of the lease as were consistent with the periodic tenancy created. Thus if in 1920 a lease for 99 years was granted orally or merely in writing, the largest estate which the tenant could claim in a court of law was usually a yearly tenancy; and his claim to this depended not on the lease but upon his possession and the payment and acceptance of rent.

(b) Effect as contract

Although such a lease itself failed to create any legal estate, it was not entirely ineffective, for it might be treated as a contract to grant the lease. A lease is clearly distinct from a contract to grant a lease: the difference is between "I hereby grant you a lease" and "I hereby agree that I will grant you a lease". Nevertheless, both law and equity concurred in treating an imperfect lease as a contract to grant a lease, provided it was made for value and was sufficiently evidenced in writing, or, so far as equity was concerned, was supported by a sufficient act of part performance.[50] Today, the requirements of evidence in writing or part performance have been replaced by a requirement that the lease should actually be in writing and have been signed by all the parties.[51] The attitude of equity was particularly important, for under the doctrine of *Parker v. Taswell*[52] equity would first treat an imperfect lease as a contract to grant the lease, and then order specific performance of that contract.[53] Once the actual lease had been granted in pursuance of the decree of specific performance, the position of the parties was the same for the future as if the lease had been a legal lease granted by deed in the first place.

(c) Walsh v. Lonsdale[54]

The rights of the parties under an imperfect lease were thus clear whenever specific performance had been decreed. What was not so clear was the position if, as was far more often the case, no decree of specific performance had been granted but the parties were entitled to obtain one. In equity, the principle is "Equity looks on that as done which ought to be done", so that the parties were treated as if the lease had been granted. But there was no such principle at law, and, indeed, it would have been strange if the positive requirements

[48] *ibid.*, s.2(5)(a).
[49] *Martin v. Smith* (1874) L.R. 9 Ex. 50; below, p. 348.
[50] See *Tidey v. Mollett* (1864) 16 C.B.(N.S.) 298; but see *Harte v. Williams* [1934] 1 K.B. 201.
[51] L.P.(M.P.)A. 1989, s.2, applying to contracts made after September 26, 1989: see above, p. 148.
[52] (1858) 2 De G. & J. 559.
[53] *Zimbler v. Abrahams* [1903] 1 K.B. 577.
[54] (1882) 21 Ch.D. 9.

of statute could have been so easily circumvented. Yet equity might intervene to restrain the parties from exercising their legal rights in opposition to their equitable obligations, and the Judicature Act 1873[55] provided that where the rules of law and equity conflicted, the rules of equity should prevail. Accordingly, in *Walsh v. Lonsdale*[56] it was held that the relationship of the parties was the same as if the lease had actually been granted.

In that case L agreed in writing to grant by a deed a lease of a mill to T for seven years, one of the terms being that T should on demand pay a year's rent in advance. No deed was executed, but T was let into possession and for a year and a half paid rent quarterly, although not in advance. L then demanded a year's rent in advance, and on T's refusal to pay, exercised his right to enforce payment by distress (distress is the right of a landlord to enter the leased premises[57] and enforce payment of any rent which is due by seizing and selling enough of any goods that are found there).

T then brought an action for damages for wrongful distress, and for specific performance of the agreement. T contended that distress was a legal, and not an equitable, remedy, and that as at law he was only a yearly tenant with no obligation to pay rent in advance, L could not distrain for the rent.[58] It was held, however, that since the distress would have been legal had the lease agreed upon been granted by deed, and since equity treated the parties as if this had been done, the distress was lawful in equity. The equitable rule prevailed over the rule at law and so even at law T could not complain of the distress. This principle applies even if the lease to T was granted while L had no legal estate in the land but only a contract to purchase it; for equity would enforce both contracts.[59]

(d) Differences between legal and equitable leases

The effect of *Walsh v. Lonsdale* is to render an enforceable agreement for a lease very nearly as good as a legal lease, and the same applies to an imperfect lease which is enforceable as an agreement for lease. There are still, however, some points of difference.

(i) Specific performance: The rule depends upon the willingness of equity to grant the discretionary remedy of specific performance, so that if an agreement for a lease is one of which the court will not grant specific performance (as where the tenant is in breach of his obligations to the landlord and so does not come to equity with clean hands[60]), the position under it will be precarious. Further, if the court lacks jurisdiction to order specific perform-ance,[61] a tenant will not be able to enforce the agreement in that court,[62] though he could defend proceedings by the landlord which ignored the agreement, as the court can give effect to an equitable defence.[63] But in any event a tenant who has gone into possession and paid rent may rely on his yearly or other periodic tenancy.[64]

---

[55] s.25(11), then J.A. 1925, s.44, now Supreme Court Act 1981, s.49.
[56] See above.
[57] See below, p. 375.
[58] See *Manchester Brewery Co. v. Coombs* [1901] 2 Ch. 608 at 617, 618.
[59] *Industrial Properties (Barton Hill) Ltd v. Associated Electrical Industries Ltd* [1977] Q.B. 580.
[60] *Coatsworth v. Johnson* (1886) 55 L.J.Q.B. 220 at 222. But see (1987) 7 Oxf. J.L.S. 60 (S. Gardner).
[61] See, *e.g.* County Courts Act 1984, s.23(d).
[62] *Foster v. Reeves* [1892] 2 Q.B. 255; contrast *Cornish v. Brook Green Laundry Ltd* [1959] 1 Q.B. 394.
[63] *Kingswood Estate Co. Ltd v. Anderson* [1963] 2 Q.B. 169.
[64] *Bell Street Investments Ltd v. Wood* [1970] E.G.D. 812.

(ii) Easements: Certain easements and similar rights may be created on a grant of a legal estate which will not be created by a mere contract.[65]

(iii) The burden of covenants: In respect of leases granted before 1996, an agreement for a lease which is enforceable under *Walsh v. Lonsdale* is not as good as a lease as regards third parties, but only as regards the actual parties to the agreement. As between the actual parties, there is privity of contract; and as the benefit of a contract is assignable, an assignee from either of them can take the benefit of the covenants in the lease. But assignees will not be bound by the covenants, for the burden of a contract does not bind assignees, and there is no privity of estate which can make the burden run with the estate, as it would if a lease (and so an estate) had been granted.[66] However, where a yearly or other periodic tenancy has arisen from the tenant taking possession and paying rent, the burden of any covenants that are consistent with such a tenancy will run with it.[67] This disadvantage does not occur in respect of leases granted after 1995, since the burden of the covenants in the lease will run whether the lease is legal or enforceable under *Walsh v. Lonsdale*.[68]

(iv) Third parties: The rights of a tenant under an agreement for a lease, being merely equitable, are subject to the same frailty as all equitable interests, namely, they will not necessarily bind third-party purchasers from the landlord. If L agrees to grant a lease for five years to T and then conveys the legal fee simple to X or, for that matter grants a legal lease or a legal mortgage to him, X is capable of taking the land or his interest therein free of T's rights.

In the case of unregistered land, X will take free of T's rights if he is a bona fide purchaser of a legal estate in the land without notice. Whether X has notice will be determined by whether T has protected his agreement as a Class C(iv) land charge. Registration of that land charge is deemed to be notice to the whole world so that X will be bound; but failure to register will render the agreement void against a purchaser for money or money's worth of a legal estate in the land, which X will necessarily be.[69] The fact that X has actual knowledge of T's agreement is immaterial in these cases.[70] In practice, however, only longer leases or leases at a fine are actually registered. In the case of tenancies for a relatively short period at a rack rent it is usual to accept a mere agreement and not to register it, relying upon the tenant's evident possession of the land to put any prudent purchaser on inquiry; and a purchaser will in any event be bound by any periodic tenancy which has arisen at common law as a result of the payment and acceptance of rent.[71]

In the case of registered land, T is in a much better position for X will be bound by the agreement not only if T has protected it on the register but also if that agreement overrides X's registration by virtue of the fact that T is in actual occupation of the land or, until the Land Registration Act 2002 comes into force, is in receipt of its rents and profits.[72] Under the present law, it is almost inevitable that T will either be in actual occupation of the land or, as a result of having sub-leased it, be in receipt of its rents and profits. (The only obvious

[65] Under L.P.A. 1925, s.62: see below, p. 425.
[66] See below, p. 394.
[67] *Doe d. Thomson v. Amey* (1840) 12 A. & E. 476.
[68] L.&T.(C.)A. 1995, ss.3(1), 28(1); see below, p. 397.
[69] L.C.A. 1972, s.4(6), (7), replacing L.C.A. 1925, s.13(2); *Hollington v. Rhodes* [1951] 2 T.L.R. 691; for land charges, see above, pp. 91 *et seq.*
[70] Above, p. 105.
[71] Above, p. 343.
[72] Above, pp. 121 *et seq.*

exceptions are where T has abandoned possession, is taking no steps to enforce the payment of rent and profits[73] or has permitted rent free occupation.[74] In those cases his agreement will be void against any purchaser for value claiming under a registered disposition.[75]) However, only actual occupation of the land will enable T's rights to override X's registration when the Land Registration Act 2002 comes into force.[76] Consequently, thereafter any tenant under an agreement for a lease who sub-leases or permits rent free occupation will be obliged to protect his agreement on the register; otherwise it will be void against any purchaser for value (other than marriage consideration[77]) claiming under a registered disposition.[78]

Sect. 2. Types of leases and tenancies

1. Classification

Leases and tenancies may be classified under the five following heads.

(a) Leases for a fixed period

(i) Certainty of term: A lease may be granted for any certain period of certain duration, no matter how long or short. Leases for a week or for 3,000 years are equally valid. Both the commencement and the duration of the term must either be certain or else be rendered certain before the lease takes effect.[79] Thus a lease for 99 years from January 1 next complies with this rule, and so does a lease from the determination of an existing tenancy for as many years as X shall name once X has named the period; but a tenancy granted during wartime "for the duration of the war" does not.[80] Although an Act of 1944[81] converted tenancies granted during the Second World War into valid tenancies for 10 years determinable after the war by (usually) one month's notice; but there is nothing in that Act to rescue tenancies for other uncertain periods, such as until the landlord requires the land for road widening,[82] or "so long as the company is trading",[83] from the rule that makes them void. The rule applies even if each party has been given power to determine the tenancy during the uncertain period,[84] and even though the tenancy is a yearly or other periodic tenancy granted subject to a provision negating the power of determination[85] for an uncertain period.[86] Where the rule invalidates a lease but a periodic tenancy arises from the payment and acceptance of rent, that tenancy will not incorporate any provisions for determination in the void lease that are inconsistent with the periodic tenancy.[87]

---

[73] *E.S. Schwab & Co. v. McCarthy* (1976) 31 P. & C.R. 196.
[74] *Strand Securities Ltd v. Caswell* [1965] Ch. 958.
[75] L.R.A. 1925, ss.20, 23, 33, 69; see *Miles v. Bull (No. 2)* [1969] 3 All E.R. 1585.
[76] L.R.A. 2002, Scheds 1, 3.
[77] *ibid.*, s.131(1).
[78] *ibid.*, ss.28–31.
[79] *Harvey v. Pratt* [1965] 1 W.L.R. 1025.
[80] *Lace v. Chantler* [1944] K.B. 368.
[81] Validation of War-Time Leases Act 1944.
[82] *Prudential Assurance Co. Ltd v. London Residuary Body* [1992] 2 A.C. 386.
[83] *Birrell v. Carey* (1989) 58 P. & C.R. 184.
[84] *Prudential Assurance Co. Ltd v. London Residuary Body* [1992] 2 A.C. 386, overruling *Ashburn Anstalt v. Arnold* [1989] Ch. 1.
[85] See below, p. 348.
[86] *Prudential Assurance Co. Ltd v. London Residuary Body* [1992] 2 A.C. 386, overruling *Re Midland Railway Co.'s Agreement* [1971] Ch. 725.
[87] *Prudential Assurance Co. Ltd v. London Residuary Body* [1992] 2 A.C. 386.

(ii) Reversionary leases: A lease which is granted to take effect in the future is known a a a reversionary lease. Before 1926, there was no restriction upon the length of time that might elapse before the term began.[88] But since 1925 the grant of a term to take effect more than 21 years from the instrument creating it is void if at a rent or in consideration of a fine; so is any contract made after 1925 to create such a term.[89] Thus the grant of a lease in 2000 to commence in 2030, or a contract made in 2000 to grant in 2001 a lease to commence in 2030 is void. However, there is nothing to invalidate a contract made in 2000 to grant in 2030 a lease which is then to commence immediately, for that lease is not reversionary.[90] An option in a lease for 35 years to renew it on its determination is similarly not invalidated.[91] Leases taking effect in equity under a settlement under the Settled Land Act 1925 (such as portions terms) are equally not affected.

(iii) Determination: The general rule is that a lease for a fixed period automatically determines when the fixed period expires; but there are statutory exceptions to this rule.[92]

(b) Yearly tenancies

(i) Creation: A yearly tenancy is one which continues from year to year indefinitely until determined by proper notice, notwithstanding the death of either party or the assignment of his interest. Continuation each year depends on the will of the parties as shown by their omission to serve a notice to quit; and in retrospect it is considered a single tenancy and not a succession of tenancies.[93] Such a tenancy may be created either expressly or by implication. Thus an express grant to A "from year to year" or "as a yearly tenant" will create a yearly tenancy. It should be noted, however, that a grant "to X for one year and thereafter from year to year" will give X a tenancy for at least two years; for he has been given a definite term of one year followed by a yearly tenancy which can be determined only at the end of the first year of the latter tenancy.[94]

A yearly tenancy arises by implication whenever a person occupies land with the owner's consent in circumstances indicating a tenancy, and rent measured with reference to a year is paid and accepted, unless there is sufficient evidence to show that some other kind of tenancy was intended.[95] A yearly tenancy also arises when a tenant under a lease for a fixed term holds over (*i.e.* remains in possession at the end of his term) and, in circumstances indicating a tenancy,[96] rent is paid and accepted on a yearly basis. In this case, the tenant will hold under such of the terms of the expired lease as are not inconsistent with a yearly holding.[97] Thus covenants to repair,[98] or to carry on some specified trade on the premises[99] and provisos for re-entry by the landlord on non-payment of rent[1] may be implied in a yearly tenancy. But a

---

[88] There were no restrictions before 1926; see *Mann, Crossman & Paulin Ltd v. Registrar of Land Registry* [1918] 1 Ch. 202.

[89] L.P.A. 1925, s.149(3).

[90] (1947) 63 L.Q.R. 20; *Re Strand and Savoy Properties Ltd* [1960] Ch. 582; *Weg Motors Ltd v. Hales* [1962] Ch. 49.

[91] *Re Strand and Savoy Properties Ltd* [1960] Ch. 582.

[92] See below, pp. 580 *et seq.*

[93] *Hammersmith and Fulham L.B.C. v. Monk* [1992] 1 A.C. 478; for joint tenants, see above, p. 303.

[94] *Re Searle* [1912] 1 Ch. 610.

[95] *Kemp v. Derrett* (1814) 3 Camp. 510; *Javad v. Aqil* [1991] 1 W.L.R. 1007.

[96] *Clarke v. Grant* [1950] 1 K.B. 104; *Longrigg, Burrough & Trounson v. Smith* [1979] E.G.D. 472.

[97] *Dougal v. McCarthy* [1893] 1 Q.B. 736.

[98] *Wyatt v. Cole* (1877) 36 L.T. 613.

[99] *Sanders v. Karnell* (1858) 1 F. & F. 356.

[1] *Thomas v. Packer* (1857) 1 H. & N. 669

covenant to paint every three years[2] and a provision for two years' notice to quit[3] are inconsistent with a yearly tenancy and cannot be implied in this way.

The payment of rent at more frequent intervals than a year will not prevent a yearly tenancy from arising by implication. The test is the period by reference to which the parties calculated the rent. Thus an agreement for "£10,400 per annum payable weekly" prima facie creates a yearly tenancy; had the agreement been for "£200 per week", a weekly tenancy would be presumed, despite the fact that in each case the tenant would in fact have made the same payments, namely £200 every week.[4]

(ii) Determination: A yearly tenancy may be determined by such notice and at such time as the parties agree.[5] Different periods for the landlord and tenant may be agreed, and it may be provided that the landlord should be entitled to give notice only in certain circumstances,[6] such as if he requires the premises for his own occupation.[7] But a term that one party should not be entitled to give notice at all is void as repugnant to the nature of a periodic tenancy.[8] In default of such agreement, the tenancy can be determined by at least half a year's notice expiring at the end of a completed year of the tenancy. The meaning of "half a year" depends on the day upon which the tenancy began. If the tenancy began on one of the usual quarter-days (Lady Day (March 25), Midsummer Day (June 24), Michaelmas (September 29)[9] or Christmas (December 25)), "half a year" means "two quarters"; otherwise "half a year" means 182 days.[10] Thus, if a yearly tenancy began on March 25, notice to quit given on or before September 29 is good, although it is less than 182 days[11]; and if a yearly tenancy began on September 29, notice must be given on or before March 25, even though it is more than 182 days. In each of these cases, the tenancy began on a quarter-day[12]; had it started on some other day, for instance March 26, at least 182 days' notice would have been required.[13] It will be noted that in neither case is the period of the notice necessarily six months, although of course the parties may agree that such shall be the notice required.

As has been seen,[14] a notice to quit for a periodic tenancy is not invalid merely because it has been given by only one of joint landlords or joint tenants.

(c) Weekly, monthly and other periodic tenancies

A tenancy from week to week, month to month, quarter to quarter, and the like (including a tenancy for some artificial period, such as for successive periods of 364 days[15]) can be created in a similar way to a yearly tenancy, namely either by express agreement or by inference, such as that arising from the payment and acceptance of rent measured with reference to a week, month or quarter, as the case may be, in circumstances indicating a

---

[2] *Pinero v. Judson* (1829) 6 Bing. 206.
[3] *Tooker v. Smith* (1857) 1 H. & N. 732.
[4] See *Adler v. Blackman* [1953] 1 Q.B. 146.
[5] *Re Threlfall* (1880) 16 Ch.D. 274 at 281, 282.
[6] *Re Midland Railway Co.'s Agreement* [1971] Ch. 725.
[7] As in *Breams Property Investment Co. Ltd v. Stroulger* [1948] 2 K.B. 1.
[8] *Centaploy Ltd v. Matlodge Ltd* [1974] Ch. 1.
[9] A mnemonic is that for these three the last digit is the same as the number of letters in the month.
[10] Anon. (1575) 3 Dy. 345a.
[11] *Doe d. Durant v. Doe* (1830) 6 Bing. 574.
[12] *Morgan v. Davies* (1878) 3 C.P.D. 260.
[13] Co.Litt. 135b.
[14] Above, p. 283.
[15] *Land Settlement Association Ltd v. Carr* [1944] K.B. 657.

tenancy.[16] In general, the position of the parties under such a tenancy is similar to that under a yearly tenancy, save that notice of termination is not half a period, but a full period, expiring at the end of a completed period, subject to any contrary agreement between the parties.[17] This is the "corresponding date" rule, under which "month" normally means calendar month, despite the differing lengths.[18] Thus in the absence of any contrary agreement, a weekly tenancy commencing on a Monday can be determined either by notice given on or before one Monday to expire on the following Monday,[19] or, since a week starting on a Monday is complete at midnight on the following Sunday, by notice given on or before one Sunday to expire on the following Sunday.[20] But for dwellings, not less than four weeks' notice in writing must be given, containing (if given by the landlord) prescribed information relating to orders for possession and legal advice; and this now extends to residential licences, with certain exceptions, such as rent free or family sharing licences.[21]

(d) Tenancies at will

A tenancy at will arises whenever a tenant, with the consent of the landlord, occupies *qua* tenant (and not merely as a servant or agent) on the terms that either party may determine the tenancy at any time. In some cases the tenant holds rent free, as where the vendor of a fee simple, owing to some delay in completion, lets the purchaser into possession of the property before the conveyance has been executed.[22] But unless the parties agree that the tenancy shall be rent free, the landlord is entitled to compensation for the use and occupation of the land[23]; and if a rent is fixed the landlord may distrain for it in the usual way.

A tenancy at will comes to an end when either party does any act incompatible with the continuance of the tenancy, as where the tenant commits voluntary waste,[24] or the landlord enters the land and cuts trees or carries away stone,[25] or either party gives notice to the other determining the tenancy. The tenancy is also determined if either party dies or assigns his interest in the land.[26] Essentially, the tenancy is a personal relation between the landlord and his tenant.[27]

If a tenancy at will is created without any agreement as to payment of rent, and rent is subsequently paid and accepted upon some regular periodical basis, a yearly, monthly or other periodical tenancy will normally arise under the rules set out under heads (b) and (c) above, unless the circumstances indicate otherwise.[28]

---

[16] *Cole v. Kelly* [1920] 2 K.B. 106 at 132; *Clarke v. Grant* [1950] 1 K.B. 104; *Longrigg, Burrough & Trounson v. Smith* [1979] E.G.D. 472.

[17] *Queen's Club Gardens Estates Ltd v. Bignell* [1924] 1 K.B. 117; *Lemon v. Lardeur* [1946] K.B. 613.

[18] See *Dodds v. Walker* [1981] 1 W.L.R. 1027; *E. J. Riley Investments Ltd v. Eurostile Holdings Ltd* [1985] 1 W.L.R. 1139.

[19] *Newman v. Slade* [1926] 2 K.B. 328.

[20] *Bathavon R.D.C. v. Carlile* [1958] 1 Q.B. 461.

[21] Protection from Eviction Act 1977, ss.3A, 5; H.A. 1988, ss.31, 32; S.I. 1988 No. 2201; *Schnabel v. Allard* [1967] 1 Q.B. 627.

[22] *Howard v. Shaw* (1841) 8 M. & W. 118. See also *Hagee (London) Ltd v. A. B. Erikson & Larson* [1976] Q.B. 209.

[23] Distress for Rent Act 1737, s.11; *Howard v. Shaw* (1841) 8 M. & W. 118.

[24] Countess of Shrewsbury's Case (1600) 5 Co.Rep. 13b.

[25] *Turner v. Doe d. Bennett* (1842) 9 M. & W. 643.

[26] *Pinhorn v. Souster* (1853) 8 Exch. 763 at 772.

[27] *Wheeler v. Mercer* [1957] A.C. 416 at 427, 428.

[28] *Javad v. Aqil* [1991] 1 W.L.R. 1007.

(e) Tenancies at sufferance

A tenancy at sufferance arises where a tenant, having entered upon land under a valid tenancy, holds over without the landlord's assent or dissent.[29] Such a tenant differs from a trespasser in that his original entry was lawful, and from a tenant at will in that his tenancy exists without the landlord's assent. No rent, as such, is payable, but the tenant is liable to pay compensation for his use and occupation of the land.[30] The tenancy may be determined at any time, and may be converted into a yearly or other periodic tenancy in the usual way, such as if rent is paid and accepted with reference to a year in circumstances where the parties intended there to be a tenancy.

There are statutory penalties for tenants who hold over after giving or receiving notice to quit:

(i) Double annual value: If the landlord gives the tenant written notice to quit and the tenant is a tenant for life or for years, the tenant is liable to pay the landlord a sum calculated at double the annual value of the land in respect of the period for which he holds over after the notice expired. This can be enforced by action but not otherwise, for example not by distress.[31] This provision applies to tenancies from year to year as well as to tenancies for fixed terms of years or for a year certain, but not to weekly,[32] or, no doubt, to other periodic tenancies.

(ii) Double rent: If the tenant gives the landlord written or oral notice to quit, then, whatever the type of tenancy, the tenant is liable to pay double rent in respect of the period for which he holds over after the notice expired; payment can be enforced by action or distress.[33]

The curiously differing terms of these aged provisions will be noticed. The rent and the annual value may be the same, but they often differ, as where premises have been let at a reduced rent in consideration of a fine.

2. Statutory modifications

Although the parties to a lease can in general create a lease for such periods as they think fit, statute has made some modifications to this position.

(a) Leases for lives

By the Law of Property Act 1925,[34] a lease at a rent or a fine for life or lives, or for a term of years determinable with a life or lives or on the marriage of the lessee, is converted into a term of 90 years, whether it was granted before or after 1925. A contract for such a lease is treated in a similar way. The lease continues even after the death or marriage, as the case may be, although either party may determine it thereafter (but not before) by serving on the other one month's written notice to expire on one of the quarter-days applicable to the tenancy, or, if no special quarter-days are applicable, on one of the usual quarter-days. Thus leases at a rent or fine granted "to A for life", "to B for 10 years if he so long lives", and "to C for 99 years if he so long remains a bachelor" are all converted into terms which will continue for 90 years unless by the proper notice they are determined on any quarter-day (not

---

[29] See *Remon v. City of London Real Property Co. Ltd* [1921] 1 K.B. 49 at 58.
[30] *Leigh v. Dickeson* (1884) 15 Q.B.D. 60.
[31] L. & T.A. 1730, s.1.
[32] *Lloyd v. Rosbee* (1810) 2 Camp. 453.
[33] Distress for Rent Act 1737, s.18.
[34] s.149(6).

necessarily the first) after the event has occurred. But these provisions do not apply to a lease which takes effect in equity under a settlement.[35]

(b) Perpetually renewable leases

A perpetually renewable lease was a lease which gave the tenant the right to renew it for another period as often as it expired; usually the tenant had to make some payment on exercising this right. A lease will be perpetually renewable if there is a covenant to renew it on the terms of the existing lease "including this covenant for renewal",[36] but not if the inclusion of the covenant for renewal is part of a separate obligation.[37] By the Law of Property Act 1922,[38] all such leases existing at the end of 1925 were converted into terms of 2000 years, calculated from the beginning of the existing terms; and perpetually renewable leases granted after 1925 take effect as terms of 2000 years from the date fixed for the commencement of the term. Any perpetually renewable sub-lease created out of a perpetually renewable lease is converted into a term of 2000 years less one day. The 2000-year lease is subject to the same terms as the original lease, with the following modifications.

(i) Termination: The tenant for the time being (but not the landlord) may terminate the lease on any date upon which, but for the conversion by the Act, the lease would have expired if it had not been renewed, provided he gives at least 10 days' written notice to the landlord.

(ii) Assignment: Every assignment or devolution of the lease must be registered with the landlord or his solicitor or agent within six months, and a fee of one guinea paid.

(iii) Breach of covenant: A tenant who assigns the lease is not liable for breaches of covenant committed after the assignment. In leases granted before 1996, the general rule is that the original lessee is liable for all breaches occurring during the term, even if they occur after he has assigned the lease[39]; perpetually renewable leases are a statutory exception to this rule which has been abolished for leases granted after 1995.[40]

(iv) Fine: Any fine or other payment for renewal for which the lease provides is converted into additional rent and spread over the period between the renewal dates, except where the lease is granted after 1925, when the obligation for payment is void.

It should be noted that the landlord has no right to determine the lease at the renewal dates. Before 1926, if L granted T a lease for 21 years with a perpetual right of renewal, it was T alone who had the right to decide each 21 years whether or not to renew the lease. This position is preserved, save that now the lease continues unless determined, instead of requiring renewal.

(c) Over-lengthy renewals

A contract made after 1925 to renew a lease for over 60 years from its termination is void.[41] This is aimed at single renewals, not perpetual renewals.

---

[35] L.P.A. 1925 ss.149(6)(a), 205(1)(xxvi); S.L.A. 1925 s.117(1)(xxiv).
[36] *Parkus v. Greenwood* [1950] Ch. 644; *Caerphilly Concrete Products Ltd v. Owen* [1972] 1 W.L.R. 372.
[37] *Marjorie Burnett Ltd v. Barclay* (1980) 258 E.G. 642.
[38] s.145 and 15th Sched.
[39] See below, p. 381.
[40] *ibid.*
[41] L.P.A. 1922, 15th Sched.

(d) Reversionary leases

A lease at a rent or a fine to commence at too distant a future date or a contract to create such a lease cannot be granted after 1925. This has already been dealt with.[42]

3. Estoppel

(a) Estoppel

On the grant of a lease or tenancy, both landlord and tenant and their successors in title are in general mutually estopped from denying the validity of the transaction. Neither landlord nor tenant will be permitted to assert that the tenancy which they have purported to create is invalid,[43] and this is so even if the landlord had no title to grant a lease[44] or if the tenancy is merely oral.[45] The tenant is still estopped from denying his landlord's title after going out of possession and so can still be sued on repairing covenants, unless evicted by title paramount, that is to say by someone with a title superior to that of the landlord.[46] But except in the case of companies within the Companies Acts,[47] this doctrine does not prevent a corporation from contending that it had no power to grant or receive a tenancy, for estoppel cannot validate an *ultra vires* act.[48]

(b) Tenancy by estoppel

One consequence of this rule is that if the landlord in fact has no estate in the land, then although the lease or tenancy can confer no actual estate on the tenant, and cannot be effective against third parties,[49] it is good between the parties to it and their successors in title.[50] Both landlord and tenant will be estopped from denying the validity of their lease or tenancy; they cannot "blow hot and cold" by claiming that the transaction was valid when entered into, and yet asserting subsequently that it was a nullity.

No tenancy by estoppel arises, however, if the lessor had a legal interest (as distinct from an equitable interest[51]) in the land when he granted the lease. If his interest was greater than the tenancy, the lease takes effect in the ordinary way; if it was equal to or smaller than the tenancy, the grant of the lease operates as an assignment of the lessor's interest.[52] Thus if L grants T a lease for 99 years, T will take a lease for 99 years by estoppel if L had no interest in the land when the lease was granted. But if L had a lease for 10 years at that time, the lease for 99 years will operate as an assignment to T of L's lease for 10 years.

(c) Feeding the estoppel

If there is a tenancy by estoppel, and subsequently the landlord acquires an interest in the land out of which the tenancy could have been created (such as the fee simple), this is said to "feed the estoppel". From that moment the lease becomes fully effective, giving the tenant

---

[42] Above, p. 347.
[43] See *Cuthbertson v. Irving* (1859) 4 H. & N. 742; (1860) 6 H. & N. 135.
[44] *Bruton v. London & Quadrant Housing Trust* [2000] 1 A.C. 406; see M. Dixon [2000] C.L.J. 25.
[45] *E.H. Lewis & Son Ltd v. Morelli* [1948] 2 All E.R. 1021.
[46] *Industrial Properties (Barton Hill) Ltd v. Associated Electrical Industries Ltd* [1977] Q.B. 580.
[47] Companies Act 1985, s.35, as substituted by Companies Act 1989, s.108.
[48] *Rhyl U.D.C. v. Rhyl Amusements Ltd* [1959] 1 W.L.R. 465.
[49] *Tadman v. Henman* [1893] 2 Q.B. 168.
[50] See *E.H. Lewis & Son Ltd v. Morelli* [1948] 2 All E.R. 1021.
[51] *Universal Permanent B.S. v. Cooke* [1952] Ch. 95 at 102 (tenancy by estoppel on letting by purchaser before completion).
[52] *Beardman v. Wilson* (1868) L.R. 4 C.P. 57; *Wollaston v. Hakewill* (1841) 3 Man. & G. 297 at 323.

an actual estate in the land.[53] This formerly created difficulties if the landlord purchased the land on mortgage. Theoretically, the legal estate vested in the landlord an instant before he mortgaged the land; and in that instant the estoppel was fed, and so the tenancy would bind the mortgagee.[54] But theory has yielded to convenience, and now the transactions are treated as being simultaneous, so that the mortgagee takes free from the tenancy.[55]

Part 3—Assignment of Leases and Tenancies

In order to effect a legal assignment of a lease, a deed must be employed,[56] even if the lease has been created by word of mouth, such as a yearly tenancy in possession at a rack rent.[57] However, on principles similar to those applicable to the creation of leases,[58] an assignment in writing will be effective in equity. In respect of leases granted before 1996, such an assignment is effective only as between assignor and assignee. Thus, unless estopped from so doing, the assignee may deny liability to the landlord on the covenants of the lease since there will be no privity of estate between them save in respect of any periodic tenancy that arises from the payment and acceptance of rent.[59] This does apply to leases granted after 1995, since the burden of the covenants in the lease will run whether the lease is assigned by deed or by writing.[60] On an assignment the assignor can reserve a right of entry to ensure compliance by the assignee and his successors with covenants in the assignment.[61] Other matters concerning assignments are dealt with below.[62]

The grant of sub-leases is governed by the rules relating to the grant of leases.[63]

Part 4—Determination of Tenancies

A lease or tenancy may come to an end in the following ways.

   (i) By expiry

  (ii) By notice

 (iii) By forfeiture

 (iv) By surrender

  (v) By merger

 (vi) By becoming a satisfied term

[53] *Mackley v. Nutting* [1949] 2 K.B. 55.
[54] *Church of England B.S. v. Piskor* [1954] Ch. 553.
[55] *Abbey National B.S. v. Cann* [1991] 1 A.C. 56.
[56] L.P.A. 1925, s.52(1), replacing R.P.A. 1845, s.3.
[57] *Crago v. Julian* [1992] 1 W.L.R. 372.
[58] Above, p. 343.
[59] *Rodenhurst Estates Ltd v. W. H. Barnes Ltd* [1936] 2 All E.R. 3.
[60] L.&T.(C.)A. 1995, ss.3(1), 28(1); see below, p. 397.
[61] *Shiloh Spinners Ltd v. Harding* [1973] A.C. 691.
[62] Below, pp. 376, 381 *et seq.*
[63] Above, pp. 342 *et seq.*

(vii) By enlargement

(viii) By disclaimer

(ix) By frustration

Sect. 1. By expiry

As has been seen,[64] a lease or tenancy for a fixed period automatically determines when the fixed period expires, with certain exceptions. In some cases the tenant may be entitled to be granted a new lease or to remain in possession as a statutory tenant.[65]

Sect. 2. By notice

A lease or tenancy for a fixed period cannot be determined by notice unless this is expressly agreed upon. Thus a lease for a substantial term such as 21 years often contains provisions enabling the tenant to determine it at the end of the seventh or fourteenth year, in which case the length of the notice required, the time when it is to be given, and other matters of this kind, depend on the terms of the lease. In the absence of any such provision the lease will continue for the full period.

Yearly, weekly, monthly and other periodical tenancies can be determined by notice. These provisions, and the determination of tenancies at will and at sufferance, have already been considered.[66]

Many periodic tenants have statutory protection against eviction.[67]

Sect. 3. By forfeiture

1. Right to forfeit

A landlord's right to forfeit a lease (*i.e.* enforce a forfeiture of it) may arise under three heads.

(a) Denial of title

If a tenant clearly and unambiguously denies his landlord's title to the whole (and not merely part) of the land,[68] as by asserting (even orally) that he or some third party is the true owner, the landlord is forthwith entitled to forfeit the tenancy.[69] But a mere denial of title in a pleading in an action merely puts the other party to proof of his case and so works no forfeiture, especially if it is withdrawn before the landlord elects to take advantage of it.[70]

---

[64] Above, p. 347.
[65] Below, pp. 580 *et seq.*
[66] Above, pp. 347–349.
[67] See below, pp. 580 *et seq.*
[68] *W. G. Clarke (Properties) Ltd v. Dupre Properties Ltd* [1992] Ch. 297.
[69] *Wisbech St. Mary Parish Council v. Lilley* [1956] 1 W.L.R. 121. *Quaere* whether the provisions as to notice and relief apply: see below, p. 360.
[70] *Warner v. Sampson* [1959] 1 Q.B. 297; and see below, p. 360.

(b) Breach of condition

If the tenant's obligations are worded as conditions, however (such as if the lease is granted "upon condition that" or "provided always that" certain things are done or not done), the lease may be forfeited on breach of condition even if there is no forfeiture clause.[71] In such a case, the continuance of the lease has been made conditional upon the tenant performing his obligations, and upon breach of one of them the lease becomes voidable at the landlord's option; but if the landlord does not treat the lease as forfeited, the tenant cannot set up his own breach in order to avoid his liabilities under the lease.[72]

(c) Express forfeiture clauses

Nearly every lease contains a list of things which the tenant shall and shall not do, and these may be framed as conditions or as covenants. The position when they are framed as conditions has just been considered. However, it is normally the case that they are framed as covenants (such as "The tenant hereby covenants with the landlord as follows . . . "). When this is done, the landlord has no right to forfeit the lease merely because the covenants are broken. He can only do so if the lease contains an express provision for forfeiture on breach of the specific covenant which has been breached or on breach of the covenants in the lease in general.[73] There is no necessary connection between the tenant failing to perform a covenant made by him and the determination of the lease; every well-drawn lease conse-quently contains a forfeiture clause which in a legal lease creates a legal right of re-entry,[74] making the lease voidable at the landlord's option if a covenant is broken.

(d) Implied forfeiture clauses

If no lease has actually been granted but the parties have either agreed that a lease containing the "usual covenants" will be granted, or have entered into an agreement for a lease containing no reference to the covenants which it should contain, then, subject to any contrary agreement by the parties, the lease must contain whatever covenants and conditions may be "usual" in the circumstances; these include an implied provision for forfeiture of the lease for non-payment of rent, but not for breach of any other covenant.[75]

2. Waiver of breach

Even if the landlord has shown that he is treating the lease as forfeited, he may subsequently prevent himself from proceeding with the forfeiture if he waives the breach of covenant; and *a fortiori* a waiver of the breach may take place before the landlord has shown that he is treating the lease as forfeited. Waiver may be express or implied. It will be implied if—

(i) the landlord is aware of the acts or omissions of the tenant giving rise to the right of forfeiture, and

(ii) the landlord does some unequivocal act recognising the continued existence of the lease.[76]

---

[71] See *Doe d. Lockwood v. Clarke* (1807) 8 East 185.
[72] See *Doe d. Bryan v. Bancks* (1821) 4 B. & Ald. 401; *Roberts v. Davey* (1833) 4 B. & Ad. 664.
[73] *Doe d. Willson v. Phillips* (1824) 2 Bing. 13. For proposals for reforming the law of forfeiture, see (1985) Law Com. No. 142.
[74] See above, p. 83.
[75] See *Hampshire v. Wickens* (1878) 7 Ch.D. 555.
[76] *Matthews v. Smallwood* [1910] 1 Ch. 777 at 786.

To constitute a waiver, both elements must be present. The landlord will be treated as having the knowledge of his managing agents or of porters who are under a duty to inform him[77]; but mere suspicion is not knowledge.[78] A waiver will be implied where a landlord, with knowledge of the breach, distrains (exercises his right to distress) for rent, whether due before or after the breach,[79] or demands or sues for or accepts rent falling due after the breach,[80] even if the rent is accepted "without prejudice"[81] or by the mistake of a clerk of the landlord's agents.[82] Waiver is a matter of law, not intention.[83] Other acts, such as negotiating a variation of terms of the lease and so recognising its continuance, may amount to a waiver, though not against a background of threatened proceedings for forfeiture[84]; and there can be no waiver once the landlord has shown his final decision to treat the lease as forfeited, as by commencing an action for possession.[85]

As would be expected, a waiver extends only to the particular breach in question, and does not operate as a general waiver of all future breaches and the same applies to a licence granted to the tenant to do any act.[86] All that is waived is the right of forfeiture for the breach, and not the breach itself.[87] A waiver is no bar to an action for damages for breach of the covenant.[88]

3. Mode of forfeiture

The normal method of enforcing a forfeiture is by issuing and serving a claim form seeking possession; such a claim form usually contains an unequivocal demand for possession, so that its mere service operates to determine the lease.[89] Alternatively, unless the premises are let as a dwelling and some person is lawfully residing in it or in any part of it,[90] the landlord can enforce his right of forfeiture by making peaceable re-entry onto the land.[91] It is usually inadvisable for a landlord to adopt this method. Although reasonable force may be used, it is a criminal offence if any violence is used or threatened when the landlord knows that there is someone on the premises who is opposed to the entry.[92] In practice, peaceable re-entry is therefore limited to premises which have been abandoned by the tenant and to commercial premises outside working hours. Only if peaceable re-entry is made unlawfully[93] does the

---

[77] *Metropolitan Properties Co. Ltd v. Cordery* (1980) 39 P. & C.R. 10.
[78] *Chrisdell Ltd v. Johnson* (1987) 54 P. & C.R. 257. Compare *Van Haarlam v. Kasner* [1992] 36 E.G. 135 (knowledge of tenant's arrest enough).
[79] *Ward v. Day* (1863) 4 B. & S. 337 at 353; 5 B. & S. 364.
[80] *Goodright d. Charter v. Cordwent* (1795) 6 T.R. 219; *David Blackstone v. Burnetts (West End) Ltd* [1973] 1 W.L.R. 1487 (rent payable in advance).
[81] *Davenport v. R.* (1877) 3 App. Cas. 115; *Segal Securities Ltd v. Thoseby* [1963] 1 Q.B. 887.
[82] *Central Estates (Belgravia) Ltd v. Woolgar (No. 2)* [1972] 1 W.L.R. 1048.
[83] See *Matthews v. Smallwood* [1910] 1 Ch. 777 at 786.
[84] *Expert Clothing Service & Sales Ltd v. Hillgate House Ltd* [1986] Ch. 340; and see *Church Commissioners for England v. Nodjoumi* (1986) 51 P. & C.R. 155.
[85] *Grimwood v. Moss* (1872) L.R. 7 C.P. 360.
[86] L.P.A. 1925, ss.143, 148, replacing earlier provisions which altered the law laid down in *Dumpor's Case* (1603) 4 Co.Rep. 119b.
[87] See *Greenwich L.B.C. v. Discreet Selling Estates Ltd* (1991) 61 P. & C.R. 405.
[88] *Stephens v. Junior Army and Navy Stores Ltd* [1914] 2 Ch. 516.
[89] *Elliott v. Boynton* [1924] 1 Ch. 236, as explained in *Canas Property Co. Ltd v. K.L. Television Services Ltd* [1970] 1 Q.B. 433.
[90] Protection from Eviction Act 1977, s.2; and see below, p. 590.
[91] See, *e.g.* *Billson v. Residential Apartments Ltd* [1992] 1 A.C. 494.
[92] Criminal Law Act 1977, s.6, replacing statutes from 1381 onwards. For another disadvantage, see *R. v. Hussey* (1924) 18 Cr.App.R. 160 (getting shot).
[93] See Housing Act 1988, s.27.

tenant have any remedy in damages.[94] However, peaceable re-entry does not deprive the tenant of any right which he may have to relief against forfeiture.[95] It is this fact, coupled with the fact that the tenant agreed to the right of re-entry being inserted into the lease when he acquired it, that is likely to defeat any challenge to peaceable re-entry which may be made under the Human Rights Act 1998.[96]

4. Conditions for forfeiture—general

The conditions under which a right of forfeiture can be enforced depend upon whether the right arises from breach of the covenant or condition to pay rent or from breach of any other provision. Moreover, in each case, first, equity, and later, statute, have intervened so as to allow tenants to obtain relief from forfeiture in certain circumstances.[97]

5. Conditions for forfeiture—forfeiture for non-payment of rent

Where a landlord has the right to forfeit a lease for non-payment of rent, two important points to be considered are the landlord's formal demand for the rent and the tenant's right to relief.

(a) Landlord's formal demand

Before commencing proceedings, whether in the High Court[98] or in the County Court,[99] the landlord must either have made a formal demand for the rent, or else be exempted from making such a demand.

(i) Formal demand: To make a formal demand, the landlord or his authorised agent must demand the exact sum due on the day when it falls due at such convenient hour before sunset as will give time to count out the money, the demand being made upon the demised premises and continuing until sunset.[1]

(ii) Exemption from formal demand: To avoid the technicalities of a formal demand, every well-drawn lease provides that the lease may be forfeited if the rent is a specified number of days in arrear, "whether formally demanded or not". The words quoted exempt the landlord from making a formal demand. However, even if a lease contains no such clause, a formal demand is dispensed with in any action for forfeiture if—

> (i) half a year's rent is in arrears, and

> (ii) no sufficient distress (*i.e.* goods available for distraint) can be found[2] upon the premises to satisfy all the arrears due.[3]

(b) Right to relief of tenant

The tenant may be able to claim relief against the forfeiture. Equity considered that a right of forfeiture was merely security for payment of the rent, so that if—

---

[94] *Hemmings v. Stoke Poges Golf Club* [1920] 1 K.B. 720.
[95] *Billson v. Residential Apartments Ltd* [1992] 1 A.C. 494.
[96] See A. Bruce [2000] N.L.J. 462.
[97] For the equitable jurisdiction, see *Shiloh Spinners Ltd v. Harding* [1973] A.C. 691; *Billson v. Residential Apartments Ltd* [1992] 1 A.C. 494.
[98] Common Law Procedure Act 1852, s.210.
[99] County Courts Act 1984, s.139(1).
[1] See 1 Wms. Saund. (1871) 434 *et seq.*
[2] See *Hammond v. Mather* (1862) 3 F. & F. 151 (no distress can be "found" if the outer doors are locked).
[3] See *Cross v. Jordan* (1853) 8 Exch. 149.

(i) the tenant paid the rent due by the date on which relief against forfeiture was ordered and interest thereon; and

(ii) the tenant paid any expenses to which the landlord had been put; and

(iii) it was just and equitable to grant relief,

equity would restore the tenant to his position despite the forfeiture of the lease.[4] These remain the financial prerequisites of relief against forfeiture being granted. (This is the case even where the rent is merely a ground rent; the tenant is not obliged to pay an occupation rent in respect of the period between forfeiture and relief being granted.[5]) However, where the landlord has gone back into possession prior to relief against forfeiture being granted, he must account for the value of his occupation. Consequently, an occupation rent will be deduced from the rent, interest and expenses payable by the tenant.[6] Originally, there was no limit to the time within which application for relief had to be made, apart from the general principle that equity would give no assistance to stale claims.[7]

The position differs depending on whether proceedings are brought in the High Court or the County Court. Proceedings must now be brought in the County Court unless they involve complicated disputes of fact or points of law of general importance.[8] The value of the property in question and the amount of rent due are relevant but are normally not alone enough to justify proceedings being brought in the High Court.[9]

Proceedings in the High Court are primarily governed by the Common Law Procedure Act 1852.[10] That Act provides that if, before trial, the tenant pays requisite amount,[11] the proceedings must be stayed. However, this provision is only applicable where at least half a year's rent is in arrears. Furthermore, where the landlord has obtained an order for possession and had that order executed, an application for relief must be made within six months of the execution of the order, in other words within six months of the landlord going back into possession. This is the case whether at least half a year's rent is in arrears[12] or not.[13] However, if the landlord has re-entered without obtaining an order for possession, the statute does not apply at all and the old equitable inherent jurisdiction of the court remains.[14] While the court tends to adopt the same time limit, it will not "boggle at a matter of days".[15]

Proceedings in the County Court are governed by the County Courts Act 1984.[16] If the tenant pays all the arrears and costs into court at least five days before the trial date, the proceedings must be stayed. If this is not done, the court will make an order for possession but will postpone the execution of that order so as to give the tenant a chance to pay; execution will be suspended for at least four weeks and the court has a discretion to make one

---

[4] See *Howard v. Fanshawe* [1895] 2 Ch. 581.
[5] *Escalus Properties Ltd v. Dennis* [1996] Q.B. 231.
[6] *Bland v. Ingrams Estates Ltd (No.2)* [2002] 2 W.L.R. 361 at paras 19–29.
[7] See *Hill v. Barclay* (1811) 18 Ves. 56 at 59, 60.
[8] C.P.R. Pt. 55 P.D. para. 2.2.
[9] *ibid.*, para. 2.3.
[10] ss.210–212, replacing L. & T.A. 1730, ss.2, 4.
[11] *Standard Pattern Co. Ltd v. Ivey* [1962] Ch. 432, criticised in (1962) 78 L.Q.R. 168 (R.E.M.).
[12] Common Law Procedure Act 1852, s.210.
[13] Supreme Court Act 1981, s.38.
[14] *Thatcher v. C. H. Pearce & Sons (Contractors) Ltd* [1968] 1 W.L.R. 748. Nor does the six months' limit apply to a mortgagee of the lease who was not party to the proceedings for forfeiture: *United Dominions Trust Ltd v. Shellpoint Trustees* [1992] 39 E.G. 144, examining the turgid statutory drafting.
[15] *Thatcher v. C. H. Pearce & Sons (Contractors) Ltd* [1968] 1 W.L.R. 748 at 756, *per* Simon P.
[16] s.138, as amended by Administration of Justice Act 1985, s.55.

or more further extensions. However, the power to grant relief against forfeiture to the tenant ends once the possession order has been executed and the landlord has gone back into possession (this restriction does not apply to those claiming through the tenant who can claim relief whenever they first become aware of the forfeiture[17]).

If relief is granted, the tenant continues to holds under the old lease[18] and execution of a new document is not required. Relief takes effect subject to any legal lease granted by the landlord after the forfeiture to a lessee who takes without notice of the previous tenant's equity to seek relief.[19] However, where such a lessee has notice of that equity, his lease is interposed between the landlord and tenant, who becomes in effect his tenant and the sub-tenant of the landlord.[20] The rent payable by the tenant since the commencement of his lease will be payable to him rather than to the landlord less an occupation rent in respect of his own occupation.[21] In practice these sums are likely to cancel one another out.

(c) Right to relief of those claiming through the tenant

Where a lease is forfeited, subsidiary interests in that lease will also be destroyed.[22] Consequently, those claiming through the tenant are also entitled to claim relief against forfeiture irrespective of whether the tenant himself is able to do so and can do so whenever they first become aware of the forfeiture.[23] In an effort to avoid late applications, rules of court oblige the landlord to serve a copy of his claim form on any persons claiming through the tenant of whose interests he is aware[24] but this will not necessarily always work.

The Law of Property Act 1925[25] specifically provides that a sub-tenant has the same right of applying for relief against forfeiture as the tenant under the head lease. Where relief is granted to a sub-tenant of only part of the premises, the court will grant the sub-tenant a term no longer than the term he held under his sub-lease[26] and will normally impose terms that will restore the landlord to his former position.[27] The sub-tenant will usually enter into a new lease direct with the former landlord under the forfeited lease on terms similar to (though not necessarily the same as) those of the old sub-lease.

The Common Law Procedure Act 1852[28] specifically provides that a mortgagee of a lease may obtain relief against forfeiture for six months after the landlord has executed a judgment for possession and a mortgagee can also obtain relief under the inherent jurisdiction and in a County Court.[29] It has also been held that a person who has registered a charging order against a lease can obtain relief against forfeiture, both in the High Court under the inherent jurisdiction and in the County Court.[30] However, he will have to do so in the name of the

---

[17] *Croydon (Unique) Ltd v. Wright* [1999] 4 All E.R. 257.
[18] Common Law Procedure Act 1852, s.212; J.A. 1925, s.46; and see County Courts Acts 1984, s.139(2).
[19] *Fuller v. Judy Properties Ltd* [1992] 14 E.G. 106 (actually an authority on L.P.A. 1925, s.146(2)).
[20] *Bland v. Ingrams Estates Ltd (No. 2)* [2002] 2 W.L.R. 361 at para. 13.
[21] *Bland v. Ingrams Estates Ltd (No. 2)* [2002] 2 W.L.R. 361 at paras 19–29.
[22] *Great Western Ry. v. Smith* (1876) 2 Ch.D. 235 at 253.
[23] *Croydon (Unique) Ltd v. Wright* [1999] 4 All E.R. 257.
[24] C.P.R. Pt. 55, P.D. para. 2.4 (cp. C.P.R. Sched. 2: C.C.R. Ord. 6, r.3(2); R.S.C. Ord. 6, r.2).
[25] s.146(4) as amended by L.P.(A.)A. 1929, s.1; see *Belgravia Insurance Co. v. Meah* [1964] 1 Q.B. 436.
[26] See *Ewart v. Fryer* [1901] 1 Ch. 499 at 515.
[27] *Belgravia Insurance Co. Ltd v. Meah* [1964] 1 Q.B. 436.
[28] s.210.
[29] County Courts Act 1984, s.139(2).
[30] *Bland v. Ingrams Estates Ltd* [2001] 2 W.L.R. 1638.

tenant, if necessary by joining him as a defendant,[31] and relief will generally only be given on terms that the lease is immediately sold.[32]

6. Conditions for forfeiture—forfeiture for breach of other covenants or conditions

Where a tenant has denied his landlord's title, it is generally thought that the landlord can immediately forfeit the lease and that the tenant has no right to relief against forfeiture.[33] Otherwise, and perhaps even in the case of forfeiture for denial of title,[34] the general rule is that forfeiture for breach of a covenant or condition other than for payment of rent is subject to the landlord's obligation to serve a notice in the statutory form and the tenant's right to relief against forfeiture. This is the case whether proceedings are to be brought in the High Court or the County Court but there are some exceptions to the general rule. The right to receive a notice and to apply for relief prevails over any stipulation to the contrary in the lease.[35] Hence a device such as an undated surrender executed by the tenant as a guarantee against breaches of covenant is void.[36]

(a) General rule

(i) Service of notice: Before proceeding to enforce a forfeiture either by action or re-entry, the landlord must serve on the tenant a statutory notice in writing under the Law of Property Act 1925, section 146.[37] The notice must—

   (i) specify the breach complained of; and

   (ii) require it to be remedied, if it is capable of remedy; and

   (iii) require the tenant to make compensation in money for the breach,[38] if the landlord requires such compensation.[39]

(ii) "Capable of remedy": A breach of a positive covenant (*i.e.* to do something) is normally capable of remedy by doing what has been left undone, such as carrying out building work[40] or painting,[41] even though this is done belatedly. However, if the covenant is negative (*i.e.* not to do something) it has been said that it can never be remedied,[42] for "that which was done cannot be undone".[43] This seems to give "remedy" an unduly narrow meaning, and it now appears that at least some breaches of negative covenants are capable of remedy,[44] though not all. Thus a breach of a covenant against assigning or sub-letting the

---

[31] *Bland v. Ingrams Estates Ltd* [2001] 2 W.L.R. 638.
[32] *Bland v. Ingrams Estates Ltd (No. 2)* [2002] 2 W.L.R. 361 at para. 37.
[33] *Warner v. Sampson* [1958] 1 Q.B. 404; reversed on other grounds [1959] 1 Q.B. 297. However, doubts were cast on this by dicta in *W.G. Clark (Properties) Ltd v. Dupre Properties Ltd* [1992] Ch. 297; *sed quaere.*
[34] *W.G. Clarke (Properties) Ltd v. Dupre Properties Ltd* [1992] Ch. 297; *sed quaere.*
[35] L.P.A. 1925, s.146(12).
[36] *Plymouth Corporation v. Harvey* [1971] 1 W.L.R. 549; and see *Richard Clarke & Co. Ltd v. Widnall* [1976] 1 W.L.R. 845.
[37] Replacing C.A. 1881, s.14, and C.A. 1882, ss.2, 4.
[38] L.P.A. 1925, s.146(1); and see below, p. 378 (repairs).
[39] *Lock v. Pearce* [1893] 2 Ch. 271 (despite the words "in any case").
[40] *Expert Clothing Service & Sales Ltd v. Hillgate House Ltd* [1986] Ch. 340.
[41] See *Hoffmann v. Fineberg* [1949] Ch. 245 at 257.
[42] *Rugby School (Governors) v. Tannahill* [1934] 1 K.B. 695 at 701 (in C.A. [1935] 1 K.B. 87); and see *Scala House & District Property Co. Ltd v. Forbes* [1974] Q.B. 575 at 585.
[43] *Rugby School (Governors) v. Tannahill* [1934] 1 K.B. 695 at 701, *per* MacKinnon J.
[44] *Rugby School (Governors) v. Tannahill* [1935] 1 K.B. 87.

premises is incapable of remedy.[45] However, an assignment is valid despite having been made in breach of covenant and so it is on the assignee that the statutory notice must be served.[46] Again, the use of the premises for prostitution in breach of a covenant against permitting user for any illegal or immoral purpose cannot be remedied merely by ceasing the prohibited use, for this will not remove the stigma attached to the premises.[47] But the breach is remediable where there is no notoriety and the immoral use by the sub-tenant can be suppressed by the tenant taking prompt action as soon as he discovers the breach.[48] The question seems to be whether the harm to the landlord done by the breach is for practical purposes capable of being retrieved.[49] The path of safety is for the statutory notice to require the specified breach to be remedied "if it is capable of remedy".[50] A notice may be valid even if it does no more than specify the breach, as where the breach is irremediable and the landlord seeks no compensation, perhaps to avoid soiling his hands with the fruits of prostitution, or other illegal or immoral activities.[51]

(iii) Time for compliance: After serving the notice, the landlord must allow the tenant a reasonable time for compliance with it. The Act does not define what is a reasonable time, but it will be measured by the time that it would take to perform the covenant, as by doing the requisite building work or decoration, or, if the covenant is negative, by terminating the breach.[52] For many positive covenants a period of three months is usually considered to be enough in normal circumstances. Even if the breach is irremediable, reasonable notice must be given so as to enable the tenant to consider his position. In such cases, two days' notice has been held to be insufficient[53] although 14 days may be enough.[54] If within a reasonable time the notice has not been complied with, the landlord may proceed to enforce the forfeiture. This he may do either in person or by action.

(b) Exceptional cases

As has already been mentioned, the above provisions concerning the necessity for serving a notice and the tenant's right to apply for relief probably do not affect forfeiture for denial by a tenant of his landlord's title,[55] but they govern all covenants and conditions (other than those for payment of rent) with two exceptions. These two exceptions are as follows.

(i) Mining leases: Cases where there has been a breach of a covenant in a mining lease providing for inspection of the books, accounts, weighing machines or other things, or of the mine itself.[56] Since the rent reserved on such a lease usually varies with the quantity of minerals extracted, such a covenant is most important to the landlord. There is consequently

---

[45] *Scala House & District Property Co. Ltd v. Forbes* [1974] Q.B. 575; and see *Horsey Estates Ltd v. Steiger* [1899] 2 Q.B. 79 (tenant in liquidation).
[46] *Old Grovebury Manor Farm Ltd v. W. Seymour Plant Sales and Hire Ltd* [1979] 1 W.L.R. 1397.
[47] *Rugby School (Governors) v. Tannahill* [1935] 1 K.B. 87; *British Petroleum Pension Trust Ltd v. Behrendt* (1986) 52 P. & C.R. 117; and see *Hoffmann v. Fineberg* [1949] Ch. 245 (illicit gaming); *Van Haarlam v. Kasner* [1992] 36 E.G. 135 (using premises for spying).
[48] *Glass v. Kencakes Ltd* [1966] 1 Q.B. 611.
[49] *Expert Clothing Service & Sales Ltd v. Hillgate House Ltd* [1986] Ch. 340.
[50] See *Glass v. Kencakes Ltd* [1966] 1 Q.B. 611 at 629.
[51] *Rugby School (Governors) v. Tannahill* [1935] 1 K.B. 87.
[52] *Expert Clothing Service & Sales Ltd v. Hillgate House Ltd* [1986] Ch. 340 at 357.
[53] *Horsey Estate Ltd v. Steiger* [1899] 2 Q.B. 79.
[54] *Scala House & District Property Co. Ltd v. Forbes* [1974] Q.B. 575.
[55] *Warner v. Sampson* [1958] 1 Q.B. 404; reversed on other grounds [1959] 1 Q.B. 297 but doubt was cast on this by dicta in *W.G. Clarke (Properties) Ltd v. Dupre Properties Ltd* [1992] Ch. 297; *sed quaere*.
[56] L.P.A. 1925, s.146(8).

no restriction upon the landlord forfeiting the lease without serving a notice, and no provision enabling the tenant to obtain relief.

(ii) Bankruptcy or execution: Cases where there has been a breach of a condition against the tenant's bankruptcy (or, for a corporation, insolvent liquidation[57]) or the taking of the lease in execution[58]; the bankruptcy of a surety for the tenant is outside this provision.[59] This head must be divided into two.

(1) *No protection.* In five specified cases, on breach of such a condition, section 146 has no application at all; the lease can thus be forfeited at once without service of a notice and without possibility of relief.[60] These cases are those where the lease is of—

    (i) agricultural or pastoral land, or

    (ii) mines or minerals, or

    (iii) a public house or beershop, or

    (iv) a furnished house, or

    (v) property with respect to which the personal qualifications of the tenant are of importance for the preservation of the value or character of the property,[61] or on the ground of neighbourhood to the landlord or to any person holding under him.

(2) *Protection for one year and after.* In all other cases, on breach of such a condition, the protection of section 146 applies for one year from the bankruptcy, liquidation or taking in execution; if during that year the landlord wishes to forfeit the lease, he must serve the notice and the tenant can apply for relief. But once the year has elapsed, the tenant is no longer protected; the landlord can forfeit the lease without serving notice and the court has no power to grant relief.[62] Yet if the tenant's lease is sold during the year, the protection of section 146 continues indefinitely.[63] This allows the trustee in bankruptcy or sheriff to dispose of the lease to a purchaser at a reasonable price, for if the lease were liable to be forfeited after the year without the service of notice or the chance of relief, it would be difficult to find a purchaser.

(c) Right to relief of tenant

While the landlord "is proceeding" to enforce the forfeiture by action or otherwise, the tenant may apply to the court for relief, either in any action by the landlord to enforce the forfeiture or by making a separate application.[64] "Is proceeding" is here used in the sense of "proceeds",[65] or "has proceeded"[66]; and a tenant may seek relief as soon as the landlord has served the statutory notice,[67] though usually it will be better to wait and see whether or not

---

[57] *ibid.,* s.205(1)(i).
[58] *ibid.,* s.146(9).
[59] *Halliard Property Co. Ltd v. Jack Segal Ltd* [1978] 1 W.L.R. 377.
[60] L.P.A. 1925, s.146(9).
[61] See *Bathurst (Earl) v. Fine* [1974] 1 W.L.R. 905.
[62] L.P.A. 1925, s.146(10)(b).
[63] *ibid.,* s.146(10)(a).
[64] L.P.A. 1925, s.146(2).
[65] *Billson v. Residential Apartments Ltd* [1992] 1 A.C. 494.
[66] *ibid.,* at 539.
[67] *ibid.,* at 539, 540, 544.

the landlord actually decides to proceed to forfeiture. Where the forfeiture is being enforced by action, the right to apply for relief is exercisable at any time before the landlord has taken possession under a judgment in his favour.[68] Thereafter no relief can be granted, even within six months of the forfeiture.[69] Where the forfeiture is enforced in person, the right to apply for relief continues for an indefinite period after the landlord's entry, though in deciding whether to grant relief the court will take into account all the circumstances, including any delay by the tenant in applying.[70]

The court may grant relief on such terms as it thinks fit[71]; and if relief is granted the effect is as if the lease had never been forfeited.[72] Relief is usually granted where the breach has been remedied, though it may be refused if the tenant's personal qualifications are important and he has proved unsatisfactory.[73] But where the breach involves immoral use, relief will be refused except in very exceptional circumstances.[74] Where premises are physically divided and separately occupied, and the breaches are confined to one part only, relief may be granted in respect of the other part.[75] Relief takes effect subject to any legal lease granted by the landlord after the forfeiture to a lessee who takes without notice of the previous tenant's equity to seek relief.[76] However, where such a lessee has notice of that equity, his lease is interposed between the landlord and tenant, who becomes in effect his tenant and the sub-tenant of the landlord.[77]

(d) Right to relief of those claiming through the tenant

As in the case of forfeiture for non-payment of rent,[78] those claiming through the tenant are also entitled to claim relief against forfeiture irrespective of whether the tenant himself is able to do so and can do so whenever they first become aware of the forfeiture.[79] It will be recalled that, in an effort to avoid late applications, rules of court oblige the landlord to serve a copy of his claim form on any persons claiming through the tenant of whose interests he is aware[80] but this will not necessarily always work.

It has been held that a sub-tenant and a mortgagee have the same right as the tenant[81] to apply to the court for relief against forfeiture while the landlord "is proceeding" to enforce the forfeiture by action or otherwise.[82] This decision supplements the specific provision that a sub-tenant has the same right of applying for relief against forfeiture as the tenant under the head lease.[83] Where relief is granted to a sub-tenant of only part of the premises, the court

---

[68] *ibid.*, at 540.

[69] Contrast non-payment of rent: above, p. 357.

[70] *Billson v. Residential Apartments Ltd* [1992] 1 A.C. 494 at 540, 543.

[71] L.P.A. 1925, s.146(2).

[72] *Dendy v. Evans* [1909] 2 K.B. 894.

[73] *Bathurst (Earl) v. Fine* [1974] 1 W.L.R. 905 (stately home); and see L.P.A. 1925, s.146(9): below, p. 331.

[74] *Central Estates (Belgravia) Ltd v. Woolgar (No. 2)* [1972] 1 W.L.R. 1048 (short-lived homosexual brothel: tenant aged and sick: value of premises not diminished); *Ropemaker Properties Ltd v. Noonhaven Ltd* [1989] 2 E.G.L.R. 50 (valuable lease of West End clip joints); *Van Haarlam v. Kasner* [1992] 36 E.G. 135.

[75] *G.M.S. Syndicate Ltd v. Gary Elliott Ltd* [1982] Ch. 1 (ground floor shop; immoral "club" in basement).

[76] *Fuller v. Judy Properties Ltd* [1992] 14 E.G. 106.

[77] *Bland v. Ingrams Estates Ltd (No. 2)* [2002] 2 W.L.R. 361 at para.13 (actually a case on forfeiture for non-payment of rent).

[78] Above, p. 359.

[79] *Croydon (Unique) Ltd v. Wright* [1999] 4 All E.R. 257.

[80] C.P.R. Pt. 55, P. D. para. 2.4 (cp. C.P.R. Sched. 2: C.C.R. Ord. 6, r.3(2); R.S.C. Ord. 6, r.2).

[81] Under L.P.A., s.146(2).

[82] *Escalus Properties Ltd v. Dennis* [1996] Q.B. 231.

[83] L.P.A. 1925, s.146(4).

will grant the sub-tenant a term no longer than the term he held under his sub-lease[84] and will normally impose terms that will restore the landlord to his former position.[85] The sub-tenant will usually enter into a new lease direct with the former landlord under the forfeited lease on terms similar to (though not necessarily the same as) those of the old sub-lease. A mortgagee is treated as a sub-tenant for these purposes even if his mortgage is not by way of sub-lease[86]; and a person who has registered a charging order against a lease also has a right to relief against forfeiture,[87] presumably the same right as he has in the case of forfeiture for non-payment of rent.[88]

Sect. 4. By surrender

If a tenant surrenders his lease to his immediate landlord, who accepts the surrender, the lease merges in the landlord's reversion and is extinguished. The surrender must be to the immediate landlord; a transfer of the lease to a superior landlord does not work a surrender but operates merely as an assignment of the lease. Thus if L leases land to T for 99 years and T sub-leases to S for 21 years, S's sub-lease will be extinguished by surrender if he transfers it to T but not if he transfers it to L. A surrender by an assignee which releases him from all liabilities under the lease will also release prior assignees, even if liable under direct covenants with the landlord.[89] But a surrender takes effect subject to the rights of others in the lease surrendered, and so they will be binding for as long as it would have lasted.[90]

Surrender may be either express or by operation of law. For an express surrender, at law a deed is required.[91] However, a surrender in writing made for value would probably suffice in equity as between the parties to it, although not necessarily in favour of prior assignees. There will be surrender by operation of law if the parties do some act showing an intention to terminate the lease, and the circumstances are such that it would be inequitable for them to rely on the fact that there has been no surrender by deed.[92] Surrender by operation of law will take place if the tenant sells the freehold as trustee of it forgetting that he also has a lease of it[93]; and if he accepts a fresh lease from his immediate reversioner, even though the new lease is for a shorter term than the old one or starts at a future date.[94] Where a lease is varied by extending the term, this operates by way of surrender and regrant.[95] Other variations, such as an agreed increase of rent, do not necessarily bring about a surrender and regrant.[96] There will also be a surrender by operation of law if the tenant gives up possession of the premises and the landlord accepts it,[97] but not if there is a mere uncompleted contract by the tenant to

---

[84] See *Ewart v. Fryer* [1901] 1 Ch. 499 at 515.
[85] *Chatham Empire Theatre Ltd v. Ultrans Ltd* [1961] 1 W.L.R. 817; *Belgravia Insurance Co. Ltd v. Meah* [1964] 1 Q.B. 436.
[86] *Grand Junction Co. Ltd v. Bates* [1954] 2 Q.B. 160.
[87] *Croydon (Unique) Ltd v. Wright* [1999] 4 All E.R. 257.
[88] *Bland v. Ingrams Estates Ltd* [2001] 2 W.L.R. 1638; above, p. 359.
[89] *Deanplan Ltd v. Mahmoud* [1993] Ch. 151.
[90] *E. S. Schwab & Co. Ltd v. McCarthy* (1976) 31 P. & C.R. 196.
[91] L.P.A. 1925, s.52, replacing R.P.A. 1845, s.3.
[92] See *Glynn v. Coghlan* [1918] 1 I.R. 482 at 485.
[93] *Allen v. Rochdale B.C.* [2000] Ch. 221.
[94] *Ive's Case* (1597) 5 Co.Rep. 11a.
[95] *Baker v. Merckel* [1960] 1 Q.B. 657.
[96] *Jenkin R. Lewis & Son Ltd v. Kerman* [1971] Ch. 477.
[97] See *Oastler v. Henderson* (1877) 2 Q.B.D. 575; but see *Chamberlain v. Scally* [1992] E.G.C.S. 90 (no unequivocal conduct by the parties).

purchase the reversion.[98] Nor will there be a surrender where a lease is determined by notice as the result of an informal agreement between landlord and tenant that the latter will not serve the counter notice which is a prerequisite of a new tenancy.[99] In such circumstances, any sub-leases will fall with the head lease.

Sect. 5. By merger

Merger is the counterpart of surrender. Under a surrender, the landlord acquires the lease, whereas merger is the consequence of the tenant retaining the lease and acquiring the reversion, or of a third party acquiring both lease and reversion. The principle is the same in both surrender and merger: the lease is absorbed by the reversion and destroyed.

For merger to be effective, the lease and the reversion must be vested in the same person in the same right with no vested estate intervening.[1] Merger may take place even if the immediate reversion consists of a lease shorter than the lease merged.[2] Thus if A, a tenant in fee simple, leases land to B for 1000 years and a few years later leases the same land to C for 400 years, the result is to give C for 400 years the reversion on B's lease. If X then acquires both C's reversion and B's lease, the 1000 years' lease will merge in the 400 years' reversion and leave X with but 400 years.[3] But there is now no merger if the person in whom the two interests vest intends that there shall be none.[4]

Sect. 6. By becoming a satisfied term

If a lease is granted as security for the payment of money, the term becomes satisfied and the lease automatically ceases when all the money has been paid.[5]

Sect. 7. By enlargement

Under certain conditions, not frequently encountered in practice, a lease may be enlarged into a fee simple by the tenant executing a deed of enlargement. Under the Law of Property Act 1925[6] this can be done only if—

(i) there is not less than 200 years of the lease unexpired; and

(ii) the lease was originally granted for at least 300 years; and

(iii) no trust or right of redemption[7] exists in favour of the reversioner; and

(iv) the lease is not liable to be determined by re-entry for condition broken; and

---

[98] *Nightingale v. Courtney* [1954] 1 Q.B. 399.
[99] *Barrett v. Morgan* [2000] 2 A.C. 264.
[1] See *Chambers v. Kingham* (1878) 10 Ch.D. 743.
[2] *Hughes v. Robotham* (1593) Cro.Eliz. 302.
[3] *Stephens v. Bridges* (1821) 6 Madd. 66.
[4] See L.P.A. 1925, s.185; below, p. 412.
[5] See below, pp. 494, 534.
[6] s.153, replacing C.A. 1881, s.65 and C.A. 1882, s.11.
[7] *e.g.* a right of redemption under a mortgage; see below, p. 494.

(v) no rent of any money value is payable. A rent of "one silver penny if lawfully demanded" is a rent of no money value, but a rent of three shillings is not.[8] A rent under such a lease which does not exceed £1 per annum and which has not been paid for a continuous period of 20 years (five having elapsed since 1925) is deemed to have ceased to be payable and can no longer be recovered.

For a sub-lease to be capable of enlargement under the section, it must be derived out of a lease which is itself capable of enlargement. A fee simple acquired by enlargement is subject to all the provisions which affected the term of years out of which it arose. This seems to be one of the few ways of making positive covenants run with freehold land.[9]

Sect. 8. By disclaimer

Most rights to disclaim a lease arise under statute. Thus tenants whose premises were rendered unfit by war damage were given a statutory power to disclaim their tenancies.[10] Similar rights were given to certain tenants of premises which were requisitioned under emergency powers.[11] The effect of valid disclaimers of this type is the same as if there had been a surrender. But not all statutory provisions for disclaimer take effect in this way; thus a trustee in bankruptcy or the liquidator of an insolvent company may disclaim an onerous lease[12] but by so doing he only terminates any future liability of himself and the insolvent person.[13] His disclaimer does not destroy the lease. The landlord can claim in the insolvency for the whole of the remaining rent payable under the lease subject to a discount for early payment[14] and to giving credit for the value of what he has received back after taking into account the cost of any necessary repairs to the premises.[15]

Sect. 9. By frustration

Leases are more than mere contracts in that they create estates in land. Nevertheless, the doctrine of frustration of contracts applies in principle to leases, though only rarely will it operate.[16] Thus a lease of a warehouse for 10 years will not be frustrated by the closure of the only means of access to it for 20 months when some five years of the term have elapsed.[17] But a lease might perhaps be ended by frustration[18] if the land were physically destroyed (such as by being engulfed by the sea), or if the lease were merely incidental to a commercial contract that had been frustrated, or where the lease was a short lease of a holiday villa which

---

[8] *Re Chapman and Hobbs* (1885) 29 Ch.D. 1007; *Re Smith and Stott* (1883) 29 Ch.D. 1009n.

[9] See below, p. 463.

[10] Landlord and Tenant (War Damage) Acts 1939 and 1941.

[11] Landlord and Tenant (Requisitioned Land) Acts 1942 and 1944.

[12] Insolvency Act 1986, s.315.

[13] *Re Thompson and Cottrell's Contract* [1943] Ch. 97 at 99.

[14] Held in 1999 to be 8.5% per annum (the rate of the return on gilts (government securities)).

[15] *Re Park Air Services Plc* [2000] 2 A.C. 172 (the rent payable under the lease was four times the market value).

[16] *National Carriers Ltd v. Panalpina (Northern) Ltd* [1981] A.C. 675.

[17] *ibid.*

[18] *ibid.*; *Cricklewood Property and Investment Trust Ltd v. Leighton's Investment Trust Ltd* [1945] A.C. 221; see the various dicta.

was totally destroyed by lightning before the term begins. Agreements for a lease and covenants in a lease may similarly, but not readily, be held to have been frustrated.[19]

Sect. 10. By repudiation

In the same sort of way, a tenancy will not normally be determined by repudiation, *i.e.* by one party accepting a breach of a fundamental term of the tenancy by the other as being a repudiation of the tenancy.[20] Thus a landlord's derogation from grant in not preventing other tenants from parking on a forecourt in breach of the tenant's exclusive right so to do will not constitute a repudiatory breach entitling the tenant to determine the lease.[21] Nor, apparently, will a tenant's prolonged refusal to pay rent entitle the landlord to determine, as distinct from forfeit, the lease. However, a landlord has been held have committed repudiatory breaches entitling the tenant to determine the lease where he wilfully and persistently refused to repair defects which had made the premises unfit for habitation[22] and where he made the tenant's unit dark and virtually unusable as a result of having leased adjoining premises to a pawnbroker.[23] It is therefore now seems to be accepted that a breach of the terms of a lease can amount to a repudiatory breach but only in extreme cases.

Sect. 11. By rescission

A lease may be set aside by the court where it was granted as a result of the fraud of one of the parties[24] or where it constitutes an unconscionable bargain.[25]

PART 5—RIGHTS AND DUTIES OF THE PARTIES UNDER A LEASE OR TENANCY

The rights and duties of the landlord and tenant under a lease or tenancy fall under five heads. First, the lease may be silent as to everything except the essential terms as to parties, premises, rent and duration. This is not infrequently the case with weekly and other periodic tenancies. Secondly, the parties may have agreed to be bound by the "usual covenants". Thirdly, the lease may provide in the orthodox way not only for the matters dealt with by the "usual covenants" but also for a number of other matters. Fourthly, there are a number of statutory provisions relating to the rights and duties of the parties to a lease. Last, there are fixtures: these have already been considered.[26]

The question how far covenants in a lease can be enforced between persons other than the original lessor and original lessee is considered separately.[27]

---

[19] *ibid.*
[20] *Total Oil Great Britain Ltd v. Thompson Garages (Biggin Hill) Ltd* [1972] 1 Q.B. 318, not citing *Wilson v. Finch Hatton* (1877) 2 Ex.D. 336; below, p. 337.
[21] *Nynehead Developments Ltd v. R.H. Fibreboard Containsers Ltd* [1999] 1 E.G.L.R. 7.
[22] See *Hussein v. Mehlman* [1992] 32 E.G. 59.
[23] *Chartered Trust plc v. Davies* [1997] 2 E.G.L.R. 83.
[24] *Killick v. Roberts* [1991] 1 W.L.R. 1146 (fraud by the tenant).
[25] *Boustany v. Piggott* (1993) 69 P. & C.R. 298 (claim by the landlord).
[26] Above, pp. 19 *et seq.*
[27] Below, pp. 381 *et seq.*

The basic remedy available for breach of covenant is damages, although distress (the right to enter the premises and enforce payment by seizing and selling enough of any goods which are found there) is an alternative in the case of unpaid rent. However, a landlord cannot either claim damages or levy distress when he has successfully forfeited the lease. The court has statutory power to order specific performance of the landlord's repairing covenants in favour of a tenant of a dwelling-house[28] and it can do so in favour of a tenant of any type of property under its inherent jurisdiction.[29] The court may also order specific performance of the tenant's repairing covenants in favour of the landlord but it will only do so where damages would be an inadequate remedy. An example is where the lease contains no proviso for re-entry and forfeiture, where the property is deteriorating and the landlord has no right of access to carry out the repairs himself.[30] In other circumstances, he will have to elect between forfeiture and an award of damages. The court will not generally order specific performance of other types of positive covenants, particularly where whether or not the order has been complied with is likely to be contentious. Thus specific performance was denied where the tenant breached a covenant to keep the premises open as a supermarket because of the difficulties of drawing an order with sufficient precision to avoid continuous and wasteful litigation. There would have been a risk of the landlord being enriched at the tenant's expense whereas an award of damages would bring the matter to an end.[31] However, the court will generally grant an injunction restraining any breach of a negative covenant, typically a covenant which is restrictive of the user of the land.

Sect. 1. Position in the absence of express provision

Except so far as the lease or tenancy agreement otherwise provides, the position of the parties is as set out below.

1. Position of the landlord

(a) Quiet enjoyment

A covenant by the landlord for quiet enjoyment (or a corresponding agreement if the tenancy is not created by deed[32]) is automatically inferred from the mere relationship of landlord and tenant,[33] unless it is displaced by the presence of an express covenant for quiet enjoyment,[34] which may differ in its terms. The implied covenant extends to all acts of the landlord and any lawful acts of those claiming under him, but not the acts of others, such as someone claiming by title paramount (such as a superior landlord[35]), nor to acts of the landlord himself if he is acting under statutory authority.[36] The covenant is not one for "quiet" enjoyment in the acoustic sense; the landlord undertakes not that the tenant will be free from the nuisance

---

[28] L. & T.A. 1985, s.17.
[29] *Jeune v. Queen's Cross Properties Ltd* [1974] Ch. 97.
[30] *Rainbow Estates Ltd v. Tokenhold Ltd* [1999] Ch. 64.
[31] *Co-operative Insurance Ltd v. Argyll Stores (Holdings) Ltd* [1998] A.C. 1.
[32] *Baynes & Co. v. Lloyd & Sons* [1895] 1 Q.B. 820 at 826 (in C.A. [1895] 2 Q.B. 610); *Budd-Scott v. Daniell* [1902] 2 K.B. 351.
[33] *Budd-Scott v. Daniell* [1902] 2 K.B. 351; *Markham v. Paget* [1908] 1 Ch. 697; *Kenny v. Preen* [1963] 1 Q.B. 499; and see above, pp. 163–165.
[34] *Miller v. Emcer Products Ltd* [1956] Ch. 304.
[35] *Baynes & Co. v. Lloyd & Sons* [1895] 2 Q.B. 610; *Jones v. Lavington* [1903] 1 K.B. 253.
[36] *Commissioners of Crown Lands v. Page* [1960] 2 Q.B. 274 (requisitioning).

of noise, but that he will be free from disturbance by adverse claimants to the property.[37] The covenant is broken if a person to whose acts it extends causes subsidence to the land by working minerals under it,[38] or in some other way physically and substantially interferes with the tenant's enjoyment of the land[39]; and this includes persistent intimidation of the tenant to induce her to leave.[40] No exemplary damages can be awarded merely for breach of the covenant,[41] though they can be if the tort of trespass has been committed.[42] In addition, a residential occupier now has a right to statutory damages if he is unlawfully evicted from his premises, whether directly or indirectly.[43]

When granting a lease, the lessor does not use the words "as beneficial owner" or, now, "with full title guarantee"; even if he did, the words would not import the covenants for title which arise from using these phrases in a conveyance.[44]

(b) No derogation from grant

It is a principle of general application that a grantor must not derogate from his grant.[45] He must not seek to take away with one hand what he has given with the other. In the case of leases, the covenant for quiet enjoyment will extend to many of the acts which might be construed as a derogation from the lessor's grant; but acts not amounting to a breach of the covenant may nevertheless be restrained as being in derogation of the grant. Thus, if land is leased for the express purpose of storing explosives, the lessor and those claiming under him will be restrained from using adjoining land so as to endanger the statutory licence necessary for storing explosives.[46]

There must, however, be some act making the premises substantially less fit for the purposes for which they were let. No action will lie if the landlord, having let the premises for some particular trade, such as for a wool shop only, lets adjoining premises for purposes which offer trade competition; for the original premises are still fit for use as a wool shop even if the profits will be diminished.[47] Nor will mere invasion of privacy, as by erecting an external staircase passing the windows of the flat demised, amount to a breach of the obligation,[48] although interference with the stability of the house by vibrations caused by powerful engines on adjoining land may suffice, and so may excessive noise, such as that caused in altering another flat in the same building.[49]

(c) In certain cases, obligations as to fitness and repair

In general, the landlord gives no implied undertaking that the premises will be fit for habitation,[50] nor is he liable to repair them. But this rule is subject to five qualifications, which to some extent overlap.

---

[37] *Hudson v. Cripps* [1896] 1 Ch. 265 at 268.
[38] *Markham v. Paget* [1908] 1 Ch. 697.
[39] *Owen v. Gadd* [1956] 2 Q.B. 99 (adjacent scaffolding).
[40] *Kenny v. Preen* [1963] 1 Q.B. 499.
[41] *Perera v. Vandiyar* [1953] 1 W.L.R. 672; *Branchett v. Beaney* [1992] 3 All E.R. 910.
[42] *Drane v. Evangelou* [1978] 1 W.L.R. 455.
[43] Below, p. 616.
[44] See above, p. 163.
[45] *Palmer v. Fletcher* (1663) 1 Lev. 122; and see (1964) 80 L.Q.R. 244 (D. W. Elliott).
[46] *Harmer v. Jumbil (Nigeria) Tin Areas Ltd* [1921] 1 Ch. 200.
[47] *Port v. Griffith* [1938] 1 All E.R. 295.
[48] *Browne v. Flower* [1911] 1 Ch. 219.
[49] *Newman v. Real Estate Debenture Corporation Ltd* [1940] 1 All E.R. 131.
[50] *Hart v. Windsor* (1844) 12 M. & W. 68.

(i) Furnished lettings: Where a house is let furnished, the landlord impliedly undertakes that it is fit for human habitation when let.[51] If this is not the case, the tenant may repudiate the tenancy and recover damages for any loss he has suffered.[52] But if the premises are fit for human habitation when let, the landlord need do no more. He is under no obligation to keep them in this condition.[53] And the tenant is not deemed to warrant his fitness to occupy the premises, such as that he is free from contagious diseases.[54]

(ii) Houses let at a low rent: Under the Landlord and Tenant Act 1985,[55] if a house is let for human habitation at a low rent, then,notwithstanding any stipulation to the contrary, there is—

(i) an implied condition that it is fit for human habitation at the beginning of the tenancy, and

(ii) an implied undertaking by the landlord that he will keep it in this condition throughout the tenancy.

This liability applies only to defects of which the landlord has notice,[56] though it extends to minor matters such as a broken sash-cord, for the question is not how difficult it is to repair the defect but whether by ordinary use of the premises damage may be naturally caused to the occupier.[57] Yet these provisions are of limited importance today as they still apply only if the rent does not exceed £80 a year in London and £52 elsewhere.[58]

(iii) Short leases of dwellings: In any lease or agreement for a lease[59] of a dwelling-house granted on or after October 24, 1961, whatever the rent or rateable value, a covenant by the landlord to do certain repairs is implied if the term is less than seven years (unless the tenant can extend it to seven years or more) or if the landlord can determine it within seven years.[60] The covenant cannot be excluded or limited by any agreement to the contrary unless the county court has authorised this as being reasonable; and any covenant by the tenant to repair or pay money in lieu thereof is of no effect so far as it is covered by the landlord's covenant.

The obligations of the landlord under the implied covenant are as follows.

(1) *Structure and exterior*: to keep the structure and exterior of the dwelling in repair.[61] This includes the drains, gutters and external pipes,[62] and also the outside walls (even if excluded from the demise[63]) and any outside steps which form an essential part of the means

---

[51] *Smith v. Marrable* (1843) 11 M. & W. 5 (bugs).
[52] *Wilson v. Finch Hatton* (1877) 2 Ex.D. 336; *Charsley v. Jones* (1889) 53 J.P. 280; cp. above, p. 335.
[53] *Sarson v. Roberts* [1895] 2 Q.B. 395.
[54] *Humphreys v. Miller* [1917] 2 K.B. 122.
[55] s.8, replacing earlier legislation.
[56] *McCarrick v. Liverpool Corporation* [1947] A.C. 219.
[57] *Summers v. Salford Corporation* [1943] A.C. 283 (tenant injured when other sash-cord broke).
[58] L. & T.A. 1985, s.8; and see ss.8(5), 10. See *Quick v. Taff Ely B.C.* [1986] Q.B. 809 at 817, 821, for unsurprising judicial surprise.
[59] *Brikom Investments Ltd v. Seaford* [1981] 1 W.L.R. 863.
[60] L. & T.A. 1985, ss.11 (as amended by H.A. 1988, s.116), 12–14, 36, 38.
[61] L. & T.A. 1985, s.11(1)(a).
[62] *ibid.*
[63] *Campden Hill Towers Ltd v. Gardner* [1977] Q.B. 823.

of access to the dwelling,[64] but not a backyard.[65] The obligation does not extend to defects such as condensation which arise from faulty design rather than disrepair.[66]

(2) *Installations*: to keep in repair and proper working order the installations in the dwelling—

    (i) for the supply of water, gas and electricity, and for sanitation, including basins, sinks, baths and sanitary conveniences, but not other appliances for making use of water, gas and electricity; and

    (ii) for space heating and heating water.[67]

This head does not apply to a central heating boiler not within the dwelling.[68] An ill-designed water closet cistern in a maisonette which floods the floor whenever used is not in "proper working order".[69]

There are two main limitations on these obligations of the landlord. First, they do not apply to works or repairs for which the tenant is liable by virtue of his duty to use the premises in a tenant-like manner,[70] such as his duty to take reasonable precautions against burst pipes when leaving the premises unoccupied during winter.[71] Secondly, the obligations do not apply to any defect in the demised premises unless the landlord has notice or knowledge of the defect, either specifically or from facts that would put a reasonable man on inquiry.[72]

Where the statutory covenant applies to the landlord, there is an implied covenant by the tenant to permit the landlord to enter and view the premises at reasonable times of the day on 24 hours' prior notice in writing to the occupier.[73]

Where a lease is granted after January 14, 1989, and the dwelling forms part only of a building, the landlord's statutory covenant is extended so as to apply to any part of the building in which he has an estate or interest. It also applies to any installations which directly or indirectly serve the dwelling if they are owned by him or are under his control, or if they are part of any part of the building in which he has an estate or interest. But it is a defence if he shows that he made reasonable endeavours to obtain adequate access to do the works, and failed.[74]

(iv) Duty of care: In some cases a landlord owes to all persons who might reasonably be expected to be affected by defects in the state of any part of the premises let[75] a statutory duty to take reasonable care in all the circumstances[76] to see that they and their property are reasonably safe from injury or damage. This duty arises where the landlord is under an

---

[64] *Brown v. Liverpool Corporation* [1969] 3 All E.R. 1345.

[65] *Hopwood v. Cannock Chase D.C.* [1975] 1 W.L.R. 373. See further *Irvine v. Moran* (1990) 24 H.L.R. 1.

[66] *Quick v. Taff Ely B.C.* [1986] Q.B. 809; contrast *Stent v. Monmouth D.C.* (1987) 19 H.L.R. 269.

[67] L. & T.A. 1985, s.11(1)(b).

[68] *Campden Hill Towers Ltd v. Gardner* [1977] Q.B. 823.

[69] *Liverpool C.C. v. Irwin* [1977] A.C. 239.

[70] L. & T.A. 1985, s.11(2)(a); and see (b), (c). For the tenant's duty, see below, p. 340.

[71] *Wycombe Health Authority v. Barnett* (1982) 47 P. & C.R. 394 (two days' absence: not liable); criticised (1984) 81 L.S.G. 3408 (M. P. Thompson), discussing lagging.

[72] *O'Brien v. Robinson* [1973] A.C. 912; *Dinefwr B.C. v. Jones* (1987) 19 H.L.R. 445; *Hall v. Howard* (1988) 20 H.L.R. 566.

[73] L. & T.A. 1985, s.11(6).

[74] *ibid.*, s.11(1A), (3A), inserted by Housing Act 1988, s.116.

[75] *Smith v. Bradford Metropolitan Council* (1982) 44 P. & C.R. 171 (patio).

[76] *Sykes v. Harry* (2001) 82 P. & C.R. 35.

obligation to the tenant for the maintenance or repair of the premises, or has a right to enter the premises to maintain and repair them, and he knows or ought to have known of the defect.[77] The landlord cannot contract out of his liability under this provision.[78] However, the tenant will be guilty of contributory negligence if he has been put on inquiry that there was a real risk that the defects have occurred.[79]

(v) Implied terms: In some cases the court may imply a covenant or obligation by the landlord as to the physical condition of the premises. Thus where a flat in a tower block is let on terms which impose obligations on the tenant but not on the landlord, the landlord will be held to be under an implied obligation to take reasonable care to maintain the common parts of the block (*i.e.* the lifts, the stairs and the lighting on the stairs) in a state of reasonable repair and efficiency, thereby supplementing the incomplete terms of the tenancy.[80] Again, where a tenant has covenanted to keep the interior of a house in good repair, the landlord may be subject to an implied covenant to keep the exterior in good repair, thus giving the tenant's covenant business efficacy by imposing a correlative obligation that will preserve the interior from the elements.[81] But where the lease sets out the full obligations of both parties, terms will be implied in it only if it is necessary to do so in order to give the lease business efficacy, and not merely because they seem reasonable.[82]

(vi) Local housing authorities: Local housing authorities have extensive powers of compelling the person who has control of a house (usually the owner or his agent) to make it fit for human habitation.[83] Many tenants avoid the burden of directly enforcing their rights by setting the local housing authority in motion.

2. Position of the tenant

(a) Obligation to pay rent

This is discussed below.[84]

(b) Obligation to pay rates and taxes

The tenant is under an obligation to pay all rates and taxes except those for which the landlord is liable. Under Schedule A the landlord is liable to income tax on the rent.[85] If he fails to pay it, the tenant may be required to pay it up to the amount of his rent, and he may deduct any such payment from any subsequent rent due from him.[86]

---

[77] Defective Premises Act 1972, s.4. See, *e.g. McAuley v. Bristol C.C.* [1992] 1 Q.B. 134 (defective garden step). See also *Targett v. Torfaen B.C.* [1992] 3 All E.R. 27 (liability of builder at common law for negligent design or construction).
[78] Defective Premises Act 1972, s.6(3).
[79] *Sykes v. Harry* (2001) 82 P. & C.R. 35.
[80] *Liverpool C.C. v. Irwin* [1977] A.C. 239; and see *King v. South Northamptonshire D.C.* (1992) 64 P. & C.R. 35 (access to rear entrance).
[81] *Barrett v. Lounova (1982) Ltd* [1990] 1 Q.B. 348. Contrast *Demetriou v. Poolaction Ltd* [1991] 1 E.G.L.R. 100, where there was no such obligation.
[82] *Liverpool C.C. v. Irwin* [1977] A.C. 239; *Duke of Westminster v. Guild* [1985] Q.B. 688.
[83] Housing Act 1985, Pt. VI, replacing earlier legislation.
[84] Below, p. 375.
[85] Income and Corporation Taxes Act 1988, s.15. This Schedule A is distinct from the former Schedule A tax on the annual value of land ("landlord's property tax") which was discontinued as from 1963–64; see Finance Act 1963, ss.14, 68.
[86] Income and Corporation Taxes Act 1988, s.23.

(c) Obligation not to commit waste

A tenant's liability for waste depends upon the nature of his tenancy. A tenant for a fixed term of years is liable for both voluntary and permissive waste, and must therefore keep the premises in proper repair.[87] A yearly tenant is similarly liable save that his liability for permissive waste is limited to keeping the premises wind- and water-tight.[88] A weekly tenant, on the other hand, is not liable for permissive waste as such, though he must use the premises in a tenant-like manner, and so must take proper care of them, for example by keeping the chimneys swept and the drain pipes unblocked.[89] The same rule probably applies to monthly and quarterly tenants. A tenant at will is not liable for permissive waste,[90] although if he commits voluntary waste his tenancy is thereby terminated and he is liable to an action for damages.[91] A tenant at sufferance is liable for voluntary waste,[92] though probably not for permissive waste.

(d) Landlord's right to view

A landlord may by statute or by the terms of the tenancy be expressly authorised to enter the premises; and if he is liable to repair the premises he has an implied right to enter them for this purpose.[93] Otherwise, he has no right to enter the premises so long as the tenancy endures.[94]

(e) Right to take emblements

The nature of emblements has already been considered.[95] A tenant at sufferance has no right to emblements, but at common law a tenant at will, a yearly tenant or a tenant for years determinable with lives was entitled to them, provided the determination of the tenancy was not caused by his own act.[96] A tenant for a fixed term of years could also claim emblements if his lease came to a premature end without his fault, such as if the landlord had only a life estate and his death brought the lease to an end. However, the importance of these rules has been greatly diminished by statute. By the Landlord and Tenant Act 1851,[97] a tenant at a rack rent whose tenancy determined by the death of the landlord or cesser of his interest was given the right to continue his tenancy on the existing terms until the expiration of the current year of the tenancy, in lieu of any right to emblements. In the case of agricultural holdings, the Agricultural Holdings Act 1986[98] provides that in such a case the tenancy continues until determined at the end of a year of the tenancy by 12 months' notice to quit. These provisions, coupled with the conversion of most leases for lives into terms of 90 years,[99] have made this subject of little consequence.

---

[87] *Yellowly v. Gower* (1855) 11 Exch. 274; for waste, see above, p. 48.
[88] *Wedd v. Porter* [1916] 2 K.B. 91.
[89] *Warren v. Keen* [1954] 1 Q.B. 15.
[90] *Harnett v. Maitland* (1847) 16 M. & W. 257.
[91] *Countess of Shrewsbury's Case* (1600) 5 Co.Rep. 13b.
[92] *Burchell v. Hornsby* (1808) 1 Camp. 360.
[93] *Saner v. Bilton* (1878) 7 Ch.D. 815.
[94] *Stocker v. Planet Building Society* (1879) 27 W.R. 877.
[95] Above, p. 52.
[96] See, *e.g. Haines v. Welch* (1868) L.R. 4 C.P. 91.
[97] s.1.
[98] s.21; for agricultural holdings generally, see below, pp. 584 *et seq.*
[99] Above, p. 350.

(f) Right to estovers

A tenant for years has the same right to estovers and botes as a tenant for life.[1]

Sect. 2. Position under a lease containing the usual covenants

1. Effect of agreement

If a lease has actually been granted, the obligations of the parties in the absence of any contrary provision in the lease are as set out above. If, on the other hand, the parties have either agreed that a lease containing the "usual covenants" shall be granted, or have entered into an agreement for a lease containing no reference to the covenants which it should contain, then, subject to any contrary agreement by the parties, the lease must contain whatever covenants and conditions may be "usual" in the circumstances, and if it does not, it may be rectified to accord with the agreement. Except in so far that they cover the same ground, the obligations imposed by the "usual" covenants and conditions are additional to those set out under the heading "Position in the absence of express provision" above.[2]

2. The usual covenants

The following covenants and conditions are always "usual".[3]

(a) On the part of the landlord

This is a covenant for quiet enjoyment in the usual qualified form, *i.e.* extending only to the acts of the lessor or the rightful acts of any person claiming from or under him.

(b) On the part of the tenant

    (i) a covenant to pay rent;

    (ii) a covenant to pay tenant's rates and taxes, *i.e.* all rates and taxes except those which statute requires the landlord to bear;

    (iii) a covenant to keep the premises in repair and deliver them up at the end of the term in this condition;

    (iv) a covenant to permit the landlord to enter and view the state of repair, if he is liable to repair; and

    (v) a condition of re-entry for non-payment of rent, but not for breach of any other covenant.

3. Usual by custom or usage

In addition to the above provisions, which are always "usual", other covenants may be "usual" in the circumstances of the case, by virtue, for example, of the custom of the neighbourhood or trade usage. In each case, this is a question of fact for the court, taking into account the nature of the premises, their situation, the purpose for which they are being let,

---

[1] Co.Litt. 41b; and see above, p. 49.
[2] Above, pp. 368 *et seq.*
[3] See *Hampshire v. Wickens* (1878) 7 Ch.D. 555.

the length of the term, the evidence of conveyancers and the contents of books of precedents.[4] Today, a right of re-entry for breach of any covenant will normally be "usual".[5] In the absence of such special circumstances, however, many covenants which in practice are usually inserted in leases and are therefore literally "usual" are nevertheless not deemed to be "usual" in the technical sense of the word. Examples are covenants against assignment, covenants against carrying on specified trades, and provisos for forfeiture if the tenant has a bankruptcy order made against him or enters into liquidation or suffers any distress or process of execution to be levied upon his goods or makes any assignment or composition for the benefit of his creditors. Such provisions are frequently inserted when (as is usually the case) no contract to take a lease has been made and the terms of the lease are a matter for negotiation between the parties. But if a contract for a lease has been made, no covenant can be inserted in the lease without the concurrence of both parties unless either the contract provides for it or the covenant is technically a "usual" covenant.

Sect. 3. Position under certain covenants usually found in leases

A number of covenants have already been considered, but certain other covenants must be mentioned as well.

1. Covenant to pay rent

Unless the lease provides for payment in advance, rent is normally payable in arrear.[6] It continues to be payable even if the premises cannot be used, for example owing to destruction by fire[7] or other calamity, or seizure by military authorities for the occupation of troops,[8] save in the exceptional case of the lease being frustrated.[9] However, this stern common law rule is frequently mitigated by an express provision in the lease, and in the case of war damage and requisitioning (but not other events) the tenant has been given a statutory right to disclaim his tenancy.[10]

The landlord may enforce payment of the rent—

    (i) directly, by—

        (a) an action for the money, or
        (b) distress;

    (ii) indirectly, by the threat of forfeiture if the lease contains a forfeiture clause.

Forfeiture has already been dealt with,[11] and there is no need to discuss an action for the money. The subject of distress is extremely intricate,[12] and all that need be said here is that in essence it consists of the right of the landlord, exercisable without application to the court

---

[4] See *Flexman v. Corbett* [1930] 1 Ch. 672.
[5] *Chester v. Buckingham Travel Ltd* [1981] 1 W.L.R. 96. See [1992] Conv. 18 (L. Crabb).
[6] *Coomber v. Howard* (1845) 1 C.B. 440.
[7] *Belfour v. Weston* (1786) 1 T.R. 310.
[8] *Whitehall Court Ltd v. Ettlinger* [1920] 1 K.B. 680.
[9] See above, p. 366.
[10] Above, p. 366.
[11] Above, pp. 354 *et seq.*
[12] See (1991) Law Com. (No. 194), which advocates the abolition of distress.

but ordinarily exercised by a court certificated bailiff, to enter the premises[13] and enforce payment by seizing and selling enough of any goods that are found there.

2. Covenant against assigning, underletting or parting with possession

(a) The tenant's rights

If the lease is silent on the matter the tenant is entitled to assign, underlet or part with possession of the premises without the landlord's consent; for during the term the property is the tenant's. However, a covenant against assignment, underletting or parting with possession of all or any part of the premises is often inserted in leases; and although an assignment or sub-lease made in breach of covenant is valid,[14] the breach will usually give rise to forfeiture or a claim for damages.

(b) Unreasonable withholding of consent

If the covenant is absolute, the landlord can enforce it if he wishes; and, although he may waive a breach in any particular instance, he cannot be compelled to do so, even if his attitude is entirely unreasonable. But if the covenant is one against assigning or sub-letting "without licence or consent" (often called a "qualified covenant") the Landlord and Tenant Act 1927[15] provides that notwithstanding any provision to the contrary the covenant is deemed to be subject to a proviso that the licence or consent is not to be unreasonably withheld. This does not permit the tenant to assign or sub-let without seeking the landlord's consent: if he does so, he is in breach of covenant even if the landlord, if asked, could not properly have withheld his consent.[16] But if he seeks consent and it is unreasonably withheld he may forthwith assign or sub-let without the consent,[17] or else pursue the safer but slower course of seeking a declaration from the court of his right to do so.[18]

The Landlord and Tenant Act 1988 has now strengthened the position of the tenant, particularly against dilatory or evasive landlords.[19] If the tenant serves a written application for consent on the landlord, the landlord is under a duty to give his consent unless it is reasonable not to do so; and, if consent is withheld or is granted subject to conditions, he must give written notice of the reasons for withholding the consent or imposing the conditions, and this notice must be given within a reasonable time.[20] The burden of proof on these matters now lies on the landlord,[21] and any breach of duty under the Act now sounds in damages.[22]

These provisions do not apply to a term in a lease requiring that before seeking to assign the lease the tenant must offer to surrender it to the landlord gratis; for in effect this is a

---

[13] See *Evans v. South Ribble B.C.* [1992] Q.B. 757 (no entry merely by inserting documents through letter-box).
[14] *Old Grovebury Manor Farm Ltd v. W. Seymour Plant and Hire Ltd (No. 2)* [1979] 1 W.L.R. 1397.
[15] s.19(1).
[16] *Eastern Telegraph Co. Ltd v. Dent* [1899] 1 Q.B. 835.
[17] *Treloar v. Bigge* (1874) L.R. 9 Ex. 151.
[18] *Young v. Ashley Gardens Properties Ltd* [1903] 2 Ch. 112.
[19] See *29 Equities Ltd v. Bank Leumi (U.K.) Ltd* [1986] 1 W.L.R. 1490 at 1494.
[20] L. & T.A. 1988, s.1(3), (4). See, *e.g. Midland Bank Plc v. Chart Enterprises Inc.* [1990] 2 E.G.L.R. 59 (delay).
[21] L. & T.A. 1988, s.1(5).
[22] *ibid.*, s.4.

condition precedent to there being any right to assign, rather than the withholding of consent under an existing right.[23] Such a term requires protection by registration.[24]

(c) Reasonableness

In determining whether the withholding of consent is reasonable, the question is whether, having regard to the purpose of the covenant, the landlord can show[25] that the withholding was reasonable.[26] He cannot rely on matters unconnected with the relationship of landlord and tenant, and although he need consider only his own relevant interests, it is unreasonable to withhold consent where the detriment to the tenant would be extreme, and disproportionate to the benefit to the landlord[27]; and contra, if vice versa.[28] The landlord now appears to be confined to the reasons given in response to the tenant's application,[29] and in any event he cannot rely on any reason which did not in fact influence his mind when withholding consent.[30] If any of the reasons given is plainly bad, this may establish unreasonableness.[31] Usually no withholding of consent will be reasonable unless it is based on the person of the assignee or the proposed use of the premises,[32] and this includes the impact of supervening statutes which would confer additional protection on the tenant.[33] Moreover, statute has provided that it is unreasonable to withhold consent on the ground of "colour, race, nationality or ethnic or national origins"; but this does not apply to "small premises" where the landlord or a near relative shares some of the accommodation with others.[34] Unless the lease provides for it, the landlord may not require the payment of a fine or other valuable consideration for giving his consent.[35]

(d) Breach

To amount to a breach of covenant against assignment on underletting, there must in general be some voluntary dealing with the property *inter vivos*. Thus a bequest of the lease is no breach,[36] nor is the involuntary vesting of the lease in the trustee in bankruptcy upon the tenant's bankruptcy,[37] or the compulsory sale of the lease under statutory provisions,[38] as distinct from a voluntary sale by the tenant's trustee in bankruptcy.[39] A mortgage made by the grant of a sub-lease is a breach, but one made by a mere deposit of the title deeds is not, nor is a declaration of trust made by the tenant for the benefit of his creditors.[40] A covenant merely against underletting is perhaps not broken by an assignment or by letting lodgings.

---

[23] *Bocardo S.A. v. S. & M. Hotels Ltd* [1980] 1 W.L.R. 17.
[24] Above, pp. 95–96, 129 *et seq.*
[25] L. & T.A. 1988, s.1(5).
[26] *Leeward Securities Ltd v. Lilyheath Properties Ltd* (1983) 17 H.L.R. 35.
[27] *International Drilling Fluids Ltd v. Louisville Investments (Uxbridge) Ltd* [1986] Ch. 513.
[28] *Deverall v. Wyndham* [1989] 1 E.G.L.R. 57.
[29] See L. & T.A. 1988, s.1(3), (5).
[30] *Bromley Park Garden Estates Ltd v. Moss* [1982] 1 W.L.R. 1019.
[31] See *Berenyi v. Watford B.C.* (1980) 256 E.G. 271.
[32] See *Viscount Tredegar v. Harwood* [1929] A.C. 72.
[33] *West Layton Ltd v. Ford* [1979] Q.B. 593. Consider, *e.g.* the Leasehold Reform Act 1967 and the Rent Act 1977: see below, pp. 592, 608.
[34] Race Relations Act 1976, s.24; see ss.1–3, 22.
[35] L.P.A. 1925, s.144, replacing C.A. 1892, s.3.
[36] *Fox v. Swann* (1655) Sty. 482.
[37] *Re Riggs* [1901] 2 K.B. 16.
[38] *Slipper v. Tottenham & Hampstead Junction Ry.* (1867) L.R. 4 Eq. 112.
[39] *Re Wright* [1949] Ch. 729.
[40] *Gentle v. Faulkner* [1900] 2 K.B. 267.

3. Covenant to repair

(a) Construction of covenant

In long leases, the tenant usually covenants to do all repairs; in short leases, the landlord frequently assumes liability for external and structural repairs, and in some cases is compelled by statute to do so.[41] Subject to this, in every case, the matter is one for negotiation. If no provision is made for repairs, neither party is liable for them, apart from statute and the general law relating to waste.[42] The extent of the liability of any party under a repairing covenant depends, of course, upon the wording of the covenant, but expressions such as "tenantable repair", "sufficient repair", or "good and substantial repair" seem to add little to the meaning of the word "repair".[43] On a letting of premises that are out of repair, a covenant to "keep" them in good repair requires them to be put into good repair.[44] If the covenant is qualified by words such as "fair wear and tear excepted", they exclude liability for defects due to reasonable use of the premises or the action of the elements, but not for consequential damage caused, for example by rain entering through an unrepaired skylight.[45]

(b) Repair

"Repair" is not confined to restoring the original structure but extends to replacing subsidiary parts of the building which can no longer be repaired, as by rebuilding a wall,[46] replacing the roof,[47] or providing new drainpipes for old. It is often difficult to draw the line between "repair" and "renewal" or "improvement". The matter is essentially one of degree, and in particular whether the works will so change the character of the building as to restore to the landlord a building that is wholly different from that demised.[48] The basic question is whether in all the circumstances of the case the requisite work as a whole can fairly be called a repair. It may be so substantial as to be beyond anything that a reasonable person could contemplate as being a repair.[49] The circumstances to be considered include the terms of the lease; the nature of the building; its state when let; the nature and extent of the repair; the nature, extent and cost of the works to be done, and who is to do them; the value and life-span of the building, and the effect of the works on them; and the comparative cost of alternative remedial works, their effect on the occupants and the likelihood of a recurrence in each case: and the weight to be attached to these factors will vary from case to case.[50] Thus to remedy an inherent defect may or may not be repair. Curing dampness in a modern high-class flat by inserting a silicone damp course will be a repair,[51] whereas it is not a repair where the damp in an aged cellar with porous bricks can be cured only by constructing new walls.[52] Premises that are still in the same physical condition as they were when first let are not out of repair

---

[41] Above, pp. 369 *et seq.*
[42] Above, pp. 48 *et seq.*
[43] *Anstruther-Gough-Calthorpe v. McOscar* [1924] 1 K.B. 716 at 722, 723.
[44] *Proudfoot v. Hart* (1890) 25 Q.B.D. 42 at 50.
[45] *Regis Property Co. Ltd v. Dudley* [1959] A.C. 370.
[46] *Lurcott v. Wakely* [1911] 1 K.B. 905.
[47] *Elite Investments Ltd v. T. I. Bainbridge Silencers Ltd* [1986] 2 E.G.L.R. 43.
[48] *Ravenseft Properties Ltd v. Davstone (Holdings) Ltd* [1980] Q.B. 12.
[49] *Brew Brothers Ltd v. Snax (Ross) Ltd* [1970] 1 Q.B. 612.
[50] *Holding and Management Ltd v. Property Holding Plc* [1990] 1 All E.R. 938 at 945 (omitted from [1989] 1 W.L.R. 1313).
[51] *Elmcroft Developments Ltd v. Tankersley-Sawyer* (1984) 15 H.L.R. 63.
[52] *Pembery v. Lamdin* [1940] 2 All E.R. 434.

merely because through some inherent structural defect the basement has been flooded, though without doing any harm.[53]

(c) Enforcement

As has already been seen,[54] the court has statutory power to order specific performance of the landlord's repairing covenants in favour of a tenant of a dwelling-house[55] and it can do so in favour of a tenant of any type of property under its inherent jurisdiction.[56] The court may also order specific performance of the tenant's repairing covenants in favour of the landlord but it will only do so where damages would be an inadequate remedy. An example is where the lease contains no proviso for re-entry and forfeiture, where the property is deteriorating and the landlord has no right of access to carry out the repairs himself.[57] In other circumstances, he will have to elect between forfeiture and an award of damages. (Both require leave to sue in respect of any property (other than an agricultural holding) let for a term of years certain of not less than seven years which has at least three years unexpired[58] and special rules govern the measure of damages.[59])

(d) Measure of damages

The measure of damages recoverable by a tenant for the breach of a repairing covenant is the cost of carrying out the repairs. However, the measure of damages recoverable by a landlord for such a breach formerly varied according to the time of the breach. If the breach occurred during the term, damages were calculated on the decrease in the value of the reversion caused by the breach,[60] *i.e.* on the difference between the value of the landlord's interest with the repairs done and its value without. Thus the longer the lease had to run, the less would be the damages. But if the breach occurred at the end of the term, the cost of repairing the premises was recoverable by the landlord[61] even if he did not propose to spend the money in making the repairs but intended to demolish the premises instead. Now, however, by the Landlord and Tenant Act 1927,[62] damages for breach of a repairing covenant are not to exceed the diminution in the value of the reversion, though if the repairs are going to be done, that diminution will usually be measured by the cost of the repairs.[63] Further, no damages are recoverable if the premises are to be demolished, or structurally altered in such a way as to make the repairs valueless, at or soon after the end of the term. There are special provisions enabling the court in certain cases to relieve the tenant from liability for internal decorative repairs.[64]

(e) Leave to sue

There are also provisions which protect the tenant of any property (except agricultural holdings) let for a term of years certain of not less than seven years which has at least three

---

[53] *Post Office v. Aquarius Properties Ltd* [1987] 1 All E.R. 1055.
[54] Above, p. 368.
[55] L. & T.A. 1985, s.17.
[56] *Jeune v. Queen's Cross Properties Ltd* [1974] Ch. 97.
[57] *Rainbow Estates Ltd v. Tokenhold Ltd* [1999] Ch. 64.
[58] Leasehold Property (Repairs) Act 1938, as extended by L. & T.A. 1954, s.51; below, p. 380.
[59] See below.
[60] *Ebbetts v. Conquest* [1895] 2 Ch. 377 (affirmed [1896] A.C. 490).
[61] *Joyner v. Weeks* [1891] 2 Q.B. 31.
[62] s.18(1).
[63] *Smiley v. Townshend* [1950] 2 K.B. 311.
[64] L.P.A. 1925, s.147.

years unexpired.[65] The lack of any provision for relief against claims for damages for non-repair often enabled landlords to force tenants to surrender their leases prematurely, and so the Leasehold Property (Repairs) Act 1938[66] provides that no action for damages for breach of a covenant to repair the property can be brought unless the landlord has first served on the tenant a notice in the form required by the Law of Property Act 1925, s.146,[67] and one month has elapsed thereafter. Further, whether the landlord is claiming damages or forfeiture, he cannot proceed without the leave of the court in such cases if within 28 days the tenant serves on the landlord a counter-notice claiming the protection of the Act; and the notice served by the landlord must inform the tenant of his right to serve a counter-notice. The court can grant leave only on certain specified grounds, such as that the cost of immediate repair would be small compared with the cost of repair in the future. An application for leave as a preliminary to proceedings for forfeiture is registrable as a pending land action.[68] The Act does not apply where the landlord, under a power in the lease, enters and carries out the repairs, and sues the tenant for the cost, for his claim against the tenant is for a debt, and not for "damages" within the Act.[69]

(f) Deducting cost of repairs from rent

A tenant who does repairs for which the landlord is liable is entitled to deduct the cost from the present or future rent,[70] though this should not be done without prior notification to the landlord.[71]

4. Covenant to insure

A covenant to insure against fire is broken if the premises are uninsured for any period, however short, even if no fire occurs.[72]

Sect. 4. Statutory protection for tenants

Three important classes of property are subject to special statutory codes designed to protect the tenant, particularly by giving him security of tenure and restricting the rent. The three classes are most agricultural holdings, most business premises, and many dwelling-houses. They will be dealt with in due course.[73]

---

[65] Leasehold Property (Repairs) Act 1938, as extended by L. & T.A. 1954, s.51.
[66] s.1.
[67] See above, p. 360.
[68] Above, pp. 99, 129 *et seq.*
[69] *Hamilton v. Martell Securities Ltd* [1984] Ch. 266; *Colchester Estates (Cardiff) v. Carlton Industries Plc* [1986] Ch. 80.
[70] *Lee-Parker v. Izzet* [1971] 1 W.L.R. 1688; *Asco Developments Ltd v. Gordon* [1978] E.G.D. 376.
[71] See [1981] Conv. 199 (A. Waite) for this and other precautions.
[72] *Penniall v. Harborne* (1848) 11 Q.B. 386.
[73] Below, pp. 580 *et seq.*

PART 6—LEASEHOLD COVENANTS

Sect. 1. General principles

Usually, the expression "covenant" means a promise contained in a deed; but in the law of landlord and tenant the expression "covenant" also includes other enforceable agreements.[74] It is necessary to consider how far covenants in leases are enforceable. As a result of the enactment of the Landlord and Tenant (Covenants) Act 1995 ("the 1995 Act"),[75] the law now differs depending on whether the lease in question was created before 1996 (" an old lease") or after 1995 ("a new lease"). However, a lease which is granted pursuant to an agreement or to a court order made before 1996[76] or pursuant to the exercise of an option granted before 1996, no matter when that option is exercised,[77] is an old lease. The rules will first be summarised and then considered in detail.

1. Enforcement against the parties to an old lease

(a) Against an original party to the lease

As between the original parties to a lease, there is privity of contract simply because the parties concerned have made a legally enforceable agreement.[78] Clearly, if two people have agreed to do or not to do certain things, their obligations bind them, whether or not their contract has anything to do with land, and whether the covenant is negative or positive. The covenants can be enforced both at law, by an action for damages, and in equity, by an injunction or specific performance. Consequently, covenants can be enforced against an original party to a lease throughout its entire term, irrespective of the fact that he has assigned his interest to a third party. However, the ability of the landlord for the time being to recover "fixed charges" (rent, service charges and any other liquidated sums) from the original lessee has now been restricted. He can now only do so if he serves notice on the original lessee of his intention so to do within six months of each fixed charge becoming due. Where a covenant is enforceable under privity of contract, there is no need to look further.

(b) Against an assignee of an original party

Where either the landlord for the time being or the tenant for the time being (or both of them) is not an original party to the lease, there is no privity of contract but there is said to be privity of estate between the parties to the lease for the time being provided that it has been created and assigned with the necessary formalities.[79] In this case, any covenants in the lease which touch and concern the land, such as repairing covenants, are enforceable both at law and in equity. But covenants which do not relate to the land are not enforceable under this head nor is the burden of any covenants in a lease which has been created or assigned only in equity. Where a covenant is enforceable under privity of estate, there is no need to look further.

(c) Against a guarantor

Any guarantor, whether of an original party or of an assignee, is in exactly the same position as the person whose liability he is guaranteeing.

---

[74] See *Weg Motors Ltd v. Hales* [1961] Ch. 176 at 193; [1962] Ch. 49 at 73.
[75] Based on Law Com. No. 174;. see S. N. Bridge [1996] C.L.J. 313.
[76] L. & T.(C.)A. 1995, s.1(3).
[77] *ibid.*, s.1(6).
[78] See the example above, p. 339.
[79] *ibid.*

2. Enforcement against the parties to a new lease

(a) Against the landlord and tenant for the time being

Liability under all covenants by the original lessor and the original lessee passes on the assignment of their respective interests to the persons to whom those interests are successively assigned no matter how the lease was created and assigned. The only exceptions relate to those covenants which are expressed to be personal to the person who entered into them, to those which require registration under the Land Charges Act 1972 or the Land Registration Acts of 1925 or 2002, and to those which are no longer enforceable.

(b) Against former landlords and tenants

Where any tenant, whether the original lessee or a subsequent assignee, assigns his lease, he will thereupon be released from the burden of any covenants which would otherwise have bound him (a subsequent assignee would only have been liable anyway where he has covenanted directly with the landlord for the time being). He will also cease to be entitled to the benefit of the covenants entered into by the landlord. However, a landlord can have recourse to the tenant who held the lease immediately before the tenant for the time being if the lease contains a covenant requiring the consent of the landlord to any assignment. In these circumstances, the landlord can give his consent only on condition that the assigning tenant guarantees the performance of the covenants by the tenant to whom he is assigning (such an agreement is known as an "authorised guarantee agreement" or an "AGA"). However, the landlord will only be able to recover a fixed charge under an AGA if he serves notice on the former tenant that he proposes to do so within six months of the sum becoming due.

On the other hand, where the original lessor assigns his interest, he is not automatically released from liability under his covenants, but he may normally, before or within four weeks of the assignment taking place, apply to the tenant for the time being to be released. If the tenant refuses his consent, the lessor may apply to the court for a declaration that it is reasonable for the covenant to be released. A subsequent landlord is not liable under his covenants anyway once he has assigned on.

(c) Against a guarantor

Any guarantor, whether of the landlord and tenant for the time being or of former landlords and tenants, is in exactly the same position as the person whose liability he is guaranteeing.

3. Enforcement against others

(a) Direct enforcement

Where covenants are not enforceable under the rules which have just been discussed, the general rule is that covenants concerning the land are not directly enforceable. This is the case as between a landlord and a sub-tenant and as between the vendor of freehold land and a person who subsequently buys it from the purchaser; this is also the case as between the landlord for the time being of an old lease and a tenant other than the original lessee where the lease has been created or assigned only in equity. To this rule there are three exceptions, the second of which is of great importance.

(i) Benefit: First, even the common law allowed the benefit of certain covenants (*i.e.* the right to sue on the covenant) to be assigned with land; and equity followed the law. One example already mentioned[80] is that of covenants for title, the benefit of which runs with the land, so that whoever is entitled to the land is entitled to the benefit of the covenants. But the burden of a covenant (*i.e.* the liability to be sued upon it) cannot be assigned; at law, if there is no privity of estate the covenantor alone can be sued on a covenant.

(ii) Restrictive covenants in equity: Secondly, equity allows the transmission of the burden (as well as the benefit) of restrictive covenants affecting the land, *i.e.* covenants which are negative in nature, restraining the doing of some act, such as building on the land. As usual, however, a purchaser of a legal estate for value takes free from such burdens if he takes without notice or if the covenants are void against him for want of registration.[81]

(iii) Mutual benefit and burden: Thirdly, equity sometimes allows the transmission of the burden (as well as the benefit) of positive covenants under the principle of mutual benefit and burden. If land cannot be enjoyed without the use of a particular benefit, the burden of any corresponding obligation can be enforced against the person who is benefitting. Thus, a covenant to contribute to the costs of maintenance of the footpaths and roads of a private estate can be enforced against the owners of all the houses on it since they cannot reach their properties without using the footpaths and roads.[82]

Where a covenant is enforceable under one of these three heads, there is no need to look further. Where it is not, it may be able to be enforced indirectly.

(b) Indirect enforcement

Where a leasehold covenant cannot be enforced directly, it may sometimes be enforced indirectly by virtue of a forfeiture clause in the lease. Thus if L leases land to T, and T sub-lets it to S, L cannot directly enforce the covenants in the lease against S. However, proceedings for forfeiture of the lease will normally impel S to comply with the covenant (such as by doing the requisite repairs), and so avoid losing his interest; for, if a lease is forfeited, the sub-tenancy falls with it. Unlike direct enforcement, this indirect enforcement is subject to the important powers of the court to grant relief against forfeiture.[83] Yet often it will be better to perform the covenant than to face the uncertainty, delay and cost of seeking relief. There seems to be nothing to confine this type of enforcement to covenants which are enforceable against T; and forfeiture clauses may be imposed on the assignment of a lease or on the grant of a fee simple.[84]

4. Liability of personal representatives

(a) Personal liability

Personal representatives of the original lessee and of his assignees (but not of their guarantors) may incur personal liability. If an original lessee or one of his assignees dies and his personal representatives take possession of the demised premises (something which the personal representatives of their guarantors cannot of course do), the personal representatives occupy the position of assignees of the lease and so become personally liable on the covenants.[85] However, as regards the payment of rent (but not as regards other covenants) a

---

[80] Above, p. 163.
[81] See above, pp. 104, 129; and see below, pp. 395, 405.
[82] Below, p. 463.
[83] Above, pp. 357, 362.
[84] See above, p. 83; below, p. 463.
[85] *Tilney v. Norris* (1700) 1 Ld.Raym. 553.

personal representative may by proper pleading limit his liability to the yearly value of the premises.[86]

(b) Representative liability

Personal representatives of the original lessee and of his assignees who do not take possession of the premises, personal representatives of the original lessor and of his assignees, and personal representatives of the guarantors of all of them incur no personal liability upon any covenant[87]; their liability is only representative. On the death of any of them, his personal representatives have exactly the same liability as the person whom they represent but only to the extent of the assets of the deceased in their hands.[88]

(c) Protection

If the deceased was an original party to an old lease or his guarantor, the personal representatives are in a difficult position since they cannot tell what breaches of covenant may occur in the future. This is also the case where the deceased either held a new lease immediately before the tenant for the time being and entered into an AGA, or is a former landlord of a new lease who has not yet been released, or has guaranteed the liabilities of any such person. Although it has long been settled that the personal representatives need not put aside part of the estate as an indemnity fund for future breaches,[89] their position used to be precarious in other respects. In order to make it unnecessary for personal representatives to seek the protection of the court in such cases, the Trustee Act 1925[90] provides that if personal representatives who are liable as such under any covenant in a lease or any guarantee given in respect of any such liability—

(i) satisfy any existing liabilities which have been claimed,

(ii) set aside any fixed sum agreed to be laid out on the premises, and

(iii) assign the lease to the person entitled under the will or intestacy, or to a purchaser,

they cease to have representative liability in respect of the assets which came to their hands. This also now applies to any liability under an AGA.[91] This does not render the assets immune from liability, for they may be followed into the hands of the beneficiaries[92]; but the personal representatives need not concern themselves with this. These provisions do not of course protect personal representatives from their personal liability if they have taken possession of the premises. However, they may set aside a fund from the estate by way of indemnity,[93] to be distributed when no longer needed.[94]

---

[86] *Rendall v. Andreae* (1892) 61 L.J.Q.B. 630.
[87] *Wollaston v. Hakewill* (1841) 3 Man. & G. 297 at 320.
[88] *Helier v. Casebert* (1665) 1 Lev. 127; *Youngmin v. Heath* [1974] 1 W.L.R. 135 (weekly tenancy).
[89] *King v. Malcott* (1852) 9 Hare 692.
[90] s.26(1), replacing L.P. Am.A. 1859, s.27.
[91] s.26 (1A) added by L. & T.(C.)A. 1995.
[92] s.26(2).
[93] *Re Owers* [1941] Ch. 389.
[94] *Re Lewis* [1939] Ch. 232.

Sect. 2. Position of the original parties to an old lease

1. Basic position

If a lease is granted by L to T, there is privity of contract between them. The effect of this is not only that L may enforce all the covenants in the lease against T while he retains it, but also that T remains liable on the covenants for the whole term, notwithstanding any assignment of the lease.[95] Thus if T takes a lease for 99 years, he makes himself liable for 99 years, even if he assigns the lease after only one year has run; thus, L may accordingly sue T for unpaid rent or for damages if the covenant to repair is not observed by the assignee. Similarly L remains liable on his covenants for the whole term, notwithstanding any assignment of the reversion by him.[96]

2. Defences

When a covenant has not been performed, the defences available to the original parties are few. There may have been such a change in the terms of the original lease that there will be held to have been a surrender and a re-grant, in which case both parties will be released. However, this will only be held where the variation affects the legal estate and increases either the extent of the premises or the term in a manner not envisaged by the original lease.[97] Other variations which are not envisaged by the terms of the lease will not bind the original parties but they will remain bound by the original terms of the lease; consequently, an increase in rent other than as a result of the valid exercise of a rent review clause in the original lease will not bind the original lessee but he will remain liable for rent at the original rate.[98] A release of an assignee from liability may also release the original lessee.[99] However, the release only of a surety of an assignee will not do so.[1]

3. Effect of rule

Save as indicated above, the rule is strict. An original lessee remains liable on covenants which, after assigning the lease, he is powerless to perform,[2] unless by apt wording in the lease he has limited his liability to the time while the lease is vested in him.[3] Otherwise he must rely on his rights to indemnity from subsequent assignees,[4] and these may prove to be of little worth.[5] As has already been indicated, if the lease contains a rent review clause, he will be liable for any increased rent that has been properly fixed under the clause, even though he has had no say in the increase.[6] However, where a lease is continued by statute beyond its original term, the liability of the original lessee will cease unless, obviously, he is still the tenant in occupation or, less obviously, the lease contains clear words to the contrary effect.[7] The position of the original lessor is exactly the same; he also remains liable on his covenants even after assigning his reversion.[8]

---

[95] *Thursby v. Plant* (1670) 1 Wms.Saund. 230. The rule does not apply to perpetually renewable leases; see above p. 351.

[96] *Stuart v. Joy* [1904] 1 K.B. 368; L.P.A. 1925, s.142(2).

[97] *Friends Provident Life Office v. British Railways Board* [1996] 1 All E.R. 336.

[98] *ibid.*

[99] *Deanplan Ltd v. Mahmoud* [1993] Ch. 151.

[1] *Allied London Investments Ltd v. Hambro Life Assurance Ltd* (1983) 269 E.G. 41.

[2] *Thames Manufacturing Co. Ltd v. Perrotts (Nichol & Peyton) Ltd* (1985) 50 P. & C.R. 1.

[3] See *Johnsey Estates Ltd v. Webb* [1990] 1 E.G.L.R. 80 (sureties).

[4] See below, p. 392.

[5] See, *e.g. Weaver v. Mogford* [1988] 2 E.G.L.R. 48.

[6] *Centrovincial Estates Plc v. Bulk Storage Ltd* (1983) 46 P. & C.R. 393; *Selous Street Properties Ltd v. Oronel Fabrics Ltd* (1984) 270 E.G. 643.

[7] *City of London Corporation v. Fell* [1994] 1 A.C. 458.

[8] See *Hua Chiao Commercial Bank Ltd v. Chiaphua Industries Ltd* [1987] A.C. 99.

This rule is obviously more likely adversely to affect original lessees than original lessors and its stringency, ill-understood by many lessees, was emphasised in the years immediately prior to the enactment of the 1995 Act when there was a slump in property values and rents being paid by tenants under existing leases substantially exceeded the rent payable under new leases. Assignees of leases, particularly companies holding commercial premises, would simply stop paying the rent and go into insolvent liquidation. Their liquidator would then disclaim the lease and their landlords would then claim the rent from the original lessees, who might have assigned the lease many years before. This was one of the principal reasons why the 1995 Act was enacted when it was.

4. Problem notices

The majority of the 1995 Act applies only to new leases. However, the ability of the landlord for the time being of an old lease to recover "fixed charges" (rent, service charges and any other liquidated sums) from the original lessee is now subject to provisions in that Act[9] which apply to both old leases and new leases. A landlord can now only recover such fixed charges from a former tenant if he serves notice, in a prescribed form, on that tenant within six months of any fixed charge becoming due. This notice informs the former tenant that the sum is due and that the landlord intends to recover that sum from him. A notice of this kind is known as a "problem notice" and is sufficiently served if it is sent by registered post to the last known abode of the original lessee.[10]

5. Overriding leases

An original lessee who pays in full any sum so claimed under a problem notice is entitled to what the 1995 Act describes as an "overriding lease", a lease for three days longer than the original lease (unless the landlord's interest would thereby be displaced) which contains the same covenants as the original lease save for those expressed to be personal between the landlord and tenant. This overriding lease is a reversionary lease and so is interposed between the interest of the landlord and the lease of the tenant for the time being[11]; the original lessee therefore becomes the landlord of the tenant for the time being. Consequently, any breach of covenant by the tenant for the time being will enable the original lessee to forfeit the lease, assuming of course that there is a right of re-entry or forfeiture, and thereby cause his overriding lease to come into possession. An overriding lease held by the original lessee of an old lease is itself an old lease[12]; so he will remain liable to the landlord for the time being for the whole of the remainder of his term. However, he will normally be able to cover the amount of any liability by assigning or sub-letting, although this will not be the case in the event of another slump in property values of the type which occurred in the years immediately prior to the enactment of the 1995 Act.

6. Direct covenants by assignees

It should also be mentioned that many covenants not to assign the lease without the lessor's consent provide that consent will not be forthcoming unless the assignee of the lease covenants directly with the lessor to observe all the tenant's covenants for the remainder of the term. A refusal of consent in the absence of such a direct covenant is reasonable. Where

---

[9] s.17.
[10] *Commercial Union Life Assurance Co. Ltd v. Moustafa* [1999] 2 E.G.L.R. 44.
[11] L. & T.(C.)A. 1995, ss.19–20.
[12] *ibid.*, s.20(1).

an assignee does covenant directly in this way, he will from then on be in exactly the same position as the original lessee[13] and will be liable to the landlord for the time being for any breach of the tenant's covenants for the rest of the term.

7. Liability of guarantors

Any guarantor of an original party to an old lease or of an assignee of the lease who has covenanted directly with the lessor is in exactly the same position as the person whose liability he is guaranteeing. Where a landlord wishes to recover fixed charges from the guarantor of the original lessee of an old lease, he is obviously obliged to serve a problem notice on the guarantor but is not also obliged to serve one on the original lessee.[14]

Sect. 3. Position where the assignment of an old lease is effective at law

Where an old lease has been created and assigned with the formalities required by the law and has neither been created nor assigned only in equity,[15] the benefit and burden of a covenant in that lease will usually pass to assignees of the lease or of the reversion. Yet the liability of such assignees depends on many factors, including the following:

(i) whether the covenants "touch and concern" the land;

(ii) whether the burden of the covenants has passed to the assignee of the lease or of the reversion, as the case may be;

(iii) whether the benefit of the covenants has passed to the assignee of the reversion or of the lease, as the case may be;

(iv) how far an assignee of a lease is liable to indemnify the original lessee;

(v) what effect a severance of the reversion has;

(vi) what rights an assignee of the reversion has in respect of previous breaches.

These factors will now be considered.

1. Covenants touching and concerning the land

The rights and liabilities of assignees of an old lease, either of the lease or of the reversion, depend on whether or not the covenant in question "touches and concerns the land" or, to use more modern phraseology, has "reference to the subject-matter" of the lease.[16] Any covenant which affects the landlord *qua* landlord or the tenant *qua* tenant may be said to touch and concern the land.[17] A covenant by a tenant touches and concerns the land if (i) it is beneficial only to the reversioner for the time being; (ii) it affects the nature, quality, mode of user or value of the reversioner's land; and (iii) it is not expressed to be personal in nature[18]; and correspondingly for covenants by a landlord. Yet the rules have been assailed as being

---

[13] *Deanplan Ltd v. Mahmoud* [1993] Ch. 151 (release of one such assignee by the release of a later assignee).
[14] *Cheverell Estates Ltd v. Harris* [1998] 1 E.G.L.R. 27.
[15] Above, pp. 342 *et seq*. For covenants in equitable leases, see below, p. 394.
[16] L.P.A. 1925, ss.141(1), 142(1).
[17] *Breams Property Investment Co. Ltd v. Strougler* [1948] 2 K.B. 1.
[18] *P. & A. Swift Investments v. Combined English Stores Group Plc* [1989] A.C. 632 at 642; and see *Horsey Estates Ltd v. Steiger* [1899] 2 Q.B. 79 at 89.

"purely arbitrary" and the distinctions as mostly being "quite illogical"[19]; it was the proposals of the Law Commission that this test should be abandoned[20] which eventually led to the enactment of the 1995 Act.[21]

Some examples of the operation of the test may be helpful: covenants in the left-hand columns below have been held to touch and concern the land, while those in the right-hand columns have been held not to do so.

(a) Covenants by a lessee of an old lease

To pay rent	To pay an annual sum to a third party[22]
To repair	To repair and renew the tools of a smithy standing on the land[23]
To pay the landlord £40 towards redecoration[24]	Not to employ persons living in other parishes to work in the demised mill[25]
To use as a private dwelling-house only	
Not to assign the lease without the lessor's consent	

(b) Covenants by a lessor of an old lease

To renew the lease[26]	To give the lessee the first refusal if adjoining land is sold[27]
To supply the demised premises with water	To pay at the end of the lease for chattels not amounting to fixtures
Not to build on certain parts of the adjoining land	To pay the tenant £500 at the end of the lease unless a new lease is granted[28]
	To repay to the tenant money deposited as security against breaches of covenant[29]

(c) Covenants by a guarantor

Covenants by a person who guarantees the liability of either a lessee or a lessor of an old lease touch and concern the land and are enforceable by assignees of the reversion and the lease to the extent that those liabilities arise under covenants which themselves touch and concern the land.[30]

(d) Estate contracts

The enforceability of covenants in an old lease which also constitute estate contracts is not determined by whether or not they touch and concern the land but by whether or not they are

[19] See *Grant v. Edmondson* [1931] 1 Ch. 1 at 29, *per* Romer L.J.
[20] (1988) Law Com. No. 174 at p. 17.
[21] Other factors determined the timing of the enactment; see above, p. 386.
[22] *Williams v. Earle* (1868) L.R. 3 Q.B. 739.
[23] *Boyer v. Warbey* [1953] 1 Q.B. 234.
[24] *Mayho v. Buckhurst* (1617) Cro.Jac. 438.
[25] *Congleton Corporation v. Pattison* (1808) 10 East 130.
[26] *Richards v. Sydenham* (1703) 2 Vern. 447. The inclusion of this is regarded as somewhat anomalous: *Woodall v. Clifton* [1905] 2 Ch. 257 at 279.
[27] *Collison v. Lettsom* (1815) 6 Taunt. 224.
[28] *Re Hunter's Lease* [1942] Ch. 124.
[29] *Hua Chiao Commercial Bank Ltd v. Chiaphua Industries Ltd* [1987] A.C. 99.
[30] *P. & A. Swift Investments v. Combined English Stores Group Plc.* [1989] A.C. 632; *Coronation Street Industrial Properties Ltd v. Ingall Industries Plc.* [1989] 1 W.L.R. 304.

enforceable as estate contracts. Covenants giving the lessee the right to renew his lease[31] or to purchase the freehold or leasehold reversion[32] are estate contracts by the lessor. So are notices by lessees exercising statutory rights to purchase the freehold or to take an extended lease.[33] On the other hand, covenants obliging the lessee to offer to surrender his lease to the lessor before seeking to assign it are estate contracts by the lessee.[34]

In the case of unregistered land, failure to protect such estate contracts by the registration of a Class C(iv) land charge will render them void against any assignee of the party burdened by the covenant.[35] In the case of registered land, however, the party with the benefit of the covenant will normally either be in actual occupation or in receipt of the rent and profits. Therefore, in the event that he has not protected his estate contract by registering a notice or a caution, under the present law he will normally have an interest which overrides registration virtue of his actual occupation or receipt of rent and profits and which will therefore bind ry assignee.[36] (The only exceptions will be where a lease is rent free,[37] the lessor is taking steps to enforce the payment of rent[38] or the lessee has ceased to be in actual occupa-n.[39]) However, when the Land Registration Act 2002 comes into force, the protection ,.en by virtue of the receipt of rent and profits will be taken away and the protection given by virtue of actual occupation will be reduced[40] although these changes are subject to the transitional provisions which have already been considered.[41] Lessors and lessees who have sub-let will then be prejudiced unless they have protected their estate contracts by registering a notice. Lessors and lessees who have neither protected their estate contracts nor have interests which override registration are in the same position as in the case of unregistered land and lose the benefit of their estate contracts as against any assignee for value (which will cease to include marriage consideration when the Land Registration Act 2002 comes into force[42]).

It should be noted that where a covenant which constitutes an estate contract is not enforceable against a successor in title to the party burdened by it, the original lessor or lessee will nevertheless be liable for damages for breach of that contract to whoever has the benefit of the estate contract. It is not a defence to such an action that the estate contract would have been enforceable against the successor in title had it been protected by registration in the appropriate way.[43] While the measure of damages is likely to be minimal in the case of options, unless the option was to acquire the interest in question at less than the market rate, the measure may well be very substantial when the claimant is a lessee who has been unable to exercise a statutory right to purchase the freehold or to take an extended lease or a lessor who has been unable to take advantage of a covenant obliging the lessee to offer to surrender his lease to the lessor before seeking to assign it.

[31] *Phillips v. Mobil Oil Ltd* [1989] 1 W.L.R. 888.
[32] *Midland Bank Trust Co. Ltd v. Green* [1981] A.C. 513.
[33] Leasehold Reform Act 1967, s.5; below, p. 549.
[34] *Greene v. Church Commissioners for England* [1974] Ch. 467.
[35] *Midland Bank Trust Co. Ltd v. Green* [1981] A.C. 513; *Greene v. Church Commissioners for England* [1974] Ch. 467; *Phillips v. Mobil Oil Ltd* [1989] 1 W.L.R. 888.
[36] *Webb v. Pollmount Ltd* [1966] Ch. 584.
[37] See *Strand Securities Ltd v. Caswell* [1965] Ch. 958.
[38] *E.S. Schwab & Co. v. McCarthy* (1976) 31 P. & C.R. 196.
[39] It has never yet been held that anyone has ceased to be in actual occupation once he has been but it must be possible.
[40] Above, p. 127.
[41] Above, p. 128.
[42] L.R.A. 2002, s.131(1).
[43] *Wright v. Dean* [1948] Ch. 686.

2. Principles of transmission

Having considered which covenants touch and concern the land, the rights and liabilities of assignees and their guarantors must next be examined.[44] As in every case when the question of enforcing legal liabilities arises, two separate questions must be considered:

  (i) whether the potential defendant is liable; and

  (ii) whether the potential claimant is entitled to sue.

In the case of the rights and liabilities of assignees under covenants concerning land and their guarantors, these questions may be expressed in the following form:

  (i) whether the burden of the covenant has passed to the potential defendant; and

  (ii) whether the benefit of the covenant has passed to the potential claimant.

These questions are governed by the common law where the lessee assigns his lease, but by statute where the lessor assigns his reversion.

3. Where the lessee assigns his lease

If L grants a legal lease to T, and T assigns it by deed to A, the common law rule laid down in *Spencer's Case*[45] is that A is entitled to the benefit, and subject to the burden, of all covenants and conditions touching and concerning the land; for there is privity of estate. In short, both the benefit and the burden of the covenants run with the land. In applying this rule, the following points should be noted.

(a) The lease must be in due form

Originally, the benefit and burden of covenants ran only with a lease by deed, but it can now run with a lease for three years or less made by unsealed writing.[46] A legal oral tenancy for less than three years has been held not to suffice,[47] but this rule may no longer be law.[48]

(b) There must be a legal assignment of the whole term

(i) Legal assignment: The benefit and burden of covenants run with the lease only in the case of a legal assignment of the whole of the remainder of the term.[49] Where instead of an assignment there has been a sub-lease, the sub-lessee takes neither the benefit nor the burden of the covenants in the lease, even if his sub-lease is only one day shorter than the head lease. Thus if L leases land to X for 99 years, X assigns the lease to T, and T sub-leases the land to S for the residue of the term of 99 years less one day, S is not an assignee and there is privity neither of contract nor of estate between L and S. T is still the tenant under the lease for 99 years, and until he assigns it, he remains liable upon it. Consequently if S does some act which is contrary to a covenant in the 99 years' lease, L cannot sue S but can sue T. In

---

[44] See generally (1991) 11 Leg.Stud. 47 (R. Thornton).
[45] (1583) 5 Co.Rep. 16a.
[46] See *Boyer v. Warbey* [1953] 1 Q.B. 234.
[47] *Elliot v. Johnson* (1866) L.R. 2 Q.B. 120.
[48] See *Boyer v. Warbey* [1953] 1 Q.B. 234 at 246; and see above, p. 342, for the tenancies which can be created orally; see also below, p. 393.
[49] *West v. Dobb* (1869) L.R. 4 Q.B. 634; above, p. 353.

practice, the covenants inserted in a sub-lease are always at least as stringent as those in the head lease, so that if a sub-tenant does some act forbidden by the head lease, this will constitute a breach of the covenants in the sub-lease and thus make the sub-tenant liable to the tenant, though not to the head lessor.

(ii) No legal assignment: If there is no legal assignment, the benefit and burden of covenants in a lease do not run with it under the Rule in *Spencer's Case*. Thus as a legal assignment can be made only by deed,[50] the covenants will not run where the assignment is made in some other way (such as by a contract to assign) and so takes effect only in equity.[51] However, the benefit but not the burden of the covenants can be expressly assigned.[52] A squatter on leasehold land is not even an assignee of the lease, and so he can neither sue nor be sued on the covenants.[53] But both an equitable assignee and a squatter may be estopped from denying liability on the covenants in the lease.[54] In the case of registered land, privity of estate may perhaps be established once the squatter has become registered as proprietor of the lease in place of the person whose title he has barred.[55]

(ii) Things *in posse*: The burden of a covenant relating to a thing *in posse*, requiring the lessee to do something entirely new (such as to erect a building) formerly ran with the land only if the lessee had expressly covenanted for himself and his assigns that the covenant would be performed.[56] This rule still applies to leases granted before 1926. However, although many leases granted before 1926 are still in existence, it is hardly likely that any such covenants remain unperformed. The rule does not apply to leases granted after 1925[57] and it has never applied to covenants relating to things *in esse* (in existence).

(c) Liability of assignees

Although the original lessee is liable for all breaches of covenant throughout the term of the lease, an assignee is liable only for breaches committed while the lease is vested in him. He is under no liability for breaches committed either before the lease was assigned to him[58] or after he has assigned it[59]; but if a covenant is broken while the lease is vested in him, his liability for this breach continues despite any assignment.[60] Thus while the original lessee of an onerous lease cannot divest himself of liability for future breaches, an assignee can do so by assigning the lease, such as to a pauper,[61] though he will remain liable to indemnify the tenant who assigned the lease to him.[62]

---

[50] Above, p. 353.
[51] *Cox v. Bishop* (1857) 8 De G.M. & G. 815; *Friary Holroyd and Healey's Breweries Ltd v. Singleton* [1899] 1 Ch. 86 (reversed on other grounds [1899] 2 Ch. 261).
[52] Above, p. 381.
[53] *Tichborne v. Weir* (1892) 67 L.T. 735; below, p. 560.
[54] See *Rodenhurst Estates Ltd v. W. H. Barnes Ltd* [1936] 2 All E.R. 3 (equitable assignee); *Ashe v. Hogan* [1920] 1 I.R. 159 (squatter); and see above, p. 352.
[55] See L.R.A. 1925, ss.9, 11, 75. The point was left open in *Spectrum Investment Co. v. Holmes* [1981] 1 W.L.R. 221 at 229, 230.
[56] *Spencer's Case* (1583) 5 Co.Rep. 16a; but see *Minshull v. Oakes* (1858) 2 H. & N. 793 (conditionally *in posse*).
[57] L.P.A. 1925, s.79.
[58] *Granada Theatres Ltd v. Freehold Investment (Leytonstone) Ltd* [1959] Ch. 592.
[59] *Paul v. Nurse* (1828) 8 B. & C. 486; but see L. & T.A. 1985, s.3(3)(a), inserted by L. & T.A. 1987, s.50 (dwellings: liability continues until tenant is notified of new landlord).
[60] *Harley v. King* (1835) 2 Cr.M. & R. 18.
[61] *Hopkinson v. Lovering* (1883) 11 Q.B.D. 92.
[62] See below, p. 392.

(d) Liability of guarantors

Where the assignment of an old lease is effective at law, any guarantor of an assignee of that lease is in exactly the same position as the person whose liability he is guaranteeing.[63]

(e) Indemnities from assignees

(i) Implied indemnity: If a covenant has been broken, the lessee and the assignee entitled to the lease at the time of the breach are each liable to be sued by the lessor. But although the lessor may sue either or both, he can only have one satisfaction: he has no right to recover twice.[64] The primary liability is that of the assignee, and if the original lessee is sued, he may claim indemnity from the assignee in whom the lease was vested at the time of the breach, whether that assignee obtained the lease from the lessee or from some other assignee.[65]

(ii) Express indemnity: In addition to this implied obligation to indemnify the original lessee, it is usual for each assignee to enter into an express covenant to indemnify his assignor against future breaches of covenant; and by the Law of Property Act 1925,[66] in any assignment for value made after 1925 such a covenant is implied.

(iii) Effect: The effect of these rights of indemnity may be illustrated thus:

A

⇓   99 years

B   ⇒   C   ⇒   D   ⇒   E

⇓   21 years

F

A has leased land to B for 99 years; by successive assignments E has become entitled to the lease and has granted a sub-lease to F for 21 years. If F does some act which is contrary to a covenant in the head lease, A can sue either B (privity of contract) or E (privity of estate). If A sues B, B has an implied right to indemnity against E. Alternatively, if on the assignment to C a covenant of indemnity was given to B, he may claim indemnity from C. C in turn may claim indemnity from D, and D from E, provided in each case that a covenant for indemnity was given on the assignment. The importance of these various rights is emphasised if one of the parties is insolvent or has disappeared. Apart from the rules relating to restrictive covenants,[67] F incurs no liability to anyone except so far as his act was a breach of a covenant in the sub-lease and so makes him liable to E.

4. Where the lessor assigns his reversion

If L, a tenant in fee simple, leased his land to T, and then L conveyed his fee simple, subject to the lease, to R, the common law rule was that with the exception of "implied covenants" (*i.e.* certain covenants which the law implied, such as to pay rent),[68] neither the benefit nor the burden of the covenants in the lease ran with the reversion: R was neither able to sue nor

---

[63] *P. & A. Swift Investments v. Combined English Stores Group Plc.* [1989] A.C. 632; *Coronation Street Industrial Properties Ltd v. Ingall Industries Plc.* [1989] 1 W.L.R. 304.
[64] *Brett v. Cumberland* (1619) Cro.Jac. 521.
[65] *Wolveridge v. Steward* (1833) 1 Cr. & M. 644; *Moule v. Garrett* (1872) L.R. 7 Ex. 101.
[66] s.77(1)(c); Sched. 2, Pt. IX.
[67] Below, pp. 453 *et seq.*
[68] See *Vyvyan v. Arthur* (1823) 1 B. & C. 410.

liable to be sued. But since the Grantees of Reversions Act 1540, sections 1 and 2, the benefit and burden of all covenants and provisions contained in a lease which touch and concern the land (or have reference to the subject-matter of the lease, to use the modern phrase) have passed with the reversion. The current provisions are sections 141 and 142 of the Law of Property Act 1925. The following points should be noted.

(a) The lease must be in due form

This requirement will be satisfied if the lease is made by deed[69] or, under the doctrine of *Walsh v. Lonsdale*,[70] is a specifically enforceable agreement[71] which satisfies the formal requirements for a contract for the sale of land.[72] (these differ depending on when the agreement was entered into.[73]) After 1925, even a mere oral tenancy is probably sufficient for, under section 154 of the Law of Property Act 1925, sections 141 and 142 extend to an underlease "or other tenancy".[74]

(b) The reversion may have been assigned by deed in whole or in part

The assignee of the entire reversion takes the benefit and burden of the provisions in the lease. Where the reversion is not assigned in its entirety, the position is not so simple. Two separate cases must be considered.

(i) Severance as regards the estate: Where the assignee has part of the reversion, as where a fee simple reversioner grants a lease of his reversion to X, the reversion is severed as regards the estate. In this case, X, as the person entitled to part of the reversion, falls within the statutory provisions, so that the benefit and burden of both covenants and conditions pass to him as the immediate reversioner.[75]

(ii) Severance as regards the land: Where the assignee has the reversion of part, as where a fee simple reversioner conveys the fee simple in half the land to X, the reversion is severed as regards the land. All conditions and rights of re-entry now become severable on the severance of the reversion.[76] The tenancy itself, however, continues as one tenancy.[77]

(c) Rights of an assignee of the reversion to sue and forfeit for previous breaches

After an assignment of the reversion, the assignee is now alone entitled to sue the tenant for rent or for breaches of covenant, whether such rent accrued or such breaches occurred before or after the assignment.[78] This is brought about by the Law of Property Act 1925 (the law was formerly different).[79] This Act also provides that rights of re-entry are enforceable by the new reversioner, provided they have not been waived. Waiver may be express or implied.[80] Waiver will not be implied merely because the reversion is assigned "subject to and with the

---

[69] *Smith v. Egginton* (1874) L.R. 9 C.P. 145.
[70] Above, p. 343.
[71] *Rickett v. Green* [1910] 1 K.B. 253.
[72] *Rye v. Purcell* [1926] 1 K.B. 446; *Weg Motors Ltd v. Hales* [1962] Ch. 49.
[73] See above, pp. 148 *et seq.*
[74] Contrast above, p. 390.
[75] *Wright v. Burroughes* (1846) 3 C.B. 685.
[76] L.P.A. 1925, s.140(1). The position is different if the lease was made before 1882 and the reversion was severed before 1926.
[77] *Jelley v. Buckman* [1974] Q.B. 488.
[78] *Re King* [1963] Ch. 459; *London and County (A. & D.) Ltd v. Wilfred Sportsman Ltd* [1971] Ch. 764.
[79] s.141, replacing C.A. 1911, s.2.
[80] For waiver, see above, p. 355.

benefit of" the lease[81]; it is "the merest *res inter alios acta*", without any impact on the tenant.[82]

(d) Liability of guarantors

Where the assignment of an old lease is effective at law, any guarantor of an assignee of the reversion is in exactly the same position as the person whose liability he is guaranteeing.[83]

(e) Enforcement after assignment

The liability of the original parties to a lease during the whole term of the lease[84] is not destroyed by assignment. Thus for covenants touching and concerning the land an original lessor remains liable even after he has assigned the reversion[85]; and an original lessee who assigns his term remains liable even to a subsequent assignee of the reversion with whom he has never had any privity of estate.[86] Further, a tenant's right to sue his landlord for existing breaches of covenant continues to exist after he has assigned the lease.[87]

Sect. 4. Position where the assignment of an old lease is effective only in equity

An assignment of an old lease may be effective only in equity, either because the lease was not created with the formalities required by the law (such as because of the lack of a deed[88]) and for that reason takes effect only in equity or because, as has already been seen,[89] a legal lease has not been assigned by deed[90] and for that reason the assignment of it takes effect only in equity.[91] In such circumstances, the rules for the running of the benefit and burden of covenants which touch and concern the land, as considered above, are only partly applicable. (That does not alter the fact that the original parties are bound by privity of contract in the manner which has already been considered.[92])

1. Covenants running with the lease

The common law rule in *Spencer's Case*[93] under which an assignee of the tenancy takes the benefit and burden of such covenants does not appear to apply.[94]

If L grants an equitable tenancy to X and X assigns it to Y, L cannot enforce the covenants against Y,[95] for there is no privity of estate which will carry the burden to Y. It would be

---

[81] *London and County (A. & D.) Ltd v. Wilfred Sportsman Ltd* [1971] Ch. 764.
[82] *ibid.*, at 782, *per* Russell L.J.
[83] *P. & A. Swift Investments v. Combined English Stores Group Plc.* [1989] A.C. 632; *Coronation Street Industrial Properties Ltd v. Ingall Industries Plc.* [1989] 1 W.L.R. 304.
[84] Above, p. 385.
[85] *Celsteel Ltd v. Alton House Holdings Ltd (No. 2)* [1986] 1 W.L.R. 666 at 672, 673; [1987] 1 W.L.R. 291 at 296.
[86] *Arlesford Trading Co. Ltd v. Servansingh* [1971] 1 W.L.R. 1080.
[87] *City and Metropolitan Properties Ltd v. Greycroft* (1987) 54 P. & C.R. 266.
[88] See above, pp. 343–346.
[89] Above, p. 391.
[90] Above, p. 353.
[91] *Cox v. Bishop* (1857) 8 De G.M. & G. 815; *Friary Holroyd and Healey's Breweries Ltd v. Singleton* [1899] 1 Ch. 86 (reversed on other grounds [1899] 2 Ch. 261).
[92] Above, p. 385.
[93] (1583) 5 Co.Rep. 16a; above, p. 388.
[94] *Marquis Camden v. Batterbury* (1860) 7 C.B.N.S. 864; *Elliott v. Johnson* (1866) L.R. 2 Q.B. 120.
[95] See *Austerberry v. Corporation of Oldham* (1885) 29 Ch.D. 750.

convenient if equity were to follow the law and make the burden of the covenants run with the land, and there are dicta supporting the view that it does.[96] There is also a broad principle that he who takes the benefit must also bear the burden.[97] But authorities to the contrary[98] have yet to be disposed of satisfactorily.[99]

The benefit of such covenants is less confined. If L grants an equitable tenancy to X, who then assigns it to Y, Y may be able to enforce the covenants against L, since the benefit of the covenants, being assignable,[1] can be passed to Y.[2]

2. Covenants running with the reversion

Where the reversion on an equitable tenancy is assigned, the position is substantially the same as where the tenancy is legal: for the statutory provisions[3] for the running of the benefit and burden with the reversion are applicable. "Lease" in the statute is defined as including an underlease "or any other tenancy", and this makes the benefit and burden run with the reversion in the same way as if the tenancy were legal.[4]

3. Liability of guarantors

Where an assignment of an old lease is effective only in equity, there is no authority as to the liability of any guarantors of the assignees but their liability is presumably exactly the same as that of the person whose liability they are guaranteeing.

Sect. 5. Restrictive covenants in an old lease

Where covenants are not enforceable under the rules which have already been discussed, the basic rule at law is that no covenants can be enforced. Thus if L grants a lease to T, who grants a sub-lease to S, there is no privity of contract or estate between L and S, and so the covenants in the lease and sub-lease cannot be enforced between them. Again, when V sells his freehold land to P, and P then sells it to Q, there is no privity of contract or estate between V and Q. Yet although in such cases covenants are not enforceable at law, in equity a doctrine grew up in the nineteenth century which made restrictive covenants relating to land (*i.e.* covenants prohibiting certain acts on the land) enforceable in equity despite the lack of any privity. Various conditions evolved, mainly in relation to freehold land, which regulated the application and operation of the doctrine; and in some important respects these conditions resemble those governing easements.[5] Restrictive covenants will accordingly be discussed after easements have been considered.[6]

For the present, it need only be said that restrictive covenants in a head lease that comply with the relevant rules may usually be enforced in equity against sub-tenants. In the case of

---

[96] See *Boyer v. Warbey* [1953] 1 Q.B. 234 at 246, 247.

[97] *Tito v. Waddell (No. 2)* [1977] Ch. 106 at 299–302.

[98] See, *e.g. Elliott v. Johnson* (1866) L.R. 2 Q.B. 120; and see the authorities on equitable assignments, above, p. 391.

[99] See the general survey of equitable leases and equitable assignments at [1978] C.L.J. 98 (R. J. Smith).

[1] Above, pp. 382, 387.

[2] See *Griffith v. Pelton* [1958] Ch. 205, where, however, the lease was legal.

[3] L.P.A. 1925, ss.141, 142, replacing C.A. 1881, ss.10, 11; above, p. 392.

[4] *Rickett v. Green* [1910] 1 K.B. 253; *Rye v. Purcell* [1926] 1 K.B. 446.

[5] See below, p. 420.

[6] See below, pp. 453 *et seq.*; and see above, p. 381.

unregistered land, such covenants are not registrable as land charges.[7] Consequently, their enforceability depends on the equitable doctrine of notice. If the sub-tenant has the right to see the head lease when he took his sub-lease, which will be the case where he was the original sub-lessee,[8] he will inevitably have notice of any restrictive covenants therein and so will be bound by them. But an assignee of a sub-lease has no right to see the head lease as a matter of law.[9] Consequently, unless he is entitled to do so under the terms of the contract of assignment or actually knows of the existence of the restrictive covenant in question, he will not have notice of them[10] and will consequently take free of them. This is also the position of a sub-under-lessee and his assignees. However, in the case of registered land, any type of sub-lessee and his assignees will automatically be bound by any restrictive covenants in the head lease.

But, although a restrictive covenant entered into by the original lessor in respect of land which is not comprised in the lease is enforceable against him indefinitely, it is not enforceable against a purchaser or a tenant of the land not comprised in the lease. The enforceability of such covenants against such persons under the general law is, in the case of unregistered land, governed by the equitable doctrine of notice[11]; thus in the normal case the purchaser or tenant of the land not comprised in the lease will take free of the covenant. In the case of registered land the purchaser or tenant of the land not comprised in the lease will automatically take free of the covenant since it cannot be protected on the Land Register so as to draw its existence to the attention of and bind them.[12]

It should also be recalled that covenants in a head lease, whether restrictive or not, may be indirectly enforceable against sub-tenants by virtue of the existence of a forfeiture clause in the head lease.[13]

Sect. 6. Position of landlord and tenant for the time being of a new lease

1. Attempts to exclude the operation of the 1995 Act

Any agreement which excludes, modifies or otherwise frustrates the operation of any provision of the 1995 Act is void[14] as is any agreement which provides for the determination of any tenancy or the imposition of any penalty, disability or liability on any tenant in the event of, in connection with, or in consequence of the operation of any provision of that Act.[15]

2. The basic rule

The burden and the benefit of all covenants in a new lease entered into by the original lessor and the original lessee (respectively described in the 1995 Act as the "landlord covenants"

---

[7] See above, p. 96.
[8] L.P.A. 1925, s.44(4).
[9] L.P.A. 1925, s.44(3).
[10] L.P.A. 1925, s.44(5).
[11] *Dartstone Ltd v. Cleveland Petroleum Co. Ltd* [1969] 1 W.L.R. 1807.
[12] *Oceanic Village Ltd v. United Attractions Ltd* [2000] Ch. 234 (a new lease but the principle must equally apply to old leases).
[13] Above, p. 383.
[14] L. & T.(C.)A. 1995, s.25(1).
[15] *ibid.*, s.25(2), (3).

and the "tenant covenants"[16]) passes on the assignment of their respective interests to the persons to whom those interests are successively assigned[17]; there is no longer any requirement that the covenants should touch and concern the land.[18] This is the case even when the assignment of a new lease is effective only in equity[19]; as has already been seen,[20] this may be either because the lease was not created with the formalities required by the law (for example because of the lack of a deed[21]) and for that reason takes effect only in equity or because a legal lease has not been assigned by deed[22] and for that reason the assignment of it takes effect only in equity.[23]

3. The exceptions

The basic rule is subject to the following exceptions.

(a) Personal covenants

The burden and benefit of any covenant in a new lease "which (in whatever terms) is expressed to be personal to any person" does not pass when that person assigns his interest.[24] In principle, this formulation appears to require some statement in the lease from which the court can deduce that the covenant is personal. It remains to be seen whether a covenant whose terms are such that it cannot be anything other than a personal covenant but does not actually say that it is is regarded as having expressed that fact by virtue of its terms alone. As the statutory formulation indicates, it is possible for a covenant to be personal to only one of the parties to it, in which case its burden, or more usually its benefit, will pass when the other party assigns his interest.

(b) Estate contracts

As in the case of old leases, the enforceability of covenants in a new lease which also constitute estate contracts is not determined by the normal rules but by whether they are enforceable as estate contracts. The 1995 Act has no effect on the enforceability of covenants which are required to be registered under the Land Charges Act 1972 or the Land Registration Acts 1925 and 2002.[25] It has already been seen[26] that covenants giving the lessee the right to renew his lease[27] or to purchase the freehold or leasehold reversion[28] are estate contracts by the lessor, as are notices by lessees exercising statutory rights to purchase the freehold or to take an extended lease,[29] while covenants obliging the lessee to offer to surrender his lease to the lessor before seeking to assign it are estate contracts by the lessee.[30] Failure to protect such estate contracts by registration will continue to render them void against any assignee of the party burdened by the covenant who takes free of them; thus an

---

[16] *ibid.*, s.28(1).
[17] *ibid.*, ss.2(1), 3(1).
[18] *ibid.*, s.2(1).
[19] *ibid.*, s.28(1).
[20] Above, pp. 394–395.
[21] Above, pp. 343–346.
[22] Above, p. 353.
[23] As in *Cox v. Bishop* (1857) 8 De G.M. & G. 815.
[24] L. & T.(C.)A. 1995, s.3(6)(a).
[25] *ibid.*, s.3(6)(b).
[26] Above, p. 388.
[27] *Phillips v. Mobil Oil Ltd* [1989] 1 W.L.R. 888.
[28] *Midland Bank Trust Co. Ltd v. Green* [1981] A.C. 513.
[29] Leasehold Reform Act 1967, s.5; below, p. 549.
[30] *Greene v. Church Commissioners for England* [1974] Ch. 467.

assignee of unregistered land for money or money's worth will do so[31] and an assignee of registered land for value will do so unless the party with the benefit of the covenant has an interest which overrides registration,[32] something which no lessor or lessee who has sub-let will have when the Land Registration Act 2002 comes into force.[33]

(c) Covenant no longer binding

Where a covenant in a new lease has ceased to be binding on the assignor prior to the assignment, because it has been released or has expired, it will not revive on assignment.[34] However, waivers of covenant which are expressed to be personal to a particular landlord or tenant will not prevent that covenant being enforced following an assignment.[35]

4. Principles of transmission

The benefit and burden of all landlord and tenant covenants which pass to assignees will pass on an assignment either of the whole or of any part of the interest in question.[36] This is also the case with any right of re-entry and forfeiture.[37] In the event that the assignor is not released from the burden of the covenants in question for one of the reasons considered below, he and the assignee remain jointly and severally liable to the other party and to anyone to whom he assigns. The tenant covenants are enforceable against any tenant who is bound by them and any mortgagee of his interest who is in possession[38] by any landlord who has their benefit,[39] a lessee of the reversion[40] (such as the holder of an overriding lease[41]) and a mortgagee of the reversion who is in possession.[42] The landlord covenants are enforceable against any landlord who is bound by them, any lessee of the reversion and any mortgagee in possession of the reversion[43] by any tenant who has their benefit and any mortgagee of his interest who is in possession.[44]

5. Partial assignments

When a lease or a reversion is assigned only in part, the position is as follows.

(a) Attribution

Whether and to what extent any covenant is enforceable against the assignee depends on whether it is attributable to any specific part of the land in question or whether it is applicable to the whole of the land.[45] Where it is so attributable, it must be complied with by whoever holds the interest in that part of the land.[46] Where it is applicable to the whole of the land,

---

[31] *Midland Bank Trust Co. Ltd v. Green* [1981] A.C. 513; *Greene v. Church Commissioners for England* [1974] Ch. 467; *Phillips v. Mobil Oil Ltd* [1989] 1 W.L.R. 888.
[32] *Webb v. Pollmount Ltd* [1966] Ch. 584.
[33] See above, p. 388.
[34] L. & T.(C.)A. 1995, s.3(2), (3).
[35] *ibid.,* s.3(4).
[36] *ibid.,* s.3(1).
[37] *ibid.,* s.4.
[38] *ibid.,* s.15(4).
[39] *ibid.,* s.15(1), (6).
[40] *ibid.,* s.15(1)(a).
[41] See below.
[42] L. & T.(C.)A. 1995, s.51(1)(b).
[43] *ibid.,* s.15(2).
[44] *ibid.,* s.15(3).
[45] *ibid.,* s.9(6).
[46] *ibid.,* s.3(2), (3).

as in the case of a covenant to pay rent or service charges, both the assignor and the assignee are jointly and severally liable for the whole amount due unless and until the liability is apportioned.[47] However, one may seek contribution from the other.[48]

(b) Apportionment

The 1995 Act permits apportionment where this is agreed by all the relevant parties.[49] In default of agreement, the assignor and assignee can agree an apportionment and, before or within four weeks of the partial assignment taking place,[50] apply to the other party to the lease to make that apportionment binding.[51] This is done by serving a notice on the other party in a specified form,[52] informing him of the assignment and the request that the apportionment should become binding on him.[53] The apportionment will then become binding unless the other party serves a written counter-notice within four weeks. If he does so, there will be no apportionment unless either the assignor and the assignee apply to the court for, and obtains, a declaration that it is reasonable for the apportionment to become binding or the other party withdraws his objections in writing.[54] Any apportionment is effective from the date of the partial assignment.[55]

(c) Forfeiture and disclaimer

The 1995 Act also provides that, where there has been a partial assignment, rights of re-entry and forfeiture are exercisable only against the part of the land whose tenant is in breach of covenant[56] and that rights of disclaimer are exercisable only in respect of the part of the land whose tenant is insolvent.[57]

6. Pre-assignment breaches

As in the case of old leases, neither the landlord nor the tenant of a new lease is liable for a breach of covenant committed before he took his assignment.[58] Nor can either the landlord or the tenant of a new lease sue in respect of breaches of covenant committed before he took his assignment[59] (the landlord but not the tenant of an old lease is entitled to do this). However, the right to sue for past breaches can be expressly assigned[60] and if it is the assignee can sue. It is thought that such assignments will become the norm, particularly on an assignment of the reversion.[61] On the other hand, the landlord for the time being is entitled to exercise any right to re-enter and forfeit the lease in respect of a breach committed before the assignment to him.[62] Where he seeks to do so in respect of arrears of rent which existed at the date of the assignment to him, any sums paid by the tenant in respect of those arrears

---

[47] *ibid.*, s.13(1).
[48] *ibid.*, s.13(3), applying the provisions of Civil Liability (Contribution) Act 1978.
[49] *ibid.*, s.26(1).
[50] *ibid.*, s.10(1).
[51] *ibid.*, s.9.
[52] *ibid.*, s.27; S.I. 1995 No. 2964.
[53] *ibid.*, s.10(1).
[54] *ibid.*, s.10(2).
[55] *ibid.*, s.10(3).
[56] *ibid.*, s.21(2).
[57] *ibid.*, s.23(1).
[58] *ibid.*, s.23(1).
[59] *ibid.*
[60] *ibid.*, s.23(2).
[61] M. & W., p. 992.
[62] L. & T.(C.)A. 1995, s.23(3).

and interest thereon in order to obtain relief against forfeiture will have to be paid to him rather than to the person actually entitled to them, the assignor. Since it is thought that the latter will not be entitled to sue for them thereafter, he may be able to recover them in equity, particularly if the assignee paid less for the reversion because the assignor did not also assign the right to sue for these arrears.[63]

7. Liability of guarantors

The guarantors of the landlord and tenant for the time being of a new lease are in exactly the same position as the person whose liability they have guaranteed.

Sect. 7. Position of former landlords and tenants of a new lease

1. Attempts to exclude the operation of the 1995 Act

It has already been seen that any agreement which excludes, modifies or otherwise frustrates the operation of any provision of the 1995 Act is void[64] as is any agreement which provides for the determination of any tenancy or the imposition of any penalty, disability or liability on any tenant in the event of, in connection with, or in consequence of the operation of any provision of that Act.[65]

2. The basic rule for former tenants

Former tenants are released from liability under the tenant covenants when they assign their lease but may remain liable to the landlord until the next assignment under an authorised guarantee agreement.

(a) Release from liability

When the original lessee of a new lease assigns his lease, he will thereupon be released from the burden of the tenant covenants and will cease to be entitled to the benefit of the landlord covenants.[66] A subsequent tenant of a new lease does not as such require the assistance of the 1995 Act to be released from his tenant covenants when he assigns on. However, as has already been seen,[67] many covenants not to assign the lease without the lessor's consent provide that consent will not be forthcoming unless the assignee of the lease covenants directly with the lessor to observe all the tenant covenants for the remainder of the term. Where an assignee does covenant directly in this way, he will from then on be in exactly the same position as the original lessee.[68] Consequently, he does require the assistance of the 1995 Act to be released from his liability to the landlord for the time being for any breach of the tenant covenants for the rest of the term; its provisions relating to release and, for that matter, those relating to authorised guarantee agreements apply to him in the same way as they apply to an original lessee.

---

[63] See M. & W., p. 993.
[64] L. & T.(C.)A. 1995, s.25(1).
[65] *ibid.*, s.25(2), (3).
[66] L. & T.(C.)A. 1995, s.5(2).
[67] Above, p. 386.
[68] *Deanplan Ltd v. Mahmoud* [1993] Ch. 151 (release of one such assignee by the release of a later assignee).

(b) Authorised guarantee agreements

A landlord can have recourse to the tenant who held the lease immediately before the tenant for the time being if the lease contains a covenant requiring the consent of the landlord to any assignment; in these circumstances, the landlord can give his consent only on condition that the assigning tenant guarantees the performance of the covenants by the tenant to whom he is assigning (such an agreement is known as an "authorised guarantee agreement" or an "AGA").[69] Where the covenant against assignment is absolute, the landlord can of course refuse consent as of right and so obviously has the right to grant consent only on the basis that the assigning tenant enters into an authorised guarantee agreement.[70] In the more normal case where the covenant against assignment is merely qualified, the landlord will be able to do so as of right only if he has stipulated that entering into such an agreement is a prerequisite of consent being given.[71] (Such a stipulation will normally be in the lease itself but there is nothing in the 1995 Act to prevent the landlord and the tenant making a subsequent agreement to this effect.) Where the landlord has not so stipulated, he can only require the tenant to enter into an authorised guarantee agreement if it is reasonable for him to do so.[72] Since the 1995 Act came into force, it has become standard practice for landlords to include such stipulations in commercial leases. However, when the tenant of an old lease exercises a statutory right to obtain a new lease, typically in the case of a business tenancy,[73] his previous lease will contain no such stipulation and the result will turn entirely on reasonableness.[74]

All or any of the following liabilities can be imposed on the assigning tenant by an authorised guarantee agreement:

(i) liability as sole or principal debtor in respect of the tenant covenants while his assignee remains tenant[75] (this renders him liable even if the terms of the lease are varied);

(ii) liability as guarantor of his assignee's compliance with the tenant covenants provided that that liability is not more onerous than liability under (i) would be[76]; and

(iii) in the event that the lease is disclaimed on his assignee's insolvency, an obligation to take a new lease whose duration and covenants are not more onerous than those of the lease which he is assigning.[77]

An agreement will not be an authorised guarantee agreement if it purports to guarantee performance of the obligations of anyone other than the assignee or to impose liability on the

---

[69] L. & T.(C.)A. 1995, s.16.
[70] *ibid.*, s.16(3).
[71] L. & T.A. 1927, s.19(1A) inserted by L. & T.(C.)A. 1995, s.22.
[72] L. & T.A. 1988, s.1 (this applies because the condition has to be lawfully imposed; see L. & T.(C.)A. 1995, s.16(3)(b).
[73] See below, p. 581.
[74] *Wallis Fashion Group Ltd v. CGU Life Assurance Ltd* [2000] 2 E.G.L.R. 49.
[75] L. & T.(C.)A. 1995, s.16(5)(a).
[76] *ibid.*, s.16(5)(b).
[77] *ibid.*, s.16(5)(c).

tenant in respect of any covenants from which the assignee is released.[78] Any such agreement is void.[79]

(c) Problem notices

However, the ability of the landlord for the time being to recover "fixed charges" (rent, service charges and any other liquidated sums) from a former tenant who has entered into an authorised guarantee agreement is now subject to his obligation to serve a problem notice. As has already been seen, a landlord can now only recover such fixed charges from a former tenant if he serves notice, in a prescribed form, on that tenant within six months of any fixed charge becoming due. This notice informs the former tenant that the sum is due and that the landlord intends to recover that sum from him.[80] A problem notice is sufficiently served if it is sent by registered post to the last known abode of the former tenant.[81]

(d) Overriding leases

A former tenant who pays in full any sum so claimed under a problem notice is entitled to what the 1995 Act describes as an "overriding lease", a lease for three days longer than the original lease (unless the landlord's interest would thereby be displaced) which contains the same covenants as the original lease. This overriding lease is a reversionary lease and so is interposed between the interest of the landlord and the lease of the tenant for the time being[82]; the former tenant therefore becomes the landlord of the tenant for the time being. Consequently, any future failure to pay a fixed charge by the tenant for the time being will enable the former tenant to forfeit the lease and cause his overriding lease to come into possession. An overriding lease held by a former tenant of a new lease is itself an new lease[83]; so he will remain liable to the landlord for the time being only while he remains the tenant of the overriding lease and for the duration of any authorised guarantee agreement which he may be obliged to sign pursuant to any covenant requiring the landlord's consent to an assignment. However, he will normally be able to cover the amount of any liability by assigning or sub-letting, although this will not be the case in the event of another slump in property values of the type which occurred in the years immediately prior to the enactment of the 1995 Act.

3. The basic rule for former landlords

A former landlord of a new lease other than the original lessor does not require the assistance of the 1995 Act to be released from his landlord covenants and there is in practice no possibility that he will have covenanted directly with the lessee to observe all the landlord covenants for the remainder of the term. Where the original lessor of a new lease assigns his interest, however, he is not automatically released from liability under the landlord covenants. He not only retains the right to enforce the tenant covenants but also remains liable to the tenant for the time being on the landlord covenants. However, except in those cases where the assignment is by operation of law (as on his death or bankruptcy),[84] he may, before or within four weeks of the assignment taking place, apply to the tenant for the time being to

---

[78] *ibid.*, s.17.
[79] *ibid.*, s.19.
[80] *ibid.*, s.17.
[81] *Commercial Union Life Assurance Co. Ltd v. Moustafa* [1999] 2 E.G.L.R. 44.
[82] L. & T.(C.)A. 1995, ss.19–20.
[83] *ibid.*, s.20(1).
[84] L. & T.(C.)A. 1995, s.11.

be released.[85] This is done by serving a notice on the tenant in a specified form,[86] informing him of the assignment and the request that the landlord covenants be released.[87] The landlord covenants will then be released unless the tenant serves a written counter-notice within four weeks. If he does so, there will be no release unless either the landlord applies to the court for, and obtains, a declaration that it is reasonable for the landlord covenants to be released or the tenant withdraws his objections in writing.[88] If he does not or cannot seek a release or fails to obtain one, he may apply in the same way to be released on any subsequent assignment of the reversion.[89] A release has effect from the date of the assignment in question[90] and also deprives the landlord of the right to enforce the tenant covenants as from that date.

4. The exceptions to the basic rules

The basic rules are subject to the following exceptions.

(a) Personal covenants

The burden and benefit of any covenant in a new lease "which (in whatever terms) is expressed to be personal to any person" does not pass when that person assigns his interest.[91] Consequently, the original lessor and the original lessee will remain liable on or will be able to enforce any covenant which is personal to them throughout the term. The fact that the original lessor is released from the landlord covenants in the way just described does not release him from liability under any personal covenant.[92] Whether the covenant is enforceable by or against the other original party or against the landlord or tenant for the time being depends on whether that a covenant to be personal to only one of the parties to it; if it is its burden, or more usually its benefit, will pass when the other party assigns his interest.

(b) Estate contracts

In the event that a covenant in a new lease which also constitutes an estate contract is not enforceable against a successor in title to the party burdened by it, the original lessor or lessee will, just as in the case of an old lease, nevertheless be liable for damages for breach of that contract to whoever has the benefit of the estate contract. It is not a defence to such an action that the estate contract would have been enforceable against the successor in title had it been protected by registration in the appropriate way.[93] While the measure of damages is likely to be minimal in the case of options, unless the option was to acquire the interest in question at less than the market rate, the measure may well be very substantial when the claimant is a lessee who has been unable to exercise a statutory right to purchase the freehold or to take an extended lease or a lessor who has been unable to take advantage of a covenant obliging the lessee to offer to surrender his lease to the lessor before seeking to assign it.

---

[85] *ibid.*, s.6(2).
[86] *ibid.*, s.27; S.I. 1995 No. 2964.
[87] *ibid.*, s.8(1).
[88] *ibid.*, s.8(2).
[89] *ibid.*, s.7(1), (2).
[90] *ibid.*, s.8(3).
[91] L. & T.(C.)A. 1995, s.3(6)(a).
[92] *BHP Petroleum Great Britain Ltd v. Chesterfield Properties Ltd* [2002] 1 All E.R. 821.
[93] *Wright v. Dean* [1948] Ch. 686.

(c) Excluded assignments

An excluded assignment is one which takes effect by operation of law (as on the the death or bankruptcy of the landlord or tenant) or which is made in breach of covenant (in practice only feasible in the case of an assignment of a lease in breach of an absolute or qualified covenant against assignment).[94] A party to a lease who makes an excluded assignment remains liable on his own covenants, but can enforce those of the other party, until the next assignment of the interest in question.[95] In the case of a tenant, fixed charges can only be recovered following the service of a problem notice and a tenant who pays a fixed charge in full is entitled to an overriding lease. No authorised guarantee agreement can arise on the occasion of an excluded assignment.[96] However, on the next assignment of the lease, the landlord who is entitled to demand an authorised guarantee agreement is able to obtain one both from the tenant who made the excluded assignment and from his assignee. Nor, where an excluded assignment is partial, can the parties to it apply for an agreed apportionment to become binding on the other party to the lease until the next assignment.[97]

(d) Contrary intention

The Court of Appeal has indicated that there is nothing in the 1995 Act to fetter the freedom of contracting parties to place a limit on the transmissibility of the benefit or burden of obligations under a tenancy.[98] Parties can obviously prevent the burden of covenants running by classifying them as personal. However, if this indication means that parties can provide that the burden of covenants will not be released on assignment, the whole policy of the 1995 Act will have been undermined. Lessors could require lessees to enter into the usual transmissible covenant to pay the rent and a personal covenant to pay the rent throughout the term, thus retaining the right to sue both the original lessee and the current tenant. However, it is likely that any such personal covenant would be regarded as an agreement which excludes, modifies or otherwise frustrates the operation of a provision of the 1995 Act and is consequently void.[99] The answer may be to say that any personal covenant which mirrors a transmissible covenant is void; this would give the original parties a choice between transmissibility and non-transmissibility but no possibility of having both.

5. Indemnity

Where a former landlord or tenant of a new lease discharges the liability of the landlord and tenant for the time being, indemnity covenants are no longer applied.[1] Where the assignor does so, he has an implied right to restitution from the assignee.[2]

6. Pre-assignment breaches

As has already been seen, neither the landlord nor the tenant of a new lease is liable for a breach of covenant committed before he took his assignment[3] nor can either the landlord and or the tenant of a new lease sue in respect of breaches of covenant committed before he took

---

[94] L. & T.(C.)A. 1995, s.11(1).
[95] *ibid.*, s.11(2)–(4).
[96] *ibid.*, s.16(1).
[97] *ibid.*, s.11(5)(b), (6).
[98] *BHP Petroleum Great Britain Ltd v. Chesterfield Properties Ltd* [2002] 1 All E.R. 821.
[99] L. & T.(C.)A. 1995, s.25(1).
[1] *ibid.*, s.14.
[2] See *Moule v. Garrett* (1872) L.R. 7 Ex. 101.
[3] *ibid.*, s.23(1).

his assignment.[4] Such breaches of covenant remain actionable by and against the former tenant or landlord as the case may be unless the right to sue for the past breaches has been expressly assigned.[5]

7. Liability of guarantors

The guarantors of former landlords and tenants of a new lease are in exactly the same position as the person whose liability they have guaranteed save that guarantors of former tenants do not as such guarantee authorised guarantee agreements. Any purported agreement with a guarantor will not be an authorised guarantee agreement[6] and may well be void as frustrating the operation of the 1995 Act. However, in the event that a landlord obliges a guarantor as well as the tenant to be a party to the lease, both could be required to enter into authorised guarantee agreements.

8. Management companies

Properties of a single landlord which are in multiple occupation are often managed by a management company which will be a party to each lease and will be obliged to perform services such as the provision of porterage and the maintenance and cleaning of the common areas in consideration of a covenant by each tenant to pay the appropriate proportion of the cost. Such companies are brought within the 1995 Act in order to ensure that tenants can neither sue nor be sued on their covenants following the assignment of their leases.[7] This is achieved by deeming covenants which are exercisable by or against a third party of this type to be tenant covenants where they are exercisable by the landlord or against the tenant and to be landlord covenants where they are exercisable by the tenant or against the landlord.[8] Thus former tenants will automatically be released in the normal way and former landlords can apply to be released in the normal way.

Sect. 8. Restrictive covenants in a new lease

All covenants in new leases which are restrictive of the user of the leased land are enforceable against any assignee of the lease or the reversion and any owner or occupier of the land to which the covenant relates, even if there is no express provision to this effect in the lease or sub-lease in question.[9] Consequently, any type of sub-lessee and his assignees, any licensee and any squatter will be bound by all the restrictive covenants in a head lease.

However, although a restrictive covenant entered into by the original lessor in respect of land which is not comprised in the lease is a landlord covenant and is enforceable against the landlord for the time being, it is not by virtue of the 1995 Act enforceable against a purchaser or a tenant of the land not comprised in the lease.[10] The enforceability of such covenants under the general law is, in the case of unregistered land, governed by the equitable doctrine

---

[4] *ibid.*
[5] *ibid.*, s.23(2).
[6] *ibid.*, s.16(1) (an authorised guarantee agreement can only be made with a tenant).
[7] *ibid.*, s.12.
[8] *ibid.*, s.12(2), (3).
[9] L. & T.(C.)A. 1995, s.3(5).
[10] *Oceanic Village Ltd v. United Attractions Ltd* [2000] Ch. 234.

of notice[11]; thus in the normal case the purchaser or tenant of the land not comprised in the lease will take free of the covenant. In the case of registered land the purchaser or tenant of the land not comprised in the lease will automatically take free of the covenant since it cannot be protected on the Land Register so as to draw its existence to the attention of and bind them.[12]

It should also be recalled that covenants in a head lease, whether restrictive or not, may be indirectly enforceable against sub-tenants by virtue of the existence of a forfeiture clause in the head lease.[13]

[11] *Dartstone Ltd v. Cleveland Petroleum Co. Ltd* [1969] 1 W.L.R. 1807.
[12] *Oceanic Village Ltd v. United Attractions Ltd* [2000] Ch. 234.
[13] See above, p. 383.

Chapter 10

Incorporeal Hereditaments

It has already been seen that incorporeal hereditaments are rights in land which do not give the owner present physical possession of the land.[1] There are two quite distinct classes of incorporeal hereditaments:

(i) those which may ripen into corporeal hereditaments. Thus a grant to A for life with remainder to B in fee simple gave B an incorporeal hereditament which became corporeal after A's death;

(ii) those which can never become corporeal hereditaments but are merely rights over the land of another, such as rentcharges.

The first class has already been dealt with.[2] It is with incorporeal hereditaments in the latter class that this chapter is concerned. Most are either obsolete or of little importance in connection with the modern law of real property, such as titles of honour, advowsons[3] and tithes.[4] The only incorporeal hereditaments which need be considered at length are rentcharges, easements and profits. They do not form a homogeneous class. Some, such as easements, can exist only for the benefit of other land, while others, such as rentcharges, lead an independent existence. In one sense, those in the former category are not hereditaments at all, for they cannot be inherited or dealt with except as appendages to the land which they benefit.

Part 1—Rentcharges

Sect. 1. Nature of rentcharges

1. Rentcharges and rent services

Periodical payments in respect of land fall under the two main heads of rentcharges and rent services. Where the relationship of lord and tenant exists between the parties, any rent

---

[1] Above, p. 67.
[2] Above, pp. 209 *et seq.*
[3] See above, p. 79.
[4] See above, p. 73.

payable by virtue of that relationship by the tenant to the lord is a rent service. If there is no relationship of lord and tenant, the rent is a rentcharge. Thus if L grants a lease to T at £5,000 per annum and X charges his fee simple estate with the payment of £2,000 per annum to Y, L has a rent service and Y a rentcharge. Since the Statute Quia Emptores 1290 it has been impossible for a grantor to reserve any services on a conveyance of freehold land in fee simple, for the grantee holds of the grantor's lord, and not of the grantor. Consequently, no rent reserved on a conveyance of freehold land in fee simple after 1290 can be a rent service. Although at law services could be reserved when an owner in fee simple granted a life estate[5] or a fee tail, it was most unusual to do so. The only rent service now met with in practice is the rent reserved upon the grant of a lease for a term of years. A rent service is annexed to a reversion, while a rentcharge stands on its own. In some parts of the country (including Manchester, Bath and Bristol) rentcharges were for long used wholly or partly instead of paying a capital sum on the purchase of property.[6]

2. Legal and equitable rentcharges

A rentcharge is real property, so that both at law and in equity it could be held for any of the usual estates or interests.[7] However, since 1925 an interest in a rentcharge can be legal only if it is

(i) in possession, and

(ii) either perpetual or for a term of years absolute.[8]

Further, a rentcharge cannot exist at law unless the proper formalities have been employed for its creation.[9]

3. Rentcharge on a rentcharge

At common law, a rentcharge could be charged only upon a corporeal hereditament. There could be no rentcharge charged upon another rentcharge or other incorporeal hereditament[10]; a right of distress would clearly be inappropriate in such cases. However, since 1925 a rentcharge charged upon another rentcharge has been valid, even if created before 1926; and special provisions have been made for enforcing payment.[11]

4. Restrictions on rentcharges

The Rentcharges Act 1977 severely curtailed most rentcharges, excepting those types which still performed a useful service. Apart from the exceptions, the Act

(i) prevented the creation of any rentcharge after August 21, 1977; and

(ii) provided for the extinguishment of existing rentcharges after 60 years.

These provisions will be considered below.

[5] A grant for life at a rent now creates a term of 90 years: see above, p. 350.
[6] See generally (1975) Law.Com. No. 68.
[7] See, *e.g. Chaplin v. Chaplin* (1733) 3 P.Wms. 229 (entail); *Re Fraser* [1904] 1 Ch. 726 (term of years).
[8] Above, p. 82.
[9] See below.
[10] *Re The Alms Corn Charity* [1901] 2 Ch. 750 at 759.
[11] L.P.A. 1925, s.122: below, p. 411.

Sect. 2. Creation and transfer of rentcharges

Subject to the Rentcharges Act 1977, a rentcharge can be created only as follows.

1. Form

(a) By statute

A rentcharge may be created either by statute, or by virtue of powers conferred thereby.[12]

(b) By instrument inter vivos

Apart from statute, a legal rentcharge can be created *inter vivos* only by a deed[13]; but a document merely in writing may create an equitable rentcharge.[14]

(c) By will

A will now operates only in equity,[15] so that if a rentcharge is created or devised by will, the beneficiary gets no legal interest until the personal representatives have assented to the gift.[16]

2. Words of limitation

If an existing rentcharge is being transferred by deed or will, the normal rule for corporeal hereditaments applies and the whole interest in the rentcharge passes without words of limitation unless a contrary intention is shown.[17] But if a rentcharge is being created by will or (perhaps) by deed, only a life interest will be created unless an intention is shown to create some larger interest.[18]

3. Restrictions on creation

By the Rentcharges Act 1977,[19] no new rentcharge can, with certain exceptions, be created either at law or in equity after August 21, 1977. The exceptions are as follows:

(i) a "family rentcharge", *i.e.* where land is charged for the life of a person or a shorter period whether under a settlement under the Settled Land Act 1925, a trust of land or otherwise[20];

(ii) a rentcharge imposed under an order of the court or a statutory rentcharge for works on land[21]; and

(iii) an "estate rentcharge", *i.e.* either a rentcharge for a nominal amount which is subject to a right of re-entry imposed as a means of enforcing covenants or other

---

[12] See, *e.g.* Improvement of Land Act 1864.
[13] See *Hewlins v. Shippam* (1826) 5 B. & C. 221 at 229.
[14] *Jackson v. Lever* (1792) 3 Bro.C.C. 605; L.P.A. 1925, s.53.
[15] See L.P.A.(Am.)A. 1924, Sched. IX.
[16] For assents, see above, pp. 199–200.
[17] Above, p. 38.
[18] See *Nichols v. Hawkes* (1853) 10 Hare 342; *Grant v. Edmondson* [1930] 2 Ch. 245 at 254; [1931] 1 Ch. 1; above, pp. 38–39.
[19] s.2(1), (2).
[20] *ibid.*, s.2(3)(a), (b) as substituted by T.L.A.T.A. 1996, Sched. 3, para. 15(1), (2).
[21] *ibid.*, s.2(3)(d).

obligations relating to land[22] or a rentcharge for the sums due in respect of the performance by the holder of the rentcharge of covenants made by him for the provision of services to, for the maintenance or repair of, or for the insurance of the land charged.[23]

Sect. 3. Means of enforcing payment

1. Rentcharge charged on land

There are four remedies available to the owner of a rentcharge charged on land if it is not paid. The first remedy, namely an action for the money, is given by the common law; the other three are created by statute,[24] and replace remedies formerly expressly conferred by most instruments creating rentcharges.

(a) Action for the money

A personal action for the rent will lie against the *terre tenant* (the freehold tenant in possession of the land upon which the rent is charged) even if the rent was not created by him[25] and exceeds the value of the land.[26] If the land has been divided, the *terre tenant* of any part is liable for the full amount[27]; but a mere lessee for a term of years is not liable,[28] for the action lies only against the freeholder.

Although the right to sue and the liability to be sued run with the rentcharge and the land respectively, the benefit of an express covenant for payment does not run with the rentcharge without express assignment.[29] Thus if a rentcharge created by A in favour of X is conveyed to Y and the land to B, Y cannot sue A on his covenant for payment if B fails to pay.

(b) Distress

If an express power of distress is given by the instrument creating the rentcharge, the extent of the right is a question of construction. If there is no such express power, and the rentcharge was created before 1882, the rentcharge owner can distrain upon the land as soon as the rent or any part of it is in arrear.[30] If the rentcharge was created after 1881, then, subject to any contrary intention, the rentcharge owner can distrain as soon as the rent or any part of it is 21 days in arrear.[31]

(c) Entry into possession

If a rentcharge was created after 1881 and shows no contrary intention, the rentcharge owner may, when the rent or any part of it is 40 days in arrear, enter and take possession of the land without impeachment of waste and take the income until he has paid himself all rent due with costs.[32]

---

[22] *ibid.*, s.2(3)(c), (4)(a), (5); see below, p. 462.
[23] *ibid.*, s.2(3)(c), (4)(b), (5).
[24] L.P.A. 1925, s.121, replacing C.A. 1881, s.44.
[25] *Thomas v. Sylvester* (1873) L.R. 8 Q.B. 368.
[26] *Pertwee v. Townsend* [1896] 2 Q.B. 129.
[27] *Christie v. Barker* (1884) 53 L.J.Q.B. 537.
[28] *Re Herbage Rents* [1896] 2 Ch. 811.
[29] See *Grant v. Edmondson* [1931] 1 Ch. 1, criticised (1931) 47 L.Q.R. 380 (W. Strachan).
[30] L. & T.A. 1730, s.5.
[31] L.P.A. 1925, s.121(2).
[32] *ibid.*, s.121(3).

(d) Demise to a trustee

If the rentcharge was created after 1881 and shows no contrary intention, the rentcharge owner may, if the rent or any part of it is 40 days in arrear, demise the land to a trustee for a term of years, with or without impeachment of waste, on trust to raise the money due, with all costs and expenses, by creating a mortgage, receiving the income or any other reasonable means.[33] If a rentcharge owner has only an equitable interest, he can grant only an equitable lease to the trustee, but the estate owner can be compelled to clothe the equitable lease with the legal estate.[34]

If the rentcharge is created after July 15, 1964, the rule against perpetuities does not apply to any powers or remedies for enforcing it.[35] If the rentcharge was created before that date the last three statutory remedies were expressly excepted from the rule, together with similar express powers conferred by an instrument.[36] Other, wider, provisions were not considered to be excepted from the rule, for example a clause which is sometimes inserted entitling the rentcharge owner to effect a permanent forfeiture of the land if the rent is unpaid for a specified period.[37]

2. Rentcharge charged on another rentcharge

Instead of the statutory remedies of distress, entry into possession and demise to a trustee, the owner of a rentcharge charged upon another rentcharge may appoint a receiver if the rent or any part of it is 21 days in arrear.[38] The receiver has all the powers of a receiver appointed by a mortgagee.[39] Thus if Greenacre is charged with a rent of £100 per annum and that rentcharge is charged with a rent of £25 per annum in favour of X, a receiver of the £100 can be appointed by X if the £25 is unpaid for 21 days.

Sect. 4. Extinguishment of rentcharges

A rentcharge may be extinguished by release, statutory discharge, merger, limitation or the expiry of the 60-year period under the Rentcharges Act 1977.

1. Release

The owner of a rentcharge may by deed release the land from the rent, either wholly or in part. A partial release may take the form of releasing all the land from part of the rent,[40] or releasing part of the land from the whole of the rent.[41] An informal release may be valid in equity.

2. Statutory redemption

Land will be discharged from a rentcharge if the landowner obtains a "redemption certificate" from the Secretary of State for the Environment (or Wales) certifying that he has paid

---

[33] *ibid.*, s.121(4).
[34] *ibid.*, ss.3(1), 8(2).
[35] Perpetuities and Accumulations Act 1964, s.11, amending L.P.A. 1925, s.121(6); above, p. 238.
[36] L.P.A. 1925, s.121(6).
[37] See *Re Trustees of Hollis' Hospital and Hague's Contract* [1899] 2 Ch. 540, criticised in Challis R.P. 190.
[38] L.P.A. 1925, s.122(2), (3).
[39] *ibid.*, s.122(2); below, p. 511.
[40] Co.Litt. 148a.
[41] L.P.A 1925, s.70.

the owner of the rentcharge a sum representing the capital value as certified by the Secretary of State.[42]

3. Merger

At common law, if a rentcharge became vested in the same person as the land upon which it was charged, the rentcharge became extinguished by merger, even if this was not the intention.[43] For this to occur, both the rent and the land must have been vested in the same person at the same time and in the same right.[44] This automatic rule of the common law no longer applies, for, by the Law of Property Act 1925,[45] there is to be no merger at law except in cases where there would have been a merger in equity, and the equitable rule is that merger depends upon the intention of the parties.[46] Even if an intention that there should be no merger cannot be shown, there will be a presumption against merger if it is to the interest of the person concerned to prevent it.[47]

4. Limitation

If a rentcharge is not paid for 12 years and no sufficient acknowledgment of the owner's title is made, it is extinguished under the Limitation Act 1980.[48]

5. Elapse of 60 years

With certain exceptions, every rentcharge will be extinguished, without compensation, when 60 years have elapsed since it was first payable or since July 21, 1977 (*i.e.* on July 21, 2037), whichever is the later.[49] But this does not apply to variable rentcharges, nor to any rentcharge, whenever created, that is of the kind excluded from the prohibition against creation.[50]

Sect. 5. Types of rent

A summary of the various kinds of rent may be useful.

1. Rent service

This is rent due from a tenant to his lord by reason of tenure; it is now encountered only in the case of rent due under a lease or tenancy.

2. Rentcharge

This is a periodical sum charged on land independently of any relationship of lord and tenant, supported by a power of distress.

3. Rent seck

This was a rentcharge with no power of distress. It is now obsolete.

---

[42] Rentcharges Act 1977, ss.8–10, replacing L.P.A. 1925, s.191.
[43] *Capital and Counties Bank Ltd v. Rhodes* [1903] 1 Ch. 631 at 652.
[44] *Re Radcliffe* [1892] 1 Ch. 227.
[45] s.185, replacing J.A. 1873, s.25(4).
[46] *Ingle v. Vaughan Jenkins* [1900] 2 Ch. 368.
[47] *Re Fletcher* [1917] 1 Ch. 339.
[48] See below, p. 555.
[49] Rentcharges Act 1977, s.3(1).
[50] *ibid.*, s.3(3), (4), (5); above, p. 409.

4. Chief rent

This was a rent service reserved on the subinfeudation of freehold land in fee simple. The Statute Quia Emptores 1290 for the most part prevented such rents being created.[51] Any chief rents existing in 1925 were extinguished by the end of 1935.[52] In some parts of the country, such as Manchester, rentcharges are sometimes called chief rents.

5. Fee farm rent

This was the name originally used for chief rents; latterly, it has been applied to rentcharges reserved on a conveyance in fee simple.

6. Quit rent

This was a rent service payable by a copyholder to his lord, whereby he went quit of his obligation to perform agricultural services; and chief rents were sometimes called quit rents. Quit rents existing in 1925 were extinguished by the end of 1935.[53]

7. Rents of assize

This term is rarely encountered today; it was applied both to chief rents and quit rents.

PART 2—EASEMENTS AND PROFITS

Sect. 1. Nature of easements

An easement may be defined as a right to use, or restrict the use of, the land of another person in some way. This definition is neither exact nor particularly helpful, for it includes certain rights which are not easements, such as restrictive covenants, and it fails to illustrate what sort of a right an easement is. Examples of easements are rights of way, rights of light and rights of water. The best way in which to amplify this imperfect definition is to examine

> (i) the essentials of an easement, and

> (ii) the distinction between easements and certain analogous rights.

1. Essentials of an easement

(a) There must be a dominant and a servient tenement[54]

If X owns Greenacre and grants a right to use a path across it to the owner for the time being of the neighbouring plot of Whiteacre, Greenacre is the servient tenement and Whiteacre the dominant tenement. Had X granted the right to A who owned no land at all, A would have acquired a licence to walk over Greenacre, but his right could not exist as an easement, for a dominant tenement is lacking. Put technically, an easement cannot exist in gross[55] (independently of the ownership of land) but only as appurtenant (attached) to a dominant

---

[51] Above, p. 407.
[52] See above, p. 28.
[53] *ibid.*
[54] *Hawkins v. Rutter* [1892] 1 Q.B. 668.
[55] *Rangeley v. Midland Ry.* (1868) 3 Ch.App. 306 at 310. See (1980) 96 L.Q.R. 557 (M.F. Sturley).

tenement.[56] On any transfer of the dominant tenement, the easement will pass with the land, so that the occupier for the time being can enjoy it,[57] even if he is a mere lessee.[58]

(b) The easement must accommodate the dominant tenement

A right cannot exist as an easement unless it confers a benefit on the dominant tenement as a tenement. It is not enough that the right should give the owner for the time being some personal advantage unconnected with his land, such as a right to use a wall on the servient tenement for advertising generally and not merely in connection with a business carried on upon the dominant tenement.[59] The test is whether the right makes the dominant tenement a better and more convenient tenement, for example a right to affix to adjoining premises a signboard for a public house.[60] There has to be some nexus between the enjoyment of the right and the use of the dominant tenement, so that the grant to a purchaser of the right free of charge to attend a nearby zoo or cricket ground cannot create an easement.[61]

Again, if X owns land in Northumberland, he cannot burden it with an easement of way in favour of land in Kent, for although it may be very convenient for the owner of the Kentish land to walk across X's Northumberland estate when he goes north, the right of way does not improve the Kentish land as a tenement.[62] This does not mean that a right cannot exist as an easement unless the dominant and servient tenements are contiguous; even if they are separated by other land, an easement can still exist, provided it in fact confers some benefit upon the dominant tenement as such,[63] as does a right for the dominant owner to enjoy an adjacent pleasure ground.[64] Nor will a right be any the less an easement merely because it benefits other land as well as the dominant tenement.[65]

In *Ackroyd v. Smith*[66] it was held that a right of way granted "for all purposes" to the tenant of Whiteacre and his successors in title was not an easement, for the grant permitted the way to be used for purposes not connected with Whiteacre. Had the grant been worded "for all purposes connected with Whiteacre" it could have created an easement. Probably the words used would be construed in this sense if the case arose today.[67]

In *Hill v. Tupper*[68] the owner of a canal leased land on the bank of the canal to Hill, and granted him the sole and exclusive right of putting pleasure boats on the canal. Tupper, without any authority, put rival pleasure boats on the canal. The question was whether Hill could successfully sue Tupper. If Hill's right amounted to an easement, he could sue anyone who interfered with it, for it was a right in land. If it was not an easement, then it could only be a licence,[69] *i.e.* a mere personal arrangement between Hill and the canal owner not amounting to an interest in land, so that Hill would have no right to sue those interfering with it. It was held that since the right did not improve Hill's land *qua* land, but gave him a mere

[56] See *Re Salvin's Indenture* [1938] 2 All E.R. 498 (dominant tenement partly incorporeal).
[57] L.P.A. 1925, s.187(1); *Leech v. Schweder* (1874) 9 Ch.App. 463 at 474, 475.
[58] *Thorpe v. Brumfitt* (1873) 8 Ch.App. 650.
[59] *Clapman v. Edwards* [1938] 2 All E.R. 507.
[60] *Moody v. Steggles* (1879) 12 Ch.D. 261.
[61] *Re Ellenborough Park* [1956] Ch. 131 at 174.
[62] See *Bailey v. Stephens* (1862) 12 C.B. (N.S.) 91 at 115.
[63] *Todrick v. Western National Omnibus Co. Ltd* [1934] Ch. 561; *Pugh v. Savage* [1970] 2 Q.B. 373.
[64] *Re Ellenborough Park* [1956] Ch. 131 (park in a square).
[65] *Simpson v. Mayor of Godmanchester* [1897] A.C. 696.
[66] (1850) 10 C.B. 164.
[67] See *Todrick v. Western National Omnibus Co. Ltd* [1934] Ch. 561 at 583–585; and see *Clapman v. Edwards* [1938] 2 All E.R. 507.
[68] (1863) 2 H. & C. 121.
[69] See below, pp. 420, 453.

personal advantage, it was not an easement and so he could not sue Tupper. The result would have been different if the right granted had been to cross and recross the canal to get to and from Hill's land. The canal owner, of course, could have sued Tupper for trespassing on the canal.[70]

(c) The dominant and servient tenements must be owned or occupied by different persons

An easement is essentially a right *in alieno solo* (in the soil of another): a man cannot have an easement over his own land. "When the owner of Whiteacre and Blackacre passes over the former to Blackacre, he is not exercising a right of way in respect of Blackacre; he is merely making use of his own land to get from one part of it to another."[71]

It should be noted, however, that the same person must not only own both tenements but also occupy both of them before the existence of an easement is rendered impossible. Thus if an easement over Greenacre is appurtenant to Whiteacre, it will not be affected by the fee simple in each plot becoming vested in one person if the plots are occupied by different lessees[72]; unity of ownership without unity of possession is not fatal to an easement. Similarly, if the fee simple in each plot is owned by different persons, the easement will not be destroyed if the plots are leased to the same tenant, creating unity of possession without unity of ownership; during the currency of the lease the easement is suspended but it will revive when the lease ends.[73]

The name "quasi-easements" is often used to describe rights habitually exercised by a man over part of his own land which, if the part in question were owned and occupied by another, would be easements. These are of some importance, for in certain circumstances they may become true easements.[74]

(d) The easement must be capable of forming the subject-matter of a grant

No right can exist as an easement unless it could have been granted by deed. This involves the following points.

(i) There must be a capable grantor: There can be no claim to an easement if at the relevant times the servient tenement was owned by someone incapable of granting an easement, for example a statutory corporation with no power to grant easements.[75]

(ii) There must be a capable grantee: An easement can be claimed only by a legal person capable of receiving a grant. Thus a claim by a company with no power to acquire easements must fail[76]; similarly, a fluctuating body of persons, such as "the inhabitants for the time being of the village of X", cannot claim an easement, for no grant could be made to them. But such bodies may claim similar rights by showing that there is a custom to that effect, such as a customary right of way across land to reach the parish church,[77] or a customary right to

---

[70] See *Lord Chesterfield v. Harris* [1908] 2 Ch. 397 at 412 (affirmed [1911] A.C. 623).
[71] *Roe v. Siddons* (1888) 22 Q.B.D. 224 at 236, *per* Fry L.J.
[72] *Richardson v. Graham* [1908] 1 K.B. 39; and see *Buckby v. Coles* (1814) 5 Taunt. 311 at 315.
[73] *Thomas v. Thomas* (1835) 2 Cr.M. & R. 34 (see especially at 40).
[74] Below, pp. 428 *et seq.*
[75] See *Re Salvin's Indenture* [1938] 2 All E.R. 498.
[76] *National Guaranteed Manure Co. v. Donald* (1859) 4 H. & N. 8.
[77] *Brocklebank v. Thompson* [1903] 2 Ch. 344.

play games[78] or dry nets on certain land.[79] There may also be a customary duty, such as a duty binding the frontagers to a common to fence against cattle grazing the common.[80]

(iii) The right must be sufficiently definite: The extent of the right claimed must be capable of reasonable definition. Thus although there can be an easement of light where a defined window receives a defined amount of light,[81] there can be no easement of unrestricted light to the claimant's land,[82] nor of privacy,[83] nor of prospect (the right to a view), for "the law does not give an action for such things of delight".[84] Similarly, although an easement for the passage of air through a defined channel may exist,[85] there can be no easement for the general flow of air over land to a windmill or chimney.[86] Again, although an easement to receive an undiminished flow of water through a defined channel may exist,[87] there can be no easement either to receive[88] or to discharge[89] percolating water such as rainwater, for any advantage or disadvantage produced thereby is a product of nature. However, sometimes rights which cannot take effect as easements may be obtained by means of the imposition of restrictive covenants[90] or under the rule against derogation from grant.[91]

(iv) The right must be within the general nature of rights capable of existing as easements: Although most easements fall under one of the well-known heads of easements, such as way, light, support and so on, the list of easements is not closed. "The category of servitudes and easements must alter and expand with the changes that take place in the circumstances of mankind."[92] But there are limits. "It must not therefore be supposed that incidents of a novel kind can be devised and attached to property, at the fancy or caprice of any owner."[93] Today, new rights are unlikely to be recognised as easements if they prevent the servient owner from doing things on his land, in the way that rights of light do, as distinct from requiring him merely to suffer something to be done on his land.[94] Nor are rights likely to be accepted as easements if they involve the servient owner in the expenditure of money, for no recognised easement does this.[95] An exception is the obligation to fence land in order to keep out cattle.[96] This has been described as "in the nature of a spurious easement",[97] or,

---

[78] *New Windsor Corporation v. Mellor* [1974] 1 W.L.R. 1504.
[79] *Mercer v. Denne* [1905] 2 Ch. 538; below, p. 421.
[80] *Egerton v. Harding* [1975] Q.B. 62.
[81] *Easton v. Isted* [1903] 1 Ch. 405.
[82] *Colls v. Home and Colonial Stores Ltd* [1904] A.C. 179.
[83] *Browne v. Flower* [1911] 1 Ch. 219.
[84] *Aldred's Case* (1610) 9 Co.Rep. 57b at 58b, *per* Wray C.J..
[85] *Bass v. Gregory* (1890) 25 Q.B.D. 481; *Cable v. Bryant* [1908] 1 Ch. 259.
[86] *Webb v. Bird* (1862) 13 C.B. (N.S.) 841; *Bryant v. Lefever* (1879) 4 C.P.D. 172.
[87] *Dickinson v. Grand Junction Canal Co. Ltd* (1852) 7 Exch. 282 at 301.
[88] *Chasemore v. Richards* (1859) 7 H.L. Cas. 349.
[89] *Palmer v. Bowman* [2000] 1 All E.R. 23.
[90] Below, p. 421.
[91] Below, pp. 453 *et seq.*
[92] *Dyce v. Hay* (1852) 1 Macq. 205 at 312, *per* Lord St. Leonards L.C.
[93] *Keppell v. Bailey* (1833) 2 My. & K. 517 at 535, *per* Lord Brougham L.C.
[94] See *Phipps v. Pears* [1965] 1 Q.B. 76 (protection of wall from weather by adjoining house: no easement); contrast *Sedgwick Forbes Bland Payne Group Ltd v. Regional Properties Ltd* (1979) 257 E.G. 64 at 70 (building divided horizontally) and *Hunter v. Canary Wharf Ltd* [1997] A.C. 655 (right to receive television signal and so prevent building envisaged as easement).
[95] See *Pomfret v. Ricroft* (1669) 1 Wms.Saund. 321; *Rance v. Elvin* (1985) 50 P. & C.R. 9 (right to passage of water through pipe but not to a supply of water).
[96] *Crow v. Wood* [1971] 1 Q.B. 77; *Egerton v. Harding* [1975] Q.B. 62.
[97] *Lawrence v. Jenkins* (1873) L.R. 8 Q.B. 274 at 279, *per* Archibald J.

more kindly, as "in the nature of an easement"[98]; and it may also arise by custom.[99] But new rights which do not involve the servient owner in expenditure have from time to time been recognised as easements. Thus in 1896 the right to go upon the land of another to open sluice gates,[1] in 1915 a right to store casks and trade produce on land,[2] in 1955 the right to use a neighbour's lavatory,[3] in 1956 the right to enjoy a park[4] and in 1973 the right to use an airfield[5] were all recognised as being capable of existing as easements.

An easement is a right over the land of another, and not a right to it. Thus the continuous occupation of the whole of a strip of land for the storage and repair of vehicles cannot be an easement, for it amounts to virtually the whole beneficial use of the land.[6] Similarly an exclusive right to a defined parking place cannot be an easement if it renders the ownership of the owner of the servient tenement illusory[7]; whether it does so or not is a question of degree.[8] But the ordinary parking of cars is a discontinuous process[9] and the right to park a car intermittently anywhere in a defined area can be an easement[10]; and so may the right of the tenant of part of a house to store coal in a shed in the garden.[11]

2. Distinction between easements and certain analogous rights

The nature of easements may be further indicated by contrasting them with certain other rights.

3. Quasi-easements

As already explained,[12] rights exercised by a landowner over his own land which, if he did not own that land, could exist as easements, are sometimes called quasi-easements.

4. Natural rights

In addition to his rights over his own land, every landowner has a natural right to support, *i.e.* a right that the support for his land provided by his neighbour's land should not be removed,[13] whether directly or by causing the subsoil to liquefy.[14] A similar right exists in cases where the surface of the land and the soil underneath are owned by different persons; the owner of the surface has a natural right to have it supported by the subjacent soil[15] unless

---

[98] *Crow v. Wood* [1971] 1 Q.B. 77 at 85, *per* Lord Denning M.R.
[99] *Egerton v. Harding* [1975] Q.B. 62.
[1] *Simpson v. Mayor of Godmanchester* [1896] 1 Ch. 214; [1897] A.C. 696.
[2] *Att.-Gen. of Southern Nigeria v. Holt* [1915] A.C. 599. The headnote calls the right an irrevocable licence, but it was clearly recognised as an easement: see at 617.
[3] *Miller v. Emcer Products Ltd* [1956] Ch. 304.
[4] *Re Ellenborough Park* [1956] Ch. 131.
[5] *Dowty Boulton Paul Ltd v. Wolverhampton Corporation (No.2)* [1976] Ch. 13.
[6] *Copeland v. Greenhalf* [1952] Ch. 488, in which *Wright v. Macadam* [1949] 2 K.B. 744 was not cited.
[7] *Batchelor v. Marlow* (2001) 82 P. & C.R. 36 (exclusive parking for 10 hours a day from Monday to Friday).
[8] *London & Blenheim Estates Ltd v. Ladbroke Retail Parks Ltd* [1992] 1 W.L.R. 1298 (affirmed [1994] 1 W.L.R. 31).
[9] *Williams v. Usherwood* (1983) 45 P. & C.R. 235 at 251; and see *Pavledes v. Ryesbridge Properties Ltd* (1989) 58 P. & C.R. 459 (car park for factory).
[10] *London & Blenheim Estates Ltd v. Ladbroke Retail Parks Ltd* [1992] 1 W.L.R. 1298 (affirmed [1994] 1 W.L.R. 31); *Hair v. Gillman and Inskip* (2000) 80 P. & C.R. 108.
[11] *Wright v. Macadam* [1949] 2 K.B. 744; contrast *Copeland v. Greenhalf* [1952] Ch. 488.
[12] Above, p. 415.
[13] *Backhouse v. Bonomi* (1861) 9 H.L.C. 503.
[14] *Lotus Ltd v. British Soda Co. Ltd* [1972] Ch. 123.
[15] *London & North Western Ry. v. Evans* [1893] 1 Ch. 16 at 30.

this right is excluded by clear words or necessary implication in some statute or agreement.

This natural right, however, extends only to land in its natural state; there is no natural right to support for buildings or for the additional burden on land which they cause.[16] But if support is withdrawn, and the land would have fallen even it had not been built upon, an action lies in respect of any damage to the buildings.[17]

Similarly, there is no natural right to have buildings supported by neighbouring buildings.[18] If no more damage is done than is necessary, a man may pull down his house without having to provide support for his neighbour's house. The right to have buildings supported by land or by other buildings can, however, be acquired as an easement.[19]

5. Public rights

An easement must always be appurtenant to land; it is a right exercisable by the owner for the time being by virtue of his estate in the land. A public right, on the other hand, is a right exercisable by anyone, whether he owns land or not, merely by virtue of being a member of the public.

The public rights which most closely resemble easements are public rights of way. The land over which a public right of way exists is known as a highway, and although most highways have been made up into roads, and most easements of way exist over footpaths, the presence or absence of a made road has nothing to do with the distinction. There may be a highway over a footpath, while a well-made road may be subject only to an easement of way, or may exist only for the landowner's benefit and be subject to no easement at all.

(a) Creation

A public right of way may be created in the following ways.

(i) By statute: This needs no explanation.

(ii) By dedication and acceptance: (1) *At common law.* To establish a highway at common law by dedication and acceptance, it must be shown

    (i) that the owner of the land dedicated the way to the public, and also

    (ii) that the public accepted that dedication, the acceptance normally being shown by user by the public.[20]

Dedication may be formal, although this is comparatively infrequent. It is usually inferred from long user by the public, the user thus being effective to prove both dedication and acceptance. But to raise a presumption of dedication, there must have been open use as of right for so long a time that it must have come to the notice of the landowner that the public were using the way as of right, thus justifying the inference that the landowner consented to this user.[21] User with the landowner's licence is not user as of right,[22] for it acknowledges

[16] *Wyatt v. Harrison* (1823) 3 B. & Ad. 871.
[17] *Stroyan v. Knowles* (1861) 6 H. & N. 454; *Lotus Ltd v. British Soda Co. Ltd* [1972] Ch. 123.
[18] *Peyton v. Mayor of London* (1829) 9 B. & C. 725.
[19] Below, p. 428.
[20] See *Cubitt v. Lady Caroline Maxse* (1873) L.R. 8 C.P. 704 at 715.
[21] *Greenwich District Board of Works v. Maudslay* (1870) L.R. 5 Q.B. 397 at 404.
[22] *R. v. Broke* (1859) 1 F. & F. 514.

that the way is being used not because the public has a right to do so but because the landowner has agreed not to treat it as a trespass in the particular case in question. Further, the use must have been without interruption by the owner. A practice frequently adopted to disprove any intention to dedicate is to close the way for one day in each year, for this openly asserts the landowner's right to exclude the public at will.[23]

The length of the enjoyment to be shown depends on the circumstances of the case. Where the circumstances have pointed to an intention to dedicate, 18 months have been held to be enough,[24] while where the circumstances are against dedication, a substantially greater period may be insufficient.

(2) *Under the Highways Act 1980.* The Rights of Way Act 1932 (now replaced by provisions in the Highways Act 1980) simplified the position to some extent by laying down a definite period of use that will suffice to show that a right of way exists. The public can still claim a right of way based on use for a shorter period than that laid down by the Act if an intent to dedicate can be inferred.

The Act of 1980 provides that a way over land (not including a river[25]) is to be deemed to have been dedicated as a highway if it "has been actually enjoyed by the public as of right and without interruption for a full period of 20 years", unless "there is sufficient evidence that there was no intention during that period to dedicate it".[26] "Interruption" means interruption in fact, and not, for instance the mere closing of the way only at times when nobody used it or was likely to do so.[27] The absence of any intention to dedicate can be shown either in one of the usual ways, as by closing the way for one day in each year, or in one of the special ways provided by the Act, namely, by exhibiting a notice visible to those using the way, or by depositing a map with the local council with a statement of what ways the landowner admits to be highways and lodging statutory declarations at intervals of not more than six years, stating whether any other ways have been dedicated. A reversioner or remainderman upon an interest for life or *pur autre vie* is entitled to the same remedies against the public as if he were in possession.[28]

The 20-year period is to be calculated as that next before the time when the right to use the way was brought into question by a notice exhibited to the public negativing the dedication or otherwise.[29]

(b) Extinguishment

When a highway has been established, it can be stopped up or diverted only by an order made under certain statutory provisions[30]; the mere obstruction of the highway or the failure by the public to use it will not destroy the rights of the public, for "once a highway always a highway".[31] And a mere closing order for a highway leaves unaffected any easement over the route of the highway.[32]

[23] See *British Museum Trustees v. Finnis* (1833) 5 C. & P. 460; and see [1986] Conv. 161 (A. Samuels).
[24] *North London Ry. v. The Vestry of St. Mary, Islington* (1872) 27 L.T. 672.
[25] *Att.-Gen. ex rel. Yorkshire Derwent Trust Ltd v. Brotherton* [1992] 1 A.C. 425 (right of navigation cannot be acquired under the Act).
[26] Highways Act 1980, s.31(1).
[27] *Lewis v. Thomas* [1950] 1 K.B. 438.
[28] Highways Act 1980, s.33.
[29] *ibid.*, s.31(2).
[30] *e.g.* Highways Act 1980, ss.116–123; Town and Country Planning Act 1990, ss.247–260.
[31] *Dawes v. Hawkins* (1860) 8 C.B. (N.S.) 848 at 858, *per* Byles J.
[32] *Walsh v. Oates* [1953] 1 Q.B. 578.

6. Licences

Licences resemble easements in that they authorise the use of the land of another in some way. But licences, which cannot exist as legal estates or interests or, probably, as equitable interests, are far more flexible and less restricted than easements. Thus they may be created without formality; they require no dominant tenement; and they may authorise the occupation of land.[33]

7. Restrictive covenants

Easements and restrictive covenants are similar in that an easement, like a restrictive covenant, may entitle a landowner to restrict the use that his neighbour makes of his land; thus the owner of an easement of light may prevent the servient owner from obstructing his light by erecting a building on the adjoining land.[34] There are other resemblances, such as the need for dominant and servient tenements, and in general the law of restrictive covenants may be regarded as being an equitable extension of the law of easements. However, certain points of difference should be mentioned.

(a) Scope

Restrictive covenants are wider in scope and more flexible than easements. As has been seen, there can be no easement entitling the dominant owner to a view or the general flow of air.[35] But by means of suitable restrictive covenants preventing his neighbour from building, a landowner can enjoy both the view and a general flow of air.

(b) Visibility

An inspection of the land will suggest the existence of many easements, but it is otherwise with restrictive covenants. Thus footpaths suggest an easement of way and pipes an easement of drainage, but no inspection of the land will reveal the existence of a covenant against trading upon it.

(c) Existence at law

An easement may be legal or equitable, whereas the burden of a restrictive covenant runs only in equity.

(d) Prescription

An easement may be acquired by prescription; not so a restrictive covenant.

(e) Positive nature

A restrictive covenant is entirely negative; it neither entitles the dominant owner nor binds the servient owner to do any positive act. Easements similarly do not bind the servient owner to do any positive act,[36] but as regards the dominant owner certain easements (called "positive easements") entitle the owner to do positive acts, for example easements of way, while others (called "negative easements") do not, for example easements of light. Certain easements thus contain a positive element which is lacking in restrictive covenants.

---

[33] For licences, see below, pp. 427 *et seq.*
[34] For restrictive covenants, see below, pp. 409 *et seq.*
[35] Above, p. 370.
[36] But see the obligation to fence: above, p. 371.

8. Rights under the rule against derogation from grant

A grantor may not derogate from his grant: where he sells or leases land, knowing that the grantee intends to use it for a particular purpose, neither he nor his successors in title may do anything to impede such purposed use, and the grantee obtains corresponding rights.[37] Thus, where a lease was granted to a timber merchant who needed a free general flow of air to dry his timber, a purchaser of the lessor's adjoining land could not build upon it so as to obstruct the ventilation required by the lessee.[38]

9. Customary rights of fluctuating bodies

These have been considered above.[39] They differ from easements in that they are exercisable by all who are included within the custom, independently of ownership of a dominant tenement. Thus the custom may extend to all the inhabitants of a particular locality, whether or not they own land.[40]

Sect. 2. Nature of a profit *à prendre*

A profit *à prendre* has been described as "a right to take something off another person's land".[41] This is too wide. The thing taken must be some-thing taken out of the soil,[42] *i.e.* it must be either the soil, the natural produce thereof, or the wild animals existing on it; and the thing taken must at the time of taking be susceptible of ownership.[43] A right to "hawk, hunt, fish and fowl" may thus exist as a profit,[44] for this gives the right to take creatures living on the soil which, when killed, are capable of being owned. But a right to take water from a spring or a pump, or the right to water cattle at a pond, may be an easement though it cannot be a profit; for the water, when taken, was not owned by anyone nor was it part of the soil.[45] A right to take water stored in an artificial receptacle, such as a cistern, is not an easement but may perhaps exist either as a profit or a mere licence, probably the latter.[46]

1. Classification of profits *à prendre*—as to ownership

A profit *à prendre* may be enjoyed

> (i) by one person to the exclusion of all others; this is known as a several profit; or
>
> (ii) by one person in common with others; this is known as a profit in common, or a common.

2. Classification of profits *à prendre*—in relation to land

A profit is not necessarily appurtenant to land, as is the case with easements. It may exist in the following forms.

---

[37] (1964) 80 L.Q.R. 244 (D.W. Elliott).
[38] *Aldin v. Latimer Clark, Muirhead & Co.* [1894] 2 Ch. 437.
[39] Above, p. 416; see also below, p. 423.
[40] *Race v. Ward* (1855) 4 E. & B. 702.
[41] *Duke of Sutherland v. Heathcote* [1892] 1 Ch. 475 at 484, *per* Lindley L.J.
[42] *Manning v. Wasdale* (1836) 5 A. & E. 758 at 764.
[43] *Race v. Ward* (1855) 4 E. & B. 702 at 709; *Lowe v. J. W. Ashmore Ltd* [1971] Ch. 545 at 557.
[44] *Wickham v. Hawker* (1840) 7 M. & W. 63.
[45] See *Mason v. Hill* (1833) 5 B. & Ad. 1 at 24; *Manning v. Wasdale* (1836) 5 A. & E. 758 at 764.
[46] See (1938) 2 Conv. (N.S.) 203. (J.S. Fiennes).

(a) A profit appurtenant

This is a profit, whether several or in common, attached to land by act of parties. A profit appurtenant may be acquired either by grant or by prescription. In general, there must be compliance with the four conditions necessary for the existence of an easement, which can exist only as appurtenant to land.[47] Thus a profit of piscary appurtenant cannot be exploited for commercial purposes; the number of fish taken must be limited to the needs of the dominant tenement.[48]

(b) A profit appendant

This is a profit annexed to land by operation of law; probably it exists only in the form of a common of pasture.[49] If before the Statute Quia Emptores 1290 the lord of a manor sub-infeudated arable land to a freeholder, the freeholder obtained, as appendant to the arable lands, the right to pasture, on the waste land of the manor, animals to plough and manure the land granted to him.[50] This right was known as a common of pasture appendant and was limited both as to the kind and number of animals which could be depastured. It extended only to horses and oxen (to plough the land) and cows and sheep (to manure it),[51] and only to the number of these "levant and couchant" on the land to which the right was appendant, *i.e.* the number which the dominant tenement was capable of maintaining during the winter.[52] It was immaterial that the land was at any particular time used for purposes temporarily rendering the maintenance of cattle impossible, for the test was not the number actually supported but the number which the land could be made to support.

No common appendant could be created after 1290,[53] for a conveyance of freehold land in a manor after that date resulted in the grantee holding of the grantor's lord, and the land passed out of the manor altogether.

(c) A profit pur cause de vicinage

This exists only in the form of a common of pasture. If two adjoining commons are open to each other, there is a common *pur cause de vicinage* if the cattle put on one common by the commoners have always been allowed to stray to the other common, and vice versa.[54] The claim fails if in the past the cattle have been driven off one common by the commoners thereof,[55] or if the commons have been fenced off,[56] or if the two commons are not contiguous to each other, even if they are separated only by a third common.[57]

(d) A profit in gross

This is a profit, whether several or in common, exercisable by the owner independently of his ownership of land; there is no dominant tenement. Thus a right to take fish from a canal

---

[47] Above, p. 413.
[48] *Harris v. Earl of Chesterfield* [1911] A.C. 623.
[49] See 6 *Halsbury* (4th ed.), pp. 199, 220; but see Tudor L.C.R.P., pp. 713–716.
[50] *Earl of Dunraven v. Llewellyn* (1850) 15 Q.B. 791 at 810.
[51] *Tyrringham's Case* (1584) 4 Co.Rep. 36b at 37a.
[52] *Robertson v. Hartopp* (1889) 43 Ch.D. 484 at 516.
[53] See above, pp. 27, 407.
[54] *Pritchard v. Powell* (1845) 10 Q.B. 589 at 603.
[55] *Heath v. Elliott* (1838) 4 Bing.N.C. 388.
[56] *Tyrringham's Case* (1584) 4 Co.Rep. 36b.
[57] *Commissioners of Sewers v. Glasse* (1874) L.R. 19 Eq. 134.

without stint (*i.e.* without limit) can exist as a profit in gross,[58] but not, as already seen, as a profit appurtenant.[59] A profit in gross is an interest in land which will pass under the owner's will or intestacy or can be sold or dealt with in any of the usual ways.

3. Distinctions between profits *à prendre* and certain analogous rights

(a) Quasi-profits

The principles that apply to quasi-profits are similar to those that govern quasi-easements.[60]

(b) Other natural rights

The same applies.[61] An example is the right of a riparian owner to the unimpeded passage of fish from neighbouring portions of the stream.[62]

(c) Public rights

The public right which most closely resembles a profit is the right of the public to fish in the sea and all tidal waters. However, since in theory the right is the Crown's, it was formerly possible for the Crown to grant to an individual the exclusive right to fish in a specified part of the sea or tidal waters; such a franchise was known as a free fishery.[63] In short, the public may fish in all tidal waters except a free fishery. But it has been held that the effect of Magna Carta 1215 was to prevent the Crown from creating any new free fisheries,[64] although any already existing remain valid and transferable to this day.

The right to fish in non-tidal water is dealt with below.[65]

(d) Rights of fluctuating bodies

There can be no custom for a fluctuating body of persons to take a profit.[66] The reason is said to be that otherwise the subject-matter would be destroyed.[67] However, if in fact such a right has been enjoyed for a long time as of right the courts will endeavour to find a legal origin for it. Two methods have been evolved.

(i) Presumed incorporation by Crown grant: The reason why a fluctuating body cannot own a profit is that the body is not a legal person to which a grant could be made.[68] However, the Crown is able to incorporate any body of persons (*i.e.* make them into a corporation), and so could, for example, grant a charter to a village making it a city or borough. Consequently there is nothing to prevent the Crown from making a grant of a profit to the inhabitants of a district and providing therein that for the purposes of the grant they should be treated as a corporation, though for other purposes they remain unincorporated. In fact, such grants have been made but rarely.[69] Their chief importance is that the court will presume that a grant of

---

[58] *Staffordshire & Worcestershire Canal Navigation v. Bradley* [1912] 1 Ch. 91.
[59] Above, p. 422.
[60] Above, pp. 415, 417.
[61] Above, p. 417.
[62] See *Barker v. Faulkner* (1898) 79 L.T. 24.
[63] 3 Cru.Dig. 261; see, *e.g. Stephens v. Snell* [1939] 3 All E.R. 622.
[64] *Malcolmson v. O'Dea* (1863) 10 H.L.C. 593 at 618; but see Theobald, *Land*, pp. 58 *et seq.*
[65] Below, p. 450.
[66] *Alfred F. Beckett Ltd v. Lyons* [1967] Ch. 449.
[67] *Race v. Ward* (1855) 4 E. & B. 702 at 705, 709.
[68] *Fowler v. Dale* (1594) Cro.Eliz. 362.
[69] See, *e.g. Willingale v. Maitland* (1866) L.R. 3 Eq. 103.

rights of this kind owned by the Crown at the time of the supposed grant has been made, provided

    (i) long enjoyment is proved, and

    (ii) those claiming the grant, and their predecessors, have always regarded themselves as a corporation and have acted as such as regards the right, as by holding meetings or appointing some officer to supervise the right.[70]

(ii) Presumed charitable trust: Even when the court cannot presume incorporation by Crown grant because the claimants have not acted as a corporation, if long enjoyment is shown the court may be able to find a legal origin for the right by presuming a grant of the profit to some corporation, subject to a trust or condition that the corporation should allow the claimants to exercise the rights claimed. Thus in *Goodman v. Mayor of Saltash*[71] the free inhabitants of certain ancient tenements had for 200 years enjoyed an oyster fishery from Candlemas (February 2) to Easter Eve each year. This right had been shared by the local corporation, which had enjoyed the right all the year round from time immemorial. The House of Lords refused to presume a grant incorporating the inhabitants for the purpose of the grant, but held that the corporation was entitled to a profit subject to a trust or condition in favour of the free inhabitants. Such a trust is charitable and so is not subject to the rule against inalienability.[72]

Sect. 3. Acquisition of easements and profits

An easement or profit can exist as a legal interest in land only if

    (i) it is held for an interest equivalent to a fee simple absolute in possession or term of years absolute[73]; and

    (ii) it is created either by statute, deed or prescription.

A legal easement or profit can be created only by deed,[74] although other documents may create a valid equitable easement or profit if made for value. Oral agreements for value could formerly do the same if they were supported by sufficient evidence in writing or part performance,[75] though now only an agreement in writing signed by both parties will suffice.[76] But in cases of part performance there may be an estoppel under which similar rights may arise.[77]

    The various methods of acquisition must now be considered.

---

[70] See *Re Free Fishermen of Faversham* (1887) 36 Ch.D. 329; *Lord Rivers v. Adams* (1878) 3 Ex.D. 361.
[71] (1882) 7 App. Cas. 633.
[72] *ibid.*, and see above, p. 238.
[73] Above, p. 82.
[74] *Duke of Somerset v. Fogwell* (1826) 5 B. & A. 875.
[75] See, *e.g. Mason v. Clarke* [1955] A.C. 778.
[76] Above, pp. 147 *et seq.*
[77] Above, p. 154; see *e.g. Crabb v. Arun D.C.* [1976] Ch. 179.

1. By statute

Easements created by statute are most frequently found in the case of local Acts of Parliament, such as an Act giving a right of support to a canal constructed under statutory powers.

2. By express reservation or grant

When a landowner sells part of his land and retains the rest, he may reserve easements or profits over the land sold, and grant the purchaser rights over the land retained. Today these transactions can be achieved quite simply, but this has not always been so.

(a) Express reservation

Before 1926, a legal easement or profit could not be created by a simple reservation in favour of the grantor. Being a new right it had to be granted by someone, and a person could not grant to himself. If, however, the conveyance reserved the right to the grantor, and the grantee also executed the conveyance, it operated as a conveyance to the grantee followed by the re-grant of the easement or profit by the grantee to the grantor.[78] The effect of a simple reservation not executed by the grantee was merely to create an equitable easement or profit.[79]

Since 1925 it has not been necessary for the grantee to execute the conveyance, as statute has provided that the reservation of a legal estate or interest shall be effective at law without any execution of the conveyance by the grantee "or any regrant by him".[80] It seems, however, that despite these words, the change merely goes to formalities.[81] The so-called reservation is still deemed to operate as a grant by the purchaser, which may have significant consequences. Where land held on trust was sold, and conveyed to the purchaser by the legal and equitable owners, a reservation by the equitable owners took effect as a grant of an legal easement by the purchaser and not as a reservation of a mere equitable easement by the vendor of the equitable interest.[82] Another consequence lies in the operation of the rule that where grants are ambiguous they are construed against the grantor.[83]

(b) Express grant

The ordinary case of an easement or profit created by the express words of a deed needs little discussion. The word "grant", though usual, is no longer essential; but not even the "grant" of a mere "licence" will create an easement.[84] The dominant tenement, if not sufficiently identified, may be inferred from the circumstances.[85] Further, an easement or profit may be created by express grant even though it is not mentioned in any deed. The Law of Property

---

[78] *Durham & Sunderland Ry. v. Walker* (1842) 2 Q.B. 940 at 967.

[79] *May v. Belleville* [1905] 2 Ch. 605.

[80] L.P.A. 1925, s.65; see also *Wiles v. Banks* (1985) 50 P. & C.R. 80 (conveying "subject to" a right may make it an easement; and see below, p. 483).

[81] *St. Edmundsbury and Ipswich Diocesan Board of Finance v. Clark (No.2)* [1975] 1 W.L.R. 468 at 478–480, commenting on *ibid.*, [1973] 1 W.L.R. 1572 at 1587–1591, where the view that the change is one of substance was maintained.

[82] *Johnstone v. Holdway* [1963] 1 Q.B. 601.

[83] *Bulstrode v. Lambert* [1953] 1 W.L.R. 1064 at 1068; *St. Edmundsbury and Ipswich Diocesan Board of Finance v. Clark (No.2)* [1975] 1 W.L.R. 468 at 477–480; but see *Cordell v. Second Clanfield Properties Ltd* [1969] 2 Ch. 9. See also below, p. 443.

[84] L.P.A. 1925, s.51(1); *I.D.C. Group Ltd v. Clark* [1992] 1 E.G.L.R. 187.

[85] *The Shannon Ltd v. Venner Ltd* [1965] Ch. 682.

Act 1925, s.62(1),[86] provides that any conveyance made after 1881 shall, subject to any contrary intention expressed in the conveyance,[87] operate to convey with the land a wide range of things and rights, including all privileges, easements, rights and advantages appertaining or reputed to appertain to the land or any part of it.[88] Thus, if a landlord grants his tenant a mere licence to use a coal shed for domestic purposes,[89] or to go through the landlord's house to reach the premises demised,[90] or to park intermittently anywhere in a defined area,[91] a subsequent conveyance to the tenant will operate to grant him the right as an easement unless the landlord revokes the licence prior to the conveyance. A right to require a neighbour to maintain fences may similarly arise.[92]

(i) Nature of rights: The section will not elevate into easements or profits rights which the grantor has no power to create by express grant,[93] or rights which cannot exist as legal easements or profits.[94] Thus it will not apply to a "right" to have a house protected from the weather by a contiguous house,[95] or to have central heating and hot water,[96] nor to a "right" of way over a courtyard during business hours when not inconvenient to the landlord,[97] or to use the landlord's passageway only while he is in occupation.[98] Nor will it apply where it is apparent that the "right" is merely temporary. Thus the first purchaser of a house in a housing development will not have the access of light to his windows transformed into an easement of light that would prevent adjoining plots of land from being built upon.[99]

(ii) Diversity of occupation or continuous and apparent: Section 62 will apply only where at the time of the grant either the two tenements are in different occupation or else the "right" is continuous and apparent.[1] What a landowner does on his own land he does as owner and not by virtue of any "right" in respect of one part of it over another.[2] But where one part is occupied by a tenant and he has been enjoying "rights" over the other part while it was occupied by the landlord, section 62 can apply to make those "rights" into easements if the landlord then grants the tenant a formal lease.[3] The section may also apply to a right which is reputed to appertain to the land as being continuous and apparent, such as windows enjoying a "right" of light,[4] a watercourse through visible pipes,[5] or a hard-beaten road.[6]

---

[86] Replacing C.A. 1881, s.6(1): see also L.P.A. 1925, s.62(2).
[87] L.P.A. 1925, s.62(4).
[88] See *Graham v. Philcox* [1984] Q.B. 747 (enlarged dominant tenement).
[89] *Wright v. Macadam* [1949] 2 K.B. 744.
[90] *Goldberg v. Edwards* [1950] Ch. 247.
[91] *Hair v. Gillman and Inskip* (2000) 80 P. & C.R. 108
[92] *Crow v. Wood* [1971] 1 Q.B. 77. For this "spurious easement", see above, p. 416.
[93] *Quicke v. Chapman* [1903] 1 Ch. 659 (grantor a mere licensee); *M.R.A. Engineering Ltd v. Trimster Co. Ltd* (1988) 56 P. & C.R. 1 (land previously sold by grantor).
[94] *International Tea Stores Co. v. Hobbs* [1903] 2 Ch. 165 at 172.
[95] *Phipps v. Pears* [1965] 1 Q.B. 76.
[96] *Regis Property Co. Ltd v. Redman* [1956] 2 Q.B. 612.
[97] *Green v. Ashco Horticulturist Ltd* [1966] 1 W.L.R. 889.
[98] *Goldberg v. Edwards* [1950] Ch. 247.
[99] *Godwin v. Schweppes Ltd* [1902] 1 Ch. 926; and see *Green v. Ashco Horticulturist Ltd*, above.
[1] *Long v. Gowlett* [1923] 2 Ch. 177; [1979] Conv. 113 (C. Harpum).
[2] See *Sovmots Investments Ltd v. Secretary of State for the Environment* [1979] A.C. 144 at 169, 176.
[3] *Wright v. Macadam* [1949] 2 K.B. 744; *Goldberg v. Edwards* [1950] Ch. 247.
[4] *Broomfield v. Williams* [1897] 1 Ch. 602.
[5] *Watts v. Kelson* (1870–71) L.R. 6 Ch.App. 166.
[6] *Bayley v. G.W.R.* (1884) 26 Ch.D. 434.

(iii) Operation of the section: The section applies to any "conveyance of land",[7] and this includes any assurance of property by an instrument, including leases, mortgages and assents,[8] but not a will or contract, nor an oral tenancy.[9] Where the section applies, the "right" in question becomes a legal easement or profit. Sometimes the section operates unexpectedly. A landlord who renews a lease[10] or sells the reversion to the tenant[11] may find that he has transformed into easements "rights" over his adjoining land which he has merely permitted the tenant to enjoy. Again, a vendor who lets the purchaser into possession before completion may find that "rights" over his adjoining land which the purchaser has enjoyed on sufferance have become easements on completion.[12] These unintended grants may be avoided by the insertion of suitable provisions into contracts, conveyances and leases, excluding the operation of the section; and most standard forms of contract do this,[13] though sometimes the subsequent conveyance inadvertently fails to do so.[14]

The relationship of the section with implied grants will be considered later.[15]

3. By implied reservation or grant

(a) Implied reservation

A grant is normally construed against the grantor and in favour of the grantee. Further, a grantor must not derogate from his grant. Consequently the general rule is that no easements will be implied in favour of a grantor; if he wishes to reserve any easements he must do so expressly.[16] To this rule there are two exceptions.

(i) Easements of necessity: If a grantor conveys the whole of a plot of land except a piece in the middle which, being completely surrounded by the part conveyed, is inaccessible, a way of necessity over the part conveyed will be implied in favour of the part retained.[17] This is so even if some of the surrounding land belongs to third parties, though it is essential that the necessity should exist at the time of the conveyance and not merely arise later.[18] The question is not whether the way is necessary for the reasonable enjoyment of the land retained, but whether the land cannot be used at all without the way.[19] Thus no such way will be inferred if there is some other means of access (such as by water[20]), even if it is difficult and inconvenient.[21] The right is based on the inference that unless otherwise provided the parties did not intend to make the land inaccessible.[22] The former owner of both plots may

---

[7] L.P.A. 1925, s.62(1).
[8] *ibid.*, s.205(1)(ii).
[9] *Rye v. Rye* [1962] A.C. 496.
[10] *Wright v. Macadam* [1949] 2 K.B. 744.
[11] *International Tea Stores Co. v. Hobbs* [1903] 2 Ch. 165.
[12] See *Lyme Valley Squash Club Ltd v. Newcastle under Lyme B.C.* [1985] 2 All E.R. 405.
[13] See *Squarey v. Harris-Smith* (1981) 42 P. & C.R. 119; and see the Standard Conditions of Sale 1990 (above, p. 124), Condition 3.4 (Encyclopedia of Forms and Precedents (5th ed.), Service Volume C (vol. 35), Form 21.1, para. 442.7).
[14] See *Lyme Valley Squash Club Ltd v. Newcastle under Lyme B.C.* [1985] 2 All E.R. 405.
[15] Below, p. 429.
[16] *Wheeldon v. Burrows* (1879) 12 Ch.D. 31 at 49.
[17] *Pinnington v. Galland* (1853) 9 Exch. 1.
[18] *Midland Ry. v. Miles* (1886) 33 Ch.D. 632.
[19] *Union Lighterage Co. v. London Graving Dock Co.* [1902] 2 Ch. 557 at 573; contrast below, p. 384.
[20] *Manjang v. Drammeh* (1991) 61 P. & C.R. 194.
[21] *M.R.A. Engineering Ltd v. Trimster Co. Ltd* (1988) 56 P. & C.R. 1 (public footpath but no road).
[22] *Nickerson v. Barraclough* [1981] Ch. 426, rejecting public policy.

select the particular way to be enjoyed, provided it is convenient[23]; but, once selected, it cannot be changed except by agreement.[24]

(ii) Intended easements: Easements required to carry out the common intention of the parties will be implied in favour of the grantor even though not expressed in the conveyance. Thus on the grant of one of two houses supported by each other, the mutual grant and reservation of easements of support will be implied if (as is usual) such an intention can be inferred.[25] A grantor who wishes to show that a reservation was mutually intended has a heavy onus of proof to discharge; thus a landlord will not impliedly reserve any right to advertise on his tenant's outside walls[26] nor will a vendor impliedly reserve the right to construct and to use an intended extension to an existing road marked as such on the conveyance in question.[27]

(b) Implied grant

If the owner of two plots conveys one of them, certain easements over the land retained are implied in favour of the land conveyed. The express grant of the land is said to be accompanied by the implied grant of the easements. Rights which will arise by implied grant are as follows.

(i) Easements of necessity: and

(ii) Intended easements: The rules which apply in these two cases are similar to those in the case of implied reservation. Thus where a landlord let his basement for use as a restaurant, and from the outset such a use was not lawful unless a proper ventilation system was installed, the tenant was held to be entitled to instal and use a ventilation duct attached to the outside of the landlord's premises as an easement of necessity.[28]

(iii) Ancillary easements: These are easements necessary for the enjoyment of some right expressly granted. Thus if there is a grant of an easement of the right to draw water from a spring, a right of way to the spring will be implied.[29]

(iv) Easements within the rule in *Wheeldon v. Burrows*: In *Wheeldon v. Burrows*[30] it was laid down that upon the grant of part of a tenement, there would pass to the grantee as easements all quasi-easements over the land retained which

    (i) were continuous and apparent,

    (ii) were necessary to the reasonable enjoyment of the land granted, and

    (iii) had been, and were at the time of the grant, used by the grantor for the benefit of the part granted.

A "continuous" easement is one giving the right to do some act of a continuous and constant nature. An "apparent" easement is one which is evidenced by some sign on the servient

---

[23] See *Pearson v. Spencer* (1861) 1 B. & S. 571 at 585; affirmed (1863) 3 B. & S. 761.
[24] *Deacon v. South Eastern Ry* (1889) 61 L.T. 377.
[25] *Richards v. Rose* (1853) 9 Exch. 221.
[26] *Re Webb's Lease* [1951] Ch. 808.
[27] *Chaffe v. Kingsley* [2002] 1 E.G.L.R. 104.
[28] *Wong v. Beaumont Property Trust Ltd* [1965] 1 Q.B. 173.
[29] *Pwlbach Colliery Co. Ltd v. Woodman* [1915] A.C. 634 at 646.
[30] (1879) 12 Ch.D. 31.

tenement discoverable on a careful inspection by a person ordinarily conversant with the subject.[31] Thus a drain into which water from the eaves of a house runs,[32] a watercourse through visible pipes,[33] and windows enjoying light,[34] all indicate the existence of continuous and apparent easements. On the other hand, a right to take water from a neighbour's pump from time to time[35] or a right to project the bowsprit of ships when in dock over the land of another[36] have been held to be outside the meaning of "continuous and apparent"[37] easements. Rights of way do not in general fall within the definition, but a way over a made road, or one which betrays its presence by some indication such as a worn track, will pass under the rule in *Wheeldon v. Burrows*.[38]

An easement is "necessary to the reasonable enjoyment of the land" if the land cannot be reasonably enjoyed without it; the test is much less stringent than for an easement of necessity.[39] It is still not clear whether this requirement and the requirement of "continuous and apparent" user are alternatives or, probably, cumulative, with the first requirement being based on conveyancing convenience and the second on the rule against derogation from grant.[40]

These rules apply to contracts to make a grant[41] as well as to grants. They also apply where the grantor, instead of retaining any land himself, makes simultaneous grants to two or more grantees. Each grantee obtains the same easements over the land of the other as he would have obtained if the grantor had retained it[42]; and similarly for two or more gifts that are made by the same will.[43]

(c) Relation to section 62

The importance of the rules relating to implied grant[44] has been considerably reduced by the operation of section 62 of the Law of Property Act 1925.[45] Yet implied grants have not been superseded by the section: the provisions overlap but are by no means identical in their operation. They may be compared as follows.

(i) Width: The section is wider than the rules for implied grant. The section applies to "all . . . rights . . . appertaining or reputed to appertain" to the land, and is not limited to rights that are necessary for the reasonable enjoyment of the land.[46] Further, unlike implied grants, the section can apply to profits *à prendre*.

(ii)   Contracts: The rules for implied grants apply not only to conveyances but also to contracts and wills.[47] The section applies only to a "conveyance", and widely though that

---

[31] *Pyer v. Carter* (1857) 1 H. & N. 916 at 922.
[32] *Pyer v. Carter* (1857) 1 H. & N. 916.
[33] *Watts v. Kelson* (1870) 6 Ch.App. 166.
[34] *Phillips v. Low* [1892] 1 Ch. 47 at 53.
[35] *Polden v. Bastard* (1865) L.R. 1 Q.B. 156.
[36] *Suffield v. Brown* (1864) 4 De G.J. & S. 185.
[37] On the origin of the phrase, see (1967) 83 L.Q.R. 240 (A.W.B. Simpson).
[38] See *Hansford v. Jago* [1921] 1 Ch. 322.
[39] Above, p. 428.
[40] See *Sovmots Investments Ltd v. Secretary of State for the Environment* [1979] A.C. 144 at 168, 169, 175; (1977) 41 Conv. 415 at 422 (C. Harpum).
[41] *Borman v. Griffith* [1930] 1 Ch. 493.
[42] *Swansborough v. Coventry* (1832) 2 M. & S. 362.
[43] *Schwann v. Cotton* [1916] 2 Ch. 459.
[44] Above, p. 428.
[45] Above, p. 425.
[46] Above, p. 428.
[47] See above.

word is defined,[48] it does not include contracts[49] or wills. Nor does it apply to a lease in writing for over three years, for, not being by deed, the lease can take effect only as a contract to grant a lease, which is no conveyance.[50]

(iii) Restriction and rectification: It will be seen that a conveyance will sometimes convey more than the purchaser is entitled to under the contract. If both contract and conveyance are silent as to easements, the narrower rules for implied grant will limit the purchaser's rights under the contract, while the more ample operation of the section may give him wider rights. Thus a non-apparent way may be outside the doctrine of implied grant but within the section.[51] In such cases the vendor can insist on the conveyance being worded so as to restrict it to the rights which the contract gives the purchaser.[52] If the conveyance has been executed, a vendor who acts promptly may seek to have it rectified,[53] except as against a purchaser without notice of the equity of rectification.

4. By presumed grant, or prescription—general principles

The basis of prescription is that if long enjoyment of a lawful right is shown, the court will uphold the right by presuming that it had a lawful origin, *i.e.* that there once was an actual grant of the right, even though it is impossible to produce any evidence of such a grant. However, it is not enough to show long user by itself: user of a particular kind is required. There are three types of prescription, namely, prescription at common law, prescription under the doctrine of lost modern grant, and prescription under the Prescription Act 1832, an unsatisfactory system that calls for simplification by Parliament.[54] Indeed in 2002 it was announced that the Law Commission is going to review this area of the law. Except so far as the Act otherwise provides, a claim to an easement or profit under any head must be supported by user complying with the following conditions.

(a) User as of right

The user must be as of right, which means that it must have been enjoyed *nec vi, nec clam, nec precario* (without force, without secrecy, without permission).[55] The claimant must show that he has used the right as if he were entitled to it. Forcible user (*vi*) occurs not only where the dominant owner breaks down barriers or commits other acts of violence, but also where the user is continued despite the servient owner making continuous and unmistakable protests.[56] Secret user (*clam*) occurred where a dock had been supported by invisible rods sunk under the servient tenement,[57] or where there had been intermittent and secret discharges of injurious chemicals into a sewer.[58] So, too, no easement can be established against an owner who, owing to absence or other reason, is able to prove that he had no knowledge

---

[48] Above, p. 427.
[49] *Re Peck and the School Board for London* [1893] 2 Ch. 315.
[50] *Borman v. Griffith* [1930] 1 Ch. 493; and see above, p. 310.
[51] See *Ward v. Kirkland* [1967] Ch. 194.
[52] *Re Walmsley and Shaw's Contract* [1917] 1 Ch. 93.
[53] See *Clark v. Barnes* [1929] 2 Ch. 368.
[54] See *Tehidy Minerals Ltd v. Norman* [1971] 2 Q.B. 528 at 543.
[55] *Solomon v. Mystery of Vintners* (1859) 4 H. & N. 585 at 602 (common law prescription); *Sturges v. Bridgman* (1879) 11 Ch.D. 852 at 863 (lost modern grant); Prescription Act 1832, ss.1, 2 and *Tickle v. Brown* (1836) 4 A. & E. 369 at 382 (prescription under the Act).
[56] *Dalton v. Angus & Co.* (1881) 6 App. Cas. 740 at 786. See, *e.g. Newnham v. Willison* (1988) 56 P. & C.R. 8.
[57] *Union Lighterage Co. v. London Graving Dock Co.* [1902] 2 Ch. 557.
[58] *Liverpool Corporation v. H. Coghill & Son Ltd* [1918] 1 Ch. 307.

of the user.[59] The whole law of prescription rests upon acquiescence[60]; and mere toleration is enough.[61]

If the servient owner has given the claimant the right to use the easement or profit claimed, so that there has been an actual grant of such a right, the user is not *precario*, and the claimant can rely upon his grant without resorting to prescription. But if the claimant has been given permission to use the right claimed "until further notice", or has had to seek permission anew each year, the user is *precario* and no easement or profit can rise from it by prescription. Similarly, if applications for permission to use a way have been made by the claimant from time to time,[62] or he has made annual payments for his enjoyment, there is evidence that the user was *precario*, for such acts are inconsistent with the claimant having a right to the easement or profit claimed.

User during unity of possession, *i.e.* while the claimant was in possession of both dominant and servient tenements, is not user as of right,[63] and the same applies to user under the mistaken belief that the claimant was entitled to the servient tenement[64] or that he had the temporary permission of the landlord. But proof that the claimant exercised his right under the mistaken belief that a valid easement or profit had already been granted to him will not prevent the user from being as of right.[65] The principle involved is that the right must have been exercised *qua* easement or profit and not, for example, under any actual or supposed right of an occupant of both tenements.

(b) User in fee simple

The user must be by or on behalf of a fee simple owner against a fee simple owner who both knows of the user and is able to resist it. In general, only easements or profits in fee simple can be acquired by prescription.[66] An easement or profit for life or for years, for example, may be expressly granted but cannot be acquired by prescription, for the basis of prescription is a presumed grant by the owner of the servient tenement, and only a grant in fee simple will be presumed. Consequently the claimant must show either that he is the fee simple owner himself or that he claims on behalf of the fee simple owner. A tenant under a lease must thus prescribe on behalf of the fee simple owner and not merely on his own behalf.[67]

As prescription rests on acquiescence,[68] a claim will fail if user can be proved only when the servient land was occupied by a tenant for life[69] or for years,[70] for the fee simple owner may be unable to contest the user. But if the user began against the fee simple owner it will not become ineffective because the land is later settled or let.[71] Further, if A leases two plots of his land to two tenants, one tenant cannot prescribe for an easement against the other, for otherwise the result would be that A would acquire an easement over his own land.[72]

[59] *Diment v. N. H. Foot Ltd* [1974] 1 W.L.R. 1427.
[60] *Dalton v. Angus & Co* (1881) 6 App. Cas. 740 at 773, 803.
[61] *Mills v. Silver* [1991] Ch. 271.
[62] *Monmouth Canal Co. v. Harford* (1834) 1 Cr.M. & R. 614.
[63] *Bright v. Walker* (1834) 1 Cr.M. & R. 211 at 219.
[64] *Lyell v. Lord Hothfield* [1914] 3 K.B. 911.
[65] *Earl de la Warr v. Miles* (1881) 17 Ch.D. 535; *Bridle v. Ruby* (1988) 56 P. & C.R. 155; but see [1989] Conv. 261 (G. Kodilinye).
[66] See, *e.g. Kilgour v. Gaddes* [1904] 1 K.B. 457 at 460.
[67] *Gateward's Case* (1607) 6 Co.Rep. 59b; *Dawnay v. Cashford* (1697) Carth. 432.
[68] *Dalton v. Angus & Co.* (1881) 6 App. Cas. 740 at 773, 774.
[69] *Roberts v. James* (1903) 89 L.T. 282.
[70] *Daniel v. North* (1809) 11 East 372.
[71] *Pugh v. Savage* [1970] 2 Q.B. 373.
[72] *Kilgour v. Gaddes* [1904] 1 K.B. 457; *Simmons v. Dobson* [1991] 1 W.L.R. 720.

There are certain modifications of this rule. First, profits in gross may be acquired by prescription at common law,[73] or under the doctrine of lost modern grant. In this case, the right is claimed not in respect of any estate but on behalf of the claimant personally. Such prescription is known as prescription in gross. The claimant must show that he and his predecessors in title to the profit (often his ancestors) have enjoyed the right,[74] instead of showing that he and his predecessors in title to the dominant tenement have enjoyed it.[75] There can be no prescription in gross for easements (which cannot exist in gross), nor can a profit in gross be claimed under the Prescription Act 1832.[76] Secondly, certain modifications are made in claims under the Prescription Act 1832. Thus under the Act easements of light can be acquired by one tenant against another tenant of the same landlord.[77] This is anomalous; it applies only to light and only to claims under the Act. Other modifications under the Act will be noted later.

(c) Continuous user

The claimants must show a continuity of enjoyment. This is interpreted reasonably; in the case of easements of way it is clearly not necessary to show ceaseless user by day and night. User whenever circumstances require it is normally sufficient,[78] provided the intervals are not excessive; but merely casual use, dependent on tolerance, is not enough.[79] Continuity is not broken if the user is varied by agreement, as where the parties vary the line of a way for convenience.[80]

The three types of prescription must now be considered in turn.

5. Prescription at common law

(a) Length of user

User of the nature discussed above must be shown to have continued since time immemorial, namely since 1189. If this is shown, the court presumes that a grant was made prior to that date. The reason for 1189 being adopted is that from time to time limits were fixed within which actions for the recovery of land were to be brought. Instead of adopting a specified period of years, events such as the beginning of the reign of Henry I or the last voyage of Henry II to Normandy were periodically selected. The last choice to be made was the beginning of the reign of Richard I, namely 1189. These periods originally had nothing to do with prescription, but the courts adopted the last date as the period of time immemorial upon which all claims based on custom or prescription depended. Modern legislation has altered the rule for claims to land, but 1189 remained the essential date for custom and prescription.[81]

---

[73] *Johnson v. Barnes* (1873) L.R. 8 C.P. 527.
[74] *Welcome v. Upton* (1840) 6 M. & W. 536.
[75] Such prescription is *"in the que estate"*: the user is by the claimant and *"ceux que estate il ad"* (those whose estate he has). See Litt. 183.
[76] *Shuttleworth v. Le Fleming* (1865) 19 C.B. (N.S.) 687.
[77] See below, p. 439.
[78] *Dare v. Heathcote* (1856) 25 L.J. Ex. 245.
[79] *Ironside, Crabb and Crabb v. Cook, Cook and Barefoot* (1981) 41 P. & C.R. 326 (way over roadside verge).
[80] *Davis v. Whitby* [1974] Ch. 186.
[81] See generally *Bryant v. Foot* (1867) L.R. 2 Q.B. 161 at 180, 181.

(b) Presumption

It is clearly impossible in most cases to show continuous user since 1189, and so the courts adopted the rule that if unexplained user for 20 years or more is shown, the court would presume that that user has continued since 1189; user for less than 20 years requires supporting circumstances to raise the presumption.[82] However, this presumption may be met by showing that at some time since 1189 the right could not or did not exist.[83] Thus an easement of light cannot be claimed by prescription at common law for a building which is shown to have been erected since 1189.[84] Consequently it was virtually impossible to establish a claim to light at common law, and many claims based on enjoyment lasting for centuries were liable to be defeated by evidence that there could have been no enjoyment of the right in 1189. Again, if it could be shown that any time since 1189 the dominant and servient tenements had been in the same ownership and occupation, any easement or profit would have been extinguished and so any claim at common law would fail.[85] To meet this state of affairs, the courts invented what has been called the "revolting fiction"[86] of the lost modern grant.

6. Lost modern grant

(a) The presumption

The weakness of common law prescription was the liability to failure if it was shown that user had begun at some date after 1189. The doctrine of lost modern grant avoided this by presuming from long user that an actual grant of the easement or profit had been made at some time subsequent to 1189 but prior to the user supporting the claim, and that unfortunately this grant had been lost.[87] "Juries were first told that from user, during living memory, or even during 20 years, they might presume a lost grant or deed; next they were recommended to make such presumption; and lastly, as the final consummation of judicial legislation, it was held that a jury should be told, not only that they might, but also that they were bound to presume the existence of such a lost grant, although neither judge nor jury, nor anyone else, had the shadow of a belief that any such instrument had ever really existed."[88] In their anxiety to find a legal origin for a right of which there had been open and uninterrupted enjoyment for a long period, unexplained in any other way, the courts presumed that a grant had been made, and so made it immaterial that enjoyment had not continued since 1189. User for 20 years normally sufficed to raise the presumption[89]; and unlike prescription under the Act, once the period has run, the easement comes into existence and is not affected by any subsequent cessation of the user.[90]

(b) Evidence

Rather stronger evidence of user is required to induce the court to presume a lost modern grant than is required for prescription at common law.[91] Further, the doctrine can be invoked

---

[82] *Bealey v. Shaw* (1805) 6 East 208 at 215.
[83] *Hulbert v. Dale* [1909] 2 Ch. 570 at 577.
[84] *Duke of Norfolk v. Arbuthnot* (1880) 5 C.P.D. 390.
[85] See below, p. 443.
[86] *Angus & Co. v. Dalton* (1877) 3 Q.B.D. 85 at 94, *per* Lush J.
[87] See, *e.g. Dalton v. Angus & Co.* (1881) 6 App. Cas. 740 at 813.
[88] *Bryant v. Foot* (1867) L.R. 2 Q.B. 161 at 181, *per* Cockburn C.J.
[89] *Penwarden v. Ching* (1829) Moo. & M. 400.
[90] *Mills v. Silver* [1991] Ch. 271; below, p. 434.
[91] *Tilbury v. Silva* (1890) 45 Ch.D. 98 at 123.

only if something prevents the application of common law prescription.[92] Since the doctrine is admittedly a fiction, the claimant will not be ordered to furnish particulars of the fictitious grant (for example as to the parties), but he must plead whether the grant is alleged to have been made before or after a particular date.[93] The presumption cannot be rebutted by evidence that no grant was in fact made.[94] But the claim is defeated by proof that during the entire period when the grant would have been made there was nobody who could lawfully have made it.[95] Thus the court has refused to presume a lost grant of a way where the land had been in strict settlement (under which there was no power to make a grant) from the time when the user began down to the time of action.[96]

7. Prescription Act 1832: Easements (except Rights of Light) and Profits

The Prescription Act 1832 ("the 1832 Act") was passed to meet the difficulties and uncertainties mentioned above, and in particular the difficulty of persuading juries to presume grants to have been made when they knew this was not the case. It is ill-drafted, but in many cases it has substituted certainty for uncertainty. The 1832 Act makes special provision for easements of light, so that the other rights under the 1832 Act will be dealt with first, and then easements of light. The 1832 Act is perhaps best dealt with by giving a summary of the effect of each section and then annotating the sections in groups.

(a) Sections 1 to 4 of the 1832 Act

Section 1: profits: No claim to a profit is to be defeasible by showing that user commenced after 1189 if 30 years' uninterrupted enjoyment as of right is shown. If 60 years' uninterrupted enjoyment as of right is shown, the right is deemed to be absolute unless it has been enjoyed by written consent or agreement.

Section 2: easements except rights of light: The section makes exactly similar provisions for all easements except the easement of light, though the periods are 20 and 40 years respectively instead of 30 and 60.

Section 3: rights of light: Easements of light are dealt with below.[97]

Section 4: periods and interruptions: All periods of enjoyment under the 1832 Act are those periods next before some action in which the claim is brought into question. Further, no act is to be deemed an interruption until it has been submitted to or acquiesced in for one year after the party interrupted had notice both of the interruption and of the person making it.

(b) The chief points to note on this group of sections

(i) "Next before some action": The 1832 Act does not say that an easement or profit comes into existence after 20, 30, 40 or 60 years' user in the abstract; all periods under the 1832 Act are those next before some action in which the right is questioned. Thus until some action is

---

[92] *Bryant v. Lefever* (1879) 4 C.P.D. 172 at 177.
[93] *Tremayne v. English Clays Lovering Pochin & Co. Ltd* [1972] 1 W.L.R. 657, not following *Gabriel Wade & English Ltd v. Dixon & Cardus Ltd* [1937] 3 All E.R. 900.
[94] *Tehidy Minerals Ltd v. Norman* [1971] 2 Q.B. 528.
[95] *Neaverson v. Peterborough R.D.C.* [1902] 1 Ch. 557.
[96] *Roberts v. James* (1903) 89 L.T. 282. See now S.L.A. 1925, s.49(1).
[97] Below, pp. 439 *et seq.*

brought, there is a mere inchoate right to an easement or profit, however long the user.[98] Further, even if there has been user for longer than the statutory periods, the vital period is always that period (such as of 20 years) next before some action. Thus if user commenced 50 years ago but ceased five years ago, a claim will fail if the action is commenced today, for there has not been continuous user during the 20 or 40 years next before the action.[99] Similarly a claim under the 1832 Act will fail if there has been unity of possession for a substantial period immediately before the action, for there has not been user as an easement during the whole of the vital period.[1]

(ii) "Without interruption": The user must be "without interruption"; but a special meaning is given to "interruption". If D has used a way over S's land for over 20 years, and then a barrier is erected barring his way, D can still succeed in establishing an easement, provided that at the time an action is brought he has not acquiesced in the obstruction for one year after he has known both of the obstruction and of the person responsible for it.[2] "Interruption" means some hostile obstruction and not mere non-user.[3] A complaint or protest against an interruption suffices to negative acquiescence if it is communicated to the servient owner; and its effect normally endures for some time after it has been made, so that there is no acquiescence in an interruption for a year merely because a year has elapsed since the last protest was made.[4]

User for 19 years and a day followed by 364 days' interruption is thus, for the purposes of the 1832 Act, 20 years' user upon which a claim will succeed. But this does not mean that 364 days is in fact deducted from the periods in the 1832 Act. To say that user for 19 years and a day is as good as user for 20 years is inaccurate, for

    (i) no action can be brought to establish an easement if only 19 years and a fraction have elapsed since the user began,[5] whereas after 20 years' user, an action can be started forthwith; and

    (ii) if an interruption commences after user for 19 years and a day, not until it has lasted for 364 days can the dominant owner commence an action to establish his easement, for not until then is there a period of 20 years.[6] If he waits another day, the interruption will have lasted for a year and his claim must fail. Thus he has only one day on which to issue his writ, whereas if he has enjoyed user for 20 years when an interruption commences, he may issue his writ on any of the next 364 days.

(iii) User "as of right": Sections 1 and 2 provide that the enjoyment must be by a "person claiming right thereto", and section 5 provides that it is sufficient to plead enjoyment "as of right". The effect is that claims under the 1832 Act must be based on user which would have sufficed at common law, *i.e. nec vi, nec clam, nec precario*.[7]

---

[98] *Hyman v. Van den Bergh* [1908] 1 Ch. 167.
[99] *Parker v. Mitchell* (1840) 11 A. & E. 788; contrast lost modern grant: above, p. 433.
[1] *Aynsley v. Glover* (1875) 10 Ch.App. 283.
[2] *Seddon v. Bank of Bolton* (1882) 19 Ch.D. 462.
[3] *Smith v. Baxter* [1900] 2 Ch. 138 at 143. For commons, see below, p. 438.
[4] *Davies v. Du Paver* [1953] 1 Q.B. 184; *Dance v. Triplow* (1991) 63 P. & C.R. 1 (2.5 years too much).
[5] *Lord Battersea v. Commissioners of Sewers for the City of London* [1895] 2 Ch. 708.
[6] *Reilly v. Orange* [1955] 1 W.L.R. 616.
[7] *Gardner v. Hodgson's Kingston Brewery Co. Ltd* [1903] A.C. 229 at 238, 239.

At common law, any consent or agreement by the servient owner, whether oral or written, rendered the user *precario*. Under the 1832 Act, this rule applies to the shorter periods (20 years for easements, 30 years for profits); but in the case of the longer periods (40 years for easements, 60 years for profits) a special meaning is given to *precario* by providing that the right is to be absolute unless enjoyed by written consent or agreement. A mere oral consent given at the beginning of the period and not renewed will thus not defeat a claim based on one of the longer periods, although it would be fatal at common law. However, oral consents repeatedly given during a period will defeat a claim based even on the longer periods.[8]

(iv) Effect of consents: The effect of consents may be summarised thus[9]:

  (i) any consents, whether oral or written, which have been given intermittently during the period make the user *precario* and defeat a claim based on either the shorter or longer periods;

  (ii) a written consent given at the beginning of the user (and extending throughout) defeats a claim based on either the shorter or longer periods;

  (iii) an oral consent given at the beginning of the user (and extending throughout) defeats a claim based on the shorter periods but not a claim based on the longer periods.

If user commences by consent, the question whether it continues by consent is one of fact.[10] In the case of a written consent or agreement, signature by the servient owner is not essential; a document signed by the dominant owner or his leasehold tenant may suffice.[11]

(c) Sections 5 to 8 of the 1832 Act

Section 5 deals with pleadings.

Section 6 provides that enjoyment for less than the statutory periods shall give rise to no claim. This does not prevent a lost grant being presumed from user for less than a statutory period if there is some evidence to support it in addition to the enjoyment.[12]

Section 7 provides that any period during which the owner of the servient tenement has been a minor, mental patient or tenant for life shall automatically be deducted from the shorter periods; further, the period during which an action is pending and actively prosecuted is also to be deducted.

Section 8 provides that if the servient tenement has been held under a "term of life, or any term of years exceeding three years from the granting thereof", the term shall be excluded in computing the period of 40 years in the case of a "way or other convenient [sic] watercourse or use of water", provided the claim is resisted by a reversioner upon the term within three years of its determination.

No more need be said about sections 5 and 6. Sections 7 and 8 are complicated and can conveniently be dealt with together.

---

[8] *Gardner v. Hodgson's Kingston Brewery Co. Ltd* [1903] A.C. 229.
[9] See *Tickle v. Brown* (1836) 4 A. & E. 369; *Healey v. Hawkins* [1968] 1 W.L.R. 1967.
[10] *Gaved v. Martyn* (1865) 19 C.B. (N.S.) 732; *Healey v. Hawkins* [1968] 1 W.L.R. 1967.
[11] *Hyman v. Van den Bergh* [1908] 1 Ch. 167; *Paragon Finance Plc v. City of London Property Co. Ltd* [2002] 1 P. & C.R. 470.
[12] *Hanmer v. Chance* (1865) 4 De G.J. & S. 626 at 631.

(i) Deduction: Where either section 7 or section 8 applies, the period deducted is excluded altogether when calculating the period next before action. Thus if there has been enjoyment of a profit for 45 years in all, consisting of 25 years' user against the fee simple owner, then 19 years against the life tenant, and then a further year against the fee simple owner, the claim fails; for by section 7 the period of the life tenancy is deducted when calculating the period next before action brought, and thus less than 30 years' user is left. But if the user continues for another four years, the claim would succeed, for there is 30 years' user consisting of 25 years before and five years after the life tenancy; since the period of the life tenancy is disregarded, the 30-year period is, for the purposes of the Act, next before action within section 4.[13] The sections in effect connect the periods immediately before and after the period deducted, but they will not connect two periods separated in any other way, such as by a period of unity of possession.[14]

(ii) Application: Section 7 applies to the shorter periods both for easements and profits; but section 8 does not apply to profits at all, and applies to the longer period only in the case of easements of way "or other convenient watercourse or use of water". Probably "convenient" is a misprint for "easement", and the phrase should read "or other easement, watercourse or use of water" as in section 2. If so, section 8 applies to all easements (except light): but the point is unsettled.[15]

(iii) Ambit: Section 7 applies to the servient owner being a minor, mental patient or tenant for life: section 8 applies where the servient tenement has been held under a term for over three years, or for life. Thus a life tenancy can be deducted under both sections, but infancy or mental illness affect only the shorter periods. If D has enjoyed a way against S's land for 25 years, but S has been mentally ill for the last 15 of those years, section 7 defeats D's claim. If D continues his user for another 15 years, however, his claim succeeds even though S's mental illness continues throughout.

Further, it will be observed that the only provision for deduction of leasehold terms is in section 8. Thus, where there had been user of a way for 20 years, the servient land being under lease for 15 of the 20 years, but free from any lease at the beginning and end of the period, an easement was established[16]: for section 7 makes no mention of leaseholds, and section 8 does not apply to the 20-year period. It will be noted that here the user commenced against the fee simple owner who, by leasing the land, voluntarily put it out of his power to resist the user: had the lease been granted before the user commenced and continued throughout, the position would have been different, for no user as against a fee simple owner able to resist it could be shown.[17] In short, a lease may affect a claim in two ways:

    (i) by showing that there has been no user against a fee simple owner who knows of it and can resist it; and

    (ii) by falling within the provisions of section 8 allowing deduction.

---

[13] *Clayton v. Corby* (1842) 2 Q.B. 813.
[14] *Onley v. Gardiner* (1838) 4 M. & W. 496.
[15] See *Laird v. Briggs* (1881) 19 Ch.D. 22 at 33.
[16] *Palk v. Shinner* (1852) 18 Q.B. 568; *Pugh v. Savage* [1970] 2 Q.B. 373; above, p. 431.
[17] *Bright v. Walker* (1834) 1 Cr.M. & R. 211.

The first of these is a common law rule not affected by the 1832 Act; the second is a creature of the statute and can apply only to claims under the 1832 Act based on the 40-year period.

(iv) Right to deduct: In section 7, the provision for deduction is absolute: in section 8, it is conditional, the condition being that the reversioner resists the claim within three years of the determination of the term of years or life. Thus if the reversioner fails to resist the claim within three years, he has no right of deduction. Further section 8 extends only to a reversioner and not to a remainderman,[18] so that it will rarely apply to the usual kind of settlement.

It will be seen from this that section 7 is wide in its scope, giving an absolute right of deduction from the shorter periods for both easements and profits; section 8, on the other hand, is very narrow, giving only a reversioner a conditional right of deduction from the 40-year period in the case of (possibly) only two classes of easements.

(v) Commons: An additional right to deduct from both longer and shorter periods is available in the case of commons. Where during the period a right to graze animals could not be exercised for reasons of animal health or because the common was requisitioned by a government department, the time of non-user is to be left out of account both in computing the periods and in determining whether there was an interruption.[19]

(vi) Difference between longer and shorter periods: In the case of the shorter periods, the only benefits which the 1832 Act confers upon a claimant are that the period for which he must show user is clearly laid down, and that he cannot be defeated by proof that his enjoyment began after 1189. The nature of the user required is still substantially the same, so that the claimant must show continuous, uninterrupted user as of right by or on behalf of a fee simple owner against a fee simple owner who both knew of the user and could resist it.

In the case of the longer periods, however, although uninterrupted user as of right is expressly required, and easements can be acquired only on behalf of a fee simple owner, the 1832 Act provides that the right becomes absolute after the required period next before action has elapsed. User against a fee simple owner who both knew of it and was able to resist it is therefore not required[20]; the only exceptions to this are those provided by section 8. Thus user of a way for 20 years against land held under a life tenancy will give no claim under the 1832 Act,[21] but user for 40 years will suffice, subject to section 8.[22] It seems, therefore, that although all prescription is, in general, founded upon the presumption of a grant, there is no need to presume a grant in the case of claims based on the longer periods under the 1832 Act, for instance where the servient owner is a corporation with no power of grant. This is clearly so in the case of claims to rights of light under the 1832 Act,[23] and in the case of other easements "forty years' user has the same effect which (under the third section) twenty years' user has as to light".[24] But the point cannot be regarded as settled, and the fact that actual

[18] *Symons v. Leaker* (1885) 15 Q.B.D. 629. But see *Holman v. Exton* (1692) Carth. 246 (remainderman "within the equity" of a statute applicable to reversioners).
[19] Commons Registration Act 1965, s.16.
[20] *Wright v. Williams* (1836) 1 M. & W. 77.
[21] *Bright v. Walker* (1834) 1 Cr.M. & R. 211.
[22] *Wright v. Williams* (1836) 1 M. & W. 77, not cited in *Davies v. Du Paver* [1953] 1 Q.B. 184.
[23] *Tapling v. Jones* (1865) 11 H.L.C. 290 at 304.
[24] *Dalton v. Angus & Co.* (1881) 6 App. Cas. 740 at 800, *per* Lord Selborne L.C.

enjoyment confers an easement of light, whereas user as of right is required for other easements, is some indication that it is light alone which requires no presumption of a grant.

The difference between the longer and the shorter periods may be summarised thus:

(i) a presumption of a grant is required in the case of the shorter periods, though possibly not in the case of the longer periods;

(ii) an oral consent given at the beginning of the period defeats a claim based on one of the shorter periods, but not one based on one of the longer periods;

(iii) the shorter periods are subject to the provisions of section 7 but not section 8: the 40 years' period is subject to section 8 in the case of easements of way and water alone, it seems, but otherwise the longer periods are subject to neither section.

8. Prescription Act 1832: easements of light

Easements of light are in some respects on a footing different from that of other rights under the 1832 Act. Section 3 provides in effect that after the actual enjoyment of the access of light to a "dwelling-house, workshop, or other building" (which includes a greenhouse[25]) has continued for 20 years without interruption, the right is deemed absolute unless enjoyed by written consent or agreement. On the effect of this, the main points to note are the following.

(a) Resemblances

Light resembles other rights claimed under the 1832 Act in two respects.

(i) Section 4 applies: Consequently, the period in question is that next before action,[26] and, with the modification noted below, "interruption" has the same meaning as in other cases[27]; and

(ii) Written consent: the rules relating to written consent are the same as for other claims under the 1832 Act.

(b) Differences

Light differs from other rights claimed under the 1832 Act in six respects.

(i) Only one period: There is only one period for light, namely 20 years.

(ii) Disabilities: Sections 7 and 8 do not apply.

(iii) Obstruction: Wartime restrictions and later planning control made it difficult to interrupt the enjoyment of inchoate rights of light with screens or other erections. Instead, a servient owner may now provide a notional obstruction. He must first obtain from the Lands Tribunal a certificate either of exceptional urgency or that due notice has been given to those likely to be affected. He may then register as a local land charge a notice identifying the dominant and servient tenements and specifying the size and position of the notional obstruction; and for a year this notice takes effect as an obstruction known to and acquiesced

---

[25] *Clifford v. Holt* [1899] 1 Ch. 698.
[26] *Hyman v. Van den Burgh* [1908] 1 Ch. 167.
[27] *Smith v. Baxter* [1900] 2 Ch. 138.

in by all concerned. While the notice is in force, the dominant owner may sue for a declaration as if his light actually had been obstructed, and for the cancellation or variation of the registration. Further, for this purpose he may treat his enjoyment as having begun a year earlier than it did; this avoids the "19 years and a day" type of problem.[28]

(iv) Actual user suffices: User as of right is not required[29]: actual enjoyment suffices, provided there has been no written consent. Thus the provision that written consent defeats the claim is the only fragment of *nec vi, nec clam, nec precario* which is left in claims to light under the 1832 Act; oral consent is no bar, even though evidenced by annual payments.[30] But there must be enjoyment of the light *qua* easement: enjoyment during unity of possession is not enough.[31]

(v) No grant: There is no need to presume a grant, because the 1832 Act provides that 20 years' actual enjoyment confers an absolute right[32]; in other words, it is not necessary to show user by or on behalf of one tenant in fee simple against another. Thus the mere fact that the servient tenement has been under lease for the whole period does not prevent the acquisition under the Act of an easement of light valid against the reversioner.[33] This has been taken to its logical conclusion, so that under the Act one tenant can acquire an easement of light over land occupied by another tenant of the same landlord,[34] or by the landlord himself.[35] In the former case, on the expiration of the lease of the servient tenement, the easement is effective against the landlord and all subsequent owners of the land.[36]

(vi) Crown not bound: Sections 1 and 2 mention the Crown: section 3 does not. A statute does not bind the Crown unless it so provides either expressly or by necessary implication,[37] and so an easement of light cannot be acquired under the Act against the Crown[38]; but other easements and profits can.

9. Prescription Act 1832: Limits to the 1832 Act

The 1832 Act does not enable claimants to establish as easements or profits rights which could not be established as such at common law. Thus a claim by the freemen and citizens of a town to enter land and hold races thereon on Ascension Day cannot be established under the 1832 Act.[39] Nor has the 1832 Act abolished the other methods of prescription. Consequently, it is usual to plead all three methods of prescription, although the claimant does this at his own risk as to costs, such as if this form of pleading needlessly increases the other party's expenses.[40] If a claim is made solely under the 1832 Act, it is liable to be defeated by showing unity of possession at any time during the period[41]; this is not so under the

---

[28] Rights of Light Act 1959, ss.2, 3; and see above, pp. 91, 392.
[29] *Colls v. Home & Colonial Stores Ltd* [1904] A.C. 179 at 205.
[30] *Plasterers' Co. v. Parish Clerk's Co.* (1851) 6 Exch. 630.
[31] *Ladyman v. Grave* (1871) 6 Ch.App. 763.
[32] *Tapling v. Jones* (1865) 11 H.L.C. 290 at 304, 318.
[33] *Simper v. Foley* (1862) 2 J. & H. 564.
[34] *Morgan v. Fear* [1907] A.C. 425.
[35] *Foster v. Lyons & Co. Ltd* [1927] 1 Ch. 219 at 227.
[36] *Morgan v. Fear* [1907] A.C. 425.
[37] *Perry v. Eames* [1891] 1 Ch. 658 at 665.
[38] *Wheaton v. Maple & Co.* [1893] 3 Ch. 48.
[39] *Mounsey v. Ismay* (1865) 3 H. & C. 486.
[40] *Harris v. Jenkins* (1883) L.R. 22 Ch.D. 481 at 482.
[41] *Damper v. Bassett* [1901] 2 Ch. 350.

doctrine of lost modern grant[42] or at common law.[43] Again, if the claim is made solely at common law, it will be defeated if it is shown that the enjoyment started after 1189. But as seen already, this would not defeat a claim by lost modern grant or under the 1832 Act. Nor should a claim be based on lost modern grant alone, for the court will not presume a modern grant if the right can be established in any other way.[44] However, a method of prescription under which it is legally impossible for a claim to succeed should never be pleaded. Thus a profit in gross should not be claimed under the 1832 Act,[45] although it may be claimed by prescription at common law.[46]

Sect. 4. Extinction of easements and profits

1. By statute

An Act of Parliament may extinguish an easement or profit expressly or by implication. Under this head must be considered the extinction of commons by approvement, by inclosure, and by failure to register the right of common.

(a) Approvement

The lord of a manor had a common law right to "approve" the manorial waste over which the tenants exercised rights of pasture. Approvement was effected by the lord taking part of the waste for his separate enjoyment. The Statutes of Merton 1236[47] and Westminster II 1285[48] confirmed this practice, but obliged the lord to leave sufficient land for the commoners. The onus of proving sufficiency was on the lord, and there had to be enough pasture for all the animals which the commoners were entitled to turn out, and not merely for those in fact turned out in recent years.[49] Since the Commons Act 1876, a person seeking to approve a common otherwise than in accordance with the strict procedure for inclosures under that Act must advertise his intention in the local press on three successive occasions[50]; and the consent of the Secretary of State for the Environment (or the relevant minister of the devolved Welsh Assembly), given after holding a local inquiry[51] is required to validate the approvement.[52]

(b) Inclosure

Inclosure involves the discharge of the whole manorial waste from all rights of common, whereas approvement applies only to commons of pasture appendant or appurtenant, and discharges only part of the land. From the middle of the eighteenth century, a large number of private inclosure Acts were passed. The policy of Parliament was to encourage the efficient production of food, which was hardly possible under the relics of the feudal system. The Inclosure (Consolidation) Act 1801 and the Inclosure Act 1845 facilitated inclosures, but

---

[42] *Hulbert v. Dale* [1909] 2 Ch. 570; and see *Mills v. Silver* [1991] Ch. 271 (cessation of user: above, p. 432).
[43] *Dalton v. Angus & Co.* (1881) 6 App. Cas. 740 at 814.
[44] *Gardner v. Hodgson's Kingston Brewery Co. Ltd* [1903] A.C. 229 at 240.
[45] *Shuttleworth v. Le Fleming* (1865) 19 C.B. (N.S.) 687.
[46] *Johnson v. Barnes* (1873) L.R. 8 C.P. 527.
[47] c. 4, now called the Commons Act 1236: Statute Law Revision Act 1948, Sched. 2.
[48] c. 46, now called the Commons Act 1285: Statute Law Revision Act 1948, Sched. 2.
[49] *Robertson v. Hartopp* (1889) 43 Ch.D. 484.
[50] s.31.
[51] As in the case of inclosure, see below.
[52] Law of Commons Amendment Act 1893, ss.2, 3; S.I. 1970 No. 1681.

public opinion was aroused by the disappearance of open spaces, and the Inclosure Act 1852 prevented inclosures being made without the consent of Parliament. The procedure is now governed by the Commons Act 1876. An application must first be made to the Secretary of State for the Environment (or the relevant minister of the devolved Welsh Assembly), and if a prima facie case is made out, regard being had to the benefit of the neighbourhood, a local inquiry is held. A provisional order is then submitted to Parliament for confirmation.[53]

(c) Non-registration

Rights of common could be lost by failure to register them under the complex provisions of the Commons Registration Act 1965.[54] The Act came into force on January 2, 1967, and it required applications to the appropriate local authority for the registration of all rights of common (except those held for a term of years or from year to year) to be made before January 3, 1970.[55] Rights of common, however created, were extinguished if they were not duly registered.[56] Registration was merely provisional, pending the determination of any objections; and these had to be lodged before August 1972.[57] Objections were investigated by Commons Commissioners appointed under the Act.[58] Their jurisdiction is subject to a right of appeal to the High Court on a point of law, but otherwise the courts have no jurisdiction to investigate rights of common save in cases of bad faith.[59] New rights of common may be created and registered in respect of land over which no rights had been previously registered.[60]

2. By release

(a) Express release

At law, a deed is required for an express release.[61] In equity, however, an informal release will be effective provided it would be inequitable for the dominant tenant to claim that the right still exists, as where he has orally consented to his light being obstructed and the servient tenant has spent money on erecting the obstruction.[62]

(b) Implied release

If the dominant owner shows an intention to release an easement or profit, it will be extinguished by implied release. Mere non-user is never enough by itself: an intention to abandon the right must be shown.[63] Abandonment may be presumed from non-user for over 20 years, but not where there has been no occasion for any user.[64]

It is a question of fact whether an act was intended as an abandonment. Alterations to the dominant tenement which make the enjoyment of an easement or profit impossible or unnecessary may show an intent to abandon the right. Thus if a mill to which an easement

---

[53] Commons Act 1876, ss.10–12.
[54] See also Common Land (Rectification of Registers) Act 1989 (dwellings).
[55] Commons Registration Act 1965, ss.1(1), 2(1), 4(6), 22(1); S.I. 1966 No. 1470.
[56] Commons Registration Act 1965, s.1(2); *Re Turnworth Down, Dorset* [1978] Ch. 251.
[57] Commons Registration Act 1965, s.5(2); S.I. 1968 No. 989, S.I. 1970 No. 384.
[58] For procedure, see S.I. 1971 No. 1727.
[59] *Wilkes v. Gee* [1973] 1 W.L.R. 742.
[60] S.I. 1969 No. 1843.
[61] Co.Litt. 264b.
[62] *Waterlow v. Bacon* (1866) L.R. 2 Eq. 514.
[63] *Swan v. Sinclair* [1924] 1 Ch. 254; affirmed [1925] A.C. 227; and see *Tehidy Minerals Ltd v. Norman* [1971] 2 Q.B. 528.
[64] *Moore v. Rawson* (1824) 3 B. & C. 332 at 339; *Benn v. Hardinge* (1992) 66 P. & C.R. 246 (175 years).

of water is appurtenant is demolished without any intent to replace it, the easement is released.[65] Similarly the demolition of a house to which an easement of light is appurtenant may amount to an implied release, unless it is intended to replace the house by another building.[66] It is not essential that the new windows should occupy exactly the same positions as the old, provided they receive substantially the same light[67]; the test is identity of light, not identity of aperture. Further, if the dominant tenement is so altered that the burden of the easement is substantially increased, the right may be extinguished altogether.[68] Acquiescence in obstructions in the servient land may show an intent to abandon, but not if it can be explained, such as by the use of an alternative but precarious way.[69]

Extinguishment by frustration seems to be possible but improbable.[70]

3. By unity of ownership and possession

If the dominant and servient tenements come into the ownership and possession of the same person, any easement[71] or profit[72] is extinguished. Unity of possession without unity of ownership is not enough[73]: the right is merely suspended until the unity of possession ceases. Similarly, unity of ownership without unity of possession effects no extinguishment[74]: the right continues until there is also unity of possession. Thus if both dominant and servient tenements are under lease, the easement or profit will not be extinguished merely by both leases being assigned to X, not will it be extinguished merely by Y purchasing both reversions; but if both leases and both reversions become vested in Z, the right is gone.

Sect. 5. Species of easements

1. Rights of way

(a) Extent of easements of way

An easement of way may be either general or limited. A general right of way is one which may be used by the owner of the dominant tenement at any time and in any manner. A limited right of way is one which is subject to some restriction. The restriction may be as to time, such as a way which can be used only in the daytime[75] or in case of fire,[76] or it may be as to the mode in which the way can be used, such as a way limited to foot passengers, or to cattle and other animals in the charge of a drover, or to wheeled traffic,[77] and the like. In construing the size and location of the right of way, the court is entitled to take into account: the terms of the conveyance and grant; the physical characteristics of the area at the time of the grant; and, where the conveyance and grant are giving effect to a contract of sale, the

---

[65] *Liggins v. Inge* (1831) 7 Bing. 682 at 693.
[66] *Ecclesiastical Commissioners for England v. Kino* (1880) 14 Ch.D. 213.
[67] *Scott v. Pape* (1886) 31 Ch.D. 554.
[68] *Ankerson v. Connelly* [1906] 2 Ch. 544; affirmed [1907] 1 Ch. 678; and see *Ray v. Fairway Motors (Barnstaple) Ltd* (1969) 20 P. & C.R. 261 (extra burden insufficient).
[69] *Treweeke v. 36 Wolseley Road Pty. Ltd* (1973) 128 C.L.R. 274; and see *Ward v. Ward* (1852) 7 Exch. 838.
[70] See *Huckvale v. Aegean Hotels Ltd* (1989) 58 P. & C.R. 163.
[71] *Buckby v. Coles* (1814) 5 Taunt. 311.
[72] *Tyrringham's Case* (1584) 4 Co.Rep. 36b at 38a; *White v. Taylor* [1969] 1 Ch. 150.
[73] *Canham v. Fisk* (1831) 2 Cr. & J. 126.
[74] *Richardson v. Graham* [1908] 1 K.B. 39.
[75] *Collins v. Slade* (1874) 23 W.R. 199.
[76] *I.D.C. Group Ltd v. Clark* [1992] 1 E.G. L.R. 187.
[77] *Ballard v. Dyson* (1808) 1 Taunt. 279.

terms of that contract but not any statements made by an auctioneer at the time when it was being entered into.[78]

A right of way can normally be used only as a means of access to the dominant tenement.[79] A right to pass over Plot A to reach Plot B cannot also be used as a means of access to Plot C lying beyond Plot B. However, in some circumstances it may not be outside the scope of the grant to use the right of way to access Plot B and then go off Plot B onto Plot C for some incidental or ancillary activity such as picnicking or strolling on Plot C.[80]

In the absence of a contrary agreement or special circumstances,[81] it is for the grantee of a way, not the grantor, to construct the way and to repair it when constructed[82]; the grantee may enter the servient tenement for these purposes.[83] If the way becomes impassable, there is no right to deviate from it unless the servient owner has obstructed it.[84]

(b) Effect of mode of acquisition

The extent of an easement of way depends upon how it was acquired.

(i) Express grant or reservation: Here the question is primarily one of construction. If the intention is not made clear, a grant is construed most strongly against the person making it, in accordance with the general rule, while a reservation is construed in his favour, for it takes effect as a regrant by the other party.[85] Thus an easement granted in general terms is not confined to the purpose for which the land is used at the time of the grant.[86] A right of way for general purposes granted as appurtenant to a house can accordingly be used for the business of an hotel if that house is subsequently converted into an hotel.[87]

If a way is granted "as at present enjoyed", prima facie these words refer to the quality of the user (for example on foot or with vehicles) and do not limit the quantity of the user to that existing at the time of the grant.[88] In cases of difficulty, the surrounding circumstances must be considered: thus both the condition of the way (for instance whether it is a footpath or a metalled road) and the nature of the dominant tenement (for example whether it is a dwelling-house or a factory) may be of assistance.[89]

(ii) Implied grant or reservation: A way of necessity is limited to the necessity existing at the time the right arose; thus if an encircled plot is used for agricultural purposes at the time of the grant, the way of necessity over the surrounding land is limited to agricultural purposes and cannot be used for carting building materials.[90]

In other cases of implied grant, the circumstances of the case must be considered. Thus where a testator devised adjoining plots of land to different persons and one plot was bought

---

[78] *Peacock v. Custins* (2001) 81 P. & C.R. 34.
[79] *Harris v. Flower* (1905) 74 L.J. Ch. 127; *Peacock v. Custins* [2002] 1 W.L.R. 1815.
[80] *Peacock v. Custins* (2001) 81 P. & C.R. 34.
[81] See *Saint v. Jenner* [1973] Ch. 275 (failure to repair results in obstruction).
[82] See *Miller v. Hancock* [1893] 2 Q.B. 177 (not affected by *Fairman v. Perpetual Investment Building Society* [1923] A.C. 74 on the duty to the dominant owner).
[83] *Newcomen v. Coulson* (1877) 5 Ch.D. 133.
[84] *Selby v. Nettlefold* (1873) 9 Ch.App. 111.
[85] For this rule, see above, p. 380.
[86] *South Eastern Ry. v. Cooper* [1924] 1 Ch 211.
[87] *White v. Grand Hotel, Eastbourne Ltd* [1913] 1 Ch. 113 (affirmed on another point, 84 L.J. Ch. 938); and see *Alvis v. Harrison* (1990) 62 P. & C.R. 10.
[88] *Hurt v. Bowmer* [1937] 1 All E.R. 797.
[89] *Cannon v. Villars* (1878) 8 Ch.D. 415 at 420, 421; *St. Edmundsbury & Ipswich Diocesan Board of Finance v. Clark (No.2)* [1973] 1 W.L.R. 1572 at 1591–1596; affirmed [1975] 1 W.L.R. 468.
[90] *Corporation of London v. Riggs* (1880) 13 Ch.D. 798.

by a railway company for conversion into a railway station, it was held that a way which had been used in the testator's lifetime for domestic purposes and for the purposes of warehouses on the land could not be used as a public approach to the station.[91]

(iii) Prescription: Where an easement of way is acquired by long user, the extent of the way is limited by the nature of the user. Thus a way acquired by long user for farming purposes cannot be used for mineral purposes or for the cartage of building materials.[92] It has been held that user during the prescriptive period as a carriageway does not authorise user for cattle,[93] although it covers use as a footway[94] (since prima facie the greater includes the less) and it extends to use for motor traffic even if the user proved was for horse-drawn vehicles alone.[95] Moreover, unless there is a radical change in the nature of the dominant tenement, the user is not limited to the number or frequency of vehicles or pedestrians using the way during the prescriptive period.[96]

2. Rights of light

(a) No natural right

There is no natural right of light; a landowner may so build on his land as to prevent any light from reaching his neighbour's windows,[97] unless his neighbour has an easement of light or some other right such as a restrictive covenant against building. The access of light to windows is sometimes deliberately obstructed in order to prevent an easement of light being acquired by prescription.[98]

(b) Quantum of light

The amount of light to which the dominant owner is entitled was finally settled in *Colls v. Home and Colonial Stores Ltd*[99]: this amount is enough light according to the ordinary notions of mankind for the comfortable use of the premises as a dwelling, or, in the case of business premises, for the beneficial use of the premises for ordinary shop or other business purposes. The quantum of light is greater where it is needed for the ordinary beneficial use of the particular building, and for a greenhouse it includes the direct access of the sun's rays.[1] In each case the test is that of the ordinary use of the dominant tenement: the dominant owner is not entitled to object even to a substantial diminution in his light, provided enough is left for the ordinary purposes. The test is not "How much light has been taken away?" but "How much light is left?"[2] An easement for more light than is required for ordinary purposes may be acquired by enjoyment of it for 20 years for purposes known by the servient owner to require it.[3] But the quantum of light to which the dominant owner is entitled is not affected

---

[91] *Milner's Safe Co. Ltd v. Great Northern and City Ry.* [1907] 1 Ch. 208.
[92] *Wimbledon Conservators v. Dixon* (1875) 1 Ch.D. 362.
[93] *Ballard v. Dyson* (1808) 1 Taunt. 279.
[94] *Davies v. Stephens* (1836) 7 C. & P. 570.
[95] *Lock v. Abercester Ltd* [1939] Ch. 861.
[96] *British Railways Board v. Glass* [1965] Ch. 538; *Woodhouse & Co. Ltd v. Kirkland (Derby) Ltd* [1970] 1 W.L.R. 1185.
[97] *Tapling v. Jones* (1865) 11 H.L.C. 290.
[98] See above, p. 439.
[99] [1904] A.C. 179.
[1] *Allen v. Greenwood* [1980] Ch. 119.
[2] *Higgins v. Betts* [1905] 2 Ch. 210 at 215.
[3] *Allen v. Greenwood* [1980] Ch. 119.

by the fact that he has used the room in question for purposes requiring but little light,[4] for a right of light is a right to have the access of light for all ordinary purposes to which the room may be put,[5] including any sub-division of it that might reasonably be expected.[6]

(c) Alteration of apertures

An easement of light can exist only in respect of a window or other aperture in a building, such as a skylight.[7] If the dominant owner alters the size or position of the window, the burden on the servient owner cannot be increased; an obstruction which would not have been actionable before the alteration will not be actionable even if it deprives the altered window of most of its light.[8] But if it is established that an obstruction is an infringement of an easement of light for one set of windows, and another set of windows (for which no easement exists) is also obstructed by it, the dominant owner can recover damages in respect of both sets of windows; for the obstruction is illegal and the damage to both sets of windows is the direct and foreseeable consequence of it.[9]

(d) Standard of light

The standard of light varies to some extent from neighbourhood to neighbourhood,[10] the test in each case being that laid down in *Colls' case*. There is no "45 degrees" rule, *i.e.* no rule that an interference with light is actionable only if the obstruction rises above a line drawn upwards and outwards from the centre of the window at an angle of 45 degrees; at most, the test provides a very slight presumption.[11] Modern standards of lighting have risen, too.[12]

(e) Other sources

In considering whether an easement of light has been obstructed, other sources of light of which the dominant owner cannot be deprived must be taken into account, such as vertical light through a skylight.[13] In one case[14] a room was lit though two sets of windows, one set facing A's land and the other facing B's land. It was held that the light received by both sets of windows had to be considered, but that A could not obscure the greater part of the light passing over his land in reliance upon B supplying a large quantity of light. Neither servient owner could build to a greater extent than, assuming a building of like height on the other servient tenement, would still leave the dominant tenement with sufficient light according to the test in *Colls' case*.

3. Rights of support

It has already been seen[15] that the natural right which every landowner has a natural right to support extends only to land in its natural state; there is no natural right to support for

---

[4] *Price v. Hilditch* [1930] 1 Ch. 500.
[5] *Yates v. Jack* (1866) 1 Ch.App. 295.
[6] *Carr-Saunders v. Dick McNeil Associates Ltd* [1986] 1 W.L.R. 922.
[7] *Easton v. Isted* [1903] 1 Ch. 405.
[8] *Ankerson v. Connelly* [1907] 1 Ch. 678.
[9] *Re London, Tilbury & Southend Ry., etc.* (1889) 24 Q.B.D. 326.
[10] *Fishenden v. Higgs & Hill Ltd* (1935) 153 L.T. 128.
[11] *ibid.,* For scientific tests as to "sill ratio", "grumble points" and 50% adequacy, see *Charles Semon & Co. Ltd v. Bradford Corporation* [1922] 2 Ch. 737; *Fishenden v. Higgs & Hill Ltd* (1935) 153 L.T. 128; *Ough v. King* [1967] 1 W.L.R. 1547.
[12] *Ough v. King* [1967] 1 W.L.R. 1547.
[13] *Smith v. Evangelisation Society (Incorporated) Trust* [1933] Ch. 515.
[14] *Sheffield Masonic Hall Co. Ltd v. Sheffield Corporation* [1932] 2 Ch. 17.
[15] Above, p. 417.

buildings or for the additional burden on land which they cause.[16] Similarly, there is no natural right to have buildings supported by neighbouring buildings.[17] If no more damage is done than is necessary, a man may pull down his house without having to provide support for his neighbour's house. However, the right to have buildings supported by land or by other buildings can, however, be acquired as an easement, particularly by implied reservation, implied grant and presumed grant.[18] Once acquired, even by prescription, an easement of support will not be lost by reason of a change of use of a building in the dominant tenement unless that change is such as to increase substantially the burden on the servient tenement[19]; in this respect the rules governing rights of support are different from those which govern rights of way and rights of light.[20]

4. Rights of water

A variety of easements may exist in connection with water, such as rights:

(i) to take water from a pump, spring or river, though this is now subject to statutory restrictions[21];

(ii) to water cattle at a pond[22];

(iii) to take more water from a natural watercourse than would be permitted by the natural rights of ownership[23];

(iv) to receive an undiminished flow of water through a defined channel[24];

(v) to receive water through a pipe situated on the servient tenement[25];

(vi) to receive the discharge of water from the land of another,[26] although there can be no easement to receive the discharge of percolating water such as rainwater[27];

(vii) to enter the land of another to open sluice gates[28];

(viii) to pollute the waters of a stream or river[29];

(ix) to discharge water onto the land of another[30] ("easement of drainage"), although there can be no easement to discharge percolating water such as rainwater[31]; and

---

[16] *Wyatt v. Harrison* (1823) 3 B. & Ad. 871.
[17] *Peyton v. Mayor of London* (1829) 9 B. & C. 725.
[18] Above, pp. 424 *et seq.*
[19] *Ray v. Fairway Motors (Barnstaple) Ltd* (1969) 20 P. & C.R. 261.
[20] Above, pp. 443 *et seq.*; see *Attwood v. Bovis Homes Ltd* (2000) 82 P. & C.R. 2.
[21] See *Cargill v. Gotts* [1981] 1 W.L.R. 441; below, p. 566.
[22] *Manning v. Wasdale* (1836) 5 A. & E. 758.
[23] *McCartney v. Londonderry & Lough Swilly Ry.* [1904] A.C. 301 at 313.
[24] *Dickinson v. Grand Junction Canal Co. Ltd* (1852) 7 Exch. 282 at 301.
[25] *Rance v. Elvin* (1985) 50 P. & C.R. 9.
[26] *Ivimey v. Stocker* (1866) 1 Ch.App. 396.
[27] *Chasemore v. Richards* (1859) 7 H.L.Cas. 349.
[28] *Simpson v. Mayor, etc. of Godmanchester* [1897] A.C. 696.
[29] *Baxendale v. McMurray* (1867) 2 Ch.App. 790; see *Scott-Whitehead v. National Coal Board* (1987) 53 P. & C.R. 263, considered [1987] Conv. 368 (S. Tromans).
[30] *Mason v. Shrewsbury & Hereford Ry.* (1871) L.R. 6 Q.B. 578 at 587.
[31] *Palmer v. Bowman* [2000] 1 All E.R. 23.

    (x) to be able to permit rain water to drop from a roof on to a neighbour's land ("easement of eavesdrop").

Easements of drainage and easements of eavesdrop are in the same position as easements of support in so far as increases in the amount of water being discharged or dropped are concerned.[32] This is presumably also the case for rights to pollute waters. Rights to take water from, as distinct from rights to discharge water onto, the servient tenement also appear to be in the same position.[33]

5. Rights of air

Although an easement for the passage of air through a defined channel may exist,[34] there can be no easement for the general flow of air over land to a windmill or chimney.[35] However, sometimes such rights may be obtained by means of the imposition of restrictive covenants[36] or under the rule against derogation from grant.[37]

6. Miscellaneous easements

There are a variety of miscellaneous easements, such as rights:

    (i) to create a nuisance by the discharge of gases, fluids or smoke, or by making noises or vibrations;

    (ii) to hang clothes on a line passing over another's land[38];

    (iii) to mix manure on the servient tenement for the benefit of the adjoining farm;

    (iv) to use a wall for nailing trees thereto or for supporting a creeper;

    (v) to extend the bowsprits of ships over a wharf[39];

    (vi) to use a coal shed for domestic purposes[40];

    (vii) to store casks and trade produce on the servient tenement;

    (viii) to let down the surface of land by mining operations under it;

    (ix) to use an airfield[41];

    (x) to enter the servient tenement to repair buildings on the dominant tenement[42]; and

    (xi) to enjoy a garden or park (a *jus spatiandi*).[43]

---

[32] *Attwood v. Bovis Homes Ltd* (2000) 82 P. & C.R. 2.
[33] *Cargill v. Gotts* [1981] 1 W.L.R. 441.
[34] *Bass v. Gregory* (1890) 25 Q.B.D. 481; *Cable v. Bryant* [1908] 1 Ch. 259.
[35] *Webb v. Bird* (1862) 13 C.B. (N.S.) 841; *Bryant v. Lefever* (1879) 4 C.P.D. 172.
[36] Below, pp. 409 *et seq.*
[37] Above, p. 369.
[38] *Drewell v. Towler* (1832) 3 B. & Ad. 735.
[39] *Suffield v. Brown* (1864) 4 De G.J. & Sm. 185.
[40] *Wright v. Macadam* [1949] 2 K.B. 744.
[41] *Dowty Boulton Paul Ltd v. Wolverhampton Corporation (No.2)* [1976] Ch. 13.
[42] *Ward v. Kirkland* [1967] Ch. 194.
[43] *Re Ellenborough Park* [1956] Ch. 131.

Certain rights are not easements but resemble them. A right to use a pew in a church has been described as not being an interest in land but an interest of a peculiar nature in the nature of an easement created by Act of Parliament[44]; and the right to require a neighbouring landowner to repair his fences exists as a spurious easement.[45]

Sect. 6. Species of profits *à prendre*

The following are the main types of profit *à prendre*. Some are usually met with as commons, and some as several profits.

1. Profit of pasture

A profit of pasture may exist in the following forms.

(a) Appendant

A profit of pasture appendant is limited to horses, oxen, cows and sheep, the numerical test being levancy and couchancy.[46]

(b) Appurtenant

A profit of pasture appurtenant is not confined to any particular animals, but depends on the terms of the grant or, in the case of prescription, the animals habitually turned out to pasture. The number of animals may either be tested by levancy and couchancy, or be fixed; it cannot be unlimited.[47] A right limited by levancy and counchancy cannot be severed from the land to which it is appurtenant but a fixed right can[48]; the registration of a right limited by levancy and counchancy under the Commons Registration Act 1965[49] is thereby converted into a fixed right and may thereafter also be severed.[50]

(c) Pur cause de vicinage

Under a common of pasture *pur cause de vicinage*, the commoners of one common may not put more cattle upon it than it will maintain. Thus, if Common A is 50 acres in extent and Common B 100 acres, the commoners of A must not put more cattle on A than the 50 acres will support, in reliance on their cattle straying to B.[51]

(d) In gross

A profit of pasture in gross may exist for a fixed number of animals or *sans nombre*. The last phrase means literally "without number" (an alternative form is "without stint"), but such a right is limited to not more cattle than the servient tenement will maintain in addition to any existing burdens.

---

[44] *Brumfitt v. Roberts* (1870) L.R. 5 C.P. 224 at 233.
[45] Above, p. 416.
[46] Above, p. 422.
[47] *Benson v. Chester* (1799) 8 T.R. 396 at 401.
[48] *Bettison v. Langton* [2001] 2 W.L.R. 1605.
[49] s.15(1).
[50] *Bettison v. Langton* [2001] 2 W.L.R. 1605.
[51] *Corbet's Case* (1585) 7 Co.Rep. 5a.

(e) Limitation of numbers

Rights of common registrable under the Commons Registration Act 1965[52] must be registered for a definite number of animals. After registration has become final, the right is exercisable only in relation to the number so registered.[53]

2. Profit of turbary

A profit of turbary is the right to dig and take from the servient tenement peat or turf for use as fuel in a house on the dominant tenement. It may exist as appurtenant, or, where it is limited to some specified quantity, in gross.[54] Where it is appurtenant, the turves can be used only for the benefit of the dominant tenement and not, for example for sale, even if the dominant owner is entitled to a fixed quantity.[55]

3. Profit of estovers

A profit of estovers is the right to take wood from the land of another as house-bote, plough-bote or hay-bote.[56] It may exist as appurtenant, or, if limited to a specified quantity, in gross.

4. Profit of piscary and other sporting rights

A profit of piscary is a right to catch and take away fish. It can exist in gross (when it may be unlimited) or as appurtenant (when it must be limited to the needs of the dominant tenement). Other sporting rights, such as a right of hunting, shooting, fowling and the like, may also exist as profits *à prendre*.[57] It is no infringement of such a right for the servient owner merely to cut timber in the ordinary way, even if he thereby drives away game[58]; but it is otherwise if fundamental changes in the land are made, as where the whole or a substantial part of the land is built upon or converted into racing stables.[59]

5. Profit in the soil

A profit in the soil is the right to enter the servient tenement and take sand, stone, gravel and the like.[60] It may exist as appurtenant or in gross.

Sect. 7. Rights of access

Under the Access to Neighbouring Land Act 1992, the court can make an "access order", giving a landowner the right of access to adjoining or adjacent land. This can be done so as to enable the landowner to do works that are reasonably necessary for the preservation of his land (or part of it), but only if the works cannot be carried out (or would be substantially more difficult to carry out) without entering the servient land.[61] An access order binds successors

---

[52] See above, p. 442, for registration.
[53] Commons Registration Act 1965, s.15.
[54] *Mellor v. Spateman* (1669) 1 Wms.Saund. 339 at 346.
[55] *Hayward v. Cunnington* (1668) 1 Lev. 231.
[56] Above, p. 56.
[57] *Ewart v. Graham* (1859) 7 H.L.C. 331 at 345.
[58] *Gearns v. Baker* (1875) 10 Ch.App. 355.
[59] *Peech v. Best* [1931] 1 K.B. 1.
[60] Co.Litt. 122a.
[61] Access to Neighbouring Land Act 1992, s.1.

in title to the servient land, subject to registration as a writ or order affecting land, or, for registered land, protection by a notice or at present, a caution against dealings (this will cease to be possible when the Land Registration Act 2002 comes into force), since the order is not an interested which overrides legislation; and both for unregistered and registered land, an application for an order is a pending land action.[62]

---

[62] *ibid.*, ss.4, 5, inserting s.6(1)(d) into L.C.A. 1972 and s.49(1)(j) into L.R.A. 1925; above, pp. 82, 106.

Chapter 11

RESTRICTIVE COVENANTS

1. No enforcement as between landlord and tenant

As has been seen,[1] lawful covenants in a lease are enforceable as between landlord and tenant, whether or not they concern land, and whether they are positive or negative. What must be considered in this chapter is the position where covenants are not enforceable as between landlord and tenant. Thus if V conveys part of his land to P, and P enters into covenants with V relating to the rest of V's land, V can of course enforce those covenants against P. But if V then sells his remaining land to W, and P sells his land to Q, the landlord and tenant rules obviously do not apply as between the two freeholders W and Q (nor, for that matter, do they do so as between a head-lessor and a sub-lessee). Whether W can enforce P's covenants against Q depends on two different questions, namely:

    (i) whether the benefit of P's covenants has passed to W, and

    (ii) whether the burden of P's covenants has passed to Q.

Only if both questions are answered in the affirmative can the covenants be enforced: the claimant must be entitled to sue, and the defendant must be liable to be sued. If either of them is an original party to the covenant, then obviously only one of these questions will arise. If V had not conveyed the rest of his land to W, the question whether the benefit of the covenant had passed to him would not arise. Similarly, if P had not conveyed his land to Q and was himself the defendant, the question of whether the burden of the covenant had passed to him would not arise.

2. Law and equity

In answering these questions, equity has partly followed the law and partly diverged sharply from it. In broad terms, the benefit of a covenant, whether positive or negative, will run with land if it touches and concerns it, and has been annexed to it. This is the rule at law, and equity has followed the law, though with some relaxations and considerable complexity in the details. But the burden of the covenant is another matter. At law, the burden of the covenant would not pass with the land affected, though this rule can be mitigated by certain devices.[2]

---

[1] Above, p. 381.
[2] See below, p. 462.

On the other hand, equity developed a doctrine known as the rule in *Tulk v. Moxhay*[3] under which the burden of a covenant attached to the covenantor's land would run with it, provided the covenant was negative in nature and not positive. The law of covenants other than as between landlord and tenant thus came to be the equitable law of restrictive covenants. This law grew up soon after the outburst of building and increase of population associated with the Industrial Revolution. Restrictive covenants became analogous to negative equitable easements[4]; like them,[5] they are extinguished when there is unity of ownership and possession for both plots of land,[6] with one important exception.[7] Most easements (other than rights of light) entitle a landowner to do positive acts affecting neighbouring land; but restrictive covenants, like easements of light, enable him to prohibit certain acts on that land. Throughout the subject, two questions must always be asked:

(i) whether the claimant has the benefit of the covenant so that he is entitled to sue; and

(ii) whether the defendant is subject to the burden of the covenant so that he is liable to be sued.

These questions will be considered separately, first at law and then in equity. For completeness, the position of the original parties to the covenant will also be considered, although the covenant will, of course, be enforceable as between them as a matter of contract.

PART 1—BENEFIT

Sect. 1. The benefit at law

1. The original covenantee

A covenant taken for the benefit of land may of course be worded so as to apply only for so long as the covenantee himself owns the land. Where this is not the case, an original covenantee who has not assigned the benefit of the covenant can always enforce it against the original covenantor, even if the covenantee has parted with the land for whose benefit the covenant was taken[8] (as in the case of easements, this land is generally described as the dominant tenement and the land intended to be burdened by the covenant is known as the servient tenement).

Anyone who is actually named as a party to the deed creating the covenant will be an original covenantee. By virtue of the Contracts (Rights of Third Parties) Act 1999, the covenant can now also be enforced by anyone for whose benefit a party named in the deed

---

[3] (1848) 2 Ph. 774; below, p. 468.
[4] See *Re Nisbet and Potts' Contract* [1906] 1 Ch. 386 at 409; *Kelly v. Barrett* [1924] 2 Ch. 379 at 405; *Newton Abbot Co-operative Society Ltd v. Williamson & Treadgold Ltd* [1952] Ch. 286 at 293.
[5] Above, p. 442.
[6] *Re Tiltwood, Sussex* [1978] Ch. 269.
[7] Below, p. 461.
[8] See *L.C.C. v. Allen* [1914] 3 K.B. 642 at 664. Damages will be only nominal.

expressly contracted.[9] However, such a person is not converted into an original covenantee for the purposes of the transmission of the benefit to an assignee. More significant for the latter purpose is the fact that under section 56 of the Law of Property Act 1925 ("section 56")[10] a person may now take a benefit under a deed even if he is not named as a party to it. For this to occur, the deed must purport to be made with the person in question,[11] and not merely to be made for his benefit.[12] Where A and B are the only parties to a deed, the difference is between A covenanting with B for the benefit of C, and A covenanting directly with C. In the former case C is within the Contracts (Rights of Third Parties) Act 1999. In the latter case C is within section 56.

The effect of section 56 is that, if V sells land to P and P binds his land by a covenant expressed to be with V and the owners for the time being of certain adjoining plots of land, these adjoining owners can sue on the covenant as original covenantees, even though they were not parties to the conveyance creating the covenant.[13] In such a case, the adjoining owners are clearly identifiable persons in existence at the time of the conveyance. However, even if the covenant is expressed to be made with the successors in title of those adjoining owners as well, those successors in title are not original covenantees, for at the date of the conveyance they are not ascertained or ascertainable.[14] Similarly, if a covenant is made expressly for the benefit of the present owner of a plot of land and his successors in title, the owner at the time of the conveyance is an original covenantee but future owners are not. They, like the successors in title to the adjoining owners, can enforce the covenant only under the rules relating to assignees.

2. Assignees

If V sells part of his land to P in fee simple and P enters into covenants binding the land which he buys, the benefit of P's covenant may run at law with V's fee simple estate in the land which he retains, so that a subsequent purchaser of V's land can enforce the covenant against P. It is immaterial whether the covenant is negative (not to do something) or positive (to do something). Thus the common law doctrine applies equally to a covenant not to build on the land purchased by P or a covenant to supply pure water to the land retained by V.[15] It is also immaterial that the covenant has nothing to do with P's land or, indeed, that the covenantor has no land.[16] For a covenant to be enforceable in this way, the following conditions must be satisfied.

(a) The covenant must touch and concern land of the covenantee[17]

It is essential that the covenant should be made for the benefit of land owned by the covenantee (*i.e.* V in the above examples) at the time of the covenant. In general, the test for

[9] This has overtaken the controversy as to whether section 56 itself enables a third party to enforce a contract made for his benefit. See M. & W., pp. 997–998 and *Amsprop Trading Ltd v. Harris Distribution Ltd* [1997] 1 W.L.R. 1025.
[10] Replacing R.P.A. 1845, s.5; see *Beswick v. Beswick* [1968] A.C. 58 at 102–107.
[11] *White v. Bijou Mansions Ltd* [1937] Ch. 610 at 625; [1938] Ch. 351 at 365; *Lyus v. Prowsa Developments Ltd* [1982] 1 W.L.R. 1044 at 1049.
[12] See *Re Miller's Agreement* [1947] Ch. 615.
[13] *Dyson v. Forster* [1909] A.C. 98. See also *Re Ecclesiastical Commissioners for England's Conveyance* [1936] Ch. 430 (where liability was equitable: below, p. 456).
[14] *Westhoughton U.D.C. v. Wigan Coal and Iron Co. Ltd* [1919] 1 Ch. 159 at 169, 170.
[15] See *Shayler v. Woolf* [1946] 1 All E.R. 464 at 467 (affirmed [1946] 2 All E.R. 54).
[16] *Smith v. River Douglas Catchment Board* [1949] 2 K.B. 500. See, *e.g. The Prior's Case*, Y.B. 42 Edw. 3, Hil., pl. 14 (1368) (covenant to sing).
[17] *Rogers v. Hosegood* [1900] 2 Ch. 388.

determining whether a covenant touches and concerns the land is similar to that which is applicable to covenants in a lease created before 1996.[18] Thus if in a lease a surety enters into a covenant with the landlord which touches and concerns the land, the benefit of the covenant will run with the reversion.[19]

(b) Annexation of covenant

The benefit of the covenant must be annexed to a legal estate in the land of the covenantee. Where the covenant benefits the land, no formal words of annexation are needed.[20] But at law, it is not enough to show that the covenantee has an equitable interest in the land retained. It must be shown that the covenant was made for the benefit of some legal estate into whomsoever's hands it might come, and not for the mere personal advantage of the covenantee.[21]

(c) Ownership of the land

An assignee who seeks to enforce a covenant made before 1926 must show that he has the legal estate to which the benefit of the covenant was attached.[22] But a covenant made after 1925 is deemed to be made with the covenantee and his successors in title, and the persons deriving title under him or them,[23] and so is enforceable by those claiming under the covenantee. Thus whether a mere tenant under a lease can enforce a covenant annexed to the legal fee simple depends on the date of the covenant. It is immaterial whether the person enforcing the covenant knew of its existence when he obtained the land[24]: what is annexed to the land passes with the land.

Sect. 2. The benefit in equity

As mentioned above,[25] the rules in equity for the passing of the benefit of a covenant are similar to those at law. Yet although they are rather less strict, they are considerably more complicated.[26]

1. The original covenantee

The position of the original covenantee in equity is similar to that at law. In particular, section 56 of the Law of Property Act 1925 applies.[27] However, if the original covenantee parts with the land for the benefit of which it was taken, equity will not enforce it against the covenantor's successor in title, since enforcement would no longer be for the protection of land.[28]

---

[18] Above, pp. 387 *et seq.*
[19] *P. & A. Swift Investments v. Combined English Stores Group Plc.* [1989] A.C. 632; *Coronation Street Industrial Properties Ltd v. Ingall Industries Plc.* [1989] 1 W.L.R. 304.
[20] See *Westhoughton U.D.C. v. Wigan Coal and Iron Co. Ltd* [1919] 1 Ch. 159 at 170.
[21] *Rogers v. Hosegood* [1900] 2 Ch. 388.
[22] *Westhoughton U.D.C. v. Wigan Coal and Iron Co. Ltd* [1919] 1 Ch. 159.
[23] L.P.A. 1925, s.78.
[24] *Rogers v. Hosegood* [1900] 2 Ch. 388.
[25] Above, p. 454.
[26] For a general survey, see (1938) 6 C.L.J. 339 (S.J. Bailey); and see (1971) 87 L.Q.R. 539 (D.J. Hayton); [1972B] C.L.J. 157 (H.W.R. Wade).
[27] Above, p. 454.
[28] *Chambers v. Randall* [1923] 1 Ch. 149 at 157, 158.

2. Assignees

For anyone except an original covenantee to be entitled to enforce a covenant in equity he must show, first, that the covenant touches and concerns land, and, secondly, that the benefit of the covenant has passed to him.

3. Touching and concerning land

The covenant must touch and concern land of the covenantee. Equity follows the law, and the legal rules apply.[29] By analogy with easements,[30] it may be said that the covenant must accommodate the dominant tenement.

4. Entitled to benefit of covenant

The claimant must establish that he is entitled to the benefit of the covenant. He may do this by showing either—

(i) that the benefit of the covenant has been annexed to land and that he owns some interest in that land; or

(ii) that the benefit of the covenant has been assigned to him and that he owns some interest in the land for the benefit of which the covenant was made; or

(iii) that there is a building scheme or other scheme of development.

(a) Annexation to land

The rules developed by equity have two requirements: first, that the benefit of the covenant has been annexed to land, and, secondly, that the claimant owns some interest in that land. Equity's rules for annexation have now been supplemented by statute.

(i) Annexation in equity: A landowner who obtains a covenant from another landowner may do so merely for his own personal advantage, or he may do so for the benefit of his land, enjoying the advantage so long as the land is his. Covenants of the first kind will not automatically run with the covenantee's land, but those of the second type normally will. The question is whether the covenant sufficiently indicates the land with which the benefit is to run, and also whether it shows that it is made either for the benefit of that land or else with the covenantee in his capacity of owner of it.[31] A covenant with the vendors "their heirs, executors, administrators, and assigns" will not suffice, for it indicates no land.[32] A classic formulation is "with intent that the covenant may enure to the benefit of the vendors their successors and assigns and others claiming under them to all or any of their lands adjoining or near to" the land conveyed.[33] Where the precise land is not identified, it may be ascertained by extrinsic evidence.[34] Express words of annexation are desirable, but they are not required if from the words of the covenant and the surrounding circumstances it appears that annexation was intended.[35]

---

[29] *Re Union of London and Smith's Bank Ltd's Conveyance* [1933] Ch. 611.
[30] See above, p. 414.
[31] See *Drake v. Gray* [1936] Ch. 451 at 466.
[32] *Renals v. Cowlishaw* (1878) 9 Ch.D. 125; affirmed (1879) 11 Ch.D. 866.
[33] See *Rogers v. Hosegood* [1900] 2 Ch. 388 at 389.
[34] See [1972B] C.L.J. 157 at 166–168 (H.W.R. Wade).
[35] *Shropshire C.C. v. Edwards* (1983) 46 P. & C.R. 270; *J. Sainsbury Plc. v. Enfield L.B.* [1989] 1 W.L.R. 590; and see above, p. 456 (position at law).

(ii) Annexation by statute: By section 78 of the Law of Property Act 1925 ("section 78"),[36] a covenant made after 1925 "relating to any land of the covenantee shall be deemed to be made with the covenantee and his successors in title and the persons deriving title under him or them, and shall have effect as if such successors and other persons were expressed". For restrictive covenants, the words "successors in title" include the owners and occupiers for the time being of the covenantee's land intended to be benefited.[37] This provision, and in particular the phrase "successors in title", is plainly apt to show that the covenant is intended to be for the benefit of the covenantee's land rather than himself personally, and so is to be annexed to the land. Yet for over 50 years section 78 remained in obscurity until in 1979 the *Federated Homes* case[38] gave it full effect. For covenants made after 1925 it is no longer necessary to show from other sources that it was intended to annex the benefit of the covenant to the covenantee's land: instead, it will be automatically annexed by virtue of section 78 unless a contrary intention appears, as where the benefit is expressly made transmissible only by express assignment.[39] Though much criticised,[40] the decision seems sound; and it is plainly convenient. As at law, the benefit of a covenant duly annexed to land passes to successors in title even if they know nothing of it; and the successors in title take only by succession and not as original covenantees.[41]

It is improbable that the benefit of a covenant not annexed to land could pass under section 62 of the Law of Property Act 1925 ("section 62"),[42] for it is difficult to see how it could be a right "appertaining or reputed to appertain" to land.[43]

(iii) Area: The benefit of a covenant may be annexed to the covenantee's land only as a whole, so that it will not pass with parts of that land.[44] But indications to the contrary are readily found,[45] and now the rule is that the benefit of a covenant annexed to land will prima facie run both with the land as a whole and also with each part of it separately.[46] But if a covenant is made for the benefit of an area of land too great to be reasonably benefited (such as "the Childwickbury estate" of some 1,700 acres), the benefit will not be annexed to it.[47] Nevertheless, if the covenant is expressed to be for the benefit of the land "or any part" of it, the benefit can run with the parts which it benefits.[48]

(iv) Ownership of land: In addition to showing that the benefit of the covenant has been annexed to land, the claimant must establish that he owns some interest in that land. He need not show that he has succeeded to the covenantee's estate in the land, nor that he has the whole of it.[49]

---

[36] Replacing C.A. 1881, s.58, where the wording was different.
[37] L.P.A. 1925, s.78(1).
[38] *Federated Homes Ltd v. Mill Lodge Properties Ltd* [1980] 1 W.L.R. 594.
[39] *Roake v. Chadha* [1984] 1 W.L.R. 40.
[40] See (1980) 43 M.L.R. 445 (D.J. Hayton); (1981) 97 L.Q.R. 32 (G.H. Newsom); [1982] Legal Studies 53 (D.J. Hurst).
[41] Above, p. 456.
[42] Considered above, p. 425.
[43] See *Roake v. Chadha* [1984] 1 W.L.R. 40 at 47.
[44] *Re Union of London and Smith's Bank Ltd's Conveyance* [1933] Ch. 611 at 628; *Re Jeff's Transfer (No. 2)* [1966] 1 W.L.R. 841.
[45] *Drake v. Gray* [1936] Ch. 451; *Re Selwyn's Conveyance* [1967] Ch. 674.
[46] *Federated Homes Ltd v. Mill Lodge Properties Ltd* [1980] 1 W.L.R. 594. So also at law: *Williams v. Unit Construction Co. Ltd* (1955) 19 Conv. (n.s.) 261.
[47] *Re Ballard's Conveyance* [1937] Ch. 473.
[48] *Marquess of Zetland v. Driver* [1939] Ch. 1.
[49] *Formby v. Barker* [1903] 2 Ch. 539.

(b) Assignment with land

(i) Express assignment: Where the benefit of a covenant has not been annexed to land, it can nevertheless be expressly assigned.[50] Such an assignment, like other assignments of rights under a contract, enables the assignee to enforce the covenant against the original covenantor. But successors in title to the covenantor are liable only in equity under the rule in *Tulk v. Moxhay*,[51] and equity will permit an assignee of the covenantee to enforce the covenant only if the benefit of it has been assigned to him together with some or all of the land protected by it. That land must be properly identified, if not from the wording of the deed,[52] then from the surrounding circumstances.[53] Although at law the benefit of the covenant cannot be assigned in pieces, yet in equity this can be done if the proper conditions are observed.[54]

(ii) Time of assignment: The assignment must, it seems, be made at the time of the conveyance of the land which is to be protected.[55] An express assignment is not required if the circumstances show that the benefit of the covenant was intended to be included in the sale.[56] But once the land has been sold, the benefit of the covenant cannot be assigned: one purpose of the covenant is to make the covenantee's land more readily saleable, and if he has succeeded in disposing of the whole of his land without assigning the benefit of the covenant, it ceases to be assignable.[57] If only part of his land has been disposed of, he can assign the benefit of the covenant when he sells any of the parts still retained, but he cannot assign it to those who have already purchased parts of the land.[58]

(iii) Subsequent assignment: The assignment need not necessarily be made by the original covenantee. If, for example, the original covenantee dies, both the covenant and the land that it benefits will devolve on his personal representatives, who may hold it as bare trustees for a devisee under the covenantee's will or for some other successor to the land. As owner in equity, the successor can sue on the covenant without joining the personal representatives,[59] and can assign it to a purchaser.[60] Subsequent owners of the land have been held to be entitled only if there is a complete chain of assignments of the benefit of the covenant to them[61]; but the better view is that the first assignment of the benefit together with the land operates as a "delayed annexation" of the benefit, so that it will thereafter run with the land without further assignment.[62]

(c) Schemes of development

(i) Mutual enforceability: Where land has been laid out in lots which are to be sold to purchasers and built upon, restrictions are often imposed on the purchasers of each lot for the benefit of the estate generally, such as covenants restraining trading on the estate, prohibiting

---

[50] *Re Union of London and Smith's Bank Ltd's Conveyance* [1933] Ch. 611.
[51] (1848) 2 Ph. 744; above, p. 453; below, p. 468.
[52] *Re Union of London and Smith's Bank Ltd's Conveyance* [1933] Ch. 611 at 625, 631.
[53] *Newton Abbot Co-operative Society Ltd v. Williamson & Treadgold Ltd* [1952] Ch. 286; *Marten v. Flight Refuelling Ltd* [1962] Ch. 115.
[54] *Re Union of London and Smith's Bank Ltd's Conveyance* [1933] Ch. 611 at 630.
[55] *Chambers v. Randall* [1923] 1 Ch. 149.
[56] *Renals v. Cowlishaw* (1878) 9 Ch.D. 125 at 129.
[57] *Re Rutherford's Conveyance* [1938] Ch. 396.
[58] *Re Union of London and Smith's Bank Ltd's Conveyance* [1933] Ch. 611 at 632.
[59] *Earl of Leicester v. Wells-next-the-Sea U.D.C.* [1973] Ch. 110.
[60] *Newton Abbot Co-operative Society Ltd v. Williamson & Treadgold Ltd* [1952] Ch. 286.
[61] *Re Pinewood Estate, Farnborough* [1958] Ch. 280.
[62] See (1968) 84 L.Q.R. 22 at 31, 32 (P.V. Baker).

the erection of cheap buildings and the like. In the ordinary way, these covenants would be enforceable only by the vendor. But much of the purpose of the covenants given by a purchaser of one lot would be lost if they could not be enforced:

(i) by those who have previously bought lots, and

(ii) by those who subsequently buy the unsold lots.

Each of these results could be achieved without any special rules for schemes of development. The first would be achieved if the purchaser's covenants were expressly made with those who had previously bought lots as well as with the vendor. The second could be achieved by the covenant being expressed to be for the benefit of the whole or any part of the land retained by the vendor, and so attaching the benefit of them to each lot sold in the future, or by the vendor expressly assigning the benefit of the covenants with each lot sold.[63]

(ii) Principle of schemes: It is, however, unnecessary for these arrangements to be made. There is a wide principle that where an owner of a defined[64] area of land deals with it on the footing of imposing restrictive obligations on the use of various parts of it as and when he sells them off, for the common benefit of himself (insofar as he retains any land) and of the various purchasers *inter se*, and the purchasers buy on this footing, then the common intention gives rise to an independent equity which binds each owner (including the vendor) as soon as the first part is sold[65]; at that point, the scheme crystallises.[66] This common intention may appear either expressly from the terms of a deed of mutual covenant[67] or of a series of conveyances, or else impliedly from extrinsic evidence which satisfies the conditions for a building scheme.[68] "Building schemes", though important, are but a species of the genus of "scheme of development".[69]

(iii) Building schemes: The conditions of a building scheme were for most part laid down in *Elliston v. Reacher.*[70] These are as follows:

(i) the claimant and the defendant must each have derived title from a common vendor or a successor in title who is bound in equity by the obligations of the common vendor[71];

(ii) previously to the sale of the claimant's and defendant's plots, the common vendor must have laid out or intended to lay out the estate in lots subject to restrictions which were intended to be imposed on all of them and were consistent only with some general scheme of development;

---

[63] See above, pp. 456–459.
[64] *Lund v. Taylor* (1975) 31 P. & C.R. 167.
[65] *Baxter v. Four Oaks Properties Ltd* [1965] Ch. 816 at 825; *Re Dolphin's Conveyance* [1970] Ch. 654; *Brunner v. Greenslade* [1971] Ch. 993 at 1003–1005, stating the principles.
[66] *Brunner v. Greenslade* [1971] Ch. 993 at 1003.
[67] *Baxter v. Four Oaks Properties Ltd* [1965] Ch. 816.
[68] See *Re Dolphin's Conveyance* [1970] Ch. 654 at 662, 663; (1971) 87 L.Q.R. 539 at 546–551 (D.J. Hayton).
[69] See *Brunner v. Greenslade* [1971] Ch. 993 at 999.
[70] [1908] 2 Ch. 374 at 384; affirmed [1908] 2 Ch. 665. The first real hint of the doctrine was in *Western v. MacDermott* (1866) L.R. 1 Eq. 499; but see *Re Pinewood Estate, Farnborough* [1958] Ch. 280 at 286, 287.
[71] *Re Dolphin's Conveyance* [1970] Ch. 654.

(iii) the common vendor must have intended the restrictions to be for the benefit not merely of himself but of all lots sold[72];

(iv) the claimant's and the defendant's plots must both have been bought from the common vendor on the footing that the restrictions were to be for the benefit of the other lots;

(v) the area to which the scheme extends must be clearly defined.[73]

The whole essence of a building scheme is that each purchaser should know when he buys his plot from the common vendor that the covenants given by him are to be enforceable by the owners of all the other lots.[74] It is not necessary to prove an express undertaking by him that this should be so, provided the circumstances show that he must have realised it. If before his purchase he saw some plan of the estate with the restrictions endorsed thereon, as in *Elliston v. Reacher*, this suffices; but the absence of a proper plan may be fatal.[75] A scheme establishes a "local law" for a defined area, and the landowners within it have both community of interest and reciprocity of obligation.[76] The reservation by the common vendor of a power to release all or part of the land from the restrictions does not negative a building scheme, nor is it essential that the restrictions imposed on each plot should be identical: it suffices if there is some general scheme of development.[77]

(iv) Sub-schemes: Where a lot has been divided into sub-lots, the scheme may be enforceable by and between the purchasers of the sub-lots.[78] Furthermore, one result of the "local law" established by a scheme is that where two or more lots come into the same hands, the covenants are not *pro tanto* extinguished but become enforceable between the owners of the lots if and when they are again separated.[79]

(v) Buildings already erected: If a fully-built upon estate is disposed of in sections, and conditions analogous to those laid down for building schemes are satisfied, the covenants will be enforceable as in building schemes.[80] Again, the principle of a building scheme has been applied to a block of residential flats, preventing the landlord from letting or using any of them otherwise than for residential purposes[81]; but the court will be slow to infer a letting scheme from the mere similarity of the covenants when each floor of a large house is sub-let separately.[82]

---

[72] Which may be hard to prove: see, *e.g. Tucker v. Vowles* [1893] 1 Ch. 195.
[73] This last condition was added by *Reid v. Bickerstaff* [1909] 2 Ch. 305: see *Kelly v. Barrett* [1924] 2 Ch. 379 at 401.
[74] See *Jamaica Mutual Life Assurance Society v. Hillsborough Ltd* [1989] 1 W.L.R. 1101.
[75] *e.g. Osborne v. Bradley* [1903] 2 Ch. 446; *Harlow v. Hartog* (1977) 245 E.G. 140.
[76] *Reid v. Bickerstaff* [1909] 2 Ch. 305 at 319, 323.
[77] *Pearce v. Maryon-Wilson* [1935] Ch. 188; *Reid v. Bickerstaff* [1909] 2 Ch. 305 at 319.
[78] *Brunner v. Greenslade* [1971] Ch. 993.
[79] *Texaco Antilles Ltd v. Kernochan* [1973] A.C. 609. Contrast other restrictive covenants: above, p. 454.
[80] *Torbay Hotel Ltd v. Jenkins* [1927] 2 Ch. 225 at 241.
[81] See *Hudson v. Cripps* [1896] 1 Ch. 265.
[82] *Kelly v. Battershell* [1949] 2 All E.R. 830.

PART 2—BURDEN

Sect. 1. The burden at law

1. The rule

As already mentioned,[83] the rule at law is that the burden of a covenant will not pass with freehold land.[84] Despite the inconvenient consequences of this rule, which contrasts both with the rule for leaseholds, where the benefit and burden of covenants run at law with the lease and the reversion,[85] and with the rule in equity, where the burden of restrictive covenants can run with freehold land,[86] it has recently been confirmed by the House of Lords.[87] Its rationale has been stated to be that "equity cannot compel a owner to comply with a positive covenant entered into by his predecessors in title without flatly contradicting the common law rule that a person cannot be made liable upon a contract unless he is a party to it".[88] Nevertheless, there are certain means whereby what cannot be achieved directly can be accomplished indirectly. There are five heads.

(a) Chain of covenants

If V sells land to P, and P covenants, for example, to erect and maintain a fence, P will remain liable to V on the covenant by virtue of privity of contract even if P sells the land to Q. P will accordingly protect himself by extracting from Q a covenant of indemnity against future breaches of the covenant to fence. If Q then fails to maintain the fence, V cannot sue Q, but he can sue P, and P can then sue Q on the covenant for indemnity. In theory, liability can be maintained indefinitely in this way; but with each sale of the land the chain of covenants of indemnity becomes longer, and more liable to be broken by the insolvency or disappearance of one of the parties to it. This indirect enforcement of covenants by means of indemnities is thus an imperfect substitute for the direct enforcement which the common law refuses to allow.

(b) Right of entry annexed to rentcharge

A right of entry annexed "for any purpose" to a legal rentcharge is a legal interest in the land.[89] It is possible, therefore, to secure the performance of covenants to build, repair, and so on, by reserving a rentcharge and annexing to it a right of entry, allowing the proprietor to enter and make good any default in the observance of the covenants, and to charge the cost to the owner in possession.[90] The right of entry is enforceable indefinitely since such rights are not subject to the rule against perpetuities.[91] Such rentcharges, which are not subject to the rule against may still be created despite the Rentcharges Act 1977,[92] which describes them as estate rentcharges. However, they can only be used to enforce covenants whose performance relates in some way to the land in question; they therefore cannot be used to

---

[83] Above, p. 453.
[84] *Austerberry v. Corporation of Oldham* (1885) 29 Ch.D. 750 at 781–785; *E. & G.C. Ltd v. Bate* (1935) 79 L.J. News. 203; *Cator v. Newton* [1940] 1 K.B. 415 (registered land).
[85] Above, pp. 381 *et seq.*
[86] Below, p. 468.
[87] *Rhone v. Stephens* [1994] 2 A.C. 310.
[88] *ibid.*, at 318 *per* Lord Templeman.
[89] Above, p. 83.
[90] See Law Com. No. 68 (1975), para.49.
[91] L.P.A. 1925, s.4(3). Perpetuities and Accumulations Act 1964, s.11.
[92] s.2(3)(b), (4); see above, p. 409.

enforce other types of covenants, such as those imposing a contingent pecuniary liability.[93]

(c) Right of re-entry in gross

As the authorities on conditional fees[94] demonstrate, the ability to enforce a right of entry is not conditional on holding some estate in the land in question.[95] It has been said to be "indisputable" that a vendor of a freehold can reserve a right of re-entry in order to enforce positive covenants made by his purchaser.[96] However, such a right will only be enforceable during the perpetuity period[97] and will necessarily take effect as an equitable rather than a legal right of entry.[98] However, given the possibility of using estate rentcharges, rights of re-entry in gross only need to be used in the case of covenants whose performance does not relate in any way to the land in question.

(d) Enlarged long lease

A more effective but artificial method is to insert the covenant in a lease which can be enlarged into a fee simple, and then to enlarge the lease.[99]

(e) Conditional benefit

A man who claims the benefit of a conveyance or other deed must submit to its burdens. Thus if a conveyance of land on a housing estate gives the purchaser the right to use the estate roads but imposes on him a liability to contribute to the cost of their upkeep, a successor in title cannot use the roads without paying the contributions.[1] Similarly, it has been held that a right of way granted in exchange for not objecting to a minor trespass by the grantor's foundations could not be withdrawn unless the trespass was remedied.[2] The liability is thus not absolute but conditional; he who does not enjoy need not submit although often there will be little choice.

The principle was subsequently extended to a case in which grants of mining rights were made to a company in return for covenants to replant the land. The company's successors in title were held liable on the covenants as having taken the benefit of the grants of mining rights.[3] However, the "pure principle of benefit and burden" (as distinct from conditional benefit and burden) distilled from this case, which would have left little of the common law rule against the burden of covenants running with land intact,[4] has since been rejected by the House of Lords, who have restricted the doctrine to cases where the condition is "relevant to the exercise of the right".[5] The party in question must, "at least in theory", be able to choose between enjoying his right with the consequential duty to perform his obligation and

[93] *ibid.* s.2(5).
[94] Above, p. 41.
[95] Co. Lit. fo.202; see *Doe d. Freeman v. Bateman* (1818) 1 B. & Ald. 168.
[96] *Shiloh Spinners v. Harding* [1973] A.C. 691 at 717 *per* Lord Wilberforce (the decision actually concerned an assignment by a lessee).
[97] Above, p. 231.
[98] L.P.A. 1925, s.1(2)(e). In the case of registered land, this will require protection on the Land Register.
[99] See above, p. 365; *Re M'Naul's Estate* [1902] 1 I.R. 114; (1958) 22 Conv. (n.s.) 101 (T.P.D. Taylor).
[1] *Halsall v. Brizell* [1957] Ch. 169.
[2] *E.R. Ives Investment Ltd v. High* [1967] 2 Q.B. 379.
[3] *Tito v. Waddell (No. 2)* [1977] Ch. 106 at 289–311 (the "Ocean Island" case).
[4] See the previous edition of this work at p. 419.
[5] *Rhone v. Stephens* [1994] 2 A.C. 310 at 322 *per* Lord Templeman; see N.P. Gravells (1994) 110 L.Q.R. 346, J. Snape [1994] Conv. 477.

renouncing his right with the consequential release from that duty.[6] Consequently, the fact that A's roof was supported by B's property did not entitle B to enforce a positive covenant to repair the roof made by A's predecessor in title. Quite where that leaves the person granted the right of way is unclear; could he really compel the grantor to remove his foundations by surrendering his right of way?

2. Summary of the position at law

(a) Enforcement

It will be observed that only within narrow limits does the common law enforce covenants outside the confines of privity of contract or the leasehold context. As will be seen shortly, equity became far more flexible and would enforce covenants in many cases where the common law would not.

This does not, however, render the rules at law obsolete, for if a covenant is enforceable at law, the claimant, on proving his case, is entitled as of right to a judgment for damages (even though they may be nominal), whereas if a covenant is enforceable only in equity the court has a discretion in deciding whether to give any remedy at all. However, since the equitable remedy of an injunction is the one usually desired, this point is not of great practical importance. Yet it should be remembered that at law it is quite immaterial whether the covenantor has any land or whether the covenant is negative or positive, and that in the case of a positive covenant, damages will usually be the most suitable remedy.

(b) Reform

The present rule against the burden of covenants running with the land at law still creates many problems. The methods of indirect enforcement of such covenants, considered above,[7] are not entirely satisfactory, and although the burden of covenants will run with land in equity if they are negative, the burden of positive covenants will not. It is now clear that the situation cannot be remedied without legislation.[8] A number of proposals have been made from time to time for enabling the burden of positive covenants to run with land.[9] The only one which has so far been enacted is of relatively limited scope, namely for the introduction of a new tenure called "commonhold", although the relevant legislation[10] has not yet come into force. Another,[11] for the introduction of "land obligations", is understood to be still under active consideration.[12]

(i) Commonhold: Commonhold is a wholly new freehold tenure which will be created when the Commonhold and Leasehold Reform Act 2002 comes into force.[13] It will not be a new freehold estate. The description which follows is no more than an outline; much of the detail of how this new tenure will work is to be contained in statutory instruments which had not yet been published when this edition had to go to press.

---

[6] *ibid.*, see also *Thamesmead Town Ltd v. Allotey* [1998] 3 E.G.L.R. 97.
[7] Above, p. 462.
[8] *Rhone v. Stephens* [1994] 2 A.C. 310 at 321 *per* Lord Templeman.
[9] See Law Com. No. 11 (1967); Law Com. No. 127 (1984); (1987) Cmnd. 179 & (1990) Cmnd. 1345 (the Aldridge Committee).
[10] Commonhold and Leasehold Reform Act 2002.
[11] Law Com. No. 127 (1984).
[12] M. & W., pp. 1010–1011.
[13] See N. Roberts [2002] N.L.J. 338.

Commonhold will only be able to be created in respect of registered land held for an estate in fee simple[14] and that land will have to be in contact with the ground[15] (there will be no possibility of "flying commonholds" with ground floor shops excluded). It will create a means of providing for freehold ownership of buildings such as blocks of flats which are horizontally divided with individuals owning different units on one or more floors (at present ownership of such units is only practicable under a long lease). The owner of each unit will also have a freehold registered title,[16] subject to the provisions of the "commonhold community statement",[17] a document which will have to be in a prescribed form,[18] although there is no requirement for standard wording. This will regulate the maintenance and user of the common parts and will specify the percentage of the annual "commonhold assessment",[19] a term which will replace what in the case of units owned under long leases is known as the service charge, payable by each unit-holder. It is this document which will ensure that the burden of what will be, in effect, positive covenants will run.[20]

Each owner of a "commonhold unit" will automatically be a member of the "commonhold association",[21] a company limited by guarantee whose Memorandum and Articles of Association will also have to be in a prescribed form.[22] The commonhold association will own the common parts[23] and will set the annual "commonhold assessment".[24] This will assess each year the funds necessary for, at the very least, the repair and insurance of the common parts. In practice, at least in the cases of blocks of flats, it is likely that the commonhold assessment will also provide the funds for the repair and insurance of the foundations, the main structure, the roof and the maintenance of them and of the common parts.

The directors of the commonhold association[25] will be able to recover payments due from unit-holders through the courts and both they and other unit holders will be able to restrain and recover compensation for other breaches of the commonhold community statement.[26] However, there is no possibility of forfeiture of a unit, no matter how blatant the breach.[27] Although court proceedings in respect of arrears may ultimately lead to the imposition of a charging order on the unit in question, that charge will not enjoy priority over pre-existing mortgages. (This contrasts starkly with the situation under the present system, where the inevitable existence of a right of re-entry and forfeiture in each lease enables the landlord to demand payment of arrears of service charges from mortgagees as a condition of not forfeiting, thus giving the arrears priority over the mortgage debts.) However, the directors of the community association are not obliged to take proceedings if they reasonably think that inaction is the best course to follow and they must have regard to the desirability of using alternative dispute resolution.[28] In particular it is expected that an Ombudsman will be

---

[14] Commonhold and Leasehold Reform Act 2002, s.1.
[15] *ibid.*, s.4 & Sched. 2, para.1.
[16] *ibid.*, s.9(3)(b), (c).
[17] *ibid.*, s.9(3)(e).
[18] *ibid.*, ss.31–33.
[19] *ibid.*, s.38.
[20] *ibid.*, s.31(3)(b).
[21] *ibid.*, ss.34–46.
[22] *ibid.*, s.34(2) & Sched. 3, Pt. I.
[23] *ibid.*, s.9(3)(a).
[24] *ibid.*, s.38.
[25] *ibid.*, s.35.
[26] *ibid.*, s.37.
[27] *ibid.*, s.31(8).
[28] *ibid.*, s.38.

appointed and regulations may require all or certain classes of community association to join an approved ombudsman scheme.[29]

Unit-holders will have an absolute right to transfer their units and will cease to be liable to the commonhold association for payments due in respect of any period after the transfer.[30] Nor can the creation of interests in the whole or part of a unit or of charges over the whole of a unit be prohibited.[31] However, it will not be possible to create interests other than leases in the whole or part of a commonhold unit unless at least 75 per cent of the members of the community association consent.[32] Further, the type of leases which can be granted will be restricted in order to prevent the reintroduction of the problems which commonhold was intended to resolve.[33] It is expected that regulations[34] will prohibit leases of residential units at a premium or in excess of seven years. Leases of non-residential units will be effective subject to the provisions of the commonhold community statement.[35]

The majority of commonholds are likely to be blocks of flats but there is no reason why buildings with shops on lower floors or, for that matter, buildings consisting entirely of shops should not also be commonholds. (However, experience in other jurisdictions suggests that commonholds will only rarely be employed in the case of purely commercial developments.) Commonholds may well also comprise townhouses sharing a communal garden and estate roads and units on business parks, particularly in the light of the current uncertainty as to the scope of the law governing conditional benefits.[36] In practice, commonhold will be almost entirely limited to new buildings. This category includes conversions of existing buildings although where these are held on long leases the developer will first have to acquire the freehold reversion, even where the lease is for 999 years. (If the freeholder is untraceable, the only possibility of setting up a commonhold will be if the lease can be enlarged.[37]) In theory leaseholders who own their freehold through a Residents' Management Company could convert to commonhold by setting up a commonhold association but this will require the unanimous consent of that company, the leaseholders and their mortgagees.[38] The inability of a majority to prevail over a minority has been criticised and the position may well be reviewed if and when commonhold becomes the norm for new buildings.

Save in the relatively unlikely case where leaseholders do unanimously agree to convert, the decision as to whether or not to utilise commonhold rather than the existing system will be entirely that of the developer. Some developers are likely to prefer the greater power and control given to their chosen management company by the existing system, in which case they will not use commonhold unless and until they are compelled to do so by market forces.

Where a developer does decide to use commonhold, he will apply to the relevant Land Registrar for the registration of a freehold estate in land as a freehold estate in commonhold

---

[29] *ibid.*, s.42.
[30] *ibid.*, s.16.
[31] *ibid.*, s.20(1).
[32] *ibid.*, s.20((3), (4).
[33] *ibid.*, ss.17, 18.
[34] *ibid.*, s.17.
[35] *ibid.*, s.18.
[36] Above, p. 463.
[37] See above, p. 365.
[38] Commonhold and Leasehold Reform Act 2002, s.3.

land[39]; the certificate of incorporation, memorandum and articles of association of the commonhold association and the commonhold community statement must accompany the application.[40] The commonhold may initially be registered without unit holders in which case the developer will retain control of the commonhold until the first person other than the developer becomes entitled to be registered as a unit-holder.[41] At that point the commonhold association will become entitled to be registered as proprietor of the common parts and the commonhold community statement will come into effect.[42] However, no unit-holder will become registered until a full list of the commonhold units is provided giving details of the proposed initial unit-holders.[43] (In practice it is likely that this list will accompany the initial application, in which case the commonhold association will immediately be registered as proprietor of the common parts and the commonhold community statement will immediately come into effect.[44])

Provision is also made for the termination of commonhold in the event of a decision to this effect by a solvent community association,[45] in the event that the commonhold association becomes insolvent,[46] and in the event of compulsory purchase.[47] It will also be necessary to dissolve a community association in the event that the unit-holders wish to sell their commonholds for redevelopment.

(ii) Land obligations: Under the scheme of "land obligations" proposed by the Law Commission,[48] a new interest in land, which could be legal, would be created similar to an easement and, like an easement, requiring both a dominant and a servient tenement. It would cover both negative obligations and three specific positive obligations and the burden of both would run with the land. The present rules for the running of the benefit of positive covenants would be abolished other than the rules governing conditional benefit. However, their benefit could nevertheless be expressly assigned and this would clearly be necessary in the case of covenants which fell outside the scheme because there was no servient tenement.[49] The three specific positive obligations would be:

(i) the carrying out on either the servient or the dominant tenement of works which would benefit the dominant tenement or any part of it;

(ii) the provision of services for the benefit of the dominant tenement or any part of it; and

(iii) the reimbursement of expenditure incurred in performing either of the obligations already set out.

[39] *ibid.*, s.2.
[40] *ibid.*, Sched. 1.
[41] *ibid.*, s.7(1), (2).
[42] *ibid.*, s.7(3).
[43] *ibid.*, s.9(2).
[44] *ibid.*, s.9(3).
[45] *ibid.*, ss.43–48.
[46] *ibid.*, ss.50–54.
[47] *ibid.*, s.60.
[48] (1984) Law Com. No.127, as modified by (1990) Cmnd. 1345, para. 3.49. See M. & W., pp. 1010–1011.
[49] As in *Smith v. River Douglas Catchment Board* [1949] 2 K.B. 500, above p. 411.

Sect. 2. The burden in equity

1. Liability—general

It has been seen[50] that the rules in equity as to the benefit of a covenant are in the main merely a more relaxed and detailed version of the rules at law. As to the burden of the covenant, however, the rules in equity came to be completely different. Until *Tulk v. Moxhay*[51] was decided in 1848 (a time when the full effects of the vast expansion in industrial and building activities were being felt), equity had gone no further than the common law.[52] In that case it was decided that a covenant to maintain the garden in the centre of Leicester Square in London uncovered with any buildings would be enforced by injunction against a purchaser of the land who had bought with notice of the covenant.

For some while the question was thought to be solely one of notice: a person who took land with notice that it had been bound by some restriction could not disregard that restriction. On this footing, it was immaterial whether the restriction had been imposed to benefit other land or merely the covenantee personally: it sufficed that there was some contractual restriction on the use of the land and that the land had been acquired with notice of it.[53] But since 1882[54] it has been accepted that equity will enforce a restrictive covenant against a purchaser only if it was made for the protection of some other land. Restrictive covenants came to resemble easements as being rights over one plot of land ("the servient tenement") existing for the benefit of another plot of land ("the dominant tenement"). In short, at a leap, the law of restrictive covenants passed from the sphere of contract to the sphere of property.

2. Liability—the original covenantor

The original covenantor usually remains liable on the covenant, even if he has parted with the servient tenement, for the common form of covenant extends to the acts of persons claiming under him[55]; but today, words limiting the ambit of the covenant to the period of his ownership of the servient tenement are often inserted.[56]

3. Liability—assignees

An assignee of land of the original covenantor is bound by the covenant only if three conditions are fulfilled.

(a) The covenant must be negative in nature

After a few cases in which the court was prepared to enforce positive covenants, the rule was settled in 1881 that none except negative covenants would be enforced by equity.[57] The question is whether in substance[58] the covenant is negative in nature: it is immaterial whether the wording is positive or negative. Thus the covenant in *Tulk v. Moxhay*[59] itself was positive in wording, but part of it was negative in nature (to keep the land in Leicester Square "in an open

[50] Above, pp. 456 *et seq.*
[51] (1848) 2 Ph. 774.
[52] Despite *Whatman v. Gibson* (1838) 9 Sim. 196, the question was regarded as still being open in *Bristow v. Wood* (1844) 1 Coll.C.C. 480.
[53] See *Luker v. Dennis* (1877) 7 Ch.D. 227.
[54] See *London & South Western Ry. v. Gomm* (1882) 20 Ch.D. 562 at 583.
[55] *L.C.C. v. Allen* [1914] 3 K.B. 642 at 660, 673; and see L.P.A. 1925, s.79(1).
[56] See *Morrells of Oxford Ltd v. Oxford United Football Club Ltd* [2001] Ch. 459.
[57] *Haywood v. Brunswick Permanent Benefit B.S.* (1881) 8 Q.B.D. 403. See [1981] Conv. 55 (C.D. Bell); [1983] Conv. 29 (R. Griffith).
[58] *Shepherd Homes Ltd v. Sandham (No. 2)* [1971] 1 W.L.R. 1062.
[59] See above.

state, uncovered with any buildings"), so that this part merely bound the covenantor to refrain from building, without requiring him to do any positive act.

The test is whether the covenant requires expenditure of money for its proper performance; if the covenant requires the covenantee to put his hand in his pocket, it is not negative in nature.[60] A covenant to give the first refusal of a plot of land is negative in nature, for in effect it is a covenant not to sell to anyone else until the covenantee has had an opportunity of buying. But a covenant "not to let the premises get into disrepair", despite its apparently negative form, is in substance positive, for it can be performed only by the expenditure of money on repairs. Among the restrictive covenants most frequently met with in practice are covenants against building on land, against carrying on any trade or business (or certain specified trades or businesses[61]) on the premises concerned, and against using residential property for any purpose other than that of a single private dwelling-house.

(b) At the date of the covenant, the covenantee must own land that will benefit from the covenant

Here again, as mentioned above, the rule was not settled at first. It is now accepted, however, that with statutory exceptions in favour of local authorities,[62] a restrictive covenant is similar to an equitable easement, and that the burden of the covenant will run with land only if the covenant was made for the protection of land belonging to the covenantee. As with easements,[63] there must be a dominant tenement which the covenant will benefit (or accommodate).[64] Thus covenants binding land in Hampstead will be too remote to benefit land in Clapham,[65] and if the covenantee retains no other land, a purchaser of the Hampstead land will take free from the covenant. Yet a landlord's reversion on a lease is a sufficient interest to entitle him to enforce the covenant against a sub-tenant, even though he has no other adjoining land.[66]

(c) The burden of the covenant must have been intended to run with the covenantor's land

A covenant may be confined, either expressly or by implication, so as to bind the covenantor alone.[67] In this case, assignees of the covenantor's land are not bound by the covenant. But if the covenant was made by the covenantor for himself, his heirs and assigns, the burden will normally be attached to his land. Although covenants relating to the covenantor's land which are made after 1925 are deemed to have been made by the covenantor on behalf of himself, his successors in title, and the persons deriving title under him or them,[68] their burden will nevertheless run only if the parties so intend; the difference since 1925 has been that such an intention will be presumed unless the contrary is expressed.[69] There is no need for the

---

[60] *Haywood v. Brunswick Permanent Benefit B.S.* (1881) 8 Q.B.D. 403 at 409, 410.

[61] Such covenants are apparently not subject to the doctrine of restraint of trade when given on the acquisition of property: *Esso Petroleum Co. Ltd v. Harper's Garage (Stourport) Ltd* [1968] A.C. 269 at 298, 309, 316, 325, 334; and see *Cleveland Petroleum Co. Ltd v. Dartstone Ltd* [1969] 1 W.L.R. 116 (covenant in lease).

[62] See, *e.g.* Housing Act 1985, s.609; Town and Country Planning Act 1990, s.106(3).

[63] Above, p. 414.

[64] See *Formby v. Barker* [1903] 2 Ch. 539; *L.C.C. v. Allen* [1914] 3 K.B. 642; (1971) 87 L.Q.R. 539 at 545 (D.J. Hayton).

[65] *Kelly v. Barrett* [1924] 2 Ch. 379 at 404.

[66] *Regent Oil Co. Ltd v. J. A. Gregory (Hatch End) Ltd* [1966] Ch. 402 at 433.

[67] See *Re Fawcett and Holmes' Contract* (1889) 42 Ch.D. 150; *Re Royal Victoria Pavilion, Ramsgate* [1961] Ch. 581.

[68] L.P.A. 1925, s.79(1).

[69] *Rhone v. Stephens* [1994] 2 A.C. 310, at 321–322; *Morrells of Oxford Ltd v. Oxford United Football Club Ltd* [2001] Ch. 459.

contrary intention to be expressed in so many words; a stark contrast between the wording of the relevant covenant and that of other covenants in the same deed will suffice.[70]

4. Effect

If these conditions are satisfied, the effect is that the burden of the covenant runs in equity. There are two main consequences of this.

(a) Equitable remedies

Only equitable remedies, which are of course discretionary, are available. The two possibilities are an injunction and damages in lieu of an injunction under the Chancery Amendment Act 1858.[71] The person with the benefit of the covenant will normally seek an injunction. However, he will not obtain either an injunction or damages if, knowing of the breach, he has taken no action for several years; in these circumstances, he will have acquiesced in the breach.[72] He is not, as in an action at law, entitled to insist upon some damages being awarded just because he has made out his case. On the other hand, lesser acts of acquiescence such as a failure to seek interim relief is likely only to deprive him of an injunction.[73] In such circumstances and also where the claimant has not sought an injunction, the primary measure of recovery is any loss in value suffered by his land. Where, on the other hand, his land has suffered no such loss in value, the assessment of damages involves the court ascertaining the sum of money which might reasonably have been demanded by the claimant from the defendant as a *quid pro quo* for releasing the covenant to the extent that it has been breached.[74] This is done by ascertaining the sum that would have been arrived at in negotiations between the parties, if each had made reasonable use of his respective bargaining position without holding out for unreasonable amounts.[75]

(b) Possibility of purchaser taking free of the covenant

The covenant suffers from the infirmity of all equitable interests, namely that it is possible for a purchaser to take free of it, in which case it will not be enforced against him.

(i) **Unregistered land:** In unregistered conveyancing, covenants made before 1926, many of which are still in force, are subject to the old rules as to notice and will not bind a bona fide purchaser for value of a legal estate without notice of the covenant, or someone claiming through such a person.[76] So are covenants in leases, whenever made, although the only persons capable of taking free of them are assignees of old sub-leases,[77] original holders and assignees of old sub-under-leases,[78] and purchasers of interests in adjoining land also owned by the lessor.[79] A restrictive covenant made after 1925 other than between a lessor and a lessee must be registered as a Class D-II land charge.[80] If registered it will bind the whole

---

[70] *Morrells of Oxford Ltd v. Oxford United Football Club Ltd* [2001] Ch. 459.
[71] Supreme Court Act 1981, s.50. The jurisdiction survived the repeal of the Act of 1858: *Leeds Industrial Co-operative Society Ltd v. Slack* [1924] A.C. 851.
[72] *Gafford v. Graham* [1999] 3 E.G.L.R. 75.
[73] *Gafford v. Graham* [1999] 3 E.G.L.R. 75.
[74] *Wrotham Park Ltd v. Parkside Homes Ltd* [1974] 1 W.L.R. 798; *Jaggard v. Sawyer* [1995] 1 W.L.R. 269; *Gafford v. Graham* [1999] 3 E.G.L.R. 75; see also *Attorney-General v. Blake* [2001] 1 A.C. 268.
[75] *Amec Developments Ltd v. Jury's Hotel Management (UK) Ltd* (2001) 82 P. & C.R. 286.
[76] *Wilkes v. Spooner* [1911] 2 K.B. 473; above, pp. 63, 97.
[77] See above, pp. 395–396, 405–406.
[78] *ibid.*
[79] *Dartstone Ltd v. Cleveland Petroleum Co. Ltd* [1969] 1 W.L.R. 1807.
[80] Above, p. 97. For lessees who cannot investigate the lessor's title, see above, p. 103.

world.[81] If not registered, it will be void against a subsequent purchaser for money or money's worth of a legal estate in the land.[82]

(ii) Registered land: In registered conveyancing, covenants in leases, whenever made, cannot be protected on the Land Register but will nevertheless bind all types of sub-lessees and their assignees.[83] However, a bona fide purchaser for value claiming under a registered disposition of an interest in adjoining land also owned by the lessor will automatically take free of them.[84] A restrictive covenant other than between a lessor and a lessee must be protected on the Land Register. At present it should be protected by a notice[85] or, if a notice cannot be registered because the Land Certificate is not at the Land Registry, by a caution against dealings.[86] When the Land Registration Act 2002 comes into force, the two possibilities will instead be an agreed notice or a unilateral notice.[87]

PART 3—ENFORCEMENT

Sect. 1. Determination

The enforceability of a restrictive covenant may be decided in any of three ways:

(i) in an action to enforce the covenant;

(ii) on application to the court for a declaration; or

(iii) on application to the Lands Tribunal for the discharge or modification of the covenant.

1. Action to enforce the covenant

Prima facie, a restrictive covenant remains enforceable indefinitely.[88] In certain cases, however, the court may refuse to enforce an action brought by the person entitled to the benefit of a covenant. Thus, if the person entitled to enforce the covenant has remained inactive in the face of open breaches for so long and in such circumstances that a reasonable person would believe that the covenant no longer applies, the court will not enforce it.[89] The same applies if the neighbourhood is so completely changed (as from a residential to a shopping area) that an action to enforce the covenant would be unmeritorious, not bona fide and brought with some ulterior motive.[90]

2. Declaration by the court

Sometimes a landowner will be content to break a covenant and rely upon being able to establish one of the above defences if an action is brought. This, however, will not always be

---

[81] *White v. Bijou Mansions Ltd* [1937] Ch. 610.
[82] See above, p. 105.
[83] See above, pp. 405–406.
[84] *Oceanic Village Ltd v. United Attractions Ltd* [2000] Ch. 234.
[85] L.R.A. 1925, s.50; L.R.R. 1925, r. 212, Ruoff & Roper, paras 3–12, 35–21.
[86] See above, p. 130.
[87] See above, p. 133.
[88] See *Mackenzie v. Childers* (1890) L.R. 43 Ch.D. 265 at 279.
[89] *Chatsworth Estates Co. v. Fewell* [1931] 1 Ch. 224.
[90] *ibid., Westripp v. Baldock* [1939] 1 All E.R. 279.

satisfactory, as where it is desired to sell or lease the land and the purchaser or lessee wishes to be assured that he is in no danger from the covenant. Consequently, provision has now been made permitting an application to the court for a declaration whether any freehold land is affected by any restriction, and if so, the nature, extent and enforceability of it.[91] This provision is often used in respect of the many covenants created in the nineteenth century which are today unenforceable through non-compliance with the more modern rules governing the transfer of the benefit of the covenants. There is no power under this head to modify or discharge a valid covenant.

3. Discharge or modification by the Lands Tribunal

In some cases a covenant may still be enforceable, but it may be undesirable for this state of affairs to continue. Consequently, a discretionary[92] power has been given to the Lands Tribunal[93] to modify or discharge the restrictive covenant, with or without the payment of compensation; and an order may be refused unless the applicant accepts reasonable alternative restrictions.[94] An applicant is not disqualified merely because he recently bound himself by the covenant, though this is a factor to be considered.[95] He must bring his case within one of four heads.

(a) Obsolete

By reason of changes in the character of the property or neighbourhood or other material circumstances the restriction ought to be deemed obsolete.

(b) Obstructive

The continued existence of the restriction would impede some reasonable use of the land for public or private purposes, and either it confers no practical benefit[96] of substantial value or advantage, or it is contrary to the public interest, and (in either case) any loss can be adequately compensated in money.[97]

(c) Agreement

The persons of full age and capacity entitled to the benefit of the restrictions have agreed, either expressly or by implication, by their acts and omissions, to the discharge or modification sought.

(d) No injury

The discharge or modification would not injure the persons entitled to the benefit of the covenant.

Both for the court and the Lands Tribunal, these powers apply to restrictions whenever made, but do not apply to restrictions imposed on a disposition made either gratuitously or for a nominal consideration for public purposes.[98] They apply to restrictions on freehold land,

---

[91] L.P.A. 1925, s.84(2). See s.84(7), below.
[92] *Driscoll v. Church Commissioners for England* [1957] 1 Q.B. 330.
[93] Lands Tribunal Act 1949, s.1(4).
[94] *Jones v. Rhys-Jones* (1974) 30 P. & C.R. 451.
[95] L.P.A. 1925, s.84(1), (1C); L.P.A. 1969, s.28.
[96] *Gilbert v. Spoor* [1983] Ch. 27 (a view).
[97] See the questions as formulated in *Re Bass Ltd's Application* (1973) 26 P. & C.R. 156 and discussed in (1979) 129 N.L.J. 523 (H.W. Wilkinson).
[98] L.P.A. 1925, s.84(7).

and to restrictions on leasehold land if the lease was made for more than 40 years and at least 25 have expired,[99] but they do not apply to mining leases.[1]

There is also provision for the county court to authorise the conversion of a house into two or more tenements in contravention of a restrictive covenant or a provision in a lease if owing to changes in the neighbourhood the house cannot readily be let as a whole, or if planning permission for the conversion has been granted.[2]

4. Implications for the Land Register

Any release, waiver, discharge or modification of a restrictive covenant should be noted on the Land Register. Where the court has refused to enforce the covenant by injunction or declared that it is no longer enforceable, the entry on the Land Register will simply be cancelled. Where the Lands Tribunal or the court has discharged or modified the covenant, the entry on the Land Register will be cancelled or modified as the case may be.[3]

Sect. 2. Town planning

In recent years, the extension of town and country planning control[4] has to some extent reduced the importance of restrictive covenants. If planning control imposes restrictions which will preserve the amenities of a neighbourhood, landowners have little incentive to impose or enforce restrictive covenants with the same object. Nevertheless, restrictive covenants have not been superseded by planning control. A landowner must see that what he proposes to do will contravene neither the private system of restrictive covenants nor the public system of planning control; and restrictive covenants sometimes extend to matters not usually dealt with by planning law. Further, a covenantee has the enforcement of the covenant under his control, whereas a landowner may be disappointed in the way in which the local planning authority imposes or enforces planning control against his neighbours. Nevertheless, the practical advice to give a landowner whose neighbour's activities are objectionable is often not to launch proceedings to enforce any apposite restrictive covenant, with consequent delay, expense and uncertainty, but to encourage the local planning authority to exercise its powers of enforcing planning control.[5]

---

[99] *Ridley v. Taylor* [1965] 1 W.L.R. 611.
[1] L.P.A. 1925, s.84(12), as amended by L. & T.A. 1954, s.52.
[2] H.A. 1985, s.610. See *Josephine Trust Ltd v. Champagne* [1963] 2 Q.B. 160.
[3] L.R.A. 1925, s.50(3), L.P.A 1969, s.28(7); L.R.R. 1925, r. 212; Ruoff & Roper, para. 35–25; L.R.A. 2002, Sched. 4, para.5(d); the new L.R.R. will presumably also deal with this.
[4] Below, pp. 569 *et seq.*
[5] For these powers, see below, pp. 574–576.

Chapter 12

LICENCES AND PROPRIETARY ESTOPPEL

Something has already been said about licences as contrasted with tenancies,[1] but they must now be considered in greater detail. In addition, something must be said about proprietary estoppel, not only as affecting licences but also in its own right.

Sect. 1. Nature of licences

In essence, a licence is a mere permission given by the occupier of land to a person to do something on that land which would otherwise be a trespass.[2] The scope of licences is great. They range from a simple oral permission given to a boy to fetch his ball from the garden to an elaborate deed granting exclusive possession of a large building for an indefinite period which would have been a lease if the period had been definite.[3] At common law, most licences could be revoked at any time, though if the licensor did this in breach of contract he would be liable in damages. A licence created no interest in the land, so that if V sold his lodging house to P, the lodgers could not resist eviction by P, and their only remedy was to sue V for damages. Normally a licence gave no right to the exclusive possession of the land. In recent decades, there has been much activity in the law of licences, and as will be seen, some basic concepts have been modified.

Sect. 2. Types of licences

Some licences give the licensee the right to the exclusive occupation of the land. At one point, this became increasingly common for flats and other dwellings where owners were seeking to avoid the occupier of the land obtaining statutory protection from eviction, which is available only to tenants and not to licensees.[4] However, the courts now ignore any provisions in the agreement between the parties which are pretences or shams.[5] Consequently, where a person has exclusive occupation of the land, he will now only be a licensee if the other essentials of a lease or tenancy are not present.[6]

---

[1] Above, pp. 340–341.
[2] See *Thomas v. Sorrell* (1673) Vaugh. 330 at 351.
[3] See above, pp. 340–342.
[4] Above, p. 340; below, p. 590.
[5] Above, p. 340.
[6] Above, pp. 340–346.

Other licences confer a right of occupation but not exclusive possession, as with lodgers and guests in a hotel.[7] There is also a wide range of miscellaneous licences, such as leave to use a concert hall for a few days[8]; permission to put pleasure boats on a canal[9]; permission to erect an advertisement hoarding or electrical sign[10]; the grant of the "front of the house rights" in a theatre, *i.e.* the exclusive right to supply refreshments and to use the refreshment rooms[11]; and permission to see a race or cinema performance.[12]

Four main categories of licence[13] require consideration: the first two are relatively straight-forward, but the other two are more complex, especially as regards revocability and as to whether successors in title will be bound.

1. Bare licence

A bare licence is the simplest form of licence. It is a licence not granted for valuable consideration, such as a gratuitous permission to enter a house or cross a field. Even if it is granted by deed, the licensor can revoke it at any time without being liable in damages,[14] though the licensee will not become a trespasser until he has been given a reasonable time to withdraw.[15] He cannot resist the licensor's claim by denying the latter's title, as he will be estopped from doing this as long as he is in possession,[16] but thereafter he is free to do so.[17] A revocable licence is automatically revoked by the death of the licensor or by any disposition by him of his interest in the land.[18]

2. Licence coupled with an interest

A licence may be coupled with an interest in the land or chattels thereon. Thus rights to enter another man's land to hunt and take away the deer killed, or to cut down a tree and remove it can both take effect as profits *à prendre*[19]; they consequently involve the grant of an interest in the land in question, the profit *à prendre*, and also a licence annexed to that interest to come onto the land.[20] The interest must be a recognised interest in property,[21] and it must have been validly created. Thus at law a right to take game or minerals, being a profit *à prendre*,[22] must have been created by deed or prescription,[23] whereas no formalities are required for the grant of a right to take away chattels, such as felled timber or cut hay. Equity will give effect to a specifically enforceable agreement to grant an interest, so that a licence coupled with a profit *à prendre* granted merely in writing but for value may be protected by injunction.[24]

---

[7] Above, pp. 340–341.
[8] See *Taylor v. Caldwell* (1863) 3 B. & S. 826.
[9] *Hill v. Tupper* (1863) 2 H. & C. 121; above, p. 414.
[10] *Wilson v. Tavener* [1901] 1 Ch. 578; *Walton Harvey Ltd v. Walker and Homfrays Ltd* [1931] 1 Ch. 274.
[11] *Frank Warr & Co. Ltd v. L.C.C.* [1904] 1 K.B. 713.
[12] *Wood v. Leadbitter* (1845) 13 M. & W. 838; *Hurst v. Picture Theatres Ltd* [1915] 1 K.B.1.
[13] This classification may not be exhaustive.
[14] *Wood v. Leadbitter* (1845) 13 M. & W. 838; *Aldin v. Latimer Clark, Muirhead & Co.* [1894] 2 Ch. 437.
[15] *Minister of Health v. Bellotti* [1944] K.B. 298.
[16] *Terunnanse v. Terunnanse* [1968] A.C. 1086; and see above, p. 352.
[17] *Government of the State of Penang v. Beng Hong Oon* [1972] A.C. 425.
[18] *Terunnanse v. Terunnanse* [1968] A.C. 1086 at 1095.
[19] See above, pp. 449–450.
[20] See *Thomas v. Sorrell* (1673) Vaugh. 331 at 351; *Wood v. Leadbitter* (1845) 13 M. & W. 838 at 845.
[21] See *Hounslow L.B.C v. Twickenham Garden Developments Ltd* [1971] Ch. 233 at 244, 254, doubting *Vaughan v. Hampson* (1875) 33 L.T.15 ("interest" in attending a meeting).
[22] Above, pp. 449–450.
[23] *Duke of Somerset v. Fogwell* (1826) 5 B. & C. 875.
[24] *Frogley v. Earl of Lovelace* (1859) Johns. 333.

A licence[25] coupled with an interest is irrevocable[26] and also assignable, though only with the interest with which it is coupled. It binds successors in title to the land in the same way as that interest.

3. Contractual licence

A contractual licence is a licence granted for value, such as a ticket for the theatre or for a football match, or an agreement to house lodgers or hotel guests. The rights under such licences primarily depend on the terms of the contract. At common law, such licences were inherently revocable even where revocation would be a breach of contract: the power of revocation was not taken away by a contract not to exercise it. At common law, such licences created no interest in the land, and like other personal contracts they did not bind successors in title to that land. As will be seen below, each of these propositions has now been substantially modified. A contractual licence is not a separate entity from the contract conferring it but takes effect as part of it, according to its terms.[27]

4. Licence by estoppel

A licence by estoppel[28] is a licence which the licensor is precluded by estoppel from revoking or otherwise failing to put into effect. Thus where at a licensor's request the licensee extended a jetty and erected a warehouse on the licensor's land, the licensor was estopped from revoking the licence.[29] Estoppel is a broad principle that applies not only to express or implied licences but also to a wide variety of cases concerning land. Thus if A builds on B's land, believing it to be his own, and B knowingly stands silently by, B will be estopped from contending that the house is on his land.[30] Again, if there is an uncertain boundary between two plots of land, and X, who owns one plot, gets the agreement of his neighbour, Y, to X's garage being erected on a particular site near the boundary, Y will be estopped from later contending that the true boundary shows that part of the garage stands on his land.[31] Estoppel may apply not only to express or implied licences but also to a wide variety of cases concerning land. It will therefore be considered in a separate section at the end of this chapter.[32] The broad principle that has emerged is that an estoppel will arise when it would be unconscionable for the licensor to rely on his legal rights.[33]

Sect. 3. Creation of licences

No formalities are required for the creation of a licence. It may arise not only from a document but also from the spoken word or the tacit acceptance of a state of affairs. But when a licence is coupled with an interest, such as a profit *à prendre*, that interest must comply with

---

[25] *James Jones & Sons Ltd v. Earl of Tankerville* [1909] 2 Ch. 440 at 442.

[26] *Muskett v. Hill* (1836) 5 Bing. N.C. 694 at 707, 708.

[27] *Millennium Productions Ltd v. Winter Garden Theatre (London) Ltd* [1946] 1 All E.R. 678, not affected in H.L. [1948] A.C. 173.

[28] See also above, p. 69.

[29] *Plimmer v. Mayor, etc. of the City of Wellington* (1884) 9 App.Cas. 699.

[30] *Ramsden v. Dyson* (1866) L.R. 1 H.L. 129.

[31] *Hopgood v. Brown* [1955] 1 W.L.R. 213.

[32] Below, p. 483.

[33] See *Taylors Fashions Ltd v. Liverpool Victoria Trustees Co. Ltd* [1982] Q.B. 133n. at 154, 155; below, p. 483.

any requirements for its creation[34]; otherwise the creation of licences is free from formalities.

Sect. 4. Revocation of licences

1. Bare licences

As has been seen above,[35] a bare licence is revocable at any time, either expressly or by the death of the licensor or by a disposition of the land.

2. Licences coupled with interests

As has also been seen above,[36] a licence coupled with an interest is irrevocable.[37]

3. Contractual licences

(a) At law

At common law a contractual licence could be revoked at any time, even if it had been granted for a fixed period which had not yet expired.[38] On revocation, the licensee became a trespasser if he entered the land, or remained on it after the elapse of a reasonable time to remove himself and his belongings from it.[39] His only redress for a wrongful revocation was to sue for damages for breach of contract,[40] and in such an action he would merely recover the price of his ticket or other consideration.

(b) In equity

The rule at law has been modified by equity, although not reversed. Equity will only intervene where the parties intended that the contractual licences should not be able to be revoked in breach of contract. This is entirely a question of the true construction of the agreement between them.[41] Where this is found to be the case, the contractual licence will be able to be enforced; an injunction will be granted to restrain a threatened revocation of the licence or the enforcement of a wrongful revocation,[42] and specific performance of the licence may be decreed.[43] Thus a ticket-holder wrongly ejected from a cinema may now recover substantial damages for assault.[44] Even though no injunction could be obtained in time, it seems that he will be treated as if he had what he was entitled to obtain.

Although the common law rule did emerge again in one case, it has not prevailed. In that case,[45] the owner of a school agreed to share the use of his premises with the owner of

---

[34] Above, p. 476.
[35] Above, p. 476.
[36] *ibid.*
[37] Above, p. 476.
[38] *Wood v. Leadbitter* (1845) 13 M. & W. 838 (ejection from racecourse), not considering *Feltham v. Cartwright* (1839) 5 Bing. N.C. 569 (licence irrevocable once acted upon); and contrast *Butler v. Manchester, Sheffield and Lincolnshire Ry* (1888) 21 Q.B.D. 207 (ejection of ticket-holder from railway carriage).
[39] See *Cornish v. Stubbs* (1870) L.R. 5 C.P. 334.
[40] *Kerrison v. Smith* [1897] 2 Q.B. 445.
[41] *Winter Garden Theatre (London) Ltd v. Millenium Productions Ltd* [1948] A.C. 173; no such intention was found.
[42] *Millenium Productions Ltd v. Winter Garden Theatre (London) Ltd* [1946] 1 All E.R. 678 at 685 (this conclusion was not affected by the subsequent appeal ([1948] A.C. 173).
[43] *Verrall v. Great Yarmouth B.C.* [1981] Q.B. 202.
[44] *Hurst v. Picture Theatres Ltd* [1915] 1 K.B. 1.
[45] *Thompson v. Park* [1944] K.B. 408.

another school. Disputes arose and, after the licensor had revoked the licence and had removed the licensee's property, the licensee forcibly re-entered the premises. An injunction was granted ordering him to leave the premises as his licence had been revoked and he had no specifically enforceable right to remain: the court could not order two people to share premises peaceably. The actual decision can be supported as preserving the status quo by evicting a person who has forcibly entered premises.[46] However, the reasoning has been disapproved[47] and it now seems that there is no right to eject a licensee in breach of contract where the parties did intend that the contractual licences should not be able to be revoked in breach of contract. This is the case whether or not the contract is specifically enforceable.[48] The grant of an injunction to restrain a breach of contract is not confined to specifically enforceable contracts.

In the absence of an express agreement that a contractual licence should not be able to be revoked in breach of contract, the courts sometimes infer the existence of an agreement restricting the revocation of a licence, particularly where there is some informal family arrangement. Thus where a man brought a house as a home for himself, his mistress and their children, and the mistress gave up a rent controlled flat in order to move into the house, it was held that she had been given an implied contractual licence to remain in the house as long as the children were of school age and the house was reasonably needed to house her and them.[49] Again, where a mother bought a house for her son and his wife to occupy for £7 a week, and the son later left his wife, the court inferred that the couple had been granted a joint contractual licence determinable only for good reason, such as the wife taking another man to live with her in the house.[50] However, in these cases it is often difficult to say whether any contract can really be inferred, and if it is, what its terms are.[51] In such circumstances it is now better to rely on the more flexible doctrine of estoppel.[52]

4. Licences by estoppel

Whether a licence by estoppel is revocable depends on the interest arising from the estoppel; and this usually cannot be known until the court has spoken. If the licence is perpetual,[53] there is no question of revocation. If the licence is determinable on certain events,[54] it can be determined only on the occurrence of one or more of those particular events.

5. Determination of licences by licensee

A licensee may determine his licence in accordance with its terms, or by abandoning it. No formalities are required for abandonment: it suffices if the licensee so conducts himself as to justify the licensor in acting on the assumption that the licence has been abandoned.[55]

---

[46] *Hounslow L.B.C. v. Twickenham Garden Developments Ltd* [1971] Ch. 233 at 250, approved in *Verrall v. Great Yarmouth B.C.* [1981] Q.B. 202. There is a full review of the authorities in the *Hounslow* case.

[47] *Verrall v. Great Yarmouth B.C.* [1981] Q.B. 202.

[48] See *Verrall v. Great Yarmouth B.C.* [1981] Q.B. 202 where, however, the contract was specifically enforceable.

[49] *Tanner v. Tanner* [1975] 1 W.L.R. 1346; contrast *Horrocks v. Forray* [1976] 1 W.L.R. 230 (no licence).

[50] *Hardwick v. Johnson* [1978] 1 W.L.R. 683; and see *Chandler v. Kerley* [1978] 1 W.L.R. 693 (implied contractual licence determinable on reasonable notice: 12 months).

[51] See *Horrocks v. Forray* [1976] 1 W.L.R. 230; *Chandler v. Kerley* [1978] 1 W.L.R. 693.

[52] See, *e.g. Maharaj v. Chand* [1986] A.C. 898.

[53] *Plimmer v. Mayor, etc. of the City of Wellington* (1884) 9 App.Cas. 699.

[54] See *Inwards v. Baker* [1965] 2 Q.B. 29 (as long as the licensee desires).

[55] *Bone v. Bone* [1992] E.G.C.S. 81.

Sect. 5. Transmission of benefit

In general, the benefit of a licence is assignable unless the contrary appears from its nature or some provision in it. This is so even for bare licences,[56] though these may more readily indicate that they are not assignable (such as an invitation to tea, or to play tennis) than will most contractual licences or licences coupled with an interest.[57] A bare licensee probably cannot grant a sub-licence,[58] but for other licences this seems to depend on the nature and terms of the licence.

Sect. 6. Transmission of burden

1. Bare licences

As has been seen above,[59] the burden of a bare licence does not pass with the land[60]; on the contrary, it is automatically revoked if the licensor disposes of his interest in the land.[61]

2. Licences coupled with an interest

As has also been seen above,[62] the burden of a licence coupled with an interest will pass with the land in the same way as the burden of the interest will pass with it. Thus the burden of a licence coupled with a profit *à prendre* will pass with the land unless the profit requires protection against the purchaser in question and has not been protected in the appropriate way.[63] If the interest in question is protected on the Land Register, the burden of the licence will be recorded as well.[64]

3. Contractual licences

(a) Principle

In principle, a contractual licence, like all other contracts, will bind the parties to it but will not bind third parties; the burden of the licence will not run with the land. Thus where A contracted to give B the right to fix posters to the flank walls of A's cinema for four years, but then sold the cinema to P before the four years had run, P took free from the licence, though A was liable to B for breach of his contract.[65]

(b) Binding successors in title

For a time this basic position was altered by a line of cases beginning with *Errington v. Errington*,[66] in which contractual licences were held to be binding on successors in title. In that case a father bought a house on mortgage, and allowed his son and daughter-in-law to

---

[56] See *Mellor v. Watkins* (1874) L.R. 9 Q.B. 400.
[57] See *Shayler v. Woolf* [1946] Ch. 320.
[58] See *Goldsack v. Shore* [1950] 1 K.B. 708 at 714.
[59] Above, p. 476.
[60] *Wallis v. Harrison* (1838) 4 M. & W. 538; and see *Terunnanse v. Terunnanse* [1968] A.C. 1086 at 1095.
[61] *Terunnanse v. Terunnanse* [1968] A.C. 1086 at 1095.
[62] Above, p. 476.
[63] See above, pp. 97, 122, 126–7.
[64] Ruoff & Roper, para. 12–35.
[65] *King v. David Allen & Sons, Billposting, Ltd* [1916] 2 A.C. 54; and see *Clore v. Theatrical Properties Ltd* [1936] 3 All E.R. 483 ("front of house" rights: above, p. 476).
[66] [1952] 1 K.B. 290. See (1952) 68 L.Q.R. 337 (H.W.R. Wade).

live in it, promising to convey the house to them if they remained in occupation and paid all the instalments under the mortgage. Before they had done this the father died, leaving all his property (including the house) to his widow. She was held to be bound by the licence on the basis that it constituted an equitable interest in the unregistered land in question that would bind the whole world except a bona fide purchaser for value without notice.[67]

(c) No interest in land

It was right to hold that the licence bound the widow, either on the basis that it was also a licence by estoppel and binding on her as such[68] or because it amounted to an estate contract[69] which was also binding on her.[70] However, it is now accepted that it was wrong to reach this conclusion on the ground that a contractual licence is an interest in land.[71] The assertion that it created such an interest in land, made without regard to binding authorities to the contrary, now has the status of a heresy that has received its quietus,[72] like the so-called deserted wife's equity.[73] Yet, although the burden of a licence which is merely contractual does not, as such, run with the land or bind successors in title, it may (as, in *Errington v. Errington*) be accompanied by circumstances which produce that effect. Including the two circumstances which were present in that case, there are a total of four. Thus a licence may be binding on successors in title—

(1) because it constitutes an enforceable estate contract;

(2) because it is supported by an estoppel;

(3) because a constructive trust arises; or

(4) by virtue of the tort of interfering with contractual rights.[74]

(d) The four bases for binding successors

(i) Estate contract: As already seen, a specifically enforceable contract creates an equitable interest in the land that will bind successors in title, subject where necessary to being protected by registration in the usual way.[75]

(ii) Estoppel: If a contractual licence is fortified by an estoppel, its burden will run with the land as in the case of a licence by estoppel.[76]

(iii) Constructive trust: If a contractual licence can be enforced by the imposition of a constructive trust, it will bind successors in title in the same way as a trust will do and will be enforceable against the whole world except someone who takes free of that trust. However, such a trust will not arise unless the court is satisfied that the conscience of the

---

[67] *Errington v. Errington* [1952] 1 K.B. 290 at 294, 298, 299.

[68] Below, p. 483.

[69] At that time an oral contract which had been part performed sufficed; above, p. 148.

[70] She was not a purchaser for money or money's worth and so was bound by that contract despite its non-registration.

[71] *Ashburn Anstalt v. Arnold* [1989] Ch. 1.

[72] *Ashburn Anstalt v. Arnold* [1989] Ch. 1; *I.D.C. Group Ltd v. Clark* [1992] 1 E.G.L.R. 187.

[73] See above, p. 98.

[74] For (1) to (3), see *Ashburn Anstalt v. Arnold* [1989] Ch. 1 at 17; for (iv), see *Binions v. Evans* [1972] Ch. 359 at 371, above, pp. 70–71, and below.

[75] Above, pp. 95, 154.

[76] Above, p. 477.

successor in title is affected, so that it would be inequitable to allow him to deny the claimant's interest in the property.[77] In relation to title to land, certainty is of prime importance, and neither inferences from slender material nor bare assertions will suffice to establish such a trust.[78] A licence is not given any greater efficacy, or made binding on a purchaser, merely because the land is sold "subject to" it; but where these words are not needed merely to protect the vendor, because the licence is in any case not binding on him, the circumstances of the sale, coupled with these words, may establish a constructive trust that binds the purchaser to give effect to the licence.[79] Thus where the trustees of an estate agreed to allow the widow of an employee to occupy her cottage rent free for her life, repairing it and cultivating the garden, and the trustees then sold it subject to her rights, and at a reduced price because of them, it was held that the purchaser was bound by a constructive trust to give effect to her rights, so that they could not evict her.[80]

(iv) Tort: The tort of wrongfully interfering with the contractual rights of another has already been considered as part of the borderline between personal and proprietary rights.[81] Though little-explored in relation to licences, the decision in the case last considered, preventing the eviction of the rent-free licensee, could probably alternatively have been based on that tort.[82]

4. Licences by estoppel

Although a licence by estoppel might be thought to be enforceable only against the party who has estopped himself from disputing its existence, it has been held that the burden of a licence by estoppel will run with the land so as to bind successors in title of the party originally estopped.[83] It has also been stated that this decision is binding on all courts other than the House of Lords.[84] Further, the Land Registration Act 2002 specifically so provides,[85] thus resolving any challenge in the case of registered land once that Act has come into force and indicating the likely outcome of any challenge in the case of unregistered land. However, that does not mean that a licence by estoppel will bind the whole world; estoppel interests in unregistered land are governed by the equitable doctrine of notice,[86] while estoppel interests in registered land require protection on the register unless their holder has an interest which overrides registration[87] by virtue of his actual occupation of the land[88] or, until the Land Registration Act 2002 comes into force, by virtue of his receipt of rent and profits[89] or his open exercise and enjoyment of an easement.[90]

---

[77] *Ashburn Anstalt v. Arnold* [1989] Ch. 1 at 22, 25.
[78] *ibid.*, at 24 (commenting on *D.H.N. Food Distributors Ltd v. Tower Hamlets L.B.C.* [1976] 1 W.L.R. 852), 26.
[79] *Lyus v. Prowsa Developments Ltd* [1982] 1 W.L.R. 1044; *Ashburn Anstalt v. Arnold* [1989] Ch. 1 at 24, 25, disapproving *Binions v. Evans* [1972] Ch. 359 at 368.
[80] *Binions v. Evans* [1972] Ch. 359; *Ashburn Anstalt v. Arnold* [1989] Ch. 1 at 23.
[81] Above, p. 81.
[82] See *Binions v. Evans* [1972] Ch. 359 at 371.
[83] *Hopgood v. Brown* [1955] 1 W.L.R. 213; *Inwards v. Baker* [1965] 2 Q.B. 29; *E.R. Ives Investment Ltd v. High* [1967] 2 Q.B. 379.
[84] *Lloyds Bank plc v. Carrick* [1996] 4 All E.R. 630.
[85] L.R.A. 2002, s.116.
[86] *E.R. Ives Investment Ltd v. High* [1967] 2 Q.B. 379.
[87] Above, pp. 121 *et seq.*
[88] L.R.A. 1925, s.70(1)(g), L.R.A. 2002, Sched. 1, para.3, Sched. 3, para.3.
[89] L.R.A. 1925, s.70(1)(g).
[90] *Celsteel Ltd v. Alton House Holdings Ltd* [1986] 1 W.L.R. 512; [1985] 1 W.L.R. 204; *Thatcher v. Douglas* (1996) 146 N.L.J. 282.

Sect. 7. Proprietary estoppel

Proprietary estoppel is a form of equitable estoppel which affects or creates rights of property. At common law, estoppel became a somewhat strict and narrow doctrine which precluded a person from denying the existence of a state of affairs that he had previously asserted. Equity both extended the doctrine and relaxed the requirements; and today it is usually equitable estoppel that is in issue. It is the type of estoppel known as proprietary estoppel that it is mainly relevant to interests in land. (The traditional distinction between promissory estoppel and proprietary estoppel is not particularly relevant to such interests because every promissory estoppel relating to an interest in land must necessarily also constitute a proprietary estoppel.)[91]

1. Judicial attitudes

(a) Traditional approach

The traditional approach of the judges has been that proprietary estoppels arise in three distinct situations, all governed by different rules:

(i) where there has been an assurance by the owner of land ("O") that the claimant ("C") will have rights therein (the "imperfect gift" cases)[92];

(ii) where O and C have consistently dealt with one another on the basis that O will acquire rights of some kind in C's land (the "common expectation" cases)[93]; and

(iii) where O has stood by and allowed C to act to his detriment in the mistaken belief that C has rights over O's land (the "unilateral mistake" cases).[94]

(b) Modern approach

Since 1976,[95] the majority of the judges have rejected the traditional approach and have regarded these three situations as being governed by a single principle. They have adopted "a very much broader approach which is directed rather at ascertaining whether, in particular individual circumstances, it would be unconscionable for a party to be permitted to deny that which, knowingly or unknowingly, he has allowed or encouraged another to assume to his detriment than to inquiring whether the circumstances can be fitted within the confines of some preconceived formula serving as a universal yardstick for every form of unconscionable behaviour".[96] This broader approach has been developed[97] into the principle that a proprietary estoppel requires:

---

[91] See Halliwell, *Equity & Good Conscience in a Contemporary Context* (1997) 19–38.

[92] *Dillwyn v. Llewellyn* (1862) 4 De G.F. & J. 264; *Pascoe v. Turner* [1979] 1 W.L.R. 431.

[93] *Ramsden v. Dyson* (1866) L.R. 1 H.L. 129 at 170 *per* Lord Kingsdown; *Inwards v. Baker* [1965] 2 Q.B. 29.

[94] *Ramsden v. Dyson* (1866) L.R. 1 H.L. 129 at 140 *per* Lord Cranworth L.C.; *Willmott v. Barber* (1880) 15 Ch.D. 96 at 105 *per* Fry J.

[95] The date of the decision in *Taylors Fashions Ltd v. Liverpool Victoria Trustees Co. Ltd* (1976) [1982] 1 Q.B. 133N.

[96] *Taylors Fashions Ltd v. Liverpool Victoria Trustees Co. Ltd* (1976) [1982] 1 Q.B. 133N at 151–152 *per* Oliver J.

[97] See Gray & Gray, p. 756; see also Pawlowski, *Proprietary Estoppel* (1996).

(i) an assurance or a representation by O;

(ii) reliance on that assurance or representation by C; and

(iii) some unconscionable disadvantage or detriment suffered by C.

(c) Significance

The practical effect of these two different approaches can be seen in relation to what are sometimes described as the five *probanda*.[98] These are (or were):

(i) that C must have made a mistake as to his legal rights;

(ii) that C must have expended some money or done some act on the strength of his mistaken belief;

(iii) that O must have known of the existence of some right of his own which is inconsistent with the right claimed by C;

(iv) that O must have known of C's mistaken belief in his rights; and

(v) that O must have encouraged C in his expenditure of money or in the other acts which he has done, either directly or by abstaining from asserting his legal rights.

Proponents of the traditional approach contend that all five of these requirements must be satisfied, not just in the unilateral mistake cases to which they are on the face of things exclusively relevant but also in all other proprietary estoppel cases. However, while the *probanda* are still occasionally applied in unilateral mistake cases,[99] the general view is that they are no longer relevant even to those cases[1] and it has been repeatedly held that they are no longer relevant to imperfect gift and common expectation cases.[2] It is the first two *probanda* which have principally been rejected in favour of a more flexible test.[3] In particular, it has been held that detriment does not need to consist of the expenditure of money or other quantifiable financial detriment, so long as it is something substantial.[4]

2. Constituents

The three elements of an assurance or representation by O, reliance on that assurance or representation by C, and some unconscionable disadvantage (or "detriment") suffered by C are "inter-dependent and capable of definition only in terms of each other"[5]; "the doctrine of proprietary estoppel cannot be treated as sub-divided into three or four watertight compartments".[6] Nor are the elements rigid requirements but guide-lines for determining the

---

[98] Laid down in *Willmott v. Barber* (1880) 15 Ch.D. 96 at 105 *per* Fry J.
[99] *Coombes v. Smith* [1986] 1 W.L.R. 808; *Matharu v. Matharu* (1994) 68 P. & C.R. 93.
[1] *Orgee v. Orgee* [1997] New Law Digest, Property Communication 107.
[2] *Taylors Fashions Ltd v. Liverpool Victoria Trustees Co. Ltd* [1982] Q.B. 133N; *Lloyds Bank Plc v. Carrick* [1996] 4 All E.R. 630; *Gillett v. Holt* [2001] Ch. 210.
[3] *Orgee v. Orgee* [1997] New Law Digest, Property Communication 107; *Gillett v. Holt* [2001] Ch. 210.
[4] *Gillett v. Holt* [2001] Ch. 210 at 232.
[5] Gray & Gray, p. 756.
[6] *Gillett v. Holt* [2001] Ch. 210 at 224.

central question, namely whether it would be unconscionable for O to rely on his legal rights.[7]

(a) Assurance or representation

O (or one of his predecessors in title[8]) must have given some encouragement to C to act in the way that he subsequently did. O's conduct may be active in that he has made an express assurance or representation to C. Or it may be passive in that he has stood silently by with knowledge that his own rights were more extensive that C believed them to be while C was acting on his mistaken belief by, for example, building on land not knowing that it was O's, or not knowing that O had a mortgage over it.[9] However, the assurance or representation must be sufficiently certain to be relied on; an offer of "financial security" will be too vague.[10]

(b) Reliance on the assurance or representation

C must have acted in the mistaken belief that he either had or would obtain a sufficient interest in O's property to justify whatever it was that he did.[11] Once an assurance or representation by O has been proved, it is presumed that C has relied on it and it is for O to rebut that presumption.[12]

(c) Unconscionable disadvantage

C must have prejudiced himself by acting to his detriment. It is for O to prove that C's detrimental acts have not caused him to suffer unconscionable disadvantage.[13]

The most obvious form of detriment is where C has incurred expenditure, as by spending money on improving property which in fact belongs to O. Thus C may have built a house on O's land[14]; or C may have built a mill on his own land in the belief that he would be able to take water for it from O's canal[15]; or C may have renovated and managed a property which he believed belonged to O on the basis that he would receive the two flats on the ground floor.[16]

Other acts of financial detriment also suffice. C may have sold part of his land, making the rest land-locked, in the belief that he would have an easement of way to the land-locked land over O's land[17]; or C may have given up his job and his council house to go and live near his father in a house provided by the father, believing that it would become C's[18]; or C, having initially been paid as a housemaid, may subsequently have cared for the members of the family without receiving wages on the basis of assurances that she could remain in the house for the remainder of her life.[19]

---

[7] *Taylors Fashions Ltd v. Liverpool Victoria Trustees Co. Ltd* [1982] Q.B. 133N at 154, 155; *Habib Bank Ltd v. Habib Bank A.G. Zurich* [1981] 1 W.L.R. 1265.

[8] *Hopgood v. Brown* [1955] 1 W.L.R. 213.

[9] *Ramsden v. Dyson* (1866) L.R. 1 H.L. 129; *Steed v. Whitaker* (1740) Barn.Ch. 220; *Inwards v. Baker* [1965] 2 Q.B. 29.

[10] *Layton v. Martin* [1986] 2 F.L.R. 227.

[11] *Ramsden v. Dyson* (1866) L.R. 1 H.L. 129 at 160, 168, 170; *Inwards v. Baker* [1965] 2. Q.B. 29.

[12] *Greasley v. Cooke* [1980] 1 W.L.R. 1306.

[13] *Greasley v. Cooke* [1980] 1 W.L.R. 1306.

[14] *Inwards v. Baker* [1965] 2 Q.B. 29.

[15] *Rochdale Canal Co. v. King (No. 2)* (1853) 16 Beav. 630.

[16] *Yaxley v. Gotts* [2002] Ch. 162.

[17] *Crabb v. Arun D.C.* [1976] Ch. 179.

[18] *Jones v. Jones* [1977] 1 W.L.R. 438; and see *Pascoe v. Turner* [1979] 1 W.L.R. 431.

[19] *Greasley v. Cooke* [1980] 1 W.L.R. 1306.

However, detriment does not need to consist of the expenditure of money or other quantifiable financial detriment, so long as it is something substantial.[20] Thus C, who had helped her mother and her stepfather throughout her adult life without remuneration on the basis that she would inherit her stepfather's property, had incurred sufficient detriment to receive his entire estate when he died intestate.[21] And C, who had worked for O, a gentleman farmer, for almost 40 years and effectively provided O with a surrogate family on the basis of assurances that the bulk of the farming business would be left to C in O's will, had incurred sufficient detriment to be able to rely on the assurances during O's lifetime once O began to transfer all his assets to a third party; C received one of O's farms outright and financial compensation for the loss of the others.[22]

(d) No bar to equitable relief

However, there must be no bar to equitable relief being given to C.

There will be such a bar as where the relief given would fetter the statutory discretion or statutory duty of a statutory body or contravene a statutory provision.[23] Where C's interest should have been protected by registration but has not been, C can claim the benefit of a proprietary estoppel in the obviously exceptional situation where both O and C have wrongly proceeded on the basis that C's interest was not registrable.[24] However, no proprietary estoppel can protect C from his failure to register an interest which was clearly registrable.[25] On the other hand, it has been held that the fact that C's acts of detriment are carried out pursuant to a void oral contract does not bar him from equitable relief where those acts are sufficient to give rise to the imposition of a constructive trust in his favour.[26] It does not appear to be entirely satisfactory that someone who has entered into a valid contract should thus be in a worse position than someone who has failed to comply with the statutory formalities at all.

It may also be inequitable for C to be given relief because of his own misconduct,[27] as where he attempts to support his claim by putting forward what he knows to be wholly false particulars of his expenditure on O's property.[28]

3. Extent of the equity

Where an equity is established, the next question which has to be considered is the extent of the equity.[29] The maximum extent of the equity arising from proprietary estoppel is that of the belief or expectation of C that O encouraged: C will not be given more than that.[30] Thus no order was made satisfying C's expectation that he would be able to live in a house for the rest of his lifetime when an order to that effect would have made C a tenant for life under the Settled Land Act 1925 with all the powers (including the power of sale) conferred on a tenant

---

[20] *Gillett v. Holt* [2001] Ch. 210 at 224.
[21] *Re Basham (dec'd)* [1986] 1 W.L.R. 1498.
[22] *Gillett v. Holt* [2001] Ch. 210. at 237–238.
[23] *Chalmers v. Pardoe* [1963] 1 W.L.R. 677; *Western Fish Products Ltd v. Penwith D.C.* [1981] 2 All E.R. 204 (town planning).
[24] *Taylors Fashions Ltd v. Liverpool Victoria Trustees Co. Ltd* [1982] Q.B. 133N (option to renew a lease which, prior to *Beelsy v. Hallwood Estates* [1960] 1 W.L.R. 549, was generally thought not to be registrable).
[25] *Lloyds Bank Plc v. Carrick* [1996] 4 All E.R. 630 (normal estate contract).
[26] *Yaxley v. Gotts* [2000] Ch. 162.
[27] See *Williams v. Staite* [1979] Ch. 291 at 299, 300.
[28] *J. Willis & Son v. Willis* [1986] 1 E.G.L.R. 62.
[29] *Crabb v. Arun District Council* [1976] Ch.179 at 193 *per* Scarman L.J.
[30] *Dodsworth v. Dodsworth* [1973] E.G.D. 233.

for life by that Act.[31] However, the parties could have avoided any risk of this by substituting a lease at a nominal rent determinable on death[32] and, since the enactment of the Trusts of Land and Appointment of Trustees Act 1996, a person in C's position will have no such powers anyway unless the land is already settled under the Settled Land Act 1925 because his interest will take effect behind a trust of land.[33]

3. Satisfaction of the equity

Where an equity is established, the final question is the relief which is appropriate to satisfy the equity.[34] The court must search for "the minimum equity to do justice to" C.[35] Once that minimum equity has been determined, the court will give effect to it in whatever is the most appropriate way.[36]

(a) Enforcement of agreements

Where the doctrine of proprietary estoppel is used to enforce agreements, no question is ever likely to arise as to the appropriate remedy. Where the terms of a proposed lease or contract have been agreed, the equity defines itself.[37] It can even extend to interlinked transactions. Thus, where C and O arranged that O would buy C's building and that C would erect a new building on O's land, which he duly did, O was compelled to purchase C's building.[38] Difficulties only potentially arise where O and C have agreed what C is to obtain but not the nature of his interest. An agreement that C was to receive the ground floor of a building could have been an agreement for the grant either of a freehold or of a long lease; C claimed the latter and was awarded a lease for 99 years rent-free.[39]

(b) Enforcement where there was no agreement

Where there has been no agreement as such, the decision as to how to satisfy the equity is more difficult. Successful claims have led to the award of a wide range of different remedies.

At one extreme, it may suffice simply to dismiss any proceedings by O for possession[40] or to grant an injunction, such as restraining O from obstructing C's improved ancient lights.[41] At the other extreme, O may be ordered to convey his land to C gratuitously, as where C has built a house[42] or carried out improvements[43] on land which O had ineffectually given to him.

---

[31] *Dodsworth v. Dodsworth* [1973] E.G.D. 233 at 236, pointing out that this had been overlooked in *Inwards v. Baker* [1965] 2 Q.B. 29. See above, p. 253, for the Settled Land Act 1925.

[32] *Griffiths v. Williams* [1977] E.G.D. 919 at 925, pointing out what had been overlooked in *Dodsworth v. Dodsworth* [1973] E.G.D. 233: see above, p. 254.

[33] Above, p. 283.

[34] *Crabb v. Arun District Council* [1976] Ch.179 at 193 *per* Scarman L.J.

[35] *Sledmore v. Dalby* (1996) 72 P. & C.R. 196.

[36] *Plimmer v. Mayor, etc. of the City of Wellington* (1884) 9 App. Cas. 699 at 713, 714. See [1986] Conv. 406 (M.P. Thompson).

[37] *Att-Gen. of Hong Kong v. Humphreys Estate (Queen's Gardens) Ltd* [1987] A.C. 114; *J.T. Developments Ltd v. Quinn* (1990) 62 P. & C.R. 33.

[38] *Salvation Army Trustee Co. Ltd v. West Yorkshire Metropolitan C.C.* (1981) 41 P. & C.R. 179.

[39] *Yaxley v. Gotts* [2000] Ch. 162.

[40] *Inwards v. Baker* [1965] 2 Q.B. 19; *Williams v. Staite* [1979] Ch. 291.

[41] *Cotching v. Bassett* (1862) 32 Beav. 101.

[42] *Dillwyn v. Llewelyn* (1862) 4 De G.F. & J. 517, where O had died.

[43] *Pascoe v. Turner* [1979] 1 W.L.R. 431.

O has also been ordered to grant lesser interests to C, such as leases,[44] easements[45] and rights of occupation.[46]

Monetary compensation has also been ordered, ranging from the return of the sums expended by C[47] through the value of the interest which C expected to receive with interest thereon[48] to the sum which C had to pay in order to acquire from a third party the strip of land on which his building was encroaching.[49] Grants of a right in or a right to occupy land have also been combined with grants of monetary compensation. Thus C has been required to pay a reasonable purchase price for O's property after deducting the amount expended on improvements.[50] On the other hand, assurances that the bulk of O's farming business would be left to C in O's will were given effect to by granting C both one of O's farms outright and financial compensation for the loss of the others.[51]

(c) Factors to be considered

In the exercise of its wide discretion, the court does not restrict itself to the circumstances which initially gave rise to the equity or to the amount of C's expenditure, but considers the whole of the circumstances down to the time of the action. Thus where proprietary estoppel would otherwise have entitled C to an easement on paying a reasonable sum for that right, prolonged obstructive conduct by O may result in C being awarded the easement without payment.[52] Again, where O knew that C's improvements to the house in which she lived were being made in the belief that O had given it to her, the circumstances justified an order that O should convey the house to C gratuitously, even though C's expenditure had been relatively modest.[53] On the other hand, where C had expected to be allowed to stay rent-free in a house for the rest of his life, his minimum equity was held to have expired where he had lived there rent-free for over 18 years, his use of the property was minimal, he was in employment and capable of paying for his own accommodation, and O was in financial difficulties and had an urgent need for the property herself.[54] In this field, equity is both inventive and flexible.

4. Proprietary estoppel and third parties

Where O is ordered to convey his land to C, C will become its registered proprietor. Where, on the other hand, C's equity has been satisfied by the grant of a lesser interest in land, that interest will have to be protected in the appropriate way if it is to be enforceable against third parties; licences will be enforceable in the ways which have already been considered.[55] Prior to any such satisfaction, C's interest might be thought to be enforceable only against O and his personal representatives. However, it has been held that an interest which is protected by proprietary estoppel is also capable of binding the successors in title of the party originally

[44] *Griffiths v. Williams* (1977) 248 E.G. 947.
[45] *Crabb v. Arun District Council* [1976] Ch. 179.
[46] *Greasley v. Cooke* [1980] 1 W.L.R. 1306; *Matharu v. Matharu* [1994] 2 F.L.R. 597.
[47] *Dodsworth v. Dodsworth* [1973] E.G.D. 233 (as a pre-condition of O obtaining an order for possession); *Unity Joint Stock Mutual Banking Association v. King* (1858) 25 Beav. 72 (lien on O's property for his outlay).
[48] *Wayling v. Jones* (1995) 69 P. & C.R. 170.
[49] *Wilson Bowden Properties v. Milner* (1997) New Law Digest, Property Communication 128.
[50] *Lim Teng Huan v. Ang Swee Chuan* [1992] 1 W.L.R. 113.
[51] *Gillett v. Holt* [2001] Ch. 210 at 237–238.
[52] *Crabb v. Arun D.C.* [1976] Ch. 179.
[53] *Pascoe v. Turner* [1979] 1 W.L.R. 431.
[54] *Sledmore v. Dalby* (1996) 72 P. & C.R. 196.
[55] Above, pp. 480–482.

estopped.[56] It has also been stated that this decision is binding on all courts other than the House of Lords.[57] Further, the Land Registration Act 2002 specifically so provides,[58] thus resolving any challenge in the case of registered land once that Act has come into force and indicating the likely outcome of any challenge in the case of unregistered land.

However, that does not mean that an interest protected by proprietary estoppel will bind the whole world. Estoppel interests in unregistered land are governed by the equitable doctrine of notice,[59] while estoppel interests in registered land require protection on the register unless C has an interest which overrides registration[60] by virtue of his actual occupation of the land[61] or, until the Land Registration Act 2002 comes into force, by virtue of his receipt of rent and profits[62] or his open exercise and enjoyment of an easement.[63] Further, a interest which is protected by proprietary estoppel is just as capable of being overreached as it would be if it had been formally created. Consequently, if C has a family interest such as a right of occupation, his interest will not be binding as against any purchaser or mortgagee who acquires O's property under an overreaching conveyance.[64] However, a commercial interest held by C such as a lease or an easement would not have been capable of being overreached if it had been formally created and, if otherwise enforceable against O's successors in title, will continue to be binding notwithstanding the fact that they have acquired O's property under an overreaching conveyance.

---

[56] *Hopgood v. Brown* [1955] 1 W.L.R. 213; *Inwards v. Baker* [1965] 2 Q.B. 29; *E.R. Ives Investment Ltd v. High* [1967] 2 Q.B. 379.
[57] *Lloyds Bank plc v. Carrick* [1996] 4 All E.R. 630.
[58] L.R.A. 2002, s.116.
[59] *E.R. Ives Investment Ltd v. High* [1967] 2 Q.B. 379.
[60] Above, pp. 121 *et seq.*
[61] L.R.A. 1925, s.70(1)(g), L.R.A. 2002, Sched. 1, para.3, Sched. 3, para.3.
[62] L.R.A. 1925, s.70(1)(g).
[63] *Celsteel Ltd v. Alton House Holdings Ltd* [1986] 1 W.L.R. 512; [1985] 1 W.L.R. 204; *Thatcher v. Douglas* (1996) 146 N.L.J. 282.
[64] *Birmingham Midshires Mortgage Services Ltd v. Sabherwal* (2000) 80 P. & C.R. 256.

Chapter 13

MORTGAGES

PART 1—NATURE OF A MORTGAGE

1. Security

Mortgages provide lenders with security for their money. Where a loan is made without security, the lender has a right to sue for the money due if it is not repaid in accordance with the terms of his agreement with the borrower but that is all. If the borrower becomes insolvent, the lender is likely to lose part or all of his money. But if the borrower gives the lender some security of adequate value for the loan, the lender is protected even if the borrower becomes insolvent, for the lender's claim to the security takes precedence over the claims of the borrower's other creditors.

A mortgage is only one type of security but it is the most important one. The essential nature of a mortgage is that it is a conveyance of a legal or equitable interest in property, with a provision for redemption, *i.e.* that upon repayment of a loan or the performance of some other obligation the interest created will be cancelled. The borrower is known as the "mortgagor" (the person who creates the mortgage); the lender is known as the "mortgagee" (the person who receives the mortgage).[1]

Mortgages today are principally regarded as the means by which an owner-occupier is able to borrow the funds necessary for him to buy the property in which he lives. However, mortgages taken out by owner-occupiers became common only in the second half of the twentieth century; the overwhelming majority of the law governing mortgages had by then already been developed in the context of commercial loans secured in order to fund business enterprises. A number of interventions by the legislature have therefore been necessary to adapt the law to the special needs of owner-occupiers.

Any loan secured by a mortgage will inevitably, at least initially, be for less than the total value of the mortgaged property; otherwise it would not provide sufficient security for repayment. However, mortgagees who lend to owner-occupiers are generally reluctant to lend more than 75 per cent of the value of the property unless additional security, such as an insurance policy, is provided. In this connection, it should be noted that the amount by which the value of the property exceeds the amount needed to redeem the mortgage is often

---

[1] The Law Commission has recommended fundamental changes in the law of mortgages: see (1986) Law Com.W.P. No. 99; (1991) Law Com. No. 204.

colloquially referred to as the mortgagor's "equity" in the property. However, this is not a technical term. In the event that the value of the mortgaged land subsequently becomes insufficient to redeem the mortgage (this is usually happens as a result of the land falling in value but can also happen as a result of the building up of substantial arrears of interest and of interest on the interest), the shortfall is in the same sort of way described as the mortgagor's "negative equity".

2. Other transactions

A mortgage must be distinguished from a lien, a pledge and a charge.

(a) Lien

A lien may arise at common law, in equity or under certain statutes. A common law lien is the right to retain possession of the property of another until a debt is paid; thus a garage proprietor has a common law lien upon a motor-car repaired by him. This lien is a mere passive right of retention, giving no right to sell or otherwise deal with the property,[2] and is extinguished if the creditor parts with possession to the debtor or his agent.[3]

An equitable lien is not dependent upon a continued possession of the property[4] and in this respect resembles a mortgage. But it differs from a mortgage, *inter alia*, in that a mortgage is a right founded on contract whereas an equitable lien arises from general principles of equity which do not permit a man who has acquired property under a contract to keep it without payment.[5] Thus a vendor of land who has conveyed away that land without receiving the full purchase price has an equitable lien upon it for the balance unpaid.[6]

A statutory lien is the creature of the statute under which it arises, and the rights which it confers depend on the terms of that statute. Railways, shipowners and solicitors have been given such rights.

(b) Pledge

A pledge or pawn consists of the loan of money in return for the delivery of possession of chattels to the lender. Although the lender has certain powers of sale, the general property in the goods remains in the borrower and the lender has possession. In a mortgage, on the other hand, the lender acquires ownership of the mortgage and the borrower usually retains possession of the property mortgaged.

(c) Charge

For most practical purposes, a charge is regarded as a species of mortgage, and is dealt with accordingly in this chapter. Nevertheless, there is an essential difference between a mortgage and a charge. A mortgage is a conveyance of an interest in property subject to a right of redemption, whereas a charge conveys nothing and merely gives the chargee certain rights over the property concerned as security for the loan.[7]

---

[2] But see Torts (Interference with Goods) Act 1977, ss.12, 13, Sched. 1, replacing Disposal of Uncollected Goods Act 1952.
[3] *Pennington v. Reliance Motor Works Ltd* [1923] 1 K.B. 127.
[4] *Wrout v. Dawes* (1858) 25 Beav. 369.
[5] See *Mackreth v. Symmons* (1808) 15 Ves. 329 at 340.
[6] *Chapman v. Tanner* (1684) 1 Vern. 267.
[7] See *London County and Westminster Bank Ltd v. Tompkins* [1918] 1 K.B. 515.

PART 2—CREATION OF MORTGAGES

Sect. 1. Legal mortgages and charges of unregistered land

The methods of creating a legal mortgage differ for freeholds and leaseholds. The modern law can only be understood in the light of the law prior to the 1925 legislation.

1. Mortgages of freeholds before 1926

Before 1926, a legal mortgage of freehold land was usually created by conveying the estate in fee simple to the mortgagee subject to a covenant by the latter to reconvey the property to the mortgagor if the principal sum lent and the agreed interest was repaid on the due date. Although at law the mortgagee was entitled to keep the estate in fee simple if that payment was not made on time, equity took the view that the property mortgaged was merely a security for the money lent, and that it was unjust that the mortgagor should lose his property merely because he was late in repaying the loan. Therefore, even if the date fixed for repayment had long passed, equity compelled the mortgagee to reconvey the property to the mortgagor on payment of the principal sum together with interest and costs. In effect the mortgagor had two separate rights of redemption:

(i) a legal right to redeem on the fixed day (at law, a mortgagor has no right to redeem either before or after the date fixed by the mortgage for redemption, but on that one day alone); and

(ii) an equitable right to redeem thereafter (equity allowed the mortgagor an equitable right to redeem on any day after the date fixed for redemption by the mortgage, a right which can be exercised only on equitable terms).

Once equity's intervention had become established, the fixed day on which the legal right to redeem arose tended to be six months after the date of the mortgage, even though there was no real expectation by either party that the money would be repaid then. In practice a mortgagor relied entirely on his rights in equity, the sum total of which was and is known as his equity of redemption.

It is important to distinguish the mortgagor's equity of redemption from his equitable right to redeem. The latter does not exist until the legal date for redemption is past and is but one of the adjuncts of the equity of redemption. In contrast the equity of redemption exists as soon as the mortgage is made.[8] It is the mortgagor's right of ownership of the property subject to the mortgage,[9] and is an interest in land which can be granted, devised and, in short, dealt with like any other interest in land.[10] It has already been seen[11] that the equity of redemption is usually of considerable value. Consequently, the equity of redemption can itself be mortgaged. But since before 1926 the interest of the mortgagor in the equity of redemption was merely equitable, any mortgage of it was necessarily effective only in equity; no legal mortgage can be created over something which exists only in equity. Consequently

---

[8] *Brown v. Cole* (1845) 14 Sim. 427; *Kreglinger v. New Patagonia Meat and Cold Storage Co. Ltd* [1914] A.C. 25 at 48.
[9] *Re Wells* [1933] Ch. 29 at 52.
[10] See *Casborne v. Scarfe* (1738) 1 Atk. 603 at 605.
[11] Above, p. 491.

before 1926 only one legal mortgage could exist over freehold property; all second and subsequent mortgages were necessarily equitable.

2. Mortgages of freeholds after 1925

The Law of Property Act 1925 provides[12] that freeholds can no longer be mortgaged by means of a conveyance of the fee simple. Only two methods are now possible:

>   (i) by the grant of a term of years absolute, subject to a provision for that lease to cease to exist when the mortgage is redeemed; or

>   (ii) by the grant by deed of a charge which is expressed to be by way of legal mortgage.

(a) The grant of a term of years absolute

When this method is employed, which is now very infrequent, the term of years granted to the mortgagee is usually a long term, for example 3,000 years. The provision for that lease to cease to exist when the mortgage is redeemed is really unnecessary, for on repayment the term becomes a satisfied term and automatically ceases.[13] In other respects, the position is much as it was before 1926. A fixed redemption date is still named, and it is still usually six months after the date of the mortgage. Thereafter the mortgagor has an equitable right to redeem in lieu of his legal right. The difficulty that a mortgagee by demise has no right to the title deeds is obviated by an express provision giving a first mortgagee the same right to the deeds as if he had the fee simple.[14]

The principal change brought about by the 1925 legislation was that the mortgagor now retains the legal fee simple. This does not mean that the equity of redemption has lost its importance; a fee simple giving the right to possession of land only when a lease for 3,000 years has expired is of little value compared with the right to insist that the fee simple shall forthwith be freed from the term of 3,000 years on payment of the money due. Indeed, the term "equity of redemption" is now sometimes used to include the mortgagor's legal estate. But the change means that the mortgagor has, in addition to his equity of redemption, a legal fee simple out of which a further term of years may be granted. Consequently, second and subsequent mortgages may now all be legal. Thus A, the fee simple owner of Blackacre, may create successive legal mortgages in favour of X, Y and Z. The term he grants to each mortgagee is usually at least one day longer than the term under the previous mortgage. Thus X may be given 2,000 years, Y 2,000 years and a day, and Z 2,000 years and two days, so that each mortgagee has a reversion upon the prior mortgage term.

The rights of Y and Z, though seemingly rather nebulous, are in fact quite substantial. Thus if A defaults and the property is sold by X under his power of sale,[15] the money is paid first to X to discharge his mortgage, the balance to Y to discharge his, the balance to discharge Z's mortgage, and any surplus to A. In short, the parties rank in the order X, Y, Z, A. Further, any mortgagee always has the right, upon giving proper notice, to insist upon redeeming any prior mortgage.[16] Thus Y might insist upon buying up X's mortgage and so succeeding to X's position.

---

[12] s.85(1).
[13] See above, p. 365.
[14] L.P.A. 1925, s.85(1).
[15] Below, pp. 504 et seq.
[16] Below, p. 523.

An attempt to create a first mortgage by conveyance of the fee simple now operates as the grant of a term of 3,000 years without the mortgagee being liable to be impeached for waste but subject to the usual provision for the lease to cease to exist when the mortgage is redeemed.[17] An attempt to create a second or subsequent mortgage in the same way takes effect as the grant of a term one day longer than the preceding term.[18] The system is thus foolproof.

(b) The grant by deed of a charge expressed to be by way of legal mortgage

This was a new creation of the Law of Property Act 1925[19] and for brevity is usually called a "legal charge". To be effective, it must be:

(i) made by deed (a charge merely in writing will have no effect at law); and

(ii) expressed to be by way of legal mortgage (the deed must contain a statement that the charge is made by way of legal mortgage).[20]

The effect of such a charge of freehold land is that the chargee (whether first or subsequent) gets the same protection, powers and remedies as if he had a term of 3,000 years without being liable to be impeached for waste.[21] Although he gets no actual legal term of years, he is as fully protected as if he had one.[22] The name "charge" is thus a little misleading because although a legal charge is by nature a charge and not a mortgage,[23] for all practical purposes it is indistinguishable from a mortgage.

Legal charges are now virtually always used. Their advantages are considered below.[24]

3. Mortgages of leaseholds before 1926

Before 1926 a legal mortgage of leasehold land could be made in either of two ways:

(i) by assignment of the lease to the mortgagee subject to a covenant by the latter to reassign that lease to the mortgagor if the principal sum lent and the agreed interest was repaid on the due date; or

(ii) by the grant to the mortgagee of a sub-lease at least one day shorter than the lease subject to a provision for that lease to cease to exist when the mortgage was redeemed.

The first method was rarely employed, for it meant that the mortgagee became liable on such of the covenants in the lease as touched and concerned the land. This was not so if the second method was employed, for then the mortgagee was only an under-lessee and there was privity neither of contract nor of estate between him and the lessor.[25] Whichever form was employed, the mortgage normally contained the usual provision that the loan should be

---

[17] L.P.A. 1925, s.85(2).
[18] *ibid.*
[19] s.87.
[20] *Cityland and Property (Holdings) Ltd v. Dabrah* [1968] Ch. 166; Ruoff & Roper, para. 23.07.
[21] L.P.A. 1925, s.87(1).
[22] See *Regent Oil Co. Ltd v. J.A. Gregory (Hatch End) Ltd* [1966] Ch. 402.
[23] Above, p 439.
[24] Below, p. 497.
[25] Above, p. 381.

repaid on a fixed date six months ahead, and thereafter the mortgagor had an equitable right to redeem.

Where a mortgage had been made by assignment, second and subsequent mortgages were made by a mortgage of the mortgagor's equity of redemption. Where the prior mortgage had been made by sub-lease, subsequent mortgages were made by the grant of further sub-leases, each normally being one day longer than the previous one.

4. Mortgages of leaseholds after 1925

The Law of Property Act 1925 provides[26] that leaseholds can no longer be mortgaged by assignment. Only two methods are now possible:

    (i) by the grant of a sub-lease for a term of years absolute, subject to a provision for that sub-lease to cease to exist when the mortgage is redeemed, the term of the sub-lease being at least one day shorter than the leasehold term vested in the mortgagor; or

    (ii) by the grant by deed of a charge which is expressed to be by way of legal mortgage.

(a) The grant of a sub-lease for a term of years absolute

The term of the sub-lease must be at least one day shorter than the term of the lease which is being mortgaged, otherwise it would operate as an assignment.[27] If the lease requires the tenant to obtain the landlord's licence before a sub-lease by way of mortgage is made, the licence cannot be unreasonably refused.[28] The first mortgagee has the same rights to the deeds as if his mortgage had been made by assignment.[29] It is usual to make the sub-lease 10 days shorter than the lease, so as to allow room for second and subsequent mortgages. Thus if T mortgages a 50-year lease, the first mortgage will be secured by a sub-lease for 50 years less 10 days, any second mortgage by a sub-lease for 50 years less nine days, and so on. But this is not essential, for the old rule[30] that a lease may take effect in reversion upon another lease of the same or greater length has been confirmed by the Law of Property Act 1925.[31] Thus, if the first mortgage was made by a sub-lease for 50 years less one day, the second mortgage would be secured by a sub-lease of the same length and so on; each mortgage would take effect in its proper order.

An attempted mortgage by way of assignment after 1925 operates as a sub-lease for a term of years absolute subject to that sub-lease ceasing to exist when the mortgage is redeemed. A first or only mortgagee takes a term 10 days shorter than the lease mortgaged. Second and subsequent mortgages take terms one day longer than under the previous mortgage, if this is possible. In every case, however, the sub-term must be at least one day shorter than the term mortgaged.[32]

---

[26] s.86(1).
[27] *Beardman v. Wilson* (1868) L.R. 4 C.P. 57; above, p. 322.
[28] L.P.A. 1925, s.86(1).
[29] *ibid.*
[30] *Re Moore & Hulme's Contract* [1912] 2 Ch. 105.
[31] s.149(5).
[32] L.P.A. 1925, s.86(2). See *Grangeside Properties Ltd v. Collingwoods Securities Ltd* [1964] 1 W.L.R. 139.

(b) The grant by deed of a charge expressed to be by way of legal mortgage

The grant by deed of a charge expressed to be by way of legal mortgage gives the mortgagee (whether first or subsequent) the same rights and remedies as if he had a sub-lease one day shorter than the term vested in the mortgagor.[33] As in the case of freeholds,[34] he gets no actual term of years but is as fully protected as if he had one, so that he may seek relief against forfeiture in the same way as a sub-lessee.[35]

5. Advantages of legal charges

There is nothing in the Law of Property Act 1925 to suggest any reason why a legal charge, either of freeholds or leaseholds, should be preferred to an ordinary mortgage. But there seem to be three practical advantages in using a legal charge:

(i) it is a convenient way of mortgaging freeholds and leaseholds together; the deed is shortened by stating that all the properties specified in the schedule are charged by way of legal mortgage, instead of setting out the length of the mortgage terms in each case;

(ii) the grant of a legal charge over a lease probably does not amount to a breach of any covenant in that lease against sub-letting, for the charge creates no actual sub-lease in favour of the mortgagee but merely gives him the same rights as if he had a sub-lease;

(iii) the form of a legal charge is short and simple.

6. Compulsory registration

Since April 1, 1998, a first legal mortgage of an estate in fee simple or a term of years absolute in unregistered land has triggered compulsory registration of that freehold or leasehold title.[36] Whether, unusually, the mortgage is created by the grant of a term of years absolute or of a sub-lease, or whether, as is now almost invariably the case, it is instead created by the grant of a legal charge, it will take effect as a registered charge.[37]

Sect. 2. Legal mortgages and charges of registered land

Subject to any restriction on the power of mortgaging which is entered on the register, a legal mortgage of registered land may be effected in the following ways.

1. Registered charges

A registered charge is the normal way in which to mortgage registered land. As seen above,[38] a registered charge is not a registrable interest, an interest which overrides registration or a right which requires protection on the register. It is *sui generis*.[39] A registered charge may be

---

[33] *ibid.*, s.87(1).
[34] Above, p. 495.
[35] Above, pp. 359, 363.
[36] Above, p. 117.
[37] Below.
[38] Above, p. 121.
[39] See L.R.A. 1925, s.3(xv), (xvi), (xxiii); and see ss.18(4), 21(4). L.R.A. 2002, s.129(1).

effected by any deed charging the land with the payment of money.[40] It does not take effect at law until it has been registered,[41] although it takes effect in equity in the meantime.[42] However, the mortgage security will not be affected by any interest which overrides registration when that interest arises between the creation of the charge and its registration.[43] On registration, an entry is made in the charges register giving the name of the person in whose favour the charge is made, together with particulars of it. At present the land certificate must be deposited at the Registry for as long as a registered charge exists, and a charge certificate is issued to the chargee as his document of title.[44] However, when the Land Registration Act 2002 comes into force, charge certificates will be discontinued and registered charges will simply be protected on the register in the same way as other interests which require such protection.[45] It will therefore no longer be necessary for the land certificate to be retained in the Registry.

A registered chargee has all the powers of a legal mortgagee, unless the register otherwise provides.[46] The priority of registered charges is governed by the order of entry in the register, unless it otherwise provides.[47] The rules which govern the ways in which that order of priorities can be altered as a result of a mortgagee making a further advance will be considered later on.[48]

2. Mortgages by the grant of a lease or a sub-lease

At present, it is possible to create a mortgage of registered land by granting a lease, or in the case of leasehold land a sub-lease, to the mortgagee with a provision for the lease or sub-lease to cease to exist when the mortgage is redeemed.[49] Such leases or sub-leases are ineligible for registration as such with a leasehold title.[50] Instead they take effect as registered charges if they are lodged with the Registry for that purpose and, once registered, the mortgagee takes a legal charge over the property.[51] If not so lodged, they take effect only in equity[52] and will therefore only bind third parties claiming for value under a registered disposition if they have been protected on the register by the registration of a notice or a caution against dealings. When the Land Registration Act 2002 comes into force, it will no longer be possible to create mortgages of registered land by the grant of a lease or a sub-lease[53] so registered charges will then be the only type of legal mortgage of registered land.

---

[40] L.R.A. 1925, s.25; L.R.A. 2002, s.23(1)(b).
[41] *Grace Rymer Investments Ltd v. Waite* [1958] Ch. 831; and see *Lever Finance Ltd v. Needleman's Trustee* [1956] Ch. 375.
[42] *Mortgage Corporation Ltd v. Nationwide Credit Corporation Ltd* [1994] Ch. 49.
[43] *Abbey National B.S. v. Cann* [1991] 1 A.C. 56.
[44] L.R.A. 1925, ss.25, 26, 65; L.R.R. 1925, r.262.
[45] This will presumably be dealt with by the new L.R.R.
[46] L.R.A. 1925, ss.27, 34; L.R.A. 2002, s.52(1).
[47] L.R.A. 1925, s.29; L.R.A. 2002, s.48(1).
[48] See below, pp. 544 *et seq.*
[49] L.R.A. 1925, s.27(2).
[50] *ibid.*, s.8(1)(a).
[51] *ibid.*, s.26(1).
[52] *ibid.*, s.106(2)(a), as substituted by Administration of Justice Act 1977, s.26.
[53] L.R.A. 2002, s.23(1)(a).

Sect. 3. Equitable mortgages and charges

1. Equitable mortgages of equitable interests

If the mortgagor has no legal estate but only an equitable interest, any mortgage he effects must necessarily be equitable. Thus beneficiaries under a trust have merely equitable interests and so can create only equitable mortgages.

The 1925 legislation has not affected the form of equitable mortgages of equitable interests. Such mortgages are still made by a conveyance of the equitable interest to the mortgagee with a provision for reconveyance of that interest to the mortgagor when the mortgage is redeemed. The actual form of words employed is immaterial provided that the meaning is plain.[54] Nor need the mortgage be made by deed, as is essential for a legal mortgage; but it must either be in writing signed by the mortgagor or his agent authorised in writing, or else be made by will.[55] The mortgagee should give notice to whoever holds the legal title to the property in question, in practice one or more trustees, in order to secure priority over later equitable mortgages of the same interest under what is known as the rule in *Dearle v. Hall*.[56]

Where a mortgagor purports to create a legal mortgage or charge but fails to do so because he has not yet acquired legal title to the property in question; in such circumstances, the mortgagee obviously does not acquire a legal mortgage. Where the mortgagor has already contracted to buy the property in question, he will already have an equitable interest therein so the mortgagee will immediately acquire an equitable mortgage. But in any event he acquires a mortgage by estoppel. Consequently, if the mortgagor subsequently acquires the legal title which he purported to mortgage or charge, that acquisition "feeds" the estoppel and the mortgagee will immediately acquire a legal mortgage or charge; this is the case whether the land in question is unregistered[57] or registered.[58]

2. Mortgages which are equitable because they are informal

Under the same principles as apply to leaseholds,[59] equity treats an enforceable contract to create a legal mortgage,[60] or an imperfect legal mortgage,[61] as being an actual mortgage. To be enforceable, the transaction was formerly required to be supported either by sufficient evidence in writing or by a sufficient act of part performance. However, for transactions after September 26, 1989, neither evidence in writing nor part performance will suffice; instead, the contract will be valid only if it is made in writing, containing all the terms, and is signed by all parties to it.[62] If it is, the contract will need to be protected as an estate contract in the usual way if it is to be enforceable against all third parties.

3. Mortgages by deposit of documents of title

Prior to this change in the law in 1989, a mere deposit of the title deeds to unregistered land which could not be accounted for in any other way would be taken to be part performance of a

---

[54] See *William Brandt's Sons & Co. v. Dunlop Rubber Co. Ltd* [1905] A.C. 454 at 462.
[55] L.P.A. 1925, s.53(1).
[56] (1828) 3 Russ. 1; below, p. 540.
[57] *Right d. Jefferys v. Bucknell* (1831) 2 B. & Ald. 278.
[58] *First National Bank Plc v. Thompson* [1996] Ch. 231.
[59] Above, p. 343.
[60] See *Ex p. Wright* (1812) 19 Ves. 255 at 258.
[61] *Parker v. Housefield* (1834) 2 My. & K. 419 at 420.
[62] Above, p. 147.

contract to create a mortgage,[63] even if not a word about such a contract had been uttered,[64] so that an equitable mortgage was created by such a deposit.[65] The deposit had to have been made for the purpose of giving a security, so that delivery of the deeds by mistake, or to enable a mortgage to be drawn up, created no mortgage.[66] But it was not essential that all the deeds should have been deposited, provided that those that were delivered were material evidence of title.[67] The mortgagee had no lien on the deeds apart from his right to retain them under the mortgage, so that if the mortgage contract was void, the deeds had to be given up.[68]

Similarly, since in registered conveyancing the land certificate takes the place of the title deeds to unregistered land, a lien could be created by deposit of the land certificate and the holder of a registered charge could similarly create a lien on his charge by deposit of his charge certificate.[69] The mere possession of the certificate provided some protection,[70] though not against transactions for which production of the certificate was not requisite, such as certain leases.[71] The lender, however, could have a notice of the existence of the deposit entered on the charges register of the land affected. A lien could also be created by giving the registrar a notice of intention to deposit the land certificate.[72] The latter procedure was useful where a loan was made in connection with the purchase of the land. Naturally the land certificate was not available until the transfer had been registered after completion of the purchase. Once registered, the land certificate would then be delivered by the registrar to the person named in the notice.

Both these types of mortgage by deposit of documents of title are still possible at present, although it will no longer be possible to create a mortgage by depositing a land certificate when the Land Registration Act 2002 comes into force[73] and charge certificates will then be discontinued prospectively. However, today a deposit of documents of title is of no effect in the absence of a contract in writing signed by all the parties.[74] This makes little difference in practice, since nearly all mortgages by deposit of documents of title have for long been accompanied by a deed setting out the terms of the mortgage, or requiring the mortgagor to execute a legal mortgage on request, thereby preventing disputes; and the execution of such a deed gives the mortgagee additional powers.[75] Such a deed will meet the present statutory requirement for a contract made in writing. But in the absence of any such writing[76] a deposit of title deeds will not now create a mortgage.

4. Equitable charges

An equitable charge is created where specific property is appropriated to the discharge of some debt or other obligation without there being any change in ownership either at law or

[63] *Russel v. Russel* (1783) 1 Bro.C.C. 269.
[64] *Bozon v. Williams* (1829) 3 Y. & J. 151 at 161.
[65] *Bank of New South Wales v. O'Connor* (1889) 14 App.Cas. 273 at 282; *Re Wallis & Simmonds (Builders) Ltd* [1974] 1 W.L.R. 391.
[66] *Norris v. Wilkinson* (1806) 12 Ves. 192.
[67] *Lacon v. Allen* (1856) 3 Drew. 579.
[68] *Re Molton Finance Ltd* [1968] Ch. 325.
[69] L.R.A. 1925, s.66.
[70] *Barclays Bank Ltd v. Taylor* [1974] Ch. 137.
[71] See *Strand Securities Ltd v. Caswell* [1965] Ch. 958.
[72] L.R.R. 1925, rr. 240–242.
[73] L.R.A. 2002 deliberately contains no provision equivalent to L.R.A. 1925, s.66; see Law Com. No. 271, para. 7.10.
[74] *United Bank of Kuwait Plc v. Sahib* [1997] Ch. 107.
[75] Below, pp. 504, 506, 511, 513.
[76] As in *United Bank of Kuwait Plc v. Sahib* [1997] Ch. 107.

in equity.[77] Thus if a man signs a written contract agreeing that he thereby charges some specific land of his with the payment of £5,000 to A, an equitable charge over that land is created.[78] The same applies where a will or voluntary settlement charges money on land.[79] An enforceable contract to create a legal charge also creates an equitable charge.[80] However, equitable charges which are not supported by a deposit of documents of title and do not arise under a trust or settlement need to be protected (as land charges in the case of unregistered land; by notice or—at present—by caution against dealings in the case of registered land) if they are to be enforceable against all third parties.

Part 3—Rights of the Parties under a Mortgage or Charge

The rights of the parties under a mortgage or charge will be considered under three heads:

(i) the rights of the mortgagee or chargee;

(ii) rights common to both parties;

(iii) the right of the mortgagor or chargor to redeem; and

(iv) the other rights of the mortgagor or chargor.

Sect. 1. Rights of the mortgagee or chargee—remedies for enforcing payment

Unless the parties have otherwise agreed, a mortgagee or chargee has five remedies available for enforcing payment. Three of the remedies are primarily directed to recovering the capital due and putting an end to the security: these are an action for the money, foreclosure, and sale. The other two remedies are taking possession and appointing a receiver. These primarily seek merely to recover the interest due, though possession is now usually sought so as to facilitate sale with vacant possession. Sale and appointing a receiver are rights which used to be conferred by the mortgage deed but are now given by statute; the other remedies are inherent in the nature of the transaction. Today, actions for foreclosure have become rare.[81] A mortgagee will not be restrained from enforcing payment merely because the mortgagor has some large cross-claim against him,[82] even if it is for a larger amount than the sum due to the mortgagee.

It may be noted that two of the mortgagee's remedies are derived from the common law (an action on the covenant, and the right to take possession), one is equitable (foreclosure) and two were formerly contractual and are now statutory (sale, and the appointment of a receiver).

A mortgagee is not obliged to take any steps to realise his security; he can sit back and do nothing.[83] However, if he does take some steps to exercise his rights, he must act fairly

---

[77] *London County and Westminster Bank Ltd v. Tompkins* [1918] 1 K.B. 515 at 528.
[78] *Matthews v. Goodday* (1861) 31 L.J. Ch. 282 at 282, 283.
[79] *Re Owen* [1894] 3 Ch. 220.
[80] *Swiss Bank Corporation v. Lloyds Bank Ltd* [1979] Ch. 548; on appeal, [1982] A.C. 584; and see above, p. 343.
[81] See *Palk v. Mortgage Services Funding Plc* [1993] Ch. 330.
[82] *Samuel Keller (Holdings) Ltd v. Martins Bank Ltd* [1971] 1 W.L.R. 43; *Ashley Guarantee Plc v. Zacaria* [1993] 1 W.L.R. 62; *Albany Home Loans Ltd v. Massey* [1997] 2 All E.R. 609.
[83] *China and South Sea Bank Ltd v. Tan* [1990] 1 A.C. 538 at 545.

towards the mortgagor.[84] Thus, where a mortgagee refused to consent to a sale by the mortgagor which, because of a fall in property values, would not raise enough money to discharge the mortgage and instead sought an order for possession with a view to letting the house until such time as property values had risen again, he was held not to be acting fairly. This was because the rent obtained would be substantially less than the interest on the mortgage which would continue to be debited to the mortgagor. Sale was therefore ordered on the application of the mortgagor[85] on the basis that the mortgagee would be free to purchase the property itself if it wanted to take the risk of what would happen to property values in the future. This decision was made in the aftermath of a substantial generalised fall in property values. Such falls in value and the consequential appearance of negative equity on a large scale have, historically, been extremely rare. Consequently in normal circumstances it is not likely that mortgagees will find themselves constrained in this way.

Where a mortgagee does decide to act, the remedies available differ according to whether the mortgage or charge is legal or equitable.

1. Legal mortgagees or chargees

A legal mortgagee or legal chargee has the following remedies for enforcing his security.

(a) To sue for the money due

At any time after the date fixed for payment the mortgagee may sue for the money lent.[86] This remedy is, of course, in no way peculiar to mortgages. It is perfectly proper for the mortgage to sue for the money due in an attempt to bankrupt the mortgagor and obtain possession of the property via his trustee in bankruptcy[87] even though the mortgagee has failed to obtain possession of the property by virtue of being a secured creditor.[88]

(b) To foreclose

(i) **The nature of foreclosure:** By giving the mortgagor an equitable right to redeem after he had lost his legal right of redemption, equity interfered with the bargain made between the parties. But equity prescribed limits to the equity of redemption which it created; the mortgagor's equitable right to redeem could in appropriate circumstances be extinguished. The process, for which an order of the court was and is necessary, is known as "foreclosure". On foreclosure "the court simply removes the stop it has itself put on"[89]; equity's interference to prevent the conveyance of the legal fee simple from having its full effect comes to an end.

Before 1926, a legal first mortgagee of freehold land had the estate in fee simple vested in him anyway so an order extinguishing the equity of redemption was of itself sufficient to leave the mortgagee as owner of the property both at law and in equity. Since 1925, a mortgagee has not had the whole legal estate of the mortgagor vested in him. Consequently it is no longer sufficient for an order for foreclosure merely to destroy the mortgagor's equity of redemption; the Law of Property Act 1925[90] therefore provides that, in the case of both

---

[84] *Palk v. Mortgage Services Funding Plc* [1993] Ch. 330 at 338.
[85] Under L.P.A. 1925, s.91(2).
[86] See *Bolton v. Buckenham* [1891] 1 Q.B. 278.
[87] See above, p. 324.
[88] *Alliance & Leicester Plc v. Slayford* [2001] 1 All E.R. (Comm.) 1.
[89] *Carter v. Wake* (1877) 4 Ch.D. 605 at 606, *per* Jessel M.R.
[90] ss.88(2), 89(2).

mortgages and charges, a final order for foreclosure (technically, a foreclosure order absolute) vests the mortgagor's fee simple or lease in the mortgagee.

The right to foreclose does not arise until the legal right to redeem has ceased to exist, *i.e.* until the legal date for redemption has passed[91] or until there is a breach of a condition required for keeping the legal right of redemption alive.[92] Once this has happened, the mortgagee may commence foreclosure proceedings unless he has agreed not to do so[93] (sometimes a mortgagee will contract not to enforce the security by foreclosure or other means until he has given some specified notice or until the mortgagor has broken one of his covenants in the mortgage). If no redemption date is fixed or if the loan is repayable on demand, the right to foreclose arises when a demand for repayment has been made and a reasonable time thereafter has elapsed.[94]

(ii) Parties to a foreclosure action: An action for foreclosure can be brought by any mortgagee of property, whether he is the original mortgagee or an assignee, and whether he is a first or subsequent mortgagee. The effect of a foreclosure order absolute in an action brought by the first mortgagee is to make him the sole owner both at law and in equity, free from any subsequent mortgages. If the action is brought by a second or subsequent mortgagee, he will hold the property subject to prior incumbrances, but free from all subsequent incumbrances. Where trustees foreclose, they hold the land on a trust of land.[95]

As will be seen shortly,[96] a foreclosure action gives the mortgagor and all others interested in the equity of redemption an opportunity of redeeming the mortgage. Consequently, all persons interested in the equity of redemption must be made parties to the action. Thus if X has made successive mortgages of his property to A, B and C, and B starts foreclosure proceedings, A's mortgage security will not be affected by those proceedings and so there is no need for A to be made a party to the action. But if the action is successful, C will lose his mortgage security and X his equity of redemption, and so both must be made parties to the action.

(iii) Foreclosure orders nisi: The first step in a foreclosure is to obtain from the court a foreclosure order nisi. This provides that if the mortgagor repays the money lent on a fixed day (usually six months from the accounts being settled by the relevant court officer), the mortgage shall be discharged, but that if this is not done, the mortgage shall be foreclosed. If there are several mortgagees and the first mortgagee is foreclosing, each mortgagee is given the alternative of either losing his security or else redeeming (paying off) the first mortgage. Sometimes the court will give the mortgagees successive periods to effect this redemption, but usually there will be only one period for all of them.[97] At the request of the mortgagee or of any person interested (such as the mortgagor) the court may order a sale of the property instead of foreclosure.[98]

---

[91] *Williams v. Morgan* [1906] 1 Ch. 804.
[92] *Twentieth Century Banking Corporation Ltd v. Wilkinson* [1977] Ch. 99.
[93] *Ramsbottom v. Wallis* (1835) 5 L.J.Ch. 92.
[94] *Toms v. Wilson* (1863) 4 B. & S. 453.
[95] L.P.A. 1925, s.31, as amended by T.L.A.T.A. 1996, Sched. 2, para. 1; above, pp. 283, 284.
[96] See below.
[97] *Platt v. Mendel* (1884) 27 Ch.D. 246.
[98] L.P.A. 1925, s.91(2); *Twentieth Century Banking Corporation Ltd v. Wilkinson* [1977] Ch. 99.

(iv) Foreclosure orders absolute: If no order for sale is made and the property is not redeemed on the date fixed, a foreclosure order absolute is made. This destroys the mortgagor's equity of redemption and transfers his fee simple or term of years to the mortgagee,[99] who thus becomes sole owner at law and in equity, subject only to prior incumbrances. In the case of registered land, the mortgagee is registered as proprietor of the land and his charge is cancelled.

(v) Re-opening a foreclosure absolute: Although a foreclosure order absolute appears to be final, it is not necessarily so, for the court will sometimes re-open the foreclosure absolute. Circumstances which may influence the court to do this are the fact that the mortgagor was prevented from raising the money by an accident at the last moment, any special value which the property has to the mortgagor (such as if it was an old family estate), a marked disparity between the value of the property and the amount lent, and the promptness of the application. Even if the mortgagee has sold the property on after obtaining his foreclosure order absolute, the court may still re-open the matter. This is unlikely, however, if the purchaser bought the property some time after foreclosure and without notice of any circumstances which might induce the court to interfere.[1]

(c) To sell

(i) History: There is no right, either at common law or in equity, for a mortgagee to sell the mortgaged property free from the equity of redemption, although of course he can freely transfer the estate which is vested in him subject to the equity of redemption. Consequently, an express power was usually inserted in mortgage deeds enabling the mortgagee to sell the property free from the equity of redemption if certain specified events occurred. However, a satisfactory power of sale is now contained in the Law of Property Act 1925.[2]

(ii) The power: Every mortgagee whose deed of mortgage shows no contrary intention has a power of sale, provided:

> (i) the mortgage was made by deed (all legal mortgages must be anyway); and

> (ii) the mortgage money is due, *i.e.* the legal date for redemption has passed[3] (if the mortgage money is payable by instalments, the power of sale arises as soon as any instalment is in arrear).[4]

When these conditions have been fulfilled, the statutory power of sale arises. Nevertheless, the power does not become exercisable unless one of the three following conditions has been satisfied[5]:

> (i) notice requiring payment of the mortgage money has been served on the mortgagor and default has been made in payment of part or all of it for three months thereafter; or

---

[99] L.P.A. 1925, ss.88(2), 89(2); L.R.A. 1925, s.34(3); there is no explicit provision in L.R.A. 2002 but the law will remain the same.
[1] *Campbell v. Holyland* (1877) 7 Ch.D. 166 at 172, 173.
[2] ss.101–107, applicable to mortgages made after 1881.
[3] L.P.A. 1925, s.101.
[4] *Payne v. Cardiff R.D.C.* [1932] 1 K.B. 241.
[5] L.P.A. 1925, s.103.

(ii) some interest under the mortgage is two months or more in arrears; or

(iii) there has been a breach of some provision contained in the Law of Property Act 1925 or in the mortgage deed (other than the covenant for payment of the mortgage money or interest) which should have been observed or performed by the mortgagor or by someone who concurred in making the mortgage.

(iii) Protection of purchasers: The difference between the power of sale arising and becoming exercisable is as follows. If the power has not arisen, the mortgagee has no statutory power of sale at all; the most he can do is to transfer his mortgage. But if the power of sale has arisen, he can make a good title to a purchaser free from the equity of redemption even if the power has not become exercisable. The title of a purchaser in good faith is not impeachable merely because none of the three specified events has occurred or the power of sale has in some way been irregularly or improperly exercised. Any person injured by an unauthorised, improper or irregular exercise of the power has a remedy in damages against the person exercising it.[6] Thus while a purchaser from a mortgagee must satisfy himself that the power of sale has arisen, he need not inquire whether it has become exercisable. However, if he has actual knowledge (as distinct from merely constructive notice) that the power is not exercisable or that there is some impropriety in the sale, he will not take free from the mortgagor's interest[7]; nor is he likely to if he turns a blind eye to suspicious circumstances.

(iv) Mode of sale: In general, the statutory power of sale is exercisable without any order of the court being required. The mortgagee may sell by public auction or by private contract, and has a wide discretion as to the terms and conditions upon which the sale is made.[8] The power is unaffected by any disposition by the mortgagor, so that a contract of sale entered into by the mortgagee will prevail over an earlier contract of sale made by the mortgagor.[9] The power becomes exercised as soon as a contract, albeit conditional, is made, so that thereupon the equity of redemption is suspended unless and until the contract goes off.[10] To prevent the mortgagee entering into such a contract, the mortgagor must tender the sum necessary to redeem the mortgage in full.[11]

It has already been seen that the mortgagee must act fairly towards the mortgagor when exercising his rights[12] but, save where there is generalised negative equity, it is not likely that mortgagees will often find themselves constrained in this way. In any event, the mortgagee is not a trustee for the mortgagor of his power of sale,[13] for the power is given to the mortgagee for his own benefit to enable him the better to realise his security. Thus he need not delay the sale in the hope of obtaining a better price,[14] nor does he have to attempt to sell by auction before selling by private contract.[15] Moreover, his motive for selling, such as spite

---

[6] *ibid.*, s.104(2).

[7] *Bailey v. Barnes* [1894] 1 Ch. 25 at 30; *Lord Waring v. London & Manchester Assurance Co. Ltd* [1935] Ch. 310 at 318.

[8] L.P.A. 1925, s.101(1), (2).

[9] *Duke v. Robson* [1973] 1 W.L.R. 267.

[10] *Property & Bloodstock Ltd v. Emerton* [1968] Ch. 94.

[11] *Payne v. Cardiff R.D.C.* [1932] 1 K.B. 241.

[12] *Palk v. Mortgage Services Funding Plc* [1993] Ch. 330 at 338.

[13] *Kennedy v. De Trafford* [1897] A.C. 180.

[14] *Bank of Cyprus (London) Ltd v. Gill* [1980] 2 Lloyd's Rep. 51; and see *China & South Sea Bank Ltd v. Tan Soon Gin* [1990] 1 A.C. 531.

[15] *Davey v. Durrant* (1857) 1 De G. & J. 535 at 553, 560.

against the mortgagor, is immaterial.[16] But the sale must be a true sale: a "sale" by the mortgagee to himself, either directly or through an agent, is no true sale and may be set aside or declared void.[17]

However, the mortgagee is under a duty to take reasonable care to obtain a proper price,[18] so that he will be liable to the mortgagor if he advertises the property for sale by auction without mentioning a valuable planning permission,[19] or if he sells the property on a "crash sale" basis without exposing it to the market for a proper period of time.[20] However, he will not be in breach if he takes a commercial decision to sell at a particular time, even though a higher price might have been obtained by delaying.[21] The duty to obtain a proper price for the property, which may be excluded by an appropriately drafted term in the mortgage,[22] is owed not merely to the mortgagor but also to a surety for the loan,[23] though not to an equitable co-owner of the land.[24] If the mortgagee sells to an associated person or company, the onus is on him to show that a proper price was obtained.[25]

(v) Proceeds of sale: Although the mortgagee is not a trustee of his power of sale, he is a trustee of the proceeds of sale. After discharging any payments properly due, any balance must be paid to the next subsequent incumbrancer,[26] or, if none, to the mortgagor.[27] A mortgagee who has a surplus will be liable to any subsequent mortgagee of whom he had actual or constructive notice who is prejudiced by the payment of the surplus to the mortgagor.[28] In the case of unregistered land, he should therefore search in the land charges register[29] to discover the existence of any subsequent mortgages since registration constitutes actual notice. It is not at present necessary to search the land register since registration there does not constitute notice, although the mortgagee must pay any subsequent incumbrancer who has notified him of his mortgage. However, it will be necessary to search the land register when the Land Registration Act 2002 since registration will then constitute notice for this purpose.[30] But a sale by a mortgagee does not affect any prior mortgage: the purchaser takes the property subject to any such mortgage, though free from the rights of the vendor, subsequent mortgagees, and the mortgagor.[31]

(d) To take possession

(i) The right: Since a legal mortgage gives the mortgagee a term of years, he is entitled, subject to any contrary indication in the mortgage, to take possession of the mortgaged

---

[16] *Nash v. Eads* (1880) 25 S.J. 95.

[17] *Downes v. Grazebrook* (1871) 3 Mer. 200; *Williams v. Wellingborough B.C.* [1975] 1 W.L.R. 1327.

[18] For building societies the duty is statutory: Building Societies Act 1986, Sched. 4, replacing earlier legislation.

[19] *Cuckmere Brick Co. Ltd v. Mutual Finance Ltd* [1971] Ch. 949.

[20] *Predeth v. Castle Phillips Finance Co. Ltd* [1986] 2 E.G.L.R. 144.

[21] *Meftah v. Lloyds TSB Bank Plc* [2001] 2 All E.R. (Comm.) 741.

[22] *Bishop v. Bonham* [1988] 1 W.L.R. 742 at 752.

[23] *Standard Chartered Bank Ltd v. Walker* [1982] 1 W.L.R. 1410.

[24] *Parker-Tweedale v. Dunbar Bank Plc* [1991] Ch. 12.

[25] *Tse Kwong Lam v. Wong Chit Sen* [1983] 1 W.L.R. 1394.

[26] See *Samuel Keller (Holdings) Ltd v. Martin's Bank Ltd* [1971] 1 W.L.R. 43.

[27] L.P.A. 1925, s.105; see *Thorne v. Heard* [1895] A.C. 495. And see below, pp. 555, 564, for the effect of the Limitation Act 1980.

[28] *West London Commercial Bank v. Reliance Permanent B.S.* (1885) 29 Ch.D. 954.

[29] See above, p. 94.

[30] L.R.A. 2002, s.54.

[31] L.P.A. 1925, s.104(1); L.R.A. 1925, s.34(4); there is no explicit provision in L.R.A. 2002 but the law will remain the same.

property as soon as the mortgage is made, even if the mortgagor is guilty of no default[32]; a legal chargee has a corresponding statutory right.[33] The mortgagee or chargee may do so without a court order,[34] even where the subject-matter of the mortgage is a dwelling-house occupied by the mortgagor although in those circumstances the court can grant relief to the mortgagor.[35] If the property is already lawfully let to tenants, the mortgagee cannot take physical possession, but instead takes possession by directing the tenants to pay their rents to him instead of to the mortgagor.[36] However, an order for possession may be refused if the mortgagee is not acting as such but is acting merely as an agent for a mortgagor who is trying to evict a tenant.[37] The mortgagee's right to possession may also be affected by the rights of co-owners of the mortgaged property, which are considered below.[38]

(ii) The practice: A mortgagee who is exercising his rights in respect of a property which is the home of the mortgagor will generally need to take possession of it in order to be able to sell it with vacant possession. In such circumstances, institutional mortgagees will, despite their right to take possession without a court order, normally seek such an order if the mortgagor is in occupation so that he has an opportunity of claiming statutory relief. Mortgagees sometimes also need to take possession in the case of commercial property. But except where there is to be a sale in the immediate future or where the property is already fully let to tenants, mortgagees are generally slow to take possession. This is because, if they do so, they will be liable to account to the mortgagor for the use of the property on an extremely strict basis, namely on what is known as the footing of wilful default. This means that they must account not only for everything that they actually receive but also for everything that they could conceivably have received.[39]

This is not a problem where the whole of the property is already let since the mortgagee will simply have to account to the mortgagor for the rents which he receives from the existing tenants; that is why there is little risk in taking possession of fully let property. However, where this is not the case, the potential problems are considerable. Where a mortgagee was a brewer and the mortgaged property was a "free" house, a mortgagee who took possession and let the property as a "tied" house was held liable for the additional rent which he would have obtained if he had let the property as a "free" house.[40] Similarly, if a mortgagee occupies the property himself instead of letting it, he will be liable to account to the mortgagor for a fair occupation rent.[41] However, he need pay no rent if through decay or otherwise the land is incapable of being beneficially occupied.[42]

(iii) Powers while in possession: While in possession, a mortgagee whose mortgage was made by deed may cut and sell timber and other trees ripe for cutting which were not planted or left standing for shelter or ornament, or contract for this to be done within 12 months of

---

[32] *Birch v. Wright* (1786) 1 T.R. 378 at 383; *Four-Maids Ltd v. Dudley Marshall (Properties) Ltd* [1957] Ch. 317 at 320.
[33] L.P.A. 1925, s.87(1).
[34] *Ropaigealach v. Barclays Bank Plc* [2000] Q.B. 263.
[35] See below, p. 508.
[36] *Horlock v. Smith* (1842) 6 Jur. 478.
[37] *Quennell v. Maltby* [1979] 1 W.L.R. 318.
[38] Below, p. 530.
[39] *Chaplin v. Young (No. 1)* (1863) 33 Beav. 330 at 337, 338.
[40] *White v. City of London Brewery Co.* (1889) 42 Ch.D. 237.
[41] *Marriott v. Anchor Reversionary Co.* (1861) 3 De G.F. & J. 177 at 193.
[42] *Marshall v. Cave* (1824) 3 L.J. (o.s.) Ch. 57, not cited in *Fyfe v. Smith* [1975] 2 N.S.W.L.R. 408 (hotel: occupation so as to preserve its business).

the contract.[43] Although he is not liable for waste, he will be liable if he improperly cuts timber; and despite his right to work mines already opened, he may not open new mines. However, if the property becomes insufficient security for the money due, the court will not interfere if he cuts timber and opens mines, provided he is not guilty of wanton destruction.[44]

A mortgagee in possession must effect reasonable repairs,[45] and may without the mortgagor's consent effect reasonable but not excessive improvements; the cost will be charged to the mortgagor in the accounts.[46]

(iv) Relief of mortgagor:

(1) *Inherent jurisdiction.* The court has a very limited inherent jurisdiction to grant a short adjournment of proceedings for possession in order to give the mortgagor a chance of paying off the mortgage in full or otherwise satisfying the mortgagee, unless there is no reasonable prospect of this occurring.[47] The court also has inherent jurisdiction to adjourn proceedings for possession pending sale of the property so that the mortgagor rather than the mortgagee can have the conduct of the sale[48] (a sale by a mortgagor in possession is likely to yield a higher price than a sale by a mortgagee who has repossessed the property). However, this only appears to be possible where the sale price will be enough to discharge the mortgagor's debt.

(2) *Consumer credit agreements.* Where a mortgage is regulated by the Consumer Credit Act 1974, which can only be the case where the advance does not exceed £25,000 and is not made by a building society or a local authority, the court has discretion to suspend an order for possession[49] and/or to make a "time order" for the payment of any sums owed by such instalments as it considers reasonable.[50] There is no formal requirement for payment within a reasonable time but the court can take this into account when exercising its discretion.

(3) *Dwelling-houses.* Where the property mortgaged consists of or includes a dwelling-house, the court has a wide statutory jurisdiction in claims for possession (other than in proceedings for foreclosure in which possession is also claimed and in the case of mortgages regulated by the Consumer Credit Act 1974). Whether the property consists of or includes a dwelling-house is determined at the time the claim for possession is made, not at the time the mortgage was granted.[51] However, the existence of this statutory jurisdiction does not deprive the mortgagee of his right to take possession of the mortgaged property and, if he does so, that jurisdiction is not

---

[43] L.P.A. 1925, s.101(1).
[44] *Millett v. Davey* (1863) 31 Beav. 470 at 475, 476.
[45] *Richards v. Morgan* (1853) 4 Y. & C.Ex. 570.
[46] *Shepard v. Jones* (1882) 21 Ch.D. 469.
[47] *Birmingham Citizens Permanent B.S. v. Caunt* [1962] Ch. 883; contrast *Quennell v. Maltby* [1979] 1 W.L.R. 318 at 322, obiter.
[48] *Cheltenham & Gloucester Plc v. Booker* (1997) 73 P. & C.R. 412.
[49] Consumer Credit Act 1974, s.135.
[50] *ibid.*, s.129.
[51] *Royal Bank of Scotland Plc v. Miller* [2001] 3 W.L.R. 523.

applicable.[52] However, institutional mortgagees nevertheless normally seek an order for possession if the mortgagor is in occupation.

Where the mortgagor seeks relief, the court may adjourn the proceedings, or stay or suspend execution of any judgment or order for possession for a defined or ascertainable period,[53] or postpone the date for delivery of possession.[54] Where the mortgagor is in arrears with his payments, the jurisdiction is only exercisable where it appears to the court that "the mortgagor is likely to be able within a reasonable period to pay any sums due under the mortgage", or to remedy any other default under it.[55] The court has power to impose conditions as to the payment of arrears and current sums and as to the remedying of defaults.[56] A common form of relief is therefore to suspend the order for possession on the basis of a revised schedule of payments gradually eradicating the arrears. Where this is done, the mortgagee may seek leave to enforce the order at any time[57] and will obviously do so if the mortgagor fails to keep to the revised schedule.

The "reasonable period" for the payments of sums due under the mortgage is normally the entire balance of the mortgage term,[58] although shorter periods are likely to be imposed where the mortgagor is not in a position to make any periodical payments or is in breach of some other provision of the mortgage such as letting the property to a tenant in breach of covenant. In the case of instalment mortgages (as most mortgages of dwelling-houses are), or mortgages which otherwise permit deferred payment,[59] the "sums due" are merely the instalments or payments in arrear, and not the whole capital sum, even if (as is usual) the mortgage makes this payable in full on any default by the mortgagor.[60] In deciding whether the mortgagor is likely to be able to pay the sums due within a reasonable time, the court must take into account not only the arrears[61] but also the sums accruing.[62] The court will have regard to probabilities such as an impending sale of the property,[63] but not to remote possibilities such as hoped-for legacies or winnings from the pools,[64] or the fruits of a counterclaim against the mortgagee.[65]

Where it is clear that the mortgagor is not able to pay the arrears and sums accruing within a reasonable time, the court is often asked to suspend an order for possession pending sale of the property so that the mortgagor rather than the mortgagee can have the conduct of the sale.[66] (It can do so both under its inherent jurisdiction and under the statutory jurisdiction.[67]) While this benefits the mortgagor, in that a sale by a mortgagor in possession is likely to yield

---

[52] *Ropaigealach v. Barclays Bank Plc* [2000] Q.B. 263.
[53] *Royal Trust Co. of Canada v. Markham* [1975] 1 W.L.R. 1416.
[54] Administration of Justice Act 1970, s.36.
[55] Administration of Justice Act 1970, s.36(1).
[56] Administration of Justice Act 1970, s.36(3).
[57] *Abbey National Mortgages Plc v. Bernard* (1996) 71 P. & C.R. 257.
[58] *Cheltenham and Gloucester B.S. v. Norgan* [1997] 1 W.L.R. 343.
[59] See *Bank of Scotland v. Grimes* [1986] Q.B. 1179 (endowment mortgage included); *Habib Bank Ltd v. Tailor* [1982] 1 W.L.R. 1218. See [1984] Conv. 91 (S. Tromans).
[60] Administration of Justice Act 1973, s.8(1); *First Middlesbrough Trading and Mortgage Co. Ltd v. Cunningham* (1974) 28 P. & C.R. 69.
[61] See *Town & Country B.S. v. Julien* (1991) 24 H.L.R. 312 (arrears over £190,000).
[62] Administration of Justice Act 1973, s.8(2).
[63] *Royal Trust Co. of Canada v. Markham* [1975] 1 W.L.R. 1416; and see *Target Home Loans v. Clothier* [1994] 1 All E.R. 439.
[64] See *Hastings & Thanet B.S. v. Goddard* [1970] 1 W.L.R. 1544 at 1548.
[65] *Citibank Trust Ltd v. Ayivor* [1987] 1 W.L.R. 1157.
[66] *Cheltenham & Gloucester Plc v. Booker* (1996) 73 P. & C.R. 412.
[67] Both inherent and statutory; see *Royal Trust Co. of Canada v. Markham* [1975] 1 W.L.R. 1416.

a higher price than a sale by a mortgagee who has repossessed the property, the court has to bear in mind the possibility that the mortgagor may attempt to delay matters.[68] Further, it has no jurisdiction to suspend an order pending sale where it is clear that the sale price will not be enough to discharge the mortgagor's debt.[69]

The statutory jurisdiction also appears to be exercisable where the mortgagor is not in arrears with his payments but is in default under the mortgage in some other way.[70] In these circumstances also the court can impose conditions as to the remedying of the default. However, serious non-financial defaults, such as unauthorised lettings of the mortgaged property, are generally irremediable,[71] in which case an order for possession will be both made and executed.

Once a possession order has actually been executed, the court's discretion under the statutory jurisdiction comes to an end; it cannot thereafter either suspend the order or set it aside and make a new order for possession.[72]

(v) Spouses and "connected persons": Where the spouse of a mortgagor is entitled to occupy a dwelling-house by virtue of the Family Law Act 1996,[73] the Act makes any payment by that spouse in respect of mortgage payments as good as if made by the mortgagor.[74] The spouse, often a deserted wife, can thus avert proceedings for possession by the mortgagee. The spouse is entitled to be made party to any proceedings by the mortgagee if the court sees no special reason against it and is satisfied that the spouse may be expected to make such payments or do such things as might affect the exercise of the court's statutory jurisdiction to grant relief.[75] These rights have now been extended in certain circumstances[76] to "connected persons" such as former spouses, cohabitants, and former cohabitants. If the spouse's statutory right of occupation has actually been registered,[77] the mortgagee must serve notice of any proceedings on the spouse.[78]

(vi) Attornment clauses: At one time many legal mortgages contained an attornment clause, by which the mortgagor attorned, or acknowledged himself to be, a tenant at will or from year to year of the mortgagee, usually at a nominal rent such as a peppercorn or five pence. Formerly this was inserted because a speedy procedure in the High Court was available to enable landlords to recover possession of the demised property from their tenants, and no such procedure was available for mere mortgagees; the attornment clause enabled mort-gagees to sue for possession *qua* landlords. But changes to the rules of court in 1933, 1936 and 1937 made the speedy procedure available to mortgagees as such, so that this reason for the use of attornment clauses has long since gone and they are now not much used. A surviving advantage of such clauses is that covenants by the mortgagor in the mortgage relating to the premises will be enforceable by the mortgagee against an assignee of the

---

[68] *Cheltenham & Gloucester Plc v. Krausz* [1997] 1 W.L.R. 1558.
[69] *ibid.*
[70] This was the majority view in *Western Bank Ltd v. Schindler* [1977] Ch. 1.
[71] *Britannia Building Society v. Earl* [1990] 1 W.L.R. 422.
[72] *National and Provincial B.S. v. Ahmed* [1995] 2 E.G.L.R. 127.
[73] See above, p. 9.
[74] Family Law Act 1996, s.30(3).
[75] *ibid.*, s.55.
[76] *ibid.*, ss.35(13), 36(15).
[77] Above, p. 9.
[78] Family Law Act 1996, s.56.

mortgagor under the rules governing the running of covenants in leases.[79] Where an attornment clause has been used, the tenancy created thereby must in the absence of contrary provision be determined by notice to quit before proceedings for possession are commenced.[80] However, no statutory protection against eviction is conferred on the tenant-mortgagor, for the relevant legislation is concerned only with true tenancies.[81]

(vii) Limitation: If the mortgagee goes into possession of the mortgaged land and remains there for 12 years without either acknowledging the mortgagor's title or receiving any payments from him, the mortgagor's equity of redemption will be extinguished and the mortgagee will acquire title to the land.[82] However, when the Land Registration Act 2002 comes into force, this right will be subject to the new rules which will govern adverse possession to registered land.[83]

(e) To appoint a receiver

(i) History: In order to avoid the dangers of taking possession and yet achieve much the same result, mortgages used to provide for the appointment of a receiver with extensive powers of management of the mortgaged property. At first, the appointment was made by the mortgagor at the request of the mortgagee, but later, mortgagees began to reserve a power for themselves, acting in theory as agents for the mortgagor, to appoint a receiver. In such circumstances the receiver was deemed the agent of the mortgagor, and the mortgagee was not liable to account strictly[84] in the same way as would have been the case if he had taken possession or if the receiver had been his own agent. A satisfactory power to appoint a receiver is conferred by the Law of Property Act 1925.[85] In the case of registered land, it cannot be exercised until the mortgagee has been registered as proprietor of his charge.[86]

(ii) The power: The statutory power to appoint a receiver arises and becomes exercisable in the same circumstances as the power of sale.[87] The mortgagee makes the appointment by writing, and may remove or replace the receiver in the same way. The receiver is deemed to be the agent of the mortgagor, who is solely responsible for his acts unless the mortgage otherwise provides,[88] or unless the mortgagee represents him as being the mortgagee's agent.[89] The corollary of this is that the receiver owes duties to the mortgagor and anyone else with an interest in the equity of redemption which include but are not necessarily confined to a duty of good faith.[90] While his primary duty is to bring about a situation in which interest can be paid and the capital repaid, if he manages the mortgaged property he must do so with due diligence,[91] although this does not actually oblige him to carry on a business previously carried on by the mortgagor.

---

[79] *Regent Oil Co. Ltd v. J.A. Gregory (Hatch End) Ltd* [1966] Ch. 402. For the doctrine, see above, pp. 381 *et seq.* All leases created by attornment clauses are "old leases", no matter when they were actually made.

[80] *Hinckley & Country B.S. v. Henny* [1953] 1 W.L.R. 352.

[81] *Steyning and Littlehampton B.S. v. Wilson* [1951] Ch. 1018; *Alliance B.S. v. Pinwill* [1958] Ch. 788.

[82] Limitation Act 1980, s.16; *Young v. Clarey* [1948] Ch. 191.

[83] Below, pp. 547 *et seq.*

[84] Above, p. 506.

[85] s.101.

[86] *Lever Finance Ltd v. Needleman's Trustees* [1956] Ch. 375.

[87] L.P.A. 1925, ss.101(1), 109(1).

[88] *ibid.*, s.109(2); *White v. Metcalf* [1903] 2 Ch. 567.

[89] *Chatsworth Properties Ltd v. Effiom* [1971] 1 W.L.R. 144.

[90] *Medforth v. Blake* [2000] Ch. 86.

[91] *ibid.*

The receiver has power to recover the income of the property by action, distress or otherwise, and to give valid receipts for it. The income so received by the receiver and any profit obtained by managing the mortgaged property is first used to discharge outgoings, to pay interest due on prior incumbrances, and to pay the receiver's commission and other expenses. Thereafter, it is used to pay the interest due under the mortgage. If the mortgagee so directs in writing, any surplus may be applied towards discharge of the principal money lent on mortgage if that is due; otherwise, the surplus is payable to the person who would have been entitled to it had the receiver not been appointed, normally the mortgagor.[92]

(iii) Limitation: Unlike a mortgagee in possession,[93] a receiver can obtain no title against the mortgagor under the Limitation Act 1980, for he is the mortgagor's agent.

(f) The mortgagee's remedies are cumulative

A mortgagee is not bound to select one of the above remedies and pursue that and no other: subject to his not recovering more than is due to him, he may employ any or all of the remedies to enforce payment.[94] Thus if he sells the property for less than the mortgage debt, he may then sue the mortgagor upon the personal covenant for repayment.[95] This is so even if the sale was by the court and the mortgagee, bidding by leave of the court, has purchased the property.[96]

However, if he wishes to sue after foreclosure, he can do so only on condition that he re-opens the foreclosure[97]; for, despite the foreclosure, he is treating the mortgage as being still alive. Consequently, if by disposing of the property after foreclosure the mortgagee has put it out of his power to re-open the foreclosure, he cannot sue upon the personal covenant for repayment.[98]

2. Equitable mortgagees or chargees

The extent to which the foregoing remedies are exercisable by an equitable mortgagee or chargee is as follows.

(a) To sue for the money due

The position is the same as for a legal mortgage.

(b) To foreclose

An equitable mortgagee may foreclose in the same way as a legal mortgagee, save that the court order will direct the mortgagor to convey the legal title to the mortgagee.[99] An equitable chargee, however, has no right of foreclosure,[1] for a charge effects no conveyance of a legal or equitable interest.

---

[92] L.P.A. 1925, s.109.
[93] *Young v. Clarey* [1948] Ch. 191.
[94] *Palmer v. Hendrie* (1859) 27 Beav. 349 at 351.
[95] *Rudge v. Richens* (1873) L.R. 8 C.P. 358.
[96] *Gordon Grant & Co. Ltd v. Boos* [1926] A.C. 781.
[97] *Perry v. Barker* (1806) 13 Ves. 198; and see above, p. 504.
[98] *Palmer v. Hendrie* (1859) 27 Beav. 349.
[99] *James v. James* (1873) L.R. 16 Eq. 153.
[1] *Re Lloyd* [1903] 1 Ch. 385.

(c) To sell

(i) Unregistered land: For unregistered land, the statutory power of sale[2] applies wherever the mortgage or charge was made by deed; other mortgagees or chargees have no power of sale, though they may apply to the court for an order for sale.[3] Although an equitable mortgagee or chargee by deed has the statutory power of sale, this probably does not enable him to convey the legal estate to the purchaser.[4] To overcome this defect, either or both of two conveyancing devices are employed.

> (1) *Power of attorney.* An irrevocable power of attorney is inserted in the deed empowering the mortgagee or his assigns to convey the legal estate.[5]

> (2) *Declaration of trust.* A clause is inserted in the deed whereby the mortgagor declares that he holds the legal estate on trust for the mortgagee, and empowers the mortgagee to appoint himself or his nominee as trustee in place of the mortgagor. The mortgagee can thus vest the legal estate in himself or the purchaser.

(ii) Registered land: For registered land, only a mortgagee or chargee who has been registered as a chargee has the statutory power of sale[6]; but equitable mortgagees may use the above conveyancing devices to sell the legal estate.[7]

(d) Possible right to take possession

Although it is usually said that an equitable mortgagee, having no legal estate, has no right to possession, on principle there seems no reason why, like a tenant under an equitable lease, he should not be entitled to it[8]; and a provision in the mortgage may give him the right to it. If the land is let, he cannot collect the rent from the tenant, for that is payable to the legal reversioner[9] to whom the tenant is bound under the rules governing leasehold covenants. An equitable chargee, who has not even the benefit of a contract to create a legal mortgage, cannot even claim possession.

(e) To appoint a receiver

As in the case of the power of sale, the statutory power to appoint a receiver[10] exists only if the mortgage or charge was made by deed and, in the case of registered land, only if the mortgage or charge has been registered as a charge.[11] In other cases, a receiver can be obtained only by applying to the court.

Sect. 2. Other rights of a mortgagee

Certain other rights of a mortgagee must now be considered. The position of these and other matters is in general the same for both mortgages and charges, whether legal or equitable, and

---

[2] Above, pp. 504 *et seq.*
[3] L.P.A. 1925, s.91(2).
[4] *Re Hodson and Howes' Contract* (1887) 35 Ch.D. 668; contrast *Re White Rose Cottage* [1965] Ch. 940 at 951.
[5] These powers are now regulated by the Powers of Attorney Act 1971, ss.4(1), 5(3).
[6] L.R.A. 1925, s.34(1); *Lever Finance Ltd v. Needleman's Trustee* [1956] Ch. 375; L.R.A. 2002, s.51.
[7] See, *e.g. Re White Rose Cottage* [1964] Ch. 483 at 495, 496; [1965] Ch. 940 at 955, 956.
[8] See above, p. 343.
[9] *Finck v. Tranter* [1905] 1 K.B. 427.
[10] Above, p. 511.
[11] *Lever Finance Ltd v. Needleman's Trustee* [1956] Ch. 375.

"mortgage" will accordingly be used hereafter to include all such incumbrances unless the contrary is indicated.

1. Right to fixtures

It is a question of construction to determine what property is included in a mortgage. However, subject to any contrary intention, a mortgage includes all fixtures attached to the land either at the date of the mortgage or thereafter; the exceptions as between landlord and tenant do not apply.[12]

2. Right to possession of the documents of title

(a) Unregistered land

A first mortgagee of unregistered land has the same right to the title deeds as if he had the fee simple or an assignment of the lease which has been mortgaged, as the case may be[13]; but under all mortgages made since 1881, the mortgagor is entitled to inspect and make copies of the deeds, despite any contrary agreement.[14] However, first mortgages of registered land made on or after April 1, 1998 trigger first registration of title so in the case of such mortgages the deeds will have to be sent to the Land Registry for the title to be registered and thereafter the mortgagor will have a registered title.

If the land is still unregistered when the mortgage is redeemed by the mortgagor (this can only be the case if the mortgage was created prior to April 1, 1998), the mortgagee must deliver the deeds to him unless he has notice of some subsequent incumbrance, in which case the deeds should be delivered to the incumbrancer next in order of priority of whom the mortgagee has notice. Contrary to the general rule that registration is notice, registration under the Land Charges Act 1972 is not notice for this purpose,[15] although as has been seen a mortgagee is bound to search before he distributes any surplus after a sale.[16] If a mortgage becomes statute-barred by lapse of time,[17] the mortgagee must return the deeds even if no part of the mortgage debt has been or will be paid.[18]

(b) Registered land

In the case of registered land, the land certificate must at present be deposited at the Land Registry for the duration of any registered charge and the mortgagee receives a charge certificate.[19] However, this will not be the case for mortgages created after the Land Registration Act 2002 comes into force; charge certificates will be discontinued and registered charges will be protected on the register in the same way as registrable interests.[20] There will therefore be no reason for the land certificate to remain on deposit at the Land Registry.

---

[12] Above, p. 22.
[13] L.P.A. 1925, ss.85(1), 86(1).
[14] ibid., s.96(1).
[15] ibid., s.96(2), added by L.P.(Am.)A. 1926, Sched.
[16] Above, p. 506.
[17] Below, p. 547.
[18] Lewis v. Plunket [1937] Ch. 306; and see above, p. 499.
[19] L.R.A. 1925, s.65.
[20] This will presumably be dealt with by the new L.R.R.

3. Right to insure against fire at the mortgagor's expense

Under the Law of Property Act 1925[21] a mortgagee or registered chargee may insure the mortgaged property against fire and charge the premiums on the property in the same way as the money lent. This power, which is given only where the mortgage was made by deed, is exercisable as soon as the mortgage is made. The amount of the insurance must not exceed the amount specified in the deed, or, if none, two-thirds of the amount required to restore the property in case of total destruction. But the mortgagee cannot exercise his power if:

(i) the mortgage deed declares that no insurance is required; or

(ii) the mortgagor keeps up an insurance in accordance with the mortgage deed; or

(iii) the mortgage deed is silent as to insurance and the mortgagor keeps up an insurance to the amount authorised by the Act with the mortgagee's consent.

4. Right to consolidate

(a) The right

Consolidation may be described as the right of a person in whom two or more mortgages are vested to refuse to allow one mortgage to be redeemed unless the other or others are also redeemed. In its basic form, the principle is simple. If A has mortgaged both Greenacre and Whiteacre to X, each property being worth £50,000 and each loan being £40,000, it would be unfair, if the value of Greenacre subsequently sinks to £35,000 and the value of Whiteacre doubles, to allow A to redeem Whiteacre and leave Greenacre unredeemed. In such a case, equity permits X to consolidate, and so to oblige A to redeem both mortgages or neither. In seeking redemption, A is asking for the assistance of equity, and equity puts its own price upon its interference, saying that he who seeks equity must do equity.

This simple concept has been elaborated to some extent; different considerations may arise where third parties are concerned, such as by transfer of a mortgage. The rules on the subject may be stated as follows.

(b) Conditions

There can be no consolidation unless the following four conditions are satisfied.

(i) Reservation of right: Unless both the mortgages were made before 1882 or unless at least one of the mortgages reserves the right to consolidate or shows an intention to allow consolidation, section 93 of the Law of Property Act 1925 provides that there is no right to consolidate. It is common practice for mortgages to contain a clause excluding the operation of section 93, so permitting consolidation.

(ii) Redemption dates passed: In the case of both mortgages, the legal dates for redemption must have passed.[22] Consolidation is an equitable doctrine and does not come into play unless and until only equitable rights to redeem are concerned.

(iii) Same mortgagor: Both mortgages must have been made by the same mortgagor.[23] Mortgages made by different mortgagors can never be consolidated, even if both properties

[21] ss.101(1), 108, replacing C.A. 1881, ss.19(1), 23.
[22] *Cummins v. Fletcher* (1880) 14 Ch.D. 699.
[23] *Sharp v. Rickards* [1909] 1 Ch. 109.

later come into the same hands. This is so even if X makes one mortgage and Y, as trustee for X, makes the other, or if A makes one mortgage and Λ and B jointly make the other.[24] But it is immaterial whether or not the mortgages were made to the same mortgagees.

(iv) Simultaneous unions of mortgages and equities: There must have been a time when both the mortgages were vested in one person and simultaneously both the equities of redemption were vested in another person.[25] If this state of affairs exists at the time when redemption is sought, the mortgagee can consolidate, subject to the other conditions being fulfilled. Even if this state of affairs has ceased to exist by the time redemption is sought because the equities of redemption are then owned by different persons, a mortgagee who still holds both mortgages can consolidate.

(c) Illustrations

There is no need to illustrate **(i)** and **(ii)**, but the following examples may be given of the operation of **(iii)** and **(iv)**.

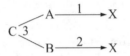

This represents the following steps:

    (1) A mortgages one estate to X.

    (2) B mortgages another estate to X.

    (3) C purchases the equities of redemption of both properties.

There can be no consolidation here, even though Condition **(iv)** is satisfied, for the mortgages were made by different mortgagors.

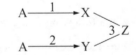

    (1) A mortgages one estate to X.

    (2) A mortgages another estate to Y.

    (3) Z purchases both mortgages.

Here Z can consolidate, provided Conditions **(i)** and **(ii)** are satisfied. Condition **(iii)** is satisfied and so is Condition **(iv)**.

---

[24] *Thorneycroft v. Crockett* (1848) 2 H.L.C. 239.
[25] See *Pledge v. White* [1896] A.C. 187 at 198.

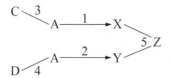

(1) A mortgages one estate to X.

(2) A mortgages another estate to Y.

(3) C purchases the equity on the first estate.

(4) D purchases the equity on the second estate.

(5) Z purchases both mortgages.

There can be no consolidation here, for Condition **(iv)** is not satisfied. It is true that at one stage (after Step (2)) both equities were in one person's hands, and that an another stage (Step (5)) both mortgages were in another person's hands; but at no one moment have both these conditions obtained. The equities separated before the mortgages came together. If C instead of D had purchased the equity on the second estate, Z could have consolidated, even though at the time of C's purchase no right to consolidate had arisen; the purchaser of two or more equities takes subject to the risk of the mortgages coming into the same hand and so permitting consolidation.

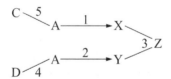

This represents the same position as the previous example, except that Steps (3) and (5) have changed places. As Z has now purchased both mortgages before A parted with either equity, Z may consolidate the mortgages provided Conditions **(i)** and **(ii)** are satisfied. In this event, if C seeks to redeem his mortgage, Z can refuse redemption unless C purchases the mortgage on D's property as well as redeeming his own mortgage.

(d) More than two mortgages

These rules of consolidation apply equally when it is sought to consolidate more than two mortgages. Sometimes it will be found that while Mortgage I can be consolidated with Mortgages II and III, there is no right to consolidate Mortgages II and III with each other, for example if only Mortgage I contains a consolidation clause. Examples containing more than two mortgages are best worked out by taking the mortgages in pairs and applying the rules to each pair in turn.

(e) Extent of doctrine

The nature of the mortgages or the property mortgaged is immaterial. There can be consolidation even if one mortgage is legal and one equitable, or if both are equitable, or if one mortgage is of personalty and the other of realty,[26] or if both are mortgages of personalty. The doctrine has even been applied to two mortgages on the same property.[27] Further, it is immaterial whether the equity of redemption has been conveyed *in toto* or whether it has merely been mortgaged; a mortgagee of an equity of redemption is a purchaser *pro tanto, i.e.* to the extent of his interest. Thus if a mortgagee has a right of consolidation, it is effective against subsequent mortgagees of the property as well as the mortgagor.

(f) Purchasers

The doctrine of consolidation makes it dangerous to buy property which is subject to a mortgage by which the purchaser will be bound after completion without first making careful inquiries. If a right to consolidate has once arisen, a person who subsequently acquires one or both of the equities of redemption is liable to have the mortgages consolidated against him. And even if no right to consolidate has arisen, a person who acquires two equities of redemption is liable to have the mortgages consolidated if one person acquires both of them. But a person who acquires only one equity of redemption at a time when no right to consolidate has arisen normally suffers no risk of consolidation.[28]

5. Right to tack

This is considered below.[29]

Sect. 3. Rights common to both parties

1. Power of Leasing

(a) Leases not binding

The most important right common to both parties is the right of granting a lease of the mortgaged property. Apart from any statutory or contractual provisions, a mortgagor can grant a lease which is binding on himself. Even if his mortgage has taken the form of the grant of a long term of years so that he has no legal right to possession, he will be unable subsequently to deny the validity of that lease and eject the tenant because of the doctrine of estoppel. However, he cannot grant a lease which is binding on the mortgagee[30] nor can a mortgagee grant a lease which will be binding on the mortgagor following redemption.[31]

Thus at common law, once property had been mortgaged, a satisfactory lease could be made only if both mortgagor and mortgagee concurred in granting it, or if the mortgage gave either or both of the parties power to grant binding leases. However, statute has materially altered this position; the provisions discussed below apply to all mortgages made after 1881 unless the parties have expressed a contrary intention, either in the mortgage itself or in some other written document.[32] (It is in fact common for mortgages of residential property to preclude the mortgagor from exercising any power to grant leases or tenancies; a lease granted by the mortgagor in breach of such a provision in the mortgage deed will not bind

---

[26] *Tassell v. Smith* (1858) 2 De G. & J. 713.
[27] *Re Salmon* [1903] 1 K.B. 147; *sed quaere.*
[28] *Harter v. Coleman* (1882) 19 Ch.D. 630.
[29] Below, pp. 542 *et seq.*
[30] *Rogers v. Humphreys* (1835) 4 A. & E. 299 at 313.
[31] See *Chapman v. Smith* [1907] 2 Ch. 97 at 102.
[32] L.P.A. 1925, s.99, replacing C.A. 1881, s.18.

the mortgagee,[33] unless he subsequently adopts the tenancy, as by accepting rent from the tenant.[34])

(b) Power to lease

A power to grant leases which will be binding on both mortgagor and mortgagee is exercisable by the mortgagee, if he is in possession or has appointed a receiver who is still acting; otherwise, by the mortgagor if he is in possession.

(c) Term of lease

A lease may be granted for not more than 50 years for agricultural or occupation purposes or 999 years for building where the mortgage in question was granted after 1925.[35]

(d) Conditions of lease

To fall within the statutory powers, any lease granted must comply with the following conditions:

    (i) it must be limited to take effect in possession not later than 12 months after its date;

    (ii) it must reserve the best rent reasonably obtainable, and with certain qualifications no lump sum payment may be taken;

    (iii) it must contain a covenant by the lessee for payment of rent and a condition of re-entry on the rent not being paid for a specified period not exceeding 30 days; and

    (iv) a counterpart of the lease must be executed by the lessee and delivered to the lessor and a counterpart of any lease granted by the mortgagor must be delivered within one month to the mortgagee.[36]

These conditions do not preclude the grant of oral leases in exercise of the statutory power[37]; such leases need not comply with the last two conditions.[38] Neither the statutory power of leasing nor any provision in the mortgage excluding these powers (as is common in the case of a mortgagor of residential property) deprives either party of his common law right to grant a lease but that lease will not bind the other unless adopted by him.[39] Further, the parties may extend the statutory powers by an agreement in writing, whether or not that agreement is contained in the mortgage.[40]

2. Power of accepting surrenders of leases

In the case of a mortgage made after 1911, if the parties have not expressed a contrary intention, either in the mortgage or otherwise in writing, statute[41] enables a surrender of any

---

[33] *Dudley & District Benefit B.S. v. Emerson* [1949] Ch. 707; *Britannia B.S. v. Earl* [1990] 1 W.L.R. 422.
[34] See *Stroud B.S. v. Delamont* [1960] 1 W.L.R. 431.
[35] In the case of mortgages granted before 1926, the periods were 21 years and 99 years respectively.
[36] See *Public Trustee v. Lawrence* [1912] 1 Ch. 789.
[37] L.P.A. 1925, s.99(17). For oral leases, see above, p. 342.
[38] *Rhodes v. Dalby* [1971] 1 W.L.R. 1325 at 1331, 1332.
[39] *Rust v. Goodale* [1957] Ch. 33; contrast *Taylor v. Ellis* [1960] Ch. 368.
[40] L.P.A. 1925, s.99(14).
[41] *ibid.*, s.100, replacing C.A. 1911, s.3.

lease or tenancy to be effected, binding the parties to the mortgage, on the following terms.

(a) Power to accept

The surrender may be accepted by the mortgagee, if he is in possession or has appointed a receiver who is still acting; otherwise, by the mortgagor if he is in possession.

(b) Conditions of surrender

For the surrender to be valid:

    (i) an authorised lease of the property must be granted to take effect in possession within one month of the surrender;

    (ii) the term of the new lease must not be shorter than the unexpired residue of the surrendered lease; and

    (iii) the rent reserved by the new lease must not be less than the rent reserved by the surrendered lease.

The statutory power of accepting a surrender is thus exercisable only for the purpose of replacing one lease by another,[42] but the power may be extended by an agreement in writing, whether or not that agreement is contained in the mortgage.

Sect. 4. The right of the mortgagor or chargor to redeem

1. Protection of the mortgagor

One aspect of equity's protection of the mortgagor's equity of redemption is to be found in the maxim "once a mortgage, always a mortgage". This is applied in two ways.

(a) The test of a mortgage is substance, not form

If a transaction is in substance a mortgage, equity will treat it as such, even if it is dressed up in some other guise, as by the documents being cast in the form of an absolute conveyance.[43] Thus, if a mortgage is expressed in the form of a conveyance with an option for the mortgagor to repurchase the property in a year's time, the mortgagor is entitled to redeem it even after the year has expired.[44]

(b) No clogs on the equity

There must be no clog or fetter on the equity of redemption. This means not only that the mortgagor cannot be prevented from eventually redeeming his property, but also that he cannot be prevented from redeeming it free from any conditions or stipulations in the mortgage.

---

[42] See *Barclays Bank Ltd v. Stasek* [1957] Ch. 28.
[43] *Barnhart v. Greenshields* (1853) 9 Moo.P.C. 18.
[44] *Waters v. Mynn* (1850) 15 L.T.(o.s.) 157; and see *Grangeside Properties Ltd v. Collingwoods Securities Ltd* [1964] 1 W.L.R. 139.

(i) No irredeemability: It is impossible to provide that a mortgage shall be totally irredeemable[45] or that the right of redemption shall be confined to certain persons or to a limited period.[46] A provision in a mortgage that the property shall become the mortgagee's absolutely when some specified event occurs is void.[47] In all such cases, the owner of the equity of redemption may redeem as if there had been no such restriction. But once the mortgage has been made, equity will not intervene if the mortgagor, by a separate and independent transaction, gives the mortgagee an option of purchasing the property and thus of depriving the mortgagor of his equity of redemption.[48] While the mortgagor is in the defenceless position of seeking a loan, or arranging for a transfer of the mortgage,[49] equity will protect him; but once he has obtained the loan or secured the transfer, this protection is not needed.

A provision postponing the date of redemption until some future period longer than the customary six months, such as for 40 years, is valid, provided the mortgage as a whole is not so oppressive and unconscionable that equity would not enforce it, and provided it does not make the equitable right to redeem illusory.[50] In one case, a lease for 20 years was mortgaged on conditions which prevented its redemption until six weeks before the end of the term. Such a provision rendered the equitable right to redeem illusory and so was held void.[51] Generally, however, the court will not interfere with a bargain made between two parties on an equal footing, even if this does postpone redemption for a considerable period.

Limited companies are not protected by this rule, for by statute a debenture may be made wholly or partly irredeemable, and even an ordinary mortgage by a company is a debenture.[52]

(ii) Redemption free from conditions in the mortgage: The mortgagor cannot be prevented from redeeming exactly what he mortgaged, *i.e.* the property free from all conditions or stipulations in the mortgage. The essence of a mortgage is a loan of money in return for security. Sometimes terms are inserted in a mortgage which give the mortgagee some other advantage in addition to his security. If this advantage is obtained by fraud or oppression, it will be set aside, but otherwise there is no objection to an advantage which ceases whenever the mortgage is redeemed, such as a provision making the mortgaged property, a public house, a "tied" house until redemption.[53] The general enforceability of advantages which end on redemption represents an advance on the attitude which the courts had at one time adopted, rendering all collateral advantages for the mortgagee void on the basis that they were a disguised form of interest contravening the usury laws.[54] After the last of the statutes dealing with usury was repealed in 1854, the courts gradually became more liberal and it is now settled that in certain cases a collateral advantage may remain effective even after redemption.

---

[45] *Re Wells* [1933] Ch. 29 at 52.
[46] *Salt v. Marquess of Northampton* [1892] A.C. 1.
[47] *Toomes v. Conset* (1745) 3 Atk. 261.
[48] *Reeve v. Lisle* [1902] A.C. 461 (option 12 days after mortgage, unlike *Samuel v. Jarrah Timber and Wood Paving Corporation Ltd* [1904] A.C. 323, where the mortgage deed contained the option).
[49] *Lewis v. Frank Love Ltd* [1961] 1 W.L.R. 261.
[50] *Knightsbridge Estates Trust Ltd v. Byrne* [1939] Ch. 441 (affirmed on other grounds: [1940] A.C. 613). Both parties were bound to allow the full 40-year period.
[51] *Fairclough v. Swan Brewery Co. Ltd* [1912] A.C. 565. Contrast *Santley v. Wilde* [1899] 2 Ch. 474, which seems unsound: see *Noakes & Co. Ltd v. Rice* [1902] A.C. 24 at 31, 34.
[52] Companies Act 1985, s.193; *Knightsbridge Estates Trust Ltd v. Byrne* [1940] A.C. 613.
[53] *Biggs v. Hoddinott* [1898] 2 Ch. 307; *Noakes & Co. Ltd v. Rice* [1902] A.C. 24.
[54] See *Jennings v. Ward* (1705) 2 Vern. 520 at 521; *Noakes & Co. Ltd v. Rice* [1902] A.C. 24 at 33.

The chief difficulty in stating the present position lies in trying to reconcile the clog held void in *Bradley v. Carritt*[55] with the collateral advantage held valid in *Kreglinger v. New Patagonia Meat and Cold Storage Co. Ltd.*[56] In *Bradley's* case the substance of the transaction was a mortgage of shares in which the mortgagor bound himself to endeavour to induce the company to employ the mortgagee as broker, and if the company did not, to pay the mortgagee an amount equivalent to the broker's fees. In *Kreglinger's* case the substance of the transaction was a loan of money to a meat company in return for an option for five years on any sheepskins which the company had for sale. The differing results in these cases can be explained in two ways. In *Bradley's* case the shares returned were fettered by the practical restriction that they could not be sold without retaining so much of the voting rights attached to them as allowed the mortgagor to continue to control the appointment, whereas in *Kreglinger's* case the property was returned unfettered. Alternatively it can be said that in *Bradley's* case the agreement fettering the mortgagor was a mere clause put in a mortgage, and so void, the basis of the agreement being a mortgage and nothing else. In *Kreglinger's* case, on the other hand, the transaction was substantially the grant of an option in return for a loan of money, with the result that the option was not merely a part of the mortgage but a separate and independent transaction and so valid.[57] The courts are reluctant to allow the doctrine which forbids clogs on the equity of redemption to upset a freely negotiated commercial contract.[58]

(iii) Unconscionable terms: The court has a general jurisdiction to grant relief against terms in a mortgage which are oppressive or unconscionable.[59] Thus where a property company sold one of its houses to the tenant, lending him £2,900 on a mortgage of the house which required repayment of £4,553 over six years, the transaction was held to be unconscionable, and the tenant was held to be entitled to redeem the mortgage on paying £2,900 with interest of seven per cent as fixed by the court.[60] Nor do the provisions commonly found entitling the mortgagee to vary the rate of interest from time to time give him a completely unfettered power to do so. There is an implied term that he cannot do so dishonestly, for an improper purpose, capriciously, arbitrarily or in a way that no reasonable mortgagee, acting reasonably, would do.[61] However, raising interest rates by more than standard market rates had risen because of commercial considerations in order to overcome financial difficulties did not amount to a breach of that implied term.[62] Further, if provisions in a mortgage, though unreasonable, are not initially unconscionable, subsequent events will not invalidate them. Thus, where a commercial mortgage for ten years was indexed to the Swiss franc, and there was then an unforeseen fall in the value of the pound by two-thirds, the court refused to intervene.[63]

[55] [1903] A.C. 253.
[56] [1914] A.C. 25.
[57] See *Re Petrol Filling Station, Vauxhall Bridge Road, London* (1968) 20 P. & C.R. 1.
[58] *Kreglinger's Case* [1914] A.C. 25 at 46; *Samuel v. Jarrah Timber and Wood Paving Corporation Ltd* [1904] A.C. 323 at 327.
[59] *Knightsbridge Estates Trust Ltd v. Byrne* [1939] Ch. 441 at 457; in H.L., [1940] A.C. 613.
[60] *Cityland and Property (Holdings) Ltd v. Dabrah* [1968] Ch. 166, as explained in *Multiservice Bookbinding Ltd v. Marden* [1979] Ch. 84 at 109, 110.
[61] *Paragon Finance v. Nash* [2002] 1 W.L.R. 685.
[62] *ibid.*
[63] *Multiservice Bookbinding Ltd v. Marden* [1979] Ch. 84.

(iv) Regulated mortgages: Mortgages under which the credit provided does not exceed £25,000[64] are regulated by the elaborate provisions of the Consumer Credit Act 1974 unless they fall within the list of "exempt agreements", which includes mortgages to building societies and local authorities.[65] Most commercial transactions and ordinary mortgages for house purchase are outside these provisions, which are aimed at improvident second mortgages by house owners for personal expenditure. There are detailed provisions requiring a mortgage within the Act to be in a prescribed form, signed by both parties, which makes the mortgagor aware of his rights and duties, and the protection given by the Act; and the mortgagor must be sent a copy of the proposed mortgage at least seven days before he is sent a copy for signature, thus giving him a "consideration period".[66] The mortgagor may repay the sums due at any time, despite any agreement to the contrary[67]; and mortgages within the Act are enforceable only on an order of the court.[68]

The Act also gives the court power to re-open extortionate credit bargains with individuals (but not companies), irrespective of the amount involved.[69] The court may set aside the bargain in whole or in part or may otherwise alter the terms of the agreement.[70] A credit bargain will be extortionate if it requires payments which are "grossly exorbitant" or if it "otherwise grossly contravenes ordinary principles of fair dealing".[71] However, whether a credit bargain is extortionate has to be determined in the light of the facts when it is entered into; subsequent rises in interest rates pursuant to a power given to the mortgagee to vary them cannot make a credit bargain extortionate.[72]

(v) Restraint of trade: A provision in a mortgage which is not oppressive, unconscionable or extortionate nor a clog on the equity of redemption may nevertheless be void on other grounds. Thus it may be invalid under the ordinary law of contract as being in unreasonable restraint of trade.[73]

2. Who can redeem?

Redemption is usually sought by the mortgagor; but the right to redeem is not confined to him and may be exercised by any person interested in the equity of redemption.[74] Thus the right to redeem extends to assignees of the equity of redemption, subsequent mortgagees, and even a lessee under a lease granted by the mortgagor but not binding on the mortgagee.[75]

3. Effect of redemption

Where redemption is effected by the only person interested in the equity of redemption, and the mortgage redeemed is the only incumbrance on the property, the effect of redemption is to discharge the mortgage and leave the property free from incumbrances. But if there are several mortgages on the property, the effect of redemption will normally be that the person

---

[64] Consumer Credit Act 1974, ss.8(2), 189(1); S.I. 1983 No. 1878.
[65] Consumer Credit Act 1974, s.16.
[66] *ibid.*, ss.58–61.
[67] *ibid.*, ss.94, 173.
[68] *ibid.*, ss.126, 173(3).
[69] *ibid.*, ss.137–139, 189(1).
[70] *ibid.*, s.139.
[71] *ibid.*, s.138(1); see *A Ketley Ltd v. Scott* [1980] C.C.L.R. 37; *Woodstead Finance Ltd v. Petrou, The Times,* January 23, 1986.
[72] *Paragon Finance Plc v. Nash* [2002] 1 W.L.R. 685.
[73] *Esso Petroleum Co. Ltd v. Harper's Garage (Stourport) Ltd* [1968] A.C. 269.
[74] *Pearce v. Morris* (1869) 5 Ch.App. 227 at 229.
[75] *Tarn v. Turner* (1888) 39 Ch.D. 456.

paying the money takes a transfer of the mortgage, as where a second mortgagee redeems the first mortgage. If several incumbrancers seek to redeem a mortgage, the first in order of priority has the best claim.[76] However, if the mortgagor redeems a mortgage which has priority over one or more subsequent mortgages, the redemption discharges the mortgage and the mortgagor cannot claim to have it kept alive to the prejudice of the subsequent mortgagees.[77] For his mortgage to them included all the rights he had, including those against the prior mortgagee. But no such rule binds his successors in title.[78]

An incumbrancer who is entitled to redeem a mortgage may usually, instead of redeeming, insist upon the mortgagee transferring the mortgage to the incumbrancer's nominee.[79]

4. Terms of redemption

A mortgage may be redeemed either in court or out of court; the latter is the more usual. If a mortgagee unreasonably refuses to accept a proper tender of the money due and so makes an action for redemption necessary, he may be penalised in costs.[80]

The mortgagor may redeem on the legal date for redemption without giving notice of his intention to do so. After that date, when he is forced to rely upon his equitable right to redeem, it is a rule of practice that he must either give the mortgagee reasonable notice of his intention to redeem (six months usually sufficing), or else pay him six months' interest in lieu thereof.[81] It is only fair that the mortgagee should have a reasonable opportunity of finding another investment for his money. But the mortgagee is not entitled to any notice or interest in lieu thereof:

(i) if he has taken steps to enforce his security, as by taking possession, or commencing foreclosure proceedings, or giving the mortgagor notice to repay the loan so as to entitle the mortgagee to sell on default being made[82]; or

(ii) if the loan is merely of a temporary nature, as is usually the case in an equitable mortgage by deposit of documents of title.[83]

If the mortgagor gives six months' notice and fails to pay on the proper day, he must usually give a further six months' notice or pay six months' interest in lieu thereof,[84] unless he can give a reasonable explanation of his failure to pay, in which case it suffices to give reasonable notice, such as three months.[85]

Even if the mortgage makes no provision for interest, the mortgagor must pay it at a rate which the court will, if necessary, fix.[86]

---

[76] *Teevan v. Smith* (1882) 20 Ch.D. 724 at 730.
[77] *Otter v. Lord Vaux* (1856) 6 De G.M. & G. 638, recognised by L.P.A. 1925, s.115(3); *Parkash v. Irani Finance Ltd* [1970] Ch. 101.
[78] *Whiteley v. Delaney* [1914] A.C. 132.
[79] L.P.A. 1925, s.95.
[80] *Graham v. Seal* (1918) 88 L.J.Ch. 31.
[81] *Johnson v. Evans* (1889) 61 L.T. 18. The mortgage deed may provide to the contrary.
[82] See *Bovill v. Endle* [1896] 1 Ch. 648.
[83] *Fitzgerald's Trustee v. Mellersh* [1892] 1 Ch. 385.
[84] *Re Moss* (1886) L.R. 31 Ch.D. 90 at 94.
[85] *Cromwell Property Investment Co. Ltd v. Western* [1934] Ch. 322.
[86] See *Cityland and Property (Holdings) Ltd v. Dabrah* [1968] Ch. 166.

5. "Redeem up, foreclose down"

The maxim "redeem up, foreclose down" applies where there are several incumbrancers and one of them seeks by action to redeem a superior mortgage. The effect is best shown by an example. X has mortgaged his property successively to A, B, C, D, and E, the mortgages ranking in that order. X thus ranks last, for example in claiming any surplus if the property is sold. Suppose that D wishes to redeem B's mortgage and, owing to the complexity of the accounts or some other circumstance, an action for redemption is commenced. Before B's mortgage can be redeemed, the exact amount due to him must be settled by the court. This amount, however, does not affect only B and D, for C, E and X are all concerned with the amount which has priority to their interests; thus if the property were to be sold, C, E and X would all wish to know whether what B was entitled to was, say, £60,000 or £70,000, for upon that figure might depend their chances of receiving anything from the proceeds of sale. Consequently, the court will insist upon their being made parties to D's action for redemption so that they can be represented in the taking of the accounts between B and D, and thus be bound by the final result.

However, it would be unfair to give C, E and X the trouble and expense of taking part in the action merely to watch accounts being taken,[87] with the risk of a similar event taking place in the future, and so the court insists that the rights of all parties concerned in the action shall be settled once and for all. A is not concerned: it is immaterial to him what is due to B, for A's mortgage has priority to B's.[88] But all the other parties are concerned, and the order of the court will be that D shall redeem not only B's mortgage, but also C's mortgage, for both those mortgages have priority to D's. Further, the rights of E and X must be foreclosed: that is, each of them will have the opportunity of saving his rights by paying off the prior mortgages concerned in the action, but if he fails to do so, he will be foreclosed. Thus if E and X fail to redeem and are foreclosed, the final result will be that D, at the price of redeeming B and C, now holds the equity of redemption subject only to the first mortgage in favour of A.

The principle may be stated thus: a mortgagee who seeks to redeem a prior mortgage by action must not only redeem any mortgages standing between him and that prior mortgage,[89] but must also foreclose all subsequent mortgagees and the rights of the mortgagor[90]; in short, "redeem up, foreclose down".

It should be noted that this rule does not apply to redemptions out of court,[91] and that there is no rule "foreclose down, redeem up"; a mortgagee who forecloses is under no obligation to redeem any prior mortgages,[92] although he must foreclose all subsequent mortgagees as well as the rights of the mortgagor.[93] In other words, for foreclosure the rule is simply "foreclose down": a mortgagee cannot foreclose a subsequent mortgagee or the rights of the mortgagor unless he forecloses everyone beneath him.

6. Termination of equity of redemption

An equity of redemption may be extinguished against the wishes of the mortgagor:

[87] *Ramsbottom v. Wallis* (1835) 5 L.J.Ch. 92.
[88] *Brisco v. Kenrick* (1832) 1 L.J.Ch. 11.
[89] *Teevan v. Smith* (1882) 20 Ch.D. 724 at 729.
[90] *Farmer v. Curtis* (1829) 2 Sim. 466.
[91] See *Smith v. Green* (1844) 1 Coll.C.C. 555.
[92] *Richards v. Cooper* (1842) 5 Beav. 304.
[93] *Anderson v. Stather* (1845) 2 Coll.C.C. 209.

    (i) by foreclosure[94];

    (ii) by sale[95]; or

    (iii) by lapse of time.[96]

In addition, the mortgagor may himself extinguish his equity of redemption by releasing it to the mortgagee, or by redeeming.

Sect. 5. The other rights of the mortgagor or chargor

The mortgagor has various other rights, including the right to have the property sold by the court, the right to inspect the title deeds where the land in question is unregistered, the right to compel a transfer of the mortgage[97] and the right to bring actions. As to the right to bring actions, even if the mortgage has taken the form of the grant of a long term of years so that the mortgagor has no legal right to possession but merely the freehold reversion, provided that the mortgagee has not given notice of his intention to take possession or enter into receipt of the rents and profits, by statute[98] the mortgagor in possession may sue in his own name for possession or for the rents and profits. He may bring an action to prevent, or recover damages for, any trespass or other wrong, and he may enforce all covenants and conditions in any leases or tenancies of the property.

PART 4—TRANSFER OF RIGHTS

Sect. 1. Death of mortgagor

On the death of a person who holds realty or personalty subject to a mortgage or charge, the person who is entitled under that person's will or intestacy will take the property subject to the mortgage or charge unless the deceased has shown a contrary intention[99] in any document, whether or not a will.[1] This rule was finally established by the Administration of Estates Act 1925.[2] However, it does not apply to a person who takes not as a legatee or devisee but, for instance as a purchaser under an option given to him by the will.[3]

These provisions do not affect any rights the mortgagee may have against the estate of the mortgagor. They merely ensure that as between the person taking the mortgaged property and the other beneficiaries, the burden of the mortgage should fall upon the former, in the absence of any contrary intention.

---

[94] Above, pp. 502 *et seq.*
[95] Above, pp. 504 *et seq.*
[96] Below, p. 555.
[97] L.P.A. 1925, ss.91, 95, 96.
[98] L.P.A. 1925, ss.98, 141, replacing earlier legislation.
[99] See *Re Wakefield* [1943] 2 All E.R. 29; *Re Neeld* [1962] Ch. 643.
[1] A.E.A. 1925, s.35.
[2] s.35.
[3] *Re Fison's W.T.* [1950] Ch. 394.

Sect. 2. Death of mortgagee

1. Death of sole mortgagee

Under the Administration of Estates Act 1925[4] the mortgagee's right to the money lent and his interest in the mortgaged property both pass to his personal representatives.

2. Death of one of several mortgagees

(a) At law

Where two or more persons lent money on mortgage of freeholds or leaseholds, the legal estate was usually conveyed to them as joint tenants. On the death of one, his interest passed to the others by virtue of the *jus accrescendi*, and the survivors could reconvey the legal estate to the mortgagor when he redeemed.

(b) In equity

In equity, however, there is a presumption of a tenancy in common where two or more together lend money on mortgage.[5] Accordingly, in the absence of any provision to the contrary, when one of the mortgagees died his share passed to his personal representatives, and if the mortgagor redeemed they would have to join in the transaction. If the mortgagees were trustees lending trust money, the disclosure of this fact would be sufficient to rebut the presumption, for trustees are always joint tenants[6]; but this would have the disadvantage of bringing the trusts on to the title.[7]

(c) Joint account clause

The practice accordingly grew up of inserting a "joint account clause" in mortgages where two or more persons lent money. This clause rebutted the presumption of a tenancy in common so far as the mortgagor was concerned and made it safe for him to pay his money to the surviving mortgagees. Since 1881 such a clause has not actually been necessary, for statute[8] has provided that as between the mortgagor and the mortgagees, the mortgagees are deemed to have advanced the money on a joint account unless a contrary intention appears. The result is that the survivor or survivors can give a complete discharge for all moneys due, notwithstanding any notice of severance which the mortgagor may have. This, however, is mere conveyancing machinery; it does not affect the position of the mortgagees *inter se*, and if they are beneficially entitled and not trustees, the survivors must account to the personal representatives of the deceased mortgagee for his share.[9] Although a joint account clause in a mortgage today is thus strictly unnecessary, it is often inserted *ex abundante cautela*.

Sect. 3. Transfer of equity of redemption *inter vivos*

A mortgagor may at any time without the mortgagee's consent make a conveyance of his property subject to the mortgage, and the mortgagee cannot prevent an order for sale being

---

[4] A.E.A. 1925, ss.1(1), 3(1).
[5] Above, p. 314.
[6] Above, p. 304.
[7] See, *e.g. Re Blaiberg and Abrahams* [1899] 2 Ch. 340.
[8] C.A. 1881, s.61, replaced by L.P.A. 1925, s.111.
[9] See *Re Jackson* (1887) 34 Ch.D. 732.

made under the court's discretionary power[10] merely because the price is less than the sums due under the mortgage.[11] Notwithstanding any such conveyance, the mortgagor remains personally liable on the covenant to pay the money.[12] He therefore usually takes an express covenant for indemnity from the transferee, although such an obligation is implied.[13]

A mortgagor who wishes to sell free from the mortgage may do so:

(i) if he redeems; or

(ii) if the mortgagee consents (as he may well do if the security is adequate or if some other property is substituted for the property in question); or

(iii) if the mortgagor takes advantage of the statutory provision enabling the court to declare property free from an incumbrance upon sufficient money being paid into court.[14]

An assignee of the equity of redemption in general steps into the shoes of the mortgagor; but he does not merely by the assignment become personally liable to the mortgagee to pay the mortgage debt.[15]

Sect. 4. Transfer of mortgages *inter vivos*

1. In general

A mortgagee may transfer his mortgage at any time without the concurrence of the mortgagor. However, for various reasons it is advisable for the mortgagor's concurrence to be obtained, such as in order to obtain his admission of the state of accounts showing the amount still due under the mortgage.[16]

Once the transfer has been made, the transferee should give notice of it to the mortgagor, unless the mortgagor has notice already, such as because he was a party to the transfer. If the mortgagor has no actual or constructive notice, the transferee cannot complain if the mortgagor pays to the transferor money due under the mortgage.[17]

2. Sub-mortgages

A sub-mortgage is a mortgage of a mortgage. A mortgagee may, instead of transferring his mortgage, borrow money upon the security of it. A well-secured debt can itself be good security for a loan to the creditor. Thus if X has lent £20,000 upon a mortgage made by B, and X then wishes to raise a temporary loan of £2,000 himself, it would clearly be inadvisable for X to transfer the mortgage to Y for £20,000 or to call in the whole of his loan. Consequently, X would raise the money by mortgaging his mortgage, *i.e.* by making a sub-mortgage.

---

[10] Under L.P.A. 1925, s.91(2); above, p. 502.
[11] *Palk v. Mortgage Services Funding Plc* [1993] Ch. 330.
[12] *Kinnaird v. Trollope* (1888) 39 Ch.D. 636.
[13] *Bridgman v. Daw* (1891) 40 W.R. 253.
[14] L.P.A. 1925, s.50, replacing C.A. 1881, s.5(1).
[15] *Re Errington* [1894] 1 Q.B. 11.
[16] See *Turner v. Smith* [1901] 1 Ch. 213.
[17] *Dixon v. Winch* [1900] 1 Ch. 736 at 742.

Before 1926, a sub-mortgage was effected by a transfer of the mortgage subject to a proviso for redemption. After 1925, this form is still available if the mortgage is equitable or is a legal charge. But where it has been created by the grant of a term of years, a legal sub-mortgage can be made only by the grant of a sub-lease or by a legal charge.[18] In general, the sub-mortgagee takes over the mortgagee's rights of enforcing payment under the original mortgage; thus he may sell the property. Alternatively, he may exercise his remedies against the mortgage itself, as by selling it. When the Land Registration Act 2002 comes into force, registered charges will not be able to be the subject of sub-mortgages.[19] However, the proprietor of a registered charge will be able to charge his registered charge by way of sub-charge[20] and the holder of any sub-charge and of any sub-sub-charge will have the same powers as the holder of the registered charge and any superior sub-chargee.[21]

Sect. 5. Discharge of mortgages

Since 1925, in the case of any mortgage of unregistered land, a receipt indorsed on or annexed to the mortgage deed, signed[22] by the mortgagee and stating the name of the person paying the money, normally discharges the mortgage.[23] Where the mortgage has been created by the grant of a term of years absolute, that term will either be surrendered or reconveyed. Where the mortgage has been created by charge, the charge will simply be cancelled. But if the receipt shows that the person paying the money was not entitled to the immediate equity of redemption and makes no provision to the contrary, that receipt operates as a transfer of the mortgage to him.[24] Building society mortgages may still be discharged by a special form of receipt, indorsed on the mortgage, which does not state who paid the money and cannot operate as a transfer of the mortgage.[25] There are certain advantages in such a receipt.[26]

Quite apart from these provisions, once a mortgage created by the grant of a term of years absolute has been redeemed, the term becomes a satisfied term and ceases forthwith.[27] But although, when coupled with this provision, it might be thought that an ordinary receipt (*i.e.* one not complying with the conditions relating to indorsed receipts) would operate as a sufficient discharge, conveyancers do not in practice rely upon such a receipt, for it is only prima facie proof of payment.

In the case of registered land, a registered charge is at present discharged by delivering the charge certificate to the Land Registry with a duly executed Form DS1, which constitutes the mortgagee's receipt for the sum due. In the case of a building society, an indorsed certificate can be used instead.[28] The Registrar then deletes the charge from the register. Charge certificates will be discontinued when the Land Registration Act 2002 comes into force; the

---

[18] L.P.A. 1925, s.86(1), (3).
[19] L.R.A. 2002, s.23(2)(a), (3).
[20] *ibid.*, s.23(2)(b).
[21] *ibid.*, s.53.
[22] See *Simpson v. Geoghegan* [1934] W.N. 232.
[23] L.P.A. 1925, s.115(1).
[24] *ibid.*, s.115(2). See *Cumberland Court (Brighton) Ltd v. Taylor* [1964] Ch. 29.
[25] Building Societies Act 1986, Sched. 4, para. 2.
[26] Wurtzburg & Mills, *Building Society Law*, paras 6.44–6.46.
[27] L.P.A. 1925, ss.5, 116; above, p. 494.
[28] Ruoff & Roper, para. 24–19; Wurtzburg & Mills, *Building Society Law*, para. 6.50. For the certificate, see above.

new Land Registration Rules will presumably provide how registered charges will be discharged thereafter.

PART 5—PRIORITY OF MORTGAGES

The expression "priority of mortgages" has traditionally referred to the situation where there is more than one mortgage on the same property. In such circumstances, the proceeds of sale of the property may not be sufficient to satisfy all the mortgages, in which case it will be necessary to determine their priority. The complex rules which have been evolved for determining priorities of mortgages are mainly applications of the rules relating to competing legal and equitable interests. These rules, which differ depending on whether the land in question is registered or unregistered, are subject to any agreement between the mortgagees, for they can alter them as they wish, without the mortgagor's consent, unless the mortgages otherwise provide.[29] In addition to these rules, there is also a process known as "tacking" which alters the priorities settled under the general rules. However, questions of priority also arise as between mortgagees and the holders of beneficial interests in the land in question. These rules, which do not depend on whether the land is registered or unregistered, will be considered first.

Sect. 1. Priorities as between mortgagees and beneficial co-owners

A mortgagee derives title through his mortgagor. Consequently, he will virtually always be bound by any commercial interests in or over the land in question, such as leases, easements and restrictive covenants. Only where any interest has not been protected in the appropriate way will the mortgagee, as the purchaser for value of an interest in the land, have any possibility of being in a better position than his mortgagor. However, the position as between mortgagees and the holders of family interests in the land is more complex. When difficulties arise, they almost invariably arise as between a mortgagee and a beneficial co-owner of the land, usually (but not always[30]) in respect of a house occupied by a married couple or by unmarried partners.

1. Overreaching

The intention of the 1925 property legislation was that on any mortgage the interests of the beneficial co-owners would be overreached into the proceeds of the mortgage advance. This will indeed happen when there is a disposition by two trustees or a trust corporation whether the beneficiaries wish their interests to be overreached or not.[31] This is so even as to any of the beneficiaries who are in "actual occupation" of registered land. (Their interests, having been overreached, are no longer "subsisting" in the land, and so cannot override registration of the title of the purchaser.[32]) Where overreaching occurs, the interest of the mortgagee will enjoy priority over the interests of all the beneficial co-owners.

[29] *Cheah Theam Swee v. Equiticorp Finance Group Ltd* [1992] 1 A.C. 472.
[30] See, *e.g. Coldunell Ltd v. Gallon* [1986] Q.B. 1184 (parents and son); *Bank of Baroda v. Shah* [1988] 3 All E.R. 24 (brother and sister).
[31] See *City of London B.S. v. Flegg* [1988] A.C. 54.
[32] *ibid.*, above, pp. 123, 124.

2. No overreaching

(a) Effect

Where a mortgage is granted by a sole trustee of land who is not a trust corporation, the interests of beneficial co-owners will not be overreached but the 1925 property legislation did not state what will happen to them. However, the courts have decided that in these circumstances the overreachable but unoverreached interests of the beneficial co-owners are treated as if they were commercial interests rather than family interests.[33] Consequently, those interests will be destroyed as against a mortgagee of unregistered land who has no notice of them and will be destroyed as against a mortgagee of registered land unless they have been protected on the register or override the registration of the mortgagee's charge.

(b) Possibility

However, it is only likely that there will be a sole trustee of land where a resulting or constructive trust has arisen as a result of contributions to the purchase price or common intention coupled with some act of detrimental reliance.[34] Beneficiaries of resulting and constructive trusts of this type will generally be in occupation of the land. If this is the case, it is only in the most exceptional circumstances (such as where the trustee has removed all signs of a beneficiary's existence) that the mortgagee will not be bound by his interest; otherwise the mortgagee will in the case of unregistered land have constructive notice of that interest[35] and in the case of registered land that interest will override the registration of the mortgagee's charge.[36]

(c) Incidence

However, a mortgage which finances the purchase of the property in question will automatically take priority over the interest of any beneficial co-owner.[37] Only where this is not the case is there any potential problem for mortgagees and in such circumstances they have been reluctant to make loans to sole owners of land unless they are completely satisfied that no one other than him is in occupation of the property in question; this approach has effectively eradicated the possibility of mortgages being obtained by sole trustees of land.

3. Partial overreaching

A mortgage which has on the face of things overreached the interests of all the beneficial co-owners will not in fact overreach all those interests in certain circumstances.

(a) Forgery of co-owner's signature

It will not do so do so if the signature of one of the beneficial co-owners was forged on the mortgage deed.[38] In such cases the mortgage takes effect only against the beneficial interest of the other co-owners who obtained it. However, the beneficial interest of the co-owner whose signature was forged remains bound to the extent that any previous mortgage paid off

---

[33] *Caunce v. Caunce* [1969] 1 W.L.R. 286 (unregistered land); *Willliams & Glyn's Bank Ltd v. Boland* [1981] A.C. 487 (registered land).
[34] Above, pp. 316 *et seq.*
[35] *Kingsnorth Finance Co. Ltd v. Tizard* [1986] 1 W.L.R. 783.
[36] *Williams & Glyn's Bank Ltd v. Boland* [1981] A.C. 487.
[37] *Abbey National B.S. v. Cann* [1991] 1 A.C. 56.
[38] *First National Securities Ltd v. Hegarty* [1985] Q.B. 850; *cp. Paddington B.S. v. Mendelsohn* (1985) 50 P. & C.R. 244.

out of the advance was binding on him or her.[39] The extent to which the remedies of the mortgagee are restricted in these circumstances has already been considered.[40]

(b) Behind the back of co-owner

Nor will it do so if the mortgage was obtained behind the back of one of the other co-owners.[41] In such cases the position is exactly the same as where there has been a forgery. The mortgage takes effect only against the beneficial interest of the co-owners who were aware of it but the beneficial interest of the co-owner who was unaware of it remains bound to the extent that any previous mortgage paid off out of the advance was binding on him or her.[42] The restrictions on the remedies of the mortgagee are also the same. However, where a co-owner knows that the property in question cannot be purchased without the aid of a mortgage, the mortgagee will be taken to have been authorised and it will take priority.[43]

(c) Undue influence over or misrepresentation to co-owner

The most common situation in which a mortgage which has on the face of things overreached the interests of all the beneficial co-owners will not in fact do so is where the validity of the mortgage is affected by the fact that it was entered into as a result of the undue influence of one co-owner over the other[44] or of some misrepresentation by one co-owner to the other. In this event, the mortgage takes effect only against the beneficial interest of the co-owner who exerted the undue influence or made the misrepresentation although the beneficial interest of the other co-owner will be bound to the extent that he or she received a direct financial benefit from the advance.[45] But it has been held the beneficial interest of the latter is not subject to such of the terms of the transaction as he or she was aware of at the time it was entered into.[46] That interest may therefore not be bound to the extent that any previous mortgage paid off out of the advance was binding on him or her. However, that will not prevent the property from being sold by the trustee in bankruptcy of the co-owner who exerted the undue influence or made the misrepresentation if the mortgagee bankrupts him.[47]

Most of the examples of mortgages being obtained as a result of undue influence or some form of misrepresentation occurred in the late 1980s at a time when general financial difficulties produced a considerable fall in land values coupled with a substantial rise in interest rates. Many small businesses fell into financial difficulties and their owners came under pressure from their banks to secure their existing overdrafts and future facilities by guarantees secured on their matrimonial homes.

The facts of the first of a number of leading cases[48] were typical. The husband's company's bank manager agreed to an increased overdraft facility on the basis that the husband would guarantee the company's indebtedness and that this guarantee would be secured by a charge on the matrimonial home. The documents were sent by the bank to a branch near the matrimonial home with instructions fully to explain the transaction and the

---

[39] *Equity & Law Home Loans Ltd v. Prestridge* [1992] 1 W.L.R. 137.
[40] Above, p. 323.
[41] *Equity & Law Home Loans Ltd v. Prestridge* [1992] 1 W.L.R. 137.
[42] *Equity & Law Home Loans Ltd v. Prestridge* [1992] 1 W.L.R. 137.
[43] *Bristol and West B.S. v. Henning* [1985] 1 W.L.R. 778; *Paddington B.S. v. Mendelsohn* (1985) 50 P. & C.R. 244.
[44] *Royal Bank of Scotland Plc v. Ettridge (No. 2)* [2001] 4 All E.R. 449.
[45] *Midland Bank Plc v. Greene* [1994] 2 F.L.R. 827.
[46] *TSB Bank Plc v. Camfield* [1995] 1 W.L.R. 430.
[47] Above, p. 323.
[48] *Barclays Bank Plc v. O'Brien* [1994] 1 A.C. 180.

nature of the documentation and to advise the couple that if they were "in any doubt they should contact their solicitors before signing". The wife was told by the husband that liability under the charge was limited to £60,000 when it was in fact unlimited, the bank gave her neither explanation nor advice and she signed the documents without reading them. The mortgage was set aside as against her beneficial interest.

A much less typical variant was for an advance actually to be obtained on the security of the residential property ostensibly for the benefit of both co-owners when it was in fact to be used for the purposes of only one of them. Thus in another leading case[49] a couple obtained an advance on the security of their matrimonial home on the basis that its proceeds were to be used for the purchase of a holiday home. In fact the husband wished to purchase shares and had pressured his wife into signing the application and the charge, neither of which she read. Given that the mortgagee had no reason to think that both co-owners were not to benefit from the transaction, it was not placed on inquiry as to the possibility of any undue influence; its mortgage was consequently binding on the wife.

Precisely when will a mortgagee be affected by any undue influence which is found to have been exerted by the debtor or by any misrepresentation which he has made? The mortgagee will clearly be affected by any such conduct by the debtor where it has used him as its agent for the purposes of obtaining the signature of the surety. However, reliance on this agency argument is highly artificial since, in obtaining the signature of the surety, the debtor is acting for himself not for the mortgagee.[50] Therefore it is only in very unusual circumstances[51] that mortgagees will now be adversely affected by this argument. It is also theoretically possible, where mortgagee and surety have used the same solicitor, for information communicated by the surety to the solicitor to be imputed to the mortgagee. However, because any information is likely to have been communicated to the solicitor before he was instructed by the mortgagee[52] and, even if it was communicated to him thereafter, probably could not be revealed by him to the mortgagee anyway,[53] this is highly unlikely in practice. Consequently, in the normal case, a mortgagee will only be affected by any undue influence or mis-representation if it is held to have notice of it.

A mortgagee was at one time[54] only put on inquiry as to the possibility of undue influence or misrepresentation where the relationship between the debtor and surety was an emotional relationship between cohabitees[55] or where the mortgagee was aware that the surety reposed trust and confidence in the debtor in relation to his or her financial affairs or was actually under the debtor's influence in other respects.[56] However, a mortgagee is now put on inquiry in every case where the relationship between the debtor and the surety is non-commercial.[57] In such circumstances, the mortgagee must always take reasonable steps to bring home to the individual surety the risks which he or more usually she is running by acting as such. If the mortgagee fails to take those steps, it will be deemed to have notice of any claim which

---

[49] *CIBC Mortgages Plc v. Pitt* [1994] 1 A.C. 200.

[50] *Barclays Bank Plc v. O'Brien* [1994] 1 A.C. 180.

[51] An example was where the employees of the bank, its debtor and the guarantor were all members of the same religious sect; see *Shams v. United Bank Ltd* (May 24, 1994) on Lexis.

[52] *Halifax Mortgage Services v. Stepsky* [1996] Ch. 207 (C.A.).

[53] *Halifax Mortgage Services v. Stepsky* [1996] Ch. 1 (Ch.D.).

[54] As a result of *Barclays Bank Plc v. O'Brien* [1994] 1 A.C. 180.

[55] The requirement for cohabitation was not rigid; see *Massey v. Midland Bank Plc* [1995] 1 All E.R. 929.

[56] *Credit Lyonnais Bank Nederland NV v. Burch* [1997] 1 All E.R. 144.

[57] *Royal Bank of Scotland Plc v. Etridge (No. 2)* [2001] 3 W.L.R. 1021.

the surety may have that the transaction was procured by undue influence or a misrepresentation on the part of the debtor.[58] This principle applies not only to co-owners who act as sureties but also to absolute owners of property who do so.[59]

Where the mortgagee is put on inquiry, it need do no more than take reasonable steps to satisfy itself that the practical implications of the proposed transaction have been brought home to the surety in a meaningful way, so that he or she enters into the transaction with her eyes open so far as its basic elements are concerned. At one time, the mortgagee would satisfy its duty of inquiry if its representatives held a private meeting with the surety in the absence of the debtor, informing him or her as to potential liability and risk and urging him or her to take independent legal advice. Only in exceptional cases where the mortgagee knew further facts which made undue influence not only possible but probable was it necessary for the mortgagee to insist on independent advice.[60] However, mortgagees came increasingly to rely on the confirmation of solicitors that such advice had been given and it was held in 2001[61] that such confirmation will ordinarily suffice in respect of past transactions.

For transactions after 2001, the mortgagee is not required to satisfy its duty of inquiry by means of a personal meeting with the surety. Ordinarily it will be reasonable for the mortgagee to rely upon confirmation from a solicitor, acting for the surety, that he has advised her appropriately. Such a solicitor acts for the surety, not as the agent of the mortgagee, and any deficiencies in his advice are a matter between solicitor and surety. However, if the mortgagee knows that the solicitor has not duly advised the surety or knows facts from which it ought to have realised that the surety has not received appropriate advice, the mortgagee takes the mortgage at its own risk.

The process of obtaining confirmation from the solicitor has been formalised as a series of requirements.[62]

   (i) The mortgagee should communicate directly with the surety, informing him or her that for its own protection it will require written confirmation from a solicitor acting for him or her, to the effect that the solicitor has fully explained the nature of the documents and their practical implications. The surety should be told that the purpose of this requirement is that thereafter the binding nature of the documents should not be able to be disputed. The surety should be asked to nominate a solicitor to advise him or her separately from the debtor, although the solicitor may be the solicitor who is representing the debtor.

  (ii) The mortgagee must explain the existing financial situation of the debtor and the purposes and amount of any new facility either to the surety or to the solicitor; if the debtor will not consent to the release of this information, the transaction cannot proceed.

 (iii) Where the mortgagee believes or suspects that the surety has been misled or is not entering into the transaction of his or her own free will, it must inform the surety's solicitor of the facts giving rise to its belief or suspicion.

---

[58] *ibid.*, see also *Credit Lyonnais Bank Nederland NV v. Burch* [1997] 1 All E.R. 144.
[59] As in *Credit Lyonnais Bank Nederland NV v. Burch* [1997] 1 All E.R. 144 (the surety was the debtor's employee).
[60] *Barclays Bank Plc v. O'Brien* [1994] 1 A.C. 180 at 196–197.
[61] As a result of *Royal Bank of Scotland Plc v. Etridge (No. 2)* [2001] 3 W.L.R. 1021.
[62] *ibid.*

Detailed guidelines have also been provided for the solicitor advising the surety.

Although transactions entered into before the process was formalised in this way are likely to come before the courts for some years yet, the existence of all these guidelines makes it unlikely that any mortgagees will be adversely affected by any undue influence or misrepresentation by the debtor in respect of future transactions. Any remedy by the surety will instead be sought from the solicitor who advised him or her.

Sect. 2. Priorities as between mortgages of unregistered land

Where there are competing mortgages of unregistered land, there are two basic rules, depending on what has been mortgaged. If a legal estate in land has been mortgaged, the rules depend on whether or not the mortgage has been protected by a deposit of documents relating to the legal estate affected; normally these are the title deeds. Mortgages protected in this way stand outside the system of registration of land charges, and depend for priority on the rules before 1926, subject to the law of land charges. Mortgages that are not protected in this way are registrable as land charges and depend on this system for their priority. If an equitable interest in any property has instead been mortgaged, the rule in *Dearle v. Hall*[63] applies, so that priority depends on the dates on which notice of the mortgages was received by the trustees or other legal owner. Additional rules govern tacking.

However, it must be borne in mind that the grant of a first legal mortgage has, since April 1, 1998 triggered first registration of title. Consequently, where the first of two or more competing mortgages is a legal mortgage created after that date, it is not likely that the later mortgages will have been created prior to the title being registered; if created thereafter, priorities will be determined by the rules that govern priority as between mortgages of registered land.

1. Mortgages of a legal estate—the rules

(a) Mortgages included

This head includes all mortgages of a legal estate in land, whether the mortgage itself is legal or equitable. The question is "Has a legal estate been mortgaged?", not "Is the mortgage legal or equitable?".

(b) Principles

The two main principles[64] are as follows.

(i) Mortgages protected by deposits of deeds: A mortgage protected "by a deposit of documents relating to the legal estate affected" is expressly excepted from the provisions of the 1925 legislation requiring registration of mortgages,[65] since the absence of the title deeds will proclaim the mortgage to anyone seeking to deal with the land[66]; "protected" probably means "originally protected", and not "continuously protected".

---

[63] (1828) 3 Russ. 1.
[64] There is a full discussion in (1940) 7 C.L.J. 243 (R.E.M.).
[65] L.C.A. 1972, s.2(4), replacing L.C.A. 1925, s.10. They are probably not registrable as Class C(iv) estate contracts.
[66] But see above, p. 103, for leases.

(ii) Mortgages not protected by deposits of deeds: A mortgage made after 1925 and not protected by a deposit of documents relating to the legal estate affected has to be registered as a land charge. If the mortgage is legal, it should be registered as a puisne mortgage (Class C(i)). If the mortgage is equitable, it should be registered as a general equitable charge (Class C(iii)).[67]

(c) Reasons for registration

The reasons for registering a puisne mortgage or a general equitable charge are as follows:

(i) Priority: Section 97 of the Law of Property Act 1925 provides that every such mortgage "shall rank according to its date of registration as a land charge pursuant to the Land Charges Act 1925 or 1972".[68]

(ii) Void for want of registration: Section 4(5) of the Land Charges Act 1972 provides that a Class C land charge created after 1925 shall "be void as against a purchaser of the land charged therewith, or of any interest in such land, unless the land charge is registered in the appropriate register before the completion of the purchase".[69] In that Act, unless the context otherwise requires, "purchaser" means "any person (including a mortgagee or lessee) who, for valuable consideration, takes any interest in land or in a charge of land".[70] Thus a puisne mortgage or a general equitable charge, if unregistered, is void against a purchaser of the legal fee simple even if he had actual knowledge of it; for where an interest is void for non-registration a purchaser is not prejudicially affected by notice of it.[71]

2. Mortgages of a legal estate—operation of the rules

The effect of these provisions must be considered under four possible heads.

(a) Each mortgage protected by a deposit of deeds

A mortgage will be protected by a deposit of deeds if the documents deposited are material parts of the title, even if they are not all the title deeds.[72] Thus two or more mortgages protected by a deposit of deeds may be created, as where the mortgagor has secretly withheld some of the deeds when creating the first mortgage,[73] or where he recovers the deeds from the mortgagee on some pretext, such as obtaining them on a short loan to show the dimensions of the property to a person concerned with a rebuilding project.[74] In such cases, the mortgages are not registrable. Four categories have to be considered:

(i) where both mortgages are legal;

(ii) where the first is legal and the second equitable;

(iii) where the first is equitable and the second legal;

---

[67] See above, pp. 94, 95.
[68] See L.C.A. 1972, s.18(6).
[69] Formerly L.C.A. 1925, s.13(2).
[70] L.C.A. 1972, s.17(1).
[71] Above, p. 104.
[72] *Lacon v. Allen* (1856) 3 Drew. 579 (equitable mortgage).
[73] *ibid., Walker v. Linom* [1907] 2 Ch. 104.
[74] *Peter v. Russell* (1716) Gilb.Eq. 122 (the "Thatched House" case).

(iv) where both are equitable.

These will be considered in turn. However, it is particularly unlikely that it will be possible to have two mortgages both protected by a deposit of deeds when the first of those mortgages is legal and was created on or after April 1, 1998. The rules governing each category are subject to the rules for loss of priority considered below.[75]

(i) Both mortgages legal: Where both mortgages are legal, priority will normally depend on the order of creation. Where two mortgages are granted by way of leases, the second will take effect in reversion on the first.[76]

(ii) Legal mortgage followed by equitable mortgage: Where a legal mortgage is followed by an equitable mortgage, the legal mortgage has a double claim to priority, both as being prior in time and because where the equities are equal, the law prevails.

(iii) Equitable mortgage followed by legal mortgage: Where an equitable mortgage is followed by a legal mortgage, the primary rule is that the mortgages rank in the order of creation; but this priority may be displaced by the superiority of the legal estate. For this to occur, the legal mortgagee must show that he is a bona fide purchaser for value of a legal estate without notice of the prior equitable mortgage.[77] The inability of the mortgagor to produce all the title deeds will usually amount to notice to the legal mortgagee that some prior mortgage already exists.[78] But if his inquiries for the deeds were met by a reasonable excuse, he can claim priority as having taken without notice. The court has accepted surprisingly frail excuses as being reasonable, such as that the mortgagor was busy but would produce the deeds later,[79] or that the deeds were in Ireland, where the property lay.[80] Instead of applying the normal rule that requires a purchaser to make a proper investigation of title, the courts have held that nothing save gross negligence will postpone the legal mortgagee,[81] and it is grossly negligent to accept the excuse that the deeds also relate to other property.[82]

(iv) Both mortgages equitable: Where both mortgages are equitable, priority depends on the order in which they were created, provided that the equities are equal in other respects.[83] Accordingly, a first mortgagee who failed to ask for the title deeds, or who, having obtained them, redelivered them to the mortgagor without pressing for their early return, may be postponed to a second mortgagee who took all proper precautions but was nevertheless deceived.[84]

(v) Loss of priority: Before 1926 it was settled that even a legal mortgagee might lose his priority in three classes of case, and the principles appear to apply after 1925, though their application to the rules laid down by statute has yet to be considered. The cases, which are

---

[75] Below.
[76] *Jones v. Rhind* (1869) 17 W.R. 1091.
[77] *Pilcher v. Rawlins* (1872) 7 Ch.App. 259; *Att.-Gen. v. Biphosphated Guano Co.* (1879) 11 Ch.D. 327.
[78] *Oliver v. Hinton* [1899] 2 Ch. 264 at 268.
[79] *Hewitt v. Loosemore* (1851) 9 Hare 449.
[80] *Agra Bank Ltd v. Barry* (1874) L.R. 7 H.L. 135.
[81] *Hewitt v. Loosemore* (1851) 9 Hare 449; *Oliver v. Hinton* [1899] 2 Ch. 264; see below, p. 538.
[82] *Oliver v. Hinton* [1899] 2 Ch. 264.
[83] *Rice v. Rice* (1853) 2 Drew. 73.
[84] *Farrand v. Yorkshire Banking Co.* (1888) 40 Ch.D. 182.

stated in terms of a legal mortgage, seem equally applicable to equitable mortgages.[85] They are as follows.

(1) *Fraud.* If a legal mortgagee is guilty of some fraud whereby the equitable mortgagee is deceived into believing that there was no legal mortgage on the property, the legal mortgagee will be postponed to the equitable mortgagee.[86]

(2) *Estoppel.* If the legal mortgagee either expressly or by implication made some misrepresentation by which the equitable mortgagee was deceived, the legal mortgagee will be estopped from asserting his priority.[87] Thus if a legal mortgagee indorses a receipt for his money on the mortgage and somebody is thereby induced to lend money on an equitable mortgage of the property, the legal mortgagee cannot afterwards claim priority for his loan if in fact it has not been discharged.[88] Again, if the legal mortgagee parts with the deeds to the mortgagor to enable him to raise money, he will be postponed to any subsequent mortgagee who lent money without notice of the first mortgage, even if the mortgagor had agreed to inform the second mortgagee of the first mortgage, or had agreed to borrow only a limited amount which in fact he exceeded.[89] Once the mortgagee clothes the mortgagor with apparent authority to deal with the property freely, he cannot afterwards claim the protection of any undisclosed limits set to this authority.

(3) *Gross negligence in relation to the title deeds.* If the legal mortgagee is grossly negligent in failing to obtain the title deeds, he is postponed to a subsequent equitable mortgagee who exercises due diligence. Failure to ask for the deeds at all would postpone a legal mortgagee[90]; it is otherwise if he inquires for them and is given a reasonable excuse.[91] If the legal mortgagee obtains the deeds, it appears that no amount of carelessness in failing to keep them in safe custody will postpone him, as where the deeds were kept in a safe to which the mortgagor had a key as manager working for the mortgagee.[92] But this seems questionable.

(b) Neither mortgage protected by a deposit of deeds

Where neither mortgage is protected by a deposit of title deeds, priority is determined by the Law of Property Act 1925 and the Land Charges Act 1972, subject to any question that may arise as to loss of priority.[93] The two statutes speak with united voice in some cases and discordant voices in others, depending on the order in which the competing mortgages have been made and registered.

(i) Concord: No difficulty arises if the first mortgage is duly registered before the second is made. Even if the first is equitable and the second legal, the first prevails, for section 97 of the Law of Property Act 1925 expressly provides that they shall rank in order of registration, and the provision that registration amounts to notice prevents the legal mortgagee from

[85] See *Rimmer v. Webster* [1902] 2 Ch. 163; *Taylor v. Russell* [1892] A.C. 244.
[86] *Peter v. Russell* (1716) Gilb.Eq. 122.
[87] *Dixon v. Muckleston* (1872) 8 Ch.App. 155 at 160.
[88] *Rimmer v. Webster* [1902] 2 Ch. 163.
[89] *Perry Herrick v. Attwood* (1857) 2 De G. & J. 21.
[90] *Walker v. Linom* [1907] 2 Ch. 104; and see *Colyer v. Finch* (1856) 5 H.L.C. 905.
[91] *Manners v. Mew* (1885) 29 Ch.D. 725.
[92] *Northern Counties, etc. Insurance Co. v. Whipp* (1884) 26 Ch.D. 482.
[93] See above.

claiming to be a purchaser without notice. Nor is there any difficulty if neither mortgage is registered. Even if the first mortgage is legal and the second equitable, under section 4(5) of the Land Charges Act 1972 the first is void against the second for want of registration, and so the second has priority. Indeed, if there are several successive registrable mortgages, none of which has been registered, the priority accorded by the date of creation will be reversed, for the last will rank first and so on.

(ii) Discord: The difficult case is where the first mortgage was registered after the creation of the second mortgage. For example:

January 1 1998	A grants a mortgage to X
February 2 1998	A grants a mortgage to Y
March 3 1998	X registers
March 4 1998	Y registers

In such a case, the order according to section 97 is X, Y; according to section 4(5) it is Y, X, for X's mortgage is void against Y. It is not clear which section will prevail. In favour of section 97, the chief point is that it is expressly dealing with the priority of mortgages, whereas section 4(5) makes unregistered mortgages void against subsequent mortgages only by virtue of the provision that "purchaser" includes a mortgagee.[94] On the other hand, the provision in section 4(5) that an unregistered land charge is void against a subsequent purchaser makes it hard to see how the registration of X's mortgage can give priority to something which, as regards Y, has no existence.[95] The problem still awaits solution (now that the grant of a first legal mortgage triggers compulsory registration of title, it probably never will be). It is thought that section 4(5) will probably prevail, since Y will have been induced to lend his money by the fact that no earlier charge appeared to exist and X could easily have protected himself by speedier registration. Even more complicated problems can be constructed, including cases of circularity, as where X has priority over Y who has priority over Z who has priority over X; but these need not be discussed here.[96]

(iii) Priority notices and official searches: At the beginning of 1926, there was the difficulty that it was physically impossible to register a land charge the instant after it had been created. Thus there was a dangerous gap between the creation of a mortgage and its registration. Further, even if a search for prior incumbrances was made, the mortgagee could not be sure that no incumbrance had been registered between the time of his search and the completion of the mortgage. These difficulties have been met by the devices of the priority notice and the official search, which have been dealt with earlier.[97]

(c) First but not second mortgage protected by a deposit of deeds

In this case, the first mortgage, by taking its priority from the date of its creation, will normally have priority over the second mortgage.

(d) Second but not first mortgage protected by a deposit of deeds

Here, sections 4(5) and 97 work in harmony. If the first mortgage is registered before the second is made, the first ranks for priority "according to its date of registration" (section 97),

---

[94] L.P.A. 1925, s.205(1)(xxi).
[95] See *Kitney v. M.E.P.C. Ltd* [1977] 1 W.L.R. 981.
[96] See (1968) 32 Conv. 325 (W.A. Lee).
[97] Above, p. 106.

i.e. prior to the second mortgage, and section 4(5) has no application. If the first mortgage is not registered when the second mortgage is made, the first mortgage is void against the second for want of registration; and even if it is subsequently registered, it takes priority from the date of registration.

(e) Summary

(i) Deposit of deeds: A mortgage protected by a deposit of deeds ranks according to the date on which it was created. The mortgagee may lose priority:

  (i) by fraud, estoppel or gross negligence; or

  (ii) if his mortgage is equitable, by a legal mortgage being made to a mortgagee for value without notice.

(ii) No deposit of deeds: A mortgage not protected by deposit of deeds should be protected by registration. If the mortgagee fails to do this, he will not, it seems, be protected against a subsequent mortgagee (s.4(5)), unless, perhaps, he registers before him (s.97). If he does register he will be protected against all mortgages made thereafter.

3. Mortgages of an equitable interest

The priority of mortgages of an equitable interest in any property, whether real or personal, depends on the rule in *Dearle v. Hall*.[98] Only since 1925 has this rule extended it to mortgages of equitable interests in land.[99] The basic provision of the rule is that the priority of competing mortgages depends on the order in which notice of them is received by the trustees or other legal owner; but this is subject to the important qualification that a mortgagee who, when lending his money, has notice of a prior mortgage cannot gain priority over it by giving notice first.

Various reasons for the rule have been given, including the consideration that as between two equally innocent incumbrancers, priority should be accorded to the one who, by giving notice, had prevented the mortgagor from representing that he was the unincumbered owner of the interest mortgaged, and so deceiving third parties.[1] Whatever the reasons, the rule is now a rigid rule.[2] As amended by the Law of Property Act 1925, the rule falls under the following heads.

(a) No notice of prior mortgage

A mortgagee who had notice of a prior mortgage when he lent his money cannot gain priority over it by giving notice first,[3] for he has not been prejudiced by the failure of the prior mortgagee to give notice and so it would be inequitable to give him priority. But if when he lent his money he had no notice of a prior mortgage, notice of it when he gives his notice is immaterial.[4] Indeed, it is just what will impel him to give notice.[5]

---

[98] 3 Russ. 1.
[99] s.137(1).
[1] See *Ward v. Duncombe* [1893] A.C. 369 at 392.
[2] See *Re Dallas* [1904] 2 Ch. 385.
[3] *Re Holmes* (1885) 29 Ch.D. 786.
[4] *Mutual Life Assurance Society v. Langley* (1886) 32 Ch.D. 460.
[5] See below, p. 543.

(b) Priority depends on notice being received, not given

Priority depends on the order in which notice is received by the trustees or other legal owner, and not on whether or when the mortgagees gave notice. Where notices are received simultaneously, the mortgages rank in the order of their creation, as where competing notices are delivered to a bank, one late at night and the other as soon as it opens the next day.[6] Notice from any reliable source suffices.[7] Indeed, one first mortgagee kept his priority by virtue of notice of the mortgage given not by him but by a letter sent to the trustee by the second mortgagee before giving his own notice.[8]

(c) Notice must be in writing

Since 1925 no notice given or received after 1925 will affect priorities unless it is in writing.[9] Before 1926, notice received through reading a notice in a newspaper sufficed to preserve priority against a subsequent mortgagee who then gave express notice,[10] though it would not gain priority for a later mortgage over an earlier mortgage[11]: less is required to preserve priority than to gain it. Whether such notice is still effective is doubtful, for although it is in writing it has not been "served".[12]

(d) Service of notice

(i) Persons to be served: The persons "to be served" with notice are[13]:

  (i) in the case of land settled under the Settled Land Act 1925, the trustees of the settlement;

  (ii) in the case of a trust of land, the trustees; and

  (iii) in the case of any other land, the estate owner of the land affected.

The person to be served is normally the owner of the legal estate, except in the case of land settled under the Settled Land Act 1925. Notice to the tenant for life of such a settlement might well be no protection, as where it is his life interest that is being mortgaged. No special provision has been made for any other cases, and so in these notice must be given to the legal owner, as before 1926.

(ii) Notice should be given to all the trustees: It has always been advisable to give notice to all the trustees for the following reasons.

  (i) Notice given to all the existing trustees remains effective even though they all retire or die without communicating the notice to their successors.[14]

---

[6] *Calisher v. Forbes* (1871) 7 Ch.App. 109.
[7] *Re Worcester* (1868) 3 Ch.App. 555.
[8] *Ipswich Permanent Money Club Ltd v. Arthy* [1920] 2 Ch. 257.
[9] L.P.A. 1925, s.137(3).
[10] *Lloyd v. Banks* (1868) 3 Ch.App. 488.
[11] *Arden v. Arden* (1885) 29 Ch.D. 702.
[12] L.P.A. 1925, s.137(2).
[13] *ibid.*
[14] *Re Wasdale* [1899] 1 Ch. 163.

(ii) Notice given to one of several trustees is effective against all incumbrances created during his trusteeship, and remains effective despite his death or retirement.[15]

(iii) On the other hand, notice given to one of several trustees is not effective against incumbrancers who advance money after the death or retirement of that trustee without having communicated the notice to one or more of the continuing trustees.[16]

(iv) If the mortgagor is a trustee, priorities will not be affected by the notice of the mortgage that he has, for this will afford no protection to subsequent mortgages.[17] But if the mortgagee is a trustee, the notice of the mortgage that he has will affect priorities, for to protect his mortgage he will readily disclose its existence to any prospective incumbrancers.[18]

(iii) Notice by indorsement: If for any reason a valid notice cannot be served (such as where there are no trustees), or can be served only at unreasonable cost or delay, a purchaser may require that a memorandum be indorsed on or permanently annexed to the instrument creating the trust, and this has the same effect as notice to the trustees. In the case of settled land, the trust instrument, and in the case of a trust of land, the instrument creating the equitable interest, is the document to be used for this purpose.[19]

(iv) Notice to trust corporation: The instrument creating the trust, the trustees or the court may nominate a trust corporation to receive notices instead of the trustees. In such cases, only notice to the trust corporation affects priority; notice to the trustees has no effect until they deliver it to the trust corporation, which they are bound to do forthwith. Provision is made for the indorsement of notice of the appointment on the instrument upon which notices may be indorsed, for the keeping of a register of notices, for the inspection of the register, for the answering of inquiries and for the payment of fees therefor.[20] In practice, little use is made of these provisions.

(v) Production of notices: Since 1925, on the application of any person interested in the equitable interest, the trustees have been obliged to produce any notices served on them or their predecessors.[21]

(vi) Distribution: In addition to securing priority, notice to the trustees safeguards the mortgagee by ensuring that his claims will not be disregarded when the funds are distributed. Trustees are not liable if they distribute the trust funds to the prejudice of a mortgagee of whom they are unaware.[22]

4. Tacking

Tacking is a process whereby the rules relating to priorities can be modified, both for realty and for personality. The process consists of allowing a mortgagee with inferior priority to "tack" (or attach) his mortgage to a mortgage with superior priority and thus to give it

---

[15] *Ward v. Duncombe* [1893] A.C. 369.
[16] *Re Phillips' Trusts* [1903] 1 Ch. 183.
[17] *Lloyds Bank v. Pearson* [1901] 1 Ch. 865.
[18] *Browne v. Savage* (1859) 4 Drew. 635.
[19] L.P.A. 1925, s.137(4), (5).
[20] *ibid.*, s.138.
[21] L.P.A. 1925, s.137(8); see also (9).
[22] *Phipps v. Lovegrove* (1873) L.R. 16 Eq. 80.

priority over any intervening mortgages. Since 1925, there has only been one form of tacking, the tacking of further advances. The former type of tacking known as the *tabula in naufragio* ("a plank in a shipwreck") is relevant only because the wider principle of which it forms part remains in force. That is the principle whereby priority for equitable interests may be obtained by acquiring a legal estate. Consequently, an equitable mortgagee may obtain priority over a prior unregistered[23] option to purchase the land if he obtains a legal charge on the land under a power in the mortgage, provided that he had no notice of the option when he lent the money.[24]

The tacking of further advances envisages the possibility that, after lending the money, a mortgagee may make further advances to the mortgagor on the security of the same property. There are three cases in which the mortgagee can tack his further advance to his original mortgage and claim priority over an intervening incumbrancer for both loans.[25] It is immaterial whether or not the prior mortgage was made expressly for securing further advances, or whether the subsequent mortgage is legal or equitable.[26]

(a) Agreement of intervening incumbrancer

The mortgagee can tack if the intervening incumbrancer agrees. Building estates sometimes provide examples of this: the owner requires more money for further building on his estate, thereby making it a better security. The second mortgagee, not wishing to lend any more money, may agree to the first mortgagee making a further advance to be expended on further building and to rank in priority to the second mortgage.

(b) No notice of intervening incumbrance

Any mortgagee, whether legal or equitable, may tack a further advance if it was made without notice of the intervening mortgage. Where the intervening mortgage is protected by a deposit of deeds and is thus not registrable, the normal rules as to notice operate. If the mortgage is not protected in this way and so is registrable, the rule that registration amounts to notice will apply and thus protect it if it is registered. In one case, however, registration is not deemed to be notice; if the prior mortgage was made expressly for securing further advances, such as on a current account (for example an overdraft at a bank, where the debt is increased and decreased as sums are drawn out or paid in), registration alone is not deemed to be notice, unless the intervening mortgage was registered when the last search was made by the mortgagee.[27] This applies to a spouse's right of occupation which is registered after a mortgage has been made.[28]

An example may make this clearer. Mortgages have been made to A (who took the deeds) and B, in that order, and A has made further advances. If when A made his further advances he had actual, constructive or imputed notice of B's mortgage, he cannot tack under this head even if his mortgage, without obliging him to make further advances, was stated to be security for any further advances he might choose to make. If he had no such notice of B's mortgage when he made his further advances, but B's mortgage was registered at that time,

---

[23] Had the mortgage been legal, not equitable, the option would have been void against it for want of registration: above, pp. 95, 104.
[24] *McCarthy & Stone Ltd v. Julian S. Hodge & Co. Ltd* [1971] 1 W.L.R. 1547, where there was held to be notice. See also [1972A] C.L.J. 34 (P.B. Fairest).
[25] L.P.A. 1925, s.94(1).
[26] *ibid.*
[27] *ibid.*, s.94(2).
[28] Family Law Act 1996, s.31(12). For the Act, see above, p. 98.

then if A's mortgage is silent as to further advances, the registration amounts to notice and prevents A from tacking. But if A's mortgage was expressed to be security for any further advances that he might make, the registration will not prevent him from tacking, and thus he need not search before making each further advance.

This points a practical moral. Even if a second mortgage has been duly registered, the mortgagee should give express notice of his mortgage to the first mortgagee, for this:

(i) prevents tacking under this head; and

(ii) compels the first mortgagee to hand over the deeds to him when the first mortgage is discharged.[29]

(c) Obligation to make further advance

A further advance may be tacked if the prior mortgage imposes an obligation on the mortgagee to make it. In this case, not even express notice will prevent tacking.[30] If in return for a mortgage a bank binds itself to honour a customer's cheques up to an overdraft of £100,000 there is no question of the bank having to search before honouring each cheque, for not even express notice will prevent the bank from tacking each further advance.

Sect. 3. Priorities as between mortgages of registered land

In the case of registered land, registered charges rank in the order in which they are entered on the register subject to any tacking (in the case of registered land, tacking is only possible in respect of registered charges). Other mortgages of legal interests rank in the order of creation, subject to any protection given by entries on the register or by deposit of the land certificate. Other mortgages of equitable interests are governed by the rule in *Dearle v. Hall*[31] so that priority depends on the dates on which notice of the mortgages was received by the trustees or other legal owner.

1. Mortgages of a legal estate

(a) Categories

Mortgages of a legal estate in registered land are either registered charges or interests which require protection on the register.[32] For priorities, there are three main categories.

(i) Registered charges: Subject to any entry on the register,[33] registered charges rank in the order in which they are entered on the register, irrespective of the order of creation.[34] This rule applies only to registered charges, and not to other types of mortgages which are protected on the register.[35]

(ii) Interests protected on the register: A mortgage other than a registered charge which is protected by an entry on the register or by a deposit of the land certificate (although such

---

[29] Above, p. 514.
[30] L.P.A. 1925, s.94(1)(c), reversing *West v. Williams* [1899] 1 Ch. 132.
[31] (1828) 3 Russ. 1.
[32] See above, pp. 497–498.
[33] See Ruoff & Roper, para. 23–39.
[34] L.R.A. 1925, s.29; L.R.A. 2002, s.48.
[35] Ruoff & Roper, para. 8–09.

deposits will not be possible when the Land Registration Act 2002 comes into force) will take priority over a subsequent mortgage, whether it is a registered charge or an interest which has been protected on the register.[36]

(iii) Interests which are not protected on the register: A mortgage other than a registered charge which is not protected on the register takes effect as an equitable interest.[37] As between competing interests of this kind, the ordinary equitable rule applies. Thus the earlier interest will take priority over the later,[38] even if the later is protected by a notice or (at present) a caution against dealings and the earlier is not.[39] At present this priority may be displaced by fraud, estoppel or gross negligence.[40] (This is on the basis that, by omitting to follow the normal practice of protecting the minor interest, the earlier mortgagee has enabled the mortgagor to represent the land as being unincumbered, and so he should be precluded from asserting his natural priority against an innocent later mortgagee.) However, priority will not be able to be displaced in these ways when the Land Registration Act 2002 comes into force.[41] But statute gives a registered charge created for valuable consideration priority over any prior mortgage of any type which has not been protected by entry on the register or (at present) by a deposit of the land certificate.[42]

(b) Deposit of the land certificate

At present the proprietor of registered land may create a lien on it by a deposit of the land certificate; and similarly for the proprietor of a registered charge.[43] However, deposits of land certificates will no longer be possible when the Land Registration Act 2002 comes into force.[44] Such a deposit is distinct from a deposit that is merely ancillary to a mortgage created by a document and creates no independent charge or lien.[45] Subject to any interests which override registration of the mortgage and to any interests protected on the register at the date of the deposit, the lien is equivalent to a lien created by deposit of title deeds for unregistered land by a beneficial owner.[46] The inference seems to be that the lien is free from prior interests which required protection on the register but which were not protected at the time of the deposit. If so, the lien will take priority over all unprotected mortgages, even if they were created before the deposit.

2. Mortgages of an equitable interest

For mortgages of an equitable interest in registered land, the rule in *Dearle v. Hall*,[47] which has already been considered[48], now applies to registered land in the same way as it applies

---

[36] *Parkash v. Irani Finance Ltd* [1970] Ch. 101.
[37] L.R.A. 1925, s.2(1); there is no explicit provision in L.R.A. 2002 but the law will remain the same. See above, p. 135.
[38] *Barclays Bank Ltd v. Taylor* [1974] Ch. 137.
[39] *The Mortgage Corporation Ltd v. Nationwide Credit Corporation Ltd* [1994] Ch. 49.
[40] See *Abigail v. Lapin* [1934] A.C. 491; *Butler v. Fairclough* (1917) 23 C.L.R. 78; and see above, pp. 537–538.
[41] L.R.A. 2002, s.28.
[42] L.R.A. 1925, ss.19(2), 20(1), 22(2), 23(1); L.R.A. 2002, s.30.
[43] L.R.A. 1925, s.66.
[44] L.R.A. 2002 deliberately contains no provision equivalent to L.R.A. 1925, s.66; see Law Com. No. 271, para. 7.10.
[45] See *Re White Rose Cottage* [1964] Ch. 483 at 490, 491; in C.A. [1965] Ch. 941.
[46] L.R.A. 1925, s.66.
[47] (1828) 3 Russ. 1.
[48] Above, p. 540.

to unregistered land.[49] The former Minor Interests Index in which entries could be made in lieu of giving notice under the rule has long since been abolished.[50]

3. Tacking

Provision for the tacking of further advances has been made only in the case of registered charges.[51] There are two categories.

(a) Obligatory

Where the proprietor of a registered charge is under an obligation, noted on the register, to make a further advance, any subsequent registered charge will take effect subject to any such further advance.[52]

(b) Optional

(i) Under the Land Registration Act 1925: Where there is no obligation to make further advances but the registered charge is made for securing any further advances that may be made, then at present before making any entry which would prejudicially affect the priority of any further advances, the registrar must give notice of it to the registered proprietor of the charge.[53] The entry will then not affect any further advance unless it is made after the notice should have been received in due course of post.[54] If in such cases the proprietor of the registered charge suffers any loss by reason of any failure by the registrar or the postal services he is entitled to an indemnity as if a mistake had occurred in the register.[55]

(ii) Under the Land Registration Act 2002: When the Land Registration Act 2002 comes into force, the proprietor of a registered charge will be able to make a further advance on the security of an existing charge if in the meantime he has not received notice from another chargee that a subsequent charge has been created.[56] Rules will govern when a notice is treated as received.[57] It will also be possible to tack a further advance where an earlier charge records a maximum figure for the total money lent provided that the amount due to the proprietor of the registered charge when the further advance is made does not exceed that maximum figure.[58] However, rules may disapply this possibility in specified cases and provide conditions for this new type of tacking which will have to be complied with.[59]

---

[49] Land Registration Act 1986, s.5(1); Ruoff & Roper, paras 8–11, 8–12.
[50] *ibid.*
[51] L.R.A. 1925, s.30; L.R.A. 2002, s.49.
[52] L.R.A. 1925, s.30(3); L.R.A. 2002, s.49(3).
[53] L.R.A. 1925, s.30(1).
[54] *ibid.*
[55] L.R.A. 1925, s.30(2); see above, p. 144.
[56] L.R.A. 2002, s.49(1).
[57] *ibid.*, s.49(2).
[58] *ibid.*, s.49(4).
[59] *ibid.*, s.49(5).

Chapter 14

LIMITATION

The fundamental principle of the Limitation Act 1980, which consolidates earlier legislation,[1] is that unless claims are enforced within a limited time, they become barred.

1. Policy

The policy which underlies the Limitation Act 1980 and, for that matter its predecessors, is that it is more important that long and undisturbed possession of land should be protected, even if initially it was wrongful, than that the law should lend its aid to the enforcement of stale claims. That legislation at present governs both registered and unregistered land and it is expected that it will continue to govern unregistered land indefinitely. But, as has already been seen,[2] when the Land Registration Act 2002 comes into force, long and undisturbed possession will only be protected if the person against whom it has been maintained does not object to the registration of the possessor as proprietor. This change has been made because of what the Law Commission has described[3] as "considerable public disquiet" over the operation of the existing law.

2. Human rights

Both under the present law and under the Land Registration Act 2002 what is crucial is the inactivity of the person against whom the necessary long and undisturbed possession has been maintained.

It has been contended[4] that the deprivation of that person's property to which his inactivity gives rise breaches the right to his possessions conferred by the Human Rights Act 1998, that the deprivation of his property without compensation was disproportionate to any legitimate public interest and breached the fair balance between his interests and the interests of society as a whole, and that the relevant limitation period (12 years) was too short. On the other hand, it was not contended that the Limitation Act 1980 was incompatible with the European

---

[1] The Limitation Act 1939 as affecting land was amended by the Limitation Amendment Act 1980, and both were repealed and replaced by the present Act.

[2] Above, p. 137.

[3] Law. Com. No. 271, para. 24.

[4] In *Pye (J.A.) Oxford Ltd v. Graham* [2001] 2 W.L.R. 1293. On appeal to the House of Lords; (2002) *The Times*, July 5, 2002, it was conceded that the Human Rights Act 1998, s.22(4) did not apply because this was an appeal against a decision made before October 2, 2002, and it was held that the absence of ambiguity prevented the courts from seeking to apply the law so as to make it consistent with the European Convention on Human Rights.

Convention of Human Rights. Nor could it have been given that that Convention itself has a limitation period and such periods exist in most if not all European jurisdictions.[5]

The Court of Appeal held that the relevant provisions of the Limitation Act 1980 do not deprive a person of his possessions or interfere with his peaceful enjoyment of them; instead they deprive a person of his right of access to the courts for the purpose of recovering his property if he has delayed the institution of legal proceedings for more than the relevant period after he has been dispossessed of his land by another person who has been in possession of it for at least that period.[6] In any event, those provisions were in the public interest and are reasonably required to avoid the very real risk of injustice in the adjudication of stale claims, to ensure certainty of title and to promote social stability. The conditions are not disproportionate or discriminatory and the period for bringing not impossibly difficult proceedings is reasonable.[7] In the House of Lords,[7a] the only relevant comment was that the question was "not an easy one".

3. Limitation and prescription

Limitation must be distinguished from prescription.[8] Two differences may be mentioned.

(a) Subject-matter

Limitation often, although not always, concerns the ownership of the land itself, whereas prescription is directed solely to the acquisition of easements and profits over the land of another.

(b) Limitation negative

Prescription operates positively so as to presume the grant of an easement or profit by the owner of the land; title is thus derived from him. Limitation, on the other hand, operates negatively so as to bar a claim to the land, thus leaving some other claimant to the land free from the competing claim. Limitation may operate differentially, barring one person but not another. Thus it may bar a tenant under a lease but not his landlord.

4. Possession as the basis of title

In English law, the basis of title to land is possession. Possession of land by itself gives a title to the land good against the whole world except a person with a better right to possession.[9] If X takes possession of A's land, X has a title which will avail against all save A; a title acquired by wrong is still a title. X has a fee simple, and so has A; but all titles are relative, and so although X's fee is good, A's is better.[10] If, however, A fails to take steps to recover the land in due time, his claim will be barred by limitation, and X's fee, freed from the superior claims of A's fee, will be good against all the world.

5. Elements of limitation

In every case of limitation, three points must be considered, namely:

---

[5] *ibid.*, at paras 55–56 *per* Keene L.J. The periods in civil law jurisdictions are periods of prescription (*q.v. infra*) rather than periods of limitation.
[6] *ibid.*, at para. 52 *per* Mummery L.J.
[7] *ibid.*
[7a] (2002) *The Times*, July 6, 2002. See above, n. 4.
[8] Above, pp. 430 *et seq.* See generally *Buckinghamshire C.C. v. Moran* [1990] Ch. 623 at 644.
[9] *Asher v. Whitlock* (1865) L.R. 1 Q.B. 1.
[10] See *Leach v. Jay* (1878) 9 Ch.D. 42 at 44, 45; *Ocean Estates Ltd v. Pinder* [1969] 2 A.C. 19 at 24, 25.

(i) the length of the period;

(ii) when time starts to run; and

(iii) the effect of the elapse of time.

These will be taken in turn.

PART 1—THE LENGTH OF THE PERIOD

1. Under the Limitation Act 1980

There are two main periods of limitation and certain additional special periods:

(i) a period of six years for actions on simple contracts (such as for money lent without security) or claims for rent, and actions in tort[11];

(ii) a period of 12 years (formerly 20 years) for the recovery of land or of money charged on land, as by a mortgage,[12] and for money due under a covenant;

(iii) a period of 30 years (formerly 60 years) in the case of Crown land[13] (the 60-year period has been retained in the case of foreshore owned by the Crown[14]); and

(iv) a period of 30 years in the case of a spiritual or eleemosynary (*i.e.* charitable) corporation sole, such as a bishop or the master of a hospital.[15]

2. Under the Land Registration Act 2002

No period of limitation will run under the Limitation Act 1980 in respect of any estate in land, rentcharge or right of redemption the title to which is registered when the Land Registration Act 2002 comes into force.[16] Instead:

(i) when a person is in adverse possession of registered land or has been evicted from that land during the last six months by the registered proprietor and he and his predecessors in title have been in adverse possession for 10 years, he will be able to apply to the registrar to be registered as proprietor[17];

(ii) the registrar will then notify this application to the registered proprietor, any registered chargee, and the registered proprietor of any superior title.[18] Anyone who is notified will be able to serve a notice on the registrar within a period to be laid down by the new Rules[19];

---

[11] Limitation Act 1980, ss.2, 5, 19. Claims in tort are subject to the Latent Damage Act 1986; and three years is the normal period for personal injuries: s.11.
[12] Limitation Act 1980, ss.15, 20.
[13] *ibid.*, s.15(1), Sched. 1, para. 10.
[14] *ibid.*, para. 11.
[15] *ibid.*, para. 10.
[16] L.R.A. 2002, s.96.
[17] *ibid.*, Sched. 6, para. 1.
[18] *ibid.*, para. 2.
[19] *ibid.*, para. 3.

    (iii) if no one serves a notice, the applicant will be registered as proprietor[20];

    (iv) if anyone docs serve a notice, the applicant will only be able to be registered as proprietor at this stage in one of the following three circumstances:

        (a) if it would be unconscionable because of an equity by estoppel for the registered proprietor to seek to dispossess the applicant and the circumstances are such that the applicant ought to be registered as proprietor;

        (b) if he is for some other reason entitled to be registered as proprietor (examples will be being entitled under the will or intestacy of the deceased proprietor or having purchased the land without having taken a transfer); and

        (c) if he is the owner of adjoining property, the boundary has not been determined, and for the 10-year period he reasonably believed that the land to which the application relates belonged to him[21]; and

    (v) a further application by the same applicant or his successors in title to be registered as proprietor after a further two-year period of possession will be successful[22] (even if he does not make a further application, earlier judgments for possession then become unenforceable against him and he has a defence to any future action for possession[23]).

The only special period which will remain is in the case of foreshore owned by the Crown; 60 years' adverse possession will be needed before the first application.[24] First registered proprietors of land registered under the Land Registration Act 2002 will be bound by interests already acquired under the Limitation Act 1980.[25]

PART 2—THE RUNNING OF TIME

Time therefore has to run both under the Limitation Act 1980 and under the Land Registration Act 2002. The Land Registration Act 2002 specifically provides that a person is in adverse possession for the purposes of that Act if he would have been in adverse possession under the Limitation Act 1980.[26] However, there are some exceptions to this basic rule[27] which will be referred to below. The running of time falls under three heads: first, when time begins to run; secondly, what will postpone this date; and thirdly, what will start time running afresh. In general, once time has begun to run, it runs continuously.[28]

Sect. 1. When time begins to run

In the case of actions for the recovery of land or capital sums charged on land, time begins to run in accordance with the following rules.

[20] *ibid.*, para. 4.
[21] *ibid.*, para. 5.
[22] *ibid.*, paras 6, 7.
[23] *ibid.*, s.98(2), (3), (4).
[24] *ibid.*, Sched. 6, para. 13.
[25] *ibid.*, s.11(4)(c).
[26] *ibid.*, Sched. 6, para. 11(1).
[27] *ibid.*, paras 11(2), 12.
[28] *Bowring-Hanbury's Trustee v. Bowring-Hanbury* [1943] Ch. 104.

1. Owner entitled in possession

Time will begin to run against an owner of land who is entitled in possession only where:

> (i) he has either been dispossessed or discontinued his possession; and

> (ii) adverse possession of the land has been taken by some other person.[29]

(a) Dispossession or discontinuance

An owner is "dispossessed" when he has been driven out of possession by another,[30] though there may be dispossession even if the owner knows nothing of it.[31] An owner has "discontinued" his possession when he has abandoned it,[32] though mere non-user will not necessarily be abandonment.[33] Neither dispossession nor discontinuance alone will start time running: there must be adverse possession as well, and it is this which is of paramount importance.[34]

(b) Adverse possession

Adverse possession is a somewhat complex concept. It depends on the squatter having possession of the land in fact, and also on his having the necessary *animus possidendi*; and in some cases these requirements may be affected by the owner's intended use for the land but this is much less frequent than it used to be.

(i) Possession: The squatter must establish that he has a degree of physical control of the land which amounts to possession in fact.[35] The nature of the requisite acts will vary with the nature of the land: they will not be the same for a buildings, a narrow strip of land, open fields, moorlands or a swamp.[36] Acts may suffice even though they do not inconvenience or otherwise affect the owner.[37]

For buildings, changing the lock of a flat and living in it thereafter as if it were the squatter's own is unequivocable evidence.[38] So is moving into the upper part of a house of which the squatter was tenant of the ground floor.[39] Adverse possession may be subterranean, such as of a cellar.[40] One half of a seven metre stretch of a party wall in Knightsbridge was possessed by the owner of the other half as a result of installing, at different times, a security camera, security lighting, an entryphone system, a wall safe and an overflow pipe and by putting a roof on top of it.[41]

For open land, "enclosure is the strongest possible evidence of adverse possession, but it is not indispensable"[42]; concreting over an enclosed area and using it as a car park clearly

---

[29] Limitation Act 1980, Sched. 1, paras 1, 8.
[30] *Rains v. Buxton* (1880) 14 Ch.D. 537 at 539.
[31] *Powell v. McFarlane* (1979) 38 P. & C.R. 452 at 480.
[32] *Rimington v. Cannon* (1853) 12 C.B. 18 at 33.
[33] *Tecbild Ltd v. Chamberlain* (1969) 20 P. & C.R. 633.
[34] *Buckinghamshire C.C. v. Moran* [1990] Ch. 623 at 645.
[35] *Buckinghamshire C.C. v. Moran* [1990] Ch. 623.
[36] See *West Bank Estates Ltd v. Arthur* [1967] 1 A.C. 665; *Treloar v. Nute* [1976] 1 W.L.R. 1295 at 1302; *Trustees of the Michael Batt Charitable Trust v. Adams* (2001) 82 P. & C.R. 406.
[37] *Treloar v. Nute* [1976] 1 W.L.R. 1295.
[38] *Lambeth L.B.C. v. Blackburn* (2001) 82 P. & C.R. 39.
[39] *Pollard v. Jackson* (1993) 67 P. & C.R. 327.
[40] *Rains v. Buxton* (1880) 14 Ch.D. 537.
[41] *Prudential Assurance Co. Ltd v. Waterloo Real Estate* [1999] 2 E.G.L.R. 85.
[42] *Seddon v. Smith* (1877) 36 L.T. 168 at 169, *per* Cockburn C.J.; *Buckinghamshire C.C. v. Moran* [1990] Ch. 623.

suffices[43] as does maintaining the garden of an enclosed area.[44] (That does not mean that enclosure will be decisive if *animus possidendi* is absent because a fence or gates were erected merely in order to prevent invasions by the public.[45]) Relatively trivial acts such as using the land for children to play on, or for tethering ponies or grazing goats will usually be insufficient,[46] though when land is virtually useless save for shooting, shooting over it may suffice.[47] In many cases, in the nature of things, adverse possession cannot be continuous from day to day.[48]

(ii) "Adverse": Possession is "adverse" only if the squatter has an *animus possidendi*, intending to possess the land to the exclusion of all other persons, including the owner[49]; no intention to own or acquire ownership of the land is needed.[50] Possession will not cease to be adverse merely because the owner, in ignorance of his title, accepts a tenancy from the squatter.[51]

However, the distribution of keys to other persons entitled to use the land indicates a lack of *animus possidendi*.[52] Nor does a tenant who occupies land thinking that it is part of the land leased to him have sufficient *animus possidendi* to maintain adverse possession as against the true owner either for himself or for his landlord.[53] An intermittent though persistent trespasser who does not seek to dispossess the owner is not in adverse possession.[54] Nor is possession adverse if it is enjoyed under a contract with the owner,[55] or under a licence granted by him,[56] even if the licensee, without rejecting it, never in terms accepted it.[57] However, the possession of a former licensee who has continued to use the land without permission in the hope that its owner would accede to his requests for a new licence is sufficient.[58]

(iii) Owner's intended use: Where the owner has no present use for the land, even very substantial acts of possession were formerly not accepted as constituting adverse possession if they did not interfere with the owner's intended future use of the land.[59] Thus in the circumstances of the case, using a strip of land as a dump for foundry refuse,[60] or cultivating the land and then erecting sheds and a fence on it for use in rearing greyhounds,[61] or using the land for farming and as part of a holiday camp,[62] have all been regarded as not

---

[43] *Burns v. Anthony* (1997) 74 P. & C.R. D41.

[44] *Buckinghamshire C.C. v. Moran* [1990] Ch. 623; *Hounslow L.B.C. v. Minchinton* (1997) 74 P. & C.R. 221.

[45] *Littledale v. Liverpool Corporation* [1900] 1 Ch. 19; *George Wimpey & Co. Ltd v. Sohn* [1967] Ch. 487.

[46] *Tecbild Ltd v. Chamberlain* (1969) 20 P. & C.R. 633; *Boosey v. Davis* (1987) 55 P. & C.R. 83.

[47] *Red House Farms (Thorndon) Ltd v. Catchpole* [1977] E.G.D. 798.

[48] *Bligh v. Martin* [1968] 1 W.L.R. 804 at 811.

[49] *Buckinghamshire C.C. v. Moran* [1990] Ch. 623.

[50] *ibid.*, see also *Lambeth L.B.C. v. Blackburn* (2001) 82 P. & C.R. 39.

[51] *Bligh v. Martin* [1968] 1 W.L.R. 804.

[52] *Battersea Freehold and Leasehold Property Co. Ltd v. Battersea L.B.C.* (2001) 82 P. & C.R. 137.

[53] *Trustees of the Michael Batt Charitable Trust v. Adams* (2001) 82 P. & C.R. 406.

[54] *Powell v. McFarlane* (1979) 38 P. & C.R. 452 at 480.

[55] *Hyde v. Pearce* [1982] 1 W.L.R. 560.

[56] *Hughes v. Griffin* [1969] 1 W.L.R. 23.

[57] *B.P. Properties Ltd v. Buckler* (1987) 55 P. & C.R. 337.

[58] *Pye (J.A.) Oxford Ltd v. Graham* (2002) *The Times*, July 6, 2002 (House of Lords reversing Court of Appeal decision at [2001] 2 W.L.R. 1293).

[59] *Leigh v. Jack* (1879) 5 Ex.D. 264.

[60] *ibid.*

[61] *Williams Brothers Direct Supply Ltd v. Raftery* [1958] 1 Q.B. 159.

[62] *Wallis's Cayton Bay Holiday Camp Ltd v. Shell-Mex and B.P. Ltd* [1975] Q.B. 94. The doctrine of implied licence in this case has now been despatched: Limitation Act 1980, Sched. 1, para. 8(4).

constituting adverse possession as against owners whose respective intentions were to dedicate the strip as a highway in the future, to develop the land when that became possible, or to use the land as the site of a garage fronting on to a road if the road was ever constructed.

Today, these cases are not accepted as establishing any separate rule based on the owner's intention. Instead, they are explained in relation to the squatter. In such cases the court will readily treat the squatter's acts either as not manifesting a sufficient *animus possidendi* or else as not showing a sufficient degree of exclusive occupation to amount to possession.[63] In particular, if the squatter knows of the owner's future intentions for unbuilt land, that knowledge may prevent acts of the squatter that are not inconsistent with those intentions from amounting to adverse possession, unless there is very clear evidence to the contrary.[64] The mere use of vacant land until the owner needs it is a frail foundation for a possessory title but, if there is very clear evidence, it will be sufficient.

2. Future interests

(a) Under the Limitation Act 1980

Under the Limitation Act 1980, a person entitled in reversion or in remainder at the time when adverse possession is taken has alternative periods: he has 12 years from adverse possession being taken or six years from the falling of his interest into possession, whichever is the longer.[65] Thus if land is settled on A for life with remainder to B, and X dispossesses A 10 years before A dies, B has six years from A's death in which to sue; but if X had dispossessed A three years before A's death, B would have 12 years from the dispossession of A. If X had not taken adverse possession until after A's death, B's interest would no longer have been a future interest, and he would have the normal period of 12 years from the taking of adverse possession. Further, if A's interest had been an estate in fee tail, then if he had been dispossessed by X, B would have been barred 12 years later. The alternative six-year period does not extend to a reversioner or remainderman whose interest was liable to be barred by the barring of a prior interest in fee tail.[66]

(b) Under the Land Registration Act 2002

No one will be regarded as having been in adverse possession during any period in which the land has been held for persons by way of succession.[67] Consequently, in all the examples above, X will not be able to make his first application until he has been in adverse possession as against B for 10 years. This apparently applies even where B is a reversioner or remainderman whose interest is liable to be barred by the barring of a prior interest in fee tail. This may be an oversight.

3. Leaseholds

The above provisions do not apply to a freehold or leasehold reversioner on a lease for a term of years where the tenant has been ousted. Irrespective of when the dispossession occurred, time does not run against the reversioner until the lease expires, because, until then, he has

---

[63] *Buckinghamshire C.C. v. Moran* [1990] Ch. 623 at 639.
[64] *ibid.*, at 639, 643; *Pye (J.A.) Oxford Ltd v. Graham* (2002) *The Times*, July 6, 2002, where the owner's expert could not think of anything else the squatter could have done with the land.
[65] Limitation Act 1980, s.15(2), Sched. 1, para. 4.
[66] *ibid.*, ss.15(3), 38(5).
[67] L.R.A. 2002, Sched. 6, para. 12.

no right to possession.[68] Thus if L grants T a lease for 99 years and T is dispossessed by X, the 12-year period runs against T from the dispossession but against L only from the determination of the lease.

A tenant cannot acquire a title to the land leased to him as against his landlord during the currency of the lease, even by prolonged failure to pay rent. There is one exception to this in the case of a lease capable of enlargement into a fee simple. If a rent not exceeding £1 per annum reserved by such a lease has not been paid for a continuous period of 20 years, five of which have elapsed since 1925, the rent ceases to be payable. Neither the arrears nor any future payment can be recovered, and the lease may be enlarged into a fee simple.[69] Further, where the tenant takes possession of adjoining land of the landlord, there is a rebuttable[70] presumption that he takes it as an extension of his lease,[71] and it becomes subject to the terms of the tenancy.[72] Similarly a tenant's adverse possession of adjoining land of a third party is prima facie for the benefit of the landlord as well as the tenant.[73] However, the tenant must know that the land does not belong to his landlord or he will lack the necessary *animus possidendi*.[74]

A landlord may be barred if adverse possession is taken not of the land but of the rent from it; for if for 12 years the tenant under a lease in writing at a rent of at least £10 per annum pays the rent to some person who wrongfully claims the reversion, and no rent is subsequently paid to the landlord, this bars the landlord's right to the reversion.[75] This rule will not apply to registered land when the Land Registration Act 2002 comes into force.[75a]

4. Yearly or other periodic tenants

Where there is a yearly or other periodic tenancy under a lease in writing, time runs in the tenant's favour from the determination of the tenancy. If there is no lease in writing, time runs in the tenant's favour from the end of the first year or other shorter period of the tenancy,[76] subject to extension[77] by written acknowledgement, or by payment of rent, in which case time runs from the last receipt of rent.[78] An oral periodic tenancy will in due course entitle the tenant to claim title under the Limitation Act 1980 or to apply under the Land Registration Act 2002 if no rent is paid for long enough. This is also the case if the tenant thinks that he is paying rent but he is not in fact doing so.[79]

5. Tenants at will and at sufferance, and licensees

Time begins to run in favour of a tenant at will on the determination of his tenancy,[80] and in favour of a tenant at sufferance on the commencement of his tenancy; for he has no true

---

[68] Limitation Act 1980, Sched. 1, para. 4.
[69] L.P.A. 1925, s.153; above, pp. 333, 334.
[70] See *Kingsmill v. Millard* (1855) 11 Exch. 313 at 318, 319.
[71] *Smirk v. Lyndale Developments Ltd* [1975] Ch. 317, reversed on appeal but not on this point.
[72] *J.F. Perrott & Co. Ltd v. Cohen* [1951] 1 K.B. 705.
[73] *King v. Smith* [1950] 1 All E.R. 554.
[74] *Trustees of the Michael Batt Charitable Trust v. Adams* (2001) 82 P. & C.R. 406.
[75] Limitation Act 1980, Sched. 1, para. 6.
[75a] L.R.A. 2002, Sched. 6, para. 11(3)(b).
[76] *ibid.*, paras 4, 5(1). See, *e.g. Jessamine Investment Co. v. Schwartz* [1978] Q.B. 264.
[77] Below, p. 559.
[78] Limitation Act 1980, Sched. 1, para. 5(2).
[79] *Lodge v. Wakefield Metropolitan C.C.* [1995] 2 E.G.L.R. 124.
[80] Limitation Amendment Act 1980, s.3(1), repealing Limitation Act 1939, s.9(1); Limitation Act 1980, Sched. 1, para. 4.

tenancy,[81] but is in adverse possession. Time does not run in favour of a licensee, for he holds by the owner's consent.[82]

6. Rentcharges

In the case of a rentcharge in possession, time runs from the last payment of rent to the owner of the rentcharge.[83] Thus the owner's rights are barred:

> (i) if no rent is paid for 12 years, in which case the rentcharge is extinguished; or

> (ii) if the rent is paid to a stranger for 12 years, in which case the rentcharge remains enforceable against the land but the former owner's claim to it is extinguished in favour of the stranger.

Similar rules apply to other rents not due under a lease. Rules must provide how the provisions of the Land Registration Act 2002 will apply to registered rentcharges.[84]

7. Mortgages

As soon as a mortgagee goes into possession, time begins to run against subsequent mortgagees and the mortgagor so as to bar their rights to redeem.[85] However, under the Land Registration Act 2002, he will have to apply to the registrar in the usual way after 10 years.[86] As regards the mortgagee's right to recover the money charged on the land, or to foreclose, time runs against him from the date upon which the money was due,[87] and when he is barred, his mortgage ceases to exist.[88] In each case, any written acknowledgment or any payment on account of principal or interest starts time running afresh.[89]

8. Claims through Crown or corporation sole

It has been seen that the Crown is at present entitled to a 30-year period instead of the usual 12.[90] If a person against whom time has started to run conveys his land to the Crown, the only change is that the limitation period becomes 30 years from the dispossession instead of 12. But in the converse case, where time has started to run against the Crown and the Crown then conveys the land to X, the rule is that X is barred at the expiration of 30 years from the original dispossession or 12 years from the conveyance to him, whichever is the shorter.[91] Thus X is entitled to 12 years from the date of the conveyance unless at that time there were less than 12 years of the Crown period unexpired, in which case he merely has the residue of that period.

Similar rules at present apply[92] to the 30-year period for a spiritual or eleemosynary corporation sole.[93]

---

[81] Above, p. 350.
[82] *Hughes v. Griffin* [1969] 1 W.L.R. 23.
[83] Limitation Act 1980, s.38(8).
[84] L.R.A. 2002, Sched. 6, para. 14.
[85] Limitation Act 1980, s.16; see, *e.g. Young v. Clarey* [1948] Ch. 191.
[86] L.R.A. 2002, s.95(2).
[87] Limitation Act 1980, s.20.
[88] *Cotterell v. Price* [1960] 1 W.L.R. 1097.
[89] Limitation Act 1980, s.29; below, p. 559.
[90] Above, p. 549.
[91] Limitation Act 1980, Sched. 1, para. 12.
[92] *ibid.*
[93] Above, p. 549.

Neither of these special periods will exist in the case of registered land when the Land Registration Act 2002 comes into force so the rules set out above will no longer be necessary in relation to such land.

9. Trusts

(a) Adverse possession by stranger

Equitable interests under trusts of land or under settlements under the Settled Land Act 1925 are in general treated as "land" and so as subject to the normal rules.[94]

However, adverse possession of trust property by a stranger under the Limitation Act 1980 does not bar the trustee's title to the property until all the beneficiaries have been barred.[95] Thus if land is held on trust for A for life with remainder to B, 12 years' adverse possession of the land by X bars A's equitable interest and, but for the provision just mentioned, would bar the title to the legal estate. But time will not start to run against B's equitable interest until A's death,[96] and the same accordingly applies to the trustee's legal estate. Consequently, after the 12 years have run, the legal estate will be held on trust for X for the life of A, and subject thereto on trust for B. This is so whether the legal estate is held by the trustee (as will be the case under a trust of land) or by A (as will usually be the case under a settlement under the Settled Land Act 1925.

No adverse possession will be possible under the Land Registration Act 2002 of land which is held for persons by way of succession.[97] Consequently, in the example set out above X will not be able to apply to be registered as proprietor until 10 years after A's death.

(b) Adverse possession by trustee

Trustees cannot obtain a title against their beneficiaries by adverse possession of the trust property; for there is no period of limitation for an action by a beneficiary to recover from his trustees the trust property or its proceeds in their possession or converted to their use, or in respect of any fraud by the trustees.[98] Thus if land is conveyed to X and Y as trustees of land for themselves as tenants in common, X cannot obtain a title to the land as against Y, no matter how long he excludes Y from the land or its rents and profits; for X and Y hold the legal estate on trust for themselves as tenants in common,[99] and X is thus trustee for Y.[1] But subject to this, the limitation period in respect of breaches of trust (such as paying the income of the trust to the wrong person) is six years.[2]

In one case a trustee's liability may be curtailed if he is also a beneficiary. If on a distribution of trust funds such a trustee receives or retains for himself trust property or its proceeds in excess of his proper share, his liability will be restricted to that excess after six years have passed, provided he acted honestly and reasonably.[3] Thus, if in distributing the trust property T takes one-third of it for himself in the honest and reasonable belief that it is divisible equally between himself and two others, his liability on the subsequent appearance

---

[94] Limitation Act 1980, ss.18, 20.
[95] *ibid.*, s.18.
[96] Above, p. 552.
[97] L.R.A. 2002, Sched. 6, para. 12.
[98] Limitation Act 1980, s.21(1).
[99] Above, p. 309.
[1] See *Re Landi* [1939] Ch. 828.
[2] Limitation Act 1980, s.21(3).
[3] *ibid.*, s.21(2).

of a further beneficiary who is entitled to share equally will be limited to one-twelfth of the trust property, once the six years have run.

(c) Adverse possession by beneficiary

Time does not begin to run against the trustees or other beneficiaries if land held on a trust of land or under a settlement subject to the Settled Land Act 1925 is in the possession of a beneficiary who is not solely and absolutely entitled to it.[4]

Sect. 2. Postponement of the period

The date from which time begins to run may be postponed or the running of time may be suspended for a number of reasons. However, the issue of proceedings, whether or not they are served, which are not pursued (because, for example, they have been dismissed for want of prosecution) does not stop time running.[5]

1. Disability under the Limitation Act 1980

If the owner of an interest in land is under disability when the right of action accrues, then even if the normal period of limitation expires, the period is extended to six years from the time when he ceases to be under a disability or dies, whichever happens first, with a maximum period in the case of land of 30 years from the date when the right of action first accrued.[6] Thus if X takes possession of A's land at a time when A is of unsound mind, A will have 12 years from the dispossession or six years from his recovery in which to bring his action, whichever period is the longer, subject to the limit of 30 years from the dispossession.

(a) Meaning of "disability"

A person is under a disability for this purpose "while he is an infant or of unsound mind".[7] For brevity and uniformity, the terms "minor", and "insane" or "mental patient", will be used.

(b) Supervening disability

A disability is immaterial unless it existed at the time when the cause of action accrued. Thus if A becomes insane the day before he is dispossessed, the provisions for disability apply, whereas if he becomes insane the day after he has been dispossessed, they do not.

(c) Successive disabilities

In the case of successive disabilities, if a person is under one disability and before that ceases another disability begins, the period is extended until both disabilities cease, subject to the maximum of 30 years.[8] But if one disability comes to an end before another disability starts, or if the person under disability is succeeded by another person under disability, time runs from the ceasing of the first disability. For example, A is a minor when the cause of action accrues. If later, during his minority, he becomes insane, the six years does not start to run

---

[4] *ibid.*, Sched. 1, para. 9.
[5] *Markfield Investments Ltd v. Evans* (2001) 81 P. & C.R. 33, see also L.R.A. 2002, Sched. 6, para. 11(3)(a).
[6] Limitation Act 1980, s.28.
[7] *ibid.*, s.38(2).
[8] See *ibid.*, s.28(1).

until he is both sane and of full age. But if he reaches full age before he becomes insane, or if he dies a minor, and B, a mental patient, becomes entitled to the land, the six years run from A's majority in the first case and his death in the second.[9]

2. Disability under the Land Registration Act 2002

Under the Land Registration Act 2002, no one may apply to be registered as proprietor during any period during which the existing registered proprietor is unable because of mental disability to make decisions of the kind to which the application would give rise or is unable to communicate his decisions because of either mental disability or physical impairment.[10] Mental disability is defined as "a disability or disorder of the mind or brain, whether permanent or temporary, which results in an impairment or disturbance of mental functioning".[11]

3. Fraud, deliberate concealment and mistake

Where:

   (i) an action is based on the fraud of the defendant or his agent, or of any person through whom he claims, or his agent, or

   (ii) any fact relevant to the claimant's right of action has been deliberately concealed from him by any such person, or

   (iii) the action is for relief from the consequences of a mistake,

then time does not begin to run against the landowner until he discovers the fraud, concealment or mistake, or could with reasonable diligence have discovered it.[12] The term "deliberately concealed" has removed the element of unconscionable conduct[13] that was required by the former words "concealed by . . . fraud".[14] The deliberate commission of a breach of duty in circumstances in which it is unlikely to be discovered for some time amounts to deliberate concealment of the facts involved in that breach of duty.[15]

The rule as to mistake applies only where mistake is the basis of the action, as where the action is to recover money paid under a mistake of fact. There is no general doctrine that making a mistake (for example as to the true position of a boundary) stops time running.[16]

Neither fraud nor mistake will postpone the running of time as against a subsequent purchaser for value who did not know or have reason to believe that there was fraud or mistake.[17]

[9] *ibid.*, s.28(3).
[10] L.R.A. 2002, Sched. 6, para. 8(2).
[11] *ibid.*, para. 8(3).
[12] Limitation Act 1980, s.32(1).
[13] See *Bartlett v. Barclays Bank Trust Co. Ltd* [1980] Ch. 515 at 537.
[14] Limitation Act 1939, s.26(b).
[15] Limitation Act 1980, s.32(2).
[16] See *Phillips-Higgins v. Harper* [1954] 1 Q.B. 411.
[17] Limitation Act 1980, s.32(3).

4. During wartime

The running of time under the Limitation Act 1980 is suspended is suspended during any period in which the owner is an enemy or is detained in enemy territory[18] and no application can be made under the Land Registration Act 2002 during any such period.[19]

Sect. 3. Starting time running afresh

Time may be started running afresh by:

(i) a signed acknowledgment in writing of the owner's title; or

(ii) part payment of principal or interest.[20]

The acknowledgment or payment must be signed or made by the person in whose favour time is running, or by his agent, and it must be made to the person whose title is being barred, or to his agent.[21] The acknowledgment must be of existing liability[22] and not merely of facts which might give rise to liability,[23] or merely that there might be a claim.[24] An order for possession will start time running afresh,[25] but a mere demand for possession will not.[26] Once the full period has run, however, no payment or acknowledgment can revive a right to recover land, for the elapse of time will have extinguished not only the owner's remedies for recovering the land but also his right to it.[27] It is otherwise in the case of other actions, where lapse of time bars only the remedy and not the right. Yet by estoppel a squatter, like any other land-owner, may preclude himself from asserting his title.[28]

PART 3—THE EFFECT OF THE ELAPSE OF TIME

Sect. 1. Title to land

1. The squatter's title to unregistered land acquired under the Limitation Act 1980

(a) No "parliamentary conveyance"

The operation of the Limitation Act 1980 is negative, not positive: it transfers nothing but extinguishes the owner's title. The owner's title is not transferred to the squatter, and so there is no "parliamentary conveyance" to him.[29] Instead, the squatter owns a new estate of his

---

[18] Limitation (Enemies and War Prisoners) Act 1945.
[19] L.R.A. 2002, Sched. 6, para. 8(1).
[20] Limitation Act 1980, s.29.
[21] *ibid.*, s.30. *Lambeth L.B.C. v. Archangel* [2002] 1 P. & C.R. 18.
[22] As in *Moodie v. Bannister* (1859) 4 Drew. 432; *Dungate v. Dungate* [1965] 1 W.L.R. 1477; *Lambeth L.B.C. v. Archangel* [2002] 1 P. & C.R. 18.
[23] *Re Flynn (No. 2)* [1969] 2 Ch. 403.
[24] *Good v. Parry* [1963] 2 Q.B. 418.
[25] *B.P. Properties Ltd v. Buckler* (1987) 55 P. & C.R. 337.
[26] *Mount Carmel Investments Ltd v. Peter Thurlow Ltd* (1989) 57 P. & C.R. 396.
[27] Limitation Act 1980, s.17; *Nicholson v. England* [1926] 2 K.B. 93.
[28] *Colchester B.C. v. Smith* [1992] 2 W.L.R. 728; see above, pp. 434 *et seq.*
[29] *Tichborne v. Weir* (1892) 67 L.T. 735 at 737.

own which by limitation will progressively improve until all competing interests are barred and he has an unincumbered fee simple absolute.

(b) Burdens binding the squatter

Even if a squatter acquires title to an estate in fee simple, he may not be able to take a clean title; for burdens which bound the land will continue to bind it in the hands of the squatter. For example, a squatter will be bound by a restrictive covenant attached to the land unless he can show that it is no longer enforceable, for instance, by lapse of time since a breach of it; for until a breach occurs the covenantee has no right of action and time does not run against him. A squatter without notice is not a purchaser without notice.[30] He will also be bound by easements and profits *à prendre* unless they have been abandoned.[31] However, a squatter who acquires title to a lease but not a title to the freehold is not in the position of an assignee of that lease. An assignee is liable to be sued for a breach of covenant committed while he held the lease even if at the time of the action the lease has expired,[32] but a squatter cannot be sued after the expiration of a lease for breaches of covenant committed while he was in possession of the land.[33] Yet during the term of the lease, he can be forced to pay the rent and perform the covenants by the threat of distress for rent or, if the lease contains a forfeiture clause, of forfeiture,[34] but he has no right to apply for relief against forfeiture[35] and he is of course bound by any restrictive covenants in the lease.

If a squatter takes advantage of some clause in the lease, such as a proviso that the rent should be halved if the covenants are observed, he cannot "blow hot and cold". If he accepts the benefits of the lease, he cannot reject the burdens. Consequently, he will be estopped from denying that he is bound by the lease.[36] But the mere payment of rent under a lease with no such clause will not operate as an estoppel.[37]

A squatter may also be bound by rights over the land that arise during the period of dispossession, as where the owner, by entering the land from time to time to trim a hedge and clear a drain,[38] or to repair and maintain his adjoining house,[39] acquires rights in the nature of easements.

(c) Barred leaseholds

If a squatter bars a tenant but not the freeholder, and the tenant then acquires the freehold, time begins to run against the freehold; but until it has run, the tenant, by virtue of owning the freehold, may evict the squatter, for the freehold is not barred, and the former tenancy has merged in the freehold.[40] Further, if instead the tenant surrenders his tenancy to the freeholder, this enables the freeholder to evict the squatter forthwith, for the surrender removes the only interest which prevented the freeholder from claiming possession of land that he

---

[30] *Re Nisbet & Pott's Contract* [1906] 1 Ch. 386.
[31] Above, pp. 442–443.
[32] Above, pp. 381 *et seq.*
[33] *Tichborne v. Weir* (1892) 67 L.T. 735.
[34] See above, p. 381.
[35] *Tickner v. Buzzacott* [1965] Ch. 426.
[36] *Ashe v. Hogan* [1920] 1 I.R. 159; *Tito v. Waddell (No. 2)* [1977] Ch. 106 at 299–302.
[37] *Tichborne v. Weir* (1892) 67 L.T. 735.
[38] *Marshall v. Taylor* [1895] 1 Ch. 641 at 648, 651.
[39] *Williams v. Usherwood* (1983) 45 P. & C.R. 235.
[40] *Taylor v. Twinberrow* [1930] 2 K.B. 16.

owns.[41] Pending merger or surrender, the better view is that the tenant who has been dispossessed and the freeholder remain liable to one another on all the covenants in the lease throughout the remaining term.[42] This will be the case whether the lease is an "old lease" or a "new lease".[43] (Of course no new lease can possibly yet have been the subject of adverse possession.) In the case of an "old lease", the original tenant will also remain liable to the freeholder.

2. The squatter's title to registered land acquired under the Limitation Act 1980

(a) A "parliamentary conveyance"

The necessary period of adverse possession to registered land under the Limitation Act 1980 does not extinguish the estate of the registered proprietor. The latter and his successors in title hold that estate on trust for the squatter without prejudice to the estates and interests of any person whose rights have not been extinguished.[44] The squatter can then apply to be registered as proprietor and must be registered if the registrar is satisfied as to his claim.[45] It is therefore now clear that the squatter does indeed acquire his estate by virtue of a "parliamentary conveyance".[46] Until the squatter has completed the necessary period of adverse possession, the better view is that his title is legal rather than equitable[47] and so he can grant legal interests out of it. Once the necessary period has been completed and he becomes a beneficiary under the statutory trust, his title then is clearly only equitable pending registration and the title which he has acquired at common law is nullified.[48] However, in the case of leases, these rules only apply where they are registered. Leases for 21 years or less are extinguished by adverse possession in the same way as estates in unregistered land.

(b) Burdens binding the squatter

Even if a squatter acquires title to an estate in fee simple, he will be bound by the estates and interests of any person whose rights have not been extinguished.[49] As in the case of unregistered land, he will be bound by a restrictive covenant attached to the land unless he can show that it is no longer enforceable and by easements and profits *à prendre* which have not been abandoned. Unlike the position in unregistered land, a squatter who acquires title to a lease but not a title to the freehold is in the position of an assignee of the lease[50] and is liable to be sued for a breach of covenant committed while he held the lease, even if at the time of the action the lease has expired.[51] For the same reason during the term of the lease, he is bound to pay the rent and perform the covenants[52] and, if the lease contains a forfeiture clause, is presumably entitled to apply for relief against forfeiture.

---

[41] *Fairweather v. St. Marylebone Property Co. Ltd* [1963] A.C. 510; but see (1962) 78 L.Q.R. 33 (H.W.R. Wade).

[42] *Spectrum Investment Co. v. Holmes* [1981] 1 W.L.R. 221; cp. *Re Field* [1918] 1 I.R. 40.

[43] Because the assignment to the squatter will be an "excluded assignment"; L. & T.(C.)A. 1995, s.11.

[44] L.R.A. 1925, s.75(1).

[45] *ibid.*

[46] *Central London Commercial Estates v. Kato Kagaku Ltd* [1998] 4 All E.R. 948.

[47] *ibid.*, at 953; cp. Ruoff & Roper, para. 29–02.

[48] *ibid.*, at 959.

[49] L.R.A. 1925, s.75(1).

[50] See *Spectrum Investment Co. v. Holmes* [1981] 1 W.L.R. 221; see also L.R.A. 1925, ss.9–11, 75; *Fairweather v. St. Marylebone Property Co. Ltd* [1963] A.C. 510.

[51] Above, pp. 381 *et seq.*

[52] *Central London Commercial Estates v. Kato Kagaku Ltd* [1998] 4 All E.R. 948 at 959.

As in the case of unregistered land, a squatter may also be bound by rights over the land that arise during the period of dispossession, as where the owner, by entering the land from time to time to trim a hedge and clear a drain,[53] or to repair and maintain his adjoining house,[54] acquires rights in the nature of easements.

(c) Barred leaseholds

If a squatter bars a tenant but not the freeholder, and the tenant then acquires the freehold, the lease does not merge with the freehold because it is either held on trust for the squatter or has already been vested in him by a parliamentary conveyance. Nor will any purported surrender of the lease enable the freeholder to evict the squatter prior to the end of the term. If the lease has already been vested in the squatter by a parliamentary conveyance, it will remain binding on the freeholder.[55] If it has not, the squatter's interest under the statutory trust will bind the freeholder as an interest which overrides registration.[56] Pending any acquisition of the freehold by the tenant or any surrender, the tenant who has been dispossessed and the freeholder remain liable to one another on all the covenants in the lease throughout the remaining term.[57] This will be the case whether the lease is an "old lease" or a "new lease".[58] In the case of an "old lease", the original tenant will also remain liable to the freeholder.

3. The squatter's title to registered land acquired under the Land Registration Act 2002

(a) A "parliamentary conveyance"

Registration of the adverse possessor under the Land Registration Act 2002 will extinguish the title which he had by virtue of adverse possession at the time of his application.[59] Thus, as under the Land Registration Act 1925, the existing title will be transferred to him so that there will be a parliamentary conveyance.

(b) Burdens binding the squatter

The Land Registration Act 2002 specifically provides that the registration of an adverse possessor thereunder does not affect the priority of any interest affecting the estate.[60] Thus the position will remain the same as where the squatter's title to registered land is acquired under the Limitation Act 1980. The only exception to this is that the estate will be vested in the squatter free of any registered charges which affected it immediately prior to its registration.[61] This is because registered chargees are among the persons whom the registrar will be obliged to notify of the application of the squatter for registration. If they do not object, there is no reason why they should retain their interests. However, in the three circumstances in which the squatter can be registered as proprietor despite an objection,[62] registered charges will remain binding on him if he is so registered.[63]

---

[53] *Marshall v. Taylor* [1895] 1 Ch. 641 at 648, 651.
[54] *Williams v. Usherwood* (1983) 45 P. & C.R. 235.
[55] *Spectrum Investment Co. v. Holmes* [1981] 1 W.L.R. 221, rejecting contrary dicta in *Fairweather v. St. Marylebone Property Co. Ltd* [1963] A.C. 510.
[56] L.R.A. 1925, s.70(1)(f), (g). *Central London Commercial Estates v. Kato Kagaku Ltd* [1998] 4 All E.R. 948.
[57] *Spectrum Investment Co. v. Holmes* [1981] 1 W.L.R. 221.
[58] Because the assignment to the squatter will be an "excluded assignment"; L. & T.(C.)A. 1995, s.11.
[59] L.R.A. 2002, Sched. 6, para. 9(1).
[60] *ibid.*, para. 9(2).
[61] *ibid.*, para. 9(3).
[62] Above, p. 549.
[63] L.R.A. 2002, Sched. 6, para. 9(4).

(c) Barred leaseholds

If a squatter bars a tenant but not the freeholder, the position will remain the same as where the squatter's title to registered land is acquired under the Limitation Act 1980.

4. Proof of title

A good title to unregistered land cannot be shown merely by proving adverse possession of land, however long the period. If A and his predecessors in title have been in possession of land for 20, 50, or 100 years, that alone does not prove that A is entitled to it; for the true owner:

    (i) might have been under disability at a relevant time; or

    (ii) might have been the Crown; or

    (iii) might have been the reversioner or remainderman under a settlement; or

    (iv) might be the reversioner on a long lease.

Consequently, to establish a good title by the operation of the Act it must be shown:

    (i) who was the true owner of the interest in land in question; and

    (ii) that he has been barred by lapse of time.

It is highly unlikely that a vendor will be able to this unless the person dispossessed left the deeds in the property or can be identified and persuaded to part with them for a consideration. But a vendor who can show these two things can establish a title which the courts will force even an unwilling purchaser to accept.[64]

In the case of registered land, a squatter who has been registered with absolute title or good leasehold title can establish a title which the courts will force even an unwilling purchaser to accept. (A squatter will usually be registered with absolute title but a squatter who bars a tenant rather than a freeholder will only be able to be registered with good leasehold title unless the freehold title is also registered.) But where a squatter has been registered only with possessory title (this will usually occur only where he has sought first registration only on the basis of the adverse possession of himself and his predecessors in title), the same risks arise as in the case of unregistered land. A purchaser can therefore only be forced to accept a possessory title if he has contracted to do so or if the squatter can show the same two things as in the case of unregistered land. (This is even more unlikely than in the case of unregistered land since a squatter who was able to show these two things would almost certainly be registered with absolute title anyway.)

5. Successive squatters

Even before the statutory period has expired, a squatter has a title good against everyone except the true owner.[65] To hold otherwise would mean that a squatter who had not barred the true owner would have no remedy against a person who dispossessed him; this might lead to breaches of the peace by competing squatters. Consequently, if a squatter who has not

---

[64] *Re Atkinson & Horsell's Contract* [1912] 2 Ch. 1; contrast *George Wimpey & Co. Ltd v. Sohn* [1967] Ch. 487.
[65] *Perry v. Clissold* [1907] A.C. 73; above, p. 547.

barred the true owner sells the land he can give the purchaser a right to the land which is valid against all except the true owner. The same applies to devises, gifts or other dispositions by the squatter; in each case the person taking the squatter's interest can add the squatter's period of possession to his own.[66] Thus if X, who has occupied A's land for eight years, sells the land to Y, A will be barred after Y has held the land for a further four years.

Again, if a squatter who is acquiring title under the Limitation Act 1980 is himself dispossessed, the second squatter can add the former period of occupation to his own. For example, if land owned by A has been occupied by X for eight years, and Y dispossesses X, A will be barred when 12 years have elapsed from X first taking possession. But although at the end of that time A is barred, X will not be barred until 12 years from Y's first taking possession, for Y cannot claim to be absolutely entitled until he can show that everybody with any claim to the land has been barred by the elapse of the full period. However, a squatter who applies for registration under the Land Registration Act 2002 will not be able to add the period of occupation of any squatter whom he himself has dispossessed unless that squatter had earlier dispossessed the applicant and the three periods of adverse possession are continuous.[67]

There is no right to add together two periods of adverse possession if a squatter abandons possession before the full period has run and some time elapses before another person takes possession of the land. During the interval, there is no person in adverse possession whom the true owner could sue; thus time begins to run afresh when the second squatter takes possession of the land.[68]

Sect. 2. Arrears of income

The recovery of arrears of income is distinct from the recovery of the land or capital money which produces it. The arrears of rent which the landlord or the owner of a rentcharge can recover by action or distress are limited to the arrears accrued due during the previous six years.[69] For agricultural holdings, distress is restricted to rent falling due during the previous year,[70] and for bankruptcy it is limited to six months' rent accruing due before the commencement of the bankruptcy.[71]

There is also a six-year period for arrears of mortgage interest.[72] But a mortgagee who exercises his power of sale may retain all arrears of interest out of the proceeds of sale, for this is not recovery by action.[73] A mortgagor who seeks to redeem can do so only on the equitable terms of paying all arrears, however old.[74]

---

[66] *Asher v. Whitlock* (1865) L.R. 1 Q.B. 1. See also *Mount Carmel Investments Ltd v. Peter Thurlow Ltd* (1989) 57 P. & C.R. 396.

[67] L.R.A. 2002, Sched. 6, para. 11(2).

[68] *Trustees, Executors and Agency Co. Ltd v. Short* (1888) 13 App. Cas. 793; Limitation Act 1980, Sched. 1, para. 8(2).

[69] Limitation Act 1980, ss.19, 38(1).

[70] Agricultural Holdings Act 1986, s.16.

[71] Insolvency Act 1986, s.347.

[72] Limitation Act 1980, s.20(5).

[73] *Re Marshfield* (1887) 34 Ch.D. 721.

[74] *Dingle v. Coppen* [1899] 1 Ch. 726; *Holmes v. Cowcher* [1970] 1 W.L.R. 834.

Chapter 15

OWNERSHIP AND ITS LIMITS

At the beginning of the twentieth century, a landowner was very largely free to do as he pleased with his own. He could usually act with impunity despite any consequent injury to others or to the environment. Thus he could erect buildings on his land wherever he wished, use them for any purpose, and alter or demolish them at will; and he was equally free to open mines on his land, or change its use. He could also evict his tenants and increase their rents whenever he wished unless prevented by the terms of their tenancies.

Today, the position has been transformed. By a series of statutes, accelerated by the effects of two world wars, this freedom has, in the public interest, been greatly curtailed. Even in 1936 it was possible to say that "the fundamental assumption of modern statute law is that the landowner holds his land for the public good".[1] These statutes are many and complex, and they can be examined here only in outline: thus what takes over 1000 pages in a recent text-book[2] is summarised in only about 50 pages here.[3] There are exceptions and qualifications to most of what is stated in this chapter. But before considering these statutes, something must be said about the position of the land-owner at common law; this is in Part 1. After that, Part 2 examines the general statutory control of ownership, and Part 3 considers the statutory protection of tenants.

PART 1—RIGHTS AND RESTRICTIONS AT COMMON LAW

Sect. 1. Rights

The owner of the largest estate known to the law, the fee simple absolute in possession, has traditionally enjoyed wide powers of control, disposition and use of the land in which his estate exists; and, subject to statute, he still does.

---

[1] (1936) 49 Harv.L.R. 426 at 436 (W.I. Jennings).
[2] Megarry's *Rent Acts* Vols 1 & 2 (11th ed., 1988), Vol. 3 (2nd ed., 1999).
[3] Below, pp. 569–619.

1. Ownership

The maxim is *cujus est solum, ejus est usque ad coelum et ad inferos*; he who owns the soil is presumed to own everything "up to the sky and down to the centre of the earth".[4] This prima facie includes all mines and minerals,[5] and any chattel not the property of any known person[6] which is found under or attached to the land, such as in the bed of a canal,[7] but it probably does not include a chattel merely resting on the surface.[8] Where land is bounded by the sea or other water which over the years gradually and imperceptibly recedes or advances, then unless the title deeds or the Land Register show that the boundary is fixed and not moveable,[9] the area of the land in the title will be increased by accretion or reduced by diluvion.[10]

2. Disposition

The owner can dispose of his land or any part of it as he wishes. Thus he may sever it horizontally, as by disposing separately of an upper floor of a building, though such dispositions raise many problems, for example as to rights of access and support. The "flying freeholds" in Lincoln's Inn are regulated by statute.[11] It is this difficulty which has led to the introduction of commonhold, the wholly new freehold tenure which will be created when the Commonhold and Leasehold Reform Act 2002 comes into force.[12]

3. Use

The owner may in general use the land in the natural course of user in any way he thinks fit. He may waste or despoil it as he pleases and he is not liable merely because he neglects it.[13]

4. Wild animals

Although wild animals are not the subject of ownership,[14] a landowner has what is sometimes called a "qualified property" in them, consisting of the exclusive right to catch, kill and appropriate the animals on his land; and as soon as the animals are killed they fall into the ownership of the landowner, even if killed by a trespasser.[15]

5. Water

A landowner has no property in water which either percolates through his land or flows through it in a defined channel. In the case of percolating water, the landowner may draw off any or all of it without regard to the claims of neighbouring owners.[16] In the case of water

---

[4] *Corbett v. Hill* (1870) L.R. 9 Eq. 671 at 673; and see *Commissioner for Railways v. Valuer-General* [1974] A.C. 328 at 351, 352; *Grigsby v. Melville* [1974] 1 W.L.R. 80 (cellar). But see below, 568.
[5] *Mitchell v. Mosley* [1914] 1 Ch. 438 at 450; for exceptions, see below, 568.
[6] See *Moffatt v. Kazana* [1969] 2 Q.B. 152 (bank notes hidden in flue).
[7] *Elwes v. Brigg Gas Co.* (1886) 33 Ch.D. 562.
[8] *Hannah v. Peel* [1945] K.B. 509; *Parker v. British Airways Board* [1982] Q.B. 1004.
[9] *Baxendale v. Instow Parish Council* [1982] Ch. 14.
[10] *Southern Centre of Theosophy Inc. v. State of South Australia* [1982] A.C. 706; see [1982] Conv. 208 (R.E. Annand); [1986] Conv. 247 (W. Howarth).
[11] See Lincoln's Inn Act 1860.
[12] See above, p. 464.
[13] *Giles v. Walker* (1890) 24 Q.B.D. 656 (thistles).
[14] *The Case of Swans* (1592) 7 Co.Re 15b at 17b.
[15] *Blade v. Higgs* (1865) 11 H.L.C. 621.
[16] *Chasemore v. Richards* (1859) 7 H.L.C. 349.

flowing through a defined channel, the riparian owner (the owner of the land through which the water flows) cannot always take all the water, though he has certain valuable rights. The owner of only one bank of a stream prima facie may exercise riparian rights up to the middle of the stream.

(a) Fishing

As part of his natural right of ownership the owner has the sole right to fish in the water. Except in tidal waters, the public has no right of fishing even if there is a public right of navigation.[17]

(b) Flow

The owner is entitled to the flow of water through the land unaltered in volume or quality, subject to ordinary and reasonable use by the upper riparian owners; and he is bound by a corresponding obligation to the lower riparian owners.[18]

(c) Abstraction

The ordinary and reasonable use which a riparian owner was formerly entitled to make of the water flowing through his land was[19]:

   (i) the right to take and use all water necessary for ordinary purposes connected with his riparian tenement (such as for watering his cattle or for domestic purposes, or, possibly, in some manufacturing districts, for manufacturing purposes), even though this completely exhausted the stream; and

   (ii) the right to use the water for extraordinary purposes connected with his riparian tenement, provided the use was reasonable and the water was restored substantially undiminished in volume and unaltered in character. Such purposes include irrigation and, in all districts, manufacturing purposes, such as for cooling apparatus. The amount by which the flow might be diminished was a question of degree in each case.[20]

These rights have now been curtailed by statute. In general, nobody may now abstract water from any inland waters, whether river, stream, lake or pond, or from any underground strata, without the licence of the National Rivers Authority. Certain quantities, however are excepted:

   (i) not more than five cubic metres may be taken, provided this is not part of a continuous operation or series of operations[21] in which more than five cubic metres in all are taken; and

   (ii) not more than 20 cubic metres in any 24 hours may be taken from underground strata for the domestic purposes of an individual's household, or from inland waters

---

[17] See *Blount v. Layard* [1891] 2 Ch. 681.
[18] *John Young & Co. v. The Bankier Distillery Co.* [1893] A.C. 691.
[19] *McCartney v. Londonderry and Lough Swilly Ry.* [1904] A.C. 301 at 306, 307.
[20] See *Rugby Joint Water Board v. Walters* [1967] Ch. 397.
[21] See *Cargill v. Gotts* [1981] 1 W.L.R. 441 ("series" judged by purposes of taking, not quantity or frequency).

for use on contiguous land for the domestic purposes of the occupier's household or for agricultural purposes other than spray irrigation.[22]

Sect. 2. Restrictions

1. Liability in tort

A landowner may be liable in tort for injuries caused to third parties by his acts and omissions in respect of things brought or artificially stored on the land, such as if water in a reservoir escapes, or if a lamp projecting over the highway gets into a dangerous state of repair and injures a passer-by. He may similarly be liable for nuisance, such as if he makes an unusual and excessive collection of manure which attracts flies and causes a stink.[23]

2. Gold, silver and treasure

The Crown is entitled to all gold and silver occurring in any mine.[24] The Treasure Act 1996 has abolished the old law relating to "treasure trove" and vests all treasure in the Crown or in its franchisee, subject to any prior rights or interests therein.[25] The Act defines treasure[26] as including:

(i) any object which before the Treasure Act 1996 came into force would have been treasure trove, in that it consists of gold or silver,[27] whether in bullion, coin or some manufactured object, has been hidden in or on the land deliberately, and not merely lost,[28] and whose true owner is unknown[29];

(ii) some coins and other objects at least 300 years old when found which have a content of at least 10 per cent gold or silver;

(iii) any object at least 200 years old when found which is of a class designated by the Secretary of State as being of outstanding historical, archaeological or cultural importance; and

(iv) any object found with any of the above.

3. Air-space

Although for centuries a landowner's rights have been said to extend *usque ad coelum*,[30] the common law has restricted those rights to the air-space up to such a height as is necessary for the ordinary use and enjoyment of the land and the structures upon it.[31] Within these limits, the continued occupation of the air-space over land without the occupier's consent, as by telephone wires, or a cornice, or branches of a tree, is both a nuisance[32] and a trespass.[33]

---

[22] Water Resources Act 1991, ss.24, 27, 221, replacing provisions in the Water Resources Act 1963.
[23] *Bland v. Yates* (1914) 58 S.J. 612.
[24] See *Att.-Gen. v. Morgan* [1891] 1 Ch. 432.
[25] ss.4, 4(2).
[26] ss.1–3.
[27] See *Att.-Gen. of the Duchy of Lancaster v. G.E. Overton (Farms) Ltd* [1982] Ch. 277 (gold or silver content must be "substantial").
[28] See *R. v. Hancock* [1990] 2 Q.B. 242 at 247.
[29] See *Att.-Gen. v. Trustees of the British Museum* [1903] 2 Ch. 598 at 608–611.
[30] Above, p. 566.
[31] *Baron Bernstein of Leigh v. Skyviews & General Ltd* [1978] Q.B. 479; but consider the authorities below.
[32] See McNair, *Law of the Air* (3rd ed., 1964), Ch. 3.
[33] *Kelsen v. Imperial Tobacco Co. (of Great Britain and Ireland) Ltd* [1957] 2 Q.B. 334.

The intermittent presence of the jib of a tower crane 50 feet above the landowner's roof level has been admitted to be a trespass,[34] and the passage of dangerous projectiles 75 feet above the land has been held to be a nuisance.[35] Aircraft are protected by statute: for no action for trespass or nuisance lies by reason only of the flight of aircraft over land at a height which is reasonable in all the circumstances, provided the proper regulations have been observed.[36]

PART 2—STATUTORY RESTRICTIONS

In addition to the many types of statutory protection given to tenants and thus restricting their landlords, there are two main types of statute that curtail the rights of landowners. First, there are the statutory provisions which restrict the use and enjoyment of land, and its development, usually without compensation. Secondly, there are the statutes which authorise the expropriation of the land itself, usually on payment of compensation. Under the first head, there is the wide-ranging system of town and country planning, together with certain miscellaneous controls, while under the second head there is a wide variety of statutes authorising the compulsory acquisition of land. They will be taken in turn.

Sect. 1. Planning control

1. Growth of control

(a) Control by schemes

At common law, any landowner was free to develop his land as he wished, provided he did not infringe the rights of others. He could erect whatever buildings he wished, however unsuitable they might be, and however injurious to the amenities of the district. Not until the Housing, Town Planning, etc., Act 1909 was enacted was there any general power for local authorities to control the development of land. Successive statutes strengthened and extended this control, principally in the Town and Country Planning Act 1932, which for the first time conferred planning powers over land in the country, as distinct from towns. The essence of this and the earlier Acts was the preparation of a scheme. Each local authority was empowered to prepare a scheme showing what development would be permitted on each part of the land: and there were powers of enforcement against those who carried out development contravening the scheme. However, this remained optional until the Town and Country Planning (Interim Development) Act 1943 was passed.

(b) The Town and Country Planning Acts

The Town and Country Planning Act 1947, which was complex and far-reaching and repealed all the previous law, had two main objects: first, a general revision and strengthening of the existing systems of planning control; and secondly, the imposition of a new system of

[34] *Woollerton & Wilson Ltd v. Richard Costain Ltd* [1970] 1 W.L.R. 411 (not followed in *John Trenberth Ltd v. National Westminster Bank Ltd* (1980) 39 P. & C.R. 104, but only on the remedy).
[35] *Clifton v. Viscount Bury* (1887) 4 T.L.R. 8.
[36] Civil Aviation Act 1982, s.76, replacing Civil Aviation Act 1949, s.40, previously Air Navigation Act 1920, s.9.

"development charges". The latter were the first of a series of attempts to prevent landowners profiting from the great increase in value of their land which often accrued without effort on their part when, for example, the spread of a town transformed into valuable building land some meadows which had previously had only a low value for agricultural purposes. The fourth and for the moment the last of these attempts was abandoned in 1985[37] but the planning provisions of the Act of 1947 remained and were repeatedly amended and consolidated until the enactment of the Town and Country Planning Act 1990 ("the Act of 1990"). Subject to important amendments made by the Planning and Compensation Act 1991 ("the Act of 1991"), the Act of 1990 is now the governing Act, with certain supplementary Acts.[38] There are also many statutory instruments, dealing with much of the detail.

(c) National Administration

In general, the central administration of the Acts is in England under the control of the relevant Secretary of State, until the general election in 2001 the Secretary of State for the Environment but now the Secretary of State for the Department of Transport, Local Government and the Regions; in Wales the central administration of the Acts has been transferred from the Secretary of State for Wales to the appropriate minister of the Welsh Assembly. Their powers are of three principal types:

(i) determining appeals and objections;

(ii) calling in specific planning applications and development plans, thus taking them out of the hands of the relevant local authorities and having them decided centrally; and

(iii) intervening in the event of default by the relevant local authorities (these reserve powers have only rarely been used).

Since 1998 policy guidelines as to the approach which local authorities should take on matters such as the protection of the green belt, housing and transport have been provided by a series of Planning Policy Guidance Notes; 25 have been issued to date. In 1999 Regional Development Agencies were created for nine regions in England to prepare economic strategies for their regions.

(d) Local administration

The day to day administration of the planning system is carried out by the elected local authorities. In some parts of the country there is only one tier of local government; what are known as unitary councils are found in Wales, in the six metropolitan areas of England and in certain other areas of England. These authorities are responsible both for the day-to-day administration of the scheme and the preparation of what are at present known as unitary development plans.[39] London has now reverted to a two-tier system: the London Borough Councils are responsible for the day-to-day administration of the scheme, but the London unitary development plan is now the responsibility of Mayor of London. Elsewhere in England there is a different two-tier system, that of the district councils and the county

---

[37] When the Finance Act 1985 abolished development land tax.
[38] See Planning (Listed Buildings and Conservation Areas) Act 1990; Planning (Hazardous Substances) Act 1990 (see S.I. 1992 No. 656); Planning (Consequential Provisions) Act 1990.
[39] See below, p. 572.

councils. The day-to-day administration of the scheme and the preparation of what are known as local plans[40] is the responsibility of the district councils but the responsibility for the preparation of what are known as structure plans[41] and control over minerals and waste lies with the county councils.

(e) Current proposals

In December 2001 the government issued a long-promised green paper entitled "Planning: Delivering a Fundamental Change" ("the green paper"), which proposes the replacement of regional planning guidelines by regional spatial strategies which will have statutory status. They will be prepared by regional planning bodies but the Secretary of State or the appropriate minister of the Welsh Assembly will implement any recommendations which arise following public examination of them. With a view to enhancing the clarity of expression of national planning policies, all the existing Planning Policy Guidance Notes will be reviewed on the model of the most recent one, which is on housing.[42] The green paper also proposes changes to the present system of plans.[43] The consultation period for the green paper had only just finished when this edition had to go to press. However, some form of legislation seems certain and it is thought that it will come into force in 2004.

2. Development plans

(a) Development plans

Under the Town and Country Planning Act 1947, each local planning authority was bound to prepare a development plan by July 1, 1951, showing the proposed development of its area.[44] These plans, which had to be reconsidered every five years, were intended to provide a prophecy of the permissions likely to be granted and those likely to be refused. But they did not themselves authorise development, and it remained as necessary to obtain planning permission after the plan had come into force as before. All development plans were subject to amendment and approval by the minister after holding a public inquiry.

(b) Structure and local plans

This system of development plans proved cumbersome, and so the Town and Country Planning Act 1968 introduced a more flexible system, involving a gradual replacement of development plans by less detailed "structure plans" which sketch the general lines of development.[45] Despite its name, a structure plan does not comprise a map: it is in the form of a written statement containing or accompanied by diagrams, illustrations and descriptive matter. A structure plan must formulate the planning authority's policy and general proposals in respect of the development and other use of land in its area, including measures for the improvement of the physical environment and the management of traffic. Structure plans require the approval of the Secretary of State or the appropriate minister of the Welsh Assembly, and may be supplemented by local plans which will not normally be under the control of the relevant central authority.[46] A local plan, which consists of a map and a written

[40] See below.
[41] See below.
[42] PPG3 (2000).
[43] See below, p. 572.
[44] Act of 1947, s.5.
[45] Act of 1968, Pt. I, now Act of 1990, Pt. II.
[46] Act of 1990, ss.36–45.

statement, provides a more detailed working out of aspects of the structure plan. It may designate any part of the area which is to be selected for comprehensive treatment at an early date. Such an area is known as an "action area", and the local plan which is duly prepared for it as an "action area plan". There are many types of local plan which can be prepared under the overriding scheme of a structure plan.

(c) Unitary development plans

The reforms of local government which led to the creation of unitary councils led to the replacement of local plans and structure plans for those areas by unitary development plans, the first part of which replaces the structure plans and is essentially strategic in its focus, while the second part replaces the local plans and is more detailed. London still has a unitary development plan under the control of the Mayor of London despite its reversion to a two-tier system of local government.

(d) Current proposals

In the green paper, the government has re-affirmed its belief in a "plan-led" system of development control but proposes to abolish structure plans, local plans and unitary development plans. They will be replaced by a new single level of plan, a local development framework, which will contain a statement of core policy and will be supplemented by more detailed action plans for local areas which are to be subject to changes of planning regime (a map will show the areas for which action plans are to be prepared). The grant or refusal of planning permission will be decided in accordance with the statement of core policies and action plans. County councils and unitary authorities will have to prepare mineral and waste plans and will determine related planning applications.

3. Control of development

(a) Development

The fundamental concept underlying the planning legislation is "development," which is defined as meaning:

(i) "the carrying out of building, engineering, mining or other operations in, on, over or under land," or

(ii) "the making of any material change[47] in the use of any buildings or other land."[48]

Many of the expressions in the definition are themselves defined by the Act of 1990, though the only phrase which need be mentioned here is that "engineering operations" includes "the formation or laying out of means of access to highways".[49] The demolition of buildings is a building operation.[50]

---

[47] See *Guildford R.D.C. v. Fortescue* [1959] 2 Q.B. 112 (intensification of use not a change); *East Barnet U.D.C. v. British Transport Commission* [1962] 2 Q.B. 484; *Jennings Motors Ltd v. Secretary of State for the Environment* [1982] Q.B. 541.
[48] Act of 1990, s.55(1).
[49] *ibid.*, s.336(1).
[50] Act of 1991, s.13.

The definition is on the face of things wide enough to catch virtually all activities in relation to land. However, its scope is reduced by the fact that what are known as "permitted development rights"[51] allow a wide range of development activities, most of which are fairly, minor, by developers such as householders and public utilities. However, the Act of 1990 makes it clear that it is development to begin using one dwelling-house as two or more separate dwelling-houses,[52] or to extend dumps of refuse or waste materials. On the other hand, "development" does not include improvements or alterations to a building which do not materially affect its external appearance, the use of any buildings or other land within the curtilage of a dwelling-house for any purpose incidental to the enjoyment of the dwelling-house as such, the use of any land for agricultural purposes; nor does it include any change from one use to another use within the same class in the 16 classes of use set out in the Town and Country Planning (Use Classes) Order 1987.[53] (Early in 2002 the government also issued a consultation paper relating to possible changes to these classes.[54]) The Act of 1990 further provides in effect that the definition does not include certain cases of reverting to a former lawful use.[55]

(b) Planning permission

(i) Permission: The general rule is that any person who proposes to develop land must first obtain planning permission from the relevant local planning authority or from the Secretary of State on appeal; and such permission may be granted either unconditionally or subject to such conditions as are thought fit, or it may be refused.[56] Any conditions must reasonably relate to the proposed development.[57] Although the refusal of permission may be a very serious matter for the landowner, no compensation is payable except in a very limited class of cases.[58]

An applicant must give prior notice of his application to certain other persons owning interests in the property; and in a few cases of development likely to offend neighbours, he must first advertise his application, so that they may be able to object before permission is given.[59] An applicant for planning permission does not need to have a proprietary interest in the property concerned: applications are frequently made by prospective purchasers and lessees. Every local planning authority is bound to maintain a register of applications for permission and the results of such applications.[60] This is quite distinct from the local land charges register.[61]

(ii) Permitted development: By the Town and Country Planning (General Permitted Development) Order 1995[62] planning permission is given[63] for various classes of developers, such as householders and public utilities, to carry out specified classes of development subject to

---

[51] Town and Country Planning (General Permitted Development) Order 1995 (S.I. 1995 No. 418).

[52] *ibid.,* s.55(3); and see *Ealing Corporation v. Ryan* [1965] 2 Q.B. 486.

[53] Act of 1990, s.55(2)(f); S.I. 1987 No. 764, 1992 Nos. 610, 657.

[54] See N. Cheshire [2002] N.L.J. 673.

[55] Act of 1990, s.57(4); and see *Young v. Secretary of State for the Environment* [1983] 2 A.C. 662.

[56] Act of 1990, s.70.

[57] See *Fawcett Properties Ltd v. Buckinghamshire C.C.* [1961] A.C. 636; *R. v. Hillingdon L.B.C., ex p. Royco Homes Ltd* [1974] Q.B. 720; *Newbury D.C. v. Secretary of State for the Environment* [1981] A.C. 578.

[58] Act of 1990, Pt. V.

[59] *ibid.,* ss.65, 66.

[60] *ibid.,* s.69.

[61] See above, pp. 91–92.

[62] S.I. 1995 No. 418.

[63] See *Cater v. Essex C.C.* [1960] 1 Q.B. 424.

certain conditions. In these cases there is no need to apply to the local planning authority for permission. The Order includes such matters as minor alterations to dwellings, temporary uses, and much development by gas, water, electricity and other undertakers. There are also wide-ranging exemptions and exceptions to the rule that demolition of buildings is a building operation.[64] Many of these permitted development rights are limited in National Parks, conservation areas and areas of outstanding natural beauty.

(iii) Special Development Orders, enterprise zones and simplified planning zones: Planning permission may also be granted by what are known as Special Development Orders, applicable to land of particular descriptions.[65] These have been used for new towns and for schemes which are controversial, such as the storage of radioactive waste. Provision has also been made for establishing schemes for "enterprise zones"[66] and "simplified planning zones".[67] The purpose of enterprise zones is to encourage business and industrial activities by granting planning permission for specified development or by making it easier to obtain permission, and by giving some tax advantages for 10 years: an example is London's Isle of Dogs, where Europe's largest office development was constructed at Canary Wharf. The object of simplified planning zone schemes is to secure the regeneration of an area by encouraging the development of derelict or unused land by means similar to those in enterprise zones, though without the tax advantages.

(iv) Caravan sites: Caravan sites proved very hard to control under the general law of town and country planning, the main difficulty being that the mere development of land without planning permission is not an offence. Sites could be exploited and the vans moved away before enforcement proceedings could be brought to a successful conclusion. To remedy this abuse, the Caravan Sites and Control of Development Act 1960[68] made it an offence in most cases to use land as a caravan site without a site licence granted by the local authority, and this is issued only if the requisite planning permission for the use of the land as a caravan site has been obtained. The licence will usually be subject to conditions relating to the physical use of the land, such as conditions aimed at preventing overcrowding.[69] The Caravan Sites Act 1968[70] is concerned with the duty of local authorities to provide caravan sites for gypsies, and deals with exemptions from the requirement for site licences.

(c) Enforcement

(i) Enforcement notices: If any development is carried out without the requisite permission, or if any conditions to which a permission is subject have not been complied with, the local planning authority may serve an enforcement notice on the owner and occupier of the land, and on the owner of any interest in the land materially affected by the notice. The notice must specify the alleged breach of planning control and also the steps to be taken (or the activities that must cease) in order to remedy the breach, and the period within which this must be done. In addition, it must specify the date on which it is to take effect.[71] A notice is a nullity

---

[64] Act of 1991, s.13.
[65] Act of 1990, s.58.
[66] Local Government, Planning and Land Act 1980, Sched. 32; Act of 1990, ss.88, 89.
[67] Act of 1990, ss.82–87, Sched. 7; Act of 1991, s.28, Sched. 5.
[68] ss.1, 2, Sched. 1.
[69] *ibid.*, ss.3, 5.
[70] Amended by Local Government, Planning and Land Act 1980, Pt. XVII.
[71] Act of 1990, ss.172, 173, as substituted by Act of 1991, s.5.

if it is defective on its face,[72] such as in failing to state the date on which it is to take effect. Other defects may make it invalid, and subject to appeal, though sometimes the defect can be cured. The notice must be served within 28 days of the date of issue, and at least 28 days before the date specified in it as the date when it is to take effect.[73] A local planning authority which suspects a breach of planning control may serve a "planning contravention notice", requiring information to be given as to activities on the land; and it is an offence to fail to comply with it.[74]

(ii) Time limit: An enforcement notice cannot be served more than 10 years after the breach; but the period is four years if the breach consists of changing the use of a building to a single dwelling-house, or if it consists of building, engineering, mining or other operations, in which case time runs from the substantial completion of the operations.[75]

(iii) Appeal: An appeal to the Secretary of State or the appropriate minister of the Welsh Assembly against an enforcement notice may be made at any time before it takes effect, and the notice then has no effect until the appeal is determined or withdrawn.[76] Wide powers are available to grant permission for the development, or to vary or quash the notice[77]; and a further appeal lies to the High Court, though only on a point of law.[78]

(iv) Stop notices: On or after serving an enforcement notice and before it takes effect a local planning authority may serve a stop notice. This prohibits the continuance of the alleged breach of planning control until the enforcement notice takes effect, thereby defeating the use of appeals as a delaying tactic. A stop notice cannot prohibit the use of any building as a dwelling-house, or the carrying on of any activity which has been continuing for four years or more. The notice must specify the date on which it takes effect, and this must be not later than 28 days after the date of service, and, in the absence of special reasons, at least three days after the date of service. In certain cases where, in the event, the notice is found not to be justified, compensation is payable.[79]

(v) Non-compliance: Failure to comply with an enforcement notice or a stop notice is an offence.[80] Further, the local planning authority may apply for an injunction to restrain any actual or apprehended breach of planning control.[81] Where any steps required by an enforcement notice have not been taken, the local planning authority may also enter the land and take them, and recover the expense from the landowner.[82]

(vi) Breach of condition notice: An alternative, and simpler, procedure for breach of conditions is now available. If there is a breach of a condition in a planning permission, the local planning authority may serve a "breach of condition notice". This must require compliance with the condition, and specify the steps to be taken or the activities which must

---

[72] *East Riding C.C. v. Park Estate (Bridlington) Ltd* [1957] A.C. 223.
[73] Act of 1990, s.172, as substituted by Act of 1991, s.5.
[74] Act of 1990, ss.171C, 171D, inserted by Act of 1991, s.1.
[75] Act of 1990, ss.171A, 171B, inserted by Act of 1991, s.4.
[76] Act of 1990, ss.174, 175; Act of 1991, s.6.
[77] Act of 1990, ss.176, 177.
[78] *ibid.*, s.289.
[79] *ibid.*, ss.183–186; Act of 1991, s.9. Registers of enforcement and stop notices must be kept in each area: Act of 1990, s.188.
[80] Act of 1990, ss.179, 187, as substituted by Act of 1991, ss.8, 9. Penalty, fine not exceeding £20,000 on summary conviction, or unlimited fine on conviction on indictment.
[81] Act of 1990, s.187B, inserted by Act of 1991, s.3.
[82] Act of 1990, s.178, as amended by Act of 1991, s.7.

cease in order to secure compliance; and it must also specify the period for compliance, which must not be less than 28 days after service of the notice. Failure to comply with such a notice is a summary offence.[83] The time limit for serving a breach of condition notice is the same as for serving an enforcement notice.[84]

(d) Additional controls

In addition to regulating development, legislation also provides a number of additional controls. Local planning authorities can make tree preservation orders which, in the interests of amenity, prohibit trees being felled, cut or otherwise damaged without the consent of the local planning authority.[85] The demolition or alteration of buildings of special architectural or historical interest without "listed building consent" will be prevented if they become "listed buildings" by being included in a list compiled by the Secretary of State.[86] Further, the local planning authority may designate any area of special architectural or historic interest as a "conservation area", whereupon the demolition of any building in that area requires a "conservation area consent",[87] and the trees are protected as if they were subject to a tree preservation order.[88] There is also an elaborate system for controlling the display of advertisements on land.[89]

4. Effect on the law of property

When the Town and Country Planning Act 1947 was enacted, some strange suggestions were made as to its fundamental effect on English land law. It was even contended that the estate fee simple in land no longer existed, but instead each landowner had merely an estate in fee simple in the existing or permitted use of his land. This view appears to have been based on the need to obtain permission for any development, and on the obligation to pay a development charge to re-acquire the development rights which the State was acquiring. The substance of the first of these changes, however, had already been made by the Town and Country Planning (Interim Development) Act of 1943 (which no one had regarded as being epoch-making), and the second of the changes and, in particular, the three later taxes by which it was successively replaced were more a tax on development than anything else. Further, on this view, no purchaser of land in, say, 1950, received more than an estate in fee simple in an existing use, and so today, despite the abolition of these taxes charges, he still has no estate in fee simple in the land. Yet again, it ignored "existing or permitted buildings" in which the landowner had the same kind of rights as in the "existing or permitted use".

In truth, the theory would not bear examination, and it has gained no foothold in the courts or among practitioners. Planning control affects the use and enjoyment of land, but not the estates or interests in it; and the various charges and taxes were a purely fiscal burden. Planning matters must be duly investigated for the protection of purchasers, but they are not technically matters of title. The right to use property in a particular way is not in itself property.[90] The estate in fee simple in land remains the same estate in fee simple as before.

---

[83] Act of 1990, s.187A, added by Act of 1991, s.2: penalty, fine not exceeding £400.
[84] Act of 1990, ss.171A, 171B, added by Act of 1991, s.4; above, p. 574.
[85] Act of 1990, ss.198–210; Act of 1991, s.23.
[86] Planning (Listed Buildings and Conservation Areas) Act 1990, Pt. I.
[87] *ibid.*, Pt. II.
[88] Act of 1990, ss.211–214.
[89] *ibid.*, ss.220–225; S.I. 1992 No. 666.
[90] *Belfast Corporation v. O.D. Cars Ltd* [1960] A.C. 490.

All that has happened is that the fruits of ownership have become less sweet; but that is nothing new in land law.

Sect. 2. Compulsory purchase

1. Powers

A landowner is subject to what is sometimes called "eminent domain", namely the right of Parliament, as part of its legislative omnipotence, to authorise the compulsory acquisition of land.

(a) General

There are many statutes, both general and specific, which authorise the compulsory purchase of land by various public and other bodies for specified purposes.[91] At first, each Act was usually self-contained, but then the Lands Clauses Consolidation Act 1845 laid down comprehensive codes of procedure and compensation. These provisions are now mainly contained in the Land Compensation Acts 1961 and 1973, the Compulsory Purchase Act 1965, the Acquisition of Land Act 1981, and the Planning and Compensation Act 1991. The individual Acts that authorise compulsory purchase are now primarily concerned with the purposes for which the land may be taken and the bodies which can take it.

(b) Planning

The Town and Country Planning Act 1947[92] extended the scope of compulsory acquisition from acquisitions for specified purposes to acquisitions made to secure the development of the land in accordance with the development plan. Under the present provisions, the Secretary of State or the appropriate minister of the Welsh Assembly may authorise local authorities to acquire any land in their areas which:

(i) is suitable for and required in order to secure the carrying out of development, re-development or improvement; or

(ii) is required for a purpose which it is necessary to achieve in the interests of the proper planning of an area in which the land is situated; or

(iii) adjoins such land and is required for executing works for facilitating its development or use.[93]

(c) Useless and blighted land

The Town and Country Planning Act 1947 introduced a process which enabled a landowner to require a local authority to purchase his land compulsorily if planning permission for it was refused or was granted subject to conditions. He can do this only if the land "has become incapable of reasonably beneficial use in its existing state",[94] and cannot be rendered capable

---

[91] In 1962 over 70 "main Acts" could be listed (R.D. StewartBrown, *Guide to Compulsory Purchase and Compensation* (5th ed.)), and in 1974 the powers were summarised under 87 heads (A.S. Wisdom, *Local Authorities' Powers of Purchase* (5th ed.)).
[92] s.38, foreshadowed by the more limited Town and Country Planning Act 1944, s.10.
[93] Town and Country Planning Act 1990, s.226; and see subs.(3)(b) (exchange for commons, open spaces, etc.).
[94] See *R. v. Minister of Housing and Local Government, ex p. Chichester R.D.C.* [1960] 1 W.L.R. 587.

of such use by carrying out any permitted development.[95] There is also a similar right where land is "blighted" by planning proposals by public authorities contained in structure or local plans,[96] such as for the construction of highways.

2. Procedure

Act which authorises the compulsory acquisition of land may of course make its own provisions governing procedure and compensation. But this is unusual, and normally the acquisition is governed by the general Acts that have been mentioned above.[97] Under these, the main steps are as follows.

(a) Order

When an authority wishes to make a specific purchase, it makes a compulsory purchase order. This does not take effect until it is confirmed by the appropriate minister; and he must hear any objections to it, usually at a public local inquiry conducted by an inspector.

(b) Notice to treat

When confirmed, the order enables the acquiring authority to serve a "notice to treat" on the owner.[98] This does not by itself create a contract for sale, though it gives either party the right to have the compensation assessed by the Lands Tribunal in default of agreement. Once the compensation has been determined, the sale is specifically enforceable as a contract.

(c) Entry

Once the compensation has been determined, the acquiring authority can obtain possession by completing the purchase. Yet at any time after serving the notice to treat and before completion, the acquiring authority can enter the land on 14 days' notice, though in this case the authority must pay interest from the date of entry on the compensation when assessed.[99]

3. Compensation

The general basis of compensation on a compulsory acquisition has generally been the open market value of the land. (The only exception to this was in the period immediately between the enactment of the Town and Country Planning Act 1947 and the abolition of the need to pay development charges.)

(a) Open market value

The open market value of land depends not only on the planning permissions that have been granted but also on those which might be granted. For these purposes it has to be assumed that planning permission will be granted:

  (i) for the development for which the purchase is being made;

  (ii) for any development within the existing use of the land;

---

[95] Town and Country Planning Act 1990, ss. 137–148, replacing Town and Country Planning Act 1947, s.19.
[96] Town and Country Planning Act 1990, ss.149–160, Sched. 13.
[97] Above, p. 577.
[98] Compulsory Purchase Act 1965, s.5; Planning and Compensation Act 1991, s.67.
[99] Compulsory Purchase Act 1965, s.11.

(iii) for any development certified by the local planning authority as being likely to be granted planning permission;

(iv) for any specified development as defined in the development plan; and

(v) for any development for which planning permission might reasonably be expected to be granted[1] if it either falls within a primary use for which the development plan allocates it, or else (if it is in an action area[2]) falls within the uses permitted in that area.

Except for action areas, (iv) and (v) do not apply to land defined by the development plan as being subject to comprehensive development.[3] Any enhancement in the value of the land that is due to the acquiring authority's proposals for other land must be excluded.[4]

(b) Other provisions

Apart from the market value, compensation may also be payable for injurious affection[5] (*i.e.* injury to other lands caused by the acquisition), and for disturbance, as well as "home loss payments".[6] Additional compensation is also payable to the former owner if the value of the land increases in consequence of a planning decision made within 10 years after completion.[7]

(c) Equivalent reinstatement

Where the land is devoted (and but for the acquisition would continue to be devoted) to a purpose for which there is no general demand or market, such as a church or school, compensation may be assessed on the basis of the reasonable cost of equivalent reinstatement[8] at the date when the work of reinstatement might reasonably be expected to begin.[9] But this basis can be adopted only where reinstatement in some other place is bona fide intended.[10]

Sect. 3. Minerals

As has been seen,[11] the Crown is entitled at common law to all gold and silver occurring in any mine. In addition, statute has deprived landowners of certain other minerals occurring in or under their land.

---

[1] See *Provincial Properties (London) Ltd v. Caterham and Warlingham U.D.C.* [1972] 1 Q.B. 453.
[2] See above, p. 572.
[3] Land Compensation Act 1961, ss.15, 16, Pt. III.
[4] *ibid.*, ss.6–9, Sched. 1.
[5] See Land Compensation Act 1973, Pt. IV.
[6] *ibid.*, Pt. III.
[7] Land Compensation Act 1961, Pt. IV, repealed by Land Commission Act 1967, ss.86, 101, Sched. 17, but revived and amended by Planning and Compensation Act 1991, s.66, Sched. 14.
[8] Land Compensation Act 1961, s.5.
[9] *Birmingham Corporation v. West Midland Baptist (Trust) Association (Inc.)* [1970] A.C. 874.
[10] Land Compensation Act 1961, s.5.
[11] Above, p. 568.

1. Petroleum and natural gas

Under the Petroleum (Production) Act 1934 there was vested in the Crown petroleum existing in its natural condition in strata, including any mineral oil or relative hydrocarbon and natural gas.[12] The present legislation is the Petroleum Act 1998.

2. Coal

Under the Coal Act 1938, all interests in coal (except interests arising under a coal-mining lease) were vested in the Coal Commission in return for compensation[13]; and these interests (including coal-mining leases) are now, following the re-privatisation of the coal industry, vested in the Coal Authority.[14]

PART 3—PROTECTION OF TENANTS

The modern tendency has been to enact legislation designed to protect tenants against their landlords. At common law, the matter was in general one of contract: provided a landlord did not contravene the terms of his bargain, he might at will evict his tenant, or under the threat of eviction secure his agreement to pay an increased rent of whatever amount he could exact. Although a number of matters such as fixtures, emblements and the like are of importance, the two crucial matters in any scheme for protecting tenants are protection against eviction, and control of rent: and these subjects will be dealt with here.

Legislation has been piecemeal. Apart from some relatively mild provisions concerning agricultural land, beginning with the Agricultural Holdings (England) Act 1875, no real system of control existed until the first of the Rent Acts was enacted in 1915. There is little common design to be found in the various statutes: as will be seen, protection against eviction is provided by a wide variety of devices, and so is control of rent.

There are three main categories, depending on the nature of the tenancy. They are:

   (i) business premises;

   (ii) agricultural land; and

   (iii) dwellings.

Although the first two heads are not simple, they are relatively uncomplicated. The third head is highly complex. Both the application of the statutes and the extent of the protection that is given depend on matters such as the type of tenancy, its length, the value of the dwelling, the date when the tenancy was granted, and whether or not the landlord is a public body. Part of the complexity, though by no means all, is due to political considerations, with successive governments introducing legislation to increase or decrease the degree of protection. Outlines of the different systems will be considered in turn.

---

[12] s.1; *Earl of Lonsdale v. Att.-Gen.* [1982] 1 W.L.R. 887.
[13] Coal Industry Nationalisation Act 1946.
[14] Coal Industry Act 1994, ss.7, 8.

Sect. 1. Business premises

1. The Act of 1927

Business premises were first protected[15] by Part I of the Landlord and Tenant Act 1927. This gave the tenant the right to a new lease (or compensation in lieu thereof) provided he could establish that by reason of the carrying on by him or his predecessors in title at the premises of a trade or business for not less than five years, goodwill had become attached to the premises by reason whereof they could be let at a higher rent than they otherwise would have realised.[16] The tenant therefore had to show goodwill which remained adherent to the premises after he had gone, something which was difficult to prove at all and normally impossible except in the case of shops; tenancies of professional premises were outside these provisions anyway. These relatively ineffectual provisions were replaced by the far-reaching terms of Part II of the Landlord and Tenant Act 1954 ("the 1954 Act") as amended in some details by the Law of Property Act 1969.[17] The closely restricted right for business tenants to claim compensation for improvements, subject to certain conditions, continues in an amended form.[18]

2. The Landlord and Tenant Act 1954

(a) Tenancies within the Act

Part II of the 1954 Act applies to any tenancy[19] where the property comprised in it is or includes premises occupied by the tenant for the purposes of any trade, profession or employment.[20] There is no requirement of adherent goodwill. The principal exceptions from the Act are the following: agricultural holdings[21]; farm business tenancies[22]; mining leases[23]; and certain tenancies granted to a servant during his employment or granted for not more than six months.[24] Tenancies at will or at sufferance are also outside the Act.[25]

(b) Security of tenure

Security of tenure is secured by the simple provision that a tenancy within Part II "shall not come to an end unless terminated in accordance with the provisions of this Part of this Act".[26] Thus a tenancy for a fixed term may continue indefinitely despite the expiration of the fixed term,[27] and an ordinary notice to quit given by the landlord will be inoperative; but the tenancy may still determine by notice to quit given by the tenant or by surrender or forfeiture.[28]

[15] Apart from nearly a year's protection under the Rent Acts: Act of 1920, s.13.
[16] L. & T.A. 1927, ss.4, 5.
[17] In 1992 the Law Commission made some proposals for reform in Law Com. 208.
[18] Below, p. 584.
[19] Whether a transaction creates a tenancy is determined by *Street v. Mountford* principles (above p. 340); *Vandersteen v. Agius* (1993) 65 P. & C.R. 266.
[20] Act of 1954, s.23.
[21] See below, p. 585.
[22] Agricultural Tenancies Act 1995; below, p. 589.
[23] Act of 1954, s.46, making reference to the definition in L. & T.A. 1927, s.25(1).
[24] *ibid.*, s.43, as amended.
[25] *Wheeler v. Mercer* [1957] A.C. 416; *Hagee (London) Ltd v. A.B. Erikson and Larson* [1976] Q.B. 209.
[26] Act of 1954, s.24.
[27] See *Herbert Duncan Ltd v. Cluttons* [1992] 22 E.G. 110 (original lessee remains liable for rent during continuation).
[28] But see L.P.A. 1969, s.4 (ineffective if during first month of occupation).

In order to determine the tenancy the landlord must give not less than six nor more than 12 months' notice in the statutory form, to expire not earlier than the date when, apart from the Act, the tenancy could have been determined by notice to quit, or would have expired.[29] If within two months of receiving this notice the tenant gives the landlord notice that he is not willing to give up possession of the premises, he may, not less than two nor more than four months after the landlord's notice was given, apply to the court for a new tenancy.[30] For this purpose, the "corresponding date" rule[31] applies in determining whether the application was made too early or too late.[32]

Alternatively, a tenant holding for a fixed term (and not merely under a periodical tenancy) may serve on the landlord a statutory form of request for a new tenancy in place of the old, to begin not less than six nor more than 12 months later; and not less than two nor more than four months after serving this request he must apply to the court.[33] If instead he wishes to leave, he may serve three months' notice in writing to expire at the end of the term or any quarter day thereafter.[34] Where he gives up occupation on or before expiry of a fixed term, there will be no statutory continuation.[35]

(c) Opposition to new tenancy

The court is bound to grant the tenant a new tenancy unless the landlord establishes one of the seven statutory grounds of opposition. The landlord can rely only on the grounds stated in his statutory notice or in a notice served on the tenant within two months of receiving the request for a new tenancy. Some of the grounds are based on default by the tenant and others on the landlord's need; and only the first three and the fifth, by using the word "ought", give the court any discretion. The seven grounds are as follows.[36]

(i) *Repair*: that the tenant ought not to be granted a new tenancy in view of the state of the "holding" (*i.e.* the premises let, excluding any part not occupied by the tenant or a service tenant of his) due to the tenant's failure to comply with his repairing obligations.

(ii) *Rent*: that the tenant ought not to be granted a new tenancy in view of his persistent delay in paying rent.

(iii) *Other breaches*: that the tenant ought not to be granted a new tenancy in view of other substantial breaches by him of his obligations under the tenancy, or for any other reason connected with his use or management of the holding.

(iv) *Alternative accommodation*: that the landlord has offered and is willing to provide or secure the provision of suitable alternative accommodation on reasonable terms.

(v) *Part of whole*: that the premises are part of larger premises held by the landlord and the tenant ought not to be granted a new tenancy because the landlord could obtain

---

[29] Act of 1954, s.25.
[30] *ibid.*, s.29.
[31] Above, p. 349.
[32] Errors of date will be benevolently construed; *Garston v. Scottish Widows Fund & Life Assurance Society* [1998] 1 W.L.R. 457.
[33] Act of 1954, ss.26, 29.
[34] *ibid.*, s.27.
[35] *Esselte AB v. Pearl Assurance Plc* [1997] 1 W.L.R. 891.
[36] *ibid.*, ss.29, 30.

a substantially greater rent for the property as a whole than for the parts separately.

(vi) *Demolition or reconstruction*: "that on the termination of the current tenancy the landlord intends to demolish or reconstruct the premises comprised in the holding or a substantial part of those premises or to carry out substantial work of construction on the holding or part thereof and that he could not reasonably do so without obtaining possession of the holding". The landlord cannot succeed on this ground if he has a right under the current tenancy to enter and do the work,[37] or if the tenant is willing to give the landlord facilities for the work without unduly interfering with the tenant's business, or the tenant is willing to accept a tenancy of an economically separable part of the holding.[38]

(vii) *Own occupation*: "that on the termination of the current tenancy the landlord intends to occupy the holding for the purposes, or partly for the purposes, of a business to be carried on by him therein, or as his residence". But this head is not open to a landlord whose interest was purchased or created less than five years before the termination of the current tenancy.

The landlord cannot have the intention required by the last two heads unless at the date of the hearing he has not a mere hope but a firm, settled intention, not likely to be changed, to do something that he has a reasonable prospect of bringing about.[39] Normally an undertaking to the court given by a responsible person or body conclusively shows an intention to do what is undertaken, such as to demolish the premises.[40] A landlord who genuinely intends to reconstruct the premises and then occupy them himself is not affected by the five years rule, for the existence of Ground (vii) does not prevent him from relying on Ground (vi).[41]

(d) Terms of new tenancy

When premises are first let to a business tenant, there is no restriction on the amount of rent that may be charged. Nor is there any power to secure any revision of the rent as long as the initial tenancy continues, unless the tenancy provides for it, as by including a rent review clause. But if the tenant obtains a new tenancy under the Act, the rent will be the open market rent and any or all of a rent review clause, a break clause, and a requirement for a guarantor may be included. In default of agreement the court will determine the rent[42] and in so doing must take into account the impact of the Landlord and Tenant (Covenants) Act 1995 on rent levels and the standard terms of commercial tenancies.[43] The rent may thus be raised or lowered, but the tenant is protected against unreasonable demands by the landlord.

The duration of any new tenancy is whatever the court thinks reasonable, not exceeding 14 years[44]; but there is no limit to the number of renewals. The court will also determine any other terms of the tenancy, though new terms will be inserted only for good reason based on

---

[37] *Heath v. Drown* [1973] A.C. 498.
[38] Act of 1954, s.31A, added by L.P.A. 1969, s.7.
[39] *Betty's Cafes Ltd v. Phillips Furnishing Stores Ltd* [1959] A.C. 20.
[40] *Espresso Coffee Machine Co. Ltd v. Guardian Assurance Co. Ltd* [1959] 1 W.L.R. 250.
[41] *Fisher v. Taylors Furnishing Stores Ltd* [1956] 2 Q.B. 78.
[42] Act of 1954, ss.32, 34, 35; *O'May v. City of London Real Property Co. Ltd* [1983] 2 A.C. 726 at 741.
[43] L. & T.(C.)A. 1995, Sched. 1, paras 3, 4.
[44] *ibid.*, s.33.

essential fairness.[45] The basic idea of the Act is thus that a business tenant has a prima facic right to continue his business indefinitely in the premises, and although there is no restriction on the terms of the tenancy under which he first occupies the premises, any renewals are controlled by the court. The court may fix an interim rent to run until the new tenancy is granted.[46]

(e) Compensation for eviction

A tenant who does not obtain a new tenancy is entitled to no compensation unless this occurs because the landlord objects to the grant of a new tenancy solely by reason of one or more of the last three grounds set out above, all of which are for the landlord's benefit. In these cases, the landlord must pay the tenant compensation equal to the rateable value of the premises, or twice that sum if the tenant and his predecessors in the business have occupied the premises for business purposes for the previous 14 years.[47]

(f) Compensation for improvements

Under the Landlord and Tenant Act 1927,[48] if a tenant of premises used for a trade, business or profession carries out improvements to the premises which add to their letting value, the tenant may recover compensation from the landlord on leaving. But the tenant must satisfy a number of conditions: in addition to making his claim at the right time and in due form, he must give the landlord three months' notice of his intention to make the improvement. The landlord may then exclude the tenant's right to compensation if he successfully objects to the improvement, or carries it out himself in return for a reasonable increase of rent.

Sect. 2. Agricultural land

The Agricultural Holdings (England) Act 1875 was the first of a long series of Acts regulating agricultural holdings. At first, the Acts were mainly directed towards securing proper compensation for the tenant, initially for improvements and, latterly, also if his tenancy was determined without good cause.[49] The Agriculture Act 1947 first gave security of tenure and protection as to rent, in place of the limited security of tenure provided during the war by Defence Regulations; the most recent Act to do so was the Agricultural Holdings Act 1986 which consolidated much previous legislation.[50] However, due to pressure for reform from within the farming industry, statutory security of tenure has been removed in respect of tenancies beginning on or after September 1, 1995 by the enactment of the Agricultural Tenancies Act 1995. This allows parties the freedom to contract on their own terms. It is hoped that this provision, together with contemporaneous fiscal incentives offered to landlords,[51] will revive agricultural leases.

---

[45] Act of 1954, ss.32, 34, 35; *O'May v. City of London Real Property Co. Ltd* [1983] 2 A.C. 726 at 741.
[46] *ibid.*, s.24A, inserted by L.P.A. 1969, s.3, a difficult provision: see *Fawke v. Viscount Chelsea* [1980] Q.B. 441.
[47] *ibid.*, s.37, as amended by L.P.A. 1969, s.11.
[48] ss.1–3, as amended by L. & T.A. 1954, Pt. III. See (1989) Law Com. No. 178.
[49] A.H.A. 1923, s.12.
[50] Principally A.H.A. 1948; Agricultural Holdings (Notice to Quit) Act 1977; A.H.A. 1984.
[51] 100% relief from Inheritance Tax on agricultural land let on or after September 1, 1995; F.A. 1995, s.155.

1. Agricultural holdings

(a) Scope

The Agricultural Holdings Act 1986 does not apply to tenancies of agricultural holdings beginning on or after September 1, 1995 unless the tenancy was:

(i) granted by a written contract entered into before that date which indicates that the Act is to apply; or

(ii) obtained pursuant to certain directions of an Agricultural Land Tribunal on the death or retirement or a previous agricultural tenant; or

(iii) granted on an agreed succession by a written contract which indicated that the Act was to apply; or

(iv) created by the previous tenant's acceptance of certain compensation provisions; or

(v) granted by a purported variation of a previous tenancy which takes effect as a new tenancy by virtue of the doctrine of "surrender and re-grant" (but not by virtue of an agreement which is expressed to be a new tenancy).

(b) Jurisdiction

The Agricultural Holdings Act 1986 confers many powers on the Minister who is for the time being exercising the functions formerly exercised by Minister of Agriculture, Fisheries and Food ("the Minister"), on Agricultural Land Tribunals, and on arbitrators. Under the Agriculture Act 1958 the powers of determining disputes which had been vested in the Minister and the former County Agricultural Executive Committee were transferred to the Agricultural Land Tribunals, which had previously had mainly appellate functions. Each of the eight areas into which England and Wales is divided has a Tribunal presided over by a lawyer appointed by the Lord Chancellor; and the Council on Tribunals supervises both the Tribunals and any arbitrators (unless appointed by agreement).[52]

(c) "Agricultural holding"

The Act applies to any "agricultural holding" created at an appropriate time. This means the aggregate of land used for the trade or business of agriculture which is comprised in a contract of tenancy for years, or from year to year.[53] An agreement for value[54] granting a licence to occupy land for use as agricultural land, or letting it for an interest less than a tenancy from year to year, is treated as being a tenancy from year to year if the circumstances are such that the land would otherwise be an agricultural holding.[55] But this does not apply to agreements approved by the Minister, or to those made in contemplation of the use of the land only for grazing or mowing (or both) during some specified period of the year,[56] even if the period is 364 days[57] or there are successive periods of three months.[58] "Agriculture"

---

[52] See Agriculture Act 1947, s.73, Sched. 9; Tribunals and Inquiries Act 1971, s.1, Sched. 1; Agriculture (Miscellaneous Provisions) Act 1972, s.21 (abolishing the C.A.E. Committees); A.H.A. 1986, Sched. 14, para. 49.
[53] A.H.A. 1986, s.1.
[54] *Goldsack v. Shore* [1950] 1 K.B. 708.
[55] A.H.A. 1986, s.2.
[56] *ibid.*
[57] *Reid v. Dawson* [1955] 1 Q.B. 214.
[58] *Scene Estate Ltd v. Amos* [1957] 2 Q.B. 205; contrast *Rutherford v. Maurer* [1962] 1 Q.B. 16 ("six months periods").

is widely defined, and includes horticulture, fruit growing, seed growing and market garden-ing.[59] On a mixed letting, such as a tenancy of pasture, an orchard and an inn, the Act applies to all or none: the test is whether as a whole the tenancy is in substance a tenancy of agricultural land.[60]

(d) Notices to quit

On the expiry of a tenancy for two years or more, the tenancy continues as a tenancy from year to year unless either party has given notice to quit not less than a year nor more than two years before the date of expiration, or unless the tenant has died before that date.[61] This provision cannot be excluded by agreement unless the term is for at least two years but not more than five, and the Minister approves a joint application by both parties.[62] A notice to quit an agricultural holding (including a notice exercising an option of terminating the tenancy agreement[63]) is invalid if it purports to determine the tenancy before the expiry of one year from the end of the current tenancy[64]; and this is so despite any contrary provision in the tenancy agreement,[65] and even if the notice was given by the tenant.[66] But there are certain exceptions,[67] and the parties may agree to treat an invalid notice as being valid.[68] Curiously, a tenancy for more than 12 months and less than 24, although an "agricultural holding" for the purpose of business tenancies,[69] escapes the protection of these provisions.[70]

(e) Security of tenure

The landlord's right to serve a notice to quit, as modified in this way, remains unaffected. But if he is given a counter-notice[71] by the tenant (or, for joint tenants, by all the tenants[72]) within one month of the tenant receiving a notice to quit, then, with eight exceptions,[73] the notice to quit becomes ineffective unless the Agricultural Land Tribunal consents to it taking effect; and only in six cases can the Tribunal give that consent.[74] There are thus three categories.

(i) No security: The notice to quit will be effective if either the tenant fails to serve a counter-notice in time, or else the case falls within one of the eight following heads and the notice to quit makes plain the head on which the landlord relies.[75]

---

[59] A.H.A. 1986, s.96.
[60] *Dunn v. Fidoe* [1950] 2 All E.R. 685; *Howkins v. Jardine* [1951] 1 K.B. 614; *Monson v. Bound* [1954] 1 W.L.R. 1321.
[61] A.H.A. 1986, ss.3, 4.
[62] *ibid.*, s.5. See, *e.g. Pahl v. Trevor* [1992] 25 E.G. 130 (five-year term until deceased tenant's grandson is old enough to become tenant).
[63] See *Edell v. Dulieu* [1924] A.C. 38.
[64] A.H.A. 1986, s.25.
[65] *ibid.*
[66] *Flather v. Hood* (1928) 44 T.L.R. 698.
[67] A.H.A. 1986, s.25.
[68] *Elsden v. Pick* [1980] 1 W.L.R. 898.
[69] *E.W.P. Ltd v. Moore* [1992] 1 Q.B. 460; above, p. 523.
[70] *ibid.*, applying *Gladstone v. Bower* [1960] 2 Q.B. 384.
[71] See *Mountford v. Hodkinson* [1956] 1 W.L.R. 422 (abusive letter), and contrast *Frankland v. Capstick* [1959] 1 W.L.R. 204.
[72] *Featherstone v. Staples* [1986] 1 W.L.R. 861.
[73] A.H.A. 1986, s.26, Sched. 3.
[74] *ibid.*, s.27.
[75] *ibid.*, Sched. 3; *Cowan v. Wrayford* [1953] 1 W.L.R. 1340.

(i) *Case A: smallholding*: the holding is let as a smallholding; the tenant signed an acknowledgment in the tenancy agreement that it was subject to this head; he is 65 or more; and suitable alternative accommodation for him is available.

(ii) *Case B: planning permission*: the land is required for some non-agricultural use for which planning permission has been given or (in certain cases) is not required.

(iii) *Case C: bad husbandry*: within the previous six months the Tribunal has certified that the tenant was not farming in accordance with the rules of good husbandry.

(iv) *Case D: unremedied breach*: when the notice was given the tenant had failed to comply fully[76] with a written notice by the landlord in the prescribed form requiring him to remedy a breach of a term of his tenancy[77] within a specified time.

(v) *Case E: irreparable breach*: when the notice was given the landlord's interest in the holding had been materially prejudiced by an irreparable breach of a term of the tenancy.

(vi) *Case F: insolvency*: the tenant was insolvent when the notice was given.

(vii) *Case G: death*: the notice is given within three months after the landlord receives written notice of the death of the tenant, or the sole surviving tenant. But there are elaborate provisions[78] which enable the Tribunal to direct, on an application made within three months of the death, that a tenancy of the holding should be given to one or more of certain near relations of the tenant who have lived by working on the holding for at least five years, and the notice to quit is subject to any such direction.

(viii) *Case H: Minister's notice*: the notice to quit is given by the Minister for the purpose of an amalgamation or reshaping of any agricultural unit, and the tenant signed an acknowledgment in the tenancy agreement that it was subject to this head.

(ii) Security dependent on reasonableness: In six cases the Tribunal must consent to the notice to quit taking effect unless it appears that "a fair and reasonable landlord would not insist on possession", in which case the Tribunal must withhold consent.[79] Each case except the fifth case depends on the purpose for which the landlord proposes to terminate the tenancy; and any consent may be made subject to conditions (which may later be varied or revoked) to ensure that the land is used for the purpose stated by the landlord.[80] The six cases are as follows.

(i) *good husbandry*: carrying out the purpose is desirable in the interests of the land as a separate unit;

---

[76] *Price v. Romilly* [1960] 1 W.L.R. 1360.
[77] See *Lloyds Bank Ltd v. Jones* [1955] 2 Q.B. 298 (personal residence).
[78] A.H.A. 1986, ss.34–48.
[79] *ibid.*, s.27(1), (2).
[80] *ibid.*, s.27(3), (4).

(ii) *sound management*: carrying out the purpose is desirable in the interests of sound management of the estate.[81]

(iii) *research*: carrying out the purpose is desirable for the purposes of agricultural research, education, experiment or demonstration, or for the purposes of the statutes relating to smallholdings.

(iv) *allotments*: carrying out the purpose is desirable for the purposes of the statutes relating to allotments;

(v) *greater hardship*: withholding consent would cause greater hardship than granting it; and

(vi) *non-agricultural use*: the purpose is to use the land for some non-agricultural use not within Case B above.

(iii) Full security: Where the case does not fall within any of the foregoing heads, the notice to quit is ineffective, and the tenancy continues unaffected.

(f) Protection as to rent

When an agricultural tenancy is first granted, the parties are free to agree whatever rent they please. However, not more frequently that once in every three years, either party may require the amount of rent to be submitted to arbitration by an arbitrator appointed by the parties or in default by the President of the Royal Institution of Chartered Surveyors.[82] The rent is to be the "rent properly payable" for the holding; and this is the rent at which it might reasonably be expected to be let, taking all relevant factors into account, including the current level of rents for comparable lettings, though disregarding any element in them that is due to an appreciable scarcity of comparable holdings.[83] Any increase or decrease awarded by the arbitrator takes effect as from the next day on which the tenancy could have been determined by a notice to quit given when the reference to arbitration was demanded.[84] Accordingly, apart from any agreement, no revision of rent is possible during a tenancy for a fixed term which is not determinable by a notice to quit. In addition, the landlord may increase the rent in respect of certain improvements carried out by him.[85]

(g) Compensation for disturbance

If a tenant quits the holding in consequence of a notice to quit given by the landlord, he will usually be entitled to compensation from the landlord,[86] even if the notice to quit is in fact invalid.[87] "Basic compensation" is equal to one year's rent of the holding, or, subject to the tenant giving the landlord notice a month before the end of the tenancy and a reasonable opportunity of valuing the farming assets, either the actual loss or two years' rent, whichever is the smaller.[88] But in Cases C, D, E, F or G above, no compensation is payable.[89] In certain cases, as where the land is to be used otherwise than for agriculture, additional compensation

---

[81] See *Evans v. Roper* [1960] 1 W.L.R. 814.
[82] A.H.A. 1986, ss.12, 84, Sched. 2.
[83] *ibid.*, s.12(2), Sched. 2.
[84] *ibid.*, s.12(2), (4). See *Sclater v. Horton* [1954] 2 Q.B. 1.
[85] A.H.A. 1986, s.13.
[86] *ibid.*, s.60.
[87] *Kestell v. Langmaid* [1950] 1 K.B. 233.
[88] A.H.A. 1986, s.60.
[89] *ibid.*, s.61.

equal to four years' rent may be payable.[90] No agreement can exclude either this or any other provision in the Act as to compensation,[91] and a provision which seeks to do this indirectly (such as by providing for the determination of the tenancy at such short notice as to leave no time to claim compensation) is void.[92]

(h) Compensation for improvements

When an agricultural tenant quits his holding at the end of his tenancy, he is entitled to compensation for certain improvements carried out by him, provided he has observed the necessary requirements. For improvements begun on or after March 1, 1948, there are three categories.[93] First, there are long-term improvements for which the landlord's consent was obtained, such as planting orchards. Secondly, there are long-term improvements for which either the landlord's consent or the approval of the Tribunal was obtained, such as the erection of buildings. Thirdly, there are short-term improvements for which no consent or approval is required, such as the liming or chalking of the land. The measure of compensation is the consequent increase in the value of the holding, or, for short-term improvements, their value to an incoming tenant. For "old improvements" (*i.e.* those commenced before March 1, 1948) there is a shorter list of improvements, including the erection of buildings and the reclaiming of waste land; and if they were made with the landlord's consent compensation is payable for the consequent increase in the value of the holding.[94]

2. Farm business tenancies

(a) "Farm business tenancy"

A tenancy is a "farm-business tenancy" within the Agricultural Tenancies Act 1995 if[95]:

   (i) it began on or after September 1, 1995 and is not subject to the Agricultural Holdings Act 1986[96]; and

   (ii) all or part of the land comprised within the tenancy has been since the start of the tenancy and still is being farmed for the purpose of a trade or business; and either

   (iii) having regard to the terms of the tenancy, the use of the land, the nature of any commercial activities carried out on the land, and any other relevant circumstances, the character of the tenancy is wholly or primarily agricultural; or

   (iv) at the beginning of the tenancy, the character of the tenancy was wholly or primarily agricultural having regard to the above factors and, on or before that date, the landlord and tenant exchanged written notices identifying the land and their intention that the tenancy was to be a farm business tenancy.

(b) Notices to quit

Where the tenancy is a tenancy for a fixed period of less than two years or a periodic tenancy other than a yearly tenancy, it can be terminated in accordance with the terms of the lease.

[90] *ibid.*, ss.27(3)(f), 60(4), 61(4), (5).
[91] *ibid.*, s.78.
[92] *Coates v. Diment* [1951] 1 All E.R. 890.
[93] A.H.A. 1986, ss.64–66; Scheds 7, 8.
[94] *ibid.*, s.64, Sched. 9.
[95] A.T.A. 1995, s.1(1).
[96] Above, p. 585.

Otherwise a notice in writing of not less than 12 months and not more than 24 months is necessary to determine the lease; in the case of a tenancy for a fixed period of two years or more, the notice must be served in accordance with the provisions of the lease[97] while in the case of a yearly periodic tenancy it must take effect at the end of a year.[98]

(c) Continuation of tenancies

There is no minimum or maximum length for a farm business tenancy which can either be a tenancy for a fixed period or a periodic tenancy. If it is a tenancy for a fixed period of more than two years, then, pending service of a valid notice to quit, it will continue as a yearly periodic tenancy.[99]

(d) Protection as to rent

If a farm business tenancy contains a provision that the rent is not to be reviewed or is to be varied by a specified amount or in accordance with a specified formula which does not preclude reduction or require or permit determination by the exercise of any judgment or discretion, then that provision will be valid[1]; to that extent the parties to a farm business tenancy have freedom of contract as to rent. Otherwise, either party may by service of a statutory notice refer the rent payable to arbitration. Any variation will take effect from the review date, which must be not less than 12 months and not more than 24 months from the date of the notice, at least three years since the beginning of the tenancy or the last review and, in the absence of agreement to the contrary, be an anniversary of the beginning of the tenancy.[2] The rent payable is that at which a willing landlord might reasonably be expected to let to a willing tenant on the open market taking account of all relevant circumstances and disregarding certain tenant's improvements.[3]

(e) Compensation for improvement

Farm business tenants are entitled to be compensated for improvements to which the landlord has consented,[4] although a refusal of consent can be referred to arbitration.[5] Improvements include not only physical improvements but also "intangible advantages" such as increases in milk quota and granted planning permissions.[6] The tenant is entitled to be paid the increase in the value of the holding at the end of the tenancy due to the improvements.[7]

Sect. 3. Dwellings

Not until 1915 were there any statutory provisions which protected tenants of dwellings. The first in a long line of Rent Acts[8] then established a system under which the rent of a dwelling could not be increased by more than a limited amount and the tenant could not be evicted

---

[97] A.T.A. 1995, s.7(1).
[98] ibid., s.6(1).
[99] ibid., s.5(1).
[1] ibid., s.9.
[2] ibid., s.10.
[3] ibid., s.13.
[4] ibid., s.17.
[5] ibid., s.19.
[6] ibid., s.15.
[7] ibid., s.20 (different principles apply to planning permissions).
[8] Increase of Rent and Mortgage Interest (War Restrictions) Act 1915.

except on specified grounds, even though at common law his tenancy had come to an end. The legislation was repeatedly consolidated and amended, control generally being expanded to meet war time shortages and relaxed in times of peace. The system was finally consolidated in the Rent Act 1977. For fifty years, tenancies protected by the Rent Acts were called "controlled tenancies"; but tenancies that the Rent Act 1965 brought into protection, with a different system for fixing the rent, were called "regulated tenancies", and the Rent Act 1977 called both types "protected tenancies". Under the Housing Act 1980 all controlled tenancies became regulated tenancies.

Subsequently, the Housing Act 1988 prevented the Rent Act 1977 from applying to any tenancy granted on or after January 15, 1989, but instead gave such tenancies (called "assured tenancies") a more limited form of protection against eviction while enabling the landlord to charge a commercial rent. The Housing Act 1996 conferred still greater freedom to landlords by providing that, in the absence of agreement to the contrary, any assured tenancy granted on or after February 28, 1997 will be an assured shorthold tenancy. Such tenancies, first created by the Housing Act 1988 enable the landlord to regain possession by giving notice.

The best way of approaching the complex of systems protecting tenancies of dwellings seems to be to consider them in two main groups. The first group consists of protection for the tenant under the main systems of the Rent Acts, or some variant of them. Under this head there are five categories:

   (i) the old system of regulated tenancies under the Rent Act 1977, which confers both security of tenure and protection as to rent;

  (ii) the newer system of assured tenancies under the Housing Act 1988, which also confers more limited security of tenure and some protection as to rent;

 (iii) the system of assured shorthold tenancies created by the Housing Act 1988 and made effectively universal by the Housing Act 1996 which confers no security of tenure but does confer protection as to rent;

 (iv) the variant system of "agricultural occupancies" for "tied cottages", which confers protection similar to that given by assured tenancies and special rights to alternative accomodation; and

  (v) the variant and partial system of "secure tenancies" for lettings by local authorities, which confers protection as to possesion but not as to rent and the right to buy the freehold or a long lease at a low rent.

The second main group consists of special systems for the protection of special categories, namely:

  (vi) residential long tenancies at a low rent which confer the right to buy the freehold or be granted a new tenancy;

 (vii) long leases and certain other tenancies of flats at a low rent with a collective right of pre-emption if the landlord proposes to dispose of the building and individual rights to a further lease at a low rent; and

(viii) a special system for "restricted contracts" which fell outside the Rent Act 1977 which confers protection as to rent and limited security of tenure.

The broad picture is that the first three categories and the last category provide the general system of control, the fourth is a special case which is very restricted, and the other three confer rights to purchase the freehold or a further long lease. In addition to these systems, there are certain procedural provisions relating to eviction and harassment that are designed to ensure that no residential occupiers will be evicted from their dwellings except under an order of the court.

1. Regulated tenancies under the Rent Act 1977

No regulated tenancy can arise on a letting made on or after January 15, 1989[9]; but large numbers of regulated tenancies had arisen before that date, and these continue to be subject to the Rent Act 1977, as amended.

(a) Application of the Acts

The Rent Act 1977 applies to every "dwelling-house" of an appropriate rateable value[10] which satisfies certain conditions. "Dwelling-house" means any house (or part of a house) which is "let as a separate dwelling".[11] Thus the existence of a tenancy is essential; this requirement excludes a mere licence from the Acts, though not a tenant at will or at sufferance. Whether the premises are let "as" a dwelling depends on the use provided for or contemplated by the tenancy agreement, or, in default, by the *de facto* user at the time in question.[12] And the letting must be as "a" (*i.e.* one) dwelling and not as two or more dwellings.[13]

The word "separate" formerly excluded lettings where the tenant was required to share living accommodation such as a kitchen.[14] However, statute has modified the rule, so that where the sharing is with the landlord the tenant is given restricted contract protection,[15] and where the sharing is with other tenants, the tenant has normal protection, subject to certain modifications.[16] Often what is structurally a single dwelling-house contains many "dwelling-houses" for the purposes of the Rent Acts, even if it has not been physically divided into self-contained flats; for one or two rooms, with a right to share the bathroom and lavatory, may for this purpose constitute a "dwelling-house".

(b) Exceptions

Certain tenancies which would otherwise fall within the Acts are nevertheless excluded. In some cases, the exception is personal to the landlord. Thus, the Crown is generally not bound by the Acts (though tenants are protected where the interest of the Crown is under the management of the Crown Estate Commissioners[17]), nor are local authorities, new town development corporations or certain housing associations or housing trusts,[18] though they are subject to a limited degree of control.[19] In such cases, the exemption does not operate in favour of other persons concerned with the property, such as sub-tenants or purchasers. Other

---

[9] H.A. 1988, s.1, Sched. 1.
[10] See below, p. 592.
[11] Act of 1977, s.1.
[12] *Wolfe v. Hogan* [1949] 2 K.B. 194.
[13] *Horford Investments Ltd v. Lambert* [1976] Ch. 39; *St. Catherine's College v. Dorling* [1980] 1 W.L.R. 66.
[14] *Neale v. Del Soto* [1945] K.B. 144.
[15] Act of 1977, s.21. See below, p. 551.
[16] *ibid.*, s.22.
[17] *ibid.*, s.13, as substituted by H.A. 1980, s.73.
[18] Act of 1977, ss.14, 15, as amended by H.A. 1980, s.74.
[19] See below, p. 605.

exceptions depend on the nature of the tenancies. Thus the Acts do not apply where the letting is rent free or the rent is less than two-thirds of the rateable value.[20] Again, the Acts are excluded where the tenancy was granted in order to give the tenant the right to occupy the dwelling for a holiday, or if the tenant is pursuing or intends to pursue a course of study provided by a specified institution, and the tenancy was granted by that or some other specified body.[21] The Acts are also excluded where the rent includes payments in respect of board or, if they are substantial, attendance[22]; payments for the use of furniture formerly excluded the Acts but no longer do so.[23]

Most of the exceptions, however, depend on the nature or status of the premises themselves. Thus for diverse reasons, public houses,[24] and parsonage houses of the Church of England[25] (such as the ordinary rectory or vicarage), are outside the Act. Agricultural holdings occupied by the farmer are also outside the Acts, though, of course, within the Agricultural Holdings Act 1986 and the Agricultural Tenancies Act 1995.[26] Although in general any land or premises let together with a dwelling-house are treated as being part of the dwelling-house, if the dwelling-house is let together with more than two acres of agricultural land, both house and land are excluded from the Acts.[27]

A further exception is for a tenancy granted after August 13, 1974, by a "resident landlord", namely a tenancy of part of a building granted by a landlord who throughout the tenancy occupies another part of the building as his residence. This does not apply to purpose-built blocks of flats unless the letting is of part of the landlord's flat, nor where the tenancy is granted to a protected or statutory tenant in the building.[28]

(c) Rateable value

A dwelling can be protected only if its rateable value does not exceed certain amounts. These amounts have varied over the years. The present amounts depend on the rateable value of the dwelling on the "appropriate day." This is March 23, 1965, or, if the rateable value of the dwelling first appeared in the valuation list after that date, the date when it first appeared.[29]

Appropriate day	*Greater London*	*Elsewhere*
A. After March 31, 1973	£1,500	£750
B. Between March 21 and April 1, 1973	£600	£300
C. Before March 22, 1973	£400	£200

Cases in Class B must satisfy the amounts in Class A as well, and cases in Class C must also satisfy the amounts in Classes A and B,[30] so that the Acts are excluded if any relevant amount is exceeded. The striking increases in the values were due partly to the Acts being extended

---

[20] Act of 1977, s.5(1).
[21] *ibid.*, ss.8, 9.
[22] *ibid.*, s.7: see *Otter v. Norman* [1989] A.C. 129. Restricted contract protection may apply in some cases: below, p. 614.
[23] Rent Act 1974, s.1.
[24] Act of 1977, s.11.
[25] *Bishop of Gloucester v. Cunnington* [1943] K.B. 101.
[26] A.H.A. 1986, s.10.
[27] Act of 1977, s.26; and see s.6.
[28] *ibid.*, s.12, as amended by H.A. 1980, s.65.
[29] *ibid.*, s.25.
[30] *ibid.*, s.4.

to larger dwellings and partly to a general reassessment and increase in rateable values. One result of the abolition of domestic rates is that for tenancies entered into after March 31, 1990, which are unlikely to be protected anyway, the test based on rateable values no longer applies, and the Acts are excluded only by a rent exceeding £25,000 a year.[31] Older tenancies are still governed by the rateable values.

(d) Statutory tenancy

The Rent Acts protect a tenant from eviction by prohibiting the courts from making any order for possession except on specified grounds, and giving him the right to continue in possession of the premises despite the termination of the tenancy by notice to quit or otherwise.[32] The Acts thus bring into being what is usually called a "statutory tenancy": this is the right of the tenant to remain in possession, despite the determination of his contractual tenancy, on all the terms of the contractual tenancy which are not inconsistent with the Acts,[33] until the court makes an order for possession against him. A statutory tenancy is not really a "tenancy" at all, in the common law sense of the word; the tenant has no estate or interest in the land, but a mere personal right of occupation, or "status of irremovability".[34] He cannot dispose of his statutory tenancy by assignment[35] or by will, and it will not vest in his trustee in bankruptcy.

Further, a statutory tenancy will cease to exist if the tenant ceases to occupy the premises as his home[36] or one of his homes.[37] Mere temporary absences are immaterial; but once an absent tenant has lost either his *animus revertendi* (intention of returning)[38] or his *corpus possessionis* (visible indication of his animus, such as the presence on the premises of some caretaker on his behalf), his statutory tenancy is at an end.[39] If a house is totally destroyed, any statutory tenancy perishes with the house, whereas a contractual tenancy could continue to exist in the ruins.[40] A statutory tenancy is thus an anomaly which fits into no recognised category of property law.

(e) Death of statutory tenant

When a statutory tenant dies, his tenancy does not pass under his will or intestacy, but his widow, if residing with him when he died, or otherwise any member of his family who resided with him for at least the previous six months (as decided by the court in default of agreement), becomes statutory tenant in his place; and two such transmissions could take place.[41] For deaths after January 14, 1989, these rules have been modified.[42] They now apply to widowers as well as widows, and also to those merely cohabiting as man and wife; and the former six months' period for residence by a member of the family is now two years' residence in the dwelling in question. But although a surviving spouse will still be fully protected as a statutory tenant, a member of the family will take only the lesser protection of

---

[31] Local Government and Housing Act 1989, s.149; S.I. 1990, No. 434.
[32] Act of 1977, s.98.
[33] *ibid.*, s.3.
[34] *Jessamine Investment Co. v. Schwartz* [1978] Q.B. 264.
[35] But see Act of 1977, s.3(5), Sched. 1, para. 13.
[36] *Skinner v. Geary* [1931] 2 K.B. 546.
[37] *Hallwood Estates Ltd v. Flack* (1950) 66(2) T.L.R. 368.
[38] *Colin Smith Music Ltd v. Ridge* [1975] 1 W.L.R. 463 (tenant's deserted mistress).
[39] *Brown v. Brash* [1948] 2 K.B. 247; *Tickner v. Hearn* [1960] 1 W.L.R. 1406.
[40] *Ellis & Sons Amalgamated Properties Ltd v. Sisman* [1948] 1 K.B. 653.
[41] Act of 1977, s.2, Sched. 1, Pt. I, as amended by H.A. 1980, s.76.
[42] H.A. 1988, s.39, Sched. 4; and compare secure tenancies: below, p. 605.

an assured tenancy,[43] and so will a surviving spouse if the deceased tenant had already taken under these provisions. Further, these assured tenancies are subject to certain mandatory grounds for possession.

(f) Grounds for possession

The court cannot make an order for possession unless the landlord satisfies one of the following two heads. First, that one of the discretionary grounds for possession exists, and also that in all the circumstances of the case, after considering the effect on both landlord and tenant of making or not making the order,[44] it is reasonable to make an order for possession.[45] Secondly, that one of the mandatory grounds for possession exists; here, there is no requirement of reasonableness. The two heads will be considered in turn.

(i) Discretionary grounds: Some of the discretionary grounds are based on misconduct by the tenant, others on the landlord's needs, or the existence of alternative accommodation. The heads are as follows.[46]

(i) *Case 1: breach.* Rent lawfully due has not been paid, or some other obligation of the tenancy that is consistent with the Acts has been broken.

(ii) *Case 2: nuisance.* The tenant, his lodger or sub-tenant has been guilty of conduct which is a nuisance to adjoining occupiers, or has been convicted of illegal or immoral user of the premises.

(iii) *Case 3: waste.* The tenant, his lodger or sub-tenant has permitted the condition of the premises to deteriorate.

(iv) *Case 4: damage to furniture.* The tenant, his lodger or sub-tenant has, by ill-treatment, caused the condition of furniture provided under the tenancy to deteriorate.

(v) *Case 5: tenant's notice to quit.* The tenant has given notice to quit and the landlord has acted upon it so as to be seriously prejudiced if he could not obtain possession.

(vi) *Case 6: assigning or sub-letting without consent.* The tenant, without the landlord's consent, has assigned or sub-let the whole of the premises, or has sub-let part, the remainder being already sub-let.

(vii) *Case 8[47]: needed for landlord's employee.* The premises are reasonably required as a residence for a whole-time employee of the landlord, and they were let to the tenant in consequence of his former employment by the landlord or a previous landlord.

(viii) *Case 9: needed for landlord or his family.* The landlord reasonably requires the premises for occupation as a residence for himself, a child of his over 18 years old, or one of his parents or parents-in-law. There are two exceptions. First, this

---

[43] Below, p. 599.
[44] *Battlespring Ltd v. Gates* (1984) 11 H.L.R. 6.
[45] Act of 1977, s.98.
[46] *ibid.,* Sched. 15, Pt. I.
[47] There is no longer a Case 7.

head is not available to a landlord who became landlord by purchasing[48] any interest in the premises after March 23, 1965. This prevents a landlord who buys the premises subject to an existing tenancy from evicting the tenant under this head.[49] Secondly, this head does not apply if the tenant satisfies the court that in all the circumstances "greater hardship" would be caused to all persons likely to be affected[50] by making the order for possession than by refusing it.

(ix) *Case 10: excessive rent on sub-letting*. The tenant has sub-let part of the premises at an excessive rent.

(x) *Case AA*[51]*: alternative accommodation*. Suitable alternative accommodation is available for the tenant, or will be available when the order for possession takes effect. This accommodation need not be as suitable[52] as the existing accommodation and may even be part of it.[53]

(ii) Mandatory grounds: A landlord who establishes one of the mandatory grounds for possession can obtain an order for possession as of right, irrespective of reasonableness.[54] But the grounds are available only if the tenant was given notice in writing not later than the relevant date (usually the commencement of the tenancy[55]) that the landlord might recover possession on the particular mandatory ground.[56] Further, in all the cases except the last three, possession must be required for a particular purpose specified by the statute. In four cases the purpose is individually specified, but for three, several are available out of the following list, namely:

(a) the dwelling is required (*i.e.* genuinely desired[57]) as a residence for the owner or any member of his family who resided with him when he last occupied the dwelling;

(b) the owner has retired from regular employment and requires the dwelling as his residence;

(c) the owner has died and the dwelling is required for a member of his family residing with him at the time of his death;

(d) the owner has died and the dwelling is required by a successor in title as his residence or for the purpose of disposing of it with vacant possession;

(e) the dwelling is subject to a mortgage which pre-dates the tenancy and the mortgagee requires the dwelling for the purpose of disposing of it with vacant possession, pursuant to his power of sale; and

(f) the dwelling is not suitably proximate to the owner's place of work and he needs the proceeds of a sale with vacant possession in order to acquire a dwelling more suitable to his needs.

[48] See *Powell v. Cleland* [1948] 1 K.B. 262; *Thomas v. Fryer* [1970] 1 W.L.R. 845; *Mansukhani v. Sharkey* [1992] 33 E.G. 65 (gift of mortgaged flat not a purchase).
[49] See, *e.g. Wright v. Walford* [1955] 1 K.B. 363.
[50] See *Harte v. Frampton* [1948] 1 K.B. 73.
[51] Though not statutory, this heading is convenient.
[52] See *Siddiqu v. Rashid* [1980] 1 W.L.R. 1018; *Hill v. Rochard* [1983] 1 W.L.R. 478.
[53] *Parmee v. Mitchell* [1950] 2 K.B. 199; *Mykolyshyn v. Noah* [1970] 1 W.L.R. 1271.
[54] Act of 1977, s.98, Sched. 15, Pts II, V, as amended by H.A. 1980, s.66.
[55] Act of 1977, s.98, Sched. 15, Pt. III.
[56] For Cases 11, 12, and 20, the court may dispense with this requirement.
[57] *Kennealy v. Dunne* [1977] Q.B. 837 (not "needed").

The mandatory grounds are as follows[58]; they are here grouped not numerically but according to the purpose for which possession is required.

(i) *Case 11: owner-occupier.* The landlord was an owner-occupier of the dwelling when he let it, and he seeks possession for any purpose in the above list except (b).

(ii) *Case 12: retirement home.* The landlord let the dwelling prior to his retirement and he seeks possession for any purpose in the above list except (a) or (f).

(iii) *Case 20: serviceman.* The landlord was a member of the armed forces both when he acquired the dwelling and when he let it, and he requires it either as a residence or for any purpose in the above list except (a) or (b).

(iv) *Case 15: minister of religion.* The dwelling is held so as to be available for occupation by a minister of religion as a residence from which to perform his duties, and it is required for this purpose.

(v) *Case 16: agricultural worker.* The dwelling was at any time occupied by an agricultural worker as such and it is required for such a worker.

(vi) *Case 17: redundant farm-house.* The dwelling is a farm-house which became redundant on amalgamation, but it is now required for an agricultural worker.

(vii) *Case 18: farmhouse required for agriculture.* The dwelling is a farm-house occupied by a non-agricultural tenant and it is required for occupation by a farmer or farm-worker.

(viii) *Case 13: holiday home.* The tenancy was granted for a fixed term of not more than eight months, and at some time during the previous 12 months the dwelling had been occupied under a right to occupy it for a holiday. In this and the next two Cases there is no need for the landlord to show that he requires the dwelling for any particular purpose.

(ix) *Case 14: student residence.* The tenancy was granted for a fixed term of not more than 12 months and at some time during the previous 12 months the dwelling was subject to a tenancy granted by a specified institution to a student at a specified educational institution.

(x) *Case 19: protected shorthold tenancies.* Protected shorthold tenancies were introduced by the Housing Act 1980[59] so as to encourage landlords to let dwellings by the assurance of possession being recoverable when the tenancy ended; but none could be created after January 14, 1989.[60] They were tenancies for fixed terms of from one to five years granted after giving the tenant notice that the letting was to be a protected shorthold tenancy. Once the tenancy ended, an order for possession under Case 19 was mandatory, provided that:

(a) no further tenancy had been granted to anyone except the tenant;

---

[58] Act of 1977, Sched. 15, Pt. II, as amended by H.A. 1980, ss.66, 67.
[59] s.52.
[60] H.A. 1988, s.34.

(b) at least three months' notice had been given to the tenant stating that proceedings under this Case might be brought;

(c) the notice was at least three months long, and it was given during the three months immediately before the date when the tenancy ended, or an anniversary of that date; and

(d) proceedings for possession were brought within three months of the expiry of the notice.

(xi) *Overcrowding*. Although not listed as a "Case", an order for possession is mandatory as long as the dwelling is overcrowded within the meaning of the Housing Act 1985 in such circumstances as to render the occupier guilty of an offence[61]; and similarly for certain insanitary or dangerous premises.[62]

(g) Rent limit

(i) Systems: There have been three stages in the control of rent. First, from 1915 to 1957, the "recoverable rent" for a dwelling within the Rent Acts consisted of the "standard rent" together with certain "permitted increases" (such as for improvements). Secondly, the Rent Act 1957 replaced the "recoverable rent" by a "rent limit", based on the gross value of the dwelling in 1956 for rating purposes. Thirdly, the Rent Act 1965 continued this system for existing controlled tenancies, but applied a new system to the "regulated tenancies" that were newly brought within the Acts. Under this, "fair rents" were to be determined by "rent officers" and registered; but until that was done the maximum rent was to be the rent payable under the last regulated tenancy during the previous three years, or, if none, whatever rent was agreed under the tenancy in question. This is similar to the system under the Rent Act 1977.

(ii) No registered rent: Where there was no registered rent and a tenancy was being granted to a new tenant, there was no limit to the rent that could be charged: the tenant's safeguard was and is his right to apply to have a fair rent fixed and registered. But if the tenancy is granted to a sitting tenant who has security of tenure, an increased rent can be charged only under an agreement signed by both parties that boldly proclaims that refusal to sign it will not affect security of tenure and that the parties may at any time apply for the registration of a fair rent. Where the regulated tenancy has become statutory, the rent cannot exceed the rent for the last contractual period.[63]

(iii) Registration of rent: An application to the rent officer for the registration of a fair rent may be made at any time by the landlord or the tenant. The rent officer, after giving the parties an opportunity to make representations, registers the rent if he thinks it fair, or, if not, determines and registers what he thinks would be a fair rent. There is a right of appeal to a rent assessment committee. For a period of two years after registration, neither party can apply for the registration of a different rent without the concurrence of the other, unless there have been changes in circumstances that make the registered rent no longer fair.[64] The landlord cannot recover more than the registered rent from a regulated tenant.[65]

---

[61] Act of 1977, s.101, as substituted by Housing (Consequential Provisions) Act 1985, Sched. 2.
[62] H.A. 1985, ss.264(5), 270(3), 276.
[63] See Megarry's *Rent Acts* (11th ed., 1988) Vol. 1, p 541–551 for these rules and variants.
[64] Act of 1977, s.67, as amended by H.A. 1980, s.60: formerly the period was three years.
[65] Act of 1977, ss.44, 45.

(iv) Fair rent: In determining what is a fair rent, regard must be had "to all the circumstances (other than personal circumstances) and in particular to . . . the age, character, locality and state of repair of the dwelling-house", any furniture provided under the tenancy, and also any premium paid for the tenancy. There must, however, be disregarded the effect of local shortages of accommodation, any disrepair or defect attributable to a failure by the tenant to comply with his obligations, any voluntary improvement carried out by the tenant, and any change in the condition of furniture.[66] The disregard of scarcity has often produced registered rents that are lower than market rents, sometimes strikingly so.

(h) Premiums

There are wide provisions[67] prohibiting any person (whether landlord, tenant, agent or middleman[68]) from requiring a premium as a condition of the grant, renewal, continuance or assignment of any tenancy within the Rent Act 1977,[69] and preventing a statutory tenant (who has no assignable interest) from asking or receiving any consideration from any person except the landlord as a condition of giving up possession.[70]

(i) Mortgages

Where the Acts restricted a landlord's rights against his tenant (such as to increase the rent) it was thought that the landlord ought to be correspondingly protected against his mortgagee. Today, there is no longer any automatic protection, but instead the landlord-mortgagor may sometimes be granted relief by the court. He can apply for relief if the mortgage was created before certain dates when the Acts became applicable to the tenancy, and the mortgage is a legal mortgage of a dwelling let on a regulated tenancy that is binding on the mortgagee. If the rate of interest under the mortgage is increased, or steps are taken to enforce the mortgage, or a lower rent for the tenancy is registered, and this, coupled with the Act of 1977, causes the landlord-mortgagor "severe financial hardship", the court may grant relief by varying the mortgage or restricting the exercise of any remedies under it.[71]

2. Assured tenancies under the Housing Act 1988

(a) Introduction

The new system under the Housing Act 1988 whereby tenancies created on or after January 15, 1989 may receive the lesser benefits of being assured tenancies exists side by side with the long-established system under the Rent Acts which has been considered above; the latter continues to apply, with some variations, to tenancies created before January 15, 1989. The two systems have much in common, but many differences.

(b) Application of the Housing Act 1988

(i) Date of tenancy: A tenancy cannot be a protected tenancy under the old law if it was entered into on or after January 15, 1989, and it cannot be an assured tenancy under the new system if it was entered into before that date. The two categories are mutually exclusive.[72]

---

[66] *ibid.*, s.70; Housing and Planning Act 1986, s.17.
[67] Rent Act 1977, s.103.
[68] *Farrell v. Alexander* [1977] A.C. 59.
[69] See *Elmdene Estates Ltd v. White* [1960] A.C. 528.
[70] Act of 1977, s.3(5), Sched. 1, Pt. II.
[71] *ibid.*, Pt. X.
[72] See H.A. 1988, s.34(1), Sched. 1, para. 13(1).

Where a tenancy was entered into in pursuance of a contract, the date to be taken is that of the contract, not the tenancy. Further, a tenant protected under the old system does not lose his protection if he accepts a new tenancy after that date.[73]

(ii) Nature of tenancy: As under the old system,[74] the Housing Act 1988 applies only if there is a tenancy under which a dwelling-house is let as a separate dwelling and the tenant occupies it as a home; but now it must be his "only or principal home".[75] With some modifications, the list of exceptions substantially follows the exceptions under the Act of 1977,[76] though the exception for board and attendance does not apply.

(c) Types of assured tenancy

Under the Housing Act 1988 there are three main types of assured tenancy, namely periodic tenancies, fixed term tenancies, and shorthold tenancies. An assured fixed term tenancy is any assured tenancy except a periodic tenancy.[77] Assured shorthold tenancies are considered below; briefly, they are assured tenancies granted for a fixed term of six months or more after a notice in the prescribed form has been served on the tenant stating that the tenancy will be a shorthold tenancy.[78]

(d) Security of tenure

A landlord can bring an assured tenancy to an end only by obtaining an order of the court for possession, made on one of the statutory grounds.[79] A periodic tenancy will thus continue indefinitely despite any notice to quit given by the landlord; and when a fixed term tenancy comes to an end, then unless this was effected by the tenant (such as by surrender) or by an order of the court, the landlord is deemed to have granted the tenant a "statutory periodic tenancy" on the existing terms.[80] This tenancy is very different from a statutory tenancy under the old system,[81] for it is, by force of statute, a contractual tenancy and not a mere status of irremovability. In addition, no proceedings for possession can be brought unless the landlord has served on the tenant a "possession notice" in the prescribed form. This must state that within one year but not sooner than two weeks (or two months, in some cases) he intends to begin proceedings for possession on one or more of the grounds specified in the notice.[82]

(e) Grounds for possession

The discretionary and mandatory grounds for possession have much in common with those under the Rent Act 1977, considered above[83]; but they are by no means identical. They are as follows.

---

[73] *ibid.*, s.34, Sched. 1, para. 1.
[74] Above, p. 592.
[75] H.A. 1988, s.1.
[76] Above, pp. 592–593.
[77] H.A. 1988, s.45(1): thus for these purposes a tenancy at will is a fixed term tenancy.
[78] *ibid.*, s.20: tenancies graboved to certain existing tenants are excluded.
[79] H.A. 1988, s.5.
[80] *ibid.*
[81] Above, pp. 594–595.
[82] H.A. 1988, s.8.
[83] Above, pp. 595–598.

(i) Discretionary grounds: If satisfied that any of the eight discretionary grounds for possession[84] is satisfied the court may make an order for possession if it considers it reasonable to do so.[85]

(i) *Ground 9: alternative accommodation.* This is substantially the same as Case AA.

(ii) *Ground 10: unpaid rent.* This is a revised version of part of Case 1.

(iii) *Ground 11: persistent delay.* Even if no rent is in arrears, the tenant has persistently delayed in paying rent.

(iv) *Ground 12: breach of obligation.* An obligation of the tenancy (apart from rent) has been broken or not performed. This corresponds with the rest of Case 1.

(v) *Ground 13: waste.* This is a modified version of Case 3, expanded to include the common parts of any building that includes the dwelling.

(vi) *Ground 14: nuisance.* This is almost identical with Case 2.

(vii) *Ground 15: damage to furniture.* This is substantially the same as Case 3.

(viii) *Ground 16: landlord's employee.* The dwelling was let to an employee of the landlord but his employment has ended. This matches the second limb of Case 8; the dwelling need not be required for another employee under this ground.

(ii) Mandatory grounds: There are in effect nine mandatory grounds for possession.[86] The first five of them are available only if the tenant was given notice in writing not later than the beginning of the tenancy that possession might be recovered on the particular mandatory ground.[87]

(i) *Ground 1: landlord's home.* Either the landlord once occupied the dwelling as his only or principal home, or the landlord now requires the dwelling as the only or principal home for himself or his spouse, and he did not acquire the reversion on the tenancy for money or money's worth. There are elements of Cases 9 and 11 here.

(ii) *Ground 2: mortgagee's sale.* Under a mortgage granted before the tenancy began, the mortgagee requires possession so that he can sell the dwelling with vacant possession under his power of sale.

(iii) *Ground 3: holiday home.* This is substantially the same as Case 13.

(iv) *Ground 4: student residence.* This closely resembles Case 14.

(v) *Ground 5: minister of religion.* This is substantially the same as Case 15.

(vi) *Ground 6: demolition or substantial works.* The landlord intends to demolish or reconstruct all or a substantial part of the dwelling, or to carry out substantial

---

[84] H.A. 1988, Sched. 2, Pt. II.
[85] *ibid.*, s.7(4).
[86] *ibid.*, Sched. 2, Pt. I.
[87] See above, p. 596. For Grounds 1 and 2 the court may dispense with this requirement.

works on it, and he needs possession for this purpose. But this ground is not available to a landlord who acquired the reversion on the tenancy for money or money's worth.[88]

(vii) *Ground 7: death of tenant.* The tenancy is a periodic tenancy and the tenant has died; the tenancy has devolved under his will or intestacy; and proceedings for possession were commenced within a year of the tenant's death.

(viii) *Ground 8: prolonged non-payment of rent.* At least three months' rent is in arrears or unpaid, both when the possession notice is served and at the date of the hearing.

(ix) *Assured shorthold tenancies.* In addition to the eight numbered grounds, there is in effect an additional mandatory ground for assured shorthold tenancies, which will be considered below.[89]

(f) Death

On the death of an assured tenant, the provisions for transmission of the tenancy[90] are narrower than those for statutory tenants under regulated tenancies.[91] They apply only to periodic and not fixed term assured tenancies. They apply only to sole (and not joint) tenants. They apply only to a surviving spouse (as generously construed[92]) who occupied the dwelling as his or her only or principal home immediately before the tenant's death, though no period of occupation is required. Members of the family have no rights of succession; and there can be only one transmission. If these requirements are satisfied, the tenancy, which is necessarily contractual, automatically vests in the spouse; otherwise it devolves under the tenant's will or intestacy.

(g) Rent

Under an assured tenancy the rent will initially be whatever the parties have agreed: there is no system of registered rents or any other statutory restriction. Unless otherwise agreed, that rent will continue for as long as the tenancy exists. But for assured periodic tenancies (and for assured shorthold tenancies) there is a limited degree of statutory control. This does not apply to other tenancies; under a tenancy for a fixed term (not being an assured shorthold) the rent payable is the rent agreed.

Under an assured periodic tenancy the initial rent will continue indefinitely unless the landlord serves a notice proposing an increased rent on the tenant. This increased rent will become the new rent unless the tenant refers the notice to the rent assessment committee, in which case the open market rent as determined by the committee will become the new rent. No such increase can be made during the first year of the tenancy, or if the tenancy makes its own provisions for increases.[93] Apart from this, the tenant has no right to apply to the committee. Assured shorthold tenancies will be considered below.

---

[88] There is some parallel here with business tenancies: see above, p. 583.
[89] H.A. 1988, s.21; below, p. 603.
[90] *ibid.,* s.17.
[91] Above, p. 594.
[92] *ibid.*
[93] H.A. 1988, ss.13, 14.

3. Assured shorthold tenancies under the Housing Acts 1988 and 1996

(a) Introduction

Assured shorthold tenancies were created by the Housing Act 1988 to replace what were known as protected shorthold tenancies. These tenancies had been created by the Housing Act 1980 to encourage the grant of residential tenancies and gave the tenant the same protection against increases of rent as regulated tenants under the Rent Act 1977 but no protection against eviction. Until the Housing Act 1996 came into force, assured shorthold tenancies could only be created expressly but since February 28, 1997 assured shorthold tenancies are created automatically in the absence of any contrary provision.

(b) Creation

An assured shorthold tenancy may have been created in three ways.

(i) Former protected shorthold tenancies: The grant of a new tenancy to a protected shorthold tenant after January 15, 1989 will have created an assured shorthold tenancy whether or not any notice to that effect has been served on the tenant unless the landlord served notice on the tenant that the tenancy was not to be an assured shorthold tenancy.[94]

(ii) Under the Housing Act 1988: Any assured tenancy created on or after January 15, 1989 and before February 28, 1997 will be an assured shorthold tenancy if it was granted for a fixed term of six months or more after a notice in the prescribed form had been served on the tenant stating that the tenancy was to be a shorthold tenancy.[95]

(iii) Under the Housing Act 1996: Any assured tenancy created on or after February 28, 1997 other than pursuant to a contract made before that date will be an assured shorthold tenancy[96] unless[97]:

   (i) the landlord serves a notice on the tenant either before or during the tenancy that the tenancy was not to be an assured shorthold tenancy;

   (ii) the tenancy agreement itself provides that the tenancy is not to be an assured shorthold tenancy;

   (iii) the tenancy has arisen by succession to a regulated tenancy under the Rent Act 1977 (other than a protected shorthold tenancy), became assured on ceasing to be a secure tenancy, arose under Schedule 10 to the Local Government and Housing Act 1989,[98] or came into being when a non-shorthold tenancy came to an end;

   (iv) the tenancy is granted to an existing assured tenant (unless that tenant serves a notice on the landlord to the contrary); or

   (v) the tenancy is an assured agricultural occupancy.[99]

(c) Grounds for possession

A landlord may obtain possession on any of the grounds on which he could obtain possession against a tenant of an assured tenancy and during the term of an assured shorthold tenancy

---

[94] *ibid.*, s.34(3).
[95] *ibid.*, s.20: tenancies granted to certain existing tenants are excluded.
[96] H.A. 1996, s.96(1) inserting s.18A into H.A. 1988.
[97] H.A. 1988, Sched. 2 inserted by H.A. 1996, Sched. 7.
[98] Below, p. 605.
[99] Below, p. 605.

those are the only grounds on which he can do so. At the end of the term, however, there is in effect an additional mandatory ground.[1] If the tenancy is for a fixed term which has ended, and before it ended the landlord gave the tenant at least two months' notice stating that he required possession of the dwelling, then provided no further assured tenancy (apart from a statutory periodic tenancy) is in existence, the landlord is entitled to a mandatory order for possession. If instead the tenancy is periodic, the landlord is entitled to his order if he has given the tenant at least two months' notice that he requires possession on a specified date, and this date is the last day of a period of the tenancy and also a day on which a notice to quit given at the same time could (apart from the Housing Act 1988) terminate the tenancy.

(d) Rent

Under an assured shorthold tenancy the initial rent will continue indefinitely unless the tenant refers it to the rent assessment committee. He may do this at any time after the grant of the tenancy. The committee then determines the rent which the landlord might "reasonably be expected to obtain" under the tenancy, but there is no jurisdiction to do this unless there is a sufficiency of similar dwellings in the locality that are let on assured tenancies and the committee considers that the rent under the tenancy is "significantly higher" than the rent that the landlord might reasonably expect. The landlord cannot recover more than the rent thus determined.[2]

4. Agricultural tied dwellings: protected and assured agricultural occupancies

Many agricultural workers who occupied dwellings owned by their employers formerly had no statutory protection because they were mere licensees, or, if they were tenants, they paid little or no rent[3]; they occupied "tied cottages" or other dwellings which "went with the job". The Rent (Agriculture) Act 1976 gave such occupants the status of "protected occupiers", with much the same protection as under the Rent Acts, though with a number of variations. The Housing Act 1988 has phased out "protected occupancies" and replaced them by "assured agricultural occupancies".

(a) Protected occupancies

(i) Definition: A person is a "protected occupier" if he has a "relevant licence or tenancy" and is a "qualifying worker" and if the dwelling is in "qualifying ownership".[4] A relevant licence or tenancy is one which would fall within the Rent Acts but for the exclusion of licences and tenancies at a low rent, and certain other matters. A qualifying worker is one who has worked full-time in agriculture for 91 out of the previous 104 weeks. A dwelling is in qualifying ownership if the occupier is employed in agriculture and his employer either owns the dwelling as the immediate landlord or licensor, or else has made arrangements with such a landlord or licensor for occupation by the employer's agricultural workers. When a protected occupier dies, his spouse or a member of his family may succeed to his occupancy, though there can be only one such succession.[5]

---

[1] H.A. 1988, s.21; above, p. 599.
[2] *ibid.*, s.22.
[3] Above, p. 593.
[4] Rent (Agriculture) Act 1976, ss.1, 2, Sched. 3, Pt. I.
[5] *ibid.*, s.3; and see above, p. 594.

(ii) Possession: On the determination of a protected occupancy, the occupier, if in residence, becomes a statutory tenant, even if he is a mere licensee.[6] Succession rights and the grounds for possession are substantially the same as those under the Rent Act 1977, with the exclusion of the agricultural grounds and a reduction in the mandatory grounds.[7]

(iii) Rent: The system of fair rents for regulated tenancies applies in general to protected occupiers.[8]

(b) Assured agricultural occupancies

(i) Definition: Normally, no new protected occupancy can arise on or after January 15, 1989. Instead, corresponding provisions are made for assured agricultural occupancies on similar lines.[9] A tenancy will not be an assured agricultural occupancy if it is an assured shorthold tenancy.[10] However, an assured tenancy created on or after February 28, 1997 in favour of an agricultural worker as defined in the Rent (Agriculture) Act 1976 will not be an assured shorthold tenancy unless a notice in prescribed form has been served on the tenant before the creation of the tenancy.[11] The default mechanism of the Housing Act 1996 therefore does not apply to assured agricultural occupancies.

(ii) Possession: Assured agricultural occupancies are treated as assured tenancies in so far as concerns the landlord's right to possession. However, there are variations: in particular, Ground 16 does not apply.[12] The spouse or other members of the worker's family have the usual rights of succession.

(iii) Rent: The parties decide the rent payable under an assured agricultural occupancy; the system of registered rents does not apply. As in the case of any other assured periodic tenancy, where the occupancy is periodic the landlord may serve notice increasing the rent and the occupier may refer the notice to a rent assessment committee.

(c) Rehousing

One special provision which applies to both protected occupancies and assured agricultural occupancies is that, if the landlord cannot reasonably provide suitable alternative accommodation for the occupier and the landlord requires vacant possession for another agricultural worker of his, then, if the interests of efficient agriculture require it, the housing authority must use its best endeavours to provide suitable alternative accommodation for the displaced occupier.[13]

5. Secure tenancies: the public sector

Where the landlord is in the "public sector", tenancies of dwellings are subject to only a partial application of statutory provisions which resemble those which apply to other landlords. Until 1980, where a local authority was the landlord, the tenant had no statutory protection either as to possession or as to rent. The Housing Act 1980 introduced a system

---

[6] *ibid.*, s.4.
[7] *ibid.*, ss.6, 7, Sched. 4; and see above, pp. 594–598.
[8] *ibid.*, s.13; above, pp. 598–599.
[9] H.A. 1988, s.24.
[10] *ibid.*, s.24(2)(a).
[11] *ibid.*, Sched. 7, para. 9.
[12] *ibid.*, s.25; above, p. 601.
[13] R.A.A. 1976, ss.27, 28 as amended by H.A. 1988, s.26 and Sched. 17.

of "secure tenancies" which gave protection as to possession but not as to rent; and this is now governed by the Housing Act 1985, Part IV.

(a) Secure tenancies

A tenancy of a dwelling is a secure tenant only while the "landlord condition" and the "tenant condition" are both satisfied. The landlord condition is that the landlord is a local authority, new town corporation or one of certain other public bodies.[14] Housing associations and housing trusts are no longer included. The tenant condition is that the tenant is an individual who occupies the dwelling as his only or principal home.[15]

(b) Security of tenure

A secure tenancy cannot be brought to an end except by an order of the court. No such order can be made unless the landlord has given the tenant a notice specifying the ground on which possession is sought, and the landlord then establishes one of the 18 statutory grounds for possession.[16] In nine cases the court must be satisfied that it is reasonable to make the order, in four that suitable accommodation will be available for the tenant, and in the remaining five both that such accommodation will be available and that it is reasonable to make the order. The grounds have much in common with those for assured tenancies.[17]

There is also provision for succession to a secure tenancy on the death of the tenant, unless he was himself a successor.[18] The tenant's spouse or, in default, a member of the tenant's family (as widely defined[19]) may take the tenancy by succession, provided that at the tenant's death he was occupying the dwelling as his only or principal home, and, in the case of a member of the tenant's family, he had also resided with the tenant for the year prior to his death,[20] whether in the dwelling or elsewhere.[21] The landlord (and not the court) selects the member of the family if they cannot agree.[22]

(c) Introductory tenancies

The Housing Act 1996 permits local authorities to elect to operate what is not as an "introductory tenancy regime". Such schemes enable landlords to give new tenants a trail or "probationary period" of 12 months and, where such a scheme is operated, every periodic tenancy which would otherwise have been a secure tenancy takes effect as an introductory tenancy.[23] During the 12-month period the landlord can claim an order for possession as of right on the service of proper notice to the tenant accompanied by the reasons for the landlord's decision.[24] The tenant can ask the landlord to review its decision and can bring proceedings for judicial review on the grounds of unreasonableness.[25] However, the landlord's action for possession cannot be defended on that ground.[26] At the end of the 12-month

[14] H.A. 1985, ss.79, 80, as amended. For numerous exceptions, see Sched. 1, and for an example, see *Tower Hamlets L.B.C. v. Miah* [1992] Q.B. 622.
[15] *ibid.*, s.81. For joint tenants, occupation by one suffices.
[16] *ibid.*, ss.82–84, Sched. 2.
[17] Above, pp. 594–598.
[18] H.A. 1985, ss.87, 88. Compare statutory tenancies: above, pp. 593–594.
[19] *ibid.*, s.113.
[20] *ibid.*, s.89.
[21] *Waltham Forest L.B.C. v. Thomas* [1992] 3 W.L.R. 131. Compare statutory tenancies: above, p. 594.
[22] H.A. 1985, s.89.
[23] H.A. 1996, s.126.
[24] *ibid.*, ss.127, 128.
[25] *ibid.*, s.129.
[26] *Manchester City Council v. Cochrane* [1999] 1 W.L.R. 809.

period the introductory tenancy automatically becomes a secure tenancy; an introductory tenancy can devolve on death but cannot be assigned.[27]

(d) Rent

There is nothing to restrict the rent payable under a secure tenancy apart from the general provision which permits local authorities to make only "such reasonable charges" as they may determine.[28] Where the landlord is a housing association or housing trust, then although the tenancy will not be a secure tenancy, nor within the Rent Acts,[29] it will, if granted before January 15, 1989, be subject to a system of fair rents similar to the system applicable to protected and statutory tenancies.[30] If granted later, it will be an assured tenancy.

(e) Right to buy

Elaborate statutory provisions[31] give a tenant who has been a secure tenant for two years or more a right to purchase either the reversion on his tenancy or a long lease at a low rent at its open market price less a discount. For a house, the discount ranges from 32 per cent to 60 per cent, and for a flat from 44 per cent to 70 per cent, depending in each case on the length of occupation. The discount has an upper limit of £50,000,[32] but the price may be left on mortgage.

6. Long tenancies at a low rent—general

Originally there were no special provisions for long tenancies; but the Landlord and Tenant Act 1954, Part I, created a system under which long tenancies at a low rent were, on expiration, converted into statutory tenancies at a normal rent. The Rent Act 1957 extended this system to other long tenancies as well, but the Leasehold Reform Act 1967 restored them to the Rent Acts and once more confined the system to long tenancies at a low rent, many of which were building leases at a ground rent. In addition, the Leasehold Reform Act 1967 gave most tenants under such tenancies the alternative right to purchase the freehold or demand a further long lease. More recently the Landlord and Tenant Act 1987 conferred on certain lessees of flats a right of pre-emption where the landlord disposes of his reversionary interest and the Leasehold Reform, Housing and Urban Development Act 1993 ("the 1993 Act") conferred on tenants of flats a collective right to purchase the freehold and an individual right to demand a further long lease. These different heads will be taken in turn.

7. Landlord and Tenant Act 1954, Part I

(a) Conditions to be satisfied

A tenancy will fall within Part I of the Landlord and Tenant Act 1954 only if it is a "long tenancy" at a "low rent" which satisfies the "qualifying condition" of being a tenancy which, but for the lowness of the rent, would have fallen within the Rent Acts[33]; thus only residential

---

[27] H.A. 1996, ss.131–134.
[28] *ibid.*, s.24.
[29] Above, p. 593.
[30] Above, pp. 598–599.
[31] H.A. 1985 (as amended by Housing and Planning Act 1986, Pt. I), Pt. V: see ss.118, 119, 127, 129.
[32] *ibid.*, s.131; S.I. 1989 No. 513.
[33] L. & T.A. 1954, ss.1, 2; Leasehold Reform Act 1967, s.39, Sched. 5; S.I. 1990 No. 434 (for dwellings with no rateable value).

tenants in occupation of dwellings of a type within the Rent Act 1977[34] will be protected. A long tenancy is a tenancy granted for more than 21 years, and a low rent is a rent that is less than two-thirds of the rateable value of the dwelling.[35]

(b) The protection

Where Part I applies, the tenancy is automatically continued unless the tenant gives one month's notice to determine it.[36] The landlord may determine it in two ways. First, he may serve a "notice to resume possession". If the tenant fails to notify the landlord within two months that he is unwilling to give up possession, the tenancy ends on any date on or after the expiration of the term that is specified in the landlord's notice. Otherwise, the landlord may apply to the court on one of the statutory grounds for possession.[37] These are substantially the same as Cases 1, 2, 9 and AA, and Ground 6, considered above,[38] though with some variations. Secondly, the landlord may serve a "landlord's notice proposing a statutory tenancy",[39] in which case the rent and other terms of the tenancy will be as agreed by the parties or, in default, as determined by the county court.[40] The tenancy will be a regulated tenancy and will accordingly be subject to the provisions governing such tenancies, including the provisions as to fair rents.[41]

(c) Housing Act 1988

A long tenancy at a low rent cannot fall within Part I if it was entered into on or after January 15, 1989, unless pursuant to a contract made before that date. The qualifying condition for Part I will not be satisfied because the tenancy is excluded from the Rent Acts both by the lowness of the rent and also by its date,[42] and not solely by the former. Nor can any tenancy at a low rent be an assured tenancy.[43] But the tenant may be able, under the Leasehold Reform Act 1967, to claim the freehold or a new lease or, under the Leasehold Reform, Housing and Urban Development Act 1993, to claim a collective right to purchase the freehold and an individual right to demand a further long lease.

8. Leasehold Reform Act 1967

The Leasehold Reform Act 1967 allows certain tenants under long leases at low rents to acquire the freehold or a new lease by paying for the land but not the house. The Act was based on the specious "principle" that under a building lease "the land belongs in equity to the landowner and the house belongs in equity to the occupying leaseholder".[44] Thus the purchaser of a building lease which had only a few years to run and so was worth little or nothing (because of the burden of repairs) suddenly found that "in equity" the house was his and not the landlord's, and that the landlord's valuable and appreciating asset in his ownership of the house subject only to the lease could be expropriated without compensation.

---

[34] See above, pp. 592–594.
[35] See L. & T.A. 1954, ss.1, 2; Leasehold Reform Act 1967, s.39, Sched. 5; S.I. 1990 No. 434.
[36] L. & T.A. 1954, ss.5, 17.
[37] *ibid.*, ss.4, 12, 13, Sched. 3.
[38] See above, pp. 595–596, 601–602.
[39] L. & T.A. 1954, s.4.
[40] *ibid.*, ss.4, 6–9, as amended.
[41] Leasehold Reform Act 1967, Sched. 5, paras. 3, 4.
[42] Above, pp. 599–600.
[43] Above, pp. 592, 599.
[44] White Paper on Leasehold Reform in England and Wales (1966, Cmnd. 2916), para. 4.

However, this has been held to be no infringement of human rights as being "in the public interest".[45]

(a) Application of the Act

For the Act to apply, three conditions must at present be satisfied.[46] (Until the enactment of the Leasehold Reform, Housing and Urban Development Act 1993, the rateable value of the house had to fall within limits which were similar to those under the Rent Act 1977[47] but this is no longer the case. One of the three surviving conditions will be amended when the Commonhold and Leasehold Reform Act 2002 comes into force.) These conditions are as follows:

(i) the tenancy must be a lease for more than 21 years at a low rent[48] (what is meant by a low rent depends on the rateable value of the property if the lease was granted before April 1, 1990[49] and otherwise on whether or not the property is in Greater London[50]);

(ii) at present, the tenant must have occupied the house as his only or main residence for the last three years, or for periods amounting to three years in the last 10 years (this condition will be replaced by a requirement of two years' ownership when the Commonhold and Leasehold Reform Act 2002 comes into force[51]);

(iii) the premises must be a "house", including semi-detached and terraced houses but not flats; in effect, any division must be vertical. It suffices if the premises can reasonably be called a house, even if part is used as a shop.[52]

(b) Claim

A tenant who wishes to claim the freehold or a lease must serve notice on the landlord in the prescribed form.[53] When the Commonhold and Leasehold Reform Act 2002 comes into force, the personal representatives of a deceased tenant will also be able to do so.[54] The tenant can do this at any time during the continuance of his long tenancy, including any period while it is being automatically continued under Part I of the Act of 1954; but if the landlord serves a notice under that Act,[55] the tenant must serve his notice within two months or he will lose his rights.[56] When served, the tenant's notice takes effect as a contract for the conveyance of the freehold or the grant of the lease; it is registrable as an estate contract, or, for registered land, it may be protected by a notice or caution.[57] In default of agreement, the price, rent and other terms will be settled by a Leasehold Valuation Tribunal (constituted by a Rent

---

[45] *James v. United Kingdom* (1986) 8 E.H.R.R. 123, construing the European Convention on Human Rights 1950, Protocol No. 1 (1952), art. 1.
[46] Leasehold Reform Act 1967, ss.1–4.
[47] See above, pp. 593–594.
[48] See above, pp. 607–608.
[49] The rent must have been less than two-thirds of the rateable value of the property.
[50] Less than £1,000 in Greater London; less than £250 elsewhere.
[51] C. & L.R.A. 2002, s.138(1).
[52] *Tandon v. Trustees of Spurgeons Homes* [1982] A.C. 755.
[53] Leasehold Reform Act 1967, s.22, Sched. 3.
[54] C. & L.R.A. 2002. s.142.
[55] Above, pp. 607–608.
[56] Leasehold Reform Act 1967, Sched. 3, para. 2.
[57] *ibid.*, ss.1, 5, 8; see above, pp. 95–96, 129 *et seq.*

Assessment Committee), with appeal to the Lands Tribunal; on other matters the county court has jurisdiction.[58]

(c) Lease or freehold

(i) Lease: A tenant who claims a lease is entitled to a term of 50 years from the expiry of the existing lease, and on the same terms. The rent will be a ground rent, representing the rental value of the site without the buildings; but after 25 years the landlord may require the rent to be revalued. The tenant must pay the landlord's reasonable costs.[59] When the Commonhold and Leasehold Reform Act 2002 comes into force, a leaseholder who has obtained an extended lease will no longer be excluded from purchasing the freehold.[60]

(ii) Freehold: The tenant is entitled to a conveyance in fee simple, subject to his tenancy but free from most incumbrances on the freehold.[61] The price is based on the open market value, as adjusted, but the method of valuation depends on the rateable value of the house on the appropriate day.[62]

(i) If that rateable value is not more than £500 (or £1,000 in Greater London) the valuation is on the basis that the tenancy will be extended under the Act, but that the tenant and his family living with him in the house will not form part of the market.[63]

(ii) If the rateable value exceeds the above figures (as adjusted for tenant's improvements) the valuation is on the basis of the house being subject to the tenancy and the tenant's right to remain as a statutory tenant without being liable for repairs, maintenance or redecoration, and with a reduction for any improvements made by the tenant, but with the market including the tenant and his family.[64]

(iii) Either way the tenant must pay the landlord's reasonable costs.[65]

(d) Modifications

With some qualifications, any agreement excluding or modifying the statutory rights of the tenant is void.[66] But there are some statutory modifications.

(i) Required for landlord: If the tenant gives notice under the Act, and the landlord then seeks and obtains an order for possession of the house for occupation as the only or main residence for himself or an adult member of his family, the tenant has no right to the freehold or a lease, but is entitled to compensation instead. No such order can be made if the landlord obtained his interest after February 18, 1966, nor if in all the circumstances (including any other available accommodation) greater hardship would be caused by making the order than

---

[58] *ibid.*, ss.20, 21; H.A. 1980, s.142.
[59] Leasehold Reform Act 1967, ss.14, 15; H.A. 1980, Sched. 22.
[60] C. & L.R.A. 2002, s.143.
[61] Leasehold Reform Act 1967, s.8.
[62] *ibid.*, s.1(4): as under the Rent Act 1977: above, p. 534.
[63] Leasehold Reform Act 1967, s.9(1), as amended by H.A. 1969, s.82.
[64] Leasehold Reform Act 1967, s.9(1A), (1B), added by H.A. 1974, s.118.
[65] Leasehold Reform Act 1967, s.9(4).
[66] *ibid.*, s.23.

by refusing it.[67] Compensation is assessed on the basis of the tenant having a 50-year extension of his tenancy, though with nothing for losing the right to obtain the freehold.[68]

(ii) Redevelopment: A landlord can sometimes apply for an order for possession if he proposes to demolish or reconstruct the whole or a substantial part of the house for the purposes of redevelopment. If the tenant has already obtained a lease, the landlord can do this in the last year of the old tenancy or afterwards; but if the tenant has given notice only claiming a lease, the landlord must apply during the last year of the old tenancy. This head does not apply where the tenant is claiming the freehold. If an order for possession is made, the tenant is entitled to compensation as in (a) above.[69]

(iii) Development by public bodies: If the landlord is a public body, and a Minister of the Crown certifies that within 10 years the house will be required for development for the purposes of that body, the tenant cannot obtain either the freehold or a lease, and the landlord will be entitled to possession when the tenancy expires. But if within two months of the service of the certificate the tenant claims the freehold or a lease, the provisions for possession and compensation under (b) above apply.[70]

(iv) The Crown: The Act does not bind the Crown[71]; but usually, as of grace, freeholds or leaseholds will be granted to Crown tenants as if the Act applied.

(v) Management: An area occupied by tenants of houses under one landlord could formerly be made subject to a scheme under which the landlord retained powers of management over the houses, relating to matters such as repairs and development. This could be done only if the appropriate Minister certified, on an application to him made before 1970,[72] that this was in the general interest in order to maintain standards of appearance and amenity, and the High Court approved the scheme.[73] Such schemes, however, did not affect the right of tenants to obtain the freehold or a lease. Schemes thus made are still operative.

9. Purchase of the reversion to flats under the Landlord and Tenant Act 1987

Part I of the Landlord and Tenant Act 1987 conferred on lessees of flats other than those holding under business tenancies, protected shorthold tenancies or assured tenancies (including assured shorthold tenancies),[74] a right of pre-emption if and when the landlord decides to dispose of his reversionary interest in the premises. More than 50 per cent of the total number of flats in the building must satisfy be lessees of the appropriate type.[75] There are no residence requirements but owners of three or more flats do not count.[76] No more than 50 per cent of the internal floor area of the premises other than the common parts must be occupied other than for residential purposes.[77] The tenants in question have to pay the price which the

[67] *ibid.*, s.18.
[68] *ibid.*, Sched. 2.
[69] *ibid.*, s.17.
[70] *ibid.*, s.28.
[71] See ibid. s.33.
[72] Or before August 1974 for houses brought within the Act by H.A. 1974: see s.118(2).
[73] Leasehold Reform Act 1967, s.19.
[74] L.T.A. 1987, s.3(1).
[75] *ibid.*, s.1(2).
[76] *ibid.*, s.3(2).
[77] *ibid.*, s.1(3), (4).

landlord has agreed with the third party purchaser; if not all the tenants participate, those who do become the landlords of the remainder.

A landlord who proposes to dispose of his reversion must serve an "offer notice" on the tenants who qualify[78]; they have two months to respond. Failure to serve a notice is a criminal offence and the tenants can enforce their right of pre-emption against anyone to whom the landlord transfers his reversionary interest by serving a "purchase notice" on him.[79]

10. Collective enfranchisement of flats under the 1993 Act

(a) Introduction

The 1993 Act conferred a right of collective enfranchisement on the tenants of certain premises. To qualify, the premises have to be a self-contained building or part of a building. At present the total number of flats held by tenants who qualify must be two-thirds of the total number[80] but this requirement will be removed when the Commonhold and Leasehold Reform Act 2002 comes into force.[81] At present buildings where more than 10 per cent of the building is occupied otherwise than for residential purposes or is common parts are excluded[82] but this percentage will rise to 25 per cent when the Commonhold and Leasehold Reform Act 2002 comes into force.[83] Buildings which contain only four flats and have a resident landlord are also excluded.[84]

(b) Qualifying Tenants

Tenants qualify if they hold their flats under a lease for over 21 years[85] at a low rent[86] or, when the Commonhold and Leasehold Reform Act 2002 comes into force, under a lease for over 50 years. (What is meant by a low rent depends on the letting value if the lease was granted before April 1, 1963,[87] the rateable value of the property if the lease was granted between April 1, 1963 and before April 1, 1990,[88] and otherwise on whether or not the property is in Greater London.[89]) Business tenancies, flats let by charitable housing trusts pursuant to their objectives and sub-leases not also carved out of a lease for over 21 years at a low rent are excluded. Owners of three or more flats do not count.[90] At present, over 50 per cent of the total number of flats held by tenants who qualify must have been occupied as their only or principal home for the last 12 months or for three years in the last 10 years.[91] However, this requirement will be removed when the Commonhold and Leasehold Reform Act 2002 comes into force.[92]

---

[78] *ibid.*, ss.1(1), 5(1).
[79] *ibid.*, s.12. See also *Belvedere Court Management Ltd v. Frogmore Developments Ltd* [1997] Q.B. 858; *Kay Green v. Twinsectra Ltd* [1996] 1 W.L.R. 1587.
[80] L.R.H. & U.D.A., s.3.
[81] C. & L.R.A. 2002, s.119.
[82] L.R.H. & U.D.A., s.4(1).
[83] C. & L.R.A. 2002, s.115.
[84] L.R.H, & U.D.A., s.4.
[85] *ibid.*, s.7.
[86] *ibid.*, s.5(1).
[87] The rent must not have exceeded two-thirds of the letting value of the property.
[88] The rent must not have exceeded two-thirds of the rateable value of the property.
[89] Less than £1,000 in Greater London; less than £250 elsewhere.
[90] *ibid.*, s.5(5).
[91] L.R.H. & U.D.A., ss.13(2), 6.
[92] C. & L.R.A. 2002, s.120.

(c) The right to collective enfranchisement

The right is to have the freehold of the premises, appurtenant property and common parts conveyed to a person or persons, usually a company, on their behalf.[93] When the Commonhold and Leasehold Reform Act 2002 comes into force, the conveyance will have to be to a "right to enfranchise" company,[94] whose definition, membership and regulations will be laid down.[95] The freeholder is entitled to a leaseback for 999 years at a peppercorn rent of any flats which do not qualify and of any parts of the premises which are not flats.[96] The right to collective enfranchisement can be blocked where not less than two-thirds of the long leases are due to determine within five years and the freeholder then intends to demolish, reconstruct or carry out substantial works of development which he could not reasonably do without obtaining possession of the subject-matter of those leases.[97]

(d) Procedure

A claim is initiated by the appropriate number of tenants giving notice to their reversioner nominating the person or persons who will be acquiring his interest.[98] The reversioner has two months to serve a counter-notice challenging the claim or claiming an intention to redevelop, in which case the nominee purchaser must bring proceedings within a further two months.[99] Any dispute over the price is referred to a leasehold valuation tribunal.[1]

(e) The price

The price payable to the freeholder is calculated by aggregating[2]:

(i) the value of the freeholder's interest in the premises, worked out by capitalising the value of the ground rents payable during the terms of the leases and adding the value of the reversion on the expiry of the term;

(ii) the freeholder's share of the marriage value, the difference between the aggregate value of the freehold and any intermediate leases prior to the acquisition and the aggregate value of those interests after acquisition (at present his share is at least 50 per cent of this difference and may well be more but, when the Commonhold and Leasehold Reform Act 2002 comes into force, it will be a maximum of 50 per cent[3] and will be disregarded completely if all the leases have more than 80 years unexpired[4]);

(iii) compensation for any loss suffered by the freeholder by reason of the diminution of the value of any other property or of the loss of any development value in the premises; and

[93] L.R.H. & U.D.A., s.1(1).
[94] C. & L.R.A. 2002, s.121.
[95] ibid., s.122.
[96] L.R.H. & U.D.A., s.36 & Sched. 9.
[97] ibid., s.23.
[98] ibid., ss.9, 13 (as amended by H.A. 1996, s.108).
[99] ibid., s.22.
[1] ibid., s.24.
[2] ibid., s.32 & Sched. 6, as amended by H.A. 1996, s.107.
[3] C. & L.R.A. 2002, s.127.
[4] ibid., s.128.

(iv) the reasonable costs of the acquisition.[5]

The date of valuation is at present the date when the price is agreed or determined.[6] When the Commonhold and Leasehold Reform Act 2002 comes into force, it will instead be when the tenants serve their initial notice.[7]

11. Individual enfranchisement of flats under the 1993 Act

Where an individual tenant is unwilling or unable to benefit from collective investment, he may instead choose to assert a right to a new lease of his flat for 90 years on the payment of a premium. At present, he must have occupied his flat as his only or principal home for the last three years or for three out of the last 10 years.[8] However, when the Commonhold and Leasehold Reform Act 2002 comes into force, he will merely have to have held the lease for two years.[9] There are no other restrictions. *Mutatis mutandis*, the procedure is comparable to that for collective enfranchisements and the premium payable is calculated in the same way as in collective enfranchisements. Comparable changes will be made when the Commonhold and Leasehold Reform Act 2002 comes into force.

12. Restricted contracts

Before the Furnished Houses (Rent Control) Act 1946, tenancies of dwellings that were let furnished or with services were wholly unprotected. The Act established a system of rent tribunals which could fix rents for such tenancies; and the Act conferred a limited and somewhat unsatisfactory degree of security of tenure. After various amendments, the present law is contained in the Rent Act 1977 as amended by the Housing Acts 1980 and 1988. The functions of rent tribunals are now discharged by rent assessment committees.[10]

(a) Application

Originally the jurisdiction extended only to dwellings that were let furnished or with services, though it applied however great the value of the dwelling. The Rent Act 1957 then excluded dwellings with a rateable value outside the Rent Acts, and the Rent Act 1974 then excluded most furnished tenancies from it, transferring them to the full protection of the Rent Acts instead; but it also extended the jurisdiction to tenancies granted by a resident landlord.[11] The Rent Act 1977 further extended the jurisdiction to mere licences, though the Housing Act 1980 greatly curtailed the provisions for security of tenure. Finally, the Housing Act 1988 prevented the creation of any more restricted contracts and it is therefore highly unlikely that many, if any, are still in existence. The subject will therefore be considered only briefly.

(b) Restricted contract

A contract is a restricted contract only if the following conditions are satisfied[12]:

(i) the rateable value is within the limits for the Rent Acts; and

---

[5] L.R.H. & U.D.A., s.33.
[6] *ibid.*, Sched. 6.
[7] C. & L.R.A. 2002, s.126.
[8] L.R.H. & U.D.A., s.39 as amended by H.A. 1996, s.112.
[9] C. & L.R.A. 2002, s.130.
[10] H.A. 1980, s.72.
[11] Above, p. 593.
[12] Rent Act 1977, ss.19–21; above, p. 593.

(ii) the contract gives a person a right to occupy a dwelling as a residence, whether as tenant or licensee, at a rent which includes payment for the use of furniture or services. The scope of this provision is much reduced by the exclusion of regulated tenancies which include most furnished tenancies. Alternatively, the contract must be a tenancy which cannot be a protected tenancy either because the tenant shares some (but not all) of the accommodation with the landlord, or because there is a resident landlord.[13]

(i) Not excepted: The contract does not fall within any of the exceptions. These include regulated tenancies, cases where the rent includes substantial payment for board, holiday residences, and lettings by local authorities or certain other bodies.[14] In particular, no contract made on or after January 15, 1989, can be a restricted contract unless made pursuant to a contract made before that date.[15]

(c) Rent

Either party may at any time refer the contract to the rent tribunal, which, after hearing the parties, may reduce or increase the rent to the amount which the tribunal considers reasonable, or may approve it.[16] The rent thus determined is registered with the local authority, whereupon it becomes an offence to require or receive more than that rent, or to charge any premium.[17] A registered rent may be reconsidered after two years, or if a change of circumstances has made the registered rent no longer reasonable, or if both parties make the application.[18] The tribunal must still consider a reference even if the tenant quits before the hearing.[19]

(d) Security of tenure

There are two alternative systems for giving a limited degree of security of tenure, depending on whether the contract was made on or after November 28, 1980 ("new contracts") or before that date ("old contracts").[20]

(i) New contracts: On making an order for possession the court may stay or suspend execution of the order, or postpone the date of possession, for not more than three months, whether the occupier is a tenant or a licensee. But unless it would cause exceptional hardship or be unreasonable, the court must impose conditions for the payment of rent and arrears of rent, and may impose other conditions.[21]

(ii) Old contracts: When an occupier has referred his contract to the tribunal, no subsequent notice to quit can take effect until six months after the tribunal's decision, unless the tribunal substitutes a shorter period.[22] This operates automatically, though it does not apply at all to a reference made after the notice to quit has been served. In that case, however, if an application to the tribunal for security of tenure is made while the notice to quit is still

---

[13] *ibid.*, ss.19–21; above, p. 593.
[14] *ibid.*, s.19.
[15] H.A. 1988, s.36.
[16] Rent Act 1977, ss.77, 78.
[17] *ibid.*, ss.79, 81, 122.
[18] *ibid.*, s.80; H.A. 1980, s.70.
[19] *R. v. West London Rent Tribunal, ex Napper* [1967] 1 Q.B. 169.
[20] Rent Act 1977, s.102A, added by H.A. 1980, s.69.
[21] Rent Act 1977, s.106A and Protection from Eviction Act 1977, s.3(2A), added by H.A. 1980, s.69.
[22] Rent Act 1977, s.103.

running, the tribunal may grant it for not more than six months, and may subsequently extend it by not more than six months at a time.[23] But this system can give no security of tenure where the contract expires by effluxion of time, without any notice to quit; nor does it apply to the recovery of dwellings under certain contracts with owner-occupiers.[24]

13. Protection from eviction and harassment

The various systems for protecting occupants of dwellings that have been considered above have been supplemented by the provisions of the Protection from Eviction Act 1977. The Act applies to all "residential occupiers", namely persons who occupy premises as a residence under a contract or legal right[25]; and it protects them against eviction without an order of the court.

(a) Eviction

Where premises are let as a dwelling and the tenancy is not within some statutory protection, the Act, with some exceptions,[26] prohibits the eviction of an occupier who continues to reside in the premises when the tenancy has ended, except by an order of the court; and this now applies to licences as well as tenancies.[27] It also applies to the enforcement of any right of re-entry or forfeiture under a lease while any person is lawfully residing in the premises or any part of them.[28] However, it does not apply to a mortgagee who is enforcing his right to possession of the mortgaged property, even if it is leased at the time.

(b) Criminal eviction

Any person other than a mortgagee who unlawfully deprives a residential occupier of his occupation of any or all of the premises, or attempts to do so, is guilty of an offence unless with reasonable cause he believed that the occupier had ceased to reside in the premises.[29] A residential occupier may now recover damages for the statutory tort of wrongful eviction.[30]

(c) Criminal harassment

The offence of criminal harassment is committed by a landlord or his agent who, without reasonable grounds, does certain specified acts with a specified knowledge. Those acts are acts likely to interfere with the peace or comfort of a residential occupier or members of his household, or the persistent withdrawing or withholding of services reasonably required for residential occupation. The requisite knowledge is knowing or having reasonable cause to believe that the acts are likely to cause the residential occupier to give up occupation of any or all of the premises or to refrain from exercising any right or remedy in respect of them.[31]

---

[23] *ibid.*, s.104.
[24] *ibid.*, s.105.
[25] Protection from Eviction Act 1977, s.1. For the details, see Megarry, *The Rent Acts* (2nd ed., 1999) Vol. 3 pp. 303–340.
[26] "Excluded" tenancies and licences: see Protection from Eviction Act 1977, s.3A, inserted by H.A. 1988, s.31.
[27] Protection from Eviction Act 1977, ss.3, 3A; H.A. 1988, ss.30, 31.
[28] Protection from Eviction Act 1977, s.2.
[29] *ibid.*, s.1.
[30] H.A. 1988, ss.27, 28.
[31] Protection from Eviction Act 1977, s.1; H.A. 1988, s.29.

(d) The Protection from Harassment Act 1997

The Protection from Harassment Act came into force on June 16, 1997 and creates a new offence of harassment, a statutory tort of harassment and a supplementary offence of putting a person in fear of the use of violence against him. Although it is not directed to harassment in a landlord and tenant context, its provisions could well apply in the context of the eviction or the threatened eviction of a residential occupier. A person is guilty of the offence of harassment if he pursues a course of conduct which amounts to harassment of another and which he knows or ought to know amounts to harassment of the other.[32] Actual or threatened harassment may be the subject of a claim in civil proceedings by the person who is or may be the victim of the course of conduct in question.[33] A person is guilty of the offence of putting people in fear of violence if his course of conduct causes another to fear, on at least two occasions, that violence will be used against him and he knows or ought to know that his course of conduct will cause the other so to fear on each of those occasions.[34]

Sect. 4. Status

1. Evolution

Most tenants today are to some degree protected by statute. In early law, leasehold tenants were regarded as holding mere contracts; it was not until the sixteenth century that they were even recognised as owning estates,[35] though they had little protection beyond the terms of their tenancies. Today, most tenancies have some claim to having travelled from contract via estate to status: for many of their important rights depend in large part not on contract but on a positive statutory protection that overrides any contract. Yet the variations between the different forms of statutory protection are so great that it is difficult to find much common ground in them; and in recent years there has been a marked reduction in the degree of the protection.

2. Rent

There are many variants.

(a) Initial control

There is now no initial control of rent. Formerly, where a rent had been registered for a regulated tenancy or restricted contract, this restricted the rent under any subsequent tenancies or contracts of this kind; but such tenancies and contracts can no longer be created.

(b) Subsequent control

Control of rent may arise at any subsequent time (under regulated tenancies, restricted contracts, assured periodic tenancies, assured shorthold tenancies and long leases at a low rent); on renewal of the tenancy (in the case of business tenancies); or after stated intervals (in the case of agricultural holdings, farm business tenancies and, once a controlled rent has

---

[32] Protection from Harassment Act 1997, ss.1(1), 2(1).
[33] *ibid.*, s.3(1).
[34] *ibid.*, s.4(1).
[35] See below, pp. 18, 35.

been fixed, in the case of regulated tenancies, restricted contracts, and assured periodic tenancies).

(c) Method

The rent may be determined by the court (in the case of business tenancies and long leases at a low rent), by an arbitrator (in the case of agricultural holdings and farm business tenancies), by a rent officer or rent assessment committee (in the case of regulated tenancies and some assured tenancies), or by a tribunal (in the case of old restricted contracts and long leases at a low rent).

(d) Level

The general level of rent is the market rent, though this is tempered in some cases by a requirement of reasonableness (in the case of old secure tenancies and old restricted contracts), and in others by a disregard of the effect of scarcity (in the case of regulated tenancies, protected occupancies and long leaseholds at a low rent and, to some extent, in the case of agricultural holdings and farm business tenancies).

3. Security of tenure

The many variants here have some degree of common ground. Security of tenure is in general provided in two stages. The tenant is, first, given the right to remain in possession in one way or another until, secondly, it is determined whether he can continue in possession, or whether the landlord has some statutory ground for claiming possession.

(a) Initial

The tenant's initial right to remain in possession may be given by making him a statutory tenant (in the case of regulated tenancies and protected occupancies); by prolonging his contractual tenancy in some form until the determination of an application to the court (in the case of business tenancies, assured tenancies, assured agricultural occupancies, and long leases at a low rent) or until the landlord obtains an order for possession (in the case of secure tenancies); by enabling the tenant to give a notice that will make a notice to quit ineffective until the landlord obtains a tribunal's consent to it taking effect (in the case of agricultural holdings); by providing that a reference to a tribunal will automatically suspend the operation of any subsequent notice to quit (in the case of old restricted contracts); or by giving the court a limited and discretionary power to postpone the operation of an order for possession (in the case of new restricted contracts).

(b) Substantive

The tenant's substantive right to continue in possession after the initial period of security may be provided by preventing an order for possession being made save on statutory grounds (in the case of regulated tenancies, assured tenancies, secure tenancies and protected and assured agricultural occupancies); by giving the tenant the right to a new tenancy unless statutory grounds preclude it (in the case of business tenancies); by continuing the ineffectiveness of a notice to quit (in the case of agricultural holdings); by enabling the tenant to serve a notice requiring the grant of the freehold or a long lease (in the case of long leases at a low rent and secure tenancies); or by enabling the tenant to apply to a tribunal for repeated extensions of the period while a notice to quit does not take effect (in the case of old restricted contracts), or to ask the court for a limited postponement of the operation of an order for possession (in the case of new restricted contracts). A tenant has no substantive right to continue in possession after the initial period of security in the case of farm business tenancies and assured shorthold tenancies.

4. Status

Both on major issues and on many minor matters, a tenant today will often look more to the rights conferred on him by the relevant legislation than to the terms of his tenancy. The diversity in the statutory rights is great, and recent years have seen some reduction in their ambit; yet it is perhaps true to say that there is still an indefinable and varied but nevertheless real status of protected tenant.

INDEX

Abandonment,
  easement, of, 442
Abstract of title,
  consideration, 159
  delivery, 158
Access orders, 450
  minor interests, 130
Access to neighbouring land,
  party walls, 335
Accumulations, rule against, 210, 240–246
  commercial contracts, 246
  corporations, 246
  debts, payment of, 245
  exceptions from, 245–246
  excessive accumulation, 243–244
    accumulation period, exceeding, 243–244
    perpetuity period, exceeding, 243
    surplus income, 244
  land, purchase of, 243
  maintenance of property, 246
  minorities, 241
  portions, 245
  Saunders v. Vautier, rule in, 244–245
  statutory periods, 241–243
    ambit of rules, 243
    choice of periods, 242–243
    periods, 241–242
    purchase of land, 243
  surplus income, 244
  timber or wood, 245
Acknowledgement,
  starting time running, 559
Action area, 572
Actual notice,
  bona fide purchaser for value, 61
Actual occupation, rights of persons in,
  Land Registration Act 2002, 127–128
  overriding interests, 123, 123–125
Adjudicator to the Land Registry, 113
Adverse possession, 123, 511
  adverse, 552
  intended use by owner, 552–553
  meaning, 551
  possession, 551–552

Advertisement, 414
  control of, 576
  hoardings, 476
Advowsons, 79, 115, 407
Agent,
  contracts, 153–154
  limitation, 559
  trusts, 295
Agricultural fixtures, 22–23
Agriculture,
  Agricultural Land Tribunals, 585
  farm business tenancies. *See* Farm business
    tenancies
  tenancies, 584–590
    compensation, 588–589
    farm business. *See* Farm business tenancies
    improvements, 589
    jurisdiction, 585
    meaning of "agricultural holding", 585–586
    notices to quit, 586
    rent protection, 588
    security of tenure, 586–588
      none, 586–587
      reasonableness, 587–588
Air, rights of, 416
Air-space, 568
Aircraft, 568
Airfield, 448
Aliens, 201
Ameliorating waste, 48
Ancient lights, 487
Animals,
  common of pasture, 422
  levant and couchant, 422
  wild, 566
Animus possidendi, 551
Annexation,
  fixtures,
    degree, 20
    purpose, 20–22
  restrictive covenants, 456
    area, 458
    delayed, 459
    equity, 457

Annexation—*cont.*
  restrictive covenants—*cont.*
    ownership of land, 458
    statutory, 458
Annuities,
  registration of land charges, 97, 101
Ante-nuptial agreements, 59
Appeal,
  enforcement notice, against, 575
Approvement, 441
Appurtenant, 414
Assents, 199–200
  vesting, 260, 265
Assignment,
  chain of, 459
  future interests, of, 212
  leases 353. *See also* Leases
  mortgages, of, 528
  perpetually renewable leases, 351
  restrictive covenants, 459
    express assignment, 459
    subsequent assignment, 459
    time, 459
  tenancies, 353
Assize, rents of, 413
Assured shorthold tenancies, 603–604
  creation, 603
  possession, grounds for, 603–604
  rent, 604
Assured tenancies, 599–602
Attestation,
  conveyance, 166
Attornment clause, 510–511
Authorised guarantee agreements, 382, 401–402

Bankruptcy,
  co-owner, 324–325
  inhibition, 132, 136
  lease,
    breach of condition, 362
    disclaimer, 366
  order, 100
  registered land, dealing with, 136
Bare licence, 476
Bare trusts,
  overreaching, 85
Base fee,
  creation, 46
  enlargement, 46–47
Beneficiaries,
  adverse possession by, 557
  conversion, 283
  doctrine of conversion and, 283
  equitable mortgages by, 498
  occupation under joint tenancy, 325–326
  overreaching interests of, 311
  rights of, under trust for sale, 283
Blighted land, 577–578
Bona fide purchaser for value,
  actual notice, 61
  better right to legal estate, 60
  bona fide, 59

Bona fide purchaser for value—*cont.*
  constructive notice, 61, 61 63
  estoppel, 62
  good consideration, 60
  imputed notice, 63
  investigation of title, 62–63
  legal and equitable rights, 58–59
  legal estate, of a, 60–61
  limitation, 558
  marriage, 59
  mere equities, 60–61
  notice,
    actual, 61
    constructive, 61–63
    imputed, 63
  personal representatives' sale to, 200
  purchaser for value, 59–60
  purchaser without notice, 59–63
  restrictive covenants, 470–471
  settled land, of, 261
  subsequent acquisition of legal estate, 60
  successors in title, 63
  value, 59
  without notice, 61–63
Boundaries,
  party walls, 332–335
Breach of covenant,
  waiving, 355
Building scheme, 460–461
Building society,
  discharge of mortgage to, 529
Business premises, tenancies of, 581–584
  alternative accommodation, 582
  compensation, 584
    eviction, 584
    improvements, 584
  demolition or reconstruction, 583
  determination, 582
  exceptions from Act, 581
  exceptions from Act, 581
  goodwill, 581
  improvements, 584
  initial protection, 581
  intention, landlords, 583
  Landlord and Tenant Act 1927, 581
  Landlord and Tenant Act 1954, 581–584
  opposition to new tenancy, 582–583
  own occupation by landlord, 583
  rent, 583–584
  repair, 582
  request for new tenancy, 582–583
  security of tenure, 581
  terms of new tenancy, 583–584
  within Act, 581

Capital money,
  overreaching,
    land, as, 87, 90
    land, capital money as, 87
    payment, 86–87, 89–90
Caravan sites,
  control, 574

Cattle, 422
Cautions,
    minor interests, 130–131
Certainties, the three, 290–291
Certainty of terms,
    contracts, 150–151
Certificate,
    charge, 499–500
Certificate of value,
    conveyance, 166
Cestui qui vie,
    life estate, 48
Chain of covenants, 462
Charges,
    See also Mortgages
    annuities, 97
    automatically imposed by statute, 94
    charge certificate, 499–500
    Class A, 94
    Class B, 94
    Class C, 94–96
    Class D, 96–97
    Class E, 97
    Class F, 98–99
    effectiveness, 495
    equitable, 95, 500–501
    equitable easements, 97
    estate contracts, 95–96
    general equitable charge, 95
    Inland Revenue Charges, 96
    investigation of title, 11
    leaseholds, 498
    limited owner's charge, 94–95
    local, 11
    mode registration, 101
    puisne mortgages, 94
    registered land. *See under* Registered Land
    registration. *See* Registration of land charges
    restrictive covenants, 96–97
    searches, 11
    statutory creation, 94
Charging orders,
    minor interests, 130
Charitable trust,
    presumed, 424
Charities,
    dispositions,
        powers, 206–207
        restrictions, 207
    inalienability rule, 240
    limitation period, 549
    perpetuities, rule against, 237
    presumed, *profits à prendre*, 424
    Saunders v. Vautier, rule in, 244–245
Charity Commissioners, 207
Chattels,
    real, 19
    settled, 274
Chief rent, 413
Cinema, 476, 478
Class gifts, 227–229
    age reduction, 229

Class gifts—*cont.*
    class and age reduction, 229
    class-closing rules, 228
    common law, 227
    meaning, 227
    statutory class reduction, 228
Clogs on equity of redemption, 520–523
Clubs,
    gifts to, 240
Co-ownership,
    See also Joint Tenancy; Tenancy in Common
    beneficiaries' position,
        bankruptcy, co-owner's, 324–325
        cautions, 320–321
        constructive trusts, 316–317
        disposition by sole trustee, 319–321
        dispute resolution, 321–326
        express trusts, 315–316
        extent of beneficial interest, 315–319
        financial trusts, 322
        occupation trusts, 321
        protection of interests, 319–321
        resulting trusts, 292–293
        sale, 322–323
    consultation, 326
    creation,
        benefit to purchaser, 313
        equity, 313–315
            executory trusts, 314–315
            loan on mortgages, 314
            marriage articles, 314–315
            partnership assets, 314
            preference for tenancy in common, 313
            purchase money provided in unequal shares,
                314
    fiduciary ownership, not, 309–310
    law, at, 308–313
        mode, 307–315
        scope of trusts, 310
        words of severance, 308
    determination, 327–332
    divided occupation, 325–326
    end of statutory trusts,
        overreaching, 312
        potential severances, 312
        registered land, 312–313
        union in one person, 312–313
        unregistered land, 312
    financial trusts, 322
    marriage articles, 314–315
    matrimonial home, 323
    occupation trusts, 321
    overreaching, 84, 311
    partition,
        common law, no power at, 327–328
        court order, 328
        sale, 328
        statutory right, 328
        voluntary, 327
    partition of land, 325–326
    party walls,
        after 1925, 332–334

Co-ownership—*cont.*
  party walls—*cont.*
    before 1926, 333
    characteristics, 333–334
    divided, 333
    divided with easements, 333–334
    ownership subject to easements, 332, 333
    release, 328
  right of survivorship, 303–304
  sale,
    co-owner, application by, 323
    creditors, application by, 323–324
    trustee in bankruptcy, application by, 324–325
  settled land, 326–327
  statutory trusts, 309
    overreaching, 311
  title,
    fragmentation, 8
    integration, 8–9
    simplification, 75–76
    undisclosed, 9–10
  union in sole tenant, 328
Coal, 580
Collective enfranchisement, 612–614
  generally, 612
  price, 613–614
  procedure, 613
  qualifying tenants, 612
  right, 613
Commercial interests, 73
  protection, 74–75
  purchasers, protection of, 75
  registered land, 74–75
  unregistered land, 75
Common law,
  basis of law of real property, 3–4
  disposition of land, 566
  life estate, 48
  meaning, 3
  ownership, 566
  restrictions, 568–569
  rights, 565–569
  use of land, 566
  water, 566–568
  wild animals, 566
Common of pasture, 422
Common, rights of,
  overriding interests, 122
Commonhold, 464–467, 566
  association, 28, 465–466
  creation, 465
  decision to use, 466
  dissolution of association, 467
  introduction, 28
  purpose, 465
  registration, 466–467
  rights of unit-holders, 466
  termination, 467
  unit, 28, 465
  use, 28–29, 46
Commons,
  approvement, 441

Commons—*cont.*
  number of cattle, 449–450
  prescription, 438
  registration, 442
  types of, 422
Companies,
  See also Corporations
  debentures, 521
Compensation,
  compulsory purchase, on, 578, 578–579
  disturbance, for, 579, 588–589
  eviction, for, 584
  improvements, for, 584, 590
  injurious affection, for, 579
Compensation scheme,
  registration of land charges, 103
Completion,
  registered conveyancing, 167
  unregistered land, 159–160
Compulsory purchase, 577–579
  blighted land, 577–578
  compensation, 578–579
  disturbance payments, 579
  entry, 578
  equivalent reinstatement, 579
  home loss payments, 579
  notice to treat, 578
  order, 578
  powers, 577–578
  useless land, 577–578
Concealment,
  limitation of period, 558
Condition,
  precedent, 230
  subsequent, 230
Conditional interest, 230
Conservation area, 576
Consideration,
  conveyance, 162
  transfer of registered land, 171–172
Consolidation of mortgages, 515–518
  conditions, 515–516
    illustrations, 516–517
  illustrations, 516–517
  redemption dates passed, 515
  reservation of right, 515
  same mortgagor, 515–516
  simultaneous unions of mortgages and equities, 516
Constructive notice,
  bona fide purchaser for value, 61–63
Constructive trusts,
  detrimental reliance, 317
  express common agreement, 316
  purpose, 316
  quantum of beneficial interest, 317
Common credit, 508
  repairs, 308
Contingent interests, 210–212
Contracts, 147–157
  agents, 153–154
  all the terms, 150–152
    certainty, 150–152

Contracts—*cont.*
  all the terms—*cont.*
    terms, 150
  certainty of terms, 150–152
    lacking, 152
    parties, 151
    price, 151
    property, 151
  correspondence, contracts by, 156
  document, one, 152
  effect, 154–155
  equity, 68–69
  estate. *See* Estate contracts
  evidenced in writing, 148
  exchange, 153
  formal contracts, 156–157
  former law, 147
  frustration, 366–367
  governing law, 147
  inquiries before, 157
  interest in land, 149
  lease contracts, 342–343
  leases, for, 342–343
  made in writing, 150
  old law, 147–148
  one document, 152
  open contracts, 156
  part performance, 148
    abolition, 154
  passing of risk, 155
  perpetuities, rule against, 235–236
  post-September 26 1989 contracts, 148–157
  practice, in, 155–157
  pre-September 27 1989 contracts, 148
  preliminaries to, 157
  purchaser to owner in equity, 154–155
  rectification, 152
  restricted, 614–616
  risk, passing of, 155
  sale of other disposition,
    exceptions, 149
    transactions included, 149
  signature,
    agents, 153–154
    requirement, 153
  Standard Conditions of Sale, 155
  terms,
    all, 150–152
    certainty, 150–152
    examples, 157
    incorporation into one document, 152
    rectification, 152
  trustee, vendor as, 155
  types, 156–157
    correspondence, contracts by, 156
    formal contracts, 156–157
    open contracts, 156
  use, 156
  usually required, where, 155–156
  vendor as trustee, 155
  void, 148

Contracts—*cont.*
  writing,
    evidenced in, 148
    made in, 150
Contractual licence, 477
Conversion, 250, 283
  title, 120
Conveyance,
  See also Conveyancing
  attestation, 166
  certificate of value, 166
  commencement, 161–162
  consideration, 162
  covenants, 163, 164–165
    enforceability, 163–164, 165
    leases, 165
    rentcharges, 165
  date, 162
  derogation from grant, rule against, 421
  details, 160–166
  draft, 159
  habendum, 166
  operation, 427, 429–430
  operative words, 162–163
  parcels, 166
  parties, 162
  post-June 1995, 164–165
  pre-July 1995, 163–164
  precedent, 160–166
  receipt clause, 162
  recitals, 162
  rectification, 430
  testatum, 162
  testimonium, 166
  third party benefiting under, 454–455
Conveyancing, 158–172
  See also Conveyance
  balance of interests, 15
  completion,
    registered land, 167
    unregistered land, 159–160
  concurrent systems, 14
  draft conveyance, 159
  draft transfer, 167
  electronic, 113
  epitome of title, 158
  law of real property distinguished, 1–2
  meaning, 158
  passing of title,
    registered land, 167
    unregistered land, 160
  registered land, 12–14
    completion, 167
    draft transfer, 167
    examination of title, 167
    Form TR1, 168–170
    inspection, 166
    passing of title, 167
    property, 171
    replies to requisitions, 167
    requisitions on title, 167
    searches, 167

Conveyancing—*cont.*
  registered land—*cont.*
    stamp duty, 171
    title number(s) to property, 171
    transfer, 168
  replies to requisitions,
    registered land, 167
    unregistered land, 159
  requisitions on title,
    registered land, 167
    unregistered land, 159
  role of conveyancer, 158
  searches,
    registered land, 167
    unregistered land, 159
  stamp duty, 171
  transfer, 168
    additional provisions, 172
    address for service, 171
    consideration, 171–172
    date, 171
    declaration of trust, 172
    execution as deed, 172
    Form TR1, 168–170
    property, 171
    stamp duty, 171
    title number(s) of property, 171
    transferee, 171
    transferor, 171
    transferor transfers property to transferee, 171
    transferor transfers with, 172
  unregistered land, 10–12, 93–110
    See also Conveyance; Registration of land charges
    abstract, delivery of, 158
    completion, 159–160
    consideration of abstract, 159
    draft conveyance, 159
    epitome of title, 158
    from contract to completion, 158–160
    passing of title, 160
    replies to requisitions, 159
    requisitions on title, 159
    searches, 159
Convicts, 201
Copyhold, 26
Corporations,
  breach of condition in lease, 362
  conveyances *inter vivos* to, 38
  joint tenancy, 304
  settlements made by, 246
Corporations. *See also* Companies
Corporeal hereditaments, 67, 407
Correspondence, contracts by, 156
Court of Chancery, 55–56
Court of Protection, 205
Covenants,
  assignment, against, 376–377
  benefit of assignable, 382–383, 455–456
  contract, privity of, 381
  custom or usage, 374–375
  definition, 381

Covenants—*cont.*
  enforceability of,
    direct, 381–382
  enforcement,
    indirect, 383
  estate, privity of, 381
  in esse things, 391
  in posse things, 391
  insure, to, 380
  landlord's and tenant's, 367–380
  repair, to, 378–380
    construction of covenant, 378
    damages for breach, 379
    leave to sue, 379–380
    meaning of repair, 378–379
  rule against perpetuity and, 235–236
  underletting, against, 376–377
  usual, 367, 374–375
Credit bargain, extortionate, 522
Creditor's notice, 130
Crown,
  easement of light and, 440
  gold and silver in mines, right to, 568, 579
  grant, 423–424
  limitation period for, 549, 555–556
  petroleum and gas, right to, 580
  tenant of, no enfranchisement, 611
Customary rights, 416, 421
  overriding interests, 127

Damages,
  repairing covenant, for breach of, 379
  restrictive covenant, for breach of, 464, 470
Date,
  conveyance, 162
Death,
  licensor, 476
  minors and, 203–204
  mortgagee, 527
  registered land, transfer of, 136
  statutory tenant, 594–595
  tenant, 602
  tenant for life, 265–268
  trustee, 300
Debts, accumulation for paying, 245
Deed of enlargement, 365–366
Deed poll, 161
Deeds of arrangement,
  registration of land charges, 101
Demand for rent, 357
Deposit,
  deeds, of, 446, 535–536
  land certificate, of, 499–500
Deprivation of property,
  human rights, 92–93
Derogation from grant, 369, 416, 421, 427
Determinable fee, 229–231
Determinable interests, 229–231
Determination of tenancies, 353–367
  expiry, 354
Development plans, 571–572
  current proposals, 572

Development plans—*cont.*
  local plans, 571–572
  requirement to prepare, 571
  structure plans, 571
  unitary, 572
Development scheme, 569
Disability, 201–207
  limitation, effect on, 557–558
Dispositions of land. *See* Contracts; Conveyancing;
    Disabilities; Intestacy; Personal representatives;
    Wills
Dispute resolution,
  adjudicator to the Land Registry, 113
  minor interests, 131
  registration of title, 113–114
Distress,
  rent under rentcharge, for, 410
  rent under tenancy, for, 375
Disturbance payments, 579, 588–589
Dominant tenement, 413–414
Double annual value, 350
Double rent, 350
"Dwelling house", light to, 439
Dwellings,
  restricted contracts, 614–616
    rent, 552–553
    secure tenancies, 605–607
    security of tenure, 553
  tenancies, of. *See* Dwellings, tenancies of
Dwellings, tenancies of, 590–617
  assured agricultural occupancies, 605
  assured shorthold tenancies, 603–604
    creation, 603
    generally, 603
    possession, grounds for, 603–604
    rent, 604
  assured tenancies, 599–602
    application of Act, 599–600
    death of tenant, 602
    possession, grounds for, 600–602
    rent, 602
    security of tenure, 600
    types of, 600
  "dwelling-house", 592
  eviction, protection from, 553–554
  harassment, 617–618
  introductory tenancies, 606–607
  long tenancies at low rent, 607–612
    conditions, 607–608
    protection, 608
    right to acquire freehold or new lease, 608–611
      modifications, 610–611
      scheme of management, 611
  protected shorthold tenancies, 597–598
  regulated tenancies, 592–599
    application of Acts, 592
      exceptions, 592–593
    death of statutory tenant, 594–595
    mortgages, 599
    possession, grounds for, 595–598
      discretionary, 595–596
      mandatory, 596–598

Dwellings, tenancies of—*cont.*
  regulated tenancies—*cont.*
    possession, grounds for—*cont.*
      reasonableness, 595
    premiums, 599
    rateable value, 593–594
    rent,
      fair, 599
      limit, 598–599
      registration, 598
        none, 598
      systems, 598–599
    statutory tenancy, 594
    termination of tenancy, 594
  rehousing, 605
  Rent Acts, 592–599
  restricted contracts, 614–616
    rent, 552–553
    security of tenure, 553
  secure tenancies, 605–607
    introductory tenancies, 606–607
    public sector landlord, 605
    rent, 607
    right to buy, 607
    security of tenure, 606

Easements, 82, 413–451
  abandonment, 442
  acquisition, 424–441
  air, 448
  ancillary, 428
  categories, 416
  conveyance, operation of, 427, 429–430
  definite right, 416
  definition, 413
  distinction from other rights, 417–418, 417–421
  dominant tenement,
    accommodation of, 414–415
    capability of grant, 416–417
    existence, 413–414
    ownership, 415
    separation from servient tenement, 414
  equitable, 97
  essentials, 413–417
  examples, 416–417, 447–448
  express, 425–427
    continuous and apparent occupation, 426–427
    diversity of occupation, 426
    generally, 425–426
    nature of rights, 426
  fencing, 416
  frustration, 443
  gross, in, 413
  implied, 427–430
    intended easements, 428
    necessity, easements of, 427–428
  incorporeal hereditament, 407
  intended, 428
  legal interest, as, 424
  licences distinguished, 420
  light, 416, 439–440, 445–446
    actual user, 440

Easements—*cont.*
  light—*cont.*
    common law claim, 433
    Crown, 440
    disabilities, 439
    no grant, 440
    obstruction, 439–440
    Prescription Act 1832,439–440
    written consent, 439
  meaning, 82
  minor interests, 130
  natural rights, 417–418
  nature, 413–421
  necessity, of, 427–428, 444–445
  overriding interests, 122, 126, 127
  positive, 420
  prescription 430–441. *See also* Prescription
  presumed grant 430–441. *See also* Prescription
  public rights, 418–419
    extinguishment, 419
  quasi-easements, 417
  registered land, 451
  release, 442–443
  restrictive covenants, 416, 420, 454
  rights capable of existing as, 416–417
  rights of way, 444–445
  servient tenement, 413–414
  soil, 417
  species, 443–448
  statutory, 425
  subject-matter of grant, 415–416
  support, 418
  unity of ownership and possession, 443
  water, 416, 447–448
  Wheeldon v. Burrows, 428–429
Electronic conveyancing, 113
Emblements, 373
  lift estate, 52
Enduring powers of attorney, 206
Enforcement notices, 574–575, 574–576
Enfranchisement,
  collective. *See* Collective enfranchisement
  engine of fraud, 296
  enlargement, of deed, 365–366
  entails. *See also* Fee Tail
  individual, 614
  limitations after, 237
  reversion on, 213
Entail, 32
Entailed interest, 32
Enterprise zones, 574
Entry, rights of, 462
  remoteness, 238
  rentcharge, 83
  rentcharges, 238, 410
Epitome of title, 158
Equitable charge, 446, 500–501
Equitable easement, 424
  registration, 97
Equitable interests, 108–110
  generally, 5
  non-registration of land charges, 109

Equitable interests—*cont.*
  overreaching, 108
  purchaser without notice, 109–110
  summary, 110
Equitable rights. *See* Equity
Equity,
  background, 2–3
  common law background, 53
  contract, 68–69
  Court of Chancery, 55–56
  creation of rights, 67–70
    capacity, lack of, 69
    formality, lack of, 67–69
    intention, lack of, 70
  estate contracts, 67
  follows the law, 57–58
  fusion of courts of law and equity, 56–57
  growth, 15
  historical basis, 53–57
  interests, 3
  legal rights distinguished, 58–59
  mere equities, 60–61
  mortgages, 66
  nature of rights,
    legal rights distinguished, 58–59
    purchaser without notice 59–63. *See also* Bona
        fide purchaser for value
  personal and proprietary rights, 70–71
  proprietary estoppel, 69
  purchaser without notice 59–63. *See also* Bona fide
      purchaser for value
  restrictive covenants, 66–67
  rights,
    creation, 67–70
    mortgages, 66
    nature,
      legal rights distinguished, 58–59
      purchaser without notice 59–63. *See also* Bona
          fide purchaser for value
    species, 64–71
      estate contracts, 67
      restrictive covenants, 66–67
      trusts, 64–66
  species of equitable rights, 64–71
    estate contracts, 67
    mortgages, 66
    restrictive covenants, 66–67
    trusts, 64–66
  treats that as done which ought to be done, 68
  trusts. *See* Trusts
  writ system, 53–55
Equity's darling, 3
Equivalent reinstatement, 579
Estate contracts, 67, 95–96, 97, 388–389, 397–398,
    403, 481
Estate owner,
  definition, 79
  overreaching, 5–6
Estate rentcharge, 409
Estate tail, 32
Estates, 24–25
  basic doctrine, 26–27

Estates—*cont.*
    classification,
        freehold, 31–33
        less than freehold, 33–35
    doctrine, 27
    fee simple. *See* Fee simple
    fee tail. *See* Fee tail
    freehold. *See* Freehold estates
    length, 26
    less than freehold, 33–34
    life. *See* Life estate
    meaning, 26
    seisin, 35–37
    time, 26
Estoppel, 62, 352–353
    equitable, 482
    feeding the, 352–353
    grant of leases, on, 352
    licence by, 477, 478
    mortgages, affecting priority of, 538
    proprietary, 69
    squatter, 560
    tenancy by, 352, 518
Estovers, 50, 450
Eviction, unlawful, 368–369, 616
Exclusive possession,
    generally, 340
    intention, 340
    pretences, 340, 341
    right, 340
    shams, 340, 341
    shared facilities, 341
Executory devises, 215
Executory interests, legal, 180, 214
Expiry,
    lease, 354
    tenancy, 35
Explosives, storing, 369
Express trusts for sale, 7

Fair rent, 599
Family interests, 73
    co-ownership, simplification of title for, 75
    overreaching, 75
Farm business tenancies, 589–590
    continuation of tenancies, 590
    improvement, compensation for, 590
    meaning, 589
    notices to quit, 589–590
    protection as to rent, 590
Farm house, redundant, 597
Fee farm rent, 413
Fee simple,
    absolute, 40, 41
        creation, 46
        meaning, 79–80
        in possession, 79–81
    base fee, 44
    condition, upon, 41, 42–44
        existence at law, 43
        flexibility, 43
        remoteness, 43

Fee simple—*cont.*
    condition, upon—*cont.*
        subsequent, 79–80
        void, effect of becoming, 44–45
    determinable, 41, 42–44, 229–231
        determination, 42–43
        existence at law, 43
        flexibility, 43–44
        remoteness, 43
    meaning, 32
    modified, 40
        nature, 44–45
    nature, 40–45
    in possession, 80–81
    words of limitation, 38–39
        corporation, conveyances *inter vivos* to, 38
        gifts by will, 39
        natural persons, conveyances *inter vivos* to, 38
Fee tail,
    barring,
        entails, 46–47
        unbearable entails, 47
    meaning, 32
    origin, 45
    present law, 45–47
    prospective abolition, 45–46
    rights of tenant in tail, 45
    words of limitation, 39–40
        conveyances *inter vivos*, 39
        will, gifts by, 39–40
Feeding the estoppel, 352–353
Fence, 416, 426
Fences, 449
Feoffment, 36
Financial trusts, 322
Fines,
    perpetually renewable leases, 351
Fire insurance, 460
Fish, 82
Fish, right to,
    free fishery, 423
    non-tidal waters, 567
    profit of piscary, 422, 450
    tidal waters, 423
Fixtures,
    agricultural, 22–23
    annexation,
        degree, 20
        purpose, 20–21
    definition, 19–20
    degree of annexation, 20
    domestic, 22
    landlord's, 22
    life estate, 52
    meaning, 19–20
    mortgages of land, 514
    objects that pass with land, 20–21
    ornamental fixtures, 22
    purpose of annexation, 20–21
    removal, right of, 21–24
        agricultural, 22–23
        devisee and personal representative, 23

Fixtures—*cont.*
  removal, right of—*cont.*
    domestic fixtures, 22
    generally, 221
    landlord's fixtures, 22
    limited right, 22–23
    mortgagor and mortgagee, 23–24
    none, 23–24
    ornamental fixtures, 22
    remainderman, tenant for life and, 23
    tenant's fixtures, 22
    trade fixtures, 22
    vendor and purchaser, 23
  trade fixtures, 22
Flats,
  collective enfranchisement, 612–614
    generally, 612
    price, 613–614
    procedure, 613
    qualifying tenants, 612
    right, 613
  eviction, 616
  harassment, 617
  individual enfranchisement, 614
  restricted contracts, 614–616
  reversion, purchase of, 611–612
Flying commonholds, 465
Flying freeholds, 507, 566
Foreclosure, 502–504
  See also Mortgages
  absolute, orders, 503
  meaning, 502
  nature, 502–503
  nisi, orders, 503
  orders,
    absolute, 504
    nisi, 503
  parties, 503
  re-opening foreclosure absolute, 504
  right, 503
Forfeiture, 354–364
  bankruptcy, 362
  breach of condition, 355, 360–364
  breach of covenant, 360
  "capable of remedy", 360–361
  clause, 355
    express, 355
    implied, 355
  conditions for, 357–360
  denial of title, 354
  express clause, 355
  formal demand, 357
    exemption, 357
  human rights, 357
  immoral use, 360
  implied clause, 355
  mode, 356–357
  notice, 360
  peaceable entry, 357
  possession, seeking, 356
  relief, 357–360
  rent, non-payment, 357–360

Forfeiture—*cont.*
  right, 354–355
  service of writ, 356
  sub-tenants, 358, 363
  waiver of breach, 355–356
Forgery, 330, 531–532
Form TR1, 168–170
Formal contracts, 156–157
Franchises,
  overriding interests, 127
  registration of title, 116
Fraud, 521, 538
  limitation of period, 558
  registration of title, 140, 141–142
  trusts, 295
Free fishery, 423
"Free" house, 507
Freehold,
  estates. *See* Freehold estates
  origins of term, 25
Freehold estates, 31–33
  fee simple 32. *See also* Fee simple
  fee tail 32. *See also* Fee tail
  generally, 31–32
  less than, estates, 33–34
  life estate 32–33. *See also* Life estate
  nature,
    fee simple, 40–45
    fee tail, 45–47
    life estate, 47–52
  remainders, 33
  reversions, 33
  words of limitation,
    conveyance *inter vivos*, 37–39
    fee tail, 39–40
    life estate, 40
    meaning, 37
    will, gifts by, 38, 39–40
Freezing injunction, 132
"Front of house" rights, 476
Frustration,
  easements, 443
Furnished lettings, 370, 552, 593
Future interests,
  accumulations, rule against. *See* Accumulations,
    rule against
  alienability of land, 209
  Cassification, 213–214
  contingent interests, 210–212, 212
  inalienability. *See* Inalienability, rule against
  Law Commission proposals, 215
  nature, 209–222
  perpetuities, rule against. *See* Perpetuities, rule
    against
  remainders, 214
    future trusts, 214
    legal remainders, 214
  reversions, 213–214
    after 1925, 213–214
    nature, 213
    vested, 213
  tying up capital, 210

Future interests—*cont.*
    vested interests, 210–212
        assignability, 212
        conditions of vesting, 210–212
        meaning, 210
        perpetuities rule, 212
        size of interest, 211–212
        subject to divesting, 212
Future trusts, 214–215

Game, 450
General powers, 232, 233
Gifts by will. *See* Wills
Gipsies, 574
Gold, 579
Good leasehold title, 119
Goodwill, 581
Grand sergeanty, 25
Grave, upkeep of, 239
Gravel, 450
Gross negligence, priorities affected by, 538

Habendum,
    conveyance, 166
Harassment, 616–617
Hedge, 560
Heirs, 32
Highways,
    public right of way, 418
        creation, 418–419
        dedication and acceptance, 418, 419
        extinguishment, 419
History,
    equity, 53–57
    formulation of principles, 15
    growth of equity, 15
    leases, 337–338
    mortgages, 511
    perpetuities, rule against, 214–215
    real property, law of, 2, 17–18
    receiver, appointment of, 511
    registered land, 12
    registration of title, 17, 111
    remoteness, rules against, 15
    social control, 17
    Statute of Uses, 15
    statutory reforms, 16–17
    trusts, development of, 15
Holding over, 350
Holiday home, 597, 601
Honour, titles of, 407
Housing associations, 606, 607
Housing trusts, 606, 607
Human habitation, fitness for, 369–372
Human rights,
    deprivation of property, 92–93
    effect of HRA 1998, 92
    European Convention on Human Rights, 92–93
    forfeiture, 357
    interpretation of legislation, 93
    limitation, 547–548
    overriding interests, 128, 128–129

Hunt, right to, 421, 450

Id certum est quod certum reddi potest, 150
Immovables, 17
Imperfect obligation, trusts of, 239
Implied trusts, 292
Improvements,
    agricultural holdings, 584, 589
    business premises, 584
    compensation, 584
    farm business tenancies, 590
    repair distinguished, 378
    settled land, 274–275
    tenant for life, by, 274–275
Imputed notice,
    bona fide purchaser for value, 63
In personam, rights, 58
Inalienability, rule against, 209, 236–240
    charity, 240
    immediate gifts, 240
    period, 238–239
    purpose trusts, 239
Inclosure, 441–442
Income, surplus, 244
Income tax, 372
Incorporeal hereditaments, 67–68, 407–451
    easements. *See* Easements
    meaning, 407
    rentcharges. *See* Rentcharges
Indemnity,
    leases, 392
    registration of title, 14, 143–145
        conversion of title, 144
        determination, 144–145
        errors, 144
        exceptions, 144
        generally, 143
        grounds, 143–144
        non-rectification, 144
        rectification, 143–144
Infants. *See* Minors
Informal leases, 343
Inheritance tax,
    personal representatives, payment by, 164
Inhibitions,
    bankruptcy, 136
    minor interests, 132
Injunction, 470
    freezing, 132
Injurious affection, 579
Inland Revenue Charges, 96
    minor interests, 130
Insurance,
    covenant in lease, 380
    mortgagee's right, 515
Interests,
    contingent, 210–212
    minor. *See* Minor interests
    vested, 210–212
Intestacy,
    administrators. *See* Personal Representatives
    personality, 198

Introductory tenancies, 606–607
Investigation of title, 10–12
    bona fide purchaser for value, 62–63
    land charges, 11
    local land charges, 11
    third party rights in land,
        registered land, 12
        unregistered land, 10–12
    vendor's title,
        registered land, 12
        unregistered land, 10
Investments, power to select, 275

Joint tenancy, 303–306
    See also Co-Ownership
    alienation of interest, 329–330
    corporations, 304
    creation, 307–315
    determination, 327–332
    interest, 305–306
    jus accrescendi, 303–304
    possession, 304–305
    settled land, 326–327
    severance, 328–332. *See also* Severance
        acquisition of another estate in land, 329
        after 1925, 331–332
        alienation, 329–330
        before 1926, 329
        homicide, 331
        mutual agreement, 330
        mutual course of dealing, 331
        notice in writing, 331–332
        present law, 332
    survivor of two or more tenants, 310
    title, 306
    trustees, 304
    unities, four, 304–306
        interest, 305–306
        possession, 304–305
        time, 306
        title, 306
    vesting, 306
        number of persons, 310–311
Jointure, 246
Judgment,
    enforcement, 100
Jus accrescendi, 4, 8, 304, 307, 329–330
Jus spatiandi, 448

Land,
    definition, 79
    functions, 4–5
    meaning, 17
    ownership and its limits, 565–619
Land certificate, 117
    deposit of, 499–500, 514, 544, 545
    possession of, 499–500
Land charges. *See* Charges; Mortgages; Registration
    of land charges
Land law,
    1925 legislation, 73–76
    structure, 73–145

Land obligations, 467
Land Registration Act 2002,
    actual occupation, rights of persons in, 127–128
    limitation, 549–550, 553, 562–563
    minor interests,
        notices, 133
        restrictions, 133–134
    overriding interests, 127–128
    rectification, 142–143
    registered land, 137–138
    restrictions, 133–134
    tacking, 546
Land registration. *See* Registration of Title
Land Registry, 116–117
    adjudicator, 113
Land tax, 83
Landlord,
    See also Leases
    duty of care, 371–372
    fixtures, 22
    view, right to, 373
Lands Tribunal, 472–473, 578
Leasehold,
    classification, 18–19
    estates less than freehold, 33–35
    fixed term,
        certain duration, 34
        duration capable of being rendered certain, 34–35
    land, as, 18
    modern distinction, 19
    modern position, 35
    reversionary, 34
    term of years absolute, 81
        absolute, 81
        term of years, 81
    uncertain period for uncertain duration, 35
Leases,
    See also Landlord; Tenancy; *and* Tenant
    See also Leasehold
    assignment, 353
        benefit of covenant, 382–383
        breach of covenant, 377
        covenant against, 376–377
        effectiveness, 353
        enforceable agreement for lease, 313
        indemnities by assignees, 392
        legal,
            assignment, 391
            leases, 391
        liability of personal representatives, 383–384
        unreasonable withholding of consent, 376–377
    authorised guarantee agreements, 382, 401
    burden of covenants, 345
    certainty of term, 346
    charges, 498
    classification, 346–350
        certainty of term, 346
        monthly tenancies, 348–349
        periodic tenancies, 348–349
        reversionary leases, 347
        tenancies at will, 349
        weekly tenancies, 348–349

Leases—*cont.*
  classification—*cont.*
    yearly tenancies, 347–348
  contract for, 342–343
  conveyancing device, as, 338
  covenants,
    assignee of original party, 381
    authorised guarantee agreements, 382, 401
    benefit, 382–383
    burden, 343, 383
    customary, 374–375
    enforcement,
      direct, 382–383
      indirect, 382–383
      new leases, 382
      old leases, 381
      others, against, 382–383
    equity, 383
    estate contracts, 388–389, 397–398, 403
    former landlords and tenants, 382
    former landlords under new lease, 402–405
      basic rule, 402–403
      contrary intention, 404
      estate contracts, 403
      exceptions to basic rules, 403–404
      excluded assignments, 404
      guarantors, 405
      indemnity, 404
      management companies, 405
      personal covenants, 403
      pre-assignment breaches, 404–405
    former tenants under new leases, 400–405
      authorised guarantee agreements, 401–402
      basic rule, 400
      excluding operation of 1995 Act, 400
      guarantors, 405
      indemnity, 404
      management companies, 405
      overriding leases, 402
      pre-assignment breaches, 404–405
      problem notices, 402
      release from liability, 400
    general principles, 381–384
    guarantor, 381–382, 382
    insurance, 380
    landlord and tenant for the time being, 382
    meaning, 381
    mutual benefit and burden, 383
    new leases,
      apportionment, 399
      attribution, 398–399
      basic rule, 396–397
      disclaimer, 399
      estate contracts, 397–398
      exceptions, 397
      excluding operation of 1995 Act, 396
      forfeiture, 399
      former tenants, 400–402
      guarantors, 400
      no longer building, covenants, 398
      partial assignments, 398–399
      personal covenants, 397

Leases—*cont.*
  covenants—*cont.*
    new leases—*cont.*
      pre-assignment breaches, 399–400
      restrictive covenants, 405–406
      transmission, principles of, 398
    old leases,
      basic position, 385
      defences, 385
      direct covenants by assignees, 386–387
      effect of rule, 385–386
      equity, assignment effective only in, 394–395
      estate contract, 388–389
      guarantors, 387, 388, 392
      in posse, things, 391
      indemnities from assignees, 392
      law, assignment effective at, 387–394
      legal assignment, 390–391
      lessee assigning lease, 390–392
      liability of assignees, 391
      no legal assignment, 391
      overriding leases, 386
      problem notices, 386
      restrictive covenants, 395–396
      reversion, assignment of, 392–394
      touching and concerning the land, 387–388
      transmission, principle of, 390
    original parties, 381
      personal representatives of, 383–384
    personal representatives,
      personal liability, 383–384
      protection, 384
      representative liability, 384
    remedies for breach, 368
    repair, 378–380
    transmission, principles of, 398
    usual, 374
  creation, 339–353
    statutory modifications, 350–352
  damages, 379
  derogation from grant, 369
  determination, 353–367
    disclaimer, 366
    enlargement, 365–366
    expiry, 354
    fixed periods, 347
    forfeiture. *See* Forfeiture
    frustration, 366–367
    merger, 365
    notice, 354, 360
    periodic tenancies, 348–349
    repudiation, 367
    satisfied term, 365
    surrender, 364–365
    variation of lease, 364
    yearly tenancies, 348
  difference between legal and equitable lease,
    344–346
  duration, 342, 346
  easements, 345
    prescription, 431
  essentials, 339–346

Leases—*cont.*
  estate contracts, 403
  estoppel, 352–353
    feeding the estoppel, 352–353
    feeding the, 352–353
    tenancy by, 352
  eviction, unlawful, 369
  explosives, storing, 369
  fitness, 369–372
    furnished lettings, 370
    low rents, 370
    short leases of dwellings, 370–371
  fixed period, 346–347
    certainty of term, 346
    determination, 347
    reversionary leases, 347
  forfeiture,
    indirect enforcement of covenant, 383
    sub-tenants, 377
  formalities, necessary, 342–344
    contracts for leases and tenancies, 342–343
    duration, 342
    equitable leases, 344–346
    informal lease void at law, 343
    legal and equitable leases distinguished, 344–346
    legal leases, 343–344
    Walsh v. Lonsdale, 343–344
  history, 337–338
  imperfect, 343
  informal lease, as, 343
  leasehold interest, 338
  lessee, 338
  lessor, 338
  limitation, 553–554
  lives, for, 337
    statutory modifications, 350–351
  meaning, 337
  mere conveyancing device, 338
  mining, breach of covenant, 361–362
  minor interests, 130
  mortgages, 495–497
    leasing powers, 518–519
    surrender of lease, accepting, 519–520
  options in, perpetuities, 235–236
  oral, 342
  over-lengthy renewals, 351
  overriding interests, 123, 126
  parties, 367–380
  periodic tenancies,
    creation, 348–349
    determination, 348–349
  perpetually renewable, 351
  possession,
    covenant against parting with, 376–377
    exclusive, tenant's 340–341. *See also* Exclusive
      possession
  premises sufficiently defined, 340
  privity, 339, 381–382
  pur autre vie, 337
  quiet enjoyment, 368–369
  rack rent, 345
  renewing lease, perpetuities, 236

Leases—*cont.*
  rent,
    cost of repairs, deducting, 380
    covenant to pay, 375
    enforcement, 375
    need for, 306
    non-payment, right to relief, 357–359
    rentcharges distinguished, 407–408
  repair, 369–372
    covenants, 378–380
      damages, 379
    furnished lettings, 370
    implied terms, 372
    improvement distinguished, 378
    low rent, houses let at, 370
    meaning, 378
  restrictive covenants in 383
  reversion, 213–214, 338, 347
  right of entry, 238
  specific performance, 344–345
  statutory modifications, 350–351
    lives, leases for, 350–351
    perpetually renewable leases, 351
  statutory protection for tenants, 380
  sub-leases,
    covenant against, 376–377
    enlargement, 365–366
    forfeiture, 358, 363, 377
  sufferance, tenancy at, 350
  term of years, 338
    absolute,
      certainty, 346
      fixed, 346–347
  term of years, fixed 338
  terminology, 338–339
  third parties, 345–346
  title, denial, 354
  variation, 364
  void at law, 343
  Walsh v. Lonsdale, 343–344
  will, tenancy at, 349
  yearly tenancies,
    creation, 347
    determination, 348
    implication, 348
Legal charge, 495, 497, 498
Legal estates,
  concurrent, 84
  generally, 5
  reduction in number, 78–84
Legal executory interests, 214
Legal interests,
  generally, 5
  reduction in number, 78–79
Lessees,
  assignment of lease, 390–392
  leases, 338
  registration of land charges, 103, 103–104
  rentcharges, 411
Letters of administration, 198
Levancy and couchancy, 449

Licences, 475–489
  agricultural, 604
  bare, 476
  constructive trust, 481–482
  contractual, 477
  coupled with an interest, 476
  creation, 477–478
  death of licensor, 476
  determination by licence, 479–480
  easements distinguished, 420
  estoppel, by, 477, 479
  exclusive occupation of land, 475
  gratuitous, 476
  limitation, 554–555
  nature, 475
  protection, no statutory, 340
    agricultural exception, 604–605
  registered land, 480
  revocable, 476
  revocation, 478–479
  shams, 341
  specific performance, 479
  sub-licences, 480
  successors in title, binding, 481–482
  tort, wrongful interference, 482
  transmission of,
    benefit, 480
    burden, 480–482
      bare licences, 480
      contractual licences, 480–482
      interest, licences coupled with, 480
  types, 475–477
Liens, 492
Life estate, 47–52
  See also Settled land
  ameliorating waste, 48
  cestui que vie, 48
  common law, 48
  embelments, 52
  fixtures, 52
  life of tenant, estate for 47–48
  meaning, 32–33
  minerals, 51–52
    leasing under Settled Land Act 1925, 51
    right to work mines, 51
    trusts for sale, 51–52
  permissive, 49
    voluntary, 49
  permissive waste, 49
  pur autre vie, 33, 48, 52
  reversion on, 213
  terminology, 33
  timber, 49–51
    estate, 50
    estovers, 50
    generally, 49
    normal rules, 50–51
    ornamental, 50
    ownership of severed timber, 51
    shelter, 50
    trees, 50
  types, 47–48

Life estate—*cont.*
  voluntary waste, 49
  waste,
    ameliorating, 48
    equitable, 49
    permissive, 49
    voluntary, 49
  words of limitation, 40
Light, rights of, 439, 445–446
  alteration of apertures, 446
  deliberate obstruction, 445
  no natural right to, 45
  Prescription Act 1832, 439–440
  quantum, 445
  standard, 446
Limitation, 547–564
  acknowledgement of title, 559
  Crown, 549, 550, 555–556
  disability, 557–558
    Land Registration Act 2002, 558
    Limitation Act 1980, 557–558
    meaning of disability, 557
    successive disabilities, 557–558
    supervising disability, 557
  dispossession, 551
  elapse of time, effect of,
    successive squatters, 563–564
    title to land, 559–564
      barred leaseholds, 560–561, 562, 563
      burdens binding squatter, 560, 561, 562
      Land Registration Act 2002, 562–563
      Limitation Act 1980, 559–562
      parliamentary conveyance, 559–560, 561, 562
      proof of title, 563
      registered land, 559–561
      unregistered land, 559–561
    unregistered land, 559–561
  elements, 548–549
  fraud, 558
  future interests,
    Land Registration Act 2002, 553
    Limitation Act 1980, 553
  human rights, 547–548
  income arrears, recovery, 564
  Land Registration Act 2002, 549–550, 553, 562–563
  leaseholds, 553–554
  length of period, 549–550
    charities, 549
    Land Registration Act 2002, 549–550
    Limitation Act 1980, 549
    special periods, 549, 550
  mistake, 558
  mortgages, 555
  negative operation, 548, 559
  owner,
    intended use, 552–553
  periodic tenancies, 554
  policy, 547
  possession,
    adverse 551–553. *See also* Adverse possession
    basis of title, 548

Limitation—*cont.*
  postponement of period, 557–559
    deliberate concealment, 558
    disability, 557–558
    fraud, 558
    mistake, 558
    wartime, 559
  prescription distinguished, 548
  registered land, 561–562
    effect of registration, 138
    further two-year period, 138
    Land Registration Act 1925, 136–137
    Land Registration Act 2002, 137–138
    procedure after ten-year period, 137–138
    ten-year period, 137
  rentcharges, 555
  running of time, 550–557
    corporation sole, 555–556
    Crown, claims through, 555–556
    future interests, 553
    leaseholds, 553–554
    licensees, 554–555
    mortgages, 555
    owner entitled in possession, 551–553
    periodic tenancies, 554
    postponement, 557–559
    rentcharges, 555
    starting afresh, 559
    tenants at sufferance, 554–555
    tenants at will, 554–555
    trusts, 556–557
    yearly tenancies, 554
  squatter,
    animus possidendi, 552
    burdens binding, 560
    possession by, 551–553
    successive, 563–564
    title, 559–564
      proof, 563
  subject-matter, 548
  tenants at sufferance, 554–555
  tenants at will, 554–555
  time,
    elapse, effect, 559–564
    running,
      adverse possession, 551–553
      beginning, 551–557
      discontinuance, 551
      dispossession, 551
    trusts, 556–557
    wartime, 559
    yearly tenancies, 554
Limitation, words of. *See* Words of limitation
Limited owner's charge, 94–95
Listed buildings, 576
Lives, leases for, 337, 350–351
Local land charges,
  investigation of title, 11
  overriding interests, 123, 127
  register, 77
  registration of land charges, 91–92
    divisions, 91

Local land charges—*cont.*
  registration of land charges—*cont.*
    failure to register, 92
    registrable interest, 92
  searches, 11–12
Local plan, 571
Long leaseholds,
  minor interests, 130
Lord and tenant, 24–25
Lost modern grant, 433–434
  evidence, 433–434
  presumption, 433
Low rent, 370, 607–612
Lunatic. *See* Mental Patient

Maintenance, accumulation for, 246
Management companies, 405
Mansion house, principal, 273
Marriage, 59
  articles, 314–315
Matrimonial home,
  mortgages, 510
  resulting trusts, 317–318
  sale, 322–325
Mental patients, 205–206
  capacity, 205–206
    after proceedings, 205
    before proceedings, 205–206
  control over property, 204
    jurisdiction, 205
    settlements, 205
  enduring powers of attorney, 206
  limitation, 557–558, 558
  prescription, 436
  settled land, 278
  tenant for life, 278
Mere equities, 60–61
Mere freeholds, 33
Merger, 365, 412
Minerals,
  coal, 580
  gold and silver, 568
  life estate, 51–52
    leasing under Settled Land Act 1925, 51
    right to work mines, 51
    trusts for sale, 51–52
  mining lease, breach of covenant, 361–362
  petroleum, 580
  right to work mines, 51
  statutory restrictions, 579–580
  trusts, 51–52
  trusts for sale, 51–52
Mines, 362, 508, 568
Minister of religion, 597, 601
Minor interests, 129–134
  access orders, 130
  beneficiary's rights, 130
  cautions, 130–131
  charging orders, 130
  classes, 129
  competing interests, 131
  creditor's notice, 130

Minor interests—*cont.*
  dealings, cautions against, 130–131
  definition, 129–130
  dispute resolution, 131
  easements, 130
  inhibitions under present law, 132
  Inland Revenue Charges, 130
  Land Registration Act 2002, under, notices, 133
    restrictions, 133–134
  leases, 130
  long leaseholds, 130
  manner of protection, 130
  notices,
    effect, 130, 133
    Land Registration Act 2002, under, definition, 133
    mode of entry, 130
    present law, 130
    rights protected by, 130
  occupation rights, 130
  priority, 545
  protection, 129–134, 545
  rentcharges, 130
  restrictions, 132–133
    effect, 132
    Land Registration Act 2002, 133–134
  searches, 134
  trust of land, 130
Minors, 301–304
  accumulation during minority, 246
  attempted conveyance to, 201–202
  death, transfer on, 203–204
  en ventre sa mère, 220
  leases, 204
  limitation, 557–558
  mortgages, 202
  ownership of land, 201
  personal representatives, 202
  prescription, 436
  settled land. *See under* Settled Land
  trustees, 202–203
  voidable dispositions, 203
Mistake,
  limitation of period, 558
Modern grant, lost, 433–434
Mortgages, 491–546
  See also Charges
  appointing receiver,
    equitable mortgages, 513
    history, 511
    power, 511–512
  attornment clause, 510–511
  charge distinguished, 492
  compulsory registration, 497
  consolidation, 515–518
    conditions, 515–516
    extent, 517–518
    illustrations, 516–517
    purchaser's position, 518
    redemption dates passed, 515
    reservation of right, 515
    right, 515–518
    same mortgagor, 515–516

Mortgages—*cont.*
  consolidation—*cont.*
    simultaneous unions of mortgages and equities, 516
  consumer credit, 508
  creation, 491–503
    equitable, 499–501
    history, 493–497
    leaseholds, 495–497
    legal,
      after 1925, 494–495
      before 1926, 493–494
      grant of term of years absolute, 494–495
      leaseholds, 495–497
      legal charge, 495
      registered land, 497–498
      unregistered land, 493–497
  date for redemption, 493
  death,
    mortgagee,
      one of several, 527
      sole, 527
    mortgagor, 527
  demise for term of years absolute, 494–495
  discharge, 529–530
    building society, 529
  dwelling-houses,
    possession proceedings, 509
    spouse's position, 510
    statutory protection,
      mortgagee, for, 599
      mortgagor, for, 509
  enforcing payment, 501–513
  equitable,
    deposit of documents of title, 499–500
    informality, 499
    interest, 499
  equity, 66
  equity in the property, 492
  equity of redemption, 493–495
    extinguishment, 526
    termination, 525–526
    transfer *inter vivos*, 527–528
  fixtures, 514
  foreclosure, 502–504
    effect, 502
    equitable mortgages, 512
    opening foreclosure absolute, 504
    parties to action, 503
    procedure, 502–503
    right, 503
  further, 495, 496
  informal, 499
  insurance against fire, 515
  joint account clause, 527
  lease,
    forfeiture, 361–362
    not binding, 518–519
    surrender, accepting, 519–520
  leasing powers, 518–519
  legal,
    charge by way of, 83

Mortgages—*cont.*
  legal—*cont.*
    registered land, 497–498
    unregistered land, 493–497
  lien distinguished, 492
  limitation, 555
  minors, 202
  mortgagee, 491
  mortgagor, 491
  nature, 491–492
  negative equity, 492
  obsolete forms, 83
  part performance, 499
  parties' rights,
    both parties, 518–520
    mortgagee, 501–513
      cumulative, 512
    mortgagor, 520–526
  perpetuities, rule against, 238
  pledges distinguished, 492
  possession, taking, 506–511
    adverse possession, 511
    attornment clause, 510–511
    cohabitants, 510
    connected persons, 510
    equitable mortgages, 513
    limitation, 511
    powers in possession, 507
    relief, mortgagor's, 508–509
    right, 506–507
    spouses, 510
    strict account, 507
    tenants, 506
  priority. *See* Priority of mortgages
  protection by deeds, 535–536
    no protection, 538–539
  puisne, 94, 536
  purchasers' position, 518
  purpose, 491
  receiver, appointment, 511–512, 513
  redemption, right of, 520–526
    effect, 523–524
    equity of redemption distinguished, 493–494
    exercise, 523
    free from conditions, 521–522
    no clogs on equity, 520–523
    no irredeemability, 521
    notice, 524
    regulated mortgages, 523
    superior mortgage, by lower incumbrancer, 525
    terms, 522, 524–525
    trade restraint, 523
    unconscionable terms, 522
  registered land, 135
  regulated, 523
  relief, mortgagor's in possession proceedings,
    508–509
  sale, 504–506
    by mortgagor, 528
    equitable mortgages, 513
    history, 504
    mode, 505–506

Mortgages—*cont.*
  sale—*cont.*
    position of mortgagee, 506
    power, 504–505
      exercise, 505–506
    price, 506
    prior mortgages, 507
    proceeds, 506
    purchaser's protection, 505
    security, 491
  spouse's position, 510
  sub-mortgages, 528
  suing for money due, 491, 501, 512
  tacking, 530, 542–544
    agreement of intervening incumbrancer, 543
    further advances, 544
      obligation to make, 546
    Land Registration Act 2002, 546
    no notice of intervening incumbrancer, 543–544
    optional, 546
    registered land, 546
    tabula in naufragio, 543
  tacking. *See* Tacking
  tenants' position, 507
  title deeds,
    deposit, mortgages by, 499–500
    possession, 514
  transfer of,
    mortgages *inter vivos*, 528–529
  undue influence, 532–535
Mortuum vadium, 439
Movables,
  meaning, 17
Murder, 331

National Rivers Authority, 567
Natural persons,
  conveyances *inter vivos* to, 38
Nec vi, nec clam, nec precario, 430–431
Negligence,
  gross, 538–539
Notice,
  actual, 61
  bona fide purchaser for value,
    actual, 61
    constructive, 61, 61–63
    imputed, 63
  breach of planning condition, 575–576
  constructive, 61–63
  Dearle v. Hall, rule in, 540, 546
  enforcement, planning control, 574–575
  generally, 3–4
  imputed, 63
  lease,
    breach, 360
    determination, 354
  minor interests,
    effect, 130, 133
    Land Registration Act 2002, under, 133
    mode of entry, 130
    present law, 130
    rights protected by, 130

Notice—*cont.*
  mortgage, redemption of, 524
  periodic tenancies, 348–349
  priority, 539
  quit, agricultural holding, 586
  severance of joint tenancy, 331–332
  stop, 575
  treat, to, 578
  without. *See* Bona Fide Purchaser Without Notice
  yearly tenancies, 348
Nuisance, 568, 569
Nulle terre sans seigneur, 24

Occupancies, protected, 604
Occupation,
  actual, for overriding interests, 123–125, 127–128
  matrimonial right of, 510
  matrimonial rights, 98–99
  minor interests, 130
  statutory rights of, 98–99
Occupation trusts, 321
Open contracts, 156
Option to purchase,
  perpetuities, rule against, 235–236
Orders,
  access, 450
  compulsory purchase, 578
  tree preservation, 576
Ornamental fixtures, 22
Overcrowding, 598
Overreaching, 210, 530–535
  actual occupation, 530
  bare trusts, 85
  capital money,
    land, as, 87, 90
    payment, 86–87, 89–90
  co-ownership, 84
  doctrine, 84–91
  effect, 86, 530
    no overreaching, 531
  equitable interests, 108
  estate owner, 5–6
  examples, 84–85
  extension, 75, 84–91
  family interests, 75
  forgery, 531–532
  LPA 1925, under, 85–86
  meaning, 5–6, 530
  partial, 531–535
    behind back of co-owner, 532
    forgery, 531–532
    undue influence, 532–535
  payment of capital money, 86–87, 89–90
  post-1996 position, 86
  pre-1977 position, 86
  rights not overreached, 8
  scope, 84–85
  Settled Land Act 1925, under, 87–90
    ad hoc settlements, under, 90–91
    generally, 87–88
    payment of capital money, 89–90
    rights prior to settlement, 89

Overreaching—*cont.*
  Settled Land Act 1925, under—*cont.*
    rights under settlement, 88–89
    summary, 89, 91
  settlements, 84, 237
  statutory trusts, 311
  subsisting interests, 530
  undue influence, 532–535
Overriding interests, 8, 9, 121–129
  actual occupation, rights of persons in, 123, 123–125
    Land Registration Act 2002, under, 127–128
  common, rights of, 122
  customary rights, 127
  easements, 122, 126, 127
  franchises, 127
  human rights, 128–129
  Land Registration Act 2002, 125–129
    actual occupation, 127–128
    transitional provisions, 128–129
  leases, 123, 126
  Limitation Acts, rights acquired under, 122–123
  local land charges, 123, 127
  nature, 121–122
  present law, 122–123
  profit *à prendre*, 122, 126, 127
  public rights, 122, 127
  rectification of land register, 141
  registered land, 13–14
  rights of way, 122
  settled land, 126
  subsisting interests, 122
  unregistered interests,
    overriding first registration, 125, 126
    registered dispositions, 125, 126–127
  watercourses, 122

Parcels,
  conveyance, 166
Park enjoyment of, 417
Part performance,
  contracts, 148
    abolition, 154
Particular estate, 213
Parties,
  conveyance, 162
Partition, 327–328
Party walls, 332–335
  access to neighbouring land, 335
  characteristics, 333–334
  definition, 332
  disputes, 335
  divided, 333
  divided with easements, 333–334
  excavations, 335
  existing party wall, works to, 334–335
  meaning, 332–333
  new party wall, 334
  nuisance, 335
  ownership subject to easement, 334
  Party Wall, etc. Act 1996, 334–335

Passing of risk,
  contracts, 155
Passing of title,
  registered land, 167
  unregistered land, 160
Pastoral land, 362
Pasture, profit of, 422, 449, 449–450
  appendant, 449
  appurtenant, 449
  in gross, 449
  limitation of numbers, 450
  pur cause de vicinage, 449
  without number, 449
  without stint, 449
Pawn, 492
Peat, 82, 450
Pending actions,
  registration of land charges, 99–100
Permissive waste, 49
Pernancy of profits, 64
Perpetual trusts, rule against, 238
Perpetually renewable leases, 351
  assignment, 351
  breach of covenant, 351
  fine, 351
  meaning, 351
  termination, 251
Perpetuities, rule against, 210–212, 212, 215–222,
    219–238
  age reduction, statutory, 223
  alternative contingencies, 226–227
  application, separate, 225
  charities, 237
  child *en ventre sa mere*, 220–221
  class gifts, 227–229
    age reduction, 229
    class and age reduction, 229
    class-closing rules, 228
    common law, 227
    meaning, 227
    statutory class reduction, 228
  conditional interests, 229–231
  contingent interests, 210–212
  contracts, 235–236
  dependence, 225–226
  determinable interests, 229–231
  development of rule, 214–215
  exceptions, 237–238
  future interests, 213–214
  future parenthood, 217–218
  history of rule, 214–215
  Law Commission proposals, 224–225
  lives in being, 219–220, 222–223
  no "wait and see" at common law, 216–217
  operation, 215–222
  period, 215–216
    alternative, 224
  powers, 231–235
    administrative, 199, 231
    appointment, of, 231–232
  prior limitation, 225
  rebutting presumption, 217–218

Perpetuities, rule against—*cont.*
  remainders, 214
  resulting trusts, 230
  rule, 215–216
  statutory reform, 215
  subsequent limitation, 225–226
  surviving spouses, 224
  tying up capital, 210
  vest, meaning of, 216
  vested interests, 210–212
    assignability, 212
    conditions for vesting, 210–212, 211–212
    divesting, subject to, 212
    meaning, 210
    size of interest, 211–212
  "wait and see",
    common law, 216, 216–217
    state, 218–219
Person of unsound mind. *See* Mental Patient
Personal property,
  real property distinguished, 17–18
Personal representatives, 198–201
  administrators, 198–199
  assents, 199–200
  chain of representation, 199
  devolution of property on, 199–200
  executor's year, 198
  liability,
    leasehold premises, 383–384
  minors, 202
  number,
    maximum, 201
    minimum, 201
  ownership of assets, 200
  powers, 200
  settled land, disposition of, 261–262
  vesting of property, 199
Personality, 17
  intestacy, 198
Petroleum, 580
Planning control, 569–577
  advertisements, 576
  caravan sites, 574, 584
  conservation areas, 576
  control of development, 572–576
    meaning of development, 572–573
    planning permission, 573–574
  development,
    control, 572–576
    meaning, 572
    permitted, 573–574
  development plans, 571–572
    current proposals, 572
    unitary plans, 572
  effect on property law, 576–577
  enforcement,
    appeal, 575
    breach of condition notice, 575–576
    enforcement notices, 574–575
    non-compliance, 575
    stop notices, 575
    time limit, 575

Planning control—*cont.*
  enterprise zones, 574
  Green Paper *Planning: Delivering a Fundamental Change*, 571
  growth, 569–571
  listed buildings, 576
  local administration, 570–571
  local plans, 571–572
  national administration, 570
  plan,
    local, 571–572
    structure, 571
  planning permission 573–574. *See also* Planning permission
  property law, effect on, 576–577
  schemes, control by, 569
  simplified planning zones, 574
  special development orders, 574
  structure plans, 571
  Town and Country Planning Acts, 569–570
  tree preservation orders, 576
  trees, 576
Planning permission, 573–574
  caravan sites, 574
  enterprise zones, 574
  permission, 573
  permitted development, 573–574
  simplified planning zones, 574
  special development orders, 574
Pledges, 492
Portions, 245
Possession, adverse. *See* Adverse possession; Limitation
Possessory title, 119
Powers of appointment,
  rule against perpetuities, 231–232
    general powers, 233
    special powers, 232–233
    validity of,
      appointments, 233–235
      power, 232–233
Powers of attorney, 206, 513
Premiums, 599
Prescriptions, 430–441
  Act of 1832, 434–441
    ambit, 437–438
    application, 437
    commons, 438
    consents, 436
    deduction, 437
    easements, 434
    interruptions, 434
    less than statutory periods, user for less than, 436
    light, rights of, 434
    limits, 440–441
    longer and shorter periods, difference between, 438–439
    mental patients, 436
    minors, 436
    next before some action, 434–435
    periods, 434
    pleadings, 436

Prescriptions—*cont.*
  Act of 1832—*cont.*
    profits, 434
    right to deduct, 438
    right, user as of, 435–436
    summary, 434
    tenant for life, 436
    term of life, servient tenement held for, 436
    without interruption, 435
  common law, 432–433
    length of user, 432
    presumption, 433
  continuous user, 432
  fee simple, user in, 431–432
  general principles, 430–432
  interruption of user, 435
  light, 439–440
  limitation distinguished, 548
  lost modern grant, 433–434
    evidence, 433–434
    presumption, 433
  minors, 436
  nec vi, nec clam, nec precario, 430–431, 435–436
  principle vesting deed, 260
  registered land, 138
  right, user as of, 430–431
Priority of mortgages, 530–546
  before 1926, 530
  equitable interest, mortgages of, 540–542, 545–546
    Dearle v. Hall, rule in, 540
    no notice of prior mortgage, 540
    receipt of notice, 541
    service of notice, 541–542
    writing, notice must be in, 541
  generally, 530
  legal estate, mortgages of, 544–545
  loss, 537–538
  meaning, 530
  overreaching. *See* Overreaching
  registered land, 544–546
  tacking, 530
  unregistered land, 535–544
    deposit of deeds, 535
    each mortgage protected by deposit of deeds, 536–538
    first but not second mortgage protected by deposit of deeds, 539
    generally, 535
    legal estate, mortgages of, 535–540
    neither mortgage protected by deposit of deeds, 538–539
    operation of rules, 536–540
    registration, 536
    second but not first mortgage protected by deposit of deeds, 539–540
    summary, 540
Priority notice, 539
Privacy, 416
Probate, 198
Profit *à prendre*, 82, 97
  overriding interests, 122, 126, 127
  registration of title, 116

Profits *à prendre*, 407
  abandonment, 442
  acquisition, 424–441
  appendant, 422
  appurtenant, 422
  classification, 421–422, 421–423
  common, in, 422
  common of pasture, 422
  common, profit in, 421
  conveyance's operation, 427, 429–430
  distinction from other rights, 423–424
  express, 425–427
  extinguishment, 441–443
  fluctuating bodies, rights of, 423–424
  gross, in, 422
  land, 421–423
  legal interest, as, 424
  levancy and couchancy, 449
  meaning, 421
  nature, 421–424
  ownership, 421
  piscary, 421, 422, 450
  prescription 430–431. *See also* Prescription
  public rights, 423
  pur cause de vicinage, 422, 449
  registered land, 451
  release, 442–443
  several, 376, 421
  soil, taken out of, 421
  species, 449–450
  unity of ownership and possession, 443
  water, 421
Promissory estoppel, 483
Proprietary estoppel, 69, 483–489
  bar to equity, 486
  constituents, 484–486
    assurance or representation, 485
    no bar to equitable relief, 486
    reliance on assurance or representation, 485
    unconscionable disadvantage, 485–486
  creation, 483–484
  extent of equity, 486–487
  five *probanda*, 484
  judicial attitudes, 483–484
  modern approach, 483
  perpetual, 479
  principle, 477
  registered land, 489
  requirements, 483–484
  satisfaction of equity, 487–488
  third parties, 488–489
  traditional approach, 483
  unregistered land, 489
Proprietary rights and interests, 236
Public rights, 418–419, 423
  overriding interests, 122, 127
Puisne mortgage, 94, 536
Pur autre vie, estate, 33, 48
Purchaser without notice 59–63. *See also* Bona fide
    purchaser for value

Qualified title, 119
Quarter days, usual, 349
Quasi profits, 423
Quasi-easements, 417
Quicquid planatur solo, sol credit, 5
Quiet enjoyment, 368–369
Quit rent, 413

Rack rent, 345
Rateable value, 552, 593–594, 610
Real property, law of,
  conveyancing distinguished, 1
  history, 2, 17–18
  meaning, 1, 17–19
  objects of learning, 1–2
  personal property distinguished, 17–18
  scope of subject, 4–15
Reality, 17
Receipt clause,
  conveyance, 162
Receipt, mortgage discharged by, 529
Receiver, 411, 513
  mortgages, 511–512
  order appointing, 100
Recitals,
  conveyance, 162
  introductory, 162
  narrative, 162
Recognisance,
  enforcement, 100
Rectification,
  contracts, 152
  conveyance, of, 430
  land register, 138–143
  Land Registration Act 2002, 142–143
  registration of title, 14, 138–143
    alterations not amounting to rectification,
        142–143
    generally, 138
    Land Registration Act 1925, under, 139–142
    consent, 140
    duplication, 140
    entitlement, 139
    fraud, 140
    grounds, 139–140
    human rights, 139
    jurisdiction, 139
    just, 140
    mortgage, 140
    non-owners, 140
    order of court, 141
    overriding interests, 141
    person aggrieved, 140
    proprietor in possession, 141–142
  Land Registration Act 2002, 142–143
    alterations amounting to rectification, 143
    alterations not amounting to rectification, 142
    effect, 143
    proprietor's fraud, 141–142
      lack of care by proprietor, 141–142
      unjust not to rectify, 142
      effect, 142

"Redeem up, foreclosure down", 525
Redemption, equity of, 493, 494
Redemption, right of, 493, 494, 520–526, 527
Registered land,
  See also Registration of land charges; Registration
      of title
  bankruptcy, 136
  charges,
    discharge, 529
    foreclosure, 504
    priority, 544–546
    sale by chargee, 513
    tacking, 546
    unregistered, 501
  commercial interests, 74–75
  completion, 167
  conveyancing, 12–14, 12–15
    completion, 167
    draft transfer, 167
    examination of title, 167
    Form TR1, 168–170
    from contract to completion, 166–168
    inspection, 166
    passing of title, 167
    property, 171
    requisitions on title, 167
    searches, 167
    stamp duty, 171
    title number(s) to property, 171
    transfer. *See* transfer *below*
  dealings with, 134–138
    bankruptcy, 136
    generally, 134
    limitation, 136–137
    mortgages, 135
    prescription, 138
    transfer,
      death, 136
      inter vivos, 135
  deposit of land certificate, 501, 545
  easements, 451
  extent of registration, 76
  Form TR1, 168–170
  generally, 2–3
  history, 12
  legislation applying to, 77
  licences, 480
  limitation, 561–562
    effect of registration, 138
    further two-year period, 138
    Land Registration Act 1925, 136–137
    Land Registration Act 2002, 137–138
    precautions, 138
    procedure after ten-year period, 137–138
    ten-year period, 137
  minor interests. *See* Minor interests
  modern position, 76–78
  mortgages, 135
  overriding interests, 13–14
  passing of title, 167
  prescription, 138
  profits *à prendre*, 451

Registered land—*cont.*
  rationale of system, 12
  registrable interests, 13
  requisitions on title, 167
  restrictive covenants,
    discharge, 472
    protection, 471–472
  searches, 167
  transfer,
    additional provisions, 172
    address for service, 171
    consideration, 171–172
    date, 171
    death, 136
    declaration of trust, 172
    details, 168
    Form TR1, 168–170
    inter vivos, 135
    operative words, 171
    precedent, 168
    stamp duty, 171
    title number(s) of property, 171
      property, 171
    transferee, 171
    transferor, 171
    transferor transfers with, 172
  trusts for sale. *See* Trusts for Sale
Registration of land charges,
  See also Charges
  annuities, 101
  basic principles, 94
  compensation scheme, 103
  conclusiveness, 14
  deeds of arrangement, 101
  effect,
    compensation scheme, 103
    lessees, 103–104
    names register, 102
    non-registration, 104–106
    notice, 102
    registration, 102–104
  generally, 93–94
  land charges 94–99. *See also* Charges
  lessees, 103–104
  local land charges, 91–92
    divisions, 91
    failure to register, 92
    registrable interests, 92
  maintenance of registers, 3–4
  mode, 101
  name for registration, 102
  non-registration, effect of, 104–106
    categories, 104
    void, 105–106
  pending actions, 99–100
  priority notices, 106–107
  reasons, mortgages, 536
  registrable interests, 94–101
    annuities, 101
    deeds of arrangement, 101
    land charges 94–99. *See also* Charges
    pending actions, 99–100

Registration of land charges—*cont.*
  registrable interests—*cont.*
    writs and orders, 100
  searches, 106, 539
  vacation of entries, 107–108
  void charges, 105–106
  writs and orders, 100
Registration of title,
  absolute title, 118–119
  application for first registration, 120
  balance of interests, 15
  basis of system, 111
  cautions against first registration, 120–121
  charges register, 13, 116
  classes of title, 118
    absolute, 118–119
    good leasehold, 119
    possessory, 119
    qualified, 119
  classification of rights, 111–112
  compulsory,
    ambit, 117
    areas, 117
    extent, 117–118
    non-registration, 118
  conclusiveness, 14, 114–115
  conferring title, 114
  conversion of titles, 120
  dealings with registered land, 134–138
  defective title, 120
  dispute resolution, 113–114
  division of register, 13
  easements, 451
  electronic conveyancing, 113
  entries on the register, 129
  fee simple absolute in possession, 115
  first registration,
    application, 120
    cautions against, 120–121
  franchise, 116
  fundamental principles, 114
  good leasehold title, 119
  history, 17, 111
  indemnity, 14, 143–145
    conversion of title, 144
    determination, 144–145
    errors, 144
    exceptions, 144
    generally, 143
    grounds, 143–144
    non-rectification, 144
    rectification, 143–144
  interests requiring protection. *See* Minor interests
  land certificates, 117
  minor interests. *See* Minor interests
  open register, 96
  overriding interests. *See* Overriding interests
  possessory title, 119
  profit *à prendre*, 116
  profits *à prendre*, 451
  property register, 13, 116
  proprietorship register, 13, 116

Registration of title—*cont.*
  qualified title, 119
  rectification, 14, 138–143
    fraud, proprietor's 141
    generally, 138
    Land Registration Act 1925, under, 139–142
      consent, 140
      duplication, 140
      entitlement, 139
      fraud, 140
      grounds, 139–140
      jurisdiction, 139
      just, 140
      lack of care by proprietor, 141–142
      mortgage, 140
      non-owner, 140
      order of court, 141
      overriding interests, 141
      person aggrieved, 140
      proprietor in possession, 141–142
      proprietor's fraud, 141–142
    Land Registration Act 2002, 142–143
      alterations amounting to rectification, 143
      alterations not amounting to rectification, 142
      effect, 143
    unjust not to rectify, 142
  register,
    charges, 116
    property, 116
    proprietorship register, 116
  registered charges, 121
  registrable interests, 115–121
    fee simple absolute in possession, 115
    franchise, 116
    profit *à prendre*, 116
    term of years absolute in possession, 115, 116
  rentcharges, 115
  system,
    concurrent systems, 14–15
    history, 12
    investigation of vendor's title, 12
    rationale, 12
    registrable interests, 13
    third party rights, 12
  term of years absolute, 115
  title,
    classes,
      absolute, 118–119
      good leasehold, 119
      possessory, 119
      qualified, 119
    conversion, 120
    defective, 120
   voluntary, 118
Regulated tenancies, 592–599
  possession, grounds for, 595–598
    discretionary, 595–596
    mandatory, 596–598
Release,
  easement or profit, of, 442–443, 443–444
  rentcharge, of, 411
Remainders, 33, 214

Remoteness, rules against, 214
　development, 15
　history, 15
Rent,
　assize, of, 413
　initial control, 617
　leases,
　　cost of repairs, deducting, 380
　　covenant to pay, 375
　　enforcement, 375
　　need for, 306
　　non-payment, right to relief, 357–359
　　rentcharges distinguished, 407–408
　level, 618
　non-payment, 357–360
　　formal demand, 357
　settled land, 272
　subsequent control, 617–618
Rent seck, 412
Rent service, 412
Rentcharges, 407–413
　action for money, 410
　creation, 409–410
　　form, 409
　　limitation, words of, 409
　　restrictions, 408, 409–410
　　statute by, 409
　　will, by, 409
　demise to trustee, 411
　distress, 410
　elapse of 60 years, 412
　enforcing payment, 238, 410–411
　entry into possession, 410
　entry, rights of, 83
　equitable, 408
　estate, 409
　extinguishment, 411–412
　form, 409
　issuing out of or charged on land, 82
　legal, 408
　lessee's position, 411
　limitation, 412, 555
　meaning, 82
　merger, 412
　　presumption against, 412
　minor interests, 130
　nature, 407–408
　on a rentcharge, 408
　perpetual, 82
　perpetuities, rule against, 411
　possession, in, 82
　registration of title, 115
　release, 411
　rent services distinguished, 407–408
　rentcharge on rentcharge, 408, 411
　right of entry, 462
　statutory redemption, 411–412
　term of years absolute, 82
　terre tenant, 410
　transfer, 409–410
　types of rent, 412–413
　words of limitation, 409

Requisitioned premises, 366
Requisitions on title,
　registered land, 167
　　replies, 167
　unregistered land, 159
　　replies, 159
Reservation, easement created by, 425–427, 427,
　427–428
Restraint of trade, 523
Restrictions,
　effect, 132
　Land Registration Act 2002, 133–134
　minor interests, 132–133
　　effect, 132
　　Land Registration Act 2002, 133–134
　　rights protected by, 132–133
　present law, 132
　rights protected by, 132–133
　use, 132–133
Restrictive covenants, 453–473
　annexation, 456
　　area, 458
　　delayed, 459
　　equity, 457
　　ownership of land, 458
　　statutory, 458
　assignee, 455
　　benefit of law, 455, 455–456
　　burden at law, 462–467
　　burden in equity, 468–471
　　entitlement, 457–459
　　express assignment, 459
　　subsequent assignment, 459
　　time of assignment, 459
　benefit of covenant, 454–461
　　assignees, 455
　　equity, 456–461
　　　annexation to land, 457–458
　　　assignees, 457
　　　entitled to benefit of covenant, 457–458
　　　original covenantee, 456
　　　touching and concerning the land, 457
　　law, 454–456
　　original covenantee's, 454–455
　burden of covenant, 462–471
　　chain of covenants, 462
　　conditional benefit, 463–464
　　enlarged long lease, 463
　　entry right,
　　　annexed to rentcharge, 462–463
　　　gross, in, 463
　　equity, 468–471
　　law, 462–467
　　rule, 462
　　summary of position at law, 464
　chain of,
　　assignments, 459
　　covenants, 462
　easements,
　　compared, 470
　　distinguished, 454

Restrictive covenants—*cont.*
  enforcement, 471–473
    action, 471
    court declaration, 471–472
    Land's Tribunal's powers, 472–473
    registered land, 473
  equity, 66–67
    following law, 453–454
    remedies, 470
  leases, 383
  negative nature, 468–469
  original covenantee's,
    benefit,
      equity, 456
      law, 454–455
    burden, equity, 468
  ownership of land, 456, 458, 469
  part of land, 458, 459
  planning control, 473
  reform, proposals for, 464
  registration, 96–97, 471
  running with covenantor's land, 469–470
  schemes of development, 459–461
    building schemes, 460–461
    buildings already erected, 461
    existing buildings, 461
    mutual enforceability, 459–460
    principle of schemes, 460
    sub-schemes, 461
  touching and concerning covenantee's land,
    455–456
  Tulk v. Moxhay, rule in, 454
Resulting trusts, 291–292, 294–295, 316
  basic principles, 317–318
  common intention, 318
  contributions, 318–319
  direct contribution to purchase price, 318
  exhaustive, trusts not, 291–292
  improvements, subsequent, 319
  indirect contribution to purchase price, 318–319
  perpetuities, rule against, 230
  purchase in name of another, 292
  voluntary conveyance, 292
Retirement,
  trustees, 299
Reversionary leases, 34
Reversions, 33, 213–214
Right of entry. *See* Entry, rights of
Rights of way,
  acquisition, effect of mode of, 444–445
  extent, 401
  necessity, 444–445
  overriding interests, 122
  prescription, 445
Riparian owner, 567
Root of title, 2
Royal lives Clause, 219, 224

Sale,
  bona fide purchaser for value, to, 200

Sale—*cont.*
  co-ownership,
    co-owner, application by, 323
    creditors, application by, 323–324
    trustee in bankruptcy, application by, 324–325
  mortgages, 504–506
    by mortgagor, 528
    equitable mortgages, 513
    history, 504
    mode, 505–506
    position of mortgagee, 506
    power, 504–505
      exercise, 505–506
    price, 506
    prior mortgages, 507
    proceeds, 506
    purchaser's protection, 505
    security, 491
  settled land, 241–242, 270
    to tenant for life, 275–278
Sand, 450
Satisfied term, 365, 494
Schemes of development, 459–460
Searches,
  charges, 11
  local land charges, 11–12
  minor interests, 134
  registered land, 167
  registration of land charges, 106
  unregistered land, 159
Secure tenancy, 605–607
  landlord condition, 606
  rent, 607
  right to buy, 607
  security of tenure, 606
  tenant condition, 606
Security of tenure, 618–619
  agricultural holdings, 586–588
  agricultural workers, 605
  assured tenancies, 600
  business tenancies, 581–582, 582
  long leases, 608
  regulated tenancies, 595–598
  restricted contracts, 615–616
  secure tenancies, 606
Seisin, 35–37, 68
  acquisition, 36
  definition, 36
  freeholder, 36
  importance, 36
  meaning, 35
Sequestrator,
  order appointing, 100
Serviceman, 597
Services, 25–26
Servient tenement, 413–414
Settled land, 247–302
  before 1926, 247–250
    alienation, 248–249
  beneficial interests, 6
  capital money,
    investment, 275

Settled land—*cont.*
  capital money—*cont.*
    payment, 263
  charge,
    grant of, 241, 272
  chattels, settled sale of, 274
  co-ownership, 326–327
  conditions of residence, 276–277
  "curtain" principle, 264–265
    errors, 264–265
    exceptions, 265
  deed of discharge, 266, 267
  definition, 251
  determination of settlement, 262, 265–268
  disputes, compromise of, 274
  documents, 258–262
    after 1925, 258–259
    basic rule, 258
    before 1926, 258
    inter vivos settlements, 258–260
    prevention of evasion, 261–262
    will, settlements by, 260
  duration of settlement, 265–268
  effect of dealing with, 252
  essentials, 252–257
  exchange, 241–242
  express trusts for sale, 7
  family charges,
    licences and equities, 253–254
    limited in trust, 253
    meaning, 254–255
  generally, 6–8
  improvements, 274–275
    repayment of cost, 275
  irregularity, protection against, 263
  leases, 241–244
    conditions, 270–272
  mansion house, disposal of, 273
  mental patients, 278
  minor, 253
    attainment of majority, 266
    entitled, 251
    joint tenant for life, 326
  mortgages, 241, 272
  options, 241, 272–273
    exercise of statutory powers, 277–278
  overreaching, 327
  overriding interests, 126
  personal representatives,
    disposition by, 261
    special, 266
  rent, 272
  resulting inconvenience, 255
  sale, 241–242
    to tenant for life, 275–278
  Settled Land Act 1925, 250–279
  Settled Land Acts, 7
  settlement, 252
  strict settlement, 247–249
  succession, 252–253
  tenant for life,
    assignment of beneficial interest, 278

Settled land—*cont.*
  tenant for life—*cont.*
    authority from court, 274
    definition, 255–256
    legal estate owner, 255–256
    minors, 256
    no tenant for life, where, 256
    position, 275–278
    powers, 251–252, 268–278
      chattels, selling settled, 274
      compromising claims, 274
      consent necessary, 273–274
      curtailment, 276–277
      exchange, 270
      exercise, 277–278
      hampering powers, 276–277
      improvements, 274–275
      investments, selecting, 275
      lease, 270–272
      mansion house, principal, 273
      notice necessary, 269–273
      ousting, 276–277
      repayment, 275
      safeguards against abuse, 269
      sale, 270
      timber, cutting and selling, 273
      transactions, effecting, 274
      unfettered, 252
    trustee, as, 252, 275–276, 268–269
    unfettered powers, 268
  timber, sale, 273
  trust instrument,
    contents, 258–259
    examination, 260, 263, 265
    pre-1926 settlements, 260
  trustees, functions of, 278–279
  unauthorised transactions, 263
  vesting assent, 260, 265
  vesting deed,
    principle,
      absence, 260
      contents, 260
      death of tenant for life, 265–268
      errors in, 264–265
      pre-1926 settlements, 260
    subsidiary, 264
  vesting instrument, 258–260
Settlements. *See* Settled land
Severance,
  absolute right, 328
  acquisition of another estate in land, 329
  alienation, 329–330
  generally, 328–329
  homicide, 331
  meaning, 328
  mode of, 328–332
  mutual agreement, 330
  mutual course of dealing, 331
  nature of right, 328
  present law, 332
  words of, 308

Shelter,
  timber, 50
Signature,
  contracts,
    agents, 153–154
    requirement, 153
  limitation, for, 559
Silver, 568
Skylights, 446
Socage, 25
Soil, profit in the, 450
Special powers, 232–233
Specific performance, 344–345
Sporting, rights of, 450
Spouses,
  occupation, statutory rights of, 98–99
Stamp duty,
  conveyancing, 171
  rate, 171
  transfer of registered land, 171
Standard Conditions of Sale, 155
Statute of Uses 1535, 15, 65
Statutory restrictions, 569–580
  compulsory purchase, 577–579
  minerals, 579–580
  planning control, 569–577
Statutory tenancy, 594
Statutory trusts, 289–290
  co-ownership, 309
Stop notice, 575
Strict settlement, 247–249
  absence of powers, 249
  alienation, 248–249
  intervention of statute, 249
  legal estate, 248–249
  powers in settlement, 248
  principal provisions, 247–248
  settlement and resettlement, 248
Structure plan, 571
Student residence, 597, 601
Sub-infeudation, 26
Sub-leases. See under Leases
Sub-mortgage, 528
Successors in title,
  bona fide purchaser for value, 63
Support,
  easement of, 418
  right of, 417–418
Surrender of lease, 364–365
Survivorship, right of, 4

Tabula in Naufragio, 543
Tacking, 530, 542–544
  agreement of intervening incumbrancer, 543
  further advances, 544
  Land Registration Act 2002, 546
  meaning, 542–543
  no notice of intervening incumbrance, 543–544
  optional, 546
  tabula in naufragio, 543

Taxation,
  income tax, 372
  inheritance tax, 164
  land tax, 83
Tenancy,
  double annual value, 350
  double rent, 350
  dwellings. See Dwellings, tenancies of
  sufferance, at, 350
    double annual value, 350
    double rent, 350
  will, at 33–34, 349
Tenancy at will,
  meaning, 33–34, 349
Tenancy in common, 306–307
  See also Co-Ownership
  before 1926, intention to create, 308
  creation, 307–315
    before 1926, 308
  determination, 328–329
  legal, non-existence post-1925, 308–309
  presumption, mortgages, 527
  settled land, 327
  severance, created by, 328–332
  undivided shares, 307
  vesting, number of persons, 310–311
Tenancy. See Dwelling houses, tenancies of; Leases,
    business premises, tenancies of; Tenant
Tenant,
  See also Leases
  breach of condition, 355
    waiver, 355–356
  business premises. See Business premises, tenancies
    of
  in demesne, 25
  denial of landlord's title, 354
  exclusive possession, 341–342
  fixtures, 22
  holding over, statutory penalties, 350
  in capite, 25
  in chief, 25
  life, for. See under Settled Land
  local housing authorities, 372
  rates, payment, 372
  relief,
    breach of covenant, 360
    non-payment of rent, 357–359
  rent, 343, 372
  rights,
    assigning, 376–377
  security of tenure, general position, 618–619
  status, 617–619
  statutory protection, 380, 580–619
  trade fixtures, 22
  waste, liability for, 373
Tenures, 24–29
  doctrine, 27
  free, 25, 27–28
  length, 26
  lord and tenant, 24–25
  modern significance, 27–29

Tenures—*cont.*
  present,
    freehold tenures, 28
    leasehold tenures, 29
  services, 25–26
  unfree, 26, 28
Terms of years absolute, 81
Terre tenant, 410
Testatum,
  conveyance, 162
Testimonium,
  conveyance, 166
Tied dwellings, agricultural, 604
"Tied" house, 507, 521
Timber, 273
  accumulating produce, 245
  estate, 50
  estovers, 50, 374, 450
  generally, 50
  licence to take, 476
  life estate, 49–51
    estate, 50
    estovers, 50
    normal rules, 50–51
    ornamental, 50
    ownership of severed timber, 51
    shelter, 50
    trees, 50
  normal rules, 50–51
  ornamental, 50
  ownership of severed timber, 51
  severed, 51
  shelter, 50
  trees, 50
Time. *See* Limitation; Prescription
Tithe, 407
  redemption annuity, 83
  rentcharge, 83
Title,
  abstract,
    consideration, 159
    delivery, 158
  abstract. *See* Abstract of title
  co-ownership,
    fragmentation, 8
    integration, 8–9
    simplification, 75–76
    undisclosed, 9–10
  conversion, 120
  deeds, retention by,
    mortgagee, 514
  denial of landlord's by tenant, 354
  epitome, 158
  investigation. *See* Investigation of Title
  number(s), 171
  passing,
    registered conveyancing, 167–168
    unregistered conveyancing, 160
  registration. *See* Registration of Title
  requisitions,
    registered land, 167
      replies, 167

Title—*cont.*
  requisitions—*cont.*
    unregistered land, 159
      replies, 159
  unity of, 306
Tombs, 239
Tort,
  liability, 568
Town and country planning. *See* Planning Control
Trade fixtures, 22
Transfer,
  conveyancing 168. *See also under* Conveyancing
  registered land, 168
    See also Conveyancing
    additional provisions, 172
    address for service, 171
    consideration, 171–172
    declaration of trust, 172
    execution as deed, 172
    Form TR1, 168–170
    operative words, 171
    property, 171
    stamp duty, 171
    title numbers, 171
    transferee, 171
    transferor, 171
    transferor transfers with, 172
Treasure trove, 568
Tree preservation orders, 576
Trees,
  overhanging branches of, 568
  preservation orders, 576
  timber, 50
Trust, 289–302
  See also Trustees
  adverse possession, 556–557
  bare, 289
  cestui que trust, duties to, 64–65
  classification,
    conveyancing, 289
    equity, 289–293
    uncertainties, 293
  constructive, 293, 316, 316–317, 481–482
  corporation, 542
  creation,
    formalities, 293–295
  declaration of, 513
  development, 15
  duties, 64–65
  enforced by equity, 64
  evidenced by writing, 294
  express, 290–291, 316
    beneficiary requirement, 291
    completely constituted, 291
    formal validity, 290
    incompletely constituted, 291
    three certainties, 290–291
  fraud, 295
  future, 214–215
  history of development, 15
  implied, 292
  incompletely constituted, 291

Trust—*cont.*
  instrument, 258–260
  land, for. *See* Trusts of land
  land, of, 7
  legal and equitable interests, 65
  minerals, 51–52
  occupation, 321
  origin, 64
  personality, 293
  post-1925 position, 66
  purpose trusts, impersonal, 239
  resulting, 291–292, 294–295, 317–319
    exhaustive, trusts not, 291–292
    purchase in name of another, 292
  sale, for. *See* Trust for sale
  for sale. *See* Trust for Sale
  settled land. *See* Settled Land
  Statute of Uses, 1535, 65
  statutory, 289–290, 309
  transfer of trust interest, 295–296
Trust for sale, 279–283
  before 1926, 249–250
  binding trust, 280
  continuance of trust, 282
  conversion, 250, 283
    limits to doctrine, 283
  definition, 279–280
  express, 7, 280–281
  "immediate", 279
  minerals, 51–52
  origin, 250
  statutory, 281–282
  trust required, 279
  trustees,
    consents necessary, 282
    position, 282
    postponement, 282
    powers, 282
  trustees. *See also* Trustees
Trustee in bankruptcy, 366
Trustees, 296–302
  additional, 299
  appointment,
    disclaimer, 296–297
    increasing number of trustees, 298
    maximum number, 297
    minimum number, 297
    number, 297
    original, 296–297
    self-appointment, 298
    settlor's power, 297
    sole trustee, 298
    vesting trust property, 300–301
  death, 300
  disclaimer, 276–277
  joint tenancy, 304
  procedure for settlements, 302
  removal, 299–300
  replacement, 297–298
    mode, 297–298
    power, 297
  retirement, 299

Trustees—*cont.*
  settlement. *See* Settled Land
  tenant for life as, 252, 275–276
  trust for sale. *See* Trust for Sale
  vesting trust property, 300–301
Trusts of land,
  consultation with beneficiaries, 286
  curtailment of powers, 285
  delegation of powers, 285–286
  dispute resolution, 288–289
  legal estate, holding, 309–310
  meaning, 283–284
  minor interests, 130
  occupation of trust property, 286–288
  trustees,
    curtailment of powers, 285
    delegation of powers, 285–286
    powers, 284–285
Tulk v. Moxhay, rule in, 454
Turbary, profit of, 450
Turf, 450

Undue influence, 532–535
Unincorporated association, 240
Unities, four, 304–306
Unity of ownership,
  easements and, 443
Unity of possession,
  easements and, 443
Unregistered land,
  commercial interests, 75
  conveyancing, 10–12, 93–110
    See also Registration of land charges
    abstract, delivery of, 158
    completion, 159–160
    consideration of abstract, 159
    draft conveyance, 159
    epitome of title, 158
    from contract to completion, 158–160
    passing of title, 160
    replies to requisitions, 159
    requisitions on title, 159
    searches, 159
  effect of conveyance, 108–110
  generally, 2–3
  legislation applying to, 77
  modern position, 76–78
  searches, 159
Use of land,
  common law, 566
  material change in, 572
Uses,
  meaning, 64
  resulting, 294
  Statute of Uses 1535, 65
  successive, 65
  use upon a use of, 65
"Usual covenants", 367, 374, 374–375

Vested interests, 210–212
  assignability, 212
  conditions for vesting, 210–212

Vested interests—*cont.*
  control over, 240
  divested, subject to being, 212
  person not ascertained, 211
  ready, interest not, 211
  size of interest, 211–212
Vesting,
  assent, 260, 266
  conditions for, 210–212
  declaration, 300
  deed, 258–259
    subsidiary, 264
  instruments, 258–260
  joint tenancies, 311
  order, 301
  tenancies in common, 311
Vibration, 448
Villeinage, 25
Void,
  leases, 343
Voidable disposition,
  minor, by, 203

"Wait and see", 201–203, 216–217, 218–219, 227,
  231
Waiver,
  breach of covenant, of, 355–356
  forfeiture, 355–356
Walls, party, 332–335
War damage, 366
Waste,
  ameliorating, 48
  equitable, 49

Waste—*cont.*
  mortgagee and, 508
  permissive, 49
  tenant's liability for, 373, 595, 601
  voluntary, 49
Water abstractions, 567–568
  common law position, 567–568
  rights, 447–448
Watercourses,
  overriding interests, 122
Way, rights of. *See* Rights of way
Wheeldon v. Burrows, 428–429
Wild animals, 566
Wills,
  intestacy. *See* Intestacy
  rentcharge created by, 409
  settlement arising under, 260
  words of limitation, 38, 39, 40
Wood. *See* Timber
Words of limitation, 409
  fee simple, 38–39
    corporation, conveyances *inter vivos* to, 38
    gifts by will, 39
    natural persons, conveyances *inter vivos* to, 38
  fee tail, 39–40
    conveyances *inter vivos*, 39
    will, gifts by, 39–40
  life estate, 40
  wills, 38, 39, 40
Words of severance, 308
Workshop, light to, 439
Writs, 53–55
  registration of land charges, 100